GET A CAMERA...
GET SOME STOCK...
GO SHOOT A
MOVIE...

THE GUERILLA FILM MAKERS HANDBOOK

This edition of
The Guerilla Film Makers Handbook
is dedicated to Dad...

'The surest way to succeed...
is to be determined not to fail...'
WV Jones

with continued support

Continuum
15 E 26 Street
New York
NY 10010

Continuum
The Tower Building
11 York Road
London SE1 7NX

First published in 2006.

ISBN 082647988X

Layout and design by Chris Jones.
Printed and bound in the United Kingdom.

THE GUERILLA
FILM MAKERS
HANDBOOK

3RD EDITION

BY
CHRIS JONES AND
GENEVIEVE JOLLIFFE

ASSISTED BY
ANDREW ZINNES, VERITY BUDDEN,
JONATHAN NEWMAN AND LUCIA LANDINO

We would like to thank all our Sponsors

Acknowledgements

We would like to thank all the contributors in this book for sharing with us their experience and expertise, helping to shed light on how films get made here in the UK. We would also like to thank everyone who has helped Living Spirit produce its first three feature films; *The Runner, White Angel* and *Urban Ghost Story,* especially those who have supported us, both financially and emotionally, while navigating the shark infested, ship wrecked waters of low-budget film making. You were our life jackets.

To all those people who said it could be done, our sincere thanks for your encouragement.

Special thanks in particular for words of advice received on a running track all those years ago.

We would also like to express our gratitude to the following for their help in producing this book -

David Barker, you are sooooo cooool! Thanks for your unending patience and encouragement.

Special thanks also to all our sponsors, without whose contribution, this book would have been 200 pages thinner.

Thanks also to the film makers who sent us their photos for inclusion in the book.

Thanks also to Mums, Dads and families.

And Jim, thanks for your illustrations.

The Guerilla Film Makers Handbook
Introduction to the third edition

It's been a decade since the first edition of the GFMH, and in that time so much has happened. Not least the expansion of the book you now hold, into this near 800 page behemoth! Like so many things in life, the big projects like movies and books, if you'd known how much work it would be, you'd think yourself crazy for even starting. It's not about the first step, or the last, but about the ones inbetween. How much we learn from our experiences. It's those experiences that guide us to the right and wise choice when opportunity manifests. And given the technological days we live in, no one has an excuse. You can make a movie. Go on, get your phone out, you can probably make a movie on that in the next 20 minutes!

Digital is here. Oh boy is it. And along with it, come welcome opportunities for new or cash strapped film makers... HD formats for under £1k, full blown post in your bedroom, online delivery is now coming fully online. But, these new bang whizzy tools and software have created a great deal of confusion. What is HD? Is HDV the same as HDCam? Can Final Cut Pro HD really cut HD? Does HD look like film? The answer to all of those questions is no. Well sort of no. Well with some tweaking and hard work and some experience and some expertise, then maybe yes. The problem faced by new film makers is the overwhelming world of possibilities that lead to endless choices. All too often, this confusion seems to distract people away from writing or collaborating on that AMAZING screenplay, and then attracting that GREAT cast, so they can raise REAL money to make a film that will enjoy a real life in the INTERNATIONAL sales arena. And worse still, the ease of access to this technology can breed a lack of discipline and creative laziness... 'It's just a camcorder after all, and they didn't use a tripod in Blair Witch...'

Let's be clear. There is nothing wrong with many of the new technological developments, it's just that none of them make it any easier to achieve the things that really matter. It's still really, really tough to write that amazing screenplay. And it's the script that is the foundation of any movie. We all know that.

This book, even more so than ever, is about maintaining an aspirational dream worthy of the tremendous journey undertaken when making a film. About making a movie that will reach, touch, move and inspire wider audiences. About creating a film career that will sustain you and your loved ones. It's about being a film maker and making movies.

So if you are reading this book now because you know, in the pit of your stomach, you have to take action, you have to make your movie, then we salute you! Go for it!

And remember, ultimately, playing safe can be the most dangerous path to walk.

Chris Jones and Genevieve Jolliffe
20:49, Dec 15th 2005, London

The Guerilla Film Makers Handbook
Introduction to the first edition

It's true that the road to becoming a successful film maker is a rocky, often bizarre and certainly unpredictable one. Neither of us expected to be writing the introduction to a book about film making on this hot July night, more likely our acceptance speech for the Oscar we would surely have been nominated for by now. That's the first lesson. Film making can take a very long time. There are exceptions the press love to quote, but on the whole, carving out a career in film making is not dissimilar to mounting an expedition to tackle the North face of the Eiger.

During our first expedition into film making, we made many mistakes. After regrouping we discovered a small group of persistent wannabe first time film makers pounding at our door, asking questions, the answer to which we had learned the hard way only weeks before. To keep these potential movie makers from consuming our every waking hour, we compiled some notes about how we made our first film and what pit falls could have been avoided. Soon after, due to great demand and overwork, our photocopier broke down. We realised then that there was a genuine need for a book about low-budget film making in the UK. Not some crusty manual written by a frustrated accountant, or an American guide that is so localised to Hollywood that it's all but useless, but a book that tells how it really is in the UK, how it's really done, what the penalties are, and what the rewards can be. And so, back in 1991, *The Guerilla Film Makers Handbook* was born.

If you have enough energy, half a brain and can convince enough people that you could be the next Orson Welles, you will become a film maker. Don't be put off by ridicule, poverty (although that can be very tough) or fear. You can do it. You will do it. Good luck.

Chris Jones & Genevieve Jolliffe - July 30th '96 (03.52 hours)

The Guerilla Film Makers Handbook
Introduction to the second edition

Since the GFMH hit the streets four years ago the film business has changed dramatically. Lottery money, the New Producers Alliance and perhaps in a small way, this book, have all paved the way for new film makers in the UK to make their voices heard.

Since the last edition we have made another feature film, *Urban Ghost Story* and like all movies it has been a labour of love. Again a Living Spirit production that was against all odds with a new set of problems, pitfalls and rewards. This time however the heavy doors of Hollywood have creaked open just enough for us to get our foot in.

In this edition you will see that there are a number of anonymous interviews. This is because we wanted the interviewees to be free to answer honestly, not politically as often that would put a person in a difficult position. So we have protected their identity.

Digital technology is also moving very quickly. It's impossible to predict how things will change but a few guesses would include DVD style distribution, international sales across the Internet, digital cinema projection (meaning you don't need a print) and most of all, origination on digital formats, of which DV is the cheapest and is accessible to all people. Undoubtedly, this liberation will spawn a plethora of dull and slow movies, but from this sea of mediocrity, a few unique film makers will rise. It's up to you to be that person, that original film maker. Be vocal. Be heard. Make your movie.

Chris Jones & Genevieve Jolliffe - April 10th 2000 (23.13 hours)

The Guerilla Film Makers
10 Commandments

Thou shalt strive, every day and in every way, to achieve excellence! Only through excellence shall thy receiveth salvation.

Thou shalt cast from thine mind the phrase, 'it can not be done...'

Thou shalt shoot, while living in PAL land, at 25fps on film, or 25P on HD, irrespective of what other soothsayers advise. They be-eth wrong!

Thou shalt never work a crew more than 12 hours a day, or 6 days a week.

Thou shalt ask if in doubt. If not in doubt, thou shalt ask anyway.

Thou shalt make a film through the legal mechanism of a limited company.

Thou shalt disregard ridicule from friends and relatives.

Thou shalt shoot the best format available, be it Super 16mm film or HDCam. Cast from thine hand thine superduper camcorder, it is the device of the Devil!

Thou shalt shoot hundreds of high quality stills of the actors and action.

Thou shalt get the best deals by paying cash upfront.

Thou shalt respect the film makers who will come after thee. Never burnest bridges other may need to use.

Thou shalt always shoot at least two takes of every shot.

Thou shalt ONLY shoot when thine screenplay is Oscar winning.

Thou shalt cut thine movie, then recut, then recut, then recut...

(yes, we know there are more than ten, but this is the GFMH Ten Commandments upgrade)

Experts Contents

7. POST PRODUCTION

8. SALES

9. WHAT'S NEXT?

10. CASE STUDIES

Tips Contents

7. POST PRODUCTION

8. SALES & DISTRIBUTION

8. SALES & DISTRIBUTION

What's on the CD?

In the back of this book you will find a CD-Rom with a bunch of fun stuff on it.

The Guerilla Film Makers Handbook PLUS!

Free on the CD is a bonus PDF document, a kind of extra to the book. It's an A5 document so you can print it into a booklet (if your printer supports that). So what's in it? There are interviews that we couldn't fit in this edition, there are interviews pulled from the second edition (especially useful if you plan to post produce your movie the old photochemical way), lists, glossaries and a whole heap of other goodies. You will need the free Adobe Acrobat Reader to read this document.

Production Forms

All the forms in the Legal Toolkit Section are on the disk, saved in MS Word Format and ready for you to use on your productions.

Contracts

All the contracts in the Legal Toolkit section are on the CD also, again in MS Word. Thank goodness, can you imagine what it would be like if you had to type them all out!

Screenplay Software

There is our new Screenplay Formatting Software too. It takes all the hard work out of formatting your screenplay. It works with all versions of MS Word up to Word 2003 (on the PC), and for Mac, we are still updating. Check our website though as we release updates every so often. There is an extensive manual with Screenplay which we would recommend you take a look at.

Budget

The new Budget Software wasn't quite ready to go on the CD, but visit our website and you should be able to download it from there when it's ready.

Plus other goodies...

If you join our newsgroup on the website, you will get info about new stuff, launch parties, software and courses.

www.livingspirit.com

Quick Guide To Low Budget Movie Making

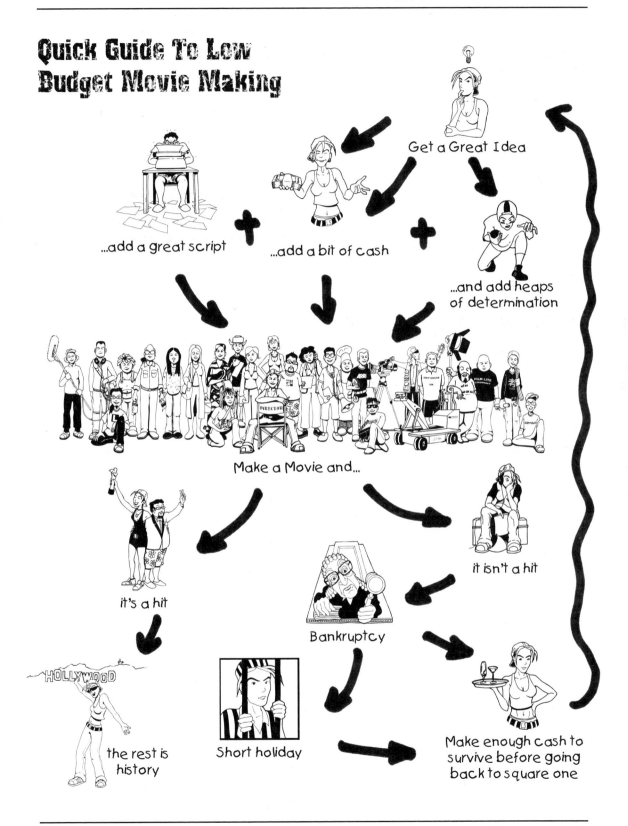

Get a Great Idea

...add a great script

...add a bit of cash

...and add heaps of determination

Make a Movie and...

it's a hit

it isn't a hit

Bankruptcy

the rest is history

Short holiday

Make enough cash to survive before going back to square one

The Guerilla Film Makers Handbook

This is a British Independent Feature film.
Its UK theatrical release was cut short due to illegal DVD piracy.
Its UK sales were SERIOUSLY damaged by illegal DVD piracy.
Next time if could be YOUR movie.
Protect our industry...
Protect your business...

If you see it, report it to FACT or the Police.
DON'T ASSUME SOMEONE ELSE WILL!
TAKE RESPONSIBILITY FOR OUR COLLECTIVE INDUSTRY,

FOR A PROSPEROUS AND SECURE FUTURE FOR US ALL!

WE ARE IN THIS TOGETHER!

FACT
7 Victory Business Centre, Worton Road, Isleworth, Middlesex, TW7 6DB
T: 0208 568 6646   F: 0208 560 6364
E: contact@fact-uk.org.uk

TRAINING

National Film and Television School

The National Film and Television School - A Skillset Screen Academy

You don't need a degree – you just need talent and a great showreel to apply to the UK's national centre of excellence in film and television training. The NFTS offers MA and Diploma courses in key professional disciplines and students learn in purpose-built film and television studios with equipment rivalling that used at the highest level in today's Industry. Working methods model professional practice, and the collaborative ethos graduates students with both professional skills in their own field and a good understanding of the other key roles involved in bringing a new film or television programme to the screen. Scholarships and maintenance grants available. The NFTS is also home to the renowned ShortCourses@NFTS, which specialises in skills upgrading for professionals.

www.nftsfilm-tv.ac.uk

Simon Fellows
Film Maker

FILM SCHOOL EXPERIENCES

Q - Why did you want to make films?

Simon - I've thought about this, if there was a period when I suddenly wanted to be a film-maker, but I can't pin point one. I had a fascination with photography, and like so many other people of our generation, *Star Wars* had an enormous impact on me, but there was no defining moment I can recall. A friend of mine said *'I'm thinking of going to film school'*, and I said *'what's that?'*, and he said, *'it was a place where you can train to do film'*. I quickly went home and did some research, and within a week I had put together a presentation and I applied. I just had a strong feeling about it, even though I didn't know where it was leading me or what I was supposed to do. I got into film school under-age by deliberately lying about my age - I've always been the youngest in whatever I have done.

Q - You are from Birmingham which isn't noted for being the film capital of the world. With that 'non film' background, do you think going to film school was a valuable experience?

Simon - We all know a lot of people who go into the film industry come from a film-in-the-family background. People I work with now, especially actors, often come from some sort of artistic or creative background. Film school can be a great place to begin if you have no obvious route into the business.

Q - Were you disappointed with the 'education' you received at film school?

Simon - Don't go to film school under the illusion that you will learn how to make films. The point of going is to immerse yourself in film, to be around other people who all want the same thing. When I enrolled, some people had done way more than me, others had done less. Within a week we were learning a hell of a lot about different levels of people's skill, understanding what the medium is, and being exposed to films and film makers work I would never have come across if left to my own devices in Birmingham. My education came from the other students on the course. The lecturers obviously have experience and could talk about some things every now and then, and they controlled the structure if you like. The film school provided the opportunity to create with the other students, with the lecturers overseeing. Rarely were we sat down and lectured, or told how to make films. I think it really is a case of getting on and doing it, that has much more value to me. To go back to my point about students that influence others, you influenced me with projects that you were developing at the school, because of their ambitiousness and their leaning towards science fiction which I was always interested in. That's what triggered me to push in those directions. In many ways the students and community are more important than the course itself.

Q - At film school, do you think there is a tendency to over obsess with technology at the expense of script, cast and other artistic disciplines?

Simon - Yes. The script is obviously the biggest issue, and we were never really taught about it. Nor were we ever taught how to deal with actors, how do you talk to them etc. Ironically, it is all about the actors and the screenplay and the combination of the two. The technical stuff is easy in comparison.

Distribution is another area of neglect, what happens in terms of the market place, is a huge grey area at film school. There are different ways that you can get into the film business, for instance you could make your low-budget films and hope that they do well at festivals as you did. Or you can get into commercials as I did. There are many routes in and I don't think I ever had a conversation or lecture with anyone at film school about the world of TV commercials. At that time, commercials was our core film industry and it's where you got to meet film technicians, crews, actors etc. When I graduated I was so naïve of the commercials business that I showed my reel to advertising agencies, not knowing that they were not responsible for the actual making of commercials, they come up with the ideas! I was never told that, which I would have thought was core. There are many avenues of work that you can go into, and TV commercials is an obvious one, so that was a bit weird I guess.

Q - So was film school good for you?

Simon - I'm going to back-peddle now. I came from a background that had absolutely no connection to film, so somebody like me needed to do it, just to figure it out. For somebody who was perhaps a little more well-versed than I was, and has access to people and equipment, film school may not be the best choice. For others, the real world may be the place to start, to get your foot on the first rung of the ladder any way you can. Whichever path you choose, it won't be successful unless you have got the push.

Q - When most people leave film school, they have a naïve concept that, maybe the BBC is about to ring them. What do you really need to get on?

Simon - Ridiculously stupid and endless optimism! During the holidays at film school, rather than actually take the time off, I wrote to a guy called Roy Field who won an Oscar for the blue screen work he did on 'Superman' - I was into special effects at the time, and this was one of many letters I wrote saying I would do anything just for the experience - and he invited me up to Pinewood Studios for a chat, which was mental in itself, I mean, I had never been there! I drove there in a clapped out Fiat Panda, had an interview and he said 'you can start straight away', and I said I would work for free and he said 'great!' I slept in the woods at the back of Pinewood studios for a month in my Fiat Panda and used to wash at Pinewood Studios toilets in the morning. Eventually he found out and he said 'we can't have you sleeping in the woods!' and gave me enough to get lodgings in a local nunnery, and so I was sleeping in a nunnery! The experience showed me that if you push, if you ask, you will get closer to what you want. I believe there is a philosophy in everything that we do, that there is a healthy balance of faith, luck and push.

Q - Some new or young film-makers take themselves very seriously. Do you have any comments about this, as clearly you are a serious film maker who doesn't take it too seriously?

Simon - I've met and worked with people on that level. I deliberately bring my character to set, and I can feel the lightness within the crew. When talent (actors) are on set, on say a 6-8 week shoot with long hours, somebody has got to generate an atmosphere of positivity nearly every day. That really helps, and it does photograph in the talent (actors), and the crew will respond better.

Q - What did you do after film school?

Simon - I knew that the jobs were in London, so I created a showreel of my film school work as I had been lucky enough to be prolific whilst there. I would visit London for two days a week, which was all I could afford, and cram in as many meetings as I could, and drop off the showreels. I wrote up lists - who I visited, who called back, who I called back, what their response was, what their tone was, what they did like about the reel, what they didn't like about the reel... This went on for four months before I got the first opportunity to join a production company. So that part of it was organised and strategised.

Then there was meeting the right person, and just at the right time, when they needed a director. You could call it fate, but I think if you push enough, the percentages of fortunate events happening around you is going to be higher.

I was aware that if you want to shoot a lot of film, commercials is an area that you can get lots of experience. But I actually got tired of them, I was frustrated that I hadn't got closer to my goal to be a film-maker. I backed away from commercials and made two short films, which was the usual put your own money and time in, break the bank, go through relationship break-ups,

Film School... Or Not?

GUERILLA FILM MAKER SAYS!

Quentin Tarantino once said something to the effect of "take the money you plan on using to pay for film school and use it to make your first film." Not all agree, here are some truths of both views to make up your own mind.

FILM SCHOOL	OR, NOT
The film industry is about networking. Film school provides you with a whole class of contacts.	No expensive tuition, so you can put all your funds into making your film.
Cheap to free equipment rental.	Some film schools only make a few of their students films a year.
Tutors are there to give advice about how the system, equipment works.	Your idea may have to wait or never see the light of day. No film school, and you can make your film whenever you are ready.
You have the opportunity to screen your work at the school film festivals.	You are not graded on work that is purely subjective.
As a student, you usually receive discounts on things like processing, rentals, and licensing fees.	No competition for equipment with other students.
You are more likely to receive grants as a student.	You have to learn everything yourself, which can cost time and money.
Expense - (The London Film School charges approx. £31k for the whole course including full production expenses and monies towards your graduation film).	Hiring professionals is expensive. No free, somewhat experienced labour pool.
Comedy and commercial work is sometimes looked down upon in film schools.	You have to make your own contacts.

then there was a gap of a year or so and I am like, *'shit, what have I done?!'* But I remained focussed. When I was in LA, and for no real reason, I bothered to pop in and see a producer who I'd met two years previously. I just thought, *'he's a good guy, I like him'*, and that led to my first feature. You could call that luck, but I needed to be in LA in the first place, and no amount of luck would get me on a plane flying to LA, I had the push to get me there.

Q - So the key is to be present as much as you can be, in a happy, optimistic, enthusiastic way, but never be demanding or overtly arrogant?

Simon - Yes, but as you say, never over-pushing. Until I had done a whole bunch of commercials, and at least two short films, I didn't really feel I had the right to push into the features market. When we graduated, I thought I was going to make a big movie *next year*, and that didn't happen. It took longer, and longer and longer. I had to realise that I had to earn the privilege of doing that,

which on reflection, was right for me. It's not been an easy path either, tons of knocks, absolutely tons, and rejections, disillusionment. Times when you think this is never really going to happen. For as much push, and strategy as you have, sometimes that luck just doesn't come, fate just doesn't twist the right way.

Q - How much can you earn making commercials?

Simon - It's no secret that advertising pays directors pretty well, for the short stint of work that it actually is. But whilst you do just put in a two day shoot, you actually have a series of major meetings prior to that, competing with treatments against a handful of other directors, not quite knowing when you have got the job, and if you do get the job, then there's the shooting and post-producing for a month maybe. So if you calculate the time spent on it, and your salary, it doesn't work out very much at all, but

Virgin Directors

Directors have different styles and methods of working with their actors and the crew. There are those that will scream and shout, and those who prefer a more relaxed working environment. There are 'actor directors' who will concentrate more on performances than the flashy shots. There are 'camera directors' who will expect the actors to do their bit while they take care of the look of the shot. And, then there are 'virgin directors', first timers who are trying to figure out which one of the above they are, or a combination of the two. Whichever, remember that great camera movement and amazing lighting will mean nothing if the acting is unbelievable, and vice versa. A good director will blend these elements together so smoothly that they appear seamless.

1. Be prepared. Know what you want for each scene and know what camera set-ups are needed.

2. The most overlooked area of directing is casting. Get the script and the cast right and you will find the journey much easier.

3. Have a read-through of your script with the actors at least once. It's important to read your script out loud as the interplay among the characters will help you to see that everything is working, and if not, you can make any changes before getting to set. If you can't get them all before the shoot, substitute with other actors.

4. Rehearse with your cast. Again, with the physical acting out of the scenes, you will get a feel for things that aren't working. It's better problems arise here than on set. Make sure that you don't over rehearse so your actors can still recreate the magic in front of the camera. The rehearsal can also help give your actors a sense of the whole story rather than just their own character. Some directors and actors do not rehearse at all, fearing that it will destroy the spontaneity of the scene.

5. Have good communication with your actors and crew so that they know exactly what you want. Use storyboards, shot lists or floor plans.

6. Know your script and therefore know the point of each scene. On set the actors may ask you for the background to each scene to help them with the emotion of their character and what their motivation is in this scene.

7. As a low budget filmmaker you are often the producer too. Make sure that when directing you let go of as much producer's work as possible! Filmmaking is collaborative - delegate!

8. Creative ideas can come from anywhere - listen to your crew and cast.

9. Don't be embarrassed to ask your crew questions if need be. It's better to get it right. As a new director, your crew members will likely be far more experienced than you.

10. Cover the scene! Make sure you have enough shots to make it work. Don't believe that your screenplay, actors and direction is so good that you won't need to edit it - you will.

11. Substance over style. Get the story right and the best performances possible out of the actors before you worry about flashy shots.

12. Rest when you can. Politely request others to get you tea, coffee and food and avoid decisions you don't have to make.

13. Keep an iPod with you so you can listen to music to take you away from the set in order to clear your mind.

14. Try and learn everybody's name, especially the actors! If people feel you're taking an interest in them enough to learn their name, they are more likely to work harder for you.

15. Be decisive! You're responsible for staying on schedule and on budget so if you're taking numerous takes because you're not sure if you got what you wanted, not only are you going to slow down production you are also going to lose the confidence of your cast and crew.

16. Actors and directors are strong collaborators, so it's a good idea to be familiar with the different kinds of training an actor may have. Avoid giving actors blank direction such as 'you're angry now' - find out how they work and help them see their character's motivation.

17. Inform your actors what type of shot you're doing i.e. if it's a close up or a wide shot. This will help them give you the right performance.

18. Keep working. Don't think that when you wrap that is the end of the shoot. Keep shooting new scenes and cutaways as you need them.

19. Have production meetings with your crew. By imparting your vision of the film to the crew and explaining what you hope to accomplish with the production, everyone will feel more like a team and a team can make for a happy relaxed crew who will deliver their best for the film.

20. Work hard and be creative, but recognise that your first film will probably be all about learning how to make it.

21. Shoot the whole script. If you don't you won't have a movie. So stay on schedule.

we love doing it. The way it works for a director is that, you have to be represented by a production company, or else advertising agencies won't accept you.

Within advertising agencies there is a team - a copy-writer and an art director - and they are responsible for writing the script and the words that go with the script, and the look of it, and they will want to hire a director. Millions of pounds go into the strategies behind big clients, be it Adidas, Nike or whoever, and they are always thinking six months ahead. The key is to get represented by production companies, because advertising agencies will look to those production companies for specific directors, with a specific skill, to hire them in for specific campaigns, be it food, cars, footwear. Eventually you become pigeon-holed into a certain genre of work, and you end up churning out the same old stuff, and any amount of artistry you had will leave you. Some commercials are amazing pieces of film, but the vast majority are about selling you stuff. The interesting thing is, through all of those strategies in terms of agencies liasing with clients, developing a concept over a process of months, story-boarding it and doing tests with audiences and one-way mirrors and stuff - when it comes to shooting it, it is the director's relationship with the agency and the client that's important. If we are talking about somebody's ability to survive and to move forward in terms of film-making, it is a healthy place to be, because you are still very closely related to film. The downside is that it will distract you from other ambitions.

Q - So you need to get out of your comfort zone?

Simon - For all the money I made in commercials, I can't say it ever resulted in much, because I always spent it on developing film projects! It bought me a flat in London but that's all really. I put a lot of money into two short films. People say *'never put your own money in!'* I think there comes a point, when if you want to further your career, make a statement, or make a film that you believe in, you have to put your money and your time where your mouth is. You have to risk some of those comforts, if not all of them.

Q - What else did you learn from commercials?

Simon - Commercials taught me to be confident in a room with powerful people. In advertising, just before you shoot something, you walk into a room with 15 people all wearing suits, and they all want to hear you talk for hours about their 30 second spot. That means that, on the first movie I got asked to do, when you are meeting somebody like Heather Graham and you may find them intimidating, you need to be calm and to be able to talk clearly through your visions. There were no guarantees when I was offered *'Blessed'*, it was subject to getting someone like Heather Graham to act in the film, and it came down to a meeting. If I blew that, then the film wouldn't have been made.

Q - What do you think of agents, as it appears you got your own jobs?

Simon - It is absolutely not the agent's job to launch your career. The usefulness of having an agent is, if you get close enough to one, that you can have a conversation about what is the next right step for you, or about the kind of material you are looking for. That agent will have an ear to the ground, in terms of what's moving in the industry, what scripts are floating around etc. Obviously they have access to talent, to writers which can be useful. If you do get fortunate enough to do a project, it is useful to have an agent to negotiate the finer points of the contract. Their job is to capitalise on your success. Over time they become a filter system for material coming in. But initially, they can give you an infrastructure that the industry understands.

Q - How would you compare your experiences in the different areas you have worked?

Simon - Commercials were exactly what I thought it was going to be like. Ultimately you learn that you can not operate as an auteur in that environment, and at every part of the decision making process there are questions brought up by others, discussions that go on for hours. Short film-making is the most satisfying, in that if you do truly develop it yourself, fund it yourself, work with a crew who wants to be there while being paid peanuts - that is the purest form of film-making. Going to a feature film, I couldn't believe how much control you are actually given, the trust and faith invested in you by the producers. On the other hand, with the power of the structure behind it, if it does want to make a decision that you absolutely disagree with, it will make that decision for you. The big difference really is that in commercials, not that many people are motivated by the film-making. In short films, everybody is motivated by the film-making. In feature films, absolutely everybody is motivated by the film-making, with due respect for the business side of things. I am amazed at how hungry the producers were for making a good film. It is incredibly up-lifting to be part of that process.

Q - Some film makers have a low regard for producers, do you share their view?

Simon - I love producers and I go out of my way to make sure they know that I will listen to them on a creative level, as much as I want them to discuss with me the financial implications of certain decisions to do with the schedule, because their influence affects me creatively. A film production is money driven and producer-driven and to forget that is foolish. I always try to work with producers creatively and openly, and remember that they genuinely want to make a good film. Of course they have commitments to bringing it in on time, which can conflict with creativity, but if you talk it through clearly you can usually balance the financial and creative interests. Sometimes you can't, sometimes it goes wrong, sometimes it goes perfectly.

Q - Some new film makers fixate on their ideas to exclusion of other people's ideas.? Is that a good idea?

Simon - There have been many occasions where somebody, perhaps a runner or grip, has come up to me and said *'why don't you try it like this?'* and they may be right, it's a much better idea. If you close yourself off or have some sort of totalitarian position, you will miss some of those wonderful little ideas that come from other people - which really is the director's job, being a focus point, for everybody to filter their ideas through, and yet be open to everybody else's input as well. Ultimately the director has to choose, sometimes you will get it right, sometimes you won't.

Q - What do you think are the key steps to success?

Simon - Be strong about your opinion, but not so strong that you don't listen to and engage with others. It is quite a cut-throat industry and you can be bitten by people who may take advantage if you are too open and trusting, so a healthy lack of trust can sometimes help. Don't be naïve, don't allow people to do something when you know in your gut you are being manipulated or lied to. It is a funny word, trust. You inevitably try to be strong and think the best, but you make mistakes again and again.

Q - What are the biggest mistakes you've made?

Simon - I have managed to deal with my career very well but the real life stuff, such as relationships and family, makes the film dilemmas pale into insignificance. When I graduated from film school, I got straight into commercials and I didn't spend time growing, traveling, developing relationships or other things like that - I didn't stop for eight years! I missed out on a lot of things that will make you grow as a person, which may benefit your film career in the long run. There is a good argument for life experience in terms of movies and story telling. It is no accident that many of the best film makers come into their game later on in life. It is easy to allow ambition to push or force you into the industry at an early age. I really only trained in film school for two years, and then I was directing TV commercials. It took me some time to figure out what I really wanted to do in life as I was so dominated by what I was doing right there and then. You miss out on your 20's and end up hitting something like a mid-life crisis a bit too early, though you still wouldn't change it for the world. Don't rush, it is not necessarily a smart thing to rush into, because ultimately your sacrifices will catch up with you, and you will need to invest some time in trying to figure those out.

Stamina is very important. Getting up every day, brushing yourself down, and thinking *'fuck it, I'm going to carry on!'* You need that quality.

Q - What advice would you offer a new film-maker?

Simon - Take the knocks.

Ray Brady
Film Maker

FILM SCHOOL EXPERIENCES

Q - How did you get into films?

Ray - I was raised in a working class family in the North. My father was a plasterer and so I started working part-time with plastering jobs to earn money. I tried university and other courses, but none were right for me. And so I ended up on building sites and became a specialist plasterer, a trade which has served me well in times of need. However, the work took so much out of me that at night I was too tired to do anything other than watch movies. I soon became quite a film buff. After some time I thought that I could do better than some of the films I saw and so I dropped out, sold my flat and went back into full-time education. I ended up on a degree course at the London College of Printing, which I believed was the best course available at the time.

After making a couple of short films I decided to make an Indie feature called *'Boy Meets Girl'*. At that time, there was very little market for short films, but if I were doing it now I think I would make a great short as opposed to a cheap feature film to promote me. A short is very cost effective and it gives you the money to promote it afterwards.

Q - How do you view your film school experience?

Ray - Even though I enjoyed my time at film school, and it broadened my education, I wouldn't go to film school now, because of the money. I think it could be better spent getting practical work as a runner, building your way up through one of the companies to get a good film trade behind you such as editing, sound recording, design etc. If you do three years on a degree course, when you come out at the end, you are still at the bottom of the ladder. So, if you are very enthusiastic about a particular career in film, find a company and start on the lowest rung as quick as you can. Be enthusiastic, turn up on time, never be late, never let anyone down, always go the distance.

There is a discipline at film school - to be told, to turn up, to listen, do this and that, and to be told off when you don't perform. Some young people need that, but as a mature student when I went back, I didn't need that.

Instead of going to film school I'd suggest acquiring maybe 15 books on film making and going through them. Read them, study them, go through them again, make notes, analyse them - that is probably a third of what you can get out of film school.

Q - Many new film-makers don't realise that it's simply not enough to be 'good' as this is one of the most desirable businesses in the world, where there is extreme competition. Enthusiasm and hard work can often go a lot further than natural talent?

Ray - Definitely. Being a hot talent is not enough, you have to find the right allies along the way. Networking and building up relationships is so important. A good foundation of people that support you is integral to success. If you work in the film business and make a living from it, rather than just have it as an expensive hobby, it can drain every penny of your income. It can also damage other areas, like your relationships if you're obsessive like I am. You need to work, and be offered work on a regular basis. So if you get out there and do it quickly, when you can afford to do it, live the life of a student, live in a squatty bedsit with no possessions, or live with parents, then you can build up a professional CV that allows you to work on a regular basis. Then in your downtime or time off, you can make personal projects with the associates that you have met on the way. Film school has become a playground for the rich, where you need the money to be able to come through it without becoming impoverished and indebted. After film school, if you actually want to make anything, you've got so little money to do it and still no professional credentials at all. Some stuff on the CV, but really it's so hard to get a decent CV, or a reel together from material shot at a film school.

If you've got very little to be paying out each month, which usually means rent, you should exploit that and get out there and make lots and lots of projects. Try working for different companies for free, get an insight into what they do, and if you don't like it, get out and find something else as quickly as you can! You will learn from all experiences, be they good or bad. And the more you move around, the broader your knowledge will be. Experience is the key.

Q - Given that so many independent short films are being made now, and even feature films, would you suggest that the cheapest film school to attend would be 'I will work on anybody else's films for free'?

Ray - I agree totally. When you pay to make your own movies, you have to invest so much, often everything you have. And no matter how much it is, it's amazing just how fast it gets spent - a little bit of make-up, a costume, film stock, camera hire etc. and then there's the unforeseen things like a clamping fee, a taxi home at midnight for a stranded crew member… It adds up so quickly. But if you are working on someone else's shoot, then you are gaining all that experience for nothing more than your time. Sometimes you may get expenses, sometimes you may even get paid.

Q - How valuable is the qualification that you get from film school?

Ray - I got a few letters after my name for my degree, which is nice, but I never use it. No-one is interested in your qualifications. Most people came out of my course with very little practical experience. They had a degree, sure, but where do you go with that? I find that some people have a prejudice against people that have gone through an educational system, like they have had a programme put in them. Sometimes they don't give them the job as they would rather have a fresh, new piece of clay to mold in their own design. Like a 19 year old runner who has more enthusiasm and is less jaded, and with less financial restraints. Some people look at you and say, *'No, you've got a degree!'*. I've done it, I've passed over people with degrees as I think they are over qualified!

Q - How should you approach making your first film?

Ray - I recommend you gather up whatever you have available to you and work your story around what you have - you've got to work backwards sometimes, especially when you are beginning, to keep it affordable. The more affordable you keep it, the further you can run with your story, because when you make your film, you are only a third of the way into it. You've got to market it, promote it and sell it, or at least get exposure for it. That takes a lot of money and people always underestimate that, putting every penny into making the film.

Q - This is a business of 'who you know' not so much 'what you know'. You can come out of film school, knowing lots, but no-one.

Ray - True, your contact book is the most important tool in your arsenal. Contacts are everything! If you don't fill that book out quick, you are going to flounder! You need to know what is going on, you can't just rely on the internet, film club meetings, or your friends. You need to be able to reach out. People are inherently lazy and they won't bother looking very hard, so if you are proactive and enthusiastic, you will be given breaks. But you won't get the break if people don't know you exist.

Q - What about financial hurdles, given that you are not rich, or mummy or daddy don't own 12 properties?

Ray - If you are not rich, the only way that you will get on, is to learn, and to get to a point where people will want to work with you. If you have knowledge and experience, then that is a valuable commodity in itself. Go out and learn, and specialise. Someone who can record sound, or is a great

Q - What kind of technical problems should filmmakers be aware of when making a first film, given they will probably be shooting digital?

Peter - *Make sure that your sound is good all the way through. I know that it is hard to find sound people who are experienced and affordable, but you could say the same thing about actors. You can see a movie that visually has some problems, maybe there can be some fixes or some re-shoots or you can cut around it, but if the sound is bad, nobody including critics, festival people, distributors, audiences will have the patience to deal with the movie. The sound recording quality on digital formats is very good, as long as the sound going in is good. Don't rely on the microphone on the front of the camera, get a good quality external microphone and someone to operate it.*

Peter Broderick
Film Consultant

Q - What advantages are there shooting digital?

Peter - *You can have a much higher shooting ratio which will help to get the right performance, coverage or shot. Lighting requirements are much more forgiving, crews can be smaller, set-ups can be faster, you have so much more freedom. You can take as long as you like. If you make your movie for $3k and it doesn't quite work out then you don't have to show it to anyone. Nowadays you can take your movie to a festival digitally so you don't have to pay for the cost of the transfer. If there's enthusiasm for a theatrical release then you can do the transfer. If not, you don't need a film print, you can still show it on TV, video, DVD, Internet etc. Video pushes the cost curve back, and with digital projection at festivals you can push it far enough*

back that completing your film should not be an insurmountable obstacle. Because the medium is so accessible, film makers will be prepared to take more risks practicing their craft and style, so we'll be in for more interesting films. Make your movie stand out. There are more and more no-budget independent films being made with the same amount of theatres. Your film can't be the same as the other 5,000 romantic comedies that are being made, you must have something distinctive to break through. Many film makers think that their chances of distribution will be better if they shoot on 35mm but it isn't so, it's the creativity in the movie, the uniqueness of the script. They should always focus on, no matter what they're shooting on, the script, direction and acting.

cameraman, or can write well - those things are really valuable commodities even from the start. Just because you are beginning, doesn't mean you don't have some of those skills inherently.

If you have a skill you can do a short gig, 3 or 4 intense weeks, then you can cruise for 2 months basically getting on with your own thing. On occasion I've dropped back to plastering whenever I've had holes in my career. It is so soul destroying and also erodes your confidence. If you are going to learn a skill to make money, make sure it is one that keeps you in the film making loop, be it on set, in the production office, or in the editing room. That's so important. The thing is, if you are out there working on a film, being involved in what you really love, there is always something to be gained, apart from a wage. There is always a way through if you have the dedication and stamina.

I've found people always want the back bone of a reel of your work to give them something to be confident in. If they haven't got that, they will always pick the other guy who has 3 or 4 really nice adverts on each reel, or 3 or 4 really nice promos. You've got to stick at one or the other, that's the one thing to decide earlier on, because if you want to make some money in a chosen area of the film business, you've got to stick with one initially, until you get really good at what you do. Then you have the luxury to try your hand at other stuff, and maybe cross over. But crossing from one discipline to another can be dangerous and damaging. People see you as neither here nor there, not committed to any particular speciality in film.

Q - In retrospect, if you could change one thing, instead of being an excellent plasterer, would you have become an excellent editor, or grip . . .?

Ray - Editor, grip, a sound recordist! There are people that I know who work on big films at the studios and I am always so envious, not just for the money, but just to be there, on set, around film making. Even though I have made several feature films, I am not yet able to spend all my time doing that as it doesn't pay my way in life.

Q - Given that whatever you choose, there is going to be a massive degree of obsession, what is the personal cost?

Ray - That's a big one! If you are a film-maker who is not making an awful lot of money, or if your career is not meteoric, if you get into debt, that can cause an amazing strain on any relationship. Often, everything in your life is about the film. The pressures can be enormous and you can become little more than a shadow in your partners life, and at the same time, you can end up hating the project itself. The strain of making it, especially with little or no money, can kill the very essence of both the story you want to tell and also your relationship. So be warned in that respect.

I destroyed my marriage of 9 years after putting so much money into my recent project, which still isn't finished - about £330k and two years of work. I've ostracised my wife, and that means I will see much less of my children, who will find it hard to understand the choices I made, and that I am not as present in their lives as I could be. In years to come maybe they will understand that Daddy's obsession with film making caused the break-up of a very strong and wonderful marriage.

Q - What advice would you offer a new film-maker?

Ray - Make films about what you know, but not about your friends. Develop skills, where you can gather a group of allies and work together. Be prepared for the long haul, because sometimes success doesn't come till very late in life. It hasn't come for me yet, and I am 20 years in and still optimistic. Things always go wrong and you can only prepare as best you can. Unfortunately, rejection is what you are going to get most. If you reject other people, be compassionate and caring as it can hurt - you will know that by then of course. Also, they may be a runner today but in a few years time they may be an executive on a production that is deciding whether to employ you or not, it can happen that quickly with some people.

* Note - as of going to press, Ray has managed to complete his movie, and by the time you read this, it may well be in the shops.

Roger Crittenden
NFTS

THE NATIONAL FILM SCHOOL

Q - What is your job?

Roger - I am the Director of the full time programme at The National Film and Television school.

Q - What kind of person wants to be a filmmaker and may be interested in film school?

Roger - At this school we train in at least 10 different areas. The motivation for being a designer for instance, is very different from being a producer, director or animator. I think the motivation can vary from thinking it is a glamorous profession to having something to say about contemporary society and to reach an audience.

Q - What advice would you offer someone who is in no way connected to the film business and who is from a cultural background where film is something that is not considered a possibility? How should they start on the journey to becoming a film maker?

Roger - Get your hands on some equipment and start making films. The technology is everywhere now, and it can produce excellent quality work. Watch as many films as you can, and films from diverse cultures and film makers. Often ambitions are formed at school and I think it is important to pursue a broad cultural education, both within education and in life. Developing an understanding of the way images work, the way sound works, the way storytelling works, is paramount. That is not just about knowing or being fanatical about a few movies. It is about appreciating storytelling traditions and the way people are moved by stories, about the way images can encapsulate moments that are special for all of us, in our daily lives. It is essential. Going from that point of having a general cultural understanding of story telling, to become a filmmaker is partly about getting your hands on some equipment and making something. In that way you can consider if your development as a filmmaker might be helped by going through some kind of course. I wouldn't want to be prescriptive about the kind of course people need, because their attitude, and where they are heading will inform an intelligent decision about whether they can afford to get that education if they need it.

Q - What do you think someone should do before they even think about film school?

Roger - The thing I find the most puzzling is that there are exciting careers in our business, which they can be just as passionate about, in areas that too few youngsters seem to understand. For instance, sound post production is a wonderful area where they can get their hands on that equipment, and contribute to interesting movies. It is finding ways of understanding the way different areas contribute to making good movies. It is very important, even if you end up still wanting to be the director, that you have an understanding of sound, as well as all the other disciplines in the film making process. It helps you focus on what kind of film maker you might be, but also helps make that decision about specifically what area you should pursue, whether it is directing or not.

Q - Most film school graduates have a bad word to say about whatever establishment they have been to. I used to do that too, but I've come to realise that my film school experience was more important than I gave it credit for. Not just because of the education, but because of the students I mixed with. One of the most extraordinary things is you get to be with a bunch of like-minded people, 24/7. Do you have any comments about the community of the film school, which can ignite higher passion, higher goals, higher achievement?

Roger - One of the things that people ask is *'what is the best and worst thing about this film school?'* It is almost the same thing because we encourage collaboration. All the people that make the film are students here (smaller roles such as runners and the actors are generally not from the school). However, because you are a microcosm, the peer group is limited and there is always a risk that those collaborations are difficult, and maybe not be the people who would naturally find common ground in the work place. But often, that very diversity is also a creative stimulant and catalyst for new ideas. Within any institution, if you label people too soon, then those people are seen by their peer group as being, for instance, the person *'who is going to record my sound'*, rather than someone who might have a greater contribution. That is a problem to be aware of.

Q - Do you think that in terms of exposure to other filmmaker's work, that students personal passions and ideas can help each other broaden as artists?

Roger - I think that is true. We now have more applications from Europe than we used to, and we are interested in making sure some of those come because of who they are, where they come from and the films they have been exposed to. That way, the level of creative stimulation within the peer group is far more effective. When Polanski was asked about what he got from the Lodz Film School, which is now a mythic film school, his answer was that there was this big staircase in the main building and *'I just remember we saw films day and night and sat on the stairs talking about them'*. I feel that what the tutors are here for, among other things, is to make sure that happens - to set it off and hope it ignites, and that the passions amongst the students create a grand slam of enthusiasm.

Q - How are the courses structured here?

Roger - It is now a 2 year MA in the 10 different areas of film and TV, everything from writing through to composing music. There is a curriculum which addresses the specialist needs of the area to which the student has signed up. There are 3 direction disciplines, fiction, documentary and animation, and there are signs that the edges are becoming more blurred, which I think is a good thing. Animation is often using live action, documentary is using dramatic reconstruction, and fiction is using techniques beyond realistic or naturalistic drama (check website for exact details www.nftsfilm-tv.ac.uk).

Q - There is always a debate over how much can be taught and how much is imprinted in your genes? Do you have any comments on that equation?

Roger - There is a whole lot of subtext in that question. The word education means *'to lead out'*. I don't think there is any point, certainly at a post-graduate level, imagining that you can force feed people with a kind of knowledge and understanding which isn't actually any use. You have to meet the student halfway rather than either waiting for them to want the information or indeed forcing it into them. That is often a difficult balance. Even the passionate student has to be provoked. As we just discussed, yes do look at a Robert Bresson film, it is not that you want to make a Robert Bresson film, but if you look at them, something might feed back into your own filmmaking. It is not about just sitting in front of a film and saying *'Ok, surprise me! Why are you supposed to be so wonderful?'* It is about making yourself available for that experience so it can inform in some way, subconsciously or however, the growth of you as the filmmaker. So what can be taught? For us, it is more about being a partner in the learning. That is what a good tutor is. The sooner you can get the student to the point of them knowing what they need to know, the more they become an active participant in their own education. I think that is essential.

National
Film ✛
Television
School

Roger Crittenden
Director, Full-Time Programme

Phone: 01494 671234
Fax: 01494 674042

E-mail rcrittenden@nftsfilm-tv.ac.uk
Web www.nftsfilm-tv.ac.uk

National Film and Television School
Beaconsfield Studios, Station Road
Beaconsfield, Bucks HP9 1LG, UK

We always talk about passion, almost obsession. There is almost a requirement of a certain kind of madness, which goes beyond passion and obsession, in a sense, because if people understand the odds of making it, they may never start out. I try to encourage students to be passionate, without it becoming obsessive. An obsession takes you away from connecting with life, which in turn feeds into your filmmaking. Often you can see in the path of filmmakers who become megalomanic - their films somehow don't connect and they lose their audience because somehow we can't connect. It is important to have that kind of perspective.

Q - Do you think a film school education puts you in good standing for getting a job in the business?

If film school is out of reach...

GUERILLA FILM MAKER SAYS!

1. Look around. Local courses will have equipment and facilities. All you need to do is get unreasonable, charming and ask and get access to it. You may find you have all the kit you need.

2. Create your own film school experiences by just going out there and doing it. Use local press to get local people interested and try to form a group. Self organise. The people with the kit in local courses will also help and get into what you are doing.

3. No matter where you live, someone local will be a successful film maker of sorts. Ask if you can mentor yourself to them, or if they would criticise your work and guide your career. Most people would be delighted if you make the right approach.

4. Do short courses, but... negotiate the fee down and try and get a sponsor. Try not to spend your own, or your families money unless you can afford it. If you are unemployed, see if you can get help there. Even if you just do a local course on how to develop web pages, it will keep you motivated.

5. If you do chose to do some short courses, do one then make a film, then do another and make another film. Never just do courses one after another. Nothing is like actually doing it, then having the chance to reflect.

6. Keep applying to film schools and ask for a bursary or seek local sponsorship.

7. Recognise that this challenge may well be the first of many hurdles. If you want to go to film school but are not determined to find a way to get in, no matter how, film making is probably not for you. How you pass this test may well be an indicator of how your career may pan out. Don't give up. Ever.

Roger - The simplest answer would be to say *'Yes!'* A good film school has its own network, and relationships with the industry and can put students in touch and actually get you through certain doors, which you might otherwise have to work very hard at getting through. I've always thought that if someone has got talent and is able to develop sufficiently through a good course, then they are likely to get to make something. Do the people who come out of film school get to do what they would like to do, rather than perhaps get a job on something else? Often our documentary students, who largely make their own independent films based on their own ideas, usually end up doing work in areas where the brief is a given one, and they deliver and the Executive Producer is the person who cuts the stuff. They have to live through that and still hope to get to the point of making their own movies.

Q - Do you think film school helps in long term career planning? Often, people are all about the 'now' and 'next week' and not about the next 5 years?

Roger - You mustn't sabotage people's passion and enthusiasm by saying *'you ought to have a long term plan'*. Just keep in mind the fact that it is a lifetime's journey - if you can make the films that Renoir made in his '80's, that would be wonderful.

Q - How much does it cost to go to film school?

Roger - Post graduate fees here, which are comparable to other schools, is £4.2k a year for Brits and £15k for overseas students. The American schools charge a lot in comparison and you are often talking about $50k a year. Australia is up there with them.

Q - How do you feel about some of the short courses that are popping up? Why come and do 2 years here, when you can learn it all in one weekend?

Roger - Some of the short courses are good value and the people who are running them are genuine, and attempt to supply a decent service. Others are more opportunistic and I think people have to look very carefully at not just the headline, but what it is and who is doing it. It is important that people do their research about who the actual tutors are, because you can read a course website and names will be mentioned as being part of the organisation, but they may well never tutor.

Q - Often new filmmakers work with what is comfortable. Their own camcorder, their friends as actors etc. Many new film makers will begin there, and that is appropriate, but they should progress and aspire to greater things - better cast, better equipment, better crew etc., even in amateur or student films. This is most apparent in casting, would you agree?

Q - What is the Metropolitan Film School?

Luke - It's an establishment for aspiring filmmakers - for the most part writers and directors, to have the opportunity to make films, learn skills relating to the craft areas of filmmaking. Equally important though is to learn how to be a professional so you have a good platform to enter the industry. It is of paramount importance that they are prepared and realistic about their opportunities afterwards, and for most people, that means entering as an assistant or in a runner position.

Q - How does what you offer differ from more traditional, longer-term traditional courses?

Luke - I think the first thing is that you get to work on many more films and spend more time in production. In traditional institutions, you spend something like 30% of your time with the tutors, and in our case it is more like 80% the time. We expect that you will turn up every day, and on a typical day, spend eight hours working – there is some sitting in classes and listening to seminars, but for the most part it is engaged in practical filmmaking exercises and filmmaking itself. The other key part is getting you into a job afterwards. Traditionally, film schools have been places where you can learn your craft, but not necessarily be prepared for the reality of the first position you are going to hold. If you want to get into this industry, you have to get a toe in the door and then you can prove yourself with all the skills that you have learned.

Q - What are the advantages of a one-year course over a longer-term program?

Luke - We can condense a great deal into a year. You spend a lot more contact time with instructors and professionals making films and doing exercises. And you are going to learn more quickly doing that. There is no doubt about that. The second part is that we have built our courses around digital technologies. That is not to say that is the only way we think films can be made - of course it's not. But what it does mean is that if we have for example an exercise in sound design or editing, all of these things can be filmed in the morning, edited after lunch, and discussed in the late afternoon. And we have found that compresses the time you would traditionally have to take to achieve the same level of learning.

Q - What should new filmmakers be doing before they apply to film school?

Luke - They need to be realistic with themselves about what they wish to achieve at the film school and what they want to do afterwards. There are a great many people who have a dream to be the next great writer, director or cinematographer, and of course within that large number some will make it, but many will not. That doesn't really matter if they are committed as there are many positions within the industry that they would find rewarding and enjoyable that aren't necessarily the person leading from the front. There are a lot of successful writers, producers and

Luke Montagu
Metropolitan Film School

directors who started off in other roles and ultimately moved over. We get a lot of people who think they are going to come out and make a feature, but that just isn't the norm.

Q - When taking this or any other course, how can a filmmaker get the most out of it?

Luke - I think they need to treat the course as if it is a job. They need to treat it with the same level or respect and commit to it and expect others to commit to them. Film making requires complete and utter commitment all the way through. You also need to spend a lot of time engaging with the people in the course and making films. One of the things they should ask themselves is if they are a writer / director. I think a lot of people entering film school see themselves as a traditional auteur and the reality is that they get in and they understand the complexity and pre-eminence of story, but the reality they discover is that it is a strength they have, or it is not. And it is absolutely fine if it isn't. They just need to realise it might be better to take on other peoples' scripts and stories and become successful directors. At this stage, the industry has changed. On the one hand, they have to be very realistic about what the industry has to offer, and on the other, we are entering a period where, for people with a rounded set of skills, it is easier and less expensive to get a feature film off the ground at reasonable production values. They need to make sure that they don't just focus on two or three key areas, but have a well rounded knowledge, or at least work closely with people who can fill in the gaps.

Q - What are the common mistakes that you see?

Luke - Alexander McKendrick who worked here at Ealing Film Studios said that student films come in three varieties: very much too long, much too long and too long. What we see with students is that they become too wedded to their script and what they shot and they find it very difficult to let any of it go in the edit. Practice as much as you can. Make films. Write. But recognise that while many people will encourage you to think that it can be learned on the job, there is a lot more that can be learned quickly if you do it in a structured way and if you learn by working with professionals who have done it before - either in a film school or as part of your team.

Roger - Yes. Go for the higher calibre of actor and don't be nervous of it. Don't feel that you are not going to be able to direct that person, as you'll be surprised how generous most of these people are when it comes to collaboration. Often the bigger the name, the more generous. What helps with that is going through acting classes yourself. However painful, every Director should experience it, it just tells you so much about what it feels like to be in front of the camera. Then your own approach to actors will be well informed.

Q - What common mistakes do you see from new filmmakers? Possibly applicants, but not necessarily.

Roger - I do think there are certain kinds of young filmmakers / student genres that it would be good to avoid. To give an example, *'the getting up in the morning film'.* I really hoped we had consigned this one to the bin, but this year there must have been at least 30! Of course some of them do go somewhere, but when you see someone lying in bed, and the frame includes an alarm clock, it is a real turn-off! Try to avoid the student / young filmmakers clichés. The other thing that worries me is that people adopt what is not only a conventional language, but is almost the *'tailored conventional language'*, as if that is the exclusive language of filmmaking, and that is based on whatever they have seen. For example, the two shot, and matching singles, that kind of unexpressive film making. It is far more interesting to see someone who has tried to do something beyond that. The conventional approach to film making has in some ways messed their heads up in terms of what they might do with cinema. It is being alive and aware of what is possible. It is not about experimental films, it is not about what we call Art-house cinema - for example, it is about the family conversation at the beginning of *E.T.* It is beautifully observed, where the camera is placed, the way that the mother and the kids relate to each other before Elliot goes out to the garden. It is extraordinarily handled. It gives you a sense of who these people are, in a beautiful way. Obviously the script works, but it is not 2-shot and matching singles, which would in a way, reduce the potential of the medium. I suppose that is the trap, because it is so comfortable. You have got your safety net because you know if you shoot both, you've got something to cut together, but of course you have only got that. It is already reducing the potential for yourself.

Q - There are always film maker war stories about how many hours and days they worked without sleep and food, so they are clearly very hard working. But often there is still a laziness of idea, they will just write a script, go shoot it, and assume it is going to be as good as Jaws. Is that something that you see a lot of in the student admission films?

Roger - Yes. Often people think that by you just turning up on the day and filming, that the translation to the screen isn't that important as long as the script is good. But of course you and I know how the importance of the director - give a decent Director and as a lesser Director the same material and you will have two very different results. Thinking through the way the images will tell the story is often underestimated. It is almost as if people will write something decent and can't wait to put it together. Some great Directors admit that they find the shooting process boring, but they still know what they are doing, and don't treat it as insignificant.

Q - What advice would you offer a new filmmaker?

Roger - Nothing that you do should be mechanical. Renoir said *'leave a door open on the set, because you never know what might come in'.* If you and I had a conversation about the movies that we remember, they will often be defined by the great moments in those movies, the moments that we remember them by. That is what the audience takes away. If you ask somebody about movies, they will always have a scene or even a moment that they refer to which has been a culmination of the magic of the medium.

Q - That is a great point and so few film makers talk about it. Any other tips?

Roger - It is not just about filmmaking, but it applies so strongly to filmmaking because of the way people are when they make films. Always take the work seriously, but never take yourself seriously. It sounds so banal, but if you don't understand this, it will probably trap you or trip you up. As soon as you think you are more important than the film, you lose sight of what you might achieve. Rudolf Nureyev, the dancer, said he was a conduit for the artistry, it wasn't him, but it came through him. That is what a great filmmaker is. He / she is actually an agent for something special, but it is beyond you. In the end you are an agent, you are producing something that is going to be an interesting, exciting and entertaining experience for others. It is not you.

Q - That is another important distinction You are not your work. Unless you know that you are always headed for an upset.

Roger - It comes back to what we touched on earlier, never underestimate what your collaborators can give you. Be open to it.

Top Film Schools, in no particular order

GUERILLA FILM MAKER SAYS!

In the UK...

National Film and Television School
Beaconsfield Studios, Station Road,
Beaconsfield, Bucks HP9 1LG
Admissions: 01494 731425 / 731413
Switchboard: 01494 671234
Web: www.nftsfilm-tv.ac.uk
Email: admin@nftsfilm-tv.ac.uk

Bournemouth University
Fern Barrow, Poole, Dorset
BH12 5BB
Tel: +44 (0)1202 524111
Web: www.bournemouth.ac.uk
enquiries@bournemouth.ac.uk

**Bristol University of Bristol, Department
of Drama, Theatre, Film & Television,**
Cantocks Close ,Bristol, BS8 1UP
Tel: +44 (0)117 9545481
http://www.bristol.ac.uk/drama/

St. Martins
London Animation Studio
2-6 Catton Street, Holborn, London
WC1R 4AA
Tel: 0207 5147373
Web: www.nfcs-createc.org.uk/las
Email: las@csm.linst.ac.uk

**London College of Communication
School of Media**
Elephant & Castle, London SE1 6SB
Tel: +44 (0)20 7514 6853
Web: www.lcc.arts.ac.uk
Email: media@lcc.arts.ac.uk

**University of Westminster
The School of Media, Arts and Design**
Watford Rd, Northwick Park,
Harrow, Middlesex HA1 3TP
Tel : 020 7911 5944
Web: www.wmin.ac.uk
Email: mad@wmin.ac.uk

University of Wales,
Newport, Caerleon Campus, PO Box 101
Newport , Wales, NP18 3YG
Tel: +44 (0) 1633 432432
Email: uic@newport.ac.uk
Web: artschool.newport.ac.uk

Napier University
Craiglockhart Campus, Edinburgh
EH14 1DJ
Tel: 0500 35 35 70
www.napier.ac.uk

Leeds Metropolitan University
Civic Quarter, Leeds, LS1 3HE
Tel: 0113 283 8000
Web: www.leedsmet.ac.uk
Email: s.golay@leedsmet.ac.uk

Northern Media School
Psalter Lane Campus, Psalter Lane
Sheffield, S11 8UZ
E-mail: chris.dawson@shu.ac.uk
Tel: 0114 225 4648
Web: www.shu.ac.uk

In Europe...

Femis
6, rue Francoeur, 75018 Paris - France
Tel: 33 (0) 1 53 41 21 00
www.lafemis.fr

**Berlin - Deutsche Film- &
Fernsehakademie Berlin GmbH (dffb)**
Erica Margoni
German Film & Television Academy (dffb)
Potsdamer Strasse 2
10785 Berlin/Germany
Tel: +49-30-25 75 91 52
Web: www.dffb.de
Email margoni@dffb.de

**Munich - Academy of Television & Film
Munich (HFF/M)**
Frankenthalerstrasse 23
81539 Munich/Germany
Tel: +49-89-68 95 73 33
Web: www.hff-muc.de
Email: margot.freissinger@hff-muc.de

**University of Art and Design Helsinki
School of Motion Picture, Television and
Production Design**
Hämeentie 135 C, 00560 Helsinki
Tel. +358 9 756 31
Web: www.uiah.fi/eto

**The Norweigian Film School
Den norske filmskolen**
Hogskolen i Lillehammer, Serviceboks
2626 Lillehammer, Norway
Tel.: 61 28 74 68
E-mail: filmskolen@hil.no

**Stockholm Dramatiska institutet
University College of Film, Radio,
Television and Theatre**
P.O Box 27090, 102 51 Stockholm, Sweden
Tel: +46 8 55 57 20 00
Email: kansli@draminst.se

**The National Film School of Denmark
Den Danske Filmskolen**
Theodor Christensens Plads 1,
Copenhagen K, 1437, Denmark
Tel: 00 45 32 68 64 00
Email: info@filmskolen.dk
Web: www.filmskolen.dk

**Brussells - Narafi (Hogeshool voor
wetenschap & kunst)**
Victor Rousseaulaan, 75,
Brussels, Belgium 1109
Tel. +32 23401020
Email. info@narafi.wenk.be
Web Site. www.narafi.be

Prague - CFE Film School
The Prague Center for Further Education
Karmelitska 18, Prague 1, 118 00
Czech Republic
Tel. +420 257534013 / 4014
Web: www.prague-center.cz/film.htm
Email: info@filmstudies.cz

**Lodz - The Polish National Film,
Television and Theatre School**
63 Targowa St., 90-323 ŁódŸ, Poland
Tel: 48-42 / 6345 820
Email: swzfilm@filmschool.lodz.pl
Web: www.filmschool.lodz.pl

Elliot Grove
Raindance

RAINDANCE

Q - What is Raindance?

Elliot - The organisation started in '92. Briefly, we do several things - training courses, a monthly magazine, the Raindance Film Festival, the British Independent Film Awards (BIFA), and this year we intend to branch out into our own production and distribution company.

Q - What happens on your courses?

Elliot - The courses are all run by instructors who are working industry professionals. We provide fresh, cutting edge information, the kind of information new film makers need, and tech craftsmanship too. The thing we notice on our courses is that many people are uninformed about all aspects of film making, be it production, editing, but especially screen writing. I think that the traditional film school route is woefully inadequate. They should be imprisoned for some of the things they teach in film school about writing and directing, because they get it so totally wrong. And if imitation is the sincerest form of flattery, then I am very flattered by the hosts of imitators out there. Raindance training courses, are, I am pleased to say, the original, and still the best. Often, the course attendees want to write, they are finishing their screenplay or they want to make a movie, and it is the same three reasons regardless of age or level they are at. First reason is they lack confidence to actually go and do it, and you know yourself having done it, it is pretty scary - you go, *'Oh my God I should have taken that job at Sainsbury's to stack shelves'*. The second reason is they self-destruct, everyone has their own pet method of self destructing. The third reason, my personal favourite, is procrastination. *'I will take this course then finish it, I will see that movie then finish it, Christmas is coming and then I will finish it'*. And they never do.

Q - And the British Independent Film Awards?

Elliot - The British Independent Film Awards were started in 1998 to recognise and honour British film and filmmakers. The event somehow seems to grow year by year, and we have a television production agreement just signed with Celador. Despite the critical success of BIFA, it is still a struggle to make ends meet financially, and people like Johanna Von Fischer and Deena Manley who work on the awards are paid a derisory amount. So we have just started a charity, the Independent Film Trust, to raise money for BIFA, and the festival. I hope to be able to make charitable donations for script development in the future as well.

Q - Tell me about the Raindance Film Festival?

Elliot - The Raindance Film Festival is now, I guess, the oldest continuously running independent film festival. The festival has grown in stature as the quality of its content keeps improving year after year. Last year we received over 2,000 submissions, and screened 60 features, 10 feature docs and about 175 short films. Our major sponsor is UGC Cinemas who have been enormously supportive. Our admissions rocketed 43% last year, due in part to their generous support. We also toured the Nokia 15 second films which we called the Worlds Shortest Film Festival through UGC.

Q - One of the things that I think is interesting is that once you put your film on a screen and an audience puts their butt on a seat it is a level playing field because they are just responding to a story, and Raindance is probably the only event in the UK where you can get your movie shown?

Elliot - Not all films submitted get into Raindance, but yes, once you get inside the cinema, even if your movie is gritty and cost £5.00, as long as it is a great story well told, you will get the audience. Raindance screens features, shorts and documentaries that are sourced from all over the world, but a high proportion of those shown are by first time British directors.

Q - As you see hundreds of new film makers movies, what general criticism would you give?

Elliot - They don't tell a story. It all comes down to a shitty script. If you want to make your first movie and break in and you want to achieve notoriety and celebrity status, then you need a great script. If you have that great screenplay, you probably won't make it with your own money, so it won't be low budget, and you will get a higher budget to make it. The minute your budget goes up you bring in all these people who interfere with the creative process, and you may even get fired. So do you make the film you want to make for less, or do you take the money and go through the hell of compromise and possibly even get fired? It's a huge paradox. And don't copy anybody - I can't tell you how many Tarantino movies I have looked at over the years, you just throw them out.

Q - And from a technical view point?

Elliot – Don't put credits on the front end, put the title but little else, it's boring. Most people put far too many credits at the front, making it far too long, just put them all at the end. Shoot in colour, you will devalue your film by 90% if you shoot in black and white. There are several first time movies in b&w, I love them, but they can't be sold because when people buy the film they want to see colour. I hear it from acquisitions executives or sales agents all the time, *'Oh, my God, it is black and white, I can't put this on TV'.* Seriously, people phone up the BBC and say that they have paid their licence fee for colour. If you send a film into us, give us a press kit. Get great stills, fantastic ones, because I am sending them out to all the newspapers. Get Beta clips of the trailer, not the whole movie, make sure that the Beta clips are at the most two minutes long, 45-60 seconds is best, and make sure that everything in those clips are cleared for TV broadcast because I might put it out on TV. On your VHS/DVD submission, put the trailer at the head. Tapes will go out for review and sometimes journalists will read the press kit, look at the trailer, fast forward half way through the movie, and base what they write on that. It's brutal but unfortunately journalists may have 30 tapes to watch in a day.

Q - Interestingly, few people ever want to sell a movie, everyone wants to write, produce or direct?

Elliot - I am Canadian and I can sit on both sides of the pond. The difference between European and American film industries is that in Europe they divide the film making process into three, financing and script development, the actual production of the movie, and then the marketing and sale of the movie. In America you make the movie and then sell the movie, and not necessarily in that order. Often you sell the movie and then make it, so at all times during the process they are aware of the sale, and film makers educate themselves as to what distributors and sales agents want, and then supply that demand. The biggest mistake I have experienced is that most film makers want millions of people to see their film which is totally wrong. The only people that you want to see your film are the acquisitions executives and there are only about 50-100 in the world that would be right for your film. You need to work out how to tantalise them, tease them so that they go absolutely mental. Once you learn how that game is played then you are going to be much better off. This is the basic reason why *Blair Witch* succeeded, they drove everybody nuts. By the time the acquisitions people saw the movie even though, let's face it, it was not a great movie, a great first movie maybe, but not great movie, they still wanted it. When they were making their movie they were thinking of the 50-100 people who could buy it, and then marketed the movie to them. Film making is so often about savvy. How do you teach savvy? You can't, it just sort of filters through you, which is why we push the networking thing, you sort of figure it out and get better with practice.

Q - What advice would you offer a new film maker?

Elliot - Find a great script. If you don't have a great script you are fucked. You can turn a great script into a bad movie, but you cannot turn a bad script into a great movie. So you find a great script, get a little bit of money, you don't need a lot especially with DV / HD, you shoot a feature, edit on a computer, you can make it for £5k, possibly less. You need to develop excellent interpersonal relationship skills, for pitching, building rapport with investors and talent. You need to develop the ability to be very firm, learn to say no. You also need boundless energy, which keeps you going through your lack of confidence, and you have to just bash through this concrete wall. The formula that seems to work in launching American film makers is that they get a stage play, and shoot it as if it is a movie in a single location. Take this kind of material and shoot it like cinema – that's what they call talent in the industry, then you can step up and start making movies with serious money and your career is launched. I mean look at *Blair Witch*, it was three actors, some trees and the amount of money you would need to buy a London Cab. That was all they needed.

Elliot Grove
Director

British Independent Film Awards
81 Berwick Street
London W1F 8TW

T +44 (0)20 7287 3833
F +44 (0)20 7439 2243

elliot@raindance.co.uk
www.raindance.co.uk

THE BRITISH
INDEPENDENT
FILM AWARDS

David Castro
NPA

Q - What is the NPA?

David - The NPA is a charitable organisation, a membership organisation, set up 13 years ago by a number of filmmakers who were not happy with the way things were going, and needed and wanted access to higher levels of production access, finance and the ability to help themselves and actually make movies. It has moved on from there where we now have an average of 800 members. We run roughly 65 events per year, most of which are free to membership. We cover all aspects of production, not just from the producing point of view, but from the triangle, which is the essential building block of any film - that is the Director, Producer and Writer. The core relationship with those people and the project is going to say whether it moves forward or not. The key relationships are also built on passion, and the one thing we do is support, nurture, train and warn people of how they can actually translate their passion into the actual production.

You can join online (www.npa.org.uk) and the membership fee is currently £75 PA, for which you get a whole load of freebies, which includes a monthly newsletter, weekly news-ezine, which gives you breaking news about what is happening in the industry. Festivals deadlines, sources of finance, new information about tax schemes that are happening or who is doing what there. The newsletter has the same kind of information, also articles from key industry figures, including Sales Agents, Distributors, Financiers, you name it. One of the biggest things that we do is we promote filmmakers themselves. Because it is all very well trying to make a film, but once you've made a film you need to promote yourself and your project. The ezine goes out to 2,500 people. The newsletter goes out to about 1,000 people, which includes industry. We are actively in support of promoting filmmakers, one of the key things about the NPA is that it is run by filmmakers, for filmmakers. So we give them the information so that they can actually help themselves. Apart from that we do core training which lasts 9 months, where we have key industry panellists, once a month, talking about every aspect that you need to know about the industry. We only use key industry people who are very kind and give their time for free in order to impart the knowledge.

Q - Most new film makers start out on their own - what do the NPA offer in terms of community?

David - The NPA is also a community and networking is at the core of everything. There are various forms of networking, with peer to peer, so we enable you to meet other people who are in exactly the same position as you are, with limited resources, sometimes limited knowledge and loads of passion. Whether you are a Writer, Director or Producer, in order that you can form relationships and then move on from there. Or facilitate direct one to ones with the industry, either through the networking, or through specific masterclasses, business breakfasts, and all of those kind of things. It is incredibly important that people get together and talk amongst themselves in an informed way, and also be informed about where the various different tranches of money are.

If you are on your own, it is difficult. Why not collaborate with people? If you look at the existing companies that have been working a number of years, they are all built on the same thing which is a team, whether it is in America, Europe or here. You need to find creative collaborators, that are not just talented, but people you can actually communicate with, who talk on the same level. Unless you find those people, you are going to find it very difficult to actually make a movie and sell it, and then do it again. You will be working with different people all the time, which again does not help longevity in terms of your company business, and certainly doesn't help your credibility in terms of how the industry perceives you.

Q - If you don't get into film school, or you can't afford film school, the NPA is a great place to start for just £75.

David - We get a lot of people who come out of film school, because the gap between coming out of film school and the reality of the ever-changing industry is so vast that it feels like a black hole. What we do is provide a bridge between that void and the industry. Virtually all of the training events we do are in the evening because we know you are going to have a job to pay the gas bill. You could easily spend £75 going to a particular festival, but unless you have the knowledge of why you are going there in the first place, what are you actually selling, is the package that you are putting together any good at all, is it professional, is it what the industry wants? You need to know this information before you go. If you want to go to a film festival and have a blast, then go and spend your £75, but don't think in any shape or form that you are going to get anything out of it other than having a good time, getting sore feet and waking up in strange beds, or a strange beach! That will happen, and if you are going to do that, then best of luck to you. The point is if you want to work professionally in the industry there are certain expectations from the industry itself, which is that you are informed, and that you do have a working, up to date knowledge of who is doing what, who is where in the industry? Certainly for what you get from us, £75 is value for money.

The NPA is a completely open access organisation. We have no bars to colour, ethnicity, gender, sexuality, any shape or form. What we are interested in is helping people with creative talent, who want to make films, to actually make their films in a professional and practical way, that they will then go on to make more and more films. Whether you want to define it as an art-house film, or as an independent film, or as a mainstream film, whatever, you must be looking at how professionally you can keep going, and hopefully become, as soon as possible, a full-time filmmaker. One of the things we are very keen on is the 9-point plan that starts in September of every year, and leads to people going to Cannes. Kodak support us in terms of we produce a Cannes Guide, an actual physical book, which is if you have never been there before, what to expect. We run a *'Cannes do'* panel event, which are people who have been there a number of times talking to you realistically about what you should be preparing for, before you go, in terms of packaging, marketing, what kind of letters of intent you need from those people you say you have got on board. Where you want to go, the whole professional aspect of that is incredibly important, because when you get to Cannes you hit the ground-running and you will be worked off your feet, if you want to be.

Q - What are the common mistakes you see filmmakers make?

David - They tend to fall into a number of separate categories, but boil down to just not being informed. If you go looking for information, if you ask for it in the right way, the industry is incredibly generous with their time. Your film is like building a house. Unless you know a little bit about every aspect of building a house, it will fall down, or it will be burgled, or you won't have a roof, or you won't be able to sell it, or the electrics will spark out etc. What we try and do is show people, in a very easy way, bit by bit, how to actually build the blocks of your film. The other way to look at it is like chocolate bars. What we kind of say is *'right, you've got a project, you've got an idea, it is just another chocolate bar, what makes it unique?'* Is it unique because it has never been done before, because of the actors you are using, because of the script, location, the genre, it can be anything, but you've got to decide. Then you have got to check it out, as to whether other people in the industry actually feel this does fit, or could fit, in a marketable place, within the industry. You need to find your core audience, it doesn't matter how niche the film is, it really doesn't matter, there is an audience, but you need to find it. You need to establish your audience from a very early stage. It doesn't matter if it is a huge chocolate bar, with lots of sprinkles on, you need to check out where your market is. Otherwise you are going to be putting a lot of time and effort in, and not get those sales, not get recognition. You are not going to win festivals, you are not going to get anything from all that time you have spent on it.

Q - What advice would you offer a new filmmaker?

David - Rather than hearing *'no'*, hear *'not now, not yet'*. If you take those *'no's'* as a negative, you will get dragged down and disillusioned by it. The point is, professionalise your passion, as one day it might be a *'yes'*. Somebody you met 2 years ago may call and say *'have you still got that project going on?'*, or you will meet them at a festival and go *'how is X, Y and Z going?'* Unless you have met them in the first place, you will never know. Get out there and meet people. Be professional. Be passionate.

Q - What is Skillset?

Skillset - Skillset is the Sector Skills Council for the Audio Visual Industries and has been mandated by government to address skills issues, in order to increase the productivity and competitiveness of the audio visual sector. Skillset Careers offers careers information, advice and guidance to both new entrants and experienced freelancers - its services include careers info on its webpages, an email service and free careers helplines. For those who need more in-depth careers guidance, there is a face-to-face guidance service with industry practitioners who've been trained to deliver careers advice and guidance. These guidance sessions are available to over 18 year olds who aren't still in full-time education, have either a media-related degree or other qualification, or at least 1 year's professional working experience in the audio visual industry. The one-to-one guidance sessions cost £30 for an hour-long session for clients with less than 2 years' experience, or £60 for an hour and half long session for freelancers with more than 2 years' experience. (for discounts, please see our website: www.skillset.org/careers)

Q - Who can you help?

Skillset - New entrants, experienced freelancers and careers advisors. Skillset Careers Advisors can help experienced freelance practitioners at times when work is lean, those who have been made redundant and are forced into the competitive world of freelancing, and we also offer new entrants, straight out of college or university with little or no industry experience, help to focus their career objectives in a methodical way. In addition, we run workshops on careers in our sector for careers advisors from publicly-funded careers agencies, so that we help them to answer more confidently their clients' queries on the audio visual industries and signpost where they can find the information they need. You can phone the free Skillset Careers helplines: 08080 300 900 in England and 0808 100 8094 in Scotland to talk to a careers advisor who receives regular training on our sector, log onto our website to email an advisor with a specific careers query or look at the careers pages for industry info. For example, the different job roles in our industry and what skills and personal qualities are required in order to succeed in them, case studies, hints and tips on how to get on etc. For a one-to-one session you need to be over 18 and have completed a course relevant to the audio visual sector and/or have some industry experience, in order to demonstrate your commitment to a career in our sector. If you fit these criteria, fill out an application form (downloadable from the website), return it to us and we'll match you with the freelance careers advisor whose industry experience most closely matches your aspirations, get back to you to set up a date and time for the session and then you come in, see the advisor (who has done some homework, based on the info on your application form) and during the course of the session, the advisor helps you to work out an 'action plan'. The great thing about the face-to-face contact is that you meet people who work in the industry in various Film/TV/Radio/Games grades, who can be insightful and pass on their working knowledge in a structured way and offer current industry news and information.

Skillset
www.skillset.org

Q - What is your view on emerging digital film makers?

Skillset - The more accessible the medium, the greater the variety of world views, life experience and story telling methods. This means that films have the ability to relate to a much broader audience. The lower cost means that there can be greater risks taken with talent and subject matter. The two factors mean that emerging digital filmmakers can work in an environment that allows them to express themselves in a highly individual way. The only downside is that filmmakers might allow themselves to become less disciplined during the film making process, less responsive to their audience and more self-indulgent, due to the relatively low-cost and practical ease of the medium. There should be room for experienced film-makers bringing their knowledge into the digital area too. It's important that people working in the industry keep their skills up-to-date and undertake training where necessary to make sure that they're confident and competent at using new technology.

Q - What common mistaken preconceptions do you see from people wanting to enter the film/TV industry?

Skillset - The common misconception is that you can enter the industry, straight out of University and start 'making films' instead of learning a 'trade' in the industry and working up to film-making. Graduates often don't seem to be aware of the realistic route to making films, and also the various roles and grades in the industry. Some new entrants limit themselves by believing that there is only one route to their desired goal. The nature of employment in the industry means that there is a constant flow of people moving from one grade to another and from one department to another. This means that there are opportunities for new entrants, but they may be in an area of film making that they hadn't originally considered. The other misconceptions is that once you have your first job, you'll never have to 'cold call', network or aggressively look for work again. New entrants don't realise that the skills they employ when entering the industry to find work will be called upon throughout their career.

Q - What advice would you offer a new film maker?

Skillset - You have to love the genre and learn as many aspects of film-making as possible. Be aware of all the background work and workers it takes to make a great film, it will give you the control, foresight and insight into what's possible. Try and make your mistakes before you get paid for them. Be prepared to go hungry for a while! Never give up and learn from any setbacks. The more flexible and multi-faceted you can be in regard to seeking work, honing your craft and progressing your career, the more successful and fulfilled you'll be.

CONCEPT

IFC. International Film Collective

Nik Powell
Producer

NOTES ON FILM MAKING

Q - What is the job of a Producer?

Nik - The producer is the boss of the movie. The job is the same as any boss, which is to do everything that is necessary to develop the film, to make the film, deliver the film, and to distribute and market it. It's hard to do all of that, to achieve the best possible result, i.e. the highest quality film, and I don't mean in production value terms.

Q - What do you think are the problems that face directors when they have to start taking on producing work?

Nik - There is only one problem and that is it distracts them from the job of directing. To direct *well* can only be done if someone is 100% focused on directing. Any distraction will inevitably lessen that director's effectiveness. To direct brilliantly, as we all know, is near impossible, so you really have no chance if you are trying to produce the movie at the same time. It also means that you are tempted not to fight for things you should have because your producer side says you can't afford them!

Q - What kind of stories make good movies?

Nik - Obviously, stories that already have proven appeal. Successful books, successful plays, successful stories in other media. You know people like it enough to lay out money for it. Then there are old stories - they need to be told from a fresh point of view. For example, a traditional story can be placed in an untraditional location, which I call 'window on the world' movies. Half the interest of the story is that it pulls you into a world that you yourself have not experienced. Whether it is because it takes place in a little Irish village, and you've never been to an Irish village, or it takes place in some exotic foreign country, or even not exotic, these are things you haven't seen before, so you are experiencing something new. That to me can be a great story. It can give you a new experience. Then again, original stories are great, too.

Q - Are there differences between stories and scripts?

Nik - People often mistake a good script for a good story, and vice versa. They are not the same thing. You can have a script, which is beautifully written, but the story is not that interesting, or at least not interesting enough for the particular market place that you are going to. You can have a really dreadfully written script, but the essential story is brilliant. Sometimes you may want to take a script on because the story is great, but you don't want to take the writer on even though he/she has invented the story because he/she may not be up to it in terms of craft and skills, to turn it into something more.

Q - What advice would you give to a person who has got a burning desire to get into films? What do you think they should do, what are the problems that they face, and how can they overcome them?

Nik - It is a big question. Everybody's circumstance is different. I am a very big fan of people who learn the industry at the coalface. Coal-face is the point at which an industry meets with the public. In the case of films that is cinemas and DVD shops. That is partly because of the way that I learnt. My old partner, Steve Wooley, a good North London working class boy, where did he start? As a ticket teller in the Scala. He sat there and watched films all day every day. He saw what worked, what didn't. He saw the scenes that people walked out at and the scenes that people didn't laugh at. In a cinema you learn how films are distributed, marketed, sold, and PR'd. You meet the filmmakers, often when they do their publicity tours and so on. You get invited to industry

get-togethers with actors, directors and producers. The coal-face is a fantastic place to learn. If you can work in a video store, or somewhere that represents a wide variety of films, not just American films, and not just English speaking films, then you really get to know the industry. There is so much bullshit written and taught about what does and doesn't work. The only real way to know is to be there.

Q - It's funny you should say that, I just went to do an interview with a Blockbuster's manager, about what makes a successful film, and he gave me so much information. I find it a valuable exercise just to go down to Blockbuster and to just look at the shelves and look at what people are picking up.

Nik - In Virgin, customers would come in all the time, asking for obscure German bands, who were making, at the time, quite difficult music. We didn't know any of the songs and most of the time there were no words. If there were, they were often in German. But, we knew that was what the customer wanted because they kept on asking for it! So we imported their records and signed them to our record label. When I started in the film business, I opened a video store in High Street Kensington in London. We quickly realised that there were films that were not available on video and my customers wanted them. So we signed the rights for them and we put them out ourselves, films such as *Evil Dead*. To me you work backwards because by the time you get back to production, you know the industry as well as anyone ever can, and that puts you as a producer in a very good position.

As a director, I would say almost the opposite. Stop watching so many films and start looking at the society around you. Look at the cultural activity around you and find the people who have impressive imaginative lateral-thinking brains. Go and see all kinds of artists doing all kinds of art because the great directors do not feed from the narrow base of just film. Even when they do feed in from the base of a film, they look at films from all over the world. Coppola, Spielberg and Scorsese were nouvelle art filmmakers. Their films are actually not about films. They are about people who are situated in a society, real or imagined. If you don't know or understand that society, or at least have a particular point of view on that society, your films are not going to seem real. They are going to seem like fabricated characters that are mechanical to watch. We are not drawn into them because you need to know them to recreate them.

Q - What would your advice be to that anxious, dedicated, wannabe filmmaker, who is going to go and do it, and get their parents to re-mortgage their home?

Nik - I think it is quite legitimate for the anxious filmmaker who wants to get going, to go and make films, but not to go and make the next *Star Wars*. It is not a fresh thing to do. The first thing to do it is to make little films that are really achievable. Spend less money. One grand rather than five, or five grand rather than twenty and so on. Make really spectacularly fresh and wonderful short films. Then go direct soaps or TV. I don't recommend going directly into film to people unless they have a particular talent, like Lynn Ramsey, where they can do that. Most of the great Brit directors have learnt their trade as directors in other mediums before they became directors of film. David Yates, who has just taken over directing Harry Potter 5, took fifteen years making outstanding television, better than most of the films that the British film industry make, until he got his shot at a feature. My thing is, learn the craft. Shane Meadows made twenty-five short films before he made *Twenty Four-Seven*. My advice to people here is there is actually more outstanding writing in TV that needs good directing, than there are feature film opportunities. The other thing is to work in the theatre where you get used to directing actors. They don't have to be famous actors. You learn how to tell a story within a confined situation. Of course there are other directing things too, pop promos, commercials, where you learn the visual side.

Q - Television is becoming very much feature film-like, in terms of the way it is made and presented to the audience. You get things like '24', which is more exciting than pretty much any British thriller in the last 10 years.

Nik - David Yates' *State of Play* was just fantastic! Television is now flowering mainly because of BBC3 and BBC4. Ch4 went young, stopped doing what its remit originally was, which was to serve a wide and diverse community. What BBC4 has done, and then it forces other people to do it, is break new ground for several series, serials and dramas that have progressed up the BBC ladder, through BBC2 and sometimes BBC1. A series like *Little Britain* on the comedy side,

judi DENCH   maggie SMITH
They saved a stranger from the sea
in return he stole their hearts
ladies in lavender
A FILM BY CHARLES DANCE

and *Casanova*, for example. You don't get to make stuff that good by just rushing off with your camera, and getting a group of friends together, and trying to make a little picture.

Q - Do you think new filmmakers should attend things like the Cannes film market, just to have a look at how all that works, before they even think about making a film?

Nik - Producers, yes. Directors, I think it is interesting for them, but directors will have a better time attending the Hay Literary festival to see what new books are coming out. They will have a better time attending a third world conference on third world debt. They are better off learning about society, whether it be our society or other societies around the world, than attending the Cannes Film festival. Same with writers. But for a producer, absolutely, they should go. At the National Film School, we send our second year producing students to Cannes each year, and they shadow active producers. So they have done a lot of classroom stuff, made films, and then they think they know the film industry. I tell them, they don't, but at least they think they do! You are halfway there. Festivals put the flesh on the bones of the industry for our visiting students, especially on the independent side.

Q - What do you think are the big problems with UK independent films?

Nik - The things that British filmmakers get wrong are the same things that filmmakers all over the world get wrong, which is anything from weak stories, to bad craftsmanship, to bad acting, to un-interesting choice of subject matter or story etc. Sometimes just bad timing - something that might have worked one year, doesn't work in another year. What I do say to people, which is not a popular point of view, is that we should play to our strengths. That is what Hollywood does, and we should do the same. Our strengths are period pieces, contemporary societal pieces, and not genre, except romantic comedies. Things that are clearly not our strengths are action movies and theatrical thrillers. We are good at thrillers on TV. We have a limited but quite a wonderful horror tradition, which has been totally livened up recently. We are good at comedy.

It doesn't mean we shouldn't do things that are outside of those strengths for the sake of innovation and pushing the boundaries. I think we are too embarrassed about the fact we do make great period movies, and we should let the World and media know that.

Q - What is your stance on the trade off between a traditional education and going to be a runner on a film set and learning your craft from that end?

Nik - There is never any one route to a particular objective, especially in career paths. Some may not be available to you, so why waste time on them. If you don't get into a particular film school, then you will have to take another route, such as being a runner in production offices or on productions. I don't have any formal education after the age of 16 myself. Obviously I am deeply sympathetic to those that go the runner route. In the US, college grads, even Harvard grads, start in the mailroom of an agency and move their way up. Film schools are good for technical courses and practical courses as well. Universities like Bournemouth, have tremendous courses for learning specific aspects of film, or programme making. Here at the National Film School, you get something that you can't get anywhere else in the UK. We have three sound stages and one big TV studio. We make thirty or forty short films a year. The producing students and the directing students have the opportunity to learn the craft of filmmaking and programme-making. They have the opportunity to learn the whole business including the marketing and distribution side. Every day

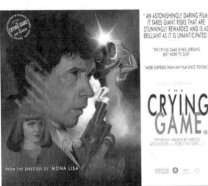

you can see successful film makers wandering around the school. It can be Stephen Frears. We had Michael Radford last week. This is aside from visiting masterclasses of the Spike Lee's of the world etc. Every day we have at least five successful filmmakers who have shown they have the craft, shown that they can make cool films, and you don't get that in places outside of film schools. Then they have the role models. The last four *Star Wars* films, shot by David Tattersall, who also shoots all the Bond movies, graduated at our school. Roger Deakins, who shoots all the Coen Brothers movies, shoots much of the great independent filmmaking, and studio things, like *The Village*, went here as well. The two biggest Brit successes of last year, *Bridget Jones 2* and *Harry Potter*, were directed by our graduates. We also have the auteurs like Lynn Ramsey and Terence Davies, so we are not turning out one particular kind of filmmaker or cinematographer, they are very, very different.

Q - What are common mistakes of directors and producers?

Nik - We all make the same mistakes. We need to choose the right subject matter or the right story. You can never get the whole thing right 100% of the time. It is ridiculous to think that one can. We can get in positions where we have to rush things and that damages the film. We also know that other things we rush turn out brilliantly, so the rushing in itself is not the sin. You can be severely damaged when there is a lack of cash flow, which is a very common problem for all British filmmakers, not just for new filmmakers, but right up to major British films.

The poor cash flow, because the powers that be will not take the risk of pre-production cash flow, hurts films in ways non-producers do not understand. A location could have taken you six months to find, but if you don't have the money to put down a deposit, you lose it! You get something less good. You upset your actors because they were going to stay in a particular hotel, and you've done a great deal, but you couldn't put down the deposit. So you lost that hotel. Then they all get grumpy and ultimately don't give as good a performance. You have to start things late because this or that doesn't arrive on the day, or maybe the piece of equipment you want doesn't arrive at all, so you have to shoot it another way. Now they say that necessity is the mother of invention, but that is ok if you know up front that you are not going to have those things. When they happen on the spot, they damage pictures. That is another common problem for all British producers. We are trying to persuade the powers that be to take more risk, so as not to damage movies. I've been fortunate that I've been able to manage without that causing a problem. We all make mistakes with the casting, whether we are casting directors, whether we are casting writers, casting crew or casting cast.

Q - Do you think if somebody has trouble making hard or fast choices, that perhaps filmmaking isn't really the right choice for them?

Nik - Yes. Producers have to decide, Directors don't. Directors can leave it right to the last moment to evaluate all the options, and then make a decision, which is highly irritating to producers and the crew! Producers have to decide which way they are going. What I always say is *'Decide but don't shut the other doors'*. You must keep moving forward, but you don't have to tell the other people if you are moving in a particular direction, so you want to leave all the other doors open because you never know when you might have to do a U-turn and go through them.

Q - What advice would you give a producer or film maker about assembling a team around them?

Nik - Don't choose people to work with you because you like them. Choose people to work with who have skills to bring something to the project that will really help you achieve your objectives. When you get together in your groups, and you are crewing up, choose the people who are going to help you solve the problems that you are going to have to make a terrific piece of work. Choose people because they have intelligence, and have the ability to work hard, which is almost more important than anything else. That way you will make better films and at the end of the day that is what it is about.

Q - What advice a new filmmaker?

Nik - As a producer, don't think you know it all. You need a certain amount of arrogance and naivety, but my thing is to learn your industry, preferably from the coal-face back. To directors and writers, I say learn your craft. No-one really gets there over night. The best way of learning your craft is to keep doing it, both in an independent situation and in a professional one. Don't shun all professional work, you will learn a lot. Even directing soaps and TV series. Respect television and theatre and commercials. Respect the other disciplines, because they produce as good a work, if not better than film often does.

Jonathan Newman
Film Maker

CAREER CHOICE
...THE GUERILLA
ROUTE

Q - How did you get into film making?

Jonathan - My family moved to LA when I was 5 and we lived in a great house overlooking Malibu beach. As a result, we had film crews using our house for location shoots a few times a year - *Knight Rider, TJ Hooker* and other crap 80s TV shows filmed at our house! I got the bug hanging out on those film sets. One night my mom made me ask David Hasselhoff if he wanted to stay for dinner. He declined. Then I started to make short films with my dad's Super 8mm film camera.

Q - Did you go to film school?

Jonathan - Yes, I did a Masters at The Northern Film School in Leeds. It was a two year program, one year of production and one year of film theory. I also studied film theory in Boston, Massachusetts.

Q - Was film school of benefit?

Jonathan - I felt the tutorage at the Northern Film School was awful though they did have a full 'hands on' approach, which is where the biggest learning curve is. However, I wish I had more knowledge of the whole process of filmmaking before I made my first short as I made a lot of mistakes with that film. Ok, it's fine to make mistakes at school, it's a learning process, but the short film was the culmination of a year's work and a year's tuition fees, and was to be the 'calling card' (as everyone likes to put it!) of that film-maker. I ended up with a crap calling card.

There's some argument to be had that you can just take that money and go and make a film (or two if you are resourceful) by yourself, outside film school. But film school is also beneficial in the relationships you make, most of whom I'm friends with today. It does also push you to take action, as it's easy to get lazy and complacent otherwise.

Q - You then made a film guerilla style. How did that work?

Jonathan - I had just returned from LA where I worked in a film as a 2nd AD. I was young and naïve, the best combination for making a guerrilla film! I decided I was going to make a short and went about raising the money. Among others, I called British Telecom and reached the right person at the right time. She agreed to give me £10k in exchange for *Video on Demand* rights to my short film. I was all set. Then I was struck by an idea. Why not really get on the map and make a feature film?! Change of plan. I wrote a script in a week, called up BT and asked if she minded if I make a feature instead. It was a go project. The money came in, I cast the film, set a date, crewed up and was on set 15 weeks later. Don't know how, but I shot on S16mm, got the film in the can and edited on a Lightworks for £10k. A lot of blagging and a lot of favours. We shot in 21 days with a dedicated crew and just used locations that were accessible to us. I managed to get James Dreyfus who was known for his TV work and also got Saeed Jaffrey for a day. If you don't ask you don't get!

Q - Why was guerilla film-making the right choice for you at that time?

Shoot For The Moon

GUERILLA FILM MAKER SAYS!

A common mistake made by new film makers is that they aim too low. Given that you rarely achieve exactly what you set out to do, but that you will get close if you work hard at it, the impact of making low aspiration choices such as shooting on miniDV or using friends as actors, can be devastating to any project.

1. Always try and shoot on the best format you can get. You can always drop back down to miniDV in a worst case scenario. Jonathan Newman managed to make a feature film, shot on Super 16mm, for £10k. Resist the urge to shoot on the camcorder sitting under your desk and go pro.

2. Always try for the best cast! Start at the top with the most amazing actors and make a polite and professional approach. They may like you. They may like your script. They may have free time. Of course they may just tell you where to go! But if you don't ask... Your best mate who wants to be an actor is better suited to a walk on part than the lead. Aim higher.

3. Redraft your script. It's not good enough! Trust us on this.

4. Get more money! You will need it. As your aspirations rise, so will your budget, and so will your charisma and ability to convince people that this is going to be amazing. Don't be afraid to ask everyone you know to invest in your movie. Remember, you are selling a dream and small investors will get to, albeit vicariously, go on that dream journey with you. They will be the loudest clappers at your premiere.

5. Be outrageous. Whatever story you tell, crank it up to greater heights. Even the title can be more outrageous. Which is a better title? 'The Texas Massacre' or 'The Texas Chainsaw Massacre'? You need to make people sit up and take notice, and for a new film maker, being the 'loudest' is often the best approach. It aint subtle but it does work.

6. Philosophically, and on every level, think BIGGER! However, don't let this go to your head. No-one likes an unrealistic, arrogant and egotistical newcomer, but a polite and dedicated newcomer with incredible dreams is a charismatic person to be around. That's who you want to be.

CONCEPT

Jonathan - I was young and ballsy and didn't know any better. I was so ambitious that I couldn't bare the thought of waiting around. I had to do it right then, right there! So the long haul of working my way up the ladder within a film company wasn't for me. Straight out of film school I was pumped up. It motivated me seeing some of my friends take action. It made me become more proactive. I convinced someone to give me this money and it was a golden opportunity. It was either, *'make another short film which doesn't really do that much for you'*, or try to get on the map with a feature which can actually sell and progress your career further. Some people think I want to be a guerilla film maker, but for me, it was not a choice. It was either my £10k film or no film. No-one chooses to make films with no money. No-one really wants to be a guerilla film maker. But it's a *make it with this* or *don't make it at all* kind of scenario.

Q - What do you need to make the Guerilla route work for you?

Jonathan - You need two things exactly. Determination, that is, the will to want to do it. And second, the ability to take action. To take that determination and turn it into something concrete. Words are meaningless without action.

Directing is the best entry level job in Hollywood today! What I mean by that is, everyone has a camcorder nowadays, and everyone has basic editing equipment on their computer. Nothing is stopping anyone with an idea from going out and making a film. Look at all the rubbish, high concept ideas that get sold at Sundance every year. If you can think of a good idea, it doesn't matter if it's shot on DV.

Q - What are the advantages and disadvantages of choosing a guerilla film as a career step?

Jonathan - Advantages - you've made a film. You're no longer just a talker or a dreamer. You've done it. You have a product which, if it's vaguely good, can probably get a sales agent, go straight to DVD and sell a few territories. You also gain a huge amount of experience which will stand you in good stead on the next production.

Disadvantages - your film is probably crap. Give up hopes of theatrical distribution unless your film is amazing. It's probably a bad script, bad performances by unknown actors and might not even get finished. Sorry to be negative, but that's the statistical reality of most low-budget films. That's why you have to go into it prepared. And you've also got to develop a great script. No low budget film ever suffered from being in development for too long. The important thing is you get going, because this is a learning curve. Your next film will be better.

Q - What happens after a guerilla film if it's not successful?

Jonathan - Depression. You're back to your desperate state of being. But don't get stopped! Don't wallow in your depression. Make another film! Maybe you'll have learnt something from your mistakes and this one will actually hit some marks. I can't think of any instance where the second film from a new or low budget film maker isn't substantially better than their first effort.

Q - You now have a feature film with distribution under your belt, has that made it easier to get the next movie made?

Jonathan - You'd think, right?! My film barely made a blip on the radar. I had some meetings, I developed some projects etc. Soon after the film, I thought I had a stroke of luck when my next script got development finance from the Film Council. We started casting and it all looked set to go. That was 5 years ago. I am still working on it now.

Q - How do you think the business views guerilla films?

Jonathan - I think the industry is always looking out for a film that may be the next *Blair Witch*, but they are few and far between. Exhibitors and distributors don't give a shit about low budget British films and they rarely get a cinema release (and for good reason, they're mostly crap). I think low budget films are a pain in most people's side. The only time a guerrilla film is ever good news is when it gets into a festival and suddenly becomes hot. Before that, it's disposable. Your best bet is to find a prolific

Short Film or Feature Film?

GUERILLA FILM MAKER SAYS!

The obvious starting point when considering a career in film is to make a short. While your short may be a great movie, it isn't a feature and you will have terrible problems trying to sell it to get your money back.

1. A feature film is a saleable product which will generate interest from buyers. A short will generate virtually no sales or revenue.

2. A feature film is three or four times longer than a short - therefore three of four times more work (not exactly true, there is a sharp learning curve.) You also need to stay alert and awake for many months longer.

3. Don't expand a short script into a feature. This almost always produces a very padded out, slow feature version of a short idea. Start from scratch.

4. If a feature film is a success, you could find yourself at the helm of a major feature film. If a short is a success, you will collect an award from a bizarre film festival that no-one has ever heard of.

5. Shorts are excellent for learning the various technical crafts of filmmaking - editing, sound, directing the camera and actors etc. Better still, work for free on someone elses short, and learn at their expense.

6. The structure of a short film is entirely different from that of a feature. Just because you can tell a story in ten minutes does not necessarily mean you can tell a story in ninety minutes. Same is true for music videos, just because you can make a great promo does not mean you know how to sustain a drama over 90 minutes.

7. If you make a great short, you could get an Oscar nomination, in which case, your career is seriously boosted.

8. Shorts are good to make up a showreel of your work and can be a good calling card for agents and executives.

9. Obviously, features are more expensive and take much longer to produce than a short.

10. With current technology, there is no reason why you could not shoot and edit a short film over a weekend. Get productive!

11. Whatever you chose to make, make sure you MAKE IT! Stop reading now and go make it happen!

home entertainment label and get it out on DVD sell-through as quickly as possible and ideally TV sales. Put the film behind you and move on aggressively.

Q - What mistakes have you made?

Jonathan - I didn't develop my script enough. I should have chosen a high concept genre like horror. I got into bed with the wrong people when I needed to finish my film and have regretted it ever since. And having done the low budget route, I got complacent and thought things would get bigger and better. You end up chasing a dangling carrot that's just out of reach. I should not have worried about the end result and just kept making films.

Q - What do you think are the most important qualities for success?

Jonathan - I think there are many qualities you need, and much of it can be contradictary. Self-belief is essential. Don't compare yourself to Chris Nolan who is currently shooting Batman - you'll just get depressed. But then if you do compare yourself to Chris Nolan, it will spur you on to make things happen!

Learn to take action - DO IT NOW! Most people don't get there because they never even start, they just talk about it. Have persistence in the face of resistance, don't get stopped by the word 'no'. To me the word 'no' actually means that I haven't shown them why they are wrong and so need to consider a new approach. Don't put all your eggs in one basket, they'll just get scrambled at the same time if things go bad. Roost many eggs and hope one will hatch into a chicken.

Very important is to not burn your bridges, make friends with everyone. Knowledge - arm yourself with it. Learn how to fish instead of looking for someone to give you the fish. If you can apply that to life - nothing can stop you raising the finance yourself. Life doesn't come to you. You have to go to life. This is it, there's nothing else, just right now. If you make it, you make it. If you don't, you don't. No one really cares about you and one day you'll end up as fertilizer for a flower crop in the countryside. Give up your personal soap opera and just enjoy what you have… and what you don't have.

Q - What advice would you offer a new film maker?

Jonathan - Go to law school before it's too late.

Soledad Gatti-Pascual
The Bureau Film Company

CAREER CHOICE
...THE INDUSTRY
ROUTE

Q - How did you start your career?

Sol - I went to film school. But this was a last resort because I started off at fifteen working in post-production companies and then at some point down the line in production companies as an assistant. We mainly did pop videos. Then I heard of The National Film School because I worked for free on a graduation film at eighteen. That was brilliant and I thought I was going to go straight into movies. Right then I didn't, but I made a lot of really good contacts. So then I was going between trying to get jobs on movies, work in production companies, work for nothing. That went on for a long time. Then I got a lucky break and worked on *Evita*, as the producer's assistant. It didn't end very well with the producer. I don't know why, really, but afterwards I was twenty-four and I knew I wanted to be a producer and went to The National Film School. It was the only place I knew that would train you to be a producer.

Q - Was film school helpful?

Sol - Yes. The process of film school was all about confidence. I realised that I had all the skills. I was probably the most qualified person there as far as production. But I lacked confidence and that is one of the key ingredients of being a producer.

Q - Did any of the short films you worked on there win awards?

Sol - Most of them won awards. It was fantastic. My film school experience was brilliant. During my time there I made four short films - two were BAFTA nominated. The first short I made, which was called *Bubbles*, wasn't made at the film school. I got a grant from the Arts Council along with my longtime collaborator, Tom Shankland, and it won seven or so awards. My graduation film was nominated for a BAFTA and won a BBC prize.

Q - What did you do after film school?

Sol - I started my company immediately. I got a phone call from my business partner, Bertrand Faivre, the day after I finished school. He got hold of me because he was the co-producer of my graduation film, *Going Down*. He was a French producer working out of France, but he had a passion for British films. I had heard of him because he was putting money into short films for French rights. He was Lynne Ramsay's producer on *Ratcatcher* and her shorts. I approached him. He liked Tom's work and he produced *Going Down*. We got on and started a company.

Q - After film school, were you ever tempted to get a job in a larger, more established film company?

Sol - No, not really. I thought I was going to go off and be an independent producer (laughs). And here I am five years later trying to be an independent producer! The opportunity to work with Bertrand came immediately and I worked on *The Warrior*. My title was production co-ordinator, but that is not what I did. Actually, it is really difficult to say what my exact job was. Bertrand is a brilliant producer, so I wouldn't say I was an associate producer, but I suppose I was like a trainee or assistant. It was a great learning curve. He was an inspiration. But after that ended, there was no more work and I had to go make my way in the world and try to make a living. I had the good fortune to be part of another great film called *Nói Albínói* by this brilliant Icelandic director, Dagur Kári and I got a co-producer credit there.

Q - What happened after that film?

Sol - The Film Council sent out a message saying that they wanted different types of companies to apply for short film schemes they were running. And one of them was this idea called Cinema Extreme, which we thought would be up our street. The definition wasn't clear, but it seemed like a good way to work with some really innovative talent, which was what we were in to. We made an application for it and we made four films. *Wasp* was one of these films and it was nominated for an Oscar, and subsequently won. Another short called *Love Me Or Leave Me Alone* I think won something like nineteen awards. *The Bypass*, won quite a few awards. *A Changed Man*, won some more awards. So The Bureau, my company, has been successful running this program and we are running it again this year. Then there was a bit of a lean period before things went crazy. We decided that we had to think more broadly about our business plan. I think we had always been quite bold in terms of what the company was about. If we were going to make a splash in the UK and survive, we had to be different. So we looked at what our talents were, which we figured out was talent spotting and then were bold about that.

Q - How do you break through as a producer in the UK?

Sol - It is all about reputation, which is often as thin as a membrane and vulnerable. You also get pigeon holed really quick. You make commercial films, you make independent films. It is difficult and as producers you are asked to do so many different things. It is virtually impossible to meet people who can do all of those things at the same time. And if you can't do all of these things, you are defective, and that is really harsh. If I hadn't met Bertrand, I would probably be a gardener. It is hard to break in if you don't have someone help you.

Q - The image of a UK independent producer is someone holed up in their flat trying to get films made and not being too successful. Why do you think that is?

Sol - I'll be cruel. There are a lot of people who think they are film makers and they are not. There are a lot of people in the middle who have a lot of talent in one area, and not a lot in the other areas. Judy Counihan of Skillset said it best. You need three separate items to be a producer - one is to be entrepreneurial, the other is to be organisational, and the last is to be creative. And if you have two of those, you can be a producer. One, no way, and very few people have all three. If you have this entrepreneurial one that is the gold dust one. Then you can do it. But then you have shit films getting made because you have brilliant entrepreneurs who don't know what they are doing.

Q - Which skills do you think you have?

Sol - Organisational and creative. And Bertrand has all three. He has business and creative talent skills. And he is organised. So to me, the producers who have been successful have either been a, lucky, b, have all three characteristics or c, have a partner. And that is why people are in their bedrooms on their own.

Q - Why do films get made in the UK?

Sol - I am beginning to think there is no rhyme or reason to why they get made. It may come down to reputation. If you have a good idea and a great reputation, you are far more likely to make a film than if you have a great reputation and you are rubbish. People can be prolific and not make good stuff. The decision making in this country is a little weird at the financier level.

Soledad Gatti-Pascual
The Bureau Film Company
tl: +44 20 7580 8182
fx: +44 20 7580 8185
sgp@thebureau.co.uk
www.thebureau.co.uk

Q - What do you think this country has a tendency to finance?

Strength In Numbers

So many successful film makers began as partners in a strong and successful team. Maybe you should build a team around you too? Maybe there is truth in the old cliché, 'two heads are better than one'.

1. Look for a partner who will compliment your skills. This way you will build quickly and never duplicate your work.

2. Look for a person who shares the same tastes in films. You have to get excited about the same things or you are two people working in the same place, but not together.

3. Trust. You must be able to completely trust your partner. And we mean REALLY TRUST! It's got to be one for all and all for one.

4. A partner will give a good sounding board. If you share the same tastes and goals, criticism will be considered and appropriate.

5. You tend to work longer hours if there is someone else busting their guts to get the film made too.

6. Everyone has off days, and when you are down, they will probably bounce up and cover for you. And vice versa.

7. Ambition and risk taking tends to increase in a partnership as each convinces the other that it can be done. Risk and ambition are cornerstones to success.

8. Fundamentally, it's tough to do it alone. We are all creatures that need company on a physical, spiritual and emotional level. Your partner will supply that. And when we say physical, you try and get a sofa upstairs if you don't have a partner!

10. All partnerships end. When it's over, don't flog a dead horse. Move on.

Sol - One thing I think the UK is blessed with is talent. We are gifted with cutting edge, new talent. So the UK will finance new stuff, but has a difficulty maintaining relationships with those artists so they can become broader and more commercial. It is almost easier here, to make your first film than your fifth or second even.

Q - Let's say you get a job at Working Title right out of secondary school, how long would it take to work your way up to producer?

Sol - If you get a job at Working Title, you should just kiss the ground and thank God. That is what it is all about. You could probably do it at Working Title rather quickly. If you are talented and you are entrepreneurial in some ways, maybe you could do it in four years if you were really brilliant and put your head down and worked.

Q - What common mistakes do you think independent film makers make straight out of film school?

Sol - That they can do it on their own. I would say that is impossible. Also, there is a common misconception about how long it takes things to get made. I did a talk at the London Film School and everyone wanted to be a director, which I thought was hysterical. And at that time we were perceived as being super successful, and I went through the amount of people who left film school in the last five years and how many of them actually made films. Maybe out of fifty people, three made films and two of them were a team. So the odds are absolutely against you. When I left film school I thought I was a golden child. I still haven't produced my own feature film. I have co-produced, though. I think that if you can say you are producing something and you are making a living at it, then you are a producer. Though, I have given up my idea of having a helipad at home.

Q - Now that you have been doing this for a while and have won some awards, is it any easier to make movies?

Sol - No. I'd say that for Bertrand, after five years of being full on, it may be a little bit easier for him. But for me, I would say it is easier because people know who I am, but that doesn't mean they are going to pick up my phone call.

Q - Does The Bureau have any relationship with Hollywood?

Sol - None, really. Well, Bertrand has developed relationships with some of the specialty arms of some of the studios. That is a different world. And we would love to be involved with it. The way I see it is that making brilliant films that win awards is fantastic and when you win, it feels great. But ultimately awards don't feed you or pay the rent. We are in this creative industry because we have a passion for film. And Hollywood is the financial epicenter of all of that. So while part of me loathes it in a very English sort of way, I respect it for the machine that it is. It has a very clear understanding of the marketplace. And that I can take to my independent world. There is no point making a film that no one wants to see because if you do enough of those, then you may never make another film.

Q - Having just returned from the States after doing the Inside Pictures program, did you find that the doors were open to you?

Sol - That program was the most amazing thing I have ever done since going to the film school. It had amazing guest speakers. That is the one thing about America that is terrific, the people there will take a meeting with you at the drop of a hat, even if they don't know you. They pride themselves on knowing everybody, everything, what is going into production. Equally, I don't think they have a life and I'm not sure I would appreciate that so much. The most important thing I got out of it was a reality check. By the end of the first day I was left with a very clear understanding of the financial machine that is the film industry. The film industry makes, globally, a huge amount of money. For all of us who say we are in the art film world, what a miniscule part of that pot we are. Like three percent and there are so many of us scrabbling around in the dirt. It also humanised people. They are all doing a job and it is just business. Sometimes I don't tell people that I am a producer because they get this glint in their eye and want me to tell them how exciting it is. I tell them I am secretary or something. Or I just tell them it is a job like any other and there is a lot of paperwork. All the glamorous travel I thought I would do, is really just staying in hotels with strangers, and it is far from glamorous. But I am doing what I want to do and I am not complaining about it.

Q - What advice would you give new producers?

Sol - Get a partner who has complimentary skills to yours. Make sure one of you has the entrepreneurial flair. You don't both need to have it, but one of you for sure must. And that one of you has the creative talent. And the two of you have a really clear career goal of where you want to be in one year or five years and how you are going to get there. Develop great relationships with directors. Go and see short films. Run after the people that you really think are amazing. That is what I did with Dagur Kári. I said I wanted to do something with him and he said he had an Icelandic language film. Don't try to tie people down with awful contracts. If you are good to them, they will want to work with you again. If you believe in a project, go for it. But on the same token, if you feel a project is a dead duck, get rid of it. And if you have some other skill in the industry, like post-production managing, try to get some of that work in order to keep things going. You will spend a lot of time in development so go to other things to refine your talent. Be nice, but firm with people. If someone is railroading you, they probably are. Take some time and get back to them. You will probably kiss a lot of frogs and make a lot of mistakes, but everyone does.

Laura MacDonald
Personal Assistant

WORKING IN 'THE BUSINESS'

Q - What is your job?

Laura - Currently I am assistant to the film director and screenwriter Martha Fiennes.

Q - What does that entail?

Laura - I started out working for her producer, so I was involved in developing her most recent project *'Chromophobia'*. After we got funding in Cannes, I moved over to assist her and saw through pre-production, production, and now we are doing post. Even though personal assisting can involve non-film duties at times, the majority of my work has been intensely creative. Martha is smart and at ease with her own place in the film world, so she has been able to delegate to me, without feeling the least bit threatened. Consequently I have experienced so much - helping her with re-writes, representing her when she is just too busy to go and take meetings, liasing with different departments, amongst many other things. Fundamentally, the job is supporting her in any way that I can.

Q - What kind of things do you do and learn, that you will carry forward into your broader, longer-term career?

Laura - I started out as a journalist, and I loved that, but I knew that I wanted to be more creative and learn how a film was developed and made. I've done a lot of script reading, which has been immensely useful in learning how a screenplay works, picking it apart, learning how to analyse what makes a good film. The biggest benefit has been to really see the machinations of production, to be able to work for producers, in the development stages, see how the money comes together, be involved with the contracts, the casting process, the hiring of each department and finally pulling all these complex components together to bring the script to the screen.

Q - So you get a real world 'film school-like' experience, and get paid to do it?

Laura - Absolutely, being an assistant to the director means you are working for the person that everybody wants a piece of - so you are always close to the action and able to learn from that.

Q - I assume you can make contacts, and you will get your phone call returned...?

Laura - Yes. This is an industry where everybody is looking to network constantly, and that is one of the keys to success, whichever film related job you choose. To be in a position where people are interested in what you are doing gives you leverage. There are no hard and fast rules when it comes to making your way into the film industry. This job has helped me immensely and people that I've met have been incredibly talented and diverse.

Q - Do you see yourself doing this in 5 years time?

Laura - No. I hope that I will be writing full-time.

Q - So, in many ways what you do now is the apprenticeship that used to exist in almost all industries until maybe 20 years ago? A stepping stone to your next level?

Laura - Yes. There are times that I have felt frustrated, wanting to go off and do my own thing. However, there is so much to learn. I think it is very easy to be pressured by the stories of Orson Welles or Steven Spielberg making amazing debut films in their twenties. Everyone works at their own pace, and as long as you keep working hard, your time will come.

Q - I refer to it as 'Quentin Tarantino Syndrome', everyone wants immediate success. Would you go along with the philosophy, 'don't get it right, get it done', and 'win an Oscar when you are 60?!'

Laura - For some people that is the way to go, others have an innate sense of self belief in what they are capable of, they are able to leap in at the deep end. I've always wanted to be a writer, but it's something I have struggled with. I know I am a better writer for being involved in development, working with producers, and working with people who are already great writers. It keeps you inspired and educated.

Q - How important are personality skills?

Laura - Hugely important! When one buys a script, the Producer also purchases the Writer or Director's ability to take meetings and communicate their ideas and vision. Good people skills are imperative as film is a truly collaborative process.

Q - Would you recommend your job to a film school graduate, somebody who's trying to break into the business, somebody who has no family connections in the business etc?

Laura - Absolutely. It teaches you discipline. You have to be efficient, able to handle someone else's life & they need to rely on you to be detail-orientated - that and a lot of passion and energy! The most important thing is having initiative, because when you have done the ground work, you can use your initiative to grow within the role and to see the potential for your career.

Q - Most people say I want to be in the camera team, an editor or another on-set job that is perceived as 'film making'. Yet your position gives you access to the real machine that makes a film possible.

Laura - Yes. You really do learn, often by osmosis, by listening to conversations, how people cope, how things work or don't work. I have been privy to so much that will help me in the future. How you negotiate is very important as you are negotiating constantly, no matter what area you are in. I always knew that the director was the person who formed the fabric of each project, but I never realised just how much rides on their vision, stamina and strength. Working closely with Martha (director) has been a completely different experience from working with Ron Rotholz and Norma Heynan (producers) - it's not simply the mechanics of how to make a film, but the magical, creative side, which is also incredibly grounded and intrinsically linked in the mechanics too! I have learnt so much by experiencing both sides.

Q - How do you get a job such as yours?

Laura - Persistence and stamina are vital. Target people that you know are actively making films, whose films you like - do this constantly. Read the trades and get to know the names of people in the industry. Subscribe to www.screendaily.com, Variety.com or indiewire.com - you will learn about industry developments, new companies, new films, new trends. . . Production companies come and go, but there is a core group of people who are constantly making good films, and you have got to try and find a way to get your CV to them. A lot of it is timing. You could send your CV to Working Title every week for a year, and if your CV arrives the day that Tim Bevan suddenly needs an assistant, you'll be at the top of the pile. Always follow up too, get that person's e-mail address, who is that assistant that you spoke to? Try and get their e-mail address, call back in a month. Always be respectful, clear and concise about what you are after, and be persistent. Try and build relationships.

Q - From your experience what do you think are the important things to focus on?

Assisting as a way in

Just dashing out to make a low budget feature may not be the right choice for you. If it isn't, maybe you could assist someone...

1. Assisting an expert or established film maker will give you a real window into how a successful film maker works. Better to learn from them than other wannabes with big ideas but no experience.

2. You will get to meet important players, and while you won't be on their level, you will at least be a face they come to recognise. In due course, they will expect you to advance your career and contact them with ideas.

3. Sitting in on important meetings will help you learn the way things work and get to grips with industry jargon.

4. On the downside, you may work long hours, do thankless tasks and generally be taken for granted. You can always jump ship.

5. If you work hard, it will be noticed. You may get a promotion quite quickly. Make yourself indispensable.

6. Start at the top! Alan Parker or Tim Bevan may not get that many new film makers asking to assist.

7. You should be able to use the office for your own endeavours. Photocopying, faxing, calls, surfing are all possible, just don't overstep your boundaries. Have a chat with your boss and let them know you want to do this in down time.

8. Read scripts! Loads will land on your bosses desk, so offer to read them and write reports. You will quickly learn what makes a great script, and if you do find that great project, you may get a promotion.

9. Beware of offering your services for free to anyone who calls themselves a film maker or producer. There are a lot of new film makers who talk a great talk but you will do little more than be their slave, learning little.

10. Don't discount Hollywood. You could get an intern position at Warner Brothers and jack into that industry. There are hoops to jump through and you just can't turn up and ask for a job, but given time, planning and dedication, it can be done.

11. Keep sending out that CV and knocking on doors. Keep your CV up to date as you never know when someone will ask for it.

12. Get a broad view of the business. Try assisting a producer, a director, a distribution company, a sales company... Experience as many aspects of the film business as you can.

Laura - The Film industry attracts a lot of different people, and some of them aren't very moral. You need to be savvy and learn quickly. You can't naively think everybody is working immensely hard to make something magical. Do your research. Sometimes you just have to be philosophical about the fact that it is often about what can you do for other people and not what they can do for you. It is a fiercely competitive business. It is also important to have advisors. Don't go blindly into selling your script, selling yourself, selling your film unless you have knowledgeable people around you. Be open to opportunity but listen to your gut instinct.

Q - And equally take advice from people who know, don't ask your mate in the pub who doesn't have a girlfriend, why you don't have a girlfriend!

Laura - Yes, exactly!

Q - What mistakes do you often see?

Laura - Your CV has to entice. Don't go into too much detail and don't ever make spelling mistakes. Show that you want a job, that you have drive. Represent yourself in the best possible light. I remember ringing up someone once, to ask them in for an interview, and I woke them on a Friday morning and they said, *'oh, I'm asleep, can you call me back?'* I thought why would I ever call you back, how could you ever think that that is a way to treat a possible business proposition? In the film industry there is a lot of misinformation, and it is a complex business. Always be as honest as you can be, but if you think it is better to keep your mouth shut, do so.

Don't ever send an important e-mail without doing a draft, do your research, and make sure you spell check, double check, triple check, because you won't get another chance. First impressions are important. If a prospective employer reads something, and they think *'they haven't thought this through, they haven't done their research'*, you won't get another go.

The key is that you have something that people want. You can't just blunder about thinking, *'oh y'know, maybe I will give this a go, but my heart is not in it because I'm not really sure'*. You need to sit down and say *'right, I think this job would be fantastic for me, because I know that I could do a bloody brilliant job, and that I would learn a lot. I love that film that you made'*, or *'I'm fascinated by this project that you are working on.'* You have got to show initiative, you have to do your research, like any other business, you can't get sloppy.

Q - What about humility. Often there is too much arrogance from new film makers?

Laura - No-one in their right mind thinks that someone wants to be a PA forever, but any employer needs you to commit and to be enthusiastic. They know that some of the things they will ask you to do, you are not going to enjoy, but you are going to do them, because your job entails a variety of tasks, each one important and necessary. You can't possibly know exactly what is required of you when you start a new job, however much experience you may have. One must grow into a position, hone your skills, learn on the job and often go through some boring tasks to establish trust and understanding. Then you will be delegated more challenging and rewarding jobs. You also need to know when to say 'no!' but when you are at an early stage of your career, trying to break into an industry such as film, you have to be ready, willing and as you say have some humility.

Q - What advice would you offer a new film-maker?

Laura - Don't forget what inspires you and what challenges you, because you are committing to a difficult, intensely competitive career. Don't ever lose sight of what it was that caught your imagination. Have faith in yourself, your talents and trust your instincts.

CONCEPT

Richard Holmes
Producer, Gruber Films

THE TRADITIONAL PRODUCER

Q - How did you originally get into film making?

Richard - Stefan Schwartz, who directed three of the films I produced, and I worked in a comedy double act based around film sketches. We realised we were never going to set the world alight, so we started to write short films. We made two in between writing feature films that never got made, tried to learn and teach ourselves, and read books about structure and story-telling in a visual medium. One of the shorts was good and that brought an investor to the table, who invested a substantial sum on a personal basis, to make a film called *'Soft Top Hard Shoulder'*, which was written by Peter Capaldi. That came out when I was 30, and now I am 42, and I've made six films, so it's been a film every other year.

Q - Did making 'Soft Top...' open doors?

Richard - The problem with the first film, is the second film. Often, you work so hard and long on that first film that the idea of having anything to do next is almost impossible. Even if you've got something that you think is developed, having made your first film, you now regard it as underdeveloped, you tend to go right back to the drawing board. Yes, it does open doors, people will speak to you, but they will only speak to you if you have got a script that they like.

Q - So really the 1st film is film school for people who didn't get into film school?

Richard - Yes, I tried to get into film school, but they wouldn't let me in.

Q - In terms of your career, you started with a low budget picture, then moved up the ladder. What would your advice be to someone who has made one or two low budget films and is finding it hard to move up the ladder?

Richard - Nothing. So much of this is down to luck. I'm not religious, I don't believe in God, and I don't believe in luck in the spiritual way, but as an example *'Shooting Fish'* or *'Waking Ned'* which are two films that I've made and have done well, have sold internationally, and were picked up by good distributors for good money - had they been made one or two years earlier or later, I suspect they would not have found a market at all. They would have been nice little films that no-one saw. The further away I get from them, the more I'm aware how lucky we were in terms of timing.

You can't rely on one project. A producer relies on their slate. Very often, through no fault of your own, a project stalls or becomes impossible, or through good opportunity becomes impossible. For instance, you have got a great script and a piece of significant talent attaches themselves to it, but says, *'I am not available till next year!'* So, what are you supposed to do this year? I would suggest that the thing that may be going wrong is that after having been very focused on getting their first and maybe second very low budget film off the ground, they become used to being monogamous. You need to spread your opportunities over at least three projects. They will be at various stages of readiness, but you can nudge each along and tickle all of them at the same time. You have got to be out there doing as much as you can, not just banging on the same doors with the same project that has been turned down.

Take a realistic assessment. It is probably going to be a year before what is a good first draft script becomes a financiable, attachable, makeable film. You have made a few films, financed in very canny ways, maybe very hand to mouth, maybe friends and family, maybe a rich benign investor, but I would try to raise some capital - you want to be able to stabilise yourself. The only way to be successful in this business is to be *in the business*. Most people fail, because they leave, not because they are bad, but because they have to give up. If you can raise a bit of capital, you can remain at the table, and that is absolutely essential, it is all about stamina in the end.

Q - Do you have any tips on how to survive?

Richard - I can only talk about myself. I did comedy and acting and enough to keep the wolf from the door. I married an actress who works, she is not famous, but she works. I came from an age when the DHSS could support you with enough money to buy food and survive, but that's really gone. You have got to eat. This is why the industry originally attracted people that can afford not to work, people with a benign parent or some kind of money in the bank. Not necessarily rich, but with enough resources so that they can tick over and pay the rent for an indefinite period. A lot of this game is *'last man standing'*, it's stamina. I recommend a second string to the bow, the ability to line-produce, consult, teach, something to keep the wolf from the door. Up until the point when I made *'Shooting Fish'* and *'Waking Ned'*, I earned almost nothing, £7k a year if I was lucky, and that was from odd bits of acting work. You need a transferable skill that can make you money.

Q - After the first 'wing and a prayer' movie, how important is your location?

Richard - For us, it is essential to live in London, although that is not a popular thing to say. I think you also need to be based in the West End, which is expensive. We have made a very conscious decision to travel to America too, for a week every two months or so. We camp out there, see agents, managers, production companies, and if we can, go face to face with talent, with the specific aim of attaching them to a specific project. Also with the aim, that if we need something quickly, if they don't know who you are, it is difficult to get them to engage, but if they have met you a few times, then they think you are real, that helps. In terms of attending markets, I think you should go, if only once. Definitely go to Cannes, you really need to know how it operates. People joke about producers hanging around at parties, and I've never done the party thing very well, but I do think it is essential to put your face about. Then people know that you are serious.

Q - Do you think being an actor has helped you in business?

Richard - In selling, certainly. I wasn't a good actor, I was the kind of actor that as a producer would dread hiring! I was lazy, never did any work, always learning my lines in the taxi to set! But I could do it and through auditioning I got confidence in selling myself and my role in the projects.

Q - In a traditional world, how does a producer put a deal together?

Richard - Producers have a mobile phone and they own a script. Very often they have written it, or a friend has written it, so they can say to the world that they control it. You have to own or control the project in some way, and for enough time, at least two years to get the project developed and set up. I would suggest British film makers should try and get some corner stone financing from the UK, ideally from a decent distributor willing to put up 10% of the budget. They are not going to write it down until things become more solid, but you know you can refer to your distributor as the person backing the film. It will give you confidence, it will give talent confidence that it is real, and it will give the other international community, financiers some comfort that a proper commercial distributor has gone for it. It could be a broadcaster. Everyone can put a tax fund or regional fund to their film, so you should really get some commercial corner stone financing to build confidence. After that it becomes a puzzle. Once a distributor is fully pregnant with it, and thinking *'I would like to distribute this film'*, then they will ring you and ask *'How's it going, can I introduce it to a distributor in Germany that I'm very close to'*, and it can get itself into motion.

gruber films

richard holmes

eOffice no. 2 sheraton street
london w1f 8bh
tel +44 (0) 8703 66 93 13
mobile +44 (0) 7803 206 348
e-mail richard.holmes@gruberfilms.com
www.gruberfilms.com

Working From Home

GUERILLA FILM MAKER SAYS!

1. Working from home can reduce your overheads and maximise your time. You won't have to rent offices and you can start work the moment you get out of bed (no tubes or traffic queues) and work late into the night.

2. Working from home can decrease your work time - it's all too easy to sleep in or get distracted into fixing the kitchen sink, etc. It's difficult to separate business from pleasure.

3. Try and have people around to keep yourself from getting bored or lonely, even schedule meetings just to stay in touch. Get on the phone and keep connected to the world.

4. Try to keep a normal work schedule during the day. Elmore Leonard stated once, that he goes to his downstairs office and writes from 9AM to noon or so, takes an hour lunch break and then goes back to the office and writes until 5pm. How many novels does he have?

5. If you intend to shoot a movie from home, rent a very big place and we mean BIG! Preferably in the country where you can't disturb neighbours. A call to the police from an angry neighbour could shut down production and force you to relocate.

6. Inviting a client or investor into your living room can have two effects. It can either make you look very amateur, or it can make you look grass roots and honest. People do like home grown talent and this is an angle which could be very effective. Just look as professional as possible and stress that working from home is a way of minimising overhead.

7. If you mess around too much, be prepared to be evicted - landlords DON'T like the self-employed. Keep it quiet.

8. Mum and Dad may say it's OK to make your film at home - just remember, they don't expect 50 friends to move in with you.

9. Get connected - broadband and a great mobile phone deal. No matter how many free minutes you get, you will use them all!

10. Exercise can wake you up when you feel burnt out. Work some kind of exercise regime into your life as an energy giver and a stress buster.

You have got to know about many aspects of financing, and you have got to know about banking, that is essential to learn in order to cash flow your film. If you are an independent producer with multi-party financing, you are not going to get a single person to cash flow the film. You might get one of the tax funds to do it, but even they go through banks. You have got to understand the requirements and the feasibility of banking, and you've got to know how to write a finance plan or a control sheet that makes sense to people.

Q - In terms of attaching talent (actors), how does that work?

Richard - I have not yet, on the basis of talent alone, been able to put a project together. Talent tends to be driven by the advice that they get. Actors just want to act. As long as the part is not crap or pornography, they are very often uncritical of what comes through the door. If it seems to make sense, and it is a good part for them, they will do it. Actors of a certain stature often rely on their management and advisors as to whether they should do it, and whether it is real. You will find most projects with an interesting director, and one interesting or good actor, will be largely without a full cast, right up to three or four weeks before the shoot, and then suddenly all sorts of actors will attach themselves because it is now actually happening. They like that certainty. Talent in the UK is often driven in a more cultural manner. Talent in America is a different game. If you will require American talent I would suggest that you get in with the agencies and managers on a regular basis, they need to know who you are.

Q - What do you feel about the producer / director / writer dynamic. There is a strong and collaborative trio there, and often people get confused about where their roles actually fit?

Richard - It really comes down to the script and the story that you are trying to make, and from where that story originates. If you are a producer who comes up with ideas for films, you can be a producer / writer, however I think that is a particularly difficult one to do, in terms of attracting a director to your project. If you are a producer who comes up with ideas, that tends to mean you are the one who commissions the writer. As a writer, not a writer / director, you can develop a script to a certain stage, then try to attach a director. There are all sorts of relationship threads set up at that point, some of which are benign, some of which are difficult to knit together. Often, if you've had an intimate relationship with the writer, and have pushed it through several drafts as a producer, the writer inevitably feels that they could direct it themselves. Then you bring this third party director in who has a profile and will help you attach talent, and therefore money - you could have friction there and you've got to allow the writer and director to form a relationship together. That may be impossible, and they may always have to relate through you. On a project that is inspired by the producer this will rarely work smoothly. However if a writer / director comes to the producer, or a writer / director team comes to the producer, then that can be completely different, and it can be benign from the outset.

Q - Who are the most important people in the making of the film, in terms of getting the film made?

Richard - Literally the writer, and then the director, those two are essential, as they will also help you attract the talent, and the interest in the project. Without those two, the thing won't fly. It doesn't mean they have to be famous, but they have to make sense for you and your project, and the kind of money you are trying to attach to it. Getting outside of the physical production, the core relationships are with your distribution and finance, and very often that's the same thing. Also it will help if you understand that they are trying to look for an upside, but also defray risk and cost at the same time. They are looking for the bargain, so that if it tanks, it is not going to embarrass them. If it goes well, they are going to look like gangbusters. You must understand where they are coming from.

In the end it's not. In the end the projectionist is the most important person on your film! I've had at least one film completely cocked up by a projectionist, whose projector broke down on the crucial screening to the buyers!

Q - Who do you need to make friends with, in the business?

Richard - No-one. There are real solo flyers in this game who rely totally on the material, and if it's good material, people will come. I'm full of admiration for people who don't whore themselves about, but to be pragmatic, you need to have relationships with writers, if you need something written, and you are not a writer but do have a great idea. It is good to know, if not agents, then agencies. Know how it works, know the key agencies in the UK and abroad. They are not mobsters, they are there to try and get the rent paid, and their clients work, and to try and build their business through talent. Also, to know the distributors and financiers. You don't have to take them to lunch, but you have to know who they are and how they operate, how the structure of companies work, if you know the top, go to the top. You need to be an everyman in certain aspects of film-making. Someone who people feel that they can come to, the responsible party, and can therefore be approached by people who have problems or ideas that can be resolved or put forward.

Q - Many new film makers get too wrapped up in the idea of shooting and not the 'putting together' of a deal and what happens after the shoot?

Things to build into your low budget film concept

GUERILLA FILM MAKER SAYS!

1. Keep characters to a minimum, and make them interesting.

2. Look for contained and controllable locations in which your story can take place. Again, minimise locations so you don't need to keep moving a crew.

3. Write for daytime rather than nighttime - night = lights = money.

4. Set your story in the present and where you live. Otherwise you'll spend resources on creating a world that does not exist, as a backdrop to the drama.

5. Avoid visual effects unless you or your brother run your own VFX company! Alternatively, create the illusion with sound or have a character tell the story of whatever the 'big moment' is.

6. Keep your story tight. You don't want to waste precious resources shooting scenes you will later cut, so edit your script aggressively.

7. Design a strong and intriguing opening for your movie. People are hooked in by mystery and intrigue. The challenge is maintaining that level of tension and tying it all up in a dramatic and surprising way.

Richard - I think the most essential thing to remember, if your film is not going to be paid for by a single source or from money in your savings account, is that you are going to have to attract commercial finance to the table. The most important thing is positioning. Sell yourself first, sell the company second and sell the project last. They want to know that you are competent, committed and passionate, and invested in it. That your company, however big or small, will deliver, you have the infrastructure and the knowledge to make it happen. Then they feel comfortable and receptive to the project itself. In terms of positioning the project, cold reading will rarely work in your favour. Therefore we work hard on pre-meetings to get people interested, so that when the script hits their desk, they are already intrigued.

Supply background material to go with it too, so they feel that this is not simply a first draft. It has been researched, there is a plan behind it, timing for it being considered etc. If they like the first 30 pages, but put it down, they might pick up this booklet and go, *'oh actually, that is very interesting, they have got ideas for casting, they have thought it right the way through'*, and then they will go back and finish the script. If they like both, then you are set.

Q - What do you think the qualities of a good producer are?

Richard - Stamina. You really do have to take the rough with the smooth - in order to do something that is fundamentally exciting and glamorous, you will have to pay in other ways. Imagination, you do need to imagine something at an ideas stage. Empathy, both personal empathy with talent, and commercial empathy with distribution and finance. Knowing when you are being ripped off, knowing what a good deal is, having basic skills of business. Try and be organised, and if you are not organised, make yourself organised.

Q - Do you have any comments about bending the truth to get films made?

Richard - What we do is often all hot air, trying to persuade people to do something based on an idea - it is very difficult, very intangible. It tends to make people desperate, and they will do and say things that may not be entirely true, but that will get them to the next stage. Dishonestly is prevalent. You do have to make quick judgments about whether what people are saying is real. I

When To Shoot

GUERILLA FILM MAKER SAYS!

1. Traditionally, January and February are slow times for hire companies. It may be to your advantage to shoot during these months as you could get better discounts.

2. If your film is set at night, it will take longer to shoot as every shot will need to be lit. If you shoot during the day, it's possible to get away with little or no lighting. Shooting from the hip during daylight is the best way to cover a lot of ground when you don't have much time and money is really tight. Consider the possibilities of moving the production outdoors as much as possible during the hours of daylight. It is easier to manage an outdoor location, and there is less to damage.

3. If shooting outdoors, remember British weather. Consider shooting abroad in southern Spain or Portugal - it isn't as expensive as you might think. Days are longer and brighter as well. Don't discount the USA too, it's a possibility.

4. Crews and actors (especially), don't like being cold and wet. Try and work around bad weather, or if the script calls for it, control the weather by creating it with wind and rain machines.

5. Be aware of day and night length - it can get very dark or very light alarmingly quickly. Keep an eye out for the clock being moved forward or back and inform all the cast and crew.

6. Avoid Christmas if possible, everyone just goes silly. Summer months are filled with important people going on holiday.

7. If you shoot over weekends over a period of months, be aware of changing seasons as leaves on trees could become a problem.

8. Big films shoot in the summer, so getting good rates on kit can be more difficult.

9. Remember, you spend a lot of money when you shoot, and then edit for some time, then spend a lot of money at the final stages of post production. Summer months are traditionally quiet for post, so plan to do it then for the best deals. Avoid the end of tax year as tax films are rushed in before the end of May, as well as movies for Cannes.

know what it's like, someone comes through the door and says, *'I want to make your film'*, and you will believe that for as long as possible. Even though other people are telling you that it is not real, they don't have the money - you want very desperately to believe. I teach my kids that most people are good, very few people are full-on *'badd-uns'!* Most people do not want to let you down, but all of us are out there trying to make people believe that it's real. As we all know, 95% of it isn't.

Q - How do you think a producer should view their career plan, as opposed to a director?

Richard - I had a partnership with Stefan Schwartz that lasted twelve years, and was extremely successful. Most relationships though, aren't forever. People die, people change, people fall out, over specific or non-specific things. Often producers feel frustrated because they struggle through their 20's to get their first film made, they make a few in their 30's, all of which are slightly experimental, in terms of learning the process. They get to their mid to late-30's, early 40's feeling that they have experience, that they have maybe one or two films that have worked. They understand it now, but they have got nothing to do - effectively they run out of things to do. It is very humiliating. As soon as you feel fit for purpose, you feel you are not being given the opportunity to do it. How do you plan? I don't think you can. All I can say is, be modest in terms of, don't get killed by your overheads, don't be flash, until you can really afford to be flash. Realise that the greatest success could be followed by four years of dark, four years of *'can't get the film made',* and for reasons that are not your fault.

I, like you, was an early member of the NPA where we used to go out and just get it done. That is fine for your 20's or 30's, but this particular game does not breed many happy people. The weird irony is, that it is not just the failure that breeds bitterness, it's success too. There are producers who have made a great film, then get no money from it and are ripped off, and it drives them bonkers. It would drive me bonkers, I've been lucky.

Or they could be abandoned by the director that they had a success with and they don't see the benefit from the success they co-launched. It is not a healthy environment for most adults. I surround myself with a great partner, who is sane, with a wife and family who are sane and stabilising, and who also take the piss out of me and what I do. It keeps me grounded.

Q - What common mistakes do you see in other people?

Richard - Naiveté. I try not be cynical, but when people come out of another career, out of distribution into production, or out of an institutionalised media company into production, and they say *'I'm going to be making a film with Joel Schumacher next year!'* - I want to say *'No, you are not, believe me that is not going to happen!'*, and I stop myself every single time, because what's the point of that? I am not trying to crush them. The key thing is the naïve belief that they are going to buck the system. Some people do, some people win the lottery, there are those great stories where people just are very well organised, and partly because they are, they get the breaks and it happens for them. Then, market realities, people just ignoring market realities, making a film that is too expensive for that particular market, or saying *'I'm not going to cast that kind of actor in it, because they don't feel right'.* Whereas that is the only way a film is going to get made. That sort of common naiveté I find irritating.

Q - What advice would you offer a new film-maker?

Richard - Never give a personal guarantee, and never build anything with a flat roof.

Gary Phillips
Sales Agent

MOVIE CONCEPT ...KNOW THE MARKET

Q - What is your job?

Gary - I work at *'Moviehouse Entertainment',* which is a film sales company. The core job of the company is to sell rights to films, internationally, on behalf of producers. Producers come to us with partially or completely financed films, sometimes they come with finished films, and we take them to the international market - through specific industry events and markets, through the festival circuit, and by going after the local distributors in each country.

Q - Given that your job takes place at the very end of the film making process, why talk to you before it's even shot?

Gary - People come to us at a very early stage and say *'I want to make this film'*, sometimes they have all the finance but they need a sales agent attached to give comfort to financiers. They also come to us to say, *'what do you think, you are the guys going out into the market place?'* And this is the eternal question to which I agonise because I don't know the answer. Then again, no-one does! It's the old William Goldman line, *'nobody knows anything!'*

However, if I were to give advice, you want people to come to you with an innovative idea, something no-one else has thought of, or a version no-one else has thought of, or a way of doing something that's new and gets people excited. It's about trying to be innovative, and original. If someone comes to you and says, *'I'm going to make the next 'Blair Witch'!'*, then it's *'No, wrong! It's been done, that was a complete fluke and no-one is ever going to make that amount again on something like that.'* Sometimes people come to us or another sales agent and we just won't *'get it'*, yet they may click with someone else - you want to work with people who understand you and what it is they are selling.

New film makers often need to be bolder, in terms of who they try to get. Actors, DP's, composers and everyone else in the process, want to be involved with good projects. If you as a first time film-maker come to us and say *'I've got this great idea, but I've got no real known cast... but I've got this DP, and he has done this, that and the other, and the music is going to be by this person because I've sold it to them, and they have got a passion for it'*, that means something. No-one sets out to make a bad film, and if they make what they say they are going to make, and they have people around them who have a track record, it can make a big difference. Some people try to get *'name'* executive producers to *'god-father'* projects, people who can help to bring the talent in, and to lend their film credibility, and that is sometimes a good thing to do.

Q - So aim high, as high as you can possibly reach, and then further?

Gary - Yes. It's about making the sum of the parts greater than the whole, and that's in all respects. It is about getting the most you can out of it, doing the best you can, being positive about it, without taking an attitude that you or the film is the best thing ever.

Q - This is an unanswerable question, but what kind of films should a new film-maker make?

Gary - OK, that is an unanswerable question. Next! For a new or low budget film maker I really believe it is about coming up with original stories, thoughts, characters, ways of doing things. I do think the market is divided into various areas. You've got kind of extreme art-house stuff going on. You have documentaries, an area that has become increasingly interesting and popular (perhaps due to miniDV making it easy to shoot and edit). Then there is the commercial fair, such as two girls and a gun, or two guns and a girl in a fast car! One area which is perceived as big at the moment is Horror. I was recently talking to a distributor friend at the American Film Market, explaining that we have been looking for one as it appears to be a growing area, and he shot back with *'Ah but Gary, there are 300 companies in this building, and 200 of them have horror films!'* So for every *do* there's a *don't!* Then of course this person went on to say *'of course most of them aren't any good'*, and *'how do you sort out the wheat from the chaff?'* It always comes back to *'nobody knows anything'*.

Q - Do you think it's likely that a new film-maker is going to make a successful business out of their first film?

Gary - It can happen, but history tells us that the odds are stacked against it. It could financially fail, yet still be successful in opening doors for the next project. I consider that if you get your money back on your first film, it's a success! For me, *'The Blair Witch Project'* was not a success, it was a phenomenon! So the realistic bench mark you should be aiming for is to break even. There are so many people out there trying to do this now, it's incredible. I left here at 7 o'clock last night, went home and watched a documentary film which was in the Sundance film festival the other week and has been offered to us. On my way home I read a script and finished it after I watched the documentary, and started another on my way in this morning. I've got two more scripts, and four more films to watch now, all of them from people who have every right to say to me, *'look, you asked to see this thing, we pitched it, and we want an answer'*. There is a lot of competition out there.

Q - Should you make and try to sell a short film instead?

Gary - From a commercial point of view in terms of film sales, there's no substantial market for short films. People say the value they have is an education in the mechanics of film-making, getting the crew, and the talent together, and making it happen. They are also a calling card to show off your skills as a film maker.

Q - So given that there is a lot of good stuff out there, is 'good' enough?

Gary - It is good enough, if it sells! Remember, we do not sell to a local distributor, or the guy who rents the DVD or buys the ticket. The challenge for us, and the film makers when conceptualising a project, is how to get a bunch of jaded industry *I've-seen-it-all-before* people excited. I always to say to film-makers, *'It is very simple, make the best film you possibly can, maybe an award-winner, something that will break out at the box office, something that is absolutely brilliant, and then I will be able to sell it!'* But inevitably it doesn't end up like that, even if they do make a good film. There are 300 to 400 companies selling films internationally, each with a whole slew of projects. It's a very tough market place. Persistence is very important, like in Dawn Steele's book, *'if you can't get in the front door, go in the back door, if you can't get in the back door, go in the side door...'* and *'don't ever, ever, ever take it personally'*, that is very important too. It's easy for me to sit here and talk about this, but I go to the market with my fantastic films and the distributors can turn round and go *'Urgh!'*, and I'd get really upset and reply, *'this film is really good, you so-and-so! You should be buying it, you should me making something of it!'*

When selling to distributors, perhaps at script stage, they now say, *'look, we've got to see some footage'*, so you show them, then they say *'we've got to see the finished film!'*, so you show them the finished film, then they say *'yeah, actually we like it, but we want to see, the poster, we want to see the trailer, we want to know how to sell it, and...'* if it's a British film they will say *'who is releasing it in the UK, how did it do?'* and you are literally having to remove as much risk as possible from the equation. They have businesses to run, and quite rightly are extremely opposed to risk. You walk down your high street and you want to buy a pair of trainers. There's a hundred shops selling them, but you only need one pair! Distributors, in many cases, handle half dozen, or a dozen films a year. Some of them more, some of them significantly more, but many handle less. And there are so many films out there, so why should they pick yours, or mine, or anybody else's? Even though we handle films with names attached, with bigger budgets, with smaller budgets, ultimately it just comes back to *is the film any good?* It always comes back to that.

MOVIEHOUSE
ENTERTAINMENT

Gary Phillips
Managing Director

9 Grafton Mews • London • W1T 5HZ
Tel: +44 (0)20 7380 3999 • Fax: +44 (0)20 7380 3998
Mobile: +44 (0)7973 627494
E-mail: gary.phillips@moviehouseent.com

TO GENRE or NOT TO GENRE

Should your film be a genre film? Here are some pros and cons to help you decide.

Pros:	Cons:
Easier to write because the genre (action, horror, comedy, romantic comedy, sci-fi etc.) has certain rules on how characters act and what they do.	*Difficult to come up with a unique story because most ideas have been done before.*
Can be easier to get funding as these films perform well irrespective of critical acclaim, as long as they deliver on the promise of the genre - a horror film will scare you, a thriller will be thrilling etc.	*Familiarity of story can be off-putting to the larger production companies and UK grant organisations.*
	It's difficult to attract big stars to these lower budget genre films, unless you get your wallet out - and you don't have a wallet!
Many genre films can be done on low budgets and within a limited number of locations.	*If no big stars are attached then distributors may pass as it doesn't compete with the big movies out there.*
A slight twist on a genre film may make your film rise up above the rest.	*Often rejected form film festivals as they prefer more "dramatic" or "indie" films.*
If it's blisteringly good, your career will be launched.	*If it's only good, or worse still, it's not good, it will not help your long term career.*

The other area that is very important is marketing. Websites where people can look at reviews, artwork, stills, watch the trailer, help immensely and are cheap and easy to do.

Q - Is a new film maker going to get 'pre sales' on their film?

Gary - No. And it's not just independent film makers who can't make pre sales. A buyer said to me recently, *'why do I need to pre-buy this film, I would only do that under very extreme circumstances, and this isn't it'.* It is so hard to tell if a film will be a success even when complete, never mind when it's just a screenplay! Buyers now have an attitude where they say *'we would rather pay more to see the finished film, than pre-buy a film for less and have it turn out terribly'.*

Q - Or even just mediocre? Or even good?

Gary - Yes, exactly, precisely! I'm not saying the pre-sell business doesn't exist, it absolutely does exist, but it depends what area you are in, if you are making films for millions of pounds, and you have big names, sure it exists, but otherwise I would not rely on it.

Q - Why would a distributor in a foreign territory not just stay with 'Troy' or 'American Pie'?

Gary - I was in a pre-market meeting with one Distributor and I said *'whose got the hot pictures?'* She went through 8 or so films, all of which were costing $40m more or less. I asked how many distributors could afford to buy even one of those films, in France, Germany, Italy or wherever? That business bears no resemblance to our world. What the distributors are looking for, in many respects, is that little jewel that cost a fraction, and turns over a huge amount, that will play to TV, will attract the video (and DVD) crowd. The video crowd will be looking for great art work, something exciting, because often people choose what they want only after physically seeing the box.

Television provides a huge proportion of potential revenue, and when a distributor comes and buys all rights in a territory, they look to sell the rights to TV, not immediately, but at some point down the line. If you are selling a film in the UK, and the film contains a huge amount of swearing, nudity or violence, then it is going to be tougher for it to be played on TV, or for it to play at a time on TV that commands a very good return. The TV buyers are going to say *'well, we can only can only play it after 11 o'clock at night, and* for that we only pay Y rather than Z!' I had a script one time, and said to the producer, 'Is it necessary to have the characters swear constantly?' You can make whatever film you want, that's not my business, but it is to sell the film. Choices you make could end up with conversations like 'It is going to be tough to get a TV placement for this, and if I do, it is only going to be worth X instead of Y'.

Once, I was negotiating a deal with a distributor in a big, foreign territory. We finished the meeting, they walked out of the room, then straight into another room with the chief buyer of that country's big television network... they put their heads together, smiled, chuckled, slapped each other on the back, and I knew basically it was a done deal. I'd sold my film to them and they had sold their film to him! That's the game.

Underlining what I've said, there is of course the McDonalds factor. You or I could walk down the road and go and get one, or we could go to Heathrow airport, fly for ten hours, and walk into a place 5,000 miles away and know if we walk into a McDonalds we'd get the same thing. When people pay their £5 to go to the cinema, they want to know 'I'm going to see a horror film, I'm going to see a chick flick' y'know, they have that expectation and they want to see that. But within that framework, which they expect, they want originality. It is like, 'I want it to be original, as long as it suits me,' there is that aspect to it.

Q - I guess that is one of the reasons we have movie stars, we like the certainty of Tom Cruise in a thriller, we know who he is and are comfortable with that, but then we like to see him do something different?

Gary - Yes. You have an immediate expectation when you hear names like Julia Roberts, Tom Cruise or Morgan Freeman for instance. For a new film maker you don't have those names, so you will have to rely on strong artwork and a great title to build interest and expectation. What is a film star? A film star is someone, who if they are in a film, and because they are in that film, you get up out of your chair, and you go to the movies. Brit film-makers often think that because you are a star on TV, that that will work on film. It's not the case, it's still like having an unknown cast for a film.

Q - Would you recommend a new film-maker go to Cannes, BEFORE making their film?

Gary - Yes. I believed people should not live in a cosseted world. Go to as many film events and festivals as you can. You don't necessarily have to go to the south of France, there are great UK places such as the London Film Festival or Edinburgh Film Festivals.

Q - After making three films, and studying others, I believe there is no tried and tested way in, it's whatever works for you. The only thing you can really change is the quantity of hard work you put in, everything else is so much down to a kind of lottery?

Gary - You are absolutely right, you can do all this stuff, you can get to the stars, and you can still get buried in the ground, and everywhere in between! In my opinion though, that is the one thing that the first time film-maker can always hold dear, that you can actually compete in the game.

Q - What advice would you offer a new film-maker?

Gary - Get out there and talk to as many people as you can, people who have done it. People in related areas, and try to understand that just because something worked today, that doesn't mean it's going to work tomorrow. Just because something didn't work today, doesn't mean it won't work tomorrow. Many really, really good films have failed. You could make a great film and it's success could largely be dictated by whether the sun was shining or it was raining on the weekend of its release. You must be able to honestly look in the mirror and say 'people are going to want to pay their £5 to see my movie'. And ask why should they? And why shouldn't they? Don't delude yourself.

Know what you are making. If it's a thriller, you should be on the edge of your seat. If it's a romance, you've got tears! If it's a comedy it should be a funny film, and that, in all cases, means *all the film!*

Liesbeth Beeckman
Producer

SHOOTING IN THE STATES

Q - Tell me about how you came to be a Producer?

Liesbeth - I've worked as a freelance production manager for the last 6 years. I was working my way up as a production co-ordinator and found that I'd really like to produce myself. When you are working on other people's projects you get to the point where you would like to do your own project. I had worked on other people's projects and put all my energy and passion in, but I just didn't have enthusiasm about their specific content. You get to the point where you want to do it yourself.

Q - When you say 'Right, I'm going to give up my freelance or full time job, and I'm going to go out and do this thing', how do you survive?

Liesbeth - Credit cards are good! The good thing about freelance work in the media business is that when you get work, you get well paid. So if you can get the work, it's not too hard to juggle the two and work off your debts.

Q - Tell me about the story of the film, what is the concept of the movie?

Liesbeth - It's a road movie about a young woman who thinks she's been cloned. She sees a girl, who looks exactly like her when she was small, and it triggers something in her head, and she decides to kidnap her and drives through the desert to her home.

Q - Is it quite art-house in its direction?

Liesbeth - Yes.

Q - So it is an art-house thriller drama?

Liesbeth - Yes.

Q - The main difference between this and other low budget Brit pics is that it's shot in the USA. Why go to the USA?

Liesbeth - There are several reasons. You always have to stand out, so the low budget productions that I made here have that same look to them. For our specific story, we needed a desert location, because the woman had isolated herself from the world, so we needed to find an isolated place. Plus because we had virtually no lighting budget, we needed a location with amazing lighting, and so we started looking at different desert locations. We looked at Spain and other parts of Europe, then we decided on Nevada as at that time, the dollar was starting to drop so comparatively you could shoot it more cheaply in the US than in Europe. Nevada still came out a little bit expensive, but then Viki, the Exec Producer, remembered when she and Isabelle (Director) went travelling through the States and they came through New Mexico and found this stunning location. So we decided to go back there and started researching.

From a cinematic perspective, because we were shooting in a visually stunning place, everywhere we pointed the camera looked amazing. The US backdrop also feels very cinematic in a way that is very hard to achieve back here in the UK and other parts of Europe.

Q - I know your picture isn't completed yet, so I don't want to reveal your budget as that will potentially have an impact on sales, but it is a low budget?

Liesbeth - Yes.

Q - Where did the money come from?

Liesbeth - Private investment. The investors are very happy with what they have seen so far.

Q - How did you move the investment money to the States?

Liesbeth - We opened a US dollar account in the UK that allowed us to transfer money to US companies and write USD checks. We also opened US credit card accounts. We then transferred money from the UK to the US so we could spend it there.

Q - Was that process quite easy to set up?

Liesbeth - Yes. Once we went on a recce to New Mexico we met with the local Film Commission, and they said we had to contact their local tax office to register as a UK company that is allowed to trade in that state. It doesn't cost anything, you just send them a letter when you are there, and they give you a tax ID number, and that is it, you are off.

Q - Is the whole picture shot in the States?

Liesbeth - Yes. Shot on HDcam. We had an amazing deal from Panavision, in Los Angeles. Before we went to the States, Isabelle went to see the guys in the UK office and told them the story and all about the film. That paved the way for the amazing deal we got in the States.

Q - Are there State incentives?

Liesbeth - Yes, we got 15% of the money we spent in New Mexico back. Each State has its own incentives.

Q - How long did you shoot for?

Liesbeth - 6 weeks.

Q - How big was the crew?

Liesbeth - Isabelle was a first time Director and she carried your *Guerilla Film Makers Movie Blueprint* under her arm the whole time, cursing its weight, but it was an invaluable guide through the project! We brought the core crew over from the UK, the DOP and assistant, sound mixer, 1st AD, and locally hired a few more such as a boom operator, make up consultant etc. The crew was around 15 people.

Q - Were you able to shoot quite a lot, quite quickly?

Liesbeth - Yes, as the days were long, the light was amazing and we had a small unit.

Q - How much preparation time did you have?

Liesbeth - The Director went over to the USA a month before we started shooting, and I came over 2 weeks before we started shooting. We did a lot of prep here in the UK though.

Q - Where did you live?

Liesbeth - We were meant to stay in a Youth Hostel with lots of rooms, a big kitchen, and we could take it over and have our base there. When we went on our recce in March we discovered it had burnt down to the ground! So we had to quickly re-think. The people from the Youth Hostel found us a local house with huge rooms and we rented that instead.

Q - How did you manage the catering?

Liesbeth - We provided the catering ourselves just by going to Walmart, buying in bulk, and making that last as long as you can. Once a week we would take everyone out to the local restaurant.

Q - What about Production design, Costume, Make-up, that kind of stuff?

Liesbeth - That was all handled by American film maker friends of ours, our contacts through the local film office.

Q - I assume you made the bleakness of the desert work in your favour with production design and the story?

Liesbeth - Yes. The local NBC channel interviewed us, and they said as a location, it was a ready-made movie set, and it is true. It is the true wild west, you still find things there from the days of Billy the Kid. It was just a matter of doing recce's.

Q - Did you need permits? Were they expensive?

Liesbeth - Compared to shooting here in London, shooting in New Mexico was both cheap and easy. People were inviting us to their house and to their land, saying *'please just come and shoot here!'*. All you would have to do is request a State Permit, free of charge, just stating which roads you will be on at which time, and they send you the permit. They can give you support as well, so if you have to stop traffic you can call the local sheriff a day or so in advance, and they would send out their Deputy.

Q - How many actors were in the film?

Liesbeth - Four lead actors and a few smaller parts.

Q - Where did they all come from?

Liesbeth - A mixture of British and American actors. One British actor played an American and did the accent.

Q - Did you have any unique problems shooting in the desert?

Liesbeth - Wind! The wind created lots of sound problems. We will need to do quite a lot of ADR (dialogue replacement in post production). The HDCam took to the extreme conditions very well. We also took a trailer to all our locations, so people could hide in the shade, drink cool water and rest etc. It was a portable rest room, kitchen, make-up, production office, everything.

Q - How did the crew and cast enjoy the experience? Making a film in the UK, especially in Winter, is just horrible, and even in the Summer it is cramped... Was all that open space and fresh air just a breath of fresh air to be in?

Liesbeth - Yes. That is how I got people excited about the project. We can't pay you very much, but you'll get to film in New Mexico for 5 weeks. We started off in Los Angeles by picking up the equipment as there are not that many facilities local to New Mexico.

Q - What were the major expenses in terms of just being in the States? What time of year was it?

Liesbeth - Literally a year ago, in May last year (2004). We booked the plane tickets well in advance, so we got cheap fares, but the main expenses were the same as here, feeding people! Also, with shooting in the States you have to get extra insurance,

Pic by Richard Smith

Pete Bryden
Filmmaker

Q - What do you do?

Pete - I like to think of myself as a creator. I've always loved the concept of creating something from nothing. I'm a musician, a writer and an artist, and I have a number of small businesses. Film and television has a definite appeal to me with the various elements of creativity that are combined in any one project.

Q - What is the show you have done?

Pete - 'Summerton Mill' is a series of 13, 4 minute animations, commissioned by the BBC and first being transmitted on CBeebies as part of Tikkabilla from September to December, 2005. It's a stop-frame animation, so it involves working with real sets and puppets, as opposed to computer screens.

Q - How did the technology work - camera, capturing etc?

Pete - When we made the pilot episode, we used my Canon XL1 on a chunky tripod. Stability is always an issue with stop-frame animation, because even a gentle tap on the camera can often result in a slightly different framing that can be difficult, if not impossible, to match up. We used the XL1 as a capture device, linking to our PC via Firewire. We captured using the Australian software Stop Motion Pro which was great, and only cost about £150 for a single machine licence. The software allowed us to view our sequences while we were shooting, to add and delete frames, and to onion-skin which is a facility whereby you can compare two shots while they sit on top of each other. We usually did a bit of tweaking in Stop Motion Pro, adding in and deleting the odd frame here and there, and then exported the complete sequence as an AVI, importing that into Premiere to replace the relevant animatic.

Because this system had worked perfectly well for the pilot episode, we decided to capture the commissioned episodes in the same way. The only difference was that we moved over to the Sony DSR-450 camera which has a 16:9 chip. This meant that we could deliver full-height anamorphic video to the BBC. Our final edits were delivered to the post production facility on a portable firewire drive and, after final checks and tweaks, transferred to Digi Beta ready for delivery.

Childrens' Animation on a Budget

Q - Do you record the voices before animating?

Pete - Each episode is narrated, with the narrator doing all the character voices. We record a rough voiceover, take it into Premiere, along with a series of animatics, edit a rough version of the episode to the exact episode length, and then replace the animatics with our stop-frame animated clips as we progress through the shoot. We record the final voiceover at the end, once we're sure that there won't be any more changes to the scripts.

Q - How do you deal with lip sync?

Pete - Our puppets have fairly static faces, as did those in some of the old classic children's programmes like Trumpton, Camberwick Green and The Magic Roundabout. Apart from the occasional blink, all expression changes are left to the imagination. It's strange, but most people don't even notice that there's no facial movement until you point it out to them. This makes it much faster to animate.

Q - How do you build sets and puppets?

Pete - The sets for the pilot episode were less substantial than those that we built before starting production of the commissioned episodes. We shot the pilot episode in a bare-walled unfinished extension at my house. The hillsides on the pilot episode sets were made from various-sized blocks of wood with chicken wire stretched over the top, a generous layer of papie mache, and then the grass and foliage on top. For the commissioned episodes, we progressed to polystyrene slabs, carved into shape which gave a much sturdier base. We built lots of detail into the sets, making everything as realistic as possible. We went as far as making hundreds of tiny red clay roofing tiles for a section of the roof of Summerton Mill. Another section was blue slate, and we had these cut from welsh blue slate, by a welsh slate cutter! Sections of the building are part-timbered and we used pieces cut from some 17th Century floorboards that I had lying around in a shed.

I made the puppets for the pilot episode using a wooden block as the main body, carved builders' foam (the sort that comes in an aerosol) for the heads, brass rods, jointed at the hips and ankles for the legs, and bundles of aluminium wire for the arms

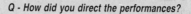

and neck. I took them down to Scary Cat Studios at Bristol before we went into full production, and they wrapped latex around my original carvings and re-cast the heads out of plastic. They also replaced the joints with more durable ball and sockets

Q - How did you light it?

Pete - We experimented with indirect lighting, and settled for a number of paper lanterns and 200 watt bulbs. The whole rig was less than 2K of lights. This avoided having to do a new lighting setup for each shot but had its problems in that tiny changes in the supply voltage resulted in visible lighting changes. We worked around this when we went into full production by running through a lighting desk, allowing us to tweak the levels to counteract any unwanted changes.

Q - How much is done in planning before you shoot?

Pete - Approximately one third of each shooting day was spent planning the shot. We broke each shot down into frames and

decided what each character and moving prop was to be doing at any time. We also had a comprehensive series of checks that we went through before each shoot. Every now and then we'd have something go wrong, like one day when we realised at the end of a shot that a lump of Blue Tac was visible on the roof of the cow shed, and another check was added to our list.

Q - How did you do the sound?

Pete - We went to a local studio to record the final voiceover. We came away with a series of wav files on disk. Ed then locked himself away in our sound studio for a few

weeks, mixing the narration and character voices, and adding all the sound effects. We had already recorded the music, and this was added to give a rough mix. We then sat down together for a few days, listening to each episode over and over again, tweaking and adjusting until we were both happy with the end result. We then sent our final mixes over to a post production facility where our video and audio levels were checked and given final tweaks.

Q - How did you direct the performances?

Pete - Ed and I worked together most of the time, directing and animating as we worked through each shoot. There were times when our assistant, James, was left to do a shot on his own. Before leaving him, Ed or I would discuss the shot and explain what we wanted to achieve. We then left him to get on with it, making his own fine-tuning decisions as he progressed.

Q - How long did it take?

Pete - We aimed to achieve 14 seconds of footage per day throughout the 10 month shooting period. We started off with me working at the front of the main set, animating the main characters, James on one of the back sets looking after background characters, and Ed at the computer desk, capturing each individual shot. James was soon promoted from assistant animator to animator, and we then had lots of flexibility. Towards the end of production, James and I animated alone in shifts, while Ed locked himself in the back room doing the sound edit.

Q - How much space did you need?

Pete - Our studio is big enough to take three 8ft x 4ft sets with room to walk between them, leaving plenty of space to set the camera up where it's needed. It's about 30ft long and 15ft wide. It was big enough, but wouldn't have worked if it was any smaller. There were times when we could have done with an extra room, perhaps just big enough for close-ups, so that two animators could have worked at the same time on different shots.

Q - Could you expand this concept into feature length?

Pete - We've been looking at the possibility of producing a feature-length film using the same production setup. It's definitely possible, and could be achieved with a relatively small budget.

Q - What advantages are there to making a childrens film?

Pete - Most people fancy the idea of writing for children. There's something about the simplicity, the innocent humour, and even an element of nostalgia that is part of the appeal. New film makers rarely think of making a low budget children's film, which is strange as there is so much programming time during the day that broadcasters need product for. Children will also make leaps of imagination that adults find harder, such as characters talking without lip sync.

Q - What advice would you offer a new film maker?

Pete - If you believe in your idea, get out there and make it happen.

because the UK public liability won't cover the US liability, so it is roughly double. That was really it, there was actually no major differences than shooting it here.

Q - How much did you spend on insurance roughly?

Liesbeth - £1,500 in total for both the UK production insurance, and the US liability.

Q - So it's still not breaking the bank?

Liesbeth - No, as I said, we actually saved money filming there because the dollar was so strong we managed to go twice as far with our money.

Q - Did you shoot production stills?

Liesbeth - Yes, though we didn't shoot any behind the scenes video for the DVD.

Q - Did you have any union problems as the US unions are notoriously powerful?

Liesbeth - No, to the contrary, they were very helpful. I think we were too low budget to be bothered about, plus we were a UK production company. We did hire some crew locally though we were unable to pay union rates. As long as you call people early enough, and you tell them what you are doing, there were very little problems. Everyone was quite happy. The film office and local film makers were very helpful in getting us through problems we didn't have any knowledge of.

Q - Do you think that, the fact that you were a bunch of European girls, helped? You must have seemed quite exotic to your average New Mexican local?

Liebeth - I am sure that it helped, yes (grins).

Q - How did you handle post production?

Liesbeth - We made the mistake of hiring the edit system locally, which just created problems when bringing the project back to the UK. In hindsight, I would have shot on 25P and taken my own Final Cut Pro over there, so I could just bring it back after the shoot. I would need to plan how to get the HDCam material digitised into the system, and when you are in another country, technical problems could cripple you. Plan.

Q - How have sales people responded to the film?

Liesbeth - We are still in post production and negotiating with sales agents. Most people comment that the film looks amazing and not at all what they expect from a low budget British film.

Q - What mistakes did you make?

Liesbeth - None worth talking about. Just the usual day to day film problems, which you sort out as and when you get to them.

Q - What advice would you offer a new film maker?

Liesbeth - You can do it, so just go and do it. Also don't get stuck making endless short films, which I see so many new film makers doing. They are a great learning experience and a great calling card, but don't just keep making one after another.

www.blue-whaleproductions.com

Ashvin Kumar
Director

OSCAR NOMINATED SHORT

Q - How did the Little Terrorist come about?

Ashvin - My first not so short short-film, *Road To Ladakh,* disqualified itself from most film festivals due to its running time of 50 minutes, and I was still hungry for a film that would be a success in the festivals circuit. *Little Terrorist* was inspired by an incident on the India-Pakistan border where a child crossed over and was subsequently returned to his village. I developed the story further by adding characters and the underlying Hindu-Muslim prejudice, which seemed to me the right way of going about it. The tonsuring of the head became a metaphor. I pretty much wrote the final draft of the script in a week in October and we were shooting end of December.

Q - How did you fund the film and how much did it cost?

Ashvin - Much of the film was made off favours, discounts and free-bees. Mainly recruiting crew from Shooting People to not only work free of cost but also fund their travel to India. The entire sound post was sponsored by Future Film in Soho. Deluxe, Computamatch (neg cutting), Fuji gave us a generous discounts. I edited the film on my G4 laptop, and we did a best light telecine for the rushes which I colour corrected on Final Cut Pro and remains the video version of the film. Sound designer Roland Heap used Pro Tools on his personal PC to lay tracks, went out into his garden in Sussex and did Foley and FX. We knew we wouldn't have money to do a proper musical recording so we took advantage of the mics and DAT on set to record the music live, and we used local musicians who were very cheap. Then the music composer, Nainita, pitched in with fusing it into a score, of course for free. British Council helped with making the prints once they'd seen the video version of the film. But production funding was organised by my own private funds and passing the hat around the family. The cash spent on the film was around £20k, but its become much more expensive now that the fallout of the Oscars, we've been forced to make more prints, spend on travel (Oscars don't pay for you to go to LA and that limo IS expensive!), festivals and so on. But I am pleased to say that since Feb 2005 whatever we've spent has been earned back via screening fees, DVD sales, royalties, telecast rights. I regret however that we have not been able to pay neither our investment or our crew back yet. And we've incurred more expenses than we would have done, had there been no Oscars.

Q - After you made it, what was your next step in getting it out there?

Ashvin - My first instinct as soon as we had a final locked picture cut on my laptop was to run off 100 copies and zap them across to as many festivals as possible. Soon after we got a confirmation that Montreal wanted it in competition but Locarno Film Festival wanted it really badly too. They promised to highlight it since it was going to be an India 'year'. That was a big decision because Locarno was in July, much earlier than Montreal (Sept 2004) which meant the film would be out there quicker. I decided to hang on because Montreal was an Oscars accredited festival and I thought that the film had a good chance. I did my research then stuck to my guns in spite of being hounded my Locarno and their Indian representative. I spent that time promoting the film and entered it into the Cannes Film Market. I got a sales agent in France to represent it. I had learned from RTL that doing private screenings was a waste of time. Instead I sent at least 300 copies to those who's radar I wanted to be in. Agents, producers, distributors, sales agents, actors, directors and so on, and was hoping that I'd get some kind of representation. And now that we've done nearly 80 international film festivals, I have to say that festivals are the most cost effective way of getting the film screened and noticed. I've always used my jaunts to Cannes as a learning experience for the big one. To understand how the international sales market works and what its all about. And using my short to engage people so one can learn from very busy professionals. So I used *Little Terrorist* as a door opener in trying to hustle people into listening / sharing. At that time, there was no nomination or festival wins.

Q - How did you get your film nominated for an Oscar?

Ashvin - We won Montreal, filled out a one page form and dispatched a print to the academy. In December I got a call saying we'd been short listed down to the last 10 and would I please send them another print. Which I did and checked the website on the 28th of Feb, and there we were… nominated!

Q - Once you got nominated for an Oscar, and the week leading up to the Oscars, was Hollywood knocking at your door?

Ashvin - Let's put it this way, when I knocked at Hollywood's door, it opened. For instance I arranged an introduction to ICM LA and ended up with representation with them. I am sure if I needed to I could approach a producer that I might want to work with and they'd do lunch or whatever they do out there. By then, however, I was in a position of having written two feature films with one of them partially financed. My aim therefore was to raise the profile of that picture, in which I am both a producer and director, and close the financing. It's something that I am working on even now, so I am not sure if it becomes any easier. I think people just start taking you quite a bit more seriously. It certainly helps if you do win the Oscar of course (which was won by *'Wasp'*). The media approaches you a little more. And everyone wants to come and look at the statue. In India they'd go berserk if I'd won. But how much of that translates into deals / finance? Not much. Money is always money. In the end, someone is going to do due diligence on your script and have to make a call. An Oscar nomination allays inherent fears about a debutant director and looks good on paper. In career terms, it just becomes that much easier and you get answers that much quicker. People take meetings with you. And ask you if you spoke with Nicole Kidman.

Q - Ok, so now you're an Oscar Nominated film director, how has that changed your life and career?

Ashvin - It's accelerated the course that I was on. The lonely, desperate world of an aspiring film maker is decidedly a thing of the past. There seems to be more security now. People return your calls. Sometimes they even pick up the phone and call themselves. And you get invited to a lot of fancy gigs, get to talk a lot about your experiences, showcase the various trials to reach here. But I am still struggling to close the finance on my picture and that is the kind of reality that brings one down to earth very quickly. People who I respect and admire want to work with me. That is the best part of it. The acknowledgement feels special. Actors and senior crew members. That kind of thing is a little harder when one's an unknown.

Q - What are you doing now and is it as a result of getting nominated?

Ashvin - No. I am making a thriller called *The Forest,* which was already in the making before this happened. Indeed, the Oscars are the reason why we had to push our shoot from April 2005 to November 2005. But there is not much I could have done with the nomination on this one, it already had a sales agent attached with an advance, an Indian cast and some of the financing in place. But if, say, I was ready to attach a Hollywood star, which is what I need to do with my next one, the nomination would have helped. The head of steam was right, and getting it into the right hands and doing the meeting right after the awards would have been possible. However, even though the script was written, I wasn't happy with it so decided to defer. It also makes me think about what all this means at the end. It's all about public perception and a bit of smoke and mirrors. How people can talk you up and get you a gig somewhere.

Q - What advice would you offer short filmmakers out there?

Ashvin - The 'market' is a real thing. And shorts are not only a great way of presenting credentials, they also provide an opportunity to enrich understanding of how the money side of film-making works. Then, being immersed in the entire process from labs to markets is a great learning opportunity, one that you probably won't get on a feature. It's also a chance of trying everything yourself once. Spending time thinking about what you're going to do with your masterpiece is as important as getting it done. Define expectations, not just a mythical *'someone will swoop down and recognise my genius'* or *'I am a writer/director, not a producer'*. It should be a concrete plan with safety nets and fall backs. I'd say just do it no matter how small or on what format. The important thing is to have it in the bag and on DVD to show.

Chris Atkins
Film Maker

HIGH DEF
AN OVERVIEW

Q - Tell me about what you have done?

Chris - I was fortunate to realise early on that the future of filmmaking, certainly low budget and independent filmmaking, was going to be digital, shooting on a digital acquisition format, HD, DigiBeta, Viper etc., rather than 35mm or Super 16mm film.

Q - When you say HD, there are several versions of what HD means, what kind of HD are you talking about?

Chris - I would advise you to shoot on a format where the definition is acceptable for cinema release. There is little point, even on a £20k movie, in shooting a substandard format. At that level, you and your crew aren't going to get paid. It's then years of work, sweating blood over it, to get completed, and the last thing you want is something that looks substandard, and that is never going to stand a hope in hell of getting a release in the market place because it was shot on DV, or the latest prosumer camera. Your film will not get a release if it looks crap.

Q - What do you consider to be the lowest quality HD format that is worth considering?

Chris - The key is to shoot images in true progressive scan mode, and not interlaced. I'd say the minimum, is currently the Panasonic DVCProHD format. We just shot *The Woman in Winter* on that, and it is pushing it in some scenes. Even though the frame size is smaller than HDV, DVCProHD has better colour sampling and a much higher data rate, 100mbit, as opposed to the HDV at 25mbit - the result is a much more robust image for post production. It is also capable of shooting slow motion as well as frame rates like 4fps for time lapse. For example, *'In the mood for love'* was shot on DVCProHD, which included lots of slow motion. The format is also better in low light than the Sony HDV format and HDCam. For all those reasons it was the right camera for that shoot. If we were shooting a normal drama in daylight, we would have used the Sony HDcam.

DVCProHD is great for shooting, but for post it is really fiddly, where HDcam is much easier to work with. It isn't about one format being better than another, it is about working out what format is best for the shoot, what cameras are best for the shoot. The size of them, the weight of them on Steadicam, handheld, what lenses do you use, there is no right or wrong answer.

Q - Having gone through post production on many HD features, what frame rate would you shoot on - 24p or 25p?

Chris - 25! 25! 25! I can thank the Guerilla Film Makers Handbook for saying that when I made my first feature. I have this argument over and over again, and I'm about to have it with my bloody DP on the next feature, and I always win because I write the cheques! What do you gain by shooting 24p? You gain the fact that the action is the same speed on set as it is in the cinema, possibly, as long as the cinema runs at 24fps. If you actually research it, cinemas run at anything from 22 to 27 frames per second, depending on how old the projector is, and how quickly they want to get people out of the cinema. Most cinemas run it at whatever speed they want anyway. The majority of people are going to see any film on DVD, be it a little low budget Brit feature or *Lord of the Rings*. So when your film is on DVD, it will run at 25fps anyway. So actually saying shoot at 24p, so that people can see it at 24fps is nonsense. So what do you lose by shooting at 24p? Lots of time, lots of money, and you gain lots of heart ache.

So you get an insignificant and imperceptible gain by shooting at 24p, and also loose a huge amount of time and money, which is not something you want to do on a low budget film. Choose 25! Post then becomes 3 times easier, you save loads of money that you can spend on music, in the art department, props, better actors, things that matter. Say to the DP, well, you can either have these nice Ziess prime lenses or you can shoot 24p, but you can't have both. Do you want 3 steadicam days, or do you want to shoot 24p? When you bring it down to that, people will suddenly start shooting 25p! Everyone is going to watch it on DVD or TV anyway, which runs at 25fps, whether you want it to or not.

Q - Another thing that isn't very often talked about is colour space. What are the advantages and disadvantages, starting again with the very low end?

Chris - HD, on the lower end formats, is compressed so that it can squeeze the picture into an acceptable data rate. One of the things that gets highly compressed is the colour part of the image. Only the very top end formats don't compress the colour space. HDCam is less compressed than DVCProHD, and DVCProHD is less compressed than HDV, and this compression of the colour becomes more of a problem in post and grading than is apparent on the shoot.

Q - Is shooting blue or green screen a problem in HD formats as the colours are compressed?

Chris - Yes it is a problem, which is why anything with 4.2.2 sampling, like the Panasonic Varicam (DVCProHD), is actually much better for green screen and blue screen. If you are going to shoot green screen in a studio, using a Genesis camera that is true RGB, it is ten times better. If you start compressing your colours, you are going to get problems getting a 'key' to remove the green screen from the shot. You are going get messy edges.

Q - What do you think a producer should be looking for in a DP (director of photography) for HD?

Chris - The most important thing is to get a DP who knows how to light. If you shoot on film, on DigiBeta, or HD, get a DP who knows how to light, then he can make HDCam look great. If you have a shit DP and you give him a 70mm camera, and all the lights in the world, he is going to make it look shit! The DP is as important, if not more important, than the format you choose. Older school DPs who have shot on film for 20 years need to have an open mind, and some do resist HD now, though that will change. A DP who can shoot and light brilliantly on film can do the same on HD. DPs already have the skills to shoot HD well, because they know about light, they know about composition, they know about framing, they know about optics, it is a gift and a skill that they learn over 20 years. That is 95% of the battle, the rest of it is just knowing about the tapes, knowing about compression, knowing about the leads, knowing about the difference between RGB and YUV, and that they can learn in a week with some camera techs.

Q - One of the problems with HD is that, being a digital camera with a tape that just slots in, anyone who has shot with a camcorder will assume it's just the same. If you gave them a film camera, they would have no idea what to do, so there is a lack of respect for the HD camera and format that results in lazy film making.

Chris - Yes. With a press of a button, it switches on and off, but you should really treat it like a film camera. It reacts to light so sensitively, especially the newer RGB cameras where they are fitting the log curve of film. It is startling how close it is to the 35mm aesthetic. People go out thinking *'Oh I've got my PD100 that has got an auto button and it looks ok'*, but it doesn't, it looks shit, because you've never blown it up on a big screen. HD doesn't make anything easier, it just makes it cheaper and makes the post easier. You still need to know how lighting and composition works. For that you should almost train on film. If you have trained on film you will respect your time on set. People who shoot on video say *'Oh let's just turnover and get loads of footage'*, and yeah, you've just shot 100 slates but 99 of them are shit, because you have no respect for your time on set. If you trained on film, it would make you really think about how you are setting a shot up, it makes you think about how you are positioning your lights, rather than this free-wheeling style of shooting you can get from video film makers.

Q - How robust are the cameras?

Chris - The Sony cameras are very robust, and I have tried to break them on numerous occasions and they never have! The tapes are robust too, though you shouldn't spool them back and forth too much in post as tapes

Suite 58
The Old Truman Brewery
91 Brick Lane
London
E1 6QL

T: +44 (0)207 053 2190
F: +44 (0)207 053 2188
E: info@s2s.co.uk
Web: www.s2s.co.uk

S2S DIGITAL FILM POST

can snag. There are new cameras and equipment that record to hard disk, which makes me nervous as I know how easy it is for data to get corrupted. I will be sticking with tape for now.

Q - How important are the lenses?

Chris - As important as on a film shoot. It is all about optics, and there are *filmised* HD lenses, the new generation of zooms, which I love, because they are very quick to use. One thing you have got to watch out for is back focus though, and that takes time. Hopping around between lots of different lenses is going to slow you down, as it would do on film. Zeiss primes are amazing, and they give nearly the same look as film.

Some people are quite snooty about the zoom lenses, but the zooms I have used are very good, and we shot all of *16 Years of Alcohol* on zooms, and we've been nominated for several cinematography awards. We also shot it at an aspect ratio of 1:2.35 (like cinemascope), thereby cropping off a bit at the top and bottom of the frame when blowing up to 35mm.

Do some tests with zooms and I am sure you will be happy with the results. Save your money and spend it on the actors and not prime lenses. Look at the project, is it going to be studio, is it exteriors, is it day, is it night, and then consider who you are taking advice from, do they really know what the hell they are talking about?

Q - Typically, new filmmakers say, 'right we are going to shoot this movie and we will cut it on Avid or Final Cut Pro', and that is the end of the conversation about its post production. What is the problem with that concept?

Chris - The problem with that concept is that unless you really know what you are doing, it only going to give you something that is of DVD quality, it is not even broadcast quality. You can cut and say *'great, we have locked picture'*, so then you have got an ungraded DV master of your film. If you want your film to do anything, you need to go back to the masters to do a conform, and do a professional colour grade.

Q - People think that as they put their movie on the computer in a 'Pro' piece of software, it is good enough quality, but actually we are back into the old 'offline' / 'online' scenario. So to break post production into 2 distinct halves, there is the offline where you make all your creative choices, and then the online where those choices are rebuilt at maximum quality?

Chris - Absolutely. Final Cut Pro and Avid Xpress Pro are both good systems to do the offline edit. I think going straight from your masters into a system is the wrong way to do it though, because it means you are fast-forwarding and rewinding you master tapes and you are having to hire an HD deck for all your digitising. I suggest you clone all your tapes to DVcam as soon as you've shot the film, in the evening - so you've got matching audio, matching time code, matching picture. If you've shot 25p, it is identical time code, if you have shot 24p, you are suddenly fucked, because DVcam, or Beta SP are PAL formats that work at 25fps. Life then gets needlessly complicated.

If you've been sensible, and you haven't been arrogant, and you've shot at 25p, then you have a DVcam tape that matches picture, audio and time code with your HD master tape. If you are very clever on set, run a sound feed from your sound recordist, back into the HD camera, which means there is no syncing audio later, it's already there on the tape.

Q - And you can reconform the DAT later as it has the same timecode as the HD tapes (time of day timecode)?

Chris - Absolutely, or you can stick with the sound off the HD tape, and export an OMF for the final mix when you are done editing. On the past 2 features it has worked a dream. In the past, I have been forced to work with some people who insist on NOT running an audio feed, which will force the assistant to waste a week of their time, spending your money and slowing down the edit, as they manually sync up from the DAT - they are idiots! Take one lead from the DAT to the HD, and you've always got the DAT as a back up. Sure, if your camera is a million miles away, shooting steadicam, unplug the fucking lead and sync that shot manually. You have got leads going out of the camera anyway, because it is going back to the HD monitor.

High Def Video

GUERILLA FILM MAKER SAYS!

Shoot at 25p, not at 24p, and not at an interlaced resolution such as 1080i.

Feed your sound directly into the camera via a sound lead. Set this link up in advance and check it, making sure recording levels can't be accidentally nudged by the camera operator.

Have plenty of blank tapes standing by as you can rip through HD tapes at an alarming rate.

Never over expose or under expose as this limits your ability to grade the image later.

Shoot a 'flat' image, planning to do your 'extreme' look in post production. You can always add to a look, but it's harder to remove a look.

Use the very best format you can get your hands on, that means start with HDCam, then DVCproHD, then HDV.

More important than the format, is the camera and lenses. Generally, the better formats will be supported by better cameras though.

Why spend £3.5k on a prosumer camera when you can rent a top end camera and lenses for the same. I know you can keep the prosumer camera after, BUT the pro cameras will distinguish you from 95% of the competition. You will also attract a higher calibre of crew. Then negotiate a better deal with the camera hire company, and pay them only £1k and spend the balance on better actors.

If your project uses a lot of slow motion, shoot with the Panasonic Varicam on DVCproHD, or any new format that supports true slow motion. If you can't, shoot any slow motion shots at 1080i, as the interlacing will give extra information that will look like film when slowed down on a computer.

If you plan to use a lot of green screen or bluescreen, don't use HDV, shoot DVCProHD or HDCam as it has better colour sampling and will make better mattes when compositing.

Plan a post production route where you can be editing within hours of ejecting the tape. Don't put this off until after the shoot. DON'T!

When editing, don't work at full HD resolution, convert tapes to DVcam and work at that resolution, using a cheaper edit station and only a few hundred gigs of firewire storage. There is no need for terabytes of data storage just yet.

Don't waste precious time and money making HD backup tapes. Just don't hammer your master tapes, and use your DVcam copies for editing. But DO look after your master camera tapes, everything is encapsulated on them.

Do your final online with professionals, and NOT at home, unless you are a professional and know what you are doing.

Research what sales agents require finished films to be delivered on.

Don't get sucked into the Avid or FCP debate. Both are fine tools and the one you should use is the one you get cheapest or free.

If you really can't afford to rent a pro camera, and you have tried and tried, use the cheaper prosumer HD cameras shooting HDV. DV is dead and we can't think of a single reason why you would want to shoot with it.

Only take advice from people who have actually got their film to the market place. And then use a pinch of salt.

So you've got an HD master tape and a cloned DVcam tape, both of which have all the audio, and then you can be cutting that evening. On these other pictures where the Editor said *'No, no, no! I don't trust that, I want my assistant to sit up all night syncing,'* they will always be at least a day behind when cutting. On my films, I shoot on HD tape with a sound feed, and once the tape ends, it's cloned onto DVCam immediately, and we are editing within 2 hours! This means when the Editor turns around and goes *'Oh shit we haven't got a close up of that'*, they know the same day, before they have struck the set, before the actors have gone home, and they can then do the missing cut away. If some ponce insists on syncing everything, then that option is unavailable.

Q - So you could even have the editor on set, with a laptop?

Chris - We've done that, and he was cutting material that was shot only a few hours earlier. The editor could say *'this is how it cuts together, I think you need another close-up'*, and the director says *'Fuck me, of course I do'*, and they just turn around and get the close up. Even shooting it the next day is a pain in the arse, when you are out on location. You know how outrageously useful it is to have a lot of cut-aways in post. If you don't have that feedback you are buggered, and a whole scene can be ruined by having to use the crappy performance take, because you don't have the right material to cut with.

Q - How important is it to have an HD monitor on set, as opposed to 14 inch colour telly from Asda?

Chris - Crucial. First of all your colour telly from Asda won't do you much good because you've got an HD SDI signal coming out the HDcam camera, so your lead won't plug into a 14 inch colour TV. You can get a down converter, but you are losing all that resolution, and the thing about HD is, what you see is what you get, almost. So having an HD monitor means the DP and the Director can look at it, and go *'that is what I'm going to get'*. Obviously you can grade it, obviously there is going to be some slight differences when you put it up on the full 2K projector, but 98% of it is what you see is what you get. It will also involve the Director more on the creative, aesthetic look of the film. You don't need a huge monitor on set, You can get a little 9" HD monitor which is very good. Another thing to remember is that these monitors clamp the blacks, guaranteed, no matter what anyone else says, though that is a good thing. It looks blacker on the monitor than it really is, so it means your blacks will come out a bit milkier on the final master camera tape, which is fine, because it gives you room to play with in the grade. If it is crushing the blacks you are fucked, you've got nothing to play with, so it is almost like it gives you a safety buffer for the grade. Go with the Sony set ups, don't fiddle with the little gamma correction side, because you will be in a world of pain. Shoot it flat, and then grade it how you want it to look later.

Q - So you never want to hit absolute white or absolute black?

Chris - Absolutely not, always keep within a 5% buffer, giving yourself the room to play with in the grade. If you want, you can crush it in the grade, and a lot of people love crushing the blacks and clipping the whites as it is a look that people go for - fine do it in the grade, DON'T DO IT ON SET!

Q - Now we are moving to phase B, which is the online, and again the mistake I've come across is, 'I've got Final Cut Pro HD, that means I can master my HD'

Chris - Because it is called Final Cut Pro HD.

Q - Precisely.

Chris - It is bullshit, as that is just the software part. The thing that you really need is an HD card, and they cost several grand. More importantly you need the storage space, not just the size, but the speed, so that's terabytes of ultrafast drives, several grands worth. You can't capture uncompressed HD into a G5, you just can't, it will drop frame after frame. You need something that can handle the data rate, 200 odd mbits a second! So you are saying that you can a) capture it, b) have a calibrated HD deck, c) have enough fast storage. You are looking at a £20K set up. Sure you can offline at home on Avid Xpress Pro or FCP, but you need to go to a professional company to do the online.

Q - What is often overlooked is the talent of the person who will do the final grading, what their experience brings to the equation.

Chris - You can offline a film and whether it is a good cut or a bad cut, that is up to the audience and the film critics out there. But when it comes to conforming the final master, there are many technical hoops you must jump through. We do conforms all the time, and they are never easy. The easier ones are the ones that shoot 25i or 25p. We double our rate if it's a 24p project, just because it is so fiddly, and you end up having to manually do the online, no matter how people set it up. No matter what Avid or FCP say, 24fps, it never works!

Shoot at 25p, then offline, lock picture, then hand it over to a post house who knows what it is doing. Give them the project on disk, from Avid or FCP, and the master tapes, and then they do an ungraded conform that just matches your offline edit. That is a technical process where they recapture all the shots in your edit at full HD res, and they add any tweaks you made, such as digital zooms, titles or cropping. You then need to grade it, adjusting the colours, contrast, brightness, gamma etc.

You also need to make a decision about what you are going to deliver your final film on too, what is this film for, is it for broadcast and TV, fine grade it to an HD monitor, but if you plan to scan out to film, you will need to do a separate grade for film scanning.

Q - To advise a new filmmaker who is cash-strapped, surely the thing that they should get right is an HD deliverable master?

Chris - Yes.

Q - The majority of their revenue is going to come from TV or DVD. Their ego is locked up in the 35mm print though.

Chris - Absolutely. I'll give you an example. On a film we made called *Feedback*, I haven't got a neg or a print of that, because I know it is unlikely that it is going to get theatrical distribution in the UK. I'd love to, I wrote and directed the sucker, I really wish it would, but I know it is unlikely. I conformed my film and graded it to a calibrated HD monitor, so wherever I show it, it is going to look the same, and when I give someone a DVD of it, it is going to look great.

When I show it in a digital cinema, like I did at Raindance, it is going to look great. Then if a big distributor turns around and says *'we want to put this out in hundreds of cinemas'*, then I go *'right, send it to the digital film lab, and tell the digital film lab to make the neg and print look like the HD master'*, which in my experience, only they can do. If you are in that independent, low budget world, grade it so that it looks great off the HD, and if you then get the money to do a blow up, go to somewhere like the Digital Film Lab, that will guarantee in writing, that it is going to look the same off the print as it does off the HD master. Then do a 1-minute test - get your DP into the cinema, get your colourist into the cinema and check the 1-minute test, which post production companies should do for free. Check that it looks the same as in the grading suite.

Sound on HD

GUERILLA FILM MAKER SAYS!

As the sound recordist and camera operator were unconnected on a traditional film set, HD features tend to carry on in that trend. This is a mistake though, as the sound recording capabilities, even on the prosumer cameras, is excellent. Now some audio evangelists may say that it isn't as good as say DAT, and they may be right, but it's good enough, especially when you consider what you get in return. Instant playback of picture and sound in sync, and an ability to digitise and start editing right away.

So here is the best way to do it. You have your separate sound recordist, recording on DAT (as a backup). They then send an audio feed, through long, balanced XLR cables, to the camera audio inputs. You will get resistance to this as it is just another cable to deal with, but stand your ground. The camera sound input recording level should be set to match the DAT output level, and then locked so it can't be changed accidentally. Both camera and DAT should use time of day timecode so that they share EXACTLY the same timecode. This will mean that later on in post, if you wish, you can go back to your DAT tapes and automatically reconform the audio from the master DAT tapes (which should take a few hours at most). In essence, the sound on the HD tapes was used as 'offline' sound, good enough for editing, but not mastering. In reality, that 'offline' sound will probably end up being used for mastering as it is that good.

Then shoot away. It's a good idea for the sound recordist to periodically check playback from the camera, to ensure there are no technical problems with the sound, and if there are, they have the DAT as a backup.

Doing this with the sound will save you around a weeks work in post, will circumvent a number of potential problems and most importantly, give the director instant playback with full HD picture and full quality sound, so judgements on camera, sound and performance can be made. Just remember, when people say the sound quality is not as good as using DAT only, your answer is, 'yes you are right, but it's good enough, and we have the DAT as a backup if there are problems...'

HD in the cinema... Before you dash out

GUERILLA FILM MAKER SAYS!

Just because you can, doesn't mean you should. HD theoretically puts the tools of film making into anyones hands. And the result is often far from pretty. Don't even think about making a feature film until you have made several short films and have mastered the technology and the craft to a very high standard. That craftsmanship will put you in the top percentages of your competition. HDV is excellent for short films that are essentially learning exercises, and potential investor sweeteners. After a few shorts, you will feel the desire to move up to a higher quality format, and that's when you will start moving toward HDCam.

Distribution is key to the success of any film. But don't get seduced into the digital cinema dream. You may be able, technically at least, to get your film ready for digital distribution in theatres, but remember, the same market forces are at work as ever. If your film cannot generate enough revenue to pay for the theatrical real estate, upkeep of the theatre, power, staff etc., (and really think about how much it might cost to run a cinema in London for instance, just think how much your rent is on your bedsit!) and it may refocus your ideas. No-one owes your movie a screen. No-one.

All too often, the HD feature has failed before it's even shot because the concept is poor or has no audience - then add a dodgy script, poor actors, rough camera work, sloppy editing, inaudible sound... you get the idea. Bad story and bad craftsmanshop. Stand above the crowd by focussing on excellence in every department, AND that means the concept and script too. HD is a bit like the easy money scam, you can find yourself investing heavily and quickly because it seemed so immediate and doable at the time.

Q - Sound is another area that people forget, because they will often say 'Well we will master to HDCam', and then they do a Dolby digital mix and then they go 'what do you mean there are only 4 tracks of sound on an HDCam?' What do you think is currently the best deliverable HD format?

Chris - I think HDSR has just started winning. HDSR has taken off in the States, and it has got 8 channels of audio, it is 4.4.4.colour space and it is a good mastering format. It is totally robust, it does all the frame rates, it does everything. Beneath that, I suppose D5, which is compressed, though it is less compressed than HDCam. HDCam is a great shooting format, Sony have got it sewn up I think, but it is not a good post format. Every generation will lose quality as it decompresses and recompresses. D5 also has 8 channels of audio, so it can handle your 5.1 mix in the first six channels, and then a stereo mix for TV on channels 7 and 8. D5 is standard in Europe now, but the way it is going, HDSR will probably supercede it.

Q - So just going back to the 24fps, 25fps, PAL, NTSC - all of these things used to be a pain, but if you make an HD master, you press a button and out the other end comes whatever format you want?

Chris - Yes. If you want to deliver to Europe, you run it at 25, if you want to deliver it to America, you run it at 23.98, and that comes out automatically at the back of the deck. There is no longer any bollocks about mastering for PAL or mastering for NTSC - that is all gone with HD Universal Mastering. So again, it makes this whole argument of 24p or 25p on the shoot a mockery. *The Godfather* re-released in the UK runs at a different speed to *The Godfather* re-released in the US. It is fine for Francis Ford Coppolla, so it is fine for you!

Q - Now festivals are moving toward HD Projection, you are no longer always shipping out a heavy 35mm print, or carrying it on the plane - you can take your movie on a tape in your bag, and if it's a short film, in your back pocket. And who knows what will happen when H-DVD and BluRay appear?

Chris - Absolutely. When people see that rather than spending £100k on 200 prints, they can spend £2k on a hard drive that they can bike around the country, everyone is going to go digital, it saves so much money for the people who have the money, which are the distributors, and the distributors run the industry. In Edinburgh this year, we were working on a film right up until the last minute. Literally 12 hours before we screened it, we did a play out to HD, jumped on a plane, went in, stuck it in the HD deck and played it - absolutely gorgeous! Everyone else who was showing their movie off a print, had to sign off their film 3 weeks before, so we got more time to work on it. Not only that, we weren't happy with some bits, so because it's digital and on tape, we could go back and we are still working on it, still tweaking the effects shots! So it enables you to screen the film in a cinema environment, before it is fully finished. If you have gone to print, that is it. On HD, you can screen it to people, get that feedback and go, *'actually that scene was a bit long, let's cut that down'* and it is not going to cost you a fortune. If you have gone to negative and print, and you've had your dub, and you want to cut 2 minutes out of your film, you can't do that easily or cheaply.

Q - I guess the key to the success of utilising the format to its maximum is to have someone in your team, who is a bit of a propellerhead? And some people think they know what they are talking about but they don't?

Chris - I have had to work with some people who have no clue what they are talking about, but think they do, and for various reasons, everyone around them believes in them, and then it all goes horribly wrong. You need someone in your team who really is a geek, not just someone who has read an article on HD on the net and think they know everything. It is constantly evolving, I am an HD expert and I don't even know half of it.

Make sure that your DP and your post supervisor have done it before. Don't be a guinea pig for someone, don't let your film become someone's try out of HD. Three years ago, you didn't have any choice, because no-one had done it. Ask questions, ask *'what frame rate, what lens, what are you delivering on?'* I've had people shoot music videos at 24fps, that are never going to go to print, so they shot at 24 because they thought that gave it the film look! They had to do their conform manually, it took a week rather than 2 hours - they were absolutely barking! Ask the right questions, spend your time, have meetings, and do tests.

If you want to shoot a feature, that camera hire company wants your business, therefore they will give you a half day test, so go in with the DP, shoot some stuff, take those two tapes, and go to a post house. That post house wants your business, so they should do the test for free. Go to the grading house, and grade it for free, go to the film house, make a 35mm print for free. Test the entire process, from start to finish, and then decide for yourself. If you still think film is better, then shoot on film. At least then you have tested it, don't go off what I'm saying in this interview. Things might have changed by next year! Do tests!

There is no right or wrong route, per say, but there is a best route for your project, and you need to find what that route is. With so many different cameras, and so many different formats, and so many post routes, you need to do your research. I think Producers and Directors need to get more technical. This whole age of *'I'm not technical, I don't understand this'* is dying out. If you are going to go with these new, exciting formats, if you want to spend £1k on your stock, rather than £50k, if you want to be able to do editing within two hours of shooting, if you want all these advantages, you have got to become a bit of a geek. Put your anorak on, just for a bit, go to some seminars, make some notes on things in this book, and go on the internet, speak to some geeks, become an anorak!

Q - A problem I have seem is the DP will make choices that are good for them, the Editor will make choices that are good for them, and at some point they will leave the project and then it is the producers problem, who has just been accepting that these guys knew what they were talking about.

Chris - Absolutely and you are sitting in a post house, who are downing tools because you said to them it is going to be a five hour conform. Now, because the Editor insisted on shooting on 24, and the DP insisted on time of day timecode, none of the EDLs match up, everything has to be done manually and it is costing a fortune. I've had that on several projects, and the Editor and DP have fucked off to their next job, using the credit of the film they just screwed up, and the Producer is picking up the tab, because the Producer wasn't prepared to get their head around it. They were lead by these people, perhaps they were in awe of them, and now it has damaged their project.

Q - What advice would you offer a new filmmaker?

Chris - Listen to everyone. Listen, listen, listen. You probably don't know a tenth of what you need to know, but make your film anyway. Listen to everyone you can, people love to talk, people like me, buy someone at Panavision a pint and listen to them for hours on end. Listen to everything they have to say, then forget it all and go and work it out yourself. Because the filmmaking process is changing so much that every 6 months everyone is wrong again. So maybe by the time this book is printed I will be wrong! Listen to everyone, then forget it, and then go and work it out yourself.

David Yates
Director, Harry Potter Five

THE JOURNEY TO BEING A DIRECTOR

Q - How did you get into film making?

David - I grew up in St. Helen's in Merseyside. It was seeing *Jaws* in the cinema that really made me want to direct, I wanted to do what Steven Spielberg did. I went back and obsessively saw *Jaws* fifteen times. After the first three or four times, I went back just to observe the audience and the way he was able to keep them involved. It just made me want to be a director. Then when I was fourteen, my mother bought me a cine-camera, so I started making little Super-8 films with my brother. I just went back home to visit my mother's grave and my very first film, *Premonition,* was shot in that cemetery, and it starred my brother who was about eight. It was about a dream he had where he walks into this graveyard and suddenly he comes across this grave and the soil started to shift and a hand came out. It was very funny. It got a laugh when I screened it to my horror. It was my best friend, Paul's hand and he was slightly overweight, so it was this pudgy hand that came out of the soil. He runs away in slow motion and then he wakes up, gets dressed and gets run over. It was a very simple horror story. I got a runner up prize on a young film maker program on TV. I became a member of local Cine Clubs and read Movie Maker magazine, which in one issue, had a three page article about the National Film and TV school and it said that if you get in, you get £2k a year to make films for three or four years. And I thought, *'Right, that is where I am going.'* You had to be in your mid-20's to get in, so I went to get a degree in politics and made little documentaries and other films. I applied as soon as I could, failed to get in, and spent a year at Media Arts College in Swindon, which was an avant garde workshop place - not like the conservative cine clubs. Then I made a film at Media Arts that got me into the Film School.

Q - How has your slower, determined path aided you in how you approach things creatively?

David - It is a marathon. I've been doing it since I was fifteen, and professionally I started in TV in '92. I think it was healthy. I think the problem with suddenly getting there is that you know less. You haven't had time to make sense of anything. For me the last four years have been very useful because I have made six or seven hours of TV a year, which is the same as three or four movies a year - that is time on the set with actors, time with scripts, time in the cutting room. It is like a hothouse for exploring how you can experiment with each stage of the process. It allowed me to make mistakes in small ways, mistakes that aren't career damaging. A young film maker getting to make a feature off the back of one short is a pretty precarious situation because they might have the talent, but they might not have the level of craft, or the stamina to do it properly. Every year I learn new things, which has been incredibly useful.

Q - What was it like going to the Film School where you could talk movies 24 hours a day?

David - It was an odd thing because we didn't talk as much as we ought to. When I went it was an unusual environment. For example, we trained at a Drama School for a week or two and there it was about working as a collective and inspiring each other. The Film School had you specialise as a producer, director, editor, etc. and it was a tricky environment. It was competitive. And I made the mistake of not going to seminars or deconstructing classic films. I just wanted to make things, so I skipped out on a lot of that stuff. I regret not taking advantage of that now, but I made things - I was very practical. My heroes were Spielberg and Forsythe and I didn't care about having this encyclopedic knowledge of intelligent European film makers. I was much more driven to tell stories and that is what I did. Also, I was there when I was 27 or so and I didn't appreciate things then as I do now. I was much more populist in my taste. I wanted to make big movies.

Q - Was that populist leaning part of your cultural upbringing?

David - Yes. I come from a part of the UK where you go to the cinema to be entertained and eat popcorn. It wasn't until my 30's that I realised that there were different ways to tell stories that were intriguing. Still at film school, I felt privileged to have those resources and get money to make films. It was an amazing experience.

Q - Tell us about some of the pivotal moments in your TV directing career and how it lead you to feature film making.

David - TV has been fantastic to me. I have been able to tell some complex and interesting stories on some pretty good budgets and tell those stories with a lot of creative freedom. You can only call yourself a director if you are doing the gig though. It's like writing. I think it is really unhealthy and precious to think that the only way to fully express yourself is on celluloid and showing it in a big theatre. It is a tough business to break into and then to maintain a long term career, which is the real goal. Not to be a flash in the pan who made a single film. My ambition is to have a career across several decades. The great thing about TV is that it allows you, in an intense way, to get better at direction. I directed eight hours of high end TV shows with really good scripts, really good actors and terrific crews, every year, over a five a year period. It is the equivalent to twelve movies! On those productions I am making the same decisions that I am on this film. I get to push things - the crew, the actors, in different ways. There are some colleagues of mine who have taken a different route and said, *'I am going to develop this because it is a movie and don't care if it is going to take one year or two years.'* And in that five years they have made one film and it has come and gone. You have a creative lifespan and there is nothing worse than wasting those years. If there is a piece of advice I would give young directors, it would be to, by all means hang out for that single film that you are desperate to make, but in the meantime direct documentaries, direct dramas, direct commercials, direct TV. Just direct! It will feed what you want to do. The danger in waiting five years to make a film is that it becomes a precious thing. It becomes do or die. And if it fails or isn't the success that you want it to be, then it is a dangerous thing. I love being prolific. It enables me to get better.

Q - Why do you think there is a snootiness towards television by some film people?

David - I don't know. They are both storytelling. Before I was chosen for *Harry Potter* by David Heyman and Warner Bros, I would go to British funding places who would tell me that they love my television work and that they would like me to do a film, but it is *'slightly different and not easy to make the transition...'* But David Heyman and Warner Bros didn't think that. They thought it was great storytelling and film making. But there is that snobbery and it is unnecessary.

Q - Why is one able to be prolific in TV and not in film?

David - In TV there is this machine that needs to be fed. Getting into that slipstream meant that I could overlap things and I've been fortunate in getting material that I want to do. Film is harder to be prolific in as there is no need for product to feed the machine.

Q - What can a film school graduate expect on their first day of their first TV directing job?

David - They are going to find a lot of people who have lost a little bit of spark. People who have been doing this for week in week out, month in month out, and they have lost the energy to raise their game. That puts the director at an immediate advantage because they are going to look at every single shot and performance, sound design, whatever, to find a way to make it better. And that mindset is going to lift them up above all the other directors who have been doing it for weeks, or months or years. When I got out of film school and was doing *The Bill*, the actors were not used to a director coming up to them and getting into the psychology of their characters or the depth of the moment they were playing. The actors found it refreshing and stimulating that someone cared, quite passionately, about making them better or more dynamic. If you go into a long running series that has a certain level of acceptance, that is where you can push it and shine. Someone said to me, *'If I do Casualty, then I am going to get stuck doing Casualty.'* I said that yeah you might get stuck if you do *Casualty,* like everyone else does *Casualty*. But if you go in and make the acting better or if you shoot it in a way that is more expressive or dramatises it, or if you make the script better in the week you have to do that, you will be noticed. And then you will get the next step along.

Q - So it is a lifelong commitment to excellence?

David - It is always pushing the envelope a bit. They shot it like that last time, but is there a way to make it more vital? You have to make the script come alive. I have never done *Casualty*, but you have a traumatic situation and all these people running around, which is an extraordinary situation. If you were there in reality, what would you observe? I bet that what you would experience as a human being would stay with you for a number of months. To try and bring a truth and reality to that is what I would do.

Q - What are your thoughts on someone being a writer-director versus having a writer and a director?

David - There are very few excellent writers out there, let alone writer-directors. It is a difficult combination. I don't know of any really in Britain in the younger generation who do it well. It limits you, too. It takes three years to direct a movie, it takes five years if you are writing it yourself. And development is the most soul damaging process in the world. When you are shooting something or you are editing something, you have something finite in your hands. When you are developing something, there is an intangibility about it. Is it going to happen this year? Oh, no the year after that? And that can destroy you if you are not careful. My attitude has always been to work with several writers and let them carry some of the load. Stimulate them and let them stimulate me. That is one way I have been so prolific. It allows me to be industrial. I have a dozen projects in development all with really good writers. When I finish *Harry Potter*, I have a line of stuff I can do instead of one thing if I was a writer-director. I have great mobility in the marketplace. If you are a writer-director, by all means continue with that because you can't ignore it, but I'd encourage you to develop other projects with other writers because that can only stimulate and challenge yourself. You get a sense of how other people do things. Don't put all your eggs in one basket.

Q - What about directors who are too technically oriented?

David - I empathise with that type of director because early on that was me. From St. Helen's to film school, all I cared about were lenses and how to move the camera. It took me five to seven years to realise that the two most important things are the screenplay and the performances. The rest is craft and an expression of that. Before I realised that, I got lost in the joy of lens types, of camera movements and crane shots. Then you discover that those things are only tools and they are limited. It is the icing on the cake. I would encourage directors to spend time at a drama school working with actors and making improvisational films. That would be a great process. You don't even need a camera. Just engage the actor. I am intrigued by the process of bringing a character to life.

Q - What is the service that agents provide for you?

David - Agents for young film makers is a tough relationship that doesn't always work. I had a frustrating relationship with my agent when I started. You expect the world. You want them to go out and get you that first feature film gig. You want them to get you that bit of TV or script development. The truth is the agent will only take to the marketplace what the marketplace will buy. And the marketplace is quite conservative. If you have two or three little award winning shorts, it is a start, but you need some luck. I think the best thing an agent can do for you besides toting your stuff around, is be there for you as moral support and encouragement. A lot of agents have so many clients, that they can't do that. All I wanted in my early stages of career was to get a call once a week to see how it was going. How is that bit of writing going? It doesn't take much to do that, but in my experience and talking to others, that doesn't happen often. It is a conservative business because things take so much money to make, even a low budget film can cost £500k! That is a lot and many financiers are reluctant to give even very talented people that chance. It is very important to be persistent and hopefully lucky. Having an agent helps at my level. I am lucky that my agents are terrific. They look long term and are script oriented, which for me is very important. They sift through the stuff that comes to me, which is often not very good, and they will pick things for me that are interesting. I value that enormously. For a young director, you need someone who you feel comfortable with and if they are not getting your work in the first instance, they are at least there for you. You want someone who is there for the long haul.

Q - Harry Potter seems to defy the usual Hollywood way of making safe bets on its film maker choices. Why do you think that is?

David - David Heyman who makes these films and Lionel Wigram, who is a Senior VP at Warner Brothers, have huge creative ambitions for this project. And Warner Brothers recognise that in order for it not to run out of steam, you need new blood to come in and push it a little bit. It would be so easy for them to be conservative and they are quite opposite; I am knocked out by them. They are inspiring people who just want this series to get better as it goes along. That is a really exciting environment to be in because

Q - Why did you start making films?

Lynne - Whilst in my final year of fine art photography, I saw Meshes in the Afternoon by Maya Deren and it really affected me, so on a whim I submitted a portfolio of photographs to the National Film School. I was going to go on to do an M.A. in photography at the RCA. But I really blew the last interview and didn't get in. I was surprised to be accepted on the cinematography course at the NFTS, I think mostly due to the fact they wanted more camera women. So without expecting to, I ended up in film school. I knew nothing about film making. I'm glad I went without too many preconceived notions and everything to learn.

Q - So did your stills experience help you in your film making?

Lynne - Yes. People who I studied photography with can see the influence of what I was doing in my stills, in the films I make. Through naivety I would do things at film school that people told me were mistakes, like use the same size lens for every shot. Or frame in a particularly oblique way. I started to recognise that these 'mistakes' could change the whole meaning of the scene, that they could be useful if used in the right place for the right reason. In Gasman the whole of the first scene is shot without seeing any of the characters' faces, only their body language which I think says a lot more about how this family interact with one another. We took the film to America where it was screened by the First Film Foundation, and a producer asked if the scene was intentional! She must have thought the camera had slipped or something. I was thinking My god she must think I'm totally stupid! But the film has been the most well received of my short films.

Q - So film school was good for learning the ropes?

Lynne - Yes. The first things I shot were absolutely rubbish! But I learnt as much as I could. I hate the attitude of camera people who think great shot, fuck the sound. You have to try to understand as much as you can about every facet of filmaking. So everything works in unison. I actually wanted to move to the documentary course because it was closer to the work I wanted to do, I often find documentary more inspiring than fiction, and on that course you were taught all-round filmmaking. But they wouldn't let me. Bastards!

Q - Two of your films won first prizes at Cannes for the shorts section. Did it change things for you?

Lynne - Gavin Emerson, the producer of Ratcatcher had the foresight to send Small Deaths, my graduation film, to Cannes. When it was accepted I was over the moon, I'd never been to a film festival before, so I took my mates who had worked on the film with me, we had a laugh and blagged our way into all the parties. Coppola was on the main jury who were also judging the shorts. I was just thinking, wow! this is madness! When I won the Prix du Jure it gave me the access I needed to make another film, before that it had been a case of don't call us, we'll call you.

Lynne Ramsey
Film Maker

When Gasman won the same prize two years later it helped get Ratcatcher into production.

Q - Did anything come out of that?

Lynne - I had a few phone calls from American agents but at the time I was thinking, why do I need an American agent? I've made a ten minute film and I'm not planning to make a film in America just yet. If you want to be put together with writers etc, an agent is great. If you generate your own material you can get a lawyer to help sort out the contracts etc. Having said that, I do have an agent!

Q - Our attitude has been to just do it, to go out there and make your movie, but you've gone a different route, making shorts, which do you think is a better route?

Lynne - I think the spirit of what you're talking about was in what I was doing. You don't have to go to film shool to become a film maker. In fact I learned how to direct after I left film school. It's cheaper and easier than ever to make films, if you have a really good idea, then do it.

Q - Did you find that you learnt a lot by doing your shorts so when it came to your feature you were better prepared?

Lynne - I made shorts because I love the short film form, I could take risks and learn as much as I could by trial and error. I explored what I was interested in as a film maker. It was a huge leap from fifteen to ninety minutes. When you get to feature level there's more pressure on you because there's more money involved. I felt some pressure to change the way I worked; We really liked your shorts but...You have to be very clear about what you're trying to achieve. I knew the things I had learned had worked and it's a big mistake to try to completely reinvent yourself. If you're doing something really low budget, you don't have the pressure of the financiers on your back so you have nothing to lose and everything to gain from taking calculated risks.

Q - How did Ratcatcher come about?

Lynne - After Small Deaths won the prize at Cannes I was approached by a scout/script editor from the BBC. She encouraged me to write a treatment for a feature. I had no idea what she expected having never done this before so I wrote 55 pages, half a feature script. It was a bit of a mess, pretty unstructured but she recognised the potential in it and commissioned me to write the script. Coming from never having earned any money, being a poverty-stricken student and having never held a job down in my life, it was a big deal for me. When they told me they would pay me £25k to do something I loved doing anyway, you could have knocked me over. I phoned my friends and family saying I'm rich! Which was a big mistake! It took me a year to write, and during that time I made Gasman, my last short film.

Q - How was it working on a feature and not a short?

Lynne - I use non-professional actors and a small documentary-type crew. I have to be comfortable as a director and I hate a big machine behind me unless it's necessary for the film. I always worked with the same crew, none of which had ever made a feature before. I spent a year writing Ratcatcher and I had a focused idea of how I wanted to make it. But it became clear that the investors were pretty jumpy about all these first-timers and non-actors. I fought and fought to keep my vision intact and work with the people I wanted. I wasted a lot of energy on some battles probably not worth fighting and was already exhausted before I started shooting.

Q - What have you learnt?

Lynne - To look at your film in terms of how much time you need on everything, and budget accordingly. If you want more time editing, cut down other areas. I could have done with more cutting time on Ratcatcher though most directors will say that. I'm more aware of my needs for the next project. Tailor the budget to work in terms of the way you make your film. A lot of money is wasted on things that aren't necessary. Be aware of how, why and where you spend money.

Q - What have you learnt about directing the camera and directing actors?

Lynne - They work best when they work in unison. Knowing when a detail is economical enough to express more about the character than you could do in dialogue. Knowing when to just let the actors roll and not let the camera get in the way. Knowing where the sound will do more work than the images. Cinema is using everything in conjunction with each other until you don't see the joins. I work a lot on instinct. If you feel there is something wrong don't do it, trust your instinct.

Q - How have you found it being a woman working in a male dominated industry?

Lynne - A few people told me I couldn't be a camera woman saying I wasn't tall enough (I'm 5'2"), but I'd tell them it was a benefit because I could see from a different perspective! It is a male dominated industry, but I think your work should speak for itself. I hate when people refer to me as a woman film maker, or worse, a Scottish woman film maker. You begin to feel slightly marginalised. I think it's great that more women are making films as they make up more than half the population. However that is not reflected in the number of woman directors. It will only make film making more interesting for everybody. The same goes for different cultures who have had little or no access to film making. The bottom line is, variety is the spice of life. I think male film makers can have a lot of pressure on them to be Steven Spielberg and that women in general are more able to communicate quickly if something doesn't work. If I make an arse of myself on a film set I'll accept it and deal with it. Leave your ego at the door. Make a good film.

Q - What mistakes do you think you've made?

Lynne - Wasting energy on battles that were hardly worth the fight. Choose your battles carefully. If something's going to cause you a lot of hassle for little or no gain, don't bother. Appear to compromise, if you have to, but with something that really matters to you, don't budge. Marketing and distribution were big eye-openers for me, remember you should know better than anyone else how to market your film. Go through the whole process even if it kills you. Be prepared for the unexpected - we had to dig up a site and make a canal, on doing so we discovered toxic waste which cost us £10k to dispose of!

Q - What advice would you offer a new film maker?

Lynne - Do something you believe in, and see it through to the bitter end. If you believe in it, other people will. Have the courage of your convictions - it comes through on the screen. Have a good idea and make sure its something that you really want to do because it takes a very l-o-n-g time.

Directing – Basic Tips

GUERILLA FILM MAKER SAYS!

1. Study films and why they work, mechanically, then recreate those sequences with a video camera and edit them. This will teach you the basics.

2. Get used to talking to actors. If you can, do an acting course so you know how to work with your cast.

3. The simplest way of covering a scene is to shoot a wide shot (master) first and then move in to your medium shots, close ups and cutaways. The wide shots usually require the most lighting and set dressing and therefore the most time setting up. When you move in, you will of course see less in the frame and therefore need to make minimal adjustments.

4. Keep consistent direction of movement. If a person walks out of frame from right to left, then they must enter the next shot entering from right to left. You may change the camera angle to make it appear that they have switched sides, but in fact, the on screen movement stays constant.

5. Do not cross the 'line of action' (see box).

6. Allow the action to send before calling 'cut!' as this will give the editor flexibility and often vital options when cutting the film.

7. Shoot plenty of cutaways, inserts and transitional shots so your editor has plenty of options to 'cut away' from the actor when needed, perhaps to help with a fluffed line.

8. Move the camera. If appropriate, tracking shots usually make the film more kinetic.

9. Change your angles. High and low shots can help create mood and break away from the CWH shot (convenient working height!)

10. Establish geography, especially with action sequences. Shoot enough wide shots so the audience can see where everything is. When you cut into the action it will have more impact.

11. Watch your rushes. You will see what is working and what isn't.

12. Learn to edit. Cutting your own work, or someone else's, is one of the best ways to learn about what to get, and what isn't needed.

13. Practice. Every time you pick up a camera, be it a full blown movie, corporate video or even your holiday video, is a chance to learn.

CONCEPT

you are not fighting a bureaucracy. You are working with human beings. Warner Brothers have a terrific commitment to the UK and have done for a number of years now. There is a certain mythology about working with American studios and my experiences were not what I expected at all. It is very early days, but I have less execs on this massive movie than I did with my little movie with Richard Curtis. I had eight execs on *Girl In The Café,* all of whom were lovely and delightful to deal with and very supportive, but still there were eight! On this, I answer to several people who I respect and give me great strength. Not what I expected. I expected conflict and fighting for control. There is something about this particular regime at Warners, who have been there for a while now, who are being very successful, which breeds confidence and the ability to trust your instincts when someone comes in and does something. I'm sure if it were a studio that was struggling it would be different. The ones that struggle usually are the ones that are intrusive and lack confidence to let the people you hire to do what they do.

Q - In the lean years, what did you do to help keep yourself focused on the goal of directing?

David - Right after film school, for a year, I didn't get any work. That was terrible. I had won all these awards, San Francisco, Chicago, and won some cash. I had a few meetings and I was terrible at it. That was one thing that film school never taught us. I would go in and get too nervous and fumble around. I got nothing for over a year and it was a difficult time. You just keep going. So I developed scripts and directed a documentary for a series called *Moving Pictures,* and that was when I got back in. That was the period where I realised it was bad to not be directing for a long time. It had been a year and a half between graduating and doing the documentary and the morning I turned up for the Moving Picture shoot, which only had a crew of two and a few interviews, I was nervous and it was tough to get back into it. So don't leave it too long. The next downtime was after I made a film called *The Tichborne Claimant*, which got some good reviews and came out in fifteen theatres and then went away after three weeks. It took me two years to make that film. Again, after a few film festivals, I thought this was it. I can make a feature film that looks good, has good performances, a good story and is told well. Here I am. I felt like I earned it now. And my phone didn't ring for another year. You just have to keep going.

Q - How much of being successful comes from just working hard?

David - I think that has a lot to do with it. I also think judgment is another thing which comes from talent. Knowing what is a good idea. Knowing what is a good script. Knowing whom to put in front of the camera. Knowing how to tell a good story. That way, when you get the break, you know what to do with it. I think all the hard work gets you through the door without question. And if you make the right choices you can get to the next stage.

Q - How do you differentiate between good and bad advice or opinions?

David - To be honest, I only ever trust my own instincts about things. Especially in choosing material. It doesn't matter what my agent thinks. It doesn't matter what my partner thinks. It doesn't matter what my mates say. I will listen to them, but ultimately there is this little voice inside me that says, *'This is the one!'* And you can't ignore it. I have had arguments with my partner and I have turned things down, and she has said, *'Are you crazy? This is going to be the next Full Monty!'* And I say, *'I can't feel it', 'I can't see it'* or *'I don't like it'.* So I go with that.

Q - Given where you came from, tell me what the moment was like when you got Harry Potter? Did you still feel like that 14 year old from St Helens when that script landed on your doorstep?

David - It was the sense that I've done it. When I saw *Jaws* I realised that was a big story, it is reaching a global audience and it is beautifully crafted. It has comedy and pathos and emotional depth. And now, they are giving me a camera with the same resources. It is an industrial process of film making that is rare in Europe because these things are so big. On this one I am learning about visual and special effects, I am learning how to manage a crew of not fifty or sixty, but three hundred. So you are gathering all that new experience that makes you grow muscles that you didn't have before. The truth of it is, and you can ask all the actors and crew I have worked with, I am still that fourteen-year-old kid. I do skip on set. I just enjoy it. There is a joy to the process because I think we are incredibly privileged to be able to tell these stories on film. Actors have told me, *'Don't lose it because that is what makes us want to do that bit more for you.'* I get moved by the stories, frequently, and the crew and actors know when you care. So if you can find that in your work as a film maker, it will pay dividends.

Q - So you are lead by your passions on set, as opposed to a tyrant who doesn't want to hear 'no'?

David - Completely. I think it is about respect and empowering people to do their best. Getting people to believe in themselves. Pushing people and taking fear out of the process. I think fear is a terrible inhibitor. I know the mythology is of the big director who scares everybody. I think that is bollocks. I think what you do is you make people feel safe and then you really push them.

Q - What are the common mistakes that you see or that you have done?

David - The biggest mistake that I see a lot of young directors make is that they feel they have to prove that they are the director. They become micromanagers. I see it when they work with actors. They seem to treat actors almost as if they were puppets rather than this extraordinary resource. It comes from fear that you will lose control if you step back a little bit and let people contribute to the process. It doesn't always get the best results. The really interesting directors have good instinct and judgment, they know what they want, and they draw things out performance-wise. They empower rather than control. The second big practical mistake that I made early on is when you choose a DP (camera person), make sure that DP is able to deliver what you want in good enough time. I had a frustrating experience where I had a very good, young DP who was all about the lighting and not necessarily about the story telling. He put lights in the actors' faces, which didn't allow them to find the truth or reality in the scene. You need to find a DP who is there for you and not for their showreel. And that can make the difference between getting your second film, in terms of the coverage that you get. If you get someone who is obsessed with lighting and slowing you down, it can work against you.

Q - What advice would you give a new film maker?

David - Appreciate that the longer it takes, the more you can benefit from that journey. It is a marathon, not a sprint. You need to figure out who *you are* in the world if you are going to say anything valuable. Get through the technical stage of enjoying the lenses and the cranes, then realise it is about a sense of understanding soul, people and stories. It is a beautiful thing to be a storyteller.

Community Based Micro Budget Film Making

Janis Sharp
Innocent Films

Q - Why make a children's film?

Janis - We've done a lot of Music and Art Therapy for kids in foster care. Many of the kids are from incredibly abusive backgrounds and have survived things that most adults couldn't tolerate. Most of these kids love films and love to escape into them. Films are often what has given them another perspective and has let them know that another kind of life exists elsewhere. Often the kids parents are drug addicts, and are mentally ill (often as a result of drugs). These kids can use films as an escape, for inspiration, to help them to make sense of the world, or just to make them laugh and enjoy the moment. Kids need to see positive reflections of themselves and to know that they're not alone, and that life can be better and their future can to an extent, be what they make it. They just have to hang on in there for a while longer. Film is a way of seeing into someone else's mind, or living someone else's fantasy and it can also be an incredible escape from reality. In the way that you can put on an album and lose yourself in the wildness and pure raw emotion of the music. Music can change your mood; a film can change your mind. To take people out of themselves for even a few hours and to possibly change their perspective on life, seems to me to be pretty special. It really appealed to me to make happy films with lots of music and to include some social comment without hitting people over the head with it. After reading your book, The Guerilla Film Makers Handbook, I was inspired and it made me believe that I really could go out there and make a film with very basic equipment.

Q - Why did you choose to tell this story?

Janis - I originally wrote a song entitled 'Lunar Girl' which was the inspiration for the film. It's about a girl who is happy living in her dreamworld until she is diagnosed as having mental / emotional problems. She's then taken to a psychiatrist and put on medication. Her view of the world changes and she becomes sad and unhappy. The theme of the film is whether 'being normal' and being a realist is preferable to being a slightly mad (but happy) dreamer. I wanted to make 'Lunar Girl' because I was sick of seeing negative, depressing independent films, many of which always seemed to me to be trying to use shock value (drug addiction, violence, abuse etc). Many independent film makers and critics seem to see poverty, mental illness and physical

disability as 'arty' or 'worthy', or at least that's how they try and portray it. These kind of independent films often win awards, the more depressing the film, the more 'arty' they apparently become. I personally think they're often a false portrayal of the reality as they don't show the humour that exists in those communities, or the dreams or the struggle to survive. Those films rarely show the extent of corruption of many of the people regarded as middle / upper class who are part of the establishment. 'Lunar Girl' was intended as a sort of musical drama for children and was never intended for the big screen, it was always a 'community project'. I wanted to make a children's film (slightly surreal) with lots of music. I ended up including some social issues including true stories of how kids became homeless and ended up living on the streets. My hope was that I'd learn a bit about film making and editing. My dream was that it would be good enough to be shown on television and that at least some scenes would strike a chord, create a bit of magic and hope in people's hearts and have some heart warming moments.

Q - How did you finance Lunar Girl?

Janis - I borrowed money from a credit card company. It cost around £8k to make and took three weeks to shoot.

Q - How did you deal with locations and permits in London?

Janis - We shot on the road in Covent Garden with hand held cameras avoiding the need for a permit. We didn't always look like a film crew so we could get away with more. The Police did move us on in Covent Garden because we were obstructing the pavement, but they turned a blind eye and told us they'd be back in about half an hour giving us the time to finish our scene. The Royal Festival Hall wanted to charge us £3,000 a day for shooting on the terraces outside their building even though we told them it was a community non profit making film, so we moved along a few yards. The security men from the Royal Festival Hall escorted us off the terraces but we got the shot first!

Q - What did you shoot on?

Janis - The Sony VX 1000 and Sony VX 2000, miniDV.

Q - How much lighting did you have?

Janis - Negligible, none mostly. We would use what lighting was available in locations most of the time.

Q - How did you deal with casting?

Janis - We advertised in Stage and sifted through hundreds of photos and CV's. We then shortlisted on look and gut feeling. Then we hired a room in Jackson's Lane Community centre (church) in Highgate for a few days, filmed the auditions and chose who best suited the roles. A very straight (and nice) actress who used to be in Crossroads asked us if she would have to strip. We asked her what sort of film she thought we were making!

Q - How much fun was it to make?

Janis - Incredible fun. A lot of the fun was in the relief of having managed to get some of the shots, dressing the doctor up as a sort of Dominatrix was fun too. The spur of the moment kitchen dance I loved. I had to sing and play guitar in Covent Garden because the singer / actor who was to play the busker didn't turn up. Initially, I wasn't happy about it but I ended up really enjoying it. Chefs across the road were hanging out of the windows and applauding. A couple who were obviously on drugs kept saying 'you're not really singing are you' (I was really singing) and they started singing along with me. A man started talking to Charli, the sixteen year old actress in the lead, not realising she was in the middle of a scene. He kept asking her 'why are you so happy?'

Q - How long did it take to edit?

Janis - We edited at home on our PC and it took about 6 months.

Q - There are a lot of very creative effects in the film, how did you do them?

Janis - These other-worldly scenes, enhanced by CGI effects achieved on relatively standard PC's, appeal to children especially. Using music as a device to further the storyline adds rhythm and movement to the pacing of the film and by deliberately opting for a more pop / rock rather than rap / dance orientated soundtrack, children and older folk were able to share a more common language together, perhaps more timeless. We did all the effects on the computer using 3D Studio Max, Particle Illusion and Adobe After Effects. We know we could do it all so much better now, better blue screen keying and rotoscoping, but hindsight is 20/20!

Q - How was the premiere?

Janis - It was screened at the NFT on the Southbank. We cringed at a lot of the beginning of 'Lunar Girl' but eventually relaxed and enjoyed it. We initially thought everyone hated it, but it was a great relief when we heard laughter during the funny bits and people cried at the sad bits. There was an incredibly warm atmosphere in the place and everyone applauded. After watching it we later re-edited it and re-organised the sequence of scenes, cut about ten more minutes out until we were a bit happier with it.

Q - Your film has been screened on Sky. How did that deal come about?

Janis - Out of the Blue. They saw it included in the British Films brochure produced by the Edinburgh Film Festival. They thought it would suit The Community Channel, so they rang us, we sent them a VHS and they've now screened it 48 times! We have had a really good reaction from viewers. We were not paid directly for the screenings, but as we wrote and performed most of the music in the film, we have earned a fair amount from the PRS, nearly paying off the film. We also sold a lot of DVD's after screenings.

Q - What has been the response to this quite unique film?

Janis - I'm well aware of the short comings of 'Lunar Girl', how technically we were very inexperienced, and how the story is corny, but I'm not ashamed of it. Some people have loved it and have said that it has changed their lives. People who like it tend to watch it again and again and again. Other people hate it and think it's corny rubbish with a big cringe factor. There are a group of Foster Children (from incredibly abusive backgrounds) aged from five to twelve years, who adore 'Lunar Girl' and know all of the dialogue inside out and see it as akin to a sort of Rocky Horror Show. They speak the lines and sing the songs along with the characters.

Q - How do you feel about the film now?

Janis - I am amazed that with no knowledge at all of film making, that we managed to get it screened on Sky Television without even asking! Charli who played the lead role in 'Lunar Girl' has now done a 14 part series for the BBC. 'Lunar Girl' was Charli's first ever acting job, so it was a pretty good showcase for her. Obviously we've learned loads and hopefully our next film will be a million times better, but as long as we enjoy what we're doing, that is what matters. I'd love to make another film and to get it screened. A film with lots of music (I love music) and a few moments that could touch people's hearts and make them feel that life is worthwhile. Now who wouldn't want to do that.

Q - What advice would you offer a new film maker?

Janis - Just enjoy it and don't give a damn what anyone else says. All of your friends who have gone to film school will fiercely criticise you even if they've never even attempted to make their own film. If you're a woman, it's fairly common for the men to get all the credit, as everyone tends to imagine that it was all their doing, due to their expertise. But as we all know; there's no better team than women and men working together, side by side and helping to portray both the male and the female angle. Filming may be about teamwork but the director should have the final say, as the director and the writer have the overall vision. Helping the actors and crew understand the vision you're working towards is all important. I think the director should also listen to the actors too. Capturing moments of emotion is what does it for me.

www.lunargirl.com

SCREENPLAY

**Screenwriter
Stuart Hazledine**

AN ENGLISHMAN IN HOLLYWOOD

Q - How did you get into films? How did you plan that out?

Stuart - I've always been a planner, and I had a new career plan every 6 months at school. At university, after making a Super 8mm short, I decided that film was what I wanted to do with my life - it was what excited me, what I was passionate about, and suddenly I was making all kinds of plans! From that first moment, I knew that I wanted to write and direct feature films in Hollywood. Up until I was about 13, the only directors in the world that existed for me were Ridley Scott, George Lucas and Steven Spielberg. I was a junkie of *Alien* and *Bladerunner*, and obviously *Star Wars* like so many others. When I hit puberty, my interests broadened into more human movies. I started watching *Chariots of Fire, The Mission*, and *Amadeus,* and a whole new vista of film-making opened up for me, but it didn't replace what I liked before, it just expanded it. I decided to start writing the stuff I enjoyed as a kid first. Hopefully I would work with a couple of big genre directors who I respected, and then once I got into directing myself I would start to move across to more adult material, the more mainstream drama that I wanted to do.

Q - Are writers often frustrated directors?

Stuart - When we say frustrated director, we're really talking about the power to decide what the film is like at any given time, so until the director comes onboard, you the writer, the director. It's like giving birth to a baby, rearing it for 4 years, then the government turns up, and says *'sorry, we now own this baby, you can come see it occasionally and give us a few ideas about what it's dietary requirements are, but it's ours now!'*

Q - Surely one advantage of low budget films is that the writer will have more power?

Stuart – That's true, though it's not to say that when you get into larger films by definition you won't have that input anymore, it is really down to the director. For instance, Roland Emmerich is known to value writers beyond the shooting script. The guy who wrote *'The Day After Tomorrow'*, Jeffrey Nachmanoff, is a relative newcomer, and he was on set every day helping with last minute re-writes. Roland didn't fire him, he kept him around and had faith in him. Other directors, and you can leave the names out, will keep you away and you will never end up on the set re-writing dialogue unless you're an established A-list Writer, it just won't happen.

Most directors will have a writer on set, the only question is, what kind of writer? Do they have the guy who came up with the idea for the story, and knows it inside out, or do they have a writer who can polish, or a script doctor? There are circumstances in which they are justified in bringing another writer on, who wasn't the originator of the script. Not all writers can do all of the things that a writer should do. There are some writers who have great ideas, and in order to acquire the script, the studio may let them write a draft, but it's really just the cost of buying the idea. The studio thinks, *'OK, this guy is unproved, fresh out of film school'*, or maybe *'he has only sold two movies before, but he hasn't stayed on the production for very long - OK, we'll take a risk on him, we'll pay a quarter of a million bucks for his idea. In our minds we are paying for his idea, but he thinks we're paying for his idea AND his writing services.'* The writer thinks, *'I'm doing a blinder of a draft,'* but they're thinking *'we'll keep him on, but we'll assume the worst case scenario, that we're paying a quarter of a million dollars for an idea, and we'll fire him when the draft comes in. We won't be disappointed if it's crap, because that's what we expect, and we will get XXX on to rewrite next week!'* That's often the case, and I think if they do indeed turn in a draft that isn't very good, it makes sense for the studio and the director to not invite that guy on set

Copyrighting Your Screenplay

GUERILLA FILM MAKER SAYS!

By law, when you write a screenplay, you own the copyright. You don't need to do anything in order to own that copyright. However... the complication comes when someone disputes that. So registration of a screenplay in the UK with some form of copyright system is a way to protect you from legal action, or prove you were the copyright owner if that action ever went to a court.

You can give a copy to your solicitor, accountant, even priest! They will all be good witnesses should you ever go to court. Some people suggest that mailing it to yourself is also protection, which it may be, but not much. In the UK, organisations such as the WCA and Raindance offer script registration services. However, the cheapest and best service is offered by the US Writers Guild. It currently costs $20, for five years and is a recognised body with weight behind it. Crucially, in the USA you do need to register for copyright, so if your work is ever going to make it to American soil, be it in an email, on paper, film or DVD, you would need to register it with the WGA anyway.

We recommend registering your screenplay BEFORE you begin sending it out. And re-registering at rewrite intervals where you have done major work, or perhaps just before production if you choose to make it as a low budget film.

You can register via their website and you don't need to be American. You fill out a form, add your credit card details, upload your screenplay (as a Final Draft, MS Word, PDF etc.) and a week or so later you get a certificate in the post. Registering with the WGA is twenty bucks worth of good peace of mind. Go to www.wga.org. You should also consider registering for copyright in Washington USA, with the Register of Copyrights. Though not initially crucial, by the time you get to sales and distribution, you MUST register as sales agents will require it. We suggest registering, with form PA, just before you shoot. Full details are at www.copyright.gov/register/performing.html, and it costs $30.

SCREENPLAY

to be re-writing it. Maybe he turned in a good draft, but his dialogue skills aren't great, maybe he's not particularly phonetic. You want a realistic sense of dialogue and you don't want to rely on your actors for that, because maybe they're just too egotistical about their line count and will end up wanting more dialogue.

You've got enough stress on the movie set without arguing with your writer, so sometimes it makes sense. Personally I think it's better to have someone who knows the story inside out. If you think your writer could hack it on set, and has enough skill with dialogue, I would say don't give in to insecurity and vanity by hiring the million dollar writer who's done big script doctor gigs before, bring in the guy that's so far proved he's worth it. But you'll get certain directors, it doesn't matter how good your script is, no matter how good your dialogue is, they just can't be bothered, they just want to bring in a big writer.

Q - As a career choice, do you think it is wise for a new or young film maker to say, 'I am going to start writing features for the big Hollywood studios', and just go for it?

Stuart - I wanted to do that and everyone told me I was insane! I was lucky to sell a script very early on, and had I had the more usual experiences of rejection that the average writer has, I'm not sure how long I would have lasted. I sold my script through a combination of some writing talent, being in the right place at the right time, picking the right idea, and luck. The odds are hugely stacked against you.

Q - How did you become a spec script writer, how does that business work?

Stuart - For me, the moment I started writing I started thinking about, *'how am I going to get in?'* I went to the BFI library and got a copy of *The Knowledge*, and I went through all the agencies in town, and I compared them to all the writers and directors who I admired, then I put little stars next to each of the agencies, to find out the agencies I was most interested in joining. I figured *Screen International* is what everybody reads, so I started reading it and I discovered that once every couple of months they had a special issue where they list all the London based production companies' development slates... and they list the credited director and producer, so you can see, *'OK, these guys only like Romantic Comedy, these guys are looking to make Hollywood stuff...'*

I would work out who the young, hot producers are, who didn't yet have huge development funds, who couldn't afford to hire big writers, but were obviously heading for Hollywood. If I could get these guys to like my stuff, then they could open the doors to Hollywood, and I could ride in on their coat tails. I picked on Jeremy Bolt, who just produced *Shopping* with Paul Anderson, and Paul Trijbits who had just produced *Young Americans* with Danny Cannon - both were working with hot young directors, and they were both flying out to LA for the first time!

So once you have your script in hand, what do you do? It's an eternal chicken and egg situation, as producers tend not to want to read your script unless it's sent by an agent. Agents don't want to read your script unless there's a reason, they don't like spending time trying to sell your script. They actually just want to take the 10%, they can be kind of lazy. So how do you break that chicken and egg cycle? My perspective is that it's easier to break in with the producers than it is with the agents. So I hit the streets around Soho, doing anything I could to get my script into the hands of producers or their assistants. When going into production companies, always assume that the person answering the phone is going to be making the big decisions in ten years time, and may already be the reader of the scripts in the production company. I ended up with Paul Trijbits company and I made friends with a girl called Harriet who was his assistant and reader. When she read my script, she liked it, and she put it on Paul's desk with a gold star, and it started to snow ball from there.

Q - What about agents?

Stuart - Rule number one, until you have an agent working for you, you are your own agent, you are selling yourself. If you don't see yourself as someone who sells, become a novelist or go and sweep streets, don't become a screenwriter. You have to sell yourself. Number two, when you do have an agent and a manager, you are still your own agent / manager, they are just helping you. Never ever stop thinking about selling yourself, you simply can't. Agent or manager, they are still splitting their time between many different people, so you still have to look at it as though nobody cares about your career as much as you do.

Q - So how do you get it to Hollywood?

Stuart - Most executives will tell you that in London the spec script market doesn't exist. As for the spec script market in Hollywood, the first thing you have to know is that how it is when you first try and get into it is not how it has been in the past. The spec script market is subject to fashion and sudden change. For about ten years, the market was almost completely created single-

Script Doctor

GUERILLA FILM MAKER SAYS!

You've felt it. You're looking at your script for the thousandth time and it's still not working. Or you think it is working, but no-one is biting and you don't know why. Instead of banging your head against your computer screen, consider hiring a script doctor!

Script doctors are professional readers (many are writers as well) who have reviewed thousands of screenplays. They will give you an unbiased critique (something your friends might not do) about story, structure, character, tone, dialogue, commerciality and format, usually in written form so that you can refer to their comments as you go through the script. Just remember not to get too defensive if they tell you to consider cutting or changing one of your darlings, or if they miss or don't understand something. Chances are the script is flawed, which is why you were having problems in the first place.

Script doctoring is not expensive (between £75-£150 depending on how detailed a breakdown you want) and can save you loads of time and grey hairs. Even if you think their ideas are not right, the doctor's points will always inspire new ideas and that is the whole point!

Always look at a doctor's bio sheet to see where they may have worked and contact them for either references or to see what type of writers they like. Most script doctors can do all genres and you may even be able to work a deal where they will help you over many drafts, much like a producer would for a flat fee. You also might want to consider getting a reader from another market, like the US, to read your project. The rules of screenwriting are the same, so the critique will be valid and give you a slightly different perspective that might make all the difference. And they're cheaper due to competition and a weak dollar.

handedly by Shane Black selling *Lethal Weapon* for a million bucks. Loads of spec scripts sold off the back of that, and the percentage of movies getting made every year that came from spec scripts as an original source was something like 60% to 70%. That is no longer the case, the number now is more like 20% to 30%. Currently there are a larger number of movies being made from book adaptations or re-makes of TV series etc.

People in Hollywood, in the absence of scientifically understanding why films fail or succeed, become superstitious and they point to omens in the sky and crap like that, and so more recently they decided that book adaptations was the thing. Every new book that came onto the book market got snapped up. That's still quite a strong market, but the edge has been taken off it in recent years by re-makes of TV series and by re-makes of Asian movies.

Q - What have you learned while in the market place?

Stuart - Don't send it out until it's ready. As brilliant as you may be - and I thought I was pretty hot when I was 25 - wait until it's as good as it can be. Beforehand, send it to as many friends as you can, and hopefully the smart friends are going to be the ones who are the most brutally honest with you. Don't give it to your gran! Get full criticism from them and listen to what they have to say.

Make sure you've done many drafts. M. Night Shyamalan had done something like 20 drafts of *The Sixth Sense* before it was made. It started out just being about a serial killer, and ended up being the story of a boy and a psychiatrist and selling for $3m to Disney overnight. Quality is essential.

Beyond that, you'll need to collaborate with your agent, relying on their wisdom. You've got to strategise with him, and work out what's the best day of the week to go out, what's your list of places to go to? Are you going to go to producers who have studio 'first look' deals? Or see if you can get a producer who is an 800lb gorilla who will go into a studio with you, and get the studio to buy your script under their producing deal? Are you going to go directly to the studio executives themselves? Or are you going to do a mixture? Generally you try to maximise the number of shots you get at buyers, especially now so many mergers have happened in recent times. Companies have consolidated so the physical number of buyers in town is less. Five years ago, there were something like 20 buyers, now there are 10 buyers or so. You can still send it to the same number of producers, and there are hundreds of producers, but ultimately the actual buyers, the source of studio coin or mini-major independent money, are physically fewer.

To maximise your shots, the first thing you would do is to come up with 4 or 5 producers who you can 'slip it to'. When I say 'slip it to' I mean let them read it outside of the 'official' system, in order that the script will not be covered by a script reader in the studio machine - the moment a script is 'covered' in Hollywood, it's entered into the studio database - so the moment they get a script, they type it into their computer and if it has already been covered, then they read the coverage instead of the script! And if some kid, just out of UCLA, who recently had a bust up with his girlfriend, is employed as a reader and doesn't like your romantic comedy as it makes him feel uncomfortable, then you're screwed - so that's why everything always gets done all on the same day, to avoid the script being negatively affected by coverage.

At the same time it creates its own reality where everyone is trying to get your script, because they're worried about it being bought by somebody else. Astonishingly, the one thing that people don't have the time or the incentive to do in Hollywood, is to form their own opinion of your script. They're always saying *'it's good, it's good'. . . is it good?'* They don't know.

So, you come up with 4 or 5 guys to slip it to, because it makes them feel special. You call some guy at a studio, say DreamWorks, and you say *'hey buddy, you liked this guy's last script, and we've got a new script that's coming in, just between you and me, I want to slip this to you for the weekend, I'm only giving it to you and a couple of other guys,'* so you create the feeling that it's rare and unique, and they've got 48 hours ahead of everybody else. Often it doesn't work anyway, but why not give yourself that chance? So you go to those guys, and if they all come back on Monday morning and say *'this is the biggest piece of shit ever!'* then you know where you stand. They'll know not to tell anyone about it, and if they do it creates troubled waters between the agent and the executive for future deals. So nobody really wants to rock the boat on that. It's all kept quiet.

Step two, beyond the 'slipping', is to go wider to producers and not to the studio. You pick one producer on every studio lot, ideally the bigger producers because the smaller producer, who has just made one successful movie and has a deal at Fox to make a few more comedies, isn't going to add much value to your script while taking it to the studio. The studios aren't going to buy it because *'Oh it's so and so, that producer'* but if you go in with Jerry Bruckheimer or Joel Silver, and Joel or Jerry says to Disney or Warner Bros., *'buy this script, or I'm going to be super fucking pissed at you!'* then you are in a better situation, because they don't want to piss Jerry off. Purists may say, *'What, they don't buy it because they like your script?'* Well duh, they probably wouldn't be buying it because they like your script anyway! They'll probably be buying because they see a gem of an idea in it, because they like some character in it, you never know what they like in your script, until after they've bought it.

Always assume they don't know what they've bought, unless some studio guy calls you and waxes lyrical for half an hour, in great detail, about how much they love your script, why they want to make it without changing a word on the page. You may have that experience with them, they'll buy it, and you'll have that creative meeting with them, and you'll suddenly realise that they have no clue what they've bought. You'll realise that they've paid you a quarter of a million bucks to enslave you for two years, to write something you never intended to write. That unfortunately is probably going to happen to you at some time.

So let's assume even Jerry Bruckheimer can't get your script bought; the third option and *'last shot'* is to go wide to every studio in town. You call all the executives and you get the script to them. You hope they like it enough to take it to the head of production, and try to persuade them to buy it. Often you'll get right to that last gate, but the head of production will say *'sorry, I don't want to buy this one'* or *'I don't know, I just don't see it...'* I've had pitches that go right up to the top, and not been able to do it, and sometimes it's nothing to do with the project. I went in with a director to New Line once and we really excited two executives over a pitch, and they went to the boss, and he just said *'buying freeze, we paid so much money for Lord Of The Rings, and I don't know if the studio is going to exist next year, because we've got so much riding on it!'*

So that's the other thing in terms of strategy; who's got money right now, who's successful, who just had a huge opening weekend, who's walking around town, showing how big their penis is to everyone? Because those are the guys who are going to want to buy a script. It's kind of like retail therapy. When you've had a big hit, you go out and buy a couple of scripts.

Also, be aware of the time of year that you send the script out. The one thing that Hollywood never seems to do is actually work! They've got Sundance in January, then it's the Oscars, then suddenly they're all building up for Cannes, then they're in Cannes, then it's the Summer, nobody does anything in the Summer! Then it's Labor Day, then you've got to give people time to get back from Labor Day, then they're off for a nice Columbus Day weekend, then there are two weeks when they work, and suddenly you're in the 3rd week of November, and it's Thanksgiving, and between Thanksgiving and Christmas it's the holiday season, nobody does anything in the holiday season! Then they're back in mid-January, and what do you know, it's Sundance again! There are actually not nearly the number of windows to get your specs out there as you'd think. The general rule is, after Labor Day, early September / October is a good time. January / February is a good time, because everyone is back from a big holiday, they're focusing, they're re-jigging, they're looking for new material.

Also there are discretionary funds in Hollywood, which control a lot of what people can buy. Producers get an annual discretionary fund from the studio and once that fund has run down, you can't buy a script. So if a script comes to them then, they're less likely to buy, or they'll pay less money. I had a spec go out two years ago and Jerry Bruckheimer's company was really interested in it. When I spoke to the guy on the phone, he said *'our discretionary fund gets topped up every September'* - it was May - *'had you sent this to us in October, we would have bought it, and we would have worked on the problems that we perceive to be in the script, within the context of our deal...as it is, we can't buy it. If you happen to do a new draft over the Summer and bring it back to us, we might look at it again.'* So generally, September and January are the months when a lot funds get topped up.

Q - Fundamentally writing a script is only part of the picture, there is a lot of strategising, a lot of plotting, a lot of horse-trading, marketeering. That is almost as important as writing the great script, having the great concept?

Stuart - No amount of strategising will cover over a crap spec script, but if you've written the great spec, then you've got to do everything you can to get it into the right position. In that world of strategy, there are a lot of legitimate things to take account of, most of which we've just gone through. But there's also a bunch of tarot card like, astrology stuff, which is just bollocks, all kinds of weird speculation.

Spec Script Case Study - The Quick And The Dead

Screenwriter
Simon Moore

Q - From a writers point of view, what first steps should you take?

Simon - The priority of the writer is to get things made, even if film people don't really see value in the end product, it's important to experience an audience reaction. Writers work in a vacuum and it's hard to get genuine feedback about a film that might cost $100m. You can sit down and write it but how on earth are you to gauge whether you are going in the right direction or not. The real route to success for me has been to write scripts speculatively and then take my chances selling them. The disadvantage of that is that you have to be prepared to go without making money. The advantage is that if and when you sell the script, you have tremendous power to negotiate yourself into a better position, role, credit and of course, money. The interesting thing is that you start off and no-one will pay you to write in advance, then when you have completed, everyone gets excited and they pay much more than if they had paid you to write it in the first place.

Q - How did 'The Quick and the Dead' happen?

Simon - I wrote the movie for myself to direct as a spaghetti western on a budget of $4m. I had sent the script to my agent who had circulated it in LA. It was a Friday night and I was out for dinner with friends. I was broke and was lamenting the fact. When I returned home there was a message on the answerphone that said somebody has read your script and they really want to do it, and they want to offer you some serious money and there is a major star attached. I had no idea which script they were talking about as I had several scripts circulating. I phoned him and it was all very hush, hush and they would not tell me who was interested in doing it. The tactical advantage that I had was that this was a film that I was trying to set up for myself to direct, and they thought that I was in the process of getting it made. I had spoken to a producer a few weeks earlier and said look, I am sorry but I have already decided to make it with someone in Britain and we are going to do it this way. And this message had filtered through the Hollywood system (laughs). So I had this crazy night where I had no money and was feeling very lost, when suddenly there was this huge pressure. Over the course of the weekend they kept offering more - they started with $370k and my agent said if they are opening with that, they will go really high - and they want to conclude the deal before Monday ...and this is Friday night. Obviously they thought that on Monday morning all the other studios would be out-bidding them, which was nonsense of course. It went on for 48 hours and I felt like I had been in a minor car crash. I was just sitting there, there was nothing I could do and he kept saying no, they are really going to offer you a lot of money, just sit tight. Then he phoned me on Sunday and said we've agreed on $1m and I

found out that it was Sharon Stone and Columbia TriStar. There was a narrow window to make the film because Sharon Stone was committed to making another movie afterward, so not only did the deal happen, but I thought it is actually going to happen as a film. So in less than two weeks I was flying back and forth to LA having meetings and the movie was happening.

Sharon Stone had decided that she wanted Sam Raimi to direct, which was a good and interesting choice. There were a group of people around Sam who were not unlike European independent film makers which was creatively good, but unfortunately, that was also part of their downfall because they had no experience of how to face the corporate might of the studio. I did ten re-writes over three months and anybody who came on board gave me notes and I just said yeah, yeah I'll do that. Script meetings were with 12-14 people, and of course the person who is in charge as far as anyone is, is not at the meeting. And so it goes on. As a scriptwriter it is hard to protect and re-emphasise the story telling, people forget the storytelling when they get involved with all the other elements that come together when making a film.

Q - How did you feel at this point?

Simon - I've had largely good experiences working on all kinds of projects, but it quickly became clear that The Quick And The Dead was not going to be one. I sat in a room in LA with Gene Hackman, who is just about my most favourite fucking actor in the world (laughs), Sharon Stone who turned up ten minutes late, and Leonardo DeCaprio. Sharon Stone being ten minutes late was the first test, you could see the sweat pouring off the executives, do we begin this read through or not, if we don't begin the read through, she has won, she is now in charge, and if you do begin the read through, your star walks through the door ten minutes late because she has got flu. I sat there thinking this is a great moment in my life, but the actual read through was terrible. It largely consisted of Gene Hackman saying out loud that was a terrible line, oh that's awful, you are going to have to change that. There were people leaning across me to Sam Raimi talking about script notes and just ignoring my presence. I was never acknowledged by any of the 'A' list cast, no-one said this is a good script and I am pleased to be doing it. I was routinely asked to leave the room for meetings and you wonder just what it is that they are talking about that you cannot hear? Actually it has nothing to do with you, it is just hierarchy. But as you know the reasons that films get made are nothing to do with the quality of the script. When shooting started and I thought I can't fucking do a hundred days of this humiliation, I am going home, it really can't get any worse, so I went up to Sharon Stone and said I am flying back to England now, and I just wanted to wish you luck with production and she said You can't go, you haven't fixed my scenes yet!

Q - How long was it between sending Quick and the Dead out, and interest coming back?

Simon - Four months. My agent always sends things to several people at once, I think that is a very good strategy. If there is no reaction, you have to re-think and re-group. I believe in consensus, if you can find one person who thinks that your script is fantastic then that is fine, but when you get four out of five people saying we like this but the ending isn't very good, or it is not a star vehicle then I think you have to listen. Unfortunately, I don't think many people appreciate how much work you have got to do in order to write a great screenplay.

Q - So should you go to LA if you want to write a Hollywood movie?

Simon - Lots of people said to me you can't sit in London and write a studio film on spec and expect to get it made - and I want to say that they are wrong because I did it and other people have done it - maybe half a dozen people do it every year. I am very much against the notion that you can calculate this business, I think that people who get on are on the whole people who have the confidence to express their individual voices. There is a danger in thinking that if you get the formula right you can sell a script. I think people still write a film and say oh, this won't sell in Hollywood, I must put it through some sort of machine, put in guns, car chases and sex. I would also say that it is just as hard to get a small movie made as it is a big movie, the studios have got to churn out loads of movies every year and someone has to make them.

Q - What advice would you offer new writers?

Simon - Films, and therefore screenplays, should be shorter. Rarely do people come out of the cinema and say gee, I loved that film, but it was too short, and almost every film you see apart from your own is too long. Writers shoot themselves in the foot by writing their screenplays 30 pages too long.

I test my ideas out on people at every stage and the way to do it is to present more than one idea. Writers often say I have got this great idea for a script tell you it and then say do you think that was good? -

then you tend to say I liked it because you don't want to upset them. The technique I have found is to present someone with two ideas and they will tell you which one they prefer. So when you say don't you think the one about my dad in Zimbabwe in the 1920s is really good? you can say no, dull as ditchwater.

The other trick is to forget the first draft. Some writers send me scripts with notes saying I know it is 30 pages too long, the end doesn't work and I have not quite got the relationship between these two people, but see what you think. That is disastrous as it encourages people to think that they can't write without your help. I put thousands of hours of work into a script and end up with something that is shootable. I believe that the first script you send to anyone should be a shooting script. You will still have to do ten redrafts but you will be building on something that is structurally sound. If you show people something that is structurally sound and you get fifty different voices and comments on it, you are not pulling down the house, you are re-decorating it. Someone could say I just love this house, I really love this house, I only want to make one change to it, I want to move it six inches to the left and that actually means dismantling the house, or you could have someone who says I really hate this house, it is really awful and you say what do you hate about it? and they say it's green and it will take a morning to paint it white. The structure is the key. You need to present a script that is as fully formed as you can make it, has been read, has been talked about, then you can enter this difficult and competitive world with a degree of confidence.

Don't demonise institutions, don't talk about them, be specific about the forces that you feel are stopping you from articulating what you want to say or what you want to do. The truth is that there are a tiny number of people who share your values, but they do exist, they are the people to seek out, they are the people that you should form alliances with and that is the way to make what you want to make.

For me, it's like predicting the weather, there are a certain number of variables you can predict, but there are so many more that you can't, nor can you predict how they may interact - the more variables that interact, the more impossible it gets to predict whether something is going to sell, and there are a hell of a lot of variables in Hollywood.

Q - How much of the stuff that is floating around in the spec script market is good?

Stuart – There's definitely more good stuff than what gets bought. They always say good material will find a way in the end, and maybe it's true, but it won't always find a way to get sold as a spec. It may die and after ten years get pulled out the drawer when someone randomly sees it. Hollywood is littered with stories of amazing scripts that ended up getting made one year, but ten years earlier when they went out as a spec scripts, everybody passed on it. *Braveheart* was passed on by everybody in town, multiple times. Don't think that if it's high quality it will sell, it's still a bit of a lottery and hard to tell why someone sees something in a script and why they like it.

Q - How much work is it to be a spec script writer?

Stuart - However hard you think it is, it's going to surprise you, it's going to be harder. It is possible to sell a script that you've written after a couple of drafts, but you have to be pretty talented for that, or it has to be the story of your life, that you're so passionate about, that it just spills out of you. People tend to latch on to the glory stories, that Chris Columbus wrote *Home Alone* in a weekend, or *Sex, lies and videotape* was written in ten days. Very very occasionally that happens, but the vast majority of scripts, come about through long man hours of slog, craft and trouble-shooting etc. Basically scripts are 1% great idea, and 99% solving all the problems with that idea.

It's not profitable for you to think in terms of maximising laziness, because if you're lazy and you just happen to write the first draft of a script and sell it, then what do you do? Re-writing is 90% of what goes on in Hollywood and you need the ability to re-write your own material in order to protect it, and to make the best out of it. The people the studios respect the most are the writers who can take an okay script that is on their development slate, and turn that script into a green light movie, something that's ready to shoot. Studios have long development slates with say, 250 scripts on that slate. They 've paid money for all those scripts, so they're assets. Assets that have problems, and what they want are writers who will turn those assets into a script that '*we now have confidence in, to get a director, to make next year, this is a green light... thank you so much Mr. young hot writer, you made us see something in this script that we never thought we would see!*' That's when you really become their friends.

Q - So they like writers that add that extra level of caffeine, to a good cappuccino? Can you do that from London?

Stuart - I work in LA, but I live and write in London, and that's the lifestyle that I wanted to have for the first phase of my career. I like going to LA, and looking at it as though I am going to market. From the moment I hit the tarmac in LA, the moment I smell the air, it is like '*right, it's selling time!*' Being from outside of LA has certain unique advantages in the sense that, as a new or young writer in LA, executives are endlessly canceling meetings. It can actually be a real help to your career when your agent can say '*you can't cancel this meeting for the third time, because he's on a plane, are you going to take this or not?*' and suddenly everyone will see you. So that can be good, but despite the fact that I prefer the lifestyle in London, you will maximise your chances of doing well by being in LA. I think there has been an invisible cost to me living in London. As successful as I have been, and as much money as I have earnt, which is much more than 90% of British screenwriters, I still think I would probably be earning more if I was in LA right now.

Q - It seems like you can earn a lot of money?

Stuart - You would think but... Say you have a writing assignment and they say they will pay you $10k for a year, to rent your script, and every time they want it re-written, they'll give you another $10k, and then if the movie gets made they agree that your ultimate fee will be a certain percentage of the budget, so maybe you end up getting $200k, but that extra $180k comes on the first day of production. What everybody forgets is that out of that $200k, which is spread over time and the biggest part may or may not appear, you have to pay your agent / manager and tax. I pay 10% to my agency, 10% to my manager, 5% to my lawyer, 1½ % in union dues (WGA), and after that 26½% is taken off my pay packet, then I go from dollars to pounds, then I pay tax, often at 40%, so you are not ending up with nearly as much as you started off with. You can survive without a lawyer, but a lawyer will come up with all those extra expenses, per diems, flights and things like that. Sometimes hiring a lawyer can feel like a waste, but they can get you really tangible benefits.

It's all about building precedent, whatever you got on your last script is used to secure a better deal on the next, as long as you can give the prior contract to the legal department of the people who want to buy your next script. Say you were hired to write for DreamWorks and paid $250k. You wrote for a couple of years and in the end the studio didn't want to go ahead and make it, they are not '*wowed*' by you. Then you get hired by Warner Bros. for another assignment and your lawyer goes to them and says '*well, his quote is quarter of a million*'. The studio legal department, business affairs says '*show us the contract, show us the precedent*', so your lawyer sends them the contract which says $250k. Then business affairs say '*Oh OK, that's fine, but the head of production on the creative side, has told us that we shouldn't pay that because your client's last script didn't do too well at DreamWorks, and it's not really that hot, and we are only prepared to pay $200k, take it or leave it!*' Then you get into a game of hard ball, and you have to decide, am I going to go with this job and come off my quote, or am I going to walk off because it sends a message to the town that I'm on the downers? There is a lot of face-saving and puffing up of the chest that goes on when it comes to contract negotiation. Most writers won't have a smooth ascent to the mountain top: you'll get troughs as well as peaks, and it's important to use your 'team's' wisdom to minimise the troughs as well as maximising the peaks.

Q - How is the money broken down?

Stuart - Generally, they will agree a certain amount to pay you for your 1st draft and revisions, then maybe they'll say *'we want a second draft and set of revisions, and then a third draft and two sets of revisions'* for which they will pay additional fees. They will demarcate say, $150k for the 1st draft, $50k for 2nd draft and $50k for the 3rd draft, and for each step, they will pay you half of it on commencement and half of it on delivery.

Once you've turned that in, there will be optional steps, so that they can continue to engage you if they like what you've done. The contract and the commitment are there in the beginning, but then it gets looser later on. So, there will be a couple of optional steps, and maybe they'll hold those optional steps in hand, until a director is on board, which is what's happening in my current project. I've done a draft, and a set of revisions, they've now said *'great, before we do any optional sets with you, if we decide to do that, we want to get a director on board, so that we can pay you for the optional sets when you're working with a director.'*

You'll agree roughly what the production budget will be, and on the first day of production (assuming it gets to production) you'll get your second fee. So, basically $250k against $500k means, $250k for the compulsory writing services, even if you are the crappest writer in the world, you'll still get paid that $250k, and if it gets made, you get a bonus $250k on the first day of shooting. Even though it's called the first day of shooting, it actually doesn't happen on the first day of shooting. The moment they bring another writer on, which frequently happens, you get into credit arbitration, and the bonus at the end is only to be given to, or shared by, the guys who the Writer's Guild determine get credit. So you get into credit arbitration on the first day of shooting, based on the final shooting script, in which you and the other writers all submit your individual drafts to a panel of anonymous arbiters from the Writer's Guild, and they will take a while to read your draft, your depositions and your witness statements. Everybody fights for their own credit, *'I re-wrote five words, therefore I deserve some credit!'.*

You will find out, probably during editing, who got the final credit, and that is when you get paid your money. Then finally at the end of this come 'residuals', which are what we call 'royalties' here in the UK. You get 'residuals' depending on how well it has done around the world. So that's how it goes... First draft, Second draft, Optional, Production Bonus, residuals.

Q - Can your residuals be considerable?

Stuart - Yes. Residuals are fairly protected and a creative studio accountant can't massage them down like they can net profit points. The best thing about residuals is that you don't have to pay a commission to your agent, manager or lawyer on them.

Q - What do you think have been your biggest mistakes?

Stuart - If you get into the industry and you are young, it is easy for you to come across as being arrogant. Even if you are just confident, especially here in the UK, it will be mis-read as arrogance. Every bad meeting that you have, where you come across as arrogant and cocky, will come back to haunt you. I have been lucky in that I've literally had over a 1000 meetings and I've only had

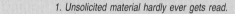

Top 10 Reasons script readers reject submissions

GUERILLA FILM MAKER SAYS!

1. Unsolicited material hardly ever gets read.
2. Story and characters are too familiar / unoriginal / unsympathetic.
3. The writing / dialogue does not have an original voice.
4. Does not produce an emotional response (not funny, scary, etc.). Especially relevant to the first 30 pages of your script.
5. Poorly structured story.
6. The company has something similar in development.
7. The genre is not what the company currently wants to do.
8. Too much gratuitous sex, violence or melodrama.
9. Depending on the company the script is either too commercial or not commercial enough.
10. Script isn't professionally presented i.e. too long, wrong format, typos, artwork on the cover etc.

Public Domain

GUERILLA FILM MAKER SAYS!

One of the greatest sources of material is in the 'public domain'. If a creator of a work, be it a poem, novel, play or even orchestral symphony, died over 70 years ago, that work is now in the public domain. That means you can use it without having to pay a copyright license fee. This law varies from country to country, but as far as we know, no country extends beyond 70 years. So that means you can produce a film based on a Shakespeare play, or a Bronte novel, without having to pay a penny. The advantage is that, for instance, if you make 'Wuthering Heights', you already have a work that is both well known and proven to work.

Beware, you cannot use other people's interpretations though, so if your Romeo and Juliet is too reminiscent of Baz Luhrmann's, you could be sued for copyright infringement - not the Shakespeare copyright, but the Baz Luhrmann interpretation. So don't copy what other people have done.

For example, go find a classic work, contemporise it, set it in an urban environment, and you have a project that is both proven to work and partly developed. You will also find it easier to attract actors as they will know that the work already has weight.

two bad meetings, but in those two meetings I was confident and quite opinionated. Anything you say in an meeting, can come back to haunt you.

Q - What do you think you need to be, in order to be a successful writer?

Stuart - You want to be someone who comes up with ideas, good ideas, someone who can pitch those ideas in a room. You need great tenacity, to just keep going and going, to be your worst critic, and to never think what you have written is perfect. You want to be able to come up with good, fully realised characters, who have established goals, that create an emotional investment in the audience. You need a good phonetic ear for dialogue. An ability to collaborate well, so you can be a team player, because film, make no mistake, is a collaborative medium.

You have to just write to the best of your ability, plus be able to work harder than you think you can. And understand that you have got to re-write, it is all about re-writing. In Britain we don't re-write enough. We don't understand how much of the success in the writing is re-writing yourself, because you should understand your story universe better than anyone, and you really should take time out to make it better.

Learn to make other people happy, invest them in the process, when someone gives a bunch of notes to you, it's an opportunity, not a threat - steer them away from their bad ideas, take their good ideas, and make them work for you, work for your script. At the end of the day, nobody cares where the ideas came from, it's your name on the credits, so if somebody else gives you a great idea ride with it. The best idea wins, which requires a certain amount of objectivity. You have to be able to step back, and emotionally separate yourself from your script once you've written it, and to go with the best idea. The opposing mentality, instead of best idea wins, is whatever I write is the best, and that is an absolutely fallacious idea, which will ending up screwing you over.

Q - What advice would you offer a new film-maker?

Stuart - Films are about imagination, so you are working in a industry that is full of imaginative, creative people, who have an imagination about who they are, and about what their talents are, and they are often hideously inflated. So try to see yourself the way others see you. That is a great skill to have in life. Do not see yourself the way you want to be, or the way you think you are, but the way others see you. Study what people say about you, and make it a goal of yours to really find out honestly what other people say, because if you are a director, and five people honestly tell you, as your friends, that you are not a particularly skilled writer, Stop re-writing scripts, just stop it! Life is too short, you're pissing off other people, annoying writers, and you're making your films worse (and vice versa with some writers trying to direct, of course)!If you can get a picture of who you are, through other people's eyes, you'll save yourself so much time. It will free you, it will liberate you, so that you can spend your time on that area to which you're most suited. The film industry is full of people who are good at one job, but they're trying to do another; it's such a waste.

Juliet McKoen
Writer and Director

Q - How did you come to write 'Frozen', which is an art-house film?

Juliet - I had worked as a film artist and wanted certain themes and motifs in *Frozen* - the use of landscape, both exterior and interior, is used tp portray emotional meaning. Another thing I wanted was to work around the themes to do with loss, obsession and grief. The script that I wrote was a long narrative dealing with all this material.

Q - So to use a label, it's not an American movie, it's a European film?

Juliet - It is definitely a European film and, at the script stage, Europeans liked it more than the Americans and the British.

Q - Given there is funding available for more arts based work than straight genre films, did you find it easier to raise money?

Juliet - No, I think it is equally difficult to make an esoteric art-house film as it is a straight genre or commercial film. They are both hugely difficult, and it is a miracle that either gets made

Q - So should you watch the market and write something you think will be successful?

Juliet - It is almost impossible to second guess the market place. Gangster films used to be in, now it's gritty social realism. By the time you read this it will be something else. By the time you make a film, it will be different again.

Q - So what project would you advise a new film-maker to choose?

Juliet - That is a difficult question. I once saw Gurinder Chadha talking about *'Bhaji on the Beach',* saying it was only shown in a few art-house cinemas. She vowed to make a project that was her own self indulgent dream project. She was going to make something commercial. I thought *'you sell-out Gurinda, you sell-out!'* But now now I completely agree with her! She made *'Bend it like Beckham'* and *'Bride and Prejudice'* which has made her a millionaire, and that was a hugely well thought out strategy. I don't see her as selling out at all, I now think she made sane and lucid choices based on the realities of the market place. I have had to make my first non-commercial movie to understand those choices, and I think she did too.

Q - Do you think Gurinder's initial choice to make an off the beaten track kind of movie, before a commercial one, actually strengthened her as a film-maker?

Juliet - There is absolutely no doubt that if you come into a project with your own voice, your own distinct slant on things, it makes you a stronger film-maker.

Q - How did you find the process of writing a screenplay?

Juliet - No, I wrote it off my own back. I love writing and find it a really seductive and creative activity. I think a lot of people give you advice about your screenplay but often this can complicate matters rather than simplify them. A good story is often about

Screenplay Formatters

GUERILLA FILM MAKER SAYS!

When writing your script, you must adhere to rigid industry specifications. You can do this manually with tabs and spacing, but it's a pain. A screenplay formatter will do it all for you so you can spend all your time being creative. The market leader is Final Draft, which varies in price, but is usually around £200ish. It's a good piece of software and used by most top writers.

(www.finaldraft.com)

*On the CD for this book there is a Screenplay formatter that we developed, as we couldn't afford Final Draft when we began making films. It's called Screenplay and works with MS Word, which is part of MS Office, and almost certainly installed on your computer. You can install Screenplay it and use it completely for free. The only restriction being that it will print the word **unregistered** in the header of the page. To remove that, you can register at www.livingspirit.com, and it costs £49.99. You can write and write and write, and only register when you want to. All your previous screenplays will then print with out the word unregistered at the top.*

As for sending your script out. The world appears to be divided. Many people still like a paper version, but sending your script via email is now becoming popular. The best way to do this is via Adobe PDF files, ideally locked and with a watermark. In Hollywood, scripts are sent out with the date and details of the person lightly watermarked on every page, so if it turns up somewhere it shouldn't, you know where it came from. This also encourages people to be more responsible with your work. Have a search on the web and you will be able to find some free PDF creation tools, rather than the hugely expensive Adobe Acrobat. www.PDF995.com is as good as any, though there are others that may be easier to use.

simplification rather than complication. I believe in the function of script editors, but I think you have to be careful to choose the right person for you and the project.

Q - How did you find the process of raising money?

Juliet - The majority of the money was tax money under section 42 & 48, which is now sadly being abandoned by the Inland Revenue and the government. It would be harder to make the film now.

Q - You shot on HD. How did you find it?

Juliet - Fantastic! Prior to this, I was a film artist, I shot my own 16mm film and I thought I would always shoot on film. Before shooting *Frozen* I went to look at some test transfers done from various formats - miniDV, BetaSP, DigiBeta and HD, transferred up onto 35mm film. I realised that I was prejudiced against digital as I had already seen a number of films in the cinemas which had been shot digitally, and I had no idea. Looking at the transfers I couldn't tell which was 35mm and which was HD, so I shot on HD. Having been a film artist all my life, it would take a lot to take me back to film now.

Q - What do you think are the advantages to making an art-house film as opposed to a genre film?

Juliet - I don't think I would personally be able to make an action thriller, gangster movie, or an epic movie like '*Troy*'. So it's not really a choice. But I would say that if you choose to make a film within any genre, don't try and buck the trends of that genre.

Q - Know the rules of the genre.

Juliet - Yes. With *Frozen* I wanted to subvert the genre, which did have its drawbacks. My advice would be to really study the market place that you are going into, whether it is commercial or art-house. Don't be too pig-headed, film-makers are so often pig-headed, and obstinate about what they want. There's no point in doing something different to what is actually marketable in the genre you choose. Having said that it is hard to be clear, as in three or four years when your film is complete, the conditions of the market place will have changed.

Q - What did you learn about the process of script to screen?

Juliet - I learnt that dialogue can look smart and funny on the page, yet on screen it's just terrible and contrived. I learnt how easy it is to cut out whole story elements without the film diminishing. Cuts can actually strengthen a film. I realised how simple you need to be to fill an hour and a half's space. I wrote something very simple and other people wanted something more complex, not so much layered because it was a layered film anyway, but more intricate. So there was conflict there. It is a bit like what I was saying about dialogue, something that seems good intellectually can become over fussy and over complex on the screen, and often you are better off sticking with the simple stuff.

Q - Keep clear in your mind the story you are telling, and gravitate back to that if you become lost in over complication, both when writing and in the editing room?

Juliet - Yes. The essence of really good art is simplicity, and what we do in the editing process is remove all the extraneous stuff, leaving something that is the core of the piece.

Q - How did actors respond to the screenplay, given that it was a more esoteric screenplay than perhaps the average episode of a soap?

Juliet - With a great deal of enthusiasm, perhaps because it was something different - it was well written, it had meaning and it had layers. A couple of canny actors pointed out that it was very bleak and, in retrospect, for my first film, I wouldn't make something so down beat. By and large, people prefer to be manipulated into an up-beat ending and a resolution, rather than having to deal with tragedy.

Q - How has 'Frozen' been received internationally?

Juliet - Strangely, it is more popular in America than in Europe, judging from the reaction from festivals, although with the script, it was the other way round. It's interesting. It really seems to speak to American audiences.

Q - How have the sales worked out for you?

Juliet - We are at such an early stage that it's difficult to judge. But what I am learning is just how tough the marketplace is, not just for art-house films, but all films.

Q - Are you going to get rich off it?

Juliet - Absolutely not! Does any independent filmmaker ever get rich? Do you remember that television series on Hollywood that said that, the whole of Hollywood would have made more money by putting their money into a building society for the last 25 years, than making films!

Q - Given that you are the director of a million pound feature film, how have you found the second film? Has it been offered to you on a plate?

Juliet - I wish! No, it's just as much a struggle as it always has been.

Q - Are you writing your 2nd film now? What is it?

Juliet - It's a funny, upbeat ensemble piece - semi-autobiographical, about a 70's house hold, a lesbian mother and her two teenage daughters. It is based on my own mother who was a lesbian head-mistress, who had a string of girlfriends and took huge risks at a time when you could be sacked for being a lesbian. I probably won't take it to final script stage, I'd like to get as far as a step outline, and then improvise with a small group of actors. Because of the nature of digital I can shoot that, which is something you can't afford to do with film.

Photos by Lee Cavaliere

Top Script Tips For Maximising Your Micro Budget
A Personal List by Juliet McKoen

Low-budget filmmaking is about maximising the use of resources and minimising the time taken to achieve scenes.

Budgets are based upon the resources necessary to realise a film. The screenplay dictates the level of budget needed to make a film.

The screenwriter greatly increases his/her chance of getting their script onto screen if s/he bears this in mind when writing.

Here are some guidelines for writing a low-budget film....

Location

1. Think about creating one main or central (interior) location in which a sizeable proportion (even as much as 30-50%) of the film can be shot. The advantage of this is it can be pre-lit & pre-dressed which speeds up shooting no end. It also helps scheduling because this set or location can act as "cover" for other exterior scenes if the weather turns against us when shooting. If you decide to set a lot of your film in a central location it helps if it is an interesting or unusual location visually.

2. Alternatively think about setting a large proportion of your film (say up to 75%) in 5-6 main locations. Again go for the interesting or unusual space.

3. Do not write large scale exterior night scenes. They're expensive to light. A limited number of Interior Night scenes and very small scale Night Exteriors are OK but remember that the crew will often be shooting theses at night. Night time shooting these is wearying for the crew and expensive budget wise.

4. Exterior Day scenes have light and weather issues that slows down shooting. Getting clean dialogue can also be very problematic. On the other hand, exterior landscapes add real value to a film by opening it out. Try, therefore, to write Daylight Exterior scenes that can be shot mute or have minimal dialogue and that are not weather dependent. Ideally, write Day Exterior scenes that can be swapped to an indoor location if it pours down.

5. Avoid scenes on trains, public transport and especially London Underground unless it can be shot guerrilla style.

6. Multiple, lengthy car scenes will require a low-loader. So minimise them or, better still, delete them from your creative vocabulary

7. Try and write scenes that can be achieved with minimal journey time from the production base (say 25 minutes). Time spent travelling a crew is time spent not shooting.

8. Unless it is the main or central location please writing scripts that use sets or locations that require substantial dressing.

9. Avoid writing scenes which will require the police to close roads. This tends to mean any major scene on a pavement and anything that requires deserted streets.

10. Limit your overall number of locations as much as you can. Try and aim for no more than 15. Restrict yourself to fewer if you can.

Cast

1. Write for a small number of main characters – ideally two, maximum three

2. Create only a handful of secondary characters – no more than 5. It is even better if all scenes with each secondary character can be shot in the same place each time.

3. In all, try and aim for no more than TEN speaking parts in all.

4. Avoid too many crowd scenes that require Extras who have to be fed, transported and directed UNLESS these are real places where we one can shoot with one or two actors guerilla style. And even then, recording good sound and getting permissions to shoot can be a real headache.

5. Avoid writing speaking parts for children.

6. Do not write parts for animals. They are time consuming to film, a continuity nightmare and usually require a wrangler.

Timescale, Period & Costume

1. The shorter the timescale that the action takes place over, the less need for costume, make up and hair changes. So think of a story that takes place over a day, a weekend, or a week. Even more economical are films that can take place over the duration of the film (1.5-2hrs)! Examples are Dinner with Andre, Run Lola Run.

2. Only write for the present day/UK. Period dramas and ones that take place overseas, on another planet or continent push up the costume and make-up budget no end.

3. Avoid characters that will need hired in costume – vicars, policemen, traffic wardens

Stunts & SFX

1. No stunts – unless absolutely necessary. They are expensive in that they increase insurance costs and need specialist crew.

2. Avoid effects unless you can think of a simple, quick, low budget way to create them.

3. Do not necessarily assume that CGI is cheap nowadays.

4. Guns and explosions cost money to look convincing and take time to film and create. So do wounds, blood and any prosthetic work.

Other

1. Do not write in the use of commercial, copyrighted music such as pop songs, theme tunes. Even a character singing a few lines of a well known song has to be cleared for use and which can be astronomically costly.

2. Avoid unusual props that will need to be hired in.

3. Remember that weather specific scenes which need rain, wind or snow entail bringing in wind, rain or snow machines and their operators to create them. If you have a scene that needs any of them try and write it so that it can be shot relatively close up. Wide shots of snowy or rainy landscapes are very expensive to dress.

4. Avoid landscapes that change rapidly – such as beaches or tidal estuaries.

5. Try not to write in changing seasons – unless these can be signified by something easy like a Xmas tree or easter egg!

6. Avoid anything that is resource heavy such as a lifeboat rescue at sea, a crew of firemen rescuing a cat, an ambulance crew attending a road crash unless you're pretty sure the producer can persuade the local services to co-operate for free or very cheaply (sometimes outside London and the big cities they are happy to do this)

7. Avoid shots that will require a helicopter, underwater cameraperson, or crane in order to achieve them.

Whatever you do enjoy yourself. Good films are based on imagination - enthralling stories, well told, inhabited by engaging characters. Rules and guidelines don't have to be restricting – they can be creatively liberating.

It is highly likely that you will have to ignore a few of these guidelines in order to tell your story. But if and when you do so - it is best to have a clear idea of how your producer can create the scene you want with minimal cost.

But whatever you do don't ignore this basic rule:

Look for a story that can be told with a small cast in a limited number of locations and preferably within a limited time-span.

Q - What have you brought into this project, from your experiences on 'Frozen'?

Juliet - The delight of making an audience laugh. There's not a lot of laughs in *'Frozen'*, but there are some. I'm satisfied with a huge number of things that I feel I did right, but there are also a number of things that I would do differently next time. The main thing that I have learnt is to start writing for a market place - whatever the market place is, not going against the rules of that market place too much. Treat the post-production period as a time when you can re-write the film and rectify your mistakes. I had to cut it quickly because of the tax implications and that didn't give me enough time to assess it, and to market test it - market test as much as you can and get people to be as brutal as you can. Do not tie yourself up with a deadline if you can possibly avoid it, and make the space to learn from people's reactions.

Q - Do you have any comments on personal cost?

Juliet - Yes, if you are interested in personal security, and a loving, intimate, stable relationship, being a film-maker really isn't for you! You are probably going to live on a low income, using your own personal resources instead of filling the drinks cabinet and buying a nice car. You'll neglect your friends, family, lovers, partners, children, everybody! The personal cost is huge, you really don't have a life in any conventional sense. If you are interested in having, what normal people consider 'a life', don't make films! You have to be obsessed.

Q - Do you have any strategies for survival?

Before you send out your script

GUERILLA FILM MAKER SAYS!

1. Never send your script out until it is the best it can be.

2. Check, re-check, and triple check for spelling mistakes and bad grammar. Simple mistakes make you look unprofessional.

3. Read the screenwriting books. All of them have something good to offer

4. Keep refining, re-editing and re-writing.

5. Don't clutter the front page. Just the name of the script, your name and contact details.

6. If you use a copier, make sure the copies are excellent. Ideally print out from your laser printer for the crispest print.

7. Everyone tracks a script. If you send it to Working Title, they will note it on their computer system and it will become very hard for you to get them to read re-drafts. Hence, don't send it out till it's as good as it can be.

8. Get as many friends with film experience, to read it and listen to their feedback.

9. Don't tweak forever. Recognise when it is ready to go out into the big bad world.

10. As Goldman says, get into every scene as late as you can, and get out as early as you can.

11. Get an agent. Most companies won't read unsolicited work. If you don't have an agent, try and keep trying, to get one. Remember, this is a marathon. Don't give up.

Juliet - As a film-maker starting out, work out how you can survive on a day-in, day-out basis. Often it's a partner or parents who are prepared to support you, or some sort of steady teaching job. However you do it, you must find a way to survive and still have time to make the projects.

Q - At what point would you say 'go make your film with whatever resources you have' instead of waiting for more money?

Juliet - Having made a film for £900k, I'm quite interested in making one for less. With a lower budget you can be more relaxed and experimental, more willing to take risks. I would say go for it, when you have enough to make it. Maybe £25k isn't enough to realise your film, maybe you need to hang out till you have £80k or £100k but maybe you don't have to hang out till you have £800k or £3m! Make it at the first possible point when you think you have got enough to realise it. There are freedoms that come with lower budgets too, a mental freedom without people breathing down your neck, and that can give you a creative edge.

Many film makers complain about not having enough money to make their film, they always want more. I think it is self-indulgent to belly-ache about money to be honest. If you are a film-maker, you are so incredibly privileged anyway that you should do it properly and within your budget, whether it is £50 or £50m! For goodness sake, I mean, get a life!

There are a lot of clichés such as *'a good script will always get made'*, which is nonsense. There are plenty of good scripts that don't get made, that's because there is no-one to promote them. There is a lack of good producers in this country because you need financial back-up as your income source is so sporadic. You owe it to yourself and your project to get it made, to find someone you can work with who has vision and passion and is capable of doing the marketing, promotion, phone calls, networking for it.

Q - What advice would you offer to a new film-maker?

Juliet - It is a process that will take over your life completely. You need huge stamina, more than you could ever imagine. Physical stamina, emotional stamina, and the stamina of not getting bored with a project. You do get bored with a feature film by the time it comes round to doing the sales deliverables and publicity, and you want to move onto something else. If you have got that sort of obsessive fixation to do it, you will be able to do it. If you are an art-house or experimental film-maker, don't be close-minded about commercial cinema. Equally, if you are a commercial film-maker, don't be close-minded about actually trying to say something or to have a vision.

Richard Kurti and Bev Doyle
Writers

WRITING FOR TELEVISION

Q - What do you do?

Richard - We are a writing team. We have made a low budget feature film, written one spec script that was sold and written eleven commissioned feature film scripts that have not yet been made. We now write high quality television genre drama which does get made.

Q - How does writing for TV differ to writing for features?

Richard - There are several areas. There's Casualty, Holby (City), Eastenders, and that TV stuff, which is very much mass produced, then there is higher budget and higher quality drama, and also mini series and TV features.

Q - How did you guys break in?

Richard - We got hired to write *Kidnapped* by a producer who had read one of our scripts called *Unnatural Murder,* that had been developed partly by BBC Films. In film there is only ever a reason to say *'No!'*, but in TV someone has to say *'Yes'* or the screen will be blank! If everyone stopped making film in the UK no-one would notice it, if everyone stopped making TV shows, we would have blank screens! So there is a huge pressure to get stuff made, and you feel there is light at the end of the tunnel. In TV, a larger percentage of stuff will get greenlit as there is higher turnover or production. Our work for TV has tended to be more cinematic and ambitious than most TV scripts.

Bev - In the film world the director is king and the writer is like ancillary to the director. It's the other way round in TV where the writer is king, certainly in American TV where often the writers are producers as well.

Richard - On some film projects, we've had directors come in and say *'OK, I call the shots and you can completely start from scratch and do it this way'*. This wouldn't happen in TV and I think writers are more protected.

Q - In terms of financial remuneration, is it equally lucrative?

Bev - Over the distance it is probably more lucrative because you get more work. If you want to make a good living writing for TV, then the way to do it is to write soaps. That is the only on-going non-stop repeat business that you can get. I'm not saying it's easy work, but it's consistent. The down side is that artistically it is very limiting as far as it's not your story, it's not your characters, and you don't really have much influence on where the story goes. Having worked on them before, I know you are not in any way a master of your own destiny. So the next level is the sort of stuff we are doing at the moment, one off drama where you are in greater control, but then you take a bigger gamble on how much work you can get.

Richard - The thing is when film does ignite, as it did with our first spec script, you may own all the underlying rights. In that instance, Miramax wanted to buy it and they got into a bidding war with Summit. Eventually they wrote a six figure cheque to us and on that one Friday afternoon, we earned more money than we had in many years of writing! And then because it is movies, just put a zero on the end and Summit sold the script on! They made far more money than we ever did from that script! So films are famine or feast and you have to ask yourself what you would rather do. Personally I would rather do years of steady paid writing than wait 4 years for that one moment when a film is going to do something - or maybe not.

Q - So how does the TV business differ, in terms of its mechanics, to the film business?

Richard - We found that in both Film and TV the only way to get on is to work on other people's ideas. If a producer has got half an idea, in their mind it's worth more than your massively and fully-formed, brilliant 26 page treatment. Producers will always get much more behind their own ideas than yours. A top TV writer was once asked why are you not doing any of your own stories, and he said *'because I won't get paid!'* Before *Kidnapped* was even shot, we were commissioned to write a three part adaptation of *20,000 Leagues Under The Sea.* And that wasn't just because of the script, it's because we worked well together, there were no tantrums, they knew that they could work with us, do business together.

Q - I assume you get re-hired because you deliver quality work, you deliver on time, you work consistently, all the kind of stuff that seems un-obvious to a lot of people?

Richard - That is very important. Delivering on time, working without tantrums, the ability to take notes, to be able to listen to other ideas, to be able to go back to your draft, rewrite and deliver a very different draft next time round. People hand in 2nd and 3rd drafts that are no different from the 1st draft, because they weren't taking onboard the notes they were given by the producers. When you hand in a draft, of course in your mind you think *'we should go and shoot it!'* But you need to make a leap of understanding why it's not right. Even now we find it hard to understand how a producer has read it, and not seen it the way we've written and imagined it. It's really important to see it from their point of view, and then in subsequent drafts deliver something that is different. Producers like to know that you are listening to them and to their problems, and that there is a partnership. I think that some writers are quite unprofessional. We hear from producers about how they have had nightmare experiences with writers where they hand over a cheque and then don't hear anything, they don't know when it's going to be delivered, and it is an insecure time for them. We work 10 til 5, 5 days a week, or 7 days a week when working to a deadline.

Bev - There is a big difference between writing for TV and writing for film. In film, no matter the genre, the bottom line is somebody's paying out money and they will want a return on that investment. Whereas, if you are writing for the BBC, very often you are writing to fill a certain brief as they need to fulfill their remit. And because the BBC is not allowed to make money back on their programs, the producer isn't saying, *'I need to make a profit'* but is saying *'I need for this to be successfully received by a certain demographic'.*

Q - Many new writers claim they are waiting for inspiration, or complain about writers block, or they will only write something with meaning... Instead of just getting on with it?

Bev - If you've got a message then screenwriting is not the place to put it. If you've got any ego, you are in the wrong business, write a novel, write a play!

Richard - There is a line in *Throw Mamma from the Train,* which is *'a writer writes',* and it's true you know! Often you just need to start writing - turn on the computer, make a cup of coffee and begin. Sometimes you just have to start writing and get the whole thing done, instead of waiting for inspiration. There is one pet project that we've had for years, and because it's the pet project, we'd never be able to agree on the treatment. All the commissioned work is like *'well, they want it by the 27th March,'* so you get it done. That pressure is really good for us and we try to get 8 pages written every day. Often we will start talking about something completely unrelated, and it is surprising how many times that will lead back to an idea for something else.

Q - How do you get into position to get those kind of commissions?

Richard - We are the world's worst networkers, we don't do the parties.

Bev - We are ugly and old! (laughs)

Richard - Yes we are unattractive and lousy shags! So it's always down to the words on the page, our professional approach, our connections through previous work and of course our agent. Without an

107

agent, we would be dead, because we can't do the socialising thing. No-one has ever asked us where we went to school or if we have got a degree. They just want the words on a page, and we are judged by that.

Bev - I started work on *Eastenders*. Then I met Richard and we wrote *'Newton's Law'*, which was our spec script that sold, and it got our entire career going. Before we sold it I gave it to my old agent and he said, *'there is a knack to writing period dialogue, and you haven't got it!'* and he fired me! So I moved to our present agent. To this day, that single script earned me more money than any other script! So don't be disheartened if you are rejected by someone, no-one can ever deliver the gospel truth.

Q - In terms of the actual words on the page, how do your TV scripts differ from standard film scripts?

Richard - For us it's identical. We just do a standard movie format. You just write film exactly like TV.

Q - What do you feel are the major philosophical differences between writing for TV and for film?

Bev - Television is talking heads, because that is all television can afford. They are still expecting characters to talk for ten minutes!

Richard - But that is not what we do, we still write more like film.

Q - Is that because TV has evolved, because of cheaper effects and the way it's shot, it can be more cinematic?

Richard - That is why we are hired, we want that 'big screen' feel. Directors are directing TV like movies now. In a film script you can push the visuals further, and to be more minimalist, say it's *'three words, and there's a look, and a sound'* Whereas in TV, they will say *'come on, tease it out for us, let's make it more explicit about what is actually going on there'*.

Bev - In most TV you've got three things that are going to happen in half an hour, that's why everyone in a TV soap will say *'I've got something really important to tell you, but I can't now, I've gotta do this!'*, because there is no way you can tell them now, as they've only got three things to tell them in half in hour!

Richard - TV is now looking for more visually-driven stories, though you often end up cutting the budget. We wrote *'Kidnapped'* without any budgetary consideration and then 6 weeks before production they said *'you know, we can't afford this, this and this!'* and we had to re-write! Remember though, we got financed on the basis of that very visual, expensive script. You aim at talking heads, you get talking heads. You aim at a movie, you'll still get pulled back down, but you will be closer to a movie.

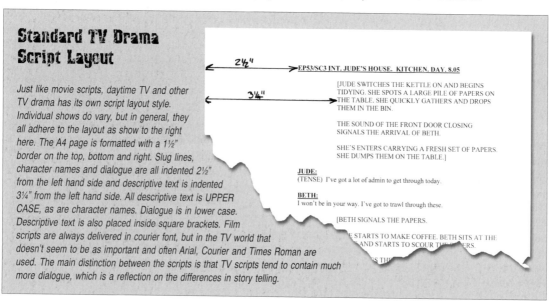

Standard TV Drama Script Layout

Just like movie scripts, daytime TV and other TV drama has its own script layout style. Individual shows do vary, but in general, they all adhere to the layout as show to the right here. The A4 page is formatted with a 1½" border on the top, bottom and right. Slug lines, character names and dialogue are all indented 2½" from the left hand side and descriptive text is indented 3¼" from the left hand side. All descriptive text is UPPER CASE, as are character names. Dialogue is in lower case. Descriptive text is also placed inside square brackets. Film scripts are always delivered in courier font, but in the TV world that doesn't seem to be as important and often Arial, Courier and Times Roman are used. The main distinction between the scripts is that TV scripts tend to contain much more dialogue, which is a reflection on the differences in story telling.

2½"

3¼"

EP53/SC3 INT. JUDE'S HOUSE. KITCHEN. DAY. 8.05

[JUDE SWITCHES ON THE KETTLE ON AND BEGINS TIDYING. SHE SPOTS A LARGE PILE OF PAPERS ON THE TABLE. SHE QUICKLY GATHERS AND DROPS THEM IN THE BIN.

THE SOUND OF THE FRONT DOOR CLOSING SIGNALS THE ARRIVAL OF BETH.

SHE'S ENTERS CARRYING A FRESH SET OF PAPERS. SHE DUMPS THEM ON THE TABLE.]

JUDE:
(TENSE) I've got a lot of admin to get through today.

BETH:
I won't be in your way. I've got to trawl through these.

[BETH SIGNALS THE PAPERS.

STARTS TO MAKE COFFEE. BETH SITS AT THE AND STARTS TO SCOUR T...ERS.

...S TH...

Writing Daytime Soaps

Q - What do you do? How did you break in?

Phil - *I am a writer who has written spec scripts and I also write daytime TV for 'Doctors' on BBC1. It's a daytime soap and it's on five days a week, and it's currently in it's seventh series.*

I toured the websites to find out what information is out there and targeted all the soaps. I managed to get in contact with a script editor from that particular show and I sent them my CV, a writing sample, and got a meeting. 'Doctors' probably has about 40 to 50 writers. Other shows like 'Hollyoaks', or 'Eastenders' and 'Coronation Street' have a more stable set of about 20 to 30 writers, but 'Doctors' in particular, turns over writers quickly.

Q - How does the process work?

Phil - *First you write a trial script, and it could be months before you hear back. If they are happy with that, you have to send in ideas for a full episode. First off you send in a two page outline, and if they are happy with that, they will ask you to expand it to 15 pages, if they are happy with that, then they will commission you. So it's a lot of work with no pay back in the first instance, and you are often sending in 2 or 3 ideas at a time. It might be that they commission one of those ideas, it might be that they don't, and frustratingly, they don't have time to give you feedback on why they accept or decline ideas. They just say, 'it's not suitable' or, 'not this time!' So you just have to watch the show and learn as much as you can about it, by absorbing as much about it as possible, and hope that one of your ideas is successful.*

You get a week to do the first draft, and I try to write it in three days, giving me time to re-read and polish. Then you send it in and wait to hear back from the script editors. It can be the next day, it can be three weeks later, and you just have to wait. Everything is conducted by phone and e-mail, so I've only met a script editor once, 4 years ago and haven't met any of them since. Once they send back your first draft with notes, you start your second draft and that can be begin with a 3 hour phone call, going through page by page, point by point, and it's generally very good feedback. You are given two days to do the 2nd draft, then from there, you may have another day to do a polish, and then you get notes for the 3rd draft, but generally the notes get less and less as you progress. Then they lock it off, and once it's locked off, it means it is going to be shot, and you are paid for that particular episode.

Q - How do you know what has happened to the characters in the past?

Phil - *All shows have a character or series Bible - a document with character biographies, where they came from, what school they went to, all their history. It also has a breakdown of locations, dates and times, and past inter relationships. You have to trawl through that and get really familiar with the characters, and that helps you to write the stories.*

Phil Mathews
Writer

Q - How much money can you earn?

Phil - *It's about £3k per episode, half at the beginning and half at the end. If you've done 4 episodes, which means you've done 2 hours of TV, then your fee goes up quite dramatically. Competition is fierce. The BBC are active in pushing for new writers, so they have days now and then where they contact agents and get all new writers down and give them a talk, and a tour of the studio, and tell them all about the show. Lots of writers do this, and write for other shows at the same time, like 'Eastenders', 'Holby' or 'Casualty', because that is the standard route for writing for the BBC.*

The main focus of writing for TV and getting work is to ensure that you have a good relationship with your script editor, because they are moving on, and will become Producers, and moving on to other shows. It's very much about relationships, because they have lots of writers on their books and they are going to want to work with the ones who are professional, who deliver on time, and are easy to get on with.

Q - Do you have an agent?

Phil - *When I started writing 'Doctors' I didn't have an agent, and it's one of the shows that you can start writing for without an agent. I got an agent after writing for 'Doctors'.*

Q - What does it feel like to be a writer of daytime soaps?

Phil - *It's great discipline and you learn to write quickly. Someone is taking your work seriously and you have to be professional about it. What is really good about it is that once it's locked off, that is it, you can't tinker with it, you can't polish it anymore, and whatever you have written will appear on screen. It is a valuable learning process, to see what you've written, how it's translated, and to know it is a finished piece of work.*

Q - What format do you deliver the final work in?

Phil - *MS Word and they have a template that you just use.*

Q - Why don't you think there are more people who want to make great TV? Everyone wants to start in film?

Bev - I think the people who want to be independent film-makers have a certain socio-economic sort of background, and they don't watch much TV, so they are not interested. The people who do watch TV, and this is a very sweeping generalisation, are so far removed from the media business that it wouldn't even occur to them that they could get involved. It's like saying *'why don't I become the head of Barclays bank!'* Film students don't want to make TV, they want to make movies! An important distinction between British and American TV is that in America they can make *ER* as they have the budget, where as here we have lower budget equivalents like *Holby City*. There is only so much high-end TV that they can afford to make here.

Q - How competitive is the TV market compared to the film market?

Richard - It's very competitive. The main difference is, in film terms there is just not the output, there are just not enough British films made to give any kind of recognised output. But there is a lot of British TV money and statistically you have more chance of getting stuff made in TV, though it's still very tough.

Q - If you were to compare your experiences making a low-budget independent film, and your experience working in television, how would they stack up, from a financial and a creative point of view?

Richard - Financially we lost everything when we made our independent film, it took us years to recover. We won't do that again. At the time we were impatient and had the independent film bug. We had to get that film out of our system. The process taught us how tough the business was and because we had been beaten up by that, we got patient! Now we wait for the right project, right deal, right money etc.

Bev - After *'Seaview Knights'* we were so low, we just assumed that no-one would ever read anything we wrote again. So it didn't matter what we wrote, so we wrote the most expensive film we've ever written. And it sold in two weeks!

Q - Is there anything that we've not covered that you think is vital or essential?

Richard - Ironically, I think it is our love of movies, and the big vision that has got us all of our TV work. Often we have gone in with an enormous and unfilmable canvas, and then we get the job! Then they say we can't do that canvas!

Q - There's that quote from James Cameron, which I will paraphrase, but you are kind of behaving like the accelerator, and they are behaving like the brakes. As long as that's a happy and constructive union, that is a very good dynamic to be in?

Richard - Yes, I don't think a writer should ever put the brakes on.

Q - What mistakes do you think you have made?

Richard - Not marrying a rich wife! If you are not financially independent, it's a tough business. When we were still just doing full-time film commissions, we had a conflict come up. We were offered a TV 2-parter that had been green lit, but they needed it fast. We also had some film work at the time, and we called the film director and said *'listen, we've been offered this fantastic gig, can we dump yours?! Are you really serious about this one getting made?'*, he said *'No, I am absolutely serious, this is going to be my next movie.'* So we turned down the TV, and then after the 2nd draft the director changed his mind and went off to do a book instead, and he just dropped us. By this time the BBC thing was made with another writer, went out on air, and we looked back and thought *'Fucking hell!'* When TV comes to you and it's green lit, they mean it's going to happen. In our experience, a film promise is worthless whereas, due to the constant need for product, a TV promise is bankable.

Q - What advice would you offer to a new film-maker?

Richard - Get a good line of credit because you are going to need it. When those letters come through the door saying *'apply for a Goldfish card now!'* Don't throw it in the bin!

Slug line, all upper case, abbreviated into INT (for interior), EXT (for exterior), followed DAY or NIGHT, followed by the scene location. Slug line followed by a line break.

Script title (optional).

Script edge, 1" from the top of the page.

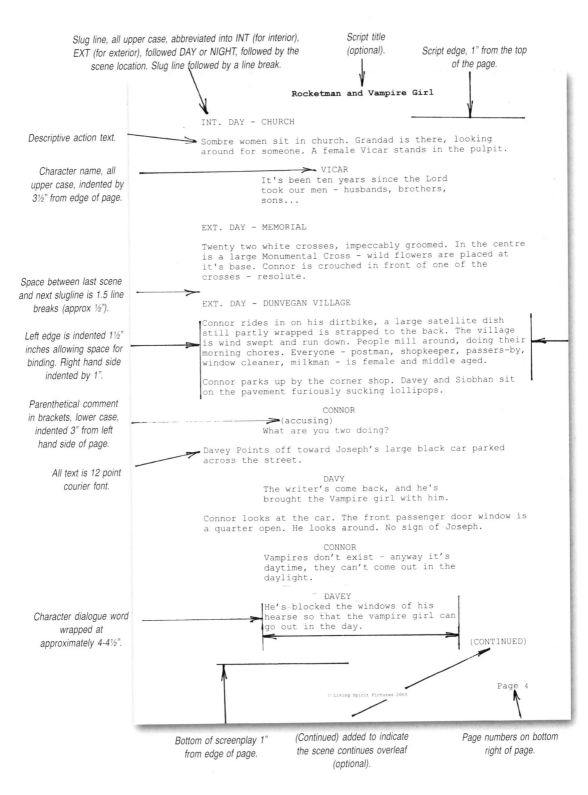

Descriptive action text.

Character name, all upper case, indented by 3½" from edge of page.

Space between last scene and next slugline is 1.5 line breaks (approx ½").

Left edge is indented 1½" inches allowing space for binding. Right hand side indented by 1".

Parenthetical comment in brackets, lower case, indented 3" from left hand side of page.

All text is 12 point courier font.

Character dialogue word wrapped at approximately 4-4½".

Rocketman and Vampire Girl

INT. DAY - CHURCH

Sombre women sit in church. Grandad is there, looking around for someone. A female Vicar stands in the pulpit.

VICAR
It's been ten years since the Lord took our men - husbands, brothers, sons...

EXT. DAY - MEMORIAL

Twenty two white crosses, impeccably groomed. In the centre is a large Monumental Cross - wild flowers are placed at it's base. Connor is crouched in front of one of the crosses - resolute.

EXT. DAY - DUNVEGAN VILLAGE

Connor rides in on his dirtbike, a large satellite dish still partly wrapped is strapped to the back. The village is wind swept and run down. People mill around, doing their morning chores. Everyone - postman, shopkeeper, passers-by, window cleaner, milkman - is female and middle aged.

Connor parks up by the corner shop. Davey and Siobhan sit on the pavement furiously sucking lollipops.

CONNOR
(accusing)
What are you two doing?

Davey Points off toward Joseph's large black car parked across the street.

DAVY
The writer's come back, and he's brought the Vampire girl with him.

Connor looks at the car. The front passenger door window is a quarter open. He looks around. No sign of Joseph.

CONNOR
Vampires don't exist - anyway it's daytime, they can't come out in the daylight.

DAVEY
He's blocked the windows of his hearse so that the vampire girl can go out in the day.

(CONTINUED)

© Living Spirit Pictures 2003

Page 4

Bottom of screenplay 1" from edge of page.

(Continued) added to indicate the scene continues overleaf (optional).

Page numbers on bottom right of page.

Josephine Rose
Script Editor

SCRIPT EDITOR and READER

Q - What is your job as a reader?

Jo - I work as a script reader and a script editor. I read submitted scripts, sometimes novels, and other materials, for various companies. I then write a report, giving a summary of the plot and outline what I think of it, and then, I do a longer synopsis, and comment on the story characters and anything that might have an impact on the development executives decision. The Script Report I write is also referred to as Coverage, especially by Americans. It shocks me the number of films that come out in the cinema that I passed on because they were poor scripts, often worse than the average script I see. Films like that get made for all sorts of reasons. Sometimes you'll read a bad script but then they'll say, but we've got Julia Roberts attached for instance. At which point everyone says *'we'll make it anyway'*. I think there are a lot of bad script readers around too, especially younger and more inexperienced ones whose criteria is not as open as it should be. It's the nature of the film industry, you've got a lot of people making bad decisions. A lot of good scripts don't get made as well. A lot of it is to do with politics that just don't belong to the scripts, it's about money and personalities.

Q - What about low budget film makers who think they can't afford a reader?

Jo - Many new film makers think, *'right I've got my script, that's fine, lets get it made...'* You would be better off investing money in script development and make a good script for less money than making a bad and under-developed script for more money. Anyone can make a decision about a script, as to whether it's good or bad, but a good person, who has read hundreds of scripts, can help you. They can break your script down, tell you what's good, where you have gone wrong, why you have gone wrong etc. It's worth it and you are not going to break the bank by hiring someone to give you feedback on a script.

Q - So paying you a small amount of money for your 'script editing' skills, to remove 20 pages from 120 page screenplay is going to reduce what needs to be shot significantly and is therefore money well spent.

Jo - Yes. Diplomatically it can be difficult because people are proud that they have physically put words on a page, but that's not good enough. Often they've got all this stuff in the script that is actually useless. I'm working with someone at the moment who tells me *'the scenes are invaluable for characterisation'*, but showing people talking isn't characterisation. Characterisation comes out within scenes that are taking the plot forward. It's things like that, that I don't think people take on board when they are starting out.

Q - How does the process of 'script reading' work?

Jo - For a company, they get their stuff each week and send me however many scripts and they pay a rate that is pretty much level across the industry. As an Indie film maker, if you just want a report, it's probably going to cost £40 to £50. So that's peanuts in terms of film making and how that report could improve your work and save you some of your production budget.

Q - One problem facing new film makers is they have not got an agent so they find it hard to get their material into the business. If you read a script that was sizzling, would you present it to some of the larger clients that you work for?

Jo - It would have to be very good, but yes, I've done that before. If I think it is worth it I could introduce them and the script to development executives. When you are starting out there is so much wasted time waiting for people to look at stuff. I think it is better to get to know people in film companies than to worry about agents. Once you get further on, you may need an agent, one who will now be hungrier for you, to represent and do deals for you.

Q - How good are scripts on the whole?

Jo - For the bigger companies I work with, Miramax, Colombia, Intermedia etc., there has already been a filtration process before they get to me, and yet some are still bad, but often those are projects that have 'talent' attached. When reading for the smaller companies or agents, the scripts can be very bad. There's some real trash floating around and I don't understand at what point some writers announce their script is finished, as it clearly is not ready.

Q - Given that such a large percentage of screenplays that hit your desk, at a so-called professional level, are below average, it stands to reason that most independent and new film makers' scripts could do with more work?

Jo - Yes. I think 100% of scripts need more work. I should say 99%, but actually I think it is 100%. Many new film makers have just finished university, they've written their script and they think that it is a work of genius. Often it is quite immature, because people haven't really thought about what story they want to tell, nor have they developed their own style. They have written a slight rip-off! I think everyone could do with getting an opinion of someone who has read a great deal and knows what is good and bad.

Q - What makes a great script?

Jo – For me, originality. There are so few great scripts. Recently, I saw *'Garden State'* - everything is very funny, but it is so well pitched, that you've got a lot of pathos coming out too, through very likeable characters. Every element of the script is coming together, in every scene. That for me was a great work. If you are going to read Robert McKee, and other books, don't just fixate on your structure. You've also got to work on strong dialogue, characters, and locations. And start from an interesting and original idea, because without that, you are never going to have anything that people are going to want to watch. A lot of things scripts are just boring. If it's a comedy, make it really funny, you don't want a couple of weak gags on page 20 and 34. It's all got to be funny. If it's a thriller, make sure that every scene is tense, that in every scene there is a surprise. Make sure that you have worked really hard on every single line, on every single page, and you haven't just got a few high points that you think are fine. I think that's part of the problem for new writers, that in their screenplay, there just isn't *enough* there.

Q - How easy is it to get a straight answer?

Jo - If you submitted your script to a film company, and were lucky enough to have a meeting, on the whole people are not going to be that frank with you. They will say *'well, it's quite funny, but not for us'*, but what they may actually think it is *'it's the worst script ever'*. Everyone is diplomatic. A lot of film makers, especially new ones, avoid having to take self-criticism by saying, *'well, they are always going to hate it, it is because they don't understand me!'* What they don't realise is that everyone is dying to read a great script. You're cynical because you have read so much rubbish, but you really hope that every script you read is going to be great. New film makers do think that they're the next great thing, which they should do, or they shouldn't be trying, but be smart. You also become better by taking the knocks, you learn through that.

Q – Whose opinion should you listen too?

Jo - Make sure you give it to someone who, when you talk to them, you're confident they are reading what you have written. I don't mean, sit there and say *'you've misunderstood me!'* If you give someone a comedy about a man cycling across the world, make sure you don't give it to someone who picks up on his pit stop in France, and says *'I think you should forget the rest, and I think you should develop France!'* Make sure you have got someone who has got the whole story, knows exactly what it is you are trying to do, and then can help you with that, and just take on board the criticism. There will be some criticisms that you will disagree, as everyone is wrong about things sometimes. No script reader, no matter how experienced, is going to be right about everything, but on the whole, they are going to have a lot to say to you that is going to help you with your project and make it far better than it probably is.

Josephine Rose   Director

ScriptScout

script consultancy

Tel: 020 7384 0304   www.scriptscout.co.uk
Email: Josephine.rose@scriptscout.co.uk

Q - Are scripts planned enough?

Jo - I think there should be a lot more planning going into scripts, before people set pen on paper. Many people outline an idea, and start writing it straight away. Then you have to go through a long development process. If people spent more time mapping out the script, then when they actually put it down on paper, they are going to avoid a lot of the filler stuff where they are trying to work out what it is they are doing. I always ask, *'why do I care about this character?'* and *'what is there that should interest me about this story?'* Often you will have a script that has a little thrillery stuff in it, but it's not really that exciting, or a little bit of comedy, but it's just not really funny. Be clear about what story you are telling.

Q - What practical advice would you offer a new writer?

Options, a Rough Guide

GUERILLA FILM MAKER SAYS!

Option - *The exclusive right to purchase a property (script, play or book) at a later date by paying a percentage of the eventual purchase price. This enables the producer to set up/develop the project with less risk than buying the property outright. During the term of the option, no one else is permitted to acquire rights to the property in question and the buyer has the length of the option period to purchase the property in full. At the end of the option period, the buyer (producer) can abandon the project (and lose the option price already paid), negotiate an option renewal, or exercise the option by purchasing the property in full (usually done just before going into production).*

Option Price - *The standard fee is usually 10% of the purchase price but is always negotiable. The option fee could be waived in lieu of the producer's efforts to set up the project. If this is the case, it's recommended to pay at least £1 to the copyright holder (usually the writer) so that money has exchanged hands in order to enforce the contract. This option price is 'applied' against the eventual total purchase of the property (i.e. if you option a screenplay for £10,000 of a £100,000 purchase, you pay £90,000 upon exercising the option).*

Other points to consider are... **The Option Period** - *Generally 18 months, but can be negotiated.* **A Non-exclusive option** - *You may give the rights to multiple producers and the first one to get it financed gets the rights exclusively. Usually no money is offered up front.* **The Option renewal period** - *12-18 months, with extra monies agreed.*

1. There are other factors that the writers can negotiate. If you're an author you could ask for bestseller bonuses where additional sums can be paid if the book is placed on certain best seller lists. If you're a stage play writer and your play wins a Tony or an Olivier Award, again you could ask for bonuses. There might also be negotiations for profit participation in net receipts.

2. Producers must make sure that if they do sign a book purchase that they also receive a publishers release. Here the publisher acknowledges that they don't own the film or any ancillary rights in the book and ensures that the buyer can exploit such rights.

3. Writers may want to reserve certain rights, such as radio and television rights, stage play rights and print publication.

4. Writers should negotiate for monies and credits should the film be so successful it launches a TV show (or any other medium) like Buffy The Vampire Slayer. Writer should also get the right to write and produce the new venture.

5. Producers (buyers) will want to make sure they can make changes to the work when adapting it. This is the bug bear of screenwriters who have no control over their Moral Rights and many a lesser movie has been made.

6. Producers will want to protect themselves by gaining warranties from the writers, making sure that the work doesn't infringe another's copyright, defame or invade anyone's privacy. They'll also want the writer to indemnify the producer, agreeing to reimburse the buyer (producer) for any breach of warranty by the writer.

7. Credits. As a member of the Writers Guild, they will negotiate your credit on your behalf. If not a member, then credit and billing must be negotiated the with producer. Make sure to protect your credit so that other writers coming on to rewrite you don't take your earned credit or billing.

8. As a Producer, make sure that you're under no obligation to actually produce a film.

9. Make sure that, in the event that the producer doesn't produce your property as a movie within a negotiated timescale, the property reverts back to you.

10. Remember, when buying an option, you must, at the same time, work out the terms of the purchase agreement. Without negotiating the underlying literary purchase agreement your option will mean nothing. The seller is under no obligation to sell to you on the terms you propose.

The Script Report

This is the top sheet that most producers see and never get past, so you want it to be good. It's pretty self explanatory. Following this there would be a longer page and half-ish synopsis of the whole plot. The reader would then rate the script with a 'pass', 'consider' or 'recommend'; and the writer would also be rated with a 'pass', 'consider' or 'recommend' assessment.

It's easy to be cynical about these reports, as you could argue that producers are so lazy that they can't even be bothered to read the script and they just get other people to do it for them. On the other hand, producers are VERY busy and there is a sea of mediocre work out there (and a lot that isn't even mediocre). If your screenplay really is THAT good, then it will rise. And if it doesn't, get persistent... or accept it may not be that good and write another. In your heart you will know which it is.

ScriptScout

Type of Material:	SP
Title:	Hollywood Nirvana
Number of Pages:	102
Author:	Henry Newman
Submitted by:	Henry Newman
Submitted to:	Josephine Rose
Circa:	Present
Location:	UK
Analyst:	Josephine Rose
Drama Category:	Comedy
Date:	22/09/2005

LOGLINE:
A man quits his high-flying city job in order to find greater fulfillment as a screenwriter. Rejection, bankruptcy and the casting couch soon take their toll and he realises that the path to creative nirvana is more treacherous than he could ever have conceived.

BRIEF:
This is a witty and well written script with strong commercial potential. The characters are engaging and the dialogue is sharp, although the plot would benefit from a tighter structure and a stronger central storyline.

	Excellent	Very Good	Good	Fair	Poor
Idea/Premise		X			
Storyline			X		
Character			X		
Dialogue		X			

SYNOPSIS:

RICHARD JONES is a high-earning city executive who is on the verge of an existential breakdown. Deciding that there is more to life than commuting and number-crunching, Richard abandons the city in search of a more spiritually enriching life as a screenwriter. He holes himself up and creates the script masterpiece that he knows will inevitably project him to the top of Hollywood's most wanted list for aspiring writers. Armed with

---

Jo - Read a lot of scripts. You can watch a lot of films but read the scripts too. It's good to read both good scripts and bad too, because you begin to recognise what distinguishes the good from the bad. You are going to write a lot of crap, so don't worry if your early work isn't good. Take advice from people, but not from everyone. Your mum is probably the last person who should be giving you advice, because, either you will get very dispirited and sulk with her, or she'll be incredibly nice about it, but not terribly useful. There are courses too, but not all are good and not everyone is suited to a course.

Q - Is script reading a means to an end for you?

Jo - I don't think anyone starts out script reading and thinks *'I've made it!'* I do it because I am also a writer / film maker and script reading keeps me afloat. Most people are script reading because they are working on something that's not paying at the moment. It is a survival strategy, but for me, it's also been invaluable in developing my writing skills. Script reading is a great way to study how to write scripts and what makes them work. Script reading is also a good way to meet people in the industry.

Q - What advice would you offer a new film maker?

Jo - Only do film if it really is the only thing you want to do, because it is incredibly difficult. Be confident and willing to learn. You are going to take a lot of knocks, you are going to meet nasty people, you are going to meet nice people, but you have got to go through that. Enjoy the learning process. Your first script is probably going to be rubbish, but hopefully after that you are going to get better. It is hard work, but if you are committed and stick around, then hopefully it will all take off.

Michael McCoy
ICM

LITERARY AGENT

Q - What is your job?

Michael - My title is 'Literary Agent'. We represent writers and directors in film, television and theatre. We spot talent that we believe could have a future making feature films, television, plays etc. and then do as much as we possibly can to push them to get that first feature made and then hopefully the 2nd or 3rd and so on.

Q - How does a new writer get represented if they've got no track record or are fresh out of Film School?

Michael - It can be a tough thing to get an agent's attention because we are so busy. A lot of my clients I found through recommendations from people who are working within the industry and have found a good script. Recently, a new writer finished a stage play and the manager of the theatre who is going to do the show passed it along to me. Now the writer has joined my list. If it hadn't have been for the recommendation, I probably wouldn't have pulled it to the top of my pile. If you can get an agent on the phone, you should be as succinct and polite as possible. If somebody comes on the phone and is bigging themselves up in such a way, then I may think that they will be a nightmare to represent. It's not going to make you want to pull that script to the top of your pile.

Q - What is it about a screenplay that gets your attention?

Michael - The first few pages have got to grab you. People say that all the time, but it's so true. You often know straight away whether the writer has got something. The whole heart of the piece has got to be on the sleeve of the script, very quickly, otherwise you just think where is this going? I love it when I can tell what the trailer or the poster will look like. Sometimes it's just a visceral reaction and you can't always explain why it is good. Also, the most polished script isn't necessarily the best script, so if there's a certain rawness to the script, an energy to it, a heart to it, that can be something to consider. Of course, the broadcasters and the people who write the cheques don't necessarily agree with me. It's such a personal thing.

Q - Does having a good attitude sway your opinion as to whether you will represent someone or not?

Michael - Absolutely. I've got a number of clients that did exactly that. They maybe made a short film, which I liked, but didn't love. In one case I saw a short and it was really accomplished but there was a bit of soul missing. But I was intrigued enough to meet the director and liked him. Now I couldn't take him on based on that short because there wasn't a lot I could do for him, however he told me he was writing a screenplay. He was really pleasant and I told him to keep in touch - and he e-mailed me after a couple of weeks to thank me for the meeting. Just somebody coming back being grateful for a leg-up is nice and people remember things like that. Six months later and out of the blue, he e-mails me saying *'I don't know if you remember me, but the screenplay I told you I was writing, I've written it! Would you take a look at it?'* Of course, I remembered him and I said *'yes'*. And it blew my socks off! Two years later it's in the can, and that was a really, good experience. He was persistent, but incredibly polite about it.

Q - How often do you read a really good spec script?

Michael - One a year might be any good. I suppose that is because everybody thinks they can do it. I wouldn't want to discourage people from thinking they can do it, but they have to be realistic.

Q - Is there a spec script market in the UK like there is in Hollywood?

Michael - I don't think there is to be honest. I think it is just tough to get people in the industry to take it seriously and to read it because generally the writers are unknown. It's not all like that, but if the idea is good from a writer that people don't know, they've gotta have something to back it up. So you will need a writing sample of some kind because the biggest stumbling block is in the screenwriting. I think we are lacking in writers who can execute their bigger, high concept ideas. Nine times out of ten it is because they aren't good at writing that genre. This is why I think often the producer comes up with the idea or concept and then goes to a writer with a track record to write it, because they feel that they know that the guy can deliver. They won't take a risk on a new writer, to wait six months for a script to arrive only to discover the guy can't spell. They'd rather just option the idea and move on to the established writer. It's depressing to hear but I just think it's realistic.

Q - So the point of writing a spec script here in the UK is really to write it as a sample?

Michael - Yes, and if it gets picked up as a spec then fantastic! That's the icing on the cake really! The other thing is a lot of producers like to be involved in the development process. If something comes in and it's ready to go, they can think there is not enough of themselves invested in it. Often, the few spec scripts that I've placed with producers go back to the drawing board and start again. In all of those cases, they ended up with a script quite different to the one they started, and not one has ever gone into production - yet!

Q - Do you use 'writing samples' often?

Michael - Yes. They help back up our claims when selling a writer, especially with writers who are new to the industry. And, I think it's enough to have one good sample. The thing that producers look for in a writing sample is to show that you can do dialogue, and characterisation. You can learn plot structure as a writer, but if you can't actually write dialogue with truthful voices and characterisation then you are not a writer. Some people come up with ideas but then they can't actually deliver on the page. *'Great ideas'* people aren't necessarily the right people to breath life into characters. And here in the UK, a good producer won't necessarily need to have a sample of the genre that he is looking for. I also don't think you need to have different writing samples of different genres. If you do, great, but there should be one really strong writing sample which people will read and go *'Wow, this guy can write!'*

Q - What is an option? How does that work?

Michael - Put simply, it's a period of time where a producer pays a little bit of money to allow that producer the exclusive right to run with that project, with the intention of taking it to the next stage, whether that is further development, production funding, casting, whatever. If the period of time expires, then the producer can pay to have the Option extended or let the rights revert back to the writer. The length of an option varies, but generally it is in multiples of six and twelve months. Twelve and eighteen month Options are the most common.

Q - Say a broadcaster comes to you and says 'We've got this great idea, who's a good writer?' and you say 'this guys terrific', and everybody's happy. What happens, how does it work?

Michael - On the business side, the producer drafts a contract for the screenplay, which will have different stages or steps. There will be a section for writing a treatment, then the first draft, first revision, second draft, second draft revisions. In these sections the payment amount and time scale are laid out. Also, should they decide to buy you out, or not want you to continue, then there are clauses for what would happen. Perhaps I'm a bit old fashioned, but I think you should stick to a writer from beginning to end. I always think that the more people who come in and cut and paste the script, the worse it ends up being.

ICM®
INTERNATIONAL CREATIVE MANAGEMENT®

MICHAEL McCOY
AGENT

TALENT AND LITERARY AGENCY
TALENT MEDIA GROUP LTD T/A INTERNATIONAL CREATIVE MANAGEMENT®
OXFORD HOUSE   76 OXFORD STREET   LONDON W1D 1BS
TELEPHONE **020 7636 6565**   FAX **020 7323 0101**

UK Literary Agencies

GUERILLA FILM MAKER SAYS!

The Agency Ltd
24 Pottery Lane, Holland Park
London W11 4LZ
Tel: 020 7727 1346
Fax 020 7727 9037
Email: info@theagency.co.uk
Web: www.theagency.co.uk

Blake Friedmann Literary, Film & TV Agency
122 Arlington Road
London NW1 7HP
Tel: 020 7284 0408
Fax: 020 7284 0442
email: 'firstname'@blakefriedmann.co.uk
Web: www.blakefreidmann.co.uk

Cassarotto, Ramsey & Associates
National House,
60-66 Wardour Street
London WIV 3HP
Tel: 020 7287 4450
Fax: 020 7287 9128
Web: www.casarotto.uk.com
E-mail : agents@casarotto.uk.com

Curtis Brown Ltd
Haymarket House
28 - 29 Haymarket
London SW1Y 4SP
Tel: 44 (0) 20 7393 4400
Fax: 44 (0) 20 7393 4401
E-mail: info@curtisbrown.co.uk
Web: www.curtisbrown.co.uk

ICM
Oxford House, 76 Oxford St.,
London, W1D 1BS
Tel: 020 7636 6565
Websitie: www.icmtalent.com

Peter, Fraser & Dunlop
Drury House, 34-43 Russell Street
London WC2B 5HA
Email: postmaster@pfd.co.uk
Website: www.pfd.co.uk
Tel:0207-344-1000

Rod Hall Agency
6th Floor, Fairgate House, 78 New Oxford Street
London WC1A 1HB
Tel: 44 (0) 20 7079 7987
Fax: 44 (0) 20 7079 7988
E-Mail office@rodhallagency.com
Web: www.rodhallagency.com

Seifert Dench
4 D'Arblay Street,
London W1F 8EH
Tel: 020 7437 4551
Fax: 020 7439 1355
Web site : www.seifert-dench.co.uk

Sheil Land Associates
43 Doughty Street
London WC1N 2LH
Tel: 0207 405 9351
Fax: 0207 831 2127
Email: info@sheilland.co.uk

The William Morris Agency
52/53 Poland Street
London W1F 7LX
Phone: 020 7534 6800
Fax: 020 7534 6900
Web: www.wma.com

For a more detailed list of literary agencies, check out the Writer's Services website at www.writersservices.com and click UK agents.

Once the deal is struck, the writer might well start on a treatment based on the idea. Financiers are very unlikely to commission a script straight away because people are much more cautious about the end product. The treatment is usually anything from a couple of pages to maybe 20 pages, and it is a prose version of the story. Certain producers and broadcasters want every single plot point. Say it's a 2-hour drama for television, they might want to know exactly how the beginning, middle and end will be. Other people are less worried about that, then will say 'Well, just give us an idea of the characters and the world', but nearly always there has to be a bit more fleshed out on paper before they then go to script. And you can see the sense in that because it's a lot cheaper to just pay for treatment than it is a full script. This way they can see if it works. Once it is turned in, the producer might give you revision notes and you go back and forth a couple of times, fine tuning the treatment. Then one hopes that the financiers will be happy with what they think they are going to get, and if they are, you start writing the screenplay and you go through the steps outlined in your contract.

Q - If you could create you own perfect writer, what would their qualities be?

Michael - Hard working would help, though equally there is no point just banging it down on the page and just getting it in. If you are just always looking for the next cheque, then it's not going to work. You've got to invest yourself in a project. The best writers are those who really care about what they are writing and listen to the advice of the script editors and the producer. You don't always have to agree with them, but listen, maybe debate and argue. It's hard enough trying to get a movie made, why wouldn't you just do it with somebody you like? That's my ideal client. Somebody who is talented, you believe in, and is really decent too.

Q - What is turnaround?

Michael - Turnaround is quite simply a way to get your project back if it has been laying dormant for a while or both parties, writer and producer, realise that the project just isn't working. Basically, the producer agrees to 'turnaround' the rights back to the writer. The way to get it back, ultimately is to have to pay for it, so if you've been paid a £100k for the script up to that point, the producer / financier is going to want that money back at some point. Ideally they get that money back when the production gets set up elsewhere, so you are not a writer having to sort the bill for £100k. They might want some interest on it, they might want a 50% premium on top of the money. These days it seems more and more a common occurrence. In my experience, in this country, the turnaround costs are never that much, because nobody can be bothered to put that much money into anything! People who don't have agents make that mistake all the time. They get some money and suddenly the copyright is passed over to the producer and there is no way of getting it back because they just don't have any rights. Options sort of safe-guard that to a certain extent, because they can't continue to run with it forever. If they paid for further drafts, that can get a bit complicated, but you have to make sure that those further drafts also turnaround at the point the Option lapses.

Q - If you wanted to adapt a book, as a writer, how does that work?

Michael - The first thing you must do is make sure you have got the rights to do so. You've absolutely got to get permission from the author to adapt and you have to get an Option. So please don't just think, 'oh I love that book', and then go and write a script on spec because you cannot sell it or make it without the rights. The number of people who come in and have written sequels to films without thinking that maybe they need to ask the producer or the originating writer whether they should have done that or not is staggering. The best way to contact the author is to go through their agent. Ask the publisher if you get stuck.

Q - Do you think a new writer should pursue a novel or a previously published work as their low budget film?

Michael - If the work is good, yes. Though most books that get good reviews seem to get snapped up these days. As a first time writer, unless there is really no interest in the book, they are going to be resistant giving somebody with no track record the rights. This is because the sums of money that first timers can afford to Option it are minuscule, and they are going to want it for at least two years to give them time to write it and to tout it around. A client of mine got a novelist to give him a free option on a

---

Screenplay Tips

GUERILLA FILM MAKER SAYS!

1. Put your characters into their own nightmare, essentially their worst fears should come true. Whatever pain they feel, we feel. Writers often have a strange love affair with their characters and so feel bad when bad things happen to their fictional characters.

2. Write every day. Whether it's first thing in the morning or by candle light, you must get into the habit of writing several pages every working day. The writers greatest fear is the blank page. Face it now.

3. Cut the world off. Switch off your phone, disconnect from the internet, shut the door, put on music (if that works for you) and write. Stop only for short loo breaks and to make tea or coffee. Never turn on the TV or just have a peek at your emails. Remove distraction and get focussed. Then do point two!

4. Make it worth reading. There is an often understood agreement between the writer and the reader. The writer says, 'listen to what

I have to say', to which the reader says, 'I will listen for as long as it's worth hearing'. So is your script really worth reading? Is it self indulgent in any way? Over wordy as you think it's smart or cool? Derivative and you think you can get away with it? In fact, can you even read it? Rewrite, refine, improve...

5. Research turns your ideas, which are essentially fantasy, into fantasy that reads like fact. If you want your fantastical situations and characters to ring true, do your research. And not just a few hours surfing. Get out there, meet people, get into their world, then you can write from a place of honesty and integrity.

6. Understand that aside from raw talent, which is somewhat indefinable and certainly unlearnable, the only thing that distinguishes success from failure, is hard work. Do not be lazy. Here it is again, DO NOT BE LAZY! Now put this book down and go and write!

short story he had written, and he made that into a short film. I wouldn't rule it out, but just be realistic in what you are going for. It might be better to try and find something which is out of copyright.

Q - What is 'out of copyright'? What does that mean, and what are the years involved?

Michael - A work goes out of copyright 70 years from the death of the author. There are some great stories out there that are now out of copyright. They might be a bit old and creaky, but you could bring them up to date. If you really don't have the ideas yourself, then take yourself off to a second hand book shop or a library and have a good rummage. Just be careful to check when the author died and make sure it is 70 years or more ago.

Q - Do writers ever get to be involved on set, when they are shooting?

Michael - It depends on the producer and the director. Some writers can be quite controlling, so the Directors like to keep them off set. A film is a director-driven medium and the writers are perhaps not as respected in film and television as they are in theatre. Then again any producer worth their salt will realise it's actually quite good to have the writer involved because they are ultimately going to bring something to the production. At the very least be there to make last minute changes.

Q - Do you think a great quality for any writer is to be collaborative?

Michael - Yes. There was a writer the other day who was insistent that the Producer was wrong. It's like if I had paid for a new bathroom, I'd be a bit pissed off if the bathroom person said *'Well actually no, you don't want to shit in the toilet, you want to shit in a bucket.'* So you say *'But I'm paying for that toilet, so I'd like a toilet not a bucket!'* and it's not 100 miles apart from when a producer is actually paying a writer to write something. You have sort of got to give the producer what he wants. If you want to be totally in control, then don't take anybody's money. Write it for free and hang on to it, though it might never get made. If you are taking somebody's money you have, to a certain extent, got to respect their wishes. They could be wrong, and if you really think they are wrong, you can fight for it. But you have got to take a step back from it and remember that the director is ultimately the person who is going to have to shoot the thing.

Q - Do you ever get involved in low budget films?

Michael - Yes. One of my clients had something in development with one of the film studios here in the UK, which was green lit by the old regime and un-green lit by the new regime. The writer/director thought *'I've got to make this'*. So he made it for £140k and we had to renegotiate with the financier turnaround costs, because the turnaround costs would have, at that budget level, been crippling. Another film that was looking set to go into production didn't happen. So the director and the producer went out and raised the finances themselves. The director mortgaged his flat and the Producer found two investors who were not in the film business, but thought this is exciting. That was made for £700k and now people are very excited about the finished film.

Q - How can a new film maker or a new writer make your life easier?

Michael - By not thinking that the agent will suddenly get your film fully financed. It's got to be a collaborative process and I think that the days of producer and agents being on separate sides are gone. We all want the same thing. If you are not working, you are not earning, meaning I'm not earning. So we do want people to have their films made. We meet people all the time, but I can't be out there hustling for that money, 24 hours a day. Be part of the process. Work together.

Q - What advice would you offer a new writer or film maker?

Michael - It sounds corny, but don't give up. If you really do believe in it and yourself, then keep going. It is not always going to be an easy ride - it can happen over night, or it can take years. Remain positive, but also be realistic about what targets you set yourself. Plan your career. If you are a writer / director, don't write something where the budget is so big that you are going to lay yourself open to being removed because after it gets over a certain level, people start to get twitchy. It's far better to write something that is manageable for you. If you are making a short film, do something that is a calling card for your for your feature film.

Q - What is your job?

Cyril - I advise IFC on their activities in Film and Music.

Q - What does IFC do?

Cyril - IFC's core business is providing development and pre-production packages for feature film projects. Which means that they have a team of consultants who take a project at script stage and produce a full studio-like report on it, covering everything from distribution, locations, casting to budget reviews and costume design etc. It can also include story boards and concept art and the Producer is often encouraged to shoot a promo. Then a CD pack is prepared and sent back to the Producer. It is as close as you can get in the independent world to do what the studios do, in terms of having their marketing, distribution, sales and TV departments look at a project and each provide their thorough assessment. The Producer then takes this package to potential financiers. It gives a detailed and independent overview of the project and its prospects so a financier can make an informed choice.

Q - So you are producing a feasibility study. How successful are those feasibility studies?

Cyril - The ratio to date has been pretty good. IFC does get involved as much as they can in actually getting the films made, sorting out various bits of finance, providing pre-production and production funding in certain cases, putting projects through its sales company. It is there to help get films made. Recent examples include Martha Fiennes' ensemble drama 'Chromophobia' or the Toni Collette thriller 'Like Minds'.

Q - At what budget levels are these films?

Cyril - There is no fixed level. The projects that IFC look at range from a $1m to $20m.

Q - On a personal level, what do you feel are the common weaknesses of projects that you see?

Cyril - I would have to say under-development, which may mean a number of things: the idea may not be particularly good (if there is one at all), or the writing falls short of delivering on that idea, or even that the entire package (script, cast, crew, budget) does not match the project's realistic artistic and commercial profile. Projects also often have too much of a local perspective or are victims of what I call this country's 'transatlantic syndrome'. That is to say that, stuck as we are between Europe and the US, and despite the huge advantages that the English language offers, British films are torn between two schools of cinema. As a result our films have a tendency to get lost somewhere in the middle and often lack a strong sense of identity. It does not help obviously that the culture of British films in this country is not particularly strong, especially when compared to say France or Spain.

Cyril Megret
IFC Development Consultant

Q - The problem is, once 'The Full Monty' has been made, you can't say 'that works, let's do it again'.

Cyril - Invariably people will try, as they have with gangster films for instance.

Q - What do you think are the strengths of the good projects that come to you? What makes a project stand out if it is good?

Cyril - If there is a sense of scope or if there is a universal aspect to it. The quality of the writing obviously has something to do with it. A sense of relevance to today too.

Q - Does it help if some of the pre-production work that you talk about has already been done?

Cyril - Yes, though if it hasn't been done properly, then it is better to start from scratch, but at least it shows a certain level of commitment and not just showing up with a script.

Q - What are the mistakes that you see? The avoidable mistakes?

Cyril - Rushing into production with an unfinished, unpolished screenplay. It's difficult to know when the script is ready, especially when you've been developing it on your own, without any market input. But it's a terrible mistake if you go in too early or too fast. You really only have one shot with a script and if two years down the line you are still flogging it, then you've burnt it effectively. If you've got the patience and the means, and I acknowledge that the latter is often the crux, you have to make sure it is ready before it goes out, that all your ducks are aligned. In an ideal world this is how it should work at least.

Q - What advice would you give a new film maker/writer?

Cyril - Watch films.

Chris Vogler
Story Guru

STORY GURU

Q - How does a writer get their first break?

Chris - There are many pathways. But you can learn from general trends and extrapolate some principles out of it. It helps to know somebody in the system. It's not the only solution but it can help as it can get your stuff read. You need to have it read by a high level executive, but to do that you need a personal recommendation.

Q - What happens if you don't have an advocate in the system?

Chris - You have to be very good, persistent and lucky. They are all necessary elements. If it does get a personal recommendation, that can be a big break for you, but you have to be good. Another element is novelty. One of the most desirable elements about a script is the buzz that comes to it because people perceive it as new. If there's something shocking or remarkable, it can set you apart. You're trying to get yourself distinguished from this vast pool of scripts that are floating around all the time. What you want is people running down the hall of the studio going, *'you've got to read this!'* An example is *There's Something About Mary*. It had an outrageousness about it and it made people within the studio eager to call their friends and ask if they had read the script.

Q - What makes a great script?

Chris - They like to say that it's character, and that does drive a lot of the Oscars. One side of filmmaking is driven by character oriented movies and everyone who has an artistic feeling about themselves responds to those, but the majority of filmmaking is oriented around good plot and situations. Also, taking us to a world we haven't been to before is an important element. A movie that can convincingly create an alternative world is also an ingredient of success. That accounts for the success of *Harry Potter* and *Lord Of The Rings*. It's true of other movies too, such as *The Hours*. It creates a unique film universe that takes you outside of your time and place, and that's a valuable service.

Q - How do you create an original screenplay while adhering to the dramatic structure?

Chris - You have to observe the forms and be aware that the audience is programmed to accept things through certain filters. They have expectations which you can totally dismantle, but within the form, you can do things that are startling. *Adaptation* is conventional in certain ways, but it is almost breathtaking in the way it presents this inner reality of the writers experience. There's a contract with the audience and certain terms have to be fulfilled. Such as to entertain us and take us out of our normal reality. There are lots of other contracts too.

Q - Have any films worked outside of the contract?

Chris - I think there are films that work in spite of the story contract, where there may be some story there, but it's secondary to the experience. This trend started with *Flashdance*. It was a minimal story that was almost besides the point as the filmmakers were giving you the sensation of the dancers and the choreography. That's true of *Chicago* too. Nobody claims that's a complex story, but the film satisfies other contracts.

Q - What do you think about filmmakers like Robert Altman and Mike Leigh?

Chris - They have found another way to get at it. Rather than to have it scripted, they improvise. It's more of a character driven emphasis.

Q - Is that less satisfying for an audience?

Chris - I think this alternative approach is more acceptable now because people are so inundated by standard techniques. It's a time where they are thirsty for new approaches. I'm thinking of a movie like *Bowling For Columbine,* which isn't trying to be a story, and it's bending some of the expectations of a doc too. You're always going to have the dance between the conservatives who play it safe, and those who applaud innovation when something new comes along.

Q - When reading scripts from new writers, what common mistakes do you see?

Chris - A common problem is the failure to identify the main character and set them apart. Everyone is presented with more or less the same value, and the writer has made the assumption that you'll figure out who the hero is. You have to give us certain signals that let us know who the main character is. More emphasis on the character and more time spent describing the main character, or they may put the character in the initial position in the story. All these things are clues that the audience is used to reading.

Q - What have you learned from reading scripts?

Chris - Often the problems are in the beginning. When the story starts to unravel after 75 pages, there was something in the first ten pages that caused that collapse. By going back and making a slight adjustment in the beginning, you can often correct that. The set up is so important. The parameters you set are critical to later on in the story.

Q - Are there any books or courses you would recommend to new writers?

Chris - I would say it's useful to take John Truby's seminar, which is good for systematically laying out the options. It gives you all the logical options. It's also useful to take an acting class as it gives you the sense of what's a realistic mouthful of dialogue for an actor. Until you've had that experience I don't think you can write good dialogue.

Q - What do you think about Mckee or Syd Field's books?

Chris - I think all these books are terrific. I endorse having a good grounding in Syd Field's work as he was a pioneer. You can get great things out of *Making A Good Script Great* and out of Mckee's *Story.* It's really useful to absorb their techniques, language and the terms that they use. Then you go off and make your own and create your own language.

Q - How does a writer get an agent?

Chris - That's a mystery to me as well. There are certain areas that remain murky, but I think the answer is to be very good and to be committed to being a professional writer. You have to get beyond the idea of *'I'm going to write one script and sell it.'* You have to present yourself as a professional who works fast, who isn't distracted by other things, and who is there at the table to work. The agent is trying to sell not just your script, but you as a worker too.

Q - What do you do in the face of constant rejection?

Chris - To deal with that you have to distinguish yourself from the rest of the pack by doing things like entering local writing contests and apply for writing fellowships. Anything you can do that signals to the buyers that you are special is very important. Winning third place in a local writing contest sets you apart. When you win something like that, it opens the door for you for a short time, so you must be ready to step through that door.

Q - What single piece of advice would you give a new writer?

Chris - Do it every day. It has to become like grieving, part of your normal routine. It can't be a special thing you do when you have a vacation.

Final Script Rewrite

GUERILLA FILM MAKER SAYS!

Before you lock your script, consider these changes to save time and money. In essence they may not change the story, but they will make it easier to shoot.

Kids
Cut 'em, or change to teenagers, for obvious reasons.

Animals
Cut 'em. Outside of movies actually about animals, you just don't need the headaches.

Atmospheres
If it says... 'Rain pours...' in your screenplay. Cut it..! Rain is a nightmare. Does it really make a difference if it isn't raining?

Night Exteriors
Rewrite and either move the scene indoors or into daytime.

Too many characters
Overwritten screenplays often contain too many characters. Merge two or three where you can, or cut if possible.

Stunts and action
Figure out how to tell the story without seeing the actual action and write it in to your script. It can be as simple as a character explaining what happened rather than seeing it.

Q - Do a lot of people crave the success more than the writing itself?

Chris - I heard a writer say that *'you'd better enjoy the writing, as that will be your life'*. It's like you're a long distance truck driver and you're ass has to be in that chair for a certain number of hours a day or it isn't going to work.

Q - Any tips on how many pages a day and the time of day to write?

Chris - No. There are certain logical ideas you might apply. It makes sense to do it early in the day so you make sure it gets done every day. Either you don't go to bed until you've done it or do it first thing. Many people operate well on the morning idea because you're not quite awake yet so you're able to tap into your unconscious and that kind of writing can be very good. One of the biggest problems people have today is distractions. Some people like to write early in the morning because the rest of the world is asleep.

Q - Is there an acceptable amount of pages to aim for per day?

Chris - People are satisfied to do a couple of pages a day. But typically when you're in production, you're expected to get 5 or 10 pages down. 10 pages is a good days work. I learned a lot about this in the editing room on an independent feature I produced. My chief realization is that telling the story became like building a ship, and the basic structure of the story was the laying of the keel, and then the individual scenes became the planks that you attach to the keel. Then it was a case of smoothing the hull and sanding and refining and taking stuff out. Streamlining became an important principle to me. I recommend that for writers too. If you ever have the chance to edit a film, it will teach you volumes about what you should have done on paper. It's important to have good characters and ideas to support the structure. Sometimes the scene is pages of talking. You can do that but it's always better if the scene is trying to achieve a specific reaction from the audience. Make them mad, make them care. You're trying to get something out of them rather than just moving on to the next scene. It may not be your destiny to have it made into a film, but it's important to tell the story anyway. It's little comfort, but every script has something to say to somebody. They have their impact even if the movie doesn't get made. There have been many times when I've read a script that I knew would never become a movie, but it gave me a piece of information that I needed at that moment. The writer had not failed.

SCREENPLAY

Q - What is the ALCS?

Jane - The ALCS - The Authors' Licensing and Collecting Society Limited - is a collection society which represents writers of all kinds, whether for film, television, theatre, play scripts, poets, books, journals anything you can think of. We licence and collect royalties on their behalf for secondary uses of their material, in whatever media and form.

Q - What typically are those secondary uses?

Jane - In the case of television, it would be cable and satellite re-transmission outside the UK for example. In the case of books and magazines and journals it would be photocopying, reproductions for educational use, those kinds of uses.

Q - Who should join the ALCS, should a Producer join?

Jane - A Producer could join, but we are primarily set up for Writers. For a Producer there is an organisation called the DPRS.

Q - How much does it cost to join?

Jane - It costs £10 a year to become an ordinary member and that £10 a year can be deducted from an actual payment. We encourage all Writers to join because we pay everyone we know whose works are being copied, and we are very anxious to make sure that we do pay those that do have some money due to them, but we can't do it if you don't join.

Q - How often do you pay out?

Jane - We normally pay out twice a year, in August and then again in February, but we can make adhoc payments if there is an urgent need for a Writer to have money in the interim.

Q - What kind of monies are we actually talking about? If you wrote a sitcom on television that did quite well, what kind of money are we looking at, because some writers will read this and immediately imagine millions of pounds!

Jane - The average of each annual payment out, is about £700, £750. Of course there are huge variations. If you took a mean, it would be slightly lower than that.

Q - Can the Producer take this money from the Writer, if the Producer got them to write the show?

Jane - That is an area of concern for the Writers. If the Producer commissioned a Writer to write and wanted to collect these royalties, we would need to be reassured that the Writer had assigned their rights to a Producer, and had understood what the financial implications of that were. In other words the Writer

Jane Carr
ALCS

is therefore the weaker party in that negotiation. We would not recommend making such a concession.

Q - Do you ever advise Writers on that kind of an issue, going into a project?

Jane - We normally wouldn't give advice on the contractual arrangements. We would probably refer them to the Writer's Guild, or the Society of Authors, if they were members of either, or both, where there is much more contractual advice, much more on what their rights would be in those particular circumstances.

Q - What common mistakes do you see?

Jane - I'd offer advice, like choosing a good agent, use the union if you need better backing. Look at everything in your contract, make sure you have read all the small print and make sure you understand it. Understand what it is asking of you.

Q - What advice would you offer a new filmmaker?

Jane - If you really want to be a filmmaker, go for it!

ALCS Ltd, Marlborough Court,
14-18 Holborn , London, EC1N 2LE

Tel: +44 (0)20 7395 0600
Fax: +44 (0)20 7395 0660
alcs@alcs.co.uk

Anne Hogben
Writers' Guild of Great Britain

THE WRITERS' GUILD

Q - What is the Writers' Guild of Great Britain? How does it benefit new filmmakers?

Anne - The Writers' Guild of Great Britain is a trade union, affiliated to the TUC, representing writers in film, television, radio, theatre, books and new media. It negotiates Minimum Terms Agreements with the BBC, PACT(independent TV and film producers), ITV companies, TAC (Welsh language independent TV producers), TMA (Theatrical Managers Association), ITC (Independent Theatre Council), the Royal National Theatre etc. The Guild advises members on all aspects of their professional lives, right from the beginning of their careers. The main benefits for new screenwriters are, among other things, a contract-vetting service (this is particularly important for new writers who do not yet have agents and who may not be able to afford legal advice), communication with other writers and networking opportunities with the industry, the weekly e-bulletin to members containing news, work opportunities, competitions, information about events etc., the quarterly glossy magazine, help and advice by phone, e-mail or letter, legal advice when necessary and a pension scheme. The Guild has a regular programme of events for writers working in every genre.

Q - Are there any Writers Guild basic agreements for feature films and television? If so, must a production company be a signatory of the Guild if they are to use these agreements?

Anne - Yes, the Writers' Guild has four minimum terms agreements for television, negotiation with the BBC, PACT, ITV and TAC. The Writers' Guild PACT Film Agreement of 1992 is currently being re-negotiated. I receive a lot of queries from Guild members' concerning low budget films. You would not believe how many so-called producers out there are offering derisory £1 option agreements. We always encourage writers to reflect carefully before entering into a legal contract. New writers are particularly vulnerable - they are often just so thrilled that someone wants to take out an option on their screenplay that they are willing to sign any contract without reading it carefully, asking questions and seeking professional advice. At my end of the telephone I get to hear all the heart-breaking stories of falling-outs, disputes, law suits and so on. So many problems could be avoided if people took the time to talk through the situation before they sign on the dotted line.

Q - What type of membership do you offer and what are the rates and benefits? (full, candidate, student etc.)

Anne - Full membership is open to any writer who has written a work for which payment has been received under written contract not less than the current minimum terms agreements negotiated by the Guild. Candidate membership is open to all those who are taking their first steps into writing but who have not yet received a contract. Student membership is open to anyone on an accredited writing course or on attachment with a theatre. Ask for an information pack to be sent to you by phone or email or post or download an application form from our website (www.writersguild.org.uk)

Q - By being a member of The Writers Guild of Great Britain, are you a member of the Writers Guilds in America (East and West), Canada, Australia, New Zealand and Ireland?

Anne - The Writers' Guild of Great Britain is part of the International Affiliation of Writers' Guilds. Each of these organisations is a separate body with its own constitution and criteria for membership. However, we have reciprocal arrangements with our fellow guilds. For example, if a member of the British Guild is offered a commission to write for television or film in America the Writers' Guild of America waives the joining fee of $2.5k. Many writers who regularly work in America are members of both organisations.

Q - Do you offer any service for registering scripts? i.e. like the service offered by the Writers Guild of America?

Anne - We do not have a script-registration service because it is not a legal requirement to register a script in the UK. Copyright exists in all original scripts from the moment when they are created in writing or recorded in any other permanent form. In the United States registration may be desirable since no legal action to prevent infringement can be taken until the work has been registered. In other major territories no facilities for official registration exist. Therefore you cannot lose your copyright for failure to register or comply with any formalities. Copyright is the right to prevent copying. The difficulty with protecting copyright is in proving that copyright exists. It is perfectly possible for two writers to produce apparently very similar works quite independently of each other and, in that case, each writer has copyright in his own work and neither can accuse the other of infringement. When a work has been published or shown to the public, then the author of any subsequent work may be assumed to have seen the previous work and is going to have difficulty denying that copying has taken place. The greatest difficulty in protecting an unpublished work is when submitting it to publishers, broadcasters, film companies, potential financiers and others. To secure the best protection make sure your work bears a copyright notice in the form © followed by your name and the year in which the work was created. This is not a legal requirement in the UK, but it is essential for the purposes of informing anyone into whose hands a copy of your work may come that copyright is claimed and by whom. Normally the copyright notice will be in the writer's name, but if you operate through your own company which contracts for your service, then it may be appropriate to have the notice in the company's name. It is also important to have evidence as to when your work was written so that if another work appears which looks surprisingly similar to your own, you can prove when your own was written. The simplest way of doing this is to send yourself a copy of what you have written (in every form it is submitted to a third party) by recorded delivery. DO NOT OPEN THE ENVELOPE. In that way you can produce evidence as to when your work was written. Copyright protects the form and expression of ideas, and, to some extent, the research and labour which has gone into that form and expression. What it does not do is ensure that the basic ideas which are more difficult to protect. The best way of protecting ideas is to get anyone who sees your work to sign a letter confirming that they will not disclose the ideas behind your work to anyone else, and will not use those ideas except by prior arrangement with you. However, it is very difficult to get broadcasters or film companies to sign such a letter since they receive thousands of unsolicited scripts, many of which may be based on similar ideas and have been created quite independently. If they agree to give confidentiality letters to all authors, they could not accept one script and reject others without being accused of breach of confidentiality by disappointed writers. Above all else do not discuss your ideas and thoughts with anyone before they are written down, and always exercise caution when discussing them with others.

Q - Can a film producer ring up the Guild and find out who represents a writer that they're after?

Anne - Yes. Or they could just take a look at the Find A Writer part of our website. The Guild has Minimum Terms Agreements (see above). An established writer is usually able to negotiate higher rates. A good agent should be able to get the best fee for a client.

Q - In the US the Writers Guild of America has a very strong presence and will determine who gets the writing credit if there are multiple writers on a film – is that the same in the UK and if so, how is that determined?

Anne - Yes, we do have a Screenwriting Credits Agreement and we do conduct credit arbitrations if and when necessary.

Q - What advice would you offer a new film maker or writer?

Anne - Read as many screenplays as possible - preferably the shooting scripts. And when you find one you really like, study it carefully and watch the film over and over. There are several websites where you can download scripts for free. I always advise writers to make use of the BBC Writers' Room website at www.bbc.co.uk/writersroom. It is full of good advice on all aspects of writing for TV and radio, interviews with good writers, news about competitions etc. You can download free screenwriting software and scripts from successful shows too. Some new writers can be unnecessarily snooty about writing for the TV soaps but it can be a terrific way to improve your screenwriting skills - and the pay is not too bad either - thanks to the Writers' Guild minimum terms agreements! Anyone who is serious about pursuing a career in writing should aim to become as professional as possible, and joining the Writers' Guild is an important step in that process.

Anne Hogben
Assistant General Secretary
anne@writersguild.org.uk

15 Britannia Street, London WC1X 9JN
020 7833 0777 Ext.201

Suzan Dormer

DPRS

THE DIRECTORS' AND PRODUCERS' RIGHTS SOCIETY

Q - What is the DPRS?

Suzan - DPRS is the collecting society representing film and television directors and administers payments due to directors as authors of their work. Payments are collected from two sources.

Firstly, from European collecting societies in countries where arrangements exist to compensate directors (and other rightsholders) for the re-use of their work. The three main re-uses where royalties may become due are cable re-transmission, video rentals and private copying.

Secondly, from UK broadcasters and production companies for the secondary use of programmes made by, for, or in association with, the broadcasters (BBC, ITV, Channel 4, Channel 5, BSkyB, S4C). These payments are as a result of a Rights Agreement concluded in July 2001. DPRS receives a fixed sum annually and has devised a scheme for allocating payments to individual directors.

Q - So nobody else can touch your royalties?

Suzan - Under the UK law which came into force at the end September of '96, the director of any work made on or after the 1st July 1994 is recognised as being a co-author of the work itself (with the producer) and co-first owner of copyright of the work (again with the producer). The other authors, including the scriptwriter and the composers are authors of their underlying work. Payments received from other collecting societies have been allocated according to the arrangements that exist in the country where the payment accrues.

Q - How much money can it generate?

Suzan - It varies. If your work was shown in Holland as a feature film and it was privately copied you could be talking £50 - £100. If it was shown on Canal+ in France again with private copying you could be talking a few thousand. The most we have collected over the years for an individual director is now going on for £150k, with the biggest single payment being around £20k.

Q - How much does it cost?

Suzan - It costs nothing upfront to register with DPRS, although we deduct a one-off registration fee of £75 (+ VAT) from the first payment. We don't have an annual subscription but levy a management fee on all money we distribute. This is currently 10% for our UK distributions and 15% for payments received from foreign collecting societies.

Q - I joined the DPRS because I found out that there was £2,800 waiting for me as my share from a German deal. White Angel also sold to Sky in the UK - how much would I, as the director, get for that Sky screening?

Suzan - Screening in the UK won't generate a penny. You have to remember that although the rights exist under UK law, there is no automatic right to remuneration.

Q - What is the deal for producers?

Suzan - Although DPRS has 'Producers' in its title this refers to individual documentary makers who produce, direct and write and frequently take an onscreen credit as 'producer'. We don't represent production companies although they are also entitled to money from the revenue that is collected from Europe. These rights are administered by societies specifically representing production companies (eg. ComPACT).

Q. Do directors need to include any particular clauses in contracts they sign?

We now recommend the following:

> "Nothing in this agreement shall prevent the director from being entitled to receive income under collective agreements negotiated by recognised collecting societies but the director shall have no claim to payment by (COMPANY NAME) in respect of rights collectively licensed."

This clause below ensures that the director receives all money due to him/her from collections the DPRS and, at the the same time, reassures the production company that they are not liable for any further payments.

Q - What other organisations should a new film maker contact in order to get as much out of their film as they can?

Suzan - Certainly the DPRS in terms of their directors and the ALCS for the writer (which also covers books). The production company should contact ComPACT.

Q - What advice would you give to a new film maker?

Suzan - Register with the DPRS now. It is in all directors' interests to sign up with the DPRS as soon as they have completed a film so that it can be lodged with the network of collection societies.

Other contacts
For Authors...
ALCS - The Authors Licensing & Collecting Society
14-18 Holborn, London, EC1N 2LE
Tel 020 7 395 0600 Fax 020 7 395 0660

For Producers...
ComPACT Collections Limited
Greenland Place, 115-123 Bayham Street, London, NW1 0AG
Tel 020 7 446 7420   Fax 020 7 446 7424

The Directors'
& Producers'
Rights Society

DP®S

20-22 Bedford Row
London
WC1R 4EB   **SUZAN DORMER**
                Chief Executive
Tel: +44 (0)20 7269 0677
Fax: +44 (0)20 7269 0676
Email: info@dprs.org

Screenplay Books

Every writer will have their favourite book, the one that got them started, the one they refer too. There is no best book though, and on the whole, ALL of them have something to offer. Screenwriting books represent a cheap and excellent way to inform and tutor, as well as keep your spirits up and your brain focussed. Buy them all and keep a selection by your PC for writers block, on your bedside cabinet for nightime reading, and next to the loo for when inspiration strikes.

The Screenwriter's Workbook (and other books) by Syd Field

The first book most people buy on screenwriting and a real eye opener for the new writer. Easy to read and understand, Syd Field's books have sold so well as his style and simple explanation makes it seem so simple and accessible. His paradigm for a movie, a graphical structure if you like, is like a coat hanger for your plot. Essential.

Story by Robert McKee

Rocket science for screen writers, McKee deconstructs the art and craft of screenwriting in such a way as to often leave you breathless with his laser like understanding of the form. It's no easy read and could be criticised for being so indepth, it starts to read more like a physics manual. But hey, who said writing a screenplay worth making was easy? Go buy it.

The Writer's Journey by Christopher Vogler

An endless source of inspiration that draws on the common rules and structures found in all forms of story. The author has a great deal of professional experience and stresses that his book is a guidebook and not a rulebook. Once you have grasped and understood the concepts in this book, it's amazing how all great movies seem to adhere to the principles. Essential.

Writing Screenplays That Sell by Michael Hague

A great starter book that really gets the juices flowing. Light-weight in comparison to Vogler and McKee but probably the best place to start if you are working on your first screenplay. Also includes details on getting agents and selling your screenplay. Practical and pragmatic.

The Elements of Style by William Strunk

Not a screenwriting book, just a simple textbook on writing. Thin and small but huge in impact. Filled with answers to fundamental writing problems. If you read and implement this little wonder, you will write more effectively. Not just scripts, but everything. You should be able to pick it up for a fiver. How else can you transform your craft for the price of a couple of coffees?

Raindance Writers' Lab - Write and Sell the Hot Screenplay by Elliot Grove

A well considered, researched and detailed book that goes far beyond the writing. The reader is encouraged to get their hands dirty by doing exercises and answering questionaires. Grove's knowledge of how the film business works on both sides of the pond helps guide the writer through the creative choices that impact on the balance between art and business.

The Seven Basic Plots by Christopher Booker

A wonderful book that took 30 years to write! Christopher Booker examines storytelling of all kinds through the ages (novels, films, opera, fairytales etc.), giving the reader detailed synopses of dozens of stories. These are distilled to the basic ingredients to answer the fundamental question of why we tell stories. It is a thoroughly mind-expanding read which anyone interested in the art of storytelling will enthusiastically devour.

Teach Yourself Screenwriting by Ramond Frensham

Without doubt the cheapest and possibly smallest book on screenwriting, but nonetheless indepth. A great book to buy if you are cash strapped, or to keep in your bag for unforeseen moments when you have half an hour to kill. Frensham appears to have culled all the ideas floating around, and has distilled them into bite sized concepts.

FINANCE

m&e
media and entertainment
insurance services ltd

Supplying specialised insurance to the film and television business
Contact Paul Cable on 020 8467 8455 and email pdc-media@netway.co.uk

Laurence Brown
Solicitor

Q - What is your job?

Laurence - My job is to make sure that the client gets the film made and transacted in the way that they are expecting, and that there aren't any misunderstandings. This is especially true when talking about money. Anything involving money needs to be properly thought through and documented, so it is clear on both sides what has been agreed.

Q - What kind of film needs your services?

Laurence - It really depends entirely on the level of the budget. A film that is made for a million pound plus should have a line in the budget for legal services, just as it should have a line in it for accounting. For films that are made for less than that, it's often difficult for us to get involved. We can do bits, we can advise on any one particular complicated small piece of it perhaps, but actually doing the whole thing, no. At that level of filmmaking you are obviously not going to be working with certain types of finance, and therefore the complexity of the finance, should be less. So you are back to your fundamentals of just making sure that you and the person giving you the money etc, are at one.

Q - If you choose to make a film, should you start a company to do that?

Laurence - Yes, you should always have a limited company to protect yourself from liability in the case of things going wrong.

Q - What are the benefits of running a limited company?

Laurence - With important exceptions it protects you personally from being sued. Also, certain types of finance require you to have a limited company. Although this doesn't apply so much at the level of the low budget filmmaker, when people do give you money, they often take security over the production company. You can only effectively take security from a limited company. Soft money, like the regional film funds, will very often require a charge over the rights to your project via your company.

Q - What are some of big legal issues film makers should be aware of?

Laurence -There are obviously various laws that have to be observed: for example if you are trying to raise money in the UK from other people on a private basis, you have to be in conformity with the Financial Services and Markets Act. The other fundamental area is copyright. Obviously what everyone is dealing with in this process, is the buying and selling of rights, throughout the whole process. You need to be aware of the different types of rights and the revenues that should flow from them.

Q - What other kind of rights issues are there?

Laurence - You need to know if the script is based on something else and if so, then get those rights. You need to ask the right questions of the writer, as to what he has based his material on. For example if it is based on a real person, you have to do an agreement with that person to acquire the rights to their life story. Obviously if it is based on another existing copyright, such as a play or a novel, or maybe if it is a remake of something, these are all existing underlying rights which you have got to clear. If you don't clear them then you may be sued.

Q - When we talk about copyright based on existing works, what if you wanted to make something based on William Shakespeare?

Laurence - That is fine, as Shakespeare is out of copyright. It is basically the life of the author, plus 70 years after the end of the year of his death. That is European Union-wide. It may be a lesser term in other countries.

Q - How much can you help a new filmmaker, realistically, who has no money or little money?

Laurence - Depends on the stage a lawyer is at in their career. I've helped quite a lot of new filmmakers because I was on the committee of The New Producers Alliance for 10 years. At my old law firm we used to give free 1-hour surgeries for people, and so we did quite a lot with low budget film makers. My new firm provides two cost legal services for PACT members. Obviously, as you get on in your career, you are required to bring more in, so you have to concentrate more on that. I think a low budget film maker can often find a more junior lawyer who may be given some latitude by their firm to give a little bit of time to help somebody. Even just having an initial consultation with somebody for an hour, or a couple of hours over a period of time, I think could be quite helpful because you can say quite a lot in an hour to somebody. Just be sure to ask the right questions and give us all the facts. And if there is something that maybe one lawyer can't answer, someone else at the firm can. For example, we have tax people here, corporate people here, who can answer those questions.

Q - Generally how do lawyers charge for their time?

Laurence - Normally in most aspects of the film process, we will give an estimate and come to an understanding. When we reach, or are close to reaching the estimate we will tell you, which is what lawyers are required to do anyway, under the rules of the Law Society. Or otherwise there can be a fixed fee arrangement. When you get to a normal sized film, and production budget, there will be a fixed or capped amount for the legal advice. Each lawyer has an hourly charge-out rate which depends on their seniority so from an internal perspective this is how the cost of work and fees are judged within the firm.

Q - What are the key contracts that a film maker needs to absolutely get?

Laurence - Some contracts are more important that others, but I think it is important to have the mindset where you do document all of your relationships, deals and job positions. Even some of what seems to be the lesser ones, can still lead to a dispute. It just seems silly to have a dispute about something when it could all have been clear. These days you can have it in an exchange of e-mails. It doesn't have to be in the form of a contract, twenty pages long etc, as long as there is clarity, and as long as there is written evidence. At the end of the day, you have to be able to point to something and say this is what we agreed, here it was. It makes agreements and responsibilities clear and commits them to paper. Further, the process of committing to writing makes you think everything through e.g. you might miss something important, which you can now add back in or discuss. That is the discipline, when you reduce something to writing.

Q - When it comes to attracting real money, how much value to that process do you think having someone like yourself involved adds?

Laurence - I think it makes the money person feel more comfortable if you have got proper professional advisors and you are going to go about it in a professional way. They know you will conform to the Financial Services and Markets Act. They know the documents that are prepared will be professional and will address the various civil and criminal sanctions. They know that the relevant documents will make them aware of the risks. They need to know that despite *Billy Elliot* and *Bend It Like Beckham,* a lot of films don't make any money, in fact lose money. If you are not upfront and honest with them, you are breaking the law. And, if you make a claim and cannot back it up with evidence, you have a good chance of losing a lawsuit. Basically you have to have a little dossier of information that you can point to, that you keep, where you can say, 'yes, I can back up the claim that I have made there, and I've got evidence', and I haven't just thought of it

FINANCE

Making a Contract

GUERILLA FILM MAKER SAYS!

A contract is an agreement between two or more parties. It can be a verbal agreement, but a piece of paper which clarifies the terms of the contract, who will do what, when, how etc. is much better. The contract is really there so that each party knows what they have to do - it's written there in black and white. It also protects you if things go wrong.

1. Remember, a contract is just a piece of paper and if someone is intent on doing something which breaks the contract, there is nothing you can do short of legal action (which you may not be able to afford). Some people will sign a contract and then do whatever they feel like doing, in their own interest, knowing you probably won't do anything. No contract can protect against this.

2. If money is involved, get it up front, preferably on signing. If not all up front, as much as possible. You don't know what might happen down the line - investors die, go bankrupt, get bored.

3. ALWAYS make a contract for everything, even when friends do work for you. If your movie is ultra successful, all those freebies and favours will cost you. At the same time, don't get hung up on huge wordy and over the top contracts.

4. When entering a deal with a company where they will supply you with goods or a service make sure they put the quote down on paper and fax you. We had one deal fall through because the chap we struck it with had died - his predecessor wasn't interested and we had no proof of the prior deal.

5. Follow your instincts - if something is too good to be true, it probably isn't true.

6. Always sign a contract before any work begins (especially actors).

7. It's obvious, but read and understand all the text of the agreement, including the infamous fine print. Never sign straight away, sleep on your decision.

8. If in doubt consult your solicitor.

9. If it comes to the choice between signing a dodgy contract and getting to make your film, OR not signing and not making your film, sign, take the money, make the movie and get ripped off. You will walk away with a very valuable experience and showreel at someone else's expense.

10. If you are going to get a solicitor involved, make sure that you both absolutely understand how you will be charged. Some charge by the half hour, so you may get a £70 bill for ringing and asking one question. Ask if you can be charged for work on contracts only, and not for infrequent advice. Keep a close eye on costs.

11. Remember, your solicitor is an advisor. YOU make the decision and you can choose to act upon, or disregard what they say. Use your instincts.

12. If things go bad, and you get on the wrong side of someone else's solicitor, don't allow negotiations to go silent or stale or you may well end up in court.

13. DON'T FORGET, in all of this legal quagmire, you are here to make your film and launch your career. Resist the urge to spend time making your contract watertight and spend time developing your script!

14. Finally, even if you think you have a watertight contract, some people are just bonkers, or have limitless legal resources, so will just screw you – even if your contract protects you. It's just a piece of paper.

after seeing an article somewhere. You have actually got a copy of the article from which you took it; you have got your source.

Q - If I have lunch with someone, and we make an agreement, shake hands on it, is that binding?

Laurence - Yes, you can make an oral contract, but the problem is: who do you believe if a dispute arises? Who do you believe as to what the terms of the contract are? It is one person's word against another. If it is an important enough arrangement that you are entering into, it is important that it be put into writing. Basically the lay-person won't be able to do it as well as the lawyer could do, it will normally be better than not having anything at all in writing.

Q - What are some ways of starting a paper trail so you have proof?

Laurence - If it is something like a 'rights agreement' that should be done in the form of a contract. It can be relatively brief. You can always do short form contracts, and anything which is quite straight forward, which doesn't need legal-type language but is just a question of confirming to somebody, 'this is what you have said, this is what we've agreed'. You can do that in an exchange of e-mails. You should print out those e-mails and keep them in a binder. Keep records of what days you spoke to people on the telephone and what was said. I sometimes find that Producers are not professional enough about keeping paper work. It is just the professionalism of running your own business, and basically as a Producer you are going into business.

Q - Do you ever introduce filmmakers to rich clients?

Laurence - We are not a finance house, but obviously we may know people who have got clients on their books that might be interested. If we can make an introduction because we can see a fit, then we will often try to do so, but is not primarily what you would expect a law firm to do.

Q - What would you say are the major sources of finance for a low budget British film, say a £1m - £2m?

Laurence - Sale and Lease Back is still around until April 2006 in terms of new films, but it is not normally cost effective to do a Sale and Lease Back on a picture under a million pounds. So the money will come from maybe regional funding, private sources, or through an enterprise investment scheme. It might come from a broadcaster or the Film Council.

Q - What are the kind of things that make films attractive to people with money?

Laurence - About the only thing that is often attractive to a private investor as far as films are concerned are tax benefits. Anything on top of that, if the film actually does well, is regarded as a bonus. They might also be interested in being an extra in the film or maybe they can go along to the premiere party. So they get a little bit of the glamour as well.

Q - How do you cope with making multiple deals for financing the film?

Keeping Investors Sweet

GUERILLA FILM MAKER SAYS!

1. Where possible, fulfil any promises made. It may not always be possible to fulfil a promise (one of the disadvantages of low budget film making), but make it a priority to do so at almost any cost.

2. Regular updates need only be a photocopied sheet of information or a well presented email, which keeps the investor in touch with what is happening. If the line of communication goes cold, so will the investor.

3. Press - this is great for keeping people happy. Everyone associates press coverage with success, but beware, this may produce a false sense of financial returns on the part of the investors. If press coverage has used artistic license, let investors know.

4. Several low budget pictures have allowed investors to act in the film in return for cash. It works and everyone is happy. Beware of problems if their scene is cut - make this possibility known in advance.

5. Send them a DVD of the final film and invite them to the premiere or any UK film festival screenings.

6. If they do make it to a screening, treat them as a VIP and introduce them to the cast and crew. They are, after all, the people who funded you dream.

7. All correspondence should be impeccably presented. Checking spelling, formatting and accuracy before sending out should be second nature but often isn't. A simple typo can send a message that your are unprofessional and uninterested in their investment.

8. If things are going badly, let them know. As long as there is trust and they can see that you have done everything possible, investors have no real come back (check your agreements though). Investors would rather know things are going badly than hear nothing at all.

7. Give them a credit on the end of the film.

8. This is a VERY long term investment, maybe 15 years. Consider how you are going to manage that commitment to keep them in touch and distribute funds if they become available.

9. If you 'make it', remember where you came from. It may not be possible to repay debts in full, but a gesture, a character named after them in a major movie or a thank you in an award speech will give at least some due credit. Without them, you may never have been able to take that first step.

Ordinary Ways To Raise Money For a First Film ...that rarely work, but can...

1. Get a bank loan - (!?) but they're not going to give it you without security, so you are really risking your own money.

2. Get venture capital investment. But hey, they aren't stupid and won't invest.

3. Speak to the British film funding bodies such as British Screen, the Lottery Franchises and Film Four. The odds are astronomical but you MUST try this.

4. Pre sell your film - almost impossible if you have no track record, unless you have big names attached.

5. Knock on the door of every single person in the film industry and ask if they will fund your dream.

6. Approach other production companies or TV companies and set-up a co-production. It's possible, but there are a lot of hoops to jump though. Some companies have successfully made UK / Canadian co-productions for instance.

7. Product Placement. Get large companies to pay you for putting their products in your film. They won't be very interested unless the production is mainstream commercial AND you have a star. They will often give you the products, but no money, which could help out in the catering budget.

9. If your script is good, and a star is in place, a distribution company may put some money in. You will have no track record, so it is unlikely.

10. Organise a European Co-production knowing that you'll spend your development budget on lawyers and accountants, but at least your movie will be made before you retire.

11. Development. At least get something going with someone like the UK Film Council, to give you some money to persue other projects as well as the one in development.

12. Most effective route by far is to be born wealthy, but hey, that doesn't work for most us. Still, you could marry into wealth!

13. Give up on this lot and move onto Extraordinary Ways To Raise Money

Extraordinary Ways To Raise Money For a First Film ...that are NOT recommended!

1. Get accounts with all the facilities houses you need to hire or buy from and work on credit. Always pay your bills, even if it is the long run. Other film makers will follow you and you don't want to burn their bridges.

2. Get a credit card with a big limit. If you use it a lot and make regular repayments, the credit card company will ask you if you want an increased limit.

3. Get friends and family to invest a little seed cash and use it to shoot a two minute trailer. It will greatly increase your chances of getting investment as the film will no longer be words on a page, but a moving image with sound (and hopefully quite good too).

4. Get friends and family to invest a little more and get your movie in the can (and worry about the debts later). It's possible to shoot a feature film for £10,000.

5. Approach ANYONE with money and invite them to invest. You will need charm, a clear vision and a good prospectus.

6. Approach ANYONE and ask them to invest, regardless of whether you think they have money or not. Many people have a little stashed away and may be prepared to gamble. If you get money off friends and relatives, make sure they understand they could lose it all (likely).

7. Let a bored, rich person pay to play a small role in the film (and then cut them out if they are bad).

8. Sell your body to science. Worked for Robert Rodriguez.

9. Write a brilliant script, sell it to Hollywood, get sacked as the director but take the money and make a new movie with your fee.

10. Masturbate. The film No Deposit No Return was funded by asking men to sell their sperm, thus making it a film 'entirely funded by wankers'. Get creative! It could raise cash AND create great PR.

GUERILLA FILM MAKER SAYS!

Laurence - The whole thing becomes a juggling act. That is why you do need to have a sort of co-coordinating and guiding mind. Again I can only really talk of the films that I am looking at, which are films of 2 million, 3 million pounds upwards. Basically, the process there is that each of the parties will appoint a lawyer who is familiar with film work. You all get into an e-mail group and you start exchanging documents, and people start commenting and saying 'look this bit doesn't work from my point of view, can you modify that', that is what they call the 'closing process'. Normally, you have a controlling document called an 'Interparty Agreement', where people deal with those things that are of common interest rather than just dealing bi-laterally with the producer. You will still have the financing party with his own agreement direct with the producer because the financing party will still require to have all the right sort of obligations that he would require from a Producer. But everyone joins together in the Interparty Agreement in order to make sure that it works for everybody.

Q - Do you think it would be wise for a new filmmaker to seek an experienced producer to act as some kind of mentor?

Laurence - Yes I do because if you are starting out, you can't have the knowledge and skills. Sometimes people are more comfortable on the creative side, than on the financing side. For example, you get people called executive producers, who specialise in coming into a project for a brief period of time and helping find some money or structure some money, so that it works for you, and giving advice on how it all fits together.

Q - Are you often involved in sales and distribution?

Laurence - Yes we do get involved at that stage as well. Those deals can get complex and you have to know what the situation is on the minimum guarantees, and on fees and commissions, the amount of P&A that is going to be spent on the movie. There is the question how many screens it is going to go out on and other obligations of the distributor. The distribution agreements also have to work if you are doing a 'sale and lease back', it has to be structured in such a way to fit in with that.

Q - Have you ever had to deal with delinquent sales agents and distributors, certainly at the very low end?

Laurence – Not so much personally. Sales agents do sometimes get bumped off projects now. That is a good point in that one of the key clauses that you need in a sales agency group is a termination clause. Basically if the Sales Agent isn't doing that well with the film, and if they haven't put any of their own money into it, they therefore are not that committed to it, you then need to get rid of them, if they are not doing a good job.

Q - Do you need to get clearance for copyrighted signs and logos that are accidentally in the background of your shots?

Laurence - I think there can be some difference of opinion about this between lawyers, as to whether something is accidentally included in a picture. My view of it is that nothing can be accidentally included because you go through an editing process and you could have chosen not to put it in. So if it is in there, then you should clear it.

Q - Can that lead to problems?

UK Film Tax Relief

GUERILLA FILM MAKER SAYS!

As of December 5th 2005, a new tax credit system for the British film industry was introduced. Its aim is to enable the UK to compete in the global film market by attracting big budget films to UK shores bringing jobs and investment, as well as a consistent flow of British films to UK audiences. The tax relief for low budget films (films budgeted up to £20m) will be a net 20%. For big budget films (£20m and above), the rate will be a net 16%. Both rates apply to the UK spend of a film's budget, capped at 80%. This tax credit will allow producers to phase tax credits so that they can take them either at the start of production, or later when they're receiving profits from the film.

A cultural test will have to be taken to access the UK Film tax relief and this is provided by The Department for Culture, Media and Sport. This test introduces a points system based on the content of the film, talent, practitioners and filmmakers and will provide a clear definition of a British film. To see the requirements, check out the DCMS website.

Laurence - Yes it can do. It can lead to expense. It is like anything, if somebody doesn't find out about it because your movie only reaches to a small scale, and nobody sees it, you might be fine. But you shouldn't really rely on that because you may be left with having to do quite a lot of damage control. I've had movies, which have employed a clearance service, and we've ended up with a binder of about one hundred different clearances in there. It can get rather lengthy. It's partly a question of common sense and judgement

Q - If the filmmaker did nothing in this instance, what would probably happen?

Laurence - It depends on the scene it is in, and whether it causes any problems. That is the main thing - does it bring e.g. the product into disrepute? Does it associate that product in a negative way? He or she could get on the wrong side of a major corporation, which has its own in-house lawyers where it is no skin off their nose to send a *cease and desist* letter.

Q - How did they deal with it in Supersize Me?

Laurence - I presume they would have dealt with it via insurance. The film would have had 'Errors and Omissions insurance', if the Line Producer has done his side properly. E & O protects you from things that you could not have foreseen such as defamation of character, chain of title and/or clearances that pop up after the film is released or as it is about to be released. You need it and most financiers who are properly advised will require it. They will make sure they are noted on the policy too, so they are protected too.

Q - How much does E & O insurance cost?

Laurence - The cost of insurance has gone up since 9/11. I think it is in the region or about $10k-$12k now.

Q - What are the common mistakes that you see?

Laurence - I think the most fundamental problem that I see with a producer is letting certain elements of the finance slip whilst they concentrate on other things, and as a result finding themselves in real grief. We normally get involved when producers are at that stage of just about getting into pre-production and getting their finance knocked into shape. That is a process where you have to be aware of time scale. Not doing things at the right time can get you into awful problems. Not asking the right questions leads to a lot of problems. That means difficult issues don't get addressed in time which can mean that you do not have time to put a plan B in place, and then basically e.g, 20% of your budget has fallen away, say 3 weeks before you are meant to start shooting, which is the nightmare scenario. Then yes someone else may give you the money, but will be aware that you are desperate, and you will get a much worse deal.

Q - What advice would you offer a new filmmaker?

Laurence - Think of your marketplace, and think international. I don't think we are making enough movies in the UK that have actually got a market place, as opposed to a movie that somebody feels that they want to make. Basically, the public is out there wanting a product. I know we can talk art-house, there are all sorts of types of film, but there isn't room for more than so many non-commercial films in any one year. A lot of films are thought to be commercial and aren't. I've had people come to me and the idea has immediately struck me as something that is of no interest outside this country. You have got to be able to sell your movie abroad to make money. So think international. I also think that because there is a steep learning curve in this business, good producers form a lasting relationship with a good lawyer and a good accountant who can guide them.

Q - How important is a good solicitor to a film project?

Helen - I appreciate that legal costs can be high, but I think what people sometimes forget is that they could be entering into an agreement where the money involved may not be substantial but the liabilities are huge. That's why it's important to have proper protection, to have somebody to say this is what you've got to watch out for. When it comes to the agreements, if you don't have very much money then you should concentrate on obtaining agreements to secure your rights in the underlying material or screenplay. Make sure that you own or have a licence to what it is that you are going to exploit. I have seen, for example, options from quite established agents which give you absolutely nothing, yet the paper says that it is an option. A proper option agreement will have the terms of the licence or assignment annexed. If you tried to get development money based on an imperfect option, a broadcaster or financier would not be interested. If you wrote a screenplay based on the underlying material you could be at risk and waste time and money if the owner then refused to grant a licence or assignment. Obviously you can go back to the person who owns the rights and say we didn't have a proper deal, but then you're in a poor negotiating position and they can be awkward. They could refuse to give you the rights or they could turn round and say Ok, we now want £10k for it! That's why it's important to have a solicitor look at those agreements and say it's ok, you can go ahead. I appreciate that most new film makers will be making a film from their own screenplay or from something a friend wrote, but it's still essential to have those rights sewn up before you shoot.

Q - Would you read the script?

Helen - Yes, I read the script because there could be areas that clients might not have thought about which could cause problems. I think it's quite good to pass it by a friendly insurance company as references to names and places should be checked to ensure there is no living person who may be innocently defamed. For example: if your screenplay contains a bent copper working for the Met - make sure there is or has been no PC of that name working for the Met. Generally if you're doing anything about living people it is an area of difficulty.

Q - Most film makers would be put off a professional like yourself due to the fear of expensive charges?

Helen - There is a certain amount of leeway that we can give, for example, if a project is likely to get off the ground, what we sometimes do is run the clock whilst it is in development, and when it goes into production and there is money available, we'll then recoup our fees.

Q - What areas do filmmakers have the most questions in?

Helen - I would say, copyright and the payment or receipt of money, the financial side is of most interest to producers.

Helen Tulley
Solicitor

Q - What happens if a production company can't pay a debt?

Helen - You can do a deal with your creditor. Ultimately, if you can't do a deal or pay, your company could be wound up by the creditor, and the creditor could end up owning your film. Unless, as a director you were found guilty of wrongful trading or unlawful trading, you won't have any personal liability - the company owes the money, not you - all the assets belonging to the company will go to pay off certain parties (Inland Revenue, Customs & Excise, secured creditors) including finally, the creditors.

Q - What happens when someone puts an injunction on a film?

Helen - They go to the court and prove that they've got reasonable grounds and evidence to warrant an injunction. The court may order the film to be withdrawn from distribution until the issues in dispute are resolved. The party seeking the injunction, if successful will issue and serve a writ on the Defendant and the matter will be decided by the courts or otherwise settled. To put an injunction on a film, if you engaged a solicitor you will be asked for money on account and it could cost £10-15k to obtain an injunction. Secondly, the person who applies for the injunction often has to make a payment in court so that if the injunction has been wrongly granted, due to evidence that later comes to light, there is money secured in court to pay the defendant, who might have suffered damages because of the injunction.

Q - What are the most common problems to resolve?

Helen - Ensuring that the producer has sufficient rights in the work to go ahead and exploit a project with the maximum opportunity to make the film (and ancillary rights) a commercial success. This also means ensuring the stream of income from the film is properly and fairly distributed. If you think about the time you are going to invest in making your film, then it does make sense to have the correct basic structure.

FINANCE

139

Christine Corner
Baker Tilly

ACCOUNTANT

Q - Why do I need an accountant?

Christine - You need accountants to ensure that your finances are properly managed and that you are receiving proper advice on financing your company and film productions.

Q - What is the job of the production accountant?

Christine - The job of the production accountant is to prepare and monitor the film production budget. They need to go through every single item and analyse what is required and then produce a detailed budget, not only looking at the costs, but the timing of each line item so that the correct amount of drawdown can be obtained from the film financiers. The actual monitoring of costs against the budget is important so that you can see how the budget is going throughout the production. Once the film is up and running, the production accountant's day to day job will be checking that all the information is coming in, processing and paying invoices and ensuring they are genuine costs that are allocated properly to the right cost code, then comparing costs with the budget.

Q - How early on in the process should a production accountant be hired?

Christine - They should be hired during the development phase to prepare the budget to enable you to raise finance. This will normally be once you have decided on the director, main cast and locations.

Q - Would a payroll company be hired to take care of the crew or can this be done by the production accountant? Is this too expensive for a low budget production?

Christine - Usually the production accountant would hire a payroll company. They are specialists and it is important to ensure that you comply with all payroll legislation. Payroll companies are not that expensive and are cheaper in the long run because there are hefty fines if mistakes are made.

Q - If a payroll company is used, would they take care of other things such as mileage, mobile phones etc. or is that handled by the production accountant?

Christine - The production accountant usually handles this.

Q - Would an on set production accountant be hired separately from an accounting firm or from within an accounting firm? Are there any agencies that provide film production accountants? Should your production accountant be qualified as an accountant?

Christine - Production accountants are hired separately from an accounting firm. The Guild of Production Accountants can recommend people. The production accountant does not need to be qualified as an accountant. The important thing is to check what films they have previously worked on. Also, check with your accountant whether they know them. If you have a completion bonder, they will recommend people.

Q - Are there any dedicated accounting programs that you would recommend to a low budget production company?

Christine - Usually accountants use Movie Magic for budgeting and cost reporting which can be expensive. Instead they could use an excel spreadsheet. They should also use a separate dedicated accounting package such as Sage, to produce the accounts for the company.

Q - What kind of complications peculiar to film making should a filmmaker be aware of?

Christine - There are many sources of finance and many ways to finance a film. A filmmaker should be aware of all sources and the costs of each type of finance. Often a film is financed using more than one source of finance, which makes the deal more complex and thus more costly from a legal point of view.

The producer needs to be aware that it is often difficult to get all sources of finance lined up at the same time and therefore some may end up not coming up with the money. The producer should never start spending money until the full budget is financed.

Q - Are you involved in negotiating deals with the actors or crew members?

Christine - We don't normally get involved with this. This is really the job of the producer and the lawyers because the legal terms, particularly if an actor takes a share of the profits, are often complicated and important to get right in a legal agreement.

Q - Do you handle any of the union (Equity or BECTU) agreements?

Christine - *Again this is the producer and/or lawyer that do this.*

Q - Do you help put proposals together, for the Lottery fund for example?

Christine - Yes, we do. We help clients in raising money through all sources, whether it is a business plan for a bank, an information memorandum for private EIS investors (see below) sale and leaseback transactions (see below) or applications for lottery or other public funds.

Q - Can you help find investors for projects? Do large accounting firms have access to private investors that you can recommend to your producing clients? Any venture capitalists?

Christine - We do not find investors for projects and as far as I'm aware none of the large accounting firms recommend films to their private clients. We can however, put producers in touch with film partnerships that have raised money from private investors. Venture capitalists do not invest in film production companies other than the very established players because of the perceived risk by the City.

Q - Are there any tax incentives to invest in the UK?

Christine - Currently, tax incentives are available for investors in two ways. The first is via the Enterprise Investment Scheme (EIS). The reliefs available are 20% income tax relief on investments up to £200k, per individual per tax year. 40% Capital Gains Tax deferral, no maximum investment. Disposal of the EIS shares is outside the scope of Capital Gains Tax if they have been held for at least three years.

The second method, which has proved popular in the last couple of years is investing via the various film partnerships (see below) that are currently being marketed, under which the 100% film write off can be taken by the individual as a tax deferral.

Q - What is Section 48 relief? Section 41 and Section 42 relief?

BAKER TILLY

CHRISTINE CORNER
Partner
Arts Entertainment and
Media Group

Chartered Accountants
2 Bloomsbury Street
London WC1B 3ST
Tel: +44 (0)20 7413 5100
Fax: +44 (0)20 7413 5101
E-mail: christine.corner@bakertilly.co.uk
DX: 1040 London/Chancery Lane

www.bakertilly.co.uk

An independent member of Summit International Associates, Inc.

VAT GUERILLA FILM MAKER SAYS!

If you make a film, you will almost certainly have to register for VAT. From that point on you will be able to reclaim the VAT on purchases, but must charge VAT on invoices to UK companies and individuals. Each quarter you balance books and either reclaim VAT or pay VAT to Customs & Excise. Books MUST be done quarterly and VAT returns sent in on time or hefty penalties may be charged. NEVER cook the books for the VAT man or you could go to prison.

PAYE

Pay As You Earn. As a director of a Limited company, you are technically an "employee" and must therefore calculate your wages on a PAYE system. This will calculate the amount of income tax and national insurance to be deducted each month and to be forwarded to the Inland Revenue (Tax and NI tables are provided by your tax office). You MUST pay the PAYE/NI due each month, or fill in a declaration if you have received no salary. If you earn less than £82 per week per individual then you will not have to operate this system. At the end of each tax year (5th April) you will have to fill in a return (P60) for each employee and an annual return (P35) for the company as a whole. Most crew on a film will be self-employed and there are certain categories where PAYE need not be applied (see Schedule D). However, it is important to check their positions with the Inland Revenue otherwise the IR might declare them as 'employees' and therefore you may be liable to pay their PAYE plus severe penalties.

Contact the Film Industry Unit of the IR for more information: **Film Industry Unit, Inland Revenue, Tyne Bridge Tower, Gateshead, Tyne & Wear, NE8 2DT:** *Tel: 091 490 3500. Fax: 0191 390 3501.*

Christine - Section 48 relief refers to Section 48 of the Finance (No.2) Act 1997 and is a 100% write-off for films costing less than £15million. This has recently been extended to films commencing principal photography before 1 April 2006 where the film is completed before 1 January 2007.

Generally, producers cannot benefit from this tax relief themselves, as they have no profits to write off the cost against. Therefore, Section 48 relief is usually accessed by producers through sale & leaseback transactions (see below) or from S48 production partnerships.

Section 42 relief refers to a three-year write-off for films costing more than £15 million in accordance with Section 42 of the Finance (No.2) Act 1992. Again, this is usually accessed by producers through sale and leaseback.

Section 41 relief is a 100% write-off for development expenditure. Again, this is something which an individual producer cannot benefit from. There are however, a few partnerships that have been created to exploit this.

Q - What is Sale and Leaseback?

Christine - The sale and leaseback of films has always been popular with the US studios on big budget movies. Since 1997, sale and leaseback arrangements have become popular for films with production budgets generally from £1m upwards. Smaller budget movies can sometimes obtain a deal if they have a completion bond, but the costs often mean it is not worthwhile. Film production and acquisition expenditure on qualifying "British Films" of £15m or less can be written off on the date the film is ready for distribution or acquired. It is not now possible for deferrals to be included as part of the production expenditure for the sale and leaseback. The film production company ("Producer") sells certain rights in the film to the Purchaser (an individual or company with UK tax capacity). The film and all rights are then leased back to the Producer by the Purchaser for a series of increasing annual lease payments over a period of up to 15 years. This length of lease is normally acceptable to the Inland Revenue, provided the Film can reasonably be expected to generate income for at least that term. The Purchaser normally requires the lease payments to be secured by the Producer, by obtaining a bank guarantee payable to the Purchaser. This is typically achieved by a substantial amount of the proceeds of the sale being placed on deposit at the guarantor bank which, when combined with deposit interest over the period, is sufficient to cover the rental payments. The difference between the purchase price and the proceeds placed on deposit is the Net Benefit to the Producer and typically ranges between 14% and 15%.

Q - Can you apply for sale and leaseback before or during the film is in production, in order to be able to incorporate the benefit of the sale and leaseback monies into the production costs of your film?

Christine - Yes, you can ask the sale and leaseback partnership to arrange for a bank to cash flow the benefit. This will normally end up funding approximately 12% of the films budget.

Q - Can you put a film through sale and leaseback if it's under £1m budget and with no completion bond company? (In addition, looking at a low cash production budget which is much less than a £1m, (say, £200k or less) but your total production budget which includes all deferred payments etc. comes to over a £1m).

Christine - It is not usually possible to carry out a sale & leaseback on films with a cost of less than £1million or without a completion bond. It is no longer possible to include deferrals in the cost of the film. The cost for sale and leaseback purposes is calculated only on cash spent.

Q - How do I make sure my film qualifies as a British Qualifying Film?

Christine - A British Qualifying Film certificate is issued by the Department for Culture, Media and Sport (DCMS). The film must conform to the following - the producer (production company) must be either a person ordinarily resident or a company incorporated and managed from a EU or EEA member state. 70% (excluding payment to one person) or 75% (excluding payment to two persons, one of whom must be engaged only as an actor) of total labour costs must be payable to citizens or ordinary residents of a EU or Commonwealth country. At least 70% of the total expenditure incurred in the production of the film must be spent on film production activity carried out in the UK. (Note not the cost of goods and services supplied from the UK). Stock footage from a previously certified film or a film not made by the same film maker cannot make up more than 10% of the total playing time. (This does not apply to a documentary film).

It's also possible to qualify under one of the seven co-production treaties with Canada, Australia, New Zealand, France, Germany, Italy or Norway and under the European Convention on Cinematographic co-productions.

Q - How can an accountant help me obtain a British Qualifying Certificate?

FINANCE

AUDITED ACCOUNTS GUERILLA FILM MAKER SAYS!

As a Limited Company, it is a requirement to submit audited accounts to Companies House and to fill in an annual return, giving details about the company's directors, secretary, registered office address, shareholders and share capital. There is a filing fee payable of £15.

If your company has an annual turnover less than £5.6 million your company may be exempt from any requirements to have its annual accounts audited. However, your investors or shareholders may request and insist on audited accounts. If you are exempt from an audit, you are still required to prepare unaudited accounts and file these at Companies House.

There are few specific tax incentives in the UK for investors in films and those which currently exist favour investment by individuals rather than companies. A new scheme, called Corporate Venturing was introduced with effect from 5 April 2000. This is similar to EIS relief but for corporate investors. Relief is an upfront tax relief of 20% on investments held for at least three years.

Individuals: The "Enterprise Investment Scheme" (EIS) replaced the BES with similar rules. The capital cost of shares in certain circumstances may be treated as a reduction against an individual's taxable income and/or as a deferral of capital gains tax (see before). Where such shares are held for at least three years, any capital gain arising is exempt but where a loss arises, this can be set against chargeable gains or other taxable income.

Christine - A media accountant can review your plans in advance to ensure that all the elements budgeted for the film allow you to qualify and will then carry out the audit and report to DCMS once the production is completed.

Q - What about incentives for filming in Ireland?

Christine - The main tax incentive under Section 481 is a tax break for investors which gives them an additional deduction against their other income. The benefit to the producer is between 12-15% depending on the amount spent in Ireland.

Q - If a completion bond company is involved on a film, do you have to provide accountant reports to them?

Christine - No, but the production accountant has to provide weekly cost reports.

Q - If the film is a bonded film, are there any kind of rules that they have to follow? (i.e. is the budget locked etc.)

Christine - The completion bonder will agree a budget with you and this becomes the locked budget. There will also be a bonded completion date agreed in advance. The completion bonder will review the progress of the film and can step in if the film is not going to schedule or budget.

Q - What reports might you be asked to do for a production company or for investors? (production reports etc.) And is this generally not common on low budget films?

Christine - Normally we will prepare a report on the final audited production cost to financiers. It depends on the financiers whether we are asked to do this on low budget films, but it is always best practice.

Q - Do you ever have to put cash flow charts together for investors or production companies?

Christine - No we do not. Usually the production accountant will do these.

Q - Should producers put a contingency into their budget and how much? Do you find that they often use this contingency or not?

Starting A Company

GUERILLA FILM MAKER SAYS!

1. There are several ways of operating, each with their own advantages and disadvantages - sole trader, partnership, co-operative, limited company etc. Take advice as to what is best for your purposes.

2. Accountants and solicitors are very expensive. Buy a good 'business start-up' book, 95% of your questions will be answered in it.

3. If your turn over is high enough, you will become VAT registered and reclaim the VAT on your purchases (currently 17.5%). You can voluntarily register for VAT registration too, so do it.

4. Limited companies cost a lot to run. You need to supply information to Companies House and if your turnover is high enough, you will also have to supply audited accounts (expensive). However, they do offer 'limited' liability in case of problems. You almost certainly MUST start a limited company for your project.

5. Some film makers opt to start a limited company for each film. This protects all their other projects should one turn into a disaster.

6. Don't underestimate how much of a pain and how time consuming doing your accounts will be. Teach your mum or brother to do bookkeeping for you.

7. Don't get hung up on being a limited company before you need to. Being the director of a limited company won't make you write a better script, but it might waste time and money. But do start a limited company before you shoot, this will give you just what it says... Limited Liability in the event of disaster.

8. The name of your company says a great deal. Think of words that project images that are positive, aspirational, professional, creative and not words or phrases like, against all odds, small with big ideas, or just plain silly names.

9. You can search for free information on any Limited company at Companies House, online at www.companieshouse.gov.uk

Northern Ireland GUERILLA FILM MAKER SAYS!

Northern Ireland has some of most extensive government programs for providing funds to film makers and production companies. The Northern Ireland Film and Television Commission (NIFTC) set up the Northern Ireland Film Production Fund (NIFPF) providing production funding in the form of a repayable loan, for a limited number of feature films and/or television drama singles, series or serials that are intended to be primarily produced in Northern Ireland between 2004 and 2007. The NIFTC will invest between £150k-£600k up to a ceiling of 25% of the overall project costs in a live action or animated feature film or a live action or animated television drama single, series or serial where the production can be clearly demonstrated to have a strong cultural relevance to Northern Ireland. Your project needs to be 65% funded to access these monies.

But there are other fiscal bonuses of shooting in Northern Ireland as well. As part of the UK it can be one of the parties of EU co-productions and is especially friendly to arrangements with the Republic of Ireland, such as Section 481. Sale and leaseback is possible as well. In addition, there are smaller grants for animation, company development, going to markets and festivals and much more. There are even grants and loans called MINI budgets for shorts and low budget films that range from £2,500-£30,000. Combine this with experienced crews, discounts on hotels and a production guide with loads of vendors, and Northern Ireland becomes a serious contender as a place to get your film made. Go to their website listed below for applications and requirements or contact them directly.

Northern Ireland Film and Television Commission, 21 Alfred Street, Belfast, BT2 8ED
T: 028 902 32444   F:028 902 39918   www.niftc.co.uk

Christine - Yes, producers should always include a contingency of 10%. Yes, the full contingency is usually used.

Q - Should budgets be padded in each section allowing for any overages?

Christine - No, they should not. Budgets should include a realistic estimate of each cost line. Financiers or completion bonders reviewing budgets will easily identify unnecessary padding. The contingency (above) is to provide for overages on cost lines or unforeseen costs.

Q - What happens about TAX, PAYE, NI on a film and will the producer deal with all of that?

Christine - Yes, or the production accountant can deal with it. They must notify the Revenue office that the film is being produced. The responsibility for the company to make sure that the books and records are kept up to date and that payments are made on time is quite significant. The question is whether the people working on the production are going to be employees or self-employed. The Revenue has published guidelines which should help and it's best to follow them rather than accept somebody's word that they are self-employed. At the end of the day, if you cannot prove that a worker is self-employed, you may be held responsible for their tax and national insurance, plus possible penalties and interest.

Q - What happens with deferred fee films with regard to paying PAYE, TAX and NI contributions to the cast and crew members?

Christine - PAYE and NI contributions will need to be accounted for to cast and crew treated as employees when the deferred fees are paid to cast and crew. They will be tax deductible in the company's accounts as and when you pay them.

Q - Do you deal with sales agents?

Christine - Generally the producer will be dealing directly with the sales agent although, initially, we might advise the producer on the terms of the contract with the sales agent.

Q - What's the easiest type of investment structure to manage?

Christine - Often it isn't up to the producer to decide on the structure, because the investor will pick the route that they think will protect them the most, and also be the most attractive in terms of tax. They may wish to invest under EIS (see above) which means they will have to invest in the company or they may wish to invest via an off shore company or merely to take a share of the film. The best scenario for you as the film producer is for somebody to put the money directly into the business without taking shares in the company, but taking a share of the profits from just one film if possible.

Q - How can a filmmaker keep costs down?

Christine - It is all dependent on day-to-day control and knowing what is going on and ensuring that costs are kept down. If, as is usual, you know that there is a specific amount of money and no more, it's in your interest to keep the costs down.

Q - What does a filmmaker need to do with regard to keeping books?

Christine - It is important to keep proper accounting records. On the simplest level, this can be done on a spreadsheet, recording each cost as it is paid out. The main requirement is to keep proper records for Customs & Excise. It is in the producer's interest to do this, as initially you will be able to reclaim VAT paid on expenses as the film is being made. Usually, you will have a separate company for each film and you should also set up a separate bank account for that company and film. This bank account needs to be reconciled with the accounting records. A simple SAGE accounting system is the best system for your production accountant to use to keep the books of the company.

Q - Is it true you don't need an audit if your turnover is under £5.6 million?

Christine - Yes, it is true, however, your backers and bankers may require an audit.

Q - What is an audit?

Christine - An audit is a review by an external, independent, Chartered Accountant of the accounting records, to check that the figures have not been misstated.

Q - Can a production company be audited at any point?

The Isle of Man Media Development Fund

Located in the Irish Sea, the Isle of Man has become a hot spot of film production due to its varied landscapes, unique architecture and access to experienced crew. But it is the Isle of Mans' favorable financial advantages that have drawn films like On A Clear Day to its shores. The Isle of Man Media Development Fund was established to make available equity investment to film and television productions shooting on the Isle of Man. Investors get up to 25% of the budget as direct equity investment, no upper or lower limits on the amount invested and full assistance in the structuring of budgets. The requirements are that at least 50% of the principal photography must be filmed on the island, at least 20% of the below the line services must be from local services, be otherwise completely funded and have a completion bond in place. Films of a commercial nature and that have sales and distribution in place or at least in strategy will be given top priority.

Applications are available at the Isle of Man website and should be submitted as early as possible so your funds will be in place when you need them. There are no deadlines. You will need to submit along with the application:
- A final draft of the screenplay.
- A long synopsis or treatment.
- Biography or filmography of all key elements including principle cast, producer(s), writer, director and Heads of Departments.
- Full budget incorporating Isle of Man expenditure analysis and where appropriate, expenditure analysis demonstrating British film qualifications.
- Finance structure including principal conditions attached to all investment.

For applications and other helpful info on filming on the Isle of Man, go to: www.gov.im/dti/iomfilm
Tel: 01624 682354   Fax: 01624 682355

TAX GUERILLA FILM MAKER SAYS!

Income Tax: Any and all income is liable to tax. If you operate PAYE then the tax for your employees will be calculated under that system. If you are self-employed, your tax bill will be payable under the self-assessment regime. If you pay taxes at 40%, then you may be required to complete a self-assessment tax return. Failure to submit this return on time may result in penalties.

Corporation Tax: Tax on profits. Where a company makes a taxable profit, corporation tax generally must be paid within nine months of the year end, unless taxable profits exceed £1.5m, when quarterly payments on account will be required. Where a company makes a loss, these losses can be set off against future profits of the same company in the same trade or may be carried back and set off against profits which have been taxed in the previous year. A corporation tax return must be filed within 12 months of the year-end, otherwise penalties will be charged.

Capital Gains Tax: A company will pay corporation tax on chargeable gains accruing during an accounting period. An individual will be chargeable to capital gains tax in respect of chargeable gains accruing to him in a year of assessment after an annual exempt amount for individuals of £8,500 in the year to 5 April 2006.

Accounting Year: This is generally set when you set up a company, but can be changed on application to the Registrar of Companies. For tax purposes, an accounting period generally ends 12 months after the end of the accounting period. Individuals are taxed in the year to 5 April.

There are five categories of National Insurance Contributions:

Class 1 - Primary: paid by employees
Secondary: paid for employees by employers (12.8%)
Class 1A - Paid by employers who provide employees with cars/fuel for private use and other benefits in kind
Class 2 - Paid by people who are self employed (£7.35 per week)
Class 3 - Voluntary contributions
Class 4 - Paid by those whose profits and gains are chargeable to income tax under Schedule D. These are normally paid by self-employed people in addition to Class 2.

If you operate PAYE then the national insurance contributions for your employees will be calculated under that system. As an "employee" you will also have to deduct Class 1 national insurance contributions from your income. However, if you are self- employed (run a partnership not a limited company, or provide your services as freelance), then you will be liable to pay Class 2 National Insurance and Class 4 if your profits and gains are over a certain limit. You may be entitled to 'small earnings exemption' if your net earnings from self-employment are under a certain limit.

Free phone Social Security Telephone No: 0845 741 3355Freephone Social Security Telephone No: 0845 741 3355

FINANCE

Christine - If the company requires an audit, the audit will be carried out at the company's year-end. It is often possible in the first period to make the year-end correspond to the end of production (the first accounting period can be up to 18 months in length).

HM Customs & Excise can send inspectors to inspect your accounting records at any time. You should always keep accounting records (including all invoices and receipts) for 6 years. The Inland Revenue may also instigate enquiries into your accounts.

Q - When does your job end on a production? Do you handle residuals etc?

Christine - The production accountant should handle residuals and all final payments. Our job is to ensure the year-end statutory accounts and corporation tax returns are properly dealt with and filed with the authorities.

Q - Would a high street accountant do as a good a job as a media accountant?

Christine - Probably not. A media accountant will understand how production works and what items can be allowed for tax, etc. The main benefit of a media accountant is the advice they can give in helping to raise and structure finance for films. It would be perfectly acceptable for a high street accountant to prepare the accounting records, look after the payroll and the VAT returns of the company as long as a production accountant was employed during the filming of each production.

Q - So once the film is made and you have a distribution or sales agent, then it's worth going to your accountant to check over the royalty agreements before you sign?

Christine - Having an accountant and lawyer go through all the agreements and documentation can make the difference between getting money and getting no money. For instance, a distributor may try to get you as the producer to pay for all marketing costs. A good accountant or solicitor would make sure that the marketing costs are capped.

Q - How is your time charged?

Christine - By the hour. It is important to use accountants and lawyers who understand the film industry. One thing film producers should always get before any work is carried out is an estimate of fees to be charged.

Q - If you have hired a production accountant separate to the accounting firm, how is their time usually charged on a production?

Christine - Production accountants usually have a daily rate and will estimate how many days are required.

Q - For a film that was budgeted at around £500k, how much should be set aside for accounting?

The Business Plan

GUERILLA FILM MAKER SAYS!

There are a myriad of ways to finance a film, but however you do it, you will need to formalise a plan. In the very first instance, this is a good idea simply because it will force you to confront a number of issues that most people avoid - like, how much is it actually going to cost? Not some vague figure plucked from the ether. Where is that money going to go and when will you need it? You need to know who is going to supply what and at what cost, and when you will need to pay those bills. How much is VATable and when you can reclaim that VAT? Then you will have to ask, when are you going to shoot, and for how long, and can you afford that time and how big is your crew and how are they getting to set and how much will it cost to feed them....? Phew! The list goes on and on. This process in itself can take months, but it is crucial that you fully understand and prepare so that you can get the most out of your opportunity.

Once you have figured all of that stuff out, you need to ask the tough questions like - who will buy this film? Is there a market for it? Are there any precedents that show it can be done? Who is going to be in it? If you ask all of these questions and more, and answer them honestly, you will quickly see why people in the business of money, such as banks and venture capitalists etc., won't touch you and your film with a barge pole. The money you are looking for is from people who believe in you and what you are doing, who are excited by it, and can afford to lose their money if it comes to it.

Once you have immersed yourself in these questions, and many, many others, and for long enough too, you will able to write a business plan very quickly. We urge you NOT to buy a business plan off the shelf or download one and modify it (though you reading one is useful to see how it is structured). The key to the success of your film is not the plan on paper, but the fact that you created the plan and therefore have thought it through.

Your plan should include pages about the film (synopsis, wish cast etc.), your company and who is in it, other data on the current market, why this will be a success, a lengthy plan on how you will make it, when, where and for how much, a cash flow etc. You can include pictures to pep up what could be a dull read too.

On a final note. You are not allowed to offer this document around as an inducement to invest. That would contravene the financial services act*. This is your business plan, but if people wish to loan you money to make your film, and take a share of the profits, then that is something else. And please, at some point, make it VERY CLEAR - you may lose all your money!

*You can put together a prospectus but you will need to work with professionals who are regulated, and it will cost many tens of thousands to do so.

The Enterprise Investment Scheme (EIS)

GUERILLA FILM MAKER SAYS!

A good way to get investors to your project or company is to get them some tax relief for their millions (especially inherited millions!). The government has set up the EIS just for this reason and it is good for risky ventures – like say, film production companies. You need to join the EISA and apply for the scheme (it costs £450). You can get a form and all the relevant details from their website at www.eisa.org.uk. Here's the highlights:

20% (of share subscription) reduction in income tax liability for individuals investing no more than 30%. The minimum subscription is £500 per company and the maximum per investor is £200,000 per annum.

Deferral of gains realised on a different asset, where disposal of that asset was less than 36 months before the EIS investment or less than 12 months after it. Not limited to investments of £200,000 per annum and can be claimed by investors whose interest in the company exceeds 30%. It is available to individuals and trustees. Where gains arise on the EIS investment, taper relief is available . Note that deferral of gains is no longer available by investing in VCTs. (Venture Capital Trusts)

No Capital Gains Tax payable on disposal of shares after three years (after five years for investments made before 6th April 2000) provided the EIS initial income tax relief was given and not withdrawn on those shares.

Helpful hints from the EISA

If you are looking to get investment, the amount you ask for determines whom you should contact.

Less than £50,000: try friends, relations or your local accountants (who may know of somebody wishing to invest in a small company).

£50,000 to £250,000: contact local accountants and the National Business Angels Network (020 7329 4141 for information pack or 020 7329 2929 for enquiries. See also their website on www.bestmatch.co.uk)

£250,000 to £750,000: contact one of www.eisa.org.uk/ Accountancy.html or www.eisa.org.uk/Legal.html members of the EISA.

Over £750,000: contact one of the www.eisa.org.uk/ SponsorsPromoters.html on the list of EISA members. Some sponsors may have a slightly higher bottom limit than this.

A further source of useful information in respect of seeking capital investment is to contact the British Venture Capital Association (Tel: 020 7240 3846 or visit their website on www.bvca.co.uk).

FINANCE

Christine - For advisors in general, including legal, I would suggest 15%. It may seem like a huge amount, but it should ensure that everything is above board and that you, as the producer, have negotiated the best terms and are protected.

Q - What are the most common mistakes that you have encountered?

Christine - Not properly estimating the budget. You should use a production accountant to prepare the budget and include a 10% contingency for unexpected costs. A good production accountant is also worth their weight in gold during the shoot, as they will control costs and prepare all the figures for the film which may be needed for investors' reports or for sale and leaseback deals. Tax, PAYE and VAT are all relatively easy to deal with, and if not dealt with properly, could cause very serious problems. If a producer doesn't wish to deal with these things, get someone in who can.

Q - What advice can you offer to new filmmakers?

Christine - Surround yourself with people who know what they are doing, whether it be cast, crew or professional advisors, they will provide you with a professional approach and advice which should prevent you from appearing too naive as an up and coming producer. Otherwise, there are people out there who will try to rip you off. Although costs will be a problem, make sure you can get every agreement checked before you sign. Lastly, filmmaking is a business which should be run professionally. There is much more to running a company than you may think. It's important to learn and understand just how a small business runs - there are plenty of good books you can get to answer most questions, plus your bank manager should be able to provide help, as can your solicitor and accountant.

Jon Farley
Bank Manager

THE BANK MANAGER

Q - What kind of bank account should a new film maker setup for their business and film?

Jon - A corporate account and not a personal account, so it's a separate entity. It is also usual for each film production to operate through a different corporate entity.

Q - We recommend starting a limited company for a film project. What do the directors of that company (the filmmakers) need to present you with so they can setup a bank account?

Jon - It's standard banking procedure really, so we need a completed application form and to identify and verify the individual(s) running the company.

Q - I'm used to having my personal bank accounts being free of charges. When it comes to running a corporate account, what costs are involved?

Jon - There are the standard banking fees for general money transmission transactions and statements etc. Beyond that, we can offer some discounts on some transactions in certain circumstances. What is important to remember is that you do not pay for time to sit and talk with your bank manager. What we can offer here in Soho Square Barclays Media Team is industry knowledge. We know the people within the industry, we understand things like Gap Finance, Sale and Leaseback, what's happening to Section 48 at the moment etc. We are purely focused on Media - Film and TV are the two largest sectors, but we've also got presence in the music, marketing and publishing industries. We understand what you are talking about, and can sometimes put you in touch with the right players within this industry. This level of expertise is clearly not going to be available from your local bank manager in a typical high street bank. You know that whenever you pick up the telephone to talk to us, you will know the person that you are going to be speaking to. We don't have a call centre mentality. We are geared very much toward the media business and understand its particular needs.

Q - So, I'm fresh out of film school, I've started my Ltd. company, I'm really talented of course, and I come in with my great script and say 'Listen my script's great, give me a hundred grand, I want to make my movie!'

Jon - That's not the business that we are in. To lend money we will need some kind of security, and that there is something tangible behind what you are proposing. So are we in the Gap Finance or Venture Capital business? No. That's not what Barclays offer. However we do have contacts that we could introduce you to, entities that could be prepared to take more of a risk.

Q - Is it a good idea to meet with your bank manager on a regular basis?

Jon - I think that is absolutely essential as communication is very important, and it's essential that we are updated on the current position of the company.

Q - If you have 2 customers, a film-maker and distributor for instance, if you see synergy, do you ever put them together?

Jon - We have done previously, yes. Of course everything is confidential, but if we see two customers who may mutually benefit from each other, we can certainly introduce them.

FINANCE

UK Film Finance Handbook: How to Fund Your Film

GUERILLA FILM MAKER SAYS!

Adam Davies and Nic Wistrich have made a marked improvement on Nic's first book 'Get Your Film Funded'. While the reader won't find any shortcuts or golden tickets to funding your movie, this book does take a detailed look at the jigsaw puzzle of film finance and breaks it down into easy to read chapters including soft money, pre-sales, gap financing and completion bonds. Everything you want to know about tax breaks, sale and leasebacks, and the public grants available to filmmakers are listed here. International funds are listed by country, and there is detailed information on bi and tri-lateral co-productions - knowledge all producers should arm themselves with. The book also includes some short interviews and case studies with various industry figures both in the UK and USA. The directory of funding organisations, listed along with contact details and general guidelines, is a useful addition to this book. Get on the phone now and get some meetings set up. Remember, this book is like a map. It details where they may be gold, but you have to dig, and dig hard and sometimes long. And you may never find gold. But if there is one thing we have learned, the winners are those who keep going.

Rather than lining the pockets of Amazon shareholders or the high street bookshops, try and buy this book direct from the authors. They will benefit significantly, and I am sure the money they make will in part go toward making their films happen. Go to www.ukfilmfinance.com

Q - Just stepping beyond the micro-budget movie... In the film business, when a producer puts a deal together from several sources, rarely will those sources - say a distributor, the film council or through sale and leaseback - stump up all, or even some of the money upfront. The film maker will then get contracts together and take them to someone like you who will loan them the money (based on the contracts) so they can cash flow the film. Is that how it often works?

Jon - All projects are different. But in that case, it would depend on how solid the contracts are. So if the contracts are signed, and there have been pre-agreements, and we've got proof of what the intent is, then certainly we can look at helping.

Q - What common mistakes do you see?

Jon - In the film business, people can be too ambitious too quickly. There is so much that people really need to do to ensure that a script will make it through to the box office. Most of the successful people that we see are the ones that have had the experience of doing it time and again. Sometimes we see brilliant and creative individuals with some excellent scripts, who then fall into pitfalls, such as not having all the finance in place, or assuming they have an actor attached when actually, when it comes to the crunch, they do not.

Q - Producers with very little money tend to bend the truth. You make a bunch of claims in order to get the whole thing to look like it's real, and once it looks like it's real, it's half way there. But if there is one person within the whole process of film-making that you never want to blag, it's the bank manager!

Jon - I agree. It needs to be transparent. It's really important that my managers and the producers are honest with each other, so we know what is coming through, what may happen in the future and if there is anything that may surprise us, then we can factor that in. Problems do occur and if there is poor communication, it makes it more difficult for us to help.

Q - Do you ever read scripts?

Jon - Yes, though we trust our customers to know what they are doing.

Q - So you don't advise them on scene 38, to 'make it tighter or rewrite the dialogue' for instance?

Jon - (laughs) No!

Q - Do you attend markets?

Jon Farley
Area Corporate Director

Media Team
27 Soho Square
London
W1D 3QR

Tel 020 7445 5766 (Direct)
Fax 020 7445 5784

Email: jon.farley@barclayscorporate.com
www.barclays.com

Barclays Bank PLC is authorised and regulated
by the Financial Services Authority.

BARCLAYS

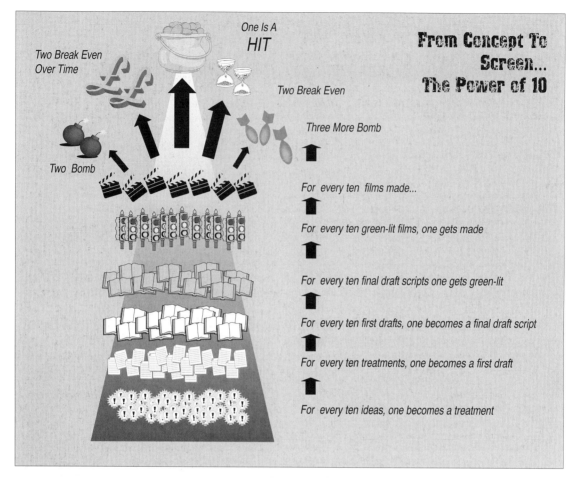

Jon - Yes. For instance in Cannes we have a boat where our customers can come on board to meet us and to meet each other.

Q - So open a Barclays account, in order to take advantage of the free food in Cannes!

Jon - (laughs) We want to make sure people realise that we are specialised within their business and that we take it very seriously. It's an environment where all the key players within the industry are present, and they may come onto a boat, say for one of the parties that we host, and we can then introduce our clients to one another. It's all about bringing people together.

Q - What could a new film-maker do to make your life easier?

Jon - Be professional, up front and honest with us.

Q - What advice would you offer a new film-maker?

Jon - Ensure that you are working with the right people, and you can trust who you are dealing with. Sometimes people fall down because they have been told things that are not true or are speculative. So you need to make sure you have a really solid plan in place, you know exactly what it happening, what's coming through, and that you've got the right people that can really help deliver what you believe in. When trying to attract finance to a project, a lot of people will say *'yeah, that sounds good'*, but then not deliver on what they have said or agreed to. Make sure you are 100% certain that you are able to deliver what you are proposing.

Q - What is a completion guarantee?

Anon - A completion guarantee or bond is an instrument whereby a completion guarantor promises to the providers of the finance for a film that the film will be completed in accordance with the budget, the timescale and the script which they have approved. It is not a guarantee to the producers of the film that those things will happen, it's a guarantee to the providers of the finance, and it's quite an important feature of the completion guarantee that the producers are not able to invoke it or call upon it. The producer will approach us with the script, budget and production schedule. We don't look at material before they have the finance for their film because reviewing the script, budget and schedule is time consuming. Once we've reviewed the material we ask the producers to come in for a meeting where we will ask them to explain particular things in the script that have struck us as being difficult or unusual such as crowd scenes, special effects, action sequences which might be logistically difficult. We'll ask them about locations, who their heads of department would be etc., so we can see whether they are people we know and feel comfortable with. It's at that meeting the producers would be able to give an account of themselves. At some stage we will also need to see the director to satisfy ourselves that he or she is a responsible individual who knows what they are going to do and they are indeed going to do what they say they are going to do. The script should be written clearly so it's apparent how everything that is described is going to be realised. Flowery language and vague generalities of what the producers hope to see on screen should be avoided.

Q - What is the lowest budget you would work with?

Anon - About a £1m. We have done a film for £750k but that is unusual. On the basis of a £1m budget, the guarantee would work out at about 5%. We also require a contingency of 10% of the direct and above and below the line costs in the budget. Very low budget film making carries so many risks that our business would not proffer if we catered for such films.

Q - When is a guarantee called in? If an actor dies? Director is arrested?

Anon - Producers will take out insurance on the cast, negative and other things, so if the lead actor dies, that would be covered by that insurance. If the director is imprisoned it would be our problem and we would take the view that either we would wait for him to come out of prison and reschedule the whole thing or we would get another director in. If a director was very slow we might have to apply pressure and tell him to get on with it, otherwise you're going to replace him. Sometimes this works, but some directors are incapable of working more quickly than the speed at which they are working. Remember, the director has assured us beforehand that he can do it within the allocated schedule so he's going to be aware that he's not keeping to his original agreement.

Q - At what point do you decide to step in?

Anon
Completion Bonds

Anon - We wouldn't usually take action right away because it wouldn't be apparent that there was a terrible problem. If projections showed the film was going to go over schedule by 50% then that would be a serious thing which would have major cost implications. It would almost certainly follow that the director was shooting too much material and we might consider cutting certain things out of the script for which you would probably need the consent of the financiers. If there were a 50% over-run we would probably decide that we wanted to exert more control over expenditure. We would probably have decided that we become counter signatories on cheques so payments are directly controlled by us. At this point we probably wouldn't replace anybody on the production team, although we might send a full time representative to keep an eye on them. We get daily progress reports while they're shooting which tells us things like how much they've shot, how many people were there for lunch etc. On a weekly basis we get reports to show how much money has been spent and how much they are projecting to spend. If the reports are accurate, which we hope they are, then we know where the production is at and can take the view as to whether we need to do anything or not. I don't think we should be regarded as ogres because that's not really how we go about our job. We're usually quite humane about anything that has to be done, even if it's fairly draconian. The producers who work best with us regard us as some sort of consultancy, able to provide advice whenever it's required. Ultimately, we can be relied upon to be there and see that the production gets completed.

Q - What advice would you offer?

Anon - Be absolutely open with us. If they are making a film and perceive anything to be a potential problem they should let us know straight away because we can give our advice to avoid them getting into difficulties. When we give a completion guarantee to financiers we also take direct contractual control over the production company and we do have very sweeping powers to step in to dismiss people, replace producers, or even move in and complete the film ourselves. It's unusual for us to take that step because the producers are often the best people to get the film finished.

FINANCE

Paul Cable
M & E Insurance Services

Q - How much should a low budget producer put in the budget for insurance?

Paul - Every film is different so the producer should call me when they are doing their budget so I can advise them what to allow for. I will ask for certain things, the script, draft shooting schedule, top sheet of the budget, and ask questions like when do you start filming? what is it about? what format are you shooting on? where are you getting your equipment from? any aspects of hazardous filming? I then approach insurance companies for a quote. Hopefully the producer is satisfied with the quote. I then issue an insurance summary, and certificates of insurance so that they can show them to hire companies.

As a bare minimum there are two types of insurance that you legally must have in this country. *Employers Liability* and *Motor Insurance*. *Employers Liability* should provide cover up to £10m *Public Liability* which is not compulsory but very much recommended should be at least £1m, motor insurance, unlimited.

For all policies, the insurers will expect the premium to be paid by first day of principal photography.

If the budget is £100k the producer should take what is called a 'production package'. This includes cover for key people going sick causing delay, the physical material - like the negative - because if you are shooting on neg, the labs won't accept any responsibility for any damage to it. The equipment should be insured on a new for old basis, so you should get an idea of the costings - if you are shooting on 35mm you may be looking at a £1m worth of equipment. You should know that irrespective of whether you are insuring the equipment or not the hire company will charge for 'loss of use' which is their loss of hiring charges during the period that their equipment is being repaired or being replaced. You need replacement values for props, sets and wardrobe. You need to know where you keep the equipment overnight. A major exclusion for all insurance companies is 'mysterious disappearance', so if you do have a claim call the broker straight away. Most of these covers run through the entire production right up to completion. An area we must discuss is hazardous filming, which includes filming from boats, aerial photography, pyrotechnics, use of animals, anything that could be construed as hazardous.

Q - A new film maker may just assume that "shot of man punching another man" is just part of the story, but it might be a red flag for you?

Paul - Yes, that is why it's useful to have a copy of the script, to spot the potential hazards and ask the producer things like *are you using a stunt co-ordinator for this fight scene?*

Q - Who would you normally liase with on a film?

Paul - I would initially deal with the producer, then the production manager.

Q - Low budget film producers are used to blagging to get everything cheaply, but insurance should not be one of those areas?

Insurance Types

GUERILLA FILM MAKER SAYS!

Employers Liability
This insurance is required by law, and protects employees from accident or damages.

Public Liability
This insurance is required by law, and protects the public from accident or damages.

Negative Insurance
This insures your master negative / Tapes during production and post. It will be cheaper not to bother and take the risk.

Equipment Insurance
This insures equipment hired from loss or damage, and lost hire charges. You won't get kit out of the door without this. Sometimes it's cheaper to buy your insurance from the equipment hire company, esxpecially for short jobs such as re-shoots.

Motor Insurance
Understand the implications of not having commercial insurance for your drivers. If they have an accident with your cast in the car for instance, you may not be covered.

Other Insurance
This insures against other potential losses, from stunts and action, to lost props or damaged locations.

FINANCE

Paul - Once someone lied about their budget, they said it was £300k and it was actually £2.5m. There was a claim and the insurer declined. The relationship with your broker is one of trust, as your broker can only support you if you tell him the truth.

Q - So a claim on insurance is based on the cost of production per day?

Paul - If your processing and running costs are as little as £500 a day and you are having to pay the first £500 under a negative insurance policy then maybe there is little need in insuring the negative. Obviously you still have the post production process where the negative could be damaged. Public Liability which you have to have, is about £250. Most equipment suppliers will insist that the producer has an insurance policy for their kit. There is also Errors and Omissions insurance which covers you for libel, slander, defamation, breach of contract, plagiarism. On major films this insurance would be in place from the first camera day, this is to give injunctive relief against somebody saying this film was my idea and bringing an action against the film producer. Clearly on micro budget films this won't be possible, but you may have to take out a policy in order to give the film to a sales agent at the end. You should always get legal advice about Errors and Omissions because it is dependent on the subject matter. The problem is that it is expensive, and the premiums range between $2.5k to as much as $15k.

Q - If you lose the free camera from Arri Media into the deep blue sea, how long would it take for an insurance claim to go through?

Paul - You should call me straight away, which is very important, and tell me how long it will take to get a replacement camera and how long this would affect the filming. If people are going abroad and they have little money and cannot afford back-up cameras I always ask them to find out how long it would take to get a replacement camera out to wherever they are. This becomes part of the insurance policy. If I have to engage the services of a loss adjuster this may take as little as two weeks but it is subject to how much invoice documentation the company gives you. If hire companies can receive confirmation from you that the claim is covered they will re-hire you new equipment.

MEDIA and ENTERTAINMENT INSURANCE SERVICES LTD
Walnut Tree House, Bickley Park Road
Bromley, Kent BR1 2AY

PAUL CABLE
Director

Tel: 020 8467 8455/77
Fax: 020 8467 8481
Mobile 07977409520
Email pdc-media@netway.co.uk

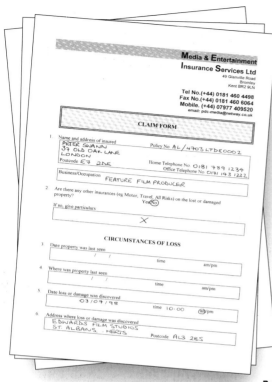

Q - What is the difference between an insurance policy and a completion guarantee?

Paul - A completion bond is there at the requirement of the financier to make sure that the film is completed. The completion bond will cover what is not covered by the production insurance.

All completion bond companies are concerned with any exclusions. We could have an elderly cast member who has a cardiovascular problem which the insurance company won't cover. The completion bond company will want to know that because if that actor does suffer a heart attack, they pick up any losses. They are there to pick up where the insurance company doesn't.

Q - What happens if mid-shoot the writer decides to change the ending of the main actor driving off into the sunset, to a helicopter chase, and the Producer neglected to inform the insurers?

Paul - If this resulted in a claim, my reaction would be that the insurance company would decline to pay.

Q - What about dangerous things like explosions and weapons? Does a stuntman come with his own insurance?

Paul - They sometimes have their own insurance. I will ask who the stunt person is, whether they are on the registry of stunt personnel, what their qualifications are etc. If a stunt person does not have insurance and the stunt goes wrong and people are injured, it is the production company's responsibility. It is also a legal requirement in this country to have a Health and Safety person. PACT has Health and Safety guidelines, and there are many Health and Safety advisors in the field.

Q - What are the common mistakes that you have experienced?

Paul - People often ring around other insurance companies for quotes to save £10 and these companies may not be aware of the film business. Then they phone me in distress because they have needed to make a claim and the company won't pay up, because the insurance was not suited to their needs, just so that they could save £10. I get calls about props or equipment damage when the production stopped filming three months ago, I need to know as soon as it is discovered.

Q - What could a new film maker do to make your life easier?

Paul - Have the conversation with me at the budgetary stage. Then contact me at least three days before filming. Tell me everything, the more that I know the easier it is to insure. So they may find the first conversation a rather painful process, but like other brokers I have things like insurance guides which explain all the types of cover that are available. Give me enough time to sort it out.

FINANCE

Q - What is the FilmFour Lab?

Peter - It doesn't really exist as a separate entity any longer - it's more a state of mind! The Lab is the film arm that carries Channel 4's values - ie. working with distinctive and forward-looking film-makers with an emphasis on UK talent. And generally on more modest budgets than before. There was also a risk that Lab films could become ghettoised, seen as not 'proper' films. So now we just have a single slate of films. As Head of FilmFour Lab, I work across the slate, providing a different perspective and taste to Tessa Ross, Head of FilmFour at whatever budget level. But we are still committed to the work of new visionary directors. We're committed to making low-budget films work. We're committed to fresh ways of looking at the world through cinema and to diverse and unexpected stories. And we're committed to different approaches to film-making - genre-bending, poetic, improvised - whatever works to tell that story as vibrantly as possible. And in that sense, the ethos of the Lab lives on.

Q - What kind of projects are you looking for?

Peter - All the projects we get involved with aim, to a varying degree, to be contemporary, smart and distinctive, and are more often than not director-led. At the higher budgets they're mainstream, classy with a top end cast - adaptations of the best contemporary literature for example. At the lower budget we look for clever use of genre to reflect today's warped and strange reality; to films which make an impact with their subject matter and approach. Horror and comedy work well for us, but only if the genre is being given a new twist. Films with fresh eyes on the world and fresh ways of storytelling, perhaps from documentarists moving into fiction, from theatre creators, from fine artists, or simply from the best new film directors.

Q - Are you looking for filmmakers who already have experience behind them either as a feature or a short?

Peter - Both at feature level. For 'Lab-type' films we welcome new directors (although they should be able to demonstrate their ability as directors) or more experienced directors branching out into new ways of working. For shorts, we have the Cinema Extreme scheme we run with UK Film Council for new directors who are a step away from their first feature - one of last year's Cinema Extreme's 'Wasp' won the Oscar for best short film. We don't really finance unsolicited shorts anymore - it doesn't make sense. But we will occasionally finance a short as part of developing a feature where the director needs to try out or prove a different vision or way or working.

Peter Carlton
Film Four Lab

FILMFOUR

PETER CARLTON HEAD OF FILMFOUR LAB

Direct Line +44 (0)20 7306 8071
Direct Fax +44 (0)20 7306 8368
For submissions www.4producers.co.uk
pcarlton@channel4.co.uk

 Channel Four Television Corporation
124 Horseferry Road, London SW1P 2TX +44 (0)20 7396 4444

Q - What kind of budgets are you working with? How are projects submitted?

Peter - This year, budgets were between £500k and £7m. We have an on-line submissions system at www.4producers.co.uk. We get about 40 submissions a week. We have 60 films actively in development and between 6 and 8 a year go into production. At the low budget end it's probably two or three a year.

Q - Do the films get a cinema release or are they intended for the FilmFour Channel and Channel 4?

Peter - Everything we do is intended for cinema exhibition in the first instance. Even our low budget films we expect to have an identifiable audience. Think of it like the music industry. Hollywood mainstream is Kylie; low-budget Lab films are garage or techno re-mixes.

Q - How long does it take for a script that you take on to reach either completion or the cinema?

Peter - Very hard to say - some things can be in development for several years - three to five years from start to premier is not unusual. But there've been some low-budget projects that we've put into production within weeks of the first pitch

Q - What mistakes do you see new filmmakers making?

Peter - They don't ask themselves 3 simple questions: 'Why am I making this now?', 'Why would anyone want to go and see it?', and 'Why should the person I've sent it to want to finance it?'

Q - What advice would you offer a new filmmaker?

Peter - Be passionate about the film you want to make. Then ask yourself why you want to do it, ask everyone you know whether it's any good, ask people in the industry to find out where, if anywhere, your project might find a place. Be very honest with yourself about whether you would turn out on a wet Wednesday night to go and see your film rather than Spiderman 3. Then be very passionate about getting that film made.

Paul Trijbits
The UK Film Council

THE UK FILM COUNCIL

Q - What is the UK Film Council?

Paul - The UK Film Council is the organisation that the British government set up five years ago to bring all aspects relating to film under one roof. That means production, development, distribution, exhibition, marketing, education - every single thing relating to film. We are also responsible for the BFI, which looks after film archiving and education and the promotion of cinema culture. The UK Film Council was set up as a strategic organisation to help the government determine and execute its policies on all those aspects. In addition, we bring to government key issues relevant to the development of the industry. And the other part of the UK Film Council, which is what I am in part responsible for, is to physically execute the tasks set by the Council's board of directors. So we have a development fund, two production funds, - Premiere and New Cinema - and a range of funding schemes run by our Distribution and Exhibition Department that focus on audience development. The annual budget of The UK Film Council is about £60m. £20m comes from what we call grant in aid, so that is pure subsidy. £33m or so comes from the Lottery. And the balance comes from the income from the portfolio of films that The UK Film Council has invested in (or previous incarnations such as British Screen). The Premiere Fund is £8m a year, the New Cinema Fund has £5m a year and the Development Fund has £4m a year. You need to be a distributor to get funding from the specialised distribution fund and as a producer or film maker you can get money from either the development fund or the two production funds, the Premiere Fund or the New Cinema Fund.

Q - How does the Development Fund work?

Paul - It is split into two major parts. The first, which is two thirds of that £4m, is spoken for by the development slate partnerships that have been awarded earlier this year. There are seven of them. They are groupings of producers, distributors, sales agents and broadcasters.

Q - So it is similar to the Hollywood studio system where you are better off going to production companies in order to access the funding?

Paul - Yes it is similar, in so far as the development slate partnerships are concerned. However, the final third of the money is set aside for people, including writers, to go directly to the development fund and on a creative level convince the fund that their project has potential. . All the funds work separately. So you have the opportunity to seek funding from any or all of the funds on the same project, but not at the same time for obvious reasons.

Q - What is the difference between the New Cinema Fund and the Premiere Fund?

Paul - If you are making a film that is aiming itself at the marketplace in all its glory, then you go to the Premiere Fund. If you want to hit the marketplace but the risk of getting there is disproportionately high, eg maybe you are a first time film maker, then you would come to the New Cinema Fund.

Q - Would a new film maker approaching the New Cinema Fund give you a treatment or synopsis?

Paul - We are a production fund (New Cinema) and we do not develop. You would go to the Development Fund for that. The money that we have splits itself as follows. We spend about £1m a year on short programmes and pilots and the rest goes to individual films - about eight or nine a year. A sizeable amount of films that we support do get made. That alone is tough enough to do without having to develop ideas from scratch.

Q - If you submit and idea to the Development Fund will they send it on to the various slate partnerships to take a look?

Paul - Yes. You will have the development fund executives here looking at it as well as the slate companies. The consortia of companies have an obligation to spend 30% of their money as matching funds to projects that come from third party producers via the UK Film Council. So in fact you have seven doors you can knock on that have extended development funds. Another thing for people to know is that in addition to the UK Film Council, each of the regions have mini-Film Councils, which are the screen agencies and they all have to a varying degree production and development funds and general support available. So the first thing to do if you are a budding film maker is to look at your regional screen agency. They may not have production money necessarily, but they may have training money or career development support so that you have a working knowledge of what you are doing and asking for when you come to us. Also, it may be more appropriate if you are based in Birmingham or Manchester or wherever to use your local film agency to develop your project to a certain level so that it is of interest to us and or the BBC or FilmFour or another potential funder.

Q - If a producer or film maker has a script and maybe some interest from actors, what happens next?

Paul - You have to apply and you can get the application form from our website (www.ukfilmcouncil.org.uk) or by contacting us directly. It asks for a lot of information about budgets and finance, but frankly in the first instance that is not what we judge it on. The judgment process begins with the reading of the scripts. It is read by one of us here, either me or one of my execs, and by an outside reader simultaneously. So the first judgement is an subjective creative one on the script and then we look at the work of the director. We get about 300 projects a year and eight get a 'yes' so there is about a 96% rejection rate. A large portion of projects are simply not good. They are under-developed, have no distinct voice of their own, and if they are in a genre, they are not even B films, they are C or D films and that is not what we do. I am constantly surprised that people do not look to see what we have done in the past. Yes, we have done a wide range of films such as slightly more mainstream comedies such as *Anita And Me* to more art house pieces as *Body Song* to feature documentaries such as *Touching The Void* or *The Magdalene Sisters*, which is a more socially oriented film. Not all of our films fulfil their potential, but they do all have one thing in common, which is, they all have something to say. And we get submitted a fair number of films that have very little to say.

Q - If you like a project, what happens?

Paul - The next thing that happens is that we would bring you in for a meeting with your director or producer and start the process. We have yet to see a project where we think it is so great that the money is given to you and you are shooting straight away. Normally, we or the film maker or both think that the film needs to be developed further. And then generally we are involved in getting the rest of the funding for the project, so we are very involved. In fact, in some instances we really do act like an executive producer, helping the film making team put the film together. We end up putting in 20% - 25% of the budget and the complete budgets of films we are involved in, usually are between £1.5m and £2.5m.

Q - Where does the balance of the budget come from?

Paul - Broadcasters typically. So BBC Films or FilmFour. Rarely ITV. An element will be tax related such as sale and lease back. Sometimes we will get money from a foreign sales agent for a small advance or a domestic release. Co-productions too. So broadly we put up 25%, the broadcaster puts up 25%, the tax break is worth about 15% and it is the last bit that is the toughest to find, particularly for the kind of films we do. It can get very complicated. Ken Loach is very good example. He has built up a good network over the years and on his last film which we co-funded , *The Wind That Shakes The Barley*, I believe it had 16 different financing partners on it. The

UK FILM | COUNCIL

10 Little Portland Street
London W1W 7JG
Tel: +44 (0)20 7861 7870
Fax: +44 (0)20 7861 7866
www.ukfilmcouncil.org.uk

Paul Trijbits
Head of the New Cinema Fund

FINANCE

THE DCMS

GUERILLA FILM MAKER SAYS!

The Department of Culture, Media, and Sport (DCMS) was set up in 1997 to control Government policy on many subjects that will improve life in the UK through cultural and sporting activities. Included in these subjects the DCMS is responsible for setting policy on UK film culture and industry issues including sponsorship of the UK Film Council and the National Film and Television School, Training in the film industry, certification of British films including co-productions, and takes the lead for the UK in the EU Media Program with the Skills Investment Fund which is administered by Skillset.

In December, 2005, a new tax relief code came into effect for investors of films determined to be British. The new rate of tax relief for low budget films (films budgeted up to £20 million) will be a net 20%. For big budget films (£20 million and above), the rate will be a net 16%. Both rates apply to the UK spend of a film's budget, capped at 80%. Films will be determined British via a point system test that is made up of three parts. A film qualifies if it scores 16 points or more out of 32.

Section A: Cultural Content
A1 Set wholly/mainly in the UK: 1 point
A2 Principal characters British nationals or residents: 1 point
A3 Based on British subject matter or underlying material: 1 point
A4 Dialogue in the English Language (inc official regional or minority languages of the UK) 1 point
Total: 4

Section B: Cultural Hubs Must be in the UK
B1 Studio and/or location shooting: 6 points
B2 Visual effects: 4 points
B3 Special effects: 1 point
B4 Music recording: 2 points
B5 Audio post production: 1 point
B6 Laboratory processing: 1 point
Total: 15

Section C: Cultural Practitioners Must be British or EEA nationals/residents
C1 Director: 2 points
C2 Scriptwriter: 2 points
C3 Producer: 1 point
C4 Composer: 1 point
C5 Principal actors: 2 points
C6 Majority of cast: 1 point
C7 Key Staff (cinematographer, production designer, costume designer, editor, sound designer, VFX supervisor, principal make up/ hair): 3 points
C8 Majority of crew: 1 point
Total: 13

Total points for Sections A, B, C: 32

SCENE 24 TAKE

closing document that we had, had a list of nine pages with different contractual parties that needed to be signed!

Q - How does the UK Film Council get its money back?

Paul - We are different from other funding bodies inside and outside of the UK because our money is equity money. It is not a straight grant subsidy and our standard position is that we recoup our money pro-rated pari pasu, which means we recoup with any other equity investor at the same time. The reason for that is that the money that flows back to us is used to fund training programs and things like that. The Premiere Fund makes back about 75% of its money and the New Cinema Fund makes back about 35%.

Q - Typically, what are the weaknesses of the projects that come to you?

Paul - Most of the time they are underdeveloped. And I understand that. Before I did this I was producer, and sometimes you just want to get going on a project. I think there is often an error in judgement in the type of material chosen. Case in point, 90% of the material we get is drama. Drama is something that most people do not go to the cinema for. They want to see comedy, a horror, a thriller, a comedy or a documentary. Drama, more than likely, belongs on television. So if you are going to present a drama and it doesn't really have a heart or a real story to tell, I think you really are struggling from the start. Struggling to convince a funder ultimately. Struggling to convince a distributor. And having a distributor is one of the key things we consider whey getting involved in a film. Struggling to get your audiences.

Q - Do you think writers don't do enough to put their characters through hell?

Paul - Yes. A lot of what I see is bland. It comes from a good place and a good heart, but that is not sufficient. If I go to the cinema it will probably cost me £50-£60. I have a young child, so I have to get a baby sitter. I will buy two tickets for me and my wife and we might have a bite to eat. That is a lot of money. When you come up with an idea, you have to think if it will get your family and

Q - What is your job?

Jenny - I run the Development Fund here at the UK Film Council. We get between 1,500 and 2,000 submissions per year. That number has stayed quite level over the years.

Q - Even though there is a perceived burst in the industry with DV and now HD?

Jenny - We haven't noticed here. It has remained consistent. We have a completely open door policy. For instance, within the Development Fund, the minimum that you can apply to us with is a treatment of between 8-12 pages. Though you would have had to put in significant amounts of work to get your 12-page treatment or your pitch document for it to be considered. I find it surprising that we have never had a submission for development that actually takes the form of something that has been shot. We are always getting scripts and the director's reel, as a demonstration of how they can do work or how they did previous work that they had done.

Q - Of the material that gets submitted, how much of it can you discount immediately as being not up to standard?

Jenny - If you want to get a piece of work taken seriously here, you have to get through several hurdles. First off you have to get through an independent reader, who is a trained script reader, and is looking at a huge number of scripts, probably for us, probably working for other companies as well. Their knowledge of the general standard is very high - they are looking for a notion of, 'Ok the script might not be perfect, obviously this is the development time, but the idea is strong or there is something in it, we can work with it'. Then it is read internally. If you make it past an executive's read here, then you must sit in a room with an executive - perhaps many times - and actually make good what you have suggested in your script or treatment. So that is three quite significant hurdles you have to get over before you are even thinking about accessing money to move things forward. On average, we have 120 projects in development here, but we don't come close to putting 120 scripts into development each year. So to answer your initial questions, we can discount about 96%-98% of what is submitted almost immediately. And just about every time, it is because the central idea of the script is not strong enough.

Q - Do you think it is fair to say that a lot of new filmmakers underestimate how much work goes into a screenplay that is worth making?

Jenny - Compared to young filmmakers in the States, UK filmmakers level of preparedness for the amount of work that they are going to have to do and their level of preparedness when they present something to you when they are asking you to fund it is significantly lesser. People don't do enough homework. Homework on the idea, so they really know what it is they are proposing, they work on the pitch and on how they are going to

Jenny Borgars
UK Film Council

sell it to you. Homework on the knowledge of how they are going to move it forward, through the development, through to financing. Homework on the notion of where it fits within an audience demographic. What are the like-minded films and what have they done at the box office? All of those notions are going to build a picture to you as the financier, to say 'this is why we want to invest...' Not just in this idea, but in the person, or the team.

Q - As you are government funded, do you think that filmmakers perceive you as only funding arty or alternative films and then tailor their presentation to that angle?

Jenny - I think there are a few myths that you are talking about there. Some of them are genuine and some need to be knocked on the head. I think there is a history associated with public funding. The previous remit for public funding in the UK was the notion of if it is commercial, the commercial sector will fund a film, why does public money need to be in it?

Lottery funding shifted this way of thinking and the UK Film Council was created. Although you still absolutely need to have a very robust argument as to why public funds are being invested, the notion of additionality is not the strongest tenant by which we work. I think you judge an organisation or a piece of public funding also by its output. It is interesting because this is the place that on one level has Gosford Park, Mike Bassett: England Manager, and The Constant Gardener on one level, and Touching the Void, The Magdalene Sisters and Bullet Boy, on the other. Some fit into the art-house niche, and some fit into a commercial niche. Within the Development Fund, it started at around 40% to 50% drama. Now our slate is probably 10%-15% drama and the rest are projects that fit within genre, or are crossed in genre.

Q - Considering that 2,000 projects go through your net every year, what are the reasons that films fail? What are the common weaknesses within the work you see?

Jenny - I don't think you can even limit it to the weaknesses in writing the script. The main weakness is in the idea. Is the idea going to appeal? Always consider when you talk about it, do people get engaged. Not reading the script, just when talking. That is always a good barometer. Then you have got to get that script to as high a level of quality as possible. The volume of films that get made here, the way that films are put together with patchwork financing, the fact that you don't really have the strong pull of distribution or someone who is saying 'we need to fill a certain gap, in a certain niche', creates an environment that is not particularly conducive to growing a generation of superb screenwriters.

So often when you are working with writers, everyone is on a learning curve because there simply are not enough successful films made out of the UK to say 'here is a model, let me follow it, here is a methodology, let me grab it'. I think there are a lot of other factors that can hamper those films. Let's say you've got the great idea and you get the great script, but then you also hit inherent bottlenecks within the industry. It is incredibly difficult to get a cast that means anything to the outside world or to financiers. It is incredibly difficult to attach a director that means anything. The budgets for films in the UK are still way too high to really justify the case for why they need to be made, and if you don't have those other two elements, it is tough to engage financiers. This is one of the reasons why we devised the new version of slate funding that we put in place earlier this year, where producers link hands with distributors and sales agents from a much earlier stage of a project. This hopefully offers us the best chance of trying to unblock some of those bottlenecks, because you've got experience plus the market being brought to bear on the material. Also significant amounts of development money can be there to make sure you can hire the best talent to make it move forward. It is starting to work.

Q - Even when they have shot the film, should new film makers continue writing the script through editing, or re-write for re-shoots?

Jenny - Absolutely, because the beauty of being able to do things in a relatively cheap way, and to shoot fast if you like, is that you can rebuild from the end backwards if you like. More and more we are thinking about that here, whether it is useful to preserve more money in the financing process for the potential of re-shooting and any of those kinds of things that are going help build up something that shows promise.

Q - Do you think a filmmaker who has already made one film has a greater chance of succeeding?

Jenny - I am always going to say, 'the project has got to be fabulous', but let's take it that the idea is great. This industry, as you know, is obsessed with what is hot. What is at the top. Anything you can do to build a case for the fact that you are the new hot thing, or you have got the magic key is going to help your case. If you are smart enough to have made something - a very low budget short, a longer piece, a trailer - that is shouting that out, then as long as you have got a good next idea and you don't have an awful script or pitch or whatever, that is going to help your cause. Hopefully, the lessons learned will help your cause.

Q - How important is getting the title of your film right?

Jenny - I wish I knew how to do titles. Coming up with that snappy title is a skill in itself. In genre films it becomes hugely important. We have a number of horror films shooting at the moment and they all seem to be one-word titles: *Severance*, *Wilderness*. We are going to do one called *Exposure*. Whether that is a trend or a right thing I don't know, but I think with genre in particular you want to brand it clearly. I think that is why the title might change during distribution, so the public knows what they are getting.

Q - Do you talk to writers about the importance of key art?

Jenny - It is a serious thing to think about what the poster is and somewhat try and work backwards from that. It is a good to get people thinking.

Q - What common mistakes do you see?

Jenny - Ideas that are not strong enough. Thinking that the only way to create drama is to look at grim and depressing subject matter. Thinking that is the only place where real conflict lies. Not thinking through who is going to see it. You can't say 'this is a teen film but I want it to appeal to 12 year olds and 25 year olds... as a result, I can't market to anybody!' Really trying to understand where it fits by looking at what else is out there, what you are up against.

Q - What advice would you give a filmmaker who, despite receiving a 'no thanks, we will pass' from you, wants to go out and re-mortgage his house to make the film anyway?

Jenny - Don't stop working on the screenplay. In the same way, if you are fully financed don't stop working on it. Understand why you are doing it - is it going to be a calling card? A calling card that is going to get me my first proper film gig? Or, is it because you're going to get this film distributed and it is going to be a hit in it's own right? Whatever it is, tailor what you are doing to fit that niche. Look at models of other films that have been made at similar budget levels here and in the US to see what you can achieve for a relatively low amount of money. You are still in an incredibly competitive world, so ensure that you know what you are up against and start thinking about how you are going to feed the pipeline.

UK FILM | COUNCIL

10 Little Portland Street
London W1W 7JG
Tel: +44 (0)20 7861 7937
Fax: +44 (0)20 7861 7862

Jenny Borgars
Head of the Development Fund

www.ukfilmcouncil.org.uk

friends to spend £50-£60 to sit through it. We will never make *Harry Potters* and *Lord of the Rings*. That is studio fare. But look at the films that do get made that do have something to say, such as *The Magdalene Sisters*. It is a real social injustice and when you come out you want to go and do something about it. Or they will tell their friends it was an amazing story and you have to go see it. Same with *Touching the Void*. Even if in your film very little happens, people have to feel compelled to keep watching.

Q - What kind of timescales are involved from the first meeting to going into production?

Paul - Well, it is a bit like how long is a piece of string, but the interesting thing is that, officially, we turn everything around in eight weeks, but really it is in three to four weeks. There is no point in making people wait unnecessarily. If it is not right for us, just say so and don't make people wait around or fill out a whole bunch of paperwork. Beyond that, the average time for everything is around six to nine months when you get to the start of your film.

Q - Is it helpful to include supplemental materials such as storyboards or design artwork with your proposal?

Paul - It is helpful especially if it really gets across what you want to convey. With the New Cinema Fund we don't only look at things that are in script form. We have gone ahead with films that have been developed in workshops. Mike Figgis' *Timecode* was written as sheet music for instance. And since we have a large array of genres and styles that we fund, this can be really helpful. I heard someone criticise us by saying, '*The problem with the UK Film Council's New Cinema Fund is that they don't know what they want. Look at all these different films they have funded*' I take that as a compliment. Our role is to be involved in a wide range of film types.

Q - What advice would you give someone approaching you for funding?

Paul - Do your homework. Then after you have done your homework, ask what is the next bit of homework you should do. Just bringing in your script is too simplistic, and the chance of it going through is slim. Look at the region in which you live and see if there is any work you could do on it there before you submit it to us, either in development or on your own. Look at the type of films we, the local agencies, BBC, Channel 4 generally support. Does your project fit into this? If you have little or no experience into the financial budgeting side of things, find someone who does. Your project may be interesting, but it may be utterly over-budgeted or utterly under-budgeted, which makes it economically non-viable. Some people have tried to make a film for £500k and it fell under the radar, but as soon as it was raised to £1.5 million, it looked like a proper film and it got made. And vice versa. Making a £4 million film where chances are the person who puts up the money will lose half, is not a good proposition. Read *The Guerilla Film Makers Handbook* from beginning to end as a start and then read it again to make sure you understand everything! Ask difficult questions that you may not want to know the answer to, eg Am I really talented? That is a good question to ask yourself. Consider your position. You may not be a writer-director. You may be brilliant at one or the other or you may be a brilliant producer, but not a writer. One of the things we do is try to get writers and directors working together because it's hard to be good at both and nearly impossible to be a good producer as well.

Q - How much success is down to just working very, very hard?

Paul - If you don't persevere, then the myriad of obstacles in the road will make your project go by the wayside. However, I think people have gotten very confused when they hear that it took someone ten years to make a film. Take Saul Zaentz, for example. People forget that he owns a hugely successful jazz record label, which makes him $millions a year, and that allows him to pursue his material. And if you've been hearing '*no*' for five years on something, then maybe something is wrong with you or your project. People never want to face their own subjectivity and that is a huge issue.

FINANCE

Co-Productions Rough Guide

GUERILLA FILM MAKER SAYS!

A good way to get money for your film is to enter into a co-production with one or more companies from other countries. You may have to shoot or edit overseas or use a certain percentage of actors, writers and directors from those specific countries to qualify, but you can fund a significant portion of your film by doing so. At present, the UK has entered into seven bilateral film co-production agreements (Australia, Canada, France, Germany, Italy, New Zealand and Norway) and has 37 under the European Convention on Cinematographic Co-Production agreement. These are constantly being updated as new countries enter into treaties in the UK - China is perhaps the next most significant player! One other thing to consider, in some treaties countries from outside the agreements (like the United States) may participate as long as they do not contribute more than 30% of the total production cost.

UK's bi-lateral treaty partners	Minimum contribution	TV & Video	Provision for co-producers from other country/ies	Provision for financial only participation	Studio and Labs	Provision for nationals from non-co-producing countries
Australia	30%	Yes	Yes	No	Normally majority country	Performers on a restricted basis
Canada	40% for bi-lateral projects #	Yes	Yes	No	Most in majority country	Lead artists
France	40% for bi-lateral projects #	No	Yes	Yes	Most in majority country	Lead artists; principal directors
Germany	UK 30% Germany 20%	No	No	No	Most in majority country	Lead artists; Writers if script completed and acquired before application for approval
Italy	40% for bi-lateral projects #	No	Yes	Yes	Most in majority country	Lead artists and principal directors
New Zealand	20%	Yes	Yes	No	Most in majority country	Performers
Norway	20%	No	No	No	Normally in majority country	Lead artists
European Convention on Cinematographic Co-production	20% for bi-lateral projects; 10% for multi-lateral, with the exception of Denmark & Iceland**	No	Yes	Yes 20%-25% for bi-lateral; 10%-25% for multi-lateral	In the states which are partners in the co-production, proportional to their investment	Creative, technical and craft team, artistic personnel and cast

Source UK Film Council

General rules for European Convention Co-productions:

The Convention requires that each co-producer must share in the total production cost. For multi-lateral co-productions each co-producers financial contribution must be a minimum of 10% and a maximum of 70% of the total production cost of the film. If it is a bi-lateral co-production, the minimum is 20%. Except in the case of finance-only co-producers, each co-producer must have an "effective technical and artistic participation" in the film, in proportion to their investment. Finance-only participation is permitted from one or more minority co-producers provided that each such participation is not less than 10% and not more than 25% of the total production cost of the film. DCMS approves 'finance only' participation by exception, where the UK producer is unable to make a filmmaking contribution. DCMS generally expects the UK producer to involve UK facilities e.g. studio, locations, cast and crew.

The members of the European Convention:

Albania, Andorra, Armenia, Austria, Azerbaijan, Belgium, Bosnia and Herzegovina, Bulgaria, Croatia, Cyprus, Czech Republic, Denmark, Estonia, Finland, France, Georgia, Germany, Greece, Hungary, Iceland, Ireland, Italy, Latvia, Liechtenstein, Lithuania, Luxembourg, Malta, Moldova, Monaco, Netherlands, Norway, Poland, Portugal, Romania, Russia, San Marino, Serbia & Montenegro, Slovakia, Slovenia, Spain, Sweden, Switzerland, The Former Yugoslav Republic of Macedonia, Turkey, Ukraine, UK.

PRE PRODUCTION

Geoff Stanton
Brinskill Management

ACTORS AGENT/ MANAGER

Q - What is the job of an actors agent?

Geoff - To promote and nurture the career of an actor. Ideally from drama school through to old age. It's very much a partnership.

Q - On a day to day basis, what does your job entail?

Geoff - Most of an agent's day is spent on the phone, literally for 7½ hours of the day! We are trying to find out what is going on in theatre, film and television as far as jobs are concerned, so we make sure we are on top of all the important productions. If we find something appropriate, we submit our clients that are available to the Casting Director and then follow up to try to persuade them to put our ideas through to the director. Of course, we prioritise by pushing the clients we think have a realistic chance of getting the job. Beyond this, there's the logistical work such as arranging meetings and auditions as well as administrative work. We have clerical staff who update all the CVs, photographs and video clips etc. I also meet with our clients frequently, not least for the contact, but to see if they've changed physically, and if we need to address that in terms of their photographs.

Q - What are some of the differences between Personal Management and straight Agency?

Geoff - Personal management companies tend to be more hands-on with the client, nurturing them and helping them decide which options to take. We give a lot of advice. For example, not necessarily taking the highest paid jobs, in order to take the one that is going to do the best thing for their career. This is because we tend to have less clients per representative. The larger agents would, I suspect, not be wanting to talk to you unless you are going to increase their profits right away.

Q - Should a new film maker be worried that their projects are going to be given less attention until they have established themselves as a well known director?

Geoff - I think there is a popular misconception that we are all cutthroat. The way we approach a film-maker, whatever the budget, is to first of all ask what do we think of the project? After that, we see if it is a vehicle for any of our youngsters. I'll give you an example, we have a young director Mark Murphy, who is doing a film and has just cast one of our clients in the lead. It's not primarily because he's our client that Mark chose him, but actually because he's not got much time and our person was the right actor. He's going to see a couple of other clients as well, in smaller parts, but he's also going with other agencies' clients. We do this not because he's our client and we are doing him a favour - that is counterproductive. If we put a good client into a bad film, it does nobody any favours. You've still got a bad film at the end of the day. We are genuinely very flexible, if someone hasn't got any money, and the project is worthy, then we will put everything into it. We also find that actors don't forget where they've came from and may want to do smaller pictures when they get more established. Billy Boyd is a good example of an actor who has gone on to make major feature films, but still wants to look at smaller projects because that's what gave him the platform in the beginning.

Q - How should a producer approach you if they are wanting to cast a film?

Geoff - So much is done by e-mail now, that's the best approach for us. It should include an introductory paragraph, a brief synopsis (no more than a page) and if possible a draft of the script. Also have a cast breakdown, because if there are no roles for our people, then there is no point reading it any further.

Q - When you say cast list, what do you mean exactly?

Geoff - A brief synopsis of each character. The briefer the better, so we can get through them faster as we read so many scripts.

Q - Writers and Directors may have a very fixed view of what that character should be, but a good Agent or Casting Director can open their minds a bit .

Geoff - True. A lovely man named Jonathan McLeish who was a BBC Casting Director came to work here. He used to cast *Eastenders*. He came to work side by side with me for about 18 months or so, and I'll never forget the day we worked through a breakdown, and I was really quite pleased with my lateral thinking. There was a character who was in his mid-30's and he was fairly vain and masculine, and Jonathan turned it completely on its head and we ended up submitting a nearly 40 year old bald guy, I thought *'I never would have gone there!'* That is just the richness of the diversity that there can be.

Q - How soon before shooting should you be approached?

Geoff - Well, as much time as possible because of actors' availability. A month or two would be great. But many independent films give me about two to three weeks sometimes!

Q - What is it that attracts you or your clients to a particular piece and makes you consider it?

Geoff - Fundamentally, the script over reputation, because you can be disappointed very easily by a well known writer's work. Every time the script is the thing that persuades the client. And it is up to the client. We don't sit here all powerful and kind of say *'OK, we've got a script in, there is a part there for you, do it.'* It's not a process where we sit on top of a hill, dictating to everyone. It's a partnership. It's not necessarily that important what I think, what's important to me is what the client thinks. They will either have their appetites whetted or not depending on what they read.

Q - On a practical level, what things can a film-maker bring to the equation to make it more attractive to the client?

Geoff - We would never want our client to be out of pocket for certain expenses. So we would always ask for transport to be taken care of once they are in production. Most of the time, you tend to find that cars are laid on these days. It makes a big difference in their performance because if they've had to wrestle their way through the great unwashed, then they are not going to be in the right frame of mind when they get to work. We generally don't insist on per diems on low budget films because you've normally got a food wagon there. If there is more money available, then that always oils the wheels, and makes things run smoother.

Q - Why are PACT / Equity agreements an attractive proposition to an Agent?

Geoff - Well, because everybody's got to eat. It's a romantic notion, but actors can't afford to do one low/no budget film after the other and expect to stay in their flat! We've had a situation recently where somebody was going to be out of their flat very shortly unless we get them a commercial, which mercifully is what we did! People cannot work for three or four weeks for nothing, no matter how much they like a project. They'll have to do voice-overs or waitressing to compensate. So, the PACT agreement is kind of designed to accommodate for exactly that situation. It establishes basic minimum figures so actors at least get a living wage.

Q - When we made our 3rd feature, we were actually going to pay our actors more. Then PACT and Equity got involved and we ended up paying them less, but everyone was happier with that. So why is this a good thing?

Geoff - Because of the security of the PACT / Equity agreement. I imagine there are thousands of situations where an agent has talked themselves out of money! I think Equity does a terrific job, not least because in any given situation we can pick up the phone and speak to a person in the department

Suite 8a
169 Queen's Gate
London
SW7 5HE

Brunskill Management Ltd

Geoff Stanton
Theatrical Agent

Tel: 0207 581 3388
Fax: 0207 589 9460
Email: geoff@brunskill.com
www.brunskill.com

Using Friends as Actors

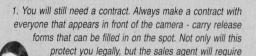

GUERILLA FILM MAKER SAYS!

Actors cost money. Even if they offer to work for free they will at some point probably ask for money for train fares etc. It is almost essential that your principal cast are pros, but if push comes to shove, friends and relatives are an option. If casting a friend or relative...

1. You will still need a contract. Always make a contract with everyone that appears in front of the camera - carry release forms that can be filled in on the spot. Not only will this protect you legally, but the sales agent will require these documents.

2. It is more likely that they will endure hardship and abuse than an unpaid actor - so if you need 'a body in the lake', ask a relative (you will still get earache, but you will be able to persuade them).

3. Equity, the actors union won't like you making a non union film - beware.

4. Unless you are sure of their skills, don't give them any important role. Be aware that they could be spectacularly awful. They may also be unprofessional.

5. Friends and relatives are great if you need a crowd - they will even come in costume (but beware of damaged egos when a costume is terrible).

6. Always consider an actor over a non actor, even if the actor in question has little or no experience. They want to be there and will have some training. There are thousands of actors just waiting for a break. Contact SBS, PCR or the Stage.

we need. And it will be a person we know well and have a dialogue with. We can iron out problems often before they have become an issue. I think Equity genuinely, is one of the few organisations where they really do have the actors best interests at heart and aren't there just to be a thorn in the side of producers and film-makers.

Q - There seems to be two kinds of low budget films. Those being made because the film makers want to make it to advance their career. They love the film, they can't get any financing, so they choose to make it this way. Then there are the more unscrupulous people who are doing it to avoid paying, to line their own pocket.

Geoff - I think we are not very tolerant of that sort of thing, whereas an actor, if a producer approached him directly and said *'Look, we will pay you, £100 a week for filming, but that's all we have got in the budget, is that OK?'* they'd sort of shrug their shoulders and say *'Yeah, OK!'* An agent would say *'C'mon! What are the circumstances?'* We have to delve deeper to find out what the real situation is in order to protect our clients from abuse. So we are the buffer inbetween.

Q - So I guess the approach every new film maker ought to have would be courteous and honest?

Geoff - Honesty is everything because the minute I smell anything suspicious, alarms go off and I shut down. You've got your work cut out for you now because I've gone from being an ally to an obstacle.

Q - That's a really interesting point, because so many people fall foul of agencies, because they see them as an enemy, as opposed to an ally.

Geoff - I'm not surprised in some instances. I think there is an awful lot of arrogance out there and in certain circumstances, people are not doing things for the right reasons. It's all about ulterior motives, or other elements that come into it. I feel that if the project is good, and the production team is competent, you should want your actors involved whether it be for no money, or for half of what they are worth. A major film star, who would normally command £50k a week, but might now do it for £20k a week. It's your job as a film maker, to persuade us that it's something that they want to do. If you are open right from the word *'go'*, that endears you anyway, and if the project is good enough, then we will see that. And most of us have a general idea of what is accepted as being good and what is accepted as being bad.

Q - Do you think it is a bad idea for a film-maker to cast actors just because they know them personally?

Geoff - Yes hugely. A writer spends months and months working out his characterisations. Who in God's name is going to put somebody in a part because they are a mate? You might as well be a plumber, sorry to plumbers out there, but certainly not a film

Jeremy - If it's a good script it doesn't matter. There's an awful lot of low-budget films with poor scripts in which I'm not interested, but if there is a wonderful script with absolutely no money, I would much rather an actor did that, than a major movie that's not very good for a lot of money. Certainly, I think English actors appreciate that, and would rather do a quality film than rubbish for bucks. A lot of new film makers believe their scripts are wonderful, but often I don't share their enthusiasm, so it is important for them to remember that if I say I don't think it's suitable, it's not because I don't want an actor to do a low-budget film, it's because I believe the script is below par. Everything stems from the screenplay - if it is good, everyone believes in it and most of your problems are over.

Q - There is a myth in film making that the agent is simply an obstacle to get around. How would you feel about film makers who contact an actor directly, either by phoning them or sending a screenplay?

Jeremy - If an actor meets film makers socially and they chat and it all works out then fine, but I know actors do not appreciate getting phone calls from desperate film makers. Nor do they like getting their post box filled with wannabe scripts.

Q - What are the main problems dealing with a low-budget production?

Jeremy - There are basic things like transport, expecting an actor to get up at four o'clock in the morning and catch a tube to Neasden to start filming. I just say that is not on, it is the producer's job to provide transport. An awful lot of low-budget films are being made by first time film makers who have no real background you can check up on so I just have to go with my gut feeling. They've just got to be honest to make you trust them.

Q - What are the main concerns of an actor, especially if the budget is low?

Jeremy - They're not being paid a lot of money so what they do want is comfort. I think pushing them all into the same car to take them to the location is not what you want to do because they need that time to be quiet, to think about what they are doing. Nor do you want to put them up in crummy hotels. I know it's difficult because the money should be on the screen, but I think the actors comfort is something that is often forgotten. Basic things like no chairs to sit on, no umbrellas if it's pouring with rain, no tents - the sort of things which often don't cost very much. Everyone else on the set is busy most of the time, rushing around doing things, but often, the actor isn't doing much and is waiting for the next scene to happen. A green room is ideal, a place where they can sit and concentrate on what they are doing without being distracted by the crew. Somewhere warm, dry and quiet, even a kettle with tea and coffee can be so easily forgotten.

Q - What is your worst experience of a low-budget film?

Jeremy Conway
Actors Agent

Jeremy - A client of mine made a film in Scotland that has never seen the light of day - it was an absolute nightmare. They hadn't scheduled anything, so he never knew if they wanted him the next day or not, that is until 10 o'clock at night - even then, they might not use him the next day as arranged. I think the most important thing is the pre planning, making sure everything is worked out well in advance and they know what they are shooting each day. Obviously things can go wrong and no-one expects any less, but one has to know what one is doing, when and where. Actors get cross if they don't know what's happening and they feel they've been mucked around, especially if they turn up and then they're not used.

Q - What are the main areas in the contract that you would be looking to nail down?

Jeremy - Definitive dates. On a low-budget production, if an actor is doing just a couple of days, I would really like the days to be nominated rather than on or about. Billing is very difficult to negotiate and terribly important for the actor. On low-budget films, when actors aren't being paid very much, I try and make sure that everyone's on favoured nations (which is when the actors get the same, nobody is going to get more). If an actor is taking a big cut in salary and suddenly discovers that one of his contemporaries is getting a lot more, it can become very difficult, but if it's favoured nations there is no argument.

Q - What can a producer do to make your life easier?

Jeremy - I think being honest and absolutely straightforward. You know when people aren't telling the truth - when I ask, is so and so's client getting more than our client? and the reply is, well no, not exactly - well, what do you mean? - the answer - well, I can't say. You just want them to be straightforward and honest and say, well yes they are getting more money, because they're doing 6 weeks more work on it. I just think that good honesty in this business pays off in the long run. Agents all talk to one another and confer on deals. An awful lot of producers, especially young producers who are starting out, have very little respect for rather senior, well known actors, and expect to meet them without even giving them a script. The actor thinks why should I, I've never heard of this person. Producers should be careful not to sound too arrogant - if they are trying to get a star to work for them, they should be extremely respectful.

Casting

GUERILLA FILM MAKER SAYS!

1. No-one is out of reach. Make a list of people who could play the parts in your picture and approach their agents. Actors can have a bad year and be eager for feature work, or may have a soft spot for the decadence of low budget film making. If you don't ask, you'll never know - and they may say yes.

2. Agents are all difficult. Their sole job is to protect their client, hustle as much money as they can and moan and groan about conditions. Agents often neglect to inform their clients of the potential job as the money is likely to be bad. Agents are paid on commission, and if the percentage is poor, why spend time and energy on negotiations if there isn't a pot of money at the end?

3. The agent's flip side is that if you have an exciting project, you are honest and upfront, then they may see your movie as a positive opportunity. Deals can be struck; for instance, a named actor is supplied along with four new faces for the experience.

4. If you have a way into an actor, bypass the agent and get the script to them. No agent will be able to stop an actor who is determined to be involved in a project. Be aware that some actors hate this approach and enjoy the protection their agent gives them from a barrage of wanabe film makers.

5. Get a copy of THE SPOTLIGHT, a book and online service with actors in Britain listed with pic. Spotlight 0207 437 7631 and www.spotlightcd.com.

6. You can get international casting information from the links on the Spotlight web site, including America, Canada and Australia.

7. There are several casting services where ads can be placed very cheaply, or even free. PCR and SBS for instance.

8. Videotape auditions, it will help you put a face to the hundreds of hopefuls you will doubtless see.

9. Be honest and up front about money and conditions - preferably on the phone when arranging an audition. It's better to know then, rather than on set if there are going to be problems.

10. If you are paying below Equity recommended levels, don't shout about it. Equity can be rather aggressive and tip the cart a little. Remember, that no matter how much Equity scream and shout, we live in a free world where people can do as they like. Just lie low.

11. Where should you hold auditions? Many agents and casting facilities have rooms for this purpose, but you can hold them in your front room if you like - we did.

12. Once you have cast a part, sort out ALL financial arrangements in a contract, before you shoot.

13. If you can afford to run with the Equity / PACT registered low budget scheme, do so. It will cost you some money, just over £500 pw and just over £100 pd, but agents love it and there are no contracts. Pretty much equals minimal headaches.

14. Using a casting director will help you get better and faster access to higher calibre talent. They also know agents and can speak the lingo. Iy you can afford it, it is money well spent.

15. Remember, your cast are the emotional vehicles through which the story is told. Alongside the script, getting the right cast is probably the most important job. Don't prioritise ANYTHING higher than casting.

maker. You have a responsibility to put the right person in the job. I should have said this at the beginning - my job is to get the right person the job. As a young film-maker, you owe it to yourselves to make sure the casting is of the highest quality because that is going to carry the script. I emphatically disagree with *'friends'* being cast because they are simply available and cheap or free. I appreciate that it has to be that way sometimes, but it is far from ideal.

Q - On a practical level, how does the interview and offer process work? Can you make multiple offers to different actors for the same role?

Geoff - No, you can't do that. Technically once you make an offer, if an agent comes back and accepts that offer, then that is binding, whether it's on paper or not. So if you did make three offers for the same part, you could find yourself having to pay three people for one actor to play the part! From the actor's point of view, what generally happens is they go into the meeting and hopefully get the job or at least a recall, and then get the job. If so, the Casting Director will phone and say *'Fantastic news, we would like to make an offer for so and so to do whatever,'* and our response varies from *'Sorry you haven't got much money,'* to *'Oh brilliant news, well get your wheelbarrow out!'* We know which Casting Directors will offer us the right money and which ones will try and come under. There are actually some who go over, but in the main it is usually under, and you have to sort of nudge them to get what's right for the actor given their experience and the available budget.

I think from an actor's point of view, they are constantly being told there is no money in the budget. Then look at the camera and think, *'well it is an inanimate object but you are paying it ten times a day the cost of me. Why is that when I am the creative element?'* The cost of talent as opposed to technicians is tiny. So as an agent you have to get them as much as possible, so they feel good about themselves on set. There is nothing worse than having an actor resenting you the experience when they are trying to deliver a performance. You have to reach that position where, as an agent, you have to push things to the point where the producer is about to walk away. I had an hour long phone call with a producer for a deal who was shouting at me down the phone, not threatening in any way, but shouting at me, really, really angry and after an hour of the conversation, he invited me out to lunch! That's kind of the process you have to go through, if you pick up the phone and say *'so and so has got the job, we are paying £500 a week, is that OK?',* any agent that says *'Yep!'* is not doing his job properly, you have got to know what is underlying that, and know that you have to push as much as you can.

Q - Many film makers never deal with professional negotiators. Do you have any advice for dealing with these people?

Geoff - You need to learn the dialogue and the terms. So when the phrase comes at you, you know how to respond to it. Then when you turn it back, the person on the other end is thinking *'Oh shit, that's not meant to happen!'*

Q - What can a film maker on a low budget film do to make an actor comfortable so they can give their best performance?

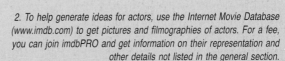

Casting Online Resources

When casting a film, you can look at hundreds, even thousands of actors. This is a huge amount of data to sort through. The web is of course a terrific and immediate resource that can help do your job more efficiently and better.

1. Join the Spotlight, a database (and books) with various Equity actors in the UK. Pretty much every working actor is listed with credits, skills, contacts etc. It is one of the tools ALL film makers will use. Casting directors often email you a link which will bring up specific actor details immediately. Fantastic! The Spotlight also has listings for Canada and Australia. Check out www.spotlightcd.com find links and purchase a CD-ROM with pictures of the actors. For America, get a copy of the Academy Players Directory.

2. To help generate ideas for actors, use the Internet Movie Database (www.imdb.com) to get pictures and filmographies of actors. For a fee, you can join imdbPRO and get information on their representation and other details not listed in the general section.

3. There are several casting services and trade magazines where ads can be placed very cheaply or for free, such as PCR. Check out PCR at www.pcrnewsletter.com, Casting Network at www.castingnetwork.co.uk, Cast Web at www.castweb.co.uk, Castcall Information services at www.castcall.demon.co.uk. Also check out Script breakdown Services at www.breakdownservices.com who have offices in LA, New York and Vancouver with sister companies in London, Toronto and Sydney.

4. On the whole, actors are not very techno savvy, so don't expect online video clips, showreel DVD's etc. Some will have them, most will not.

Pic (left) - Spotlight online.

Method Acting & Classical Acting

GUERILLA FILM MAKER SAYS!

Broadly speaking, actors can use one of two main techniques to elicit their performance. These are classical acting and method acting - essentially, pretend to be it (classical) and try to be it (method). These are the powertools of their trade.

Classical Training

A style that was used by Shakespeare and the Greek Classics for their plays. Many of the great theatre actors such as Laurence Olivier and John Gielgud come from classical training, as are some of the greatest film actors such as Judy Dench, Jeremy Irons and Anthony Hopkins. With classical acting, sometimes called technical acting, the actor does not let the character envelop their 'way of being', rather they rely on a planned performance using specific acting tools such as precise speech and movement to get the desired performance. In classical training, the actor uses external factors to analyse a character.

Method Acting

(Also known as the Stanislavski System which Lee Strasberg adapted to create 'the Method') refers to immersing yourself in the role and actually becoming the character, if only to a small degree. Actors can use relaxation techniques to allow them to access emotions. Method actors often use sense memory to stimulate the emotional response, where the actor recreates or relives a past experience they've had, one that has a similar emotional response to what is required by the scene. They will access their five senses to recall how things felt at that time in order to bring it to life in the present. They become one with the character and will frequently stay in character until they are done with the project. This method is very internal and can be very rewarding as well as frustrating. Robert DeNiro, Al Pacino, Anne Bancroft, Marlon Brando and Dustin Hoffman all came out of this school of acting.

Geoff - The actor needs to be given the space to prepare, and you can't expect them to jump off the tube, come racing in, sweating, take off his jacket, be padded by the make-up girl, and go into his emotional scene. He might be able to, if it's a rushing to work scene, but if it's a completely different scenario, he would have to have time to settle, think about what is about to happen and prepare himself mentally. Also, Directors need to be people people. So often you hear stories about mistreatment of an actor say in the audition process where an actor will walk in, walk up to the desk and stick out a hand, and the Director will not even look up. I've seen it. You just think, *'what are you doing?'* This person is supposed to be giving you their best, and you are putting them on edge the minute they walk into the room. So some people are on a power trip, and that is something that filters through, in the end, I'm not saying there is a black list, or Directors that we won't have our people working with, but you certainly hear stories that recur about people.

Q - Are there places where you keep an eye on projects that are coming up?

Geoff - We get a lot of feedback from our actors who hear on the grapevine. We see all the professional casting reports. I have to be honest, when it's busy, as it is at the moment, we don't have the time to go out searching for low budget films because there are other priorities. But the direct approach is best and we would prefer a company to phone us up, and say, *'we are doing some films, would you mind sending us a brochure of your client list, or e-mail us your client list'*. We would be only too happy to. Of course before anyone commits to anything we will need to see the script and the synopsis and so on, so we've got nothing to lose and everything to gain by doing it.

Q - Why not bypass the agent, and then just go to the actor?

Geoff - Because actors are the worst negotiators in the world. They want to do the job, and the minute the Producer or Director starts talking to them about the job, they will be trying to see if they will fit into the role. If you start talking money, they start to glaze over, and they will say *'Speak to my agent, speak to my agent!'* It's generally not the done thing, for a very good reason, they are very vulnerable.

Q - If somebody is making a picture, should they come and meet you?

Geoff - In an ideal world, it would be nice, but generally we don't have time for any pleasantries.

Q - Is that one of the reasons why you would work with a Casting Director, because you have existing relationships?

Geoff - Yes. If we know Gail Stevens is casting a television production, we would unhesitatingly submit any of our clients, as long as the role was large enough. If it were an unknown casting person, Director or Producer we would need to have as much information as possible to make a judgment as to whether it was something we wanted to be involved in. So yes, if it was a major film and they wanted a client to play a lead and take up 4 months of the year for very little money, then it would probably get to the stage where we would meet and talk things through. If there are any concerns, then it's much better to have a face to face meeting.

Q - One of the mistakes that I see so often in independent films is that they didn't start casting from the top and then work down.

Geoff - Yes, why not start big? They might say yes. But you must make sure they are right for the film. You have to cast your leads first and match everybody from there otherwise you have got problems. For example, if you stick a mammoth actor in a smaller role against a lead who is weaker, you've got a problem on your hands. So, yes you actually have to cast down sometimes, and lighten a character because it's not going to work in reality. A good Casting Director will prevent that from happening. Again most of our day is spent talking to Casting Directors, so I obviously have a bias towards them, it's a very well-oiled process.

Q - How do the contracts work when it comes to lower budget stuff?

Geoff - Well, they are usually in the form of a letter of agreement. In a few cases a lawyer's contract. We have a natural aversion to those as we'd much rather the money was spent on the production than on lawyers. There must be thousands of examples out there on the Internet of contracts you can manipulate yourself. Just make sure it covers certain elements. The Equity contracts are good. They are very well thought out, so I would always try and get hold of an Equity contract to look at and base it on that, if not use it. Even on low budget films you should try and work with Equity as it keeps everyone happy and the process can run much more smoothly.

Q - How does payment of an actor work?

Geoff - Normally, it's very simplistic. They get paid on the Thursday of the week they are filming. If they are only being employed for 2 days, then what generally happens is they shoot the 2 days and are paid very soon afterwards. Sometimes you can have problems getting the money, but if you get any of those instincts before hand, i.e. if you like the person who sold you the project, you love the project, your actor was going to be terrific in it, all was well with the world, and they say to you *'this is filming on February 3rd, we'll have the money in your bank account the following Wednesday, is that OK?'*, I say *'Yes, absolutely fine.'* If they had been a plonker from the word go, I would say *'he's not filming, until you pay him!'*

Q - What advice would you offer a new film maker?

Geoff - Everyone in the industry, successful or otherwise, will have an abundance of advice to give. Be selective and bear in mind a lot of it will apply to what has worked in the past, which may not necessarily work for your film. Don't be afraid to push boundaries. Learn from the past, but don't live in it. Also, you *need* a sense of humour, so if you haven't got one, get one! And be passionate about what you are doing, and if you can't be - stop doing it!

Catherine Arton
Casting Director

CASTING DIRECTOR

Q - What is your job?

Cathy - I'm a Casting Director. That means a variety of things, but mostly that I help the Producers and Directors find cast for their film, or television programme.

Q - When should you be approached on a low budget film?

Cathy - From a production's points of view, probably as soon as possible. If you do get a 'name' attached, that can help you with the financing.

Q - What do you need to do your job?

Cathy - I need the script and a very strong sense of what the budget is. I need to know contingency, in regard to budget too. I need them to think both ways, best case scenario casting, worst case scenario casting. I'd really love them to have an ideal A-list Hollywood cast list, if they could have their dream cast, who would it be, it really helps.

Q - How important is nailing down dates in the schedule?

Cathy - It is important, but you do have to go with the flow and be aware of the Production requirements. Things do go wrong. You have to get availability from the actors, so if are going for a name, they are very often booked up for a very long time. If you are hoping to shoot season dependent scenes, then in theory you need to get it pinned down too, etc.

Q - How do you charge for what you do, by the day, or by the job?

Cathy - Each job is a different story. I try very much to be fair and go with the budget, and there are points at which I won't go below, but by the same token if it is a beautiful script from a new Director, and deserves to be made I'll work as hard as I can to help and get it made.

Q - So when you get the screenplay do you or the Producer or Director draw up a cast list of the characters, what do you do from that point on?

Cathy - I do a *cast report*, which means, from the perspective of casting, I write a synopsis of the script, and then I define, in regard to budget, the type of actors I feel will be attracted to the script and why. Then I start to make suggestions and see what fits.

Q - Is the reason that people hire you because you have existing relationships, you have your eye on new talent?

Cathy - Yes.

Q - Do you hold auditions?

Cathy - Yes. I do generals for myself, so I can see who is new. I also go to new shows, school showcases etc., to spot new talent. During auditions, each Director has a different method, or thing that they prefer. Sometimes I will just do a basic casting, the first casting by myself with a cameraman and go from there, shortlist, and show the director the tapes.

Q - The Director isn't always available as they are busy doing stuff?

Cathy - Yes. Some Directors enjoy interviewing and know what they want, some have a very actor-friendly perspective on things, some of them are ex-actors, so they love to be there and see what kind of commitment an actor can give to the part immediately. It is that immediacy thing. Some Directors just like to sit back and hand me a note saying *'Ask them this'!*

Q - What would actors supply to you, in the early stages of casting?

Cathy - A CV and photograph. Possibly a reel of their work, but that's rare.

Q - What is Spotlight?

Cathy - Spotlight is a very useful industry guide where the majority of British actors and some international actors can put their headshot and details. It exists in book form and via the internet, which is more popular now as its so accessible and has a database. It has a search feature, so if you are looking for a male, 20-year old, black actor who can roller-skate, you can search for that.

Q - Can the production get access to that as well? So that you can make phonecalls and say 'Quickly look at this person on Spotlight, without having to post a photo?

Cathy - You can send them a shortlist.

Q - Do you do the deals with the actors or does the production?

Cathy - Both.

Q - What are the common areas of negotiation with an actor when you are talking to an agent?

Cathy - Obviously dates, whether it is Equity or not, payment, billing tends to be a big one, per diem (daily allowance money), nudity is another, hours they will be expected to work, days off etc.

Q - Do you think it is fair to say that some actors are just not worth working with on a low budget film?

Cathy - Absolutely. The time you can waste pandering to an actor's ego can be enormous, but I have to say that it is very rare that that happens. In my experience, most actors are a delight to work with, and have a passion and love for the art. Some of them get a bit confused, especially when they get a lead in a low budget feature, they suddenly start comparing themselves to Julia Roberts, or Brad Pitt, and assume that it should be on the scale. I think that you have to make it very clear to the actor and agent once they are interested in doing the project, the nature of the project, and spell out even what is seemingly obvious to you.

Q - Can a production help in the casting, I'm thinking in terms of maybe they have got existing relationships, or what about small roles, extras, that kind of stuff? Who takes care of all that?

Cathy - Normally I get an extra agency involved or they have one already. As you well know, you can get friends and family and investors to fill those parts too.

CATHERINE ARTON
casting director

catherine@acacasting.com

Extras

GUERILLA FILM MAKER SAYS!

Low budget films are often let down by simple things, such as, there not being enough extras in a scene, or just plain old bad or the wrong extras. On lower budget films you are almost certainly going to pull extras from friends and family, but if the scene needs more people, you may need to look at extras agencies.

1. New film makers tend to be younger, and populate their backgrounds with students of the same age and look. This is a dead giveaway. Try and find older people to populate your backgrounds.

2. Untrained extras may look at the camera, turn up inappropriately dressed etc. Write up a sheet of do's and don'ts and send to them all.

3. Empty shots make the film look cheap. Use extras for screen clutter. Just make sure they look appropriate.

4. To find extras, contact extra agencies such as The Casting Collective (www.castingcollective.co.uk or Real People (www.realpeople.co.uk) or internet sites like www.ukscreen.com or www.freshfaces.com. The union that covers background artists, walk-ons and doubles in film and television is BECTU's sub division, FAA (Film Artiste's Association).

5. A new background artistes agreement using the FAA/PACT agreement will have come into play by November 1st, 2005. This raises the basic day rates of extras (£69.03 / day and £86.80 / night), calculates overtime in half hour increments, provides for supplemental payments if the extra makes costume changes and provides provisions for holiday pay. Go to www.bectu.org.uk or www.pact.co.uk for more information.

6. Extra casting agencies have lists and access to the 'right looking' people for your shoot i.e. school kids, medical professionals, professional musicians, actual firemen, actual police officers etc. People who genuinely look the part and therefore make your film look more 'real'.

7. Before securing your extras, make sure they've been informed of how long you anticipate them to be on set.

8. If there are a large number of extras from one source, provide free transport to move them to and from the location.

9. Make sure there are enough loos available and that food, tea and coffee, and water are on hand at all times.

10. Remember that your extras are going to have to do a lot of waiting around and will get bored very easily. If you can afford to, entertain them in between shots and make sure they have a green room.

11. Your extras might not show up, so be prepared to have a backup plan.

12. Make sure you have at least one but preferably more designated production crew members to take care of all the extras, providing them with call times, what to wear, what to bring etc.

Provide your extras with release forms and make sure they sign this before they appear on camera.

Q - As new filmmakers tend to be young, they can often fill all those background parts with mates from university, and suddenly everyone in front of the camera looks like they are 19?

Cathy - Yes, that happens a lot, and I think it is unfortunate. Everyone has older family, get them involved.

Q - Can a filmmaker do the casting themselves without using a Casting Director?

Cathy - Absolutely.

Q - What are the problems that you see in that process?

Cathy - I think there is a naiveté in what to expect from agents and actors if you do that. You can get tongue-tied and intimidated by their knowledge because they know more than you do.

Q - Agents can be quite intimidating, as they are professional negotiators.

Cathy - Yes they are, they are generally extremely good business people, and they know the meaning of the dollar.

Q - What is the deal with Equity in terms of, if you make a low budget film. Should you be Equity, do you need to be Equity?

Cathy - No. Though I think Equity is a very important body for both film makers and actors. By the same token, perhaps there could be more leeway in nurturing and helping the new filmmakers get their very first foot on the ladder of making a film. To put them through the same hoops, as somebody like Sam Mendes, is I think not fair, and I think we need to nurture our new talent a little bit more.

Q - How do you approach big names, say you want Kevin Costner?

Cathy - Go to his agent, unless I know somebody who knows him, in which case . . .(laughs)

Q - What is the procedure for going for somebody like that?

Cathy - Same as any other, if you start to get intimidated by the idea that they are a big name you will fail, but if you just go ahead and treat them like any other actor, you have much better odds. It is just a mindset. You contact their agent, ask their availability, and then say *'I have a script that I'm very interested in sending to them'*, then you just keep pressing to get the script sent.

Q - Are scripts sent by paper in the post now, or is it done more electronically?

Cathy - Both.

Q - What is the process when you make an 'offer', what does that mean when you offer a part to an actor?

Cathy - If you make an 'offer' to an actor, you are legally bound to use that actor, and it is quite a process to 'un-offer'. It is considered extremely bad form to pull out, and you will get a bad name.

Q - What are the common mistakes that you see?

Cathy - Sometimes a filmmaker will mistake an actor's enthusiasm for talent, and because they seem to see eye to eye on the project they go *'Yeah, this guy understands me, this is great!'* Then they get them in front of the camera and they don't pull it out of the hat. A lengthier audition process can be useful. I don't want to be negative, but also very often a filmmaker will try and be someone they are not, out of insecurity they will try and yield certain power during the audition process, and it does not create the best environment for the actor. What they should be aiming to do is create the most friendly, nurturing environment to get the best work out of the actor, without going over the top, to really see what the actor can do. Actors are frequently very excited or nervous and they wouldn't be there if they didn't want the part.

Q - Frequently filmmakers are terrified that someone will find out that they don't know what they are doing?

Cathy - Yes, and the actors have the same fear on the other side (laughs). I think it is very useful for a filmmaker, before the audition process, to either read one or two acting theory books. Just to get a bit of jargon, to get what they want out of the actor.

Q - Do you think it would be wise to put Directors through an acting class, or even auditions?

Cathy - Yes. Both.

Q - What advice would you offer a new filmmaker?

Cathy - Always remember the reason why you wanted to get into film, and keep your passion, and do it from the heart. Don't do anything because you think you are pleasing somebody else. Do it from the heart, because it appeals to you.

PRE PRODUCTION

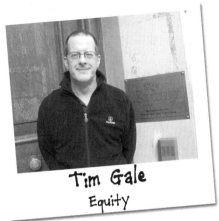

Tim Gale
Equity

Q - What is Equity?

Tim - We are the Trade Union that represents actors, singers, dancers, stunt performers & stunt co-ordinators. We have 45,000 members who are all professional performers with either substantial work behind them or who have been suitably trained. We negotiate collective agreements with employers' organisations which determine the relationship between producers and actors/ stunt performers etc.

Q - What is the procedure for making a film with Equity agreements?

Tim - Equity has a cinema agreement with PACT which has provisions for film agreements and registered low budget films. To access our agreements a film must be registered with PACT, through PRA Ltd., the Producers Rights Agency, and it is they who issue the contracts. The producer supplies to both PACT and Equity a copy of the budget for the film which has been audited and verified by a film chartered accountant. The producer then pays 0.25% of this budget to PACT as a levy, even though they do not need to be a member of PACT. The budget must also reflect that in excess of 5% of the budget is spent on the performers. The producer will lodge the performers' fees in an Escrow bank account which is held for each artist and is currently a maximum of two weeks fees @ £2500 per week (ie the max held is £5000 per artist). However, if you are using an artist for two days @ £150 per day, then only £300 would be held. These fees are the same for a low budget film. When principal photography is finished, there is a two week turn-around to check artists have been paid and then the Escrow is returned.

We only accept letters of financial guarantee from the Studios (Warners, Disney etc.) or the major TV companies (ITV, BBC, C4). Equity would then release contracts to the producer who would then be able to hire the chosen performers. The contract is 20 pages with fees that are calculated on a weekly or daily basis. The producer does not pay the performer out of the money in Escrow. The money held in Escrow is a guarantee until after the shoot wraps and the performers have been paid and then the money is released back to the producer. Usually for low budget productions, is it usual that no-one is paid more than anyone else and other than a 75% for cinema and UK free TV use fees, other uses are not pre-purchased until after the film has recouped between 1.75%-2.75% dependent on its registered budget. Agents may also negotiate extra things like credit billing on the film and poster, per diems for the cast etc.

Q - What are the Equity agreements for low budget? i.e. the PACT/Equity low budget cinema agreement? (what are the budget ceilings etc.)

Tim - We consider films budgeted under £3m to be *Low Budget*, films with budgets under £1m are considered *Very Low Budget*.

Q - To use an Equity agreement, must you be registered with PACT and must your accounts be certified by the Guild of Film Production Accountants? And if so, how do you do that?

Tim - You only have to register with PACT if you're going to be using the *Low* and *Very Low Budget* agreements.

Q - Do you have any agreements for films under the budget of 250k?

Tim - No, the *Very Low Budget* agreements apply to this budget. However, for features and shorts budgeted under 250k the budget is not required to be certified by the Guild of Film Production Accountants. Instead you just submit a summary of the budget.

Q - Within the agreements, do actors receive a share in the profits of a film or a share of the proceeds from sale to TV, video and DVD rentals and sell through?

Tim - Yes, for films under £10m, actors receive an non-negotiable 2% share in the profits of the film (2% of the producers' net profit). For films over £20m, actors receive a royalty from the theatrical release and also from sales to TV, Video/DVD rental and sell through.

Q - How much is a day rate and weekly rate for an actor?

Tim - Minimums; on very low budget; £150 per day & £600 per week. Minimums; on low budget; £175 per day & £700 per week. Standard feature film minimums; £380 per day & £1520 per week. There are no half day rates.

Market/Medium & Territory	Use Fee	Initial Use Period/Extent of Use
Theatric North America and Non-Theatric Worldwide	37.5%	Unlimited
Theatric World **excluding** North America and Non-Theatric Worldwide	37.5%	Unlimited
Videogram	90%	Until the amount of 50% of Production Cost has been earned in worldwide wholesale Videogram receipts less those excluded items set out in the definition of Distributor's Gross Videogram Receipts.
UK Premium Pay, Pay Per View and On Demand Television	25%	Four (4) years from first Use in this market
UK Network Terrestrial Television	20%	The earlier of five (5) years from first Use in this market or after three (3) transmissions
UK Secondary Television	5%	Four (4) years from first Use in this market
USA Major Network Television	25%	Unlimited
USA Non-major Network Television	10%	Unlimited
USA Pay Television	20%	Unlimited
World Television excluding UK and USA	10%	Four (4) years from first Use in this market

Q - What is the standard work week schedule for an Equity member?

Tim - Five day week. 10 hour day including one hour for lunch. Minimum 12 hour overnight break.

Q - As well as the day rate and weekly rate, what are the pre purchased rights for USA/Canada and rest of world, theatrical and Video and TV?

Tim - I will supply you with a breakdown (see box above).

Q - Are these pre purchased rights included in all agreements i.e. even in the very low budget agreements? If certain rights have not been pre-purchased, can you pay these if and when the film is sold or do you HAVE to pay for this upfront? Or is there a certain percentage that the film must recoup until this is paid?

Tim - Under the low budget arrangements beyond either the 75% or 50% use fees purchased, there are no further use fees payable until the production has recouped 2.5 times its production budget if not more than £1m, 2.25 times its production budget if not more than £2m, 2 times the budget when between £2m & £3m. Statistically an insignificant number reach this level.

Q - On a low budget production, are actors generally paid the same?

Tim - In my experience, yes but there is no rule on this and there can be differentials in actors' pay even in low budget films.

Q - What are the benefits to actors for becoming an Equity member?

Tim - Members receive expert help & representation in relation to their working lives as well as specially negotiated insurance rates. If a member is having problems with a production company not paying, in addition to advice, we can provide legal advice and even legal work. There's an Equity pension scheme that members can join too.

Equity
performing for you

Tim Gale
Films' Organiser

email   tgale@equity.org.uk
web   www.equity.org.uk

Equity
Incorporating the Variety Artistes' Federation
Guild House • Upper St Martin's Lane
London • WC2H 9EG
T 020 7379 6000 • F 020 7379 7001

Q - With regards to stunt members, what happens with compensation in case of a fatal accident?

Tim - This would depend on whom liability for the accident lies with.

Q - What are the different schedules in your agreements?

Tim - Theatrical release, Video release, TV etc. The actor is paid a basic fee for doing the work, then the producer must purchase the rights to use this in a variety of different areas – theatrical release, video release, TV etc. – these are the use fees.

Q - If you plan to have only a TV/video release, but you then get picked up for theatrical, can you and must you convert your agreement to theatrical?

Tim - Yes, this is covered within the agreement – most productions would usually have pre-purchased both theatric & video rights.

Q - Is there a way that Equity can track a film in foreign territories? (I.e. to see where a film has sold to make sure that use fees are correctly covered.)

Tim - We do have means of checking use abroad but I can't for security grounds detail these here. I would point out that selling a film in a territory not paid for & then failing to pay the artists would constitute fraud, a criminal offence. We would not hesitate to report & have prosecuted any fraudulent use of our members' work.

Q - What is the BECS?

Tim - Recently new initiatives have come out of Europe that give performers legal rights to payments when their work is rented or lent on video/dvd or audio tape. To ensure that UK performers receive monies arising in the UK and Europe from these new legal rights, The British Equity Collecting Society (BECS) was setup in 1998. However performers must sign up to BECS as rights are held individually so BECS must have your mandate in order to act on your behalf and collect any monies due. Signing up costs nothing and performers can withdraw at any time. BECS now has agreements with collecting societies in Switzerland, Denmark, Belgium, The Netherlands, Greece and Norway. In the past year BECS distributed over £800,000.00 to British performers and hopes that this figure will continue to rise in the coming year

Q - In cases where minors are used, what's the issue with pay and Equity contracts there?

Tim - We do not represent children under 16.

Q - If you had someone who was a walk on and had no speaking role, do they have to be an Equity member?

Tim - Equity does not represent walk-ons & background artists in film although we do in TV – the FAA represents film extras.

Q - What are the general rules and regulations in an Equity agreement for actor's accommodation, transportation, ADR in post etc.?

Tim - Accommodation is outside the terms of the agreement – this should be agreed with artists/agents before signing the contract. ADR is payable on low budget films at the rate of £71 per four hour session.

Q - What information does Equity require from producers?

Tim - We require cast lists and after principal photography the artists' report. This lists the time & salary each artist received on the film and is used to work out what they are owed out of the 2% net profit/royalty.

Q - What power does Equity have? Can it shut down a production?

Tim - We try to persuade our members not to work without equity contracts. No we cannot shut down a production if it's working with non-union contracts. Under European law no trade union can force or coerce an employer to use union members so a filmmaker is free to hire non equity members. The equity contract not only helps in stating the rate of pay but also protects the performers and their rights. There is a special attention list that Equity publishes quarterly where either individuals, companies or agencies are listed because they have either owed or still owe money to members. We advise our members to consult Equity before accepting engagements with or through any of the names on this list. We also tell members to consult us when they are offered a non-Equity contract.

We also can recommend that our members not work in a variety of circumstances and we have powers under Health & Safety legislation to close down places of work if H&S is not being cared for properly. This has happened on occasion but only when there were serious breaches of safety. It only would happen if there were immediate dangers to cast and crew that could not be resolved on the spot – for example, if asbestos was found on a location or a biohazard. Most other H&S issues can be improved with only small disruption to the filming. This misuse of course would have to be proven in a court of law.

Q - How can Equity help low budget film producers?

Tim - Through the registered Low Budget Film arrangements with PACT. Being registered with Equity makes the agents more likely to feel that the production is going to be run in a professional manner than if not using Equity contracts. Therefore it creates less problems with the agent and also less fighting about the rate. Everyone realises that it's a standard rate and a standard contract. Also because of this, agents can help film producers find well known performers with successful careers to take part in certain productions because they like the production company, the producers, the director etc. and ultimately it could also help their actors so agents are much happier to use Equity contracts.

Q - How early on should a producer come to you to sort out the Equity agreements?

Tim - Unless circumstances dictate otherwise, producers should make contact at least four weeks before filming commences. Filmmakers can call us to get quotes of the rates when putting together their budgets. Unfortunately these rates are not available on our website (www.equity.org.uk).

Q - What are the common problems you encounter with producers?

Tim - Failure to understand the contracts that they are using. The contracts are not guidelines; they are a set of legally binding obligations on both parties. Therefore the terms & conditions are as stated within the contract and the producer needs to be au fait with these in relation to the work to be done. If part of the agreement is not understood, advice should be taken from PRA or Equity. There are always some non-Equity productions but in my view these are largely semi-professional in nature. Using Equity contracts helps everyone; the agents, artists & producers all benefit from using a well-known set of rules & regulations that protect the latter as much as the former.

Q - What advice can you offer producers/filmmakers?

Tim - Talk to us, we're not here to make life difficult for filmmakers. We recognise that it is in everyone's interest that films get made and I'm always happy to discuss issues and try to help.

PRE PRODUCTION

Stephen Biggs
'Whizz Kids

WORKING WITH KIDS

Q - What is your job?

Stephen - I run a children's casting agency and drama company.

Q - How does one go about casting a child in a film?

Stephen - Well, the first thing you have to do is know what you want or who you want. Sometimes we will get a brief, but once a casting director comes on board and sees a whole range of children, that brief changes. They may want to see a whole new age range for example. So know what you want from the outset, and then contact a good casting agency. Some are stand-alone agencies who see the children for ten or twenty minutes and they are on their books and that's that. There is hardly any further contact except for things that may come up for them. Some casting agents take it a bit further and actually work with the children and really they know the kids. There is nothing worse when the casting agency sends a child to the casting director and they are not suitable. It is embarrassing for the child. You have to know your kids. We have classes all week, Monday to Thursday evening and all day Saturday. Also consider location because if you are doing a project that involves two or three weeks filming in London, then you probably want a child from London instead of Manchester because you will have to deal with things like accommodation.

Q - What are the broad rules for using children in each age bracket?

Stephen - First, the rules are, a child that is up to five years old is five hours a day. That is set in stone. Five years to nine years is seven and a half hours. Nine years and older is nine and a half hours. Playing down, where a sixteen-year-old plays thirteen could work, or a seven year old to play five for instance. The main thing about the hours is that it is during the day. You can get night shoot clearance, but that gets a bit more complicated. Try to think about using children during daytime, especially if they are younger. Toddlers and babies should be used in the late morning after they have been up and about for a while, not just after being fed. And remember, even though we say children as adults, they are still children and be aware of that. They can only take so much direction in a short space of time. And if they say they are hungry or need to go to the loo, you have to accommodate them.

Q - Do children cost more than adult actors and are there any problems for a film maker to consider when hiring children as actors?

Stephen - Strangely, in the main, they are roughly half the price of an adult actor. Which is strange for me, as that they work just as hard or even harder than the adults. One thing to consider is to get a sixteen-year-old that can play down to a fourteen-year-old. But remember, when you choose them for the part but start shooting six months down the line, that sixteen year old is now seventeen.

Q - If the story concerns an intimate portrayal of the life of a thirteen-year-old, should you get one who might be really in touch with the emotions?

Stephen - Perhaps. But a really good sixteen-year-old actor could portray the emotion you would want in a thirteen-year-old. Maybe even better.

Q - Does talent level in a child change dramatically from year to year?

Stephen - Yes, and the danger is that if a child is wanted then there is a huge demand for how that child looks at that point in time. Two years down the line, whatever made that child popular, the cuteness or whatever, may have moved on. So the core thing with children is to work on the skills, as those things stay with them. The superficial stuff, when that isn't there, the skills still are. And it is a difficult transition to go from a successful child actor to a successful adult actor. We have a mission statement, if when the child reaches the age of eighteen and they want to go to drama school or arts school, we want them to be prepared to make the decision.

Q - What is the process when a filmmaker comes to you looking for actors?

Stephen - Usually it is a casting director who comes to us with what is required from the director, and we try to find that person. We may have a conversation with the producer about the storyline, the concept of the characters and then give a slight steer as to what kind of child they should be looking at. Once we know what they want, we would show them a range of suitable children. I would suggest that they go to other casting agencies too. There are certain publications they can use like PCR or Cast Call, where they can advertise and get them straight through. If it is a lot of children, it is best to work with one casting agency because, say if you have fifty children on a shoot, we can arrange a bus to take them there and back. So see a few agencies that you trust and then see the children.

Q - How do you suggest a director should audition a child actor?

Stephen - I'm not sure it should be too different from adults. Most twelve and thirteen-year-olds can handle being directed like adults. You can say things like, *'Can you give that to us again, but with a little more mischievousness? Or with a little more anger.'* Any actor worth their salt would be able to understand that. And a director would need to talk to them like that from the start of the film anyway. So I don't think there should be too many concessions unless they are younger, but nothing too extreme. Maybe you have to spell it out a little more, explain it in greater detail. Our child may only be doing four pages out of eighty, but if our child knows the whole story and where that child fits in, you will get a better audition. Often it evolves into where the first stage of casting is just a few words and the second stage is them reading the whole script.

Q - What is a child-acting license, what are the restrictions and how do you get one?

Stephen - It is literally that - a license for a child to work as a performer. The rules and restrictions are a bit of jungle at the moment. Slowly it is evolving, but it is a jungle and people can interpret it differently. The legislation that is there is based on common sense and most people can use their common sense. For instance, if you have a period drama that has a child in make up and costume for three or four hours and the child is loving it, it is a great experience for them. You will have to break for lunch and whatever, but that child could be filming well into the evening. And if you are halfway through a scene, with half an hour to go, and the time to pull the child has come, technically you have to pull the child. But that would upset the child who has been waiting for the scene, it would upset the film crew and the director. I would like to think there is some flexibility there based on common sense.

Right now the cut-off age is sixteen-years-old, at the end of GCSE's academic year - so that means even if they are sixteen, it is only in June that they are finished - then that child is not of compulsory school age, no matter how old they are. So before that they will need a license, which you get from the local educational authority of where they live. The license has about seven pieces of paper that need to be completed. They need a photograph of the child, a birth certificate, school clearance forms, a form signed by the production company, a form signed by the parents, a form signed by the doctor, and a master form that we fill in. We have destroyed several rainforests with all the paperwork that we have used and it is often for one child that runs around in the background of a shot. And each authority has different requirements. Some say they need to see original copies of all the forms rather than faxed copies. The maximum time to get a license is twenty-one days, which actually in practical terms is not very practical! I can't imagine when filmmaker knows twenty-one days ahead of time that he needs a child, let alone the locations that are required on the form.

Q - What is the role of the chaperone?

Child Performers Licence Restrictions - ENGLAND

AGE	9 to 16	5 to 8	UNDER 5
Maximum hours at the place of rehearsal or performance	9.5 hours	7.5 hours	5 hours
Hours	7.00am - 7.00pm	9.00am - 4.30pm	9.30am-4.30pm
Maximum period of continuous rehearsal performance	1 hour	45 minutes	30 minutes
Maximum number of hours for the entire performance or rehearsal	4 hours	3 hours	2 hours
Rest and meal breaks	If present for 4 consecutive hours (including presence for educational purposes whether or not tuition takes place at place of performance): 2 breaks, one meal break for at least an hour, the other breaks at least 15 minutes	If present for more than 3.5 consecutive hours (including presence for educational purposes whether or not tuition takes place at place of performance): 2 breaks, one meal break for at least an hour, the other breaks at least 15 minutes	Any time not used for work but be used for meals or rest.
	If present for 8 consecutive hours: 3 breaks, 2 must be meal breaks of at least an hour each, the others at least 15 minutes.	If present for 8 consecutive hours: 3 breaks, 2 must be meal break of at least an hour each, the others at least 15 minutes	N/A
Education hours	3	3	NIL

Stephen - It is someone who puts the child first. Someone who can say, *'The child is fine. I know they worked hard, but they are fine...'* or, *'I know we are within the hours, but the child needs a break'*. What I have noticed in the last five years is that the awareness of the child on set has been growing. Most productions now have a second or third person, like a runner, who will be with the children to keep them happy, or getting them water or whatever.

Q - Where do you find tutors and chaperones?

Stephen - Each educational authority has a list of licensed chaperones and tutors. And then there are professional tutors who go around teaching. And when you are doing your budgets for children, you must consider the chaperone. If it is a low budget, no-budget or student film, often the mums and dads would go along and do the job. But children are not the same as when their parents are around. They can then, without parents present take bigger risks, make mistakes, shout and they can let themselves go. Even in a dramatic situation, with a parent there, it is not quite the same. It is different if it is a stage production because everyone is there. You've got to go and do it. So even for low budget movies, a chaperone might be better.

Q - Are there things that can be done when filming to keep a child character within a scene, but as they are shooting beyond their hours, do it without them being present?

Stephen - Yes. You can frame them out of a shot so we know they are there, but they are not on screen.

Q - There is a moment at the end of Aliens where Ripley is running through the ship with the little girl holding onto her. Well, that little girl is actually a dummy and if you look closely you can see it clearly.

Stephen - Yes, there was another one where there was a child in a car with a big wheel spin and it was done with cameras going all around the car, not the car actually moving. So you think the child is in danger, but he/she is not. You can use doubles too, and we have pictures of twins in our book. Again, that can be a dangerous road because they can look the same, but they might give the same standard of performance.

Q - Can children handle the edgier material such as bad language or sexuality that might be in independent films?

Stephen - Usually they are fine. I think parents think of their children as younger than they actually are. Scenes with swearing or sexuality are not a problem provided that we know about it ahead of time, so we can tell the parents. Same thing goes for gore or violence. Just tell us about it so we can alert the parents. Again it is all about common sense and I think these days people use common sense more than five or six years ago.

Q - Are there any things to consider if the child is in a lead role?

Stephen - Just be aware of the challenges, especially if it is a younger child, because they don't have the experience of acting at that level. Also they can be unpredictable because they are kids. But don't be put off because of their age or their abilities or licensing laws. Children can add depth to any film.

Q - What are the restrictions when you have to take a child out of school?

Stephen - If it is during weekends or holiday time then it is no problem because it is not during school. We try to restrict filming to four days a term to two weeks a year a child can be taken out of school without requiring extra tuition. If it is more than that, then, they will need a tutor. And that is potentially expensive. So if you are going to use a child try to use them during summer or Christmas holidays and/or weekends. The bottom line is that the schools have the ultimate say so.

Q - What are the parents of child actors like in your opinion?

Stephen - I don't mind the parents who are 'pushy' because they are on your side. What I don't like are the parents who are apathetic. We could be hyping a child up and you get somewhere and you phone up and the mother says, '*I don't know whether he can do it.*' And you just feel all your energy drain away whereas a parent who is on the side of the child, is on your side as well.

Q - What would be some good cost effective and sensible ways of keeping children occupied during takes?

Stephen - Film makers want their children to act like kids in front of the camera, but off camera to act like adults. If you can do that, great. But even the best of the kids are going to need time to get back into kid mode in front of the camera. And vice versa. It doesn't happen suddenly and that is something to be aware of. If it is during term time, they will have homework to do. If it is holiday time, then we bring a whole range of things for them to do. We bring cards, we bring books and the like. If it is longer term,

Child Performers Licence Restrictions - SCOTLAND and WALES

AGE	9 to 16	5 to 8	UNDER 5
Maximum hours at the place of rehearsal or performance	8 hours	7.5 hours	5 hours
Hours	9.00am - 7.00pm	9.00am - 4.30pm	9.30am-4.30pm
Maximum period of continuous rehearsal performance	1 hour	45 minutes	30 minutes
Maximum number of hours for the entire performance or rehearsal	3.5 hours	3 hours	2 hours
Rest and meal breaks	If present for 4 consecutive hours (including presence for educational purposes whether or not tuition takes place at place of performance): 2 breaks, one meal break for at least an hour, the other breaks at least 15 minutes	If present for more than 3.5 consecutive hours (including presence for educational purposes whether or not tuition takes place at place of performance): 2 breaks, one meal break for at least an hour, the other breaks at least 15 minutes	Any time not used for work but be used for meals or rest.
	If present for 8 consecutive hours: 3 breaks, 2 must be meal breaks of at least an hour each, the others at least 15 minutes.	If present for 8 consecutive hours: 3 breaks, 2 must be meal break of at least an hour each, the others at least 15 minutes	N/A
Education hours	3	3	NIL

you can put a video on a laptop. And they have to like their own company as well. It is often difficult for one child and no other children around and that is something for a film maker to consider. They do better when there are two kids.

Q - Do you find it helpful for the adult actors to spend time with the child actors?

Stephen - Yes, the really talented young actors that we have get on better with the adult actors than with their own peer group.

Q - Do directors usually know when they have gone too far or do you have to step in?

Stephen - I have been doing this for fifteen years and I can count on one hand the number of times I have had to step in and say, *'That's enough.'* I wouldn't say it to the director. I would talk to the second assistant director and he or she would have a word with her/him. Some directors push adults any way they can, but they don't know when to stop. The problem is that a child wouldn't say *'stop it',* whereas an adult might.

Q - What do you think are the common mistakes made by productions when dealing with children?

Stephen - With younger children, though you can talk to them as adults, you need to plan your shoot as if they are children. For instance, the first day on the set instead of saying, *'They are here... let's go!',* some time should be spent explaining the whole thing to the child so that they get to know the cast and the crew. Maybe some sort of initial party or get together would be a good idea. The other thing to do is to make your casting briefs as specific as possible. Some of the briefs we get are very vague: fourteen-year-old boy with dark hair who can act. Then the child gets there and there is a row of fourteen-year-old, dark haired boys and they are in with audition for only minutes. Then maybe the video will go to the director. And you don't hear anything if it is a *'no',* and that is quite hard for children to take because there is no feedback. It is quite understandable because these people see one hundred children and are they supposed to write one hundred letters? Still it can be emotionally difficult on a child to go up to London, get all hyped up for a video shoot and then nothing. Or worse, you make several trips for callbacks and then don't get it. Sometimes there is a lack of communication with the child. Very early in the proceedings you should sit down with the child and very casually, as you and I are doing now, explain to them what it entails to make a movie. That way, they really understand what is going on and know where you are coming from.

Q - What advice would you give a new film maker ?

Stephen - Some of the children that we have want to act and some of the children *have* to act. Those that have to act have got to do it no matter what it means. They are naturally devoted and naturally focused. More often than not, they are talented, but they will do anything to act. I think a film maker has to be the same way. If he has to make films then he should!

Q - What is Shooting People?

Stu - Shooting People is a network of filmmakers, primarily an emailed daily digest. It exists to make easier the process of getting films made, so as to enable people to achieve what they want, in a much more streamlined way. An example could be someone might be crewing up a production and needs to find people to collaborate with, or you could post questions about issues that your are unclear about. Over time it has evolved and we now put on events, run a few different events a year, competitions, as well as publishing books and running a website resource and archive etc.

Q - So it's like having a massively extended family of friends who are all in the business - possibly at your level, or above you or below you - and you get to ask lots of questions? Gone are the days of stepping out of my bedroom and saying 'I have no idea what to do, who to talk to, I feel very alone', there is really no reason to feel alone?

Stu - Exactly. Over time we have grown on from that, to cover different areas. We started out primarily as a filmmaking website, but now we are helping out with Documentary, Writing, Casting, Animation, and different genres like Music video. We are getting bands involved who want to get music videos made as well, that has been quite a successful off-shoot. Also we are going international, our New York list is steadily growing for instance. So you sign up for the lists you want and every day, they will come through to your mailbox in the morning with an edited digest of messages relating to that subject. You can post onto those lists and ask a question, and if it is relevant it will get posted onto the next issue. Then it will get an audience of thousands of people who will see that the next morning, and be able to help you with whatever you are posting for.

Q - For someone who is very cash-strapped, or from a particularly socially-compromised background, who can't go to film school. . . Do you think that joining Shooting People (SP), maybe joining the NPA (New Producers Alliance), buying a bunch of books, blagging a camera and shooting a film is a viable alternative? I am not saying it is the same as film school, but it is a really good way of kick-starting yourself into something that you want to do for a maximum of a few hundred pounds all in?

Stu - Absolutely, yes. Taking that approach means that you can get out there immediately, to start finding different people to collaborate with, to start making things happen. We see that as a great way for people to get into achieving the thing that they want in the industry. Quite a lot of what happens, happens behind the scenes. People will post and find people to work with, and what happens from that point, happens in the background. Ashvin Kumar, who made the short film 'Little Terrorist', crewed the film from SP, then they went off and they shot it, and it got nominated for an Oscar. To watch that process, from the original posting on the list, to being nominated for an Oscar, is amazing.

Stu Tily
www.shootingpeople.org

Q - Who set it up and why?

Stu - It was born in 1998 by Cath LeCouteur and Jess Search. They had just finished making their first short film and were struck by how difficult it had been to find the people to work with and to get questions answered. That was the motivation for setting it up in the first place.

Q - How much does it cost?

Stu - To be a member is £30 a year.

Q - How can filmmakers best use SP?

Stu - You should approach SP as being a community of people that you can help with the things they want to do, they can help you with things that you want to do. You can ask questions or search our database of questions and answers going back many years.

Q - How can the first time filmmaker be assured that what they are getting is good information, or highly opinionated waffle?

Stu - We have editors on our lists, who come together and check that whatever gets posted is relevant and interesting. We do encourage debate on the lists as there are some subjects for which there isn't a 'right' answer. These debates can last many days. Each list has an Editor who will be working in that industry, and have a depth of experience in that field. So inaccuracies are not posted.

Q - What advice would you offer a new film maker?

Stu - I would say that the most important things are to not be daunted by it, get out there, communicate with people, make contacts and believe in your ability and use whatever resources you have available that are going to help you be successful in making films. To be successful in making films, you are going to have to blagg stuff, be convincing to sell your ideas, to use whatever is available to get that thing made. SP is a useful thing to join to get started on that.

Tim Dennison
Lighthouse Entertainment

PRODUCER / LINE PRODUCER

Q - What is the budget of a low budget film?

Tim - There are 2 categories of budget. The British low budget film is a couple of million quid, where it is bonded, and as soon as it is bonded, you've got to put all your rates in at a certain level. I would class independent filmmaking, as unbonded, and is generally below a million quid to make.

Q - If you assume that somehow you have managed to get a bit of money, you have put a deal together, what do you, as the producer, do?

Tim - As in any film, you have to set the parameters. If for example, when you go out to raise money, you have to know how much you need, or the minimum you can make the film for. So to do that you need to have a screenplay which is at a level of development that is suitable for shooting. Then you must do a budget and a schedule, just to work out the overall dynamics, to give yourself a blue print of how you will do it. You will need to sit down with the Director and say *'How are we going to achieve this, with this amount of money?'* To a certain extent that blueprint then sets the tone for everything else.

As is often the case, a project begins with the Producer optioning a project for no money, say £1k, £3k, whatever, they then spend a year and a half developing it, constantly trying to extend the option, which depends on what the relationship is like with the writer, and after two years, you are still nowhere - and so you say *'right, sod this, what is the minimum we can do this film for?'* Sometimes on that £2m, traditional UK low budget, bonded picture, you say *'right, hardcore facts, forget union rates, if we get all heads of department for £500 a week, 2nd ADs for £350, and the tea boy for £150, rewrite to make it more shootable, then shoot on HD ...'* and you basically pair it down to the bare minimum, just to be able to shoot the film.

Q - I know every film is different, but there are some broad parameters for a low budget, independent film, where it is do-able, but not to the point where everything is so compromised that it becomes either crap or unsaleable. What do you think is the minimum budget, minimum shoot time, before it becomes silly?

Tim - I think you have to pay people something, even if it is only £100. I think that as soon as you go below the £300k threshold, there can be some ramifications that may appear on the finished article. However, in saying that, it also depends on the screenplay, if you have a screenplay which has got brilliant dialogue, is set in 3 rooms, and you can shoot it over 3 weeks, and you pay people a couple of hundred quid to do it, then it could be made for £100k.

Q - Once a picture is up and running, what is it that you do? Assuming that you will take on the Line Producer roles as well as Producer role?

Tim - I will use a recent film that I did as model, where the budget was £300k. I had done a budget and schedule and knew the money was in place. The story was set, predominantly in one location, as is the case with so many low budget films. Finding that location became central to making the budget work, and after looking at many places, we found it. We were then able to set dates for pre-production, and at £300k, your prep time is going to be around 6 weeks. My key thing then was to sort out the heads of departments, the DP, Production design etc., and we were paying the crew, on average, around £300 a week. In an ideal world I would have a 'second me' in the production office! The problem is nobody is as good as oneself, whether other people think you are a load of shit, is irrelevant, you know what you have to do, and sometimes telling other people what you need to do can waste time when you could be doing it.

So finding a Production Manager to assist would be fairly crucial to putting the project together. As soon as you say, *'OK, prep starts June 5th'*, and that 6 weeks commences, and you have done a cash flow, then the train begins, and you can't get off (laughs). At this level, the biggest challenge is just the sheer workload, and you can only do so much in a day before your mind becomes overloaded and ineffective. So that is why it is good to have a Production Manager, a Production co-ordinator, a Production secretary, which would be the norm in any £2m picture. It is good to have that network behind you so that you can off-load work. You want to avoid the situation where you spread yourself so thin that the net suddenly develops a couple of holes, and things aren't done.

At the end of the day, my task is to service the Director. As irritating as it can be, as Directors can be, the Director's job is to demand, and get what he wants, and can go to the extent of being quite arrogant about it to get what he needs. It is the Producer's job to, in the most diplomatic fashion, provide that, in any form necessary, within the budgetary remit. That can be quite a testing time. There is a slight difference between a Line Producer and a Producer, because a Producer can say to the Director, *'No you can't do that'* or *'we don't have enough money to do that, you are going to have to rethink the way you want to shoot that'*. Whereas to a certain extent, a Line Producer works under the Producer, and is more of a go-between.

Q - That's an interesting point about the dynamic between the Producer and Director. Do you think that is why it would be wise for a new Director to try and get involved with a more experienced Producer, even if it is only in an advisory capacity? Simply because most new Directors push so hard, so far and they waste time and resources pursuing a fanciful goal that isn't that important?

Tim - Yes is the straight answer. Sometimes you get Directors that are so frustrated with trying to get their film going that they actually take on the producing role as well, which in my opinion is a total no-no. So you do need to find a Producer to come on board. The more experience they have, will in turn lighten the load for the Director. They will also guide the Director into making some sound decisions. For example, a novice Director might over shoot a scene, purely to compensate for not being 100% confident on how it is going to cut together. If you are a Producer that has got some experience, you can sit down with the Director and comfort them to a certain extent and say *'we've got 'X' amount of stock that is going to allow you to shoot 'X' amount in a day'*. Try and storyboard it with the Director, even if it is stickmen storyboards. At least you are rehearsing how he is going to shoot it, and to a certain extent, it is getting the Director to make choices before getting to set. In theory, this should relax him because he is actually working out in his own head how he is going to do it, which in theory should help you when you are shooting it.

Q - In your experience on low budget films, is the script ready to shoot?

Tim - I think that if there are problems in the script and they are not addressed before it is shot, they will come and bite you on the arse when you preview the film. I often think that low budget films are underdeveloped. Because as a Producer / Director you are trying to build a body of work, you want to make your film as quickly as possible. It is sometimes rushed into development, rushed into financing and it will show. There are times when a Producer will look at a screenplay and say *'we have got too many locations here, we've got £300k and you've got 45 locations!'* You can rewrite, with the same dialogue, or capturing what the scene is saying, but merge locations. You can only get to that once you have done the schedule and you will see how many locations you have got.

If you are doing low budget, you will often hear that you have got to do it in one location for obvious reasons. Just make sure that that dynamic works, that you can sustain a film in one location, yet keeping it fun and punchy.

Q - How do you go about doing a budget and a schedule?

Tim - To a certain extent you need to do a schedule first, because the schedule will dictate how many weeks you are going to film.

One needs to break down the script, and highlight all your key locations. If you are not governed by cast, by Julia Roberts being in it and shifting things around her (and you won't on a budget of £300k!), then locations will dictate the schedule, with actors taking second place. For a £300k film, you are going to shoot 6-day weeks, so you just try and structure it accordingly. Once you have done that, you can then do your budget. You have got to sit down with the Director and say *'Do you want to shoot on high definition, what is the level of cast you are going to get, how do you plan to shoot it?'* Are you working with a contingency, a contingency is normally 10%, but on £300k you sometimes slash that to 5% just to get the figure in at £300k. Then you just have to workout what you will need if the schedule works out at 4 weeks, 5 weeks... You have to workout what elements you need for that 5 weeks. Are you filming on location, have you got location costs, do you have to put up actors, crew and cast, feeding people etc. The core thing is you have to be smart with your money as £300k doesn't go far, and you have minimal ability to go over in any area, so you have to put all the money up on screen. To do that, you need to maximise shooting hours, ideally everybody being in the same location. As soon as you start travelling and moving people around, it takes time.

Q - Do you think it would be wise to almost make a film in your head as a Producer / Director before you even get to set, so you can confront those compromises?

Tim - From my side of things, if you have got no money to make your film, you need to give yourself lots of preparatory time. The prep time is there to work out all your problems before they even develop, this is why storyboarding is useful, because it is a way that everybody can rehearse in their head what the Director is trying to achieve - costume, wardrobe, make-up, all departments can see what they have got to achieve. I think that is really crucial in pre-production time. Pre-production is communication. Have regular meetings where everyone, from each department, can ask questions and openly address problems. As soon as somebody says something from one department, somebody from another department will chip in and say *'Hang on a second we thought we were making that, are you doing that?'* So pre-production is sometimes more crucial on low budget than it is on regular budgets.

Q - What kind of problems do you see during the shoot? What are the common problems you have to deal with?

Tim - Tiredness. Especially if you are night shooting, or if you go from nights to days. You have got to keep aware of people's politics too, and keep a smooth running ship. There is always the weather factor if you are on location, which is why you schedule weather cover scenes. Predominantly, it's about staying on budget and on schedule. Of course, you have always got a major problem if you are looking at the rushes and thinking *'fuck, we have got a problem here! (laughs)'*

Q - Once the shoot is finished, that whole family, the camaraderie, the whole crew and pre-production staff, they all disappear, and you look at your bank balance and you realise you have spent more than you should have done. Then you enter post-production which is a horrendously expensive stage, at the very final steps at least. What mistakes have you encountered in post-production that are easily avoidable?

Tim - I think that locking the edit takes longer than you anticipate. With the best will in the world, the edit can go on and on and on. Sometimes through insecurity, script problems, fixing problems on the shoot, and even having distance to address overall pace. I actually like the time when you have wrapped the crew and you return to a small team of people. It is far more relaxed and controllable, but one of the pitfalls is that you can take your foot off the gas, and before you know it, you are a month in, and they are only halfway through scene 2! You have to manage your post-production schedule as you do the main shoot.

Q - One of the things new filmmakers rarely take into consideration is cost of sales and distribution deliverables, which is a budgetary cost, but it is not part of the pure filmmaking process - do you have any comments on that?

Tim - When you are making the film, you just want to get the thing shot, and that is an achievement in itself. If the film is going to be the success you think it is going to be, you will need certain elements to service the world sales, commonly called deliverables. Currently this is coming in at about £80k! On the last film, we shot on HD, so that £80k includes a 35mm blow up (£30k), trailers, your errors and emissions insurance (£7k). All these elements, financially, you have to find. You could say to the Sales Agent, *'OK we don't have the money to do a trailer, would you pay for it?'*, so the Sales Agent will pay for it, and obviously they will pay money

Negotiating Tips

Getting your film made will rely largely on your ability to negotiate amazing deals, or creatively work around problems, or just plain work hard! Most of all, remember, no-one owes you a break, so be humble and charming.

1. Everything is negotiable. Every list price you will ever be quoted will have another figure next to it which is what the person you are negotiating with is allowed to go down to. The trick is to find out what that figure is.

2. Find out from friends what kind of deals they got - it's a good yardstick.

3. Set up an account with the company and stretch the credit as far as you can. It is cheaper than a bank loan. Always keep in touch with the company you owe money to, never lie and never ever try and get away without paying. Good will can be stretched if you are civil, have a good reason for not paying, and can offer a schedule of payments within a set time frame.

4. When approaching people for deals or freebies, be polite and DON'T try and hustle. Most people who are in the Industry have been in it for many years and can spot ignorance and arrogance a mile away. Both these qualities are not desirable. Go to a person for help and advice - everyone likes to help someone out, it makes them feel good inside. Follow up thank you letters will often get a repeat performance if it is needed.

5. Many things can be begged, borrowed or stolen. If there is any opportunity for a company logo to be featured on screen, they will probably supply you with free samples of the product. Cars, costume, cigarettes etc. These can all reduce your budget. They may even pay (product placement).

6. Be thorough, ring around and get the best quotes. You will get a feel for who will be able to help you.

7. Many companies, not related to the film industry will often render their services for free just to be involved in the production (for the fun) or for a credit on the end titles. Tickets to the premiere can be a good bribe.

8. Go into negotiations with a maximum you will pay and don't go over it. If you are prepared to walk out without making a deal, you are in a very strong position.

9. If you can pay cash on delivery, you can push harder for a bigger discount. This is the best way to get the biggest discounts. Avoid doing non VAT declared deals (cash in hand) - it may seem like a good idea at the time, but when Customs & Excise or the Inland Revenue ask you where the money went, you may have problems (you should be VAT registered anyhow in the UK).

10. If you can't get a discount, get something thrown in for free.

11. Remember to say thank you afterwards. If you can, send a bottle of booze or even chocolates and flowers. Whatever the gift, it will be appreciated.

12. Take whoever you are doing the deal with out for a drink and build a relationship. After your shoot, start taking the credit controller out for a drink, as you probably can't afford to pay and you need to extend good will to as near breaking point as you can.

13. Find out when a hire companies off season is and use them during that period. They will frequently reduce prices on equipment and services.

14. Especially in the post production phase, try using facilities after hours or in non-peak hours. In addition, see if you can hire the assistants of the main editors or telecine operators, peolple who want the opportunity to move up the ladder.

15. Go to the hire company and introduce yourself personally. People like having a face with a name.

16. Make sure you get all quotes in writing and faxed over to your office. Ask them to list the equipment or materials, the service and the dates and the exact agreed amount. This will help avoid any misunderstanding and make it harder for the company or individual to retract their offer.

plus money for the mark-up to do that. Suddenly what you as an independent guy could do for £2k, a Sales Agent would charge £8k for! If you go to a trailer making company, they will quite easily charge you £15k for a trailer. So you have to be aware of how you cash flow for your deliverables, and if you've scrimped and scraped just to get the film shot, cut, dubbed, as a lot of people do, don't think you can relax when it's done as there is still a lot of work to do and pay for. You really need an advance from a Sales Agent to cover the cost of the deliverables. Of course that advance is then just another tranch of money which puts you a step behind recouping your budget.

Q - You have made quite a number of lower budget British pictures, some of them very low, some of them not so low, and some of them you would have been paid well, others not so well. After the film is complete and entered sales, from how many of those films have you seen money - that is, money from actually selling the film?

Production Value

GUERILLA FILM MAKER SAYS!

While the director isn't directly responsible for production value, the job is split through other departments such as, camera, production design, script etc. It is the directors job to make sure that production value does not turn into production failure. If the production values fail, the whole credibility of the world in which your story is set, and therefore the audience suspension of belief, can be compromised. It can be as small as typos in a newspaper headline, or a background artist who looks out of place.

1. Fill the scene with as many props as possible without it looking cluttered.

2. Do not use cheap wigs and costumes unless you are doing so for comedic reasons. They never look good.

3. Try to use practical lights in a scene to highlight props and set decorations. This can be anything from a desk lamp to buttons and dials that light up on a submarine control console.

4. In exterior situations, shoot during 'golden hour' to get the best light. Often in the UK that's golden minute!

5. Always shoot wide shots of your locations as it makes your film look bigger.

6. Cast people of different ages in your film, if appropriate, so it does not look like a student film maker using his friends.

7. Find creative ways of moving the camera to make the film more dynamic. Don't fear going hand held when appropriate, it can add energy.

8. Stunts can be a lot cheaper than you think, and make a film pop with excitement. Brainstorm with a good stunt co-ordinator on how to get more bang for your buck.

9. Make sure you have enough close ups and cutaways. Eye light in close ups always looks good.

10. Try to get permission to use the real thing whenever possible. A real corner shop will look better than one you build on a set.

11. Try to get as many extras as possible for crowd shots and public locations (like a car park or train station) in order to make the scene look bigger and more real. If you are restricted on extras, shoot on the long end of the lens to compress down the space you need to fill.

12. For night shoots, wet down streets with a hose in order to make a scene shimmer on film.

13. Pay particular attention to the colours in front of the camera (costume, location, props), and try not to have clashes unless you want it.

Tim - In a word, none! Next! (laughs)

Q - So the key is, whatever money you are going to get, you get upfront and during the shoot as some kind of fee?

Tim - Yes. It is crucial to say that.

Q - What do you think about HD?

Tim - HD is excellent. I'm of the film era, I used to have a film post-production company, but I can't fault HD. There are so many advantages. The films that I have done on HD have been transferred to 35mm and no distributor has said, 'oh it's shot on HD'. The only thing I would warn people of though, is, if you go to the trouble of mastering to HD (before you spend £30k making a 35mm neg / print) you will want to screen it for distributors and sales agents in HD, and the screening facilities are hugely expensive compared to standard 35mm screening rooms - 35mm would cost me a couple of hundred pounds where HD is closer to a grand. That will change though as HD becomes more prevalent.

Q - How do you feel about making low budget films?

Tim - Although the journey of making films is a fucking rocky one, there is a good part of me that prefers doing a non-bonded picture, where you have more control and freedom. Working with people that are not doing it for the money, who are doing it for the fun and camaraderie. That is on the sentimental side. On the business side, it is fucking hard to make low budget films work as a business. There are two kinds of producers. There is the more technical kind of guy, more hands-on, which is more the category that I come into. Then there is the guy who is more of the schmoozer, political animal, that is not particularly interested or needs to know the mechanics of making the film, they just need the key element of the script, the relationship with the Director, the Agent, and those are the dealmaker producers. It is a business at the end of the day. I admire people like Jeremy Thomas who has been around for a long time, but has still kept his autonomy, and still does low budget stuff. He is putting money together, project by project, piece by piece, patchwork quilt financing! You kind of have to work out who you are and where you see yourself.

Often I think you need more of an accounting brain than a producing brain. You also need another brain or mindset to be dining with bigger players in the UK funding scene, so you can move in those circles. If you are not in that circle it is fucking tough to get in. I do think everybody should do their own low budget film. If it is not a success, fine, but you learn so much by doing it yourself. I've learnt many lessons and I am still learning, just by trying to do my own things.

Q - What are the most common mistakes that you see Producers making?

Tim - Often, it is only when it is too late and you have kind of learnt from the error that you know how to fix it, but it's usually too late. Over budget, over schedule, are obviously the most common problems, hence, get somebody with some film knowledge to look over the budget and see if it is feasible. If you go to somebody who has just done a $20m picture, they would say *'fuck that pal, you are wasting your time!'* If you get a film off the ground, in itself, in it's own right, it is commendable. When I look at some films, I suppose I question, ponder, think *'how the fuck did they get that made?!'* You look at the script and you think *'Christ, I can't see any commerciality in that!'* It's not a criticism, and if they have got the balls to get it up and running, good luck to them.

Q - What advice would you offer a new filmmaker?

Tim - My girlfriend thinks I am crazy (laughs), but if you have got the film bug, you will make films, and it is very difficult to get out of it. To a certain extent you have to be selfish, it is a selfish business. That selfishness will often take out other chunks of your life. You have to be prepared to go to all lengths. Any producing person will often question themselves as to why they are doing it, what are they doing, how are they doing it... most often, *why aren't they doing it (laughs)!* I do think that when it goes well it is fun. But boy, when there is a drought it is fucking painful! Your girlfriend has left you, you are bankrupt, and it is not pleasant. Sitting in a creditors meeting, trying to explain yourself and how you've run up a £70k debt, and that you scheduled the film for 5 weeks, and you were 5 weeks in and you had shot a third of it! You do think *fucking hell!* With all the downside, the plus side is that I think there are lots of good people in the business. There are two sides to every coin. If you want to do it, have a good crack, make your own film.

PRE PRODUCTION

Martin Spence
BECTU

Q - What is BECTU?

Martin - BECTU is the Broadcast Entertainment Cinematograph & Theatre Union, with about 26,000 members in the entertainment industries. In film and TV side, we represent permanently employed members at the BBC, ITV, film studios, film labs, post-production and facilities houses, etc. And of course we also represent around 10,000 freelances who make up much of the production workforce.

Q - What is the PACT/BECTU Freelance Production Agreement?

Martin - This is an agreement with PACT that sets out minimum rates of pay and a framework of other working conditions (hours, travel etc.), and acts as a benchmark across a wide range of film/TV production.

Q - What can you offer your members?

Martin - Collectively we negotiate agreements with employers on members' terms and conditions of employment. These include the PACT/BECTU Agreement mentioned before, freelance agreements with other employers such as the BBC Natural History Unit, and major staff agreements with the BBC and ITV. In addition we give a range of individual services and benefits. For instance, we issue a regular bulletin called "Early Bird" to alert freelance members of upcoming job opportunities - while making it quite clear that we are not an employment agency.

We can help with career development, training needs, and qualifications by putting members in touch with other organisations - Skillset, Skillset Careers, FT2, regional skills panels, and so on. We also advise on rates of pay, contract queries, insurance cover, the do's and don'ts of working abroad and on whether the prospective employer is known to us as a dodgy customer. And of course we give support when a member has a problem - e.g. an employer won't pay them for the work they've just done. Sometimes this means us dealing directly with the employer on the member's behalf. Sometimes it means getting our lawyers involved. It all depends on the circumstances, and it's all paid for by the member's subscription. Finally, we help out on essential but boring-sounding stuff such as insurance - freelance members can get Public Liability Insurance through their union membership - tax, NI, and so on.

Q - What is your Script Registration Service?

Martin - This is a service where members can register a treatment, script, or design with us, to protect themselves against copyright theft.

Q - Is this free to members and what is the process to submit a script?

Yes it's free to members. All they have to do is send in their script in a sealed envelope. We can then provide dated confirmation that it existed in a particular form at a particular point in time.

Q - What benefits can you offer Producers?

Martin - We are a trade union. Our role is to represent the interests of our members as workers in relation to their employers. Producers, in general, are those employers. So it's not really our role to offer benefits or services to them. There are other organisations - PACT, the NPA - which do that. Having said all that, we do have Line Producers and Production Managers in membership, and when they find themselves in dispute with their employers, then of course we will advise and represent them like any other member.

Q - What are the BECTU rates?

Martin - We have negotiated minimum pay rates with PACT: these are on our website - www.bectu.org.uk - click on Agreements and follow the links. We issue recommended rates for work on Commercials, also at the website. And we have information on current going rates in different types of production which is available to individual members.

Q - How do members join?

Martin - The easiest way for freelances is to go to the website and click on "Join". If you're freelance you can join online.

Q - Does BECTU have agreements that Producers can use for crew?

Martin - Yes, the PACT/BECTU Freelance Production Agreement.

Q - Does BECTU have any particular agreements for crew working on low budget productions?

Martin - The PACT/BECTU Agreement is a minimum terms Agreement. It is intended to provide a minimum set of pay-rates and conditions for all film/TV productions with mainstream or commercial exposure or potential. Many experienced freelances command personal rates a lot higher than those on the PACT/BECTU ratecard - and quite right too. For Producers who want a good, experienced, reliable crew, the PACT/BECTU Agreement provides an absolute minimum benchmark on rates and conditions.

Q - Are there any agreements or advice for crew who are working on UK co-productions that are shooting overseas?

Martin - We have negotiated a standard insurance package for overseas work with PACT, and we regularly advise members on other issues related to working abroad.

Q - Can BECTU negotiate deferrals with a Producer?

Martin - Absolutely not. Deferred pay deals are bad news, and 100% deferrals are unlawful, a breach of the National Minimum Wage, and we don't have anything to do with them.

Q - What is BECTU's policy on crew working on non BECTU films? What if the film production company can't afford to pay the union's recommended crew fees?

Martin - There's no such thing as a "non-BECTU film". If members are working on a production, and need our assistance, then we will do whatever is necessary to help them. If we're looking at a low-budget film which is not being made under our Agreement, and a member agrees to work below the union rate, then so long as the contract itself is legal that's their choice. We may not like it but there it is. We believe that members who regularly do deals of this sort only undermine their own career prospects.

Q - Can BECTU shut down a production/ blacklist or expel it's members who work on non BECTU films?

Martin - Again - there's no such thing as a "non-BECTU film".

Q - Does BECTU help its members with any payment disputes?

Martin - Yes, all the time. We are experts in the arcane science of debt collection.

Martin Spence

373-377 Clapham Road, London
SW9 9BT United Kingdom
Tel: 020 7346 0900 Fax: 020 7346 0901
Email: info@bectu.org.uk

**BROADCASTING ENTERTAINMENT
CINEMATOGRAPH & THEATRE UNION**

Q - Can BECTU help film Producers find crew for their productions? Likewise with Health and Safety crew?

Martin - Yes we can help with crew via our online crew directory - Crewbus (www.crewbus.org.uk) - which is a good place to look for freelance talent. We certainly provide basic advice to some especially naïve Producers on the do's and dont's of health and safety - even though this isn't really our job. And we invest a lot of time working with the Health & Safety Executive and industry employers on practical health and safety arrangements. But if you are asking whether we would recommend a particular individual to a Producer as a Health & Safety Adviser, then the answer is No. That would put us in a very invidious position.

Q - What is the magazine that you offer your members?

Martin - The BECTU magazine Stage Screen & Radio comes out ten times a year. It contains the 'Ask First' list where we identify companies which have failed to honour their obligations to our members. Usually, though not always, this means they have refused to pay for work done. The 'Ask First' list is widely consulted in the industry, not only by our members but by facilities houses, post-production houses etc., who are keen to avoid getting stung by rogue production companies.

Q - What common mistakes do you come across?

Martin - Dangerously long working hours, and ridiculously low pay for newcomers - sometimes no pay at all - are the biggest problems. I wish I could describe them as "common mistakes" but I'm afraid it's worse than that - they are now part of an ingrained culture. Many Producers genuinely think that this is the only way to make films. Of course it isn't, and nor is it the way to develop a skilled and stable workforce.

Q - What advice would you offer new Producers / Filmmakers?

Martin - Our starting point is that the film/TV industry is just that: an industry, not a hobby. Within that industry, we do our best to ensure that the people whose skills underpin the whole business are properly treated and properly rewarded. Low / no-budget filmmaking is encouraged by colleges offering a glut of superficially attractive media courses, regardless of the fact that the number of graduates vastly exceeds employment prospects in the industry. The low / no budget production sector exists because a lot of young people coming off media courses see no other way to get started. And because a few grubby characters who like to call themselves "producers" want to make a few bob by ripping these same eager young people off. These are the ones who insist on going into production even though they can't, or won't, raise the budget to pay for it. We all know how they try to square the circle, by begging or borrowing money from family, friends, or ads in 'Loot', by calling in favours, by offering "deferred pay" deals to prospective crew members. We have three problems with this. Firstly, low/no-budget production undermines pay rates, budgets, expectations and standards right across the industry. It plays right into the hands of the worst, most brutal, cost-cutting employers. Secondly, to get people to "defer" all of their pay is actually illegal as a result of the National Minimum Wage. Thirdly, there is increasingly little justification for it, because the industry is slowly putting the pieces back together in terms of skills, training and career patterns. We have a highly-regarded training co-ordination body in Skillset. And we have new money coming into the industry to fund training and tackle the looming skills crisis - most importantly, the new Skills Investment Fund in the feature film sector.

So my advice to would-be new filmmakers is that film and TV is not a hobby, but an industry. If you seriously want to make a career in this industry - to earn a living in it - you've got to put in the groundwork, get the careers advice, decide on your line of attack, research the training opportunities, do the training, build your network, work your way up. You may even get to make "your film" - but on real money, rather than a wing and a prayer.

Q - What is your job?

Andy - Research and Legal Liaison Officer for BECTU - with responsibility for health and safety policy issues.

Q - Who should deal with Health and Safety issues on a set?

Andy - The production company/employer - i.e. the producer - carries ultimate legal responsibility for health and safety. Against this background they may delegate some specific heath and safety tasks to key individuals (e.g. production managers, heads of department) within their respective areas of operation. The self-employed will often be regarded as employees for purposes of health and safety regulations. If something goes wrong, it's the producer that will be sued.

Q - What are the common areas for health and safety?

Andy - Excessively long working hours on shoots, including prep and wrap time and travel to locations, is a major problem, with consequent concerns about fatigue leading to accidents. Other common health and safety areas are physical hazards such as lifting and shifting of heavy loads, camera cranes, falls from height, electricity. Hazardous substances such as chemicals. Environmental hazards such as temperature, noise, unsafe locations and hazardous tasks such as camera tracking backwards or working alone.

Q - How much is common sense?

Andy - Common sense will only get you so far. Creatively driven film-makers tend to have their minds on priorities other than health and safety. It's better to give some thought to health and safety in advance of the production rather than relying on common sense to get you through.

Q - What happens if there is an accident and it's found to be a health and safety issue?

Andy - Deal with the injured person straight away - through first aid and medical help if needed. Then there is a legal requirement to record and report work related accidents. The injured person has the right to take independent advice and, if they consider someone was at fault, to make a legal claim. If the accident was serious, the Health & Safety Executive (HSE) may investigate.

Q - What about food preparation?

Andy - If food is prepared on site, health and safety regulations require suitable standards of hygiene governing where the food is prepared and where it's eaten.

Q - Where can film makers get more detailed information?

Andy - The HSE produces a great deal of useful information, including a series of information sheets for the 'entertainment

Andy Egan
Health and Safety

industry' (www.hse.gov.uk; HSE Infoline 08701-545500). BECTU provides information for its members, including the BECTU Health and Safety Handbook and 15 separate Health and Safety cards for different film occupations. (www.bectu.org.uk; tel 020 7346 0900) The BBC Health and Safety website is useful for health and safety in our industry (www.bbc.co.uk/ohss).

Q - What would you say to a film maker who is making an ultra low budget film and doesn't consider health and safety a major issue?

Andy - It will certainly be a major issue if you get sued when someone suffers an injury. Far better to invest a bit of time and effort in advance into sorting out health and safety.

Q - Stepping back from rules and laws - what things do you think lead to accidents happening?

Andy - In respect of employers - a lack of thought about health and safety and in particular about risk assessment (i.e. the duty to assess risks and identify precautions). In respect of individuals, long hours of work and the pressure to get the job done rather than raise awkward questions.

Q - What common mistakes do you see?

Andy - Waking up to doing a risk assessment only after the accident, rather than preventively in advance. Working on, for creative reasons, just a little too long. Scheduling for a shoot that's too short and for daily hours that are too long.

Q - What advice would you offer a new film maker?

Andy - Educate yourself on basic health and safety and get insurance cover.

BECTU

Andy Egan
RESEARCH OFFICER

373-377 Clapham Rd, London SW9 9BT
Tel 020 7346 0900 Fax 020 7346 0901
email: aegan@bectu.org.uk

BROADCASTING ENTERTAINMENT
CINEMATOGRAPH & THEATRE UNION

PRE PRODUCTION

Tim Willis
PACT

Q - What is PACT?

Tim - PACT is the Producers Alliance for Cinema and Television - the UK trade association that represents and promotes the commercial interests of independent feature film as well as TV, animation and interactive media companies.

Q - What kind of services does PACT offer?

Tim - We have a range of services for our members such as the business affairs surgery run by PACT's business affairs advisor Rowena Evans, as well as subsidised legal services provided by a leading city law firm; we offer financial support for film and TV companies who are attending key international festivals and markets and in addition we provide industry conferences, networking events, training. But our most important service for independent filmmakers is through the PRA, the Producers Rights Agency, which negotiates and maintains Film and TV agreements with broadcasters and Unions. It provides PACT members with model contracts and supplies help and advice.

Q - How much does membership cost ?

Tim - Producer membership is turnover related. If your turnover is under £500k a year, then it is £825. If it's between £500k-£2m, it would be £1,175, if between £2-£5m, it would be £2,115, £5-£10m it would be £2,350 and then over £10m, £2940. If you're a start up filmmaker with under £100k turnover and a limited company, you can join for £415 inc. VAT. However you'll have to upgrade in two years or if your turnover exceeds the £100k.

Q - What is the Production Levy for feature films and TV?

Tim - PACT has two principal sources of income - your annual membership subscription and a production levy on the budgets of feature films and television programmes made by PACT members. As soon as you are commissioned by a broadcaster, or begin production of a feature film, you should complete the on-line production information form at the following address: http://www.pact.co.uk/mbr/pra/pra_info_form.asp The production levy is due on the first day of principal photography and the production budget is defined as direct costs and overheads (so excluding the production fee and any contingency or completion guarantee). You should be aware that it is a condition of PACT membership that you pay the production levy due on any work in accordance with the Memorandum & Articles of Association. The production levy for feature films is calculated at 0.25% of the production budget up to a maximum of £1,000 for the first £1 million and thereafter 0.5% on the balance, up to a ceiling of £4,500 (ex VAT). For television productions the production levy is calculated at 0.5% of the production budget, up to a ceiling of £4,500 (ex VAT). The production levy must be included as a line item in your production budget and you should notify PACT so that we can invoice you directly. For television productions fully funded by the BBC, Channel 4, Five, or where the BBC fully funds a feature film, the production levy is remitted directly by the broadcaster to PACT. You should confirm with the broadcaster that it will be paid and therefore will not form part of your production budget.

Q - What is the PACT / Equity low budget scheme?

Tim - PACT and Equity operate a registered low budget film scheme. To qualify, a film needs to have a budget of less than £3m. For films budgeted above £250k to £3m you need to get your budget certified by an accountant who is a member of the Production Guild. The benefit of registering your film is that in addition to paying artists the daily/weekly rate, you would only need to pay either an additional 50% or 75% (depending on budget) to acquire worldwide all media rights that would otherwise cost 280% of their fee.

You are not limited in where and what media you show your film, but there is a hold back period for one year from its first theatric release before you can show it on UK television. If you are unable to secure a theatric release then the period is 15 months from the date of delivery of the film to its principal financier. Once the budget has been certified you must send a copy of the accountant's letter with the top sheet of the budget and a letter from your company stating that you wish to register the film under the low budget provisions. For films with a budget of less than £250k a budget summary from you will suffice. You would also have to send a letter in which you identify the financiers of the film, the commencement date of filming, where it was to be filmed, and for how long. You also need to confirm the number of cast roles and that all of the Artists would be contracted under the terms of the PACT Equity Cinema Agreement. Once this information has been passed to our offices it would normally take three to four days for registration to be agreed.

Q - Do you have to be member of PACT to access the Pact/Equity low budget scheme?

Tim - No, but you do have to pay the Levy.

Q - Do you provide other agreements?

Tim - PACT / PRA have negotiated many agreements with relevant counter parties to cover the rights and obligations of producers in relation to musicians, writers, crew and cast with all the relevant guilds and unions. A list of the agreements, model contracts and guidance notes which PACT members can access include: The PACT Equity Cinema Agreement, The PACT/Bectu recommended minimum pay rates and agreement, The PACT/Equity TV agreements, Writers Guild agreements as well as those covering minors, composers, locations, producers, directors etc.

Q - Are there any pay rates or minimums for Producers?

Tim - There are no establish pay rates or minimum rates for producers. Pay rates are all negotiable.

Q - Can PACT help its members with legal advice and/or business services?

Tim - PACT's business affairs service is intended to provide advice on all matters relating to developing and putting together a production to exploiting your rights. If you wish to obtain advice on service agreements for cast and crew, employment issues etc during production, you can approach the PRA. PACT's Legal Service, operated in association with Davenport Lyons, is designed to allow independent production companies with a modest turnover access to first class professional advice. The scheme is designed to make expert advice available at times when producers are struggling for finance. The rates offered will not be made available, either directly or indirectly, to broadcasters or other financiers, and once an allowance for legal advice is made in development budgets, or a television programme / feature film is commissioned or funded, the fee level would be a matter of agreement between Davenport Lyons and the client. The arrangements for invoicing for such fees would also be a matter for Davenport Lyons and the client to agree directly. An important principle of the PACT Legal Service, and one reason why the service can be offered at such an economical rate, is that all legal advice is paid for in advance by means of renewable bond lodged with PACT. The Legal Service will be charged to members at a rate of £75 per hour, excluding VAT and disbursements.

Q - Can you register your script for copyright protection with PACT?

Tim - One of the traditional means of registering copyright is to post a copy of your work to yourself; solicitor or bank manager by registered mail to be retained unopened. If you are a PACT member, an alternative is to use our copyright service. Before the work is shown to anyone, the material to be registered must be sent to David Alan Mills, Membership Officer, PACT, 2nd Floor, The Eye,1 Procter Street, London. Pact will date stamp each page of the work and retain a copy in case of dispute. The original will be sent back to you with a covering letter confirming receipt. This service is free of charge to members. If there is a copyright dispute the individual / organisation may approach the Pact business affairs advisor for advice.

pact.

Procter House
1 Procter Street, Holborn, London WC1V 6DW

Tel: 0207 067 4367
Fax: 0207 067 4377
web: www.pact.co.uk

Tracey Wilson
Storyboard Artist

STORYBOARDS

Q - What is your background?

Tracey - I went to art college, and then worked as an illustrator, doing children's books, advertising, that kind of work. Gradually I got interested in doing film work but wasn't sure how to get into it. I always had a fascination with film. The first time I ever heard that they used artists was when I picked up a book about ILM and saw the drawings by Ralph McQuarrie. I realised they actually used sketch artists, and so I began to pursue that. I started doing pop promos and commercials and got into it that way, and then got onto a feature film.

Q - What was the first feature film you worked on?

Tracey - The first film I did was *Dragonheart,* but just before that I did work as an illustrator on a film called *Crusade,* which fell through. On *Dragonheart* I had to learn as I went along. I couldn't tell anyone that I hadn't done it before, but the director knew apparently. They told me it would be for three and a half weeks in Slovakia, but it ended up being for four months.

Q - What is the job of a storyboard artist?

Tracey - Storyboards are like a map to help the rest of the crew know what the director wants, and to inspire everybody. It's a series of drawings that represent that shots that the director wants. I would of course work closely with the director to create them. It's like a map that enables people to tie everything together. Storyboards are the first visualisation of the screenplay. A lot of the job is thinking, I'd say only 20% of it is drawing. The rest of it you've got to sit down and construct a sequence and think about what's going to work. When you're short of time, you are often forced to draw quick *line work*, but if you have more time, it's nice to render the story boards so they have more of a feeling rather than just the actions.

Q - What is a concept artist?

Tracey - A concept artist works for the production designer, and they draw how the set is going to look, and design everything to do with the set. Whereas the story board artist draws the action. You work primarily for the director. We all collaborate of course, but the director would be the one to hire the story board artist and the production designer would choose the concept artists. Sometimes they overlap, if they can't afford a concept artist, the story board artist may be asked to do concepts as well.

Q - How soon are you brought in?

Tracey - Usually, just after the producer and the director are on board. Often you're the first person to be hired.

Q - Is there a certain style to doing the storyboards?

Tracey - No, everyone's got their own style. Some people will do more action films, other people will do more romantic comedies. It depends on what your illustration style suits. You'll abbreviate certain words like POV for point of view and MS for a medium shot. There are direction arrows which help too. I have worked for a couple of directors who refuse to have arrows on their drawings, which I think is a bad idea, as it doesn't help people see which way something's moving. By the time the boards are locked and you get to set, the boards are turned into a kind of flick book for quick reference.

Q - Do you literally do every shot the director wants?

Tracey - It depends on the director. Usually to begin with, we start on the big sequences that they know are definitely in the script and will cost a lot of money. Some directors just want the main effects sequences story boarding, and some want to lock down all the dialogue sequences as it's like a security blanket for them, so they've got something on paper and they can say *'well this is what I asked for'*. If they don't get it, they can prove it.

Q - Are they always just black and white sketches?

Tracey - Usually, but if it's an important scene, we can do colour key frames as well. But usually, for speed reasons, we do them in black and white. Also you get a lot more drama from black and white, as there's a lot of light and dark. When you want to pick something out and show more detail, then it's nice to do those key frames in colour, so they can work out how everything's going to look and work with the art and design departments as well.

Q - How big do you end up drawing them?

Tracey - We usually do three frames on an 8.5" x 11" page. On average, you're likely to do about ten or twelve pages a day, that's pages, not frames. Then you may also rough out more frames too.

Q - Does it go onto the computer at all?

Tracey - Often they make 'animatics' from the storyboards, but some people have started storyboarding on the computer using software. They look pretty good, but I find it's often quicker to draw something than do it on the computer.

Q - Have you worked on low budget movies?

Tracey - Yes. There tends to be more work to do on the smaller ones because you're the only one on it. On bigger projects there's usually two of you minimum. Often you work harder as they expect you to do a lot more in terms of character design as well, whereas if you're on a bigger film, that's usually handled by concept artists. When you're working for an independent director, they'll often call you at nine in the evening, or they'll try to get you to work a weekend without realising you don't get paid for weekends. It's just a bit more loose.

Q - How long do you think it would take to board a low budget drama?

Tracey - With smaller projects I've done it in six weeks. There's a lot of it that doesn't get covered, but pretty much all the big sequences do. I've also worked with people who've had a spec project that they want to present and I've just done a few boards for them in two weeks.

Q - Have you ever found that the location is different to what you had drawn, and so the story boards are abandoned?

Tracey - Yes, you can do all these boards and then see the film and it's nothing like what you drew. On the other hand, it's nice when you see the film and it is shot for shot what you have drawn.

Q - Would you work with the stunt co-ordinator?

Tracey - I've worked with stunt co-ordinators. On *Die Another Day*, we had to work closely with the 2nd unit director and the stunt co-ordinator on some scenes. I had to draw a sword fight, so that was tied in with the stunt co-ordinator and various fencing moves.

Q - Do you find action sequences hard to story board?

Tracey - It depends on the sequence. For example, with a fight scene you tend to just do a few key frames as the scene needs to be properly choreographed and this involves the stunt coordinator. I worked on a project where they wanted all the fight sequences storyboarded shot by shot. So the stunt guys did rehearsals which we taped and then the story board artists drew them up from the tapes. Action sequences, in general, are fun to draw.

Q - Are there differences doing story boards on films laden with effects?

Tracey - Yes. They like you to establish, in the storyboards, what could be a matte painting or what could be CG or a model. We write a note by each frame saying, 'this would be model,' or 'this would be 2nd unit'. That helps them to break down the sequences.

Q - Does the director sit with you and say, 'I want that shot here?'

Tracey - It depends on the director. I've worked on projects where I've been given shot lists, where the director's said, 'I want this shot, this shot and this shot', and figured it all out. But often the director doesn't really know what he wants until he sees it. He has an idea, but he likes you to be a catalyst for new ideas. So they give you the script and you go away and come up with a couple of ideas. I find it takes about three weeks to get into their head, to get to know what they like and don't like. There have also been cases where you work with a director who didn't like what you were doing, it wasn't that you are doing anything wrong, it was just the fact that you didn't really fit. Often the director doesn't want to hire a storyboard artist, and it's the producer's that make them. Then again, I've worked with some lovely directors who are very open to ideas, and if you come up with a good idea, they will let everyone know it was yours.

Q - Do you need to understand what look different lenses will give?

Tracey - Yes, it's good to know about lenses. If the director wants a certain lens, like a 50mm lens, then you'll know what he's going to be seeing through that lens and you can draw it accordingly.

Q - You must have a lot of directors referring to specific shots from movies as well?

Tracey - Yes, more than people realise. A lot of stuff's repeated in an indirect way. They never want the same shot, but they'll say they like that shot in that movie. So you have to think of something that's similar, but is also as good as that. You're often asked to draw a character to look like an actor. If there's someone who's a big box office hit, they like the boards to look like him or her.

Q - How do you present storyboards?

Tracey - If you're at a production meeting, everyone is handed a copy of the sequence or they are pinned on the wall, and you go through them. Often the director doesn't want anyone to see the boards until they're approved.

Q - What happens in those meetings?

Tracey - It's with all department heads. They want to make sure everybody's clear about their tasks and what the director wants. It's at that point an effects guy will say *'You can't have it explode that way, you've got to do it this way'*, and so we'll change the boards accordingly. This meeting would be pretty far in advance of the shoot. If you have a four month prep period, you'd probably have a big meeting at least once a month, and then more frequently in the last few weeks. It just helps to figure out as much as you can before the first day of shooting. At least have the first few weeks of shooting boarded and settled and sorted out. Obviously it's going to change from day to day, but if you can have a more or less clear idea of the basics, that usually helps.

Q - Would you recommend all directors use story boards?

Storyboard Abbreviations

MCU
Medium close up, (head and shoulders).

CU
Close up (head), actors need to be aware that a close up might mean that they can move around less in the scene as the camera will need to follow them. It's common to shoot a wide or mid shot and then 'crash in' for a close up of the same angle (there may be minimal relighting), and the camera may not even be moved. Either a zoom lens would be zoomed in or a prime lens will be swapped for a longer lens to get the close up shot.

BCU
Big close up. Any movement will be exaggerated, so an actor opening his eye's wide will seem like a surprise, or an extreme shock has occurred. Actors will not be able to move around too much as they will quickly move out of shot.

ECU
Extreme close up (eyes or anything extremely close), This is more of an effect shot, the actor's eyes as a killer approaches for instance, the bullet going in the gun chamber, the number flashing on the cell phone for instance.

EST
Establishing shot or master shot, often used to introduce a scene or location to the audience. Generally, this is a wide shot of a building or landscape or an introduction to the location in which the scene is set.

MS
Medium shot, head and upper torso, versatile and basic shot.

LS
Long shot, a wide shot which is generally includes a character's whole body and immediate surroundings.

ELS
Extreme long shot, a very wide shot where a character's would seem tiny in the frame. Great for establishing shots.

MLS
Medium long shot, in between a LS and an ELS, character is relatively small in the frame and you see much more of their surroundings.

High angle/Low Angle
Camera is looking up at the subject or looking down at the subject. High angles looking down can dominate and low angles looking up can imply power. Beware of production problems when using these shots - looking up might shoot 'off the set' etc.

Dutch Angle
An extreme tilt of the camera. Used to make things look weird or crazy.

Storyboard Abbreviations cont...

Pan and Tilt
Moving the camera horizontally or vertically.

Zoom
A zoom lens is used to zoom in (closer to the subject) or out (away from the subject). The advantage of a zoom lens is that the camera does not move and so there is no need to refocus. To get a smooth zoom you will need to hire a special zoom control unit. Zoom shots can look a little odd because we cannot zoom our eyes and so our brain knows that this is a trick effect. NEVER allow an operator to perform a zoom manually, it must always be motorized.

OS - Over shoulder, the camera is looking over someone's shoulder. Often used in conversation coverage.

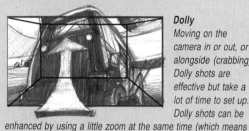

Dolly
Moving on the camera in or out, or alongside (crabbing). Dolly shots are effective but take a lot of time to set up. Dolly shots can be enhanced by using a little zoom at the same time (which means your track could be shorter).

Other abbreviations include...
OC - Off camera, this refers to dialogue / sounds off camera.
VO - Voice over.
POV - Point of view, shot from your main character's point of view, such as looking down the dark corridor.

The storyboards featured here were drawn by Andrew Yap, email him at andrews_battle_hymn@yahoo.co.uk   www.corneredreality.com

Tracey - Whatever they're comfortable with. I do believe, however, that storyboards are an essential talking point when you begin a project. Not only do they help with budgeting and storytelling, but they capture the mood and emotion of a script, and are a good visual representation of the directors ideas.

Q - What are thumb nails?

Tracey - The director will give you a little sketch, and you'll go away and produce something much better. I worked with one director who had a white board and would quickly draw up, shot by shot, what he wanted. Of course there were bits missing and I'd go away and fill in the spaces too. If the shots have already been figured out, it makes my job a easier. It's nice to know what's going on in a directors head, if they can put pen to paper and do something, it doesn't mater how scribbly, it will help.

Q - Do you have any advice for new film makers?

Tracey - Watch as many films as you can. That helps with regard to story boarding, and directing as well. Keep a library in your head. As a story board artist you are often asked to pull up a certain shot from a certain film and it's good if you know that film, and when you're drawing a sequence, it's nice to remember how they did angles in various scenes. The more you see, the more you remember. A lot of people don't know what they want until they see it, or they know only what they don't. That's not unusual. Then they change their minds a lot too. That is part of the creative process too. But it helps, especially if you have little time and money, to have some initial idea of what you want.

The Crew And What They Do

Producer

Head of the production, the first one on the film and the last one off. Generally, they are the ones who have found the screenplay and are involved in all aspects of the film making process. They raise the finance for the film, and are answerable to financiers. On a low budget film, more often than not, they will be also doing the job of the line producer, such as scheduling and budgeting.

Executive Producer

Usually the person who has made the film possible in either putting together the finances and/or creative package. Also, used as a credit, given as a 'thank you' for funds or services that have made the film possible.

Line Producer

Assigned by the Producer early on to help produce the film's budget. Takes care of the main deals with facility houses, keeping in control and in line with the budget. Not necessarily needed on a low budget movie where the producer and/or production manager will do the job.

Unit Production Manager (UPM)

Needed early on. One step below line producer. Helps the producer prepare the production schedule. Makes sure the director has everything he or she needs at an affordable price, keeps in contact with the accountant. Visits the set daily to be aware of everything that is happening in order to make things run smoothly.

Production Coordinator

Works with the UPM. Makes sure there is a smooth flow of information between departments both verbal and written. Prepares call sheets with 2nd AD, schedules, orders equipment, and co-ordinates transport.

Production Secretary

Hired early on by the producer for secretarial administrative skills.

Production Assistants (PA)

Assistants to the production team, where job varies from being a typist, running errands, carry equipment, etc.

Runner

Runs for everything needed, fulfils a variety of chores from messenger to miscellaneous buyer to getting food. Sometimes a PA and the runner are one and the same.

Production Accountant

Takes care of monies throughout the shoot. Arranges for payments, expenses, petty cash, etc. Keeps an eye on how the shoot is going with regards to the budget.

Location Manager

Organizes location scouting and takes care of everything associated with shooting on location, i.e. getting permissions and permits, hotel bookings, bathrooms, rental cars, notifying local police, authorities etc. Acts as liaison between crew and location owners. May have location scouts as assistants.

Director

The creative decision maker throughout the filmmaking process who directs the cast and crew from pre to post- production. Responsible to the producer for transforming the screenplay into the finished film.

Second Unit Director

Aids director in shooting certain shots, generally those that don't require sync sound or the principal actors, i.e. cutaways, establishing shots, insert shots, etc. Receives instructions from the Director of what needs to be shot and how to shoot it.

First Assistant Director (1st AD)

The link between the production office and the set. Must ensure that everything is available that is needed on the day. Keeps in close contact with the director and the production manager as he/she must know everything there is to know about the script, locations, actors, sets, production schedule and how the director intends to shoot. Aids thedDirector, keeping up the energy and strength of the crew, pushing them within sensible limits to keep the show moving at a good pace.

Second Assistant Director (2nd AD)

A backup to the 1st. Writes the call sheets in conjunction with the production coordinator, arranges cast calls, pick ups, extras, stunt calls, deals with payments to extras and is present when cast arrives and is available to sort out production problems if and when they arise on set.

Third Assistant Director (3rd AD)

Assists the 2nd AD and acts as a runner.

Casting Director
Oversees finding the cast, works closely with the producer and director. Has a good knowledge of agents and their clients after building up good relationships with them.

Continuity
Observes and records details of a shoot such as costume, props, and blocking to make sure that shots match during varied takes and that all shots are completed.

Storyboard Artist
Prepares detailed panels of shots as requested by the Director. On low-budget shoots this may not be deemed necessary.

Director of Photography/Cinematographer
Head of the camera team who collaborates with the director to establish the visual style of the movie. Familiar with camera and lighting equipment and film stocks. Contact person between the lab and production.

Camera Operator
Operates the camera. Familiar with equip., camera movement and an eye for framing.

1st Camera Assistant/Focus Puller
Loads film, keeps the image sharp by following focus, changes lenses, sets exposure, 'checks the gate' after each shot.

2nd Camera Assistant/Clapper Loader
Loads film into mags, cans exposed film and short ends, fills out camera reports.

Grip/Key Grip/Dolly Grip
In charge of operating dollies, cranes, laying track, moving cameras - all heavy work, so this person needs to be strong. If needed, they design or construct special rigs and camera mounts. The key grip heads this crew. Dolly grips specifically handle moving the camera on a dolly along track.

Gaffer
Chief electrician in charge of equipment and connection to power supply. Works closely with DP, explaining and delegating the lighting design. Works with Best Boy, generator operator and electricians (sparks).

Best Boy
1st Assistant to the gaffer.

Electrician
Moves and maintains the lights. Organizes power from the generator. Sometimes called "sparks."

Production Sound Mixer
Records the production sound, wild tracks, and ambience. Will either have their own kit, or will hire one from a sound house.

Boom Operator
Works with the production sound mixer either holding the boom microphone or arranging the necessary mics for a particular scene. Takes care of sound recording sheets, which will be used during editing.

Make Up Artists and Hair Stylist
Breaks down script for special make up or cosmetic makeup, i.e bruises, wounds or shaved heads, etc. Each artist will have their own basic kit and will take care of hiring wigs, special effects and prosthetics. Keeps continuity notes.

Costume Designer
Designs the costumes. Breaks down the script, working out costume changes according to story days, meets actors to discuss requirements. Usually, the first people from production to meet the actors. They must shop, hire, or make the costumes and have good social skills to have a good working relationship with the actor. Can have a costume assistant.

Dresser / Assistant
Sets up a working wardrobe. Arrives before actors to set up costumes, supervises their dressing, checks continuity throughout the day. Stands by with wet weather gear or warm clothing depending on conditions.

Production Designer
Works with the director and DP on visual style of the movie. Responsible for sets either in the sound stage or on location. Ensures the "look" of the set and props are as desired.

Art Director
Oversees the ideas of the production designer, arranging furnishings, liaising with the construction manager and art dept.

Set Designer
Responsible for the selection of props and supervises the dressin of sets. Prepares prop lists and works closes with the prop buyer in organizing the dressing and striking of sets. Makes continuity notes. On low-budget shoots, the set decorator and the art director may be the same person.

Leadman
Answers to the set designer and heads the swing gang (the people who set up and take down the set) and the set dressing dept.

Prop Master
Physically puts and removes furniture and props on the set. Keeps tabs on all props and looks after them during the shoot.

Prop Buyer
Responsible for finding appropriate props from specialist sources. Purchases, hires and maintains a record of art department budget. Organizes collections and returns of hired props. On low budget shoots, prop buyer and prop master may be the same person.

Prop Maker
Designing, building and operating any props. On low budget shoot, this may also be done by the production designer and/or the art director.

Construction Manager
Responsible for building sets within art department budget. Organizes materials and extra crew if necessary. Schedules building and striking of sets in conjunction with the production designer.

Painters/Scenic Artists/Carpenters
Work with construction manager on building and striking sets.

Stills Photographer
Shoots production stills for use in press kits, publicity and advertising.

Unit Publicist
Works with still photographer making sure the "right" shots are taken to publicise the film. Takes care of getting publicity while shooting, prepares press kits and makes sure that sufficient material is obtained during the production to publicize the film later on.

EPK Producer
Shoots a documentary of the making of the film for publicity purposes and for the DVD release of the film. Interviews the major creative forces behind the film including the actors, screenwriter, director and producers.

Caterer/Catering Company/Craft services
Oversees all catering (food and drink) requirements on the film.

Drivers
A team of drivers for ferrying crew, cast, equipment. Not necessarily required on a low budgets as job is doubled up with other crew members.

Stunt Coordinator
Oversees, plans and executes all stunts and action throughout the film. Coordinates with stunt performers and special effects coordinator.

Special Effects Coordinator
Oversees, plans and executes special effects throughout the film, including atmospherics (rain, wind, smoke) fires, explosions, etc. Works with the stunt coordinator.

Post Production Supervisor
Oversees entire post-production process. Not necessarily required on a low budget film. On low budget film these duties may fall to the editor/ producer/director.

Editor
Once dailies are received from the set, the editor will assemble the movie. Works closely with the director.

Assistant Editor
Aids Editor with preparing picture and sound, synchronizing dailies if necessary, logging, maintaining good files and records and storage of all movie elements. On low budget films, not necessarily needed.

Sound Editor
Assembles production tracks, effects, music, recording extra effects, gets effects from libraries, organizes Foley and ADR. Ensures all location atmospheres are covered with wild tracks. Takes film to final mix with editor anddirector. Should hear and approve the final optical soundtrack.

Negative Cutter
Cuts the negative of a movie and conforms, or matches, it to the final cut of the film as decided by the director, editor, and producer and anyone else who may be involved. Final prints of the film are made from this conformed negative.

Foley Artist
Creates footsteps, sound effects, clothes rustle, etc. that match the cut movie filling empty scenes.

Composer/Musician/Music Copyist
Hired for the original score of the film and composes music in accordance with the director's wishes.

Music Supervisor
Hires musicians, locates and clears required additional music tracks.

The Film Makers Compromise

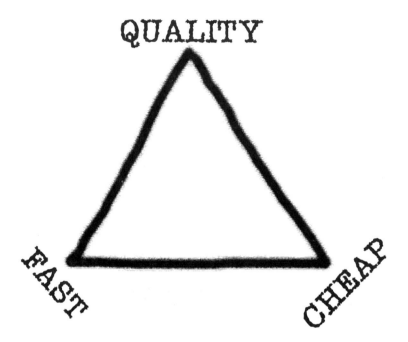

Study this simple triangle. Whatever film making discipline you apply, you can only ever have two corners, and always at the expense of the third corner. As an Indie Film Maker, almost certainly you are going to need QUALITY and CHEAP, and it will never be FAST. Knowing this, plan, plan, plan...! You can't do it FAST, so you must be prepared.

PRODUCTION

BMG ZOMBA
PRODUCTION MUSIC

BMG Zomba is made up of 8 of the major production music labels in the world including Atmosphere, Bruton & Chappell. This unique and unrivalled collection of eclectic works, talented composers and enthusiastic and experienced staff, gives you access to an unrivalled source of musical styles to facilitate the television and media industries. You can also rely on an experienced Music Research department, whose knowledge of the repertoire and enthusiasm for the creative application of the music helps clients make the most of the world's largest production music resource.

Louise O'Malley
Production Accountant

PRODUCTION ACCOUNTANT

Q - What is your job?

Louise - I am a production accountant. First of all, I monitor the money and the budget that is either put together by myself or the production manager. At the same time we are setting up the equivalent of a small business registering the company for vat etc, working out staffing levels for the accounts dept, discussing and setting up authorisation process

Q - Is the reason for the small business model so that from an insurance point of view, if the production goes belly up, that nothing else will go with it?

Louise - It might be part of the reason. There are many other practical reasons to set up a limited company to be commissioned to produce the film.

Q - Who owns the limited company?

Louise - The company directors. Sometimes that is the producers, exec producers – on occasion it might be someone paid to be a company director.

Q - What are the tax implications of creating a company and an asset and then dissolving the company? Where does that asset go?

Louise - That is taken care of in all the master agreements. So before you even start filming, when your finance comes together and is signed off, there will be a clear path as to what rights will be going where and at what time. It is different for each project.

Q - When do you normally come on board a production?

Louise - In an ideal world your accountant should be the first person on, with the producer and production manager There are two reasons why your accountant has to be on so soon. One is that you need to get your budget in shape as soon as possible. And the other is that these finance plans are so complex now that you need someone constantly number punching.

Q - So on a film that is £3m, one would have that money in the bank before you started shooting?

Louise - One would hope so! In theory you should. In practice, because things are so complicated, pre production cashflow is either borrowed at huge cost or funded usually equally by the financiers.

Q - Where does someone find a production accountant?

Louise - The Production Guild.

Q - How do you differ from a regular high street accountant?

Louise - It is different because you are dealing with a creative elements, that you estimate before incorporating into the budget. It is very much based on experience.

Q - What equipment or space do you need to do your job?

Louise - A small office, a broadband line, a computer for each member of the accounts dept - a few filing trays, a bit of stationary and you are off.

Q - Who do you work with most closely during production?

Louise - The producer and the production manager.

Q - Who deals with the writing of cheques?

Louise - The accountant does that. But the accountant will ask the producer what preferences they have, such as whether they want to sign off on everything or see everything. But the accountant will suggest what the levels of authority are. And on the whole, you are left to make that judgement. It is very important that the less experienced should see everything until they are more confident.

Q - Who deals with the petty cash?

Louise - The accounts assistant, cashier or I will deal with that if they have gone out for lunch. We all have to be able to do each other's jobs in the accounts department. But the actual signing off of the petty cash should be done by the production manager.

Q - Do you see people, cast and crew, trying it on with petty cash or is that just a fearful film maker's myth?

Louise - No. I mean, everyone is going to maxmise their opportunity to be reimbursed, but nobody puts in huge expenses these days. Any unreasonable claims would be easy to spot.

Q - What is the process that you go through to run a proper payroll service?

Louise - You can employ a payroll service, which is the most efficient way of doing it, but you are paying a weekly sum of money to the payroll service. They will do all your returns for you, which is very bulky. Or you can go buy software off a shelf and run your own payroll,

PRODUCTION

Office Tips!

Aside from the obvious stuff, such as a computer, printer and a desk, here's a list of the stuff you will need in your production office. You must also network your computers. It's easier than you may think and will mean you can share resources such as your printer and internet connection. Finally, try and get a professional office, on an industrial estate or in a studio. It will add kudos, separate your film life from home life, and will be cheaper than you expect.

Phone with answerphone	Fax	Petty cash box (lockable)	High shelving (put up before
Fridge	Good chairs	TV/VCR/DVD (for showreels)	you get too involved)
Tea and coffee	Office supplies (lots of paper	Radio / CD player	
Water cooler	and toner)	Backup device (DVD-R) with	
Microwave	Courier service account	software	
DSL connection (wireless)	Extra keys to office	Digital camera	
Heavy duty punch for scripts	Paper shredder	Networked computers	
Spare mobile phone charger	Filing cabinet	Cheap and fast laser printer	
Photocopier	Stamps	Cheap colour inkjet printer	

Keep Your Receipts!

GUERILLA FILM MAKER SAYS!

V.A.T (Value Added Tax) is the Government's sales tax and is currently set at 17.5% on sales and purchases of VATable goods (there are some VAT exemptions, listed below). If you operate a company or partnership and have registered for VAT, you can either pay money or reclaim money from the VAT office, depending on your sales, minus your profits - if you have made more sales than purchases, you will probably pay the VAT difference to the VAT office. If you have made less sales than purchases, you can probably reclaim the VAT difference from the VAT office. In short, when you make a movie you spend spend spend! So you will be in a state of constant reclaim of VAT (so that's 17.5% of the money you spend, not including the items that don't attract VAT). Only when you sell your film will you charge VAT, which could be several years down the line, if ever! It's not too complicated and there are lots of simple books on how to organise your accounts. You should strike up a long term relationship with a good accountant too, not a media accountant, just a plain old high street one. They will be able to advise you and free you up to keep working on your movie.

What is a surprise to most people is what you can claim back... Here's a few ideas...

Research *- This includes cinema tickets (checking out other directors / writers / actors), DVD/VHS/CD rental or purchase, magazine and newspaper subscriptions (for story ideas).*

Equipment *- TV / VCR / DVD / computer / copier hire or purchases can be claimed. In fact, any equipment that is used for your film making business can be claimed (camera equipment, lighting equipment etc.) as well as stock, tape, battery consumables etc.*

Vehicle *- You can deduct a portion (based on the percentage you use it for work or personal reasons) of your car expenses, which includes maintenance, fees, petrol, parking etc.*

Office *- If you have office space, your rent and utilities can be deducted against your end of year tax and the VAT can be reclaimed (if VAT was charged) each quarter. If you have a home office, the percentage of the whole house that your office takes up is the percentage of your rent, utilities and insurance you can claim. Of course, any fax, telephone, internet or mobile phone charges can be claimed as long as they are for business purposes. Any other VAT on office consumables such as stationary, software, and delivery companies can be reclaimed too.*

Travel *- Hotels, airplane fares, rental cars, business meals and other location expenses can be claimed as well as long as you are not being reimbursed by someone, though VAT is not charged on most transport, nor is it charged when you are not in the UK.*

Clothing *- Only costume rentals can be claimed and adult clothing when used for costume.*

Non VAT items *- Food and drinks, transport, vehicle purchase, books, kid's clothing, postage, bank charges, overseas purchases etc. The VAT office can help you with a detailed list too.*

To register for VAT visit www.hmce.gov.uk

As a final note, don't be complacent with your VAT and receipts. Don't abuse, misuse or even bend the rules. If you do, you could end up in prison. Just keep all your books tidy, in order and up to date.

but I wouldn't advise anyone to do that. It is very important that each recipient gets a piece of paper saying exactly how their wages are made up.

Q - Are most crew members hired on a freelance basis and have their own companies and give you an invoice?

Louise - There is a split. The heads of department are Schedule D and all the assistant grades are PAYE. There is a bit more flexibility now, but you have to stick to the guidelines. The worst thing is to agree with someone with a status which they are not fully entitled to and then they go onto the next film and they say to the producer, *'well, they let me have (x) status on the last project.'* So you have to be very careful to make sure you are all doing the same thing or you will have people abusing the system.

Q - So you have conversations with every cast and crew member and have a paper trail?

Louise - They are given a start form that says PAYE/Schedule D on it and if they tick the wrong box we advise them correctly. We also issue a memo to let them know procedures with petty cash and purchase orders

Q - Why are people given per diems instead of just getting paid a fee that includes a per diem?

Louise - I think that will happen in the future. For the time being though, your per diem is your out of pocket living allowance. So in theory, if you get lunch at work and you are away from home, you need the value of your meal and you need your rent paid either directly or given to you.

Q - Are there any tax implications to that?

Louise - Yes there are. There are allowed allowances in the guidelines, and if you go over that, you have to get dispensations or pay tax on it. The implications of going to a distant location, and coming back again to your original base are complicated and not really designed with the film industry in mind

Q - A sound recordist might be Schedule D, but what if they want to charge their equipment to the company?

Louise - There are two things. First we would need a list of all the equipment that is coming on the set for insurance purposes. We need to make sure that they are insured if they are providing it. The other vital thing is never to agree to pay for someone's equipment unless you know you can use it. Some people think it is a given they can have their *'box allowance'* for whatever is in their box. That is not the approach to take. It is, *'you can offer us that, but we will phone the supplier and get our discount price, and that is what we will pay you for your box.'*

Q - What do you spend most of your daily time on?

Louise - People. Thinking ahead and being prepared for emergencies.

Q - What do you do before production?

Louise - You start with budgeting and re-budgeting, almost all the time. You are setting up your payroll system. You are setting up your petty cash system. You are checking all the contracts of the people who are going to be contracted. You are determining whether your cast are having withholding tax taken from them. You are getting involved in taking out the insurance policies. You are invariably discussing things with the bond companies. Nearer to production, you have a lot of staff starting and all their forms have to be checked against the budget. A lot of petty cash goes through in small amounts, and that has to be checked. Basically you are building a department that has to service a company the size of the film. There could be one of you or there could be six of you, depending on what that film demands.

Q - What about during the shoot?

Louise - If you have a good team with a good production manager, by the time you start shooting, you should have done everything. So what you are doing now is checking your progress reports and looking at your daily costs - flagging it if you can see something happening that you haven't got enough money for. It is all in the prep. If you shorten your prep, you shorten the opportunities you have to make everything go as you want it.

Q - How much are you involved in the post process?

Louise - You have to tidy up and the accountant is in for the longest time. The accountant is the one who takes all the fiddly things at the end and deals with them. If it is not done neatly, it will haunt you forever. It is boring but you have to tie up every lose end. Never should a project be remembered for not tidying up after themselves, as that is how we all get bad names.

Q - What are some of the more common problems in tidying up that can come back to bite you?

Louise - Mostly it is if people don't fill in their paperwork. Also claims for things such as petrol or mobile phones that employees have held on to from the start. It is not just the delivery of the film that counts. There is a much bigger delivery that goes on behind the scenes. The only time to collate the paperwork is when we are in production. It is very difficult to collect the paperwork a year later.

Q - What paperwork does the producer end up with?

Louise - From the accounts dept, there are copy cost reports, possibly weekly cheque lists and anything else they wish to see.

Q - What advice would you give to a new film maker who is making their first film and cannot afford to hire a professional accountant?

Louise - I think they should have a bookkeeper in. The bookkeeper cannot budget so the producer and the production manager will have to do the accountant's side of budgeting and cost control. But a bookkeeper could come in and install a Sage system, which costs around £140, and you can then see what you spent everywhere. Even if people are working for nothing, you still have to keep records for them for health and safety. You can't have someone working for you for three weeks and not know how many hours they have worked. It doesn't have to be a film person.

Q - What software would you recommend?

Louise - A lot of people load Sage (also try Quickbooks). Another way to save money is that sometimes your personal accountant will do it for you. That is a very good idea for a low budget film.

Petty Cash Problems

GUERILLA FILM MAKER SAYS!

Managing the cash budget is a major task throughout production and mismanagement could easily lead to disaster. Negotiate a weekly petty cash float for each department and ensure that they complete a form to explain what was spent, when and where, with receipts and contact numbers. Sometimes there is no receipt (pay phones, parking meters, etc.) so then a receipt must be drawn up, listing the expenses and the date. At the end of each week, petty cash receipts should be handed in for payment. Where possible, try to use cheques as this creates an accountable paper trail.

Per Diems
An allowance given to actors and some crew prior to the day or week of work. This is to cover any 'out of pocket' and will be a contractually agreed amount. Per Diems are seen as a perk but are standard throughout the industry. Per Diems are subject to income tax.

Mobile Phones
Mobile phones are always needed on a film set, however if the production company has agreed to reimburse the use of mobile phones, then it's difficult to keep costs under control. Restrict mobile phone use to certain crew members and cap the usage. Request that the crew members submit their bills containing all work related calls (circled) to the production office, before reimbursement.

Mileage/Petrol reimbursement
Generally petrol receipts are reimbursed, but sometimes an agreed rate per mile can be paid instead.

Restaurant meals
Keep an itemised receipt with a business card of the restaurant along with their VAT number. Credit card receipts alone are not good enough.

Car Allowance
Sometimes, key crew who will be using their own cars, will request a car allowance. This is essentially a rental fee for the use of their vehicle.

Kit/Box Rental
Certain crew members may have negotiated kit rental with the production. i.e. a make up artist may include his or her own make up equipment under kit / box rental.

Bribes
We don't like saying it, but sometimes you've got to grease a palm or two. This cannot be accounted for, unless the person whose palm is being greased will give you a receipt! In the end, any money without a paper trail behind it, such as a receipt or invoice, will need to be accounted for. Often this will mean the producer will need to accept the 'money' and pay tax on it, effectively meaning the bribe was paid out of the producers pocket and not the films budget.

Accounts Software

GUERILLA FILM MAKER SAYS!

Doing your accounts is a nightmare for we creative folk. But it is a necessary evil. You must make sure you dot ever 'i' and cross ever 't' from a financial perspective, file your accounts on time, submit your VAT returns accurately and on the whole, keep your paperwork up to date and in order. Software helps enormously. There are a number of accounts programs out there, but most are way too complex for a small business like a low budget film company.

Programs like 'Sage' are way too over complex, and all you really need is something to track your cash transactions, your bank transactions, issue invoices and calculate your VAT. The rest should really be done by an accountant. We use 'Quicken', but 'MS Money' is also a good contender. Ask around your freelance film making friends and see what they use. A word of caution.

Whatever program you choose will probably be the one you stick with, so make an informed choice and don't just go for the first package that comes across your desk.

Q - Is putting inexperienced people on a sophisticated program like Sage a recipe for problems?

Louise - That is why you would go the bookkeeper route. To have someone who knows how to operate that system. Or go the accountant route. You are right, why should a film maker become well versed in Sage? You don't have the time to do that.

Q - What are the qualities that make a good producer?

Louise - Realism. The ability to have a good relationship with their director, but to be able to tell them that they cannot have something and to stand your ground. Do not hide from blossoming problems. You have to have a lot of guts and a lot of energy. And you have to be prepared to give 24/7.

Q - What are the common mistakes that you see from new film makers?

Louise - The one thing I see time and time again amongst the new film makers is that they are adamant that they know what they are doing. And no matter what advice you give them, they are sure they know what they are doing, and invariably, they mess up, and you watch them messing up, and it is very frustrating. Don't be frightened to ask. Don't think that you know everything. Surround yourself with good people and use them. Don't find them threatening.

Q - What advice can you give a new film maker?

Louise - Shadow an experienced Producer. It sounds boring but if you are in the right environment and you are actually with the producer of the film, day in and day out, you are learning.

PRODUCTION

Zoe Edwards
Production Co-ordinator

PRODUCTION CO-ORDINATOR

Q - What is your job?

Zoe - I am a production co-ordinator, who is someone who is responsible for the prep. Making sure that the right people are there at the right time. Making sure that the right supplies, contacts, film stock and facilities are there on the first day. Making sure all the insurance and legal and medical matters/side of things are dealt with. And making sure that all of this happens on a daily basis. I am the link between the floor (crew) and the production office.

Q - On a lower budget shoot do you take on any responsibilities of the line producer or UPM?

Zoe - Yeah. As time goes on, you learn who supplies you the best radios (walkie talkies), who supplies you the best mini-buses, who is going to do you the best deal so you can do those other jobs. It is all contacts and I am employed because of my little black book. You always strive to have the best production team around you. You want to make it as smooth as possible.

Q - So you would end up saving a new producer more than he would pay you on a shoot?

Zoe - Yes. The more line producers you work with the more information you have. And after only doing this for three years, I know the people that I can call up and I get a good deal.

Q - At what point do you normally come on board?

Zoe - Depending on how long the shoot is. For a four week shoot, I get six weeks prep.

Q - Who hires you?

Zoe - The line producer. I am their right hand.

Q - Where does someone find a production co-ordinator?

Zoe - You phone someone like me and ask if I know of anyone who is not working. You get our numbers from *The Knowledge* or go to imdb.com and look for names and then try to find someone that has worked with them and contact them. It is a very small network.

Q - What are the main skills that a production co-ordinator needs?

Zoe - Being organised. I think it is so important to be lovely to everyone. You have to treat everyone the same because you never know whom you are talking to. The guy who looks scruffy when he walks in is probably one of the producers. You have to hold it all together. If there is a problem, you deal with it. You have to work long hours and be prepared to have no life for long periods of time. You have to be dedicated to it. Your phone is never off and you can't let that bother you.

Q - Is there ever any tension between the office and the floor?

Shooting Abroad - Carnets

GUERILLA FILM MAKER SAYS!

A carnet is basically proof that a bond is held in your home country on the production equipment and will not be released until it is returned. It keeps people from buying goods in one country where they are inexpensive and selling them in another for a tidy profit and / or to avoid paying taxes on the goods and certain countries require them if you want to shoot there. There are certain companies that process carnets for a fee that is based on what country you are going to and how soon you need it. You will have to pay a bond for your equipment, which is a percentage of its declared value (this can be on what it costs to replace it new or used). When you get your carnet, make sure it is stamped and signed every time you leave or enter a country. If you don't, you may have to present the equipment to a Customs Inspector and pay a fine. And if they happen to catch you months after the fact while doing paperwork, you may have to rehire the identical equipment to show them. Nightmare!!! Once home, return the carnet documents to the issuer immediately and if posting, send it registered.

You don't need a carnet to shoot in any EU country, but you should have an itemised list of all your equipment with serial numbers listed on company letterhead. You do need a carnet for the US, Canada and Australia as well as most of Asia and South Africa.

Zoe - It is very easy to get a divide between the production team on the floor and the production office. If people don't trust one another, then things aren't going to get done and for me, the production office door should always be open. Someone should be able to walk in an ask for wetsuit boots and we should go get them.

Q - Do you get the sense there are more females in your job because most of the people you talk to on the phone are male?

Zoe - That is absolutely true. You want to have balance in a production office. And most of the production assistants that I have worked with in the office are girls. And then you try to get a boy runner to balance out the office.

Q - What tools do you need for your job?

Zoe - A computer, a printer, an internet connection, a phone and a mobile. And a filing system. That's about it.

Q - What kind of paperwork do you generate?

Zoe - Cast and crew contacts. All insurance documents. Action vehicle insurance. The call sheet comes through me and gets sent out to the executives. And the progress report, which is an evaluation of what has happened the day before. How much stock was shot the day before. A 2nd AD report, which says what people or animals have been in and a continuity report that says we shot three minutes of script today. Then I take the stock log, which says that we shot 3200 feet of footage and that ratio gives the cost, which goes to the financiers. I also create a complete summary, on two pages.

Q - Who do you work with mostly?

Zoe - In the office, it is mostly the line producer who goes off to set in the morning and comes back during the day. The accountant, the assistant production co-ordinator, the production runner and the 2nd AD on a daily basis.

Q - How do you get the best deals?

Zoe - It is in partly knowing what is achievable and a bit of back scratching. You can try your darnedest to do something that doesn't involve money, and then bring the suppliers business down the line, so loyalty is important too.

Q - Which crew members cause you the most problems?

PRODUCTION

Zoe Edwards

production co-ordinator
zoeedwards@ukonline.co.uk

Zoe - None specifically. The AD, you have to get on with. You must also get on with the 2nd AD, who is essentially doing my job on the floor and is in charge of all the artists.

Q - What do you do before you leave a project?

Zoe - You have to make sure that you have all the signed documents, which are all the signed contracts from the crew and cast. You have to have all the clearances done for logos and newspapers that unexpectadly creep into shot (or are cleared beforehand) etc., so that when they turn around and say that we can't put their name in our film, we can go back and take it out of the shot or obscure it in a way that becomes non-specific. Marie Claire, in my experience, is one of the companies that always says no for instance. You learn who says yes and who says no. They will sometimes ask for a synopsis of the show and they will say, *"Sorry, we don't want our product used in this context."* And it is different between films and television as far as what you can show.

Q - What conversation would you have with someone who wanted to do what you do just before they worked on their first low budget feature film?

Zoe - I would say, *"You will love it if you put your heart and soul into it."* It is such a buzz. But you have to have nothing to go home to. It's true! You will be there until one in the morning. You can't walk away from it and you have to be totally committed from day one. On a practical level, I would tell them to be organised and structured. And also to remember that no matter how many e-mails or conversations that you may have had with people in getting something done, someone may not have passed on the information. So keep double checking everything, or it will come back to you.

Q - Do you deal with cast agents at all?

Production Budget

GUERILLA FILM MAKER SAYS!

Your budget is the financial representation of everything you will need to do, buy or make to fully complete your film. Movie Magic is the industry leader, though a bit OTT for a low budget film. Excel does just fine, or our own Movie Tools Budget does a fine job too (see www.livingsprit.com) You may end up making several versions of your budget, depending on your financier's needs. For example, your £100k version that gets sent to private investors, would be beefed up to £3m if you talk to the BBC. Either way, think about these things when putting your figures together.

1. Figure out how many days you are going to be shooting as it will effect how long you will need to hire equipment and keep actors.

2. Your first budget should be how much it costs to make the film properly, i.e. with a full union crew, a full compliment of days, proper visual effects, etc. This will give you a starting point from which to cut back.

3. When trying to find out prices, call several different hire companies and get their rates. They will want to know the number of days and the budget as it will effect their ates. Try to see if they will beat each other's prices.

4. Separate your budget into pre-production, production and post-production sections.

5. If you can swing it, include things like festival dues and delivery requirements in the budget as well.

6. The easiest way to reduce your budget is to get rid of people - cut redundant actors and crew, who then don't need transport, catering etc.

7. If you can afford it, hire an experienced line producer to read your script and come up with a budget in the price range you want.

8. Most unions, such as Equity, have different rates for low budget films. Find these out and plug the numbers into your budget.

9. When cutting back, put silly prices in your spreadsheet and then see if you can actually make that work, by thinking laterally or by ringing around and asking for favours.

10. Remember, a philisophical point, for micro budget films, it's not how much do you need, it's now much have I got, and how can I best spend that? Make the movie now, not one day someday with some money you might get.

The Wrap

GUERILLA FILM MAKER SAYS!

Preparing for the end of a production is just as important as being organised for the beginning of one. This is where hidden costs, damaged equipment and forgotten items can come back to bite you if you are not thorough. So, make sure you budget enough time to do it properly. Also, it is a time when you should be thanking all those people who helped you through those glorious days on set and in the office. And there are the people who could make your post-production life easy, or a living hell, if you don't take care of them now.

1. Leave enough time to strike sets completely and thoroughly (could be several hours or a few days). This includes making sure all utilities are turned off and the property is clean. If you are on a sound stage, a good stage manager can make your life easy here.

2. Return all rentals to their houses ASAP so you don't get charged for extra days or late fees.

3. Collect release forms from everyone so that you are covered.

4. Collect all keys, mobile phones, computers, PDA's and any other office or mobile equipment that you can be charged for. It's amazing what can go walkies.

5. Do all your exit paperwork, such as final pay cheques, camera reports, lab reports, petty cash reports etc.

5. Make sure to have contact numbers for everyone, just in case you need to get in touch with them should you need to, and for the premiere.

6. Take a cast and crew photo for publicity and to give to your hard working cast and crew.

7. Throw a wrap party. Many local restaurants will cut you deals on food, drink and hospitality / dining rooms if you bring a lot of people.

8. Send small gifts to everyone who helped you, and follow up with a call to thank them personally. They made a significant difference and let them know that.

9. There are often lots of items that could be turned into cash. Props to sell on eBay, unneeded kit to sell to the next new film maker, unused film stock to sell to other productions. Turn as much as you can back into cash for post production.

10. On low budget shoots, the warp often spells the start of nightmares. All the problems you said you would fix in post will now come back to haunt you.

Zoe - Yes. I have a lot of contact with cast agents. A lot of the publicity requests come through me and I have to keep everyone sweet.

Q - What common mistakes do you see?

Zoe - Not being told things that you are meant to know. It has to filter down from the producer. And not knowing that you need a cherry picker on Wednesday for instance, will cause problems. Having said that, I generally know what we need from the production meetings. And it equally needs to filter up from the bottom too. If I have a great assistant, then I know the information is going to get out to a hundred people no problem.

Q - What advice would you give a new film maker?

Zoe - Never lose sight of what you are trying to achieve because in this business it is very easy to be battered down by other people who supposedly know better.

Jeremy Pelzer
Studio Director

STUDIO HIRE

Q - What is your job?

Jeremy - I'm responsible for the day to day running of Ealing Studios, securing the 3rd party clientele, looking after productions that come in and out of the studios, running the team that manage the studios and overseeing the redevelopment of the studios.

Q - What are the advantages to shooting in a studio as opposed to on location?

Jeremy - Controlling the shooting environment and all the facilities that come with being in a studio including dressing rooms, make-up and hair etc. Production offices get the benefits of having telephone, DSL broadband, and all the associated items that you expect with a swift set up provided for them on the lot. You are part of the studio community, which provides networking contacts. A key issue for productions is always security and being able to produce without prying eyes. Stage work is obviously slightly different, so it is simply the option of being able to create sets, light them, shoot them, day for night, night for day, however you see fit, building the sets to your own particular needs.

Q - And of course there are things like, if you are shooting on a stage, and the scene is shot at night, you don't actually have to shoot it at night.

Jeremy - Absolutely, shooting on a set means you are able to work during reasonable hours yet shoot in an environment which could be day or night. This removes practical factors, which you are always going to face if you are out on location.

Q - When a film crew moves into any given location it becomes an attraction and a distraction to the crew. How is it different at a studio?

Jeremy - With every film crew there are catering wagons, assorted trailers, lighting trucks, camera trucks etc. The logistics that location managers have to go through on location is quite massive, and often for a fairly short period of time. You require permission from the local authority, from local residents, from all the other associated parties that might be interested in that location and the consequence is that problems often occur. The beauty of the studios is you don't have to deal with many of those issues.

Q - From an insurance point of view, one of the things I experienced when we made our last picture is that when you hire equipment there is always the issue of where is that equipment going to be overnight?

Jeremy - Certainly. Insurance, along with health and safety, has become an increasingly dominant and important area for any film maker to deal with. The beauty of filming within the confines of a studio is that insurers are familiar with the studios, their set ups, and the security associated with it. Insurance companies are happier in general to underwrite productions that shoot at stages because there are likely to far fewer claims than if you are all parked on the street, etc.

Q - How long does it take to build a set?

Jeremy - It's entirely dependent on the type of set. Stage work can range from building a small interior room to a three-story lighthouse as we experienced recently. Or it could include building Harry Potter Hogwart's dining hall to building a massive external 'Gotham City', such as *Batman* did. You have got to anticipate that firstly you need a designer on board. It's going to have to be drawn and drafted carefully by an art department in conjunction with a construction manager and a construction team. So even the simplest sets, you are probably going to be looking at a week to two weeks. But obviously the more complex the set becomes, it can stretch to 3 or 4 months. If there's elements of special effects, or if there are other bits and pieces involved in it, it becomes more time consuming.

Q - What's the procedure, and how long does it take to strike a set?

Jeremy - I'd say for low budget films, they could be struck in 2 to 3 days. There are two types of striking. One is just to strike it - dispose of it. Sets are not designed to last forever. Even external sets built on back lots aren't designed past the requirement of that particular film. However some production companies, for various reasons, want to pack strike sets, which is the second type. If you are pack striking, you are going to re-assemble it somehow, and connect it all back together, which would involve a further element of construction to make it seamless again. Pack strikes can a long time.

Q - What happens to all the bits that get thrown away?

Jeremy - Where things can be recycled, they will be, but often the cost of de-nailing a set piece can outweigh the cost of ecologically disposing of it. Quite often a production will put up for sale some of the more salvageable and attractive items.

Q - When building a set, is there any consideration about how much space you need to leave between the set and the wall?

Jeremy - Usually you require at least one metre. But at the top of your consideration is where your camera position is going to be. If you are shooting from outside into the room, you can design sets specifically to meet the requirements of your script, so you are going to leave plenty of room around so you can to light it. Generally, you want to do this from the outside in, so you leave room for all your lighting.

Q - Is there a rough equation of how big a set you will need?

Jeremy - No, there is no set rule of thumb. Invariably designers will try and maximise the square footage of the stage. So if its a 9,000 square ft stage, they'd be looking, if they could, and if there was a requirement and a script for it, to build a set something in the region of 7,000 sq. ft, and work around it. Alternatively, a designer may look to construct two or more smaller sets and move between them.

Q - What happens about power?

Jeremy - The studio supplies three phase power facilities. Such power is largely there for the lighting. Where power on stage is concerned, they require enormous amounts, which is just charged back to the production by the unit. It is metered at the beginning and metered at the end.

Q - Can people bring their own generators?

Jeremy - They can. It's often not very cost efficient. Three-phase power off the grid inside a studio environment is the general norm and is very stable.

Q - What happens if you need to build a set, and you need to see the world outside that set?

Jeremy - Different productions have different means of doing it. Increasingly green screen and blue screen are used and then they shoot a smaller insert

Jeremy M Pelzer
Studio Director

EALING STUDIOS

Ealing Green London W5 5EP
T +44 (0) 20 8567 6655
F +44 (0) 20 8758 8658
www.ealingstudios.com

PRODUCTION

unit on location. Historically and conventionally you are looking at a large painted backing. They would erect a large cyclorama and, with very skilled scenic artists paint a cityscape, or a landscape behind, so that when you are looking out and it's lit, it's as good as. You can get such things as translight backings now, which effectively are large reproduced photographs that are very cleverly formed with gaps and translucent elements, so that you can then light it from behind You can transfer from day to night and the lights will come up so actually you get almost a time lapse effect.

Q - There is a notion that studios are going to be expensive, but in the longer run it actually works out cheaper and more efficient to try and base the whole production in one place. Is that true?

Jeremy - Yes, productions come together at fairly short notice, and have an extremely hectic schedule for the duration of their prep and shoot. Always, whether it be TV drama, low budget feature, short film, high-end feature production, I think there is a real benefit and efficiency involved in being able to come in for a service environment, that is used to your industry, that's used to supplying you with your requirements, setting you up within a day for pre-production, and then assisting you throughout the process through post and signing off at the end of it, saying 'Thank you.' Everybody goes away happy.

Needless to say, we have a wealth of short-term production clients, who may not use the actual stage facilities, but will base their production, even if they are entirely location based, within the studios, because of the services that we offer. Where low budget is concerned, there are real benefits for exactly the same reason. An enormous tool that everybody has to use on a feature film production is the telephone. If you are going to get into the shenanigans of setting up contracts, licenses, which may be 12 months etc., it is much easier to walk into a studio, have a phone on your desk that works and you just pay for the usage that you have for a short period of time. On location you are going to be talking location fees, contractual fees, location finding and all the assorted costs of actually running a unit on the street. In the studios, you're probably looking at an experienced designer and a construction team, combined with an art department, props, set decorating of a larger scale than you get on location. However, you do get to shoot in a place that is authentic. So, it's six of one, and half a dozen of another. The more intricate your script, or the more complex the effects or the shots, you are better off probably doing it in the studio.

Q - And of course within 100 yards of the stage, there is a cutting room, if you need to go and check shots.

Jeremy - It's much, much easier to piece the whole thing together. You can flick back to the cutting room to look at the dailies from the previous two days. And, with your art department, if you have got more than one stage, more than one set, you can be prepping the next set, whilst shooting on another. It's very easy for the director to come off set for an hour to go look with his designer and art department at the complexities of the next set. This way the next day's shoot or next week's shoot is all lined up correctly. It avoids enormous amount of travel, by all involved.

Q - What happens if you overrun?

Jeremy - Most producers can't afford to overrun, but there is always an element of pick-ups or re-shoots. All producers talk to the studio on a daily basis in relation to their schedule. We will never book, or rarely book, a client in the day after a schedule of a previous client. Invariably we will sit down and work out an appropriate solution with the producers to any overrun.

Q - What happens with catering usually?

Jeremy - Most studios have catering facilities. At Ealing, we also have many restaurants on our doorstep at Ealing centre. Studios will provide catering facilities for it's longer-term clientele. Short-term productions often have a desire to use their own catering firm because most films involve an element of shooting on location. They will have their own location caterers when they are out and about and it's a far more cost effective deal to be able to then bring them into the studios. All we do then is provide them with the facilities to park up the catering truck, with a dining area.

Q - Is there anything that we have missed?

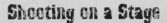

Shooting on a Stage

GUERILLA FILM MAKER SAYS!

1. Shooting in a set means you can make your set exactly as you want it. The downside is of course, you have to make it!

2. Sound is usually very good as stages are sound proofed.

3. Facilities such as parking, changing rooms, production office, cutting room, canteen, toilets, are usually just around the corner. This is a MASSIVE advantage.

4. You are responsible for all the light on the set - there is no sunshine to move, cloud cover, rain or night time. You can completely tailor your lighting and know it won't unexpectedly change.

5. Whether your film is set at night or during the day, shooting on a stage means you can operate sensible daytime hours without messing up the collective cast and crew body clocks.

6. Stay on schedule. If you slip, have a contingency plan in place with the studio management so you are not turfed out on the scruff of your neck.

7. Unlike a domestic residence, stages have comparatively limitless power, but it can be expensive.

8. There will be 24 hour security so you can leave your kit there, and it will save on insuranec too.

9. Bigger studios may have a lot of downtime between bigger productions. you may be able to slip in and use that time.

Jeremy – I'd like to reiterate what colleagues have said in the past, which is if you are thinking about shooting in a studios, you should be talking to the studios early on in relation to what your requirements might be; where we might be able to help you in pre-production. The studios provide a hub, a network to the industry at large. We are very well connected to all the different lighting camera companies. We can advise people about who they should be speaking to in the local area in relation to their production.

Q - How can a new film-maker get the best out of you and cause you the least irritation?

Jeremy - I think the new film maker has to sit down with us, as early as possible, and has to make a conscious decision whether or not it's a stage picture or a location picture. There after, to look at all the different facilities we might provide that film maker, and even if there is no stage requirement or build requirements, to look at where we might help them. They need to retain some sort of flexibility in lieu of the fact that we will probably look after them financially somewhat more than we would the bigger clients. If it's short film or a low budget feature that only requires a week of shooting, and they are looking for a financial discount because of the fact they are new and emerging, and they simply don't have the budget, they need to be flexible with us. If they've got some flexibility and fluidity within their schedule as to when they shoot it, it allows us to then slot them in between our more commercial clients.

Q - What common mistakes do you see from film makers?

Jeremy - Not terribly many in relation to the way in which films are structured and scheduled. Even the less established film makers will probably have surrounded themselves with experienced professionals, whether it be their DoP, their 1st assistant director, their editor, their producer, their UPM. If anything, it's more often than not trying to cut back the number of days early on in the production, and then resulting in an overrun or a requirement for re-shoots because shots weren't necessarily completed as properly as they ought to have been. Normally most productions will get into problem areas simply on the creative content, and actually on the way they shoot, which is the nature of any creative industry.

Q - What advice would you offer a new film maker?

Jeremy - Persistence and guts. Keep hammering at it. Nobody in the industry has got where they are through luck or through resting on their laurels. It's a hard craft, but if you are prepared to put in the time, you will be rewarded.

PRODUCTION

David Colenutt
Location Manager

LOCATION MANAGER

Q - What is your job?

David - I am a location manager. My job is to find and manage locations. I am usually brought on between 5 and 6 weeks before it shoots. On bigger budgets that's nearer to ten weeks.

Q - Do you work from the script, or with the Director, how do you begin your job?

David - Usually I just begin by breaking down the script, and then have a conversation with the Director about what exactly is wanted from each location on a creative level. I then sit down with the Production Manager and go through what money we have available. I will see if I can get any more money from another department. If there are already props in a location for instance, I may be able to get some of the production design budget.

Q - So there is a negotiation that goes on, that is mutually beneficial. Do you ever get involved in script re-writes to save money on locations?

David - Yes, it can happen, especially on low budget films. It is common sense sometimes and I can suggest alternative story locations if we find a location is too hard to find or too expensive.

Q - How do you find Directors take those suggestions?

David - The smaller the budget, the more co-operative they are as they know that they are on a limited budget.

Q - What are your views on locations for micro budget films?

David - It is kind of take what you can get. Write your screenplay to accommodate the resources you have.

Q - What are the main considerations you have when you are looking for locations?

David - The actual creative element. How it looks always comes first, and logistics come second.

Q - What are those logistical issues?

David - Parking, access - how much hassle it is to get to and from the location, how easy the owners will be, how close the unit base can be, how much time it takes travelling from the unit base to the shooting location, if it is a congestion charge zone etc. Of course, on site toilets are essential, as you will not be able to hire honey wagons (portable loo) on low budgets. Sound is a big consideration when picking a location - is the location next to a main road, is it on a flight path? This can make sound unusable. Power is another consideration. Will you need to hire a generator? Which on low budget films you don't want to do. You need to find access to the local power.

Q - How do you go about securing a location?

David - We usually get as many options as possible, several possible locations for each story location. Usually you show photo's of everything you have got, then pick 2 or 3 of the best and go round and have a look in person. The director would then choose, and then you would sort out contracts.

Q - What is that procedure with contracts and negotiation?

David - I always mention the budget on the phone before even considering a location so as to avoid wasting time. After a location is chosen, you go back and finalise the money. Sometimes you can re-negotiate and try and get a bit of money off, of course, knowing in the back of your mind that you have back ups, just in case they change their mind.

Q - How often is it that locations tend to fall through?

David - Not a huge amount. Obviously, the lower the budget the more you are at risk. On average, one location may fall through on a film. You generally keep two or three locations in your back pocket, in case something happens with a certain place.

Q - What is the Director's availability to check locations, like in the weeks leading to the shoot?

David - Not great. To plan recce days is important, because you have got to take a whole day to see everything, which kills a whole day for the director. Plus you don't really want to be visiting locations that probably won't be used, it is just a waste of everyone's time. Generally you start with pictures and eliminate from there.

Q - Do you take digital photos, and e-mail those?

David - Yes. The director usually sees all the photos beforehand, and usually they are sent by e-mail.

Q - Do you think 90% of the choosing process can be made with digital photos?

David - Yes. If you have taken a photo well enough, you can get a real sense of what the actual place looks like.

Q - How much can locations cost?

David - With the film we are on at the moment, we are trying to get a huge open-plan office in which most of the film is set. A decent figure for that would be £1k a day. You can get options on that from the Film Commission, and Film Libraries and various other places. The budget for this film is quite low, so we only have £300 a day for an office. £300 for an office is tough, but just about possible.

Q - What are the organisations who can help in terms of liasing between you and the final location owners?

David - I usually use the London Film commission quite a lot, another one is the BFI. Then there are the actual boroughs in London. Each film officer runs each borough, and they are hugely important. No matter where you film, almost certainly you will have to talk to film officers, even if it is on private property.

Q - What about just going and doing it guerrilla style?

David - Some times it is best to let sleeping dogs lie. If you are filming on the road for half an hour with a crew of five, you may best be served to say nothing and just go and do it. There are so many

DAVID COLENUTT

Location Manager

davidcolenutt@hotmail.com
+44 (0) 77 0808 9033

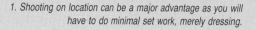

Shooting on Location

If you have no budget, shooting on location is probably the only option for you.

1. Shooting on location can be a major advantage as you will have to do minimal set work, merely dressing.

2. Space can be a major problem as even the biggest of rooms will become sardine like with a full crew.

3. Shooting outdoors can be a problem as there is no way to control the weather. Consider shooting in a place like Spain where there are long days with great light. The locations will be cheap too.

4. Always try and get permission to shoot wherever you intend to be. Sometimes, if you can foresee problems, it is best to simply dash in, shoot, and get out as quick as possible. If someone turns up to find out what is happening, try to get them interested and involved, and claim complete ignorance.

5. Getting to and from difficult locations can be very costly in terms of time - one hour travelling is one hour less shooting. Don't underestimate the chaos of moving thirty cast and crew just one mile down the road.

6. Use movement orders. This is a piece of paper with a photocopied map (the route picked out with highlighter pen), explicit directions and mobile phone numbers for those who get lost.

7. Facilities for the crew on location can be a problem - a place to eat and sit will be needed, and a loo must be provided - you can't ask your star to squat in the bushes.

8. Closing down streets in the UK is difficult. The police will be as helpful as they can, but they have crimes to stop and don't relish the thought of holding the hand of a new producer.

9. When choosing a location, don't forget the sound. There isn't much use shooting a period drama next to an airport (unless you can post sync the dialogue).

10. Film crews trash locations. Clean up after yourself, leave muddy boots outside, ban smoking inside etc. Remember, you may need to return to the location if there is a problem with the negative - try not to burn your contacts.

11. Think creatively - many locations can double for several different parts of your story. This will minimise the time you waste moving between places.

12. Shooting in London is tough as many councils have got smart and will charge you just to take a camera out on the streets. Be aware that parks, streets, schools and the like will probably all carry a price tag that is small to your average production, but crippling to a micro budget movie. Avoid paying at all costs.

13. If you are away from a city, you may need to pay excessive travel costs or even accommodate cast and crew. Ouch!

14. Beware of the cool location that is impossible to either light or get cameras into, Buildings with big windows cause lighting problems, turrets with narrow stairwells are tough for carrying kit, anywhere in London will cost you simply in parking alone.

boroughs and a lot of them are very different in their financial demands, and sometimes you choose to avoid some just because it costs so much to shoot even the tiniest little things on tiny little roads.

Q - What about outside of London?

David - It is all split up, North-West Screen, Southern Screen etc. If we were shooting in Cornwall, or Bristol, probably the first port of call would be to call South-West screen, and say *'how can you help?'*

Q - Is there a centralised place on the Internet where you can get all that information?

David - The Film Council will have that information.

Q - What happens about insurance?

David - Generally we are insured up to £5m or £10m in Public Liability, so if something happens to the location, then it is covered. Of course you will need to work professionally and not do anything that would void the insurance, such as burning stuff without prior agreement with the insurers and location owners.

Q - How much does that insurance cost?

David - Every one is different of course, and dependent on the script. It can be a couple of grand I think.

Q - What happens about security?

David - Yes you have security, especially when vehicles are involved, which is usual, even if it is low budget. For instance if you have to leave vehicles with equipment, parked overnight somewhere, you should have security there, patrolling it all night. Security companies usually provide their own vans and they often sleep in them as well.

Q - How much does security cost?

David - About £10 an hour is quite good, more often like £12, £13 an hour.

Q - Does it get more complex if you are shooting at night or with things like rain or fog?

David - Yes. It is just a bigger, more expensive, more risk, more risk assessments, more people to tell about it, more calls. More paperwork!

Q - What kind of paperwork do you generate?

David - There is usually quite a lot. There are various contracts and agreements, and location letters, saying we are going to film from this date to this date, and how much it will cost etc.

Q - You don't need a massively over-complicated contract, you can even write your own contract?

David - You can get stuff off websites like Shooting People (www.shootingpeople.com), that is just one page. Usually location owners are quite happy to have that contract. Keep it simple.

Q - Talk me through what would be a typical day.

David - I'd get up pretty early, because you have got to be the first one there. So I would be up around 5am, to be at a location for 6ish. The catering people would arrive around the same time, then soon after a lot of other vehicles and staff will arrive and costume, make-up will set up. Then the caterers will be parked, and will try and get breakfast ready for about 7am. Once they are all parked and up and running, you are usually OK. That is pretty much your job for the day, you are done, unless you get a shout from the 1ˢᵗ AD, saying they need help with something.

Later, you may spend time putting up signs on the street for the next day's locations. You may also go and check out new locations, perhaps one has fallen through, perhaps there has been a script re-write.

If there is a location move, there will be a movement order, which is a piece of paper saying the address, the new location, with very specific details of how to get there, how long it takes, how far is the nearest hospital, ambulance, contact details for myself and the location owners etc. That is usually distributed with the call sheet each day, for the next days shooting, and handed out to the crew before they leave.

EXT. RUN DOWN
PUB —
LOC - DEW
DROP INN
E. LONDON

Q - What does the Unit Manager do?

David - The Unit manager is basically the person who stays on set for the whole time and manages it. You work more closely with this person than with anyone else on set. So if I need to go off and prep a location, then the Unit manager will be the person who stays with the crew, to make sure everything goes smoothly.

Q - In your experience, do film crews trash locations?

David - They are usually conscientious, but sometimes some damage may occur, not on purpose, but it is a film crew, it is 25 people, wandering round a house. Sometimes there can be damages.

Q - Does insurance cover that?

David - Yes.

Q - What common mistakes do you see?

David - The movement order would be quite important. If you got that wrong you can lose a lot of time with lost cast and crew members. Unit signs should be made up in advance, so you are not caught out before a shoot.

Q - Generally if it is all organised properly, it tends to run smoothly?

David - Yes. Once you are on set, and you start shooting for the first day, you should have few problems. Don't get complacent though.

Q - What can a film maker or screen writer do to make your job easier?

David - Write easier locations! On low budgets, be creative and at least consider seriously alternative story locations. Something that seems easy in the script may be a location nightmare - I recently had to find a Leisure Center for 5 days shooting - this was a very big problem on a low budget as they had classes scheduled that they would not move without compensation that we could not afford. We ended up shooting in a hall instead and dressing it.

Q - Gone are the days where you can ring people and they would go 'Oh my God, a film'?

David - Yes, pretty much. People are very savvy now.

Q - What advice would you offer a new film maker?

David - Write something or direct something or produce something, or work on a film that is actually good and means something, and hasn't been done before.

Location Permits

GUERILLA FILM MAKER SAYS!

Sometimes you just can't grab shots guerilla style – you actually have to set up lights and close down streets. You need a permit to do these things, especially in big cities. If shooting in the UK, find your area below and contact that office and they will sort you out. Some permits are free, some cost, some are quick to get hold of and some take ages - so give yourself plenty of time to get them. And make sure you keep copies of the permit nearby in case that cranky neighbour calls the police on you. If shooting abroad, contact the city government you are going to for their requirements. And find someone who speaks the local language if necessary so "language barriers" do not translate to "film shut down."

For Derbyshire, Leicestershire, Lincolnshire, Northamptonshire, Nottinghamshire, Rutland:
EM-Media
35-37 St Mary's Gate
Nottingham, NG1 1PU
Tel: +44 (0)11 5910 5564
Fax: +44 (0)11 5910 5563
Email: emily.lappin@em-media.org.uk
Web: http://www.em-media.org.uk

For Greater London:
Film London
20 Euston Centre
Regents Place
London, NW1 3JH
Tel: +44 (0)20 7387 8787
Fax: +44 (0)20 7387 8788
Email: info@filmlondon.org.uk
Web: http://www.filmlondon.org.uk

For Cumbria, Durham, Teeside, Tyne & Wear, Northumberland:
Northern Film and Media
Central Square,
Forth Street
Newcastle Upon Tyne NE1 3P
Tel: +44 (0)19 1269 9212
Fax: +44 (0)19 1269 9213
Email: locations@northernmedia.org
Web: http://www.northernmedia.org

For Cheshire, Greater Manchester, Lancashire, Merseyside
North West Vision
233 The Tea Factory
2 Wood Lane
Liverpool, L1 4DQ
Tel: +44 (0)151 708 2967
Fax: +44 (0)151 708 2974
Email: lynn.saunders@liverpool.gov.uk
Web: http://www.northwestvision.co.uk

For Bedfordshire, Essex, Cambridgeshire, Hertfordshire, Norfolk, Suffolk:
Screen East*Southway
Leavesden, Hertfordshire, WD25 7LZ
Tel: +44 (0)1923 495051
Fax: +44 (0)1923 333007
Email: jess@screeneast.co.uk
Web: http://www.screeneast.co.uk

For Berkshire, Buckinghamshire, City of Oxford, Hampshire, Isle of Wight, Kent, Surrey, Sussex, Channel Islands:
Screen South Room 33, Admin Building
Pinewood Studios,Pinewood Road
Iver Heath, Buckinghamshire, SL0 0NH
Tel: +44 (0)1753 656 412
Fax: +44 (0)1753 656 412
Email: film.commission@screensouth.org
Web: http://www.screensouth.org

For Herefordshire, Oxfordshire, Shropshire, Warwickshire, Staffordshire, West Midlands, Worcestershire:
Screen West Midlands
31-41 Bromley Street
Birmingham, B9 4AN
Tel: +44 (0)121 766 1470
Fax: +44 (0)121 766 1480
Email: info@screenwm.co.uk
Web: http://www.screenwm.co.uk

For Yorkshire, Humberside
Screen Yorkshire, Studio 22, 46 The Calls
Leeds, LS2 7EU
Tel: +44 (0)11 3294 4410
Fax: + 44(0)11 3294 4989
Email: kaye@screenyorkshire.co.uk
Web: http://www.screenyorkshire.co.uk

For Cornwall, Devon, Dorset, Gloucestershire, Somerset, Wiltshire:
South West Screen, St Bartholomew's Ct
Lewins Mead, Bristol BS1 5BT
Tel: +44 (0)117 952 9977
Fax: +44 (0)117 952 9988
Email: info@swscreen.co.uk
Web: http://www.swscreen.co.uk

For Northern Ireland:
Northern Ireland Film & Television Commission, 3rd Floor, 21 Alfred House
Belfast, BT2 8ED
Tel: +44 (0)28 9023 2444
Fax: +44 (0)28 9023 9918
Email: info@niftc.co.uk
Web: http://www.niftc.co.uk

For Scotland:
Scottish Screen
2nd Floor, 249 West George Street
Glasgow, G2 4QE
Tel: +44 (0)14 1302 1700/1723/1724
Fax: +44 (0)14 1302 1711
Email: louise.harris@scottishscreen.com
Web: http://www.scottishscreen.com

For Wales:
Wales Screen Commission
66 Parc Gwyddoniaeth
Cefn Llan,Wales
Tel: +44 (0)2920 333300
Fax: +44 (0)2920 333320
enquiry@walesscreencommission.co.uk
Web: www.walesscreencommission.co.uk

PRODUCTION

Pic by Jeremy Larkin, from London Voodoo

Bill Mayell
First AD

ASSISTANT DIRECTOR

Q - What is your job?

Bill - Generally, my job is to plan the shoot, organise and control the set, and take that weight from the director, so he can concentrate on directing. I filter through all the questions that he would normally get and then decide which ones are most important to bring to his attention. It gives him the room to direct instead of having to be a manager.

Q - At what point do you get involved on a project and what are your initial duties?

Bill - For a lower budget film, I would say about a month to six weeks before shooting. I read the script several times. Then I get the storyboards or shot list in front of me, and I go through them with the director, and we will talk through the whole film. Then we plan, by running through scenes and locations, sometimes with the location manager, and sometimes you are the location manager! It also depends on the nature of the film. If it is a horror film, then there are prosthetics and the like to set up.

Even when we have a good firm plan in place, as soon as we start to shoot, things are going to happen. The old Russian general Zukov said, *'As soon as you enter war, your plan is gone.'* So part of the plan becomes having contingencies set up for when things go wrong. So I would start off by saying what contingency would I have if it rains one day. Perhaps, I would have another location to go to or have cutaways to do. Don't ever waste your time.

Q - Do you advise the film maker on ways the script could be rewritten to make it more doable?

Bill - I think it is unusual for a 1st AD to do it. But I have done that, and it usually depends on your relationship with the director. It's easier for the more experienced people to let that happen, whereas the younger people are less likely to consult with you. I have actually gone to the stage of working things out with a director and saying *'you can't do that, but you can do this'*. And he has actually listened and at the end of the day, we have something in the can that we can edit. I think that is part of the reality of being a filmmaker - you can have some great ideas, but if you can't get them in that one night, if you only have one night, then what is the point?

Q - What are some of the key conversations you would have in those four weeks of pre-production and whom would you have them with?

Bill - The conversations would be with the director and all the heads of the different departments. One of the main topics would be logistics. What do you need at the various locations that we are going to be at? Part of our job is to actually visit those locations and look for potential problems. For example, I remember doing a feature film that involved a lot of military equipment. We were turning a London car park into Tiananmen Square. When I first heard this, I had no idea how that was going to work. So I went to the car park and, in looking around, the first thing I thought was that OK, people use this car park on Saturday night, and we are here first thing Sunday morning. Everyone who comes out after drinking is going to have their car parked here, and they might decide to take a cab home instead. So the first thing that clicked in my mind was to get someone to move cars if we have to. And Sunday morning we turned up and there were twelve cars parked across the car park and so we had them moved out. That sort of thing logistically is what you need four to six weeks for.

Q - What is a schedule?

Script Timing

GUERILLA FILM MAKER SAYS!

When line producers and 1st ADs are trying to schedule a film's production, they need to know how long each scene will take to shoot. This will tell them how long the total shoot will take and thereby determine how much money they need to budget for production costs for each scene (and thereby the whole film). The way they start this calculation is by figuring out how many pages each scene takes up of the script. This is called script timing.

The way it works is that a screenplay page is divided up into eighths from top to bottom. If a scene takes up half the page, then its script timing is 4/8 of a page. If it takes up one quarter of a page it runs 2/8 of a page, and so on. Do not reduce the fractions (e.g. 4/8 should not become 1/2) in order to keep things consistent. If a scene lasts more than one page it will be listed as a whole number and then the fraction (1 3/8, 3 5/8 etc.). A good rule of thumb for low budget filmmaking is that you can usually get through 4-5 pages a day, so a 100 page screenplay will take somewhere between 20-25 days to shoot, but it's not uncommon to squeeze a movie into 19 days over three weeks.

Bill – The schedule is a plan if you like, a list of shots and scenes in the script, broken down into an order to best utilise resources. For instance, we may only have an actor for one day, so all their shots would need to be scheduled on that one day. Add to that a problem like, we only have a location for one day, and half the scenes of the one day actor are there, but also in other locations, you can see how it can become a complicated and logistical nightmare.

Based around a shot list, I will draw up a schedule of the shots we are going to do and the locations we are going to be in a specific area. That schedule will then be used by all the departments to schedule their own activities that they have to do. For example, the schedule will go to the costume department and they will see that, on the first day, they need an 18th century dress at 2:00pm. So I don't get the actress ready until 2:00pm and the costume department does all their preparation in the morning to get it ready for 2:00pm. All of the departments' work is based around the schedule. I can make an ideal schedule that is logistically brilliant, but artistically, a director might say, *'I don't want to shoot that scene at that point...'* And he has every right to say that. So then we say, *'OK let's move the scene to here...'* But then the DP might say the light is going to be wrong for that time of day for that scene, so let's move it there. So we all sit around and discuss what we think will be the best way to shoot that day's scenes.

Q - How do you do a schedule, who does it?

Bill - Script rewrites we normally do on the day. I normally do the schedule. I do it after I have read the script and looked at the storyboards if there are any. Then I show it to the director. Then the producer may have some input and then I will move to the DOP, who will definitely have some input. Then I take it away and rejig it in order to come up with the best compromise - at least to a certain extent. At the end of the day, we have to get it in the can and on the day, and either the director, the DOP or myself will have to compromise. Part of my job is to look after the crew and all of their interests.

Q - In your experience, if you are getting behind schedule and the director is digging in to get his shots, what kind of disaster can that spell?

Bill - Things don't get finished. And unless you cover the screenplay, you don't have a movie. Often compromises are forced upon you, maybe it's rain, money or a difficult actor, and a smart director will roll with the punches rather than fighting a battle they cannot win. In a worst case, it's always about getting enough shots to make the script work in the cutting room.

Q - Who is on your team?

Bill - I can have one assistant or I can have many. So that would be a 2nd AD or a 3rd AD and then some runners. Sometimes there can be two 1st ADs if the project is big enough.

Bill Mayell
First Assistant Director

07803 024402
bill@carmelcrest.co.uk

PRODUCTION

Story Days

GUERILLA FILM MAKER SAYS!

Story Days are the number of days through which your story is told. It is not the amount of time over which the film is set in the story. It could be 1 story day, as in Training Day, or Die Hard, or 20 story days set over a 50 year period in a biopic - the 20 days are the specific days over the 50 year period, that we as viewers, visit the story and characters.

Department heads need to know the story days, in particular, costume and make up. It's essential that your Story Days are calculated when breaking down the script for scheduling as you're going to be shooting out of sequence (almost certainly). If a fight scene halfway in the film results in your lead actor having a scar for the rest of the movie, it's important that your makeup department knows that all story days after the event should include the scar, possibly at varying levels of healing on different story days. Remember, the scar will not be referred to in the screenplay except on occasion, and certainly not in every scene for makeup to be prompted when reading the screenplay. Equally, the costume department need to know when to change costumes to indicate a passage of time, and simply not later that day. On a low budget movie, it's advisable to minimise your story days, so that your actors are not spending much time changing costumes and wasting valuable production shooting time.

Story Days can be included in your screenplay, in the slugline which, for example may read...

    SCENE 23   INT. JIMS FLAT - NIGHT   SD4

This is scene 23, set inside Jims flat at night, and it takes place on story day four.

Q - What do the 2nd AD and 3rd AD do typically?

Bill - They are my eyes and ears. I normally use my 2nd AD to liaise with actors and crew if I am too busy with the director. I normally use my 3rd AD as a runner. They would be at a higher pay scale than just a runner though.

Q - Who would draw up each days call sheets and the paperwork?

Bill - Generally, I do all of that. If I am too busy then the 2nd AD would do it.

Q - Take me through a typical day of what would happen, say, shooting a conversation scene with two or three actors?

Bill - Ninety-nine percent of the time I am the first one to arrive at the set or location. I meet with the director, the producer and the DOP before we get underway, and see if there have been any major changes, especially to the first shots of the day. Then I would make sure that everyone was in their appropriate places. For example, the actors are in make up and the guys are setting up the first shot. And once we are set up, then we would walk through the day's business by going through the schedule and the script. We call it walking the course. That is normally led by me and involves the director and the DOP - sometimes the producer. And between the three of you, you get a really good idea of how it is going to work. Politically, it can be really awkward to push the day along, especially in front of a crew. Then after that, the day begins and everything that goes into a day's work. The first scene may take longer than we think or it might go quicker. It may start raining and we have to move somewhere else. But I have those contingencies written down and ready to implement if needed.

Q - Do you have any observations on working with DOPs who are either very fast or very slow?

Bill - I do admire DOPs very much and many of my friends are DOPs, but they do sometimes feel that they are the most creative cogs in the whole process. Gordon Willis who shot *The Godfather* said that he never realised how difficult directing was until he did it, and I think that the more experienced DOPs know that too. If you have a DOP who is willing to do things quickly and not compromise too much over the look of things, then I think that is going be a savior for everybody. He can help everybody, the whole crew throughout the whole shoot, the cast isn't going to be standing around because the lights are not working. Generally, I think they can make or break a movie.

Q - Who deals with background artists?

Scheduling Problems

GUERILLA FILM MAKER SAYS!

One of the first things your 1st AD and Director will tackle together is the scheduling of the film. Or, in other words, when do we need to be at certain locations and how long will we be there for? The first factor in this equation is scene length as, generally, you will need to get all your shots in one location before you move on to the next. Some scenes move faster than others, so here are some things to bear in mind when calculating your total days or to watch out for in order to keep things moving.

Simple dialogue scenes

These can move quickly. If you have just two characters facing each other while talking, you can shoot a master, and their close ups very fast. If up against it, cover the whole scene in one shot, for example if you know that only one of the character's reactions are important.

Complex dialogue scenes

These move much more slowly because having multiple characters may mean multiple cameras and more complex lighting setups. Also, you have more people to cover with close ups. If you know how you plan to edit the film later, you can shoot specific shots and leave what you know you won't use. However, this may limit your options in the edit if it does not work as planned.

Action scenes

All action scenes, especially those with stunts, take longer than you will expect as aside from setup time, they may need to have many different angles for editing. Stunt scenes take even longer because they must be planned down to the smallest detail, always putting safety first. If you can afford it, have a second unit shoot these scenes.

Cutaways and establishing shots

Close ups of newspaper headlines and sides of buildings really make your film flow and take very little time to shoot. If you don't get them during the primary shoot, get a skeleton crew together and pick them up on weekends after principle photography wraps. These are also good things to give to the second unit.

Night and Rain

The rule of thumb is that it will take you four times as long to shoot any scene that involves night or rain. Setting up lights in the dark is difficult and you will need more of them. Rain screws up everything from lights to continuity to the crew and actors' mood. Rewrite avoiding both if possible.

Day or Night

You may be able to shoot interior night time scenes by blacking out windows and vice versa. Always try and block locations together, then block day or night scenes within that location together, then see how that fits with other elements like actors or special props etc.

Track and Cranes

Any way that you move the camera other than on the tripod or on your shoulder, will take twice as long because of setting up track and repositioning equipment. The good news is that moving shots make your film more dynamic and you may only need to shoot a simple walking dialogue scene from one angle, which doesn't take as long to film.

Production

It takes time to move trucks, equipment and people from place to place. Changing costumes and sitting in make up slows people down. Sets may need to be redressed and cameras reloaded. Then, there is lunch! Factor these things in and also don't forget wrap time.

Other things to consider are...

A slow camera crew, bad planning, police problems, actors screwing up their lines and not hitting their marks, technical problems, interpersonal dramas, multiple location changes, late crew, and exhausted crew members who are tired at the end of the day because they've had to deal with a production that doesn't know how to budget their time correctly... we could go on...

Remember the Golden Rule... STAY ON SCHEDULE!!!

PRODUCTION

Scheduling

Making a schedule is a complex and lengthy process. Unfortunately it often gets left until the last minute, not through laziness, but because of script rewrites and production problems changing the way in which the film will be shot. The idea is simple, to organise the scenes in the screenplay in such a way as to get the most out of your time and money when you shoot. Usually this starts with grouping locations together, then day and night within those locations. But actor availability may mean you are unable to do this. And so the juggling begins.

Start by breaking down your screenplay, listing the scene number, location, DAY/NIGHT, INT/EXT, scene length (1/8th of a page, or 7/8th of a page etc.), characters in the scene etc. and a brief description. Enter this information into a program such as Movie Magic Scheduling or ShowPlanner, or onto strips for a strip board, or most cost effectively, onto 3x4 index cards. You may also want to make a note of things that occur within that scene that will impact on how much you can shoot, such as child actors, stunts, visual effects, special effects, special make up, weather conditions, animals, special props, extras etc...

If using index cards, use highlighters to colour code certain elements, such as stunts, VFX, animals, night and day, cast members etc. Or, if you're using a scheduling board (strip board), you will have colour coordinated strips that can be used i.e. blue could be used for interiors, green for exteriors and so on. On a production board, black strips are used in between shooting days. On a computer program such as Movie Magic, it will print production board strips on white paper, which are then ready to be put into plastic sleeves that come in a variety of colors. These plastic sleeves are then inserted into a production board. OR, your production board strips are printed onto your already color coordinated paper to be fitted into your production board.

The Production Board

This was the industry standard until computers came along. It's still widely used as once you understand how it works, it is simple, effective and transportable.

4x3 cards

The cheapest way of organising your schedule. Transfer all the info from your screenplay onto the cards and then arrange them into the best possible shooting order.

SC 56/58 (SD3) INT/NIGHT		1/8
DAVEY & SARAH PREP FOR GOING TO HOUSE WITH CONNOR		
DAVEY SARAH	SARAHS BEDROOM	TV WITH VAMPIRE FILM

Movie Magic Schedule

Industry standard, powerful, but you will not be able to install and start using if you have no prior experience. It's quite complex and it isn't cheap either. ShowPlanner from CompanyMove is a good and cost effective alternative.

How many weeks to schedule?

This depends on what type of movie you're working with. Is there a lot of action? Are you working with kids? Both can extend your shooting days. Or is it a simple walkie talkie? Generally, for an independent movie, where you're looking at perhaps 90-120 pages in total, you'd be looking at either a 3-6 week schedule, depending upon your budget. And you'd be looking at a 6 day week, not a 5 day week.

Second Unit Scenes

These could be establishing shots, scenes without any principal actors, scenes with your main actors in the distance where you could use doubles, cutaways where an actor picks up a book - all should be singled out in the schedule.

Create a number list for Cast

Assign numbers for your actors so you can create schedules with Day out of Days, Call sheets, production reports etc. so, your hero is #1 for example.

Have a Back-up Plan

Always make sure that you have a backup. If you've scheduled to shoot on location in the beautiful sunshine, but it just so happens to pour with rain that day, then arrange for an interior shoot. This is called a 'Cover Set'.

Floating Scenes

There may be days where you slip behind schedule and you'll have to reschedule that last scene of the day that you just couldn't manage. If you can't find the right place to replace the scene, then place it as a floating scene. This can then fit either as part of your back up plan (as above) or if you're lucky to get ahead of schedule on a day, you'll know immediately what you must cover to catch up.

Cont...

GUERILLA FILM MAKER SAYS!

Cont...

Cutaways and Establishing shots

These are your establishing shots of buildings, landscapes, close up of a newspaper headline, close up of fingers tapping a keyboard etc. Break these out from the main shoot and if running behind schedule either put as a floating scene, give it to your second unit or in a worst case, do them as a pick up after the main shoot.

Shot in Order or Juggled?

Remember films are hardly ever shot in sequence. It is the AD's job to juggle all of the elements - cast, actor's availability, locations etc. to make the schedule efficient. The AD must also allocate travel time between one location to the other, work closely to the union rules (if it is a union film), work closely to the rules when working with minors, animals etc. The AD must be aware of where to place important scenes, for example, the big kiss of your movie or an extreme emotional scene. Is this wise to schedule at the beginning of the movie when your actors don't know each other, or towards the end of the schedule when your actors are feeling more comfortable with each other, but also exhausted? It's a fine line and a very complex job.

The Breakdown Sheets

Once you have your final schedule (although remember it's always changing with rewrites etc. throughout the shoot), transfer the information onto Breakdown sheets. Each sheet represents one scene. Each breakdown sheet must be numbered and dated in sequence.

Now that you have your schedule, other paperwork can be drawn up such as 'Actor Day out of Days', Call Sheets, Shooting Schedules etc. Scheduling programs such as Movie Magic and ShowPlanner will create this paperwork for you once the information has been entered.

(see detailed charts in the Toolkit section towards the end of the book)

Bill - Me. If someone is walking across the road or through scene, I'll usually choreograph that while the director is talking to the main actors. Often the 2nd AD will help me with that, too.

Q - Who draws the line with set safety?

Bill - Me. We are all responsible. But I am in charge of the set in that regard. We all work with professionals and we would all like to think that they would put a sandbag on a light and know how to take down leads. But in today's world, it is the number one factor before we start shooting - is anyone going to get hurt? And it is up to myself and everyone to keep our eyes and our ears open. I caught two runners up a ladder just recently, maybe sixty-five feet in the air and the ladder was just barley touching the girder. They were trying to take down a light for the DOP. The slightest movement would have killed them! So I had them walk slowly down the ladder and everything was fine. So it's everyone's responsibility to watch out for everybody else.

Q - Do you think most film makers think about health and safety?

Bill - You have to be careful. Filmmakers get into the industry by working really hard and working long hours, and they get tired. From my perspective, I sometimes have to say, *'that's enough. You are doing something that is silly and danger is involved.'* You have to say no, and I am the one who has to do it. Directors try to push it because they want to get it done. But if in your heart you feel it is dangerous, you have to stand up and say no. And if a another crew member comes up to you and says that something might not be right, you have to have empathy and then say whether you are comfortable with it or not.

Q - What do you think makes a great AD?

Bill - Firstly, you have to love the process of film making because it is not glamorous - it is hard work. After that, you need good organisational skills because that is how you come across to people and issue orders to them. Your people and diplomacy skills have to be very good. You have to have a thick skin because often people like to blame you. I have heard stories of producers blaming the 1st AD because they are buffering the director.

Q - What kind of equipment do you need to be an AD?

PRODUCTION

Bill - I have a laptop computer with Movie Magic Budgeting and Scheduling software. I don't own walkie-talkies, I usually get them hired through the production company because of the logistics and they are also reliable then. I usually take a camera with me if we are going to locations. Sometimes I will take a compass with me so I know which way the sun is going to be shining.

Q - Would it be a good idea for a production to hire a photocopier rather than use the local printing shop?

Bill - Yes. It is essential and much cheaper.

Q - When you are on set, do you call "action"?

Bill - Well, I would say 70% of the time I do it. I guess it is a bit of a myth that people think it is the director who yells it all the time.

Q - Do you find that most directors are mentally ready for the next shot once they have called 'cut'?

Bill - Half are, but I always am. I know what is coming next and I may lean over and whisper into the director's ear that *'this is enough and we have to move on'*. Some guys are really good and know we have to crack on and others will look at me and ask what is next.

Q - Some people start to resent the 1ˢᵗ AD because they think he has something personal against their department when in fact all he is doing is trying to meet the demands of the director and the schedule.

Bill - I think it is important to remember that when things do get stressful and people do lose their temper, and everyone does because they all want to do so well, and they are under so much pressure, it is essential to remain calm. I rarely raise my voice to a

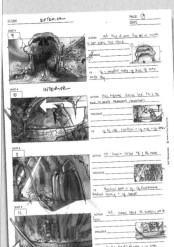

Script Planning

GUERILLA FILM MAKER SAYS!

If you had all the time in the world and the most perfect conditions, you would be able to plan every shot of your film down to the smallest detail. However, low budget filmmaking never gives you either of those conditions as you have limited time to shoot and those frequently occurring prop/location/actor/money/mother nature problems are always nagging at you. While you can plan for the best, you may find yourself winging it in order to get everything done. These five examples show you how much information you could offer in five different levels of planning for a scene.

Shot list
A simple description of the shot that relates to the action. You can make these fast and will work in any location under any circumstance. However, you have the least amount of visual information to convey to your crew.

Plan
If you are not good with drawings, you can sketch out an overhead camera plan (much like a blueprint) of where the camera, props and actors will go.

Director's Storyboard
Drawn by the director and limited by their artistic abilities. Often a storyboard artist will use these as a base for the actual storyboards.

Full Storyboard
A full illustrated picture of the shot drawn by a storyboard artist. If you have time and money to do this, it will give you the opportunity to easily convey the visual information to the crew.

Previsualisation
A technique where a you shoot your movie in a temporary way, with no real props, locations or full lighting. Often used for effects sequences, but slowly becoming a more accepted way of pre-planning. But lets face it, for most new film makers, the previsualisation IS the movie!

Coverage

GUERILLA FILM MAKER SAYS!

A good director knows what they want to shoot, before they get on set. If they know that in the final edit of the film, 'the monologue scene' will always be in close up, then they will not waste time and money shooting a wide master for coverage. However, should you find yourself working on a studio film, you may be required to shoot much more than you think you need so that the executives feel comfortable with the amount of coverage the editor will have to use in order to tell the story properly. If you are working on a low budget film, you have to be much more economic with your shots, yet still have enough to tell the story powerfully and effectively.

1. Always shoot a master shot of the scene. This establishes location and always gives you something to cut back to.

2. Shoot singles (either medium wide or close up) of the actors in the scene. This way you can edit their performance to improve dramatic impact.

3. Get as many cutaways and insert shots as possible. This will help tell the story and give the editor more options.

4. Even if you are happy with your first take, always do a second take for safety. You never know what can happen, such as the lab screwing up the processing or the film getting torn.

5. When you go to a new location, shoot an establishing shot. This orients the audience to location and gives your scene a jumping off point.

6. Never cross the parallel line of action to the camera. Doing so will make the actors seem to flip flop location on the screen, and it will disorient your audience.

7. Ensure reverse shots match one another. For example, if you are shooting two 'over the shoulder singles' of two people talking, the two actors' eye lines should appear as if they are looking at one another and not off at some weird angle.

8. Get all your shots on one object or actor (master, medium shot, close up) at the same time. This will reduce relighting time.

9. If part of a take is good, but the rest is bad, you may not have to do the whole shot over again. You can 'pick up' from just before the mistake and continue through to the end, but you will need a bridging shot (insert), such as a reaction from another character to cover the join.

10. Shooting lots of coverage can wear down a crew. Keep your eye on their fatigue level so you know when to call it a day.

11. Learn to work within your budget and schedule. Neither are limitless and on low budgets, they are VERY limited. Extra takes could mean you have to drop scenes. Always be aware of the longer term impact of your choices.

12. Learn how to edit and work on other peoples films. You quickly learn what you need and don't need.

13. Know the rules before you break them. Oh and just to confuse you more, there are no rules!

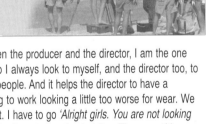

temper level. I always have to remain calm. If there is a big shouting match between the producer and the director, I am the one afterwards who has to calm everyone down and tell them where they are going. So I always look to myself, and the director too, to remain calm. The other thing is that it is often my job to spell out the bad news to people. And it helps the director to have a relationship with say, actresses who might be staying up a little too late and coming to work looking a little too worse for wear. We both know it, but I am the one who has to go up to them and let the actress know it. I have to go *'Alright girls. You are not looking your best. Let's get to bed a little earlier tonight...'* And it is how you put it across. You have to be nice, but firm. The same thing goes for the crew. *'Guys, we are going to have to work late tonight and there is no overtime. But we have to do it.'* If they respect you, they will moan and they will kick their heels, but they will do it.

Q - What scenarios lead to either shoots running late or shots getting aborted?

Bill - Poor planning. If you are shooting at night and you have no provision for rain and it rains all night, then the night is lost. The same thing for the day. If you put all your eggs in one basket, you can lose the whole thing. If you don't have the money to do it, you don't want your production to go tits up. Have contingencies. Have a plan to do something else if things go wrong. Outside of that, if you are shooting someplace that you don't have permission to use, then the police can shut you down and ruin everything. If you don't have your health and safety policy and there is an accident on set - that can cause problems. It is all down to planning.

Q - What are your duties after a project is wrapped?

Ross Novie
www.company-move.com

Budget Scheduling Software & Scheduling Tips

they can't drink milk and now you have to wait thirty minutes to get a milk substitute from the store. Communication is key because you really have to share the schedule with the director to get ideas of what the director wants to do, the production designer as to what sets will be ready and when, and with the DP who might want certain things with lighting at certain times. The first draft of my schedule is always a starting point of the discussion.

Q - When people are scheduling a film, what are the key things they need to think about before they start?

Ross - The overall point of properly scheduling is giving the director the most time to direct. Getting the most money on the screen. Scheduling is all about grouping together your sets and your expensive resources, which can be cast, special equipment, locations or extras, in the most efficient manner. It always seems that you start out with a script where you have this ideal schedule where you do the least moves, cast is kept to a minimum and then reality sets in and you end up scrambling it around. The better you are at scheduling, the more you can go beyond what the script is and start shaping the budget and the script to meet in the best possible place. When I am scheduling shoots, I look for locations that have a lot of multiple uses. So if you are at a restaurant, maybe there is a building around the corner that you can shoot an apartment scene in. Then maybe the street has a look you need, or there is a park nearby. That way you can do lots of scenes and maybe several days in that same space without having to move the trucks or strike everything. Independent film makers really want to think about making the script help shape what the practical locations are. For example if you have a conversation that takes place in a restaurant, but there is a really visually interesting church around the corner, then as long as it still serves the story, think about having the conversation take place in the church. Now this is a little bit of a taboo in higher budgets where you follow the script. But on the lower budgets it really makes you think what every scene is about.

Q - For low budget film making, how fluid is the schedule and how much contact do you have with the creative personnel?

Ross - There are so many factors with a schedule that an experienced 1st AD, Production Manager or Producer can anticipate before they happen. And Murphy's Law applies to it as well. If I read a scene and in the scene someone is drinking a glass of milk, it is guaranteed that the actor is lactose intolerant! I know it and I have seen it. So I ask the actor if they are before we start shooting because it is one of those things where you get on set and then it's the milk drinking scene and the actor says

Q - Why should a new film maker invest in scheduling software?

Ross - Just like any artist, you have to know the rules before you break the rules. In my last short film, I stole locations from all over the city. I know how to do that because I am an AD, where to go and what to say if someone comes. When I was a first time film maker, I would get busted in five minutes because I had no idea. If you are doing a short film, then $500 for Movie Magic scheduling software is overkill. My software may be overkill for a short film. But if you are doing something with any sort of complexity, you want to do it in the most efficient way possible. In fact, it becomes more incumbent for you to schedule it better because you have less resources to cover problems. You don't have the luxury of dancing around problems that larger productions can. A software program like mine, CompanyMOVE, allows you to organise your thoughts, plan the shoot and communicate it to other people, and that also has a secondary effect of giving people confidence in the project because there are a few things that will show your project as one of professional calibre, and one of them is scheduling software. It is an industry standard of presenting how you are going to shoot. You want call sheets to show what you are shooting that day, which in our program is integrated so that you don't have to spend a ton of time creating them. And there are 'schedules' and 'day out of days' so the actors know when they are working.

Q - What are some of the highlights of CompanyMOVE that film makers should take advantage of?

Ross - First off, it is less than half the cost of Movie Magic, and if you belong to certain organisations, you can get even bigger discounts. We have integrated production reports and call sheets, which is great for smaller shoots where you might not have the time or personnel to do a call sheet or production report. Secondly, there are important legal documents to have in case something goes wrong and it

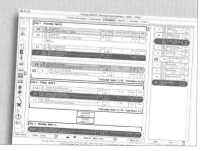

looks professional. In our program, you just type in the times and all these documents are spit out. Having to retype all that information into a Word or Excel document wastes time and doesn't make sense. In Movie Magic, I find things are counter-intuitive. To find out what is happening, you have to read back a day. So we use icons and very clear indications as to what is being shot on what day. We use drag and drop functionality, which a lot of the other programs don't have. We have cast blackout so that you don't accidentally schedule someone who isn't shooting on certain days. It seems simple enough, but if you are juggling eighteen different actors' schedules, you can forget things and end up scheduling the movie around something that can't be. We have really geared our program towards independent film makers.

Q - What are the common mistakes that you see new film makers make as far as scheduling is concerned?

Ross - You never want to put your biggest work at the end of a schedule. You never want to start with the hardest thing either. You want to ramp up and get some good days under your belt. So some nice dialogue scenes to get the crew into a rhythm. But

soon thereafter, you want to tackle your bigger work so that if something goes wrong you have time to fix it. And try to finish light in case you have to carry scenes over from earlier in the shoot. And within a day, people move faster in the second half, but you want to put your important work in the first half of the day. Never leave important scenes for the end of the day or you will end up rushing through it. And never shoot inserts until the end of the day unless it is absolutely unavoidable. There is nothing more demoralising to a crew than standing around waiting for someone to shoot a piece of paper.

Q - What advice would you give a new film maker?

Ross - Get friendly with a very bankable star and put that star in your movie. That will get your film in doors it wouldn't normally. I am not talking necessarily about Brad Pitt, but you need someone.

Pic - Darren Gerish © PPFI Ltd

Bill - It depends on the director. Some directors insist that I get in the cab with them and leave. That doesn't happen very often, but when it does it's great. Usually, I stay afterwards and make sure that all the actors are OK and that everyone is on their way home. I'd talk to the production manager to make sure that things are fine. I'd make sure the set is cleared or if sparks are still working, I would leave them to it. Occasionally, there may be some follow up paperwork over the next few days. Often I am lucky enough to be invited in to see the rushes on the other side of it. But generally it is a couple of days wind down.

Q - What advice would you give a new 1st AD or someone who finds themselves in the role and has never done it before?

Bill - Especially on low budget shoots, try to keep everyone's enthusiasm up. Try not to look at it as a job, but try to push things along enthusiastically. People feed on enthusiasm. Be positive. When things go wrong, be positive, not negative. It is very easy to bring a whole job down if you are negative, especially if things aren't going quite right and you are not getting the shots you want. Always be the one who is positive and moves things along to the next set up. Enjoy the whole process. Enjoy sitting behind the camera and watching two actors act out a great scene together. Enjoy that the camera is rolling. There is no better job.

Q - What diplomatic tricks do you have up your sleeves?

Bill - A big one is just to let people talk. Let them vent and get it out of their system. Once it is out, speak calmly to them. Never raise your voice to them. Avoid producers that have got a lot of money, don't know what they want to do and then decide to go into the media. They are the ones that drag down a production. Movie sets should not be playgrounds for the rich.

Q - What are common mistakes that directors make?

Bill - I have seen some really funny things happen where a director doesn't listen and they do what they want. That is the biggest mistake new directors make - not listening to experience, but that usually goes away once they have some experience of their own.

Q - What advice would you offer a new film maker?

Bill - Go out and do it. It is great. The good times completely outweigh the bad times. Do it because you want to contribute something and try to do things differently. Be innovative and try to push the boundaries.

PRODUCTION

Olivia Williams
Actor

THE ACTOR

Q - A director and actor can be alike, interested in telling stories through drama, almost as though they are different sides to the same coin. What makes a person want to be an actor?

Olivia - I think it begins with how you are as a child, and I wasn't the one putting on the plays, I was the one with the hairbrush as the microphone. The desire to perform / show-off was very evident, and that absolutely does not make you an actor, and could probably make you a bad actor. I'm not saying it made me a good actor, or showed that I would be good at it, but it is what pushed me to that side of the camera or the curtain. I have subsequently thought a lot about directing and producing, partly from the sheer frustration of an actor, having no power or control over your final product, particularly in film. I think it is worse on film than it is on stage. At least once you are on stage, unless armed security come on stage, they can't stop you doing it the way you think it is right, where, as you know producers and directors can change what you did on set through editing.

I think there is a need for a Director to have a kind of omniscience, to have an interest in every single detail of the entire story, you have to have a very holistic mind. I love picking a pathway through a script, and finding a character's route, story and arc, though I find it very difficult to have an opinion about everything and everybody, which is perhaps another reason why I am an actor and not a director. When I read a script, I only ever see it from my character's point of view.

Q - What attracts you to a project? Clearly there are two aspects to it. First of all is the money, but if you remove that from the equation, and say the money is nothing to do with the choice, what is it that attracts you to a part? Can Indie films offer an actor something mainstream films can't?

Olivia - I was faced with this the other day when I was asked to be involved with a very interesting script, written by an extremely bright and clever woman. The story was about a young girl, a coming of age story mixed with a psychologically messed up story about her brain at the time. They wanted me to play her mother. Now, there is the attraction of being involved in something because it is good, but what made me shy away from it in the end, was that no attention had been paid to making this mother character real, and to have a story of her own. My point was that the character was badly written, though the script was good, the idea was good, the role for the girl was good - but the mother role was ill-conceived. I don't mind being a minor character but I look to my character to have an arc of their own, something that happens to them that gives you something dramatic to do, that has an influence on the plot. One of the practical reasons, is so that you don't end up on the cutting room floor, and secondly so that you are not being brought in as totty. I'm pretty well past the totty age, but there was a stage where I was just being brought on because the character needed to have a girlfriend so that they could have a nookie scene, and she could say *'Don't go!'* or *'Don't leave me!'*, and you could cry. I think a mainstream actor who gets well-paid to play good roles will do a small movie, as long as you pay attention to their character. Give them an arc, give them a story, and try and read the script purely from that character's point of view, but not from the actor's point of view, don't try to persuade the actor to do it. Having smoke blown up your arse is very irritating when you are trying to make an intelligent and valuable point.

Q - It is an interesting point, and I often suggest new filmmakers ought to write films with strong female leads, because you can access a greater talent pool.

Olivia - Absolutely. Don't write it for females, write it for a male and just change the name to a girl. Why not? And it can be done so often. Also think about the peripheral characters, the doctors, the lawyers, the policeman, they don't specify sex or for that matter race. Your lead does not have to be a good-looking bloke in his mid-twenties to thirties. He doesn't have to be white, and he doesn't have to be a he. There are a lot of established actors out there who can greatly enhance your film, once you move away from the stereotypes.

Q - The moment you embrace that philosophy, you start to get further away from convention and cliché. Everything that the audience expects is kind of there, but in a way that the audience doesn't expect. That's new and fresh and exciting for everyone.

Olivia - Yes. You would just get an enormous amount of support from those of us who aren't 25 to 35 good-looking blokes, and there are quite a lot of us out there. A good note for script writers and film makers generally is pay attention to your smaller characters. It doesn't mean that they have to have a speech, but giving your smaller characters depth and an arc will greatly enhance your chances of getting better actors, and also improve your story and drama.

Q - You must read a lot of scripts and will have developed an eye for good material. For new film makers, your creative input into the screenplay could be very valuable?

Olivia - You've hit a real nerve with that, because very often a project is attractive, but not quite right. I keep on coming back to this recent project because it was nearly so good, that I nearly said *'Yes'*, on the basis that I thought we could sit down and tinker with this and make it right. I've done that before, and every time I have been wrong. You can't tinker with it, there isn't time when it comes to it.

I would say to everybody, make sure it is right before you go into production, and make sure you've done your changes. What I've found, and I can see why it happens, is that I've said in what I think are the clearest terms, what I think the problem is, and how it can be made better, and then the Writer or Writer / Director goes away, tinkers with it, comes back and in the process they have lost something and the screenplay is even weaker than before. So I would suggest you watch out for the amount of people giving you advice, because it can fuck with what was special. I shouldn't say this about my fellow actors, but actors can muck it up, and can make it a lot worse. The reason I say sort it out before you go into production, because you don't want this fight on set. If you have got an actor who is insisting on changes, lock down your changes before you go into shooting, because an actor can waste a lot of time by saying *'I thought you were going to change this'*, all while you are standing there with the lights on, the location booked and the clock ticking. Get all your changes agreed, to an almost legal level before you go on set. Particularly if you have a tricky actor who says they are unhappy with the script.

Q - It's not always possible, but do you think the director and actors should spend time together, not just rehearsing, but also talking, perhaps more philosophically, about the project and themes it contains?

Olivia - I think it is very important. You have to be prepared though, as my foul language comes out (laughs), you have to be prepared for a lot of wank. I can't think of another way of saying it. You have to be prepared for a lot of pretentious talking, and you need to put time aside for it.

Rehearsing can be difficult, because so often in a screenplay there is little dialogue. It is just one person saying *'Hey'*, and another person saying *'Hey'*, and then you go *'let's try that again'*. It can be a bit painful, though if you ever hear something like *'Oh yeah, we will sort that out on set'*, *'I'm not happy with that'* or *'oh yeah we can improvise it'*, I would suggest dealing with it before you get to set. Give the actor time to say what they are thinking, and check that you are on the same page.

During the shoot, directors often come in when you are in the make-up chair, and that is a very vulnerable place for an actor to be. You may already be feeling nervous as perhaps the person who is doing hair and make-up is heading down the wrong path, and then the Director comes in and says something. You can have a tremendous sense of falling down a black hole, that it is all going wrong. I would definitely have good chat beforehand, and it doesn't have to be a formal rehearsal stage, maybe a quiet restaurant or by coming round to somebody's house. Talk about your vision, and even how you are doing the shots. Not with a view to that being up for discussion, but just so that the actor knows what to expect. Often you just don't have time on the day, so it can be very important. The actor might be expecting a big close-up of her own for some lines, but if you say *'Oh yeah, we are going to do that with your back to the camera',* it can be surprising.

Q - On low budget films, actors can be often seen like props and denied some of the tools that will reward the film with better performances. Such as a place to prepare, not hair and make up, but mentally. Also, an actor fighting their way on the tube may not arrive in the best of emotional states...?

Olivia - I don't think this is just about actors being needy and spoilt. When shooting a drama there is a co-ordination of an unbelievable number of people, with a staggering array of equipment, and you are trying to get them all to get to the same place, at the same time, doing the same but slightly different things. That is your biggest logistical problem, and at an early hour in the morning. It may seem that an actor asking to be driven somewhere is a lot, but actors are people who are not necessarily used to office hours or a 9-5 job. If you want them there on time, I'm afraid you are going to have to get them there. I really feel very strongly about this and believe it is worth the investment.

Q - Do you think that the problem can arise because we are all in the same boat, cast and crew, and we are all going down the same river together, but fundamentally, actors are a completely different breed of person to almost everyone else on the crew, and actors have very different needs. If you want to get the best out of an actor you need to treat them differently to the crew and give them the space they need?

Olivia - Yes, though I don't want to sound precious about this. Remember, the crew probably all know each other, and know how to get to location, and they have bonded as a group. And it can be a very lonely thing as an actor as you turn up into that environment - we all want to be wanted, we want to be loved, and it can be quite isolating. If you want an actor to be in the best state of mind, when they turn up for makeup and hair at 5am, at least get them a minicab. If the director is your mate, and you've been part of the process, and everyone is easy going, and can prepare by having a cigarette and a coffee, that is fine, but if you don't know the people, it helps when people try hard to make you feel welcome.

Q - Actors are as human as everybody else, even though there is almost like a veil between you and everybody else. It is not a real veil, but it is perceived?

Olivia - We are like normal human beings, just quadruple the insecurity and the vanity. If you absolutely exponentially multiply those two, and then you've got your average actor.

Q - What do you think independent filmmakers, as storytellers can offer you, that you don't get from the bigger projects?

Olivia - I would say a character with an arc, something transforming that happens to a 37 year old woman, that doesn't involve her husband leaving her or losing a child. Things that are thrilling to act, a dramatic event, or more off-beat plot stories. Something that I find depressing to read is when a character's appearance is described in too much detail, because when I read it, I think I can't do that. If she is supposed to be luscious, with a gorgeous waist and a fabulous pair of legs, I would think *'alright, they are going to need someone else then'.* Take care when writing, and if you go into too much pervy detail about what you are looking for, a lot of actors and actresses just go, *'I can't live up to that'.*

Q - In terms of 'on set', the way it is run, what do you think are the common mistakes that you see, that make it harder for you to be the best that you can possibly be?

Olivia - Squabbling. Get your chain of command right, establish it before you ever go out there. Everybody should know what the 1st AD said, and the 1st AD should be making it possible for the Director to direct. Have your rows in private, before you get out there, do not do it in front of other people.

Q - A film should be almost militaristic in the way it is run?

Working With Experience

Actors are one of the most underrated asset to any film. And if they are considered important, it tends to lean towards putting the deal together... This actor is known so they will add to the attractiveness of the overall project, which is true. But for low budget films, access to that calibre of actor isn't always possible. However, there is a wealth of extremely experienced actors out there who would be interested in talking to hard working, passionate and interesting new film makers who will make their film happen, rather than let it sit in development hell. Actors want to act as much as film makers want to make films. The money is important, but to most, the work takes precedence.

1. Don't fear approaching any actor, no matter their stature. They can say no. But they may say yes. They may like you, your film, the genre, they may have some free time...

2. Cast older actors with more experience. Their faces will be familiar, their experience will be invaluable. Even actors who are not known but are experienced will raise the standard of work.

3. Never try and pull rank on an actor with 30 films under their belt, especially if this is your first foray into film. Equally, fight passionately for your ideas. The directors job isn't to come up with the best idea, it's to select and utilise the best idea, wherever it comes from.

4. Cast women. We have a surplus of extremely good actresses who no longer fit in clichéd stereotypes that most work comprises of. They are no longer young enough to be the pretty girlfriend of the hero, nor old enough to be mother of hero. This talent is almost completely untapped in the UK and the USA. It can be as simple as gender swapping all the characters in your screenplay. Try it!

5. Experienced actors also have experienced friends who they can call if they like the project. The secret is to be passionate, modest, interesting and utterly professional.

6. Get to know agents. This is one reason to make a few short films in quick succession. The agent will see that you make things happen, and that you are on the way up. You will also be on first name terms with them.

7. Work with a casting director. They have contacts you don't and can add credibility.

8. Cast unusual actors. Look for faces that are interesting, not just pretty or charismatic. Part of what makes an actor stand out is their differences. Ugly can also be very beautiful.

9. Above all, respect what an actor can bring to the role. They may be neurotic and difficult, but that is part of the package. They are trained to deliver raw emotion. Your job is to channel that in the right direction and capture it on camera.

10. Cast your film right and it will almost make itself.

Pic from 'Frozen'

PRODUCTION

Olivia - If you think it is going to be cool and laid back, or that you can just breeze in and do it, you are absolutely wrong. You will earn my undying hate, if I have to get up early, and look good, and be ready to go on camera, my lines learnt by 8am, and then some fuckwit is late. There are no excuses.

Q - I agree. The logistics of a well run set create the opportunity to be creative. If you don't create that opportunity, you just end up with the mechanics or covering the scene, which rarely results in a great piece of drama.

Olivia - Work it all out with your AD - they are the most amazing people who are so organised. You want all the actors going through make-up, while you are setting up the set and shot. It is like school where you have a timetable. In order to get a shot on camera by 9 o'clock, you probably start at 5am.

Q - One of the things that is often overlooked in terms of importance, especially on low budget films, is costume, props and make-up. How important is the authenticity of those things to you as an actor?

Olivia - I can't say I've ever had a problem with dodgy props, though I would say that with costume, I'd prefer to provide my own than wear a poor one, and I have worn my own clothes in movies. I don't think that is unreasonable to ask actors to do. You feel

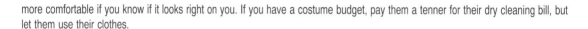

Blocking

GUERILLA FILM MAKER SAYS!

Blocking a scene refers to figuring out how the actors and camera will physically move through a scene, and it is done on set or location just before shooting it. Blocking allows the director and the heads of various departments, as well as the actors, to see where potential problems might arise. For instance, the camera team may realise that a light is in their shot during a tracking move, or an actor may not feel comfortable delivering a certain line at a specific spot on the set. Blocking also allows for the camera team to mark the floor with white camera tape, to give actors a specific point to stand on, so the camera team know the camera will be in focus (this is where the phrase 'hitting your mark' comes from). Resist the temptation to drop blocking. Five minutes blocking may save an hour trying to figure it out on the fly.

more comfortable if you know if it looks right on you. If you have a costume budget, pay them a tenner for their dry cleaning bill, but let them use their clothes.

Hair and make-up can set things off on a really bad footing. I don't wear make-up on a daily basis, I use it purely for purposes of filming. There are many make-up artists who are moving from music video or fashion into film making and their idea is to try out the latest make-up product... Sometimes, having the wrong makeup artist can be worse than having nobody.

Q - Of course you would be an ideal person to ask, about good make-up artists.

Olivia - Absolutely. Come to me first, because the point about make-up in film is that you are not trying to make someone look like Kylie Minogue. A film may need children, men, black people, old people etc., and someone who has come from music videos may not know how to deal with a wrinkled face or a child's face, or how to do a decent bullet wound in 5 minutes. The greatest make-up artist I know can cover up your spots if they need covering, or can make a pimple in 30 seconds if you need to be more spotty. You are not looking for someone to make you beautiful, you want someone who can make you ugly, who can make someone look tired and look like they've just been born. You really have to think very carefully because sitting in a make-up chair, watching someone fuck up your face, sets you up on a very bad foot for the day.

Q - Inexperienced filmmakers can see actors as a bit of a problem, because they can come with an amount of baggage, like being picked up in the morning, fussy about how they look and what they wear... It is a seen as a problem, therefore the actor is a problem. Yet fundamentally the relationship between the screenplay, the Director and the Actor is the core creative relationship. Actors are probably the most important collaborator in the process. People can get fixated on the Camera, the Sound, the effects, when it is your eyes that they are looking into, not at the great set behind you. What would you say to that new filmmaker?

Olivia - Involve the actor in the process. You are very often the last person on board, and nobody tells you what is going on. Talk to them, tell them what your vision is, how you want it to look, what atmosphere you want to create. That is a personal view and there might be some actors who don't want to know what you are doing, who want to try and pretend that there is no camera there. The De Niro or Day-Lewis school of acting, where the actor is *'the person, and it is your job to capture me being that person at that moment'.* You will encounter an entirely different set of problems with that approach and you had better make sure that they have the space to do that.

Q - Do you think it would be a good idea for Directors, perhaps even Writers, to do a 3-week acting course, so they know who Stanislavski and Brecht are, to just experience being an actor, so that when they come to set, they are not just fixating on camera?

Olivia - Yes, I think that would be a good idea. I think many people don't understand what is possible, what an actor can do for you. I don't mind saying *'Do you want me to cry? Do you want there to be tears? Do you want me to gasp, do you want me to sob? Do you want me to be hysterical? What do you want?'* Watch performances on film, and watch nothing else, don't look at the lighting, don't look at the lens, don't think about what the f-stop is. Watch the actor and think about what choices they have made, and what they are capable of. If you have hired an actor because you liked their performance, watch the performance, and tell them what it is that you like about it. From that they will be able to extrapolate what it is you want from them. Some actors aren't like this, but I particularly, I see myself as a sort of conduit for the Director's vision, and it can be very depressing if you are saying *'I am your conduit'*, and they've got nothing to say to you. Tell me what you want.

Q - What advice would you offer a new actor, going into a low budget film?

Olivia - I'd give them a list of things they need to pack into their bag. Several books and a newspaper, your own towel, lavatory paper, your favourite teabag or coffee. Go incredibly well prepared to be entirely self-sufficient. Put your armour on, because your ego may well get bruised on the day. I would say this to everybody starting out, do what you are told. Which is not a popular piece of advice, but while I was a fighting and embattled actor, I was a very unhappy one, while I was constantly saying *'my character wouldn't do that, this isn't right for my journey, what if, what if'*, I was in a state of conflict, and I didn't act well, because I was not thinking about the character. I would say try and relax and have a calm about you, where you greet everyone, you say *'hello'* to everyone, call everyone *'darling'*, if you can't remember their name. Try and stay calm and polite in your exterior, while the chaos goes on, so that when the camera rolls you are thinking about nothing but your character. I find if I am worrying about hopeless transportation arrangements, I'm worrying about the row going on between sound and costume on site, because sound want to put a mic on you, and costume say they can see the mic.... You just have to stand and breathe, and exempt yourself. Try not to be part of the row, try not to be part of the crisis.

Q - That is also one of those areas I guess where often the filmmaker forgets that you are a person.

Olivia - Everybody does. The filmmaker is not so bad, it is usually Sound and Costume particularly. Sound asks ridiculous things like *'Can you walk across the room without making any sound with your feet?'*, or you are having a row and the script says *'Slam your glass down on the table'*, but you can't slam the glass down on the table when you are saying a line, so you have to shout, then slam the glass down with silence and then carry on speaking. And you are having a row, but you are not supposed to overlap the dialogue, because it makes it difficult for the editor.

Q - I find that really tragic, because anything that inhibits the performance will removing a layer or quality, empathy, energy...

Olivia - It is absurd. Another great tip I had from Bill Murray... He said *'If you've got a funny line, make sure it is recorded properly on set, go to the Sound guy and say, is the sound good on this, as you will never get a laugh on a dubbed line, never ever.'*, he always made sure if he was saying something funny, that there were no aeroplanes, no barking dogs... Know what you are doing. I've been on set on huge movies, and even then, I have experienced the film makers turning up and saying *'OK, let's see how we are going to do this'*. If you are making a movie where the entire thing is in a room with 2 people fighting and it has got to be very organic, then you can do that. But most of the time, when you have locations for a short period of time, you've hired a bus or a horse and carriage or something, you cannot do that.

Q - What advice would you offer a new filmmaker?

Olivia - Become a lawyer. That is what I should have done. The advice to follow your dreams is extremely dangerous, and not all dreams come true. I think that is when my blood would boil is when I saw a documentary about *Britney Spears* and her Redneck roots, and there are so many people peddling *'Follow your dream, because if you work hard enough, and you want it enough, your dream will come true'*. They usually don't. They might, but just work your arse off, do your very best. Follow your dream and if it doesn't work out do something else.

Philip Cooper
Arri Media

CAMERA HIRE

Q - How do you hire?

Philip - Camera hire is normally based on a daily rental charge, however we also have weekly rates too. Equipment orders will only be accepted from a member of the production team, never by the camera crew. If we were not strict on this policy we could get into the situation where we have shipped extra cameras out and no one wants to pay for them because they weren't authorised. Be aware!

Q - Let's talk about film first. What is the difference between Super 16mm and 35mm?

Philip - 35mm film is larger than S16mm so the image is clearer and sharper. It's also the same format that is used in cinemas for projection, but it's more expensive to shoot on. We would like more things shot on 35mm but the success of S16 is apparent in films like *'Lock Stock and Two Smoking Barrels'* which are blown up to 35mm and then go theatrical. S16 is very attractive to low budget film makers. It's also more compact and lighter so you don't require so much crew.

Q - What is in a basic camera kit?

Philip - Between 16mm and 35mm it is a very similar package. The camera kit would comprise of 3 x 400ft magazines, follow focus, mattebox, batteries etc. It would then go on to include a set of prime lenses, possibly a zoom, a fluid head, tripods and even a video assist. Dependent on where you hire your camera kit from, it's a good idea to check exactly just what you get for your money. But don't forget consumables - you always need that gaffer tape, empty film can and clapperboard!

Q - If you have four lenses as suggested, could you hire an extra body and share the lenses in order to have a second camera?

Philip - Yes, you may even find it's a requirement from an insurance perspective, but if you do intend to use it as a second camera you will need all the extra equipment like head, tripods, filters and magazines too.

Q - Do you hire creative filters?

Philip - Yes. There are many choices of different filters such as promists, soft FX, diffusions etc, depending on the type of look you're after. For instance, if you want to give the film an 'older look' you could use a sepia filter.

Q - Why have so many lenses?

Philip - Why not! It's great to cover every filming possibility, however cost will always outweigh the practical side. Generally primes are faster, ideal for handheld work and give great results but if you can't afford to have a certain focal length in your primes set, then use the zoom.

Q - If you're a new film maker shooting on S16mm, what camera should you hire?

Philip - From us it would be the Arri SR2. They're a robust and reliable camera that's easy to use. You could achieve a movie like *'Lock Stock...'* with an SR2. There are other S16mm cameras too, like Aaton. You should make sure everyone knows about the equipment before you use it, there are always things you pick up by coming to see us. We expect a camera team will come and test the cameras here, and familiarise themselves with the kit.

Q - As a producer, you do live in fear of lost or damaged cameras as they are so expensive.

Philip - If we were to add up every zoom bar that has been lost or damaged then I'm sure we could have purchased a brand new lens. Filters are easily scratched if not taken care of correctly. This can all be avoided if the crew look after the equipment in a professional manner in which case there should be no damages!

The camera team is encouraged to go to the rental company to shoot tests and familiarise themselves with the equipment before finding out the hard way on set.

Q - What happens about insurance?

Philip - In the event of loss or damage we look for the cost of replacement plus 13-weeks loss of hire. We won't let any kit go out until we have received a copy of their insurance policy, which must include this. The majority of productions will always have their own insurance; however if not we can always recommend an insurance company for you.

Q - If a low budget film maker came to you and said 'I am going to pay you on day one of principal photography' would you give them a better deal?

Philip - Definitely. It's a great incentive for us and puts the production in a good position regarding price. No one likes to chase bills, it wastes everyone's time. If you haven't got much money be honest. Don't be afraid of getting us excited - we love movies. Show us your scripts, tell us about the project, who is already onboard. It could help us make the right decision in pushing your film forward.

Q - How quiet are cameras and what can you do with a noisy camera?

Philip - Cameras are quieter now than they have ever been. However in confined spaces, such as a bathroom scene, we would always recommend using a soft Barney.

Q - What happens about slow motion?

Philip - The SR2 or SR3 standard cameras will go to 75fps, the high speed SR2 and SR3 to 150fps. Faster than that and you are in to specialised cameras like the 16mm photosonics with a speed up to 500fps. For ramping high speed but keeping the aperture constant, the ARRI ICU can be used. For a TV drama, items like these would be hired on a daily basis to keep the costs down.

Q - What is anamorphic?

Philip - Anamorphic is a 35mm system where the taking lenses contain elements that squeeze the image by 50% horizontally, allowing an image twice the normal width to be photographed on regular width film. The reverse process is used to restore the wide screen image when it is projected. This system produces what many regard as a visually pleasing look with very little grain. The lenses tend to be physically larger than spherical ones and being slower, require more light. A typical working stop would be between 4.0 and 5.6.

ARRI
MEDIA

PHILIP COOPER
GENERAL MANAGER

Media Film Service Ltd, 3 Highbridge, Oxford Road, Uxbridge, Middlesex, UB8 1LX
Tel: +44 (0)1895 457100
Fax: +44 (0)1895 457101
E-Mail: pcooper@arrimedia.com
Web: http://www.arrimedia.com

PRODUCTION

HD - The Technology Carrot

GUERILLA FILM MAKER SAYS!

Every day seems to bring a new technology or debate. Is HDCam better than Film? Is HDV better than DVCProHD? Is Avid better than FCP? Should I shoot 720p or 1080i and do the film look in post? Of course there is never a definitive answer, and certainly not one that will apply over time, even a short period of time. It's always getting better, faster, cheaper...

So how do you make your choices?

Two philosophies stand true. First, professional film makers need technology that delivers images that meet exacting standards, and robustness that means the kit can be relied upon in all conditions. As such, what they use would be a good choice for you. Rather than taking the easy option and shooting on your camcorder, professionalise your film and see if you can shoot HDCam, even Super 16mm. The images you get will not disappoint you. The crew you attract will be better than the one you would if you shoot on a camcorder.

The second philosophy is that, the lower the shooting format quality, the more time you will spend trying to pull out an acceptable image to meet creative standards and also international delivery standards. Yes, you can just go out and shoot your film on a Sony Z1, and that may be an appropriate choice for many film makers, but is it the right choice for you and your project?

Finally, whatever choice you make, ensure you have the whole process - production, post production and delivery - covered, including sound. You must know what you intend to do so that you don't get into trouble in post production.

HD (that's everything from top end HD and HDCam, down through HDV and DVCProHD) is a wonderful technology, but the many variants around now, and no doubt the ones in the future, can often confuse matters unless you fully understand the impact of your shooting format and post production route. Plan, test, plan, test.... before committing to a major project.

Don't ask what is the best format, ask what is the right format for your story and production.

Q - What is video assist and how does it work?

Philip - Video assist is a small video camera that sits on the side of the film camera feeding a picture to a TV monitor which the director can watch. It's great for the director because they can see exactly what movements the camera operator is making, what they are doing. The disadvantages are that it could slow the production down due to other members of the crew getting involved watching the monitor and giving their input. More DoPs and directors ask for the video assist in the early stages of their career for safety measures. On the more recent features we have serviced, video assist isn't being used at all. Not only does this save them time but also money. All video assist really does is show you the frame and tells you if the operator has captured in frame what you had hoped but don't be fooled by the colour or lighting as it is only as good as the monitor you are watching it on!

Q - HD is now a viable shooting format. Most people understand the advantages, but film cameramen often talk about the quality of lenses. Does HD have the same kind of lenses?

Phil - Cameramen who come from a film background, who are used to using prime lenses, can continue to use those lenses. Broadcast cameramen are more used to zoom lenses and may ask for those. The optics have improved with the zoom lenses and are now excellent. There are also HD lenses which are that bit better for the job, but you pay a premium for those. For low budget films, a good quality zoom lens is ideal.

Q - Technology seems to be updating the cameras all the time?

Phil - Technology changes in all areas. Not only in digital, but also in film. Digital technology does change more rapidly, compared to film though.

Q - Because of that rapid change, more than ever, renting, opposed to buying, makes sense for a production company?

Phil - Yes.

Film Camera Kit

CAMERA BODY
(Arri SRII pictured). The heart of the camera. All the other parts in the camera kit are attached to the body.

MAGAZINE
Film is loaded into the magazine, commonly called a 'mag', by the assistant camera person. Three 'mags' are normally supplied. One 400' mag will run for approximately 10 minutes (at 24fps with Super 16mm).

FLIGHT CASE
All the kit is mounted in separate flight cases for protection. Can be bulkier than you expect and the small ones can be easily mislaid.

LENSES - ZOOM LENS
Common length is 10-100mm, giving a fairly wide shot to a good close up. Cheaper zoom lenses can be heavier, are physically longer, and need more light than prime lenses.

LENSES - PRIMES
Usually supplied in a kit of three or four - common prime lenses are 9.5mm (very wide), 12mm (wide), 15mm (mid), 25mm (mid/long) and 50mm (long). Much shorter and lighter than a zoom, usually gives a crisper image and needs less light for exposure.

MATTE BOX WITH BARS
Affixes to the camera body and protects the camera from stray light entering the lens and creating lens 'flare'.

BATTERIES
A charger and several batteries should be supplied as standard. Ensure batteries are recharged as soon as possible as you just can't plug the camera into the wall.

INTERVALOMETER
Used to control the speed of the camera so that it can shoot at extreme intervals such as 1 frame a second, or hour. Used for time lapse shots.

APERTURE CONTROL
Used to control the opening or closing of the aperture electronically and smoothly. Used in conjunction with a variable speed control, sequences where the speed changes mid shot are achievable.

SPEED CONTROL
This device allows the camera to be used at various speeds, usually from around 5fps to 70fps. Note, the camera speed can be set independently of this device, but not altered with ease or during a take.

FOLLOW FOCUS
Device used by the assistant camera person or focus puller to alter the focus of a lens during a take, so that when an actor moves they stay in focus.

ZOOM CONTROL
Device to control the zoom lens so that it can zoom in and out smoothly and at the right speed. If you intend to use zoom shots, you MUST use a zoom control as no operator will be able to perform a smooth zoom.

LIGHT METERS
Device used by the DP (Director of Photography) to measure the amount of light in a scene. They come in two basic varieties.

Spot meter
Used much like a camera lens and gauges the amount of light reflected off a selected area of the subject.

Incident light meter
Used to measure the amount of light falling on to all sides of the subject. This is the most common type of light meter used.

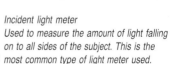

FILTERS
Colour correction filters to convert between tungsten and daylight are essential. Effects filters are only rented on the day needed and cheap semi pro photographic filters will usually do the same job for a fraction of the price.

Film Camera Kit... cont

PHASE ADJUSTER
Used to alter the frame rate of the camera so that it can be used to film television screens. Without this device it is possible that a dark band or bar will appear on the TV.

EYEPIECE EXTENSION
Useful for when the camera is mounted high or low, or in an awkward position.

CHANGING BAG
Used to load and unload magazines with the film. Remember you will need empty cans when shooting so that you can unload film, perhaps with short ends being re-canned.

HIGH SPEED CAMERA
If you want to do slow motion shots of up to 150fps, you will need to hire a special high speed camera body. Note that this HSRII is grey in color. You can use your existing lenses and tripod/head with this body.

TAPE MEASURE
Used to measure the distance between the focal point on the camera and the subject. Aids in focusing to ensure the image is sharp. Don't make the common error of mixing up feet and inches with centimetres and metres on the tape measure or the lenses.

CONSUMABLE STUFF
Compressed air for cleaning, torch for checking the gate, camera tape, gaffer tape, clapper board, camera report sheets, dulling spray (to reduce reflected highlights), empty cans, stickers for the cans etc.

VIDEO ASSIST
Device that connects to the camera so that the director can watch the shot on a small TV monitor. The quality is as good as the kit and can be recorded for instant 'playback'. Don't expect too much out of old kit.

BARNEY
A blimp that covers the camera body and deadens some of the sound. Leather coats draped over the camera will also help.

HEAD
The camera sits on the head. The better the head, the smoother the action. Rent the best head you can afford. Ensure you have the right bracket to connect the camera to the head.

LEGS
The tripod - comes in two sets, tall and short.

SPREADER
Connects the base of the tripod for use in places where the tripod spikes will damage the floor, or just won't hold fast.

TRANSPORT
You will need a large estate car or transit van to drive all this kit around. Ensure one person is responsible for all the kit being packed away and checked so that no equipment is accidentally left. Think about where you are going to park overnight and if the equipment will be loaded and unloaded at the end of each day.

THE CAMERA ASSISTANT KIT
This will include all manner of bits, including tape, compressed air, WD-40, filters, lens cloths, pens, scissors, screwdrivers etc. Most of this kit usually lives in a bag that hangs of the hip of most camera team members.

Q - What are the common problems you come across with digital cameras?

Phil - There are a lot of ways to set up the equipment. Some of the DigiBeta and HD cameras have set-up menus that control the white balance, and different aspects of the digital images, and you may have to set those up. We can always reset the cameras to the manufacturers defaults before they go out. Equally, when you come in and shoot tests, you can figure out your settings then. We can also advise at that point, rather than on the end of the phone when you are on set and under pressure.

Q - Are there any other operational issues that are common with HD?

Phil - The cameras are very much of a broadcast background, so they are camcorders and probably not as robust as film cameras.

Q - Do you ever have a back-up on set?

Phil - A lot of productions will take a 2nd back-up body. You don't need to take a lot of accessories, just the back-up body itself. Make sure the camera is set up exactly the same as the main camera package itself. Lower budget films won't do this of course.

Q - What about sound? Digital, unlike film, can record sound.

Phil - Most people use the old fashioned way of recording sound separately, though yes, you have the option of recording sound through the camera system. If you are going to record sound onto the tape through the camera, make sure everything is happily set up and have your camera team and sound team work it out in advance. Certainly for the low budget side of things, recording through the camera is an ideal way to go forward.

Q - How important is an HD monitor on set?

Phil - It is very important and, unlike video assist on film, it is a true representation of what you are getting on tape. Most productions will take 2 monitors, one for the camera team and one for the director.

Q - What do you think are the most common mistakes that Producers make?

Phil - We try to spend time with crews and production people, testing equipment. We'd like to feel that they understand equipment. So we try to encourage Producers and technicians to learn about equipment, it is very important. Not only should a crewmember come down and look at the equipment, but the production staff should come down and understand what they are actually buying. It is really important to understand why they need those pieces of equipment in the first place. Budgets are always cut, but by a producer coming down and seeing the equipment, they can then understand why 'that lens' or 'that piece of equipment' is so important.

Q - What advice would you give to a new film maker?

Philip - Honesty is the most important thing. Getting people to support you on a lie will get you into trouble. Visit the rental house and have a look at what equipment is available and understand how it works. Testing the equipment before the shoot will prepare you for the shoot ahead. Don't be afraid to ask any questions. Speak to us, we like to work with the crew so don't get scared off. Come down and see what we have, you can pick up some brilliant ideas and not only can we help make that shot work but also give you enough confidence and support for a smooth shoot.

PRODUCTION

Mark Furssedonn

Panavision UK

GRIPS HIRE

Q - What is grip equipment?

Mark - It's all about camera support and movement. We can supply anything from a top hat so that you can get low shots, up to camera cranes which give you aerial shots looking down on the action. Essentially, we supply the equipment that allows the camera to move in a controlled manner. We also hire camera equipment.

Q - What is the most versatile piece of grip equipment?

Mark - The camera dolly is the bread and butter of grips every day hire. It's a support which can run on track or rubber tyres, depending on the model. They are heavy and therefore stable, producing smooth moving shots. Some models have hydraulic arms enabling the camera to be moved up and down in shot. Most Producers normally hire track and dolly.

Q - Are there any particular extras that would be very useful?

Mark - Track is the most common, but there are tongues which can offset the camera, a snake arm which drops the camera down lower, a small jib arm to give crane effects etc. Most of the advanced dollies come with a full set of accessories. You will need a minimum of a Mercedes Sprinter van to move it all around in as well.

Q - What are your main considerations when hiring kit out from the grips point of view?

Mark - Who the grip is. We generally know how good the grips are and if you've got a good grip, you'll probably never hear from him during the shoot. Whereas the opposite applies to the less experienced grip - he'll be ringing every day asking questions. All our kit is in good condition when we send it out and it should return in that condition - unfortunately, it doesn't always return in good condition and sometimes we may have to make a charge if serious maintenance work is needed. The grip must maintain and service the kit to ensure that it stays in good working order.

Q - What's your policy for insurance on the equipment?

Mark - We ask the client to supply their own cover and we need to see documentary evidence as proof of cover. No equipment goes out without full cover.

Q - What are the most common problems you have to sort out?

Mark - It depends who you get on the phone. With the Producer, the most common problem is that they don't have enough money in their budget. The crew come to us with technical problems - something is not working - maybe they are not doing something correctly. We try to help wherever we can.

Q - Does grip equipment differ between 16mm and 35mm and the larger digital cameras?

Mark - No, that is the advantage of our equipment. We can put anything on it, any camera - 35mm, 16mm, video, all can be mounted. You would probably hire a slightly more lightweight dolly for 16mm than 35mm.

Q - What other types of equipment can you supply?

Mark - It's never ending really. We actually design equipment for specific shots so you could put a camera on the front of a roller coaster or on a camel's back for example. We have cranes, we put cameras on helicopters, we have put a crane on the back of a tracking car and driven down the motorway at high speed. The list is endless.

Q - What kind of cranes are there?

Mark - We have everything from a 9' to a 50' crane. Cost wise, the smaller the crane, the cheaper it is to hire. We also have electronic telescopic cranes which can telescope in and out during a shot. Nowadays, cranes tend to be used with a remote head instead of a camera man sitting on the end. The head is remote controlled and we can supply it as part of the package as well as the remote lens control. All our cranes have a dolly base which would run on track.

Q - Cranes can be dangerous if abused, what is your policy?

Mark - We would never send a crane out without one of our technicians. I would always advise that in addition to our technician the production company should supply two experienced grips but we can't stipulate that, only advise. At the end of the day, they are dangerous and we have people's lives in our hands. Because we have to pay the technician, it can make the hire of cranes more expensive than say dollies. All our cranes are regularly checked for fatigue by an independent company.

Q - Give me a short run down of the different bits of kit.

Mark - The Fisher 11 Camera Dolly is one of the most versatile and well manufactured dollies available. It covers all cameras, 35mm, 16mm and video. As with all dollies, track is extra and is hired in sections. The dolly comes as a package which includes comprehensive accessories. The Super PeeWee 4 is of American manufacture and is probably the most popular dolly at the moment. It is good for 35mm, 16mm and video shoots on both location and in the studio. It may be slightly lightweight for some 35mm cameras though. The Panther is a German made dolly which is operated electrically and has a centre column that moves up and down so you can actually get up and down movement in shot - you can also put a small crane on to get high shots at 12'-14'. An example of a small bit of grip equipment would be a turntable which can be used to put a camera in the centre of a table for 360° pans.

Q - What about vehicles?

Mark - We have car rigs and accessories and we can supply various types of rigs to mount the camera anywhere on a car, the bonnet, roof, looking at the wheel, looking at the bumper, the driver. Boats, trains, helicopters - we've done it all over the years. If we haven't got a rig to suit, then we'll build one for a specific shot. There is also a range of tracking vehicles that are fully equipped with various mounts and platforms for the camera, and wherever needed, the crew. These are used for high speed car shoots, chasing horses down a race track etc. Some vehicles can also be mounted with cranes, again using the remote head, others just for a camera crew to sit on with the camera mounted on the tripod to shoot off the back of the vehicle. We supply a trained driver as it's very dangerous at high speeds.

Q - How has gripping equipment advanced in the last few years?

Mark - Recently there has been growth in the rental market for telescopic cranes with stabilised heads. Directors can now ask for more sophisticated shots because of this technology. Fifteen years ago grip equipment was lumps of metal and lumps of wood. Now it's carbon fibre, special lightweight alloys and significantly enhanced electronics for control. Manufacturers are constantly developing new technology to enable the director to be more creative and productive. Of course, all this kit costs more to hire because it's new.

Mark Furssedonn
OPERATIONS DIRECTOR

Direct Line: 020 8839 7318
Mobile: 0410 313102

PANAVISION
LONDON

PANAVISION LONDON,
METROPOLITAN CENTRE,
BRISTOL ROAD, GREENFORD,
MIDDLESEX UB6 8GD
TEL: 020 8839 7333
FAX: 020 8566 6123
E-MAIL:
mark.furssedonn@panavision.co.uk

Q - How has HD impacted on the grips market?

Mark - HD is still a camera and as such it makes little or no difference to gripping equipment.

Q - What can a Producer do to make your life easier?

Simple Grips Shots

GUERILLA FILM MAKER SAYS!

There are a few 'classic' grips shots that can, if carefully placed, add real impact to the way you choose to tell your stories...

1. Track in - this is when the camera slowly creeps in on the subject. It can give a sense of getting closer and focussing in on the subject. It's often used when a character is given a piece of devastating news, and when combined with a terrific performance, gives a GREAT moment. A tracking shot looks different to a zoom as the camera is physically moving instead of the lens simply changing its focal length. Part of why a tracking in shot works is down to the fact that we all track all the time, simply by walking, and zoom shots look weird as no-one has Six Million Dollar Man zoom lens eyeballs! Tracking out can also give a sense of closure or loss.

2. Crabbing - this is moving the camera left or right on a track and dolly. Often the impact of this dynamic shot is lost because the film maker failed to place anything in the extreme foreground, and when the shot is viewed, the physical movement is diminished. Watch good movies and you will see this shot, and you will also see stuff that is placed in the foreground to enhance the effect of the movement.

3. Crane Shots - oh how every director loves crane shots, and how boring they can be unless they are needed for the drama, or extremely well executed. Again, the effect can be lost unless there is some foreground objects to enhance the movement. Often, this can be a tree, as the camera cranes down to join the actors walking along the pavement.

4. Track with the subject - this is where the camera follows the subject, perhaps from the side as two people have a conversation, perhaps from the front and at the same speed as the actor, to give them presence, or perhaps creeping from behind... The big problem with this is that you may need a huge amount of track to cover the drama. Often these shots are best accomplished with Steadicam or by hand holding the camera.

5. Steadicam - a whole separate section in its own right, and often confused with more traditional grips. Steadicam is a rig that is strapped to the camera operator that allows the camera to move freely, even over uneven ground such as rocks or steps. Steadicam requires a trained operator.

6. Car rigs - used for when you want to shoot your actors in a car and on the move. Often the car is towed or parked on a kind of trolley called a low loader, so the actors are not in control of the vehicle when it is being pulled along. More and more, these shots are being replaced with green screen digital effects and shot in a studio, as they are safe, more controllable, and the director can easily see the performances.

There are of course, thousands of variations on these shots. Watch movies and deconstruct how the shot looks, how it must have been filmed, the effect it produced, and how successful it was within the whole mise-en-scene.

On the flip side, don't get hung up on all your fancy shots. Good solid drama will always be the best friend to cash strapped film makers who need to shoot fast.

Mark - Have greater knowledge of the equipment available. In general they do not know enough about the current equipment and this has an affect when they're budgeting. Most professional Grips are excellent but there are occasions when production companies employ grips who don't know enough about the equipment. We often get calls from guys on location actually asking us how to operate the equipment. Obviously we tell them, but this should not be the case.

Q - What are the most common mistakes made by a Producer?

Mark - Budgeting. I understand that there is never enough money and I know that it is not always their fault but a problem they inherit. To the Producer, a Grip often appears to be little more than manual labour, therefore the level of professional hired for a production can be poor. Gripping is a highly skilled profession.

Q - What is Steadicam?

John - *Steadicam entails putting a rig on a person which holds the camera steady, enabling the operator to walk over rough ground, follow the action and still keep the camera movement smooth. It fills the gap between tripod and the encumbrance of a track dolly. Sometimes you can also get shots that you would not get on either.*

Q - Can you strap a Steadicam onto any camera operator?

John - *No. Steadicam is specialised kit requiring training and experience. It takes time to learn how to use Steadicam, especially to get the challenging shots directors demand.*

Q - Are there any considerations with regard to the cameras?

John - *The most dynamic shots use wide lenses. On longer lenses you don't tend to see the Steadicam motion as much. It will handle both 35mm and 16mm comfortably and there is even a smaller Steadicam for DV cameras (SteadicamJR).*

Q - Is it possible to shoot a whole film on Steadicam without a tripod or track and dolly?

John - *I've shot a whole film on Steadicam so yes it can be done. But you still need to understand the nature of drama and using Steadicam exclusively isn't often the best way to tell your story.*

Q - How much does it cost?

John - *A full size Steadicam in feature film mode with operator will cost £800-£1000 per day. The lighter Steadicam with operator will cost you about £500 a day. It does cost money, but it can save a lot of time and can enable you to get more shots in a day. I am always willing to help out with new film makers as long as they are professional and honest. Often I have time between bigger jobs, and if I like the people and the script, I get involved. But don't try and con me into a deferred payment because the only way I work on deferred payment is that you pay me now and I work for you in a few years time. People say 'no, you don't understand' and I say 'no it's not me that doesn't understand, I understand all too well'. If you come to me saying that you have no money, you're being up front. If I can help you, I will. Steadicam operators are usually hired by the week or day.*

Q - How do actors respond to the camera moving around?

John - *A common mistake is to think 'Oh, I don't have to rehearse the actors, all I have to do is set them off and leave the Steadicam operator to blunder his way through, catching the spontaneous drama'. That's the worst of all worlds because the actors don't know where the camera is, the camera operator doesn't know where the actors are going to be, and nobody hits anything. You still need to rehearse your shots and work out what is going to happen just like you would in a normal tracking or tripod shot. Those rehearsals give the actors the confidence to say 'ah, I know where I am supposed to be now and I know where the cameras*

John Ward
Steadicam

going to be at that moment'. And the operator also knows where the actors are going to be so he can keep them in frame.

Q - You don't look through the camera when using Steadicam - how do you see what is in shot?

John - *I can see, however in low light situations it is often not as easy to see the actors as it would be through the viewfinder. It's important to remember that even though you can move the Camera around with speed and fluidity, lights, crew members and passers-by can often creep into shot. Rehearsals are vital.*

Q - What mistakes do you encounter with new film makers?

John - *They tend to be uninspired with the movement and think in terms of a dolly-like tracking shot and I end up walking in a straight line. The great thing about Steadicam is it can go around things and it really opens up a set. It makes much more of your locations. The other thing they expect is that you move in and finish on a pin head - absolutely rock steady. Steadicam moving in onto static objects is not as good as a dolly, and it never will be. There's always a place for a dolly and tripod as well as Steadicam because each fill the gaps the others leave. Strangely enough, it's using the Steadicam more dynamically is something that you usually to talk people into.*

Q - What common mistakes do you come across?

John - *Trying to construct the shot because you've got a Steadicam rather than make the shot work in dramatic terms and then realise you need the Steadicam to cover it. You should let the action and drama take you along and then decide what the best way to cover it would be legs, rig, dolly, hand held or Steadicam etc. If you really do want Steadicam, before you get on set it's a good idea to study movies that have used Steadicam very successfully.*

Q - What advice would you offer a new film maker?

John - *Make sure the project holds up dramatically - if it is a good story and you have good actors - the rest is relatively easy.*

johnward@jwfilms.demon.co.uk

PRODUCTION

Eddie Dias
Lighting Hire

LIGHTING HIRE

Q - What would be a good, basic lighting kit?

Eddie - The BBC used to have the best idea, they used to give a fixed package to the cameraman and send him off to shoot on location - *six weeks and there's your lights.* It really shouldn't be any different with feature films. The lighting cameraman had a 60kw package including a large source, either a 12k or 6k, a couple of 4ks, four 1.2ks, a couple of 5.75ks, that's the HMI package - and the tungsten package maybe two baby 5ks, four baby 2ks, four to six pups, some small lights, mizars, blondes, redheads - and that would cover them for all eventualities. They would also take a 60kw generator.

Q - With that lighting set up, what kind of personnel do you need to service it?

Eddie - You could have a two person camera crew, camera operator (lighting cameraman / DP) and camera assistant, who would pull focus and clapperload. You're going to have the gaffer, chief electrician and the best boy. The gaffer usually sits on the cameraman's shoulder, the cameraman explains what he actually wants and the gaffer will relay that to his electricians and tell them what they need. The best boy's job is to liaise between the lighting office and the production office, making sure he's got adequate crew, cranes are going to be there in place etc. - making sure that they're covered for all eventualities. If extra equipment needs to be ordered, the gaffer doesn't need to be tied up ordering it, that's the best boy's job.

Q - So in terms of servicing the lighting you're going to have a gaffer, best boy, plus two or three sparks?

Eddie - Yes, one of those sparks will be driving the lighting vehicle and one driving and operating the generator.

Q - Would you normally have a generator with that kind of kit?

Eddie - Yes. You're not always going to be able to plug into the mains. Plus, many lights just can't be plugged into a socket on the wall. If you want to use all your lights at one time, you can do that with a generator without having to worry about a good solid electric source.

Q - And you supply the sparks as part of your package?

Eddie - Yes, we have to by law. Once you get to a vehicle that's over 3.5 tonnes, which is basically a transit van, you then have to have a licence to operate heavy goods vehicles - so every 7.5 or 16 tonne vehicle is on our operator's licence. The people driving the vehicles are paid by us, the onus has to be shown to be on us from a safety point of view.

Q - What's the situation if a producer hires out your people and they overrun?

Eddie - They carry on into overtime which would be paid at an agreed rate. The average daily rate is £150 - £200. If they're doing an extended day they have a set fee, if they're doing a night shoot, they have a set fee on top. It's always good to set up those parameters beforehand. We understand that films will sometimes overrun slightly, and if there's a bit of give and take, for instance if they finish early another time, we can be accommodating. As long as people are clear on that beforehand. People have lives outside the film industry. It may be very important to the producer and director, but an electrician, rigger, painter or a carpenter, isn't going to be taken on for their artistic abilities - to them it's just a job, at the end of the day they've got to bring the bacon home and put it on the table.

Q - If we scale it down a bit, if we think small, what kind of lighting kit would you suggest to keep the costs down?

Eddie - We have made feature films on very tight budgets, but it's like going into a rent-a-car company and asking for a JAG with only £30 a day to spend. They'll turn round and give you a bargain basement car, you've got to expect the same in equipment hire. We had a production come to us and said we *'know we haven't got a lot but this is what we need'*. I welcomed them to my bargain basement and told them that they could have anything they wanted from there. So they took it and four weeks later, the equipment came back and the film was made. They didn't do any special effects or high speed shots so they didn't have to worry about flicker free lighting or strobing.

Q - What is flicker free lighting?

Eddie - If you're taking daylight lights - HMI's - you're susceptible, if you're changing camera speeds, to flicker. If you're shooting at 25fps (50i or 25p digital) there's no need to worry. Most productions now hire flicker free lighting which is obviously more expensive. For the lower budget films you can take non-flicker-free lights, they'll be cheaper to rent. If you do use more expensive flicker free lights, there is a ballast unit which gives you a high frequency hum. If your sound man says *we're getting a hum on the sound*, then we can supply special ballasts that don't hum.

Q - With non-flicker-free lighting, can you run slow motion at all?

Eddie - On film, yes you can - what you do is adjust the shutter angle in the camera. A lot of cameraman are scared of doing this but there's a simple calculation you can do, and all cameramen should know this - after all, you're paying the cameraman for his expertise. For example, if you're shooting at 52.778 fps, then adjust the shutter angle to 190°, if you shoot at 40 fps, put your shutter angle at 144°. With digital you will be able to see what flicker you may be present on the monitor so mistakes don't tend to get made as they could with film..

Q - Would you advise an inexperienced producer who has an inexperienced, artistic cameraman to sit on him like a ton of bricks?

Eddie - Yes, or it will cost you. A lot of inexperienced cameramen want to be creative - but if you're on a low budget, you can't necessarily afford that. You need someone who is going to deliver the goods, to the technical standard needed, on time.

Q - How does the process of booking and paying for lights work?

Eddie - Anybody who's waving money around, instead of asking for credit or thirty days, is going to get a good deal. The scary thing for us is somebody saying *'we're doing a low budget film'* - immediately you tense up! (laughs). As soon as someone says low budget, it scares people - don't say low budget, say *'we haven't got a big budget'*.

Q - What do you do about insurance?

Eddie - We ask the client to insure everything (plus 13 weeks loss of hire). Things do get broken and lost, we're usually quite lenient on the odd bolt and screw and there are some things we can equate to wear and tear. But if something is blown over in the wind, then the production company has got to accept that damage. We also ask to see a certificate of insurance. We can insure the equipment, but we're not insurance specialists and we have to charge a premium rate. You'd probably be better off taking out your own insurance.

Q - Does insurance cover bulbs?

Eddie - Yes, unless of course, the damage is through misuse. A 12k HMI bulb costs £2,000 and if they're misused or burnt incorrectly, it affects the bulb's life considerably.

Q - And what are the most common mistakes that could be avoided?

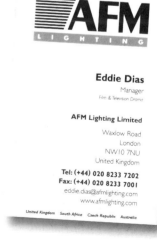

Eddie Dias
Manager
Film & Television Drama

AFM Lighting Limited

Waxlow Road
London
NW10 7NU
United Kingdom

Tel: (+44) 020 8233 7202
Fax: (+44) 020 8233 7001
eddie.dias@afmlighting.com
www.afmlighting.com

United Kingdom   South Africa   Czech Republic   Australia

PRODUCTION

Lighting Equipment

Gels

Put over the front of lights to change their colour balance - orange to turn day-light into tungsten balance, blue to turn tungsten-light day-light balanced. Also trace and spun to diffuse light.

Spare Lamps

Keep lots of spare bulbs. You should not be responsible for bulbs that blow, unless your crew was negligent.

Torch

If you want a torch in shot, your normal one won't do, you need to hire an extremely powerful one from an effects or lighting company.

Extension Cables

Can't get enough. Make sure that the cables you get can handle the power. Rent extra.

Expendables, Gloves, Clothes pins & Gaffer Tape

Pins are used to attach gels to barn doors, gloves are a necessity with hot heavy lights, and gaffer tape will stick pretty much anything to anything.

Stands

Used to mount lights. You'll also need various poles and stands. Make sure you have enough for your lights.

Bounce Boards

Used to reflect light. Some are small and hand held, used to fill actors faces in daylight. Large sheets of foam core are ideal and cheap. Use nets to reduce the amount of light emitting from the lamp.

Grip Truck

A 3 ton grip truck is ideal as comes with loads of extras.

Practical Light

A light that usually lives within a scene and is usually tungsten blanched, table lamps, desk lamp, ceiling lights – loaded with a standard bulb from 100-275 watt (beware of melting lights at 275 watts!) Beware of fluorescent lights as they have an odd colour balance and may turn out green or pink on film.

Sun Gun

A hand held light, usually battery operated. Ideal for shooting with small crews where only a little fill light is needed. In a pinch, cheap battery operated camcorder lights will do a similar job.

Pepper Light

Very small 200 watt tungsten light. Used for highlighting small areas or creating small pools of light. Also used to place an attractive highlight dot in actors eyes.

Red Head

Blunt instrument and working horse of micro budget film. 750 watt tungsten balance usually coming in kits of three. Ideal for small shoots and close up shots. Don't expect too much out of them though! Can plug into the wall.

Blonde

More powerful version of the Red Head at 2k / tungsten. Ideal to use with a Red Head kit. Can plug into the wall.

Fresnel Light

Large tungsten light, from between 1k - 10k. Used for studio lighting. Fresnel means the light uses a lens which focuses the light in a given place. May need an adapter to plug into the wall. Larger lights will need specialised power sources such as a generator or studio power source.

HMI Lights

Comes in various guises. Daylight balanced and very powerful. All lights come with a ballast which sits at the base of the light or can be hidden away. Come in two varieties, flicker free and non flicker free - non flicker free means shooting at 25fps but is cheaper. Rating from 0.5k to 20k.

Lighting Equipment ...cont

Flags
Black cloth within a metal frame, mounted on a stand. Used to block light when the DP is creating shadow or darker areas.

Kino Flos
Use high frequency ballasts that are flicker free and avoid hum of standard ballasts. Produce daylight, tungsten and soft, even light. Very versatile and inexpensive to run.

Clamps and bits
Misc. clamps and arms for affixing lamps, flags and reflectors in places where a stand is not appropriate. Get more than you think you need.

Distribution Box
Used to distribute power to several lamps from a single power source.

Sandbags and weights
Used to weigh down stands for safety, when the lamp is heavy or when there is wind.

Generators
Large vehicle which houses a sound deadened (not sound proof) generator. For low budget shoots, if you can limit your power consumption, you may not need a generator. Pic shows a towable Movie Quiet®20KW Generator.

Eddie - There are weekly consumables that the crew will go through. If the cameraman wants to adjust the colour (and colour temperature) of the lighting, he'll do that with CTB, blue transfer gels, orange transfer gels, neutral density gels, frosts and diffusers. When you're given a quote, 90% of the time, it's plus consumables. Always bear in mind that there are consumable costs on top of that - if you've got a generator and a truck and another truck, you've also got fuel to think of, which can be quite considerable. Even when crews are shooting in a studio, they often draw power from a generator as studio power is very expensive, sometimes five or six times more expensive than what comes out of the wall. We can give advice about how much should be budgeted for this kind of consumables. Don't be afraid to ask if you don't know something - if you ask a company for their advice they will give it to you open heartedly.

Q - How has the digital film making revolution impacted on your business?

Eddie - Even though cameras have become smaller and lighter, film stocks faster, lenses faster and overall, the technology for capturing images has improved, people are now taking out more lights than ever. Standard TV drama is now lit with a package that we would have expected to go out on a feature film just ten years ago. I think it is because the final results now have to be of a higher quality. Audiences expect more and sales agents and distributors are now demanding HiDef masters. There are also new inventions that crop up regularly, and everyone wants a go with the new toys, perhaps to give them a visual edge. We also hire out Kino-Flos lights in pretty much every rental package now, where ten years ago they were not so common.

Q - How about lighting for micro budget films?

Eddie - Even though you can shoot a movie on a cheap(ish) camcorder now, as they did with '28 Days Later', it would be a mistake to think that it will look amazing unless you pay attention to the lighting. If you want your shots to look good, you need adequate and appropriate professional lighting, and the time to set up properly.

Q - What advice would you offer a new film maker?

Eddie - Make films that people will want to see. We have brilliant writers and great crew and we make too many films that nobody wants to pay money to watch.

Jon Walker
Film DP and Lighting

FILM DIRECTOR OF PHOTOGRAPHY

Q - How do you approach the look of a film?

Jon - The *look* is more than just the photography, it's a joint effort between the set design, costume, make-up and other creative departments, they can all enhance the final look of the film. As well as being a 'science' combined with an 'art', lighting has an element of 'philosophy' in it, *what do I show? what do I hide? Should the scene be bright and happy or dull and sad?* The Director of Photography (DOP) can literally change the tone of a scene by the quality and style of the lighting used.

When a person watches a film they should be oblivious of the technical processes involved in making the film. If they are distracted by the editing, the sound effects or the lighting then something has probably gone wrong. The job of the technician on a film is to re-create reality, or the illusion of reality. Both film and video are now very good at copying reality, however, they are not as accurate as the human eye and by understanding this, a good DOP can manipulate the medium to create a natural look. A DOP needs to understand four very important things. First, film stock (and even more so Digital cameras) is far less sensitive to light than the human eye. Second, film produces an image about 1.5 times more contrasty than the original scene. Third, our eyes and our brain adjust for different light temperatures and situations; the amount of light striking the eye can vary greatly and yet the eye and the brain can even it all out. You can read a book with a torch or on a blazing summer day where the quantity of light coming from the sun is hundreds of times greater than with the torch. Lastly, we don't just see with our eyes; we interpret what we see with our brains.

Q - What do you think of the new digital formats?

Jon - They have clear advantages - cheap stock, instant playback, married sound (if you do it that way), extremely cheap entry level equipment, tight integration with new editing technology. And a few disadvantages - cheaper cameras are not as good as film makers often expect them to be and their use can encourage lazy film making, the camera's are not as robust and the image can have a very different 'look' to film if care is not taken in the shooting and post production. Overall, it's just a change in film making styles and it's still all about a good story told well. Depending on the production I would still like to aim for film, though I can see that HD is more often than not, going to be a smarter choice from a production perspective. Like vinyl, I think film will always be there for the purists, and will enjoy occasional revivals, but digital is here to stay. It's the future... and the present.

The most exciting aspect of the digital revolution is that you can shoot on film and post produce entirely digitally, which opens up a vista of possibilities.

Q - If shooting film, how important is the lab?

Jon - The best place to start when you are just about to shoot on film is to go where the film is going to end up, the laboratory. An understanding of what the lab can and can not do is crucial - you need to know what grading can do for you and the technicians may be able to tell you something about the film stock you are using that isn't immediately obvious in any tests you might shoot. The most important principle when dealing with the labs is communication. They will only do what you want if you tell them what you want and you can't assume anything. The lab is a very powerful tool if you bother to find out how it operates.

If you are not grading the film digitally then a good relationship with the film-grader is essential. They can change the look of the film in a way that could completely destroy the effect you had intended, on the other hand, if you help them they can make your film look fantastic - it's vital that you sit down with the grader and watch the film, discussing exactly what you intended when you lit the

GUERILLA FILM MAKER SAYS!

Depth Of Field

This refers to the area in the frame that will appear to be in focus. If you have very little (shallow) depth of field, then not much is in focus, whereas a lot of depth of field means almost everything is in focus. Shallow depth of field generally is effective for close ups for the subject seems pulled out of the background forcing the audience to concentrate on it. However, in these situations focus is critical for you can lose it very easily. Large depth of field is great for establishing shots. Two main items affect depth of field, the length of the lens and aperture setting. Here are some rules of thumb to follow...

Length *The shorter the lens (wide angle) the more depth of field you will have, and conversely, the longer the lens (telephoto) the less depth of field you will have.*
Aperture *The more light you let through the lens, the more depth of field you will have. So, at F-2 you will lose almost all of your depth of field while at F-22 you will have great depth of field.*

By combining a different focal length lenses and changing the amount of light reaching the lenses either through lighting or with filters you can manipulate the depth of field for creative purposes. In addition, the type of film you are using can effect depth of field. Small format films stocks like Super 8mm and Super 16mm tend to have greater depth of field, while larger formats like 35mm and 70mm have less depth of field.

film. The grader hasn't read the script and may never hear the sound track - how are they supposed to know what you intended if you don't tell them?

If you're post producing digitally the flexibility you have for imposing a look on a film and enhancing the pictures are enormous. (As long as you've produced a good negative).

Q - What is the most important technical aspect of photography?

Jon - A properly exposed negative - it sounds obvious, but because modern negative emulsions are so flexible there can be a temptation to over rely on their latitude. I've shot a number of films on Super 16mm which were subsequently blown up to 35mm. To get the best result I slightly over exposed the negative - this resulted in a dense negative, producing a final print where the low key and night scenes have good solid blacks. If I had not done this the blacks might well have looked milky (where the blacks look grey and the grain of the film becomes so obvious it can be distracting).

Q - What is the difference between 35mm and 16mm?

Jon - Simply put, the 35mm frame is much bigger so you're spreading your image over more grain to get a sharper, richer image. But this does mean you need a bigger lens to get more light onto the film. The problem is that to get a decent depth of field you need a small aperture. For instance, on 16mm you could probably shoot at f2.8, but to get the equivalent depth of field on 35mm you'd need at least f4-5.6. This means that for 35mm you need up to four times as much light and a bigger, heavier camera, all of which will add to your budget.

Q - How noisy are cameras?

Jon - Properly blimped 35mm cameras are extremely quiet. 16mm can be noisier, but modern cameras are still very quiet. If there's a real problem, you can resort to covering the camera and blimp with coats, but that's an operator's nightmare. Film stock varies. Most noise comes from the misalignment of the sprocket holes and registration pin. 16mm is more prone to this as it is so much smaller. You should always take some of the stock you intend to use to your camera hire company and run tests so that if adjustments need to be made, they can be done then and not on set.

PRODUCTION

Jon Walker

jon@capstone.plus.com

Film Frame Rates (slower and faster)

GUERILLA FILM MAKER SAYS!

A major drawback of digital formats is thay they can't handle slow motion very well. What few cameras can do it, don't offer very high frame rates, which means slow motion must be 'created' in post production, which is never as good as if it were shot in slow motion on set. In this area, film is still king. On any action, especially things like a glass being dropped and breaking, or a stone being thrown through a window, shoot slow motion as the action happens so fast in reality, that it can be almost unseen in shot.

Slow Motion

True slow motion (also known as over-cranking) is where you run the camera at a faster frame rate than the normal 24 fps, such as 48fps. When projected at 24fps, the action would run at half speed - slow motion. While most cameras can do some slow motion (often up to 50fps or 75fps), high speed cameras are needed to capture dramatic shots.

Fast Motion

The opposite of overcranking, undercranking, refers to running the camera at a slower frame rate than the normal speed of 24fps, such as 12fps, which produces fast motion when replayed at 24fps. In the old days, chase sequences would often by under cranked so to make the cars move faster than they were actually going (the trick still works as long as you don't undercrank too much, say 21fps to slightly speed up some action).

Ramping

This is where the camera ramps from one speed to another, in shot. For instance, 24fps to 100fps. The effect is that the shot begins in normal speed, then slows down and turns into a slow motion shot. The catch is that as you speed up or slow down you need to adjust the exposure to compensate, so you will need to have an Iris Control Unit (ICU) too.

Time Lapse

This is a technique where single frame exposures are taken over a prolonged period, at say 1fsp or 1 frame per minute. It's used to film subjects that move too slowly to be seen with the naked eye, for instance, a flower bud opening, buildings demolished and rebuilt, or the sun rising and setting, hours in real time, seconds when played back on film. There are a variety of gadgets that enable you to do this, but the most common is to use an intervalometer, which allows you to set the frame rate for a given time period.

Post Slo-mo

The other way to create slow motion is to film at regular speed and then to slow it down in post-production. The effect can be jerky or even slightly blurry if done digitally. Where possible, always shoot in slow motion on set if you want it in slow motion in your movie. This will save money in post too. Of course if you shoot DV or HD, this may be impossible.

Q - How long does it take to change a roll of film?

Jon - A few minutes although you should always have pre-loaded magazines available so that you're never waiting on set. But if you've just got one cameraman who's doing the lighting, operating and loading, as you might on a low budget film, it's going to take much longer.

Q - What are gels and filters used for?

Jon - There are two basic areas. One is to correct light so it looks natural. For example, if you're filming inside and you've only got redheads and daylight is coming in through the windows, then you'll need to put a blue filter (gel) over the redheads to make the redhead's 'orange' light look blue to match the daylight. Daylight is 'blue', and tungsten lights (anything that has a filament) is generally 'orange'. Tungsten balanced film stock (the most commonly used) produces accurate colours in tungsten light. Daylight balanced stock produces accurate colours in daylight. Video cameras have to be switched between colour temperatures as well and tend to have all the tungsten and daylight filters built into them.

The other use of filters is to create an effect. You might want blue moonlight so you put blue gel on your redhead, or you want to have warm skin tones, filming with a candle for example, you'll put half an orange (filter) on the front of an already warm light.

Q - What about Day for Night?

Jon - Essentially you underexpose. On a film I did recently we shot some sequences in a house during the day, but it needed to be night. I simply added a bit of extra back light and under exposed by about 4 stops. I also put lots of neutral density grey filters over the windows so they wouldn't be too bright. On viewing the shot film the normal background light was basically black, the bits I added were highlights and it looked as though it was shot at night. If you're filming outside, as long as you don't have sky in the shot you can do day for night, but as soon as you get the sky in shot it's no good. The sky is so bright even when underexposed it tends to dominate the scene. The best time to film day for night is the magic hour - which is just before it goes dark. There's enough light to pick up details but it's definitely night.

Q - What is trace and spun?

Jon - The smaller the source of light, the harder the shadows produced. Most film lights have 'small' filaments and therefore produce hard shadows, which isn't very flattering on people's faces. If you put spun or trace, which is actually like tracing paper but fireproof, over the light, it 'widens' the source of light and produces 'softer' shadows.

Q - What are practical lights?

Jon - Practicals are lights that actually exist in the scene. For example an angle poise light is a practical. You can either use domestic bulbs, 60-100watt which might be enough, or you can buy 150-250watt bulbs (photofloods) that screw into the same socket. They give much more punch and are a good way to light moody interior scenes very quickly and cheaply - but be on the lookout for smoke rising because domestic lighting is not designed for the heat produced by high wattage bulbs and can catch fire.

Q - Would it be feasible to film an entire low budget movie using practicals?

Jon - Yes, if you were really low budget, I would suggest shooting on slightly faster stock because this requires less light, something like 250ASA, and add a couple of red heads to the list. Modern video cameras can produce great results in low light conditions.

Q - What is the basic lighting kit you can get away with to make a low budget movie?

Jon - If look isn't your primary concern and you just want to get something exposed then you could go for a kit that an average ENG crew would use - a battery powered light that's used in the field (a PAG light or SUNGUN) to fill up shadows. A couple of redheads for indoors and plenty of practical bulbs. This isn't going to look too pretty though. If you do want to create a 'look' then lighting is very important and a basic lighting kit should include at least one big light (2.5k HMI min.) as well as a range of smaller but controllable lights (fresnel lights 500w and 1k). I find I use everything I have got. If a DoP is always struggling to get enough light on the scene because of the lack of lights, making the film look good as well may be asking too much.

Q - What about stock mixing?

Jon - Some stocks you can mix and some you can't but I would try to avoid it. Mixing speeds (ASA) is the same, it can be done, but it's best avoided.

Q - Shooting outside usually means you don't need lights, although you may need a little fill light - what are the basic elements of actually lighting a shot?

Jon - The three most important lights are the Key Light, the Fill Light and the High Light.

The Key Light is the most important - it's the 'modelling light' and it's usually the main source of light, and sets the mood and texture in the scene.

GUERILLA FILM MAKER SAYS!

Lens & Focal Length

Telephoto
The background is crushed and the figure appears more normal. There is less spillage of 'set and props' to the left and right.

Wide
The background is more distant and the figure appears more distorted - depth is enhanced with objects closer to the camera appearing much larger than those slightly further away.

PRODUCTION

The positioning of the key light is dictated by the requirements of the scene - for example, the sun is the key light in a room where the only source of light is the sunlight coming through the window. Outside, on a clear day, the sun is the key light producing bright highlights and strong dark shadows. On an overcast day with heavy cloud cover, the sun is still the key light, but it is completely diffused by the clouds producing a very flat look, soft shadows and not much contrast between highlights and shadows.

When you light a scene the first question to ask is *what is the most important source of light in this scene?* It may not be obvious; you might be in a tunnel or in a sitting room at night with various light sources (lamps, candles, etc.). Often the job of the DOP is to enhance an existing 'key light'. The scene might be set in a room where the only light is coming from a candle set between two actors facing each other at a table. Without extra lighting the film will come back from the lab with a candle flame surrounded by complete darkness - remember film is not as sensitive as the human eye. So what do we do? We want to create the subtle look of a candle lit atmosphere without killing it by using too much extra light. By adding a slightly diffused key light that just adds to the candle light we can achieve a look on film that matches what the eye sees. The key light should be placed at the same height as the candle and on an axis. That means that when you look through the camera, the light from the key light looks as if it is coming from the candle. When you view the film you now see the flame and the actor.

Sun lit interiors can also be tricky. Overcast days can mean that without added light the windows are bright but the interiors are very dull (overcast light tending to come from above). The difference in contrast between the exposure needed inside the room and the exposure outside (through the window) is too great to be accommodated by the limited latitude of the film stock. The easiest solution, in order to simulate the look of a day lit room, is to place a very powerful and diffused key light outside the window. The further away from the window this light can go the more even the light in the room (the exposure drop is proportional to the distance from the light source - the further away the less difference it makes). The key light's colour temperature is the same as the daylight, but the key light only adds to the amount of light coming into the room; it does not add to the outside light so the contrast between inside and outside has been reduced and can now be captured on film, (important if the scene requires that both inside and outside the room be seen). The more diffused the key light can be the less harsh the shadows inside the room should be.

Q - What if there isn't a single main source of light?

Jon - Sometimes you may have to deal with multiple key lights - a simple case would be a tunnel with overhead lighting at regular intervals. The scene requires the camera to follow the actors as they walk down the tunnel. The overhead lights may only be domestic 100 watt bulbs and provide very little light for the scene. By replacing the 100w bulbs with 275w or 500w photoflood bulbs (which look the same), you don't change the look of the scene, but it is now bright enough to expose film.

Q - How does the fill light help?

Jon - If the key light 'creates' reality by enhancing the natural light sources, the fill light is the tool a DOP can use to give film the 'latitude' that the eye has.

Take the candle on the table again. Turn off the key light and look at what you've got. The candle light decreases rapidly the further from the flame you get. There's a ring of light around the candle on the table, the actor's faces are darker but still clearly visible and the walls, maybe 10 feet away, are just visible - not totally black. Now turn on the key light(s); you might have set a key light for each actor and put a light over the table shining down to simulate the ring of light produced on the table by the candle. Now film the scene. You should expose for the light on the table so that this is correctly or just under exposed and the actors (whose key light is slightly dimmer) look correctly and proportionally darker. However, the scene looks too contrasty and the background walls are completely black, this is not what we saw with our eyes. The solution to this problem is the fill light.

A way to understand fill light is like this; If you were sitting in a room with light coming through the windows, but the room was painted black, all the objects in the room would be side lit from the window, and the other side would be dark. The walls reflect none of the sunlight back onto the objects. If, however, the room is painted white the objects in the room would be lit by the light reflecting off the walls, as well as from the window. The objects would appear to be lit from all around. The white walls are acting as a fill light. The fill light must supply an equal amount of light to the whole scene without adding shadows to it. In the case of the candle scene, the easiest way to do this would be to bounce light from a powerful light off a white reflector placed just behind the camera. Reflected light is the softest light you can achieve and the position behind the camera means that any shadows created appear directly behind the subject and therefore are invisible to the camera. Experience is the best guide as to how much fill light to use. If there's too much the scene will lose all the texture provided by the key light and the scene will look over lit and flat. To the naked

Simple Lighting Setup

Even the simplest of shots needs to be lit properly, or it will look like your average home movie. This simple mid shot of an actress required four lights - key light, fill light, rim light and a background light. The overhead diagram to the left illustrates where each light was positioned.

Key Light

The key light 'models' the subject and is often the most important light in the scene. It is often the foundation on which all other lights are based. In this case it is a light placed to the front left of the actress, perhaps representing a window light source (in the story of the shot).

Fill Light

This light is designed to 'fill' the harsh shadows created by the Key light, to create a more natural and rounded look. It will pick out detail and texture where otherwise there would be only dark shadows. In this case, it is placed close to the camera.

Back Light

To add another dimension, in this case, a light source is mounted behind and above the subject. It hits the back of objects and the actress and gives a nice impression of three dimensionality.

Background Light

This light has been positioned to illuminate the background of the scene to create a more natural look. Without it, there would be a fully lit actress sitting against a very dark background.

PRODUCTION

eye the addition of fill light will make the scene look slightly over lit and flat, however, remember that film is more contrasty and less sensitive than the eye. The use of the fill light reproduces the sensitivity of the eye on film. By using fill light the candle scene now looks on film as it did to the naked eye.

Outside on an overcast day the need for fill light may not be immediately obvious. However, overcast days, where the light is essentially overhead, can produce dark eye sockets on your actor. A simple piece of white polystyrene or a photographic reflector placed below the actor's face just lifts the details in their face, removes the harsh shadows and creates a softer more attractive look.

Sometimes providing a bounced fill light behind the camera is not possible. In a tunnel for example, the overhead lights provide the necessary quantity of key light, but also produce harsh and ugly shadows. There might also be pools of darkness between the lights. A light mounted on the camera might be the solution. The light is close to the camera so that shadows are kept to a minimum and by diffusing and dimming it the dark areas and shadows on the actor's faces are reduced without becoming obvious to the viewer. As long as the distance between the camera and the actors doesn't vary too much, the quantity of fill light will remain constant producing a natural look. If this distance is difficult to maintain then a hand held light (on the same axis as the camera)

Lenses

GUERILLA FILM MAKER SAYS!

Prime Lens

This is a lens of a fixed focal length. They are usually sharper than Zoom lenses, have a lower f-stop and are better for low light interior scenes. However, depth of field can be very shallow when the lens is wide open and focusing can become critical. These are often referred to as FAST lenses. 16mm, 25mm, 50mm and 75mm are the standard primes for Super 16mm and 35mm. On 16mm, the 25mm lens reproduces a perspective similar to that seen by the human eye. On 35mm, the 50mm lens does the same job. For 16mm, Zeiss-Distagon Super speed lenses are recommended, which come in focal lengths of 9.5mm, 12mm, 16mm and 25mm. These lenses are faster than the standard primes and are therefore sharp even when you're shooting wide open. Depth of field can be very shallow when the lens is wide open and focusing can become difficult.

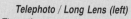

Wide Angle (left)

Lenses shorter than 25mm are considered wide angle. Wide angle lenses have a greater depth of field, but can distort the subject if it is too close to the camera.

Telephoto / Long Lens (left)

Those that are two or more times longer than 25mm are considered telephoto, or a long lens. These can keep your subject large in frame at greater distances - great for dangerous stunt work where you don't want the cameras on top of the action. Long lenses have a shallow depth of field and can create an out of focus background. Telephoto lenses can be used to photograph the sun setting and heat hazes. Bear in mind that long lenses are extremely vulnerable to camera vibration.

Close up or Plus Diopters

Also used to film close up objects. They are mounted in front of the lens like a filter. They enable closer focusing with all lenses and require no exposure compensation. The higher the number of a plus diopter, the closer you can focus. Conversely, as power increases, the quality of the image deteriorates. With a close up diopter you can no longer focus on infinity. Great for shots of eyeballs, the phone book or postage stamps. (pix - above without close up diopter, below with close up diopter).

Zoom Lens

These lenses do not have fixed focal length as you can move between wide angle and telephoto. The most popular Zoom lens for Super 16mm is the Angenoux 12-120mm and the 10-150 Angenoux. All zoom lenses require the same procedure for setting up a shot - open the aperture fully, zoom all the way in on the subject and examine the sharpness. After focusing, REMEMBER to return to the proper T stop. For smoother zooming, you can use a motorised zoom control.

---

might overcome this problem. Discussing the positions of the actors should also ensure optimum lighting - if they stop and talk in a dark patch the scene might not work.

Q - What is the back light?

Jon - The back light makes actresses look beautiful, bad guys look mean and can get around the problem of providing a light source where, in reality, none would exist; a forest at night for example. Subtlety is the key in most cases. Like the fill light, overdoing the high light can destroy the 'real' look of the shot.

In the candle scene we've created a realistic look on film, however, the actor's close-ups look a little dull. A light placed behind and slightly above the actor produces a highlight on the head. As long as it's not too bright the 'real' look will not be spoilt, however, the depth and texture of the shot has been enhanced - the high light separates the subject from the dark background and a sense of 'space' has been created.

Key lights and high lights can sometimes be the same. In a room lit by various lights - angle poise on the table, standard light by the sofa - one actor's key light might be the other actors high light.

A real problem for a DOP is where in reality there would be no light at all. For example, a narrow unlit street at night or the woods at night have no natural sources of light for the DOP to enhance. Front lighting the subject with a key light would destroy the 'night time' look. A well placed back light is the solution to this problem. The intensity of this back lighting can help set the mood, harsh strong back light can create a powerful look suitable for action and a more gentle diffused back light might create the illusion of moonlight. Back lit smoke and shiny wet surfaces can be very effective in creating mood.

Q - Why do you put coloured gels on lights, or coloured filters on the front of the camera? What is colour temperature?

Jon - Light is essentially radiation produced as a result of heat (red hot and white hot). A domestic light bulb produces light when its filament is super heated, as the light source gets hotter the spectrum of light goes from red to blue. Candles burn at a 'low' temperature and are orange, the sun is very hot and produces white/blue light, (sunsets and dawn are coloured by aberrations in the atmosphere; a bit like putting a coloured gel over a light).

The human eye and brain balances these different colour 'temperatures'. Within a range 3200 Kelvin (about 3273°C) which is orangish and 6000 Kelvin (6273°C) which is bluish to the eye, a piece of white paper is seen as white! However, film doesn't interpret what it sees. Given that you film within these two light temperatures the lab can probably grade the colours correctly. Most film stock is balanced to produce accurate colours in Tungsten light, which is 3200 Kelvin and is produced by heating a filament (Incandescent). If this film is used in daylight everything looks blue. Although the grader at the lab can correct this, a filter put on the lens to correct the colours at the time of filming provides a more evenly exposed negative and therefore a better looking picture.

Mixing light sources with different colour temperatures unintentionally could cause considerable problems. You might use Tungsten light inside, but the windows and outside are daylight. The result would be either correct colours inside but a blue exterior or a orange interior and a correct exterior. You can deal with these differences by using coloured gels on the lights to produce a constant even light temperature for the scene. If in doubt, light your scene with one type of light source. Overhead striplights come in all sorts of different colour temperatures, the commonest are 'tungsten' sometimes called 'white' and 'daylight'. Because the spectrum of the light they produce is uneven - 'tungsten' is not true tungsten and 'daylight' not true daylight - when filming, make sure that all the striplights are the same type and you might rig up a 'light box' using the same type of lights for use as a fill light or key light. The lab can then make the small changes necessary to correct the colours.

Q - You mention grading, what can the lab do to correct problems?

Jon – There are essentially two types of grading, film grading which varies the amount of light passing though the negative onto another piece of film to produce a properly exposed and colour corrected positive picture or using digital grading where the film negative was either scanned or telecinied into a computer and then all the picture manipulation is done by changing the numbers.

Visual Tricks

Day for Night
Although not done often these days, mainly because it is tricky to do effectively, there may be occasions when you have to shoot day for night. When shooting day for night exterior, the best place to have the sun is behind and above the subject or behind and to the side. This is because you want to create as many dark areas (shadows) you can. If the sunlight is 90° from the optical axis, grad filters are helpful in darkening the skies. Underexpose 1½ to 2 stops on the wide shots and 1-1½ on close ups. Make sure you inform the laboratory on the camera report that you have shot day for night. Day for night is much better when shooting at dusk as the low angle of the sun creates longer shadows. Day for night interiors are much easier to control, but require a lot of grip work to block out the natural daylight. Black out windows slightly in front of the actual window and then throw some green light on the window from the outside.

Shiny Streets
Wetting down the streets can enrich night exteriors, creating high contrast textures that reflect the lights, whether or not it's supposed to be raining in your scene. But it can be expensive if you need large areas wetting down.

The Magic Hour
This is the time of day when the sun is below the horizon (pre-dawn and post-sunset), but there is still light in the sky. The light is soft and golden and can make your subjects look amazing. Magic hour is very short, so be ready to work very quickly.

Sunset
Long lenses, anything between 500mm-1000mm, are used to capture a perfect sunset. The lower the sun in the sky, the more atmosphere you're shooting through, and the richer it will look. The same can be said for shooting the sunset on a smoggy day. This will give you a beautiful orange orb. Shooting a blazing sun in a clear sky can be too hot and therefore not pleasing on film. Graduated filters can be used to create more of the orange glow. Make sure to balance the light in the background and foreground, as they will change as the sun goes down and changes color temperature.

Lighting Types

One way to create the 'look' of your film is to play around with the lighting. Moody film noir will have harder shadows and higher contrast, whereas a docudrama would have low contrast (flatter) lighting. Get together with your DP and Gaffer to discuss ways to come up with interesting lighting schemes using the items below.

Hard Light

Hard lights, such as a Fresnel, produce an intense, bright light that creates hard shadows that tend to be dark and sharp edged and can be used to emphasise more depth in the texture such as the wrinkles on a face. These lights tend to be used as key or back lighting.

Soft Light

A gentle, subtle light that's non-directional and produces a scattered light that creates softer shadows and is typically used as fill lighting. One way to make soft lighting is to use a hard light and bounce the light off, or through, diffusion, such as a silk bed sheet. Soft light doesn't necessarily mean that it's a flat light, which refers to a low contrast ratio throughout the scene.

Bounce Light

Bounce light is a type of a soft light that is great for softening shadows and subtly filling in areas of an actor's face. You can bounce light off of anything reflective, such as foam-core, silks, a bed sheet, wall or ceiling. Overhead bounce is 'safe' in that ceilings are more frequently colour-neutral and lighter than walls.

Umbrellas

Umbrellas with a reflective surface on the inside are used for quick conversion of hard and broad light sources into softer ones.

Reflectors

These add sparkle to people, products and props that are back-lit, in deep shade, or that have an excessively bright background. Similar to bounce boards but used in exteriors, reflectors provide fill. One example would be shiny boards, mirror like, aluminum surfaced reflectors that are used primarily for lighting dark or distant backgrounds, such as tree foliage, where uneven light won't be noticed.

Chimeras

A wireframe, cloth box with diffusion at one end that attaches to a light and helps soften it. Originally used in still photography.

Nets & Scrims

Both are used to control the intensity of light. Nets are netting stretched between a metal frame that is attached to a C-stand and placed in front of a light. Scrims are usually round metal screens placed on the light itself. Both come in singles, which reduce the light one stop, and doubles, which reduce it by two stops.

Gels

Used for colouring or colour correcting light. Comes in full, ½ and ¼ strengths.

Silks, Spuns and Muslin

Various types of diffusion. Silks are large white sheets. Spun and muslin are cottony, cloth-like substances. All are usually hung within square or rectangular metal frames and soften light.

Flags

Used for stopping light from getting onto the subject. They are generally made of black cloth held within a metal frame and are attached to a C-stand.

Barndoors

Metal flaps that attach to the light itself for directing the light in a certain direction.

China Balls

A paper lantern light that creates a soft light like candlelight. They can be very beautiful, but are hard to control.

Cheating

Tricks used on set to help make the lighting look more realistic. For example, raising a table on blocks to bring it closer to an actor's face in order to tighten the composition or moving people and furniture away from the walls to reduce shadow on background problems and make it easier to use back light.

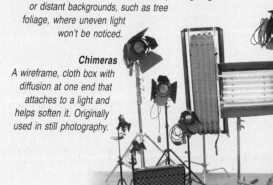

Grading shouldn't be over relied upon to correct your mistakes, although it often can, it is to even out the small difference in exposure and colour that occurs when scenes are shot in different places and at different times. For example, you might film in a field all day, but in the final edit a shot from the beginning of the day is cut next to a shot from the middle of the day. Nature cannot be controlled and the colour temperature of the light might change, clouds form and you might even have to shoot some close-ups in the studio later.

The grader film can 'even out' the colour differences so that from shot to shot, the flesh tones and the colour of the grass stay the same - the scene has continuity. The grader has a 50 point scale for the three colours - red, green and blue - with which to grade the film. The closer to the middle of the scale the negative is, the more variations the grader can make; this is why properly exposed negative is so important. If you shoot tungsten film in daylight without a correction filter (Wratten 85), the negative will have too much in the blue layer and not enough in the red. The grader will have to compensate by putting in less blue and more red light at the printing stage; if the negative is under or over exposed the grader's chance of correcting the problem completely will be seriously reduced.

The digital grader and radically change the film look, increase and decrease contrast and enhance different areas of the picture, secondary grading can mean that different parts of the pictrure are treated differently.

In either case grading is like 'polishing' the film or video and if you can afford to do it is worth all the time and money you can spend on it.

Q - What should you do in advance to ensure problems are ironed out?

Jon - Shoot tests. Film stock is a tool; it is the mechanism whereby the image is captured, copied and then transmitted. Film is made of several layers of light sensitive material - when light strikes it there is a chemical reaction, the more light the more reaction. Not enough light - no reaction and you get nothing on the negative (black), too much light and there's a complete chemical reaction and nothing on the negative (white). Most scenes you shoot will have varying degrees of light and dark; it is important to understand the sensitivity of the film. Your eye may be able to see into the shadowy areas, but will the film negative pick up that detail? Both stocks available in the UK - Kodak and Fuji - are different; their grain structure may not be exactly the same and their sensitivity to different colours may vary. Contact the manufacturers who are usually more than happy to supply a free roll of any stock for tests. Design a series of tests that help you to access the characteristics of the film. A test scene should have a selection of different light and dark areas; you should know what the reflective quality of each area is (a spot meter may help), and by shooting a range of exposures you can see what they look like and how they relate to each other. Talking to the lab is crucial and shooting tests are a great way to gain experience in a short period of time. I have always tried to shoot tests in advance of tackling tricky situations. For example, filming a TV screen and incorporating it into a scene so that it looks as it would in real life is tricky. Shooting tests enables me to experiment and therefore get the best results.

Q - How much input should a director have with the look of the film?

Jon - It's vital to read and discuss the script with the director. It sounds obvious, but it's so often overlooked. A film should have a style and the photographic look should not radically change during the film unless the story requires it.

Q - What are the most common mistakes made by the production?

Jon - Expecting stunning images with very basic lighting and crew. Getting a good image takes time and resources and that means money. Outdoor locations at night take a long time to light, it's really hard work especially when you don't have enough lights. You're adding time, tiredness, and don't forget it's colder, long cable runs, all sorts of problems.

Possibly the quickest way to shoot a low budget film would be entirely outdoors during the day - with a few good poly boards and reflectors you can be shooting shot after shot after shot.

PRODUCTION

Nic Morris
Director of Photography

DIGITAL DP

Q - What is your job?

Nic - I am a director of photography. I started very young as a DOP on documentaries and I was lucky enough to work at the BBC where I got a good spread of work. I did hundreds of documentaries and pop promos, then went into commercials and fortunately, some of the directors took me across into drama. I did 2nd unit on *Alien 3* which was a nice start.

Q - Can HDCAM look like 35mm film?

Nic - If you look at 35mm and Hi Def, side by side, you really have to do a double take to see the difference. Just about everything that I have shot, has been using the HD Panavised cameras. The Panavision film cameras work as a very efficient film making tool - the matte boxes and the accessories are all designed for the focus puller to work quickly - and you also have really superlative lenses, lenses that you can take to the wire and you can use wide apertures so you can get that shallow depth of field. Both of these advantages are present with the Panavised HD cameras.

But I think it is wrong to try and make it look like film. I think rather than spending time trying to make it look like film with film effects, I think you should be true to the medium that you are using. Which means that if you are shooting on MiniDV or Super 8, you use that medium and don't try to pretend that it is something else.

At the high end of HDCam, and Genesis, it is a different medium, it is not film. There is monitor sitting there, and it is not just 'low quality preview', it is full quality and therefore can be used as a quality control thing as well. And that is a double-edged sword. I prefer to have quality control in the evening at the lab, as during the shoot, it interferes with the pace of work and sometimes you are not in ideal viewing conditions. Actually our waveform monitors are the most important tools to have on set.

Q - HDCam cameras have a multitude of frame rates. Which one would you tell a low budget British feature film DOP to use?

Nic - For a low budget film, it comes down to the workflow. As a DOP you are in charge of maintaining the visual quality of the picture and you should be checking in with the editor all the time. Within the HD realm, that means understanding workflows and the implications of them. If you honestly think that you are going to have a major theatrical release in America, then I would say 24p. If, being realistic, your film is likely to go to a small theatrical release and DVD / TV, I would say 25p. If you are in a 50hz environment, as we are here in the UK, 25p does make everything much easier. So for a low budget film, you can save yourself a lot by going 25p rather than 24p.

Q - Some people believe that if they shoot at 25p they will not have the "film look"?

Nic - The flim 'look' is about progressive scan and not the shooting frame rate. I think there is mythology here. Stuff that is originated at 24fps will be watched on television every night at 25fps in Europe. And it goes the other way too, stuff shot at 25fps can be viewed in a cinema at 24fps and no-one notices. I think you need to take a cold hard look and figure out what is going to be the most cost effective for you. Are there any technical reasons here? Are we in a 60 Hz environment (USA) where we have to shutter down to get 25 to work? Or are we in a 50 Hz environment (UK) where 25p works without hiccup? There are really good reasons to stay 25p within Europe.

Q - Is there more or less kit in shooting HD versus Super 16mm or 35mm film?

Nic - It is interesting, I was shooting an HD production and we had monitors and cables and cameras and then I did a rather lovely little film about Sussex and music with a friend of mine. We had an Arri III, a set of prime lenses and a tripod. Recently, I went to the Viper presentation and we looked at the pictures, which were wonderful, but there were roomfuls of equipment! And we thought, wow our 35mm was very lightweight. OK, we didn't have a crew and it was landscape, but it did bring it home that yes, there is a lot of kit in HD to make it work well. And the cables slow you down.

Q - So even without having to load the camera or getting hairs in the gate, sometimes HD can be a slower process?

Nic - It depends on what level of monitoring you want on the set. And it depends on what kind of quality control you have at your lab. I shot 'Without You' with Julian Simpson after 'The Criminal', and it was budgeted for a DV, two man crew shot over six nights in Leeds. I wanted to shoot HD on this and thought they couldn't afford it. I told them I wouldn't change anything, just the camera. We shot with Panavision HD and then downconverted. So apart from the downconversion, the costs were the same, save for the more expensive camera. And we shot a really good drama with a two-man crew and no real back up. Just one small monitor. And that is coming back to the experience from shooting Digibeta all those years where you have the confidence in ones skills without having to resort to the comfort of checking monitors. And if you have that level of confidence with a system, you can do it.

Q - One difference between the two is that with film, everyone thinks that if the lighting is OK and the camera is set up right, it will look OK. But with video, you have that damn monitor to look at?

Nic - True, but on a mid to low budget feature you have to take some of the responsibility for quality control when you are the DOP. And if you don't, probably nobody else will and you could find yourself with an embarrassment. For example, on one production we had problems with dead pixels. A dead pixel is something really hard to see, and one or two you can get away with, but it becomes very costly in post-production if you don't see them and you don't correct them. If you do spot them, you can do a quick and simple repair at a small cost and they are gone. But that is a case where we had a good quality monitor and we were studying it and we noticed them. If we were working with a nine inch monitor and we were working on the fly we wouldn't have noticed them. But I agree with you. When you become an experienced DOP, at least I think, that I do my best work when I am doing it by intuition. Sort of let the force be with you. And that doesn't change for me whether I am shooting on film or digital.

Q - Are HD cameras equally tough and robust to their mostly metal film counterparts?

Nic - It doesn't look it, but they seem to be tougher than they look. I have mounted them on cars and done all the things that we do to film cameras. There is a wonderful old quote from the Mitchell days where he said, *'Just give me a camera that a blacksmith can fix.'* But we are not in that era, even with film cameras. They all have electronic boards and synch boards. I had to shoot some infrared stuff recently, and the amount of infrared LED's I had to disable so as not to fog the film was amazing. I also think that a professional crew will not allow a camera to be maltreated. That is something at the lower budget end where the less experienced crews don't look after the cameras as well.

Q - Do you generate the same amount of paperwork that you would on a film shoot like camera reports and the like?

Nic - In my own work, I use the disciplines of film and television working styles. We would shoot frame leaders. We would get some sort of quality control back from the lab. We would keep camera sheets and those would go to the editors. It is also to identify a problem. When shooting film, we keep a log of mag numbers, so that if there is a scratching issue, you can take that mag out of service until you have resolved it. And there are similar practices with HD camera bodies, tape batches and lenses.

Q - For a low budget feature, what would be the minimum HD kit that you would need?

NIC MORRIS BSC
Director of Photography

dop@nicmorris.com
Contact Lou Coulson's Agency
on 020 7734 9633

The Rule of Thirds

If you look at an object, your eye is automatically drawn to points on it one third of the way in from the left or right and one third from the top or bottom. For this reason, when you frame your shots it is best to place objects on these points, or along the lines themselves. This makes for attractive framing.

The easiest way to do this is imagine a tic tac toe board drawn across the frame. Where the lines intersect is where you put the object. For example, if you have a person holding a gun looking right to left, put the person one third of the way in from the right hand portion of the screen with their head (or, eyes if it is a close up) one third of the way from the top. Place the gun one third of the way in from the left and one third of the way from the top or bottom depending on which way they are looking. This is also why, when you have one character talking to another that is off screen, they are always slightly off center.

Nic - I am more than happy to make a film with one camera and with one lens, but it must be a good lens and a well-calibrated camera. I am a believer in zoom lenses now. But they have to be good ones. If you can get a good zoom lens that has not come through the ENG way, because most of the Digibeta cameras that we are using for films these days are the same machines that were used for news a few years ago. And while they do have great optical ranges, but they also have nasty things like their aperture goes up and down as you zoom. They are not as sharp at the far ends of the zoom.

Q - And what would that lens and camera be?

Nic - If I had a choice, probably the Panavision system just because I am used to it. I am sure that the Arriflex D-20 will also be good. It also depends on what you are doing. I just did something on HDV, and while I wouldn't be comfortable blowing it up and projecting it ninety feet across, it might be the best thing for your project if it is not going theatrical. I say, look at the script and see what it needs and maybe one camera and one lens is right for it, and maybe a range of primes is right for it. When you are starting to move towards drama, you cannot run on automatic and expect that there is just one answer to a problem or one way to go. You can't stick with the same equipment and lighting list every time. There are two variables with a film - the script and the director. And if you are going to do a great job as a DOP, you need to get inside the director's head and understand the kind of film he wants to make.

Q - Can HD shoot slow motion?

Nic - Yes, kind of. There is the Tornado camera. While it is not up to HD standards, you can up-res it on a Quantel EQ. It will run very high speeds. That camera was developed from a single chip industrial motion-capture camera and the problem with frame capture rate there is getting the information down onto tape or disk fast enough. And with solid state, in a year or two, we will be getting cameras that can do it too. There is also DVCProHD which can shoot up to 60fps, though again, is not up to HD specs.

Q - How do you deal with the limitations of electronically captured images - for instance, video has less latitude than film?

Nic - That all has to do with camera set up, and as a DOP working in Hi Def, that is probably the single most important thing that I do. I have to understand and know the camera and be able to set it up in a way that won't necessarily give the most exciting pictures on set, but will give the best bandwidth in post production. So what I am looking at in all photography, film, stills, digital, is tonal gradation. Between the black and the white, you have as many as possible shades of grey. And that is the Holy Grail. That is why something looks great. That is not to say that in a down and dirty harsh action movie, I am not going to push everything to the limit. Of course I am because it is true to the script. But in a period drama, or in a light comedy, I am going to set up the camera differently. I know that some people try to set up the camera so that it looks perfect on set, but I don't think that is the right way to go. I do it on commercials and on some dramas where I am not confident in the amount of money that will be available in post-production. But on a feature film with a reasonable budget, I have enough confidence that the editor is really going to pay attention to quality control. So my job is to maintain the look. I am not saying just shoot everything grey. In fact, I think you would be surprised at how little grading is needed. I am looking to avoid loss of detail in highlights or shadows at that shooting stage. Maybe at the digital intermediate stage, you can lose those details, but not when shooting, because the more information you have going into the process the more you will have going out the other end.

Q - What are the settings that you would recommend?

Nic - It's hard to say because they are changing all the time. They are also different from camera to camera, or if you are going to use one that is Panavised. But what I would say is that if you are going to be a DOP, work out what the issues are. And don't work it out by playing with the menus, work it out by talking to people further up the line in post-production. In general, all the disciplines that film teach you will still apply. Don't over-expose. Don't underexpose. Don't clip the whites. As a film cameraman, the most important instrument that I have is my exposure meter. So that the concept of correct exposure is correct to the script and correct to the look and feel and emotion that you want. It is not correct to what someone in Rochester, NY at Kodak says that you are exposing. And in fact, they make their stocks so that you do have a lot of latitude for what you want. If there is one frustration in electronic film making as opposed to film, is that with film I can expose something in a way that I am pretty sure that when I watch rushes in the morning, as long as the lab is good, I will get rushes that are very true to what I want in the finished film. If I under or over expose it half a stop, the lab knows that I have probably not made a mistake. The assistant cameraman will have put a grey scale on the front so they know that is how I want it. I will have control over the authorship of that negative. I seek to do that in the electronic domain, but it is harder because there are a lot of things in the workflow further down the line that kind of normalise what you have done. You are not trying to get a perfect oscilloscope trace. What you are trying to do is get a picture that is true to the emotion and mood of the piece, but also one that has enough bandwidth there to allow you to go through the degradations that you will go though.

Q - Should you shoot tests?

Nic - Yes. I shoot tests on a feature right the way through. For an HD feature I shot recently, I shot tests and even had them scanned onto film so we could check, not only my own cameras and lens, but the whole post-production workflow as well. I am testing it to see what it does to my camera original and to see what compensation I have to make when shooting.

Q - Are there any differences in how one would choose to light film or HD?

Nic - I was at a film festival in Poland some years back where we had an awful lot of Oscar winners in that room. And the chap from Sony, who had not really worked out that this was a cameraman's festival and there were a lot of camera men about and was used to talking to producers said, 'The great thing about HD is that you don't need to light.' He was lucky to get away with his life that night! The thing is with film, with 500ASA and a T1-3 lens, I don't really need to light. I could shoot you now, in this domestic living room that is softly lit, and still get a good image. Film still has the edge in sensitivity. 500 ASA on a large format has very smooth grain and looks quite nice. I am sure that will change in the digital worlds and the speeds will come up. So for some

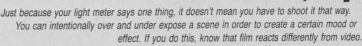

Over or Underexposing

Just because your light meter says one thing, it doesn't mean you have to shoot it that way. You can intentionally over and under expose a scene in order to create a certain mood or effect. If you do this, know that film reacts differently from video.

Shooting on Film - *Over exposure is good, under exposure is bad, because with over exposure you will still have an image on the negative, which you can manipulate in post if you decide to change your mind.*

Shooting on video (HD) - *Under exposure is just about acceptable (but not too under-exposed), over exposure is bad, because video cannot recover as well from 'clipped' images.*

Pic - D © Black Mole Productions Limited 2005

PRODUCTION

GUERILLA FILM MAKER SAYS!

Cheap Special Effects Filters

If you can't afford to hire expensive effects filters, gelatin filters can be used. Stills photographers use them with a special plastic holder which snaps onto the front of the lens. Split diopters, graduated, star, close up, and diffusion - all can add to the image if used subtly. Best of all, they're cheap.

Polarising

Much like your polarising sunglasses, it you place the camera at a right angle, this filter can radically reduce reflections in a window. Obviously useful when shooting through glass on sunny days.

Split Diopter

This is essentially half a close up lens. It allows the extreme foreground and backgrounds to be in focus at the same time. It's a weird effect, but very pleasing in the right circumstances. Often a vertical object such as a door, tree or wall is used to disguise the transition from one focus plane to the other.

Graduated

Used to create heavier skies, for that Ridley Scott look. Many colours are available, including neutral density which can be used to simply darken the sky so that it does not over expose and burn out, thereby losing detail in the clouds.

Close-Up

Most camera lenses don't get very close to a subject. So if you want that extreme close up, you are going to need a close up filter. They look a bit like a large magnifying glass, and come in different strengths. Buy the strongest.

Mask

Binoculars and a keyhole are perhaps the most common type of mask. They work best on the longer end of the lens and can be done in the lab instead, although that will cost significantly more. Mask shots tend to look cheesy.

---

projects it might not be right to light due to what the script demands. My normal style is to be quite glossy and polished and for that you need quite a lot of light. You light for emotion and for creating a visual narrative.

Q - Any advice on handling sound with HD?

Nic - The obvious thing is to get the best, most experienced soundman you can who is confident with HD workflows. But it depends at what budget level you are looking at. When we did *'Without You'*, we went straight into the camera and worked the same way we would have with a Digibeta and a breakout box (SQN) and going back in. There are some clear advantages to that in terms of post-production cost. The advice about testing applies here, too. Test the sound all the way through. During the HD projects I have worked on, if sync problems occur, it's usually because someone has changed something without checking with the heads of department. I tend not to run the sound into the back of the camera mainly because it is one less cable and it slows you up when moving. You have to disconnect from the sound guys and they have to wrangle up the cables, move the camera and reconnect the sound. But below a certain budget level, it is the right thing to do, and certainly for very low budget films.

Q - How important is tape management?

Nic - There is no reason to lose the disciplines that you have in a film style of working. Clearly as a tape costs fifty quid instead of seven hundred quid, there is a chance to be much more relaxed about it. But the tapes could deteriorate if they are left to get very hot in a car, or if they are somewhere very humid. So it is good to know about your stock and get them to the lab as soon as possible. As soon as that tape goes into that camera, it becomes infinitely more expensive and all good clapper loaders will want to get rid of it as quickly as possible - either to the lab or the post-production suite.

Q - What experiences have you had with HDV?

Nic - I just shot a corporate video in New York using HDV for the first time. I got to take the

The 'Line Of Action'

Camera 1

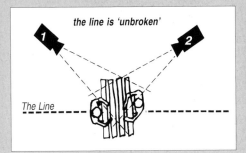

the line is 'unbroken'

The Line

Camera 2

Camera 1

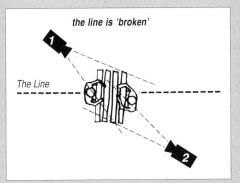

the line is 'broken'

The Line

Camera 2

The Line Of Action, or 'line', is an imaginary line drawn through the action of a scene so that the audience understands the layout of the world in the scene they are watching. In these two examples you can see when the line is OK and when it is broken.

The top diagram shows two camera angles on a scene. Camera 1 is on the left of the scene and pointing right. Camera 2 is on the right of the scene and pointing left. When the two shots are cut together it is clear who is sitting where and the line remains unbroken. The people appear to be looking at each other.

The lower diagram shows the same scene with cameras on the left and right, but this time, camera 2 has moved across the line of action. Note how the two resulting shots show the characters sitting on the right of frame and looking left. Cutting these two shots together will jar. In this instance the line is 'broken'. The people don't appear to be looking at each other.

The 'line' is a very simple concept but desperately easy to break. If in doubt, make short video movies and practice by actively breaking the line and examining just how awkward the shots will look when cut.

camera home for a few days and play with it - the Sony HVR Z1E. It looks like the Sony PD-150 camcorder. It is about £3500k and is a good camera. But I think that one of the problems that I see is that you look at advertising for DOP's and they say they are HD specialists, but in truth they are MiniDV specialists who have bought an HDV camera. That is a frustration to people who work on the high end of HD. And while HDV is a remarkable format and doing some very clever things, it is not the same thing as recording on a D-20 or a Genesis. However, it is clearly a nice format compared to standard DV. What are some of the main differences? Well, apart from money, the controllability in the menus is a real difference. There are some really fundamental things that you just can't change. And a result of that, everything that comes out of the camera looks kind of the same.

Q - Do you agree that some of the drawbacks of HDV are the non-progressive scan and restricted colour space?

Nic - Yes. Though the progressive scan issue is going to disappear quickly. You always get the odd film that breaks out. It is a little bit like saying I am going to pay the rent next week because I bought a lottery ticket. Yes, it does happen, but to go into a film thinking that you are brilliant, the script is brilliant and that you can shoot it on anything and think you have an equal chance of

Colour Temperature

GUERILLA FILM MAKER SAYS!

Saying film stocks are sensitive to light seems obvious, but there is more to it than you might think. Light contains all colours of the spectrum, and while the human eye can compensate to see most artificial light as white light (except highly coloured lighting), film stock is not so clever. Depending on what light source you're filming under and the type of stock (tungsten or daylight), you might end up with a colour correction nightmare. The key to reducing these mistakes is to understand Colour Temperature, or the colour of light.

When light is at given intensities, it gives off different colours. This is measured in degrees Kelvin (named after the British scientist who devised a way to measure the amount of red and blue in a light source by comparing it to the colour of what is called a 'black body' – an instrument that is dead black when it's cold but changes colour when it's heated to various temperatures.) At one end of the scale is 'warm light', which oddly enough has a lower temperature reading (2,900-3,400 degrees K) and gives off a red orange hue. Tungsten lights and household incandescent lights fit into this category. At the other end of the scale, light is said to be 'cool' or 'blue' and has a higher colour temperature. Daylight at noon is around 5,600 degrees K as are H.M.I lights (Halogen-Metal-Iodide). Here a bluish tint colours all objects. Just as a visual for these two concepts, imagine heating up a piece of metal – as it starts to get hot it glows red, then as the heat increases, it glows white.

Light in the early morning and at sunset have a 'warm' colour temperature, HOWEVER you still need to treat it as daylight because all light from the sun is daylight. Lights can also be between red and blue. For example fluorescent lights tend to give off a greenish hue. As an example of a possible problem area, imagine you have found a great office location with huge windows - it may be a great location but it's also a DP nightmare. What if you have tungsten lights being mixed with daylight through those HUGE windows? The solutions would be... black the windows and frame them out, gel the windows to rebalance the daylight as tungsten balance, or gel the lights to rebalance them as daylight balanced.

*Film stocks are balanced for either **DAYLIGHT** or **TUNGSTEN**. Using daylight film under 'blue' lights (the higher colour temperature) or using tungsten film under 'warm' lights (the lower colour temperature) will create normal coloured objects. If you were to shoot daylight film with 'warm' lights, everything will look orange. Conversely shooting tungsten film stock under 'blue' lights will make everything look blue. This can be corrected by placing filters over the camera lens or gels over the lights (see filters and gels for more info).*

__Video.__ On video cameras, there is the white balance - an electronic way of telling the camera what kind of lighting is being used. Always ensure that all light sources in a shot are balanced the same, either all daylight or all tungsten.

getting distribution, that is naïve. The increase in HD television broadcasting, America is starting, Sky is doing a 750 line lower quality version, is going to drive up the quality level requirements of the original material, not down. You need to future proof your project, so it will not be obsolete when you are done. If you have the production costs, you need to ask yourself what are the real differences between HDV and something a little better. Having said that, if you have a project that is going to be very real, then it is a perfect medium for it.

Q - So for a new film maker who has scraped together £50k to make a film, do you think it is better to buy a Z1, or go to a rental house and try to get them to give you a deal on a HDCam package for the same amount of money?

Nic - I think you want to produce the highest quality negative that you can. That is what I am employed to do. That highest quality negative could be MiniDV, if it is appropriate to the project, then it should be MiniDV with no dropouts and the best bandwidth. I think we are going to be flooded with Z-1 films soon. 90% of it won't be very good because the story is not very good or the acting is bad. I would encourage new filmmakers to raise your production value above the level of all the other people who are doing shoots on Z-1s. Maybe it is reworking the script or getting better actors, and maybe it is shooting on film or going with better options in the HD arena. How can you raise your film above the others?

Q - When you master to HD, do you make one master for TV and one master for film? Or do you do one for both?

Nic - Ideally you would make one for each. Just as a feature film that originated on film, you would have a lab grading session or digital intermediate and you would have a telecine session for TV masters. And the look that I get on a telecine session is different than the look I get on film. One of the joys of the cinema is the idea of having people in a dark room with a screen, and that means that you can play dark, low key scenes with great lenses and it looks wonderful. We are not there yet with HD, though we will be soon. But within a dark room you can make a very strong, striking print. If you did the same on a DVD or for television output, most people wouldn't see it. You can still have a low key scene, but you do not have the same grade that you would have for film. It might be possible to modify a master grade from a master and take it in different directions. But I would do different things.

Q - Do you think all with the new technologies, with seemingly infinite numbers of ways to make things, has actually made things more complicated and created a greater chance of ending up with a film that you are not happy with?

Nic - There is a lot of misinformation and confusion with post production workflows. But even so, people with limited knowledge of the area are able to burn to DVD a good, finished product. And that is very enabling. To think that I could edit my showreel on my laptop or watch rushes there too - the technology is fantastic and it is only going to get better. But even though it sounds like a lot, there really are only two editing packages - Avid and Final Cut Pro. So in one way, it is as restricted as it ever was.

Q - What are the common mistakes that you see in new DOPs?

Nic - There is a mastery of detail that you do not need in other areas, and that is sometimes missing, such as in shooting reverses. Reverses need to match their opposite shots and if you are not careful you can light yourself into corners. For example, on one side you have a high key, sexy shot that you cannot match in the reverse for various logistic reasons and it looks bad when cut together. When I started at 21, I was shooting documentaries on film. In all light conditions in all situations, you were exposing film - sometimes reversal film, and you became very comfortable with shooting and exposing film. And now this is the first generation of cameramen who will not have been exposed to much film. They come up through the Digibeta or TV drama stage. I don't know what the future holds for Super 16mm, which for me, is still a superior format to HD.

Q - Are there some practical things that a DOP can do to make themselves better?

Nic - Understand the mechanics of the crew. The crew dynamic is vital and I think a lot of inexperienced DOPs, rather than engaging with other people, showing leadership and explaining things, will end up doing it all themselves because it is easier for them. I think that surrounding yourself with good crew and having faith in them is a sign of maturity. Also, if you are going to work fast and the most cost-effectively, having the right amount of crew is important. Working film students, for example sort of fall over everything together instead of having defined roles. I think it is more difficult at the micro budget end of film making where you are not paying people or asking for favours and it tends to be very egalitarian. I am all for egalitarian, calm sets, but I think it is important that people have defined roles. Today I will load for you, but tomorrow on my shoot, I want you to take on 2nd AC clapper responsibilities. The next film you will be the focus puller. And you should have an understanding of what those roles mean. We are coming to a new generation of assistants who don't understand the complexities of their jobs or how big they are. So really learn what every job is within the camera department and really use people.

Q - Do you think it someone who wants to be a DP should work for an experienced one for a while to learn how to do it?

Nic - Yes, the traditional way of working your way up through the department as a loader to focus puller, to operator, is very effective. I see the focus pullers that I work with, using lunchtime to show the trainees how some of the equipment works all the time. There is a real tradition in the camera department, as there is in most departments, that if someone took the time to show you, you should do the same to someone else. That is a fabulous way to do it. All the jobs are different and it must be very difficult to come up as a DOP when they haven't worked on a film set in the other grades. And I think that is why I am seeing these slightly less effective atmospheres on the set. There is less structure. Seeing a feature film crew working quickly and quietly is quite a thing to see. It is impressive. And you wouldn't be able to slot into that unless you have experienced it, at least for a little while.

Q - What advice would you give a new film maker or DOP?

Nic - Embrace HD for what it is. Don't pretend that it is film. Don't pretend that it looks like film. But don't make it look like Digibeta, either. But the real advice is to look ahead. To not get so immersed in the project that you are working on right now or for the next two weeks, but to take a step back and think in ten years time, this is where I would like to be and work backwards. Then it is not this instant gratification thing. You take a longer view and it will make you so much more effective.

PRODUCTION

Martin Gooch
Assistant Camera

ASSISTANT
CAMERA

Q - What is your job?

Martin - I work in the camera department as a Camera Assistant. But, that can mean many things. First of all, it depends on whether you are shooting on tape, or on film. If you are shooting on film then you will have a Clapper Loader and a Focus Puller. In America that is known as the 1st AC (Focus Puller) and the 2nd AC (Clapper Loader). On tape (digital or analogue) they usually just have a Camera Assistant.

On the day of the shoot, your first job is to make sure that the camera is there, up and running and ready to shoot. The DP is a link between many departments - lighting department, which is the Gaffers, Sparks and Best Boys, the Grip department which is the Grip, the Dolly Grip, and the Key Grip, and the Camera Department. The DP is the fulcrum around which these departments work and he tells everyone what to do. If you are on a really big film you could have several cameras on a large truck. So you are there to make sure there is a camera that the DP wants to use, it's working and is ready for the required shots, otherwise you get a smack!

Q - On a low budget film, shot on film, what would be the various duties that you may get asked to do?

Martin - Well first of all, turn up in the morning, have a bacon sandwich and a cup of tea and a chat, and find out where and what you are doing, whether you are inside or outside, is it hand-held, are you on a crane etc., then go and find your camera. If you are on low budget you won't have a camera truck so you will need to get all your boxes out of where they are stored or have been transported (usually by car). Ideally, beforehand you should label all your camera boxes (silver flight cases) so when you are running around and you can't get to the box, you can say to someone, *'can you go and get me the 400ft magazine box?'* (a *magazine holds the film and locks onto the camera).* They can then go and see its label, pick it up without opening 100 boxes and bring it back. And you can guarantee that if they open a box in a search, they won't close it properly and then when you pick it up, just as the beautiful make-up girl is walking past, everything will fall out and it will be very embarrassing, and ruin your chances!

Take out your camera, put up the sticks (tripod), put on a head (tripod head), put on a base plate (which screws to the camera), make sure that is firmly fixed, put the camera body on and then put a battery in before you put all the rest of it in, so you can run it and make sure it works. How embarrassing is it if you put all the camera together and it won't even turn over (run). You've wasted half an hour, when you could have phoned Arri and say *'It won't work!'*, and they will say *'have you pressed that little button?'*, and you will go *'Oh yeah, thanks!'* It's all about being ready and never holding anyone up unnecessarily.

Q - In terms of film, what are the common problems that occur with the cameras?

Martin - Commonly, not checking your loop size when loading a new magazine, which will cause the camera to jam or film snap. It takes time to load a magazine, even if it's only 3 minutes, it is still time, because you have got to go to the loading bay or the bag or the room, unload it and put it back in again, and every time it snaps, there is invariably little bits of film dropped inside the mechanism, which you may not even be able to see, and even if you spray it with Ken-Air, they may not actually come out. Always take as long as you need to lace up a film. Often, someone is running around, usually the 1st AD is shouting at you, the actress has burst into tears, or it's about to rain - but it doesn't matter, because if you turn over that camera and the film snaps, you will have to do it all over again and you will look like an idiot. If it's taking a long time, just calmly say *'I'm sorry, it will be another moment here'.* It is vital to get that right.

Q - What about changing mags (magazines), unloading, reloading and labeling cans and report sheets etc?

Martin - If you are lucky, before your shoot you will have a couple of days to look at the kit and make sure everything is working. You can practice your work, such as changing mags - it's like being a runner in a relay race, to practice with your Loader and your Focus Puller, how to load a magazine. Remember, all eyes are on you at that point - the actress is in place, the camera is set, make-up and costume are happy - everyone has been hurried into place only to find they have to wait a moment for you as you need to change the magazine!

Say for example you are in a tight stairwell, you will need to know which hand the Loader is going to hand you the magazine, it really helps - an efficient changeover will mean it's fast and there is a reduced chance of any dust or crap falling into the camera. I know this is really basic stuff, but some people never do it. I've seen people drop magazines on the floor which could cause internal static flashes, which in turn could cause some sparkle on the film - and break the mag!

Q - Going back to unloading and reloading film stock, and the procedure for putting it back in cans, and labeling it, how important is that whole process?

Martin - Labeling your cans is vital. People spend millions of pounds making a film, and if you are the Loader, you can really fuck it up! You can lose the film by putting it in the wrong tin, and mislabeling it, or you can put it in a tin and not label it and it will get thrown away, or you might re-load it into another camera. I know this sounds unlikely, but I've seen it happen. Not by me of course, I'm still available for work, and my number is...! (laughs)

The camera department is all about being organised and being prepared. You should know what is coming up next, and the same goes for your magazines, you should have all the labels written out - so when you are having lunch, write out some labels. As soon as the shot negative is in a can, stick on a label that you have written on already, then all you have to do is write, how much is in it, like 400ft, 25ft, and the roll number etc.

Q - With each can, there is a corresponding report sheet - what is on that sheet?

Martin - You have your negative report sheet, and on a big film, you usually write one sheet per roll. You should always write and send a sheet to go with each can, because otherwise when the lab get it, they don't know what it is. It is just a tin of film, they don't know what to do with it. They need to know if it needs to be cleaned, developed, does it need to be telecined, if so what sort? And who it is from and where it should go.

Q - What about other duties such as operating, focus pulling etc., is that your job?

Martin - The Director of Photography is responsible for the lighting and the positioning of the things that you are filming. The Camera Operator is responsible for the framing and the moves. Obviously the DP and the Operator can be the same person. The Focus Puller is not just responsible for the focus, which is why focus pulling is something of a misnomer. They are responsible for the camera to be ready to run, to make sure it actually works. They are responsible for lacing up the film, making sure that the gate is clear of dirt and hair, making sure that all the bits below the camera - the sticks, the dolly etc., all work. They coordinate with the Grips to make sure everything fits together and works and is in the right place. They make sure the camera is balanced and that the camera doesn't run out of film, which is also the Loader's job, but the Loader may be away, loading, or getting a cup of tea or something.

It is awful to have a big take, and then to run out of film just before it ends. There is no excuse for it, because you should have timed the rehearsal and can check if there is enough film left in the camera. Then of course you are responsible for the lens and setting the stop (aperture) which regulates how much light comes in to expose the negative. You are responsible for keeping the front of the lens clean, so there is no dirt or anything. Also keeping lens flair out. Then of course there is focus, so your job is to make sure things stay in focus, and to work out which thing is in the frame you want to stay in focus. Usually it will be the actor, so maybe the foreground is soft, and the

Martin Gooch

camera assistant
goochling@hotmail.com

PICTURE NEGATIVE REPORT

No. 12519

LABORATORIES COPY

CONTINUED FROM SHEET No.	—	SHEET NUMBER	1	CONTINUED ON SHEET No.	—

THE SHEET NUMBERS MUST BE QUOTED ON ALL DELIVERY NOTES, INVOICES AND OTHER COMMUNICATIONS RELATING THERETO

PRODUCING COMPANY: ARRI MEDIA
STUDIOS OR LOCATION: LOCATION

PRODUCTION: "FILM TEST"
PRODUCTION No.

DIRECTOR: P. COOPER
CAMERAMEN: S. NELSON
DATE: 14/07/02

STATE IF COLOUR OR B & W: COLOUR

ORDER TO: TECHNICOLOR
LABORATORIES

STOCK AND CODE No.: 5246 250D
LABORATORY INSTRUCTIONS RE INVOICING, DELIVERY, ETC.: NEG DEV + CLEAN, RUSH PRINT TO LOCATION AS ARRANGED
CAMERA AND NUMBER: ARRICAM ST
CAMERA OPERATOR: S. NELSON

EMULSION AND ROLL No.: 513,014 (1)

MAG No.	LENGTH LOADED	SLATE No.	TAKE No.	COUNTER READING	TAKE LENGTH	'P' for Print B & W / COL'R	LENS F/L & STOP	ESSENTIAL INFORMATION	CAN No.
1	400'	1	1	0'	30'	P	T2.3½ 25mm	EXT. DAY	1
			2	30'	30'	P		ND 0.6	
			3	60'	10'			81 EF	
			4	70'	30'	P		¼ BLACK PROMIST	
		2	1	100'	25'	P	T4 85mm		
			2	125'	25'	P			
			3	150'	30'	P			
		3	1	180'	50'	P	T4 18mm		
			2	230'	50'	P			
		4	1	280'	30'	P	T2.8½ 25mm		
			2	310'	30'	P			
			3	340'	20'	P			
			4	360'	30'	P		10' WASTE	
				390'					
2	400'	5	1	0'	40'	P	T4 35mm		2
			2	40'	40'	P			
			3	80'	50'	P			
			4	130'	20'	P			
			5	150'	30'	P		220' S/E	
				180'					

FOR OFFICE USE ONLY

TOTAL CANS: 2

TOTAL EXPOSED	550'	TOTAL EXPOSED	550'	TOTAL PRINTED		TOTAL FOOTAGE PREVIOUSLY DRAWN	0'
SHORT ENDS	220'	HELD OR NOT SENT	—			FOOTAGE DRAWN TODAY	800'
WASTE	10'	TOTAL DEVELOPED				PREVIOUSLY EXPOSED	—
FOOTAGE LOADED	800'	SIGNED				EXPOSED TODAY	550'

The Camera Report Sheet

This document is usually filled out by the assistant camera person. This one is for a movie shot on film, opposed to video/digital (which would differ slightly, though is essentially the same), and is used by the laboratory and editor later on down the line. Each night, a copy of this document will be taped to the exposed film cans and sent to the lab (or if shooting on tape, a copy will be sent with the tapes to the cutting room). You will get a pad of these triplicate sheets from the hire company when you hire your cameras.

The sheet details shots, takes and notes on what is expected from the lab. It also details information like roll numbers, stock types and contact details etc.

background is soft, and the actor is sharp, especially on a long lens. You do that by measuring the distance from the object you are filming and the camera gate where light is focused. If the camera moves on a track, or the actor moves, the distance between the camera and the object will change. That is why you see guys with tape measures putting marks down on the floor, or using local marks like a static object, a TV, a chair - and during the shot they will gently re-focus, using these markers on the floor and on the lens, so the actor stays sharp and in focus.

Q - How does all this differ when it comes to an electronic camera, a digital camera?

Martin - When you are not shooting on film, you don't need a Clapper Loader, because there is no film to take away and load in darkness, you have just got a cassette that you can keep in your pocket, and load in the camera. Generally, you only need one camera assistant. There is no report sheet to fill in because invariably they will just take the whole tape, and watch it all the way through. The main difference for the Focus Puller is that generally non film lenses have a greater depth of field so there is less focus pulling to do. Things stay in the field of focus for longer. This is one of the things that subtly changes the look of digital over film.

Q - What are the other primary practical differences between film and electronic cameras?

Martin - With film there is always 10 times more stuff, there is always one more box than you think there is going to be. Tape cameras are lighter too.

Q - Do you think there is less discipline on a tape shoot?

Martin - Absolutely. One thing that I've noticed, is that actors are more focused and serious when it is a film camera. As soon as you tell them *'this is film, not tape'*, they know you can't shoot as many times, you can't carry on running because every time you do a take it costs lots of money.

Q - A lot of the time, people start out wanting to make a feature film on film, then become seduced into some electronic way of shooting it. Do you have any comments on how they can modify the technology to make it look more like film on set? Do you think it is a good idea to hire film lenses?

Martin - One of things that people do that makes it look shit, is do it hand held. If you have got tape, one thing straight away you can do is to do controlled moves either on a tripod or a track and dolly. Controlled moves is really the way to make it look filmic, nice tracks, and think about your shots carefully. Don't do zooms as optically it's more akin to TV than feature films. Bringing down the depth of field usually helps too, so things in the background are soft, and the actor is sharp. That is a very film look. You can also do that by putting in filters, like a Promist, which gives it a 'look'. Ultimately, you can't take a tape and make it look like 35mm (circa 2005). If you could there would be no 35mm. One day we may be able to do that. We can get very, very close, but there is no film filter just yet. You can also light it properly which will make it look more filmic.

Q - In terms of the discipline of the set, and attracting a higher calibre of technician, and therefore higher calibre actor. Everything cranks up if you shoot it on film?

Martin - That is true. The thing is, the better your picture quality, the more likely you are to get it sold. If you can shoot it on film, always try to shoot it on film. There is nothing worse than spending all that money, get all those favours in, spend 6 months to make it, then wishing it had been shot on film. Surely it is better to spend another 6 months looking for the money? They shot *'Lock Stock and Two Smoking Barrels'* on Super 16mm, so you can make a wicked film on that format.

Q - Is it a good idea to go to the hire company before you hire the cameras?

Martin - Absolutely. On a big project they will give you as much as 2 weeks in the rental house just to do tests - you do a steady test, to make sure that the film is traveling through the gate smoothly and it isn't wobbly. You do light tests on

T-stops and F-stops

GUERILLA FILM MAKER SAYS!

A camera lens has an iris, or aperture, just like your eye. The aperture, mechanically controlled by a ring on the lens (and sometimes electronically on digital cameras) is used to control the amount of light passing through the lens to hit the negative on a film camera, or CCD on a digital camera. The markings that are used to set the iris are called F-stops, and on some lenses, T-stops, and they directly relate to the readings on the DPs light meter.

F-stops

F-stops are referenced by numbers (always white markings etched into the ring of the lens) with F-2, F-4, F-5.6, F-8, F-11, F-16, and F-22 being the most common. The lower the number (toward F-2), the more 'wide open' the lens is said to be (with less available light). The higher the number (toward F-22) and the lens is said to be 'stopped down' (with more available light). The amount of light entering the camera between adjacent F-stops is either halved (going toward F-22) or doubled (going toward F-2). For example, F-8 allows twice the amount of light into the camera that F-11 does. Likewise, F-5.6 would let in four times as much light as F-11. F-stops are calculated by a general mathematical equation that is the same for all lenses, no matter what type.

T-stops

T-stops are similar to F-stops and even have the same reference numbers - except that they start with a T (T-2, T-4, T-5.6, etc. and are also etched onto the ring, but in color). The difference is that T-stops are calibrated for each individual lens as opposed to a general mathematical formula, thereby creating a more accurate reading for the specific lens you are using. This takes into account light loss from it passing through the lens itself. Also, zoom lenses and long prime lenses will have T-stops, but short prime lenses will usually have only F-stops.

the magazines to make sure there is no light infiltration. Do scratch tests to make sure the film isn't getting scratched. Then you do all the lens calibrations, because if you look at a lens it will have all these numbers - infinity, 10ft, 5ft, 3ft, 2.1ft etc., but how do you know it is right, unless you test it? Sometimes they are well out, especially older lenses, as they may have been in hot countries or somewhere cold perhaps, and the elements will shift and move. Also on your first day, it will save you so much time as you will know where everything is, you know it all fits together, you won't go *'Where the bloody hell is the pan bar?'*, and then look all around and everyone is waiting for you, because you can't find it!

Discipline. A film unit is like the army, it is made up of loads of different things, it has got logistics, its got foot soldiers, you've got gunnery, artillery, medics... In the film industry you've got camera, sound, lighting, make-up, props, art dept., etc. Everyone does their own thing. We don't have anything to do with the make-up dept., but we are working with them. So it is all about being disciplined and actually turning up, knowing where all your stuff is, doing it properly and efficiently, in a safe way, not being an idiot. You will always have more shots to shoot than you can shoot in a day.

Q - Should a new film maker ask to be part of the camera team to learn how a set works?

Martin - No, I'd say go and be a runner first. The problem is there are so many people trying to get in, there isn't very much work. The British film industry made 89 feature films last year, that is rubbish! The Americans made 2,000! The French made 500, come on! I think Bosnia Herzegovina made more than we did! I started off as a runner, then you get to see which department you really like.

Shooting Ratio

Shooting Ratio is the ratio of how much film you shoot to the amount of time on screen. For example, if you're going to make your film on a 3:1 shooting ratio means that for every minute of film that makes it into your movie, you're going to shoot 3 minutes of footage - throw away 2 and keep 1. A 400' can of Super16mm = about 10 minutes. Therefore, to make a 90 minute film you need 9 cans multiplied by 3 (if shooting ratio is 3:1) which equals 27 rolls, which equals 10,800'. The same ratio applies to 35mm except that a 1000' roll of film runs for approximately 10 minutes. Here you would need 27,000 feet for a 90 minute film an a 3:1 cutting ratio. Of course, the lower you plan your shooting ratio, the less expensive it is for stock and processing. The downside is that you have less of a chance to compensate for bad takes, technical problems, cutaways and experimentation. It's going to be hard to shoot at 3:1, even 5:1 is tough. Most low budget films end up somewhere near 8:1 cutting ratio.

1. Save stock wherever possible. It's expensive to purchase, and expensive to process.

2. Work out your system between sound, camera and clapper loader/cam assistant so the camera starts turning over at the last possible moment. Just a couple of seconds wasted at the head of every shot will accumulate on a feature shoot.

3. Don't get too anxious to call cut. Often in the cutting room, you will need that extra second on the end of a shot. When you feel the shot has ended, wait a beat before calling cut.

4. Know in your heart if you have got what you need in your first take. Takes that are not needed waste time as well as stock.

5. If you get a hair in the gate, you should re-shoot. If stock is very short and you are having to get everything in one take, don't bother to re-shoot, (unless the hair is massive - many major features go out with hairs in the gate.) In the cutting room you will always use the best take, regardless of technical problems that camera operators will moan about, such as hairs, flare, soft shots and wobbly camerawork.

6. Rehearse as much as possible. Block the scene for the cameraman so he knows what is going to happen and when. If the scene could be spontaneous in terms of performance from the actor, allow the cameraman to widen the lens so there is more space in frame to accommodate the unexpected. This will avoid losing the frame or focus, forcing a retake (which will probably be wider anyway).

7. If you are shooting 35mm, you will only develop and print the shots you want. If you shoot 16mm or Super 16mm, you will print everything.

8. Storyboards will help, but it is likely that too many shots will be boarded and that when it comes to shooting, not all shots will be possible due to the location being different, a script rewrite or simply a lack of resources.

9. Shooting on tape formats such as DV or HD often means that directors will say 'leave it running while I just...' This can mean hours and hours of wasted footage that doesn't cost much in terms of tape, but will cost you severely in the cutting room in wasted time and frustration. Whatever the format, remain disciplined about shooting absolutely no more than is needed.

HD Tapestock

Shooting HD means you have tapes and not filmstock. Aside from the sensitivity to light, film stock and HD master tapes should be treated very much the same - with great care and attention!

1. *Label all tapes clearly and after recording, make sure they are write protected.*

2. *Keep tapes in an orderly manner, stored on their edge (not flat). Don't let them get too hot or cold either, and keep them away from dust and high powered magnetic sources.*

3. *Only use high quality, new tapes, that have been error checked. You can get error checked re-used tapes from Creative Video Associates (www.cva.co.uk) which are guaranteed.*

4. *Maintain accurate and unbroken timecodes on each tape.*

5. *Tape is fragile, so avoid unnecessary spooling back and forth in the edit. Ideally, clone your master tapes or down-convert to DVCam and do an 'offline' edit. Do not drop or throw tapes.*

6. *In the long term, master tapes should be checked and fast forwarded / rewound every five years or so.*

7. *Don't underestimate how many tapes you will accumulate. Develop a system for storage.*

Q - What are the common mistakes you see?

Martin - Not listening to the camera department. Most Directors only ever get to be on set when it is their film, and they are not on other people's films, where as camera people spend their whole life on set, they are never in the office, they are never invited to pre-production meetings, they work with loads of Directors.

Q - What specific mistakes have you come across within the camera department, where they could have been avoided?

Martin - Keep notes, keep track of everything. Know what equipment you've got and make sure you know what all the little bits in all the little boxes do. Don't go home on the first night and find that you've forgotten to put in a particular cog. The camera may work without all the right bits on it, it just may not work very well. I've seen people put a lens on a camera, and a big zoom lens can cost £20k, and not lock it properly - they turn their back on it and it falls off, the weight changes on the camera, and the whole camera flips over. I've seen it happen. Like if someone gave you a rifle in the army, you want to know how it works, because there is nothing worse than you firing it, and it jamming - same with the camera. Try and be psychic and guess what the next shot is going to be. So if you are filming in a house, and you know after the next shot you are filming in the garden, get the assistants to move the stuff outside, or go and find out where the shot will be and find out if there is a place for your kit that is out of the way. Always try and be prepared. You don't want people waiting for you. Time is our greatest asset. Without time you can do nothing. If you are losing time, you are ruining the film.

If you don't know how to do something, say you don't know how to do it. Then spend 5 minutes working it out. Never ever let anyone rush you as that is when you make mistakes. If you are loading a magazine and people are banging on the door, just load your magazine, put the tape on it, write it out, then come out.

My philosophy is, if you are working in the film industry, you are very lucky because there are millions of us who want to do it, a lot of us who love it, and would kill to get on a film. If you are working on a film, and it isn't fun, and you feel sick in the morning, you don't want to go to work, something is wrong. If you don't like it, go and find what you don't like, and sort it out. If your Director is an asshole, talk to the rest of your camera department, if you are not getting on with someone, you have got to sort it out. If you are scared of not knowing how to use a piece of equipment, say *'I'm really sorry, I haven't used the remote control shutter speed thing before'*, because you will only get caught out. Then you will ruin it, and if you ruin a shot, you've ruined it for everybody. You are there to make a good movie and enjoy it being made.

Q - What advice would you offer a new film maker?

Martin - Go and get a proper job!

PRODUCTION

Joe Allen
Gaffer

GAFFER

Q - What do you do?

Joe - I'm a Gaffer. The role of the Gaffer is to carry out the Director of Photography's (DP) wishes, to co-ordinate the efforts of the Sparks and to give the DP the look that he/she wants on film. That is usually about setting up lights, placing gels on the lights, laying cables, setting up flags, checking power, loading and unloading lighting equipment from the lighting van etc. It is a very physically demanding job for myself and my crew of sparks.

Q - Do you ever take directions from anyone other than the DP on set? What if the Director started ordering you about.

Joe - I would listen politely, because they usually have their own views and ideas of what they want, but ultimately I would not change anything or do anything lighting-wise without talking to the DP and getting permission. I don't work for the Producer, I don't work for the Director, I work for the DP.

Q - What is the difference between a Gaffer and a Spark?

Joe - As head of the lighting department the gaffer has responsibility for the job in hand and has a general overview of what is required by the DoP, the sparks take their direction from the gaffer.

Q - So the Sparks only take orders from the Gaffer?

Joe - Yes. There has to be one person who is responsible for co-ordination, responsible for Health and Safety, and that is usually the Gaffer. The Gaffer will know his/her onions with regard to Health and Safety electrically, and know how to achieve what the DP needs with the minimum amount of effort. There are a hell of a lot of good Sparks out there that could quite easily Gaffer, but choose not to take on the responsibility.

Q - How many Sparks do you have working under you?

Joe - It depends on the budget. Try to allow your Sparks to work in pairs. It makes life, in any kind of work, a lot easier if there are two of you. Heavy lights or equipment are easier to move in pairs, and from a health and safety aspect, it makes sense. If we are talking real guerilla film making, it would be me plus two. Obviously there are circumstances where there really is absolutely no budget and all you have got is a key light, some pepper lights and maybe a Dedo kit, in which case, you can really do it on your own.

Q - Are you responsible for hiring the Sparks?

Joe - Yes definitely. I've done jobs where that part has been taken out of my control and problems have occurred, and I have made a decision that will never ever happen again. I will turn a job down rather than have labour that I haven't chosen. Especially on low budget productions, your team have to be on your side, because you are going to be asking for a lot more out of your Sparks. So you need to know that those people are behind you and performing to their best abilities. Inevitably in guerilla filmmaking, you will be working longer than the union regulated hours, and you'll be getting less pay than you would do on normal jobs. So therefore your team has to be with you and behind you, otherwise you cannot achieve the result that the DP wants. If you don't achieve a high standard of lighting, i.e. what the DP wants, then he/she won't use you the next time, so therefore they won't get used the next time. You have to have people who have a little bit of common sense, and are prepared to put their all in, no matter the job, no matter the budget.

Q - How important is it to be qualified as an electrician, to work on a film set?

Joe - If you are not qualified as an electrician, it means that you will not be trusted, and there are clear health and safety issues there. I will not trust a non-qualified electrician with certain aspects of the lighting game. There are times when you need to tie into the mains equipment, and you couldn't let a non-qualified electrician go near any kind of 3-phase switch gear. You couldn't let an unqualified lighting technician go near anything electrical, other than plugging things in. That kind of power can kill instantly and everyone needs to take utmost care.

Let's get one thing clear, no matter how small the budget is, the Gaffer is responsible for the safety of everyone in his/her team. In fact the Gaffer is responsible for anybody, and everybody that works on that set, as far as electrical power is concerned. We've all had to serve our apprenticeship by doing low or no-budget films and often they can't afford fully qualified electricians. I don't have any issues with that, as long as the people in my team understand and take on board that electricity kills, and that ultimately I am responsible. As long as they play by the rules that I set out, I've got no problem working with some unqualified electricians.

Q - Is there some kind of a union that Gaffers belong to?

Joe - I am a member of BECTU. One of the main benefits of membership is that a Public Liability Insurance, which all gaffers need, is included for a nominal fee.

Q - Why do you have to take insurance, and why isn't that covered under the Producer's insurance?

Joe - The Producers do have an insurance and mine is just a 2nd layer. I've never really questioned it, because I have had it all the time, ever since I've been a Gaffer, just purely for personal piece of mind. If anything goes wrong, I want to make sure that I am personally covered. Producers being the breed of people that they are, will tell you anything you want to hear, to get the job done, because that is all that they care about. If they say, *'don't worry, we've got full insurance'*, that doesn't cut it for me really.

Q - The crew are often the 1st people to get grumpy on a badly run set. What is the limit, before you feel that the filmmaker is taking the piss?

Joe - I insist on hot food in the lunch break, and an 11-hour turnaround for my crew, that is at least 11 hours off between when you finish work to when you start work.

Q - So what would be a normal working day?

Joe - A normal working day is 12 hours, which destroys any chance of a happy family life, or a social life. I know that it is a major issue with all crews. A good production company will tie your travel in, so you will get time in that 12 hours for travelling. I also believe that it can be counter productive to work 6 days a week, 12 hours a day. Especially when you are doing a 6 week feature - genuinely, you are not giving the production your best. After the first 3 weeks, everybody is fucked. I think it is counter productive. The bare minimum should be an 11 day fortnight, so at least every 2 weeks, you get a full weekend off. In my book, it should be a 5 day week. The 12 hours a day I have no problem with, as long as you are getting a 2-day break.

Q - Let's say, at the end of the day, you hit the 12-hour mark, the Producer asks the crew to stay longer to complete a shot, what do you do?

Joe Allen
Film and Television Lighting Gaffer

T 020 7401 9841
F 020 7771 2778
M 07976 265 860
joeallengaffer@hotmail.com

Joe - Firstly, I would want to know why, and whether it is just unnecessary greed on the part of the Producer, or Director - everybody needs sleep, you can't avoid that fact. A lot of inexperienced Producers will be running around chasing their arses, doing stuff that is unnecessary. Often, people below them are afraid to question the almighty hand of a Producer, so we will find ourselves knackering the crew in a totally unnecessary way. This destroys morale, and can cause accidents. This is why the 1st AD, the DP, Producer and the Gaffer will usually have a meeting and try to establish how we can do it without overrunning. Obviously this depends on the length of the job. If it is the last day on a low budget film, you are almost guaranteed that they are going to ask you to over run. The question is how long, not whether or not it is going to happen. Hopefully you can work towards a common goal, of everybody being reasonable, because let's face it, this is a job.

Secondly, I want to know what they are going to do about how that affects my turnaround.

Thirdly, I have to go to my crew. I am responsible for them, but I don't own them, and they have their lives too.

Q - Do you get paid over time?

Joe - I rarely ask my chaps to work over time, unless there is something in a brown envelope or some other compromise, such as a later call time the next day. If we need the last shot, to make the whole thing make sense, and we lose our main actor, we lose our location, we lose absolutely everything, and they've got absolutely no money, then of course I will go to the boys and explain the situation. We just put in this amount of time, this amount of effort to get this result, and if we don't stay late, then we are not going to get that result, and the whole thing was a waste of time. It is about being reasonable, and adult.

Q - What are the common mistakes that you see on a film set?

Joe - The most common, painful and time-costing mistake a new film maker can make is to think that he/she doesn't need a First Assistant Director. A 1stAD can be irritating on set, but they are pivotal to the smooth running of the overall shooting process and

---

Gels

GUERILLA FILM MAKER SAYS!

A common way to change the colour of light, other than a colour correction filter on the front of the camera, is to use gels on the lights (as well as windows and other light sources). Gels are made of flexible, transparent heat resistant plastic, that comes in small sheets and large rolls. They're reusable and fairly durable, but crease easily, can be noisy in windy locations and will need replacing if they become paler due to the heat of the lights. Gels are mounted on lights in gel frames or can just be attached to barndoors with clothespins.

CTB (Colour Temperature Blue)
Converts tungsten light to daylight. These can also be referred to as booster gels as they boost the colour temperature. The gel will cut out about 1 1/3 stops of light. Also available are 'dikes' (dichroic filters). These are blue glass filters that correct tungsten light to match daylight. These cut about 1 stop and must be fitted to a particular light.

CTO (Colour Temperature Orange)
Warms daylight to tungsten light. 3/4 CTO gels are roughly equivalent to an Wratten 85 camera filter, and will cut out 2/3 of a stop of light. Both come in fractions ranging from 1/8 to one full f-stop. These gels are also available as a combination with Neutral Density filters which can be extremely useful when you want to diminish window light.

Other coloured gels are available for creating a variety of effects. For instance... Green - This can be used to create fluorescent lighting. Yellow - This can be used to create light coming from a street lamp. Pale yellow can be used to warm up a HMI that is too blue. Blue Frost - This changes tungsten to daylight while adding diffusion, therefore preventing further loss of light by having to add a camera filter.

They can be purchased in full, 3/4, 1/2, 1/4, and 1/8 gradation, from deep colour to pale, to make large or slight changes in colour for matching the light sources. Remember, the deeper the gel colour, the less light is emitted.

Gels are expensive and big productions tend to use it and discard it, so if you are around the bins on the studio backlot, you my be able to save your self some cash by operating midnight raids.

the most important person to get right when crewing. If I am asked to do any kind of low budget film, or short film, the first question I ask is 'who is the 1st AD?'. If they haven't got one, I don't do the job! In my view the 1stAD is the most important person on set, they will force the Director and the Producers to make realistic compromises, and they will make sure that you go home and get your turnaround.

You will find Directors are more often than not, unrealistic - about what they want, and what can be achieved with the manpower, budget and equipment available. In my experience, if you've got an experienced DP, 1stAD and Gaffer, they will get together and help the Director get the most out of the available resources. All to often I have seen a film go wrong because the Director was not prepared to compromise, and the DP, 1stAD and Gaffer were not strong enough to make the Director aware of the fact that, by trying to achieve 10, he/she was actually going to achieve 1. Whereas if he/she had taken advice and compromised, he/she may have achieved a 6. The relationship between the DP, 1stAD and the Gaffer, is in my book, quintessential. If they are all playing ball, and acting as a team to resolve issues rather than allow them to snow ball, it can all go a lot more smoothly.

The most common mistakes occur from a lack of planning. It is very easy to think 'yeah, great, that is not a problem', and not plan for it. It is only when you really start to plan, that you realise exactly what problems you are going to come up against. So, lack of planning, lack of interaction and discussion between the heads of department. Big headedness and inter-departmental rivalry is a also killer. You've all got to be understanding, you are all working for the same goal, you have all got to compromise, especially with guerilla filmmaking! You have got to watch each other's backs.

Talking to Gaffers or people responsible for lighting, you must never lose track of the fact that firstly you are dealing with something that you can't see, and something that can kill. Ultimately if you are putting your name to it as a Gaffer, it doesn't matter what the budget is, it doesn't matter how fly-by-night it is, you are legally responsible. So my advice is never rush into something, and never do something that is going to compromise your electrical safety and integrity. Far better a Director lose a shot than someone lose their life!

For example, if you've got to light one side of a road at night, you've got to be careful that you don't shine that light into driver's eyes. When you are racing around, trying to get the last shot before day break, or before the clouds open up, and there are a million and one reasons why you've got to get the shot now, you can forget something simple like that. Never compromise safety. It only takes a split second for a boy racer to come tearing around the corner, breaking the law for a start, and going far too fast, on a really quiet street, gets blinded by your light and could kill half of the crew. You would never forgive yourself, you would never work in the film industry again, and you could quite possibly end up in prison or with a large fine. Never be afraid to tell a Producer, Director or anybody to *fuck off* because you are responsible! Always use the right safety equipment, especially when using electricity outside in the rain. There are very simple plugs and connectors to use that are safe - RCDs - short for a Residual Current Device. If a problem occurs, it trips the current before it can do any damage. My personal policy is ANY electricity that is used outside is backed up and protected by an RCD.

Never be rushed and intimidated into doing anything that you don't feel is safe. That can be from electrical safety, including rigging things high up, to putting heavy lights on ridiculously tall stands that are just not designed for those lights. The most important rule is, always think, and always calmly make your decision. Understand that YOU, as far as health and safety are concerned, are the boss.

Q - So in summary, given your years of experience and wisdom, what advice would you give a new filmmaker?

Joe - Never come to work with a hangover!

PRODUCTION

Rachel Baker
Fuji UK

FILM STOCK

Q - What different gauges are available for film makers to make a feature film?

Rachel - 16mm and 35mm. The Standard 16mm format is not really used for features now, but that is not to say that it cannot be used, it is just that Super 16mm is much better at the job. However, 35mm is the international feature film standard. Super 16mm is now very popular for low budget features that plan to do a digital intermediate. Shoot film and post digitally, delivering a digital 35mm negative at the end.

Q - What's the difference between 16mm and Super 16mm?

Rachel - The only difference between 16mm and Super 16mm is that Super 16mm must be perforated on one side only. The Super 16mm format allows for the picture area to be exposed to the absolute edge of the non perforated side which when blown up to 35mm (aspect ratio of 1:1.85) gives 40% more visual screening area than standard 16mm. So you could say the negative yields 40% more useable picture area whilst staying on 16mm film. Both standard and super16mm formats can be captured on single perforated film.

Q - What length is 16mm delivered in?

Rachel - The standard lengths are 400 foot and 100 foot rolls. A 400 foot roll lasts just over 10 minutes at 25fps.

Q - What is film speed, or sensitivity?

Rachel - The film speed or Exposure Index(EI) relates to the film's sensitivity to light. To put it simply, the higher the EI, the less light is needed to properly expose the negative. Daylight photography with harsh sunshine would cope admirably with the slower speeds of stock, for instance EI 64 or 125. Other speeds such as EI 250 can be used for daylight exterior photography but can also be used for twilight or dusk shooting. There are higher speeds such as EI 500 which is mainly used for night photography where there are very low light levels.

Q - Am I correct in saying, the slower the speed of the film, i.e. the lower the EI, the less grainy the film looks?

Rachel - Yes, to some degree. In the past, a cameraman would select lower speeds to keep the grain finer, as opposed to choosing higher speed with increased grain. Recently, things have changed and high speed stocks have improved dramatically. Several factors have brought that about, one of which is demand from productions with restricted budgets and low light levels.

Q - What is the best average all round stock for shooting in Britain?

Rachel - From a personal point of view, I would go for the mid range EI 200 to 250 but other cameramen may select another speed like the 125. That is true for both 16mm formats and 35mm.

Q - What does the colour balance of film mean?

Rachel - All light has a colour, interior light bulbs are 'orangey' whereas natural daylight is 'blueish'. Your brain can make adjustments for your eyes, but a camera can't adjust the film stock. There are two balances of film stock, *Tungsten* which is generally used for shooting indoors with lights, and *Daylight* which is generally used outdoors for shooting in natural light. Different lights also have different colour temperatures or colour balance. *Tungsten* balanced stock is designed primarily for use with tungsten lights - If you have selected HMI lights then it would generally be accepted that you use a *Daylight* base stock because of the colour temperature of these lights. With HMI lights the colour temperature is a lot higher than tungsten and they yield a very daylight looking light.

Q - If you find yourself having to shoot with tungsten stock whilst filming outside, or daylight stock whilst shooting inside (with tungsten lights), what can be done?

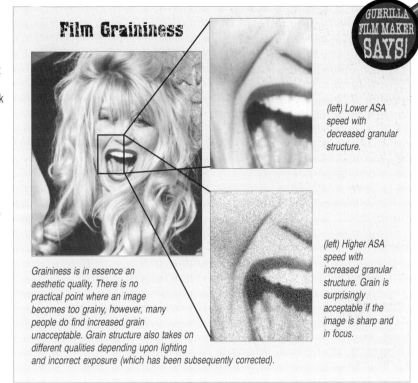

Film Graininess

(left) Lower ASA speed with decreased granular structure.

(left) Higher ASA speed with increased granular structure. Grain is surprisingly acceptable if the image is sharp and in focus.

Graininess is in essence an aesthetic quality. There is no practical point where an image becomes too grainy, however, many people do find increased grain unacceptable. Grain structure also takes on different qualities depending upon lighting and incorrect exposure (which has been subsequently corrected).

Rachel - With tungsten stock outside one should always use a WRATTEN 85 filter on the camera (which should be supplied with every camera kit), otherwise known as a Daylight filter. This filter changes the 'colour balance' of the light entering the lens and exposing the negative. It isn't the end of the world if the filter is not used - indeed there are some leading cinematographers who do not use that filter and still get a lovely result. The negative is technically exposed incorrectly, and the exposure latitude is reduced but once it is graded at the labs, it can fall within the realms of acceptability. You can also change the colour temperature of the lights by using specially coloured gels on the front of the lights, and these are often used to create a particular "look".

Q - What are the advantages of shooting 35mm over Super 16mm?

Rachel - 35mm is a global standard gauge that's recognised instantly. Super 16mm isn't (unless it is subsequently blown up to 35mm). Plus the negative is two and a half times bigger, sharper and also has two and a half times less grain on screen.

Q - What are the main problems shooting Super 16mm and blowing up to 35mm?

Rachel - When blown up, Super 16mm is very good. It's economic to shoot Super 16mm, but as step printing is so expensive, it's possible you could have shot on 35mm for the same price, if not cheaper. It could be a false economy. Now digital post production is common, shooting Super 16mm and posting digitally is a very attractive option. In post there is no attempt to recreate the look of film, as it was originated on film in the first place.

Q - In what length is 35mm delivered?

Rachel - 35mm comes in 100 foot, 200 foot, 400 foot and 1000 foot lengths. 1000 foot lasts about 11 minutes at 25fps. The EI speeds are the same whether 35mm or 16mm is being shot.

FUJIFILM

Fuji Photo Film (U.K.) Ltd.,
Fujifilm House, 125 Finchley Road,
London NW3 6HY, U.K.
Tel: 020 7586 5900

Fax: 020 7483 1419
Mobile: 07774 608709

Rachel Baker
Sales Manager
Moving Image
Email: rbaker@fuji.co.uk

PRODUCTION

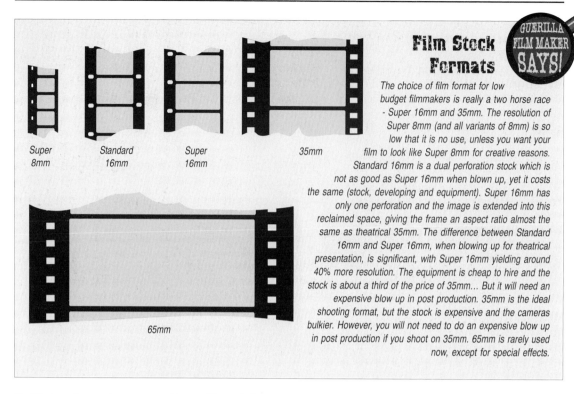

Super
8mm

Standard
16mm

Super
16mm

35mm

65mm

Film Stock Formats

GUERILLA FILM MAKER SAYS!

The choice of film format for low budget filmmakers is really a two horse race - Super 16mm and 35mm. The resolution of Super 8mm (and all variants of 8mm) is so low that it is no use, unless you want your film to look like Super 8mm for creative reasons. Standard 16mm is a dual perforation stock which is not as good as Super 16mm when blown up, yet it costs the same (stock, developing and equipment). Super 16mm has only one perforation and the image is extended into this reclaimed space, giving the frame an aspect ratio almost the same as theatrical 35mm. The difference between Standard 16mm and Super 16mm, when blowing up for theatrical presentation, is significant, with Super 16mm yielding around 40% more resolution. The equipment is cheap to hire and the stock is about a third of the price of 35mm... But it will need an expensive blow up in post production. 35mm is the ideal shooting format, but the stock is expensive and the cameras bulkier. However, you will not need to do an expensive blow up in post production if you shoot on 35mm. 65mm is rarely used now, except for special effects.

Q - What are the most common problems with stocks?

Rachel - Long term storage outside the manufacturers warehouse. The life of the base negative can be affected by long exposure to heat whilst still in its tin. In places of high temperature like the desert, faults with the negative could occur because of the extreme heat. Always store the negative in the way the manufacturer recommends on the tin i.e. in a fridge.

Q - Once film is exposed, must it be processed as quickly as possible?

Rachel - No, it can stay as long as a year without any problem as long as its kept at room temperature and doesn't go over 60° Fahrenheit. However, it is advisable to process exposed footage as soon as possible.

Q - Is the X-ray machine at airports a film makers myth?

Rachel - With current levels of Airport Security there is always some risk of X-ray. Don't pack unexposed or unprocessed film in baggage that is to be checked in. Checked baggage may be subject to high-intensity X-ray examination which could ruin the film. If the film is included in hand baggage it is more likely, but not guaranteed, that X-ray examination will be at a lower intensity which does not harm the film. Although all this appears quite formidable, please bear in mind that the number of instances of X-ray fogging we have experienced over the years has been very small indeed.

Q - On a low-budget film people are tempted to use outdated stock or short ends - is there any way a producer can be confident that this stock is fine?

Rachel - If you are in doubt about the stock, you could send it to your lab for a clip test. The laboratory would cut off a few feet from the end of a roll and produce a gamma test which would determine whether the stock was still within the realms of commercial acceptability.

Q - If one roll was all OK, would it be safe to assume that the whole batch would be OK, as long as they were all stored together?

Rachel - If they were all stored together with the manufacturer, then yes. If not with the manufacturer, then not necessarily - it would be wrong to assume that all the cans were OK, but it would be a fair bet.

Q - At the beginning of rushes, I see a colour chart - what is that?

Rachel - The colour chart is put on the front of each camera negative roll to assist in rushes grading at the labs - it ensures that the labs are printing the way the cameraman had intended. We can supply those charts to a production, as well as the labs.

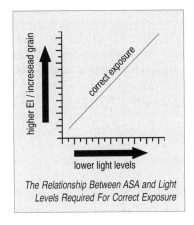

The Relationship Between ASA and Light Levels Required For Correct Exposure

Q - What are edge numbers?

Rachel - The edge numbers are a series of numbers generated at the time of manufacturing the stock. These numbers are unique to any particular roll and are used when negative cutting. All stocks now carry digital bar codes which are an electronic edge number. These are used to speed up post production and are mainly used with non linear editing systems.

Q - Does Fuji do deals for bulk purchase?

Rachel - Every single purchase is different - it depends on so many circumstances. Everyone is different. Always give me a call in the first instance, and we'll take it from there.

Q - What common mistakes have you experienced with regard to selection of stock?

Rachel - The main problem I have encountered is that of pressure when a new cameraman is given his first bite of the cherry. He's under enormous pressure to make the right decisions and choose the right stock - half way through that decision may have been proven to be the wrong stock but he should always bear in mind that modern Fuji stocks such as the new 'ETERNA' range, can be very forgiving.

16mm & S16mm Blow Up To 35mm

GUERILLA FILM MAKER SAYS!

Standard 16mm - Only the middle part of the negative can be blown up to 35mm losing some 20% at the top and bottom of the frame.

Super 16mm occupies a wider negative which can be completely blown up to 35mm without loss. The combination of a larger negative and NO part of the image being cropped away yields 40% more negative to blow up to 35mm.

35mm theatrical print with 1:185 aspect ration. The Super 16mm aspect ratio fits comfortably whereas the standard 16mm has to be cropped at the top and bottom which limits further the amount of negative that can be blown up to 35mm.

Adrian Bell
Sound Recordist

SOUND RECORDIST

Q - What is your job and when do you come onboard?

Adrian - As a sound mixer I record (mainly) dialogue and some sound effects for films. I come on board when the line producer gets his heads of department together. This is usually when the script is just about being finished, and probably between about a month or two before production.

Q - Who's normally in your crew?

Adrian - Three in total - a boom operator plus a sound maintenance engineer and myself. As you go down the scale in production size you'd end up with just the two of us, myself and a boom operator. If it's a micro budget it would just be the one sound mixer with a bag over his shoulder and winging it with a mic, documentary style.

Q - Are there disadvantages if it's just the one sound mixer?

Adrian - Yes, you don't have time to think. You can't preplan very much because you're spending your time covering what you need to cover at the time. Obviously the physical aspects of boom swinging and mixing are difficult as well as making sure recording is going down to the camera or recorder ok. You can't do running repairs by yourself as well as recording so you're just short of time. The physical side of it is quite difficult as a one man band and for drama, it is not advisable at all.

Q - On an average budget picture, what kind of equipment would you use?

Adrian - A hard drive recorder, an eight track mixer, four radio mikes, a couple of boom mics, and maybe a couple of extra mics to plant or hide on set.

Q - Are producers surprised at how much equipment you have?

Adrian - Yes, most are completely blown away with how much we have! When we roll up at the location we hear, *'Why on earth have you got a van like that for?'* They get it when you start using it all, as you get into the nitty gritty of production. I try and travel with the amount of equipment I'm going to use and some of it will be a back up. There's enough there for breakdowns with spare cables and boxes of batteries and stuff like that, but pretty much it's all there to be used.

Q - On a low budget film when you have a boom swinger as well as you, what equipment would you have then?

Adrian - I'd record onto DAT, or go straight in to the camera if it's a video format, then add a four channel mixer and carry it all over my shoulder. One boom mic and say, two or three radio mics. This is similar to how I record documentaries too.

Q - Isn't it simpler to shoot it all on radio mics?

Adrian - Not necessarily, but recording with a mulitrack recorder does offer the flexibility of recording everything separately on location, and we're getting into the habit of recording everything separately. The boom is recorded separately and all the radio mics are recorded separately and we also supply a two track mix which is used for the cutting copy for the editor. But you would not be doing that on a micro budget film as you wouldn't have the equipment or the extra crew needed available.

Q - Rather than providing too many choices in post which will mean you'll need more money, is it best on a low budget film to focus on getting two really good tracks of audio?

Adrian - Yes, definitely. One track for boom and the other for mixed radio mics. I don't think there are any hard and fast rules about using just radio mics. They do however have a certain quality to them as there's a lot of compression on them and there's sometimes distortion, but I've used them in documentaries and they work absolutely fine. The major factor of working in drama with radio mics is positioning them to stop clothing rustle. Sometimes the artist might be wearing costumes that you can't actually get a radio mic on them, they're in a bathing suit or in a very skimpy top and it's difficult to place them. But as the quality goes, it differs - you could have the same thing being done all day long and it might sound different in the morning than it does in the afternoon. It just depends on where you place them, that the batteries are good, what the location is like, if there's any other radio interference around. So I would always recommend trying to get the best sound on a boom mic, but that obviously has limitations on the shot.

Q - Do most sound recordists come with their own kit?

Adrian - Yes.

Q - What are good quality microphones?

Adrian - Condenser microphones which are powered by 48 volt phantom power. Sennheiser gun mics, schoeps gun mics. As far as recording dialogue, I use Sennheiser MKH 50's or 416's and maybe a Sennheiser MKH70 for exteriors if there is a lot of background noise. That's got a bit of colouration to it, so it's not as rounded as a 50 or 416. We also use a Shoeps CCM41 & CCM8 stereo kit for recording atmos and effects. These are my staple mics, but there are a number of other manufacturers mics to consider too. Experiment & listen!

Q - With radio mics, is there a problem with interference, mobile phones etc?

Adrian - We always have a rule printed on page one of the call sheet on all the shoots I've worked on, where we don't have phones on set. It's bound to be the one take, say a 5th take of dialogue where someone's phone goes off and if they're standing between you and the artist, it's almost certain to cause interference. And you can't clean it out. Once it's embedded in the track it's very difficult to take it out so we always try and discourage that. That interference occurs even if the phone is set to silent ring. All phones must be switched off.

Q - On low budget films would you say it's good to focus on the dialogue tracks and not worry about the extra atmos tracks?

Adrian - Yes, definitely. As far as atmos goes, editors prefer to use the two seconds between the board going on and the first line of dialogue or after action is called, as opposed to hunting around for wild track atmos'. Quite a lot we won't get time to do that anyhow as the crew is de-rigging and on to the next scene. Yes you try and get wild tracks where you can whether they're used or not. Whether they're useable is another question.

Q - If the location is too noisy, is it wise to re-record the performance for sound only in an ADR style, silent environment, directly after the take, with the actors still in the moment of the performance, but without the actors watching picture?

Adrian - Yes, if time permitting and if the artist is happy to do it, we will always try and re-record that piece because that artist has that scene in his head and is normally very happy to do multiple takes of the scene at the time. If they turn up to do it four months later in a studio, they'll be in a different frame of mind, and may have shot another four movies since, so it's much easier to do it right there and then. As soon as they've accepted the take for camera, we would just do the take, which would take a minute or a minute and a half depending on what the scene is. And as far as the logistics of the day, it takes minimal time to do that and it really covers your backside. Nine times out of ten, when you edit it, it will fit sync perfectly.

Adrian Bell

Film & TV Sound
M: +44 (0)7836 322802
E: mail@adrianbell.net

Q - Do you often find when you get to location that everybody thought about the lighting and the beauty of the shot, but nobody thought about the sound?

Sound Equipment for Low Budget Shoots

Recording device
DAT, Digital Audio Tape, is now the defacto. For low budget productions, cheap semi-pro machines are affordable to buy, never mind rent. Beware of distortion and of non professional connectors that don't deal with the rigours of film making very well. Resist the urge to use ¼" tape.

Recording device
MiniDisc isn't ideal, especially when DAT is so affordable. However, it may be used at a push, especially for weekend re-shoots where only a few lines of dialogue may be used.

Headphones
Essential to use high quality 'cans'. Enclosed earpeices mean you hear more of what is going down onto tape, although some recordists prefer the open type.

Microphones
Undeniably the most important part of the sound recordists kit. They include...

Tie Clip Mic (powered)
Can be concealed on an actor when a normal mic isn't appropriate. Radio mics are expensive and excellent, but beware of radio interference with cheaper ones.

Directional Mic (powered)
Several mics produce excellent results and a nominal hire charge will get you the best mic available. Rent. Sennheiser 416 is a good workhorse.

Large Diaphragm Mic
Ideal for recording foley sessions or close mic. singing. No use on a film set.

Omni-directional Mic (unpowered)
Cheap and cheerful and pretty much no use except in emergencies for guide tracks. Avoid.

Camera Mic
If shooting digital you may have a camera with a mic. This mic is useless for production sound but ideal for recording guide tracks for sync only.

Jammer / Baffle
Fits over the mic to protect it from wind. Usually comes with a 'furry' jacket that reduces wind noise even more. Essential.

Cables
Must be high quality and shielded. XLR cables are the professional norm and cheap semi-pro cables should be avoided and one short cable just isn't enough. Extra important if feeding sound to HD for recording.

Batteries
Batteries must be replaced regularly. You can't wait for the battery to go down as quality might be compromised. Buy in bulk before shooting.

Stock
Whatever format you record sound, make sure you have enough stock for the shoot, plus a few extras. Work on recording a one hour tape a day and always label clearly.

Connectors
Most cheap semi pro equipment will use ¼" jack plugs which are unbalanced. Pro kit will use XLR connectors which are balanced and more suited to the job. If you have both, you will need an adapter to convert between the two. Before you shoot, make sure you can connect everything up as needed.

Leather Jacket
Used to put over the camera in order to help deaden noisy cameras.

Sound Equipment for Low Budget Shoots ...cont

Telescopic Mic Boom Pole

Used by the assistant sound recordist to place the mic over the actors, getting the mic as close as possible. Must use lightweight pro kit, fishing rods and clothes poles just don't cut it.

Mixing Desk

On complicated jobs where multiple mics may be used, you may need a small portable mixing desk. This does add headaches though and isn't ideal for low budget productions.

Adrian - Every time (laughs!). Normally I'd be on the location technical recce anyway, so I would already be aware of any potential problems. Ideally, problem rooms would have been rigged with black drapes or some kind of sound baffle, but if it's a big room, we'd have drapes up in the room or we'd use polyboards on the side or we'd take baffle boards on the set. They're used to stop the reverb around the room. But generally, on most shoots, sound hasn't been thought about so that's why a recce for us is very important.

Q - Do you think that by not thinking ahead about the sound, it marginalises the sound recordist as well? Everyone can see when the camera isn't right because it's out of focus or wobbly, but when there's a sound problem, it's more objective and often the sound recordist's complaints are seen as an annoyance...?

Adrian - It depends on the director and how sound conscious they are. If they're listening to what is going on, they can hear interference or a radio mic not working properly, or they can hear why you're complaining about the soundtrack. If they're not, and quite a lot of directors don't listen to the sound but listen to the performance live, they'll subconsciously say, *I'm going to use take 4, so why do we need to go for take 5?* But actually, what they'll end up doing is using take 5 picture and using take 4 sound and treating that sound like ADR. Yes it's a compromise. It's much more obvious to see visual problems than to understand why you need to go for another take for sound.

Q - In the days of film, the camera would clatter away and that would have some impact on mic location, is there any equipment in the HD world we're in today that causes problems?

Adrian - Yeah, the cameras themselves are very noisy (laughs!) Nothing's changed, it's just a different noise. A lot of the post production houses have got used to removing a lot of camera noise with whatever tricks they use. The DigiBeta and HD cameras are notoriously noisy with fans. When we started the production I'm on now, the Panasonic monitor on set had a fan in the back of the monitor, which was being used by the cameraman to frame up and look at lighting. Fortunately you could turn the fan off. The more you get into the digital age, there are things such as playback equipment which is one bloody big hard drive whirring away, and they're looking at me like some lunatic because I don't want it on set. The director wants it 'cos he wants to watch playback, the focus puller wants it so he can check his focus on a take, so if it's off set it takes longer for people to go off and monitor stuff. The more you get into HD, the more toys and the more noise.

Q - What problems do you encounter with cast and crew?

Adrian - If you're working with a very unhelpful DP, you can have problems with lighting shadows due to boom shadows. Then you might have a situation like the shoot I'm on now, where we were asked to shoot close up and wide shots simultaneously. This meant there was no way we could get a boom in. Which for me, meant that the sound was going to be compromised because the only sync sound that would be useable would be on radio mics. So as long as everybody understands what that compromise is and it's been explained to them very clearly then I'm happy to go along with it. But I virtually get it signed on a dotted line that I cannot get a boom in anywhere and that they're happy to go with only radio mics, which also might mean a lot may have to be ADR'd. With the cast, yes, they can be very temperamental too. For instance, they might decide to not wear a radio mic until they're about to go for a take, in which case it's not possible for us to get a rehearsal in. Artists do like their mics unplugging when they come off set and it can be quite difficult depending on what they're wearing. It's always good to liaise with the costume department to find out what they're going to be wearing. Leather jackets are a pain in the bum, silk blouses are notoriously difficult. They'll still buy the costumes but we'd try and do as much as we can before we start day one.

Q - Do you think the artists don't like to have that radio mic on them all the time as they could be recorded having private conversations or even sitting on the loo?

Adrian - Yes, they probably think that, and yes of course it's possible. But I always fade off artists when they walk off set and I think most artists know that you do that. There's a non-spoken kind of trust that that kind of thing doesn't go on and most of them would accept that they have to wear radio mics for a fair amount of the time.

Q - What are sound recording levels and why should you bother with them? I mean, on my camcorder I have automatic levels...

Adrian - It's absolutely imperative to line up your equipment, especially with digital recording kit. You must make sure you have the levels lined up at the start of the day's work and at various points along it. This means you line up your recording equipment with your camera equipment and wherever it's going from thereon in, and that you clearly mark at what level you've set your line up to so everyone knows along the post production chain what it's set to. If you don't do that, you'll encounter many problems in post. For instance, you might be under-recording your own takes on location so when it ends up at the production house if they can't see a line up tone, they won't know where you've set it to. Then they'll re-set it to normal levels and end up doing all kinds of things to it. But notoriously with digital equipment there is no saving grace so it's imperative to line up.

Q - How do you deal with very dynamic performances?

Adrian - With digital kit, it's probably easier not to do so much riding of the fader. In analogue days,when using ¼" tape recorders like the Nagra, there was a lot of "riding" the faders because the signal to noise ratio was generally lower. The ideal was to get as much signal onto that tape as possible. Analogue tape is a very noisy format so when you're recording low level, to bring that dialogue up to an acceptable level in a film you'd be bringing up the noise level too. In a digital format, you do that to an extent but you do not have quite as much noise associated with it, so you can afford not to ride the faders as much. My priority as far as dynamic range is, to not over record, so I would always under record than try and get more volume out of a quiet spoken artist. Yes, there are limiters on the camera and on the mixer, but you try not to use them.

Q - Would you ever record the same performance on two channels, one recorded much lower than the other?

Adrian - If I had time to do that, it would be fantastic, but I generally don't. In fact in some instances, if it's on a radio mic or if it's on two booms, they might take the performance of the artist from the other mic that's not directly on them.

Q - Most people think of the mic being on a boom over the actors, and obviously on radio mics hidden in clothing, are there other places where you place mics?

Adrian - Yes, lots. We can put microphones anywhere. We have mics specifically that we use for planting around the set. It might be in a flower vase, in the visor of a car, or strapped to a gear-stick in the car, or behind the ear. Sometimes we go into theatre mode where you put mics in the hairline rather than on their body. So yes, sometimes we put mics just out of shot on stands or on the floor. It could be anywhere really.

Q - How do artists respond to radio mics strapped to their ear?

Adrian - A lot of them have done theatre before. They may not have seen it in film, but generally they're ok with it. Again there's a lot of liaising between costume and makeup and if they have hairpieces it's a lot easier obviously.

Q - How important is the clapperboard to the sound recordist?

Adrian - I think even in the digital / time code age, the clapperboard is the single most important piece of equipment on set today. Not only is it the easiest method of syncing sound and picture rushes, even with automatic time code synching - I'm told by post production houses that the clapperboard is still by far the easiest way to sync rushes, but it's also fundamental to on set discipline. It's a mark that makes the crew quiet, and the actors know instinctively when they're on.

Q - You mentioned time code. What is time code and why do you use it?

The Slate/ Clapperboard

GUERILLA FILM MAKER SAYS!

Slates mark the beginning of each filmed take and allow the editor to synchronize the sound track with the picture. The slate displays the scene number, take number, director's name, DP's name, name of production company and name of film. Each shot is given a slate number, and each slate can have any number of takes. Scene numbers are NOT used on the slate. When shooting a take, the clapper loader reads aloud the slate number, then the take number, before clapping down the hinged part of the slate at the beginning of each take - 'the clap', making sure that the slate is in frame. If using the traditional clapperboard, numbers can be written on camera tape and stuck to the back of the slate which can be used quickly when needed.Remember to give as much pre roll as possible before each slate (7 seconds is the minimum) and to number sound rolls consecutively.

'Timecode Slate ' or 'Digislate'

This is when a timecode generator feeds code to the sound recording device (usually a DAT machine) as well as feeding an identical code to the time code slate (which is connected to the sound recording device). The time code slate has an LED screen comprised of hours, minutes, seconds and frames. When the slate is clapped, the time code at that instant is held for a few frames on the display. This time code is usually read visually in the telecine and entered into the computer. The system then locates the same time code number in the audio and the shot is then 'in sync'.

A 'Smart Slate' has it's own built in timecode generator and is better because there's no need for a connection between the slate and the DAT recorder. A 'Dumb Slate' is an older method that has no internal time code generator so it receives its time code from another machine, most likely the sound recording device (the DAT) via a cable or preferably through a wireless transmitter. Make sure that the time code numbers are easy to read, particularly in bright sunlight. Always record the 'clap' just in case there's a problem with the timecode.

The Smart Slate has 5 running modes for generating time code.

1. Free Run/Time of Day: here the internal time code generator works like a clock with the actual time of day. It runs continuously whether the audio is recording or not.

2. Free Run/User Set: here the user chooses the starting time for the time code generator and it doesn't correlate to the time of day. The hour digits are used to signify sound roll number.

3. Record Run: this is when the generator stops when the audio recorder does i.e numbers work like a tape counter and pauses during pause or stop. Again the hour digits are used to signify sound roll number.

4. External Mode: a continuous time code from an external source that's being regenerated onto the tape.

5. Jam Sync: the recorder synchronises its internal time code generator to match the starting numbers from an external source. When the external is triggered the internal time code will keep in step with it. Always Jam Sync every few hours to make sure sync isn't drifting.

In-camera Time Code

When filming with time code capable cameras, the camera and the audio recorder record the identical time code. This enables the telecine machines during telecine to read the time code and automatically sync it to the audio code.

Head Slate

Slates that are done as normal, at the beginning of each shot.

Tail Slate

This is a slate done at the end of the shot, which may be used when you need to be less disruptive with actors etc. Traditional clapperboards are done upside down to indicate a tail slate. The assistant also yells out 'tail slate' when marking the slate.

M.O.S. Slate

(originated when a German director in Hollywood asked for the shot 'mit out sound' and the camera assistant wrote M.O.S. on the slate). When recording without sound, write M.O.S. on the slate and do NOT raise the hinged bar.

Voice Slate/Voice I.D

At the beginning of each tape, the sound recordist or assistant will record the necessary technical information such as the roll number, the title of the film, the production company, the director's name and any other useful information.

The Tone

After having recorded the voice I.D., the sound recordist will record 30 seconds of tone (minus 8db for analogue / minus 18db for DAT) from the built-in tone generator of their audio recorder or mixer. This tone is used to calibrate the level of the playback machine in the transfer process. Every recording MUST be slated whether sync sound or not. Ie. such as 'spot effect for scene 25, car idling, take one' or 'wild track for scene 12'.

Assuming you shoot 25fps / 25P, you can use 25fps timecode, which makes life a lot easier for everyone!

PRODUCTION

Getting Good Sound

GUERILLA FILM MAKER SAYS!

It has been said that sound can be up to 80% of the movie going experience, so it should not be neglected. Unfortunately, many inexperienced filmmakers forget to properly budget or prepare for recording sound, stating that they will 'fix it in post'. Thinking this way usually means many £thousands in post-production time, versus a moment of cast and crew time on set.

1. Hire the best sound recordist you can. Inexperienced sound recordists may be paranoid and request further takes when they are not needed, or not know how to fix problems.

2. Everyone is a perfectionist. Learn to recognise when the sound is good enough.

3. When looking for locations, bear the sound in mind. Traffic and planes are usually the biggest culprits, as are air conditioning units. Most natural sounds can be covered up and disguised in post-production.

4. Blimps and barneys are good at filtering out most camera noise, but they will not get rid of everything.

5. Always get at least 30 seconds of room tone at each location so your dub mixer can lay down a decent ambient track.

6. Post sync dialogue (looping / ADR) is a pain and expensive. Try to avoid it by either getting it right during the take or wild without the camera rolling, so it can be dropped in during post.

7. If you cannot use a boom mic due to space constraints, try using lavaliere mics hidden within the set (like a flowerpot or table lamp).

8. If you can afford it, try using more than one boom mic to record the sound so that you are completely covered. Also, get as many wireless lavaliere mics as possible for your actors.

Adrian - Time code is a reference signal of 25 frames per second or 24 frames per second depending on whether you're shooting for film or TV. If shooting at 25fps, each second is split into 25 frames, and for each frame of picture and on every one of those frames there is a timecode reference, which means for each frame for sound and picture they can be locked together using that timecode reference.

Q - If you are shooting HD, you have an audio track on the camera, so why not just put the audio onto that audio track?

Adrian - We do that as well. Whether it is DigiBeta or HD, we always put the sound down on the two tracks of the camera-recording format. That for me is a backup, which I know is going down on the tape. In post-production, that also gives an easy way to get sound into the Avid.

Q - What is an SQN and how often do you use it?

Adrian - There are three or four manufacturers of four channel, battery operated location mixers. They are used for more portable situations. So if we have a lot of location moves or if we are in cramped conditions, say in a car, where we can't get our normal rig in, we would use a small SQN mixer. An advantage of using an SQN is that I can go straight into my hard drive recorder. The one that I used also had a good range of inputs and outputs on it, so if I want to send a feed to director, or if I want to send power to certain microphones, I can do that. It is a really good workhorse tool.

Q - If I were making a low budget feature, would it be a wise post-production move to ditch DAT, or use it as a backup and just go straight from the SQN to the HD tape as long as everything is lined up?

Adrian - Yes. In fact that is probably the way I would do it. The lining up of your recording mixer to the camera line up is fundamental because you need to know what the camera is receiving. You do get a 'confidence feed' off the monitoring back of the camera (so you can listen to what is recording on the camera), which is a secondary check. But fundamentally you need to check the meters and make sure they never get changed by the camera team.

Q - What is overlapping?

Adrian - It is when you do takes of a scene with two or more actors and they are talking over each other. In a quickly spoken scene, they do tend to overlap each other. So you may be trying to splice these two pieces of sound together where they are overlapping each other's dialogue. That becomes very difficult to cut because where you want character A's dialogue clean, and character B is speaking over it.

Q - As the sound recordist, do you do any of the sound editing, sound mixing or collecting sound effects from libraries?

Adrian - No. What I do is that I look at the script before production and look for suggestions on how the film is going to be played out - what else is necessary to bring that soundtrack to life. Depending on the budget, if there is a post-production supervisor or sound designer, then we talk to them about what they might need.

Q - Anything else that we haven't covered?

Adrian - When you are looking at the various budgets of filmmaking it is very easy to put the headphones on and look at something that has been shot on a small format or a cheap format with cheap equipment and it sounds fantastic. And remember, you're looking at it with your headphones on and watching a nine inch monitor. But what you must bear in mind is your final delivery. Where are most people going to see this? If it is going to be on TV, then you need to make sure that the quality is going to be acceptable on TV. If it is going to be in the cinema, then you really have to be on your toes about the quality of the background as far as sound goes. If the director wants to use your dialogue in the cinema, I have to be very careful about what gets recorded and I have a much stricter on set discipline as far as background noise and crew chatter, sirens, dogs barking, etc. than I would on TV. I know what I can get away with on TV. And certainly the time constraints of TV are much tighter.

Q - Do you think it is fair to say that when most filmmakers start out they are obsessed with the image and oblivious to sound?

Adrian - I think it is very easy for a director to do that because they are so involved in the script and how they 'see it' in their head before shooting.

Q - What advice would you give to a new sound recordist?

Adrian - Try and visit as many film sets as possible. Try to talk to some sound recordists and see what is involved; what equipment is being used. See what you might want to use and get some experience on that. Use some favours and try to get a hold of that equipment and test it before you start shooting.

Q - Is it a good idea to apprentice yourself to a sound recordist for a while?

Adrian - I think that is a good idea and I encourage that. I don't think there are many other ways to learn the industry as there is very little formal training now.

Q - What technology causes the most failures and problems?

Adrian - Headphones. It might be radio mics as well. But headphones on a day to day basis.

Q - How can filmmakers make your life easier?

Adrian - Get me on board earlier. Get me a script earlier. Show me the locations earlier. Get the main crew members together so we can get to know each other earlier.

Q - What common mistakes do you see?

Adrian - Actors pulling wires out of their radio mics. They don't know how to unplug it so the cable just gets ripped out.

Q - What advice would you offer a new filmmaker?

Adrian - Watch more films. And be absolutely passionate about what you do.

PRODUCTION

Linda Haysman
Costume Designer

COSTUME DESIGN

Q - What is your job?

Linda - I'm a Costume Designer, which means I'm responsible for everything that visually goes on the actor's backs! Ensuring everything that somebody wears will clearly depict the character the actor is playing.

Q - So your job is to put them in clothes that are appropriate to the story, to help them be the character? At what point do you normally get involved?

Linda - Quite early on. Probably one of the first members of the design team - costume, make-up, set design - is the set designer, because it takes longer to prep sets than it does say costume or make-up. According to how much budget they have, and what the actual time involved is, and whether it's a modern or a period show, the costume designer is brought in anywhere from three weeks to many months in advance. Most of the time you are on board before actors are cast, sometimes you are not. Basically you should in place, having read your script, and broken it down, and knowing what your game plan is as far in advance as is needed. You will have your own ideas, have incorporated the Director and Producer's ideas, then when you ring the actors you get their input.

Q - How much prep time would you need, if it were a simple contemporary show, with just a few characters?

Linda - I think about three weeks are comfortable. Things can get hairy even when you have enough prep time but you don't get your cast confirmations, which means you can't contact your actors, you can't get measurements and you can't start really.

Q - So you can't get everybody sorted out until they are in place?

Linda - You do get going, yes, because you can go and do research and find out what is in the shops. You would go and find out what the look of things are, and prices of things. There is always stuff you can do even before you get names. But you cannot fit costumes until actors are cast. And of course they may have an input on how they think they should look too, which when time is short, could complicate matters.

Q - What are the departments you work closely with?

Linda - With make-up and set design, mostly make-up. When you are shooting, the AD department too, for sheer logistics. They are the ones that you are in contact with as to knowing where your actors are and bringing them to the set.

Q - What do you need with regard to the screenplay? I mean they give you a script, what happens to / from that script from your department's point of view, what do you do to the script?

Linda - You are reading the script first for the story, but at the same time you are reading it for anything that gives you a visual description of an actor. An actor's characterisation, it's not just the fact that Johnny's in a red shirt for this scene, it's the fact that Meg comes on as a prostitute, or a single mum, or Mrs. Roth from next door has been a farmer's widow for X amount of years. Whatever it might be, you look at the characterisations, and you are also reading it for content, of anything that effects costume. For example, if there is a fight scene, if somebody gets thrown into the river, immediately there are going to be doubles, or if somebody goes through a window, there is going to be blood and doubles or triples of their costume.

If you've got a stunt man, you will need to match the character's to the stunt performer who may be a different size. If there are uniforms, you will be noting the number of police, ambulance men, if it's a modern story etc. I would go through the script with a highlight pen and mark everything I thought relevant.

Q - How does it work when you've got your cast list, and you are having fittings?

Linda - The first thing you would do is ring your actors and find out what their measurements are accurately from them. By the time you reach a fitting, you have looked out a number of costumes pertaining to their characters for each scene. So you have a whole rail of costumes which you have prepared including shoes, and hats and coats etc. During the fitting between yourself and the actor, you would decide on the things you both think work for this character, and the things that obviously fit. It's about moulding a character from the clothes chosen, so that the audience can read immediately where the character is at, and who they are. That's consistent all the way through the show. So even though a person changes clothes; suddenly they go from a Goth to someone who is really neat and middle-class with a nice house in Surrey. They have got to be believable all the way through, they are still that character. So you are finding clothes that will actually work day by day, scene by scene. You are seeing whether you can get away with singles, doubles or whatever is necessary according to the action that happens. You might find a fantastic characterful jacket in the market, but you need to double it - so now you've got a problem. The actor or director might love it but you may need more than one, because of something that happens to the character in the story. You've got to then decide do you let go of this lovely piece or do you try and make doubles, or do you go for something very similar that, you can buy off the shelf so you can buy as many as you like?

Q - On the surface it sounds like a really good idea to just go to Oxfam and see what they've got, what problems come with that?

Linda - The problem with that really is time. Again you can find some great stuff in 2nd hand shops, but you have a budget to manage. When you shop, you inevitably always go to shops where you can take clothes back if they don't work, or if the actor doesn't like them, or they don't fit. If you go to Oxfam and you buy a load of stuff, if it doesn't work or it doesn't fit, you are stuck with it. You could put it on extras if you like, but it ties up your budget every time. Also trying to find the right thing in Oxfam, from shop to shop to shop, is like a needle in a haystack and it's time consuming.

Q - Why don't you get actors to just wear their own clothes?

Linda - That is possible, and does happen on shows, but it's best if you actually provide a costume as then you have control of the costume, and at the end of the day, it goes back on their rail and you have it safely. It is not at home, where they can forget it for the next day's shoot. Or if you are on set and they are wearing their own clothes, the Director decides suddenly let's break it down a bit more, he starts asking you to spray it or slash it, and it's their own costume, they are going to be a lot more bothered than if it were just a costume obviously! So it's not always a good idea, unless you are on a really low budget.

Q - Where do you get your costumes generally, I'm not talking about the uniforms, but just general costumes?

Linda - If it's a modern day show, you mostly buy. So you do your research, you go to the shops, and according to your character, to their income bracket, you know whether a character is going to be going to Littlewoods or going to Harrods so you would tailor your costume selection according to that. You can go shopping and take your actor with you, because then that means you have the say then and there, and you fit them, everyone agrees and everyone is happy. You can also hire items, even modern items which is very useful. For example if you have got a scene that is like Ascot or a very expensive party, you don't want to go and spend £400 on a single item for just one scene, where as you can hire it and spend under £100, and it is going to look fantastic, including jewellery, and it goes back afterwards and that's that.

Linda Haysman

Costume Designer
e-mail   linda@capstone.plus.com

PRODUCTION

Q - Is that the same for Ambulance and Police uniforms etc?

Linda - Yes, you would always hire, because the hire companies are the most accurate, and also companies have got a lot tighter now. You can no longer hire London Transport costumes through costumiers, it has to go through London Transport. Security is tighter now and you can understand why, because if there is any security threat and people can get hold of station staff costumes, LT has to know if staff are genuine. They have had to clamp down.

Q - What kind of space do you need to work in?

Linda - It depends on what you have got, and what you need. Obviously some kind of office, you need a desk and a phone, and in your preparation you need a space where you can line up rails that can be moved around. You need a fitting room where you can dress actors comfortably. You also need washing facilities, which often happens on a filming van, which is specifically designed for costume, or make-up, sometimes a combination vehicle. They vary in size according to the kind of show you have got, and how many rails you need.

Q - What equipment do you need?

Linda - Mostly when you are filming, you obviously need stuff that is going to be quite portable, that you have access to when you are on set, and there is also a base box of things that you actually have on the caravan, or on the filming truck. You have everything to do with haberdashery, all sorts of sewing materials, and anything that can mend costumes should they break. You've got hangers, an iron and an ironing board, washing machines and facilities, laundry facilities. Pens, markers, all office equipment, sellotape, various odds and sods.

Q - What kind of hours do you do, compared to other crew members?

Linda - Long hours. It depends on the shoot, but typically you'd be there two hours before shooting and possibly an hour after wrap, and that could be a modern show. It depends on the cast and if you have got big days with lots of extras – sometimes you can be in really early. If you are doing a period show, you could be up and in your caravan, getting things ready from 5am to shoot at 9am. At the end of the day you have to ensure that the costumes that are required for the next day are lined up, and accurately prepped, so that they are clean, ready and labeled. Everyone has got their costume, accurate jewellery, everything that is correct for continuity. Then you have got to do laundry, ironing and be ready to go for the next morning.

Q - Do you have an assistant?

Linda - Yes. Unless it is a tiny show, you would always need help. The thing about having a assistant is that in prep, it is somebody else that can make phone calls for you, someone who can organise, who can run around getting fabric samples, doing research. An assistant is also very good when it comes to extras, because you can't be expected to see to the main cast and work with

Story Days

GUERILLA FILM MAKER SAYS!

Story Days are the number of days that your script (film) encompasses on screen. For instance, it could be 1 Story Day as in Training Day, 7 Story Days as in Seven Days and Seven Nights, or 9 Story Days spanning a 25 year period (the story takes place over 25 years but we the story tellers, visit the lives of the characters on 9 specific days in that 25 year period). A story day is indicated by an obvious change of time in the storyline, or by literally moving on to the next day. Your department heads need to know the story days, but in particular, costume and make up. It's essential that your Story Days are calculated when breaking down the script for scheduling as, with most shoots, you will be shooting out of sequence. Therefore, if in an action movie there's a big fight scene halfway in the film, which results in your lead actor having a noticeable scar for the rest of the movie, it's important that you don't forget the scar in the latter scenes. In this case, the Story Day (that will now be on breakdown sheets and continuity sheets) will notify your make up department to what condition your lead actor is in, so that mistakes are avoided. On a low budget movie, it's advisable to minimise your story days, so that your actors are not spending time changing costumes and wasting valuable shooting time.

Costume

They say clothes make the man (or woman), and in filmmaking that is especially true. Your costumes need to look natural and seamless for the world that you create, as audiences are sensitive to this. Inadequate or inappropriate costuming will make an audience turn on you, even if they cannot pinpoint why things look off. The best way to avoid this is to have trained pros handling wardrobe.

1. If working on a low budget, most likely you'll be working with actor's own clothes. If this is the case, make sure the costume department keeps hold of the various costumes for the duration of the shoot.

2. On a low budget shoot, directors may lose sight of the costume and may only comment on it when it's entirely inappropriate. Have second set of creative eyes on it.

3. Consider making or buying seconds and thirds of the same costumes in case the originals are damaged either in the filming process (get wet, fake blood splattering on them, ripped in a stunt) or the cleaning process (shrinking in the dryer, bleached).

4. Oxfam and charity shops are fantastic places to find cheap wardrobe - especially if you need something period or really worn looking.

5. Be careful with your use of colour. Flamboyant wardrobe looks great for something out of a Baz Luhrman flick, but may be inappropriate for a social drama.

6. On the flipside, big, bright and flamboyant costumes can look bold and exciting, thus adding to production value. It works for Pedro Almodóvar!

7. When doing nude scenes, offer the actor the possibility of wearing a flesh body wear costume. If they don't mind stripping off, have someone from the costume department waiting in the wings ready with a robe.

8. The costume department sees actors long before most everyone each day, and they can judge their mood. Always talk to your costumiers to see if there are any potential problems on the horizon that you can deal with early. Likewise, make sure your actors trust your costume department.

9. The Costume Department is usually the first of the general crew to arrive in the morning and the last to leave at night as they can only go after they've washed, dried and ironed clothes so that they're ready for the next day. Be nice to them.

10. Keep your eye on the weather forecast. Have thermal underwear and blankets ready for your actors if it is cold, umbrellas and towels should it be raining and cool spray if it is warm.

11. Keep your actors safety in mind. Fly spray and suntan lotion can save you a lot of headaches later.

12. Try not to rush costume changes as actors want to feel right in the new 'skin' they are putting on.

13. Make sure actors have a space to change that is more than a toilet.

14. Continuity can be a big problem with costume as actors may make small, improvised modifications, such as loosening a tie. That will need to be corrected when doing the next take. Use digital cameras and make notes to keep track of all the changes.

15. Make sure your actors do not take any of their costumes away with them. This will end up costing when the rental house charges you for missing items. Likewise, make sure your actors don't mishandle the clothes during changing (such as rolling them up into a ball and tossing them in the corner of the dressing room) as damaged items will also be billed to your account.

16. Minimise costumes. As long as they are appropriate, they wont add too much to your film, and unnecessary clothing changes adds to the budget and eats shooting time.

17. Not all actors have the character in mind. Some will just want to look good, which may not be right for the character. Be aware.

PRODUCTION

extras as well. Even if it is 5 extras on the day or 100, you need help doing that. You need somebody that has got a good eye, has experience in costume and an interest in costume as well, so they are able to match and compliment your vision, they have got to tune in to what you are doing.

Q - What kind of paperwork do you generate?

Linda - Quite a lot. You are making lists, writing down what you require, notes about characters, what the Director has said, you are writing down scheduled times when your fittings are going to be arranged. Then you have got notes to people like the costumiers, who are the people that you hire from. You have got notes to costume makers, about what you want made etc. That is all in prep, you are constantly making notes about research, trying to keep files on what you are trying to hire from this place and that place. It is quite a lot of paperwork. When you hire costumes in, you have a whole inventory about what you have hired, everything from jewellery to shoes, every piece, every single item should be on a sheet somewhere. That has got to be checked in, and checked out when you are at the end of the film, so you can make sure everything is there, to avoid incurring a charge if you have got missing items. By the time you start to shoot, you will have prepared a continuity book, which is an accurate record of what every actor is wearing for every scene, on every story day. So at any one time, you have a good cross reference to what an actor has worn and on which day, therefore when you are lining up, you actually see that 3 weeks ago, we shot this scene when so and so was in the pub, and now they are coming out of the pub, and now they are walking over the green and are going to be hit by a car, you have to make sure you have the same costume. A continuity book is a very important thing, it has got to be worked out and labeled up, it has got to be prepped before you actually start shooting, so you know accurately where you have put your pictures and where you have written your notes.

Q - So you take continuity photographs aside from the continuity department?

Linda - Costume and make-up do their own continuity. It is specifically geared towards their needs, as opposed to what the continuity person would do.

Q - Talk me through a typical day on a simple drama.

Linda - I would get myself to location and meet my team at the costume caravan - so you meet your assistant and wardrobe assistants, or your dressers. You would know what time your actors are coming in, you get there in good time to make sure that everything is ready. Remember, you've lined up the day before, so all the costumes should in theory be lined up on rails and ready. Your wardrobe assistants take the costumes to the separate dressing rooms on location, or they might be in the studio, to where the actors are going to get dressed.

You are there to make sure that each costume is in their room in good time before the actors arrive. You then have got to tie in breakfast with that, sometimes you are working so hard that you don't even get breakfast, that is where the AD's come in, they might get you a bacon roll if you are lucky! You would ensure that everybody is happy, you would go to the artist, check they are there, they are happy and everything fits, and that they don't want a change of anything. If they didn't like that jacket, could they have another one? Then you would go onto set, checking your continuity photos and notes to make sure everything is correct. You also take weather stuff - for example you might have wet weather cover items, umbrellas, rain-macs, and if it is cold, you would have blankets, hot water bottles, hand warmers, whatever is necessary.

You would ensure the smooth running of the show on set. Someone is always watching the filming, be it yourself or your assistant, ensuring that every person in front of the camera looks correct before the camera turns over. You are watching the rehearsals to see how things happen, how costumes move, especially if there is anything like a fight scene. Seeing what the actors do, an actor might take the costume off, or put a costume on in a scene. So you are watching how that goes. You are as concentrated and as involved as any other member of the crew, behind camera watching what goes on. If it is a busy show, the designer doesn't always get to be there, or is unable to be there, because you are still prepping other costumes or characters not yet confirmed! Your day may start by making sure everyone is happy, everyone is in the right costume, everything should run smoothly and then off you go shopping, meeting other actors and doing fittings, always checking with the shoot to make sure if it is OK.

Q - Do you think it is fair to say, if you left an actor to do their own costume design, they would just turn up looking as good as they possibly could?

Linda - It depends on the actor, because most actors, especially experienced ones, are marvellous to work with, because they are very happy and pleased to get things right, and they really will want to do that. They are not that interested in looking good as it were, they are interested in getting the character right, and if that means wearing an old grey mac, or something really unflattering, they will be prepared to do that, and that is fantastic, because that is when such synergy brings the best to the screen. Some actors however, will want to look good, and even though they want to look right, they will have other agendas going on. It's like being pushed by a cross-wind, it always pushes you into a direction where they actually look best, as in the back of their minds they are worried about what they look like as opposed to who they are in front of the camera.

Q - What kind of costumes do you hire out?

Tim - *We hire out any costume and any uniform from the beginning of time through to contemporary. We have production facilities within the company so we can make up any outfits - whatever needs making, we can get made. We have over a million costumes in stock.*

Q - In terms of budgeting, is there a great price difference between a very basic costume and something that is extremely elaborate and extravagant?

Tim - *No, with films you tend to have a set price per costume that's dependent on the number of weeks and number of costumes hired. We'll always start with a book price, and then we'll discuss it with the producer or the accountant. When we're making up a costume, the prices can vary - if it's a simple outfit it will be a lower price and if it's a complex outfit it will be a much higher price. It depends on how much handwork, what sort of fabric and how much time is involved.*

Q - How do you usually hire out, is it a daily rate, a monthly rate, a weekly rate or by the production?

Tim - *For a film, it basically works out by the number of weeks and the daily rate wouldn't apply. Unless of course, a costume is only needed for a day or two.*

Q - Who usually comes to you first?

Tim - *Initially, a designer will come with a production, sometimes the producer but at the end of the day we always deal with the producer when it comes down to the money as they are paying the designer.*

Q - If a producer comes to you with a low-budget period drama and assuming nothing needs making up, would you be able to offer a good deal?

Tim - *Yes, we'll always do a deal. We view each project as it comes along. One does negotiate prices and there are times when one does low-budget films. What a producer should do is ring up when they are budgeting, ask us for an estimate and work backwards from there.*

Q - What are your terms for hire?

Tim - *Normally we like to get 100% before the production shoots, in other cases, it might be staggered payments that tie in with deliveries we've got. It really depends, but there is always an upfront payment.*

Q - What's your policy for insurance?

Tim Angel
Angels the Costumiers

Tim - *That's the responsibility of the production company and they have to insure the goods to the value that we specify.*

Q - What are the common mistakes made by new film makers?

Tim - *I think the first thing they do is think that a place like this is too expensive for them to afford, so they try and find all different ways of doing it. The easiest way to deal with that is to ask the question at the beginning, come and see us. We might say no, but we might say yes. Even if you've got no money you should at least try and follow the path that the people with money have rather than try and cut the corners.*

For a low-budget contemporary film, they'll probably employ somebody who'll think 'Oh, I can't afford to hire anything' and they end up in Oxfam, charging around everywhere - and if they're first time people, that takes away a lot of their creativity. As a producer you're getting bills from Oxfam, Marks & Sparks, wherever, whereas if somebody actually asked the question the worst thing that could happen is we say 'No, you can't have all that', or 'we'll cut some of the crowd number'. There's usually a way.

Q - So your advice would be, regardless of the budget, come in here with a wish list if only to have 'no' said to you?

Tim - *Yes, if you can get the best, why go for second best. There are problems for us though as we don't have unlimited resources. If we are inundated with requests for Victorian gowns and a low-budget producer comes to us wanting Victorian gowns, we're less likely to do a competitive, low-budget deal. Also, there is a cost to simply organise and put clothes together and therefore there is a point when it just becomes uneconomical for us to do a production.*

Q - Do you have any tips for low-budget producers?

Tim - *Come and discuss things at the beginning as it makes everything much easier.*

Costume Design Books

**Costume Design 101
by Richard La Motte**
A well-written 'how to' for someone wanting to know more about what it takes to make the costumes in a movie come together.

The Costume Designers Handbook: A Complete Guide for Amateur and Professional Costume Designers by Liz Covey & Rosemary Ingham
The bible of theatrical costumers, this book follows the process from script to production, also containing a chapter on the profession.

Costume Design: Techniques of Modern Masters by Lynn Pecktal and Tony Walton
A combination of great interviews conducted with 18 leading contemporary costume designers, explaining how to go from sketch to costume, with stunning illustrations of the finished products.

Q - How reasonable do you think new, and inexperienced film makers are when it comes to the time it takes for make-up and costume changes?

Linda - It is a learning curve. If there is any way of scheduling to avoid costume changes then great, I would do that, but it isn't always possible. Sometimes we can see things in the schedule and may make suggestions to help. However, changes are often unavoidable due to other facts such as location or actor availability, so you are going to have to lose time somewhere, whether it is moving the camera, or redressing the set, or sending an actor back to a caravan, or doing a quick change in the next room on set. Remember, no-one will take longer than they need to.

Q - On low budget films, is if often that people forget things like, you can't just ask your lead actor to drop his trousers in the middle of the street?!

Linda - Yes, you have got to have a respect for actors and for what they are doing. So therefore, you have got to understand some that people are used to roughing it, to a certain extent, but beyond that there is going to be a degree of creature comfort that everybody deserves. So yes, dropping the trousers in the middle of the street isn't the best thing to do. Some would be game, and others wouldn't, and you can understand why. Think ahead, towels if they are going to get wet, umbrellas for rain, hot water bottles for when they are cold, standing by off shot with a warm jacket if they are exposed to the elements.

Q - On a more general, philosophical note, tell me what you think costume design ought to be. On an obvious note, it is literally about putting people in clothes, on a deeper level, how can your department augment the story-telling?

Linda - I think it is extremely important and it's not often recognised just how important both costume and hair and makeup are. If you think about it, we all read each other visually very quickly. We give off visual signals all the time before any audible signal. So for example, if you are on the train, you can make a judgement about the kind of person opposite you, who they are, where they are coming from, what their social and economic status is, what their education might be, even their taste in music - and how do you tell that? Mostly from what they are wearing, and how they wear their hair. These are signals that we give off to each other all the time, very effectively. It is this subtle form of signal giving when we are telling a story. We are trying to put before them a character that feels right. You can do so much with clothing that actually helps that actor along, and tells their story. It tells the audience who this person is, before they have even opened their mouth.

Q - What can young film makers do to make your life easier?

Linda - First of all, appreciate the importance of costume design and of how an actor looks. Don't think of costume and makeup as a subsidiary department, that is, at worst a necessary evil and at best a thing that they can think about later. They can understand that it is very important, and very visual. What comes along with that is a level of respect for the department.

Another misconception is that clothes grow on trees! They don't. Things need to be sourced, sorted out, hired and bought, and that takes time, money and effort. If you suddenly write a scene and you think, well we need some really expensive costumes here, but we can only afford very little, can we do it, well no, I can't! The other thing to realise is that you can't make a silk purse out of a sow's ear. If you don't allow the money and time that is required for what it is that you want, then you are going to get a poor result, and that is not the designers fault. If you have a very low budget, consider this impact on costume at the script stage.

Q - What kind of mistakes do you see?

Linda - Sometimes with costume, people don't often get the colours right. It is amazing how blind people can be to colours, in that they will put the wrong colours on people. Sometimes you see a character who is wearing something fashionable, and might be right for the part, but it doesn't suit them. I think what is important is to get something that is right for the character, but if you can be clever enough to make sure it actually brings the best out of the actor or actress, then you are laughing. A lot of ways in which people go wrong, especially with a character who is fashionable, is that they will put them in the latest fashion, but it looks awful on them because their figure isn't flattered by what they are wearing. It might be a ra-ra skirt, but if they have not got the figure for it, then don't put your actress in it. Unless of course you want to make a statement about that, then you would do it in a very bold way. Take into consideration that not everything you put them in is going to work for them, as a person, even if it is the current fashion.

Q - What advice would you offer a new film maker?

Linda - We are on your side. We are not there to be used as a kind of subsidiary thing, we are not there as a necessary evil, so if you consider us as such, then you are on a loser from the start. Recognise that every member of your crew is a member of your team and you are the team leader. They have all got something very valuable to contribute to the making of your film. So if you belittle their involvement, or belittle their input then you are impoverishing your whole accomplishment. If you have a good attitude when you start, crews will go with you through the rest of your career, and you will always be respected, even if you don't agree with them, you will always share respect with every member of your crew, a runner, a dresser, they are all very important no matter what job they do. Don't get annoyed with say somebody in the Costume Department, if they are going in to check something before a take. As long as they are being subtle and sensible about it, and not annoying any of the actors or getting in the way of the lighting or whatever, as long as they do it appropriately, then allow them to do their job, they are doing what they need to do, and in the end – enriching your film.

PRODUCTION

Sharon Holloway
Make-Up Designer

MAKE-UP DESIGNER

Q - What is your job?

Sharon - I am a make-up designer for film. I also do make-up prosthetics and special effects.

Q - What is make-up, why do it, why bother?

Sharon - My priority is always the actors, because this is about adding to their character, and anything that assists that actor to play that character convincingly is important. It doesn't necessarily mean theatrical make-up, but if the make-up and hair is right for the character, and it helps that actor give a better performance, then I've done my job properly. The second aspect is added production value. Again, if it is right for the film and for the characters, then it will only add to the overall production value.

Q - It is not just about making people beautiful?

Sharon - No. Quite often it is the opposite, because you can have very attractive actors, who are playing parts against type, and so again, everything that you do that assists that, the way they look and the way they feel about their character is the skill of the job really.

Q - How do you get jobs?

Sharon - I started out trailing Internet sites like *Shooting People, Mandy,* and *Talent Circle,* picking up as much unpaid work as possible, and through that you make more and more contacts. A certain amount of my work is still through the Internet sites and resources, but, most of it is now through connections I have made, when those people I originally worked with on small scale stuff, have also moved on and then it becomes word of mouth.

Q - What are the departments that you work with, that you liaise with, when you're making a film? How early on should you be brought in?

Sharon - It depends on the scale of the film, so I would expect for a feature of a reasonable budget, at least two weeks, because I work so closely with the costume designer. Their research, fittings, buying and sourcing of costumes will have happened partly before I start my work, but there is an overlap. If there are specialised things to do, in terms of prosthetics, or wig-fitting, or all those other things which take time, then obviously the longer the better. For a 4 or 5 week shoot, it would be unreasonable to expect a make-up designer to do all of what is necessary in a few days. The whole process starts with the script, breaking it down, and then when you know who has been cast for each character, you can plan, even before you go out and buy a single make-up product.

I also work with the production department, in terms of scheduling, because that may have an impact on make-up, how many artists are going to be needed on a particular day etc., because when there are big scenes we tend to pull in extra help. But most of my work, in getting ready for a film is done with the costume department. As I said before, when developing that character visually, everything has sort of got to work together and fit together, and both myself and costume designer have seen work on screen where the two departments clearly haven't been working in harmony.

Q - So in an ideal world, there is a synergy between make-up and costume, but also in the broader sense of design, to give a consistency and a reality to whatever the story is?

Sharon - Yes, and if there is a strong visual that is being designed by the production designer and the art department, then that is something you also want to work in harmony with. It is about getting down to the nuts and bolts of creating characters, and creating a world on screen for them to inhabit.

Q - Do you have any tips on maximising your effectiveness or problems to avoid?

Sharon - If you are shooting out of sequence, then you can be toing and frowing unnecessarily, but unfortunately, that is the way films are made. The continuity issues of different script days, with make-up and hair, is a necessary beast to consider. For an example, if someone has got a scar or tattoo, sometimes it can just be confined to a scene and it's a one-off. By talking to costume and the director, for the remainder of the film the actor could be wearing clothes that obscure it, which means there is only one day that something like that is going to be needed. There may be things that can be cheated with the way that a shot is going to be done, so it's important, either for me to see storyboards or to talk through certain tricky scenes with the director, so that we can minimise the time that is needed to get the effect. An example is where somebody is having their hair cut, it might be cheated in the actual shot, or maybe the actor seen is just cut out, and you have got a *'before and after'* which is easier to deal with, because all these things take time. So, as you say, this is all an illusion, and there are many ways of cheating things, and that has to be considered, because it is not always time well spent. Anything can be done, but the amount of time, work, preparation and cost that is involved needs consideration. There is always an easier way round it.

Q - Is there friction between your department (and costume too) being expected to perform faster than is possible? As make-up and costume is kind of invisible, everybody wears clothes, everybody looks the way they do, everybody expects it almost to be instantaneous?

Sharon - Yes, and it is something which I find baffling, that when you get to big budget films, you can see that every attention to detail is paid, in terms of how actors look. No-one would scrimp and save on make-up and costume at that end. And yet at the low-budget end, perhaps because people are inexperienced, and directors don't really understand the process, they think *'well, people get dressed the morning, they put make-up on in the morning'*, and it is a bit of a battle to put yourself on the same footing as say the camera crew, who would never be told, *'right, we've got to get that shot even though the light is wrong, there is a big shadow.'* It seems perfectly acceptable to expect clothes to be thrown on, and people to look perfect all day. If I do make-up at half past six in the morning, where that actor is shooting for 12 hours, inevitably I've got to constantly supervise, and maintain that make-up and that hair, because of continuity, and because you can't keep taking the actor back to the make-up room to start all over again, you are literally standing in the middle of the set 'checking' the actor with the entire crew as an audience for as many as you can justify. And so it is very important, that particularly 1st ADs respect that, what time make-up and costume need is necessary, and it is a battle getting that time.

Q - With simple effects, how long will it take?

Sharon - Well, with smaller scale special effects, I think, I've got a good idea of how long something is going to take me, and I will be honest about that. If I can do it quicker, then I can do it quicker, but there is nothing worse than being rushed with any make-up, let alone with a prosthetic make-up, because you are trying to cheat something to look very real. But is has obviously got to be done properly or it will get re-shot or cut out.

Q - Do you think it is worth doing tests?

Sharon - That is helpful. Sometimes I get an opportunity to do test make-up, not necessarily to be filmed, but just to be sure that I'm going in the same direction as the director. Quite often on low-budget productions you don't have the time. Prosthetics screen tests should always be done to get that right. It's all in the planning, if you know what something is going to entail,

sharon holloway
make up artist

mobile: 07966 303354
e-mail: sharon.holloway@btinternet.com

PRODUCTION

you know how it is going to look, you know how long it is going to take, and all those things are clear from the start, when it comes to actually do that work on that day on set, things usually run a lot smoother. If you have got something that is going to be a continuity issue throughout the film, getting it right the first time is the thing. Because if you don't get it right the first time, then you are stuck with continuity issues on make-up which makes life more difficult.

Q - Any tips on using blood?

Sharon - Yes. I think you need a lot of red to show on screen, when it comes to make-up and effects. With prosthetics quite often they are covered in heavy red shades, and to the eye it looks completely different to how it looks on screen. So when it comes to blood, what might look accurate and authentic to the eye in the make-up room, can barely be seen on screen. When we have anyone getting dirty, bloody, or clothes being torn, the costume department are normally in on that, and geared up for perhaps having clothing doubles and so on. Always use blood that washes out of clothes. It keeps you well in with the costume department.

Q - Talk me through a typical day, on a typical drama, nothing fancy, not many characters...

Sharon - Well, I am usually one of the first to arrive on set. My room may have already been set up, but if it is a new location, and I've got a whole make-up kit to set up and get ready before the actor sits in a chair, then I would certainly be there half an hour before I'm actually due to start make-up. So this can be very early in the morning. The actor comes in, usually they are breakfasting or having coffee, and it's a bit of a push / pull to get them in the chair, and get them sat down. I will have an idea of how long things are going to take, if it's the first day of the shoot, things will always take longer because, once you know what you are doing with make-up or hair-styles, what works, then it becomes a lot easier to do.

Usually the actors will go onto set before I have completed, for blocking the scene, and whilst that is being lit, the actor gets given back to me to finish off. So once we are on set, I'd usually place myself within sight of the monitor, have everything with me on set that I would need for doing checks, keeping an eye on what they are doing rehearsal-wise, see the camera rehearsal, and do any final checks before they go for the first take. So, I need to have a good relationship with the 1st AD, so that they call for final checks every time they go for a take, and most of those times I'm happy, and I don't need to go in. So that really goes through the course of the day, then there maybe other make-ups to do, if actors have been staggered, so I'd usually like an assistant to be on set looking after actors, if I'm away from set.

Then at the end of the day, getting the actors cleaned up is very important. Some actors will go home with their make-up on, but I'd prefer them to get properly cleaned up, especially if we are on a longer shoot, because we have got to keep their skin in good condition, and that is all part of the job. If we are using prosthetics then that can take as long to take off as it does to put on, and quite often, the make-up department is the last to leave. So with a 10-hour shooting day, make-up can end up working 12 to 13 hours. At the end of the day, there are brushes to clean, and things to wash, like the costume dept., they may have shirts to wash and iron. Then just get yourself ready for the following day.

Q - What happens about continuity, do you have your own continuity?

Sharon - Yes, usually I'll look after that, and we will have a folder with make-up notes, and photographs, which we can work from ourselves. The script supervisor, or continuity person, will obviously keep half an eye on an actresses hair on set, but they're concentrating on other things, and so I look after hair and make-up continuity. If you have got one actor in the film who has got the same look all the way through, that is relatively easy to deal with, unless they have got particularly unruly hair, but if you have got actors in different costumes, different hairstyles and so on, then you are going to have quite a large continuity file, because you really do need to know how things are changing. The other issue on a long shoot, is men with short hair cuts, they will need constant hair cuts during the shoot to keep it at the same length.

Q - What kind of space do you need to work in?

Sharon - Lots please, as much as I can have! If you are shooting in a film studios, or a television studios, everything is there, the mirrors, the workspace, the sinks, it is all laid out and that is like a dream. But quite often on a low budget shoot, you are in a room

Make-up & Hair

The Make-up artist is just that - an artist. Likewise a hair stylist has style. It takes a special skill to know how to apply cosmetics and sculpt hair for film. If you put this in the hands of amateurs, what may look okay for a Saturday night out on the town will look garish on a 40 foot screen.

1. Often on low budget movies, the Make-up designer and Hairstylist are usually the same person. If you can separate the two, do so, because one doesn't necessarily know the skills of the other. Then there's the work load. If you want your lead actress to look stunning throughout the film, that will take time, no matter how amazing you think she looks in the flesh.

2. Don't assume your make-up artist can do all make-up such as special make effects like blood, cuts, bruises, prosthetics etc, as they require different skills. Make sure to ask a make-up artist what they can do before you hire them.

3. If working on a low budget, ask your hair stylist or make-up artist to be creative with the actor's natural hair to avoid unnecessary wigs or facial hair.

4. Some cosmetic companies will offer free or discounted make-up in exchange for a mention in the film itself. Get your product placement person on this ASAP.

5. If dealing with gore, special make-up or complicated wigs, it's a good idea to do camera and make-up tests. What you might consider looks realistic in real life can look really fake on screen and vice versa.

6. Remember that make-up is where your actors start their day. If they're made up in a relaxing fashion, then will leave feeling good and ready for their shots.

7. Your make-up artist can keep an eye on the actor's deeper feelings and fears and report back to the producer. You have a spy who is both on your side and the actors side.

8. Make sure you have enough time allotted for your actors before they go on set. Depending on the complexity of the make-up, this could take anywhere from 15 minutes to several hours.

9. Make sure that the hairstyle is not too 'over the top' for each character. You don't want your hairstylist trying out a new design if it's for a working class mom living on a housing estate.

10. Consider hiring extra help on days when you have a lot of extras or principals in a scene. It may save you a lot of time.

11. Make sure your actors are out of make-up each day and their skin cleansed. You don't want to contribute to a bad complexion.

12. Make sure to have enough room for your make-up and hair departments to work freely.

13. Schedule time during prep for your make-up and hair people to meet the actors to discuss any issues or ideas.

14. Make sure the 1st AD has make-up and hair check for imperfections just prior to the first take, and also to keep an eye on sweating and degradation in the make-up under the hot lights.

15. Polaroids or digital photos of the actors should be taken from all angles at the end of each shot to ensure continuity.

16. The make-up department will create a character breakdown for make-up notes, a make-up story order (i.e. how many changes there will be not just from day to day but within each day), their own continuity sheets which they will use throughout the shoot.

17. Give them time and respect. Make-up artists are often pushed around by bossy crew members with big cameras because they are female (mostly) and their job is can often be seen as not being as important. They will rarely ask for more time than is absolutely needed, so when they ask for it, give it.

Pic by Jeremy Larkin, from London Voodoo

PRODUCTION

that you are trying to turn into a workable space. It is extremely hard, although it's been done - working in a small space, with nowhere to put anything down, bad lighting, no on tap water. You cope in those situations of course, but inevitably it's harder work and everyone gets more stressed. It really should be something that the production team discusses with make-up as to what is needed, and do the best they can to prepare that space, because an actor may be in a chair for 45 minutes to an hour, or an hour and a quarter, and you, as the make-up artist will be working in that space non-stop, and you do need a lot of space to be able to get round the actor, to be able to use hair dryers, and to have decent lights, and set things up, and somewhere that is clean as well! I've been into places where I have had to clean them before I've even got a single piece of make-up kit out.

Q - Do you think a wise production would make sure that the space is as warm and comfortable as possible, because it does tend to be, especially on low budget films, a bit of a haunt for actors as they don't really have a space to go to?

Make-up Artist Books

Grande Illusions by Tom Savini
For those who love special make up effects, especially from the horror genre, this book is for you. It teaches you how the effects Savini has done in movies, such as The Burning, The Prowler, Dawn of the Dead, Friday the 13th, and Creepshow all came together. There are two volumes, Books I and II.

The Complete Make Up Artist, 2nd Edition by Penny Delamar
An essential for anyone who wants to become a successful make-up artist in film and TV. Written for those learning about media make-up, this book provides a wealth of information, activities and advice.

The Technique of the Professional Make Up Artist by Vincent J. R. Kehoe
Covers all of the current studio make-up methods and lab techniques, with text and art contributions from some of the leading experts in the industry. Kehoe clearly explains the differences between applying make up for TV verses film, interior versus exterior and studio lighting versus natural daylight.

Sharon - Getting off to a good start to the day obviously bodes well, and if the first thing that an actor does is to come and sit in the make-up chair, then that first half an hour, or an hour of the day could really make a difference as to how they feel when they go out on set. Actors tend to gravitate towards the make-up room. I think largely because what we do in make-up is so personal and intimate in a way that no other person on the crew can quite replicate. You see the actors raw, at their worst, you are touching them, you are looking at them throughout the day, keeping an eye on how they look, or how they feel, so naturally they are going to gravitate towards the make-up department. They know that we are going to look after them.

Q - And as you spend so much time together, make-up can often get a 'vibe' for how the actors are doing.

Sharon - Absolutely. One of the great things about the job is the contact with actors, because we do build up good relationships for the duration of the shoot. A good producer will obviously respect, not just the actor and what the actor is going through, but you and what you are going through, and so a happy make-up crew and happy actors is obviously a big bonus to any shoot. Over the course of a shoot, when the production crew see that there is a good relationship between the make-up department, costume department and the actors, and they are happy, then they will start to understand what an important job we do, not just in getting actors on set to look right, but also in oiling the wheels of the production.

Q - Smart actors know that your job is entirely about making them look right?

Sharon - And the good thing is, that if they trust you, that you are going to be looking out for them, and on set if you notice anything, you will go in without fuss, and alter it, change it, they do not need to worry about how they look. If they know you are keeping an eye on them, they become less self conscious.

Q - How long does it take to do a 'simple' make-up for a general scene?

Sharon - For most straight make-up for men, including a little bit of hair styling, it would probably take about 15 minutes, and that is quick! The average female make-up would take about 40/45 minutes, and then their hair can be anything up to another half an hour. So for some key female leads on the film, they can be in the chair for an hour and a quarter if you are doing it properly. There are lots of variables, and the more you do make-up the quicker you get.

Q - What about hair, beards and moustaches?

Sharon - With facial hair, it is always better if it can be the actor's own, but sometimes they don't have to time to grow it, because they may be on another production right up to the start of your own. So then it will probably be a hire from somewhere like the BBC. You can't always get the actor to do a fitting, so you have to have a pretty good idea of what is going to work, and see the actor in order to then choose a piece, which has not been made to measure, but will be the best that you can do in the circumstances. On average wig hire is about £50 a week, and beards are about £25 a week, and moustaches are about £12 a week. It can be an expensive way of doing things, but if it is absolutely necessary for that character, then that is obviously something to consider from the budget.

Q - From a low budget point of view, it is better if you can modify the screenplay so you don't have to deal with it?

Sharon - Yes, there is the hire cost and there is also the time to fit every day. Things do take quite a long time to do, particularly with wigs.

Q - What mistakes do you see on a regular basis, especially on lower budget stuff, when people are pushed?

Sharon - One of the reasons I've mentioned the 1st assistant director is because if you have got a good 1st AD who knows how to run a set, and knows that make-up needs to do checks, then you have not got a lot to worry about. But on low-budget productions, they will shoot things without giving warning, or you may have one make-up artist who can't be on set all the time, because they have got other make-up to do, which often means that shots are taken of actors, where they're hair has moved, or their make-up needs checking, and it hasn't been done, and it all seems fine until you actually get into the cutting room, and then you will see the difference, the continuity mistakes.

There are other things we have already touched on, which is getting make-up people in to production so late in the day, without proper preparation time, so that expectations are far in excess of what can realistically be done in that time. And, trying to work in a space which is not appropriate adds to stress, which can cause friction on set. I don't know if these are so much mistakes, as rather not thinking things through, not planning things through, because no matter how much money you have got, it doesn't really cost time to talk things through with people. Planning can make such a difference to a really stressed out shoot, where people don't know what is happening, people don't know what is round the corner, don't know what next shot it coming up, and things are being changed and no-one is being told. That is just a recipe for disaster. So I always think if you have got more money then that is fantastic, but actually having a well run shoot, where people are communicating, and people are respected is far better than having a lot of money.

Q - What advice would you offer to a new filmmaker?

Sharon - Whatever job you are doing, what is important is not that you know every detail, about what everyone else does, but that you try and learn, and understand where it fits into the picture, because filmmaking is a collaboration and you will get far more out of your experience if you are genuinely working in a team across all departments.

PRODUCTION

Kave Quinn
Production Designer

PRODUCTION DESIGN

Q - What is the role of the production designer?

Kave - The Production Designer helps the director translate their vision of the film onto film, by collaborating with the design of the 'look'. This includes designing the sets, adding to or changing the locations, overseeing the dressing of these areas in conjunction with the Set Decorator and overseeing the special effects and action props, including vehicles. All this has to be carried out with the close association of the Director and DP, and also the Producer in case of budgetary problems and logistical problems.

Q - What is your background?

Kave - I initially trained as a fashion designer at St Martins School of Art, and started as a costume designer, changing to art direction after about 4 years. Also I did a lot of student films at the National Film and Television School, even though I didn't go there! And I did a draughting course at the same time. I then became Assistant Art Director to a number of designers and gained experience working with them on a number of films until my first break with *'Shallow Grave'*. I certainly didn't follow a set path on becoming a Production Designer but the best way to gain knowledge regarding draughting skills, drawing skills re visualising sets and budgeting skills is best gained by working as an assistant to a designer in as many roles as possible.

Q - Who makes up the art department?

Kave - That is dependent on the size of the film. There's normally a Designer who's the head of the department. Then, an Art Director. They're responsible for over seeing construction of any sets that are being built and or locations that are being used and may require construction. They also assist in running the art dept and all the departments that the art department oversee i.e. prop department, set decorating dept, special effects etc. There's a draughts person who produces the construction drawings; an assistant art director who's responsible for many elements e.g. draughting details, maybe not whole sets, graphics and generally assisting the designer, art director, set decorator. There's a set decorator who's responsible for finding the dressing for the sets or locations... a prop buyer who's in charge of buying the props, a prop master who takes care of organising the dressing to go into each set or location and removing it when that set or location has been filmed....and a team of standby people such as standby art director. Then there is the construction team with a manager and team of carpenters and painters to construct sets and change locations.

Q - How do you structure each project and what is the first job you tackle?

Kave - The first thing I do is to go through the script and break it down into key elements, e.g. the characters, the plot, the mood and pace. I would then try to formulate the way I feel I could visually enhance the script. I would be in close communication foremost with the Director, the Cameraman and the Producer - to see if my ideas are possible and within the budget.

Q - What do you think is important as far as location scouting goes?

Kave - If a film is to be shot with some or all the scenes set in locations, location scouting is key to the design of the film. You must work very closely with the scout so you can achieve the right look.

Q - How important is attention to detail to you?

GUERILLA FILM MAKER SAYS!

Props and Set Dressing

Just about everything you see on the screen, barring the actors and special effects, fall under the broad umbrella of props and set dressing. Props (short for 'properties') refers to all physical objects that are handled by the actors or featured in the script, such as a cigarette, a car, food, coffee cups, candles, newspaper headlines etc. Set Dressing refers to background decoration of a scene i.e. furniture, paintings etc. Props and set dressing may cross over at times and may even include wardrobe when referring to something specific such as glasses.

The person in charge of props is called The Prop Master, and they handle the selection, the cataloging and maintenance of these objects. The Set Dressing is overseen by the Set Decorator who is responsible for physically creating the vision of the Production Designer and the Director from the drawings created by the Art Director. The set decorator's next in command is the Lead Person who supervisors the set dressers (called the Swing Gang). If sets aren't dressed on time, it can put the whole movie behind schedule. Here are some things to think about so that this doesn't happen:

1. Make a list of all props and potential set dressing from your script as early as possible. This will give you enough time to gather or create them.

2. Be aware of TV programmes or web sites that will appear in the script as these will either require you to get the rights to the show / site or to hire someone to generate them. Even the web browser needs clearance.

3. Likewise, photographs, newspaper headlines, magazine articles and books etc. will need ample prep time for their creation.

4. If there is a prop that is prominent in a scene such as a box of cereal, try to get product placement to fill this need. However, if you can't get this because you have put the product in a negative light, you will need to create a new fictitious brand.

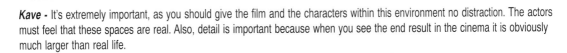

5. Make sure everything is as realistic as possible. Use authentic props and set dressing. I.e. Use a real gun (from your armourer) instead of a plastic one, use real flowers and not plastic ones.

6. Be well organised and have a choice of each prop ready in case it doesn't fit the production designer or director's vision - also you might need multiple props for multiple takes or, in case a prop is damaged. This is especially true for food and stunt props.

7. Make sure that each prop is always readily at hand.

8. If you have an action vehicle in your script (i.e. a car, boat etc.) make sure it's properly insured. Also it may be more cost effective to rent a vehicle from an actual place of business than a specialised action prop house. This obviously depends upon the use of the vehicle within the film.

9. Keep an eye on your props so that they don't end up going home with your crew.

10. Always return your Props and set dressing on time to avoid late fees.

11. Appoint someone to be responsible for checking each shot so as to avoid unwanted logos and copyright material. This will mean the job of clearances later on will be easier, perhaps even unneeded.

Pic from Djamel's Eyes by David Casals-Roma

PRODUCTION

Kave - It's extremely important, as you should give the film and the characters within this environment no distraction. The actors must feel that these spaces are real. Also, detail is important because when you see the end result in the cinema it is obviously much larger than real life.

Q - What is the relationship between the production designer and the DP?

Kave - The relationship with the DP is to visually map out and plan the look of the film with camera angles, use of different lenses and lighting changes. All this is done in conjunction with the Director who may have a clear outline of this already. Generally the designer starts on the production before the DP and drawings etc are sent to the DP for their thoughts etc. On 'Layer Cake' the DP, Ben Davies, was brought in at the same time as me and it made making decisions and tackling problems a lot faster.

Q - How do you create a colour palette?

Kave Quinn
Production Designer

kavequinn@onetel.com

Props Hire

Q - What is a Prop House?

George - It is a hire company that rents props to television, film, theatre, dressing displays and photographic shoots. We have been here for forty years so we have a lot of experience. We are specialists in 'smalls' which means that we have props ranging from pens and pencils to TVs, radios, bicycles, stuffed animals, kitchen equipment, games, mannequins, Americana, neons, musical instruments, prams, even a yeti. We have over half a million varied items. Other companies specialise in other things like furniture, modern or period, tanks, armoury, weapons, costumes, curtains, etc. If it needs to be in front of the camera there is a specialist out there for it. We also buy and make up new props all the time. When the World Cup was on we made the only existing World Cup replica.

Q - How does the rental system work?

George - Every item has a value, the first week's hire is 10% of the value, thereafter you go on a sliding scale, the longer you have the prop, the cheaper the weekly rate. The minimum charge is £15 + VAT. Selecting the props means walking around the warehouse and putting post-it labels on the large objects, and putting the smaller ones on a shopping trolley. Then we give you the quote and we go from there.

Q - So if a Production Designer comes to you with a list of say 300 things you would do a deal?

George - Yes, we try and work with people's budgets. We are here to work with the customer, and the bigger the hire the more we can do for them.

Q - What about transport and insurance?

George - They should have their own transport. I would rather they checked with us about the sort of vehicles they plan to use, so we can suggest an alternative if we feel the props will suffer. We can also recommend good companies for transport. The customer organises their own insurance. Sometimes a customer will not insure and then if there is any loss or damage they will have to pay for it out of their own pocket. Some people just insure over a certain value, i.e. insure anything over £1k. We always suggest that their driver checks props when they are returned to avoid any misunderstanding. The problems tend to occur when the production has cut corners and not hired good vans and drivers who take their responsibility seriously, or they won't let the driver spend time at the various prop stores checking everything. Prop hire companies welcome anyone who takes the time to check everything and pack it sensibly for transport.

Q - What common mistakes do you encounter?

George Apter
Studio and TV Hire

George - We need official orders on paper and often this doesn't happen, even with the biggest companies. Everyone needs to know what and when they are ordering and how much it will cost. Productions often rent for one week and then end up needing the prop for several weeks, therefore escalating the cost. Props get stolen or lost because they don't have an experienced props masters, props get damaged when they don't employ proper couriers.

Q - What advice would you offer?

George - Get professional and work in a professional manner. Don't lie, you will do far better if you tell us what you have rather than pretending that you have lots of money.

Either come to us with a list of what you want or an amount you want to spend and we can tell you how the deal will work. Be honest. I prefer film companies where the producer is frank and tells me when he can pay rather than fobbing me off with empty promises. We are all in the same industry, no one really wants to put someone else out of business, keep in touch, keep them updated.

NOTE - STV now have a great website with lots of pics that really show you just how much stuff they have. It's also got a searchable database. www.stvhire.com

Kave - The time that you're plotting out and breaking down the script is when you start to formulate a colour palette. Influences can come from a specific reference e.g. a painting, a photo, or just from your or the director's imagination. With *'Layer Cake'* I wanted to have a monochromatic colour palette with strong primary colours coming through in props, sets, costumes at significant points in the film.

Q - What have been your greatest challenges?

Kave - One of my greatest challenges was trying to build and dress the set for *'Shallow Grave'* on the budgetary restrictions we had. In *'Shallow Grave'* the main set was the large flat that the chararacters lived in and it was supposed to be on the top floor, so we needed to elevate the set about 4' off the ground to give a feeling when you can see out of the large Georgian windows that we are high up. Adding this under a large set adds a big unseen cost to the set on a very low budget film. But because we made the flat to feel as big as an Edinburgh Newtown flat, this helped in the filming because we didn't need to float out so many walls.

Q - What are the challenges when working on a low budget film?

Kave - Trying to achieve a specific look within the confines of a tight budget and having viable alternatives if a more expensive one is not achievable.

Q - What are some of the unique qualities of the directors you've worked with?

Kave - Their clarity of thought and determination to achieve their vision.

Q - What advice would you give to new Designers?

Kave - Listen to what the Director would like to achieve, add to this and enhance, but remember it is ultimately their vision.

Q - What mistakes have you come across on low budget films that could be avoided?

Kave - Having an unrealistic budget to match too overambitious design requirements. As mentioned earlier, if you don't have a big budget, think of clever ways of achieving a good production design for little money...

Q - What advice would you give to new filmmakers?

Kave - Try to push out the boundaries but also have a practical eye on things, even early at the scriptwriting stage, so when in production and realising your vision, there aren't too many compromises made.

Production Design

If there's no consideration for production design, your film can look uninspired, messy and unfocused. By stylising the look of your film, you can make it stand out. Even on a low budget, spending more time and money on what goes up on the screen, will go a long way.

1. Allow your production designer and concept artists the freedom to use their own ideas. They're generally experienced at this and can take your vision to new levels.

2. Building models of your set can help with the communication between the director and the production design team as to what needs to be changed or added. It can also help the director and DP envision where the camera and lights will go, so the set builders can compensate with removable walls etc.

3. It may be advantageous to create a maquette (a small model) of certain people, creatures or objects, in order to fully visualise what they look like. This is especially true if you're working in a fantasy world. On a side note, bringing these objects into a finance or studio meeting, can help enhance your vision.

4. Consider the colour palette of your film with the Production Designer, the DP and Director. The locale and tone of your story will affect this choice. For instance, if your movie is a comedy set in the Caribbean, you might want to use saturated colours. Changing the colour palette throughout the film can be an effective way of creating mood.

6. Keep a consistent colour theme in order to avoid a jarring mish mash of hues that make no sense. This applies to everything in the movie, from props to costumes to locations etc.

7. Get everyone on the same page. Often, production designers may come up against costume designers or the DP over the choice of colours. Help everyone see the importance of this. This most often occurs when budgets are very tight and time is short as filming can turn into 'just get it shot now!'

PRODUCTION

Verity Scott
Production Designer

Q - What is your job?

Verity - I am a production designer. The art department falls into two departments. You have the production designer who is sort of the big boss who comes up with all the ideas. And then there is the art director who has to visualise those ideas and then go out and buy the props and build the sets under the guidelines of the production designer.

Q - On cash strapped films, the production designer and art director get rolled into one?

Verity - Yes, I would do both jobs. If you can rope some people into helping, that is fantastic. Sometimes you might need a carpenter for a day if you can stretch it. Otherwise you rope in runners.

Q - How early do you get involved in short films and low budget films?

Verity - Anything from a month to three days.

Q - What do you do in that month or three days?

Verity - I figure out what the production needs. I dissect the script and prioritise what are the main things you need. And from your budget, if you have one, you have to go out and source these things, whether they are going to be specific props that you are going to have to make or find. Or if there are specific colours that the director is trying to put forward, then you have to find them. Then there is working out a time schedule of how long it is going to take to find the things you need before actually going into production.

Q - At lower budgets, what can a director do to get the most out of you, so that you can be creative, or at these levels, is it just that you want to make it look real at that's hard enough?

Verity - It is quite difficult to put your artistic stamp on stuff when there is no budget. Working closely with the DP to get the lighting right is important, because that can often make or break your art design. And trying to pick out what you think are the nicest parts of the project. For example, it might be a bouquet of flowers that the person has to hold. You want to make sure that it is really, really nice. The sets can be scrappy and the locations don't have to be perfect, but if something stands out, then it puts your stamp on doing it.

Q - Do you ever get into conversations with the producer, director or screenwriter about cutting things because it is not doable?

Verity - Yes, but they generally don't listen. You can scream until you are blue in the face, *"How the hell do you expect me to do this with no money?!?"* At lower budgets, it is basically beg, borrow and steal.

Q - How closely do you work with the director in the prep?

Verity - I like to work quite closely with the director because you are all trying to get the same vision across. The DP is important on a low budget shoot because his lighting is so important to what you are trying to produce. The last couple of days leading up to the production I

Prop Problems

GUERILLA FILM MAKER SAYS!

Not all props are easy to get hold of - some are a real problem...Think ice cubes under hot lights for instance. Television and computer screens cannot just be filmed, you need clearance to use what is on the screen (if you didn't create it) AND then you need special equipment to allow the camera to film the screen itself (unless you shoot at 25fps / 25p). Who will take care of vehicles? Do the characters drive? Can the actors actually drive? Are there any animals and where are they coming from? Who will look after them? Most common problems relate to special props within the story, a newspaper headline that was forgotten etc. Remember a poor prop can destroy audience 'suspension of belief'. Food is always a problem, especially if an actor is expected to eat it! And then there's the stunts, action and FX stuff, a whole department unto itself. Consider all these problems and props before you get to set. Often they can be modified in the screenplay, removing a production problem without compromising the drama.

will talk to the director everyday, but up until then, you talk mostly to the producers and the location managers just to work out where you will be filming.

Q - On low budget films, do you deal with the props?

Verity - Definitely. And even when I have projects with budgets, I like to have a hold over what props I am getting. But on low budget stuff, you have your props list and you have to go out and get them. You don't have the luxury to go to a prop house and say I'll have one of those. It is more what can I get out of my father's garage. Or sending an e-mail to all your mates stating what I am looking for and seeing if anyone can help me.

Q - How important are good props?

Verity - Very important.

Q - Do you go along with the adage that one dodgy prop can destroy a film?

Verity - It depends on how key it is to the project. I think in all cases, try and get the best that you can because you personally will know if something doesn't look right and that is more annoying because you know you haven't produced something that looks great.

Q - Any tips on the aesthetic of props?

Verity - One key thing is using the space that you have, as creatively as you can, because you want to cut back your budget in any way, whether it is building props or using that location. Oxfam and second hand shops are very useful in sourcing things, but you really have to trail around to find them. But it makes you a better designer because you have an understanding that it is not something you are going to find instantly.

Q - Do you ever get involved in working on clearances, such as making sure Kellogg's don't mind their corn flakes being in shot?

Verity - You have to be very careful. Generally you have to disguise labels or put them at angles so it doesn't say Corn Flakes because you can get in real trouble. But if you give people enough time, it is quite easy to get things cleared. Graphics are important as well. So say you do have a Corn Flakes box, then you can design your own box and then you can get away with whatever you want.

Q - And that's the same for newspaper headlines or signs outside a building, are those props sometimes left longer than they should be?

Verity - Yes. It is always a last minute job. You have to do them as early as possible because there is always someone who is going to need a newspaper prop. They are a nightmare to do and you need to learn Photoshop really well.

Verity-Jane Scott

Production Designer

e-mail: verity@verityscott.co.uk

web: www.verityscott.co.uk

mob: +44 (0) 7814 869978

PRODUCTION

Q - Do you get involved in the choosing of locations?

Verity - Usually I'm told that 'this' is what I have to work with. But it is nice if you can say to the location manager 'this is what I am looking for' and if you can find it, my job will be easier. You do get to go on location searches sometimes.

Q - What tips would you give on building and dressing sets on a micro-budget?

Verity - You don't have to use the best quality materials. Often finding things in skips is just as good. If you need 'flats', you can make them rather simply instead of hiring them. Use the cheaper end material and just make sure they are put together properly. See if there are any props at the locations that you can use.

Q - What kind of props do you find have the best production values as far as filling space?

Verity - Drapes and scarves. Bits of fabric are useful. Bits of office supplies and furniture - pens and papers or a laptop. Modern day stuff is great. And don't take for granted that it is going to be there all the time, as often times, it is not.

Q - How do you combat the 'white wall' syndrome in low budget films, where there is a blank space between two characters?

Verity - You can paint the wall or put a picture up on it. Stick a fire exit sign in there. Anything really, that is at head level behind the person, to break up the frame a bit. I wouldn't want to see a wall that is bare. It sticks out like a sore thumb.

Q - What things give you the most problems in props?

Verity - Special effects on a small budget can be quite difficult because I am expected to be able to deliver them instead of a special effects guy! And if you don't know how to do it, then you have to work out a way of doing it. One scenario in which I am not sure how I got away with it was that we had to shoot the back streets of Soho and it had to appear as if it had been raining. But we were shooting at the beginning of February and it hadn't been raining. We had a problem because the lead character had to come into this scene with shadows everywhere with lots of reflections. I am fortunate enough to have a friend who is a fireman. We got clearances from all the local fire brigades where we were filming and he got his fire hoses and went into the mains on the street and sprayed everything down instead of hiring someone. At 6am, he had gone home and I had to wet down the streets. So I went into a shop and filled up buckets from their basement, and also used a street cleaner to wet down the streets. Special effects have to be right and they have to be safe and they are my biggest problem.

The Skip GUERILLA FILM MAKER SAYS!

A micro budget Production Designers dream. One man's rubbish is another man's treasure. And a skip can be a treasure chest for the production designer who has to build the impossible with a budget that would barely buy lunch.

1. Skips are often filled with wood, the main material needed in construction. Don't be proud, scavenge.

2. Don't buy materials from a DIY shop, find a local timber merchant or building supplier where you can buy at trade prices.

3. Everything is reusable. Don't be tempted to get a skip! Keep everything in storage until the shoot is over. It's guaranteed that if you junk something, the next day it will be needed.

4. Keep a close eye on tools, they are expensive and have a tendency to go walkies.

5. When it comes to the person who is going to oversee the construction of any sets, find someone who is ready to 'go for it'. The construction supervisor is like the caretaker - at the end of the day, whatever they say, goes.

6. Think about re-using sets and locations. One room could be redressed to be three different rooms! A few posters, different curtains, a false plywood wall and a lick of paint is all you need to create the illusion.

7. An advantage to shooting in a film studios is that you may be able to scavenge flats and timber from the other productions as they strike sets.

Set Building

GUERILLA FILM MAKER SAYS!

1. It isn't cheap to build a set, but if you can afford it, it's well worth it, especially if most of your movie is set in one main location.

2. Make sure you leave enough time to build, it can take weeks.

3. Make sure you have enough skip space for the strike. You should be able to break your set in a day, but it does produce an enormous amount of junk.

4. Get enough tools and the right tools for the job. You might save a bob or two on cheap saws, but powerful electric ones would speed everything up enormously.

5. Raid skips nearby for wood that you can use. Often you can buy the materials from a set that is about to be struck, it's good for them, it's good for you.

6. Watch out for wandering tools. Hammers, drills, nails etc., all just seem to go walkies on their own.

7. Buy from the trade suppliers and not big DIY stores. Get your production manager on the phone searching out the best deals for timber. Get them to deliver.

8. Make sure your set is 8 feet high or you might find tall cast members heads popping over the top. We had this problem with Andreas Wiesniewski on Urban Ghost Story, so you'll notice he sits down for a lot of the movie!

9. The secret is in the dressing. Make sure you fill your set with props, don't rely on the four walls to do it all for you.

10. Build as many flying walls as you can, it makes it easier to shoot and dress.

11. Try and reuse sets. Once one room has been shot in, could it be repainted and dressed to be another location altogether?

12. Sets are potentially dangerous places. Make someone responsible for Health and Safety and check that they do the job. One dropped hammer from 15 feet can shut you down and end a life. Take care.

Q - How quickly can you knock together a smallish set like a bedroom?

Verity - If you have all the furniture, then you can build something in a day.

Q - On a low budget film, ideally how many people would you work with?

Verity - You need one right hand man who would be your assistant. It is always useful if you have a runner who has carpentry skills. And by that, I mean someone who can hammer a nail into a piece of wood, not create sculptures! You don't have to be technically minded, you just have to have common sense. But depending on the set build, I would say two, up to six people, is right.

Q - What tips would you offer a new production designer?

Verity - Stick to your guns. Believe in what you have designed and make it as simple as you can. Use the locations you have to their maximum potential. When the crew turns up, they may tell you that your designs have to change and you have to be kind of dogmatic because you have been talking with the director and know what he wants.

Q - What are the common mistakes you see filmmakers making?

Verity - Making things look tacky. Chintzy furniture and ghastly colours. Not paying attention to detail. I know you are on a low budget, but try to get the nicest stuff you can. It is about positioning things so that when the camera is looking at it, it doesn't look thrown together. Low budget stuff is difficult, but it can be the most satisfying.

Q - What advice would you give a new film maker?

Verity - Keep a close eye on your budget, because if you are good with it, people remember you and it can lead to paid work, and budget management is a good discipline to have.

Elizabeth Tremblay
Script Continuity

SCRIPT SUPERVISOR

Q - What is your job?

Elizabeth - I make sure the movie cuts together, and also make sure the director has all the shots he needs and that the script is covered. When shooting a scene, I watch for continuity with costume, props, hair and make up and continuity of action. Continuity of action involves knowing what hand the actor was smoking with, when did the actor smoke and when did he get up to speak to the other actor and where. Making sure the actors say the right lines. I also have to log everything that we shoot. Every job is different and a lot depends on the experience of the director, DP and 1st AD you work with. The better at their job they are the easier time I'll have. I'm usually hired from a month up to 2 weeks before a film. I've also been hired months in advance by directors I know.

Q - Do you time the script?

Elizabeth – Yes, and it's my least favourite part because it takes a long time, and there is always a lot of pressure on the total estimate timing, especially if it's for TV. In reality it's only an estimate and you never know how the director is going to work, and most of the time you haven't seen the locations.

Q - Does the one page equals one minute rule generally work?

Elizabeth - Yes but sometimes 1/8 of a page, that is only a simple description, can be up to 45 seconds.

Q - Do you have to watch for actors ad libbing?

Elizabeth - Yes, but I can't always write it all down. I sometimes ask the actor to write it down for me if I don't have time to write it down, or if it's too much new stuff, so I can send a copy to the editor.

Q - Do you note the continuity for shots?

Elizabeth - I do a continuity sheet for every shot that we shoot. It includes taking down the lenses, what size the shot is, how many takes we do, how long they are and then I have to make comments to each take the director likes and what is wrong with the takes that didn't work.

Q - Do you give the editor all your continuity shots?

Elizabeth - Yes, plus the marked up script and the wild lines recorded throughout the shoot, and any other notes the director gives me to edit.

Q - How do you separate it?

Elizabeth - I have to do a sheet per shot, and then I have to do the marked up script also called tram lines, which shows the editor what shot covers what part of a scene. Not my favourite part either!

Q - Do you take polaroids?

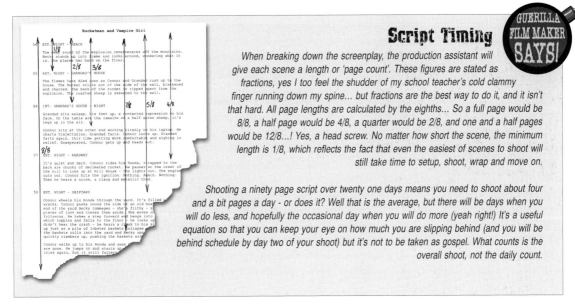

Script Timing

When breaking down the screenplay, the production assistant will give each scene a length or 'page count'. These figures are stated as fractions, yes I too feel the shudder of my school teacher's cold clammy finger running down my spine... but fractions are the best way to do it, and it isn't that hard. All page lengths are calculated by the eighths... So a full page would be 8/8, a half page would be 4/8, a quarter would be 2/8, and one and a half pages would be 12/8...! Yes, a head screw. No matter how short the scene, the minimum length is 1/8, which reflects the fact that even the easiest of scenes to shoot will still take time to setup, shoot, wrap and move on.

Shooting a ninety page script over twenty one days means you need to shoot about four and a bit pages a day - or does it? Well that is the average, but there will be days when you will do less, and hopefully the occasional day when you will do more (yeah right!) It's a useful equation so that you can keep your eye on how much you are slipping behind (and you will be behind schedule by day two of your shoot) but it's not to be taken as gospel. What counts is the overall shoot, not the daily count.

Elizabeth - I used to but now I'm a digital girl. It's so much easier than Polaroids. We take shots right before the take, and after if I have to match positions or if something changes. I also take them to match costume, hair, make-up and props. I use it as a continuity log and back-up so if any department is ever in doubt of something I have the pictures to match.

Q - Is eyeline something you have to be aware of?

Elizabeth - Absolutely and it's always nice when the DOP and director are knowledgeable with eyelines. I did a film last year where neither the director or the DOP knew about eyelines and they both operated the cameras, it made my life difficult for two months. It's part of their job to know too, so it's always frustrating if they don't know because it makes my job harder and I don't think it's fair that the pressure should only be on the script girl to make sure eyelines work!

Q - Do you have to note down where the camera is?

Elizabeth - Yes, but I only make little drawings in my notes. It's not like I have to make drawings of where exactly they were on set.

Q - Do the directors also keep an eye out for this stuff?

Elizabeth - When they are good!

Q - What common mistake do you come across with filmmakers?

Elizabeth - That's a hard one! All filmmakers are different but the biggest one is to alienate your crew. I've worked on films where the directors were so nasty to crew and actors that everybody hated them, and nobody wanted to give them what they wanted because of that, and their film suffered from it. It's also something you can see in the final cut.

Q - What advice would you offer new filmmakers?

Elizabeth - Do your homework. Be nice and respect your crew and you'll get much more out of them.

Elizabeth Tremblay
Script Supervisor

zabeth75@hotmail.com

PRODUCTION

Steve Read
1st Place

PRODUCT PLACEMENT

Q - What does your company do?

Steve - We were established in 1991 to provide the free loan of editorially correct branded products to UK made TV and Film, and have since become a leading specialist product placement agency. We continue to provide the free loan of products to production companies, but also broker partnership deals between productions and brands and provide innovative product placement solutions.

Q - How does product placement work?

Steve - Product placement works in a variety of ways. At its most basic level it is the free loan of branded products for use as props in film and TV. It can also be a source of revenue for production companies whereby brands pay to have their products included in a film. Increasingly, product placement is about a partnership between the production and the brand whereby, in return for the inclusion of a product in the film, the brand provides advertising for the film by basing a marketing campaign around it.

Q - What kind of products are typically placed in almost all productions?

Steve - Product placement is about matching the product to the scenario within the film, and to the film's audience, rather than the type of products themselves. It is that which dictates what items are placed rather than the products themselves. Almost everything from mouthwash to cars is actively placed, if the scenario is suitable.

Q - What about bigger stuff like a TV or car?

Steve - We regularly place larger and more valuable items. For more expensive items such as cars and computers, there is often a limited amount of stock made available for product placement opportunities. Independent film makers will find themselves up against major features and TV productions who also want to use the products. The economics of the market mean that a brand or an agency will almost always choose to provide items to major productions rather than independents if there is not enough stock to satisfy all opportunities.

Q - Do companies pay to put their product into a film?

Steve - Yes, but only if it is a good strategic marketing fit. Independent film makers need to be realistic. Companies will always consider what the return on their investment will be. Whilst brands may be willing to pay big money to have a Hollywood A lister use their product, this is based not only upon the associative value gained from their brand being in the hand of a star but also upon audience numbers and demographic. If you can't guarantee an audience, and more specifically an audience of people realistically likely to buy the product, a brand manager is unlikely to pay hard cash, unless they happen to be related to you!

Q - How much do they pay?

Steve - How much is paid is based on the potential return on investment, in a similar way to TV advertising. An agency or brand manager will look at the amount of time the product will be seen on screen, the associative value gained from that placement, and the quality and quantity of the audience. It is rare for an unproven director without distribution to be able to get money from a brand.

The potential viewers need to be of the demographic targeted by the brand. A predicted audience of young adult males may potentially bring in money from a computer games company but is unlikely to bring in any money from a makeup brand. Sounds obvious but it is surprising what productions ask for.

Q - If they don't pay, what is in it for the filmmaker/producer?

Steve - Firstly, saving on art department budgets through the free loan of products. Productions have been known to almost fully dress sets with free, product placed, items. If the product is seen in a good light you have also set up valuable contacts for the future. It never hurts to get an agency or brand on side. Secondly, advertising. Hollywood films can spend more on marketing a film than producing it. The tie in marketing deal is a great solution for both parties. Productions get their film advertised on the back of a brand and vice versa. Many large Hollywood deals see no money changing hands but rather a mutual marketing deal.

Q - When should a producer contact you?

Steve - If there is a chance of a brand becoming integral to the plot, then at the script writing stage is not too early. We represent many technology brands and are often willing to discuss innovations in things such as mobile telephony, computer security and computer gaming that could feature in plot lines. Final product placement deals rarely take place without the agency or brand having seen the final shooting script, but it never hurts to be in contact early and find out what brands are looking for from product placement. As an independent film maker you will often find yourself turned down as brands look to be involved with guaranteed success.

Q - If a producer contacts you with an idea to get, for example, Coca-Cola into their film, is that something you arrange?

Steve - It is always worth contacting us. Although we work for the brands rather than the productions, we would be nothing without good relations with productions, media strategy agencies and brands themselves. With contacts throughout the production and advertising industry we are a good place to start.

Q - I've heard that in the US, companies pay to have their product in a film, is it the same here?

Steve - Product Placement is widely used in the UK, although mainly concentrating on unpaid placement of editorially correct props in TV. The TV market provides a shorter lead time and a more proven audience. Product placement is all about positive associations and a gritty Brit flick about drugs or family angst rarely results in a product placement frenzy. American films and TV shows can reach vast audiences. That is where the big money comes in to play. We are leading the push in the UK to get productions and brands to collaborate on innovative product placement deals.

Q - How much competition is there for a company such as yours?

Steve - There are few specialised product placement agencies in the UK. We represent major brands to TV and film. We do not represent competing brands. We wouldn't represent Coke and Pepsi for instance, so there is room for other agencies to represent brands that compete with the brands we represent.

Q - Why can't I go directly to the advertiser for their product?

Steve - You can, although if they have a product placement agency they will pass you on to them. The benefit of using an agency is that they will pitch you directly to the person making the decisions, saving producers hours of fruitless phone calls. An agency will also look for ways to marry up your picture with a brand marketing strategy and suggest innovative ways that product placement could work.

Q - Do you charge a fee if a producer contacts you?

PRODUCTION

What's in shot?

GUERILLA FILM MAKER SAYS!

It seems that pretty much everything is now a copyrightable image, logo or creative 'work'. The law is very open to interpretation, and to make matters worse, regardless of the law, if big business isn't happy with something in your film, they could just pursue legal action to the point, where, even if you are 'in the right'. Remember, you may not have the resources or will to fight a battle with a big company.

1. If at all possible, avoid showing corporate products or logos. It may be that featured props need to be redesigned (a new label on a jar for instance) or simply held or rotated in such a way as to obscure the name or logo.

2. Be aware of story props - if a character chokes and dies after eating a particular brand of food, the manufacturer is going to take a dim view. Work out these problems in the screenplay beforehand.

3. Beware of copyrightable work in shot, such as magazines, posters, artwork etc. There will be less of a potential problem if the object is out of focus, in a non specific pile, passing through frame quickly, than if it is held in shot and clearly visible. It must be clearly identifiable to be a problem.

4. Many companies will be happy to have their products featured, as long as its not in a negative light. Contact product placement companies in advance to set this up. If you get your product from a placement agency, they generally have been cleared for use. Make sure there are no 'exclusive' clauses where you are disallowed from showing competitive brands. Make sure that the items featured are used ONLY in the way intended. No use complaining when a beer company sues because your serial killer uses the empties to slash characters throats.

5. There will always be stuff that slips though and someone will have to get on the phone and find out whose image or prop has been used, and then get the necessary clearances.

6. The nightmare scenario is when a prop is featured without anyone in the crew either noticing or caring, and that prop is then 'disallowed' by the company who owns it. Editing, digital replacement or reshooting will then be needed.

7. On the whole crews are very good at spotting things that may be a problem. Just ask a few key members to keep an eye on stuff, even the camera operator as they can see exactly what's in shot.

8. Copyright laws also apply, so artwork created by people who have been dead for over 75 years should be cleared for use (check with your lawyer).

9. Advertisments which exist before the crew arrive can be used as background dressing without formal clearances, but never featured in shot or in dialogue.

10. The making up of fake props sounds like a good idea, but it can harm the 'reality' of your story as viewers will be aware of the items they commonly see being replaced by lookalike props, created by the design department. Most props can be cleared given time.

11. To get clearance, ideally before shooting, contact the manufacturers and negotiate with them to allow you to use their products in shot.

There is a clearance form in the documents section at the end of this book.

Pic by Darren Gerish © PPFI Ltd

Steve - We work for the brands, finding them appropriate productions in which to place their products. The only time that a fee is charged to a producer is if we broker a reciprocal deal between a brand and the production. Some agencies work in the reverse way, charging productions an upfront fee to find them free products and marketing money. It is up to producers whether they want to pay to have an agency at their beck and call or not. You may find that experienced props buyers and art directors will do much the same job. Remember that even if the agency is working for the brand and not the production, they wouldn't get very far without keeping both sides happy.

Q - Are there legal restrictions to what can be shown and how?

Steve - There are not as many rules governing movies as there are TV (although if you are involved in productions for TV do keep an eye on the Ofcom rules governing product placement and branded props as they are subject to change). The legal restrictions come mainly from the brands themselves protecting their brand image. If you go through a product placement agency they can ensure that all the legal clearances for the brand are in place before shooting begins. Agencies and brands will often require productions to sign paperwork that confirms the discussions regarding how a brand is to be shown, covering things such as no association with illegal or antisocial behaviour etc. There are guidelines concerning marketing to children that many brands sign up to voluntarily and you may find yourself subject to unwanted attention if you appear to be heavily pushing a junk food brand or a mobile phone company in a children's film.

Q - What common mistakes do producers make when it comes to including products in their films?

Steve - Thinking that merely seeing the product on screen is enough. Brand managers and audiences have become much more cynical in recent years. A brand manger will not be swayed simply by seeing their product on screen and will equally not be happy if a product is crow barred into a scene. Blatant product placement can be off putting to an audience and actually have a detrimental effect for a brand. To be really worthwhile to the brand the product needs to be associated with an aspirational character in a seamless fashion.

Another common mistake by productions is not keeping in contact once filming is underway and after filming has wrapped. Do send stills from the set featuring the product. Do send footage of how the product is appearing. And most importantly do invite the agency and / or brand manager to an early screening. Remember if a brand has invested time and money, even if it is only the free loan of a product, they want to see the results.

Q - What advice would you offer a new film maker?

Steve - Be realistic. Product Placement is no longer an easy buck. The reality is that most major brands and agencies will concentrate their product placement energies on major films with either a big name star or a big name director. To be taken seriously take a long hard look at what positive associations your film could offer a product. Produce a Product Placement pack to email or send to agencies such as ourselves, or directly to brand managers. This pack should include a synopsis of the film, details and pictures of the cast, biogs of the main crew and, most importantly, details of distribution and target audience. If you have time, target your contact to the brand or brands in question. Don't just tell us about your film, tell us how our products could benefit from association with the film. Also look beyond the big brands. If your film is likely to have a regional release target regional companies. If it's likely to reach only a niche audience look for products that fit that niche. Consider going to brands that are also up and coming in their field, artists, bands, designers etc. who might not bring in money but could bring in press or media coverage. Above all be honest, if you take a product or cash saying that it will feature make sure it does and in the manner discussed. Brand managers and agencies have long memories, if the product is used by the bad guy, ridiculed or associated with the wrong kind of character you will find it hard to get money or deals in the future, even if you become the next big thing.

PRODUCTION

Terry Forrestal
Stunt Co-ordinator

STUNT CO-ORDINATOR

Q - What are the most common stunts for low budget films?

Terry - Fights. No matter the genre there's always some kind of fight, be it between lovers, friends or a bar room brawl. An experienced co-ordinator can choreograph that making sure it works for the drama and the camera; whereas young or inexperienced people have a tendency to overcomplicate things. This is especially problematic when you have actors trying to perform action sequences without professional guidance as this is not what they're trained to do.

Q - Are any stunts a real problem?

Terry - All stunts need proper organising and preparing, so from a low budget persepctive, all stunts are a potential problem. Many areas are specialist such as motorbikes, high falls, cars and horses. Most stunt people should be happy to fall out of a saddle, but pulling a horse down is a potential leg breaker.

Most injuries are caused by motorbike crashes and car knock downs. High falls don't hurt, unless you get them wrong; then you're very dead. It's knowing how to shoot the hard things that makes them easier and much less dangerous.

Q - What basic precautions does a film maker need to take?

Terry - Clearly preparation and discussion are essential. The first and foremost precaution that any young producer should take is not to listen to all those people around them who aren't in the film business who say *I know a fireman and my kid brother's mate can race motorbikes*. Use professional people, look at their CVs, don't listen to anyone who cuts short on safety, and if they do, get rid of them.

Whether you're low or big budget, you're responsible for health and safety, not just morally, but by law. If anyone gets hurt you could be dealing with a serious offence.

Q - The rule here is to find a way of achieving what your drama needs without doing a major stunt?

Terry - Yes, if necesary, cut away to a driver's face for the car impact and use a loud sound effect for instance. There are some co-ordinators and stunt performers who are happy to help out on low budget films because many people see new film makers as the future of the industry. Who knows, help them now and in the future they may give you a fully paid job.

Q - How involved is a stunt sequence?

Terry - It depends on the stunt. A serious stunt such as someone catching fire and falling out of a window will need some dedicated support - the art department will need to build the window, a special effects team will need to handle the glass and the fire, official paramedics will be needed, one to drive and one to do the tending should something go wrong, the fire brigade etc.

Even something that seems simple, such as two lovers on a lake having an argument and one falls in can need full prep. You'd need the boat people, divers, the water needs to be tested beforehand in case there is a metal pole sticking up for instance. Also, film makers

Second Unit

GUERILLA FILM MAKER SAYS!

Key to the success of many stunt and special effects sequences is the second unit team, and the second unit director (often a good friend of the main director who is helping for the fun and experience of working with a pro stunt team or special effects team). Planning of shots in meticulous detail, and the critical timing and execution required to pull off a stunt effectively and safely, can rarely be achieved by the main unit on a low budget feature. This is because the main unit is under massive pressure and is used to cutting corners and rushing through shots. Stunts are not shots where you can cut corners or rush.

Have a second unit team that plan while the main unit is shooting other sequences. When it comes to the stunt, allow the second unit to take over the main unit and do what they have spent so much time planning and preparing. They will have thought of all the angles and problems. Of course main unit personnel can be around to help and advise, in particular the DP, for lighting. But camera placement and direction of action should be nailed down by this point.

need to remember simple things like hot tea and coffee, towels and blankets if someone is going to fall in a lake. It's an easy oversight, but it can cause very bad feeling. Every film unit must have a unit nurse by law. Speak to the co-ordinator, they'll tell you what you need.

Q - What happens about weapons - a killing weapon in a story can also be a killing weapon in real life?

Terry - More than likely you will need an armourer, like the guys from Perdix Firearms. Anything that's a practical weapon that actually fires out of the barrel must by law be taken away from set and put in the hands of a registered armourer who has a section 5 licence. When weapons are not in use, actors and extras and to a certain extent stunt people should not be allowed to handle them. Only at the last minute will the armourer load the weapon and shout *gun loaded* to let everyone know about the potential hazard. It may seem over-precautious but even blanks at close range have killed people before.

However, dummy weapons, made of plastic or blunt knives for instance, can be used and kept by the props master. If you're out and about, the location manager must inform local police and civilians that weapons will be on the streets. It has happened in the past that the police have swept in on what they thought was a robbery only to find a bunch of actors.

Q - What happens about stunt insurance, above and beyond other normal insurances?

Terry - All Equity stunt people have their own insurance covered by Equity. If a stuntman is injured and it is not the fault of a ridiculous demand from the director or producer, the production company is not liable. If I decide on a stunt and how to do it, then it goes wrong, then it is not the fault of the production company but my responsibility and it would end up on my insurance. However, if for example, an inexperienced A.D. wasn't doing their job correctly and at the last minute a pedestrian, dog or pushbike comes from nowhere and the stunt performer is forced to swerve and has an accident then they'd have a right to claim.

Q - What are 'adjustments'?

Terry - Adjustments are a long standing tradition in the stunt business. The risk factor and potential for serious injury increases according to the severity of the stunt - accordingly a stunt person would want to be paid more. Also, each time you perform the stunt you will be repaid.

Q - What about camera tools like slow motion?

Terry - Many tricks with the camera are used to help the overall effect of a stunt. Slow motion is a great tool. Stunts can happen very quickly and a little slow motion can slow the action down so that you can see it more clearly. Many stunts are shot in slow motion and audiences don't even know that it is slow motion, they

PRODUCTION

Stunts and Pyrotechnics

GUERILLA FILM MAKER SAYS!

Although stuntmen and SPFX guys may seem a bit cavalier about their craft, rest assured they are fully aware of how easily their work can turn fatal. Many have migrated to stunt work from other dangerous professions, such as the Marines, and they know exactly how to avoid or minimise injury, while still making the effect look like the real thing.

1. Approach a stunt co-ordinator as soon as you can so that they have the maximum amount of time to come up with ideas for your stunts or SPFX, and more importantly, enough time to figure out the safest way to do them.

2. To find a stunt coordinator, ask other filmmakers for recommendations and then call those people to talk about your film. Call the biggest people in the field, they might not do it, but they will turn you over to a respected colleague who will. Also, there are a few stunt person agencies you can solicit as well.

3. Stunts are dangerous. Don't push a stuntman to do his job quicker, or with less safety equipment. Remember, they are putting their life on the line for you.

4. Stunts aren't as expensive as you may think. A good stunt can make the film look like it cost much more than it actually did.

5. If a stuntman or pyrotechnician is eager or very willing to reduce safety standards, be wary. They may not be fully qualified and therefore a liability. Don't mess, get a qualified person to do the job.

6. Be careful with blank firing weapons. Metal fragments can become stuck in the barrel of the gun (from previous firings because someone did not check or clean it properly). The power of firing a blank round is more than enough to shoot this object at a deadly speed. The last thing anyone wants is a repeat of the Brandon Lee tragedy on the set of The Crow.

7. Try and organise all your stunts into one shooting block. This will minimise time wastage by dedicating the production to stunts and effects during this period.

8. There are many books on the subject of homemade (safe) effects and cheats, some of which are excellent, safe and could save you lots of money. For example, to simulate a helicopter flying over at dusk can be achieved by panning a bright light over the set and mixing the sound effect over it or bullet hits produced using compressed air from a garden spraygun.

9. Sound is a major consideration with stunts and effects. A good 'whack' sound in a fist fight can hide a dodgy stunt. Track lay these sequences with extra care and attention.

10. Digital effects are now very cost effective, and techniques such as wire removal for high falls may well be within your budget. Ask for a quote.

11. For large stunts, you will have to provide a fire engine and paramedics on the scene. You will need costly stunt insurance as well.

12. Actors are comforted when a stuntman is around for potentially dangerous scenes. It says to them that they are protected, that you take their safety seriously, and that you are a professional. If the situation is relatively low impact and merely involves a degree of physical acting, try a trainee stuntman to lend a hand on set.

13. Always ask for advice. Stuntmen and pyro technicians know many cheap ways to achieve what may seem impossible to you as a new filmmaker.

14. Before embarking on an expensive and time consuming stunt or effect, ask yourself if you could actually cut away from it or cut out of the scene, just as it is about to happen. For instance, see the lead up to a car crash, then hear the impact over a shot of the face of a grieving relative at the funeral. It's a lot cheaper if you don't have to film it, but if you do go down this route, make sure it's done cleverly and that you're not cheating and disappointing your audience out of something they might expect.

15. If you get the stunt right the first time, DO NOT go for a second take. Two reasons. You will be undermining your stunt co-ordinator's authority and you will be unnecessarily exposing them to additional risk. The latter is what happened to Harry O'Connor, a master stuntman in the filming of XXX where he died repeating a stunt.

16. Editing is key to many stunts. Make sure you have enough shots and the right shots. You can never have too many cameras rolling on a major stunt.

think that it happened at that speed. Similarly, under-cranking the camera slightly can make some stunts look much faster, such as a car knock down.

Q - What is your relationship to the first assistant director?

Terry - I work very closely with the first AD as the set must be completely controlled. I know that stunts are very exciting to watch but you should try to avoid letting people get over excited as it can be very distracting. Making sure everyone knows exactly what is happening and keeping everyone a safe distance is also essential. Clarity and co-ordination are essential.

Q - Can you advise on better ways of achieving the same ends in the drama of the script?

Terry - Nothing should be impossible for a good stunt co-ordinator given enough time and money - but you often don't have either of those. I can advise about possible script changes to take advantage of a simpler, safer and therefore cheaper stunt that might have equal impact. Again, if money is tight, be creative about getting around the story without having to show the stunt - that's the cheapest and safest way by far!

The flipside is that often I can suggest ways of making something that seems fairly mundane in the script into something more spectacular.

Q - What common mistakes do you encounter?

Terry - In general, overall inexperience of young or new crew members. For example attitudes to saftey, and another classic is the person doing the budget. The latter often leads to conversations like *I didn't realise that was a stunt* or *What? This isn't a stunt picture.* Usually I then say *well if it isn't a stunt picture, why are you talking to me?* An old lady with a walking stick who trips and falls, that's a stunt.

Virtually everything has been done before, check out other movies and make what you are doing different somehow. Hire a professional - the people to go for are Equity stunt registered performers and co-ordinators, and remember you need Health and Safety on the set - by law, no matter what the budget. Lastly, remember, even though a stunt person is highly trained, they are putting their life on the line for a production and you must respect their experience and decisions.

Q - What basic advice would you offer a film maker?

Terry - This isn't a glib answer, I will quote my school motto - *'think well on it'.*

Some time after this interview was conducted, Terry was tragically killed in a base jumping accident.

PRODUCTION

Johnny Rafique
Elements Effects

Q - What is your job?

Johnny - My job title is Special Effects Supervisor. I work with practical effects, that is, effects that occur on set and in front of the camera. We often co-ordinate with post production effects people who work on effects digitally, either enhancing or combining our work with other elements.

Q - When do you normally get involved?

Johnny - That depends on the production. The sensible productions call us at their script stage, the non-sensible productions call us on a Friday night and say *'We need a wind machine on Saturday morning!'* You get everything in between. I always suggest film makers get us involved at the very beginning and we don't charge for those initial meetings. So why not?

Q - One thing I've heard consistently is 'come and talk to us, we are free for a chat, ask us all the questions...'

Johnny - It is the most sensible solution, and because we do it day in day out, and we are here in our workshop playing with things all the time, trying to make something new and interesting, we can offer excellent advice and plan to save money and produce the needed effects. We want every job we do to be fantastic so it can be an advert for us. We are constantly looking at new things to do. They might think an effect is completely out of their ballpark because it is too expensive or complicated, but if they get onto us at the script stage, we can read through the script, and offer suggestions. Then they can make their minds up. It is just another string to their bow that they can accept or decline.

Q - As a general rule do you think it is better to get it right in front of the camera than to try and create or fix it in post production?

Johnny - Yes. It saves everybody's time and effort if you can look at it on video playback, and you know you've got it, you've only got to do it once. If you watch the first take back and it has got everything you want on it, leave it, and move on.

Q - How often do you hear that dreaded phrase, 'Oh we will fix it in post!'? How often should the film maker hold fast and go again with the practical effect rather than trying to fix it digitally?

Johnny - Practically speaking, yes you do hear the Director, Producer or the 1ˢᵗAD say *'Oh we haven't got time for that, we will do it in post'*. You know that although they feel they haven't got time to do it on the day, one more take might give them exactly what they want. Post production will cost them an arm and a leg. In a lot of instances we know better, because we are the people who do it day in day out, on the floor. There are other instances, when the digital guys know better. That is the sort of thing you need to get out in the open at the beginning of all production meetings. You really can save time and effort on a film during pre-production. One good meeting can save you a whole day's wasted film making. The things that the digital guys can do are changing every single day. Every day they come up with *'we've got a button for this, we've got a button for that'*, and some of them are fantastic, some of them are in their infancy, and they are not as good as they could be yet.

Q - Can you help inexperienced film makers get the most bang for their buck?

Johnny - We can take them by the hand and explain all the ins and outs of it. If they've got us on board, the stunt guys and the post production guys are on board all at the same time and at the same meeting, it can become very easy - as long as there is no-one there with a massive ego who is just going to cause problems. To get the best results, film makers should just let us do what we do best. When we do get to the shooting stage there is always a point where we have to say to the 1st AD, you're handing over to us now and the 1st AD will say *'Johnny's in charge'.* There is a point where they are more experienced at what they are doing, and there is a point when we are more experienced at what we are doing. It's important to recognise when that hand over needs to take place.

Q - What happens about quotes?

Johnny - We run through the script and annotate it with everything that we think is necessary. Hopefully someone on the film is doing a similar thing, and then we come together, and see if there are things in there that they've missed. We will come up with our ideal figure, and then we will negotiate. We may have to start trimming back on how spectacular things are, or trimming back a number of things. If you trim back a number of things, and just go for the big things, you can still have the same visual impact, but you just lose out on a couple of things, a few bullet hits are acted rather than seen on screen for instance.

Q - That is a really interesting point because so much can be done with editing, acting, all the other stuff. Do you ever get involved in terms of saying, 'look these are your main moments, we should make these really great, and the other stuff, let's work on those and do them in a non-special effects sort of way, in order to do something great'?

Johnny - Yeah. You look at some of the great genre films that have been made and there have been no special effects whatsoever. It was either before that there was the capacity to do it, or they just didn't have the budget to do it. Script, acting, editing etc., can all make a movie stand alone. There is a definite point where you have to do something, or it won't have the impact or reality that is required. If they concentrate on those moments, then they can get a much better bang for their buck.

Q - How closely do you work with other departments and what departments are they?

Johnny - First of all, we work with the Production Designer and the Art Director, because what we are doing is related to their job. The Production Designer is in charge of the overall look of things, and therefore whatever we do, must tailor the look of the whole film. Of course, we work closely with the camera department too. A good DOP knows how he/she wants to light things, but sometimes we have to help some of them who haven't had much experience with rain, explosions or fire for example. It might be that we spend a day in a field where they can just have a look at the intensity of different kinds of explosions, because a gas explosion will have a different intensity of light to a petrol explosion. If it is a big sequence that must be done in one take, those kind of preparatory tests are essential.

Q - How prepared are Directors generally?

Johnny - If the DOP and the Production Designer can explain what their vision is, then we should be able to put that vision together without them having had the experience of doing it before. We are there to hold their hand and make it all happen. A lot of the time, if you come across 1st ADs, who've done this sort of thing before, it makes things so much smoother. The 1st AD is in charge of scheduling and the inexperienced ones will look at a special effects sequence and say *'we've got all this script to get through first, and there is no dialogue going on in the special effects shot, so we'll do it last'.* Then the shooting day goes on and on and the special effects time is reduced. What then happens is the effects are not as good as they should be, or they end up being re-done at greater expense. It just causes problems in terms of health and safety apart from anything else. We will

PRODUCTION

obviously do our best, but if not enough time is available, you sometimes don't get the sequence that is wanted.

Q - On a low budget film, with all good intentions, people will storyboard, but in reality that may become impossible. Having said that, do you think it is important to storyboard the key sequences with effects?

Johnny - That is a difficult one, because sometimes by storyboarding you limit what you are actually going to get. Because we are breaking up the sequence into certain things, we have to get from A to B to C to D to E, when what might be better would be to go from A to E and see what happens in between, because a lot of the stuff we do is fluid, and sort of runs as it happens. Having said that, if we know what A, B, C and D all are, at least it gives us a better idea of how we get to E, in the style we want it to. It does help us but it is not essential.

Q - One issue that I come across with inexperienced film makers is they don't realise how quickly an effect can happen.

Johnny - Generally, our sequences can happen very fast (not the setup time, just the execution time). You can make it more dramatic by having more cameras, even if it's a DV camera or a GSAP (aka Zap) camera, often setup where you can't get close to the action for safety reasons - it doesn't matter that the definition is not that fantastic. It doesn't even, in certain circumstances, have to be broadcast quality, because it is such a quick instant of time on the screen and it can help you out of an editing problem, and it can certainly make a sequence more interesting.

Q - What about of slow motion?

Johnny - On film you can hire a camera that will shoot slow motion, though rarely do people shoot 'slow mo' enough. To get that real slow motion look on an explosion, you should be shooting at something like 200 frames a second. On digital and HD formats, it's more of a problem though there are new cameras and technologies always emerging. A company just down the road has a fantastic high speed video set up and they can shoot thousands of frames a second.

Q - Typically, what are the pyrotechnic requirements for your average movie?

Johnny - They usually like to have an explosion of some sort, whether it is inside a building, outside, in the middle of nowhere, a car blowing up - they like explosions as they are a fantastically visual thing. It looks fantastic on the screen, and it looks like a million dollars. It is actually quite a cheap and simple thing to set up, compared to a large water sequence or a train crash. Bullet hits are almost a daily thing for us. A lot of what we've been doing recently involves using flames for lighting as it gives such an attractive 'look'.

Q - When you are using pyrotechnics, clearly there are safety issues. Are people surprised by how much control is needed?

Johnny - It starts with the choice of location. They will say, *'we are doing an inner city thing, and we'd like to blow a car up, and we just want to put it in front of this post office please,'* and the council is not going to let you do it, the road people aren't going to let you do it, the police are not going to let you do it, and the fire brigade is not going to let you do it, so we are not going to let you do it! They will think it is only a little explosion, *'surely we can get away with it?'*, because you see it in so many big films. You see these fantastic explosions in confined spaces, but in reality it is a set, or it is somewhere where stuff really doesn't matter, such as a derelict site. Choice of location is something where people often make mistakes.

Time to set up is another thing. They say *'how long does it take you to set up?'* and we say *'it will take us 4hrs in total, but 3hrs 45mins we can do before you get to your sequence'*. But for that 3hrs 45mins we still need everyone to be out of the way, so while the production could be shooting in that time, they must not, in any way, be in our way. Although we can do everything in advance, we still need people to be out of the way while we are setting things up. A good 1st AD will know this and schedule accordingly.

Q - What are the safety people you need in place?

Special Effects - Rough Guide

If your film calls for something to enhance the reality of a scene or requires you to create the illusion that the impossible or improbable really occurs, then a cool special effect may be what you need. While special effects may be costly and dangerous, careful planning and a seasoned SPFX man can alleviate those concerns while adding a huge about of production value to your project. Here is a list of special effect types you can use to make your film pop. But beware, if it goes wrong, you could waste a huge amount of time and effort on something that, if it just isn't good enough, you will need to cut. Nothing destroys the audiences suspension of belief like a dreadful special effect.

Pyrotechnics
Fire, smoke, flares, fireworks, explosions, debris - anything which burns, smolders or explodes, such as a campfire that burns at the same rate for continuity, and is smokeless and safe.

Models & Miniatures
Small versions of a real object, i.e. the Whitehouse in Independence Day. Also forced perspective models, hanging miniatures, objects that are difficult to film or control, like a virus or an atom.

Mechanics
Anything from a rig to control milk pouring out of a jug on cue and at just the right rate to a massive rig to knock down a wall (if it needs to be done mechanically rather than pyrotechnically).

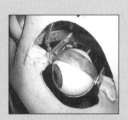

Action Prop/Animatronics
Making creatures up which have realistic movement, operated by radio control servos, cables, or computer operated these days.Also, any object to be constructed that must perform movement.

Breakaways
Glass (bottles, windows), and crockery, hand props and furniture (balsa wood is used for those chairs that are to be broken or thrown) and structural breakaways (walls collapsing, a roof cave-in etc.)

Prosthetics
A latex piece that is attached to an actor that sometimes requires body and face casting enabling artists to sculpt 'onto' actors faces and bodies.

Water
Anything taking place on or in water i.e. water flooding a submarine or a sinking ship, shooting in water tanks, miniature damns.

Firearms
Weapons, firing blanks, bullet impacts, bullet squibs, bullet hits, bullet holes, arrows, knives.

Atmospheric
Rain, mist, wind, snow (falling and dress), hail, wind, fog, smoke, ice, dust storms etc.

Miscellaneous
Rocker units (i.e. a boat in heavy seas), earthquakes, cobwebs, volcanic lava, quicksand etc. Anything else you can imagine!

PRODUCTION

Johnny - Number one call is the fire service. We tend to use the same guys who provide us with a fire engine and trained fire crew on the day in question. We have off duty officers or ex-officers who are there to look after us and everyone else. Obviously, you have to notify the police in the area because any loud bang is going to be called in by somebody, and the police need to know that, even though they wont attend. Paramedics should be employed by the film production, and we usually advise that any day we are doing anything with fire, water or even the slightest danger, that the unit nurse should be up to a paramedic level.

Q - What are the things in a script that Producers often don't realise are pyrotechnics?

Johnny - They will go through the script and see the car explosion, the bullet hits etc., but the things they won't see are log fires, fires in a grate, steam in the bathroom…all the little things that people just take for granted. Because they are shooting a sequence with a shower in it, they think that will have steam in it. In reality, the water may be cold as the steam could cause problems with the cameras. Pyrotechnically, one of our stock in trades is a fire in a grate, and we set the whole thing up with gas and a copper pipe and sit there for the day turning the fire on and off (laughs).

Q - Let's talk about atmospheric effects - the complexities, snow, mist, rain etc.

Johnny - The most complicated of all those things is smoke. Everyone takes it for granted and, no disrespect to the props guys, they just give the props man a smoke machine, or the lighting department a smoke machine and they think they've got things covered. The difference between bad smoke and good smoke is enormous. Anyone can push the button down on a smoke machine, and fill the room up with smoke, and it will just look like a room full of smoke. Someone who has been doing it for many, many years, will be able to trickle it in here and there, and move it around properly so that it comes from the right place. When you are outdoors and they are trying to shoot a sequence where you need wind and smoke, and it is howling a gale, it becomes an enormous and labour intensive job.

Q - What about rain, how do you do that?

Johnny - How long is a piece of string? On the lowest budget, someone will call me up and say *'we need rain and it's just on a window, can you do it, it is only going to take 10mins'* and I say *'it might take 10mins in your production, but I guarantee you it is going to take a day of our time, because we have got to get there, we have to sit around and wait for it to happen, and we have got to prep it all, and get things ready'*. In those instances where they really haven't got the money, I just say, *'find a garden hose, and fire it up into the air and let it come down onto the window!'* If you haven't got the money, it is really not worth wasting it on having us standing around for a day to do rain on a window. The more complicated or better-looking rain sequences create a very complicated, time consuming and money-eating process.

Urban Ghost Story, *the third feature film made by the authors, employed a forced perspective model - a small sign six inches long, suspended on fishing wire in such a way that from the camera viewpoint, it appears to be much larger and attached to the side of the building. Note operator's hand holding the sign in the right picture.*

Q - Does it involve very large rigs?

Johnny - Yes. Enormous rigs. You have got to have cranes and platforms, and time to string in over head bars and all that kind of stuff.

Q - And of course the use of rain complicates the sound department, and there is electrics, and all sorts of nightmares - and then people want it at night!

Johnny - Every time we do it, we will get there and we will talk to locations about where we can park the pump. They will say *'Yep, you can park it there,'* and you say *'are you shooting sound?'* and they will say *'yes'*, and you say *'well, the pump is 15 yards away from your microphone and it is going to be screaming its head off as it pumps 6 bar worth or water, so we need to get it 100 yards away for the sound recordist to be happy, and even then he/she will still probably have to run a wild track!'*

Q - What about snow?

Johnny - Snow is enormously time consuming and backbreaking, but it can look fantastic. There are so many different kinds of snow. I think there are 65 different types of snow now as everyone is constantly researching new ways of doing it. If you are doing big, fantastic, complicated snow you should talk to Snow Business. We do snow and have our own snow kit but if it were an enormous sequence, we would defer to Snow Business. I think anyone in his or her right mind would.

Q - What about wind?

Johnny - Wind comes from, at the bottom end, a hairdryer all the way up to enormous turbine wind machines. We tend to go as far as a 4ft Volkswagen wind machine, then after that, Effects Associates have got these enormous Cheetah wind machines, with V8 engines on them - that are fantastic pieces of kit!

Q - What is it that seals the illusion of all of these effects, is it the leaves in the wind.

Johnny - Yes. It is what you can get in front of the camera. You cannot obviously see wind unless there is something in it. If you are doing a sequence where you put too much stuff in, it draws attention and the audience can sense an effect. It is a difficult balance. There are things we've done where you want to put in some material and you say *'well it's fluttering the clothes a bit, but it's still not selling it as being an enormous gale'*. Short of getting a much bigger wind machine, you could do it with either a bit of smoke or debris that whips across camera, which makes it appear windier than it is. The big wind machines will cost you a lot of money so for low budget you should tailor your shots so that you can get away from the big wide shots, then you can get close into your actors and use a 6ft wind machine rather than a 16ft wind machine.

Q - What about models? Are they on the decline now with digital effects?

Johnny - Definitely. Back in the good old Thunderbirds days you could always tell a scale fire or water - they are natural things and they have an organic size and shape to them, so you can always see when there is a miniature shot. With digital effects these problems are gone, though you'd be surprised how many miniatures are still made and combined with digital elements.

Q - What are the common things that appear in the script where the Director and Producer probably haven't thought 'Oh, we need a model for that'?

Johnny - Normally in fight sequences where there is a gun or a knife or a chair, you will need safe, soft props. It is a difficult thing to quantify because there are different things that turn up in every script.

Q - I guess that will include break away glass and bottles etc.?

PRODUCTION

Johnny - Break away glass usually tends to be the one that film makers see in the script because they immediately think of a bar brawl, they want breaking glass, because it seals the illusion. The script says a guy has got to land on a table in a fight, so they budget for the glass, but they don't budget for doing the break away table.

Q - Do you deal with weapons?

Johnny - We do to a certain extent but often we defer to an armourer, and there are those who we work with all the time. If someone comes to us with a sequence where there's just one weapon involved and it is fairly simple, we'll say *'yes, we can take care of that'* and we will get an armourer on board. We then get one of our armourers who can come in and handle the gun for the day. So to the Producer or Director's mind it is a problem solved, and we deal with the armourer on their behalf.

Q - How much control do you need with that? One thing a lot of people don't get is that a blank is still a live round, it is still a gun with a live round in it.

Johnny - In all of these things, safety is always the number one priority. Brandon Lee is the obvious example. There was nothing dangerous about that sequence apart from the fact that he got killed. It is never dangerous until it goes wrong. At that point it is enormously dangerous and lethal, so yes, you have to start from scratch with the most careful safety precautions.

Q - Of course if you are running around on the streets of London with weapons, even if there is a film crew next to you, there is always going to be someone who thinks that something else is going on. . .?

Johnny - Yes. I heard of a job where they were doing a shoot out in a motorway service stop, and they warned everyone on one side of the services, but not the people from the other side. What they saw, through two plate glass windows, was a guy with a gun running around and shooting. It caused an enormous panic. You want to avoid that kind of situation.

Q - What happens with things like car crashes? What are the implications of that?

Johnny - First off, you have to think how big this car crash is in the story, how much damage are you going to do with the car and its occupants? Then you have to think, in real life, how much damage would occur to the car and the driver / occupants. If a car rolled into a lamppost, for example, then you can set it up quite simply, you can have a car with no driver and we can just push the car into the lamppost with a piston or a rig. That is a fairly simple thing for us to set up. Usually though, a car crash will involve stunt driving so we are talking about ambulances, paramedics and a fire crew, just in case something goes wrong. You can do 80mph worth of damage with a 30mph accident, if you prep the car correctly. If you need to have a really enormous serious accident, you can do it by having an enormous serious accident or you can do it by having a low speed, controlled collision with a car that is designed to crumple in all the right places to make that impact look larger that it would normally be.

Q - Do you think that some film makers get a bit too excited about special effects, everybody loves a bang!

Johnny - Definitely. It is important that everything serves the story, be that camera, editing, acting, and effects are no different. Every story has a different set of requirements.

Q - One of the grey areas – are, when does it stop being an effect and becomes costume, make-up or props etc?

Johnny - It is all a cross over. Prosthetics seem to be a part of our business. We don't specialise in prosthetics, so if we have a prosthetics part in our sequence, we get someone who really knows how to do that stuff. He/she is either his or her own department or they become part of the make-up department, or they become part of the effects department. It doesn't matter to me, whether prosthetics comes under make-up or under special effects. As long as it is all done properly. We can help in that respect, and they can help us as well. Planning and co-ordination between all departments is essential.

Q - What should you use for movie blood?

Johnny - The main problem you come across with blood is colour, viscosity and staining. You can get the colour right, and it stains, you can get the viscosity right and it doesn't wash off. If you get all three right, you are doing very well. There are a few commercially made bloods which are enormously expensive, and you just couldn't practically use them for a sequence where you have 60 litres of blood in a pool, as some horror films do. Everyone has their own recipe and we have our own too.

Q - There is an equation I have found - whatever happens on set, once you get it in the cutting room, it is never quite as big - so if you have some blood on set, when you get it in the cutting room, it often doesn't seem like there was enough. No matter how big the explosion, in the cutting room it's nothing special?

Johnny - Yes. An experienced director will have come across the problem, and know it is going to be a problem. You have to be willing to listen to people who know what they are doing. There are a lot of special effects men out there who can do a fantastic explosion, and they can make it look fantastic in terms of what is actually happening, but aren't that interested in what the camera man is doing, or what the director is looking at. That is fine if you have a camera man and director who really know what they are doing and know what their finished product is going to look like. I think you come to a place where everyone needs to have the whole thing in mind, everyone has got to have that same finished vision in their heads to achieve it properly. This is what I was saying about camera angles. If you add in two extra cameras, put one of them right in on the explosion you can't fail to get something big and spectacular that is going to completely fill the screen. If it is a surplus shot then fine, it has only cost you one camera for one day, but if you miss it, you've got to set the whole day up and re-do it with a full crew.

Q - What are the common mistakes that you see?

Johnny - Not back-lighting rain is my biggest annoyance! We come in, set the rain up, put it up in the air, and there is often the comment *'can we have more, we cant' see it, we need more!'* You don't really need more, you just need to back light it. It just comes down to experience in doing rain sequences and back-lighting them properly. You can get away with a very small amount of water, if it is lit properly.

There can be friction between camera and special effects departments, I don't know why. It's experiences like where we've had cameras that haven't been turned on by stunt men, we've had operators who have failed to load their cameras properly, and we've had special effects men who haven't put their charges in properly. Everyone is inclined to make a mistake now and again. As long as it is a mistake that is rectifiable and not dangerous. You can all laugh about it at the end of the day.

Q - What advice would you offer a new film maker?

Johnny - Don't do it! (laughs) Talk to everyone you can as early as you can. There are so many people out there who have done it before, and know how to do it, and know what the pitfalls are. If you can get hold of those people before you start, then you can save yourself weeks and weeks of heartache.

Secrets Of Hollywood Special Effects by Robert E McCarthy is a great, hardback book for new film makers and aspiring special effects technicians producing a low budget film. It is incredibly detailed and covers a huge amount of effects. It's so detailed in fact, that often new film makers could be put off as it looks more like a physics manual than a film making book.

David Manning
Animal Ark

WORKING WITH ANIMALS

Q - What is your job, what does your company do?

David - I consider myself a Naturalist, which is the person who works with animals and not the person who takes their clothes off a lot! I run a business that supplies, handles and co-ordinates animal requirements for Film and Television productions, photo shoots, parties, government organised events etc.

Q - Why not use your own pets for a film?

David - You can if you want, but you might find your pet is not suitable for the job as it isn't trained. It might be afraid of the huge crew, or bite one of the actors. The dog probably isn't insured too. Other than that, some people do.

Q - What kind of animals are most often required?

David - Dogs and cats are the bulk of work in film and TV. Horses, farm animals too, and then you get onto the exotics, the monkeys or zebras, and spiders and snakes.

Q - In terms of bang for your buck, if I were an independent filmmaker, and I was thinking 'I want to make a children's film, featuring an animal', what is the easiest animal to work with, and most cost effective?

David - Probably a dog. There are a lot of well-trained dogs available to the industry and very good handlers to accompany them onto set.

Q - If budget is a concern, what kind of animals can you re-write and change to avoid problems?

David - You may want to re-write or even remove anything that is covered by the 'Dangerous Wild Animals Act', so venomous snakes, gorillas, monkeys, giraffes, anything big, powerful and potentially dangerous, is also potentially very costly.

Q - So even in the American show 'Friends' when Ross has a little monkey that would be a problem?

David - It would be a problem for a small, self-financed independent filmmaker. For a studio or TV show, such as 'Friends' it would not be an issue at all.

Q - What are the common misconceptions that you come across, especially with inexperienced Producers, or maybe inexperienced 1st Ads?

David - Whether you are a prop maker or an animal supplier, the one thing that people comment on is budget.

Q - How does one go about casting an animal? Say a dog in a lead role.

David - It varies. On a commercial, we may simply cast by e-mail or MPEG. A lot of my regular clients trust my judgement and I can just turn up and do the job. On a feature film, on say *'Phantom of the Opera'*, we supplied poodles. We first sent e-mail images of the dogs, but eventually they did come into the studio to meet the Director, to have a face to face. There are also other considerations. You may find a wonderful dog that lives in Glasgow, and you are shooting in Shepperton, so that it is not going to happen. Part of my job is to find an animal that is suitable for the role, also one that lives within a reasonable distance of where the production is going ahead.

Q - How much more work is it to work with animals?

David - Possibly a lot more than you may think. A posh breed like a poodle will probably need bathing and grooming before the shoot, so that there is some work the day before the job. There is also the journey to collect the dog, the journey to the studio, the journey back to the dog's home after the job, then the journey back home for the handler. It is not like putting a bit of camera equipment back in the case and locking it for the night.

Q - In terms of working, is it like children, you can't keep them on set for 18 hours a day, and expect them to perform?

David - Absolutely. Certainly you wouldn't want to keep them for 18 hours on set anyway, it is never going to give you the best out of the dog or the handler. A lot of the time, my job is trying to minimise the time the animal needs to be on set. For the welfare of the animal, but also for the benefit of the production.

Q - How much time should be allowed for handling and preparing?

David - It depends how complicated the shot is, and how many angles they are working it from. Some animals, such as trained pigeons or a cat, may need some pre-production training, or time on set prior to shooting, just to familiarise them with the new stage. For the vast majority of animals, for a horse, a snake, a frog, you need 5 minutes.

Q - One of the reasons people come to someone like you, is that an animal in it's own environment, I'm sure is comfortable, but suddenly putting it on set with 30 people stood around it, is a different thing?

David - Particularly if someone were trying to use someone's pet, but a trained animal, an animal who works in films shouldn't be phased by that at all. We are often called to do re-shoots where people have tried the secretary's cat or their friend's dog. That can be very costly for productions, having to re-shoot a whole scene just because of the animal.

Q - Does a Producer have to get any kind of a license to use animals?

David - The handler or the agency should be covered by what is called *'The Performing Animals (Regulation) Act 1925'*. They should check that the animal agency that they are using, like any other company or supplier, has *'employer and public liability'*. Other than that you talk to someone, you get a feel for whether they are right for the job or not.

Q - If you had a dog as a lead character in a film, do you need doubles?

David - Sometimes. It depends on the scale of the project, sometimes a double may be essential if you are working a cat over a long period. It could die, fall ill - all sorts of things can happen. Most productions that I've worked on have not needed a double.

Q - Do animals often get ill, or stressed, or refuse to perform because they are put in that environment?

David - Generally not. Over the years we have never needed to claim on our insurance policy. There have been very few incidents where an animal has been

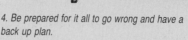

Working With Animals

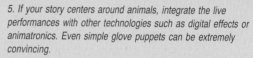

1. If you can, don't do it, especially on low budgets, where too much time and resources will be wasted trying to get an untrained animal to perform.

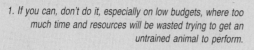

2. Consult with a trainer about what kind of animal you have chosen. Could your hamster be a rat? You cat a dog? These choices could impact on costs significantly.

3. Use a professional. You will then at least get useable footage, and ideally just what you need.

4. Be prepared for it all to go wrong and have a back up plan.

5. If your story centers around animals, integrate the live performances with other technologies such as digital effects or animatronics. Even simple glove puppets can be extremely convincing.

6. Make sure that the animals welfare is looked after.

7. Consider the locations and how that will impact on an animal. For instance a cat on a noisy street isn't going to be very happy.

8. If it's low budget, re-read point one and cut the animals out of your script!

scared of something on the set. When it has happened, it is where we haven't had information from the production company like *'there is going to be an explosion, a car is going to bash through the wall'*, things you really need to know before you put your animal on set.

Q - I assume you get a copy of the script anyway?

David - It may be a breakdown of a scene, you may get a full script, but it does depend a lot on the production.

Q - Assuming it is not a major character in the film, would it be a good idea just to give you a copy of all the scenes in which the animal operates, as opposed to the whole script.

David - A breakdown, a storyboard, something useful to give you background, into that particular job is good. Normally when you are discussing the job with a Production Assistant, you try and get as much of that information as you can.

Q - How do you deal with animals that need to be aggressive for the scene?

David - We can find animals that are trained to behave in that manner, without actually being aggressive. You don't want an aggressive, potentially dangerous dog on the set. You want a dog that looks aggressive and potentially dangerous.

Q - We are sat in a room where there is a myriad of animal bits and bobs, where does all this lot factor into your job?

David - One part of our business is supplying props to the film and television industry. Fibreglass animals, taxidermy bears, insects, bugs, and equipment. It gels very well with the business. If you are doing a commercial with a cat, you will often use a stuffed cat for focusing or lining up, for checking the shadows, things that a photographer or cameraman might wish to do before the real cat comes on. Also many times you'll film with a live pigeon or a live crow that has to be run over or shot, that's when we use our taxidermy doubles. It is essential. It is very much part of the business now.

Q - The whole area between special effects and the use of animals is starting to merge - with animatronics and digital effects. How does that whole thing merge from your perspective?

David - It is part of the evolution of the film industry. CGI is reality. On a CGI segment they may just hire a stuffed chicken, and use that as the template to create their digital chicken, without ever actually hiring a live chicken! Other productions will do both, hire both, to get a bit of natural movement, still using the stuffed one for whatever it is these technological guys do.

Q - Often film sets are very stressful environments, do you think bringing that dog into that environment de-stresses the environment or increases the stress?

David - A lot of the time it decreases stress because there is so much hanging around, it gives someone a focal point, you can pat the dog. I find with almost whatever animal you arrive with on set, it is a point of conversation.

Q - What are the common mistakes that you see?

David - One of the worst is if a company supplies half a dozen different animals from half a dozen different animal agencies, because there is not so much 'in-fighting' between the animal handlers, but there are issues like, does this dog get on with that dog? And will the horse be scared of the frog, or the snake or the owl. It makes it more complicated as an animal handler when other people are managing other animals on the same set. Other than that, generally in my experience people do look after animals as there is a lot of concern for their welfare.

The most important thing I've found over the years is the relationship that a Supplier like an Animal agency builds up with the Buyer, the Producer, and the Director. That is actually what is important. It is easier to work with somebody who you have worked with before, than to work with somebody new. You often both know where you are coming from and what is expected of you, and how things are likely to pan out.

Q - What advice would you offer a new filmmaker?

David - Build a good team around you, find people you trust and keep them. It is all about relationships.

Jaap Buitendijk
Unit Photographer

STILLS PHOTOGRAPHER

Q - What is your job?

Jaap - I provide the photographs that are used to publicise a movie. When you see images from a film, in a magazine, on the internet or on a DVD cover, you might think that these are somehow lifted out of the movie itself, but technically that is barely possible, and when you do it, it doesn't look very good. Also, a composition that works as part of a moving shot doesn't necessarily translate into a good still image. In a still you have to condense a much greater story into a picture, rather than having the luxury of being able to edit many different shots together. Both technically and in terms of content you do need a photographer to take photographs rather than somehow picking frames out of a movie.

Q - What do you think makes a killer image?

Jaap - If I had to generalise, it is a shot that shows the lead actor, in a context that is representative of the movie. For example, if it is a sci-fi film it would be obvious that is set in the future. But there should also be dramatic content, by showing a relationship between the protagonist and something or somebody else.

Q - Often new filmmakers see stills as a pain in the arse, putting a camera into a Production Assistant's hand, saying 'Oh just snap some shots off'. What is wrong with that approach?

Jaap - I think it is pretty disastrous. You will probably end up with pictures that are a record of what happened on that day, as opposed to pictures that actually tell a story with dramatic content. It is that dramatic content that will make people interested in the movie and that is key.

Q - Is it a smart idea for a cash strapped Indie Film to say, 'I can't afford to hire a photographer for the whole shoot, but I'm going to nominate 5 days where we can...' Then would you suggest going through the script to find the best 5 days?

Jaap - Yes, though it is not ideal, and certainly from my point of view I would try to avoid the jobs where you are just rolled in on key days. If money has to be saved then it may be a way of getting some usable material. But the reason I don't like it is threefold. Firstly, because of re-scheduling, days often change. Secondly you can't really predict when an amazing shot is likely to happen; The best moments often take you by surprise. Thirdly, you don't become part of the process, you don't become part of the crew, you are an outsider, and I think it is a real advantage when you are there everyday - you blend in, and the cast feel comfortable having you around.

Q - Do you think an inexperienced crew may not see the importance of stills? Everybody is focussed on getting the next shot and they don't really want to stop for the stills.

Jaap - You have to be careful as a photographer when you choose to hold things up, when you choose to ask for a little extra time to get a shot, because you weren't able to get it on the take. My mission on set is to become a part of what is going on, and to not be in the way. To take up as little time as possible, to be noticed as little as possible, and to still get the shot. That way, when you *do* ask for a moment just for stills, it will generally be given to you.

Q - Are stills shot digitally now?

Jaap - I shoot almost entirely digitally because I prefer it.

Q - I assume because digital cameras are silent, you can also shoot during takes.

Jaap - Digital 'snap shot' cameras are silent, but the high-end digital cameras still work in the same way as a traditional camera, so the shutter and mirror make a 'click' noise which would interfere with sound during a take. However as a film stills photographer you do have what is called a 'blimp', which is essentially a box with foam walls. You stick your stills camera inside this box, and you fit a tube around the lens and you end up with what looks like a roadside speed camera! It kills the noise sufficiently to shoot during takes, and this is a 'luxury' that photographers who are starting out may not have. It makes all the difference of course, in terms of how unobtrusive you can be, and what kind of material you can get, because if you don't have it you are restricted to rehearsals only. Often during rehearsals people wear their costume coats, or their hair still has clips in it, and you are more likely to have to ask for some things to be set up afterwards.

Q - Do you get involved in setting up shoots for still only?

Jaap - Yes. It's called a 'special shoot', and it's usually quite an involved affair. It is done in a photographic studio, which means you are lighting it, and it probably means you are using medium format cameras, as opposed to smaller format digital film cameras. It is a big photo shoot that is often used for poster purposes. It doesn't mean you can't make a poster out of the unit stills, but when you go to the trouble of setting up the big shoot it tends to be because people have a concept that they want on the poster.

Q - How much time do you spend taking photos of the crew?

Jaap - Perhaps 10% or so. Those shots may be used in trade magazines, specialist magazines or asked for by the production company. People like to see pictures of themselves making a movie which is fair enough as nobody else is likely to be allowed a camera on set, so you are expected to photograph people at work.

Q - Do you think it is important to get the 'Director directing the film' photo?

Jaap - Yes, this is perhaps the most obvious example of a behind-the-scenes picture.

Q - At the end of the shoot do you just hand over the stills?

Jaap - I don't retain any rights as I get paid per week and usually sign all rights away. I can use the photographs to promote my photography, although of course you can't show any images from a film not yet released. The only control you have is that you can take out material that you don't want to be used, because they are clearly bad, out of focus or for whatever reason. I can identify the images that I like, but it is up to others to decide what gets used.

Q - What tips would you offer someone with basic photographic knowledge but no film skills experience?

Jaap - Blend in, so you don't get thrown off the set. This will give you a chance to get a good shot. Don't be a prima donna, and don't be too upset when you miss a shot; you are part of a team effort, and you can't expect to have everything go your own way all of the time. If you want to be a world famous photographer then you are in the wrong place.

Q - What advice would you offer a new filmmaker?

Jaap - Make movies that you believe in and are passionate about. It's the same for photographers; make sure you are passionate about whatever it is you photograph. Don't do it just to earn a living.

JAAP BUITENDIJK

jaap@jaapphoto.com
www.jaapphoto.com

Steve 'Barney' Barnet
Location Catering

CATERING

Q - What is your job?

Barney - Location catering. We are with the film crew on location, or in the studios, and we take care of all their catering needs during the day, or night, depending on when they are filming.

Q - What is a typical day's work for you?

Barney - Get up nice and early, usually at 4am, so we can cook and prepare breakfast. We then prepare and serve lunch and dinner. Throughout the day there is tea and coffee, biscuits and fruit baskets. A long day on average is 14 or 16 hours a day.

Q - Why spend money on a crew? Why can't they feed themselves?

Barney - Sometimes they are in locations where there is nothing available, and I suppose you could ask them to bring a packed lunch - I'm sure if they had to ask the artist to bring in packed lunches they wouldn't be too happy! We are a lot more flexible than a restaurant, they may say they want lunch at one, but because they are filming, they won't come till two. Or they may want it earlier, we have to be flexible to cope with their changing schedule. That is why we are there. The producers also know that dining will be efficient and wholesome and they need never worry about it.

Q - How much can it cost?

Barney - It can cost from £12 a day, out to £25 a day, possibly more depending on requirements. That is per head, for a basic day's catering. It varies between film, TV and commercials. The menus can vary.

Q - Who do you liase with in order to find out how many heads that you are catering for on a daily basis?

Barney - For the number situation we deal with the 2nd Assistant, but the job itself is normally booked through a Line Producer, Producer or the Production Manager.

Q - How do you deal with over-runs?

Barney – If a shoot goes overschedule we can normally cope as we have four mobile kitchens, but there are times when we can't. In that case another company comes in to finish the job.

Q - So effectively you are a kitchen on wheels?!

Barney - Yes. We are self-sufficient, with generators and water tanks. We can pull up anywhere, and cater for up to 250 people in a day without any external help.

Q - What are the facilities that you require?

Barney - Beyond a days shoot we will need access to power over night, and water to refill.

Q - What about rubbish at the end of the day?

Barney - Rubbish is now a health and safety issue, and usually the Location Manager has someone pick it up, or provides a skip, because we can't carry it on our vehicle.

Q - Would you say there is more to on set catering than most people actually think?

Barney - Yes.

Q - What is good food to keep a crew going on cold winter nights?

Barney - Hearty food, stews and soups. Film crews are like an army and as the saying goes, an army runs on it's stomach. If they are well fed they are normally quite happy. Obviously in the winter we do more wholesome food, the Summer is more salads.

Q - What mistakes are made in pre production?

Barney - Most productions, not all, but most, will try to under-budget, which is not easy because people are so much more demanding nowadays. A big cost now is just water and drinks.

Q - How important do you think it is to have a space where people can sit and eat?

Barney - Often there are dining buses or marquees. You will need somewhere undercover where people can sit and eat.

Q - Is it fair to say that the cast and crew look forward to stepping up to that little hatch?

Barney - I think they find it very enjoyable to see what is on the menu. Hopefully they enjoy it, and the time and effort that has gone into its preparation.

Q - What mistakes do you think people make during the shoot?

Barney - They don't always inform us of how the shoot is going, what time everything is required. It is always best to let us know exactly what is going on so we can adjust accordingly.

Q - What advice would you give a new film maker?

Barney - Don't do it! Seriously though, get the budget right!

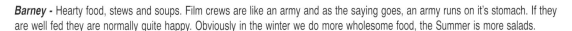

PRODUCTION

Bon Appetit

'Film and T. V. Location Catering'

BARNEY

2 Convent Road, Ashford, Middlesex, TW15 2EW
Tel / Fax: (01784) 256368 Mobile: 0831 852874

Catering

GUERILLA FILM MAKER SAYS!

A film crew looks forward to only one thing - lunch! It is best not to engage their wrath by providing dodgy grub or too little.

1. A film crew works better on a full stomach, especially if they are out in the cold. Tea, coffee and cold drinks should always be made available, with someone making sure that the key personnel (who are working harder than the others) have their drinks brought to them.

2. Feed a crew as much food as you can. Have energy snacks such as fruit, pastries, sweets, crisps, nuts, bread, all constantly available.

3. Film caterers are expensive but they do provide a wonderful service. Try negotiating them down to a price per head that you can afford.

4. If you can't afford a film caterer, find someone who is used to catering for large groups and employ them full time for the duration of the shoot. They may bring their own equipment and will certainly have good ideas. Catering students can also be a good option, but they will be inexperienced and unprepared for the barrage to which they will be subjected.

5. Large sandwiches are a good lunchtime filler - easy to prepare and distribute. However, beware of crew boredom with this culinary treat. Try and make up a simple menu (also catering for vegetarians) and give people an option. This will prevent arguments, and give them something to look forward to.

6. On the whole, actors are fussier than crew, and often expect to be treated better than you can afford. Be aware of this very important factor.

7. Sweets and beers after a hard weeks shoot can offer a good emotional bribe to get back in favour with a disgruntled cast and crew.

8. Concentrate on foods that are easy to prepare, cheap to produce, and fast to distribute and clear. Draw up a list of meals and outline them in a schedule. This will allow certain meals to be rotated.

9. If possible, give your crew a small amount of money each day and ask them to feed themselves. This works well if you are close to shops, a canteen or a pub. This way they get a choice, and you get zero catering problems. Make sure they can be fed quickly though as they may end up in a pub with an overloaded kitchen.

10. Product placement is always a good way of getting a couple of boxes of chocolate bars and crisps.

11. Some cast and crew will expect breakfast. It's your choice, but as soon as you give it to them, you will have to cater for this extra meal every day. Ask them to eat their cornflakes and toast before they leave home. Yes, it's unpopular, BUT it's your job to put your meagre budget onscreen.

12. If cast and crew are away from home for a location shoot, you will need to cater for all their needs, breakfast, lunch, dinner and supper for night shoots. This quickly becomes VERY expensive.

13. Make sure that food is not left out too long or in the sun or uncovered for insects to get into. You don't want your crew coming down with salmonella. Check health and safety regulations.

14. Find out if your cast and crew are allergic to any foods which either you must avoid or provide a substitute for them.

15. Many people are now vegetarian, especially we arty types in the film biz. Keep this in mind.

16. It's obvious, but if you are shooting in a confined place, avoid farty foods for lunch!

POST PRODUCTION

Paul Collard
Ascent Media

THE LAB

Q - What is your job?

Paul - I am Vice President of Film and Digital Services. Effectively, my role reflects the change in the industry where there is so much interface between film and digital now, you have to be able to carry the service from film to digital and back again or digital to film and it has to be a smooth process.

Q - What percentage of films these days do you see shot on a film format?

Paul - A surprising number are still shot on a film format, and there are a lot of virtues of shooting Super 16mm, which is a relative economic way of shooting things as opposed to 35mm. And the reason for this is that film is still regarded as an ideal medium to shoot because it has this very wide capture range of image brightness, and a very good range of colour reproduction. This is why costume dramas look so good on film for example. The fact that you are shooting on a smaller frame does not alter those characteristics - it is still a piece of film. The only thing to deal with is the blowing up of the image where the image structure has a deteriorating effect as opposed to shooting on a larger format. But that is offset by the amazing developments in film technology and the finer grained emulsions that are around today. Even at high speeds (ASA) you can retain good grain quality. We have seen the possibilities of shooting on S16mm where previously you could have only shot on 35mm, and this is then added to in the improvements in the transfer machines. So the telecine machines are better. So between the two, you can get a doubly good picture. But if you shoot electronically it is all bound up in the head end of the camera that only change when a new generation of technology comes out with upgrades. So the people who want to make a film that is visually filmic are sticking with shooting on film.

There is a whole new generation of film makers who are shooting on video, that came up through the DV and camcorder formats, and feel more comfortable there. I see electronic film making as an extension of film making rather than replacing film. There are of course some productions that need to shoot HD because they have a high shooting ratio, where it is cheaper to shoot on tape. But in post, while we are dealing with two things - film or digital aquisition - the two are different but come together very quickly, once you get into post production, and the same process will apply to both formats.

Q - Is the old photo-chemical process of making internegs and interpositives etc., a dead choice for new film makers?

Paul - It will be, but just not yet. A film that is simple, with straight cuts and simple visuals can still make an effective film by going the traditional route. And that is sometimes used. It is still cost effective to actually cut your negative, compared to the digital route in post-production. If you had a straight drama feature and there is nothing fancy going on, then it is currently the best way to go, and it should not be discounted (2006). It is all about getting the end result that you want, by the most cost-effective means. If you can get good deals on cameras and stock, then you can save money because the middle part of the post process is much more expensive in the digital formats. But if you need to do effects or transitions that cannot be done photo-chemically, then you have to go digital.

Q - If I wanted to shoot Super 16mm and post digitally, how would I do that?

Paul - Basically, you would 'offline cut' your pictures and sound on an Avid, using Beta tapes (or DVCam) that you digitise into the Avid. You would then produce an EDL and that would be used to do a neg pull of the shots that you are a going to use. The neg cutter actually produces an over-length neg cut. Those shots would be scanned or transferred, depending on if you were going to

Choosing a Lab

1. Lab contacts are usually very friendly. It's a good idea to go and look around a lab just so that you know roughly how everything is done.

2. Make sure that you will have a lab contact. This will be one person who will be your point of contact when discussing issues through pre production to final print.

3. Keep in contact with the lab and try not to run up a big debt. When the film is ready for delivery, the lab could withhold the neg until payment is made. This is a problem and should be avoided. Find out who the accounts person is and keep them happy.

4. Try and get an all in deal where you agree to a fixed price for a fixed amount of footage, including all sound transfers, stock, and even courier charges for dropping off the stock and dailies.

5. Double check what the lab tells you with regard to any processing issues. Your cameraman can be a useful source of information here.

6. Get some figures from other production companies to see if the deal is competitive.

7. You will probably edit on a non-linear system. Make sure the lab telecines your footage with ALL the technical information onscreen such as roll number, keykode, time code, etc. Ensure they know what film speed you shoot at, the sound sample rate and your aspect ratio (film format).

8. If shooting HD, the lab will come into play at the final stages if you need a 35mm print. If not, the lab will be replaced by a specialised HD mastering and grading company.

do an HD finish or a 2k finish. From there on it is an editing and conforming processes within either a 2k digital space or in an HD digital space.

Q - What would be the process if you shot HD?

Paul - Again you would cut offline with Beta tapes, which you would digitise or if you shot HDCam, the editor would digitise directly from the HDCam tapes. But you have to remember you can't be working those tapes hard because they are your original masters, and that is why people make Beta or DVCam offline tapes so they can work with them without fear. Then they will make their cut on the Avid. The timecodes that come out are the same codes that are on the master tapes. So those master tapes would go into an online master suite or be digitised on an HD Adrenaline, and then would picture grade it, add titles and any effects created by other companies. Finally you would re-record it back to 35mm. After the conforming stage, you still need to go for a colour correction stage. What is interesting about all digital formats is that more time is spent on film grading than when grading film in a traditional photo-chemical environment. You have more tools and you spend more time in the digital world. Most feature films take ten days to grade - a reel a day. In the old days when there was just film, a feature would take two days.

Q - Even though Final Cut Pro and Avid Express have colour correction features, would you still recommend that film makers come in for a professional grading?

Paul - Yes. We have more expertise at it and sales agents may say your attempt was not good enough. Whatever you do with your film, you have to bear in mind that it will be judged as any other film. If it isn't right, you have to fix it or lose the sale. And you usually have to do it rather quickly because there is a time limit to the sale remaining open and you could end up spending a lot of money on it if it is not right in the first place. So the processes of pro grading, Q/Cing (quality control) and sign off are crucial when you are trying to make a sale. The stringent nature of Q/C-ing has come to the fore in recent years and HD delivery is now one of the requirements of feature films. If you do it right first time, you won't need to go back and it will cost less in the long run.

Q - What, in your terms, is a universal master?

Paul - An HD-D5 is most common now. That may change though.

Q - How do you deal with the audio?

Ascent Media Group

1 Stephen Street
London
W1T 1AL
Tel: +44 (0) 20 7 131 5780
Fax: +44 (0) 20 7 131 6132

paul.collard@ascentmedia.co.uk

Paul Collard
Vice President of
Film and Digital Services

The Technological Mine Field

Gone are the days of a single tried and tested film post production route. It's now digital technology throughout, HD, editing on computers, mixing formats, home editing, multiple shooting formats etc.... the list is endless, the combinations seemingly infinite. So how do you chose the right post production route for your film?

1. There is no right route, but there is a best route for your film. That should be a balance of artistic aspiration (what do you want it to look like), technical excellence (what's the best kit you can get and the best crew to use it) and budget (what can I get for what I have). As for DV? For drama, it's a dead format and should not be used, except for tests and exercises.

2. If shooting in the UK, shoot your film at 25fps (if shooting film) or 25p (on HD), or if no progressive mode is available, you will be forced to shoot at 50I (probably 1080i). Let's put to bed once and for all, a debate borne from misinformation and confusion. 24p or 24fps DOES NOT give you a 'film look'. DO NOT, and we mean NEVER, shoot a low budget film at 24fps or 24p as it will consign you to a more costly post production route and a myriad of headaches you can't afford. In the UK, when making a low budget film or short film, SHOOT AT 25fps or 25P (HD).

3. Plan your post before you shoot. Make sure it all works. Make sure your editor understands it all. Make sure YOU understand it in concept. Ask lots of questions. Draw a flow chart for your project, not a generic project flowchart you are going to copy, and make sure everything is covered. Don't forget sound.

4. Make the distinction between the shooting format and the distribution format. You can shoot on any format and end up on any format. Shoot HD end on film, shoot DV, end up on HD... Any combination works. Generally though, whatever you shoot on, you will in the first instance, need an HD Universal master (current favourite is D5 HD) and a 35mm negative from which you can make 35mm prints (this will become redundant at some point as we switch to 100% digital distribution).

5. Chose your shooting format based on what best serves the story. Do not discount film as either too expensive, to difficult or old hat. None of those views are true. Film still has the 'look' most people want, it has immense exposure latitude and it is a desired format used by a higher calibre of cast and crew. Do not discount HD as it's 'not film', as it has some major advantages. Choose the format for the story.

5. Do not confuse top end HD formats, such as HDCam, with low end formats like HDV. They are not the same and when shown side by side, the difference is staggering. It's not just about frame size, but about the technology inside the camera. Often, low end formats end up looking like hi-res home movies.

6. Consider the traditional photochemical post production route as it is still cost effective and viable. Shoot film, neg cut, grade and print, all in the lab. This is most suited for simple dramas where there is limited editing and no special effects. You will still need to make an HD Universal master at the end for sales and distribution.

7. There is no doubt, HD is here, and over time it will supercede film in all areas. Just ensure that when you say HD, you know what specific technology you are referring too. Remember, shooting any digital format will tempt you into a significantly increased time in a post production facility in order to maximise the visual image. Do not think that HD is necessarily cheaper than film. In the long run, your film will probably cost around the same, whether you shoot film or HD. Do the maths, for the WHOLE process, and you may be surprised. Remember, you will shoot much more on HD which will make post longer and because of what you can do, you will spend greater time picture grading in very expensive suites. These are the hidden costs.

8. Whatever software you choose, make sure it can do what you think it can. It may have the characters HD in the name, but can it handle what you think it can, in the way you think it can? You may need more hardware and almost certainly will need more storage than you think.

Paul - 5.1 sound is pretty much the norm these days with a stereo TV mix too. D5 has eight tracks of audio so can handle all six tracks of your 5.1 mix, in a non-encoded and uncompressed format, as well as a stereo mix for TV.

Q - Given that most independent films go to DVD instead of into cinemas, is it fair to say that most film makers should spend more time and money getting an impeccable HD master?

Paul - There are a lot of film festivals around the world, and unless they all go digital, you are going to need one 35mm print that you can show. Whereas there could be many barriers if you have a digital master because most of these festivals are not going to be able to afford a D5 machine to play your Universal Master. The lifeblood of an independent film maker should be taking their film print of their short or feature around the world, to all the festivals. This may all change in time when there are more digital theatres in the UK, Ireland, Europe and potentially the festivals.

Q - Do you see a lot of HDV projects coming in?

Paul - HDV cameras are inexpensive and produce great pictures. We did a trailer for an experienced DP who was testing the camera. Then we put it on D5, cut it and transferred it with an Arri Laser to 35mm and made a print, and it holds up really well. There are some issues in how you move the images out of the HDV format and into another format as it doesn't have conventional video outputs. There is no reason why you couldn't use Final Cut Pro HD or Avid Xpress HD and squirt the data straight into it and then edit it. Then you have to put it onto film via a universal master, which is a hurdle that needs to be overcome. It is seductive to think you can make a feature this way, but you need professional interfaces and professional colour technicians to get it right. Most projects will fall down without them. So more money may have to be spent at the end of the production chain.

Q - What are the common mistakes that you see?

Paul - You still have to pay attention to focus. You can fix almost anything, but if something isn't sharp, you have problems. It is key, especially once you get onto large format presentation such as a movie screen. The second one is making sure that your sound post production is good. Make sure that your graphics and titles are at the highest resolution possible. If you don't then they look like absolute rubbish when you blow them up.

Q - What advice would you offer a new film maker?

Paul - Talk to as many people in the industry about all the possible ways you can make a film and don't rule them out. Find out what is the best route for you. Bear in mind that you may shoot very cheaply, but it may cost you a lot at the end. Capture the best images you can in-camera, because in the long run, it will save you money.

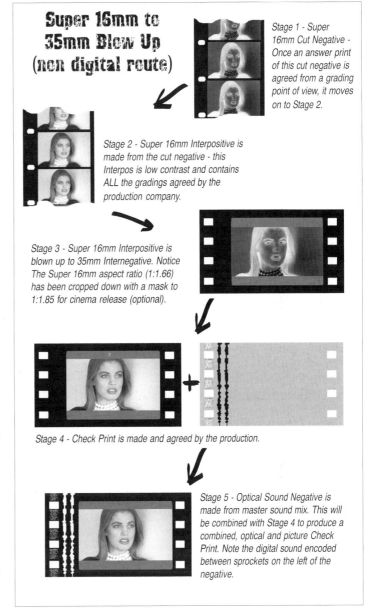

Super 16mm to 35mm Blow Up (non digital route)

Stage 1 - Super 16mm Cut Negative - Once an answer print of this cut negative is agreed from a grading point of view, it moves on to Stage 2.

Stage 2 - Super 16mm Interpositive is made from the cut negative - this Interpos is low contrast and contains ALL the gradings agreed by the production company.

Stage 3 - Super 16mm Interpositive is blown up to 35mm Internegative. Notice The Super 16mm aspect ratio (1:1.66) has been cropped down with a mask to 1:1.85 for cinema release (optional).

Stage 4 - Check Print is made and agreed by the production.

Stage 5 - Optical Sound Negative is made from master sound mix. This will be combined with Stage 4 to produce a combined, optical and picture Check Print. Note the digital sound encoded between sprockets on the left of the negative.

POST PRODUCTION

HD Mastering Workflow (shooting on HD or Film)

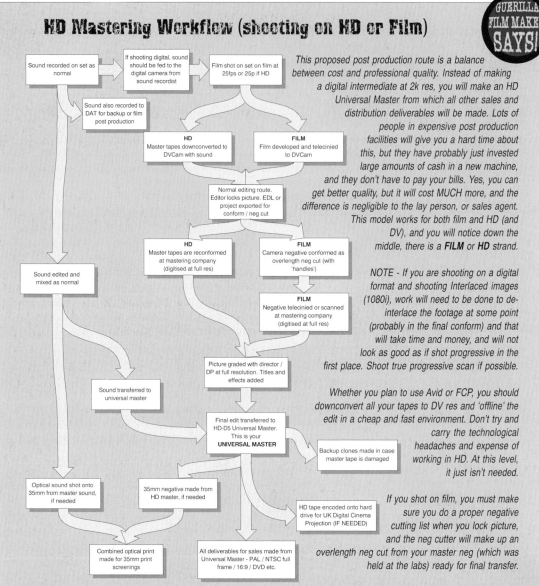

GUERILLA FILM MAKER SAYS!

This proposed post production route is a balance between cost and professional quality. Instead of making a digital intermediate at 2k res, you will make an HD Universal Master from which all other sales and distribution deliverables will be made. Lots of people in expensive post production facilities will give you a hard time about this, but they have probably just invested large amounts of cash in a new machine, and they don't have to pay your bills. Yes, you can get better quality, but it will cost MUCH more, and the difference is negligible to the lay person, or sales agent. This model works for both film and HD (and DV), and you will notice down the middle, there is a **FILM** or **HD** strand.

NOTE - If you are shooting on a digital format and shooting Interlaced images (1080i), work will need to be done to de-interlace the footage at some point (probably in the final conform) and that will take time and money, and will not look as good as if shot progressive in the first place. Shoot true progressive scan if possible.

Whether you plan to use Avid or FCP, you should downconvert all your tapes to DV res and 'offline' the edit in a cheap and fast environment. Don't try and carry the technological headaches and expense of working in HD. At this level, it just isn't needed.

If you shot on film, you must make sure you do a proper negative cutting list when you lock picture, and the neg cutter will make up an overlength neg cut from your master neg (which was held at the labs) ready for final transfer.

That neg, or your master HD tapes, will then be taken to a facility where they will capture the HD or telecine the neg, onto a digital workstation. All your picture grading will then be done. Titles and effects will also be added. If shot on film, dust and scratches will be removed. This is a lengthy process. Once that is done, your film will be transferred onto a single HD tape, with the sound coming in from the final mix at some stage during this phase. There are competing formats for HD mastering, but HD-D5 is currently the best balance of quality and cost, though HDCamSR may well have overtaken by the time you read this. There may also be new mastering formats. Do some research. The tape should be mastered at 25P if you shot at 25fps or 25p (and you should have).

From that single tape, known as a UNIVERSAL MASTER, you can make everything else - PAL and NTSC tapes, DVD, full screen, pan and scan, you name it, you can do it. You can also, if you really must, make a 24fps version of your film with NO quality loss.

From this HD master you should be able to make a Digital Print, for UK Digital Cinemas (a digital file of your movie, designed for playback on a digital cinema server), as well as a 35mm print (should the technology for theatrical presentation and film festivals still exist).

Common Video Formats

Betacam SP

Cassette analogue component format. Commonly used for rushes for offline editing. Not suitable for mastering. Maximum running time of approximately 110 mins.

Digital Betacam

A 'compressed' (2.5:1 compression) digital version of Betacam SP - made by Sony. Common format that is ideal for Standard Definition (SD) delivery as tapes can easily accommodate a feature film. Robust, with a relatively low tape and running cost. Excellent format for delivery of movies for TV / Video etc. Content is usually copied from an HD Universal master.

MiniDV and DVCam

Super common digital format, ideal for ultra micro budget video production, documentary and offline video editing. Superb picture and sound in relation to the cost, but not suited to mastering or archival of video masters. Uses compression at 5:1 and has limited colour space in the signal.

HDCam

The current 'best' format for shooting HD, in terms of quality and cost ratio. Shoots in 1080 interlaced and progressive modes. Can shoot 24p, 25p, as well as 50i and 60i for HD video for PAL and NTSC TV respectively. When shot properly, it rivals film in aesthetic look. Ideal shooting format, but not commonly used for final mastering as it only has a limited number of audio tracks. Hot on its tracks is HDCamSR, an improved version that is better for mastering as it carries eight audio tracks. Pictured is a samll camera tape, but larger tapes are used for mastering

HDV

The consumer version of HD, highly compressed with lots of compression artefacts. Colour space in the signal is very compressed making it poor for green screen and creative picture grading, though it is very hi res and cheap. A much better alternative to DV for shooting a micro budget film. Not suited to mastering due to the high compression. Can capture images in 1080i or 720p (Camera dependant).

DVCProHD

Excellent Prosumer HD format that uses DV tape. It runs the tape faster than DV and has a much higher bit rate. It also shoots everything at 60fps, so slow motion is possible. It does not shoot 1080 HD, rather 720 and upscales in post production to 1080. Ideal for shooting low budget features. Great shooting format, not so good for mastering.

HD-D5

The current 'best' format for mastering, in terms of quality and cost. HD-D5 is a component 1080 format with 8 channels of sound. It has been adopted as the common format for making a UNIVERSAL MASTER for sales agents. UK low budget features would be mastered in 1080P / 25P, with 10 bit colour sampling. Smashing baby!

Domestic Formats and Obsolete

Low Band Umatic, HiBand Umatic, 1", VHS, SVHS, 8mm and Hi8mm can all be requested at various stages of production and are commonly used for preview tapes and sync tapes. Other formats also include D1 and D2, excellent in all ways, just superceded and expensive to run.

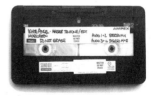

Eddie Hamilton
Editor

THE EDITOR

Q - What is a Film Editor?

Eddie - The editor is the person who takes the footage shot by the crew and cuts the shots together to tell the story in the best way possible, shot by shot, a scene at a time, making sure the cuts flow smoothly and the audience understands the story and emotions being communicated by what they're watching. They have the responsibility to ensure that everyone's best work gets up on screen – a combination of the best performances, lighting, makeup, costumes, and sets. The editing process is also the last chance to correct any mistakes made during the shoot. If the script has problems, you have to fix them with re-structuring or ADR (lines recorded by the actor in a studio after the shoot). Similarly, if an actor's performance is disappointing, you have to cut around it. George Lucas says that editing is the most important part of the film making process. You really can radically change a film for the better in the cutting room. If there is life in the rushes and you have a good story to tell, taking the time to find the moments that work and then piecing them together to create a decent movie (even if it is totally different from the original script) is very rewarding.

So it's very creative, but it also requires an immense amount of organisation. Every single frame of film has to be carefully logged when it arrives in the cutting room so that it can be found at a moment's notice. Any inaccuracy can cause problems and if not spotted can cost a lot to put right. The editor is also an ambassador of diplomacy. Sitting in the same room as the director working on their masterpiece for months takes its toll – emotions get charged, especially if there is a producer who disagrees with the director. The editor should serve the director's vision, but must speak up if he thinks the director is mistaken. It's important to try and stay objective and see the film fresh each time. Sometimes you have to be ruthless with the cut to improve the film. It's not personal. Everyone wants the best film at the end of the day.

Q - How do you edit film?

Eddie - Traditionally, cutting film meant having a room filled with rolls of film and magnetic tape (the rushes), looking through these on a machine called a Moviola or Steenbeck, then literally splicing the film together shot by shot with clear tape. The system worked well, but it had disadvantages. It took time to locate a trim (an offcut from an edit) and if you wanted to change the cut it wasn't easy to return to a previous version. Plus, the more you handled the cut reels, the dirtier, dustier and more scratched they became. The advent of fast, cheap computer technology changed all that.

The leading computer-based film editing system is the Avid Film Composer (with Apple's Final Cut Pro HD hot on it's heals). Avid is one of the simplest, fastest, most feature-rich system on the market today. All the rushes reside in digital form on the Avid's hard disk drives, giving instantaneous access to any one of the hundreds of shots that make up a movie. The Avid allows you to keep several versions of a sequence to compare them, and the image quality never deteriorates or gets scratched, it physically can't. Because you work from video, the resolution is not as good as working on film, but this will change in the coming years and the positives massively outweigh the negatives in my opinion. There are other benefits of using a computer to cut a film – you can produce dissolves and other visual effects to see how they look in the cut. For test screenings you can produce an incredibly rich soundtrack with sound effects, temporary music and ADR. Every frame of film has a timecode associated with it and the Avid takes care of that all the way through the editing process (as long as the information you give it in the first place is correct).

Q - What is a good edit?

Eddie - Well, there is no simple answer to this – whole books have been written on this very topic by people who've had a lifetime of experience editing films!

The Editor's Job

GUERILLA FILM MAKER SAYS!

1. Label the tapes as they're returned from the lab, or from the set (if digital). Organisation is your best friend.

2. Digitise the material onto the editing system. It's very important to ensure that you digitise timecode and that the timecode on the tapes is accurate. Check, check and check again.

3. Break down the footage into the various shots and takes and sort them into bins for easy access. Make sure you can read and easily understand the labels for the bins.

4. Once digitised, store the original in a safe place. Your exposed negative film should be stored at the lab until you decide to cut your neg. If shooting digitally, consider cloning your camera tapes and send them to a relative for safe keeping.

5. For your first assembly, order the scenes the same way as the screenplay had planned. If there is a scene that is missing or contains visual effects that will be added later, place a title card in those areas stating what should be there.

6. Don't worry about your first assembly being overly long, badly paced, or tonally off. These will be fixed in the next passes.

7. Re-edit, reorder, screen, then help with the reshoots... Keep doing this until you truly have the best edit of the film. Export and EDL for final neg cut or digital conform.

8. Tidy the sound and co-ordinate with the sound editors.

9. Visit the labs for viewings of test prints, visit the final mix to advise on sound, visit the final conform to advise on color correction on HD / video.

Q - OK, so what makes a cut between two shots work?

Eddie - The cut should be fluid (unless deliberately being obtuse). The flow and rhythm of the cut should not interrupt the audience's passage of concentration. It should feel natural. For me, it's a gut reaction, some kind of instinct. As you play through a take you feel the cut should be HERE, or you sense an edit needs a couple more frames on the outgoing shot. When you watch it back you just intuitively sense if a cut is working or not.

There are some grammatical rules to follow (though these should have been taken into account when shooting the film). When cutting between shots try not to cross the line (the imaginary eyeline between the actors on screen – see elsewhere in the book). If you do, it will feel wrong. Just try it. You can sometimes get away with it if there's no option and you're careful but generally it's a bad idea (unless it's a deliberate directorial choice as in 'Moulin Rouge!', for example, where Baz Luhrmann crosses the line constantly). If someone or something exits frame right, they should enter the next shot frame left and vice versa. Picture a car chase along a road. If the lead car zips off to the right of the camera, it always enters to the left of the camera (unless you pick up the chase at an entirely different location). Try imagining it the other way. Of course, in some totally frenetic action sequences almost anything goes, but especially on a low budget movie it can look incompetent if you do this the wrong way.

When cutting dialogue I often find a natural place to cut to another character is on punctuation, where there's a natural pause in the delivery. I have read a theory that says it takes at least two frames for the audience's eyes to travel from one part of the screen to another between cuts. I would tentatively agree with this – if I'm editing a conversation I tend to trim the incoming shot back a couple of frames and find the cut feels smoother. Another tip, all subconcious emotion is shown through the actor's eyes. Even the subtlest movements give away a character's thoughts.

Lastly, make sure each cut is *motivated*. If the scene is playing well, don't cut for the sake of it.

Q - What makes an edited scene work?

Eddie - As you have no doubt discovered when writing or reading a script, most scenes have a beginning, middle and end and are designed to carry the plot forward, developing the characters along the way. This may seem obvious, but you should take it into account when cutting a sequence together. How does the scene start? Where

EDDIE HAMILTON
FILM EDITOR

email: eddiehamilton@email.com
website: www.eddiehamilton.co.uk

POST PRODUCTION

Editing Tips

Whether you hire and editor or cut your project yourself, the cutting process can be both rewarding and frustrating. You will love seeing your film come to life, but may cringe at shots or sequences that don't work, or at bad acting that you let go on set (at the time you blamed the actors, but now you suspect it's more to do with your script and you now regret not spending time on that extra script rewrite!) The key here is to keep going to your first cut, then have a few unbiased people watch it so that you make changes or schedule reshoots to fix problems you could not see as you. Then repeat these two steps over and over until you get it right. While the length of editing varies by budget and time constraints (one month to a year), a general rule of thumb for a low budget picture is to allow 12-16 weeks for picture lock. Remember that the editor hasn't been on set and therefore isn't aware of how painstakingly long it took to set up a certain shot, or how difficult it was to get that perfect take.

1. Hire your editor during production and have them begin editing from day one of shooting. The editor will see your movie come together and can inform you of problems as you go along (such as needing more coverage or cutaways), problems that will then be simple to fix and far more economical than fixing them in post.

2. Establish a relationship with the lab (this goes for the director and the DP as well) prior to shooting and have meetings with them as necessary. This will iron out problems that may arise, such as what to do if the footage comes back dirty.

3. Whether shooting film or digital, make sure the sound and picture are synched together before sending the dailies to the editor. You are paying him to cut, not to sync sound for weeks.

4. Make sure your editor has all the necessary post paperwork - camera reports, continuity reports, sound reports, lab reports, etc.

5. Generally, it's a good idea to keep the actors out of the cutting room. Scenes may not have gone as planned, and insecurities may flare up which may adversely effect future performances.

6. Kill your babies. That scene, the one that looked beautiful, with amazing acting… If it doesn't advance the story, then you need to leave it on the cutting room floor.

7. If you're not sure about a scene, take it out and see if you miss it. You can always put it back in.

8. If you have to make major changes, note the scenes on index cards and stick them to the wall. This will keep you from getting lost.

9. Music and sound effects will enhance a scene that is tedious, but they will not fix the heart of the problem.

10. Dropping the ends of scenes sometimes helps, it can create a question in the audience's mind - what's going to happen next?

11. Don't be afraid of inventing new scenes, or lines of dialogue, getting the actors back and having a mini reshoot. If the audience doesn't understand something fundamental, you can fall back on the blunt instrument of explanatory dialogue.

12. Take a break before locking picture. When you come back to it, you will see the movie with new eyes and increased energy.

13. If you are faced with a long dull scene or a shot that you can't cut away from, try hacking it with an unusual cut. It might work.

14. Listen to the people who view your rough cuts. While they might not know exactly what is wrong, they know what is working for them and what isn't. Don't fall into the mistaken position of believing you know better because you are the filmmaker.

15. Don't take anything personally. Whatever opinions you or your editor express, you are both just trying to make the film better. It isn't worth losing a friendship over.

16. Most Important! Sort out your entire planned post-production route before you shoot. Both FCP and Avid Xpress Pro can handle the job. Don't get sucked into the 'Avid is better than FCP' and vice versa devate. They are both excellent tools. What is important is the cuts the editor makes, not the software used. (Avid Film Composer is pictured below).

Test Screening

GUERILLA FILM MAKER SAYS!

Even if a festival deadline is fast approaching, you should have a test screening of your film. Showing your movie to an impartial audience is a vital way to tell if the mechanics of your story are working. While the opinions of the people watching your film are just that, opinions, for the most part, if a problem keeps being raised, you should attend to it. Hold a test screening with a DVD-R, pair of speakers and video projector.

1. Have your editor copy the whole movie with all the sound, sound effects, temp music onto DVD-R. Where titles or scenes are missing, put up a card explaining what should be there. This is what you will screen.

2. Pure human emotion is always the best indicator of how things are going, so watch and listen to your audience. See if they're shifting in their seats, are they fidgeting or looking visually bored? Has anyone fallen asleep? Are they laughing in the right spots? Looking at their watch?

3. You may have several test screenings. A small one with people whose opinions you respect would be a good starter, and this will fix immediate problems. These can be people in the industry who can see technical problems that a general audience may not get. Once you make these changes, then have a larger test screening. Invite friends of friends who aren't in the industry and who would be your target audience for your movie. Avoid family as viewers as they may not tell you the truth.

4. Remember a test screening is all about finding the problems. Don't expect anyone to praise your film, and if they do, ask them what they hated about it. Invite them to be as harsh as possible.

5. If you can't afford a video projection venue, then find someone with a huge TV and buy everyone pizza. Try to create as much of a theatrical experience as possible, so take the phone off the hook and switch off the mobile.

6. Draw up a questionnaire and ask them to fill it in. Do this before you get into a general discussion in order to reduce 'group think'. Have a big box of pens at the ready.

7. Have a freeform discussion at the end of the screening, and ask questions about the things you suspect may be a problem.

8. Your distributor or studio may require a test screening of their own so they know how to market your film and how much to budget. This will be with a complete unknown group in your target audience, and from all walks of life, to hopefully represent the audience who will eventually be viewing your movie.

9. This can be a harsh environment for actors and directors. Don't let actors attend, and warn the director that it's going to be rough.

are we? Who's here? Has time passed? Subconsciously the audience will be asking these questions when the scene starts. Unless you're setting out to confuse them, you should try and set the scene as soon as possible so that they can get on with digesting the plot and characterisation. Sometimes, you can start with an exterior of where we are (e.g. a crowd outside the cinema for a premiere before cutting inside to show who's attending). Or maybe start on a detail and reveal the situation, (e.g. a digital counter counting down from 30 seconds, track out to reveal a small bomb under a table, track out to reveal two characters having dinner unaware of their predicament). These are obvious examples but the audience immediately knows what's what.

Now, consider what the function of the scene is. Which character do you want the audience to identify with? Whose story is this? What plot details must the audience understand so that we don't lose them? For example, consider a scene where a woman is asking a man to marry her. She might beat around the bush a bit, nervous. At the start of the scene we might stay on a medium two shot showing both the actors. Then she plucks up courage – do we go in for a close up? Maybe. Do we want to show her extreme anxiousness? Or do we want to see the man getting intrigued about her emotional turmoil? The answers are never clear cut, but if you know what the audience needs from the scene, it can certainly point you in the right direction. All the time you're listening to your gut feeling about whether the flow of the cuts feel right. At the last minute, the woman can't do it. She's trying to win a bet with a friend by getting engaged before the week is out but decides it's not worth it. The scene builds to this moment and without an explanation she leaves. The man is left standing wondering what he did wrong. Do we stay on a close up of his confusion, do we see his POV (point of view) of the woman walking away, or do we cut out to a wide shot of him standing alone and bemused? Any of these will work, depending on what you want to say. But for sure the scene has drawn to a close. We've had a beginning, middle, and end. Very few or even no words have been exchanged, but we've understood and the edited scene has done its job.

Q - What makes a movie work as a whole?

POST PRODUCTION

Eddie - When you've finished the first cut of a film, the fun really starts. Just cutting the scenes and putting them in script order is only half the battle. If I'm cutting during a shoot I normally have a first assembly ready a couple of days after the wrap party. The editor and director will watch this and as a general rule it's very average and probably poor – it's too long, the pace is all over the place and there will probably be sections missing such as special effects or second unit shots. But this is to be expected – every editor I've spoken to says the first assembly always looks terrible. However, it's also exciting because it's the first glimpse that all the work so far has been worth it.

First you work through the film with the director getting the scenes how he or she wants them. You've been cutting alone so far, according to what you think works. Of course it's their film and they may have other ideas about how to approach a scene. It's a long process of going through the rushes re-working each scene according the director's taste – with your input where necessary. Then you take a look at the film as a whole. Are the characters introduced correctly? Is the plot working? Does the pace lag anywhere? Is it too fast? As a rule, the film is probably too slow. How many people have seen a film that's too slow? Then ask yourself if you have ever complained about a film because it was too fast or too packed. Sometimes what worked well in the script seems redundant on screen. Sometimes the performances are lacking something. Maybe the relationship between the two lead characters is misfiring somewhere. Maybe a character is unnecessary now. Maybe some of the jokes just aren't funny.

What do you do? Well, work through the problems. Can I move some scenes around to get the pace more even? Can I intercut some scenes? Can I cut out this joke altogether? Can I shoot some pickups to act as clever cutaways or help with the plot? Slowly but surely you'll work out the answers over several weeks and months of cutting. Then screen your cut to a select audience of articulate people whose opinions you value and who aren't afraid of being brutally honest about the film. You want to fix problems, not have your ego stroked. Watching your movie with an audience is like watching it afresh. You suddenly sense when they begin to fidget. You sense when they're gripped. You know if a joke has hit the mark. Ask them questions afterwards. You'll soon find out what the problems are. There'll be comments like – *But isn't he her brother?* – and the characters aren't related at all! The audience will come back with all kinds of comments that you hadn't even thought of because you're too close to the film.

Back to the cutting room for more changes, more careful honing. You will probably have to cut some scenes you love because they just don't "play" to the audience or aren't needed in the film any more. Screen the film again for a larger number of people. Get them to fill in a questionnaire. Read the forms and listen to what they're saying. Don't take them as gospel, but don't ignore them. Gradually you will get closer to the day when you lock picture.

There is a saying that films are never completed, just abandoned. This is partially true because you will never be 100% happy with the end result. The director will have had this vision for the film that can never be matched. You will always have to compromise. But with patience and creativity you will find the movie hiding in those rushes and it will take on a life of its own. The audience will watch it and forget that they're seeing dozens of cuts flickering across the screen – they will be engrossed in the story being told and then you'll know you've done a good job.

Q - What common mistakes do you see?

Eddie - The way to avoid mistakes is to ensure you understand the entire post production process from the moment the neg leaves the camera right up to the premiere. Make sure you know about processing, telecine, timecode, digitising, neg cutting, opticals, sound tracklaying, mixing, grading and delivery requirements. These are all places where you can trip up and it will cost you time and money to fix, neither of which you will have a lot of, probably. Ask an editor to explain these things to you and if he or she doesn't know, don't give them the job.

Q - What advice would you give to a low budget movie maker?

Eddie - Don't rush into production without really working on the script and developing it until you know it's the best it can be. If in doubt about any technical aspects of film making, ask - people will be happy to explain. Know who the audience is for your film and don't bore them. Have test screenings (even small ones), because they will help you understand where your film needs more work. Finally, if you're shooting on film anywhere that uses PAL, SHOOT AT 25 FPS. It will save you ENDLESS headaches later in post production. Good luck!

Hans Venmans
Avid

Q - What is Avid?

Hans - Avid is a company that makes editing tool in various flavours, for various different applications and markets. New film makers will be most interested in Avid Xpress Pro. The most important thing about Avid is the heritage of the software, when compared to other systems. The software was designed, in the first place, for professional editors, and has been honed by professional editors over the years. The key things with Avid, aside from it being a professional tool, developed hand in hand with professional editors, is that it is very stable and has excellent media management. People who I speak to who have been editing on Final Cut Pro or the other systems for instance, comment on the fact that the Avid system is much faster to edit with. The interface is much more geared towards doing the job that you want to do, for an independent filmmaker, that it is very important. Other manufacturers focus on flashy effects, lots of layering and compositing, often at the cost of the basics. Most of what story telling is about is cutting shots together, fine-tuning the edits, pruning the edits etc. I know it sounds like a sales chat, but that it is what I hear from people who have used other systems.

Q - What system should a new film maker go for?

Hans - Xpress Pro, which is the software-based system. They can both offline edit and online edit on that system. But for large scale independent films, the best use of the system is as an offline edit tool. So you shoot HD, Film or any other format. Then downsample the tapes to either DV or HDV, edit the film, then take the project to a full blown suite and online it there. If on film, you can generate a cut list for the negative cutter too. Many people get excited at the proposition of cutting in HD, but the equipment overhead of cutting in full blown HD can be very expensive. Low budget film makers should down-res their work to DV25 (or HDV), offline and online with expert graders later. A project that you create in Xpress Pro is compatible with the whole Avid family. We call that 'Total Conform'. It means that your project, which is obviously your edit, the effects that you may have used, the layering that you've used, even the physical media, is compatible and transferable to other Avid systems.

Q - HD has actually made the whole market and workflow even muddier?

Hans - Yes, but at the same time more interesting. The new native shooting formats, such as HDV and DVCProHD, allow a filmmaker to have pristine quality images and sound, within the confines of the basic computer system, because the data-rates have now come down so much that you can make it work on the same data rates as you would have done before with DV.

Q - What if you wanted to use the top end HDCam or HDCamSR?

Hans - I would advocate an offline edit, then an online performed by experts in a dedicated environment. They will have better and faster equipment, but most importantly, they will understand what is possible in terms of the image and picture grading, and they will also adhere to the rigorous sales and distribution standards required in the professional marketplace. You can't just burn a DVD and expect to sell that to TV companies around the world. The other problem with the lower end HD formats, especially HDV, is they are highly compressed and are designed for acquisition. It wasn't designed to go to various generations as it would if you mastered yourself, with grading and layered effects. DNxHD, which is a Codec we created and is free for anyone to use, can help here too. It allows you create your effects at higher bitrates than the 25MB/s of native HDV, usually around 150MB/s, so the artefacts of rendering and compositing are reduced. It's just a higher quality way to work than at native HDV. DNxHD is the perfect solution for somebody who needs to do compositing or true online finishing inside their home system.

Q - People get all excited about HD at home - but how can you monitor exactly what you are doing, especially when it comes to picture grading?

Hans - That is a very good point. The problem is a good quality HD monitor costs an absolute fortune, I don't think any independent filmmaker would be able to afford one. The second problem is because of the Codecs, you probably won't be able to play it out in its native format, unrendered, so you can't actually easily watch it, even if you were able to afford a nice HD monitor.

Q - So get a couple of widescreen LCD monitors, and you run the software on one.

Hans - And view the playback on the other.

Q - Should you back up regularly?

Hans - Yes. Every night. Keep a memory key on you and save the whole Avid project to that key every night. You should also think about your master tapes. Do you have a backup, and if so, they should be stored somewhere else. Consider what would happen to your film if there was a fire. Could you recreate it? If you backed up your project and you had cloned tapes someplace else, even in the event of a disaster, you would be back to where you were within a few days.

Q - What advice would you offer a new filmmaker?

Hans - Look at the entire post production workflow and choose your editing system accordingly. Try to do as much as possible yourself, but don't over-stretch yourself.

Rob Hall
Assistant Editor

Q - What are your responsibilities in the cutting room?

Rob - I work as a First Assistant Editor on feature films. This means it is my responsibility to ensure that everything in the cutting room runs smoothly, efficiently and on time - from start to finish.

Q - What do you do before shooting starts?

Rob - In the run up to a shoot, the editor and myself will plan thoroughly to make sure that the cutting room workflow is in place - that the kit will be ready and that it will actually work technically, which is becoming a more complex task as features are being shot digitally - the technology advances so fast that the standards also change fast - liaising with the camera department and the sound recordist are essential and it's wise to get test footage beforehand if possible. Test everything right through from digitising to outputting material for the sound editors (get them to OK it). You should also make sure the telecine / dubbing house will be giving you the right format tapes with all the correct burn-ins (timecodes etc), etc. Everything done at this stage saves time and trouble later on.

Q - What is your role during and after a shoot?

Rob - Once shooting starts, it's my job to digitise the dailies tapes (picture and sound), sync up, label the shots and do playouts of the entire day's sync dailies for all those that need them. I cannot emphasise how important it is to make thorough checks at every stage of the process. The dailies tapes will also come with documentation that must be filed properly, as should the continuity notes. The only other daily task is simple: do everything the editor needs done while he's cutting! This can include making playouts of cut scenes, gathering and cutting in temp sound FX, mocking up temp visual FX, producing lists / images for pickup shots that are needed, filing any further documentation received, labelling EVERYTHING, dealing with and reporting problems (for example, neg scratches or digital dropout), making daily backups of the project and last but not least, making cups of tea!

The end of the shoot signals a change in job - there are no more dailies tapes (except for pickup shoots later on), but lots more playouts and temp sound FX work to do. Most features these days have a good number of visual FX shots in them and I'm in charge of tracking these shots and liaising with the various VFX houses that may be involved. This can become a very big job if the number of visual FX shots gets into the hundreds. Negative may need to be cut and scanned for visual FX work long before the cut of the film itself is locked, all of which must be ordered and tracked. Sound editors and a composer will also become involved, requiring copies of each cut, as will the director and the various producers.

Q - Is assistant editing a good way to become an editor?

Rob - Being an assistant is a perfect way to learn how to become an editor. First, you have an editor working with you that you can watch and learn from; second, the editor should know about EVERYTHING that goes on in the cutting room, because they are ultimately responsible for anything that goes right or wrong. You won't know if your assistant isn't performing if you haven't ever done it yourself - the editor's reputation is often dependent on work performed by their assistant. Of course, the essence of editing is actually cutting, and it's up to you to make time to edit anything you can in your spare time - short films, promos, showreels, or just practising on scenes from the film you're assisting on. Some editors may allow you to edit a small scene in the film, but don't expect it!

Pickups and Reshoots

For the most part, it's best get all your shots during principal photography. However, there might be some that you can't get due to time constraints, some that you realise after viewing your first assembly or a test screening that you now need, or some that were screwed up the first time around and need to be redone. Going back to "pick up" or "reshoot" shots is extremely common, and should be budgeted for both in cost and time. Some pickups, such as close ups of fingers on a keyboard, a wide establishing shot of a location, a match igniting, or a coffee mug being placed down are very simple and can be done over a long weekend with a minimal crew. Even getting a certain look from an actor that resolves a loose end is fairly easy; only complicated by time schedules and continuity issues (making sure they are wearing the same shirt they wore the day of the original shoot). Larger reshoots of whole scenes or sequences can be more complex and more expensive (you'll need most of your full crew), but getting your film right is so much more important both creatively and psychologically.

Q - If you've assisted on bigger budget movies, would you be happy to work on low budget movies as an editor?

Rob - If offered the chance to edit a low budget film, I would definitely be very interested and, provided I was not on a job and had not agreed to do a job that would clash with it, I would take it. There are two types of assistant editor - those that want to become an editor and those that are career assistant editors. Although being a career assistant can be both rewarding and a stable income (especially if you associate yourself with a successful editor), I am one that aims to become an editor outright. If it doesn't work out, there's always the fallback of assisting again.

Q - What does feature film assistant editing allow you to offer as an editor on a low budget film?

Rob - As an assistant attempting the switch to becoming an editor, I would bring the experience of running a cutting room from start to finish for a feature film - emphasis on 'feature film' - an editor that has only worked with shorts and promos beforehand will not necessarily take into account the scale of what they are about to undertake. Don't underestimate it. It requires excellent structure and organisation, both within the project and in the cutting room in general. Very high standards in all areas are needed, with great attention to detail, all on a large scale. This is absolutely vital, since a lack of organisation inevitably leads to constant impediments to the actual purpose of an editor - to edit. The faster you can find a shot, a sequence, a document or whatever, the less interruption to the editor's train of thought (and the director's, since he will work closely with you after the shoot). Working as an assistant for an established editor also allows you to work in bigger budget movies at an early stage of your career - this is all to your advantage as it can be an intensive learning experience!

Q - What problems can arise in the cutting room?

Rob - There are always mistakes made by everyone during a project, including the assistant editor. These can be incorrect key numbers and timecodes, shots out of sync, bad labelling, a bad telecine, anything. However, it is the assistant's job to always check everything, absolutely everything, that comes to them and is given out by them. If you've made a mistake, it will never leave the door (or be given to the editor) because you will have always checked it first. If you've found someone else's mistake, get them to correct it - they will appreciate it. These checks take time, but it is always quicker in the long run, without fail.

Q - Why is your photo so scary?

Rob - While working on *Resident Evil - Apocalpyse*, I was given the opportunity to be a zombie and got shot in the head!

Q - What advice would you give to a new film-maker?

Rob - Set yourself a very high standard and NEVER compromise it in anything you do. Any time there's an option of taking an easy way out by producing shoddy work, remind yourself of your standards and remember that it's keeping to them that will set you apart from the crowd. Not that many people do this, but not that many people make it to the top.

Rob Hall
FILM EDITING
email: roberto2104@email.com
web: www.robhallediting.com

Becky Bentham
Hot House Music Ltd

MUSIC SUPERVISOR

Q - What is the job of a music supervisor?

Becky - The job of a music supervisor can consist of track research (taking a brief and finding suitable tracks for particular scenes that work creatively and within budget), track clearance (negotiating fees for use of the music and producing licenses), selecting artists to record specific tracks and concluding their deals, hiring a score composer, preparing budget breakdowns, hiring specific music personnel (Engineers, Studios, Conductors, Orchestrators, Programmers, Copyists, Technical assistants, writing rooms etc), co-ordination of score and source material, attendance at recording sessions and fixing record deals.

Q - What kind of rights do you need to clear to use music in a film?

Becky - You need to clear sync rights, which are the publishing rights to have their music synchronised against the picture. And you need to clear Master rights, which is the recording that the song comes from and lastly you must pay any re-use fees due to musicians.

Q - How do you find out who owns the particular rights?

Becky - Firstly you'd contact the MCPS/PRS. The information they give you can be a starting point of giving you the name of who publishes a song and which record company owns the song if you know the performer, but may require further investigation once conversations get underway. For instance, maybe one publisher is listed with the MCPS/PRS but in talking to that publisher you may find that additional publishers own part of the track and would therefore need to ensure you clear their share too.

Q - With film, is the music licensed for a certain number of years or in perpetuity?

Becky - The license fee should allow the filmmakers to use the track within their film in perpetuity because once your film is finished that music is locked in.

Q - What do you need to be aware of in terms of royalties?

Becky - Royalties are generated from music performance on radio, television, cinemas as well as live performance and also from the duplication of tapes, records and CDs. These are collected and distributed by the MCPS/PRS and their sister societies worldwide. In the case of soundtrack CD's the Artist/Producer royalty payable to the Composer is prorated over the number of tracks on the CD. The Record Company would usually negotiate the Artist/Producer royalties with Composers/Artists/Producers.

Q - Can you get good deals with record companies?

Becky - Unless the film is a guaranteed success with well known Artists on the soundtrack it is fairly difficult to get a good advance on film soundtrack deals at the present time.

Q - If you want an original score, how do you go about getting a composer?

Becky - To get a composer you will need an idea of which style of music you are looking for then either contact a Music Supervisor who will give you suggestions of suitable composers or if dealing direct, make a shortlist of composers who may be suitable, then contact their agents to check availability before setting up meetings with the director. The composer's agent will most likely need an idea of music budget and schedule so they can assess if a requested composer would be able to work within the required parameters.

Q - At what stage should you bring in a music supervisor and/or composer?

Becky - A music supervisor should be bought on at the earliest opportunity as quite often the producer is left with too little money in the budget once they get into post production to deliver their ideal soundtrack. With a music supervisor involved early on they can be given advice on how much their 'ideal' soundtrack will cost and whether they can reserve adequate funds or if they need to scale down their preferences. The composer should be given approximately eight weeks from delivery of locked picture to delivery of score but on larger scale Hollywood movies the composer is sometimes given a number of months and on very low budget European features it can be as little as a couple of weeks!

Q - Is it generally a flat fee for the composer?

Becky - In the US it is not uncommon for the Composer to receive a flat fee and for the Studio/Production Company to fund third party costs separately. On some US based projects and most European projects the composer is offered a 'Package' fee whereby the fee covers payment to composer and all third party costs. It is possible on European projects, where the commissioning fees payable to composers are significantly less than fees paid in the US for the composer, to retain all or some of the publishing income.

Q - What should you budget on a low budget movie (budgets of up to a million) for a composer?

Becky - Ideally 10%, but this is rarely the case.

Q - If the composer attains the rights to music and the producer sells the film to Germany, does the producer then have to pay the composer royalties?

Becky - No - the composer would most likely collect their royalties direct or via their publisher so there would be no need for payment to come via the producer.

Q - Is it expensive to hire an orchestra?

Becky - In the UK we work under the PACT/MU combined use fee for films which has four scales of fees payable to musicians. These range from £51 per hour to £104 per hour (these rates are reviewed each year) and fee is determined by total number of musicians hours used. UK musicians do not receive residuals under this agreement. Some composers record at various locations in Europe and the cost for this is cheaper than the UK.

Q - Do you find that many new filmmakers use their friends who are in bands? Are there problems generated with this?

Becky - Sometimes a friend of a filmmaker who is in a band can be an opportunity to get a good deal for a known name. Other times it can be a disaster!

Q - Does a music supervisor have any involvement with the contracts?

Becky - Music supervisors can negotiate contracts on behalf of the producer as required.

Becky Bentham

Hot° House Music Ltd
Greenland Place, 115-123 Bayham Street,
London, NW1 0AG
+44 (0)20 74467446
www.hot-house-music.com

POST PRODUCTION

Music Rights

GUERILLA FILM MAKER SAYS!

To use music in your film, there are three distinct legal rights you MUST acquire before locking and mixing the sound. Failing to do this could result in a film that no one will sell, buy or even screen in a festival.

RECORD / MASTER RIGHTS
Copyright in the recording of a song or composition owned by either a record company or the entity that has paid for the recording and thus owns the master tape. Different record companies may hold the copyright to a recording in each separate country.

PUBLISHING RIGHTS
Copyright owned by the author or composer of the work, literally the notes on the page. These become public domain 50-75 years after the death of the composer dependent on the country. These rights are controlled by a music publisher on behalf of the composer or author. Where there is more than one writer, then two or more publishing companies may own a share of the work.

SYNCHRONISATION RIGHTS
Rights granted to a filmmaker to 'synchronise' the copyrighted music in conjunction with the film. Publishing rights granted for the composition or song by a music publisher on behalf of the composer or author. Record / Master rights granted by the record company to use a recording of that song or composition.

Q - Is there a place where producers can go to get a list of record companies?

Becky - There are various trade manuals listing all record companies such as Music Week that publishes the Music Week Directory which also lists the artist's manager.

Q - When is the best time to talk to the record company?

Becky - Unless it is a big budget picture with loads of known names and a known composer, when conversations can take place fairly early on, then the best time to approach a record company is when the final mix is complete and the film is ready to be screened. This way the record companies can assess how successful the film could be and therefore how big a public will hear and buy the soundtrack.

Q - Do new bands generally do film scores for free for exposure?

Becky - It is rare to get a signed band for free as their representatives won't want them working for nothing but new bands can be hired for very good rates in return for exposure.

Q - How does library music work? Do they have set rates?

Becky - Library music, also known as Production music, is charged on a 30 second basis e.g £475 per 30 seconds if the overall film budget is less than £10 million. This can be a cost effective way to licence music into a lower budget film.

Q - What is the music cue sheet?

Becky - The music cue sheet is prepared (usually by the music editor, or in the absence of one by the publisher). This is a listing of each music cue in the film, listing cue number, title, timing, author, publisher, type of use, artist etc.

Q - Who should you give the cue sheet to after it's finished?

Becky - Information from the cue sheets will be registered by the publisher with the collection societies. Also a copy is given to each publisher that you've used and will also be given to the film's distributor.

Q - What's the difference between background and featured music?

Becky - Featured music is where the people on screen can hear the music. i.e. music at a party, music coming from a radio etc. Background music is used to assist the images but cannot necessarily be heard by those on screen.

Q - Are there any other rights you need to clear? Say for instance, if an actor sings a song in the film?

Becky - No. If you re-record a copyright track with a new Artist for use in a film then you would still need to clear the sync rights with the Publisher.

Q - If you want to use the lyrics of a song within your script, can you do that without clearance?

Becky - No. You must clear lyrics with or without music if they are in copyright.

Q - Can the title of a song be used as the title of a movie?

Becky - It is possible but the publisher/estate should be consulted at the earliest opportunity for discussion.

Q - If you use a film clip in your movie that has music in it, do you need clearance?

Becky - Yes, you will need to clear any film clip used in a movie.

Q - What are needle drops?

Becky - Needle drops are existing commercial tracks which can be licensed into a movie.

Q - If you had an actor singing in a film, do they get the musical performing rights?

Becky - If they are listed as the Artist then they would be entitled to artist royalties if the track ended up on a soundtrack album.

Q - What is the extra fee you have to pay in America if your film is released there? Will a sales agent take care of this?

Becky - Performance royalties are generated when film music is played in a cinema. In the US there is no performance income from the cinemas so the producer has to pay a fee, by law, to the PRS in the UK for using a UK recorded score in America.

Q - What mistakes have you encountered with new filmmakers?

Becky - Too little money for what they intend to achieve. Too little time.

Q - What advice would you give new filmmakers?

Becky - Involve a Music Supervisor early on to give some indication of cost for the desired soundtrack or start discussing alternative suggestions. Too often, the director has lived with his wish list for some time before a Music Supervisor is contacted and then maybe he/she can't afford tracks they have lived with for many weeks. It can then be difficult for them to find a suitable alternative.

POST PRODUCTION

Rupert Gregson Williams
Composer

MUSIC COMPOSER

Q - What do you think makes a great score?

Rupert - For me personally, it is a good tune. If someone writes a fabulous tune that I can remember, that does it for me. But that comes from a slightly selfish, unfilmic standpoint.

Q - When does a composer first get involved in a film?

Rupert - Often at script stage, especially if I have a good relationship with the director. Sometimes it can be as late as six or seven weeks before the final mix. For example, for *Hotel Rwanda,* I was hired four weeks before the premiere. But if it is a long-standing relationship, then I love to get involved very early in the process.

Q - Why were you hired so late in the game with Hotel Rwanda?

Rupert - There was a problem with the original composer. But even then they held off making a decision on a composer and put it off until then.

Q - Do you like being able to read the script before you start working?

Rupert - Yes, if it's before the film is shot. If they have started shooting, then I would rather get my hands on some rushes or watch them with the director at the end of the day and talk about it.

Q - How much time would you ideally like to do a film score?

Rupert - Jeff Softer, a top engineer who has mixed many of my movies, told me that there is no point in writing anything before the final cut, because they are only going to get you to change it anyway. I would love to have six to seven weeks, maybe two months. But sometimes it gets crammed into the last fortnight.

Q - Who hires you?

Rupert - If it is a lower budget film, in my experience, it has been the director who has the most power. If it is a studio film, then the producers are very much more involved. So, from my point of view, it has always been a budget thing.

Q - How important is the relationship between the director and the composer?

Rupert - Very important. One of the most important for the director, I'd say, because it is the last thing that gets layered onto the film. So the director can lay a lot of his emotional baggage onto the composer, and that can put pressure on the composer to make or break the way the film is going to end up.

Q - What would you say is the relationship between the film editor and the composer?

Rupert - It is very important because of the speed of editing. There is a massive relationship between the tempo of how it is edited and the tempo of the score you write. I have always found that the scores that are the easiest to write - where it just flows - is when I have some relationship or a link with the editing.

Q - What is a temp score?

Rupert - During editing, the director and editor will lay in some temporary music from other films to give a feel for what they are after. It's also useful for test screenings as it gives a more complete experience to the viewer.

Q - Have you come across directors who have fallen in love with their temp score and will not give you the freedom to come up with something new?

Rupert - Yes, I have had a few battles. It is OK if someone temps with John Williams because then it becomes a challenge to find something that is better. It is only a real problem when they temp it with their own stuff and you are encouraged to copy it. It then becomes a challenge to turn the director around to like what I have done.

Q - Does a film have to have memorable themes?

Rupert - My instinct is to say yes, a film needs a strong theme, but it depends on the movie. I would always lean towards a great theme that people can relate to and give some sort of emotional benchmark for the film. But then, it would be stupid to say that every film needs a big theme or a big melody because that is obviously not the case. Sometimes a big melody would overstate what the director is doing. But for my money, that is where I start - to make a theme that will have emotional resonance with the rest of the film. And that will help me down the line.

Q - How do approach scoring a movie creatively?

Rupert - The first thing is to watch it and to figure out what are the strong points and the weak points of the film. Then to watch it again with the director and to feed off of anything creatively that he or she wants to get from it and what they think you might be able to bring to the party. The more scores I do, the more I procrastinate and think a lot more, whereas I used to go headlong into it the first day and really try to punch a hole in the score, trying to make my mark with a big tune in the first couple of days. Now I think a lot more about it and sit at the piano.

Q - Do you always start by sitting at the piano?

Rupert - Once again, it depends on the film, but if it is something that needs a melody, yes. There have been a couple of films where it has been a sound that I am after. For *Hotel Rwanda*, I was not after a tune. I was after a sound of vicious tribalism and couldn't do that at the piano. So I used a distortion pedal and samples of a big drum.

Q - In order to start scoring, what do you physically need from the film makers?

Rupert - I ask for a QuickTime file of the film in its individual reels, with burnt-in timecode for visual reference. And in that QuickTime movie, I will ask them to put the dialogue on the left side and sometimes I will ask them to put the temp on the right side - on Channel 2. Then I will import that into my computer and be able to control the level of the dialogue and totally wipe out the temp if I have to.

POST PRODUCTION

Spotting and Timing

GUERILLA FILM MAKER SAYS!

After the temp track has been cut, the director and composer figure out where and how the real score will be placed in the film. The first part of this process is called spotting and second part is called timing.

Spotting	Timing
Literally the 'spots' where you want the score to be. Written down as spotting notes which contain very general 'in' and 'out' cues as well as any specific instructions about the score such as when certain themes are to come in, or if there is to be an absence of score. The final version of these notes is called the master cue list.	A precise (to the 1/100 of a second) list of the music cues that is given to the composer to execute. In addition, this 'cue sheet' contains descriptions of each shot, which includes its cuts and lines of dialogue. This is rarely done for low budget or indie films.

Q - What format do you record and deliver the score in?

Rupert - It is recorded and mixed in ProTools, usually in 5.1. I may also supply a stem mix where it can be re-separated and therefore remixed in the final dub.

Q - Do you always go to the dub?

Rupert - If I can, yes. It is vital to go at the beginning and at the end of it.

Q - Does the producer or director switch the music around a lot?

Rupert - Yes, it happens a lot. It usually happens at the end of a dub when all the insecurities start creeping in and a director is just trying to fix a problem that could have been fixed at script stage. But the dub is a good time in the last throes of the film where if the production team or the director sees something that is not happening or the emotion isn't coming across, then they can find another cue from somewhere else. So things can be fixed in a positive way.

Q - And if you are there you have some control over what cues are used?

Rupert - Yes. But it also depends on the budget. On a lower budget film, the Foley mixer may also be taking care of music. On a bigger budget, you will have a music editor who will always be there fighting your corner, who has a mobile phone and is always in direct contact with you while you are writing the last bits of the score. And they say, *'You should come over now!'* That is a good thing.

Q - What does spotting the picture mean?

Rupert - It means once you have got the job and have watched the movie a couple of times in the privacy of your own studio, you sit down with the director and watch the film from the beginning and discuss where there should be music - at what spots the cues for music should happen. But not only where should the cue come in, but also what sort of cue should it be. In spotting sessions, one of the things that usually comes up is what themes are really needed in the score. So you might find out that what we need is a real family theme. If it is a love theme, then there has to be a theme where there is tension between two people. Then you start to get your building blocks for the score.

Q - When does the composer get paid and what kind of percentage of the budget should be set aside for the composer?

Rupert - I don't know about percentage. Usually you have a flat fee that you charge. And usually you set it up in three payments. The first would be at the spotting stage, the second payment would be a couple of weeks before recording and then the last payment would be a couple of days after the last recording of the final mix. When you actually earn your quoted price, then you are getting into studio films where they are willing to pay. And if your film is successful, then your quote will go up.

Q - Should first time film makers aim high and approach well known composers to see if they are interested in working on their film?

Rupert - Absolutely. Go for it. If your film is interesting and you have no money, there is every chance that a composer that you couldn't afford might be interested enough to take it on.

Q - Should film makers approach new composers for scoring if you don't have a lot of money?

Rupert - In the beginning, I did a lot of jobs for nothing. And then I did some films where I spent all the budget on just those extra few strings or that extra percussionist so that the score would sound half decent and I would get a job again, and so the director and I would have something to be proud of. I have a couple of composers who work for me that do not have a lot of credits and if they frown because they have to pay to play, I always encourage them to do it. It is the only way to get into it, unless you are very lucky.

Q - How expensive is it for a film maker to hire an orchestra? Is it out of the realm of possibility for a low budget film?

Rupert - There are a few ways of looking at it. It depends on what you call 'an orchestra'. England and America have the finest orchestras and recording facilities in the world. But they are expensive. There are other places in the world where you can record that are not as expensive. I have recorded in Munich and in Bratislava. I used them three or four years ago because they were cheaper, and they sounded like they were cheaper. But now because people have been using them more often and people are cracking the whip a bit over there, they are actually quite good. And they are a quarter of the price of the English orchestras. So that is one way of getting around it. The most difficult thing for a composer to write is for a small line up of musicians, say twelve strings and single woodwinds, and then make them sound efficient. That's where a proper composer comes into his own. It is easy to throw the kitchen sink at something and make something sound great by having a seventy-piece orchestra with loads of brass and percussion. But have them write something for a string quartet and that sort of separates the men from the boys. But if you give it a lot of thought and back it with some samples or computerised sounds, then you can make a small line up sound excellent. But it is all in the writing.

Q - How good is the quality of samples these days?

Rupert - Fantastic. And what is remarkable is you can have a director sit in your room, press the start button on the scene and have them listen to the music (computer sampled) that is very close to what it is going to be like when recorded. Then you can put in the dynamics and emotion to make it great. There are no mistakes. He is hearing what you are going to produce on the day in the studio. That saves a lot of money in the budget. If the director hears it later and says that it didn't sound the same as he heard it in the studio, then either you have really crap samples or they weren't listening. A few years ago, there were still some composers who wrote everything on the piano. That is trust. But if they have notes and start wanting changes, that is going to cost money. A standard rate for a musician is £120 for a three hour session and if you spend an hour discussing it with the director in the control room, that is going to cost money.

Q - Do you physically write the score yourself?

Rupert - No. I hand it off to an orchestrator. He gets a sequence out of my computer, which has everything I want. Every individual instrument that I want to use. It doesn't look very pretty and doesn't have the dynamic marks for soft and loud on it. Some of the notes run into each other and it doesn't play smoothly. So I hand it off to a guy and he makes it play smoothly and makes it look pretty. Then he hands it off to a copyist who breaks down the score into every single player who plays a part on one piece of paper, which ends up on the stand. And then that is divided into each individual instrument part - the cello part, the violin part. The copyist is married to the photocopier.

Q - Do you hire the orchestrator?

Rupert - Yes. The orchestrator and the copyist, I hire myself or get the studio to hire them for me. In my case, I have a long-standing relationship with a person who has orchestrated all my stuff for the last six years. He is a writer himself and we work very quickly. That is a great relationship to have. And for the musicians, I let a music fixer know what I want and they will hire them. There are only two or three effective people in London - one of whom I go back many years with. Their job is to make sure the musicians are sitting in their chairs ready to play on the day you want them.

Temp Music

GUERILLA FILM MAKER SAYS!

While you are editing, and before your original score has been written, you will want to put some music tracks down to help set a tone and find the pace of scenes and your overall movie. You will find yourself browsing the soundtrack section in music shops and plundering the collections of music score collectors, in search of the appropriate feeling score to use as a guide. Music editors sometimes call this 'tracking'. At this point ANY music is fair game as you do not have to pay royalties (as the film will never be screened publicly in this unfinished form). Many film festivals will accept temp music in your submission for entry, with the stipulation that you will have permanent score in place should you get into their event.

However, beware when it comes to temp music. On one hand, it can be very helpful to your composer to have famous music tracks as temp music in order to give them an example of what you want from the score. On the other hand, you may grow too attached to that style of music and not open yourself up to alternative ideas. All too often, new filmmakers lay in some temporary John Williams or Jerry Goldsmith, and not surprisingly, it improves their film. BUT, neither John Williams or Jerry Goldsmith, nor the London Symphony Orchestra, is likely to do a low budget indie film.

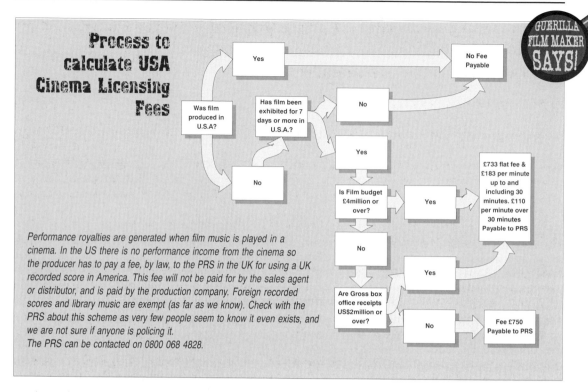

Process to calculate USA Cinema Licensing Fees

GUERILLA FILM MAKER SAYS!

Was film produced in U.S.A?

Yes

No

Has film been exhibited for 7 days or more in U.S.A.?

No

Yes

No Fee Payable

Is Film budget £4million or over?

Yes

No

£733 flat fee & £183 per minute up to and including 30 minutes. £110 per minute over 30 minutes Payable to PRS

Are Gross box office receipts US$2million or over?

Yes

No

Fee £750 Payable to PRS

Performance royalties are generated when film music is played in a cinema. In the US there is no performance income from the cinema so the producer has to pay a fee, by law, to the PRS in the UK for using a UK recorded score in America. This fee will not be paid for by the sales agent or distributor, and is paid by the production company. Foreign recorded scores and library music are exempt (as far as we know). Check with the PRS about this scheme as very few people seem to know it even exists, and we are not sure if anyone is policing it.
The PRS can be contacted on 0800 068 4828.

Q - Who takes care of hiring the studio you are going to record at?

Rupert - In the case of the bigger films, like this DreamWorks film I am working on, the production co-ordinator booked a whole load of time. And we discussed whom I wanted to mix it and engineer it and she went off and made it happen. On a lower budget, you do it all yourself and if you don't, problems start to happen because no one is there to stay on top of these things. Someone will slip up somewhere if you don't take care of it yourself.

Q - Do some film makers tend to overscore a movie?

Rupert - No. Not necessarily. I have three great relationships with directors who are mates of mine. One of them wants me to go over every single moment of his film. I think it is just insecurity because by the time I get to the end of the dub, I have left half of it as is. One of them is scared of the score. So he has to be taken through the process really carefully. He feels that if he has a really good performance out of the actors then there is no need for it. It will affect the scene so much that it becomes a third actor. I have seen them all.

Q - What can a producer do to make your life easier?

Rupert - Pay me more! No, there really haven't been many mechanical problems. They are usually diplomatic problems. So an executive producer might want to have a say on the film, but doesn't want to upset the director, and so they will get on the phone and have secret liaisons with you. They do write the cheques, but some diplomatic policing would be something a good producer can do.

Q - Have producers ever come in and changed what the director wants score-wise?

Rupert - I can think of three or four times when that has happened, where producers have undermined directors. They see it as protecting an investment, so you can see where they are coming from, but you also see it as a creative relationship with the director, so it can kick off all sorts of problems as you try to appease two separate groups. From a commercial aspect and from an art perspective, that can be quite tricky.

Q - Is it a good thing if the director is knowledgeable about music?

Rupert - I would love to say it is the kiss of death, but no, it can be a fruitful relationship.

Q - Are there scenes that can work really well with just sound effects?

Rupert - Yes. Recently, I just spotted music in a three-minute scene that I had been battling over. So I called the director and said it just isn't happening. He had fallen in love with some temp music he found. So after several months, we tried playing it without music and it worked. And sometimes if a scene is really hot and electric, then by introducing music, all you are doing is telling your audience to do something else other than just watching.

Q - Do you have any control over the soundtrack album?

Rupert - If it is a score soundtrack album, then I have control. But if it is a soundtrack album where the studio has a deal with a record company and they place some songs for a deal on the film, then I don't. They may put some of my cues on the soundtrack and they may ask me which ones they should use, but I don't really have much control over it.

Q - What are the qualities that make a great film composer?

Rupert - I think they have got to have some sort of understanding of film. Not just an understanding, actually, they have to have a love of film. Otherwise, they are missing the plot somewhere. I don't think it is necessarily a musical thing. I think some of the greatest musicians and composers aren't that adept in a musical way, but they can create amazing and complimentary film scores.

Q - What are the common mistakes directors and producers make when it comes to music?

Rupert - The only thing I can think of was on a comedy I did a couple of years ago. We encouraged the director to make a massive comedic statement with the music. We had him do lounge 'big'. It was quite fun writing it, but there was a problem with what it was doing to the film. And this was seven weeks before the final mix. I worked for four weeks on this lounge score that I felt was ruining the film, but that the director was convinced it was right. One Sunday morning, I told him he had to come down and watch the film with all my lounge stuff in there. We watched it and at the end we looked at each other and said, *'Shit, what are we going to do?'* We have four weeks left. Fortunately, I had enough time to rewrite the whole score and finish it. So I guess the lesson there is to make sure that you have enough time to score in case things go wrong.

Q - What advice would you offer new composers?

Rupert - In this day and age, don't be obsessed with equipment. It is a common problem. The main bit of advice is to make tea in the studio of someone who is actually doing the job. It is a very lonely process spending those years writing music for corporate videos and commercials. It's all well and good writing stuff that you think could go well in a scene, but the only way you are going to understand the business is to be there where the mechanics actually happen, with a composer who has done it before. And seeing the whole creative process with the director from the beginning to the end. Writing a scene is good practice, but the nuts and bolts is watching a working composer doing it. Every single composer that I know has been an assistant to another composer.

Q - What advice would you give to a new film maker?

Rupert - As a composer, when I am approached by a new film maker, I would like to do things in stages and to be cut some slack to do my own thing. And then to be torn back to their vision after a while rather than having pressure right from the start to do the bidding of the film maker. That makes you put something into the film of your own and if it doesn't work, it can be discussed and trashed if necessarily. Give the composer a bit of space.

POST PRODUCTION

Andrew Sunnucks
Audio Network

OFF THE PEG MUSIC

Q - What is Audio Network?

Andrew - It is a company that was formed out of Boosey & Hawkes (music publishers), originally out of my background as a music publisher. Robert Hurst, the Finance Director there, and myself, realised that there was a tremendous gap in the industry and that the music industry wasn't supplying music in the way the media industry wants to use it.

Q - How does clearing the rights to use music work?

Andrew - If you were going to use a commercial track you would have to find out who the record company was, and you would need to find out who the publisher was. Sometimes the rights would be out of copyright, so you can use certain elements, but that in itself is a hugely complicated thing, particularly working out what is, and what isn't in copyright, which can also differ from country to country. My background is in clearing those rights and negotiating my way around a labyrinth of publishers.

Q - Which can take how long to do?

Andrew - Frequently it can take weeks or months to clear a track. In the situation where a composer is dead, you might suddenly find that his estate is controlled by 4 or 5 different people, all of whom are around the world who are not talking to one another. You have to have the permission of every single person, within that estate, before you even start to try to clear the recording. Anyone who has tried to clear music knows it is a nightmare. I was out in Los Angeles working on a thing over there, and I spoke to a Producer, who said *'the music industry makes its product more difficult to use than any other part of the filmmaking process! It is a nightmare, it is high time the music industry reconfigured itself to find a way of making it simple, easy, quick and straightforward!'* The main point that they made is that you can no longer think of the world as a series of territories. It is a global business, and you have to think of it as a multi-platform industry. It is one thing to talk about territories, then when you start on platforms, you get into a whole different realm of clearance. Most filmmakers say *'We want to use this piece of music in our production and we want to make sure that we can then go off and exploit that production in any way that we want, without having to go back and clear individual rights with individual rights owners'.* Publishers have never liked to hear the term *'buy out'*, so that has always been a problem. In the 1950's to some extent that problem was helped by the introduction of library music. Library music at least holds the rights for the music and the sound recording. So potentially it is a one-stop shop.

Q - How much does that cost, for example?

Andrew - It depends on what kind of application you are going to use the music on, and what medium you want it cleared for. It is a more efficient process, but it is still expensive, especially for the lower budget films. There is some very high quality music in libraries, and there is an awful lot of total crap. So it is a matter of wading through that to find what is good, what is bad.

Q - So how does your company differ?

Andrew - We acquired all the rights, everything, from the music that we record. We buy the performances, we buy out the publishing in the recordings. Crucially we don't vest all our rights in organisations like the MCPS. The MCPS at the moment controls the pricing structures, the library music and they aren't allowed to depart from that. The MCPS then has a rate card, so everybody knows that all library music costs the same amount of money. So if you want to use library music, you work out how much you are using and then you work out where you want it for, what media you want it for, and then you can clear it. The problem is that when a lot of films are made, they don't necessarily know where it is going to be sold, they don't know what media it is going to be on, and the filmmaker is taking the risk up front, to clear things that they may or may not need in the future. We realised that there was no point in trying to make money out of producers, who often have very little money, though sometimes they have lots of money! If we could get our music used in loads and loads of films, we would make money from broadcast royalties. We persuaded a number of top composers to get involved, and recorded their work to the highest standards. Now, producers of low budget feature films can buy a world, blanket licence to use any of the music in our library for £180, no matter how much they use in any one production. Multiple production licenses are available too. The music is available off CD and from the Internet.

Q - So you can use as much music as you want from your library and it is cleared for the world?

Andrew - The only additional thing that we do is that if the film is then sold on DVD, as retail, we have a small additional charge. As an example, the maximum this would ever be, for 50,000 copies, is about £300. If you are selling over 50,000 copies of the film it shouldn't be a big issue.

Q - So I have paid my £180 to you, I've used your music, what kind of paperwork do I have to do?

Andrew - The usual thing, you just fill in a music cue sheet, which would always accompany the film anyway. It is so that there is a record of who composed it and so on, so that the composers get their royalties.

Q - Then there is no dealing with the MCPS at all?

Andrew - No.

Q - What about using music for promos or showreels?

Andrew - The most common question I get asked is *'can I use my music for free on my show reel?'* The answer is that if you ever use any music in any form whatsoever, you have to pay for it, and there is no getting away from that. Then they normally say *'well, does it really matter?'* It is a bit like when somebody might park on a yellow line, well you could say *'no, it doesn't really matter, but if you get caught, you will have to pay for it'*.

Q - So even in a private setting, such as a show-reel, which no one is going to see except for a private audience.

Andrew - The thing is you have got to have a licence, so if anyone does come in and throws tomatoes at you, you can show that you have got permission. It might be that you call up the publisher and they let you do it for free. It is very important that people realise that there is a potential at the moment for a lot of litigation.

Q - What happens if you use music and you haven't cleared it?

Andrew - It depends where you are found out. In the United States, if they can construct an idea that you have in some way damaged the music, and the way that it has been used, there is *'punitive damages'*. In the United Kingdom that doesn't happen, you simply have to pay the record company or the publisher what you normally would have paid for the use of that music, plus a bit. It is something that you really don't want to get into.

Q - What are the timescales for copyright?

Andrew - The rule in the UK at the moment is that a musical work comes out of copyright 70 years after the composer has died. But people often forget that the recording will be in copyright, and the recording stays in copyright for 50 years after the recording was made.

audio network plc
www.audiolicense.net

Andrew Sunnucks
Director

School Farm Studios, Little Maplestead, Halstead, Essex CO9 2SN, England
Phone +44 (0) 1787 477277 Fax +44 (0) 1787 477609
Email a.sunnucks@audionetworkplc.com

POST PRODUCTION

Q - So for example I can use Beethoven, but if it is played by the Royal Philharmonic Orchestra . . .

Andrew - You would need to clear it. If the Royal Philharmonic Orchestra played it more than 50 years ago, and you were using the original recording, you could use it. But if that recording had been re-released on a CD for example, there would probably be a copyright in the re-mastered version of the recording that was made 50 years ago. Also things that people assume are out of copyright are often not, such as *'Happy Birthday to you'* which is in copyright until 2016.

Q - That is 70 years after the composers death?

Andrew - It is a controversial one, but it was originally a song called *'Good morning to you'*, and then it said *'Good morning good teacher',* and then in 1900, it was released in a songbook for children, with *'Happy Birthday'*. It was a small change in the music, a dotted quaver, which became a copyright, it made the whole thing a copyright work. The old dear who did that died and then her sister had a claim that she had a hand in writing the words. She didn't die until 1946, so it stays in copyright until 2016.

Q - What about incidental music, music that is perhaps playing on a television or on a radio in a film?

Andrew - A big danger is *'incidental inclusion'*. There was a big row at the Oscars a few years ago because music was playing as the actors walked down the red carpet. The film crews couldn't exclude the music during their interviews, and of course the record companies and publishers were sitting there rubbing their hands. I'm not sure what the outcome was, but there was a major barney, because certain people were saying that this was very unfair, because they couldn't exclude the music. If you use music in any way at all, you have to clear it. Sometimes you will be in a situation where you simply can't find out what it is - but quite often you can find out what it is from mobile phones, Shazam and things like that. They are incredibly effective to find out what it is. If you really can't, the important thing is to have a very clear paper chain of inquiries and letters, and you can prove that you've attempted to find out what the music is, and attempted to clear it.

Q - What mistakes do inexperienced composers make when writing music for a specific film?

Andrew - A lot of composers understand music very well, but they don't necessarily understand film very well. The classic would be not getting the composer to talk to the sound guys, so a music cue is written for an explosion, which would fight with the sound effects and may well be removed in the final mix. Think about the frequencies that are going to be used in the final film - a music track, a dialogue track, a sound effects track, and get mixed together, which can be a recipe for a bit of an audio muddle.

Q - What advice would you offer a new filmmaker?

Andrew - Make sure that all music you use is cleared for the world, because it will come back to bite you in the bum. If you have a successful film and you suddenly find that you can't clear the music, you will be into having to replace the music, and that is very expensive. Editors cut to music tracks, and they often cut to their favourite thing from home and everyone falls in love with it, because you see images and music together, and the two lock in. To unlock them later, to disassociate them, is next to impossible. So my heart sinks when I hear *'we love this track by whoever, but we can't clear it, we can't afford it, can you do something like it?'*, and I know whatever I do, they will say *'Oh it is not the same as the original!'* I always go in with my new music and say *'right, you are not allowed to say anything, you are not allowed to comment, until you have heard it 6 times!'* It is amazing, they always come back with *'when we first saw it, we really weren't sure, but actually now I look at it again, I think it works really nicely'*. Music is an extraordinarily powerful tool for the Director. If you imagine a beach scene, little children playing, and you put *'We're all going on a summer holiday'* over that scene, then image what that brings up? Then you replace in your own mind the theme of Jaws, and you know the kids have had it! The scene is exactly the same pictures, but there is a subliminal instruction to the audience, of how they should be responding to a scene. Alfred Hitchcock said *'when the music and the pictures are doing the same thing, one of them is being wasted...'* Whenever we are doing music, quite often when people have had images and put music up against them, it is amazing how almost any kind of music in some way will work. You can suddenly put The Archers theme tune over the shower scene in *Psycho* or something. I'm not saying it is going to work very well, but it will make you look at that scene in a completely and utterly different way.

Think and plan what you are going to do with the music. Don't leave it to the last minute.

Jo Tizard
Music Publisher

Q - What is your job?

Jo - I run Trackdown Music which specialises in TV and Film Music Publishing. We provide an experienced, personal music publishing service which gives thorough attention to royalty collection worldwide. Trackdown's catalogue covers a wide range of productions including TV drama series, documentaries and theatrical films.

Q - What is the role of the music publisher? What do they do?

Jo - As a publisher of specially composed music, my role is to protect the copyright and ensure that royalties are paid. This involves proper registration of the works with the rights societies and ensuring they have the cue sheets, tracking performances of the films and soundtrack album and video releases, and collecting any royalties payable. If appropriate, I would also look for opportunities for further exploitation of the music.

Q - What are the various music clearances?

Jo - To clear a commercial recording, you need a synchronisation licence from the publisher and a licence from the owner of the sound recording. To clear library music, both the use of the music copyright and the sound recording is cleared via one licence from the library or its agent - usually the MCPS in the UK. Specially composed music is cleared via the commissioning agreement with the composer which may or may not include the clearance of any performances on the recordings.

Q - What are mechanical royalties?

Jo - A mechanical royalty is payable for every copy of the music made for sale to the public - this can be in the form of a soundtrack album, VHS, DVD, video game, etc.

Q - Do most film makers cut a deal with the composer for a share of the publishing right royalties?

Jo - I don't know what proportion of film makers do get a share. In my opinion, it is unreasonable for film makers to expect a share unless the commissioning fee is generous. However this is entirely a matter of negotiation between the composer and the film maker.

Q - Who collects the royalties? How does that process work?

Jo - In respect of performance royalties, the composer collects his writer's share direct from his performing rights society, and the publisher collects the remainder. Mechanical royalties are usually collected 100% by the publisher. Under PRS rules, the composer cannot receive less than 50%. The split is agreed between the composer and the publisher and varies from deal to deal.

Q - Why is a music cue sheet important?

Jo - Performance royalties and video mechanicals cannot be paid without a cue sheet. This contains all the details of the music included in the film - music title, composer, publisher, performers, record label, CD number, duration, use of music - so that the correct rights owners can be paid.

Q - How do film makers get a soundtrack deal?

Jo - By contacting record companies, particularly those that specialise in soundtrack CDs. The composer's publisher may also be able to help. It is a difficult market unless you have a sure blockbuster, which of course all film makers have!

Q - At what stage should a producer come to you?

Jo - As early as possible if he would like help to find a composer for his project.

Q - What is a music contractor? Who hires the musicians and studio for a score?

Jo - A music contractor books the musicians. He / she will provide a costing for hire of the musicians and correct rates to pay for the rights needed, including all the extras like leader's fees, porterage, travel subsidies, etc. The contractor will book and pay the individual musicians. Who hires the musicians and studio depends on the commissioning agreement - if the fee includes all musicians and studio costs, then the composer will book them, via a music contractor if necessary. Many composers have an agent who needs to be contacted early. Agents can also suggest suitable composers if the producer needs help with this. For major film projects, a producer could hire a music supervisor to take care of all the music requirements.

Q - Any common mistakes you've seen film makers make that could be avoided?

Jo - Yes - negotiating the commissioning agreement as the composer is writing. Completing this before he starts work will avoid any last minute awkwardness.

Q - Any advice to filmmakers?

Jo - Discuss with the composer well in advance what time he will need to write and record the music so delivery dates are achievable.

POST PRODUCTION

James Fitzpatrick
www.tadlowmusic.com

ORCHESTRA HIRING

Q - What is your job?

James - My job consists of three main elements. Music Supervision / Music Production which is doing and overseeing the whole job, Orchestral Contracting services which is hiring an orchestra, and I am also an Agency for Composers, Orchestrators, Conductors & Recording Engineers. Taking each element separately. Firstly, Music Supervision / Music Production. This job applies both to film, TV, video game scoring and record production and is where a production company or record label hire my services to advise on choice of music for film or album and then supervise the hiring of composer, conductor, orchestrator / arranger, copyist, engineer and select musicians, singers etc. that I might need to produce a complete score or album recording. I then produce the actual recording sessions as well as supervising the mixing, editing and mastering of score or disc. In other words I have overall charge of the music production. Secondly, Orchestral Contracting services involves some of what we just discussed but generally I take a more *'back seat role'* by booking, at the request of either the composer or production company, the orchestra, studio, musicians, etc., and then generally the composer is in charge of the actual recording, with help, advise or supervision from myself if needed.

Q - Why hire an orchestra?

James - I still believe in keeping music live. An orchestra can bring so much more to a score than just samples or electronics. An orchestra has passion, dynamics, feeling and humanity. That's not to say that I don't like electronic scores. Far from it. Each film has to have the most appropriate score to fit the on screen action...and some films, like *Halloween* are perfect with a simple synth score. What would *Lawrence of Arabia* be like without Maurice Jarre's classic score?

Q - How does the composer supply music to be performed?

James - Mostly these days the composers will supply music on either Finale or Sibelius software. Due to time restraints the composer might not be able to do the orchestrations and copying (extraction and printing of orchestral parts). So, that is where Tadlow Music comes in. If the composer does not have either an orchestrator or copyist, these can be recommended or supplied by Tadlow music.

Q - What are the different sizes of orchestras one can hire?

James - Any ensemble from solo musician to 100 piece orchestra and 60 piece choir. Size of orchestra does not affect quality. This is all dependent on the quality of the music. If it is well written it will be performed well, if the music is poorly scored or orchestrated then it will get the performance it deserves! The main thing is to have the correct balance of strings against the rest of the orchestra. Violins make a very small sound whereas trumpets are very loud. The most difficult aspect of an orchestral recording is making sure that you are not having to mike the strings too closely because there are not enough string players booked when set against a full horn, brass, woodwind and percussion section.

Q - Can you produce good quality music with a small orchestra? How can this be achieved?

James - Yes, but that all depends on the scoring and orchestration. However if you want a score to sound like *Star Wars* you can't achieve it with just 20 musicians, you need upwards of 70.

Q - How can one hire an orchestra with a limited budget?

James - Again it all depends upon the size of ensemble required. If you want a big symphonic sound, but only have the budget for a string quartet, then there's not much I can do for you! On low budget films, one of my main jobs is to find out a client's expectations and balance that against the budget, and work out how best to use their limited resources.

Q - What recording technology is used? How important is the engineer?

James - Various recording formats are used but the most common in the business is Pro Tools...24 or 48 track. A good recording engineer, who knows the recording venue well, is vital to the orchestral session. I've seen a fine orchestral performance that is ruined by sloppy or inexperienced engineering, not only for the recording stage but also in the mixing, editing and mastering.

Q - Is it cheaper for a producer to hire an orchestra outside of the UK? For instance, in the Czech Republic?

James - I work in both the UK and Europe. So, where possible, I try to steer things in London's direction. But, if a composer just doesn't have the budget for London, but still requires a quality orchestral score then I can take them to Prague where I work with 4 different orchestras and studios. London can work out to be 4 or 5 times more exepnsive than a place like Prague.

Q - Does the composer / director ever attend?

James - The majority of the time the composer will be present at all the sessions, and it is helpful if the director is present too. It all depends on the size of the production. On a film like Polanski's *Oliver Twist,* which I have just worked on, the control room was absolutely full with not only Roman and composer Rachel Portman, but also producers, the music editor, the click track / streamer technician, the recording engineer and his assistants. On TV scores it is just the three of us, composer, engineer and myself!

Q - Can the music be used for trailers and promotional work?

James - The score would have to be recorded as a 100% buyout. This would have to be negotiated and cleared with a London orchestra but is included in the cost of the Prague orchestras, so there is a clear advantage for low budget productions.

Q - Can the producer sell a soundtrack album?

James - Again, if the recording is done as a 'buyout' then the production company own the master rights to the music.

Q - What are the common mistakes producers make when it comes to music?

James - Not allowing enough time to get a great, rather than OK recording or performance. Leaving too little in the score recording budget after spending too much on the source music. Hire a composer like you would the lead actor. Get the right person for the job. If you want an orchestral score, get a composer well versed in that. If you want a rock or jazz score then don't hire a classical musician. Most importantly do your research and don't just go for a fashionable name. Spend time researching and listening to other scores, or get companies like mine, to advise and supply musical examples.

Q - What advice would you offer a composer?

James - Preparation is the key to any successful recording. Don't leave things to the last minute or to chance. When you arrive on the scoring stage make sure all the music is ready for the musicians to play. Time is money, and especially on a low budget production recording session, you can't afford to have musicians sitting around not playing while you are correcting major errors in either the composition, orchestration, copying or synchronisation.

MCPS & PRS

GUERILLA FILM MAKER SAYS!

The Mechanical-Copyright Protection Society (MCPS) and the Performing Right Society (PRS) both collect royalties for their members when their works are used. The MCPS mainly collects royalties in respect of the mechanical copyright in musical works, such as from the right to copy the work and the right to issue copies of the work in public. The PRS collects royalties from music users in the UK and around the world who every day publicly perform, broadcast and include music in cable production services. PRS collects the royalties by issuing a licence to the music user (usually charged on an annual basis).

POST PRODUCTION

Pete Burgis
Foley Artist

Q - What is your job?

Pete - I am a Foley artist. My main job is to provide sound effects, i.e. footsteps and general sound effects for the post production part of the film. Foley is a device within post production to replace or create new sound effects for the film that were not recorded or recorded badly, or that were CGI'ed so there were no sound effects.

Q - Is there a reason why a human does this and not sound effects of a computer?

Pete - Yes, because we can get a more organic sound, a more real sound than a computer can. You can imagine an editor trying to lay thousands of footsteps for a movie. You could take six months where as I can do it in real time. And also since I am a human I can trip or scuff my feet more naturally. An editor can do this too, but it would take them forever to get a natural organic flow to a character. I can add dimension to a character as well. I can work sympathetically to a character's performance. So the sounds that I can create can be designed for a specific person or individual.

Q - Why is it called Foley or 'footsteps' in the UK?

Pete - The word 'Foley' comes from America. In the old days when they didn't record sounds very well, a chap called Jack Foley realised that there weren't enough noises in a film, so he went into a studio to recreate those missing sounds. In America they called it 'Foley walking'. In this country we call it footstepping because the bulk of the work on the movie we do is just that. In a film like *Troy*, you have 50,000 people running up the beach and so you want to make that thunderous.

Q - For simple character drama and low budget films without space ships and dragons, you bring the human dimension to the sound?

Pete - Absolutely. It gives the director and the editor choices as to what they can do. They can choose to hear footsteps or not hear them to see what the effect is.

Q - What would a film be like without footsteps?

Pete - I think it would be a very boring movie if music and dialogue were the only things an audience could hear and be moved by. Music is a great mover, but if it is a very quiet scene and the music is just fading out and you want to add something to the end of that such as a sigh or a chair creak, it makes it more interesting. The difference between film with and without Foley is quite startling, even the 'lay' viewer can sense something is missing. We cover everything in a film. Whether it is needed or not, whether it is asked for or not, because further down the line they are going to sell it to a foreign market. That full sound mix, minus the dialogues is called a Music and Effects mix. In particular, the clothing movement is perfect for covering up dialogue holes (for the M&E) and in the full mix, things like ADR (replaced dialogue) where creating an atmosphere around an ADR line is needed to fill in the sound gaps.

Q - How much detail do you go into when doing Foley?

Pete - We go into minute detail depending on the film. For *Girl With A Pearl Earring*, it was very quiet and the soundtrack had to

The Props Room

GUERILLA FILM MAKER SAYS!

To the side of the foley studio there is often a room that is filled with all manner of props. A great Foley artist will take items and use them to recreate sounds - and not just the sounds appropriate to the item. There is a famous story about 'The Exorcist' and a Foley artist who recreated the famous head turn scene sound effect using a leather wallet filled with credit cards. Remember, it doesn't need to be real, just sound real.

sound like a painting. So it was very macro. We were mixing paints together in extreme close ups (close mic). We work on everything from a mouse crawling across the floor, to a plane crash.

Q - Would you say that Foley is good value for money in making the film sound of good quality?

Pete - Absolutely. I can replace a whole soundtrack for a fraction of the cost it can take to record on the set. That takes six months and I can do it in six days. For a first time film maker a Foley artist can help produce a soundtrack that can sound like it cost them millions to produce.

Q - What is the minimum time someone should budget for Foley?

Pete - For just general footsteps moves and a kind of an atmospheric feel to the thing, I like to do twenty minutes of footage a day. That can go up or down depending on if I make a mistake or don't like what I have done, I am human after all, and I may have to do it over. Or if the director wants to try different things, then it can take longer.

Q - Are there different groups of sound effects that you do in the process?

Pete - Yes. Generally we do the track for the feet first - a whole reel or per scene. Then we'll do a movement track to go on top of that. And last we will do a sound effects track of anything they come into contact with, such as a door.

Q - Is there a special studio that you record Foley in?

Pete - As a Foley artist I would recommend that you use a Foley stage, not necessarily the Shepperton Foley Stage which is a huge aircraft hangar soundstage and it has yards and yards of concrete and every sound prop you could imagine. You could do it in a small TV studio as long as it doesn't have a raised floor where everything sounds boxy and hollow as if you are only walking on wood. You need some concrete there so you can get it to sound like a road surface. I have recorded Foley in ADR booths, but you are not going to get the best quality.

Q - How is it that you are able to make just about any sound imaginable?

Pete - Practice and an understanding of sound. The tricks come from when you stop trying to make a noise and start thinking about the actual components of the sound. And the more you do, the more you realise that many objects make the same sound. Unfortunately, there is no training course or apprenticeship to become a Foley artist, you just have to go out and try to make the sounds.

Q - How important is the Foley recording engineer?

Pete Burgis
foley artist

peteburgis@hotmail.com

Pete - Very important. They have to have a good understanding of Foley and its uses. British movies record Foley different from the Americans who are different from the French. The French like to record Foley that sits right on top of the movie as soon as it comes out of the theatre, whereas in the UK, we tend to record the Foley flat and it moves onto an editor who will add atmosphere and a bit of echo in the final dub. There are ways to create a wooden room for example, which relies on wooden panels up and placing microphones in a certain way. That is down to the recording engineer. Artists don't wear headphones as it is more important for us to hear the noise we are actually making, so you need an engineer to monitor that.

Q - What elements does a film maker need to supply you with?

Pete - Of course they need to bring the film into the theatre and you should talk, in advance, with the engineer about exactly what they require. But for me, there's nothing really. If there is something very specific such as a car crash, the director might say that he has a specific recording of the exact car that is being used and give that to me. Or if there is a prop that is unique to the movie, then we may ask them to bring it in.

Q - Are you in perfect sync when you do the recording?

Pete - I try to be spot on as it saves time in the edit suite, but I average about 2/25 of a second off, one way or the other (two frames either way). It is not just about the actual footsteps being technically in sync, it is the feel of the run of footsteps. I may be off a few frames on the track, but overall if it feels right, that is what matters. As a person it is very difficult to see sync because often you can't see the feet so it is a body language thing. Time in the Foley studio is of the essence so we cannot sit there and study a scene for half an hour and besides, I feel it gives a very natural and spontaneous feel to the Foley to just watch it and do it.

Q - What is ADR?

Pete - ADR - Advanced Dialogue Recording is not the job of the Foley artist of course. ADR would be dine if there was a problem on the day where the dialogue was unusable for some reason, ruined by a sound on the set or if the actor didn't get the proper feel to his lines and the director wants to replace them, then you do ADR in a studio with actors. You are then left with the dialogue only and need to add Foley - footsteps and moves - to help seal the illusions and add life to it.

Q - What are some of the common things you use to create sounds?

Pete - Most studios will have traps in the floors that can be lifted up and they have concrete in one, marble in another, earth in another. We will bring in turf to lay down. For snow, we use all sorts of things like cotton wool - if you squeeze it you get a wonderful squeak like snow. We have used real snow and ice and crunched it up to get a good mountainside sound. We just did *Batman Begins* and for the ice scene where they are fighting on a frozen lake we used marble with salt on it and got this wonderful sound.

Q - For a first time or student film maker shooting on a really low budget, possibly no budget, do you think it would be a good exercise for them to get a microphone and a computer and do their own Foley?

Pete - Yes. And they could do a really good job because they might have a really small recording device they could take back to the places where they shot. So if they shot in a mate's flat, they could go back there and record Foley and then you don't have to worry about acoustics at all. They should call up a Foley artist or engineer and ask them about it because you could easily build your own rudimentary studio with a microphone and computer, and if you are prepared to invest the time, you could do quite a good job.

Q - What are the common mistakes that you see?

Pete - Generally, over-recording or under-recording Foley. Also, recording Foley without considering what it is going to be used for.

Q - What advise would you give a film maker?

Pete - Get a good artist who can get you the best sounds possible. The art of Foley is not being able to hear that it is there. Be creative with sound and respect how it can help your film and the story you are telling.

Andrew Stannard
BMG Zomba

Library Music

Q - What is production library music?

Andrew - Music that has specifically been written and recorded for Film, TV and advertising. It is off the shelf and is easy to clear. It is all composed with pictures in mind, as a resource for filmmakers.

Q - Is all library music badly composed stuff from the 1980's?

Andrew - No, though it has a history of being pretty bad synthesised music that someone has written in their bedroom with a really basic keyboard set up. But it has completely changed in the last ten years. It is the same quality as any other musical recording, we even record full scale orchestras.

Q - So I could have a piece of Wagner in my movie for the cost of library music?

Andrew - Yes. Our catalogue now includes all the classical artists. Wagner, Bach, Beethoven, performed by many orchestras, including the Royal Philharmonic. That is all available for you to use and you are paying a much lower rate than you would if you recorded it or bought it from a music label. We also have full scale orchestra recordings of other film genres, such as Hammer Horror. Our library includes stuff going back to the 50's, so we even have Carry On music. And the 1970's cheesy stuff, like The Sweeney, is in demand right now.

In the UK, the main libraries are BMG Zomba, KPM, Extreme, DeWolfe - the people that you first think of. But then there are hundreds of small libraries. The thing with the smaller libraries is that occasionally you get good music, but they can be quite narrow on what they can provide, and the quality of their production might not be so great.

Q - So what happens when I call you to buy a piece of music?

Andrew - The whole idea of production music is that it is meant to be as easy as possible. So you ask us if we have it and if we do, we send it to you. Then it is a one stop shop. The payment goes through the MCPS, so you don't have to worry about writing off or writer consent, doing deals etc. And you can do it online now so it is paperless.

Q - And how much would it cost?

Andrew - All music libraries charge the same (managed by the MCPS). You buy it in 30 second units (or part thereof). At the moment, for worldwide rights for a feature film up to £10 million budget, it is £475 for 30 seconds. That is for general clearance and trailers (the tarriffs are all online). You are not going to find anything cheaper than that. If you go to any commercial catalogue it is going to cost much more.

Q - How do I access all your music to try it out?

Andrew - It is all on our website and you can audition every single track and you can download in WAV, AIFF and MP3 formats. We first need to give you clearance, so don't expect to get a download immediately because it is copyrighted material, but once you do, you can download whatever tracks you like. You don't even have to wait for the post. So we are really handy in last minute edit situations.

Q - Do you get some famous composers like Hans Zimmer?

Andrew - Absolutely. Our library has a history of employing well known artists. We have artists like John Barry, Ennio Moricone, Coldcut and Amon Tobin who have recorded for us.

Q - Once a company has your library, they just find what music works, fill out an MCPS form and pay the bill?

Andrew - Yes. Once you sign the code of conduct with the MPCS, which is just a formality, you are away. You send the MCPS your cue sheet electronically and then they invoice you. And it is a quick process. Once you have sent off that application, you don't have to wait long to get it back.

Q - Can I release a soundtrack of my movie on CD?

Andrew - This can normally be done, but we do have to check that all the performers requirements have been met. You just contact us and we'd take care of everything (there may be additional charges too).

Q - What mistakes do you see new filmmakers making?

Andrew - They think that library music is copyright free and doesn't have to be paid for which is a massive error. They get confused between us and a company where you buy a CD and you can use the music for free. In a worst-case scenario, some people think they don't have to clear music at all.

Q - What advice would you offer a new filmmaker?

Andrew - Listen to your heart, stay true to your ideas and be ready for the long haul.

POST PRODUCTION

Paul Hamblin
Sound Design

SOUND DESIGN

Q - What is sound design or sound editing?

Paul - Essentially, sourcing sound effects, either from libraries or custom recording, then track laying them against the picture. On a more aesthetic level it is about looking at the picture and making it shine, enhancing the light and shade through sound. The soundtrack should always move the story on in an elegant and clever way.

Q - Isn't sound just dialogue, sound effects and music?

Paul - Not at all. Of course it is those things, but it is so much more. The main role of sound is to make a scene run in real time as opposed to all the bits of dialogue that get joined together. It can smooth the edges. It also tells the story outside the picture frame, creating a world that you can trust and believe in.

Q - From a low budget filmmakers point of view, sound can be used to create production value?

Paul - Yes, you can have helicopters passing over, or bullets flying everywhere when on the set there was just an actor in an army uniform having dust thrown at him.

Q - Is the pacing of the sound important?

Paul - Without question, you can be economical in order to create contrast. *The Matrix* was masterfully handled from this point of view, often there was a great deal of stuff going on in the image where there was little sound, but enough to keep it alive. By keeping it kind of empty they achieved great clarity and character whilst allowing the hard bits to have real impact. They also had a good idea about focus and the sound can focus the story. In life, your ear will guide you to any individual thing that you want to listen to at any particular time. You should try to achieve that balance in your film. Use the sound to guide the story, perhaps a scene where one character is talking to another, but really listening to another who is behind them for example. You could drown it out in the mix, or subtly mix it so that the audience understands, from, their own personal experience, what is going on.

Q - What is interesting here is that when you listen to the soundtrack of a movie it sounds so effortlessly mixed?

Paul - It is often a massive amount of work with enormous attention to detail. It takes a lot of effort and is labour intensive to make something seem simple.

Q - Where can you source sound effects?

Paul - The sound effects libraries give you a lot of choice. It is also easy to go out and record your own, but not in London as the skyline is generally too noisy. A lot of people now have DAT recorders or even minidisk recorders that produce excellent quality, provided they have a half decent microphone.

Q - What should a new film maker do if they have little or no money for sound editing?

Paul - If they have any acoustic appreciation about them they could do it on basic computer equipment using semi professional software like Adobe Premiere, Avid Xpress or Final Cut Pro. This will allow you to lay multiple tracks alongside each other and against a digitised picture. However, you need to go in to a dubbing theatre and mix it in the end as you need to produce an optical soundtrack for cinema release, but in

44.1 kHz or 48 kHz?

The sampling rate is the measurement of the level of the sound signal. The higher the sampling rate, the better the quality will be. Frequency is a measure of how frequently the waves of sound pressure hit the ear and it's measured in Hertz. There are two sample rates that are used in the industry: 44.1 kHz and 48 kHz. 44.1 kHz is the sampling frequency rate, set when they invented CDs, and was arrived at by doubling the upper limits of human hearing plus-a-bit (22.05kHz). Humans can hear sounds up to approx 20 kHz (sounds above this are audible to dogs and bats but not to humans). To capture the full range of sound, you need to record at least double. 48kHz is the standard for most post production and as it's a higher frequency rate, it will be a higher quality. You won't get any compatibility problems if everyone is working with this. Obviously you may need source music or sound effects from a CD where you can sample rate convert from 44.1kHz to 48kHz (easy with most editing software), or even play it in via analogue inputs.

CDs / Mini Disks- 44.1kHz.
DATs – Both 44.1kHz and 48kHz.
DA88s - 44.1kHz and 48kHz.
HD DA88 - 96kHz.

DigiBeta - 48kHz.
DVD - 48kHz.
Computers - 44.1kHz and 48kHz.

terms of putting the sounds in the right place, pulled off CD or recorded yourself, as long as you spend enough time, you could create an excellent soundtrack.

Q - How long will it take to track lay a low budget feature?

Paul - Give yourself as much time as you can. I wouldn't be thinking of three weeks if you are going to do it properly and by yourself.

Q - What are the common sound mistakes that you come across?

Paul - Preparation - people put good sound effects in place, very abstract sometimes, but they put them on one track, or break them up in a disorganised way. It's important to keep effects separate so the mixer can do their job. For instance, keep gun shot sound effects on one track, telephone or RT effects on another so that each go on a seperate fader. The channel on the mixing desk can then be equalised to get the optimum effect from that type of sound.

Q - What about things like sound and music fighting?

Paul - The tendency with big scenes which have dynamic music is to go for big sound effects. If everything fights, it can make the sound mushy or hard. Advice to the sound editor who puts the sound effects in place is not to be too precious about whether it gets used in all its glory or not, because the film should have an organic and natural feel at the end. Another common mistake is to do with sounds off screen, when the sound is telling the story outside of the image. If you have got a tram in vision coming right at you and you have a poor sound effect, the combination of sound and picture will make that sound effect work. However, if you don't have the tram in shot, the lack of character in the sound effect can make it hard to identify. Sounds off screen create fantastic atmosphere when they are good and can distract when they are not.

Q - What advice would you offer new film makers?

Paul - Try and make your film in a way that gives you time to pay attention to the detail. You said at the beginning of this chat that the difference between four weeks sound editing and having seven weeks is amazing, especially considering what it costs. The difference it can make to the film is massive because it is not just about doing obvious stuff, it's about what else is happening off screen, the details, having time to reflect on how well it is working and then to make the necessary adjustments. You know the way an artist will break up a straight line by something really rather clever, well we are doing the same sort of thing with sound, and that is when it will feel like a natural thing. People have more of an idea about sound than they imagine, provided they are remotely musical. What I feel is that the main role of sound is to provide the focus for the film. In places it can stand on its own right in a high fidelity or ballsy kind of way, and can reach out and touch you. But mostly its role is to guide the ear and the eye through the film, and I guess a good camera man would say the same about the way that they frame.

POST PRODUCTION

Tim Cavagin
Re-recording mixer

FINAL MIX

Q - What is the final mix?

Tim - It is where the dialogue, music and sound effects meet each other and get mixed into what you hear in the cinema. Hopefully the director, editor and producer all want the same thing and don't have different ideas and will stomp their feet and refuse to budge from those ideas.

Q - What materials do you need to do a final mix?

Tim - Normally we have a BetaSP for the picture so that we can run the sound alongside it. With regard to the sound element, it's important to check with the theatre in which you are mixing to see if they can handle the digital audio format you have chosen. We prefer the sound to come to us on hard drive because there is more flexibility with hard disk recording than there is with tape recording.

Q - Let's talk about the different types of sound that there are, firstly dialogue tracks?

Tim - The dialogue that is recorded on location will never be bettered in terms of performance. Provided the background sounds are not atrocious I would always advise the director to use this production sound. However, there are times when you can't use the production sound, because of background noise such as aircraft, in which case you are going to have to use ADR. This is where you replace the dialogue, but invariably, it lacks the sparkle of the original performance as the actor isn't giving the same energy levels, so it's best avoided. Every sound effect and every atmosphere in a room can be put on afterwards, the most important thing, especially with a low budget movie, is to make sure that your dialogue is as clear as possible. The sound recordist should spend all of his time concentrating on that fact. Forget about the door slams in the background, forget about the atmospheres of the room, forget about multi-track recording, just get the dialogue between the people in front of the camera, as cleanly and simply as possible.

Q - One of the things we did on Urban Ghost Story is that whenever we had an ADR scenario, as soon as we called 'cut' we would take the actors to a quiet room that was padded with duvets and ask them to re-perform it. They were not looking at any picture for sync, but nine times out of ten it would fit and the energy level would be there.

Tim - If you can get an actor after he has finished shooting the take to go off to your little room that you may have sound proofed then I think that that is a very good idea. As you say they are fresh from the shoot, the lines fresh in their head, and they know what they have just done so they can give a very similar performance.

Q - What happens about sound effects and atmospheres?

Tim - Sound effects are the colouration of the film, they enhance the production sound which can be flat, you need to spike up the sound. There are obvious effects such as doors closing, cars starting, but they can be used creatively to enhance the drama and story. You can get effects from CD libraries, or record them yourself. Atmospheres, a continuous sound that runs through a scene, are also used to enhance production sound, but you have to be wary of over egging the pudding. When you pre-mix your production sound you spend a lot of time sucking out the noisy backgrounds. There's no point in layering new atmospheres to create a mushy sound. Unless of course you are creating an other worldly atmosphere in which case you can use creative licence. If it's a normal contemporary atmosphere I think that it is very dangerous to put too many atmospheres down as the ear can only take in a few things at a time.

Q - What about music?

Tim - If at the end of the day you think about the sound track to a film as a bucket, you can only fit so many things in that bucket. Once

Track Groups And What They Mean

Dialogue Tracks *(mono)*
Keep dialogue tracks clean and bright, where needed use ADR (dialogue replacement), but be mindful that ADR can sound pretty bad.

Sound Effects Tracks *(mono and stereo)*
Track lay an effect for as many things as you can. Differentiate between effects that will stay mono and are from the perspective of the characters (such as doors and switches), and effects that will be in stereo and add acoustic punch (such as police sirens and thunder claps).

Atmosphere Tracks *(stereo)*
Don't be afraid to lay several thick atmosphere tracks and mix them as they can provide a very attractive stereo image. Use atmospheres to help create continuity during a scene, and also to help illustrate that a scene has changed by switching to a different atmos track.

Foley Tracks *(mono)*
The movement of the actors in the scene need to be brightened by a foley artist, a person who will add these with expert precision and clarity. Don't be afraid of going a little over the top, very rarely do you make a loud swishing sound when turning your head, but you do in the movies.

Music *(stereo and mono)*
Always in stereo (except when it comes from a prop in a scene such as a TV) and sparingly placed. Avoid drowning out your sound mix with music and use it only when you really need it.

Tools
A mixer will have tools like echo and reverb (used for churches, canyons etc.), a noise gate (that can kill sound below a certain level, excellent if you have too much reverb), a notch filter (to help get rid of continuous sounds such as a fridge or the camera). Don't let these tools lull you into a false sense of security, get it right in the track laying.

it's full, everything else becomes a waste of time. The dialogue is obviously very important, then the music and then the effects. In say a large sci-fi movie you want the sound effects upfront, you also want the music upfront and you also want the dialogue upfront - something has to give. So you to start chipping away at things to find the right balance otherwise you have a wall of noise that is unintelligible.

Q - In terms of quantity of music is it common to over-score?

Tim - A good score will really help the film and a bad score will really drag a good movie down. Too much music will suffocate a film, you have to allow for it to breathe, to allow the dialogue and the effects to have their space, otherwise you are in danger of swamping everything with music, a common problem especially with inexperienced film makers.

Q - What tools do you have at your disposal, other than the mixing desk?

Tim - We have a variety of tools. For the dialogue we use compressors which keep the dialogue within a certain dynamic, cutting the top off the loud bits and bringing up the quieter bits. If you raised the dialogue track to raise the whispers, then a shout would almost deafen you, so the compressor raises the whispers and catches the shout so they sit happily on the ear. We have dynamic equalisers which you can tune into a certain frequency, so if your dialogue has a noisy background, you can tune into the 'noise' frequency and this machine will just suck out that frequency in between the lines of dialogue. This can help clear up a noisy track. We also use reverb to match dialogues and to give sounds greater space. If two people are talking in a room and you want it to sound like a cathedral you can add reverb. A common problem with dialogue is a thing called 'essing'. When people pronounce their s's the ssss is annoying at times, and can start to hurt the ear. So we have a de-esser, which tunes into the frequency of that person's s's and decreases them. We also use exciters. If somebody is talking and they are not projecting very much, as long as the background isn't too high we can make it more dynamic and punctuate it with an exciter. We grab certain levels and raise them just to make it a little bit more dynamic. There's a tendency to over use these tools because they are so great and you think *isn't that a fantastic machine! I can suck out all this* and then you hear your soundtrack back you think *Oh No! I*

TWICKENHAM FILM STUDIOS
St. Margaret's · Twickenham · Middlesex · TW1 2AW · England
Tel: +44 (0)20-8607 8888   Fax: +44 (0)20-8607 8889

Tim Cavagin
RE-RECORDING MIXER

POST PRODUCTION

Post Production Sound

GUERILLA FILM MAKER SAYS!

1. Make sure that you previously recorded the best production sound you could - especially when it comes to dialogue. This will reduce the amount of ADR (it never sounds as good and it gets expensive) and other post tricks you will have to do. If an actor blows a line, or you are not sure, have them record it wild without the camera running and drop it in later.

2. Put your actors' voices on separate tracks so your re-recording mixer can set their levels once for each track instead of having to move faders up and down as each person talks.

3. Put your effects on different tracks from your dialogue and music so you can adjust them separately.

4. A good ambience track (atmosphere / environment) will act like filler in the cracks, smoothing over your edits. Choose your atmospheres with care.

5. Think of sound effects that might occur offscreen, such as a dog barking or a ship's foghorn, which could fill out your soundscape and perhaps help add tension or mood to your film.

6. A heavy ambient / atmosphere track can cover many natural sound problems.

7. If you decide to record your own sound effects, don't do it in an apartment that is noisy or located on a busy street.

8. Many household items can be used for creating sound effects. Slapping a raw steak on a counter makes a great punch sound.

9. Your various tracks should compliment each other, not compete, so don't have important sound effects and a really loud music score at the same time.

10. Too much music can make the audience 'music deaf' and so your score ends up having no impact. A rough guide is no more than 30 minutes of music in a 90 minute movie.

11. If you need to edit some music, cut on the beat. In some instances, you can just crossfade your music and it will be fine.

12. Always do a Foley track as it really helps fill out your soundscape. It's also vital for your M&E mix for international sales.

13. Get to know your dubbing mixer before you start working so that you can talk about what kind of sound and effects you want. Also, defer to his or her expert opinion when you are in doubt. They do this day in and day out and know what will and won't work.

14. Your final mix should be done in a studio that handles feature films as opposed to TV programs or news. While these other studios may be cheaper, you will not get the best-shaped sound and end up in the more expensive suite anyway. Most of all you are paying for the person whose fingers are on the faders, not the cool kit.

15. Make sure to save enough money to pay the recording studio / dubbing studio so that they will not keep your tapes hostage.

16. Appreciate the power of silence. Sometimes the best tension is created when nothing is being heard.

17. If you plan to track lay yourself, don't underestimate how much time it will take. Six to ten weeks is a good guide. You are not experienced and don't have a huge SFX library to hand.

18. Work out how you are going to get your audio to the mix. Avid can export an OMFI file which is often the best way, but do tests as without them, it won't work on the day.

have sucked all the life out of it! It's always a compromise, you want to suck backgrounds out but you do not want to suck the life out of your dialogue.

Q - What is Foley?

Tim - Foley is performed by a Foley artist, a person who stands in front of a screen and watches the film, then re-enacts the footsteps, door openings, glasses being put down, clothes rustles, leather creaks etc. They are important to enhance the location sound, but their primary job is for M&E used for foreign sales. If a film gets sold abroad, any sync sound with dialogue is unusable, so that is when foley becomes very important.

Q - What is the M&E mix?

Tim - It's the Music and Effects mix for the foreign markets, of great importance to world sales. It is everything in the final mix minus the sync dialogue so that abroad they can re-voice their dialogue into it. If you don't do the M&E properly it bounces back and you have to do it all over again.

Q - If you forgot an effect, could you drop it in there and then?

Tim - It depends on the dubbing theatre, but on the whole, as long as it is simple, yes. Check with the theatre though as they may not have an effects library. Instead of slowing the dub down it would be better for your editor to go off, get those sounds and come back once he has those sounds in synchronisation to the picture. We could then drop them into the mix. Because it's costing a lot of money, it's best not to slow the mix down. The most important thing to get right is the dialogue because without that you are lost. Proportionally, the time spent mixing in a four week mix would be four days spent pre-dialogue mixing, two days Foley pre-mixing, five days effects and atmos pre mixing, then six days final mixing. If you then said that you had a one week mix I would say decrease those amounts by four times.

Q - As digital audio tools on a computer are getting cheap and common, how much work can you do at home?

Tim - We had a film with a very low budget. I pre-mixed the dialogues, then they had already done all their work at home on their digital system for the effects and atmospheres. They had done an effects and atmospheres pre-mix and I sat here with sixteen faders set at zero, just making the odd adjustment. It was a very fast way to work. Aside from the computer you'll need a way to monitor the sound at home. It doesn't need to be superb, just a good amplifier and speakers, a way to listen to all the effects in relation to each other.

Q - How does the final mix get from your master tape or file, say a DA88 or OMF, onto the print?

Tim - Your lab will take the master mix and shoot an optical version of it which will then be married to your print. Aside from the analogue stereo tracks, there are several other digital formats that you can use but you will have to pay a separate licence fee for them. As long as your film is not going to be distributed theatrically, you can use the Dolby SVA surround system for free. If you do get a deal for a theatrical release you will then have to pay the licence fee to Dolby.

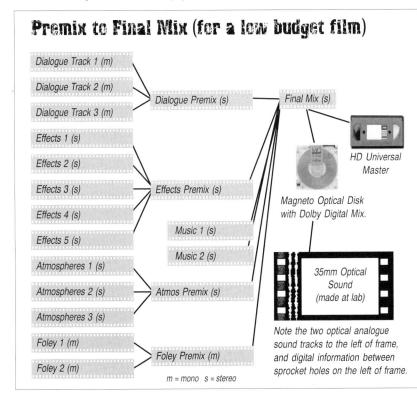

Premix to Final Mix (for a low budget film)

Dialogue Track 1 (m)
Dialogue Track 2 (m)
Dialogue Track 3 (m)
→ Dialogue Premix (s)

Effects 1 (s)
Effects 2 (s)
Effects 3 (s)
Effects 4 (s)
Effects 5 (s)
→ Effects Premix (s)

Music 1 (s)
Music 2 (s)

Atmospheres 1 (s)
Atmospheres 2 (s)
Atmospheres 3 (s)
→ Atmos Premix (s)

Foley 1 (m)
Foley 2 (m)
→ Foley Premix (m)

→ Final Mix (s)

HD Universal Master

Magneto Optical Disk with Dolby Digital Mix.

35mm Optical Sound (made at lab)

Note the two optical analogue sound tracks to the left of frame, and digital information between sprocket holes on the left of frame.

m = mono s = stereo

When completing your mix, it can all get a bit confusing as there are so many different mixes and formats. In essence, you will deliver audio files to the HD mastering company, a Magneto Optical disk of the Dolby Digital mix to the labs (that's the surround mix), who will use that to make the optical sound for the 35mm prints. This mix will later be used on your DVD too. You will also have another disk or tape (DA88 format if tape) that will have a stereo mix for broadcast TV, and an M&E mix for foreign sales. You may also have a 'stem' mix, which is a disk or tape that has the mix but in all its separate channels, should you or anyone else, wish to go back and change it. Delivery on disk is becoming more popular, usually as a Pro Tools session.

POST PRODUCTION

Q - Who should attend the final mix?

Tim - In the theatre I'd expect to see the picture editor, sound editor, director, and producer, no more. Any more and you'll have a constant cross pollination of ideas as everyone has their own little agenda, everyone wants to hear their own little things and it is just not possible.

Q – How do you get the best deals?

Tim – When a dubbing theatre is busy you're not going to be able to match the £300ph that fully funded productions pay. What you can do is agree to come in during downtime. You might have to have a day here, then not mix for a few days and you might be pushed out by a paying job. Most theatres are accommodating because they might as well be earning some money than nothing at all. If they've done a deal they probably won't let the tapes out without the money upfront.

Q – What are the most common mistakes that you come across?

Tim – On a low budget film the most common mistakes I come across are in fact over track laying. People who have far too many tracks for the time allocated, it is all right coming in saying I have got thirty two tracks but if you have only got two days you are not going to be able to mix those tracks, it's just not physically possible, you have to cut your cloth accordingly. Another problem is when people bring in their own tracks and they do not give you any separation, they do not checkerboard the sounds or dialogue. This means that I can't get in and apply an EQ or mix easily. This can make the final mix much longer or force creative compromise. I would say to all editors who are laying up tracks, think where you are laying them and *if I was me mixing it, would I be happy with what I have here?* Indecision is a

The Final Mix

GUERILLA FILM MAKER SAYS!

This is when all your sound effects, music and dialogue are mixed into one. It's the most exciting moment of the whole process, as your movie seems to leap to life.

1. Mixing studios are expensive. Make sure you are prepared, your charts are clear and any or all creative decisions have been made.

2. Mix in stereo at the least. You can opt for analog Dolby, which is a surround sound system, free for TV, video and festivals, but you pay for cinema. There are other digital formats, each with a fee for use. Dolby Digital is the most widely used format and the preferred format.

3. Get to know your dubbing mixer. Push them to be satisfied with 90% and don't waste time trying to get that last little effect absolutely perfect. Often a film will mix itself, so avoid trying to get that last 10% out of the mix, it will cost you 90% of your time.

4. If you are on a tight budget, it's possible to mix a feature film in 3-5 days (with M&E). Don't let the mixers persuade you into 3 weeks.

5. If camera noise is a problem, most of it can be filtered out, but not all. Either post sync the dialogue or lay in a heavy ambient track over it, e.g. a plane flying over, or a printing press.

6. A good Foley artist will work wonders. A Foley artist is a person who adds the clothing rustles, footsteps, keys jangling in pocket etc. Spend a good two-day session here and you will have a much livelier sound track.

7. Cheap computer software and hardware can be used. Most PCs / Macs can record in 16 bit digital stereo. Sound effects can be recorded and cleaned up in programs like Cool Edit Pro (free download from the web) and editing systems like Premiere / FCP / Avid Xpress can be used to track lay sound effects. This isn't ideal and presents the few technical headaches, but it is possible, especially if you are technically minded.

8. Produce a Music and Effects mix (M&E) at the same time as your master mix. The M&E is a mix of the film without any dialogue, to be used for re-voicing in foreign territories. This is essential and you will be unable to sell your film without it.

9. Work out what of stock you need for your master mix and buy it before you go to the studio. They will try to sell you their tapes / disks at an increased price. Alternatively, do a deal including stock. Don't underestimate how these charges can add up.

10. The Dubbing Theatre is the best environment you will ever hear your film. What may seem like an over the top sound effect may be too subtle on a TV speaker. Make sure all plot sound effects or dialogue are clear and correctly emphasised.

35mm Print Audio

The sound for your film can be encoded onto the print in several formats. Each use a form of surround sound, but you can mix in simple stereo.

Twin Analogue Tracks *containing a stereo mix. Can use encoded Dolby or DTS SVA mix to give left, center, right and surround. This is the cheapest and universal format. The quality is very good. If money is tight, this sound format alone will be more than adequate.*

Dolby Digital *- Surround digital mix with left, center, right, left surround, right surround and sub bass channels. Encoded and stored between the sprocket holes on the film.*

SDDS *- Sony's digital format. Eight channels, left, center left, center, center right, right, left surround, right surround and sub bass. Encoded and stored on the extreme left and right of the film. If one side is damaged, the other side which is offset, will drop in to ensure the sound never disappears.*

DTS *- Surround system recorded onto CD Rom with left, center, right, left surround, right surround and sub bass channels. A time code like signal is encoded on the print which controls a CD Rom with the audio stored on it. One print can be used with different sound mixes being supplied on different CD Roms.*

common problem too because the dubbing stage is the last stage before the film goes out. The dub is the point where you have to make up your mind about all those things you have been putting off and a lot of people are uncomfortable about that. Come in with a firm idea of what you want. If you have a firm idea of how you want things to be, don't be afraid to tell the mixer. It's much better than a director turning to the dubbing mixer and saying *'it's not how I want it, I can't tell you how I do want it, I can just tell you that it is not how I want it'.* That's the worst thing in the world. Often they haven't had enough time, *we haven't slept for seventy-two hours* they say. It happens on the low budget films, it happens on the big budget films. Give yourself enough time. If you think it's going to take four days allow six. Give yourself time and a half and you can't go far wrong.

Q - What advice would you offer a new film maker?

Tim - Many low budget films come in and you can see that they would be so much better if the editor and director had been ruthless and cut aggressively instead of leaving it long and baggy.

Howard Bargroff
Re-recording mixer

SOUND POST

Q - What is your job?

Howard - My job is to take the sound from the edit and turn it into a finished sound mix.

Q - At what point should you be contacted about taking that material and making the final mix?

Howard - We sometimes get involved when they are shooting, but more commonly it's at some point in post production. Usually, we are contacted too late to be of most use.

Q - How important is it to get a good sound recordist on set?

Howard - It is certainly worth investing in a good sound recordist. You will save yourself a fortune if it is recorded properly in the first place, and the end product will be that much better.

Q - If I've just done an edit on my Avid Xpress at home, and it sounds pretty damn good, why should I bother coming to you?

Howard - It may sound good at home, with your small speakers, but our job is to make it sound good in a cinema. You have got to make your material resilient to being played back on huge JBL speakers, in a room like the Empire Leicester Square, or some cavern somewhere. If you listened to your home mix in that kind of environment, things will jump out of your edit that you've never heard and will be a shock to the system.

Q - Say I've made myself a low budget independent feature film, and I come to you guys and say 'Listen we've done our Avid or FCP cut, we want you to do the sound mix', what happens from that point on, assuming that you can cut a deal?

Howard - The first thing that we would ask is *'How much money have you got?'*, because the workflow that follows will be dependent on the price.

We would want an OMF (exported files from Avid / FCP) from the editor of the sound, assuming you are working with an editor who is technically savvy, and not one who has loaded the material in just off the analogue tracks of the beta! That is very important. Using an OMF, we are able to just pick up from where the editor left of. The OMF is always the starting point for us.

Q - So when you are doing your edit, with regard to the sound, tidy it up, clean it up, and if you are going to track lay in effects, make sure those are the effects that you want, not just pulled out of some TV show?

Howard - Yes, that will save us a lot of time and therefore your money. So clean up the dialogue tracks, lay in appropriate sound effects, checkerboard dialogue so it is easier to mix, generally be very tidy and organised.

Q - Should people do test exports?

Track Laying Yourself? GUERILLA FILM MAKER SAYS!

Sound is an area where low budget films often fail, yet they need not. The technology is cheap and all it really requires is a little know how and a lot of time consuming work. Sound Effects CDs are an excellent source of high quality stereo recordings of pretty much everything you could imagine. These are the same recordings as used by multi million dollar productions. And you can use them too! If you can't afford to buy the disks, try asking the studio where you plan to do your final mix and see if you can use their CD library. Be creative with sound and try and fill your soundtrack. You can track lay the sound in your film with a number of semi-pro and domestic computer tools such as Adobe Premier, Avid Xpress Pro and Final Cut Pro. Using either SPDIF digital input / output, and by pulling effects directly off CD, you can stay 100% digital, maintaining acoustic excellence without a silly price tag. You will need a good computer, large and quiet space, good amplifier and speakers and a high quality microphone. Best of all, both Avid Xpress Pro and FCP export OMF .

Howard - Yes, just export some sound and picture and let us have it ahead of the mix. We can then isolate and deal with any problems or mistakes. And if you are pushed for money, keep your tracks as simple as you can too.

Q - How do you project the picture?

Howard - We usually run a Beta tape with burnt in time code. If you run tests, you could also happily export Quicktime files too, but do run tests as not all Quicktime files work as expected. Whatever the format, it must have the correct timecode, so you can't run from formats like DVD.

Q - Unlike some other sound facilities, you can also track lay the sound for the film makers. Do you have lots of sound effects?

Howard - We've got an enormous sound library, plus if the budget is there, new recordings can be done, and new recordings are done on most projects. Library sounds are not always the best sounds to use, they are just easy. For instance, things like thunder are very difficult to go and record.

Q - So that process of track laying, how long would it normally take?

Howard - It depends on the budget. Anywhere between a week and twenty weeks. The more organised you are, the more creativity you are going to get for your money. It is now becoming how long have we got, and then you get into the dubbing, and the creative triangle of *cost*, *time* and *quality* comes into play - you can have two sides of that triangle, but never three.

Q - If you were a micro budget filmmaker, and you said 'right, I want to tracklay it all myself, and I'm going to spend two months doing everything, making sure it's all labelled and organised in my timelines, I will have a clear idea of what I want, I will have done tests and all the technology works... tell me what you would do then?

Howard - I would always attempt to get the dialogues as good as possible, as clean as possible, because I think a good, fast flowing mix, stems from good dialogue tracks. If you have cleaned everything out, and all your acoustic holes have been nicely filled, then that is the core of your film onto which you can hang sound effects. From that point on, the mix should just flow into place, as long as that ground work was done first by the film maker. The best people to have in the final mix are directors and editors that know exactly what they want, people who have prepared. It just makes life easier for everyone.

POST PRODUCTION

Audio Tracks In Detail

GUERILLA FILM MAKER SAYS!

Even a low budget film should have excellent sound. As long as you spend time selecting good effects, laying them in, acoustically annotating everything on screen (and some things off screen), then adding good ambience tracks, detailed foley and finally a considered and rich score, you are in for a great sounding movie. We spent a great deal of time on the sound for our third feature film, Urban Ghost Story, but at the same time, knew we didn't have limitless resources. The example below is all the tracks from reel five of the movie

1. Dialogue Tracks (mono) - The sound of actors' voices recorded on set. It is important to get this as clear and crisp as you can so that less sweetening or ADR will be needed later. In this instance there are three mono checkerboarded dialogue tracks. Note how each track is for an individual character so the mixer can easily access each.

2. Set FX (mono) - These are sounds that we recorded live on set, broken apart from the dialogue so that they can be used in the M&E mix. This is stuff like footsteps, a door slamming, or water running. There are two tracks of set effects here.

3. Panic (mono) - This is a single 'just in case' track. Used for audio you probably won't use, but might have to in case of an emergency or creative epiphany.

4. ADR (mono) - Also known as looping. Re-recording of actor's lines that were not properly picked up on the production. Two tracks here. All our ADR was recorded wild, mostly on-set after the shooting finished, but sometimes in the actors' apartment.

5. Foley (mono) - A recreation of all the actors' movements in a film, from their footsteps to clothes rustling. Will also be a large part of the M&E mix. In this instance there are two foley tracks.

6. Spot Effects (mono) - These are all the character and story driven sounds. Door slams, car tyre screech, telephone ring etc. Two mono tracks here.

7. Spot Effects (stereo) - Used for wider sounds such as a gunshot, police siren or a sword being swung etc. We had four stereo tracks as many effects needed building from several layers.

8. Ambiance (stereo) - Continuous 'background' sound that appears throughout the film. Not usually recorded on set, but pulled off of library CDs. A full atmosphere track can really make your film sound rich. Spend time and get these right. We had four tracks as it was a spooky ghost story.

9. Music (stereo) - Either composed, taken from a library or some other source. Can be in the background or foreground. Too much music can be really annoying. One track here but you would normally have at least two or more.

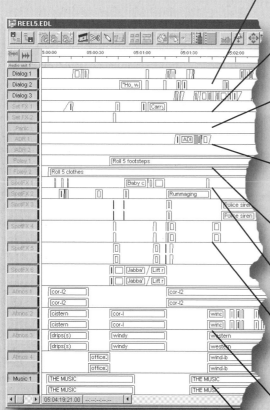

Cinema Surround Layout

This is a pretty average 'small theatre' that will playback surround sound encoded soundtracks. Usually this means Dolby Digital, or its analogue little brother now called Dolby (which used to be Dolby Surround). Note how all the front speakers are mounted behind the screen. Next time you are in a cinema, go right up to the screen and you'll notice that it is filled with tiny holes to allow the sound to pass through more easily. In some cinemas you can even look around the edge of the screen and see the speakers! Not all cinemas are kitted out like this, many of the smaller screens and independent cinemas have either their own version of surround sound, cobbled together from bits. And then there are the flea pits! Only recently I visited an independent cinema (that shall remain nameless) that was still reproducing sound in mono, that's one speaker! And being a low budget film, these are the theatres you inevitably end up screening your movie in.

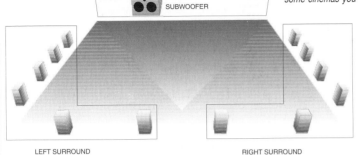

Q - As an alternative to coming to you guys and doing the whole mix, do you think it would be a good philosophy for a savvy, technologically, creative filmmaker to say 'You guys do the dialogue premixes, and we will do all the rest'?

Howard - I'm not saying that sound effects are easy to lay and mix, they are not, they need to be done properly, but if there is one thing that is going to make a film sound amateurish, it is badly recorded or mixed dialogue tracks. So yes, that would be possible.

Q - What is the best way to get the best deal out of a sound mixing facility?

Howard - Flexibility. Understand that if someone is helping you out, if a paying job comes in, you will be moved, and you mustn't complain. Often, a short film, which should be a simple job, takes much longer as the film makers are learning how to do it, and that can be quite painful. Simple things like changing the edit mid mix without understanding the implications of that choice are common.

Q - What tips would you offer somebody who has made a film school project and is thinking about sound for the very first time?

Howard - Try and get across some salient moments with the sound. Don't worry about it being technically superb, but do try to use the sound creatively. Watch the picture and listen to the sound, and see if it is working, if it is complementary. Ask yourself, 'I know I've spent a long time developing this bendy sound, but is it right?' If it is not, try something else. Really, really watch the picture, make sure the sound is right for it. Personal introspective honesty is worth its weight in gold.

Q - What are the common mistakes you see?

Howard - Badly recorded sound. We hate having to use ADR, as everyone does. The most common thing is not being savvy on set, and not listening to your sound recordings. If sound is important to the film, it needs to be shot with sound in mind as well, which doesn't always happen.

Q - What advice would you offer a new filmmaker?

Howard - Half the film is sound, so when you are shooting, remember that and you will save yourself a lot of aggravation.

POST PRODUCTION

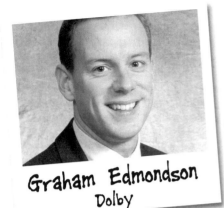

Graham Edmondson
Dolby

Q - What is Dolby Stereo, Dolby Surround etc.?

Graham - Dolby Stereo and Dolby Surround are often confused, but in fact relate to pretty much the same thing. Both are four channel systems using Left, Centre, Right, and Surround channels. But due to restraints in recording mediums (e.g. the physical width of a piece of film) and broadcast systems (e.g. TV two channel systems), the four channels have to be squeezed into two channels using Dolby matrix encoding technology.

Q - So what's the difference between the two?

Graham - Purely marketing names really, Dolby Stereo was the term used when this format was used in the cinema, and Dolby Surround was the term used when this format was used for TV and video systems. Dolby SR is a professional noise reduction technology, but since it is added onto the Dolby Stereo track on film, it is often simply used to describe this track as well.

Q - What is Dolby Digital?

Graham - While Dolby Stereo and Dolby Surround are pretty much the same thing, but called different names, at least Dolby Digital is called the same thing when used in both the cinema and at home. Dolby Digital expanded on the four channels of sound and increased this up to six channels of sound with the addition of two channels of surround (often called "stereo surrounds") and a subwoofer channel. In the cinema, Dolby Digital is added onto the film in digital data blocks, which are located between the film's sprocket holes. By leaving the Dolby Stereo analogue track exactly where it was on the film - every cinema could receive the same film print - if the cinema was equipped with digital playback then it would play the Dolby Digital track, if not then it would play the Dolby Stereo analogue track. In the home, Dolby Digital is the standard on DVDs and more broadcasters are also starting to broadcast in Dolby Digital. It's the same six channels of sound that you would hear in the cinema.

Q - How is Dolby Digital encoded on the film?

Graham - All Dolby approved dubbing studios (contact Dolby for a current list) have equipment installed that encodes the six channels of audio onto a single MO disk (a computer disk) that can then be sent to the film lab. The film lab uses this MO disk to shoot a sound negative, which contains both the Dolby Stereo analogue track, and the Dolby Digital track between the sprocket holes. Once the negative is made, the prints are produced as normal the digital soundtrack will play back in the cinema. Because it's digital audio, the sound quality that is heard in the cinema should be identical to what was recorded in the dubbing theatre.

Q - What is meant by 5.1?

Graham - Although we say that Dolby Digital uses six channels of sound, in fact the subwoofer channel only reproduced very low frequency bass sounds (explosions, rumbles etc). Because this isn't a full frequency channel, it quickly got referred to as only a .1 of a channel. Hence six channel sound very quickly became known as 5.1 channel sound.

Q - What does it cost a filmmaker to license Dolby? And must you have a license for a feature film if you use Dolby? What if you use Dolby for a short?

Graham - It is a common misconception that there is a license fee to pay to use a Dolby technology for a film's soundtrack - there isn't. However, Dolby do insist that a Service Agreement is signed for each film, and there is an associated fee for this.

Q - So what does the Service Agreement include?

Graham - It includes the use of the Dolby equipment that has been installed into the approved dubbing studios. It also includes 16 hours of a Dolby consultant who is assigned to your film and will help you technically through the soundtrack production process, whether you choose to use those 16 hours in a dubbing studio, assisting with the laboratory transfers and printing, or checking and aligning cinemas for your first important screenings. And with everything carefully controlled and aligned at all stages, it gives peace of mind that what you eventually hear in the cinema was exactly what you did indeed intend to hear. If your film is less than 45 minutes, it's considered by Dolby as short film. If you choose just the Dolby Stereo analogue soundtrack format for a short film then there's no associated Service Fee cost. But if you choose Dolby Digital as well for a short film then there is a minimal charge to mainly cover the cost of producing the MO disk (for theatric release and not DVD).

Q - Is a representative of Dolby present at every film mix?

Graham - Yes, as part of the Service Agreement a Dolby Consultant will be at your final mixing stage. The Dolby Consultant will spend time before a mix checking the alignment of the dubbing studio and the equipment, and will then stay for the final mix to check everything is in order before the MO leaves for the film lab. Getting things right at this stage is crucial to avoid costly mistakes when the film lab starts making negatives and prints.

Q - What is Dolby Digital Surround EX and what are its advantages?

Graham - Dolby Digital Surround EX expands the number of surround channels from two to three. This means that the back wall of the cinema becomes its own surround channel, with the other two surround channels on each side wall. Why is this necessary? Well many sound mixers feel that this gives them greater artistic control to be able to accurately pan sounds around the back of the cinema, or flying sound effects from the front to the back - giving the impression of sound going right over the audience's heads. The third surround channel is encoded into the regular Dolby Digital track, and cinemas need an extra box to be able to decode this extra surround channel. This first film to use this format was *Star Wars Episode I*.

Q - What is the different between Dolby Digital, DTS, and SDDS?

Graham - All these three digital soundtracks in fact give similar digital audio quality to an audience in the cinema. Like Dolby Digital, Sony's SDDS system is actually printed on the film itself - this time on each outer edge of the film (this was pretty much the only space left on the film). By contrast however, DTS choose to put their six channel digital soundtrack on a separate CD which plays from a DTS box hooked up to the sound system. DTS managed to fit a thin strip of timecode information onto the film itself and it uses this to synchronise the CD soundtrack to the film.

Q - How does a filmmaker go about getting an agreement with Dolby?

Graham - Simple, just look up Dolby's contact details on their website and ask to speak to someone in the Production Service department. All inquiries from North and South America are dealt with out of Dolby's Hollywood office, and everywhere in the world is dealt with out of Dolby's UK office.

Q - What is Dolby's relationship to THX?

Graham - Another misconception is that Dolby and THX are rival sound formats In fact the truth couldn't be further away. Dolby and THX have worked very closely together for years to improve cinema sound. THX offers a set of requirements that cinemas must meet to be THX certified. This includes room acoustics, proper equipment selection, and a few THX products that integrate within the sound system. Dolby provides the technologies that record the soundtrack onto the film, and plays them back in the cinema. If you end up with a cinema that is replaying a Dolby Digital soundtrack, into a THX certified cinema, you're going to end up with pretty awesome quality.

Graham Edmondson
Development Manager
Production Services Group

Dolby Laboratories, Inc.
Wootton Bassett · Wiltshire SN4 8QJ · England
Tel. (44) 1793-842100 · Direct Line (44) 1793-842116
Mobile (44) 7768-375909 · Fax (44) 1793-842101
Email gce@dolby.co.uk
www.dolby.com

Mike Milne
Framestrore - CFC

DIGITAL EFFECTS

Q - What is your job?

Mike - I work at *Framestore-CFC* and have two jobs. My first is really a legacy from having started the CG department here 14 years ago, so I sit in meetings and on committees and get involved choosing teams. My real job is running the team that makes visual effects for Long Form TV such as *'Walking With Dinosaurs'*.

Q - What are digital visual effects?

Mike - The first major catagorisation is in two parts, between computer-generated images and computer manipulated images. They are both equally important and both equally revolutionary in the film business. The fact that you can source lots of material from live action (camera), then combine it and manipulate it in computers, in what we loosely call 2-D, is one half of it - that covers things like changing the sky if it wasn't sunny enough, to more complex things like crowd replication (for instance, filling a football stadium with 100,000 screaming fans, when in fact you only filmed 50 extras in different costumes and in different places).

Then the other half is where you are generating images from scratch, which have no existence outside the computer, where you are using the computer as a camera to photograph unreel objects. Obviously when you combine those with live action, you are using the 2-D side as well. I don't think you can separate these two sides. There are two groups of people who do it - CG and 2D - but they are inseparable, in that you can't really have the CG without having a 2-D manipulation and vice versa, unless you are doing something like *'Bug's Life'* or *'Toy Story'*, which is all CG.

Then in CG, you've got some broad areas. You've got replacement for stuff that would've been done physically before. So you have got pyro-technics, and *'Perfect Storm'* tidal waves, and volcanoes, and various effects that would have been done by live action effects, scaled up miniatures etc., and are now done by particle systems. You also have 'set' extension, which again is something that would have previously been done by miniatures (where a set is made to appear bigger). Set extensions can be anything from making a street longer to building an entire city. Virtual stunt work, where you are replacing something that would be done by real actors, and I include in that both a single person falling off a building all the way up to entire armies of Orcs. Effectively they are all virtual stunts. You would have hired the Spanish army and dressed them up in costumes 30 years ago, now you get a software package called *'Massive'*, and use that instead.

Then you have got one that stands out on it's own - CG characters. At one end of that is the Tyrannosaurus Rex in *Jurassic Park*, that is a CG character and it works fine, you believe it, there is nothing that it does that you think *'Oh that's not real'*. Before it would have been done by Ray Harryhausen or a man in a suit.

At the other end of the character work you've got Gollum. Again, Gollum works - the facial stuff was great, the fact that you are taking an actor's performance and enhancing it and adding 10% to it is good, though I thought that the body was unsatisfactory and there were a lot of the movements that you felt weren't convincing. But a fabulous piece of work and no doubt that will get better. It is an area of the business which is controversial because people think we are going to have virtual actors populating our movies. To them, I say, *'yeah, but who is going to achieve the performance?'* When you think that you've got films that stand or fall on whether Brad Pitt is any good or not, or you can get a film that is really not that good, and it becomes brilliant because Johnny Depp is in the lead, as he just has staggering charisma and can carry a movie with him - those are elements that we don't know how to quantify. We don't know why performances are good or not, and so we pay massive amounts of money to the sort of people who can achieve them. So who exactly is going to perform the virtual actor's job? In the case of Gollum, it's a very good actor, Andy Serkis. The electronic side of it just enhances the performance. That is fine, we can understand that is an actor performing, we are just simply stretching the performance. New performances from totally digital characters, I think it is some time away.

Q - What about old school special effects, perhaps enhanced slightly with digital technology, things like forced perspective models, matte paintings, wire removal, that kind of stuff? Surely that is ideal for low budget films?

Mike - Matte paintings have moved entirely into the digital field now, and the sort of people who do them are identical to the sort of people who used to do them, except they use PhotoShop rather than glass and oil paints. The difference is they can now do 2½D, which means they can wrap their 2D matte paintings onto simple geometric, shapes, and move the camera. In the old days, you could do a tiny bit of movement on the camera, if you kept the matte lines where they should, but now you really can do a lot with digital matte painting that you couldn't do only a few years ago. It has just freed up camera movement. Being able to shift the camera round 2½D I would say is the most important weapon in the low budget filmmakers visual effects arsenal, because you get a lot of bang per buck on that.

Forced perspective models have fallen away in that there is no need to do forced perspective anymore. The idea was to save on the materials, and the set space. Now, you shoot your little bit of set with your actors on it, against bits of blue or green screen. Then you whack it into a digital set extension, or a digital matte painting. Though there may be instances where an in camera forced perspective model may be a prudent budgetary choice.

Q - Let's imagine a typical independent film with not very many effects, but some stuff. A bit of fixing of shots, a bit of CGI - many new filmmakers may say, 'let's shoot the movie and figure out the effects later in post'. What is wrong with that approach?

Mike - They are not taking advantage of the expertise of the Special Effects people who could tell them in advance for free, how to maybe avoid some of the special effects, so that they are not special anymore, and they can get them in camera. Quite honestly, they can go round to a special effects place and get that advice for free before they start the movie.

The second thing they are missing out on, which they would have to pay for, is to have the set supervision. So you have a CG expert, usually a compositor or a 2-D expert supervisor, on set while you are filming. They can make sure that what is shot is usable. Even if you think you know how to do this stuff, mistakes get made and problems arise. For instance you get your green screen, put your actors in front of it, film it, you go back and the special effects people say *'Sorry mate, we can't use this, you had the green screen so close to the actor, that you are getting spill all over him, and we can't get a key'*. Or there may be any number of other reasons why the shot won't work. If you go early to an effects house, you can acquire an advisor on the set, who not only can tell you all about the stuff, but they will pick up the camera, and carry it to the next location as well! They will help on the set, so that's two lots of help there!

Finally, lack of planning and consultation could mean that you will spend a lot more money in post-production. You will find you don't have the elements that the compositors need, often things that would have been easy to get on location - *'just turn the camera sideways and shoot a bit of that'*. If you don't have it, suddenly your work has tripled later, or you have to go back and shoot more.

Q - So that's things like background plates I assume?

Mike - Yes, clean background plates are absolutely essential. Also important are on-set measurements - often that kind of information is not written down, not even the camera lens. Certainly if you have got any CG that has got characters or creatures in it, you need to know where the ground is so that the animators can convincingly animate feet being positioned on the ground. Things like that need to be measured on the day.

Q - In the absence of measurement, you have to keep guessing until it kind of looks right?

MIKE MILNE
director of computer
animation

19-23 Wells Street
London W1T 3PQ
Tel 020 7344 8000
Fax 020 7344 8001
mike.milne@framestore-cfc.com
www.framestore-cfc.com

Mike - Exactly. It takes ages in a Soho studio, at a high rate, rather than out on location, when you can do it in a couple of minutes.

Q - With expensive high tech kit like a tape measure and a pen and paper?

Mike - Yes!

Q - What is a typical decision making process like, I'm thinking now about the enthusiastic Director who wants to make 'War of the Worlds' for £6, and the Producer who is pulling their hair out - what are the dynamics of that scenario?

Mike - I think the way the relationship should work, is that the Producer should go to a bunch of people who do effects, and get a feel for whether they are the right company to do it. I think that is all done face to face, just clocking what they are like, whether they seem to be enthusiastic about the project, whether they think they are capable or if they are not what they are cracked up to be. It is always is going to be more expensive than you think!

Then you have to show a treatment to the people who are going to do the effects and discuss how the effects might be achieved. From there, the next stage is the simple storyboards which don't have to be drawn by a brilliant artist, they can be thumbnail sketches by anybody. Just showing basically what the shots are. At this point you can pinpoint anything that is really going to be difficult. The effects people can say, *'if you move the camera a bit around on this shot, you can save all that money, because you don't have to see where the feet touch the ground... you don't have to see this bit of the set extension for that shot, it can be hidden, it can be an out-of-focus piece of one of the other shots that we just stick there'.* That is the most important stage, the rough storyboard where you sit down and plan to save money. Then you will know how the effects are going to be done, you will know how much money you are going to spend, that is really where it works. Provided there is some chemistry going on between the people doing the effects, and the Producer and Director.

Q - All the pictures that I have done have been genre films and I worked extensively with a stunt co-ordinator. As a Director I would often say 'You tell me the best way to do this' rather than me saying 'I want this . . .'. Is that true in the Special Effects world as well?

Mike - Yes, because that can come at the treatment stage, even at the thumbnail storyboard stage. That is the point at which the effects person can say what is cheap and achievable.

Q - If a new filmmaker is savvy, do you think they could produce amazing visual effects work for a very low budget?

Mike - Yes. It just means that you can't go to a big effects studio to do it, because there will be costs associated with that. I saw a 30 minute film made by a guy up in Alaska, and the whole thing is CG. He produced an entire film in CG, single-handed, in around 6 months, on a budget of $8k, which were his living expenses. You are far more likely to get it with enthusiastic people working out of a garage, than you are from a big effects company.

Q - There are those people knocking around?

Mike - Yes. More and more.

Q - How important is recording the lenses used on set when planning to composite later?

Mike - It is getting easier. Lens matching what was shot on set with the computer tools we have here is now fairly straightforward. Even if you don't have a record of what the lens was, provided you've got a couple of reference pictures, which can be digital stills, and they don't have to be through the camera lens, you can usually get a program to tell you what the camera lens was (of course making a note on set could take ten seconds).

Q - Would you make a paper diagram of where the lights that lit the shot would be?

VISUAL EFFECTS

Visual effects seem like they would be very expensive, and they can be. However, you can do a lot of interesting things with relatively inexpensive software, that can enhance your film - such as removing a boom microphone, stabilising a shaky camera move or animation. Preparation is your biggest cost cutter, so plan ahead by storyboarding your VFX shots and talking to a visual effects company or supervisor as soon as possible.

Motion Control

A technique where a camera is placed on a motorised head / dolly that is computer controlled. It enables you to perform a camera move over and over again in exactly the same way. The camera move co-ordinates can then be imported into a 3D program so the software can generate new elements that perfectly match the on-set camera move. The 3D elements and on-set footage can then be composited together. (pictured is the Juno from www.mrmoco.com)

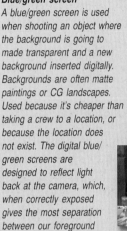

Motion Capture

A technique used to record the exact movements of a real object and translate them to a digital character. Most common is an actor in a specially designed suit with motion capture sensors attached to it, which the computer can capture to record the movement. This data is then applied to a computer generated 3D object which will then inherit the real world and life like moves that animators find so difficult and time consuming to imitate (pic www.metamotion.com).

Animatics (previsualisation/ 'previs')

Animated video story-boards for visual effects, which make a more accurate representation of what will eventually be filmed or created in the computer. It helps everyone understand 'the shot' and can be used in the edit as a temp shot for timing.

Rotoscoping

The frame-by-frame painting or tracing of an image. A matte is created for separate elements within the same image, so that they can be manipulated independently of each other. It is very time consuming and labor intensive process as it has to be done by hand. Famously used to animate Snow White.

Blue/green screen

A blue/green screen is used when shooting an object where the background is going to made transparent and a new background inserted digitally. Backgrounds are often matte paintings or CG landscapes. Used because it's cheaper than taking a crew to a location, or because the location does not exist. The digital blue/green screens are designed to reflect light back at the camera, which, when correctly exposed gives the most separation between our foreground element and the blue/green

screens. DP's usually like to shoot blue when working with actors as it gives the most pleasing flesh tones. Green screen requires less light to best separation exposure and there is less film grain in the green channel, which makes for cleaner edges. Make sure actors are not wearing the similar tones to the blue / green screen. The key with shooting blue / green screen is even lighting and as much distance between the screen and subject as possible (to avoid light spilling from the screen and onto the back of the actors). This means you will need a big space to shoot in.

2D compositing

Two-dimensional (flat) image creating where no shading is used, like blue/green screen techniques. Generally, this takes less time to create and is therefore less expensive.

3D compositing

Three-dimensional image creation where the objects appear to be alive within the film, such as animation like 'Spiderman' or the mouse in 'Stuart Little'. Large use of shading and simulated light sources to create this effect, which takes longer and costs more.

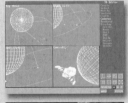

Mike - We used to, but no longer do. If you are in an artificially lit environment where there are lots of different light sources, the simplest thing is to put a reflective sphere in that shot. Even if you are not using image-based lighting, it gives you the locations of the main light sources. A white ball does that too. It tells you where all the light is coming from.

Q - What are the advantages and disadvantages of the various shooting formats that you come across?

Mike - The problem with TV cameras, as opposed to a film or a progressive scan digital camera, is that it records the image in fields. The moment you muck around with the shot in any way, you get artifacts caused by the fact that the original picture was grabbed in two fields for every frame. It mucks everything up, and it makes life hellish. That is avoided using Progressive Scan, which the new high-resolution DV cameras and the Hi-Def cameras are using. That is fine and there is no penalty for using those. In terms of film formats, there is no problem with 35mm and Super 16, though with ordinary 16mm you can have stabilisation problems when you are trying to composite. 16mm is best avoided for composting if possible.

Q - If you were to embark on a major low budget project that had a significant amount of post CG work, would it be wise to shoot it on progressive scan HD as opposed to 16mm?

Mike - Super16 is OK. The problem with HD progressive scan is that of your equipment costs in post-production. They are both equally good formats and ultimately there is probably not much in it. You can also zoom into the picture a bit on HD (or film if you plan to telecine to HD) and reframe a bit. If your final output it TV only, rather than theatrically released film, then you have no problems at all on either of those formats.

Q - Many new film makers spend a lot of time and energy getting their film into a cinema for one week when 300 people turn up to see it. We suggest you could bypass all of that and sell to TV and DVD only. That makes effects much more doable?

Mike - I would say that right at the moment, you can save a huge amount of money by doing your effects at TV resolution. Even if you have sourced it on film or HD. If you plan to complete at TV res, you have got so much freedom to reframe or do digital moves in post, because you have got more information than you need in the frame. Then for you one theatrical release, where a few people are going to watch it on a wet Thursday somewhere, you can bump it up to 35mm - sure it will be softer, but it will still look wonderful. If your main output is on DVD then why worry! Eventually films will be shown digitally, but then you will be shooting and mastering in HD of some sort, and the costs are going to be much the same as they are now for doing it on film.

Q - In that scenario, where you post produce everything to TV-res, would you work in a 25p environment on the computer if you could get everything shot in 25p - as opposed to 24p or 25i?

Mike - Yes. Effectively, whatever you shoot on, all your source material is converted into single frames with no fields. Then all the work is done at TV-res, but on single frames, rather than 2 fields. If you've shot on film, you get that anyway. If you've shot on progressive scan you get that anyway. If you've shot on video, then you do lose information because you have got to somehow combine those fields into one. They call it Film Look, but you are effectively throwing information away if you do that. It is better to shoot true progressive scan or on film if possible.

Q - Once you are in that world, a huge amount of homegrown visual effects become possible with After Effects and even plug-ins for AVID and FCP?

Mike - Absolutely. Even though we all see the death of the TV format sometime in the next decade, as everyone will move to a higher resolution format of some sort, at the moment, it is still the most cost-effective way, it really is.

Q - The technology is so pervasive and therefore cheap...

Mike - It is all there. It is everywhere.

Q - Typically what materials would be supplied to you to do effects work?

VFX Shooting Formats
Bad   Good

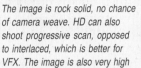

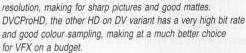

DV / HDV

All variants of DV, miniDV, DVcam etc., use image compression, which in turn adds 'noise' to the image, which is not too noticeable by a viewer, but the computer will see it. To make matters worse, the way DV encodes colors is quite poor, so it is not very good at blue / green screen. Best avoided for VFX. HDV, the High Definition format on DV can be bad too. It compresses the colour part of the signal very highly, making it best avoided for green screen. It also has lots of compression artefacts.

HDCam and DVCProHD

The image is rock solid, no chance of camera weave. HD can also shoot progressive scan, opposed to interlaced, which is better for VFX. The image is also very high resolution, making for sharp pictures and good mattes. DVCProHD, the other HD on DV variant has a very high bit rate and good colour sampling, making at a much better choice for VFX on a budget.

35mm

Special film stocks are produced on 35mm for blue/green screen work, which is ideal. The image is rock solid (as long as the camera is not faulty or the mag has been badly loaded). Film grain is usually not an issue too. The incredible resolution of 35mm means that you can often 'zoom' into an image digitally and pull elements, or even create entirely new shots without too much noticeable loss of quality.

Super 16mm

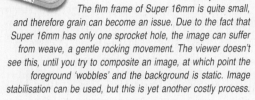

The film frame of Super 16mm is quite small, and therefore grain can become an issue. Due to the fact that Super 16mm has only one sprocket hole, the image can suffer from weave, a gentle rocking movement. The viewer doesn't see this, until you try to composite an image, at which point the foreground 'wobbles' and the background is static. Image stabilisation can be used, but this is yet another costly process.

Mike - If we are using live action and we are putting CG objects onto live action backgrounds we will need live background plates, clean plates with actors, plates without actors, bits of blue screen etc. Then there are what we call elements. An element would be a special shoot where you've shot people throwing talcum powder at a black wall, or spraying steam from hose etc., and we can then composite that into the shot. For instance if your actors are supposed to be in the snow, but shot in a blue screen studio, they need to have breath coming out of their mouths, so we will shoot some steam coming out of a hose and use that at various points to make the steam come out of people's mouths. Elements are things like that.

We like measurements from the set too, so please don't forget them. If we are doing full CGI stuff, then we need production drawings or models, sculpted models that are cast in resin of creatures or whatever it is we need to build. If it is set extensions, there will be production drawings of the set, the bit that was built, and production buildings of the bit we have got to build to extend on. If it is putting a medieval city onto a hill in the background of a shot, then it will be some photographic reference of what a medieval city might have looked like, artist references of some sort so the matte painters can paint it.

Q - If you are going to do some kind of composite like that, a simple locked off shot is going to be the easiest way to do it. What if you wanted to do some camera movement?

Mike - This is a very important point. Effects are always easier on a locked-off shot. Most importantly because of the 2-D aspect, rather than the 3-D aspect. We've now got tracking software that allows us to track any camera move, handheld or otherwise. There are a lot of caveats about that, but there is no need to go into them now. Then you can render out your computer animated elements to sit in the shot perfectly, but the problem is, you can't composite them, because foreground stalks of grass get in the way between you and the CG, and you have got to hand paint out every bloody blade of grass or leaf that gets in the way, so that compositing becomes a nightmare when you have got a moving camera. So, the way to get around this is to do as much of your camera movement as possible in post production. The way you can do this is to shoot tiles. What that means is, the camera is on a tripod and you shoot your principle action, and you then shoot 30 seconds panning the camera left, right, up, down, and you make a 9-tile with your action in the centre. Then we can stitch that together afterwards - you've then got a locked off shot that is huge and then we can put in any camera move you want - but it's a nodel move, that is a pan or a tilt or a zoom - the camera can't dolly in for instance.

The place where we used that in anger was on 'Walking with Dinosaurs', where we said they should not shoot more than 5 or 6 actual moving camera shots per episode. The other 150 shots, we put post-moves on. That worked brilliantly.

The easiest post-movement to do is camera shake. So if you shoot your shot with the camera locked off, we can then give it a slightly hand held feel by moving in by 10% and putting a bit of dipsy doodle onto the camera. We actually recorded off air, a couple of episodes of a famous US TV show where hand held work is used, and we then used tracking software to track the camera moves and then put those camera moves onto static camera shots from 'Walking with Beasts', just to give a kind of natural feel. In other words, rather than it being a CG artist's idea of what the camera move might be, it was a real one. I'm not suggesting that you have to do that, but all sorts of shots can be brought alive by adding the odd subtle camera move in post.

Q - What seals the illusion is the imperfections of physical shooting, it is the camera wobble, it is all the stuff that makes us know it is a camera, and a cameraman, and not a computer tracking something.

Mike - There is a term that we use called 'spliny' - when something is spliny it means that it looks mathematical. So that you get a camera move and it is done by a computer animator and it has this cold, mathematical look.

Q - When you do shots, and you put them all together, talk me through the process of the Director coming in, and saying 'Yeah, I like it' or 'No, there are changes', all the way through to completing it.

Mike - Here is where you can throw away a lot of money. In Hollywood film, the Director has to have absolutely fascist control of everything, because if it loses $100m it is his fault. So for that reason, everything is invested in the Director knowing how not to lose $100m. Which means that the Director sees everything at every stage, and approves it. When you do a shot, you take it right to completion, and you show them the final lighting and everything, and if they then say 'no, I don't like it, do it again', you have to go back and do the whole lot again - and you keep doing that over and over. You end up spending say $50k per shot.

I spent time thinking up ways how we could save money for Long Form TV where there isn't that budget or directorial control. What we do is we take the Director's control away in points where we think it is unnecessary, because perhaps in this environment, we are not going to lose that sort of money.

We start with a rough block animation of the shot, so that's literally grey cubes composited with the live

Visual Effects Quote Procedures

1. Look through your script and locate all the scenes that may require visual effects. For low budget films, reconsider if you can rewrite to avoid the effects.

2. Create a breakdown sheet that lists the scene, effect and the priority of how crucial the effect is to the story.

3. Research visual effects houses. Most visual effects houses have the same equipment - the major creative differences will be the ingenuity of the visual effects artists. Try to find facilities that have done effects that are similar to yours. Call them and ask for demo reels. Be careful here for smaller houses may have done work on big films, but may only have done small portions of the scenes they show. Ask them specifically what they did on each shot.

4. Find four or five visual effects houses that you like and ask them for a quote. Do not tell them what your visual effects budget is, as they will try to make their work fit that number as opposed to just giving you a bid. It's OK to tell them what the overall budget of the film is, however. Send a copy of the breakdown sheet and the script for their review.

5. Get their bid and have them send a breakdown on how they would do each shot. Be wary of houses that significantly underbid all the others for they may not be able to deliver on time and on budget.

6. Once the bids are in, if they are excessive, find ways to cut, change or alter your visual effects so that they are less expensive. For example, CGI animals may be more expensive than hiring an animal wrangler and the real thing and shooting green screen. Change 3D effects to 2D, or try to find a way to make them mechanical effects that you can do on set. The cheapest of course is cut! How much you really need that effect?

7. Once you choose a facility, take them on, or have them either become or work with your visual effects supervisor.

8. When doing effects, you will need to be available to check work in progress. The more you do this, the less chance there is of them doing work that is either inappropriate or unneeded.

9. Remember, visual effects people are artists, not just people who press keys and move a mouse. Treat them as such.

action background for instance. The Director can take that away for the rough-cut (picture editing the actual drama). Then we come back and do a bit more work on it, so that the animation is finalised, but you still are just looking at simple grey, shapes. This is normally called Pre-viz or Moving Layout. At this point, the Director should be able to make the decision about whether the action is final, because even though they are not seeing it in full Technicolor with all the bells and whistles, actually everything we are going to put into it in terms of motion is there. If it is a creature, the whiskers are going to move, even if they are just bars on the model for now, the tail is going to move exactly as you see, it just doesn't look finished. You have to make the decision at that point, to sign off on the motion, on the animation. It is the same way with set extensions and things like that, you will see where they are, they will be blocked out but they won't be fully finished. Once the Director approve this, there is no need for us to keep going through the approval process again and again.

In return we give the Director a lot more leeway in the final output. We generate all of the detail that is needed to make the final shot without directorial involvement, and then render out that final shot 5 or 10 different ways and supply to the compositing artist a whole bunch of things that allows the Director to change their mind about more or less everything except the movement. So that we give, for instance, key lighting from different angles, we give shadows from different angles, we give reflection passes, shadow passes, highlight passes - all are given to the Director who can then play in the composite to get the balance right. If that isn't enough, you've then got one further step in the final colour grading. That process will result in a good balance between the highest quality results produced but in the most cost effective way.

Q - If you are clever about what you do, you can actually re-use effects in a slightly different way in order to kill 2 birds with one stone?

Mike - Absolutely right, and that is the secret to a lot of this stuff. You don't ever want to be in a position where you have to use the same shot twice. But you can repeat an action without repeating a shot, just as you would film the same action from several different angles (typically seen in stunt work to minimise danger to the stunt performer). We can do that in CG, so that you can take an animation, view it on a longer lens, or a shorter lens, or from a different angle, and make use of it several times. 'Walking with Dinosaurs' was based on that exact trick, because that is what happens in real life with animals. They do the same thing over and over again anyway! So once you have animated the behaviour of an animal you've done the job, and then you can see it from whatever angle you want to see it.

Q - What are the common mistakes that you see?

Mike - The first one we have covered, not thinking about it in advance or consulting it in advance, remembering that a lot of consulting is free. The second mistake that people make is that they assume that the effects are going to be much better than they are. Often they assume that they are going to see *Jurassic Park* when actually they can only afford *Muppets!* Expectations can be too high. You need to be realistic so that you can talk about real improvements that you can make, rather than imagining in your mind that it is going to look like something unaffordable. You should always underestimate how good it is going to be.

Q - What advice would you offer a new filmmaker?

Mike - Don't try and make your work important. If you do, nobody will want to watch it. In a way, avoid being pretentious. Don't worry about how important it is, forget about that bit of it and it will end up being much better.

Q - Serve your audience and not your ego!

Mike - That is another perfect way of putting it.

Jason Wheeler
Negative Cutter

NEGATIVE CUTTING

Q - What is your job?

Jason - I am a negative cutter, which means the physical reconforming or preparing of original camera negative for the final mastering stages of post production.

Q - So you take the original camera negative and make it match what the film maker edited on their Avid or FCP?

Jason - Yes.

Q - When an editor makes edits on the computer, how do you know where to look for those exact shots on the lab rolls?

Jason - When the film is telecinied to BetaSP or DVCam for offline editing (on Avid or FCP), a physical punch hole is made at the head of each lab roll. That hole then gives everyone a link between the physical world of film, and the electronic world of editing. Unique timecode is laid down with the pictures when they are telecinied onto tape. The editor will then digitise those tapes, along with the timecode, and edit the story.

When the editor locks picture, they generate an EDL (edit decision list) which is a list of the timecodes for every shot. It tells us exactly where each shot is from (on which lab roll and where on that roll), how long the shot runs for, and where in the final reconstruction of the edit it will go. We then take the negative and log it all, using the punch hole at the head of each roll as a kind of starting point, and we cut the neg to match the EDL. We normally ask for a viewing tape too, so we can eye match each shot, just as a visual backup.

It is important to not start the neg cutting phase until you have absolutely locked picture and know you will never go back and start to re-edit. This is particularly important on Super 16mm, as there is no space between frames to make a cut, so when we do make a cut, we will need to destroy the frame preceding or after each shot.

It is also essential that you understand how timecode relates to your film, and that the software you are editing, can 100% accurately deal with that timecode AND export a readable EDL or cutting list.

Q - The traditional photochemical route is still viable for a low budget film, though probably only short film makers will use this route. Are there any special requirements when cutting super 16mm for blow up to 35mm photochemicaly?

Jason - Yes, stability is important because it's single perf only. Super 16mm is often blown up to 35mm so the joins have to be very smooth and seamless. It is vital to find out if the negative cutter has worked with Super 16mm before and that he is set up for it, otherwise you could end up having to go to great expense and re-neg cut the whole picture. Super 16mm is cut A and B checkerboard. Every shot is on an alternate reel so that the joins don't show and you can have dissolves etc. With 16mm and Super 16mm you have to have an overlap which effectively destroys the frame before and after every shot. The important thing to remember about 16mm when in the cutting room or edit suite is that you must always lose one frame at the beginning and one frame at the end of every single shot of your film - that's the absolute minimum requirement. Also, laboratory printing machines can only do dissolves at the rate of either 16, 24, 32, 48, 64, 96 frames. They can't do anything else - if you want it done at any other length you have to have it done optically which will produce an interneg. Also, when you're doing A and B roll, you have to leave on 16mm at least 20 frames between a cut and the

Anatomy Of An EDL

GUERILLA FILM MAKER SAYS!

CMX 3600 is the most common and robust cross platform EDL that we have come across. Make sure that when you supply your EDL it is on the correct format disk, most cutters use DOS format. Note also that a CMX 3600 can only handle 999 cuts. You will probably never see your EDL in this format as it's almost always electronic... But then if it can go wrong... Better to at least understand the process when you consider that sharp blades are about to come into contact with your master negative!

Edit Number - this is the chronological number given to each and every cut.

Video - As it's a picture only EDL, each of these will be V for video.

The Lab Reel / Beta SP source in point column - the time code where a shot actually begins.

The point on the assembled master negative time line where the shot begins.

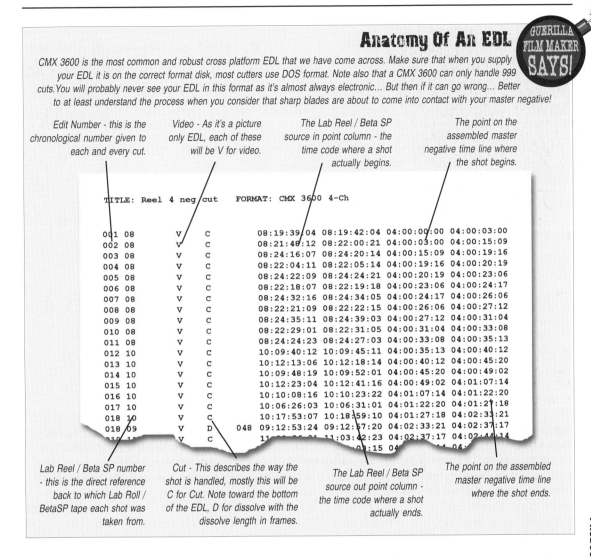

```
TITLE: Reel 4 neg/cut     FORMAT: CMX 3600 4-Ch

001 08        V   C        08:19:39:04 08:19:42:04 04:00:00:00 04:00:03:00
002 08        V   C        08:21:48:12 08:22:00:21 04:00:03:00 04:00:15:09
003 08        V   C        08:24:16:07 08:24:20:14 04:00:15:09 04:00:19:16
004 08        V   C        08:22:04:11 08:22:05:14 04:00:19:16 04:00:20:19
005 08        V   C        08:24:22:09 08:24:24:21 04:00:20:19 04:00:23:06
006 08        V   C        08:22:18:07 08:22:19:18 04:00:23:06 04:00:24:17
007 08        V   C        08:24:32:16 08:24:34:05 04:00:24:17 04:00:26:06
008 08        V   C        08:22:21:09 08:22:22:15 04:00:26:06 04:00:27:12
009 08        V   C        08:24:35:11 08:24:39:03 04:00:27:12 04:00:31:04
010 08        V   C        08:22:29:01 08:22:31:05 04:00:31:04 04:00:33:08
011 08        V   C        08:24:24:23 08:24:27:03 04:00:33:08 04:00:35:13
012 10        V   C        10:09:40:12 10:09:45:11 04:00:35:13 04:00:40:12
013 10        V   C        10:12:13:06 10:12:18:14 04:00:40:12 04:00:45:20
014 10        V   C        10:09:48:19 10:09:52:01 04:00:45:20 04:00:49:02
015 10        V   C        10:12:23:04 10:12:41:16 04:00:49:02 04:01:07:14
016 10        V   C        10:10:08:16 10:10:23:22 04:01:07:14 04:01:22:20
017 10        V   C        10:06:26:03 10:06:31:01 04:01:22:20 04:01:27:18
018 10        V   C        10:17:53:07 10:18:59:10 04:01:27:18 04:02:33:21
018 09        V   D   048  09:12:53:24 09:12:57:20 04:02:33:21 04:02:37:17
                  V   C        11:         11:03:42:23 04:02:37:17 04:02:44:14
                           03:15 04:
```

Lab Reel / Beta SP number - this is the direct reference back to which Lab Roll / BetaSP tape each shot was taken from.

Cut - This describes the way the shot is handled, mostly this will be C for Cut. Note toward the bottom of the EDL, D for dissolve with the dissolve length in frames.

The Lab Reel / Beta SP source out point column - the time code where a shot actually ends.

The point on the assembled master negative time line where the shot ends.

beginning of an optical or the end of an optical and a cut, and you must always leave a minimum of 4 frames between the end of one optical and the beginning of the next.

Q - For low budget productions, originated on film, we propose doing an overlength neg cut and then conform to HD. What would your involvement be in that process?

Jason - We would take the source negative, log it, then associate the time code with the punch hole and negative. We would then get an EDL from the cutting room and we would convert that to our format, and then cut the negative with 'handles'. As the negative would be scanned to a server for grading, or telecinied to HD, we would leave a little extra (usually 21 frames) on either end of every shot, hence the phrase handles. This process also means you can easily re-use shots in the edit, something that would have required optical effects in the past. Our software automatically deals with re-used shots and overlapping shots and it all just comes out in the wash.

We would supply to the facilities house that is going to do the scanning or telecine of the film negative, both the cut neg and a new EDL (which now matches the new lab roll of cut negative). They would then probably scan / telecine the whole neg, with the handles and the computer would drop all the shots into the right place. The handles would give you a little play in the final conform, to tweak each edit should you want or need to. The picture would be graded, effects and titles added, and depending on the film stock used, you may use some picture noise reduction to remove unwanted grain. Any dirt and scratches, which should be minimal, can also be fixed at this stage.

Something we recommend is that before the telecine, the negative should be given a re-wash. Because you are working with an actual film element, it can statically attract dust particles, so they need to be cleaned.

Q - How often are mistakes made?

Jason - Rarely, but it can and does happen. Usually it is because there has been a weak link in the chain, perhaps an inexperienced editor or a telecine house in a foreign country. If all the post is done here in the UK, with professionals, mistakes are almost unheard of.

Q - What happens to all the un-used negative?

Jason - It is usually stored someplace safe. You do need to consider what you will do with it long term. Especially documentaries, as unused footage may be sold to other shows at some point in the future.

Q - How do you charge your time?

Jason - It is usually charged by transmitted minute. So if a show is 50 minutes, then I charge at £70 a minute. Additional cost would be for pulling shots visual effects etc.

Q - How long do you take to cut an average low budget feature?

Jason - Two to three weeks. But if there are effects shots that need to be pulled, we would probably start earlier than that as the editor would request certain shots be pulled, from flash frame to flash frame (the entire shot), and sent to the SFX house.

Q - What happens if I want to change the cut after you have finished cutting the negative?

Jason - It depends what format you are on. If we have cut with a handle then we can easily extend up to the handle. And with 35mm we can cope too as there is space between frames to rejoin shots. But on Super 16mm, it's a problem as frames are destroyed when we join shots. You want to try and avoid re-editing after you have neg cut.

Q - What are the common mistakes that you see from film makers?

Jason - Budgeting. If they are students and they are trying to do it for a penny, it is hard to charge them the going rate and we are always willing to talk about doing a deal, but it always seems like a shock to them that we charge them at all!

Q - What advice would you give to a new film maker?

Jason - Shoot film.

jaw.wheelr@gmail.com

GUERILLA FILM MAKER SAYS!

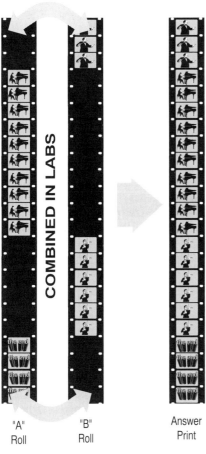

COMBINED IN LABS

"A" Roll   "B" Roll   Answer Print

16mm & Super 16mm A & B Roll checkerboarding (traditional photochemical process)

The A & B roll cut negative rolls are printed to produce a single positive print. A & B rolls must be used in all 16mm formats as there is no room in between frames to make a clean join between two shots. By using two rolls with black spacer, a whole frame can be used for the join. The black spacer covers the join and creates a 'window' for the incoming shot on the alternate roll. This process is still viable, though many film makers are now doing an 'overlength neg cut' where the computer scans and pulls the shots instead of them being cut together exactly.

16mm Negative Join In Detail

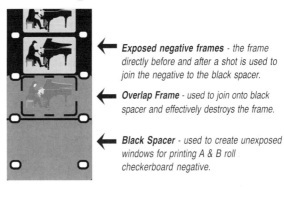

← **Exposed negative frames** - the frame directly before and after a shot is used to join the negative to the black spacer.

← **Overlap Frame** - used to join onto black spacer and effectively destroys the frame.

← **Black Spacer** - used to create unexposed windows for printing A & B roll checkerboard negative.

Punch Hole and Timecodes

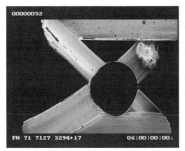

(left) The punch hole at the start of each lab reel represents the absolute point from which all negative cuts are calculated. In this instance, this frame is from lab roll 52 (top left) with a timecode starting at 06:00:00:00 (six o'clock). Note the Key Kode details in the bottom left of the frame.

(right) Beta SP rushes frame. Lab roll 52, Timecode frame 06:05:58:24, Key Kode reference bottom left of frame.

Ian Buckton
Capital Effects

TITLES and OPTICALS (DI)

Q - So what is it that your company actually does?

Ian - The majority of our work is creating titles for film and television, along with DI work (digital intermediates), where a whole feature negative is scanned onto a computer, then assembled, graded, titled, effects added, then put back onto film again (and possibly mastered to HD too). That bypasses the various lab processes there used to be. Everything is done under one roof. The final thing we do is laser subtitling for foreign language films.

Q - There are essentially 2 forms of independent film. Those with a full budget and can do the whole DI route. Then there are those that are going to finish to tape only, by that I mean HD or another digital format, and they are almost certainly going to be cash-strapped. When it comes to the titles they are just going to say 'Oh we will do it on the Avid or FCP'. Now that is fine, if all it is ever going to do is be on DVD or TV?

Ian - Exactly. Yes but check with your sales agent or broadcaster beforehand.

Q - But the problem comes when somebody says 'I really like your film, let's release it in Brazil in the cinemas'...

Ian - It would depend on if it were being released on film or digitally. If the film was mastered in DigiBeta for instance, the image may be acceptable to transfer to film, though we would need to recreate the titles at a higher res. If it were mastered to HD and done properly, we can then take that and put it onto film without much extra work.

Q - The mistakes many new filmmakers make is say 'well it looks fine on my TV'?

Ian - When you project it up on a screen which is 45 feet wide, that is when you start to see problems.

Q - What do you need to consider when planning your titles?

Ian - The first thing they have to do is always produce a textless background, no matter what. If somebody does pick it up at a film festival and they say *'That is fantastic, we want to localise it and dub it into another language'*, then you have then got the ability to reproduce the titles again, in that new language. If you ever have titles on top of picture, you will need to supply that footage 'clean', without titles, for sales abroad.

Q - What do you need from somebody in order to do the titles?

Ian - What the film maker needs to think about is are they are going to do a full set of main and end titles? Not everyone needs to do that, some people just put the main title on the film, and back-end everything, which may be appropriate for an independent film where you have got to grab the sales agents and audience quickly. Don't get over complicated with the titles. Blockbuster movies go big time with their title sequences, they can afford it and an audience expects it. If you have got a nice simple film, keep the titles simple. You see lots of really nice title sequences where the title is just sitting there. Also, make sure that your backgrounds, if you are going to run background images with your titles, are not messy and that they are not moving or wobbly. When you have a title on screen it is absolutely rock solid, and any movement in your camera, whether it be shake, sideways pan, up and down, it will just look bad. Try and avoid movement, and if you are going to have movement, such as tracking shots, make sure that they are absolutely smooth, and allow for where your title is going to go. So pre-plan the whole sequence that you are going to put together, don't just put a load of scenes together and slap titles over it.

Q - Are there any fonts that don't work quite as well as others, or colours that should be avoided?

Ian - Everything is acceptable on film, though people tend to avoid black titles. Generally, titles are white with drop shadows, or white with a casing. Any colours are acceptable, but as it will go to video eventually, you should avoid primary colours as the colours will bleed on a TV and look bad. You also need to avoid serif type faces (such as Times Roman) as the very intricate fonts can, on TV, fall between scan lines and flicker unattractively. Solid fonts such as Helvetica or Ariel are more attractive and less problems occur.

As for the speed of the end roller, it is generally the same, regardless of the length of your film. Get creative with your main titles if you like, but not with the end roller, let the roller do what it does and in the time it demands. The only way I feel is appropriate for making an end roller interesting is to put outtakes in them (in a box), people love to see crazy things happening! It's the best way to get an audience to sit through the entire end credits.

Q - If the titles are white on black, you don't even need to do text-less background?

Ian - No, if they are white on black you don't have to produce any textless backgrounds.

Q - How do filmmakers supply the actual titles?

Ian - The best way is a Word document, laid out like titles, and in order. Of course, check and double check before sending to us if you want to save time. There is no point spotting spelling mistakes when the titles are on film. That will be costly to fix. We do not check for name spelling, that's your job. We have virtually every single logo (such as Dolby Digital etc.) that is going to be on a roller already in house, so that is not an issue.

Q - Optical effects, such as a slow down or a reframe, used to put the fear of god into me as they never matched and were a pain to integrate into the film.

Ian - I was a Film Optical Cameraman so know all about that. Digital has replaced that whole technology now. The great thing now is that you take your clients original camera negative, scan it, and then you can do almost anything you want with it. You can put titles over it, you can put effects over it, and you can composite a thousand people into it if you want to, but when it is transferred to film, it is the same quality as when it went in.

Q - So all of the effects that you have got in any basic post production suite, such as Avid or FCP, you can replicate in your facility, and improve on...?

Ian - There is nothing that can't be done now.

Q - So things that used to be a really big problem, like making a shot slow motion, is much better now?

Ian - Yes. We can interpolate footage shot in real time and slow it down and speed it up. There are limits, so don't expect John Woo style slow motion from a standard speed shot. We have so many digital tools it is quite amazing. However, if you have the ability to do so, you should shoot slow motion in camera.

Q - And they are getting better every day?

CAPITAL

FX

IAN BUCKTON
DIRECTOR

2ND FLOOR 20 DERING STREET LONDON WIS IAJ
T +44 (0)20 7493 9998 F +44 (0)20 7493 9997
ian@capital-fx.co.uk   www.capital-fx.co.uk

POST PRODUCTION

Ian - Absolutely. I still get stunned with the kind of things that we can do. I think sometimes even the operators do too.

Q - So in many ways your company is replacing the laboratory?

Ian - To be honest with you, the only thing you need a film lab for is developing the original camera negative, developing what we produce, and making quality answer prints and show prints etc.

Q - When a filmmaker makes a film, and shoots on film, and they want to do the digital intermediate, do they still go through a negative cut, of sorts?

Ian - There are two ways of doing it. You can do what is called an over length neg cut, where you cut the negative down, leaving handles on either side of shots. Or you can just bring all the negative in and scan the shots you want. The advantage of the over length neg cut is that you will spend less time spinning back and forward in the expensive environment of a film scanner. It will save money to do that if you shot a lot of footage. If the film is very talky, with few edits and takes, it will probably be better to just scan the neg without a neg cut.

Q - If you are familiar with desktop tools like PhotoShop and how to use Avid, you've got a good mental angle on what you can achieve with your digital tools?

Ian - Yes, very much so. *Combustion*, and the other tools we use, are all just extensions of those tools.

Q - You can buy Combustion yourself, or After Effects, and do your own work? So in many ways, the limitation of what you can achieve is down to your budget, or how much work you are prepared to invest?

Ian - Yes. Though I would advise against getting over complicated, especially in Post, as that can end up being the focus, instead of a really great story well told. Look at the limitations of the tools you have before you walk into Post, and don't assume that everything can be fixed in Post, because it can't. Look at Post Production as a way of enhancing, not a place to recreate what went wrong on set.

Q - Are there any things that you would recommend avoiding?

Ian - If you plan to conform and grade digitally, don't over expose or under expose your original footage. That is critical, especially on HD or other digital camera formats.

Q - Film has a very high latitude, which HD does not have?

Ian - High end HD does have a high latitude, but lower end digital formats certainly do not (such as DVcam, HDV, DVCProHD). Whatever you shoot, you can still expose it correctly! Once it goes into Post Production, if it has got all the information there, you can do something with it. Be creative in the filmmaking process, but don't over do it, because if you want it fixed, then it is an impossibility if the information isn't there in the shot. You can add all your 'look' in post.

Q - Once you have done all your work digitally, how does it get back to film?

Ian - The data is rendered and is then sent to the film recorders and it is scanned out to film.

Q - Can you make an HD master tape from that?

Ian - Yes. You can make any format from that, because it is film resolution.

Q - Gone are the days of multiple masters? Do it properly once and you will never need to do it again?

Tape to Film Transfer

David Hays
E-Film, USA

Q - What is tape to film?

David - The tape to film process is taking images captured on film or video (digital) and manipulating and storing on digital tape. These digital images are then transferred to 35mm film. Tape to film is used by many different types of productions. Independent producers sought the digital capture mediums (DV, DigiBeta HD etc.) as a less expensive way of telling their stories without the cost of film. Others captured on 16mm and 35mm and use digital post production to off line the film, create visual effects, and for color timing the film using video post production tools.

Q - How do you transfer to film?

David - At E-Film we evaluate the Master tape, frame by frame, to ensure you are within your aspect ratios and verify there are no dropouts or other anomalies that may affect the transfer process. The shooting computer up-rez's the files (if they are PAL or NTSC) to 2K (approximately four times the resolution), and then an Arri Laser Film Recorder shoots a red, green, and blue pinpoint laser to expose the 5242 film (fine grain intermediate stock). The negative is then processed as you would a normal negative and a daily print is made.

Q - What happens to the sound in the transfer?

David - Sound is treated as a separate element, usually mixed to a DA88 tape format based on cut reels of less than 20 minutes. If a digital sound master is needed ie: SDDS, SRD, DTS, then an MO disk needs to be created prior to shooting the optical sound track. This optical track is actually a piece of film that only has the soundtrack on it and looks like squiggly lines on the left hand side of the screen. Yes, 'squiggly lines' is a technical term! Other information that is on the optical track is what looks to be a bar code in between the perforations. This is the digital sound which is read by a device also attached to the projector. When the optical track negative is married to the picture negative you have a release print for theaters.

Q - What are the best formats to shoot on?

David - You should match the type of format to the type of film you want to make, or the type of equipment that is available to you at the time. I have had dozens of film makers come through our facility and have looked at Mini DV through HD and 35mm prints from a negative and each one has reacted differently to what they feel works best for their production. Some choose DV because it is more suited to their film or they might actually own

the camera and some choose HD because of visual effects and need the resolution for certain shots. It is also feasible that you can use multiple formats in your film to get a story point across.

Q - How does HD compare to SD when transferring to film?

David - High Definition can significantly change the look of a film. It is a much higher resolution than Standard Definition which captures 720X486 for NTSC and 720X576 for PAL, but HD captures information at 1920X1080 lines of resolution. Just in terms of pixels transferred to 35mm film, HD is better quality. The film negative can capture a much wider and more resolute range of image than any type of digital capture. So when working with a film negative you may have more latitude when color timing, either in the laboratory, or in the digital environment than you have with Hi Definition. HD has a great deal of information but you must expose this image properly and cleanly to be able to manipulate these digital images to their fullest. Some film makers have been able to create looks using filtration in the matrices of the camera as well as filtration on the lens, with great results. Keep in mind that this can 'lock' you into a look that you may not like on final color correction or film record out.

Q - Should you avoid anything when shooting on video?

David - Avoid fast camera movement when the subject is stationary. If you know you have a certain look you want to achieve or there will be situations that may affect the outcome when transferring to film then definitely shoot tests.

Q - What should a filmmaker supply for the transfer?

David - It is best to break all of your reels out into separate reels 20 minutes or less. The reel breaks are creative and a part of the editorial process. The reels usually come to us on DigiBeta for NTSC and PAL and on HDCam or HD-D5 for HD. The sound should be delivered on an MOdisk or DA88 also corresponding to the image reel breaks.

Q - Should all colour correction happen on the tape before the film transfer rather than grading the actual film print?

David - Yes, as this alleviates the necessity to try to colour time (grade) the film in the laboratory process. You want to have the balance of the images done in the digital realm and any other special colour timing should be done at this time. The idea with tape to film is to have the transfer facility replicate what you have created in your digital timing.

Q - Are rolling titles created on video suitable?

David - No because usually they are created on a field updating basis to create the roll causing strobing and double images on each credit. To create titles effectively use traditional film opticals or as single frame digital card created in software.

POST
PRODUCTION

John Claude
Midnight Transfer

Q - Telecine used to be about taking film and putting it onto videotape. It's now more than that, and encompasses telecine, scanning, autoconform from HD, grading... What used to be work done at the lab photochemically, has now migrated to companies like yours, offering a more 'lab like' service, but bridging the electronic and digital worlds.

John - Yes. We are historically a dailies (rushes) facility where we transfer footage to a video tape format for offline editing the next day. Things have grown from there, and we now offer a complete workflow, working at film res throughout (from dailes to final master) but now in completely the digital domain. Ideally, that way the grading done during the dailes can form the basis for the final grade. However, that is probably financially out of reach for new or low budget film makers.

Q - What route would you suggest a guerilla filmmaker use to post produce their film?

John - If you were shooting film, you would transfer your rushes to an SD (standard definition) format, probably BetaSP or HDCam, for offline editing. If HD, you would downconvert your rushes to BetaSP or DVCam for offline editing too. In both instances, if shooting in the UK, it makes life a lot easier of you shoot 25fps on film or 25P on HD. Remember, when you offline edit on your FCP or Avid, you must also understand the role of timecode, and make sure that everything is rock solid and accurate.

Q - So in the past, a film maker would come to you to do a telecine from a low contrast 35mm print or interpos, onto DigiBeta. Now that doesn't often happen and you get will involved earlier?

John - Yes. Although we still do that kind of telecine. If the project originates on film, we can scan in the film from the overlength neg cut. That is an automated process, and we can work at various resolutions, up to 4k, which for a low budget feature is probably going to be too expensive. We could also work at 2k or at HD 1080.

If the job comes in from HD, we would autoconform all the material into the computer from the editors cutting list. Either way, we end up with very high quality images on the computer here. From that point we begin the grading process, the adding of special effects and titles etc.

The great thing about this process is that once we have the material in our computers, we have immense control over the images. In some ways, it doesn't matter what your originate on so much these days. I can scan in from 16mm, from 35mm, 3 perf 35mm, or from any other film format. Or else I could come in from an HD tape format, and just digitise straight into the *Baselight* grading environment, then do a very powerful non linear grade, with all sorts of secondary grading layers, shapes and mattes. Another major innovation is the actual physical grading environment. We now project the job in a theatre, so you can see just what it will look like in a cinema when it's completed. Our Barco 2k digital projectors are highly calibrated and set up to our very rigorous standards, so you can be sure that what you see is what you will get. We break it down into three parts financially; scanning costs, grading costs and the film output cost (and the transfer to an HD Universal Master) .

Q - Just to play devil's advocate, another mistake independent filmmakers make is that their ego gets the better of them and they say 'I've made a cinema film, therefore I will not bring this film to market until I have a 35mm print!' When actually their film may not have theatric potential?

Mastering Tips

GUERILLA FILM MAKER SAYS!

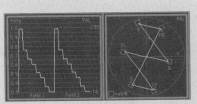

The waveform monitor and vectorscope

These used to measure the video on a technical level. The video level must not peak over 1v or under 0.3v or it will be rejected. Many software editing tools come with software scopes, like this one from an Avid. Generally, these are a guide and are not as accurate as a dedicated scope.

Bars

There are 30 seconds of bars before your picture starts, which are used to line up the video levels on the scope. The white to the left is just under 1v, the black to the right is just over 0.3volt. Essential to get right or your movie will be rejected.

Clock

This is needed so that the tape can be cued up for broadcast or duplication. Normally the clock will countdown from 30 seconds to 0 (the start of the show) and will fade to black at 3 seconds before the start of the show.

TV Safe and Title Safe

The TV safe area, the outer box, is used as a guide and your drama must stay within it. Many TVs will crop off right up to TV safe. Title Safe, the inner box, is a guide for the maximum extent to which you should place your titles onscreen.

John - I think that is a huge mistake and we hear it a lot.

Q - But what you can do now is master to an HD Universal Master, giving you a great balance between quality and budget. And who knows when all cinemas will go digital?

John - Yes, though film and HD do not use the same colour space. Having said that, as long as you make a decision early on and grade with the correct look-up table (LUT), you should be able to get the best of both worlds. If you grade for HD, with a clever 'film output house', you can do the conversion to film at the final stage.

Q - It makes no sense for a guerilla film maker to master to any format less than HD now, would you agree?

John - Yes. HD-D5 is very good, but HDCamSR is the format of choice, and you are going to have access to that format for many years to come. But remember, if you shoot on film, never let go of the original negative because that is always going to be a valuable piece of archive material.

Q - Have you seen any HDV in this environment?

John - I have seen HDV shot on a camcorder, and it looks quite bright in the high lights, and it looks too much like video for my liking.

Q - Prosumer camcorders are designed to be viewed without need for grading, as it's designed to look good on a TV straight away. That limits what you can do though and you will end up with something looking much more like video?

JOHN B CLAUDE
MIDNIGHT
TRANSFER
179 WARDOUR STREET
LONDON W1F 8WY
TEL 020 7534 3400
FAX 020 7534 3401
john@midnight-transfer.co.uk
www.midnight-transfer.co.uk

POST PRODUCTION

John - Yes. I have also seen some DVCProHD and that was much better, though granted that was shot on professional camera. I still think however that in terms of an aesthetic look, most people who do love the look of film would still agree that most HD formats haven't actually emulated that yet. If you really want it to look like film, perhaps your best choice is to shoot it on film, rather than shooting HD and spending too much time in post tweaking it to make it appear more like film.

Q - Are there any problems you come across? Surely with all this amazing equipment, you can do anything?

John - There is a slight danger that with all the tricks and toys available in post, people will latch on to that mentality of *'don't worry about it, we can do it in post'*. While that might be true, it is budget dependent, and it can be time consuming, so it is really important that the DP still light correctly. To be fair, the DPs that I've worked with in the suite, have not really changed their approach on set, which is crucial. Nobody is trying to cut corners or is getting lazy on set. Even though you can do a lot more in post, none of the DPs seem to be getting too overwhelmed or too carried away with the palate available to them. Most people still want it to look filmic, they still want it to look theatrical. They don't want it to look like a 30 second car commercial with too many tricks, too many grading looks on it.

Q - What are the tricks to producing the perfect negative, or the perfect HD master tape, to get the most out of working in this environment?

John - Shoot with as much contrast as the scene requires, but try not to push the highlights or crush the blacks - keep it safe. Also, don't push in any particularly strong direction with the blacks or the highlights, and the colour saturation or colour balance, as those are the things that are very easily done in the grade. Even with camera filters, don't get too worried about putting one on, unless it is a basic polarising or colour correcting wratten 85 filter.

Q - What are the common mistakes you are starting to see?

John - It has become a bit of a minefield for the layperson. There are so many different HD formats and there are stories circulating of people who make errors in the final stages and either end up clipping the whites or crushing the blacks without realising it. Silly things like that, even in big Hollywood releases. It is important to work with a colourist who understands the destination, and to really plan your post route carefully.

Q - What do you think is the best shooting format for low budget films?

John - HD is the low budget format of choice for acquisition. So hire a DP who understands how to light for HD, ideally one who has shot HD, and try and do a couple of tests. See that you are getting something that you are happy with before you embark. Super 16 is also very well suited to low budget films wanting the true film look, and we've done a number of those already this year. Also 35mm 3 perf gives you a film saving up front, even 2 perf!

Q - What is the most popular delivery HD format at the moment? In terms of cost, value and quality?

John - HD-D5, but HDCamSR will probably overtake it given time.

Q - What advice would you offer a new film maker?

John - Understand the technology available because it is evolving quickly, and if you want your product, for want of a better word, to have any sort of longevity or impact, then you should really know what sort of technology you are going to use to best achieve that. Bear in mind your first film always costs about as much as a house and no matter how low budget you think you are going, it is always going to cost more, so you would be well advised to be pragmatic, flexible with the technology available, and to know how you could make savings within that framework.

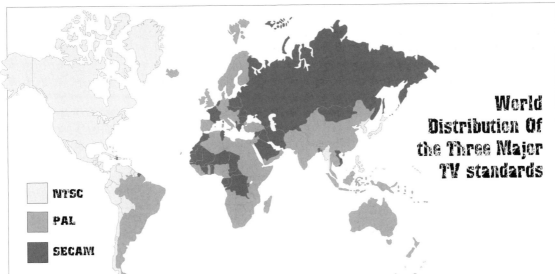

World Distribution Of the Three Major TV standards

NTSC

PAL

SECAM

Abu Dhabi - 625 PAL
Afghanistan - 625 PAL/ SECAM
Albania - 625 SECAM
Algeria - 625 PAL
Andorra - 625 PAL
Angola - 625 PAL
Antigua - 525 NTSC
Argentina - 625 PAL N
Australia - 625 PAL
Austria - 625 PAL
The Azores - 625 PAL
Bahamas - 525 NTSC
Bahrain - 625 PAL
Bangladesh - 625 PAL
Barbados - 525 NTSC
Belgium - 625 PAL
Belize - 525 NTSC
Benin - 625 SECAM
Bermuda - 525 NTSC
Bolivia - 525 NTSC
Bophuthatswana - 625 PAL
Bosnia/Herzegovina - 625 PAL
Botswana - 625 PAL
Brazil - 525 PAL M
British Virgin Isles - 525 NTSC
Brunei - 625 PAL
Bulgaria - 625 SECAM
Bukina Faso - 625 SECAM
Burma - 525 NTSC
Burundi - 625 SECAM
Cameroon - 625 PAL
Canada - 525 NTSC
Canary Islands - 625 PAL
Central African Republic - 625 SECAM
Chad - 625 SECAM
Chile - 525 NTSC
China - 625 PAL
Colombia - 525 NTSC
Congo - 625 SECAM
Cook Islands - 625 PAL
Croatia - 625 PAL
Cuba - 525 NTSC
Curacao - 525 NTSC
Cyprus - 625 PAL/ SECAM
Czechoslovakia - 625 SECAM
Denmark - 625 PAL

Djibouti - 625 SECAM
Dominican Republic - 525 NTSC
Dubai - 625 PAL
Ecuador - 525 NTSC
Eire - 625 PAL
Eqypt - 625 PAL/ SECAM
El Salvador - 525 NTSC
Equatorial Guinea - 625 SECAM
Ethiopia - 625 PAL
Faeroe Islands - 625 PAL
Fiji - 625 PAL
Finland - 625 PAL
France - 625 SECAM
French Polynesia - 625 SECAM
Gabon - 625 SECAM
Galapagos Isles - 525 NTSC
Germany - 625 PAL
Ghana - 625 PAL
Gibraltar - 625 PAL
Greece - 625 SECAM
Greenland - 625 PAL
Grenada - 525 NTSC
Guadalope - 625 SECAM
Guam - 525 NTSC
Guatemala - 525 NTSC
Guinea (French) - 625 SECAM
Guinea - 625 SECAM
Guyana Republic - 625 SECAM
Haiti - 625 SECAM
Honduras - 525 NTSC
Hong Kong - 625 PAL
Hungary - 625 SECAM/ PAL
Iceland - 625 PAL
India - 625 PAL
Indonesia - 625 PAL
Iran - 625 SECAM/ PAL
Iraq - 625 SECAM
Israel - 625 PAL
Italy - 625 PAL
Ivory Coast - 625 SECAM
Jamaica - 525 NTSC
Japan - 525 NTSC
Jordan - 625 PAL
Kampuchea - 525 NTSC
Kenya - 625 PAL
Korea (North) - 625 SECAM/ 525 NTSC

Korea (South) - 525 NTSC
Kuwait - 625 PAL
Laos - 625 SECAM/ PAL
Lebanon - 625 SECAM
Leeward Isles - 525 NTSC
Lesotho - 625 PAL
Liberia - 625 PAL
Libya - 625 SECAM
Luxembourg - 625 SECAM/ PAL
Macedonia - 625 PAL
Madagascar - 625 SECAM
Madeira - 625 PAL
Malawi - 625 PAL
Malaysia - 625 PAL
Maldives - 625 PAL
Mali - 625 SECAM
Malta - 625 PAL
Martinique - 625 SECAM
Mauritius - 625 SECAM
Mexico - 525 NTSC
Monaco - 625 PAL/SECAM
Mongolia - 625 SECAM
Morocco - 625 SECAM
Mozambique - 625 PAL
Namibia - 625 PAL
Nepal - 625 PAL
Netherlands - 625 PAL
Netherlands Antilles - 525 NTSC
New Caledonia - 625 SECAM
New Zealand - 625 PAL
Nicaragua - 525 NTSC
Niger - 625 SECAM
Nigeria - 625 PAL
Norway - 625 PAL
Oman - 625 PAL
Pakistan - 625 PAL
Panama - 525 NTSC
Papua New Guinea - 625 PAL
Paraguay - 625 PAL M
Peru - 525 NTSC
Philippines - 525 NTSC
Poland - 625 SECAM
Polynesia - 625 SECAM
Portugual - 625 PAL
Puerto Rico - 525 NTSC
Qatar - 625 PAL

Reunion - 625 SECAM
Romania - 625 SECAM
Rwanda - 625 SECAM
Sarawak - 625 PAL
Samoa (Eastern) - 525 NTSC
San Marino - 625 PAL
Saudi Arabia - 625 SECAM
Senegal - 625 SECAM
Seychelles - 625 PAL
Sierra Leone - 625 PAL
Singapore - 625 PAL
South Africa - 625 PAL
South West Africa - 625 PAL
Spain - 625 PAL
Sri Lanka - 625 PAL
St. Kitts & Nevis - 525 NTSC
Sudan - 625 PAL
Surinam - 525 NTSC
Swaziland - 625 PAL
Sweden - 625 PAL
Switzerland - 625 PAL
Syria - 625 SECAM
Tahiti - 625 SECAM
Taiwan - 525 NTSC
Thailand - 625 PAL
Togo - 625 SECAM
Trinidad & Tobago - 525 NTSC
Tunisia - 625 SECAM
Turkey - 625 PAL
Uganda - 625 PAL
United Arab Emirates - 625 PAL
United Kingdom - 625 PAL
Uruguay - 625 PAL M
USA - 525 NTSC
Former USSR - 625 SECAM
Vatican City - 625 PAL
Venezuala - 525 NTSC
Vietnam - 625 SECAM/ NTSC
Virgin Isles - 525 NTSC
Yemen - 625 PAL/ SECAM
Former Yugoslavia - 625 PAL
Zaire - 625 SECAM
Zambia - 625 PAL
Zanzibar (Tanzania) - 625 PAL
Zimbabwe - 625 PAL

POST PRODUCTION

Ivan Palmer
DVDi

DVD PRODUCTION

Q - What is your job?

Ivan - We author DVDs.

Q - What does a film maker need to give you in order for you to make a great DVD?

Ivan - High quality assets of the film such as a good quality master tape. A good idea of what the film is so that they know what style they want for the menu design. Obviously we watch the film, too so we have an idea ourselves. And then we juggle ideas between the two of us to figure out. Also they need to have an idea of what extras they want on the DVD and why. Sometimes people want too much on a disk.

Q - Is it a good idea for them to give you a flow chart of what they want and how they want it to happen?

Ivan - Not necessarily because we can do that ourselves anyway. And we do that once we know what the assets are.

Q - What are the best formats the assets can come on?

Ivan - Currently, Digibeta tape. If we get something that has been MPEG-ed already, we don't know how well it has been done so we can't be responsible for how it is going to look. DV is fine for the extras too.

Q - Is it a good idea to know what 16x9 does before you decide to use it on the DVD?

Ivan - Yes, 16x9 is the better option these days because it is how people are viewing things. Most people have widescreens of some kind. You are making use of the whole screen you paid for. It is still 4x3 but just stretched. I find it surprising how many producers and film makers don't understand 16x9 because it is vital - it is the most important element of your project that goes on the DVD other than the audio file. People don't understand the difference between 16:9 and 4:3 letterbox because it is the same shape.

Q - Most independent film makers will master their film in Region 0 so it can play anywhere in the world. Should they then master it in PAL or NTSC, and is there a difference in quality between the two?

Ivan - There is a difference in quality, PAL being noticeably better to my eye. For the casual viewer, they wouldn't see this and may not care. I would lean towards PAL myself, but I don't think it is so important. It is safer to do a world disk in NTSC as that should play on most setups. The disk is only for Europe, you should do a PAL disk.

Q - Take us through the process of putting a DVD together from the first meeting, through encoding to the final steps and how long would it take?

Ivan - How long it takes depends on how much content you want. You can do a DVD in a few hours or a few months and we have done both. A lot of it comes down to the approval of the assets and making sure everyone is happy with it.

Q - Is it fair to say that the more organised a producer is, the cheaper it will be?

Ivan - Totally.

Q - Do you do test disks?

Ivan - Yes. We can do a DVD5 or a DVD9.

Q - Once everyone signs off on the project, do you give them a DVD to take off to the DVD factory?

Ivan - That depends on whether they are duplicating or replicating. If they are duplicating, we just give them a disk, which will be their master disk from which they will make copies. If it is to be replication, they will probably want a DLT tape.

Q - What kind of copy protection can you put on a DVD to stop casual piracy?

Ivan - You have the options of CSS and Macrovision. CSS doesn't cost anything but if you go to Macrovision, you have to pay for it and it the costs are per disk.

Q - Is it common to go get Macrovision?

Ivan - Very few of our clients use Macrovision these days.

Q - Your office is filled with computers and doesn't look any different from mine. Why shouldn't I just use Adobe Encore or Apple iMovie to make my 10,000 DVD release?

Ivan - Go ahead and have a go, but be aware that if you run into trouble then it could be costly to fix. I don't know anything about film making but I know about making DVDs. I get phone calls all the time from people who say they have done it in DVD Studio Pro or something similar and have problems and they ask if I can help them out. Sorry, but it's going to cost you.

We have to restart a lot of projects because without full knowledge, people might forget something like audio compression, MPEG compatibility, the use of all the scripts that are approved by the DVD forum etc. Certain consumer products for making DVDs can include scripts that are not available in the common player. So your disk may work in a computer but not on 25% of the DVD players in the world. Players are mass produced these days. In the old days, they stuck close to the forum, but now some disks won't play on certain players and we have to go back and figure out why. So it is about going to someone who understands the DVD forum and what they are trying to achieve and what the standards are in the world.

If you are making a film for a select number of people, then go ahead and use those tools. Especially for home movies. You are paying for piece of mind. It should work and if it doesn't, you can shout at me, *"this doesn't work in Japan!"* and then I will have to eat humble pie and fix it.

Q - What are the common technical mistakes people see when they make their homemade disks?

Ivan - Most mistakes can be worked out through trial and error, but something like navigation can be a nightmare if you don't understand how scripts work.

Q - What are the common mistakes that you see in the assets that come to you?

Ivan - Mislabeled ratios. People bringing in a master 4:3 letterboxed version and thinking it is 16:9. People are now becoming complacent about safe areas too, and they are assuming that anything outside those areas cannot be seen. Make sure you understand about title safe and picture safe areas and that neither is guaranteed to be out of vision.

POST PRODUCTION

DVDi
NEW MEDIA SOLUTIONS

Ivan Palmer

DVDi Limited 132 Cleveland Street
London W1T 6AB
T: +44(0)20 7692 7710
F: +44(0)20 7692 4120
E: info@dvd-i.com
W: dvd-i.com

DIY DVD GUERILLA FILM MAKER SAYS!

If you want a great DVD for your movie, and you do, then that means YOU will need to oversee the production. Leave it to the distributor or anyone else and you will no doubt get an uninspired collection of extras. We would all like out films to be seen on the big screen, but the way technology is going, it's likely that this DVD is going to be where many agents and studio executives see your movie. So make it special.

You can produce all the extra bits on miniDV - 'The Making Of...', 'Directors Commentary', 'Deleted Scenes' etc. So get interviewing yourself, and make it snappy and entertaining. Get a great 16:9 transfer of your movie, clean it up and remove dust and sparkle. Make sure you have a great Dolby Digital mix (the licence is free for DVD), create some great menus in Photoshop etc. If you feel so inclined, you could master the whole thing yourself, though in practice, we would recommend letting a dedicated company with a track record do this. If you give them detailed notes (ideally a flowchart), all menus and backgrounds on disk, and all the video elements on tape (clearly labelled with in and out timecodes), then you should be able to cut a GREAT deal. Maybe as little as £300, even less...

They will burn you a DVD-R for you to test (if it's a dual layer DVD9 disk then they will burn two DVD-R's or recompress to fit on a DVD5 for testing only), and when you are happy with the job, they will export it all to a DLT tape which will go the factory that will press your disks.

Q - Do you have problems with people wanting over complicated menus?

Ivan - Yes. People are used to seeing websites, done in Flash, where you can go over a button and everything moves, and then you have to explain that you are really going back to the basics on a DVD. You can only highlight these four colours and that is all you can do. I think people are often surprised because they come from the creative side and they have genuinely great ideas that unfortunately due to DVD standards, we cannot put into practice. It is the same with movie subtitles. They want them to look like they do on TV, but it is a DVD player and it handles the subtitle creation.

Q - What does the future hold for an HD DVD format?

Ivan - I think that eventually we will all be on video on demand. That might be awhile away because we all still buy CDs, yet we can download music and people still like owning that physical thing.

Q - How can film makers make your life easier?

Ivan - Talk to us in the beginning. We would much rather give free advice to someone, even if they go somewhere else!

Q - With the featurettes and director's voice overs, some producers think they need to go to a big producer for that. Is there any reason someone couldn't just make it in Adobe Premiere and put it onto Mini-DV as long as they know what they are doing?

Ivan - Yes, you could.

Q - What advice would you offer a new film maker?

Ivan - Don't try and make money. Hopefully you will and good luck to you, but there's too much heartbreak in it if that is what you are in it for. And that is from a runner to a writer to a producer. Do it because you are passionate and it is what you want to do. Then there are clichés like don't give up. Don't be afraid to sell out. If someone offers you £5m to make something cheesy, do it. At least you should get some experience.

SALES &
DISTRIBUTION

Guerilla Films is probably the only distribution company ever to be run by an award winning actor and producer, David Nicholas Wilkinson. Originally set up to distribute Wilkinson's own films, over the years more and more filmmakers have asked guerilla to take on there films. Since 1999 the company has only distributed British & Irish films. The lowest budget film is £55k, and the highest cost $16 million. The company seeks to secure all rights - cinema, DVD and TV however they will take split rights on certain films. Because of the companies creative background it will only take on a few films per year and works hard at promoting them rather than the scattergun release hundreds and some are bound to succeed *ethos*.

Contact 020 8758 1716

Lise Romanoff
Vision Films

INTERNATIONAL SALES AGENT

Q - What is your job?

Lise - I am a sales agent for producers of independent feature films, documentaries and music related programming. It is my job to sell feature films, on behalf of the filmmakers, to distributors, video companies and TV channels around the world.

Q - Is there a type of film that sells the most?

Lise - It is not genre that is most important, it is star names. So casting is still number one. Thrillers and action will still sell better with lesser names, but you need bigger names for romantic comedies and dramas.

Q - Why do you think that US independent films do better than British independent films?

Lise - Here in the US you have Lion's Gate, Focus Films, New Line, Miramax and a bunch of other distributors that can get independent films into theatres widespread and do a lot of press. There's fewer independent companies in the UK that will put that kind of muscle behind the release of their picture. I am impressed with companies like Lion's Gate who take smaller genre films like *Open Water*, get it out there, on screens, on billboards, on buses and buildings, create hype and gives it a chance to be a success.

Q - What do you need from a producer to sell a movie?

Lise - It should still be shot on 35mm film for maximum potential. Filmmakers still aren't lighting and directing DV and HD well enough yet. They tend to make them look like home movies. They don't think of it like a theatrical feature. They don't do dolly moves and they don't do the sound and lighting properly. So they are terrible movies and it is the film making process which is bad, not the medium. I think film makers need to be trained in film. And producers should still cut their negative if possible or go to Hi Def for final mastering, because that is the way of the future. They need to have a 16x9 Hi Def universal master, and they have to do 5.1 Surround Sound. If you want your movie to last, even a little low budget movie, you need to do this.

Q - Is there anything on the delivery list that producers usually have problems with or haven't thought of?

Lise - Images. They have to have a photographer on the set. You can't pull video stills and expect to get good key art. They are only good for the back of the video box at best! I would say have your still photographer on the set for 5-10 crucial days so that you have something to give us of the main actors. They should be digital stills, too, not 35mm film. You need a dozen of all the key actors. And get some close ups even if you have to have them pose. If you can, get a graphic designer to read your script and come up with some ideas ahead of time and create a mock campaign.

Q - Do film makers get their own Errors & Omissions Insurance?

Lise - Yes, it is not a sales agent's responsibility.

Q - Are film makers aware of E&O?

Lise - No. But you can get it after you make your first sale that requires it... It costs around $5k-$10, unfortunately the pay TV digital channels only pay between $15-$35K for the licence fee and they demand E&O. Foreign doesn't require E&O generally. Some might ask for it, but if we don't have it, then they write in an extra indemnification clause in lieu of it.

Q - Do you find that sound is a major problem with low budget movies?

Lise - Bad sound mix can make or break a film. Many producers don't create M&Es or even know what a full M&E is. They separate the music and the effects, but there are a lot of holes. They don't do the ambient sound. What happened to that old school thing in film making where before everyone left the room, they recorded *'room tone'?* And, if they don't have an M&E, they have to go back and make one, which is an additional expense. Also, many producers don't know what the specs are for the channel they are going to sell to. Their blacks may be crushed or the film isn't colour balanced. They do unsupervised telecine to cut corners and save money. Today's standards are so high. Producers should take a course in post-production and delivery, and be concerned with the technical quality of the film, not just the content.

Q - Can a film maker come to you with a screenplay in the hope that you will find funding?

Lise - Generally not. But recently, a producer named Steve Nemeth came in with a project called *What We Do Is Secret*. Steve did *Dogtown and Z Boys* and *Fear And Loathing in Las Vegas*. This is the Darby Crash story. Darby was in a punk rock band called The Germs and he killed himself so it has the drama of *Sid & Nancy* and *The Doors*. It has cast attached in Lucas Haas, Shane West from ER and Bijou Philips. Pat Smear from Nirvana and The Foo Fighters is doing the soundtrack. So this film came to me with all the right elements in place. And they had three quarters of the financing in place. So if something like that comes in, I can go find an equity partner. In this case it was out of Japan. We'll take an executive producer credit and fee, and will sell the available rights in the rest of the world.

Q - Is there a standard list of sales minimums for each country so a film maker can know what to expect?

Lise - There are two sets of numbers. There are the ones for those films that have theatrical potential. If not, then it goes into the other. Actually there is a third category for cult films in which the numbers are higher than the movies that don't make theatrical - especially for DVD and late night TV. Theatrical numbers are always by far, the highest. Of course, it is always dependent on the film itself and the cast.

Q - What is a standard deal that a producer gets with a sales agent?

Lise - It is not *'what does the producer get with the sales agent?'*, It is *'what does the sales agent get from the producer?'* It is a commission off the top of gross receipts, which is the gross sales less bank wire fees. We get a minimum of 10% and a maximum of 30%, depending on the project. On library product, I get 25%-30% average. On new product, because there are more zeroes involved at the end of the day on each sale, we go 20%-25%. But that is the because of the way that we work where we don't charge back a lot of our expenses to the producers. In the instance where I go down to 15%, then I am charging back the typical stuff that sales agents charge like market fees. But if you get a higher commission, you still charge back expenses directly associated with that film such as flyers and ads in the trades, but not for general overhead costs. If we put an ad in the trades for five films, you will get one fifth of the cost charged back to you. If we build a DVD trailer reel with thirty films, then you get charged one-thirtieth of the total.

Q - But can't those expenses get out of control? What about caps on expenses?

Lise - It could get out of hand and producers do get into trouble. If you want to put caps, then it hurts you in a sense because you are saying that we cannot advertise or push the picture after a point. If you are nervous about expenses getting out of control, then perhaps it is best for you to give a higher commission so that less things get charged back to you. I don't charge most overhead expenses because if a film that doesn't sell well all of a sudden gets $5K sale, it will be eaten up. And having been a producer, I know how bad that is. Plus here is another way to look at it. If you see that I have only charged you for twenty screeners of your film in a year, you know that only twenty buyers have seen it. I find that producers like to see that I am charging them back for fifty screening cassettes because it shows that I am actively trying to sell their film.

SALES

Q - Do you ever say that there are some guaranteed marketing expenses?

Lise - Initially there are always some expenses. When I first take on a film it always costs me $5K to get that film to market. I have to pay a designer to create a flyer etc. In some cases, if the design comes to me then you don't have that expense and all I have to do is make the mechanical artwork. If it originally comes in PAL, then I require that you make me an NTSC copy as well, but I make it when I get the first NTSC sale. If it comes in NTSC, I make the PAL because I know my lab will do a good job that will pass Q/C (Quality Control). Do I recoup that off producer share? Yes, but that is why I am so fussy about what I take on because it costs me a lot to take on a picture including my time and energy, which I don't charge back.

Q - Do you create trailers?

Lise - I never create trailers. The producers do that. But I should say the market ones are usually longer than the ones you see in the theatre. Maybe two minutes and show more story.

Q - How many markets are there that really matter?

Lise - There are eight to ten. AFM, Cannes, MiPTV, MIP-COM, DISCOP, Asia-TV Forum, The LA Screenings and I go to the VSDA. I don't take a stand at VSDA, but I go sell to video companies in the US. The markets are between October and June and the selling is pretty even throughout the year except Summer when it slows down a little bit.

Q - How long does it take to see returns on a film?

Lise - Six months. You might get lucky and get a big sale in the first month. But usually in the 1st quarter, you sell Turkey, Indonesia and Thailand and the distributor makes back their commission and expenses. By the end of the 2nd quarter, we've sold the larger territories and the producer should get their first cheque. Then it builds for 2 years, then tapers off to a small, steady flow of revenue.

Q - What is the typical length of a license?

Lise - It is anywhere from one to five years on TV and three to seven years on video and seven to fifteen on all rights.

Q - What is the shelf life for a movie before you have exhausted all sales opportunities?

Lise - It is continuous because when a license expires, it can be resold. I have taken on films like *Hellmaster*, which was a 1992 release. They shot it on film and spent a million dollars, which was a lot back then for a little horror film. It had good key art. But it never had a US DVD release or a worldwide release. So I had them do a director's cut for me so that I could take it back to market. I would rather have a good older film than a bad newer film.

Q - What is the likelihood of an advance for your film?

Lise - It is back to that toss up of whether you give that sales agent a higher commission and less expense or vice versa. If you get an advance, then you have to give them more favourable terms like no caps on expenses or much longer terms to be locked in with them. When a producer asks me for an advance, I e-mail them back and I say good luck and really carefully consider what you will be getting for that. What I offer is the services of a really good sales agent, so you know that you are going to be making money by the end of second quarter. If not, I will give the film back. I also usually ask for two years to start with, which is still short term in the big picture of things, and if producers are happy they then sign long term with me.

Q - For the typical film you handle, would you say that the amount of money you would get at the end of the second quarter be lesser than, equal to or greater than any reasonable advance you might get?

Sales Agent Deliverables

Not all of these items will be needed by a sales agent, but most will. The cost of making up this extensive list of items could feasibly cost more than the production costs of an ultra low budget film. Speak to your sales agent and negotiate an exact list, with a budget for making up that list, BEFORE you sign any sales agreement. This is a LOT OF STUFF! Also bear in mind the whole digital distribution situation. Until the entire planet goes digital, 35mm will remain a serious element in any sales agents delivery list.

Release Print
35mm com/opt print (Combined optical print). This is used by the sales agent to screen the film at markets in a cinema environment. A 90 minute film will be 5 reels long.

35mm Interpositive and 35mm Internegative
Made from the original negative. You have already made this in order to produce your final print, and will be held at the lab. (90 mins is 5 reels)

35mm Optical Sound Negative
Made from master sound mix. You have already made this in order to produce your final print, and will be held at the lab.(90 mins is 5 reels)

Sound Master
Master sound mix, probably supplied on either DA88, time coded DAT, hard drive or MO disk. Some agents may request a 35mm sound master which you should avoid. This sound mix will also be on the DigiBeta on tracks 1 and 2.

Music & Effect Mix (M&E)
Master M&E sound mix used for foreign territories to re-voice the film. Supplied on either DA88 or time coded DAT. Some agents may request a 35mm sound master which you should avoid. This sound mix will also be on the DigiBeta on tracks 3 and 4.

Textless Title Background
35mm Interneg / Interpos / print of sequences without title elements. Used by territories to re-title in their native language. Video versions of the textless backgrounds will also be needed.

35mm Trailer
Including access to interneg, interpos, optical sound, magnetic sound master and M&E mix. It is common now to produce the trailer on DigiBeta and digitally copy the video onto film. The quality isn't as good but it may be adequate and certainly cheaper and easier to produce.

Video Tape
Full screen (not widescreen) perfect quality Digital Betacam of the film, including stereo sound (on tracks 1&2) and M&E (on tracks 3&4). You may want to make widescreen versions and 16-9 versions too, but these will probably be subsequent to the full screen version. You may need to supply a BetaSP so that the sales agent can make VHS copies.Should also include the trailer, in full screen (not widescreen) perfect quality, including stereo sound (on tracks 1&2) and M&E (on tracks 3&4). You will also need a trailer with textless backgrounds too.

Video Tape Textless Backgrounds
Full screen (not widescreen) perfect quality Digital Betacam of textless background sequences, including stereo sound (on tracks 1&2) and M&E (on tracks 3&4).

Universal Master
25P HD master tape (Usually HD-D5) transfer of your film, fully graded and cleaned. Hi res and true 16:9 image, means it can be used to make ALL the different tapes required for international sales. Also includes all audio tracks (Dolby Digital 6 discrete tracks) and a stereo track for for broadcast TV. This would replace ALL other video tapes required in this list. All textless backgrounds can be included at the end of the tape. THE HD MASTER IS POSSIBLY THE MOST IMPORTANT ELEMENT TO GET RIGHT FIRST.

Stills set
100 full color transparencies will be requested but you can get away with 20 as long as they are good. May be possible to supply these on CD-R / DVD-R now, but they must be very high quality scans professionally done or from a high quality digital camera.

Screenplay transcript
Final cut including all music cues. This isn't your shooting script, but an accurate and detailed transcription of all the dialogue and action. You will need to sit down with your PC and a VHS and do it from scratch.

Sales Agent Deliverables... cont

Press Kit and reviews
Copies of the press kit, on paper and disk, and copies of all press and reviews. Don't give them the bad reviews.

EPK- Electronic Press Kit
BetaSP or DVCam tape of interviews with actors and principal crew. Shots of crew at work, plus clips from film and trailer. You will also need a split M&E version so that interviewees voices can be dipped down allowing a translation to be spoken over the top.

Music Cue Sheet
An accurate list of all the music cues, rights etc. See the music cue sheet later in the book. Used by collection agencies to distribute music royalties.

Distribution restrictions
Statement of any restrictions or obligations such as the order in which the cast are credited etc.

US Copyright Notice
Available from The Registrar of Copyright, Library of Congress, Washington DC, 20559, USA.

Other Miscellaneous Paperwork...

Chain of Title
Information and copy contracts with all parties involved with production and distribution of the film. This is needed to prove that you have the right to sell the film to another party. Usually the writer, director, producer, musician, cast and release forms from all other parties involved.

Certificate of Origin and Certificate of Authorship
Available from solicitor. You go in, pay a small fee, swear that the information is correct, they witness it and you have your certificates.

Certificate of Nationality
Available from the Department of Culture Media and Sport, Dept., of National Heritage, Media Division (Film), 2/4 Cockspur Street, London, SW1Y 5DH.

Credit List
A complete cast and crew list, plus any other credits.

Errors and Omissions Insurance Policy (E&O) - A policy that
indemnifies distributors and sales agents internationally. Available from specialised Insurers (approx. cost £7k). You may be able to negotiate around this, agreeing to supply it if and when it is needed by any specific distributor.

Lab Access Letter
A letter giving access to materials held at the lab to the sales agent. Remember, if you haven't paid your lab bill yet, they may not give you this letter. This also applies to any digital mastering company who has created your HD masters.

Lise - The money you would get over the first year would be equal to the advance and then you would surpass it. And that would be for an advance for $50-100K. That may seem like a lot, but if you have a name in your film how much have you spent to make it? You are taking a chance that you might not ever see another dime.

Q - Do you think producers worry about not having enough money for delivery requirements so wouldn't it be great if I could get an advance to cover them?

Lise - Yes. But again, it is a toss up.

Q - Would you advise spending a little more on talent since that is the thing that really sells a film these days?

Lise - Yes. If a name costs them $10K for a cameo, then you should do it. And on the $500k budgets, you should be able to get a name. Or, spend $50K more and make it right and have a better chance of making it all back. And also your name has to be a name internationally to sell that way. If you have a big TV name in the UK in your film and no one in the US knows who that person is, then they are not a name. Then again, if you have, say, a big German star and can get a big deal in Germany that makes your money back, then that is a way to go, too. Then you have the rest of the world to make a profit though you will have to lower your expectations for those territories.

Q - Does it help if film makers go to the markets with you?

Lise - The only way it helps is that the film makers can see what really goes on and they will leave me alone. I had a friend act as a hostess at one of the markets and she was great. When film makers see that sometimes they don't even get a chance and there is very little we can do, it's a buyer's market, they leave me alone. Which leads me to another thing, by going to a market, Producers can learn how to pitch. You need to have your movie down to a really short pitch. If you can't do it in two minutes, than neither can I. If I can say romantic comedy with Rob Lowe and Peter York and it is an angel / devil thing, great, the buyer gets it and can instantly make a decision whether to buy it or not.

Q - What are presales and how do they work?

Lise - Presales are when someone will buy a film before it is made. They are harder and harder to get these days. Buyers have been hurt more often than not because the film doesn't turn out as well as they thought and they paid too much. So they will not pre-buy unless they really know the producer or there are so many stars attached, that they know they are going to make their money back. Or it has to have a hook. You can do a conditional presale where they put down a small deposit that goes into an escrow account so they can guarantee that they can get it back. But that doesn't help you produce the movie. You need to get a buyer to trust you enough to cash flow your production.

Major Film and TV Markets

GUERILLA FILM MAKER SAYS!

With the demise of MIFED, there are only two major film markets left on the schedule - Cannes in May and The American Film Market (AFM) in November. Although there are a host of mid sized film festivals and markets that may step up to fill in the gap, the way of the film market is changing. Sales are all year round, not necessarily just at a market. Major film festivals sans market have now become attractive places to meet in person and do business at the same time as enjoying the festival atmosphere - therefore festivals such as Toronto have attracted distributors who are hiring out theatres for screenings and office suites to do business. Companies can choose the specific festivals that will suit their needs. However ultimately markets and festivals create a buying frenzy which is more difficult to do throughout the year or if your film isn't in a festival. Here are some festivals/markets that may emerge as a third major market.

MIPTV
Television market for world buyers.
Cannes, France
Mid April
www.miptv.com

MIPCOM
Television market for world buyers.
Milan, Italy
Mid October

NATPE
Primarily US market, but some international.
Host city changes (New Orleans most recent)
Late January
www.napte.org

LA Screenings
Los Angeles, USA
Cannes competitor primarily for USA based sellers.
Mid May
www.videoageinternational.com

AFM - American Film Market
Los Angeles, USA
Primary feature film US market for world buyers.
Late February
www.afma.com

Cannes Film Market and Festival
Cannes, France
Primary feature film Euro market for world buyers.
Mid May
www.cannesmarket.com

Sundance Film Festival
Utah, USA
Festival, not a market but attended by buyers.
Late January
www.sundance.org

Berlin Film Festival
Berlin, Germany
Festival, not a market but attended by buyers.
Early February
www.berlinale.de

Toronto Film Festival
Toronto, Canada
Festival, not a market but attended by buyers.
Early September
www.e.bell.ca/filmfest

The Venice Film Festival
Venice, Italy
Festival that may replace MIFED market.
September
www.labiennale.org

The European Film Market
Berlin, Germany
Berlin International Film Festival's sister event.
February
www.berlinale.de

The Hong Kong Filmart
Hong Kong, China
Premiere Asian film market
March
www.tdc.org.hk

Rotterdam Film Festival
Rotterdam, The Netherlands
Festival, not a market
January
www.filmfestivalrotterdam.com

Pusan Film Festival
Pusan, South Korea
Festival, not a market
October
www.piff.org

Karlovy Vary
Czech Republic
Festival, not a market
July
www.kviff.com

Buenos Aries Film Festival
Buenos Aires, Argentina
May become the major South American market
April
www.bafici.gov.ar

Bangkok Film Market
Bangkok, Thailand
January
www.bangkokfilm.org/market.aspx

San Sebastian International Film Festival
San Sebastian, Spain
Has an informal market.
September
www.sansebastianfestival.com

SALES

Estimated Sales Breakdown

All sales are negotiated and calculated in US$

TERRITORY	Max	Min	Probable	Actual
Benelux	$25k	$10k	$20k	$20k
Canada	$50k	$20k	$20k	$20k
UK	$50k	$20k	$10k	$10k
French Canada	$25k	$10k	$10k	$0k
France	$60k	$15k	$20k	$0k
Germany	$75k	$25k	$50k	$50k
Greece	$10k	$5k	$5k	$0k
Italy	$60k	$10k	$20k	$20k
Iceland	$10k	$2k	$4k	$0k
Israel	$10k	$2k	$5k	$0k
Portugal	$10k	$2k	$3k	$0k
Spain	$60k	$15k	$20k	$20k
Scandinavia	$50k	$20k	$20k	$20k
Czechoslovakia	$10k	$2k	$4k	$0k
Hungary	$10k	$2k	$5k	$0k
Poland	$10k	$2k	$2k	$0k
Romania	$10k	$2k	$2k	$0k
CIS	$15k	$5k	$5k	$0k
Former Yugoslavia	$10k	$2k	$3k	$0k
Turkey	$10k	$2k	$4k	$0k
Egypt	$10k	$2k	$2k	$0k
Arg/Chile/Uru/Para	$20k	$2k	$5k	$5k
Brazil	$20k	$7k	$10k	$0k
Colombia	$10k	$2k	$5k	$0k
Mexico	$15k	$5k	$5k	$0k
Peru/Equa/Bol	$10k	$2k	$2k	$0k
Venezuela	$10k	$2k	$2k	$0k
Central America	$10k	$2k	$2k	$2k
West Indies	$10k	$2k	$2k	$2k
India	$30k	$10k	$10k	$0k
Pakistan	$10k	$2k	$4k	$0k
Hong Kong	$15k	$5k	$5k	$5k
Indonesia	$10k	$2k	$3k	$3k
Japan	$100k	$20k	$50k	$0k
Korea	$80k	$40k	$50k	$50k
Malaysia	$10k	$2k	$2k	$2k
Philippines	$15k	$5k	$5k	$0k
Singapore	$10k	$2k	$2k	$0k
Taiwan	$25k	$5k	$5k	$0k
Thailand	$10k	$2k	$5k	$0k
Burma	$10k	$2k	$3k	$0k
South Africa	$25k	$10k	$10k	$10k
Australasia	$50k	$10k	$20k	$20k
USA	$200k	$20k	$50k	$20k
TOTAL	$1285k	$336k	$501k	$279

It is almost impossible to give sales estimates for a film that does not exist, so we based these figures on a genre driven film, shot on S16mm or HD, with no real stars. It looks pretty good and is OK. It's not going to win any Oscars, that's for sure. We came to these figures after talking with sales agents and other film makers. Of course the sales agents talk it up, the film makers inject reality.

The figures quoted in the first three columns represent Max., Min. and Probable sales based on the assumption that the film is actually sold in a given territory. The fourth column, Actual, is based on what sales are likely to be achieved in total (that's the film makers talking there!) Genre films also sell more consistently.

Remember, it is very possible that you may only achieve two or three sales, say the US, Germany and Korea. Treat any more sales as a bonus. Remember also, these sales dollars are not what would go to the film maker, the sales agent will slice their commission off the top, then their expenses. And to make matters worse, the money will come in over a five year period in dribs and drabs.

Sales Agent Tips

GUERILLA FILM MAKER SAYS!

1. Consider the viability of your film as a salesman - would I want this film and if not, why? First films are usually the fruit of a long held dream. From that perspective, if you feel the desire to make it, don't worry about commercial viability. As long as the film isn't awful, and you don't spend too much money, you should get it screened somewhere. Plus you will learn soooooo much! Your first film is all about learning.

2. Sales agents are tough to deal with - they are professional hardcore negotiators. If they sign your film, they will more than likely want it for 15 years, 25% of sales, plus expenses, and refuse a cash advance. The upshot is that you will probably never get paid. You MUST try to get a cash advance, reduce the number of years and percentage. The first one is unlikely to happen, the last two are very negotiable.

3. Keep some territories and windows for yourself. If your sales agent messes you about, this will mean you can approach distributors in a different country and make a direct sale. You will get a lesser fee because you are not a sales agent, but it's better to get 100% of £10K than 100% of nothing.

4. Alongside your film, you will have to supply a huge amount of delivery items (see the Delivery List). These are important and often overlooked. Without these items, no sales agent will touch the film or they will fulfill the delivery list and charge you for doing so. Take care of it yourself. Study this list and make sure you know what each thing is, how much it costs and where you will get it.

5. Think about whether you want to shout about how little you shot the film for. Saying it cost too little might hurt your sales as in the eyes of a buyer, a film is worth what it cost to make.

6. Attending one of the big film markets like Cannes or the AFM will broaden your outlook of sales agents and of how films are marketed and sold. GO TO THE NEXT ONE!

7. At film markets, look at which ones sell your type of film and target those.

8. Get a performance clause in your contract. If they don't do a certain amount of sales in a certain amount of time, you can void the deal.

9. Cap their expenses so that they have to get written permission to spend more than you agreed initially. Otherwise they could be free to charge you whatever they want.

10. Be tough from day one. Insist on reports as agreed, prompt payment and accurate information. Make them understand that you will not tolerate complacency. If you make yourself a nuisance, which is well within your rights, they might actually give you what you want.

11. You do not have to go with a sales agent from your own country. If the one who shows the most enthusiasm or offers you the best deal is in the US or Australia, go with them.

See also points to look for in sales agents agreements in the legal toolkit toward the end of the book

Q - How important is it to launch a film at film festivals?

Lise - It helps if you get some critical acclaim and a couple of laurels. If you have a film with low budget and medium names, but it has some critical acclaim, the buyers will take a chance on it. I usually don't get involved in any of that! I get in touch with film makers after they have done the festival circuit and come back down to reality. If their film becomes a hit like El Mariachi or The Blair Witch Project fantastic! And I don't want to take a film from a producer and ruin a studio deal for them. If they don't, then hopefully they will come back to me. One piece of advice would be to not let your rep (Producers Rep) take complete control because nobody can sell your film better than you. You should work with your rep. So it is always up to the producer to see it all the way through. Unless they are lucky enough to be going on to their next project. But even then they are taking a risk on their asset.

Q - Do you work out selling strategy with the producers?

Lise - I let them know how much advertising I am going to do because that is pre-negotiated. If they want something special like a big ad campaign in the trades, then I will weigh it out with them to see if it is cost effective. And the same thing goes if they want a theatrical release. I tell them, if you didn't take it to the film festivals or distributors didn't want it then, how do you expect me to get you a theatrical release? Again, I try to give Producers a reality check.

Q - Is there a book where all the sales agents are listed?

SALES

Distributors and Sales Agents - When Disaster Strikes

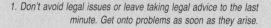

All films start out with good intentions, but then again, we all know that the road to hell is paved with good intentions...! We hope that you never find yourself in a bad situation when selling your film, but if you do, think about these following points...

1. Don't avoid legal issues or leave taking legal advice to the last minute. Get onto problems as soon as they arise.

2. If you think your distributor is being dishonest, at the minimum, write them a letter stating what you think is wrong. Be nice at first and then get progressively more adversarial if they resist. Copy the letter (cc:) to your solicitor so that the distribution company knows you are involving them.

3. A contract agreement cannot force someone into action, but a good one has get out clauses if someone is dishonest, you could get money or your film back.

4. Have your contracts made in your company's name instead of your own so that any bankruptcy or legal action does not affect you personally.

5. Have a clear paper trail of who said what and when. Print emails and keep ALL correspondence in a file.

6. Have a bankruptcy contingency clause in your agreements stating that if your distributor goes under, the film copyright reverts back to you.

7. Arbitration favours the wealthy. If you don't have any money, avoid going to arbitration if you can, and sue them instead.

8. Sometimes the only recourse is to ride out the deal and get your film back that way. If it is a valuable title, you will still be able to sell it. If it is too old and no one wants it, try a gimmick like making a director's cut or adding new commentary features to attract sales agents.

9. If you are owed money by a company that goes under, stay on the person's bankruptcy proceedings. People will try to get away with things if they are not checked.

10. Actors and crew cannot take their names off films if they have a contractual obligation to be named.

11. As a last resort, you can get an injunction to stop a film from being released. They are VERY expensive and should only be done if you know you are right and the end result will be hundreds of thousand or even millions of pounds.

12. Bankruptcy does offer you an out to your problems, but you will have a bad credit rating for a long time, which may effect your ability to get a mortgage or a car loan.

13. Unfortunately, all too many film makers find themselves in these kinds of problems. Often the only solution is to walk away. Remember, no matter the financial situation, you still made the movie, and the experience and the actual film as a tool for attracting new partners is more valuable than the meager returns you may be forced to fight over.

Lise - The trades during markets where they list all the agents is the best. Variety, Screen and Hollywood Reporter.

Q - How does a first time film maker get a sales agent?

Lise - E-mail all of us with a pitch of your show. I wouldn't waste money on sending out screeners unsolicited. If you can make an e-mail pitch with some pictures and a trailer, great. Always get references for a sales agent from producers whom they have generated revenue for, but make sure that their film is comparable to yours.

Q - Should a UK film maker get a US sales agent because they have better contacts?

Lise - Not necessarily. Go to a sales market and walk the halls and see the person's booth. You will see all the UK people right next to the US people. Talk to them and decide whom you think is best for your film.

Q - How often do you report to your producers?

Lise - They get a statement from me 45 to 60 days after the end of each quarter.

Q - If nothing happens sales-wise after the first year do you return it?

The Quality Control (Q/C) on delivery items can be stringent. Dust particles, scratches, bumps - anything technically imperfect could stall a deal. This company actually found a negative scratch on White Angel that Living Spirit had never seen in 62 screenings!

FOUR MEDIA COMPANY
2820 W. OLIVE AVENUE, BURBANK, CA 91505-4455   818.840.7100
QUALITY CONTROL REPORT

Title: White Angel
Series: Part 1 of 1
Client: Colimar Ent.   Eps. # :   4MC ID. # : LS700724
                                W.O. # : 134615   P.O. # : 370   TRT : 95 : 26
☐ PASS   ☒ Fail   ☐ Hold   Comment: AUDIO TICKS ON CH 3&4

Inspected By: Valerie Moore-Porter

Lise - Sometimes. But I have had some sleepers and they hit when I started to give up. So probably after a year if nothing happened I would give it back...then again, I would have a financial negative on my books. But if it is a small negative of $5K or so, I would give it back and tell the producer good luck and find another sales agent.

Q - Is there anything in a sales agent contract in particular a producer should look out for?

Lise - Look out for weird language concerning when terms would or wouldn't be extended. So you know you have a clear out at one point in time. And also make sure that they have to give you copies of all the agreements they have entered into on your behalf. I think it is really wrong for a sales agent to provide you with the short terms and not give you the full contracts. Especially if you decide to go elsewhere, how are you going to know the terms of the previous sales and create an accurate availability list.

Q - How does packaging work and is it a bad thing for a film maker?

Lise - No, it is a good thing for little films because you are not going to get your film sold otherwise. That is how I sell these older titles - in packages of five to ten films. And then the allocations are divided equally unless you have a Nicole Kidman picture and a Hugh Grant picture and eight 'no name' pictures, then it only makes sense to do allocation within the package. It is really interesting in negotiating a package because I'll say I need more for these films, then I will allocate more for them and the producers get to see in the agreement what is up. Otherwise, if all the films are the same, they will be split down the middle.

Q - What kind of deal would a video label give you?

Lise - They give an advance against royalties. Usually it translates out to a dollar per unit sold to the producer. So if they think they are going to sell 10,000 units, you will get $10,000 advance with a 15% royalty. But if they are selling them into stores so cheaply, then their wholesale cost has to come down - probably to $5. So your 15% of $5 is $.75 and if they sell 10,000 units, then you will get through $7,500 of your advance. And that is why advances tend to be low. But I am still getting advances for producers up to $100k, which means they are planning to sell a lot of units. When I am looking for advances from companies, the first question I ask is how many units do they think they will move? Then it comes down to how bad do they want that title? They may give up more than 15%. Or they may pay you more up front.

Q - What is a good number of units to be sold?

Lise - Each company is different. Some have motivations to only move 2000 units, others will move 10,000 – 20,000 and the studios won't take on a movie unless they think they can move 50,000 and up. And this goes for TV licensing as well. You have to know the company. If it is a little digital channel that only has an audience of 100,000 people compared to the big terrestrial channels that have millions of eyeballs then, you are going to get a lower license fee. So my job is to understand to whom I'm selling so I know what license fee to get, so that I know I am getting the best deal possible. It also matters what time period they are going to air it in and how old the film is. Older films get smaller fees.

Q - What advice would you give new film makers?

Lise - Get a name in your film and get proper training on how to make a film so it looks like something I can sell.

SALES

Fyn Day
Cannes Virgin

CANNES VIRGIN

Q - What is your job?

Fyn - I'm a writer, which used to involve sales and marketing copy, journalism, and even technical authoring, in other words anything that paid, but since my debut novel (*The Alice Factor*) was published in 2003 I've been able to focus on fiction. I'm currently writing a second novel and editing someone else's manuscript, but the majority of my ambition lies in writing for film. Eventually I'd like to write-to-sell, not write-to-produce, but in order to establish a track record I'm actively involved in collaboration with others in raising the finances to produce a film from my script.

Q - Was this your first time in Cannes (2005)?

Fyn - Yes

Q - Why did you think you needed to go to Cannes?

Fyn - When I worked in sales and marketing I became involved in a number of trade exhibitions. I imagined Cannes to be something similar, but replacing a bunch of plumbers, builders and decorators crammed into Earl's Court convincing you that their service was just right for your perfect home, there'd be a bunch of distributors, producers and financiers offering their services for my perfect film. This I now know is not the case, but this was the notion I had, that it would be just another trade fair, a trade fair for filmmakers, and since I was interested in making a film then it seemed a good place to be.

Q - What was your objective?

Fyn - From the point of view of someone selling a script I knew my product wouldn't be ready until next year, but I didn't want to go to Cannes when doing business would be critical with no idea of how Cannes worked. So, my true objective was just to familiarise myself with the Cannes process. In fact it turned out that this objective was based on an erroneous premise, because from the point of view of someone raising finances to produce a film my product was actually ready enough to do some business... and I would have done more had I understood the Cannes process.

Q - How easy was it to gain entrance? How did you do it?

Fyn - It was extremely easy to gain entrance. I was alarmed by some stories of what was going to be necessary to gain accreditation but these appear to have been unfounded. Either that or I was extremely lucky. I just went to the accreditation office on my first morning, queued for less than five minutes, showed them a business card which describes me as Managing Editor of Running Legend Film Ltd, and paid in advance for however many days temporary accreditation I wanted. It was cheap, quick, and gave me access to everywhere I wanted to go. Having said that, the way I did it was not necessarily the best and did not garner all the advantages that other routes to accreditation might provide - a free copy of an extremely comprehensive guide to the Cannes festival for instance, which would have proved invaluable.

Q - What did you think you would get from your trip?

Surviving Sundance

GUERILLA FILM MAKER SAYS!

If you are reading this book chances are your trip to the Sundance Film Festival will not be subsidized by a studio, agency or production company (if you are, buy us a drink, will ya?) Here are some tips for making your life easier and a little less expensive while still having a good time in Park City, Utah.

No one needs to register to attend the festival, but you should try to buy as many tickets to films online before you leave. If you can't, then you can get them at several kiosks around Park City, but you will have to get them a few days in advance as they sell out rapidly. You an also scalp tickets, beg or stand in a "stand by" line where if people don't show up to a screening, they will start admitting people from that line.

Flights from London to Salt Lake City will run in the region of £350-£400. If you don't plan to drive during the festival, it's best to grab a free shuttle from the airport into Park City – once in Park City there are loads of free shuttles to take you around. If you're thinking of hiring a car just a word of warning - driving in Park City and certainly parking in Park City is a nightmare. If you do insist on driving, remember that it snows a lot during January in Utah so think about renting a four wheel drive. If you're also considering taking in a trip to LA around the same time, bare in mind it's either a 12 hour drive or around $200 for a return flight from LA to Salt Lake City if you book way in advance.

Staying in Park City is a lot of fun. If you want a hotel in the town, book it as soon as you can as they go fast. Also, many people rent out their homes and apartments to festival goers. They are not cheap,

but if you can get 10 friends to all go in on a house together, then it's not that expensive. If you have a film in the festival, Sundance will be able to put you in contact with other entrees who want to split a place.

Every night there are tons of parties in and around Park City. The big ones that are sponsored by places like Miramax or talent agencies are tough to get into. But, if you keep your ears open and talk to enough people, you may be able to schmooze a pass. Other parties happen in people's hotels or rented houses – again talk to people and you can find out where they are. These are also great ways to get free food and drink. If you are lucky, you might end up in a hot tub at 3AM with a bottle of champagne!

If you do have a film in the festival, be prepared for a lot of work on the days leading up to your screenings. You will have to do some publicity – hopefully a lot of interviews with media. You should be prepared to personally publicize your film somehow. Posting flyers can only be done on designated street walls, but you can pass them out at other screenings and parties. If you can think of a cheap stunt to pull to get people into the theatre – even better!

If you have any major problems or concerns, go to the Sundance main office and they can sort you out. They usually have food, coffee, water, internet access and other goodies there as well.

Pic courtesy of www.sundanceguide.net

Fyn - Insight, an appetite for more, and a tan.

Q - What were your first impressions?

Fyn - My very first impression was *'Ooh, this is going to be a lot easier than I expected'*, but that was soon replaced by confusion, frustration, and disappointment. The halls actually did resemble Earl's Court and Olympia, but the exhibitors were the ones with the movies, not the buyers. It was like being a sweet manufacturer attending a sweet shop fair where you expect all the exhibitors to be sweet shop owners wanting new sweets for their shop, only to find all the exhibitors are actually sweet manufacturers themselves. There you are looking for allies and you're faced with wall-to-wall competition. On several occasions I asked myself *'Does the world really need another movie?'* - but of course it does; it needs mine.

Q - What were the real shocks for you?

Fyn - Besides the rain and limited glamour? Yes, the apparent lack of trade show organisation, but this was partly due to my timing and temporary accreditation. I floundered at first, not really knowing where to find the people I was looking for. There were plenty of published guides but none of them had what I wanted in them. In my naivety I wanted a section headed *'Here's Where All the Financiers Are'*, and a map to the *'Hall of Distributors'*. Actually, the comprehensive guide that I didn't get free with my temporary accreditation (and could not acquire elsewhere for love nor money) did have the real world equivalent of these. And I have learnt since, that the buyers tend to do their bit early in the festival. I didn't arrive until the mid Cannes, by which time they had mostly bought and gone. Another shock was how sore my feet got as I walked miles. Most of the people I wanted to talk to weren't in the

SALES

Useful Websites For Sundance

www.sundance.org

Accommodation help:
Resort Quest Park City: www.resortquest.com
Tel: 1-435-646-6606
Toll Free number: 1-800-243-2932

Park City Condo Rentals: www.condoparkcity.com
info@condoparkcity.com
1-888 4 Park City (1-888-472-7524) or 1-435-658-2227
(offers free transport from and to Salt Lake International
Airport and your condo, also offer 2 free local Park City taxi
rides to the condo unit per day).

Travel help:
Express Shuttle: 1-800-397-0773 and 1-801-596-1600
(provides round trip shuttle service between Salt Lake
International Airport and the Festival in Park City). Vans
depart the airport every 30 mins.
Park City Shuttle: 1-800-724-7767 and 1-435-658-2227
www.parkcityshuttle.com

**Sundance
A Festival Virgins Guide**
Much like the Cannes guide, it's
everything you need to know in
one pocket sized volume.
Essential and cheap.

Get it now from
www.sundanceguide.net

trade halls, they were in suites in a variety of hotels spread along the *'Boulevard de la Croisette',* the vast bustling beach promenade.

Q - Was it productive?

Fyn - Having discussed shock, disillusion and sore feet it might be surprising to hear that it was absolutely productive, much more so than I anticipated. And it could have been even better. You must be prepared to pitch and get knocked back. Courage and belief are equally as important as careful planning and familiarity. The 'money men' themselves admit that they need to get involved in quality productions earlier and earlier or risk losing out to their competitors. I am closer now to making this film than I would have been had I not gone to Cannes.

Q - Where did you hang out?

Fyn - The main arenas for the festival and market (the 'Marché du Film') are the 'Palais des Festivals' and the 'Riviera'. I spent many an hour here, and walking up and down La Croisette. At the rear of the 'Riviera' was a terrace of national pavilions, these were well worth a visit and I used the UK 'tent' as a base and a venue for meetings. There was another Brit-based meeting area at one of the hotels where a bar terrace had been set up. I learnt too late that in the evenings the place to hang was the Majestic, apparently deals really were being struck in the relaxed surroundings of this hotel bar and there was no telling whom you might meet.

Q - Did you form any relationships that will help you?

Fyn - I am the cautious solitary writer-type, perhaps too conservative to be in people's faces in the way I felt expected to be, but film is a collaborative process, much more so than say writing a novel, and just by talking with people in the quieter moments, and being honest about my project, my degree of experience, and my ambition, I did form the kernel of some valuable relationships. Again, I'm too cautious to say that any of these will bring short term reward and they involve busy people who probably wouldn't appreciate a name check here, but I do have some follow up appointments, which can be nothing but a positive sign.

Q - Do you think you will re-think your project after your Cannes visit?

Fyn - If by the project you mean the film itself, then no. But if you mean how we go about getting it made, then yes. I'm a writer. I've been writing for twenty years or so. I have a masters degree in creative writing, I've read extensively on writing for film, attended Robert McKee's Story seminar and Syd Field's master class and have a sufficient body of published work to have confidence in my writing. But what do I know about finance strategies, sales and leaseback, tax breaks, completion bonds and development funds? There's more value to the 'money men' than their money, there's their experience as well, and if they tell me I'm going about it the wrong way, then I'm willing to listen.

Q - Did you achieve your objective?

Surviving Cannes

GUERILLA FILM MAKER SAYS!

Oui, it is May. It is time to go to the French Riviera and see who will win the Palme D'or! Champagne, croissants, caviar! Cannes is a rollicking good time, full of decadence and luxury for those who can afford it, or those who can schmooze their way into the hot spots. Even if you can't or don't, Cannes is a spectacle unto itself, with hundreds of screenings, a full fledged film market and so many stars buzzing around it will make your head spin.

The first thing you need to do to prepare for going to Cannes is to get accreditation (your pass) to the Festival. There are three types of passes you can get:

Professional Pass

This is available to all practising film industry professionals (producers, directors, writers, actors, agents, technicians, composers, film lawyers, film accountants and facility houses) and is FREE. This gives you access to the Palais and the Riviera complexes enabling you to attend all the screenings in the official program and sidebar and enabling you to enter the major hotels where companies reside.

Market

This is only available to companies and there are registration fees attached. You receive a blue badge that will give you access to market screenings and events.

Press

If you can get this, then you have free range of the festival. Consequently, this is hard to get unless you're working for a media that's been accredited by the Festival press office and you're a media representative who holds a national press card or you have been specially commissioned by a media organisation.

Applications for accreditation are available from mid January each year from the accreditation department of the festival. The Deadline is generally early April. Although applying for accreditation used to be completely free, there is now an administration charge and you must apply to the correct organisation to deal with your accreditation.

Festival Accreditation for foreign producers

Unifrance. 4, villa Bosquet, F-75007. Paris. Tel: 47-53-95-80 Fax: 47-05-96-55 (you must provide evidence of industry qualifications of at least 3 films that you have worked upon. Evidence could be flyers, posters, business cards.

Market Accreditation

Marche du Film Service des Accreditations, 3, rue Amelie. F-75007. Paris. Tel: 53-59-61-41 Fax: 53-59-61-51
www.cannesmarket.com

Press Accreditation

Press Office of the Festival de Cannes, 3, rue Amelie. F-75007. Paris. Tel: 33(0) 1-53-59-61-85 Fax: 33 (0) 1-53-59-61-84
press@festival-cannes.fr

Getting Tickets for films

If you're a festival attendee, you can get tickets for films in and out of competition. Tickets are released each morning for films screening that day and the following morning. The ticket office is run by Unifrance and can be found in the Village International France area, located at Espace Pantiero (by the Ferry Port). Ticket office opens 10-12am and 2-4pm every day. You need to get in line from 8.30am at the latest each day to guarantee a ticket. For films screening in other sidebars (Un Certain Regard, Directors' Fortnight, Critics Week), you need to line up outside the venue approximately an hour before screening. You need either a festival, market or press accreditation to get in. For Market Screenings, you need market or press Accreditation for entry, although sometimes you can talk your way in.

It might be in your best interest to stay outside of Cannes so that you can take a breather from the chaos. You will have to rent a car, but they are not that expensive, neither is parking in Cannes. Visit Cannes Festival Virgin Guide at www.cannesguide.com for a list of hotels and immediate online access to Hotels in or around Cannes, as well as bus, train and taxi phone numbers. For additional information, such as screening times, go to the festival's website at www.festival-cannes.com.

Once at the festival, go around to all the hotels and meet with as many companies as you can, to find out who does what. Your next script sale might be a few feet away. Hang out at the American Pavilion, which is a great place to meet people and to find out where all the parties will be held. If you have a film in the festival, be prepared for a media assault. Lack of sleep and repetitive question answering will wear you down. If you are advertising or marketing your film, be aware that posting flyers is illegal and they will be torn down immediately. If you decide to do this anyway, don't put anyone's name, the company name or any contact information on the flyer. Try and find alternative methods of creating a buzz, such as one filmmaking team who wrote screening times of their project in crayon on the sidewalk.

Cannes - A Festival Virgin's Guide

Buy this book! It's cheap, small and has just enough information to not scare you too much, but keep you out of trouble too. Essential for any first timer to Cannes!
ISBN: 0-9541737-1-6
By Benjamin Craig (www.cannesguide.com)
Cinemagine Media Publishing   www.cinemagine.com
Photo courtesy of www.cannesguide.com

SALES

Nicole Valdizan Sacker
Film Maker

AFM Virgin Experiences

Q - How long did you spend at the AFM (American Film Market)?

Nicki - I attended the AFM for the first time this year, although I only went for the first three days of it. It was a very informative experience for me as a filmmaker to attend it because I hadn't ever attended an event like it before. I also made some potentially good contacts through the experience, which is partially what the whole thing is about anyway.

The first day I was a bit overwhelmed by the sheer size of it. The entire Loew's hotel in Santa Monica (all 8 floors and every single suite) as well as the first three floors of Le Merigot hotel, weres taken over for the 8 day duration of the AFM, November 2-9, by financing companies, distributors, exhibitors, film commissions and others.

Walking through the crowded hotel corridors and lobbies was a bit like walking through LAX or London Heathrow with the cacophony of foreign languages being spoken all around me. It was all business, and I felt almost out of place being a filmmaker there. What I found out after talking to various people was that there is an unspoken code of etiquette about the AFM.

The first three days are purely for sales agents and buyers to meet and buy / sell their film to each other - sales are being made for domestic as well as foreign territories. Many of the agents will have had appointments set with each other months in advance. The financiers do not want to listen to a filmmaker trying to pitch their project to them in these first few days, so don't even go there. The next two or three days are for sales yet again, but possibly for people who didn't get organised enough to book meetings with the sales agents and buyers in advance. In the last three days of the AFM, everyone is a lot more relaxed with the anticipation and the adrenaline of the selling frenzy soon to be behind them, so this is where the financiers will be more open to listen to a filmmaker pitch them on their new projects.

Sometimes pre-sales will be made at this point. Pre-sales are a dream for any filmmaker as it is a great way of partially

financing your film, but pre-sales are very hard to come by as most financiers won't want to purchase a film that hasn't even been made yet, and risk the film being a turkey once completed. The only films that get some of their financing via pre-sales are ones with A-list and possibly B-list actors, and even then, most financiers are hesitant at such a gamble. Most financiers like to 'buy' a finished film because they can view it first to decide for themselves if they like it.

Q - Are there any other events going on?

Nicki - There are hundreds of films being screened either in private screening rooms at either hotel or in some of the 9 or 10 movie theatres in the Santa Monica area.

There are some great seminars and panels too. I went to only one of them because I was a bit 'paneled out' after having just attended 4 days of panels at the Intl. Women in Film summit prior to the AFM. I attended the Financing Seminar, which was 3 and a half hours, with a 20 minute break in the middle. Continental breakfast was included, although the breakfast left a lot to be desired. Among some of the most interesting speakers on the financing panel were Mike Medavoy of Phoenix Pictures, Tom Ortenberg of Paramount Classics, and Ashok Armitraj of Hyde Park Entertainment.

Q - So there are contacts to be made?

Nicki - Yes, and I ran into some familiar faces from the industry and met some new faces too - networking is always a good thing.

Like a lot of other filmmakers, I have a history of being resistant to the business side of things and yet we work in 'show business', not 'show art', so the sooner we embrace the business side of things, the quicker we'll find success. And what better way to be immersed into the film business than experiencing the AFM from the inside.

Passes to get into the AFM are pricey (around $250 / day pass or $700 / week pass) so I wouldn't go unless I had a business reason to be there, or a film I was trying to sell. But I am certainly wiser now as a result of attending the AFM.

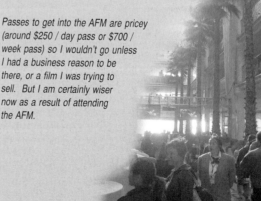

During Cannes week, sales agents and distributors descend on the south of France and take over any free space where they can promote the films they are selling. It's worth going down to Cannes, even if you don't have a project, to experience the insanity that is international sales.

Fyn - Insight, yes. Appetite, yes. Tan? Maybe next year.

Q - On reflection, what did you learn?

Fyn - I learnt that Cannes is a lot of hard work, but an absolutely necessary calendar date for anyone involved in filmmaking. I learnt a few mistakes not to make next year, but no doubt next year I'll make a few new mistakes to ensure that the learning process continues. I detected less of a major budget / minor budget divide than I expected. There is a definite distinction between the two, but there's recognition that this year's low budget heroes might be next year's big budget bosses (and vice versa). I learnt that despite the cynicism and crass commerciality, film is a people business. It's you they either buy or they don't buy, not just your product. To put yourself at increased risk of success you need to put yourself among the people.

Q - What mistakes did you make?

Fyn - I went at the wrong time and have already corrected this error for next year by blocking out my calendar. I stayed at the wrong hotel, that is to say it was a very nice hotel and I was pleased to have done so well at such short notice, but the reason probably that I was able to find a vacancy at this very nice hotel with such short notice was because it was a dreadfully inconvenient location. This is more important than just not wanting to be bothered with a daily commute – the last public transport back to my hotel was too early to spend meaningful time in the evenings at bars or parties where people do business with people; this was a bad misjudgement. As an aside, I should say if your solution to this is to travel massive distances by taxi, then obviously you don't need film funding - just about one Cannes cab fair would cover most independent film production budgets.

Q - What advice would you offer a new filmmaker?

Fyn - Three things. The first is to plan ahead. Try, if at all possible, to go for the duration with your accreditation already in place and accommodation at close quarters. Be prepared to pitch to anyone you meet, taking your project seriously but yourself not too seriously. Make some appointments in advance, but don't make too many in a day. Allow for some down time and hang out with as many people as you can. Respect everyone, not just those you think could be useful. And be flexible enough to accept that all your plans might come to nothing.

The second is to be open. That means both being open to the experience that is Cannes but also giving Cannes the experience that is you. Don't bullshit or misrepresent yourself, don't say you can deliver anything that you can't, and don't be afraid to take on board the odd paradigm shift. Faith in yourself is essential but a good man knows his limitations. Don't fight the way Cannes works even if it doesn't meet your expectation; work with it.

The third is to employ me as a script consultant.

SALES

David Wilkinson
Guerilla Films

Q - What is your job?

David - I distribute films in the UK, getting them in cinemas, video shops, retail outlets, TV companies, oil rigs, hotels etc., then collecting and distributing the payments back to the film maker, should there be any left. I am different from the large distribution companies as I am mainly interested in the low-budget (sub £500k) end of the film market and therefore I have to work in unconventional ways. That said I do have a few $10 million plus films. I am in my 10th year of selling my films via the Internet. I believe I was the first UK distributor to use the medium for selling films. I have sold films around the world to an audience that I would have never reached any other way, which offers great opportunities for filmmakers.

Q - When should a producer come to you?

David - The best time for a producer to come to me is when they have completed their first rough assembly. I can usually tell from that point what is going to be the reaction to the movie. I also like to be involved at the post-production stage of a film and sometimes I can raise finishing funds as with I did with *'Retribution'*. Usually most producers don't come to me until late in the process, often 1-2 years after they finished the film. They write a letter to one of the majors before they produce the film enclosing a screenplay. That major will write back something like *'your film sounds interesting but we cannot commit at this time, however as soon as you have made it please send us a copy to view before sending it elsewhere...'* This is standard.

Sadly most filmmakers believe this. The majors take very few completed British films. If they do it's normally for DVD only. It does happen that they will take it for the cinema but it is rare. Most majors have so much coming from their US parents that they have to dump some of these films straight to DVD as they do not have the slots to release them in the cinema. They do not really want new films but by the same token they do not want to turn down the next big hit.

The problem is the filmmaker presents the film to each major, one at a time. In one case it was 18 months before the producer had a no from all of them. By this time it was very late to start talking to all us small distributors. Approach everyone at once.

The rule of thumb is that you release a film in the year of its copyright date or the year after. If not it is really hard to place it. Everyone tracks films and we all know when they are completed.

Q - Do you ever offer any kind of advance?

David - I am begining to pay them, though this is only something that has happened recently, not because I am mean, but because of the market place. For first time films it's almost a given that we will not put up an advance. It is hard enough persuading cinemas to take it on and very expensive to make up prints, pay for BBFC classification, master DVD's, make posters, pay for advertising etc. However as I have said I do raise finishing money for films.

Q - What is P&A?

David - It is an industry term for Prints and Advertising, in essence, the cost of releasing your film to the distributor. It can mount up very quickly as so many items are unmovable.

Q - Say I did a 5 print release which took £150k at the UK box office, how much of that will I see as the filmmaker?

David - Of that, 17.5% VAT in the U.K. goes to the government. The balance is then usually split, 75% / 25% in favour of the cinema and that is then paid to distributor. If the film does really well you might hit the house nut figure in which case you will start to see considerably more, perhaps even 90% of that equation, but this is very unusual, especially for independent films. Out of that 25% from the cinema the distributor will deduct their fee, usually around 35%, and then whatever is left pays off the P&A. I don't know of a micro-budget film in ten years that has paid off its P&A and made a profit.

Q - So in reality theatrical release is really to raise the value of the film, like a very expensive marketing exercise that will lead into the real money that is in TV, video, pay per view, overseas sales etc?

David - Yes, it is very important. Overseas sales are where the real income is found. Overseas distributors and broadcasters tend to take on films that have been released in the cinema in the country of origin even if they never release them in the cinema in their own country. Also more and more UK broadcasters will not take films from me unless they have been screened in the UK cinema.

Q - How do sales to video rental work?

David - At the time of writing, the conventional video rental market has almost disappeared. 20 years ago, there were around 30,000 outlets doing some form of video rental. Now it's more 3,000.

There is now 'shared revenue' on video rental. You used to just sell the video to the store for a fixed price and that was it. Now the theory is that for every £1 the video rental store takes, 75% goes to the store and 25% to distributor. This is fine if your video is *The Matrix* because you will receive a considerable income. In the past video companies paid an agreed fee (this practice is still around but seems to be going out fast) which meant that you would get a definite return. In the future it will be down to whether or not a particular film rents well. Generally low budget films do not appeal to a mass audience. Your local video shop should be able to give you details of how similar films have performed. Talk to them as their advice could be invaluable and on the whole they're very helpful.

At the time of this question the rental market is changing and I doubt it will be around in its present state for that much longer.

Q - Talk me through a deal for say a £150k film?

David - I would want a license on all UK and Irish rights for 15 years. We would take a 35% commission for cinema and also charge a movement fee for every time the print moved from one cinema to another. There are cases when you only get £20 from the cinema because it played so badly, which isn't even enough to move the print. Any P&A that we had put up we would get back from the net income and that is usually about 65%. Many distributors pay a royalty of 25% of the net dealer price for video rental and 12.5% for sell-through and DVD. With TV we charge a commission of 35% unless the producers have provided some or all of the P&A. This is up for negotiation. We pay a more even 50-50 deal after we have recovered costs.

If there are any unpaid losses from P&A from the theatrical release this will come out of the producer's share of the revenue of video, DVD and TV. This is the BIG problem that all low budget British films face. They have a very difficult time making the P&A back let alone making their distributor a fee to cover their overhead. There are many films I have wanted to take on but cannot because of the losses we would incur with just the P&A. We always expect to lose money in the cinema on low budget films and hope to make up those losses from video rental / sell-through and DVD. TV becomes vital for a company like mine. Sadly with a number of the films we wished to distribute we sent copies to all the UK broadcasters but none agreed with our view that they were good films. We had to reluctantly turn them down. I have spent the last 5 years trying to persuade UK broadcasters to license more UK films. In France or Germany almost every film shown in the cinema is bought by broadcasters in their own country. In this country it is not the case.

Before you start your film you need to know what a UK film is worth. Study the gross box office figures for British films, it can be quite distressing to find out just how little some films actually took. For more up to date and in-depth figures you should look at Screen

guerilla films ltd

email david@guerilla-films.com
url www.guerilla-films.com
post 35 thornbury road, isleworth
middlesex tw7 4lq uk
tel 020 8758 1716 fax 020 8758 9364

david nicholas wilkinson
chairman

SALES

Finance which you can find at the BFI Library. Search out a UK film that is similar to yours and work out how well it actually did.

Q - What materials should a producer bring to you?

David - Photos. photos photos! 80% of the films that we have do not have enough or good photos. I would love everything including a 35mm trailer, otherwise I have to pay for one to be made. I have in the past paid £17k to get a trailer cut and I don't want to do that again. I want access to the negative at the lab, the digibeta / HD masters. I need lots of stills. It is the single biggest mistake I see repeated again and again; people come to me with 5 stills and expect it to be enough. I need lots. Producers don't seem to have any idea of the importance of having the actors available for promotion. I want the leading actors, the director and the writer available for promotion and if they have disappeared it makes it very awkward. The press will take a greater interest if they can interview someone who is reasonably well known.

If youre leading actor refuses to be interviewed then you are in real trouble, journalists are always looking for a story that is different to the one that you want to give them. You must remember that they are used to interviewing the stars of *The League of Gentlemen* or *It's All Gone Pete Tong,* because it is part of the lead's fee to promote the film around the world. So they will not read the best into your film if you can't provide them with your actor who used to be in *Emmerdale*. You should have a clause in your contracts with your actors for publicity. You must not blow your chance with doing publicity while you are shooting because it could be two years before your film reaches the cinema. Journalists will not give you a second chance. You can ask them to hold their piece until your movie comes out but they may not. For low budget films free marketing is vital.

Q - How often do you do your accounts?

David - Every three months. After two or three years I tend to drop that to every six months. Of course if a large cheque from TV comes in I will pay that out straight away. I did this with you on *Urban Ghost Story.* I recall you were very surprised.

Q - What is the FDA?

David - The Film Distributors Association. They look after us, make sure we behave and organise your screenings for the press. They schedule the official press screenings. It is then up to the distributor to organise and pay the costs. These are official FDA screenings which no one can clash with so that no distributor can arrange a competitive screening at the same time.

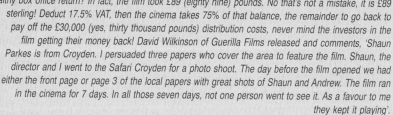

Offending Box Office

In 2001, film maker Andrew Rajan embarked on his debut feature, 'Offending Angels'. Andrew is a trained actor and was frustrated by the lack of opportunities he faced, so decided to make a feature film, write and direct, and star in it. He secured the finance to make it, shooting on Super 16mm film, with a plan to release in the cinema (blown up to 35mm). He also managed to attract a great cast, including Andrew Lincoln (from 'This Life' and 'Teachers') and Shaun Parkes (from 'The Mummy Returns'), plus a bunch of other excellent actors. The film was completed and a premiere raised the profile of the film by raising nearly £10k for charity! Then came the theatrical release. The P&A spend was around £30k, and the film was released in cinemas on four prints. Reviews were not good, but given that £30k was spent on P&A, that the charity event raised awareness and that the film had such an excellent cast, you would expect a healthy box office return? In fact, the film took £89 (eighty nine) pounds. No that's not a mistake, it is £89 sterling! Deduct 17.5% VAT, then the cinema takes 75% of that balance, the remainder to go back to pay off the £30,000 (yes, thirty thousand pounds) distribution costs, never mind the investors in the film getting their money back! David Wilkinson of Guerilla Films released and comments, 'Shaun Parkes is from Croyden. I persuaded three papers who cover the area to feature the film. Shaun, the director and I went to the Safari Croyden for a photo shoot. The day before the film opened we had either the front page or page 3 of the local papers with great shots of Shaun and Andrew. The film ran in the cinema for 7 days. In all those seven days, not one person went to see it. As a favour to me they kept it playing'.

So why did this film not perform? Let's rephrase. Why did only 15 people or so, pay to see this film? In part, it could be the reviews? Or the film concept (guardian angels coming to earth to help some hopeless lads find the meaning of it all)? Or the way the release was handled? Whatever the problems, it is an indicator of how hostile and hot the theatric market place actually is. The movie should be out on DVD now, so you can see what you think of the movie and why it may have failed.

Q - What is the BBFC? What are the classification tariffs?

Sue - The BBFC was set up by the film industry in 1912 to classify films on behalf of the local authorities in the UK, who are the bodies legally responsible for classifying films. We have been classifying films on their behalf ever since, but they retain the right to overrule our decisions at any time. We are funded entirely by the fees which we charge for classification. We classified 562 cinema films last year. In 1984 the Video Recordings Act was passed which requires that all videos, and now DVDs, be classified by the BBFC. Last year we classified over 11,000 of those as well as film trailers, video trailers, and cinema adverts.

Q - What are the classification categories?

Sue - The tariffs are U, PG, 12A, 12, 15, 18. In the case of U, the film is suitable for audiences aged four and over. For a PG any child may be admitted to the film or be able to rent or buy a video unaccompanied by an adult, however, PG warns parents that some scenes may be upsetting for younger children. For a 12A, no one under 12 may see a 12A film unless accompanied by an adult but in the case of the other categories, no person under the age indicated will be admitted to a cinema or be rented or sold a video. More detailed information of these classifications can be found on our website - www.bbfc.co.uk.

The Board employs around 75 people and of those around 30 actually watch the films and videos. They are made up of people of all ages and a range of backgrounds, including teachers, lawyers, social workers, academics etc who apply for the job of 'examiner' which are advertised in the UK national press.

Q - How long does it take and how much does it cost?

Sue - For a straightforward decision on a cinema film where there are no classification issues the average turnaround is around 3-5 working days. Our fees are based on the length of the work and a 90 minute film would cost around £660 plus VAT. There are concessionary fees and we actually charge less for foreign language films on the basis that fewer people will go to see them, and so they will make less money. There is a fee calculator on the website so anyone wishing to know what their film is likely to cost, including concessions, can check it out.

Q - How do filmmakers submit their films?

Sue - Information about the exact submission process is on our website, but there are some forms to fill out, the classification fee must be paid in advance, and the film is sent to our offices so we can watch it. We can handle film prints and we watch them in our own cinema to simulate the cinema going experience. As far as DVD submission is concerned the material is supplied on video although we are piloting receiving it on DVD. If it is a film for cinema release we prefer to see a film print. If it is for video / DVD release we take it on video.

Q - Can you submit the film before its full completion?

BBFC
The British Board of Film Classification
Sue Clark

Sue - Yes but only for advice. We need the completed film, complete with credits before we can issue a certificate.

Q - What happens with trailers?

Sue - They also have to be classified by the board in the same way and are submitted and watched in exactly the same way as a film. The same with advertisements as all cinema material is rated U to 18.

Q - What is likely to be rejected? How does the BBFC recommend cuts?

Sue - A full set of our classification guidelines is on our website. We would reject anything which is illegal and we have a very clear policy on sexual violence in particular, but other things might lead to a work being rejected, it is impossible to say categorically because it would depend on the treatment of the material as well as the content. As far as cuts are concerned, it would depend why the work was being cut. In some cases we would supply a detailed cuts list which the distributor would have to comply with to get the certificate, in other cases we might only indicate that certain material would need to be 'toned down' if the distributor was looking for a lower category for instance.

Q - When should filmmakers approach the board with their completed films?

Sue - The sooner the better. If a work needs to be cut, leaving it too close to the opening date could jeopardise the opening as we have to see the work again to be satisfied that the cuts have been made.

Q - Does the film have to be resubmitted again with the new cuts with another fee? Do you have an appeals board?

Sue - No there is no additional fee if the film has to be viewed again because of cuts. We do not have a formal appeals system for cinema because the ultimate responsibility lies with the local authorities. If a distributor really cannot accept our decision they are free to get a local authority ruling.

Q - What advice would you offer?

Sue - Check the guidelines if a particular category is required - it is no good putting a lot of strong language in a film if you are hoping to get a 12A for instance.

www.bbfc.co.uk

SALES

BBFC

The British Board of Film Classification rates films based on their content so that parents know what movies are appropriate for their children. It's likely that you will be able to guess what certificate your film will receive, just be aware that most film makers think their film is a bit 'older' than it actually is. So you may think it's an 18 cert film, but ends up getting a 15 cert. The certificate also sends out a message, for instance, 18 cert films do not play well outside of major cities. Remember also, the cert you get for the cinema release is NOT the cert you will get for the DVD, it may be different. For instance a horror film may just get a 15 cert for the cinema but get an 18 cert for DVD.

U - Universal. A film for any age. There can some very mild bad language, occasional natural nudity with no sexual context, mild sexual behavior like kissing and only very mild violence or threat of menace. There can be no references to illegal drugs unless the project is clearly an educational one citing anti-drug message.

PG - Parental Guidance. Any unaccompanied child may attend, but parents are advised to consider whether the content may upset younger or more sensitive children. Similar to Universal in language and nudity. Sexual activity must be discreet and infrequent. Moderate violence is allowed as long as it is not graphic. Weapons may not be glamourised. References to drugs must be innocuous and carry a suitable anti-drug message.

12 - No one under twelve admitted without an adult. Strong language allowed, but infrequent. Nudity allowed, but sexual context must be brief and discreet. Violence must not dwell on detail. More liberal uses of drug and horror are allowed.

12A - No one under twelve admitted. Similar to 12, but pushes the envelope more in content.

15 - No one under fifteen admitted. All themes are allowed. Strong language allowed as long as it is not overly aggressive. Nudity in a sexual manner allowed as long as it isn't too detailed. Violence may be strong, but cannot dwell on pain or injury. Threat or menace are permitted. Drug use is permitted as long as it does not promote or encourage its use.

18 - No one under eighteen admitted. Adult themes and graphic language, violence and sex.

R18 - Restricted eighteen. Basically, porn.

For more information, go to the BBFC's website at www.bbfc.co.uk. You can download the certifcates for your artwork at www.bbfc.co.uk/downloads/logos.html

Ten years ago three screenings would be fine but now you have to screen the movie perhaps 10 times to make sure everyone sees it. The journalist's workload often makes them request the movies on video, clearly the wrong medium to see the film. Sometimes I arrange a special screening just for one person as I would prefer them to see it in the cinema than on DVD, I prefer to send VHS with timecode as they are far harder to pirate.

Q - How big is the UK market on a global scale?

David - Europe is broken up into three types of territory, big, medium, and small. These definitions are based on how well films do in these territories. The head of the EU Media Film Programme told me a few years ago that she now considers the UK to be a small territory. British films do best in Europe, however you can have a British film, with a British cast, crew and money, it can sell to every country in Europe except for the UK! You must not be put off by this. The UK is only 5% of the world market. Unfortunately if you have not released in the UK, overseas distributors seem to think that there is something wrong with your movie.

Q - What mistakes do you see regularly?

David - I have been a producer myself and have made so many of these mistakes. It is a general perception to think that all you have to do is make a film and it will be sold / distributed / screened on TV etc. Every year every distributor in the world is offered far more films than they could ever take on. One year, I looked at 41 low budget British & Irish films and I have taken on 3 of them. Very few of those other ones have been picked up for the cinema. The large and medium distributors will have invested, co-produced or pre-bought a number of films before they are made. A great deal of their time and funds will be tied up with these films and much as they might like your completed film, most will just not have the resources to get involved with it. Most first time low budget films will be lucky to obtain a theatrical release. In 1997, of the 1000 non-studio films made in the USA, 60 had a theatric release and only 14 of those had a substantial release. In other words 940 either went straight to video / cable / TV or else they did not have any release.

Small films can be successful; it's all a matter of approach. Steven Lewis Simpson's 'The Ticking Man' was made for £30k. On paper that was recouped and more from licenses to small DVD companies around the world, hence the reason I became involved in his next film 'Retribution'. Steven has studied the market. I have already put in place finance for another film with him.

As the only UK distributor who only distributes UK/ Irish films (including co-productions) I always try to see every British films made and carefully consider it. I specialise in low budget films and ones that other distributors think difficult. Simon Rumley, a filmmaker I admire and someone I really like as a person, invited me to see his film The Truth Game. It was at a distributor screening and his goal was to secure a cinema release that year. I turned up the screening at Mr Young's and found that only one other distributor attended. Therefore I was in a way, one of the two most important people for him in the audience. To my surprise the screening room was packed with Simon's friends and assorted hangers on. By the time I arrived all the seats were taken. I had to sit at the front on the floor. Simon noticed this and did nothing. I suffer from a very bad back as a result of an accident and I also hate sitting too close to the screen. I should have left but he had gone to a great deal of trouble and expense to arrange for us distributors to see the film he had worked so hard on. After 15 minutes I wanted to leave. This was nothing to do with the film, but my back hurt so much I began to lose interest in the film. After 30 minutes I could not wait for it to finish. I would not leave. I had recently been reported in the press as saying "I will never walk out of a film. If the filmmakers have gone to so much effort and trouble, not to mention expense, the least I could do was watch their film". I think Simon had read the article.

When it was over Simon asked me what I thought. I lied and said something complimentary. I could not remember much about it. Needless to say I did not take the film on. He never did get a cinema release and I do not think it has sold to TV in the UK. Years later I saw it again on DVD. I liked it. I would have released it on 3 prints and it could have become part of a TV deal I did for a series of British films.

The experience summed up a lot of filmmakers view of the their films. You are not making a film for you and your friends. You are making it for a paying audience. I am sure that Simon thought that by having a friendly audience in attendance it would improve his chances of finding a UK distributor, but it did not. These days I tend to walk out of more films.

Example UK Theatric Release For Low Budget Feature

GUERILLA FILM MAKER SAYS!

Basic Costs	
BBFC Certification	£1,000
Prints	£5,000
Posters	£4,000
Trailer	£4,000
PR	£4,000
Advertising	£5,000
Shipping	£1,000
Fly Postering	£1,000
Misc	£500
Balance	£25,500

Gross Box Office	£150,000
Minus VAT at 17.5%	£127,659
25% paid from Cinema to distributor	£31,915
Minus distributors fees at 35% (£11,170)	£20,745
Minus Expenses Above (£25,500)	-£4,755
Balance (yes you owe the distributor!)	-£4,755

This example is for a fictitious film where everything has been done cost effectively. It is for a five print release, and quite frankly, it's done astonishingly well at the Box Office. More than likely it will have taken maybe £10k, instead of £150k. If that were the case, you can see how much money would be owed at the end! Any distributor would offset losses at the box office with sales to video and TV in all their various forms.

As for the digital screening debate, well you could possibly deduct the cost of prints and replace with digital costs at maybe, £1,000. The cinema costs, advertising, PR would all remain the same though. You would still not break even. And that is if the film takes £150k remember, which is EXTREMELY unlikely. To further amplify that sobering thought, it is worth noting that 40% of ALL films, from any country, released in the UK, gross less than £100k at the UK box office.

SALES

When People Go To The Movies (days)

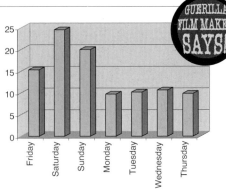

The chart to the right is an annual average of UK cinema attendance in 2004 (broken down into days). You can immediately see why exhibitors watch the weekend figures so closely. Roughly two thirds of cinema tickets are sold on the Fri / Sat / Sun weekend, the rest of the week generating around a third of sales. Knowing this, you may consider when to ask your cast and crew (who should bring everyone they know) to come and see the film. Ideally, Fri / Sat / Sun, but not in the evening if possible, afternoon showings are better as it's less likely your screenings will sell out, resulting in a possible situation where you could turn Joe public away.

Source CAA, Nielsen EDI / UK Film Council

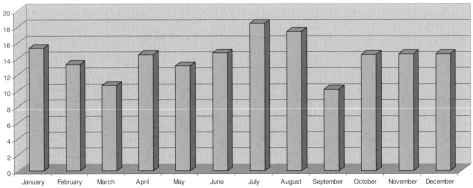

When People Go To The Movies (months)

The chart above shows the annual admission figures for the UK (in millions) for each month. In 2004, there were 171.3 million admissions. It's easy to see where the busy months are, where the Bonds, Harry Potters, Star Wars movies complete. But clearly March and September are quiet months. So do you release then, where there is possibly less competition? September is probably dipping as that is the start of the Academic year and students make up a large portion of the cinema going public.

Source CAA, Nielsen EDI / UK Film Council

I frequently receive emails from filmmakers wanting production funding, finishing funds, distribution etc., and then I see it is cc'd to dozens, sometimes hundreds of other film financiers, sales agents, distributors and broadcasters. A scattergun approach looks lazy, impersonal and unfocused. I am much more likely to respond when people say things like *'I visited your website we think that your company would be the best home for our film'* or *'we have long admired the work you have done'.* Flattery goes a long way in this business.

We all know that you are likely to go to many companies at the same time, it's the nature of the business, however why advertise the fact? Most of us will not think we must view this ASAP because look who else they have sent it to. We are more likely to think forget it, why bother, someone else is bound to beat me to it. They work so hard making the film they lose sight of the fact that they must continue to work both hard and professionally to sell it.

Q - What advice would you offer a new film maker?

David - Perseverance is the most important thing that you need to get your project off the ground. I once managed to sell a movie to a TV company and this took me nine years. They took it eventually just to shut me up. I think the reason why a lot of poor films reach the marketplace and the cinemas is because the people involved have not let go of it and pushed and pushed and pushed to get it out there. Every film has an audience even if it is only your mum and dad, so you have to be realistic. You have to step back and look at it for what it is. Put that script on a shelf for six months and come back and hopefully at that point you have managed to distance yourself from it and you can see where the inherent flaws are. Make sure that your Brit flick is not so full of topical British issues and very British jokes because these will not travel to Taiwan. Try to see the bigger picture.

As a filmmaker you must absolutely believe in your film, however you also need to be realistic about it. Try to look at it as an outsider. Watch videos of similar films to yours, then watch your film or read the script. BE HONEST. Why will anyone pay £5 to see your film? At the time of this interview (May 2005) there are 38 films being released in the cinema in this month alone. There are a number of films being held over from previous months. Even the most ardent film fan will only see a small percentage of them. In September 2005, in the run up to the Christmas market, 784 new DVD's were released in the UK. The majority of these titles were feature films. Most film makers seem to think that if a films fails in the cinema, it will do extremely well on DVD. This is rarely the case. I used to handle a British film with one of the biggest UK stars of the last 50 years. It was a $12m production with good reviews. However, in the five years I had the rights, we did a very small number of sales. No matter what I did, I couldn't shift it. The bottom line was, none of the retailers thought the film worthy of much shelf space. They didn't dislike the film, it's just that with so many others on offer, they could not justify stocking it in large numbers or for a long period.

Also know your limitations. I know one first time filmmaker who has become his own distributor and sales agent. He is not having to do this because the film has been rejected everywhere. He has not shown it to anyone. He just thinks he can take on these roles although he has no experience in selling or distributing. He is failing badly. The problem is that he will realise this too late. By the time he approaches an established company to act as either the Sales Agent or Distributor he will have blown it.

Q - New digital formats mean anyone can make a film. Surely that's a good thing?

Low Budget Films Distributor Share

In 2004 there were nine major distributors in the UK, most handling the Bond, Harry Potter, Bridget Jones and Hollywood style movies. The only distributor here worthy of note for low budget film makers is Momentum, as they have a track record of UK low budget film releases and a savvy interpretation of the market. In 2004 they released 18 films, grossing £18.4m in total, which is an average of just over £1m each film. The average is of no real use to an individual film or film maker, aside from assessing the market value of the types of film any given company releases. And if we were in bed with UIP at £6.03m per picture, releasing 42 films a year, we'd all be much happier.

Now your film and my film, that is if it's a low budget indie film, is likely to land in the 'others' category. Even though the 'other' distributors numbered over five times as many (52 in all) as the top nine, and release more films (288 in all) than the ten majors (who release 230), their average taking for each film is less than £150k. That staggering statistic means that on average, your film would capture less than 1% of the marketplace when released. That's LESS than 1%! Check out the pie chart and look at YOUR little one percent slice!

So who are these 'other' distributors? Companies like Guerilla Films and Redbus float at the very top of the pile, but the majority of producers or companies in this group are on a vanity release (as no commercial company would release the film). And don't get excited about that £150k average. Some of the films released by these distributors will be taking significantly more than £150k, illuminating the sad fact that most new film makers movies tend to take somewhere between £5k and £50k at the box office, usually around the £15-£20k mark (and remember, 17.5% of that goes to the VAT man, then the balance is split 75/25 in favour of the exhibitor (that's the cinema), the 25% going to the distributor who then takes their fees and uses the balance to repay the costs of the release.) Realistically, new film makers almost always get zero returns from the theatrical release.

How do you make a difference? Write a great script. Cast it brilliantly. Get enough money to do it justice. Make the best movie out of that mix as is possible. Get the best distributor you can. Help the distributor do the best job possible... So if you thought making a film was hard, releasing and making a film a success is off the scale.

Company	Films	Gross	Average
UIP	42	253.4	6.03
Warner Bros	22	125.1	5.69
Buena Vista Intl	42	122.9	2.93
20th Century Fox	23	91.2	3.97
Sony Pictures Intl	29	85.1	2.93
Entertainment	20	67.4	3.37
Pathé	23	23.4	1.02
Icon	11	19.2	1.75
Momentum	18	18.4	1.02
Others (52)	288	42.9	0.15
Totals	518	849	1.64

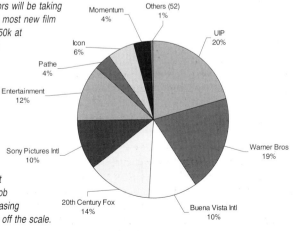

SALES

Distribution Pointers

GUERILLA FILM MAKER SAYS!

Much talk has (for some time now) been made about things like Internet Film Delivery and Digital Cinemas. But, and this is a big but, cinemas will always have staff, rent, rates and lighting, meaning that the expensive part of theatric distribution will remain similar to it's current 35mm status... And as for the Internet, let's wait and see, but we think it's going to be a LONG time before that technology, in any significant way, will rival DVD and Theatric distribution. If you want to reach a wide audience, sadly, things not only remain the same at the time of printing, but they will probably do so for years to come. Let's hope and pray we are wrong! So if you are going to work with an established distributor, here are some pointers to look for in the deal.

1. Cash Advance. Rarely given, usually only if the film needs completion money, in which case the distributor/agent might take a higher commission.

2. Number of Years for the rights to be licensed to the Distributor / Sales Agent: From 5 - 35, standard is 5-10 years. NOT in perpetuity. Try to have the initial term be relatively short (say 2 years) with automatic rollovers should the distributor deliver a certain amount of revenue in that time and / or deliver a specified release (so they just can't sit on the film and do nothing). If those performance requirements are not met, all rights would automatically return to the film maker.

3. Extent of Rights being requested by Distributor / Sales Agent: i.e worldwide, worldwide excluding domestic to be negotiated between the parties.

4. Fees / rate of commission: Usually between 20-25%. Sometimes 30% depending on the extent of input by Distributor/Sales Agent and this should be limited so that the Distributor takes only one commission per country.

5. Ownership: Make sure you, the producer, will still own the copyright to the Film. If you are licensing the rights to certain territories you will remain the copyright owner.

6. CAP on expenses: Make sure there is a maximum limit (a ceiling) on expenses and that you are notified in writing of any large expenses i.e. over a specified amount, that you are able to refute if necessary.

7. Direct Expenses: Make sure that overhead of the Distributor and the staff expenses are not included in Distribution expenses and will not be added as a further expense.

8. Sub Distributor Fees: Make sure that these fees are paid by the Distributor/Sales Agent out of its fees and not in addition to the Distribution expenses.

9. Consider your position on Net Receipts: i.e. monies after Distributor has deducted their commission and fees subject to any sales agreements you enter into with a Distributor. Make sure this is clearly delineated in the contract with no loopholes. Remember that taxes should be taken out of gross receipts not net receipts.

10. Errors and Omissions Policy: See if this is to be included in the delivery requirements as this could be an added unexpected expense. Distributors are often willing to absorb this cost and recoup from gross profits. It is important that you as the film maker are added as an additional named insured on the policy.

11. Cross Collaterisation: Where the Distributor will offset expenses and losses on their other films against yours. You don't want this.

12. P&A (Prints and Advertising) commitment from the Distributor: Negotiate total expenses that will be used on P&A in the contract i.e. a fixed sum. Include a floor and a ceiling.

13. Domestic Theatrical Release: Negotiate what print run is expected, and in what locations. Specify what locations so that you don't find a clause in your contract such as 'your film will be released in three of the top one hundred markets'.

14. Distribution Editing Rights: Limit for only censorship requirements although if you are dealing with a major Distributor this will not be acceptable.

15. Producer's input in the marketing campaign.

16. Trailer commitment: will this be another hidden additional cost? Make sure theatres have this in plenty of time.

17. Release Window: Get Distributor to commit to release the film within a time frame after delivery of film to Distributor.

18. Audit Rights: The Producer has the rights to inspect the books with a ten-day notice re: the distribution of the film. The Film maker should receive statements (either quarterly or monthly) from the distributor with any payment due to the film maker.

19. LIMITATION ON ACTION: You want to make sure that you have enough time to act on any accounting irregularity that you may discover. Fight to have at least a three- year period from receipt of a questionable financial statement, or discovery of any accounting irregularity, whichever is later, in which to file a demand for arbitration.

Distribution Pointers ...cont

GUERILLA FILM MAKER SAYS!

20. If the Sales Agent intends to group your film with other titles to produce an attractive package for buyers, ensure that your film is not unfairly supporting other films or that you are receiving a disproportionate or unfair percentage.

21. Make sure that the rights revert back to the Producer in case of any type of insolvency or if the Agent is in material breach of the agreement.

22. Check the Delivery requirements very carefully.

23. Indemnity: Make sure you receive reimbursement for losses incurred by you as a result of distributor's breach of the terms of the agreement, violation of third party rights, and for any changes or additions made to the film.

24. Lab Access Letter: Distributor should not be permitted to remove masters from the lab nor take possession of the original negative and any other original materials. They may have a lab access for supervised use of the negative and other materials for duplication or promotional purposes.

25. Termination Clause: If the distributor defaults on any of its contractual obligations, the film maker should have the right to terminate the contract, and regain rights to license the film in unsold territories as well as obtain money damages for the default. The Film maker should give distributor 14 days prior written notice of default before exercising the right to termination.

26. Arbitration Clause: This ensures that any contractual disputes may be solved through binding arbitration with the prevailing party entitled to reimbursement of legal fees and cost by the losing party. For the best results, the parties should submit such action to binding arbitration with a licensed UK Arbitration entity or if it's a US company, with the AFMA (American Film Market Association) arbitration division. The Distributor will fight for Arbitration to take place near them locally. If they're not local to you, either fight for arbitration to occur locally to you or in a place of equidistance to the two of you.

27. Film maker Warranties: Film maker warranties in regard to infringement of third party rights should be to the best of the Film maker's knowledge and belief, not absolute.

28. LATE PAYMENTS/LIEN: All monies due and payable to the film maker should be held in trust by the distributor for the film maker, and the film maker should be deemed to have a lien on film maker's share of revenue. The distributor should pay the film maker interest on any amounts past due.

29. SCHEDULE OF MINIMUMS: For each foreign territory for which a distributors or foreign sales agent who licenses foreign sales rights, there should be a schedule of minimum acceptable license fees per territory. The distributor is not permitted to license the film in each territory for less than the minimum without the film maker's approval.

30. FILM MAKER DEFAULT: The distributor should give film makers 14 days written notice of any alleged default by film maker, and an additional 10 days to cure such a default, before taking any action to enforce its rights.

David - It is a good thing but it is also a bad thing. The biggest problem the film industry has now is that there are just too many films in the world. Around 500 films are distributed in the UK in the cinema every year. Many of these films, I would estimate 200, do not even make back there P&A let alone any of the production investment. However over 3,000 films are made each year. With digital formats, the number of films made will hugely increase. Most people, broadcasters, cinemas etc., only have a finite amount of time to view / screen films. With more films in the marketplace it will become much tougher to sell them.

On average, there about 100-125 new DVD titles coming out each week. This should go down once everyone's back catalogue is on DVD, but there will still be more titles released than most stores can feature. Take a large DVD store in say Wolverhampton, they could only put something like 10-20 new titles on their shelves and only then for a short period. They just don't have the shelf space for everything. Yes Amazon would feature everything but just because it is on their site it does not mean someone will buy it. Every DVD is competing with over 35,000 others. By 2010 that could be almost 100,000 titles.

When you make your film, you will be able to secure fantastic deals across the board, from actors to facilities companies, working for much less than their normal rate, in some cases for free, for a number of reasons. This will not happen when it comes to sales and distribution. As an example, film makers are always trying to get me to negotiate low advertising rates with Time Out (London). Time out charge me £1.5k for a half page B&W advert that will run for a week. There is nothing that I or any film maker can do to reduce that. They are a commercial organisation and that is their charge.

SALES

447

UK Box Office 2003

This is a chart of UK films, or UK co-productions, and how they performed at the box office in 2003. Many of the films were UK co-productions purely to take advantage of UK tax laws at the time, so there a good few you can discount as not really being British. Still, it's fascinating to see just how much they took at the box office. In previous editions we also listed their budget, but getting that information now is too hard, and when you do get it, frankly, we don't believe it! There are a number of sub £150k films where producers and sales agents have sworn blind that the budget was two point whatever million pounds! Clearly a commercial 'modification of the truth' designed to take advantage of old tax laws. So rather than give inaccurate budget info, we have omitted it altogether.

Go through the list, see what movies you recognise, what you don't, check them out on IMDB, then see how much they took. This will give you an idea of just how 'hot' the UK theatrical marketplace can be. We have calculated average ticket prices at £5, which then gives you a rough idea of just how many people turned out to see the movie.

Lastly, remember, these are gross figures... 17.5% goes to the VAT man, the balance is the split 75 / 25, with 75% going to the cinema. The distributor then takes their commission of say, 35% out of that meagre 25%, then they pay back all their costs such as advertising, BBFC classification, posters, trailers, PR, prints (digital prints will only save a fraction of the cost of delivering a film to the cinema when it switches to digital). If there is anything left, you will get your money, but let's face it, it's very unlikely anything will be left. You will get used to feeling like a chef who baked an amazing pie. Everyone feasted before you, and literally, nothing, not even scraps, were left for the creator.

Title	Distributor	Country of Origin	Box Office Gross £	Approx tickets sold
Actors, The	Momentum Pictures	UK/US/Ireland	£458,220	91,644
Aileen: Life And Death Of A Serial Killer	Optimum Releasing	UK	£12,702	2,540
Alien - Director's Cut	Twentieth Century Fox	US/UK	£543,350	108,670
American Cousins	Bard	UK	£24,054	4,811
Blackball	Icon Film Dist.	UK	£889,238	177,848
Bodysong	Pathe Distribution	UK	£12,933	2,587
Bollywood Queen	Redbus	UK	£50,246	10,049
Boy David Story, The	Ratpack	UK	£1,444	289
Bright Young Things	Icon Film Dist.	UK	£1,085,470	217,094
Buffalo Soldiers	Pathe Distribution	UK/US/Germany	£1,098,522	219,704
Calendar Girls	Buena Vista	UK/US	£20,427,788	4,085,558
Citizen Verdict	Georgia Films	UK	£9,593	1,919
Cold Mountain	Buena Vista	UK/US	£9,118,817	1,823,763
Concert For George	Pathe Distribution	UK	£11,413	2,283
Core, The	UIP	US/UK	£1,591,786	318,357
Devil's Gate	Independent UK	UK	£2,908	582
Draughtman's Contract, The (reissue)	ICA Projects	UK	£1,741	348
Emotional Backgammon	Buccaneer	UK	£1,046	209
Evelyn	Pathe Distribution	UK/US/Germ/Ire/Neth	£1,445,396	289,079
Feardotcom	Columbia tristar	UK/Germany/Lux/US	£57,931	11,586
Fogbound	Blue Dolphin	UK/Netherlands	£1,033	207
Four Feathers	Buena Vista	US/UK	£164,725	32,945
Good Thief, The	Momentum Pictures	UK/France/Can/Ire	£325,514	65,103
Hard Word, The	Metrodome	Australia/UK	£67,912	13,582
Heart Of Me, The	Pathe Distribution	UK/Germany	£239,779	47,956
Heartlands	Buena Vista	US/UK	£72,228	14,446
Hoover Street Revival	Metro Tartan	UK/France	£14,075	2,815
Hope Springs	Buena Vista	US/UK	£1,062,100	212,420
Hours, The	Buena Vista	UK/US	£4,697,689	939,538
I Capture The Castle	Momentum Pictures	UK	£1,043,230	208,646

Title	Distributor	Country of Origin	Box Office Gross £	Approx tickets sold
I'll Be There	Warner Bros.	UK/US	£30,688	6,138
In America	Twentieth Century Fox	UK/Ireland	£1,900,096	380,019
In The Cut	Pathe Distribution	US/Australia/UK	£1,051,871	210,374
In The Name Of Buddha	Miracle Communications	UK	£50,500	10,100
In This World	ICA Projects	UK	£147,623	29,525
Innocence	Capers Matcine	UK/Australia	£6,058	1,212
Intermission	Buena Vista	UK/Ireland	£2,142,126	428,425
Italian Job, The	UIP	US/UK	£7,713,411	1,542,682
Johnny English	UIP	UK/US	£19,650,225	3,930,045
Last Great Wilderness, The	Feature Film Co.	UK/Denmark	£27,672	5,534
Late Twentieth, The	Timeless Pictures	UK	£4,442	888
L'homme Du train	Pathe Distribution	UK/France /Germ	£437,681	87,536
Live Forever	Helkon Sk	UK	£22,066	4,413
Love Actually	UIP	UK/US	£36,450,860	7,290,172
Max	Pathe Distribution	UK/Can/Germ /Hungary	£133,309	26,662
Miranda	Pathe Distribution	UK/Germany	£8,641	1,728
Most Fertile Man In Ireland	Ian Rattray Films	UK/Ireland	£4,799	960
Mother, The	Momentum Pictures	UK	£280,494	56,099
Mr In-Between	Verve Pictures	UK	£7,846	1,569
Mrs. Caldicot's Cabbage War	Arrow Films	UK	£16,415	3,283
Mystics	Momentum Pictures	UK/Ireland	£12,666	2,533
Ned Kelly	UIP	UK/Australia	£524,022	104,804
Nicholas Nickleby	Twentieth Century Fox	UK/US/Germ/Neth	£1,244,263	248,853
Nine Dead Gay Guys	Guerilla Films	UK	£12,685	2,537
Noi Albinoi	Artificial Eye	Iceland/Germany/UK/Den	£115,510	23,102
Octane	Buena Vista	UK/Luxembourg	£19,061	3,812
One And Only, The	Pathe Distribution	UK/France	£113,150	22,630
Otherworld	Miracle Communications	UK	£1,272	254
Petites Coupures	Artificial Eye	France/UK	73,897	14,779
Pianist, The	Pathe Distribution	UK/France/Germ/Poland	£2,972,334	594,467
Puckoon	Guerilla Films	UK/Ireland/Germany	£5,991	1,198
Pure	Artificial Eye	UK	£26,947	5,389
Revenger's Tragedy	Metro Tartan	UK	£42,278	8,456
Ripley's Game	Entertainment	UK/US/Italy	£1,011,364	202,273
S Club Seeing Double	Columbia tristar	UK	£2,317,357	463,471
Safety Of Objects, The	Entertainment	US/UK	£8,231	1,646
Shape Of Things, The	Momentum Pictures	US/France/UK	£60,006	12,001
Shoreditch	Georgia Films	UK	£2,272	454
Song For A Raggy Boy	Abbey Home Entertainment	UK/Ireland/Den/Spain	£479,243	95,849
Spider	Helkon Sk	UK/France/Can/Jap	£326,414	65,283
Spin The Bottle	Buena Vista	UK/Ireland	£362,842	72,568
Steal	Redbus	UK	£40,331	8,066
Summer Things	UGC Films	UK/France/Italy	£132,238	26,448
Swimming Pool	UGC Films	UK/France	£715,155	143,031
Taking Sides	Guerilla Films	UK/France/Germ/Austria	£9,576	1,915
Ten Minutes Older: Cello	Blue Dolphin	UK/Germany	£1,615	323
That Girl From Rio	Helkon Sk	UK/Spain	£488	98
Thirteen	UIP	US/UK	£276,411	55,282
This Is Not A Love Song	Soda Pictures	UK	£1,709	342
To Kill A King	Pathe Distribution	UK/ Germany	£262,102	52,420
Tomb Raider 2	UIP	UK/US/Germ/Jap/Neth	5,297,335	1,059,467
Touching The Void	Pathe Distribution	UK	£2,217,479	443,496
Underworld	Entertainment	UK/US/Germ/Hungary	4391553	878,311
Veronica Guerin	Buena Vista	UK/US/Ireland	£3,304,231	660,846
What A Girl Wants	Warner Bros.	UK/US	£873,699	174,740
Wilbur Wants To Kill Himself	Icon Film Dist.	UK/Den/Swed/France	£127,340	25,468

SALES

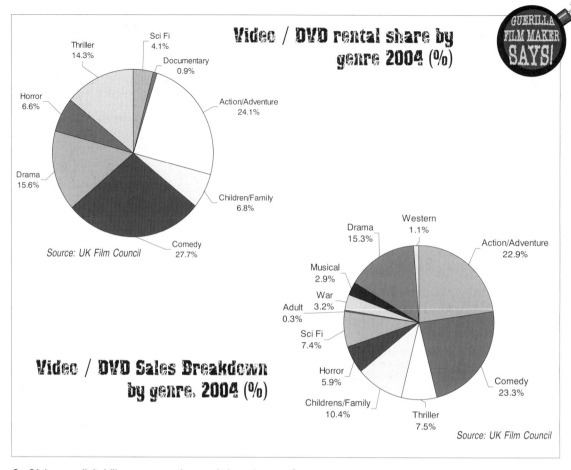

Video / DVD rental share by genre 2004 (%)

- Thriller 14.3%
- Sci Fi 4.1%
- Documentary 0.9%
- Action/Adventure 24.1%
- Horror 6.6%
- Drama 15.6%
- Children/Family 6.8%
- Comedy 27.7%

Source: UK Film Council

Video / DVD Sales Breakdown by genre, 2004 (%)

- Drama 15.3%
- Western 1.1%
- Action/Adventure 22.9%
- Musical 2.9%
- War 3.2%
- Adult 0.3%
- Sci Fi 7.4%
- Horror 5.9%
- Childrens/Family 10.4%
- Thriller 7.5%
- Comedy 23.3%

Source: UK Film Council

Q - Of the new digital films you see, what are their weaknesses?

David - Content. A film that is going to stand out has to be really good. So many I see are half good. Everyone seems to rush into making the film. I have one film, featured in your book, that nearly had a very, very high price paid for from a broadcaster, but in the end, it was decided that it was just not a good as it could have been, and as a result they decided just not to take it. They are offered thousands of films a year from all around the world and therefore can be very choosy.

Q - What advice would you offer a digital film maker on a micro budget?

David - Bring in someone on your film with an established track record in film. Ask them how you can make it better. All films can be improved. First time filmmakers are nearly always blind to their own film but hugely censorious about other first time filmmakers. They think all other first time films are crap and theirs is a work of genius. I was in Cannes one year and some first timers came to me with a film I liked. Before we started they had a go at two films I distribute, saying they were 'shit' and 'should not have been made', and that 'their film was so much better'. I walked away. They have spent the last two years trying to get me to change my mind as I am the only UK distributor to show any interest in their film. Don't be a twat. First time filmmakers are more opinionated than anyone else in this business. It's not a quality that will ensure longevity in the film business. I think it's the single biggest reason that most first timers fall by the wayside.

Make the best film you can. Listen and evaluate advice. If someone criticises you, do not take it personally. They may have a valid point. I have been in the business for 35 years, produced a dozen films that have won many awards, I have distributed over 100 feature films and yet I still get things wrong. Everyone does. Sadly most first times will never acknowledge this - until it is too late.

Digital Theatres - Arts Alliance Media

Richard Phillips
www.artsalliancemedia.com

Q - What is your job?

Richard - I'm the head of Technical Operations for Arts Alliance Digital Cinema. I'm responsible for all technical aspects of our digital cinema projects. We are a systems integrator. We sit between the existing film distributors and existing exhibitors, and offer the interface that enables them to take advantage of digital technology, so that might include recommending and installing equipment, maintaining that equipment, training the operators, preparing digital content for distribution, upgrading equipment as standards change etc.

Q - What's the advantage of Digital Projection to filmmakers?

Richard - The main advantage is that they can potentially get a much wider release of their film without the additional cost of extra prints. Because the digital prints are so much cheaper to make, they can potentially release simultaneously on lots of sites across the country. There are also advantages in terms of the image quality, and most people now agree that digital presentation looks at least as good as 35mm, and in most cases better. It doesn't suffer from degradation and wear and tear in the same way as film prints. The way that scheduling at cinemas has evolved is really a result of the fact that they have to book prints and then run with those prints for a release window. There is no reason why, with digital technology, that shouldn't change. A typical digital cinema server may store many movies at the same time, and they could show them at different times throughout the day, much more easily than if they had to reload their film platter with another print in between shows. It offers more flexibility, especially for special events like The Rocky Horror Show on a Friday night.

Q - What is a digital print?

Richard - The electronic copies of film that are distributed for digital projectors (vs the old celluloid prints)have become known as digital prints. We use the term digital print because it is something that people understand. They understand the concept of a print, they understand that the film has to somehow be sent to an exhibitors site. And we do send the digital files physically, on removal hard disks, and it's not sent over the Internet or via satellite. It is language that is easily transferable, but what it really means is a hard disk with all thefiles. Some of the films are quite small, it depends on the complexity of the material. I was looking at Casablanca this morning, and that is a 28gb file.

Q - So I've made my low budget independent feature film, I want it to go into the digital system somehow, what do I supply, and who do I supply it to?

Richard - We will in due course match the standards that Hollywood has been moving towards with DCI. DCI stands for Digital Cinema's Initiative. The main Hollywood studios got together and came up with a set of standards that they wanted the rest of the world to use as a replacement for 35mm film. Currently (2006), we ask for an HD master of the film, then we would encode that to the digital cinema master at our offices in Olympia. We create the digital prints from that. We accept all formats though we express a preference for HDCamSR, because it is higher quality, but HD-D5 and HDCam are also acceptable.

Q - Will film makers be able to show other formats, such as DVD, BluRay, HDVD?

Richard - The systems that we install also supplies an interface that will allow cinemas to connect standard definition DVD players, and also DigiBeta players, for running those sort of independent events, festivals etc. In theory, it should be able to play anything, assuming the venue has a player.

Q - What about piracy?

Richard - The movies are encrypted when they are sent out, so they are no use to anyone who intercepts them. The system also gives extra tools for content owners to manage when and where their content is shown. They can give us instructions to generate security locks for particular venues, particular screens, with particular playout windows. It would not play at other times, in other screens or other venues. There is also digital watermarking, so it is possible to embed invisible signals into the content at the time of exhibition, that are then recoverable from any attempts at pirating that content, so you can pinpoint where and when the content theft took place. A lot of the effort of the DCI was put into the security side of standardisation, and it is very secure. They are using the same protocols as the guys who run ATM machines. They take it very seriously.

Q - Who is going to control the content? Who chooses what gets shown?

Richard - As far as we are concerned it is still up to the distributors and exhibitors to agree between each other what films are going to be shown and when, it is not for us to get involved in that. We are just the technology enabler.

Q - What advice would you give to a new filmmaker?

Richard - Follow your instincts and do what you want to do.

Ian Rattray
Ratpack Films

FILM BOOKER

Q - What is your job?

Ian - My job is to get films into cinemas. Among other things, I am a film booker.

Q - Who do normally you get involved with - the Film makers or distributors?

Ian - It can be both.

Q - At what point do you get involved?

Ian - Usually at the last minute, when they've finished editing and they suddenly think *'What are we going to do with this?'* I try to get involved as early as possible, even at script stage.

Q - Is that because you can advise on market realities?

Ian - Yes, even simple things like the BBFC certificate, making a film that is going to be an 18 certificate but that is commercial death for small towns. Perhaps your film is aimed at 15 year old boys, but it is going to have an 18 certificate so it is going to miss its target audience.

Q - Do new film makers come to you?

Ian - It happens all the time. I will give you an example, I've just released a film called *'New Town Original'*, on behalf of New Town films, who I met through losing my wallet! They found it in the back of a taxi and then sent it back to me! It's chance meetings like that. Or someone will recommend a film.

Q - Do you think more films deserve a theatrical release?

Ian - No! Normally the average UK independent film is not good enough to be released in cinemas, or simply does not have theatrical potential. It's a very tough market. Of course I know that comment won't stop anyone trying, and if the film is good enough, it should rise to the surface.

Q - What do you think are the common mistakes a new film maker makes when they think they have made a good theatrical movie, but they have not?

Ian - It is a very difficult thing to quantify, but essentially you know in your gut when you see it. I just have to be honest with them and tell them what I think. Not every film deserves to be released, and a lot of films that get released don't deserve to be released. It's also true that some films that should be released are never released.

Q - If a new film maker comes to you with their film, they are effectively acting as the distributor. How does the process work? What do you do on a day to day basis?

Ian - The first step is to screen the film for the exhibitors - that's the cinema owners. If some of the exhibitors like it, then you have got to put a release date on it, and that is a bit of black art as you can never know how the dynamics of the release schedules for films will work. Nor can you tell how the public will react to the weather for instance, so aside from the strengths or weakness of the film, there are other factors too. For instance, there is no point putting your film out in the same week as a similar film. You have got to be prepared to move around, and if it comes to it, you must move the date of your release to get some distance from something else.

Q - What happens about the PR?

Ian - You need a marketing campaign for which you will need a film PR person. That is the easiest way to get coverage for your film without it costing too much. You are paying for the PR person who will get you features, articles and reviews, but you are not paying for newspaper ads or television space. It is crucial to have something to hang the film on - cast, poster, title, concept - that goes back to when you are making the film you have got to think about who you are actually making the film for.

Q - What do you need from the film maker in order to release the film?

Ian - I need a poster, a marketing campaign, a trailer, and of course the film. I need as much information about the film as I can possibly be given. The crucial thing for first time film makers is to remember to get strong and emotive images to give to the press.

Q - Generally as an independent film, are you going to make a million pounds at the box office?

Ian - No. Think of the theatrical as the shop window for your DVD / TV and International sales - it is in many ways a PR exercise and if the film manages to break even in the cinemas, well you treat that as a huge success. On an average, if your film took a £1m at the box office, you would get about £300k of that back.

Q - How do you get paid?

Ian - Two ways. I get paid on a flat fee, or a get paid from a percentage.

Q - Which is the best deal for the independent film maker?

Ian - I would go for flat paid fees, because if their film does take off, it will cost them a lot.

Q - Do you get involved in TV and DVD?

Ian - No.

Q - How is the revenue from the cinema release calculated?

Ian - It is calculated on what you call the *'house nut'*. Each cinema has an individual house nut and every cinema is different. It is based on how many seats you have. As an example, if the house nut is set to £1k, if you took £1k, the first 17.5% would got to the VAT man, then the balance would be split 75/25 in the exhibitors favour, the distributor getting 25%. Once the film takes more than £1k the balance shifts to the distributor who then gets 75% and the exhibitor keeps 25%.

Q - So the key to a financially successful independent film is to cram that cinema, as much as you can, not release on as many screens as you can, but focus on filling each screen?

Ian - You want to have a high screen average, that is what everyone quotes about the film, the screen average, screen average, screen average!

Q - What makes a film stand out?

Ian - Subject matter, performances, pace, and the look of it. Just a well made film that keeps you held there.

Q - How important is the poster, trailer and title?

Ian - It is everything. The poster art is what everyone sees first, they may not actually stare at it, but they will register it. You must have a catchy title. That is so important. The trailer is also very important. These days you can get the trailer out on the Internet and DVD as well as the cinema. It is very important. Talent (cast) is crucial too. The talent that you use to make the film, and to promote the film, is what journalists pick up on.

Q - If a new film maker is doing a release through you, how involved should they be?

Ian - Be involved but listen to what people tell you, because you are working with people who have done it before, they have learned their lessons and they are going to help you avoid making the same mistakes.

Q - So given that you accessible, why would any film maker use a distributor?

Ian - If you do it right yourself, you should get more back. Then your money comes straight back to you and it doesn't get to a Distributor who then charges you a fee and their expenses.

Q - Would you recommend working with a distributor for the DVD release, or would you do it yourself?

Ian - You can actually do a DVD yourself quite easily, as long as you get the guy who gets them into HMV to work with you. It is companies like Golds who actually sell them to the shops, not you, so you have got to convince them to pick the film up. You can make the discs yourself, it is not difficult or expensive. It will be easier to do with a distributor, but it's not impossible to do it yourself.

Q - All of this begs the question, what is the distributor doing? Because if the distributor rings you up and says, book the film, then rings a PR agent and says do the PR... I'm not trying to put distributors out of jobs, I'm just saying new film makers could maximize their profit by doing it all themselves?

Ian - Yes, but if the film goes through an established distributor, he can get the right people to turn up to watch the film. You can't do that on your own. That is the key bit of knowledge that I have.

Q - Who are these people?

Ian - These are the people who put the films into the cinemas. They are key. Each have different tastes and are looking to book films for specific theatres - so there is no point trying to get an action thriller booked into the Notting Hill Gate theatre in London for instance.

Q - What common mistakes do you see?

Ian - Film makers have an amazing belief in their films and they never give up. There has to be a stage where they accept it is not going to work. It's time to move on to your next project. Get a good editor too. I'm not a great believer in Directors / Writers / Editors doing everything. Editors are very good at what they do and you should let them edit your film to be as tight as possible. There is nothing worse than an overlong and drawn out film.

Q - What advice would you offer a new film maker?

Ian - From my point of view, think of who you are making the film for, you are not making it for yourself, you are making it for people to sit and watch in the cinema. That is what you have got to think about from the beginning. You can have the best film in the world, but if people are not interested in it, they are not going to come and see it.

Reuben Barnes
Soho Screening Rooms

Screening Rooms In London

Q - What are preview theatres?

Reuben - Preview theatres or screening rooms are theatres, which are for hire to show films provided by the customer for commercial purposes - i.e. to sell a film to sales agents or distributors, or to do test screenings or press screenings. It's a place where you can professionally present your work to a group of people you invite. We can screen 35mm in all its aspect ratios, with full Dolby and Dolby Digital. We can also project video, usually off Beta SP, DV and DVD. The smallest theatre costs £80 an hour, the medium £100 an hour and the largest £110 an hour. There is an extra £20 per hour for all theatres after 6pm. The smallest theatre seats twenty-five people, the medium sized theater seats forty-one and the largest forty-four. Most preview theatres are about these sizes. If you want larger you can hire a cinema on a Sunday morning for instance.

Q - What are your observations after seeing many new film makers films?

Reuben - It is different making a short to making a feature. Features are about pace and storytelling, Shorts are about grabbing your attention and looking good. It is a really tricky one. The thing about HD is that I was so anti-HD and everything that goes with it, 'Oh no, it won't change, I love film!', but I've seen the stuff they are doing now on HD and it is phenomenal.

Q - In terms of when you present material electronically, either DVD, or DVCam etc., what are the technical problems that you usually run into?

Reuben - With DVD the problem is obviously if people have scratches or fingerprints, the DVDs can skip. With tape we don't really have problems. Only price-wise, obviously hiring the equipment. There are so many different HD types. I've got a list of about 10 different formats of HD on my wall. You have to be really quite clear of how you want it.

Q - When you speak to distributors you obviously see the same old faces over and over again every year. What do you think their reaction to independent films is?

Reuben - I think that they probably enjoy those kinds of things far more than anything that Hollywood can produce. Hollywood films have become so formulaic now and you will be pushed to find one that is really good. Little independent films, when they work, are just phenomenal. I'd say 90% of stuff I'm showing is independent stuff. If it works, it is brilliant. What I consider a great film for film festivals is not possibly a film that would do well on the market though. Whenever the film festival guys come to see me, they all ask me whether I've seen anything good. I say 'Well this film is great, but I don't know if it will make a lot of money, but as a festival film it will get your audience really excited'. I would say most of the distributors I get, mostly acquisitions people, are just interested in seeing things that are either slightly different or are going to make money.

Q - Everyone in sales and distribution knows your facility, and others like it, and they are comfortable coming here. So rather than trying to set up some strange venue, is it going to help you film by screening at a proper preview theatre?

Reuben - If we were being honest, I would say we are the filmmakers' number one. I still have all the massive directors on my books and they all insist on screening here.

Q - What times are best for distributors?

Reuben - Mid morning and mid afternoon are the best times for distributors. However, press shows and test screenings fare better at lunch time or early evening, when you can offer the viewers something to eat or drink.

Q - What about food and drinks?

Reuben - We supply both food and drinks on request, with a little warning. You can bring your own food and drinks if you like.

Q - What are the common technical mistakes that you encounter?

Reuben - Missed reel changes due to a print not being 'spotted'. It's also worth remembering that prints get dirty quickly, especially if they have been used at film festivals, so don't expect it to look crisp and clean if your print has been around the block (although it can be helped a little by ultrasonic cleaning).

Q - What advice would you offer a new film maker?

Reuben - Just get out there and shoot it. But don't start filming until the script is absolutely right. We often see disappointed film makers who only realise they didn't work hard enough on the script when the sales agent walks out ten minutes into the screening. It doesn't matter what your budget is, just get out there and do it. If it works it works. You have got to be really tenacious. I've been projecting and doing all this kind of stuff for 15 years and I have seen people literally going from runner to being a producer or director. You have got to take the knocks and keep coming back.

Reuben Barnes
The Soho Screening Rooms,
14 D'Arblay Street, London
W1F 8DY

Tel: 020 7437 1771
Fax: 020 7734 4520

SALES

Robert Kenny
Curzon Cinemas

EXHIBITORS

Q - What is your job?

Robert - I am the general manager at Curzon Cinemas. I oversee everything that goes on here. The exciting stuff is events such as Q&As and festivals, but also the more mundane stuff like ordering new lamps for a projector or organising the artwork in the bar.

Q - How do you get a film into your theatre?

Robert - When someone makes a film it is very difficult to get that film screened unless you have a distributor for it. A distributor will put a lot of money behind the promotion of the film and we work closely with distributors. It is a two way process. Curzon Cinemas work with smaller distributors who usually have foreign language films or more specialised film. Sometimes we will work with a US studio if they have a crossover film. Sometimes we screen films that do not have a distributor by negotiating directly with the film maker or the producer. We will only do that if we get really excited about the film.

Q - How would a film maker who does not have a distributor get you to screen his film?

Robert - I work with a lot of talented colleagues who's judgment I trust. So, when I get a tape or a DVD in of a film, I will give it to them and ask them to watch it and then tell me what they think about it. If it fits in with what we are trying to do, we'll try to work a way to show it. It could be part of a festival or a late night show. If we like it, we will try to find it an audience. Usually, the film makers are really motivated and they do as good a job as a distribution company in promoting that film. Four years ago, we were one of the first to screen *McLibel*, which was about one of the longest running trials in British history. We screened it three or four times in the last few years because the director keeps on adding bits onto the end, and every time we get fantastic response to it.

Q - When you screen films like that, do you find them a loss making exercises?

Robert - I don't think we do it to make money as such. We do make a small profit. For example, *Paradise Lost*, which was distributed by Luke Morris of Warp Films, screened as a late film and got over a hundred people in to see it when it started at eleven o'clock at night. It was two and a half hours long. A lot of that was down to Warp Films being good at what they are doing. When we are showing films like this, we are showing it to have something different on our screens.

Q - Can the cinemas afford to show movies that make losses?

Robert - It is a balance. If we were solely in the business of making money, we would show Hollywood films. But Curzon Cinemas is a privately owned company that has two cinemas in the West End. We made a conscious decision to show films that are different. We do have rent to pay, so we do have to make some money and I won't hide the fact that we sell popcorn, ice cream and we have a bar. Those things subsidise what we really want to do, which is to show challenging and meaningful films. It is not a situation where we would show a Turkish film or a Lithuanian film and say we need to sell two hundred seats for the next two weeks. We are usually happy to get thirty-five people in for a main show on a Tuesday night. We will show cross-over art house films like *The Motorcycle Diaries*, but we will play alongside it films from new film makers.

Q - If a film maker comes to you to exhibit a film directly, what kind of profit split can they expect?

Robert - A general rule of thumb, we would negotiate a sixty percent split to us and a forty percent split to the film maker. This is mainly because we have the overhead - the building, the lighting, etc. But that is not what we would get from a normal feature film. Exhibitor cuts in the UK are very high compared to the rest of Europe. My colleagues there get something like a fifty-five percent split and are astounded that I get between sixty percent to seventy-five percent when I deal with a distributor. It is a convoluted financial equation that determines that amount. Is it on my biggest screen or my smallest? Is it in its first week or its ninth? Stuff like that.

Q - How closely do you work with distributors?

Robert - We are in constant dialogue. They will have a slate of films that they want us to see and then we negotiate things like release date and which screen it will be on. We usually know all of this a few months before the film gets screened and you have to be in touch constantly to organise that.

Q - If you screen a film directly from a film maker, who pays for advertising?

Robert - Each case is negotiated individually between us and the film maker. And it really depends on what is involved. Warp Films are very good about getting a buzz out about a film and they have Warp Records so they can use that to help promote things. However, we get posters made at our cost. We will put things in our program and the film maker won't get charged by us because that is part of our advertising. We will also do e-mail blasts to our customers.

Q - How has digital and HD projection changed exhibition and the Curzon chains?

Robert - Not as markedly as it will in the near future. The UK Film Council has something called the Digital Screen Network where they are using Lottery money to award digital projection equipment to one hundred and fifty cinemas around the UK. We had to make business plans to say how we would use the equipment and how we would promote specialised films. The point of it is not so much updating theatres as giving specialised, non-Hollywood films a venue to be seen. At the moment, we have been told how many theatre screens are going to get the digital equipment. For 'phase one', they have chosen two locales, Lancashire and Yorkshire, out of central London to put six digital theatres. Most of the rest are in the West End and they will generally get the films on the first day of release.

Q - Is digital projection better than traditional projection?

Robert - The equipment that the UK Film Council is getting into theatres is very good quality. I went to see a film in a multiplex in Wandsworth a few months ago and I cannot tell the difference. They were used at the NFT, whose audiences are notoriously difficult to please, and they got a 96% approval rating. The purists believe that 35mm is the best and can never be beaten, and I can see that, but it will be the same thing as the vinyl versus CD argument that happened twenty years ago. And soon they will be running alongside each other. I think that films will still be delivered on 35mm, but in twenty years time it may be more of a niche market.

Q - Will not having 35mm prints streamline the exhibition process?

Robert - Our projectionists are going to be over the moon! A two hour film is broken down into five or six reels and they have to tape them together in the right order and the right way around, screen the film and then at the end of the run, break it down and send it on to the next venue. Then that projectionist has to do that same process all over again. With digital we get an HD tape that is delivered to site, then we download the movie and they press a few buttons and there is the film. Then we just send the tape onto the next cinema. The advantage to people who watch films is that hopefully the image is not going to deteriorate over a number of years. Every Sunday we show a double

Robert Kenny

Curzon Soho
93-107 Shaftesbury Avenue
London
W1D 5DY
020 7734 9209

Curzon Mayfair
38 Curzon Street
London
W1J 7TY
020 7495 0503

SALES

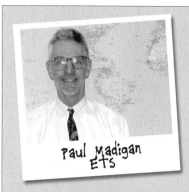

Paul Madigan
ETS

Checking your TV screenings

9.45pm'. You can also ensure that you get your collections from other agencies such as the PRS or the DPRS. It also enables distributors to know when the programme is available to re-sell because it has played its contract through. For instance if you sell three screenings over two years, if the film is screened three times in the first month, it is available for re-sale and you don't need to wait twenty three months. Remember, the TV station won't volunteer this information. We have a 157 publications come into the office on a weekly basis, typically TV guides. Our translators go through them all and enter the details of all the shows into a huge database, currently holding 600,000 titles and 5 million entries since '93. With regard to costs, $200 gets you a report for a year - a print out of when and where your show screened (also available on www.etstv.com).

Q - What is ETS (Essential Television Statistics)?

Paul - Since '93 we have tracked where and when films and programmes play on a daily basis on 144 channels in twenty countries. So we would be able to tell you if and when your feature film or programme had played in one of those twenty countries.

Q - So you can track if your film has been screened or sold without your knowing?

Paul - Yes, it's an independent source of information that enables you to go to your sales agent and say 'I know that this played on television in Switzerland on Jan 11th 1998 at

Q - How often do producers get their report and say "Oh, my god, I did not know that it was showing there"?

Paul - It is not uncommon. A lot of producers never know what happens. They just sell it and don't follow through. They don't look upon it as an asset. Asset management is not perceived as part of the producers job.

Q - What common mistakes do you encounter?

Paul - The inability for creatives to realise that they own assets, they just don't see the true value of those assets. A film is like building a house, it has to be built correctly, you have to maintain it, you have to follow through and of course if you get it right at the start you then have an asset that buys you many lunches over the years. Some never wake up to it. Some wake up to it who have been out there for years and they get quite a surprise when they get their money.

Scheduled Transmissions Report

Title: Urban Ghost Story (1998)

Period: January 1, 2001 to September 30, 2005

Country	Channel	Date	Start	End
DENMARK	DR 2	11/09/02	20:05	21:40
DENMARK	KANAL 5	09/11/01	21:00	22:35
DENMARK	KANAL 5	13/06/03	21:00	22:40
NEW ZEALAND	SKY TV MOVIES	08/06/01	00:00	01:30
NEW ZEALAND	SKY TV MOVIES	18/06/01	12:30	14:00
NEW ZEALAND	SKY TV MOVIES	19/06/01	03:45	05:15
NEW ZEALAND	SKY TV MOVIES	22/06/01	08:15	09:45
SWEDEN	CANAL +	11/04/01	23:35	01:00
SWEDEN	CANAL +	23/04/01	17:45	19:10
SWEDEN	CANAL + GUL	02/04/01	23:05	00:30
SWEDEN	TV 5	03/02/03	01:05	02:40
SWEDEN	TV 5	29/10/03	02:55	04:20
SWEDEN	TV 5	29/07/04	01:40	03:10

Source: ETS Ltd.

E|S

Paul Madigan
Managing Director

ESSENTIAL TELEVISION STATISTICS

Pinewood Studios Iver Heath Bucks SL0 0NH UK
Tel +44 1753 630990 Fax +44 1753 630860
paul@etstv.com www.etstv.com

bill of previous films or really old films from the 50's and 60's and that is dependent on the quality of the print. Then again, the people who come to see these old films like the graininess or the streaks because that is what they expect. The other thing digital projection will do is make hard-to-get films easier to show. For example, we can't show *Gone With The Wind* because there is no 35mm print available. But if the rights owners put it on HD tape, then we could show it very easily.

Q - How often do film makers approach you to screen their films?

Robert - Including short films, probably ten to twelve a week, which is why I don't have time to watch all of them. We get a lot of short films and programme them often. When I first came to Soho, I had two people working with me, Nicky Tucker and Joe Bateman, and we realised that we had a lot of short film makers wanting to project their film, but they didn't have the money to pay for the rental fees. So we chatted and over a period of time we realised we could do something to support film makers. Now once a month we have seven consecutive days where, between six o'clock and seven o'clock, we will show a programme of short films.

We try to get someone who has a sponsor or a rich uncle who can pay three to four hundred pounds to hire the screen for an hour. Many times this sponsor is an agency that represents short film makers, like Dazzle or an organization or a film festival. We both advertise and then split it sixty / forty. And some of the events are public and some are private. We don't do one offs, that is one seven minute short film because people will not come out for that. It gives us a little more work to do, but it is worth it because some people have gone on to bigger and better things. The guy who owns Curzon is Roger Wingate and he is all for nurturing new talent whether it be short film making or screenwriting or theatre. And it filters down to things like the short film programs.

Q - If a film maker came together with a package of films, would you screen them?

Robert - Yes. I know that some of the people we worked with who represent certain organisations will then put one of their own films in and I have no problem with that. You tend to find that an audience for short films is fifty percent public and fifty percent friends and family.

Q - Any common mistakes that film makers make in relation to exhibition?

Robert - They are generally pretty savvy in knowing that we are a feature cinema and that is what we do first and foremost. We put all the other stuff around the edges as it makes us stand out from other cinemas. I guess the other big mistake film makers do is not knowing how to get it to us. They have made a film and don't know what to do with it. I usually tell them to go find an agent, and they will represent it for you. We have a short film summer school, which is a four day seminar of screenings and master classes and get all the industry people down here. So like the UK Film Council, New Producers Alliance, Leap Frog, etc., come down for four days to help spread their knowledge to film makers. And also to get the public involved as well. You might not care how a HD camera works, but you can see the films themselves.

Q - What advice would you give new film makers?

Robert - If you make a film, get it seen. If it is in a cinema, great. If it is in a festival, great. Get it seen in a pub or bar that run short film programs. For feature films, you are going to get a lot of rejection even when a distributor comes on board. You have to keep going. You have to have confidence in your own abilities. Network to the max. Get DVD copies of your film and put it in peoples' hands. There is a lot to be said for guerilla marketing on a film. You can do a lot by word of mouth.

SALES

Jim Angell
F.A.C.T.

F.A.C.T.

Q - What is FACT?

Jim - FACT - the Federation Against Copyright Theft - is the investigation authority that represents major film companies that are based in the UK. Most of them are American-lead, but we represent Momentum, BBC, Sky etc. We are financed by the major film companies. A lot of the film product has to go to various companies for editing, post production, printing and even destruction. We have to accredit those companies on behalf of the major film companies and that includes a security audit, to make sure that their product is safe and accountable. Although we are non profit any fees we acrue from this service goes back into the fighting fund to fight film piracy.

Q - How much piracy is going on?

Jim - The worrying thing is that some of the product is available as a pirate DVD before cinema release, or just as it enters cinema. Often it is shot on a camcorder by somebody sitting in the cinema with a covert camera, or a member of the cinema staff is coerced to allow somebody to record it. It is then electronically put onto a DVD-R and off it goes.

Q - What are the main areas of concern for a film maker while making a film?

Jim - Look at security from the word go. From writing the movie to the end result. So if you have got something that you've put onto film, make sure it is secure all the way through. If it goes somewhere to be edited, make sure that the company who is editing is secure. I know it is difficult to actually look over somebody's shoulder all the time. The editing company should be FACT accredited to ensure that we check the security on your behalf. After that, it is when it comes out into cinema, or a pre-cinema showing, by making sure that the people who view it are looking at the film and not taping it or doing anything that they should not be doing. What happens now with the majors is that they put markings on their film, so if it is copied elsewhere there is an audit trail and they can actually trace back to the cinema that it was shown at. Often an advance DVD, such as an Academy Award Screener DVD goes out and then somehow, it falls into the hands of counterfeiters and it all kicks off. Once it goes to a distributor, or to a replicator, to go out to the public, it is very difficult to protect it fully. Steps should be taken prior to all this because obviously with release windows, your film can be shown here in January, but it won't come out to a DVD till June time. So you've got this gap and what we are finding is that the more popular the film, the quicker that the pirates want to put this out because it has reached it's popularity. For instance, *Shrek*, that was a stunner. Universal lost a lot of money from that because it came out in the States in May, and we had it over here on a pretty good format within a couple of days. It didn't come out in the UK until October time. Then it was on a DVD in time for Christmas. The damage has been done by the time it has gone to a replicator. So it is the security before replication.

Q - What kind of impact do you think organised crime is having on the film business?

Jim - It is having a major impact because it is financing other forms of crime. We can talk about a guy in a market, he is not what I call a 'Del-boy' character. He is not your friendly guy who is trying to sort you out something a bit cheaper. The people selling these films are basically thieves. They are stealing from the film industry. We all think of film piracy as a victimless crime, but there is a victim to every crime. The major companies are the recipients of the criminality. It has a knock-on effect all the way through. You have got your rental, your retail chains, your cinemas and all the people working trying to put these films together who will be affected. Of course what will happen is that it won't affect them next week or the week after, but in a year's time. Or when one of the majors decides to do an audit on how many films they have sold in the UK of so and so title. They think *'well hang on a minute, I thought that was a popular film'*, well it was, but it was pirated.

Q - I heard that 'The Football Factory' was doing well in the cinemas, until the 3rd week, then it died, and that coincided with the streets being flooded with pirate DVDs of the film? Of course, Football Factory is a British independent film too.

Jim - That is correct. We had a lot of enquiries with that, and Momentum couldn't understand why suddenly it took off, and then bang, it stopped. As you rightly say, we picked up a lot on eBay, and through market places as well. This is a prime example of how a potentially good film has suddenly been stopped in it's tracks, through piracy.

Q - What other security mistakes do people make in terms of film distribution?

Jim - Well, again if you are looking at security, which is obviously a big issue, at the cinema it is making sure that when the film goes in that it is kept safe. When the film goes out it is obviously logged back, so there is no losses anywhere. Whilst it is being transmitted within the cinema itself, make sure there are sufficient people employed within that cinema network to make sure that there is no 'wrong-doing' occurring within the cinema. I know it is difficult, and all you see is just black with the little green lights on the stairs. If you do see someone doing something, bring it to the attention of the cinema manager, and the cinema manager can then call the police. Whether it is a film from one of the big studios, or with one of the small guys, it is their pride and joy that is going to hit the pirate scenes. If you go and spend £5 to buy a counterfeit copy, do you know where that £5 is going to? The answer is, no you don't! You are looking at this situation where you have got product that, as you rightly say, may be a good quality. The majority isn't, but I would be lying if I turned round and said to you that some of it that we see is not of a reasonable quality, it is watchable, but it is a gamble. People like to gamble, and it is difficult to try and change that mind set. So where is that £5 going? Is that £5 going back to organised crime? Does that mean that that £5 is going to the guy on the market stall, who is living a life of luxury but is claiming social security benefits that are being taken away from people that are needy? Is it being pumped into some sort of drugs set up? We are not talking about an odd £10, we are talking thousands and several hundreds of thousands of pounds. That money never stays in the UK. It has never had tax taken from it. It has never had VAT taken from it. This is money that is being sent back to the Far East somewhere to either go back in to other counterfeiting exploits out there, or it is going into somebody's pocket that is involved in some more organised crime.

Q - So what should I do when I am down at Camden market and I see some guy flogging clearly pirated DVDs?

Jim - Report it to the police, Trading Standards and us. We have a website that you can just tap in and report it. These people are replicating in a machine that you can buy for a few hundred pounds and they just copy it and sell it. One disk in and it records seven at a time! So in ten minutes you have got seven films. If you start at the beginning of the week, by the time the weekend comes, you have got a nice market stall. To them, it's like printing money, only it's the film makers money they are stealing.

Q - Is there anything you can do if it gets on the Internet?

Jim - We have authority to do internet investigations within the UK on behalf of all the UK members. We have a good working relationship with eBay, and with the other auction sites. If you got somebody who is persistant we will instigate an investigation, then we will collate evidence and take it to a police authority who will then get a search warrant, and we will get that person arrested and taken before a court. It is as simple as that. We are not going to have sand thrown in our faces.

Q - What advice would you offer a new film maker?

Jim - Be vigilant at all stages. You can only do so much as these people are organised criminals. If they want something, they'll get it.

Q - So as future film makers, if we see pirated DVDs or someone filming in a cinema we should report it?

Jim - Yes, and don't assume someone else will report it. It's your business at the end of the day.

SALES

Jim Angell
Director of Operations

Federation Against Copyright Theft
7 Victory Business Centre
Worton Road
Isleworth, Middlesex TW7 6DB

FACT

T: 0208 568 6646
F: 0208 560 6364

E: jim@fact-uk.org.uk

Jason Thorp
Fox FX

Q - So what is your job?

Jason - I'm Vice President of Broadcasting at the Fox FX channel, so I run the channel, which involves buying all the programming, and occasionally commissioning. We run out of LA and we are owned 100% by Fox Entertainment, but we are essentially left alone as to operate the way we choose as we know our market. There are only 12 of us here, so it is a relatively small operation. The vast majority of our product is bought in from the States.

Q - If a new film maker came to you with the right product, would you consider it?

Jason - We have just bought some UK produced completed product. If we like the film, we will pay for it, though the fee is relevant to the kind of audience it would attract.

Q - If an independent producer put together a strong commercial picture that was suitable for your channel, and they offered a premiere before DVD release, would that be interesting to you?

Jason - For us the most important thing is the first showing in our environment. If it is a UK TV premiere that is perfect for us, it then becomes really PR-able. We can get the press behind it, we can make a bit of a song and dance about it. Buying that window is probably what we pay most for, however the kind of deals we are doing now may involve investing at a much earlier stage for a later window. We will take the UK first run and pay a premium for that. Obviously we will be competing with the likes of Sky.

Q - What kind of product is it you look for specifically?

Jason - We are targeted at 25 to 44 year old men, slightly more up market. We are looking for something that is commercial enough to get bums on sofas. Something with an edge, with something unique about it. We are not going to air a cheapy action film or cloned horror movie - we can always access the studio library for relatively commercial titles and pay very little money. For us, investing in the smaller independent films actually means less viewers for more money, but it does create PR and press to help build the brand.

The majority of our product comes from the 6 major studios. The problem with that is they have so much power and they can demand a premium, so it will go to Sky, then to a free TV window. Often the smaller channels like us will only be able to consider a title five years after the theatrical release. It is difficult for us to compete on that level. That is why we may consider an indie title. We just pick our fights with titles that we think really deliver on the brand.

Q - Do you consider low budget films?

Jason - Absolutely. It is not about the budget, it is about the way the film works, what it says, the cast, and the script.

Q - How much would you pay approximately?

Jason - For a completed title ready for full delivery, it could be anywhere between £10k and £50k. If it is a first run product, it could be more. It is entirely dependent on the film itself. It is about coming to an agreement that works for both of us really. For us it is about an honest and open discussion.

Q - From my perspective, it is an incredible conversation we are having. What I often hear from sales agents and distributors is that my film is worth 50p! That is outside of David Wilkinson at Guerilla Films. David seems to be the only person who is actually telling the truth and doing something about it for British micro budget films. Would you talk directly to a producer or do you prefer a distributor?

Jason - We will talk to anyone who picks up their phone and calls with a serious proposal.

Q - Do you think it would be wise for producers to approach other channels, in the way that he / she may approach you? Are other channels open to direct deals?

Jason - I think they are. Just be aware and realistic about the value of your property. Make sure that when you talk to these people that you have drawn some lines in the sand.

Q - What would you require in order to close a deal?

Jason - When we shake hands, we will agree on a price and strike up a very simple one-page deal memo, to lay down the terms. It is a legally binding document. A payment schedule, which normally involves a percentage up front, then payments paid right across the license period, will also be agreed. From the film maker we will need a digibeta master that has been fully QC'd (quality control) independently.

Q - When you pass on a movie, what are the main reasons for that rejection?

Jason - On the independent sector, there is a lot of pretentious material out there. It is for us, all about that gut feeling - I enjoyed that or I didn't enjoy that. We want to do what we can in terms of supporting film, especially independent film, but for us it needs to be entertaining. We are in an entertainment genre, so you just need to say *'Yeah, I enjoyed it!'*

Q - What do you think are the strengths of the Indie film business?

Jason - Everyone is so much more lighter footed. You can literally have a conversation, look at a title, and a deal can be done. If you are doing a deal with a major, it is two months minimum. It is just that ability to come to a mutual agreement, and shake hands on it, and get on with it.

Q - What kind of mistakes do you see?

Jason - We reject a lot of material. When people put stuff in front of you which I think they know is not up to scratch, you do think why are you wasting everyone's time? The criteria are fairly clear, it needs to be good, different, entertaining, technically excellent and most of all, work in terms of our brand.

Q - What advice can you offer a new film maker?

Jason - Make it entertaining. It does not matter how serious the subject matter is, how wordy it is, just make it entertaining. That is what it is all about.

SALES

2nd Floor, Shepherds Studios East
Richmond Way, London, W14 0DQ
Phone +44 (0) 20 7751 7600

FOX INTERNATIONAL CHANNELS UK
A UNIT OF FOX ENTERTAINMENT GROUP

Jason Thorp
Vice President
Broadcasting and Marketing
e-mail: jason.thorp@fox.com

A NEWS CORPORATION COMPANY

Merlin Ward
Writer and Director

SALES
REALITY
'OUT OF BOUNDS'

Q - Tell me what were you doing before you became a filmmaker, and how did you end up being in the film business?

Merlin - I'd always dreamed of being an actor in movies. As an actor I was quite lucky as I worked a lot, and then I ended up in a soap opera called *'Crossroads'*. After that, surprise, surprise, I couldn't get any work. I was recognised everywhere but no one wanted to hire an actor with that baggage. So I flew to LA, because I had always dreamed of going to Hollywood, and I bought Syd Field's books, like everybody does, and I wrote a screenplay by the numbers as it were, which I got optioned by a British Producer. For years I worked as a writer, getting things optioned and writing on commission, but for one reason or another, nothing ever got made. I was immensely frustrated because I thought I've worked with all these big companies and players and they can't even get the scripts made and my film just lies in development. So I decided that I had to become a Producer. I'd written this script which I thought could be done very inexpensively, which turned out to be *'Out of Bounds'*, and I showed it to Michael Cowan at the Spice Factory, and he liked it, and then introduced me to David Rogers of Great British Films, and together the three of us made it.

I describe myself as a story teller / film maker, rather than a Director. I think it is a different viewpoint, and now, if somebody asked me what I do in the film business, I'd say Writer first, Producer second, Director third. I noticed at the BAFTA awards this year that everybody mentioned the producers, what a wonderful job they had done with the money, they know how bloody hard it is!

Q - Most people think of new film makers, as being young film makers. Do you think that your other experiences and life experiences served you well when you made the leap into being a producer?

Merlin - My background certainly helped me, I was grown up enough to know that I didn't know anything really, so I hired people who did. A great DP, Camera operator, I had a superb cast, everybody was really experienced in the industry and I didn't have the arrogance. Maybe that is why being over 40 was a real benefit. I hadn't been to film school. I didn't know very much about track and dolly, lighting or anything like that. I know a great deal more now of course, but at the same time, on the next film I will be doing exactly the same. I'll hire the best people that I can afford, who can make sure I don't cock up.

Q - What was the official budget?

Merlin - The actual budget for the film is £680k minus 20%, so I had about £500k to actually shoot with.

Q - So you put together a high-class picture, which I guess is stamped with approval because the BBC bought it and screened it. BBC1 isn't going to screen a low budget piece of rubbish. So surely the expectation is that it is going to be a success in the international market place?

Merlin - I was realistic enough to know that it was more suited to a Friday, late night television slot, than it was to opening at the Empire, Leicester Square. What I did expect from the international sales was that the prices that people were prepared to pay, in some of the smaller territories, were going to be higher than they eventually turned out to be. Nor was I prepared for the astonishing level of low expectation and cynicism from the sales people who had taken it on. At times it seemed like they didn't know what they had taken on, and I am not sure if they ever even watched it through. Though they did pay a company to do a very good trailer for it.

It is still very hard to fully understand how sales and distribution operate, especially when you live with the dream of making a movie all your life. To meet people who don't really care about it, it is just a product to them, is distressing. As an inexperienced person you are not used to using the word product. Their cruelty can be quite shocking when you first experience it.

Q - Is that because your agenda was to tell a great story well, and theirs was to sell the movie any way that they could?

Merlin - *Out Of Bounds* pressed a number of buttons for the sales agents which is why they were interested in taking it on. It was good enough that they could create a very good trailer. But what they really wanted was for Sophia's character to have stripped off! Speaking as a Producer now, a number of years later, I would never go as far as some other film makers, but I am more interested in saying *'let's not handicap ourselves'*, let's do a little bit more to attract sales.

Q - When you get to sales, we are all serving a new master. Instead of serving the story telling master, we are serving the sales and distribution master, and that is something most film makers feel slightly uncomfortable about. One can sit self-righteously in front of your typewriter and say 'I'm not going to sell out when I write this script', but when you get to making it, all those 'sell out' elements come into play. And perhaps sell out is the wrong word? I think it is knowing what you've made, and knowing what the expectations of the marketplace are for what you have made. If you could go back in a time machine and visit yourself two months before you shot the movie, what would you say to yourself about making this particular movie?

Merlin - There is probably not a lot that I would actually change with the actual film itself, partly because I was very fortunate to get the cast that I did, and the actual shooting of it was fine. Sure I haven't got anybody naked in it, and maybe that would help sales, but that wasn't an option. One of the areas I would definitely go back to is all the things to do with the DVD and stills. It was left to somebody in PR who didn't do a very good job, so I had no interviews with actors for the DVD documentary, nor on set footage, and what stills I did have were very poor. I had to fabricate a lot or take them off the tape. I was unaware of how important all those things are to the sales process.

Q - What happened about sales and distribution once the film was complete?

Merlin - The problem is that you sign a contract and you actually believe that your sales agent is going to adhere to the contract. You say *'can I have a sales report?'* and they say *'we are busy with so and so, we will get one out in the next few weeks'*. I find that happens all the time, and years go by, and you have not had any sales reports at all. It is like you sign the movie to them and they have the attitude that it is not even your movie, it is their property now and you are just an annoyance. That is the way a lot of sales agents treat small independent companies. Of course, they don't treat big people like that because they want to work for them again.

They'll attach as many costs as possible and try to do their best to make sure that you don't receive anything - at least that's what it feels like. The amount of energy I spent with my first sales agent, just trying to get him to send a cheque - and when they eventually sent a cheque it was a round figure, so I felt it was as though they thought *'let's just send them a cheque for this amount to keep them quiet'*, as how could it just be a round figure?!

Before you sign a contract with a sales agent, you have really got to structure it and plan, so that you are protected, so that there are automatic clauses to do with the rights reverting back to the film maker, should certain circumstances arise. They will scream at you *'No other sales agent would ever do a deal like that'*, but it is better to not do any deal with a sales agent than to do the deal that most of them want to do where you sign away your movie for 15 to 20 years, and then they just flick you a V sign after you've signed.

You need to look at several contractual areas such as making sure you have copies of all contracts that they do with any buyers. Now they don't want you to see those because they think it is giving away their sales contacts. But you must have copies of all contracts, sales reports if possible, and monies owing to be paid promptly as well. Give them targets to hit too, such an amount of sales within a year or the rights revert.

SALES

There is no doubt about it that, as with your experiences, there are sales agents who will do a good job and others who will not. The thing is, they need to be helped. First, you need to give them a film that they can sell. Like a child, you need to give them borders, they need to know the areas which they cannot cross. They need to know that if they don't do as they have signed in the contract, they will lose the picture. Once they know the borders, they can be very good. Once you get a bit further down the line in your career, they can be very helpful in putting together deals. They are very much half of the producing process and can bring certain territories to the table.

From the sales agent's point of view, they will say, we can only operate with what we've got. It is a crowded market. Unless you've got elements attached (such as casting a named actor), it is a hard sell. If you want to get a foot in the door you've got to think about what will sell and is marketable. Genre films help, such as suspense, or something that has a ready market - more sophisticated filmmakers don't enter that area often. This is why I chose it. I didn't want to make slasher movies, but I do like films like *The Sixth Sense* and *The Others* - spooky movies, which is why I made *'Out Of Bounds'*, a spooky boarding school movie.

Q - You've been involved in selling to some territories yourself. How did you do that?

Merlin - As an example, I formed a relationship with ZDF, a major German broadcaster who paid a good price for the film early on. I said I was planning on doing another movie and they said *'Well, we will buy it!'*, and I said *'Would you put some money up in advance?'*, and they said *'No. We'd like to see the finished movie and then we will buy it'*. So I said *'Would you buy it off me?'*, and they said *'Yes! You don't need to go through a Sales Agent'*. That struck home. So yes you can sell the film yourself, but you do need contacts and it's hard work.

Q - A big problem is that most new film makers want to make films and not be involved in sales, and then complain when it all goes wrong?

Merlin - There are so few truly gifted people who can be both creative and good businessmen. If you are writing the script and organising everything, it is difficult to also be the hard-nosed business guy who is dealing with people who are so experienced at screwing other people. Some people are very hard negotiators and it can be a meat market, which can be a shock for a new film maker who has rose tinted glasses! You learn so much on the journey that it's hard to believe you were as naive as you were when you began. It is like JK Rowling wants to re-write the first Harry Potter book, because she wrote it when she was just starting out on that journey. It is not right in her eyes. I understand that, I really do. If she does re-write it, she can make loads more money out of it. For us, it is difficult to move on, the films are our babies.

Q - How would you find out who could buy your film internationally, if you were not going through a sales agent?

Merlin - The simplest thing is to read the Cannes guide - the big thick one you get if you have a stand, a suite or attend the producers network, which can cost upward of £300. It details everybody in the world who could buy your film. They are gold dust.

Q - Does it make sense to make that investment?

Merlin - If you think about all the time you've spent writing a script, then you've spent all that time raising the money, trying to get it going, then all the energy making it, involving all those people, then editing.... and then most people think it is the end of their job and they hand the film over at the first market and think *'fantastic, it is not my problem anymore!'* They really should not think like that because it will probably turn into a bigger problem when sales don't materialise.

Q - I can't agree with you more. Independent film is a viable business if you are prepared to work hard at it. The problem is that it is not a viable business if people treat it as a purely

artistic or self indulgent venture. They go ahead, they make the thing, but they are not prepared to sell it, then they complain that the people who do sell it don't give them any money. You have got to sell it yourself, or let go and accept there will probably not be any returns?

Merlin - The ideal is the middle path where you work closely with the sales agent. I'm selling *Out of Bounds* myself because we just thought we would give it a go, for the hell of it. Ideally, I will try and find a sales agent who will sell it for me, but also do it the right way. Report back to me. Make sure I have got in the contract incentives, as well as penalties, but incentives to do it right. You've still got to keep a very close eye on your movie. So far that has not happened and I am still selling it myself.

Q - Has your film made profits?

Merlin - No. It has returned somewhere in the region of £220k so far.

Q - So, it's all about going in with your eyes open? There have been times when I've looked at contracts or been in meetings with sales agents and distributors and I've chosen to believe them. Whereas experience would tell me that I shouldn't have believed. It is not empirical fact, it is belief. Yes, believe, but also have a contract and nail them to it?

Merlin - Yes. Be prepared to walk away with your movie.

Q - If you are able to hand it over to a sales agent, your life becomes free again. You can get on with that next movie now - and that's a very desirable thing?

Merlin - I suppose if you want security and still to make movies, then you should work in television - get all your satisfaction, get the money, and you don't have to worry about sales.

Q - The BBC bought 'Out Of Bounds' and screened it. How did that happen?

Merlin - I sent the BBC a tape, and about 18 months later, they came back. In the meantime Sophia Myles' profile had been raised considerably. By that time we'd done a UK deal with David Wilkinson at Guerilla Films, and he was planning on releasing it on DVD first of all, then trying to get a TV sale, and then the BBC popped up. Because of David's good relationship with the BBC, we got a good deal, and what was so gratifying about that deal with the BBC, was that the BBC paid the money properly, and we got it within days of David Wilkinson receiving it. That was one of the sweetest things that has happened to me in my career. We've seen it on BBC1, and got paid immediately.

Q - What advice would you offer a new filmmaker?

Merlin - The hardest thing to accept when you are 22 is that getting successfully into movies could be a 30 year time frame, and not a 3 year time frame. I would advise getting some kind of job in the industry so that you can get the pleasure of being in the business and not on the outside. I would definitely try and find a job so that your creative soul is being fed, while your body is also being fed. I was formally an actor, so I was waiting for the phone to ring for someone to hire me, and as a screenwriter, I was waiting for somebody to make my film. I feel like I've waited far too long.

SALES

Geraldine Higgins
British Council

BRITISH COUNCIL

Q - What is the purpose of the British Film Council?

Geraldine - The aim of the British Council's film department is to promote the British Film Industry, that is films and film makers. We are trying to promote young filmmakers, exciting filmmakers; we also promote the more older, established filmmakers. We are just looking for new talent, feature films and short films.

Q - What is your specific job within that organisation?

Geraldine - I predominantly cover film festivals throughout the world, which at the moment my remits are in Baltic, Scandinavian, some of the former Eastern European countries and parts of Africa. We take British film makers and films to these territories where the local population may not get the opportunity to see British films. We work with our British Council offices to maybe organise a British film week at these festivals, or to identify someone who can go out and do a workshop, a seminar, or script-writing, directing, animation etc.

Q - At what point should a new feature filmmaker come to you and say 'Hello, we exist!'?

Geraldine - What they should be aware of is that the British Council currently acts as, or offers a preview service to certain features on festivals. I'm talking Cannes, Venice, Toronto, Berlin, Sundance, etc. Those festival selectors will contact us and say *'We are coming to the UK for a few days, can the British Council put together some films for us to look at?'* So we contact the people that we are aware of and say *'Look, the selector is coming in, is your film ready? Are you finished, do you have a print? Are you interested in showing it to this selector?'* But if it's a young film maker who has made a film, and for some reason it is not on our radar, then they can go to ww.britfilms.com and register their feature films with us so we know you are out there.

Q - Are you still working on 35mm prints?

Geraldine - We do (2005). There are some events that will show Digibeta and BetaSP, and some will start to show HD I am sure. But you have to ask if they have actually got good quality projection facilities to be able to screen a digital film? Most of the festivals realise they are dealing with lower budget films, and they will appreciate that the film makers probably shot it digitally and can not afford to make a 35mm print.

Q - Do you help film makers financially in getting them to these festivals?

Geraldine - Depending on the film festival, especially if it is one we work with regularly, we may be able to get a travel grant for them to go, though this is not as common as it used to be.

Q - Of course the festival itself may have a deal with an airline?

Geraldine - What we find is most festivals will cover accommodation costs. What they don't appear to be able to stretch to is an airfare. Now, if it is a major festival, such as Cannes, we would assume that the sales agent, producer or production company could find the airfare. If it is a smaller festival, we might be able to find a few hundred pounds.

Q - What do you think makes a film successful on the festival market?

Geraldine - I would hope that festival organisers are looking for something that shows talent, that shows a young / exciting director who has flair, imagination and is brilliant at working with actors. It also comes down to something that just catches their attention. Sometimes it is a film that most people think is very commercial, and other times it is a film that people put into the art-house category. Though I am certain that what they are looking for is something that is exciting.

Q - How can new filmmakers help you help them?

Geraldine - When they have made a feature film, they need to get it onto the Britfilms.com website where we have the British films catalogue. That website gets 50,000 hits a month. So if you are a film maker, and you have made a low budget feature film, and you don't have a sales agent, this is free publicity. All you need to do is contact us, give us the details of your feature film and we will put it up on the website. It also means we are then aware of it. So when the festival selectors come, we ask *'do you want to show the film to them?'*

Q - Should a new filmmaker send you a DVD, or invite you to a screening?

Geraldine - Yeah. Either, or. I would prefer to see the film on the big screen, but if you have a 35mm print, a DVD is fine.

Q - What about short films?

Geraldine - We specifically work with between 50 and 60 short film festivals around the world. They are the ones we consider the most important. What we will do is the filmmaker will send us their short and then we will look at it. If we think that the short will be of interest to one of the festivals, we will take on a lot of the administrative work. Which means we are alerting the filmmaker to the fact that this festival deadline is coming up, and they need to fill in the entry form and send the tape to us. We will then ship the film if it is selected for the competition. We pay the freight to send the film out to whichever country. More importantly for the young film maker who has made a short film and has never seen their film in a festival before, and it is now in competition, we can possibly give them a travel grant. We have a small sum of money set aside for the short film festival circuit to enable filmmakers to go out and enjoy the experience of the short film festival. Also we track people who move from shorts to features. David McKenzie, Lynn Ramsey, they all started off as short filmmakers whose careers we have followed, and now they are making feature films.

Q - How many UK feature films were made last year?

Geraldine - I think we are talking 100 plus. Unless it is a major film festival, I don't think they are particularly concerned with the format on which the film was shot. I think they just want to see what is out there, and what you can do.

Q - There is a preconception that somehow because you are government-funded that the kind of films you are interested in are politically correct. Is that true?

Geraldine - No! We are interested in seeing a film that is well made, directed, and written. The fact that the storyline may be considered controversial, problematical, *'Is this creating a good or bad image of the UK?'* is not a primary concern. If they are touching on a subject matter that might be considered sensitive, or one that might be showing the UK in an unflattering light, we are not going to censor and say we won't support that film.

Q - Do you ever advise about sales agents?

Geraldine - Not as such but you can check Britfilms.com to see which companies have been around for some time and therefore are more stable and which films are being handled by which agents.

BRITISH COUNCIL

Geraldine Higgins
Film Programme Manager, Film and Literature Department

British Council, 10 Spring Gardens, London SW1A 2BN, UK
T +44 (0)20 7389 3066   F +44 (0)20 7389 3175

geraldine.higgins@britishcouncil.org
www.britishcouncil.org   www.britfilms.com

SALES

Festival Do's and Don'ts

GUERILLA FILM MAKER SAYS!

1. Do research on as many festivals as you can before you start to submit. Find out what kind of films they program, when they program, who attends and what resources they have available to entrants and if they have competitions – you may walk away with a prize.

2. Contact The British Council festival department as they will offer much assistance including preview screenings in London and helping you get to that international premiere. They will also inform the international festivals of your film and before you know it, you may receive invitations to attend festivals around the world.

3. Choose your World Premiere wisely – you only get one.

4. European festivals should generally be free to enter and so are most international festivals except for the US (where entry fees are between $25-$50). If your film is selected for some of the bigger festivals, you may likely find that the festivals will call you requesting you and the filmmaker to attend. Certain festivals may also pay for a screening of your film.

5. If invited to a festival, they will cover ALL costs like flights, accommodation and shipping of the prints. However, just in case the festivals do not take care of these expenses (and the British Council can't help financially), you should budget for your stay at certain festivals that you'd like to attend. Put money aside for hotel, food and transportation. You can always get a bunch of friends together and pack one hotel room. Makes for great stories.

6. Do not pay to be part of the festival program. You should be included since they have chosen you to be in the festival.

7. Make your application as early as possible and send a press pack with stills (including a shot of the director).

8. Once you've been selected, send a pile of press packs to the festival in advance (including stills and a shot of the director), they will then set up interviews with their press. Take a Beta SP tape with clips (in both PAL and NTSC). Don't leave that tape at the festival or you will never see it again!

9. Do advertise your film as much as possible yourself. Bring press kits, VHS tapes, DVDs, flyers, posters (some festivals forbid postering buildings and passing out flyers), hats and anything else you can slap the name of your film on. Be creative as well. If your film is about cowboys, dress one of your friends up as a cowboy and have him walk through the festival handing out flyers.

10. Do get a press agent, but ONLY if you are going to be at one of the larger festivals were there will be a lot of press. It also may be helpful for the larger foreign country festivals as the agents will be more familiar with the press agencies.

11. Do make sure that your print is in a format that the festival handles and that any special requests, such as HD players, are taken care of two weeks in advance.

12. Do schmooze with the festival operators to find out where the free food, booze and best parties are. If you are cunning, you can survive on this free food. Pack doggy bags.

13. Do not freak out if the projector blows up or the sound drops out of your film. Remain calm and professional. Usually it is a volunteer running the projector with very little training. Don't blame them. Also, an agent or producer may be in the audience and if he sees you go ballistic here, they may think this is how you will be on the set of a major job when things go south.

14. Do not stay too far away from the festival center. The pace of most film festivals, especially the larger ones, is draining. Having to drive half an hour or more to your hotel at the end of the night just sucks.

15. Remember, if it's a free trip, go for a festival where you actually want a holiday – you could get a week in Asia all expenses paid.

16. If you're going to a festival where the language is different from your own, try to get the festival coordinators to find you a translator.

17. Do research on the festival and the country that you are traveling to. You don't want to end up in the middle of a coup or a typhoid outbreak.

18. Don't get too tied up going to festivals. You can just go to what feels like a few and before you know it, a year has gone by, you're no longer a hot new filmmaker and you've blown your window of opportunity.

Film Festival List

www.britfilms.com, run by the British Council is a great film makers resource. It has several lists and search engines that allow you to find just about everything going on in the UK Film industry. You can find out what films are in progress and who is working on them, you can search for film directors, find out what training courses are being offered around the county and search for all sorts of hire companies and crew. Most useful at this stage however, is the Directory of International Film and Video Festivals. It's an exhaustive database of almost every festival in the world, and it allows you to sort by genre, deadline, month or country so you can plan your festival submissions. Go to www.britfilms.com

Q - What is the value of going to a film festival?

Geraldine - Contacts. You can come here and meet potential investors or a potential co-producing partner. You may even be looking for a director to direct your film. The one thing I would say to filmmakers coming to a festival for the first time is you have to prepare before you come here. Everyone is in a rush. They don't have time to listen to someone ramble for hours. You have got to have a really, good short speech about what you can do for them. You might be lucky enough to get 5 minutes, and if you haven't prepared yourself for that 5 minute meeting, they are going to show you the door. If you are trying to find a sales agent, check out what type of genre those sales agents buy, then concentrate on the ones that buy the genre that you are trying to sell. If it is a horror film, look out for the agency who concentrates on horror films. It is expensive to go to the festivals and the markets, so you need to have researched before you set foot out of the country.

Q - What do you see are the common weaknesses in independent films or independent film makers movies?

Geraldine - Often it seems to be, you've made the film, and then you don't know what to do with it. It seems like, you've spent all this money, you possibly have re-mortgaged your house, and now you have sat back and gone *'I've finished my film'*, and you are expecting people to come to you when actually your job has just started. Now you have to sell it. You have to find a sales agent. If you haven't got a sales agent, you have to sell it yourself. It is incredibly hard work and time consuming, and it can be very expensive. I think if there is a problem with some independent film makers, it is the lack of appreciation of the amount of work involved once the film is made. You really need to be thinking about your research and what kind of sales agents you want to approach when you are in post-production, and getting a screening. Then inviting as many as you can to a UK screening to try and get someone attached as soon as possible.

Q - Do you feel, often with first time/new filmmakers, that they could improve their film with a re-edit?

Geraldine - I don't think that is a criticism of only first time film makers. I think some of the more established film makers can also fall victim to being precious. But, after all it is their baby and even the best film directors around have admitted that they have been a little bit over-generous, lingering on a particular scene. I don't think there is a standard running time for a feature film. As long as you have got the audience engaged from start to finish, they will forgive you if it is three hours long.

Q - What are the common mistakes that you often see?

Geraldine - Only thinking about your publicity material once you have finished the film. I sometimes get the impression that people have not spent enough time thinking about images and press packs - getting the ammunition that you will need if you are going to go to a market or a festival on your own to interest prospective buyers. You need to put together a really good press pack. It doesn't have to be too long. And label everything - your posters, DVDs, VHS cassettes! I can't tell you the number of short films where we get a cassette with no title on it.

Q - What advice would you offer a new filmmaker?

Geraldine - Don't be disheartened. If you feel like you are being rejected all the time, keep trying. If you have got the courage and the confidence that you have made a film that you feel deserves to be seen, then keep battling away to get people to actually see it.

Sandra Hebron
London Film Festival

FESTIVAL ORGANISER

Q - What is your job?

Sandra - I am head of festivals at the BFI and the artistic director of the London Film Festival. I oversee the BFI festivals, which are the BFI/London Times Film Festival and the London Lesbian and Gay Film Festival. And as the artistic director of the London Film Festival, I have the final say in terms of what the selection is, so as my title suggests I determine the artistic direction of the festival, and I play a large part of selecting the individual titles. I am also responsible for making sure that the festival happens by managing the festival team.

Q - What are the differences between screening a film at a festival or just going to your local theatre?

Sandra - I think the key difference is that in a festival you are watching a curated programme. You are watching a selection of films that some people, somewhere, have selected because they think they are appropriate, relevant, interesting, necessary to show them. So it is not the same as going to see a film that has found its way into theatrical distribution. The second thing that is typically different is that usually at the festival there will be someone there to talk about the film either beforehand or immediately afterward. Those people might also be taking part in other panels or discussions. So the sense of the festival is always that it is about more than just the films. It is about creating an environment, where people see films that they wouldn't be able to see otherwise. Also to create a context for the film and encourage discussion about what these people are seeing. That sounds terribly earnest and improving - it is not necessarily about that as sometimes it is about being wildly enthusiastic and raving to other people about what you've seen.

Q - So it is a place where film lovers can come out of the closet and be completely crazy about movies?

Sandra - Absolutely. It always pleases me that all of us who work on the festival actually love the festival. We might be completely exhausted or frustrated during the course of it because the days are long and the work is hard, but actually it is the most exciting thing to do. Programming a festival is the equivalent of reading a really good book and telling someone else that they have to read it too. You want the audience to have the buzz about a film that you had when you watched it. You have just put in the 29th DVD that you have to look at after rejecting the first 28, and you go, *'Oh, my goodness! That's great!'*

Q - How many feature films get submitted to the LFF, and are they submitted on DVD now?

Sandra - No. It is a real mixture. And we are open submission. Anyone can send in anything and reasonably expect us to watch it. We also solicit a lot of submissions. We are constantly tracking films and seeing what is being produced in any part of the world. The films that aren't ready for us to look at one year, will be kept in a database and carried forward to the next year. We pull in all the submissions for consideration, which means sometimes we will be watching on DVD, often we will be going to other places to watch films. All told, we look at about 2000 features and somewhere close to 1200 shorts.

If as a film maker your film is rejected, you are perfectly at liberty to ask why, but if you are going to ask why, be prepared for me to tell you. Obviously, we wouldn't do that in a way that was completely crushing. Actually, it is like a job interview, if you don't get the position, it is not a bad idea to ask for some feedback. Of course some film makers really just want to tell us how great their film is instead of really listening to what we have to say. Some of the common mistakes would be, making the film far too long, especially with shorts. There is a reason why old cinema shorts used to be eleven minutes long. There is a tendency now for people to stretch things out a little more than they should, and from a programming point of view, a film that is twenty-three minutes long, even if it is perfectly realised, is hard to programme. This applies to feature films as well. Don't think that more is more. The other common problems that we see, especially with drama, is that the acting lets it down. You may have a really good script, but often films are made with very little money and you get your pals to be in it or stitch together a cast as best you can. Then you probably have a director who doesn't have a lot of experience working with actors.

Q - What is it that catches your eye about a film, that makes you want to programme it?

Sandra - It is all about a good story, well told. That is quite subjective, but it is usually something that has originality - something that I haven't seen before. Every year there seems to be a certain set of films that you avoid. I remember that we once had an unwritten rule where we would never programme another American film where a couple set off on a road trip across America and they pick up a dodgy looking character. There are those terrible fashions in film and that is something to be wary of. In terms of what catches the eye. The well made part doesn't necessarily mean made with a lot of money. A film could be made in a rudimentary fashion as long as the film maker has something to say. There is nothing worse that watching a film that has a reasonable budget and is well executed, but it is about nothing. I used to be a film maker before I was a programmer and the reason I stopped making films was that I didn't have anything that I had a burning desire to say.

Q - Is there a competition at the London Film Festival?

Sandra - We don't have a competitive section. We have a number of awards that we give and most importantly, they are about recognising new talent. There is the Sutherland Award, which is for the most innovative and original first feature. That is a long standing BFI Award that has been won by everyone from Bertolucci to Scorsese to more recently Lynne Ramsey. We have the FIPRESCI Prize, which is for the best first or second feature. We have the TCM Shorts Award. We have the UK Talent Award, which is for up and coming UK writers, producers or directors. This year for the first time we will have a Documentary Feature Award. Then there is the Satyaijit Ray Award which has its own independent jury and is for a film that the jury feels has something in common with Ray's own form of film making.

Q - How much time do you need to be given to get a film into selection?

Sandra - Ideally, people should just make the deadline! Of course, we need to watch it and make a decision, which could take as little as a few hours. But our deadline really is about a month before we have to make the programme, and usually people get their films in on the deadline or just after. If people send things in early, say in January, and I could tell straightaway that we want it, I could tell them immediately - that would be easy. Sometimes, though, I might think 'maybe...' and then want to see more. So there is no real hard and fast rule. It would be inadvisable for a new film maker to chance their luck - the later they leave it the more pressure there is on us and the more likely it is for us to say that this film is interesting, but perhaps we don't have space for it. But as long as people meet the deadline, they will get a fair viewing. Information on submitting can be found at www.lff.org.uk

Q - A film festival is a great opportunity for first time film makers to make their presence known. How can they maximise their exposure?

Sandra - Everyone who gets into the festival gets an allocation of tickets and you could use those for your friends and family and have a bit of a knees up, and that would be a perfectly valid thing to do. However, if the film makers have aspirations beyond that, then they should talk to the people here, who look after the film makers, and find out how to get important industry people to their screening. We have over six hundred industry delegates and a lot of press delegates and we can act as a broker for making suggestions. There's no need to be insufferably pushy, but don't be afraid to ask. If you are presenting a film at the festival then someone is going to come on stage with you to introduce the film and have some questions to ask at the end. If there are points you want to get across then say so. If you have never done this before, then we are absolutely there to make sure that no one feels uncomfortable or foolish on stage. New film makers tend to have one of two approaches. One is to be deeply grateful and think that we are so fantastic for putting the film on. Well, at the end of the day, we didn't make the film. The film makers are more important than we are in a festival. We are there to push them forward and people need to recognise that it is a competitive environment and if their film gets through, that we have confidence in them. The other brand of film maker is the pushy person who thinks they are doing you a favour when they turn up. They are harder to deal with as they ask for less help and they are likely to get less out of us.

Q - Do you find that many film makers don't have the proper support materials, like stills, posters and press packs?

Sandra - Yes. When you are shooting, do get decent production stills, even if you are sacrificing sandwiches to get them. Because at least, if you have those, you have something to start with. People need to think about the life of their film after it is made. The press office is there because they know about festivals and the press, so ask their advice on which interviews to say yes to. New film makers will probably say yes to everything. We run the film maker's breakfast where journalists are there to meet as many film makers as possible.

Q - Do you have relationships with other festivals where if a film doesn't fit your programme and fits another, you will recommend it on behalf of the film maker?

Sandra - There are two levels at which that happens. The formal level is where, at the festival, we have amongst our industry delegates, representatives from other festivals. They can be from overseas such as LA, Istanbul, New Zealand - it is quite international. People will come here to look at films for their festivals. Things also happen informally. Because I go around the world looking at other films, I talk to other film festival programmers and directors and we do share opinions. And we have definitely passed people and films on. Last year, there was a film that wasn't for us, but I passed on to another festival because it

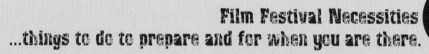

Film Festival Necessities
...things to do to prepare and for when you are there.

GUERILLA FILM MAKER SAYS!

PREPARE:

Get your airfare, accommodation and rental car (if necessary) squared away early. See if the festival has some deals worked out for film makers.

Save some cash so you can have a good time and relax.

Get business cards printed to pass out.

Create a website to promote your movie online.

Create stickers, flyers, a press kit (b&w, colour and digital photos), posters and postcards to pass out at the festival with times and locations of your screenings. The press kit is the most important followed by flyers and postcards.

Take several copies of the film's EPK (electronic press kit) to pass out to distributors. DVD is fine, DVCam is better.

Make a trailer to include with the press kit.

Pack some fancy clothes for parties.

Don't forget your mobile. If you are going overseas, call your wireless company to see if you can get a better international rate.

Have a next project to talk about!

If you can afford it, get a publicist to help you create a media strategy (do this only for the big festivals like Edinburgh, London, Cannes or Sundance)

WHEN THERE:

Meet as many people as possible – film makers, distributors, journalists, agents, etc. Get their business cards and pass them yours!

Create a buzz for your film – pass out flyers and postcards. Do a cheap (or, not so cheap) publicity stunt. Get your actors and friends to go and help you and do as many interviews with the media as possible.

If you can afford it, throw a party for your film. Team up with other films to reduce cost.

Find out where other parties are – then crash them!

Use your digital camera to take pictures of you there to put up on your website.

If you are on a budget, hang out at the film festival office, everyone goes there and they usually have free food.

Hand out your movie / promo items to journalists, distributors.

Follow up every meeting, either there or when you get home.

Talk about your next project and try to get as many people to read it as possible.

Don't be too quick to sign any contracts with representation while you are there. Make sure you've read and understood everything, having had a lawyer go over the contract if necessary (not all agents provide contracts).

Collect ALL press and reviews

Support other film makers by watching their work and cheering! HAVE FUN!

was more their thing. It is also good for film makers to know that we tend to share information about them as well as their films, which is a polite way of saying don't be a nightmare at festivals.

Q - Any advice on meeting other film makers at festivals and the value of that?

Sandra - In a sense, I really hope that film makers do meet each other, and we try to make it easier. If you are not part of the 'in crowd', then festivals can be just the most horrible, lonely experience. Everyone seems to know everyone else and they are having a grand old time getting invited to parties that you don't know about. That is how I felt my first few years of going to film festivals. So we do make sure that we have people who look after the film makers and make sure they are getting introduced to people. We try every night to have some social activity open to film makers. It is hard, you need to have confidence when everyone seems to know everyone else. But as with all these things, the best thing is just to ask in advance so you know what is possible.

Q - What is the festival circuit and how do you get on it?

Sandra - In every part of the world there is at least one major film festival going on each week. So if film makers generate some buzz, they can find the film and themselves being passed on from one festival to the next - that's the festival circuit. So how you get on it is obviously by having a film that is well received.

Q - Are film festivals great places for talent to be spotted by distributors and producers?

Sandra - Yes. Amongst the number of delegates there are a lot of buyers and sellers, but there are a large number of development execs, and they will come along to screenings to find new talent. It is the most competitive part of their jobs. They will come to the buyer and seller screenings or come to public screenings to see how films play in front of an audience. And a lot of that is off their own initiative. At the same time, we do a lot of work on getting people to come and see certain titles. The film festival is big and giving direction towards particular films is sometimes necessary.

Q - What are the common mistakes that you see from film makers?

Sandra - You can generalise and say that people don't get their scripts right or the boom is in the shot, but in the terms of the selection process I can't categorise what makes my heart sink. I find it really hard to believe that there are things that, if you do them, mean that your film will be good or it will get selected. There is no surer way to make a dull film! So the worst thing is seeing something that has been made a thousand times already that year. Of course, I shouldn't say, '*don't make those films just because they might not be of interest to the festival*', because people have to learn how to make films, and how do you learn? You learn by doing it. The mistake is in thinking that every film made should be seen by a paying audience. I don't come from a commercial background, but I do have to think about the audience, but I don't believe film makers should tailor their films that way.

Q - The instant genius syndrome can kick in where film makers aren't given the chance to learn?

Sandra - That is where digital is important because it gives people a way to try things out and practice their craft. That means our submissions go up and that means more films that aren't right for the festival get rejected too. But they may have been right for the person who made it. And maybe their film isn't right for the festival, but there is talent there and we file that fact away to see what they make next.

Q - What advice would you give a new film maker?

Sandra - Treat people as you would like to be treated yourself. Extend a certain amount of courtesy to everyone. It is that old cliché, for everyone you pass going up, you will pass them on the way down. And something else that I have been harping on in my answers is not to be afraid to ask. Most people are kind of flattered to be asked for their knowledge and expertise in an area. None of us ever got anywhere completely on our own - we all ask for help.

SALES

Julia Jones
DDA PR

PUBLIC RELATIONS

Q - What is your job?

Julia - My job is to publicise and create the profile for a film. I come on board as early as possible, ideally in pre-production because that is the time when you really need to start planning your publicity. If you haven't done it during production, and you leave it until you are in post, you've missed many opportunities. I advise on stills, I work on written materials, production notes, the EPK, and all the supporting materials to promote your film. These are essential elements as they are seen before the film is released.

Q - So how early should you get involved?

Julia - As soon as the cameras roll, you should have someone on board doing your publicity.

Q - How important is it that right from the get-go, everybody knows what kind of film they are making?

Julia - I think it is very important. An audience will want to know what they are going to see. If you are vague, that puts you in a weaker position. Clarity is essential.

Q - How important is the cast to the publicity?

Julia - Very important. It falls into two areas. You've either got "names" and the phone is going to start ringing because the press know that you are in production and a major part of your job is fielding requests and prioritising. At that level you have also got to deal with personal publicists. The second area is if you have unknown actors. Journalists are often quite open to doing stories on rising stars. Here, your role is to create a profile for new talent. Your cast is essential to your publicity campaign.

Q - One area new filmmakers really screw up is stills. What have you got to say on that?

Julia - Tell me about it! I've been in situations with low budget movies where somebody will say *'my friends, friends, nephew can shoot on a throw away camera from Snappy Snaps!'* If you are taking the time and energy to plough money into making a film, with no stills to support it, how are you going to sell it? Once the production period is over, it is too late, you can't suddenly recreate it, and catching those moments is so important.

Q - What kind of image should you be looking for? Given people don't have endless budgets, what would be the best way that you would suggest getting images that are good enough to support the marketing of the movie?

Julia - Go through the script with a fine toothcomb and choose the scenes where you know you're likely to capture iconic images. If you have an eye for it, you can see what's going to get used. On a low budget, it's not a case of shooting stills everyday. Tear that script apart, and go *'Ok we've only got X days, so let's choose those days very carefully, so we know we will get the right images for the right scenes'.* You are better off getting somebody really experienced on for a few days than having someone inexperienced for the whole shoot.

Q - I assume they are all done digitally now?

Julia - Yes most of them are.

Q - I think the word you just used which is key is iconic. It is not just a shot of the actor walking down a street, it is 'that' moment.

Julia - And you might spend 5 weeks waiting for that moment to happen. You have to be ready to capture it.

Q - That image may then become the key image for the advertising campaign that everyone sees when they think of the movie. It often ends up being integrated into the poster, then that fits in with the title, and everything clicks if you get it right?

Julia - Exactly. It is part of the jigsaw.

Q - What is a Press Pack?

Julia - A Press Pack consists of the production notes, including a long synopsis and short synopsis of the movie; the story of the film, how it came to be, the process, history behind it and how it was financed. The casting process, the director's vision, and the look and the feel of the project, general production information, locations, info about costumes, production design and anecdotal stories from filming. Quotes from the actors about their character and anything that adds colour and essense. If they've been shooting in some fantastic location, stories from that are useful. Journalists read the production notes and pull out information to write features and diary stories. Stills are also part of the overall press pack.

Q - Traditionally that was printed out on paper, with 10x8 Black and White photos. I assume it is done electronically now, as well as on paper?

Julia - Yes. Once you get to the release process, the key set of stills will be put on Image Net and people will just download them.

Q - Amongst most filmmaker teams, at least one person is a geek, and there is no reason why you shouldn't have a website almost to rival Peter Jackson's King Kong website, technologically it is not very hard to put together. Of course it serves two purposes, I assume not only is it a talking point for the movie, but the simple delivery mechanism for stills, PDF's etc?

Julia - A decent website makes the project look serious, and increases the overall kudos.

Q - If you get some new, young filmmaker in your project who wants to do websites, just let them do it, as long as they do it brilliantly.

Julia - Definitely.

Q - What is an EPK?

Julia - An Electronic Press Kit. A behind the scenes documentary, including interviews with all the actors, heads of department. The EPK crew also shoot extensive background footage of key scenes, rehearsals etc. It basically tells the story of the production on camera. The distributors utilise this material for their release publicity, supplying it to TV stations.

Q - So when you are watching Sky movies, and you've got that 7-minute behind the scenes making of X, that is all pulled out of an EPK?

Julia - Yes.

Q - On a low budget film, there is no reason why they can't shoot it on one of the higher end DV formats?

)))
dda public relations ltd

Julia Jones
Senior Vice President

192-198 Vauxhall Bridge Road
London SW1V 1DX

Main: + 44 (0) 20 7932 9800
Fax: + 44 (0) 20 7932 4950
julia.jones@ddapr.com
www.ddapr.com

SALES

Julia - Absolutely.

Q - On an independent film, rather than leave it to the producer, or even the director to take care of that DV EPK shoot, should you create a little unit and do it separately, so they can get it right?

Julia - Yes. Someone is always going to be interested in doing that, because it is quite a fun job. If you've got someone who is creative, just let them run with it. You'll be amazed at what you can get.

Q - Can you have too much publicity, or badly timed publicity?

Julia - Yes you can. You can have too much too soon and people can start to get bored of a project way before the release. It's a very fine balance and if you haven't got enough, you don't have that early buzz. I think you always have to drip-feed, have a certain amount during production to whet people's appetites, and then have the majority held for the release campaign.

Q - I guess one of the reasons why people hire somebody like yourself is because you know exactly who to drip-feed that information to, and at what point. I could loftily announce that I could do it myself, but I've just got the Daily Express phone number from their website, I don't know who to speak to, when to talk to them? You do.

Julia - Absolutely, you have a whole set of journalists who are tried, tested and trusted. That is the thing, you can call up a newspaper, and say *'come and do a set visit on my film'* and you get some random person from a newspaper who exposes your whole story, and starts writing stuff about your lead actor. Journalists who are approved, who work with film companies all the time, know that we need them and then they need us, so we all work together and we trust them. They are not going to stitch us up, because they know that they won't go onto the next film. There's a community of publicists and journalists who work together regularly.

Q - What is a good strategy for an independent film? Assuming they've not got a sales agent already.

Julia - You must have all your publicity and sales support materials lined up so that you've got all your supporting materials - stills, production notes, EPK, so when you do start approaching sales agents, you look professional and they will take you seriously.

The Press GUERILLA FILM MAKER SAYS!

1. Try and get a PR agent on board. If you cannot afford one, go ask for advice and do it yourself. It's not too hard, but you have to be quite charming, persistent and put in the hours.

2. Doing press for a film is pretty much a full time job, especially in the run up to the release - don't try and take on too much.

3. A press pack is vital. It should contain a synopsis, cast and crew bios, production notes and four or five good stills, including one of the director.

4. Work out the unique selling angle of your film and play on that. If the film is controversial, stir it up even more.

5. An electronic press kit (EPK) is also helpful - a copy of video taped and loosely edited interviews with cast and crew with long clips from the film and shots during production. Usually supplied on BetaSP / DigiBeta or possibly DVCam.

6. Journalists will almost always hunt out the story. If you don't want it to be printed, don't tell them - EVER.

7. Magazines will work with long deadlines, contact them as early as possible.

8. Your story will probably only break once, so try and time it for maximum effect i.e. the weeks leading up to your release.

9. Local press, TV, newspapers and radio are easy to get and can help solve pre production problems.

10. Avoid talking about the budget and focus on the film and it's unique selling point.

Handling Interviews

GUERILLA FILM MAKER SAYS!

If you wanted to be in front of the camera, you would have been an actor. However, as the filmmaker or producer, you will have to do interviews in order to publicise your project, so after all that avoidance, you will finally feel the glare of the lights. Remember, there are three main types of media - print (inc photos and internet), radio (inc podcasting etc) and TV (DVD etc.) Each require a different approach. Think about what you are doing before you turn up for the interview.

1. Have a list of questions which you can offer an interviewer who might not be prepared. You will have well rehearsed answers for these questions.

2. You will be asked the same questions over and over again. Have responses that are concise, intelligent, humorous or profound. If you can swing it, try to get the interviewer to show you the questions in advance.

3. If you are being recorded, pause before answering. This will give the editor a clear editing point.

4. Try to answer the question with the question in the answer. For example... 'What was working with an elephant like?' is answered, 'Working with an elephant was fantastic...'

5. Refer to the film by name. Avoid referring to it as "the film" or "the project". If people don't know what it is called they won't go to see it.

6. Wear something interesting so that at the very least you will stand out.

7. It is not a bad thing to avoid answering confrontational questions, especially if the reporter has a grudge against you or a hidden agenda. Politely decline to answer or shift the conversation back to the film itself. However, creating controversy around a film can help at the box office.

8. Always have your publicity stuff on you - press pack, EPK, stills, posters, etc.

9. Telling good, relevant stories is always better than giving boring standard information.

10. Make sure you know how long the interview will last so you can organise yourself to get the maximum amount of information out in the time.

11. Have business cards printed up and give one to the interviewer so that they can contact you for more information - and get your name spelled correctly!

12. The interviewer may want you to say something particular or in a particular way. Try to be flexible here and let them put words in your mouth - as long as they are accurate!

13. If you don't want something to get into the press, don't say it to them.

14. Always be complimentary of other film makers and their work, and of the people you have worked with. If you have nothing nice to say, don't say anything.

15. Try to avoid talking about the budget of your film unless it was a remarkable feat, such as you made it for £2k generated by having medical experiments done to you.

Q - Whenever I've spoken to sales agents, they just roll their eyes and say 'For God's sake have some stills, get organised'

Julia - You can't afford to mess up your stills. A sales agent needs to service their distributors and if all you've got is a couple of out-of-focus shots, they can't promote the film in their international territories.

Q - Most new filmmakers don't have sales agents on board because they haven't got a proven track record and the project isn't strong enough in terms of casting and the screenplay. Do you think it is important to differentiate that there are two different kinds of marketing campaigns that go on, one is to the public, to bring awareness about the film. That is generally going to happen during the release of the film, theatrically or DVD. But the other one is a campaign aimed at the industry and sales agents, to promote both the film and the film makers?

Julia - Absolutely, and it is all the more important to get trade coverage. If you've got an exciting new, young filmmaker, and you get a piece in Variety, or Screen International, or Hollywood Reporter, all those sales agents, prospective distributors are going to read about them and they're more likely to want to know more about the project.

Q - And, in fact, you could argue that it is even more important than getting all your stuff ready for the DVD and the theatrical release?

SALES

Publicity on Set

GUERILLA FILM MAKER SAYS!

People get a buzz from being on a film set. This includes the press, which you can use to your advantage, but only while you're still in production.

1. Invite local newspaper, TV and radio reporters down to the set for a first hand look at moviemaking in action. It will get them excited, especially if you are shooting in a small community that doesn't get such 'glamour' every day.

2. Do interviews now, which means using your cast while you have them. It is much easier than trying to get them back later when they are on another project, and god forbid, if they fell out with you, or most commonly, the film stinks and they are embarrassed by it.

3. Having a constant flow of press coverage will make your investors happy.

4. Create CD-ROMS / well maintained web site, of still photographs of the director and principle cast in action. Hand out disks to the visiting reporters to make their lives easier, and email them web links for downloads.

5. Collect and archive all articles about your project. It will come in handy later to help promote future projects and add credibility to your next project. Get into the habit of recording your TV and radio appearances as rarely will you be able to get copies out of them.

Julia - Absolutely. You've got to secure your release, so hitting the industry by hitting the trades is vital. Coverage in the trades can help you secure your theatrical release, and sending promotional material about the film, images, and background info to the sales agents.

Q - If a film is picked up, all the PR about the film will probably be re-done anyway, by experienced agencies? All they need to do then is just supply them with the raw stuff, and they will shape it into a campaign?

Julia - Yes, and they'll mould the whole thing, and create an overall release strategy. I think clarity is important, from the outset, you need to know how you are trying to pitch it. If I was a sales agent and somebody came to me with *'well, it is kind of this and kind of that'*, with no proper pitch or written materials, or images, I would probably pass. Presentation is vital.

Q - Who organises screenings for journalists, in the run up to a release of a film?

Julia - That is all organised by either the distributor or the PR Company. It all has to go through an official process, because there are so many films being screened over the course of a year. You have to apply for a magazine screening so all the distributors then get their magazine slot, that will be 4 months before release. Then, at staggered intervals, you will do a Fleet Street screening, a radio and TV screening, a multimedia screening, so it is all very targeted and very specific, and timed implicitly.

Q - What do you think are the qualities of a terrific publicist?

Julia - You've got to be a people person. You have to be able to write, and have an eye for good stills. To do unit publicity you need to be a diplomat and be able to get on with everyone. To do release publicity you've got to be very tenacious, because you are hitting the phones the whole time, and you've got to be more of a sales person, like a "dog with a bone". Journalists get so many calls every day, they are being pitched stories constantly, so you've got to be a good sales person.

Q - One thing that strikes me about publicity for the release, is that you can't get more of a coalface atmosphere than that! You are really at the front line, and at that point, the filmmaker can often become aware of all the weaknesses of the film, because they are in the hottest environment they will ever be in. Do you have any comments about the quantity of stuff people are being bombarded with, every day, and making your film stand out in some way. What possible reason would you have for seeing this little indie film as opposed to say, 'Lord of the Rings' or 'King Kong', or 'Star Wars Episode 3'?

Julia - I think a lot of it has to do with who is doing your PR. It is all to do with contacts, if you've got an agency or an individual who is respected and has got very good contacts you will get a better response. Because the journalists are getting so many calls, so many e-mails, so much stuff through the post, actually picking up the phone and having a personal contact and being able to explain *'this is really worth seeing'* is one of the most important things. As we're all aware, good word-of-mouth is the most powerful tool in a campaign.

Q - Let's say an independent filmmaker with a great concept, great script, good cast, everything in place, has managed to secure a tiny amount of money to make the film, say £150k - would it be wise to make the film for £150k and then try and go for it, and see what happens. Or would it be wiser to make it for £100k and then spend £50k on PR later on?

Julia - As long as it is not going to compromise the project. I would say definitely spend money on PR and ensure you have good stills and support materials. The big studios often spend many times more the budget of a film PR.

Q - How do publicists generally charge their time?

Julia - It is usually a flat fee. Even if they have little or no money, before shooting a young producer is better off calling up a freelance publicist or an agency and just saying *'Can you help me out?'* There are many publicists who are happy to help young filmmakers. I've done it myself. I think to wait until after the shoot is a big mistake.

Q - What makes a great poster?

Julia - It has got to be eye-catching and intriguing. I think simplicity as with most things, is the way to go.

Q - Which again, for me, leads right back to the very moment when you sit in front of your word processor, and you say, 'what is it I'm going to make?'. You need a really simple strong idea that is going to leap off the page, which is going to excite people on set, and then it's going to self-market because it is that great killer concept.

Julia - I think the greatest ideas are the simplest. The more complicated and contrived a story becomes, it confuses people. Simple, stylish and clever is the most effective approach.

Q - How important do you think it is to hold a glitzy premiere?

Julia - You don't have to spend an absolute fortune, as long as it's cool, and you get the right people along, and it becomes a talking point. You don't need to do a massive party, and have stunts and fire-eaters, you can just do something really contained, but stylish. That's just as effective.

Q - Then an after premiere party I assume?

Julia - Yes, at a venue that is going to be fun. It doesn't have to be wildly expensive, but it should have a cool element and people must want to go to it. If you've got a few names there, invite the paparazzi along - they don't care whether it is a tiny, micro budget movie as long as you've got a few faces there.

Q - What are the common mistakes that you see?

Julia - Not having enough materials to support the release of the film. It is a cardinal sin, it is like you might as well not bother. In the age that we live in now, and the audience's hunger for behind the scenes information is even greater.

Q - What advice would you offer a new filmmaker?

Julia - Be nice to people. Treat other people how you want to be treated yourself and you will go a long way. I don't think you have to be a ruthless asshole to get on. What goes around, comes around. If you upset someone, they might be in some amazing position one-day, and you might need them!

SALES

Nigel Floyd
Film Critic

FILM CRITIC

Q - What is your job?

Nigel - I review films and write features about films and the film-makers.

Q - What is unique to low budget films from your perspective?

Nigel - If you are an independent film maker and you think that your film should be given an extra star just because it cost £100k as opposed to £100m then you are barking up the wrong tree. To some extent you get brownie points for having gone out there and done it, because most critics have never made a film. But in the end you have got to judge the film as a film. It is hard because you have split loyalties - I want to encourage film makers because I know how hard it is for them to make the film and I want them to succeed; but you also have a responsibility to the readers, especially if you write regularly for a publication like *Time Out.* The readers need to know that the reviews are consistent so they can make a judgement about which film to spend their time and money on.

Q - Film makers complain that making a low budget film isn't a level playing field. But the minute that you get it on the screen, it is a level playing field because the audience responds to it purely as a story and they don't care about the budget.

Nigel - Yes, take *Following,* it's a very strong, nicely played, well constructed film, and the reviews were very good. It wasn't because it was made cheaply that the reviews were good, it was because it was an interesting take on something new and the ideas were up there on the screen - not handed down clichés, but of fresh and original ideas. On the other hand, so many films are appalling and it doesn't matter how much it cost or how much publicity money the distributors throw at them, they will not get any better. As a critic I would prefer to see something fresh and interesting.

Q - What should a film maker give to you to make your job of reviewing their film any easier?

Nigel - This is an area where people fall down very badly. The three most important things for any independent film are STILLS, STILLS and STILLS. Most independent film makers think that if they spend long enough making the film it will sell itself. Films don't sell themselves, they have to be sold, and one of the things that sells a movie, and particularly the way that magazines and websites are constructed now, is images of your movie. These should be taken by a professional photographer during the shoot. When the art director at *Total Film* or *Time Out* sits down to lay out the page, if they have four crappy B&W grainy images from a little independent movie and one monster pic from the latest Schwarzenegger film, with shades, sparks flying, hardware and muscles, then they are going to choose the Schwarzenegger pic. They don't think in terms of film or story telling quality, they think about how a picture is going to look on the page. You can get the press involved early on, get them on set and get them involved in the idea of what the movie is about. You may spend a year editing without any money, but if journalists were on board at the beginning, then there is a likelihood that when the movie is screened they will look more favourably upon it because they are somehow involved.

Q - It's human psychology that you would be inclined to be more favourable if you like someone, and more damning if you don't like someone?

Nigel - Yes. Personalities ought not to be an issue but the fact is that when you do an interview and you get on with the film maker, they are making an effort to engage with you and talk about the film, then there is a tendency to feel more positive towards them and their film. Another common problem is poorly organised screenings. If you can afford it, employ someone to organise screenings on your behalf. If not then hire out cinemas early in the morning and get people along.

What's in the Press Kit?

COVER
Movie title, contact, press quotes, credits and film festival awards.

SYNOPSIS
The story of the movie, with a few pics to spice it up.

CAST & CREW
Bios of main cast and crew, with pics and brief quotes about the making of the film. Also, full cast and crew listing.

NOTES
The story of how the film got made, where, why and when.

REVIEWS
Copies of all your good reviews that you have collected so far. Don't include bad reviews!

Credits
Complete cast, crew and technical credits.

If I receive two invitations and one of them comes on a scrappy photocopied piece of paper and the other comes on a nice printed ticket, the chances are that I am going to think to myself, *I need to go to this one, this is the one that look's like it is going to do the business, this is the one that is actually going to be out there*. You need people saying hello as you come in, getting names and phone numbers, so that afterwards you might have a ring round to ask people for their opinion, or send them an email asking for a few words about their reaction.

Journalists also need well presented, reliable and detailed information about the characters, actors, principle crew. Also background information on how and why the film was made. This is usually in the form of a press pack, and it must be professionally presented. If I receive a press kit for a small independent film and it looks like they have taken the trouble to use some computer graphics or a still or something on the cover, or to use an icon like the *Blair Witch* stick man, then I have a sense that they are involved in selling the film to me. You don't want to plead *please feel sorry for us, because this only cost £3k* but you can be factual and put in interesting stories and anecdotes, stuff that journalists might pick up on. Then when they do an interview they can say *that was an interesting story about that night when you were trying to do the big effects scene and everything went wrong*. So in a sense you can lead journalists into areas you want to be given exposure.

One thing that is guaranteed to make journalists feel good about your work is to offer them a drink at the screening, nothing heavy, just a beer or coffee, and perhaps a few sandwiches. In a way it is a lot like art direction, you shouldn't notice the hospitality, but when it is not there, you notice it immediately. So you wander in, are greeted by someone, get a drink, watch the movie - which starts on time and is well presented - then at the end people are standing around thanking you for coming - it is very simple manners. Then you get home and look at the press kit and you go *oh, yes, I see, so that's the guy, oh yes he did this, oh yes, he was involved in that other movie*. And when you sit down to write your review you have it all at your fingertips.

Q - Do journalists talk to each other?

Nigel - Yes. Naturally you gravitate towards the people that share your likes and interests. Word of mouth within that community is almost as important as the word of mouth out there in the audience at large. Again, if people have a choice between three screenings in one evening and they have heard that there is this really interesting low budget independent film that has good word of mouth, they might be inclined to see it above the two bigger competitors.

Q - If your film is going to be released by a small distributor, or if you are going to distribute yourself, how can you get as much good press as possible?

SALES

inside her womb? Long on atmosphere but sh n momentum, the meandering plot is fleshe t by Theron's delicately nuanced perfor nce. Ravich's slick direction, meanwhile, fills interiors of the couple's apartment with a ing menace. Sadly, this slow-burning sus se is rapidly extinguished when too much is aled at just the wrong moment. (Nigel Floyd) *E: Plaza*

Nigel - You can't start early enough. In a sense, you need to cultivate the journalists, not schmooze them or be sycophantic, because that can be counter productive, just act professionally. I have seen many low budget independent films pissed away because they made a pretty good film, with a few problems, but had no idea of what to do when it came to being presented.

It's important to have a hook - something that captures the imagination of the journalist, a background story, an interesting tale that happened during the making of the movie, something that might make it stand out as a story. If the arts editor of a TV show says *we have got to do something about films this week,* and they look down the list and there are a couple of sub-titled movies which they can't do because it's breakfast TV and then they say *Oh, there's this little independent movie,* like yours perhaps, *there's a story here.* Not every film is going to have that magic ingredient, that built in hook, but it is up to you to find one. Some new directors tend to present themselves and their movie in such a way as to antagonise people - *here's my film, it is brilliant, I am the best film maker that has ever been* - it's not surprising then that if the movie is on the edge, critics will tend to lean toward a bad review. It's also important to make yourself and your cast available to journalists.

Q - Should you approach everyone with your film?

Nigel - New film makers tend to hit everyone, which is counter productive and wastes energy and resources. For instance if you have a low budget horror comedy then you are not going to target *Sight and Sound* or the *Sunday Times,* you are going to target the sort of publications that are sympathetic to that kind of movie. Similarly if you have made an action picture you are more likely to get coverage in *Total Film* or *Empire* than you are in *Women's Realm*. You have to think about which publications you will target.

Q - What is the SFD (Society of Film Distributors)?

Nigel - The SFD co-ordinates the times and dates of screenings for journalists. They try to organise things so as to avoid conflicts, such as two screenings of different films, both for magazines but at the same time. They organise separate screenings for magazines, TV and radio, London and suburban newspapers, and the national press. As an independent film maker you are not part of that club, so unless your film is being distributed by one of the majors, finding a slot is going to be a major headache, but not impossible.

Q - What is lead time?

Nigel - It is the time between a journalist seeing a film, writing about it, and then the magazine actually going to press and hitting the streets. You have to understand that the lead times for different publications are very different, so if you are dealing with a glossy magazine that is published monthly, like Maxim, the lead time can be as much as two months. Magazines like Total Film and Empire have slightly shorter lead times, and daily newspapers will just want to see the film a week or so before it's release.

Q - What is positioning a film all about?

Nigel - It is a cynical word, but movies are 'positioned' and a lot of thought goes into it. The campaign for *East is East* took a low common denominator approach, *it's the mutt's nuts* and *it's the dog's bollocks.* It was a brilliant campaign as it side stepped what the movie was really about and got people to go and see it. I know that they spent months working out how to position an Asian comedy in a multiplex environment. You need to figure out who your audience is, how to get to them and what will make them want to see your movie. Your movie, *Urban Ghost Story,* is not an easy film to position. On one hand it addresses social issues but on the other hand it appears to have some kind of supernatural element. You don't want people coming expecting a ghost story, but at the same time you don't want to overplay its social realism because then people will be equally misguided. Not all films have a single *Star Wars Episode One: The Phantom Menace* kind of simplicity about them. In some ways this is where journalists can help and if they like the film they can get behind it. You can also think in terms of an icon too, which will normally be derived from the movie concept and probably some stills. *Blair Witch...* the image of the stick man became a kind of icon. Show that image to anyone now and they will say *The Blair Witch Project.* The Pi symbol from the US Indie film *Pi* also became synonymous with the movie.

Q - What about the Internet?

Nigel - *Blair Witch* was clearly helped by the swell of support from the Internet site and the build up before it came out. It is very cheap

Setting up Press Screenings

GUERILLA FILM MAKER SAYS!

1. Give yourself enough lead time. Magazines, television and newspapers usually start thinking about stories 3-4 months before they appear in their publications or on air. Contact them around this time to get things rolling. But, also remember that you only get one story out of them, so make it count!

2. Create a press release. This is usually a one sheet, 2-3 paragraph statement that tells the press the basic details of your film like when the film will screen along with an RSVP contact number. Contact the publications that you want to show up and ask for the fax number or e-mail to their news desk.

3. Book a theatre. Make sure they can screen whatever format you are going to show your film on and make certain there are enough seats for the amount of people you invited. Although standing room only would be a good sign!

4. Have press packs made for the screening. This should contain all the basic information that the press needs to write a review about your film. This consists of production information, a synopsis, bios of the key cast and crew and still photographs of the director and key cast members. You can include statements from other people who may have been crucial for the inspiration for the film, such as the author of a book on which it was based.

5. Have a hospitality area set up. The press love free food and alcohol, and putting them in a good mood before they see your film can't hurt.

6. While not necessary, having the director, producer, writer or actors around for a Q&A session can be beneficial and a lot of fun.

7. Try to get a few "ringers" in the audience (friends, relatives) who will laugh or clap to create a positive atmosphere, which may sway a reviewer's opinion. DO NOT OVERDO THIS! EVER!

8. Don't be so concerned about getting your film screened on the big screen by journalists. Many might not make it, so have DVD's available. Some film critics might have their own particular requirements, such as insisting on watching the film in a screening room all to themselves.

9. Find the hook of your film that sets your film apart from others and then stress that to the press.

10. Follow up your press screenings with phone calls to the journalists to thank them for calling and to take their temperature as to how they enjoyed the film.

11. Remember that your low budget film is being judged the same as Hollywood blockbusters. Expect criticism.

12. Remember that there is really no bad publicity. Invite as many publications as you can for the smaller organisations are just as passionate about film as the larger ones and may give you more good reviews from which to choose.

to set one up and is a good way of getting information to journalists. Always put your website address on posters and press kits, and make sure it's easy for a journalist to send you an email.

Q - Is there a list of journalists I can contact to see my film?

Nigel - Someone once phoned me, someone that I hardly knew and said *would you let me have your contacts list of all the journalists in the film industry* and I said *yes, if you pay me £2000*. Information is power. Those details are held on databases at PR companies and are very valuable to them. It is a major part of their business, knowing who is who and who can do what for you.

If you don't have a PR agency working for you, you will have to go and buy all the magazines and newspapers, write down where they are and then contact each of them. There is no guarantee that you will get to the right person either, whereas a PR company will already have a relationship with the right journalists and know exactly who is right for the project. I would advise approaching a major PR company if you are a low budget film. They know they will not get blood out of a stone, but if you are professional and they like you and the movie, they may be inclined to help and do a deal with you. If you can't afford to employ them, then maybe you can buy an hour of their time and say *can you give me some pointers here, because I don't have any money, but what sort of things could I do?*

Q - What advice would you offer a new filmmaker?

Nigel - It all comes down to stills, stills and stills. Then the press kit, then screenings, in that order. The stills you have got to do while you are shooting, the press kit has to be prepared before you get to the screening, and the screening has got to be run professionally.

SALES

Christopher Fowler
Creative Partnership

Q - What is it that the Creative Partnership does?

Chris - The Creative Partnership advertises films. It handles the marketing and advertising of feature films in the UK, internationally, and in North America.

Q - While a micro-budget / independent filmmaker may not be able to employ your services, because they simply don't have the budget, they can certainly look at what you do, and emulate what you do as best as they can. Can they come in and talk to you as well?

Chris - I think that is one of the changes since we last spoke. We know every film that is being made in the UK, we keep an eye on everything as it is approaching the start gate and then going into production. Under the old system if someone had a super low budget movie, they could come in and sit and talk to us, we would keep track and we would help them out. They probably wouldn't have any money to put in the P&A, but we would kind of see them through it. They would cobble something together, and then get a small independent release. These days, the independent scene has pretty much vanished from the UK Theatrical world. Independent film viewers have become DVD buyers, so a lot of those films that would have opened in a couple of screens, now, if they are good enough, go on to DVD. We are seeing a lot lower through-put of small British independent films. If they do come through, it is normally because someone bigger than them has a vested interest in them. Therefore they are putting up the P&A money, so there is a good chance that when they come through the door, they will have a budget. We will talk to low budgeters no problem, but the days when people arrived with simply no idea at all, and no money to implement it, are pretty much gone.

Q - So what would your advice about marketing be, to a new film maker who is about to make a film, or has just completed one?

Chris - I think number one is find your demographic and stick to it, because the market is very segmented. There is no point making a kid's film with a ton of swearing. There is no point making a gangster film right now when the cycle has ended. You need to find what your demographic is going to be and tailor it to the certificate you want, in advance, because that is what everyone else is doing. We sometimes act as advisors for this sort of thing.

For example on the film *Wilde*, we found that there were UK websites for Oscar Wilde, run out of Universities. So we said, your key audience is actually younger than you think, so you have got to get a 15 for this. In fact, prior to production, a couple of sex scenes were reduced. They were kind of repetitive anyway, and there was already enough in there. It got its 15, and it found the right target market and did really well. The other thing was positioning it in advance. Everybody knew it was *Wilde*, the story of the first modern man, a 20th century man in the 19th century, and it was a very appealing subject. When you've got that, we start to create an image, and the first shot was him wearing a white suit as he walks through a whole crowd of people in black suits. It was all about individualism and being brave enough to be individual. Once you have got that as a hook, everybody knows what they are doing, what you are meant to take away from the finished product, so we all started from the same page. It was really helpful to have a producer and director who were completely amenable to us having a hand in that, it helped us really shape it.

Q - Do you think that is a common problem with new and young filmmakers that they kind of go off on this journey, they don't quite know what they are making?

Chris - Yes. I think they don't do enough back-end work. I think a lot of the kids I have talked to, they know the films of Goddard and Eisenstein, just as much as they know Carry-On movies, which is great, but they haven't really thought about distribution. They don't know what they are going to say to exhibitors for example. Go and talk to exhibitors, because it is really interesting, they have a completely different take on what plays and they will give you the grass roots on what they are looking for. If you don't connect your ideas with the business side of it, you are pretty fucked.

Q - In terms of putting together the key elements, what are they, the poster, trailer, anything else?

Chris - If it is an independent film being shot in the UK, we normally try and do a special shoot, while the cast is still together. Get all the stills, get all the material done. Our biggest single problem is access to material, because so many films now contain CGI, and so many films run very late to the gate. We are now running on *Fantastic Four*, and we are working right up to just prior to when the film hits without having seen it, because it is not completed yet. This is really common. The trouble is if you wait for it to be completed, before you pick up your special photography, you are too late. It needs to be done while the film is in its early stages. Also you lose people, they go off and do other things, have a hair cut, get a sun tan, they look different. You need to keep everyone together longer to get special materials for sales. We are just preparing *Stormbreaker*, based on the teenage spy books. The very first thing that has been done is to shoot the major cast, tons of poses, because those poses will be digitally worked for posters, all the print and press material will spin out of the shoot, so get that lot together.

Q - Do you have any comments on the title of the movie?

Chris - If it feels like there is a real problem with the title, for a specific reason, like it is too reminiscent of something recent, or if it is too vague, if it gives you absolutely no direction, we normally recommend changing it. I was just doing that this morning on a film. That is really the director or writer's call. Quite often it happens, though not as often as it used to. I think those kind of things are basic stuff that will be looked at from the outset. The sales agent needs to know exactly what they are selling. The worst thing to do with anything in film is to change it midstream. The day you start shooting is the day you start building an awareness.

Q - What do you think is the very minimum you need to put together for a very low budget independent film, in order to take it to market? To secure a sale, with enough of those elements in place so that the distributor and sales agent can do their jobs properly?

Chris - The barest minimum would be synopsis and stills. You can get away with special photography and a synopsis. Though there is no reason why you should not be able to put together a press pack and promo / trailer yourself.

Q - If someone is going to do their own trailer, poster, key artwork themselves, what advice would you give them about doing those two jobs?

Chris - I'm worried when the film's editor cuts his own trailer as they are normally too close to the film. Don't try to invent the wheel and say *'this film is going to be advertised in a way that no other film has been advertised'*. The guy who did the FCUK campaign said he was going to change the rules on cinema advertising and treat them like regular ads. He did the posters for *Layer Cake*, the girl in suspenders, and an iron on a jeep. But the iron on the jeep means nothing if you haven't seen the film, and weakened the audience perception of a terrific movie. The campaign was changed in mid-stream to a traditional campaign. Film advertising is kind of old fashioned but it is that way for a reason, because certain things

Christopher Fowler

Creative Partnership
13 Bateman Street
London W1D 3AF

Tel   020 7439 7762
Fax   020 7437 1467

chrisf@creativepartnership.co.uk
www.creativepartnership.co.uk

SALES

work, and public perception of how things look on posters, that is why when advertising agencies want to copy a movie poster they know exactly how to do it. There are certain elements in place, they are there for a reason.

Get somebody with an outside view to say what they think the film is, because when you have spent 16 weeks sitting in front of it yourself in the edit, the last thing you should do is then try and work out what someone, who knows nothing about it at all, can take from it.

Q - With regard to putting together a poster, what do you think the common mistakes people make, the people who sit at home with Photoshop, who can't afford to get someone to do it. What would your advice be to them?

Chris - We don't actually see that very often. It is very rare that somebody comes in with a Photoshop piece of art. Because normally even the smallest film, if it has got a chance in the market, will have somebody on board.

Q - That is the key distinction that a lot of new filmmakers probably don't get, that if you are putting your own artwork together, really you are putting it together to attract a distributor, or a sales agent, who is going to take your film to the next level, and all of that will then get replaced.

1. The First Poster
Produced in pre-production to give the film an identity. Note the film is called 'An Urban...' We dropped the 'An' in post production. The image also echoed a keyhole, implying a gateway to other worlds. It's quite a commercial image, but perhaps graphically, too far removed from what audiences expect from film advertising visual grammar. It was ditched once the film was in post.

2. The First Sales Poster
Once the film was complete, we became very aware that we couldn't just sell the movie as a horror film. The title alone was enough to let audiences know that it was within the horror genre, so we needed to pull the artwork away from expectations of 'Scream' or Texas Chainsaw...' The image we went with was printed in a deep red, and we felt it was a quite cryptic graphic. This was also used in the UK theatrical release. We soon became convinced that it was deeply flawed. It was ultimately ditched.

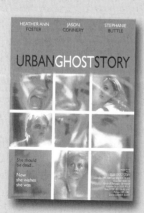

3. The Second Sales Poster
Once we moved to our second sales agent, we switched design too. We based the new art on the original 'keyhole' design. It was sleeker and simpler, with stark use of red and blue. Sure it was a harder selling image, but at that point, the film was not selling internationally. We decided to go down the 'it's a horror film' route. The image was well received by the sales agent and sales picked up.

4. The New UK Image Test
Unhappy with the UK cinema (aka The First Sales) poster, Chris designed a new image featuring the little girl looking over her shoulder. We all liked it as it implied the sense of other worlds and something following. It also featured Heather, the central and strongest performance in the film. It was however, perhaps a little refined and the film title was not large enough or bold enough. The image was re-invented by the new UK Distributor.

Chris - This is not about the consumer, it won't get to the consumer until way way down the other end of the process, and the distributor has a plan for your movie. So you are attracting a sales agent, you are attracting someone who sees the potential of what you've done, in order to make more copies of it to sell around the world.

Q - Do you have any comments when you see an independent film - do you see anything regularly about the film that would be easy to fix?

Chris - The general rule of thumb is repetition. They tend to edit it slightly on the long side, you just need to tighten it up. You rarely get a film that is so tight that is under-length. That is the main thing. Sometimes people will make a film that plays a lot younger than they realise. There was a film a few years ago called *'Shooting Fish'*, where they thought they had made a tough, gangland flick, and I thought they had made *Banana Splits:The Movie!* They couldn't see that it played really young. Dave Stewart made a film called *'Honest'* with the Appleton girls, and to me, it played like kids TV with guns. What you have to do with those films is take out some of the high-end nastiness, and aim it properly at their audience, because actually it is playing younger than you realise. A lot of films play younger than the makers realise, mainly because they have had the project in their minds for a long time, and the world is moving very fast.

Q - What are the most common mistakes that you see?

Key Art Design

GUERILLA FILM MAKER SAYS!

Most films have a single image that somehow captures the essence of the story, genre, cast and target audience. Think of posters that work well and everyone will all think of the same thing... Jaws (the shark and girl), Saw (the severed foot)... The problems come when the film makers are not entirely sure what box to put their film in. Our third film, 'Urban Ghost Story' is such a film. Most people seem to like it when they see it. but that has never been the problem for us. Getting them to pick it up and watch it has been the problem! This is because it's a low key, social realist ghost story. Now we can't market a ghost story to the people who like Ken Loach social realist films, nor can we market a horror movie as a slice of social realist arthouse film! Nontheless, people seem to like the movie when they actually see it. So how do you sell such a difficult concept in a simple and hopefully iconic fusion of image and words? Below and left are the various ways 'Urban Ghost Story' has been marketed and what we feel about the various images after the fact. You can judge how successful each is.

5. The UK DVD
After our distributor went bankrupt, we found ourselves in a new office with a company who wanted to re-design everything. That included the DVD cover. They wanted to go much more 'urban' and 'teen'. The image was reproduced in a deep browny red and drew heavily from Chris' last design. We all liked it, though felt it was a bit too 'teen horror'.

6. The USA DVD
Designed by MTI home video, this cover was put together completely without our involvement. It's certainly a genre image, and while we liked it, again, we were uncertain it accurately represented the film. That said, the film has performed quite well in the US marketplace. We have also received some annoyed emails from Americans complaining they couldn't understand the film or the accents!

SALES

Chris - Copying someone else is the most horribly obvious one. You get one hit, then you get 4,000 misses, each a copy. After *Lock Stock and Two Smoking Barrels,* for the next 3 years of my life, I had to sit through so many shit, awful, repetitive gangster films. You see an awful lot of script clichés, where people actually think they are doing something fresh and original. Perhaps their film history doesn't go back very far. In a way, that doesn't matter, because film works in a 7 year cycle maximum. So everything is being constantly reinvented from 7 years ago, and that is fine, it doesn't matter if it is just similar to a film that was made 10 years ago. But you really shouldn't recycle clichés. We still see *'Alien'* rip-offs. I've got a script on my desk this morning, which has got space men saying *'I've got a bad feeling that something awful has happened to the first crew we sent down...'* The other thing that we tend to see an awful lot of is gorgeous lighting over script quality, where they have got a great cinematographer, a good eye, and it has been edited to death, but there is nothing behind it. People are getting quite savvy to that now. People can spot when something is under-funded, and has been bailed out by a few decent lighting rigs. The answer to that question is over ambition in trying to make it look bigger than it is.

Q - So your advice would be to concentrate on a good story well told, as opposed to a glossy, Hollywood style movie that doesn't quite pull it off?

Chris - I get shivers when somebody tells me it is going to look great. I want them to say that it is going to move audiences.

Q - The irony is it doesn't really matter what it looks like, as long as there is a brilliant story, so play to your strength, if there is no money don't try and create 'money'.

Chris - To be honest it can look like shit without harming the films prospects. *The Blair Witch Project* looks like it is printed onto greaseproof paper. As long as it is compelling.

Another mistake we see on a practical level is to just decide who is going to pick up the tab before you start spending on the marketing. Sometimes the sales agent or the distributor will share the cost between them. What happens then, is you tend to get caught in the middle. They are both saying, *'he agreed to pay',* so decide in advance and lock down who is going to pick up which bill.

Q - What advice would you offer a new filmmaker?

Chris - Kill yourself now! (laughs) Don't use your own money! Get a cast-iron script that you are so happy with that you don't want to cut the work. Never go into production without it all finalised on paper. Never go in without knowing where your money is going. Ideally come out the end of it with something left over. Storyboard everything, and know what effect every scene should have on an audience.

Q - What is your job?

Chris - I am the creative director for a design company. So for the film community we do things like key art, posters and DVD covers.

Q - What elements does a film makers need to bring to you in order for you to get to work?

Chris - Whatever people can supply is fine. Sometimes people give me 7,000 pictures. My favourite piece I ever did I was only given one piece to work with though. Supply as much as you can and then don't worry about it.

Q - How do you approach creating the 'image' for a film when the director may have one vision and the distributor may have another?

Chris - I would approach that by trying to please all aspects of the committee by giving them what they want, and what they want, and what they want! And also supplying them with what they really should have if they trust that my understanding is more than equal to any problem they think they might have. Design is not a problem, its a way of reacting to the world

Q - What can you add to a good image that a film maker has made for themselves?

Chris - Generally all they need is refinement. They have a vast understanding of film making, direction, colour and composition. We translate that and combine it with our innate understanding of posters and other ways of marketing film. If they have a brilliant idea, I won't say that it is shit, I will say that it is fantastic and I will refine it. And they will be charged less. Most of the time, they will look at my refinements and say it works. Sometimes they don't listen. I have worked on films where they didn't listen though and then the result is often poor.

Q - When you are working, are you going by instinct mostly?

Chris - I've been doing this for 19 years so I would say it is not instinctive, it is more intuitive by now. If I want to make a film, I don't do it myself, I go to a film maker who knows how to make one. If I want to make a poster, I come to someone that knows how to make it and trust their understanding.

Q - Generally, how many designs would you go through before everyone is happy?

Chris - The most I would generally present would be three. It is often that they want five and in those situations, I would still present three. Usually it is the first one that hits the mark.

Q - How can film makers save money by making your life easy?

Chris Charlston
Artwork Designer

Chris - By trusting me and giving me time and a deadline. Even if I get bad elements, I can makes something work. Some of my best work has come from poor elements supplied by the film makers. If you get only a few images, you have to create something from scratch, and will therefore be highly tuned.

Q - What are the common mistakes you see in key art?

Chris - Usually it is letting the software create the art for them, rather than using the software as an artist would use a paintbrush. If a new filter comes out in Photoshop, you will see it everywhere. It is not their idea. It is the idea of the people who have made the program.

Q - What advice would you give a new designer who has been given the job of doing his mate's low budget feature?

Chris - Go down to Blockbuster where they arrange the videos and DVDs alphabetically and see what will be around your movie by title, and see what they look like. Also find out what genre it is and see what the current releases within that genre are, and try to make your design allude to that genre. Don't pastiche. See what you are competing against and make your image better than that. And have all your logos in the right place and size.

Q - What advice would you offer a new film maker?

Chris - Outsourcing. You are the film maker. You may be able to make a great film, but that doesn't mean you can make a great DVD. Trust people's skills. You hire a good soundman because he is good with sound and you hire a good editors because they're good at editing. But when it comes to things that you are not good at, find someone who is and it will increase the quality of the product.

eeso

www.eeso.co.uk   Chris Charlston

14a Iliffe Yard
London SE17 3QA   07900 906 285
                      cc@eeso.co.uk

SALES

Dave Hughes
Creative Partnership

MAKING A TRAILER

Q - What is your job?

Dave - My job is to write, produce and edit trailers for movies. Not just movie trailers, it is anything that can market and sell a movie. Whether that is selling it to cinema-goers, distributors, sales agents, video consumers etc., both here and abroad.

Q - There are two levels to the trailer for an independent film. The first trailer is to entice somebody from sales and distribution to pick up the film (and also market the film makers to the film business) and then that sales or distribution person is then going to move it to the next stage, and make a trailer for the end consumer. These trailers are different as they serve two distinct jobs.

Dave - Yes. Initially we are talking about a sales promo. The first thing you don't have to worry about with this trailer is being too long or too short. It can be as long as it needs to be, though often it's between three and five minutes. I think *The Lord of the Rings* one, for the first film and before it was finished, was 45 minutes long and shown at a special preview theatre in Cannes. That was New Line putting that together with a captive audience wanting to see it. With a low budget film you are not likely to get a captive audience for 45 minutes! So less is more. There are more and more low budget independent movies out there, so you have got to find a great hook for your movie. What is the unique selling point of your movie? If it is a genre picture, what makes it different from the other 40 low budget genre movies that are coming from England alone this year? As well as making it original you've also got to prove it can work in the existing market place. Distributors are reluctant to take on brand new ideas. So they need to be able to know it can work in a traditional way as well. Give the audience what they expect just not how they expected it, as Goldman says.

Because of the nature of those sales promos, so much shorthand is used, be it the voice-over, captions, montages etc. There is going to be an air of familiarity to it. There is a structure to the way these things are done for a reason, because it works. Though it's always great when you can break a rule and bring something fresh to the table.

Q - What do you think makes a great promo, or a great trailer?

Dave - A great movie.

Q - Assuming that they have not got a great movie, how do they make a great promo for their not so great movie?

Dave - It is difficult to discuss that without having a specific example. One thing to be aware of is that with a promo, you are basically pitching to industry people. You are dealing with the most cynical audience who is ever going to watch anything you make. Flashy montage editing, snazzy graphics, great use of music, they have seen them all before and it won't impress them. You have to find what is fresh and exciting about your movie and push that. So how do you make a good promo for a bad movie? If you have got a real stinker, then you have to push the fact that, worst case scenario, it is going to be good for *'straight to video'*. Think of the film you were trying to make when you were starting. Say you wanted to make a horror movie, something like *Evil Dead*, or *Se7en*, then go and watch those trailers and use them as your template. Watch as many trailers and promos as you can so that you understand the form. Also you don't have to worry about lying in a promo, because everybody does it. Everybody.

Q - I have heard music from top composers used in sales promos where the film maker could never afford that music. How can they do that?

Dave - At this stage of the game, as the promo is not for commercial use, you can use any music you want. The chances are the sales people you are showing it to will know that the music you used is not going to be in the movie, and they will probably have heard the music before in another promo, because these guys would have seen many hundreds at any one market.

Q - Often new film makers don't know exactly what they have made - it's a fusion of ideas and genres. How important do you think it is to seal in the mind of the viewer exactly what this film is?

Dave - I think it is vital. Distribution companies and sales agents take many movies to the markets, with the bigger companies as many as twelve new movies at a time. These markets are normally in huge rooms where each company has a stand that is four by four meters, in which they will have a TV and posters, and they can screen your promo. Next to them will be another stand with posters and TV, and next to them the same, and so on. Everyone is playing their promos at full volume. You have got a handful of tired, hot and disinterested buyers who's phones are going off... and that's the sales environment! You have really, really got to get them in the first 2 or 3 seconds, make them feel that they are comfortable, they are not confused, they get what is going on. A lot of the people watching this won't speak English necessarily, because the sales company is servicing foreign markets too. You have got to hook people quickly, and in the worst environment for watching a trailer or promo possible.

Q - In terms of putting together a promo, I assume you just work off videotape, and create a DVD for this kind of international sales?

Dave - Yes.

Q - There is no reason, technologically at least, why they couldn't do that at home, on Final Cut Pro, or Avid?

Dave - That's what the pros use, so yes.

Q - What do you think are the creative issues involved with the director and editor of a film putting together their own promo, do you think that works?

Dave - I would ask a director or editor friend to make the promo for you for two reasons. First, you get a whole set of fresh eyes on it. You can be too close to your own movie. There is a reason why the most important directors in the world, who have Final Cut on their movies, with near limitless resources, decide not to do their own trailers - because there are people who do this better than they could. It is not that people are better filmmakers or anything like that. It is just that these people specialise in it, and they can watch their movie and say *'If I take a line from scene 1, and put that next to line from scene 48, it condenses it all down and all of a sudden something really interesting and exciting has happened.'*

Q - Having been involved in sales myself, one of the things I have seen is that you can end up selling the film on the trailer alone. People may spin forward and watch five minutes of the movie from the middle, or watch the whole movie in fast forward, and then say 'I'll buy it'. For a sales promo can you reveal the whole plot, almost compressing the whole movie into five minutes? Obviously this is something you would never do in a consumer trailer?

Dave - I think if you have got a really great plot, if there is a big twist at the end for instance, sure I would do it for sales promos.

Q - Do you think it is important to do a Dolby Digital mix at this level?

Dave - No, just do a stereo mix. Quality is not as important as you might think as these are film savvy people who are used to seeing work in progress.

Q - Can you then use the sales promo for the consumer promo for DVD and cinema? What are the creative and technological differences between the two?

Dave Hughes

Creative Partnership
13 Bateman Street
London W1D 3AF

Tel 020 7439 7762
Fax 020 7437 1467

daveh@creativepartnershop.co.uk
www.creativepartnershop.co.uk

SALES

493

Dave - Creatively, with sales promos, you should allow certain scenes to play out a little bit so that the buyers can get into it. It is not just flashy editing, you should show that real direction has gone on and show that the actors can act etc. When you come to the theatrical trailer, all the fun and games begin. All that flashy editing that you couldn't rely on in the sales promo as the buyers are aware of all the tricks, you can now use. If you used a lot of voice over in the sales promo the buyers can think *'these guys ain't got a story'*. Whereas if you put a voice-over on the trailer in a movie theatre, it is authoritative!

Technically, delivery of a sales promo is a video online, and transfer to DVD. For a theatrical trailer it gets much more technical and can involve film elements, HD elements, creating film res animated titles, doing a full mix and M&E mix etc. It can get very expensive. A lot of low budget movies are shot on tape now, so what you can do is master a promo to DigiBeta or HD and scan that onto film.

Q - Would it be wise to master your movie to HD, fully graded etc., and then make an HD master of your trailer from that?

Dave - Yes. You also need to be aware that if you have any captions in your trailer, or if you have text over an animated background, you need to supply those elements separately for the international market so they can translate and recreate captions in their own language.

Q - Do you ever see bad promos?

Dave - If it is bad a promo, you tend to blame the movie and conclude it must be a bad movie. But that could just be the 'trailer making brotherhood' sticking up for each other!

Q - What common mistakes do you see?

Dave - The worst thing you can hear is if someone comes in says the director has cut a promo that they really like. You instantly think *'oh dear!'*, not because they haven't made a terrific picture, but because they can just be too close to it. When film makers cut their own trailers you often get 90% of the promo covering stuff that happens in the very first 15 minutes of the movie, then they realise *'actually we have got to do this thing in 2 minutes max'*, and then they cram the rest of the movie into the last 30 seconds.

Q - What advice would you offer a new filmmaker?

Dave - Just make the best film you can make.

WHAT NEXT?

Abigail Payne
Solicitor

LONG TERM LEGAL

Q - What is your job?

Abby - I am a partner in Harbottle & Lewis's film and television group. Harbottle & Lewis is probably the largest Entertainment law firm in London - handling all aspects of the entertainment industries. This year is our 50th anniversary. My specialist area is film. Our clients range from sales agents, to film funds, sale and leaseback companies, household name production companies, agents, through to first time producers.

Q - If someone calls you up asking a question, do they have to pay?

Abby - No, I try and be as helpful as I can on the phone and usually take an initial meeting with no charge. I have been helped in my career by people being generous with their time and I try and do the same.

Q - If someone has finished a feature film, what do they do next?

Abby - Usually producers call us before signing or issuing book option agreements, screenplay agreements or other development agreements - so we'd normally be involved throughout development and production. Of course a producer may decide to shoot a film which they've financed themselves involving friends without our initial involvement - in which case they might not involve us until they needed to tidy up the contracts in order to attract a distributor. This can only really work with private investment though. If the film involves financiers such as the BBC or Pathe etc, then they normally require a lawyer to be doing all the legal work from the initial stages.

Q - Is it a mistake not to have a lawyer attached when the film is financed through private investment?

Abby - If all contributors to the film are good friends of the producer, and provided things go well, then it's probably not fatal. The important issue is the identity of the director, writer and lead actors. If the producer also wrote and directed the film, then not too much can go wrong because the producer will be the owner of the rights anyway. The producer can simply transfer the underlying rights to the production company later - as they are within his control. The problems really occur when there is a breakdown in the relationship between the producer and the writer and/or director. Although the producer may have financed the film, any exploitation of it will depend entirely on the company having acquired the copyright. The acquisition of the underlying rights is vital.

Q - So what do you do when someone brings you a finished film?

Abby - We normally start by asking producers a series of questions, such as '*who financed the film?*' For example, the producer will normally need us to draft investment agreements with third party financiers reflecting how much was invested and the recoupment terms/net profit share etc I normally ask about the proposed recoupment schedule and net profit participations, which will need to be reflected in the paperwork. I also ask about the underlying rights - which will need to be contracted properly. I would also question whether all rights in the screenplay are being transferred to the production company or whether certain rights in the screenplay are being reserved to the writer such as radio, stage, book publishing etc. I also need to know whether the screenplay is original or an adaptation of a book, in which case the film rights in the novel will also need to be acquired. Contracts for the actors and crew will also need to be issued and normally also a composer's agreement. I also ask about sales and distribution. Has a sales agent been appointed? Have any territories been sold? Producers normally appoint a sales agent for the whole world. The sales agent will then sell off individual territories to local distributors during film markets. The sales agent normally provides sales estimates and the producer and the film's investors will have the right to approve any sales below those estimates.

What are the common problems between the sales agent and the producer?

Abby - I guess the main point of contention is lack of sales! In some cases, the film may simply sit on the shelf for years. Producers tend to want to be in control of the exploitation of their films and if there are very few sales they may feel they can do a better job selling the film themselves! I think the main mistake that producers make is to grant the sales agent too lengthy a sales term. I therefore normally negotiate for a provision in sales agreements stating that if a certain number of major territories have not been sold within 18 months of delivery, then any unsold rights at that point will revert to the producer. This is quite a good compromise, as 18 months will give the sales agent sufficient time to go to attend four or five markets. Of course, a sales agent is likely to resist this provision if it is putting up a minimum guarantee. However, a minimum guarantee is unlikely on lower budget films so producers may get a little more control, in which case producers should try for something like a seven year term, with a right of reversion after 18 months, as described above.

The sales commission will be negotiable, but producers should try for approx. 10% in North America and 12% for the rest of world. Although sales commission can be as high as 20-25% if the sales agent is putting up a minimum guarantee.

Other problems can occur if the main salesperson leaves the company or the sales agent becomes insolvent or ceases trading. Producers can get around this by providing for a right of termination if any of these circumstances occurs.

Q - What do you do about sales expenses?

Abby - Sales expenses tend to be capped and any expenses incurred above the cap are subject to the producer's approval. There is normally a definition of "Expenses" setting out the type of expenses which are permitted. Expenses need to be reasonable, direct and out of pocket. Expenses should exclude office overhead and the salaries of the employees of the sales agent. For a lower budget film, expenses should be capped at around US$100k - although this might be increased to US$250k for a film with a budget around £10 million.

Q - What do you do if you think the sales agent is ripping you off?

Abby - The sales agent is accountable and they have to supply a detailed breakdown of their expenses, before they can recoup them. If producers feel that expenses are not genuine or that the sales agent is not declaring all the income it is receiving, then producers can always organise for the sales agent's books to be audited.

The mistake producers often make is not to appoint an independent collection agent. The producer should if possible avoid any revenue passing through the sales agent by using an independent professional collection agent such as Fintage House or Freeway or the NFTC. The sales agent will direct each local distributor in each territory to pay the advance and any overages directly to the collection agent which will then administer the revenues in accordance with the recoupment schedule The sales agent will then only be entitled to be paid commission and expenses by the collection agent once it has properly accounted to the collection agent for these. Collection agents take a small upfront fee out of the revenues - a couple of thousand dollars, and then charge a commission of around 1 - 1.5% of further revenues which they receive.

Q - What do you do if the sales agent does not provide you with accounts?

WHAT NEXT?

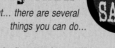

Going Under

When that dreaded letter from the solicitor finally comes, and you cannot pay, and you see no way out... there are several things you can do...

1. Offer a deal - your creditor could be interested if they believe that they won't ever get paid unless they take this offer. Stumping up half or even less of what is owed is better than nothing, and they may take it, but you will have to pay there and then.

2. Offer to pay off a small amount of money per month. If it is vaguely reasonable, they will accept.

3. No one wants to force you to go bust, it costs a lot, takes a long time and often, no one wins.

4. If you do want to go into insolvency, let them push you into it. They will then have to pay the liquidator or receiver rather than you.

5. If you go into liquidation, you will have to supply all your books and records which will be scrutinised. Make sure you didn't do anything illegal or undeclared.

6. If serious negligence or fraud is discovered, you will be barred from being a Ltd. Company director again.

7. Hopefully you will have made your film under a Ltd. Company. If you didn't, you could be made bankrupt personally, and everything you own can be taken, bar the tools of your trade.

8. Keep talking to your creditors and it may never get that far.

9. Seek legal advice immediately - let's hope the company forcing you into liquidation isn't your solicitors.

10. Going bankrupt gives you a bad credit score. Bankruptcy details remain on people's ratings for up to six years, although it should take a year of good credit practice to return a rating to health.

11. In reality, these extreme measures only come into play if a, you are seriously unlucky or incompetent, or b, you are a crook. More than likely, you will be on the receiving end of someone going under, in which case they will be offering the deal or waiting for YOU to force them into liquidation.

Abby - Maybe ask your lawyer to send off a stiff letter! Normally we negotiate a termination clause into the sales agreement so that if the sales agent breaches any term of the agreement and fails to rectify that breach within 14 days, then the producer can terminate. The rights would then revert back to the producer.

Q - Is an independent producer ever likely to see revenue back from their film?

Abby - It can happen, but it normally takes months or even years. I find that producers sometimes believe that a low budget film means it will be easier to recoup the budget and get into profit. However, it doesn't always work like that. Without names as actors, it is harder to obtain minimum guarantees from the sales agent or the local distributors. Minimum guarantees are paid on delivery of the film. In the absence of minimum guarantees, the producer has to wait for revenue to filter down from exhibitors and television broadcasters to the local distributor and then to the sales agent or collection account which can take months or years. If minimum guarantees are payable, these go directly into the collection account on delivery of the film. Producers tend to underestimate the amount of commission deducted by exhibitors and distributors (in addition to the sales agent's commission!) which all eat into the revenue. People also underestimate the amount spent by local distributors on prints and advertising (known as "P&A") accompanying a theatrical release. This can frequently run into millions. As these sums are spent by the local distributors rather than the sales agent, they are excluded from the "cap" on expenses referred to above. P&A needs to be recouped by the distributors before they pass money on to the collection agent. Hopefully this goes some way to explain why net profits are so rare!

Q - So are there any shortcuts to getting revenue faster from films?

Abby - Try for minimum guarantees from local distributors wherever possible. Some producers try and sell their films directly to local distributors without using a sales agent. This obviates the need for sales commission and expenses to be deducted, although producers need to have very good international contacts and a lot of free time and determination to take this on successfully!

Q - What are producer's net profits?

Abby - In the UK, we tend to use a very transparent definition of net profits, unlike in the US where producers are given a share of "adjusted gross". "Adjusted gross" tends to be a studio definition of net profits, and the definition can go on for pages and pages! In the UK, net profits tends to mean those revenues received into the collection account which remain after the deduction of the collection agent's fees and expenses, the sales agent's fees and expenses, the recoupment of any production investments such as bank loans and private investments and the recoupment of any deferred fees. You then hit "Net Profits". Net Profits tend to be split 50% to the financiers and 50% to the production company. So when people talk about "the producer's share of net profits" they mean the 50% share payable to the production company. The production company normally pays some of its share of net profits to the talent, such as the writer, director, actors etc.

Q- From a legal standpoint, what do producers need in place when delivering to a distributor?

Abby - They need to have all contracts with contributors signed and all rights cleared so that no further payments or residuals (other than net profits payable from the producer's share of net) become due to contributors, such as actors, crew etc following the exploitation of the film. The chain of title will also need to be perfected. Some distributors require producers to take out errors and omissions insurance.

Dealing with Debt

GUERILLA FILM MAKER SAYS!

Now that you've maxed out your credit cards and spent your family fortune to make your film, you've got to survive and think of paying it back. The big problem here is that you thought you were going to sell your film, but now realise that even if you do sell it, it's going to be months, perhaps years, before you will see any money, if at all! It can be a daunting time, especially if you have rent, car loans, utilities and that unavoidable need to eat. Here's some tips on how to make some cash so you can still finish your film or work on your own projects.

Get a job
Seems easy enough, pays the most, but takes up a lot of time when you could be working on your projects.

Temping
Takes up a lot of time, the pay's not that great, but you have flexibility to choose the gigs you want. Plus you meet a lot of people going to different companies which certainly could help if you stick to entertainment companies.

Script Reading
Great for that little bit of extra cash. You can get around £30 for writing coverage on screenplays that company directors don't want to read. Contact production companies, agencies and web based services to see if they are hiring.

Medical research
Robert Rodriquez did it to make El Mariachi. Donate your body to research clinics and you can earn some cash for testing drugs and the like. Of course, Robert is also missing part of his triceps, so make sure you know what you are getting yourself into.

Extras work
Doesn't pay very well and you stand around a lot, but you are on a film set and if you are smart and charming enough, you can network.

Wedding Videos
These days everyone wants their wedding filmed. Capitalise on this (especially with relatives) and make some money shooting and editing nuptials. Works for bar mitzvahs, births and just about any other family celebration. Money can be made by selling duplicate DVD's too.

Corporate Video
Commercial businesses, especially those involved with sales, know the power of a promotional video. While not great art, they are short, pay well and are good for keeping your skills sharp - you just have to deal with pleasing a client who might not know what they are doing, have really bad taste or want endless changes. These videos are almost always mastered to DVD and web based streaming technologies now, so some techy knowledge is needed.

Learn a film trade
Whether it's assistant directing, sound recording or assistant camera, if you can learn a proper film trade, you can make a living in the business, and at least you will be on the set and not someplace else dreaming of filmmaking. Sound Recordists are always hard to come by, so if you feel inclined to learn that discipline, you will probably always be able to find some work. Remember, the worst day on set is better than the best day stocking shelves in a supermarket or delivering pizza.

WHAT NEXT?

What to do if you're arrested

GUERILLA FILM MAKER SAYS!

Sometimes problems occur on a film set - not having a permit for special effects, weapons, animals etc., upsetting a local business or bribing the wrong person. Hopefully, you won't have to spend a night in a cell, but if it looks like you might...

1. Never admit guilt, in fact don't say anything while being arrested. Stay calm and listen to everything the police say.

2. Whatever you do, DO NOT piss off the police officer. More often than not, they're just doing their job.

3. When you get to the station, you are offered a phone call and a solicitor. Use them. If you know a good solicitor or someone who can get you one, CALL THEM IMMEDIATELY. If not, the government will supply you with a solicitor for free.

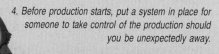

4. Before production starts, put a system in place for someone to take control of the production should you be unexpectedly away.

5. DO NOT say anything until your solicitor arrives. You don't know what angle the police are looking for, so keep quiet.

6. You have the right for your solicitor to be present during your interview and you can stop the interview at any point to talk to your lawyer.

7. Assuming you are innocent, or at least relatively (!), co-operate as much as you can, but always with the lawyer's 'say so'.

8. Unless you are charged, they cannot take your photo or prints.

9. Make sure you find out all the charges against you and discuss with your solicitor whether they are criminal or civil and how serious they are - this will let you know if you are fighting a ten year prison stretch or a £50 fine.

10. In the moment, it can feel MUCH worse than it actually is. Just stay calm and try and keep in mind, it will pass. On the other hand, carrying a criminal record around with you can have long term repercussions.

Unless you've killed somebody or absconded with the entire production budget, you should be out of the cells within 24 hours at the most.

Q - What is errors and omissions insurance?

Abby - it is an insurance policy which protects the distributor and anyone named on the policy from a claim for breach of copyright, defamation etc. The insurance company will normally run the legal proceedings and compensate the insureds. The excess on the policy is normally US$10,000.

Q - What are the problems with selling your film directly to UK distributors?

Abby - The main issues are the same as with a sales agency agreement. For example, how long is the term? Will the distributor provide a minimum guarantee? What will their commission be? The commission and fee structures for UK distributors vary enormously and can be quite complex. A producer might also decide to distribute directly in the UK - by which I mean splitting off the rights and granting TV rights to a broadcaster, DVD rights to another entity and theatrical rights to another.

Q - If you do a movie on a historical figure and there may be a book out there about that person do you need the rights? Is history in the public domain?

Abby - Both historical and current events are in the public domain. The issue though lies in what research material the producer or writer uses. If a producer makes a film based on a historical figure and relies heavily on a biography written by a particular author and structures the film in the same way as the biography is structured and takes the same viewpoint, then there is an argument that the film is really an adaptation of the book - in which case the rights to the book would need to be acquired. But if the producer uses lots of different research material and creates its own structure, then there should not be a problem. Deceased persons cannot be defamed in the UK under UK law, although if any of the characters are still living, the producer could run a risk of a claim for defamation in certain circumstances.

Q - What kind of mistakes do film makers most frequently make?

Abby - Mistakes with chain of title are the most frequent ones to occur - not acquiring the rights to a book or not realising an option has run out. Or falling out with the screenplay writer before acquiring the rights in the screenplay. A typical mistake is to acquire an option on a book or screenplay which is not really a binding option - merely an option to agree terms at a later date. Unless the terms for the exercise of the option are clearly set out, the option is likely to be unenforceable. Option agreements do not need to be lengthy - they can be effective on one or two pages - so long as the terms for the exercise are clear. Options are normally exercised by the production company issuing the writer or author with written notice and paying a specified sum. This might be something like 2% of the budget. A classic problem is where the option runs out before the producer finalises the budget. It is therefore always useful to put in a fixed figure for the "floor" for the exercise trigger fee, with any balance payable on the first day of principal photography.

Q - What mistakes are made in relation to music?

Abby - Films need to be fully cleared, which means that further sums do not become payable to contributors other than a share in the producer's net profits. One classic mistake is to promise a composer a video royalty calculated on video sales - and then fail to pass the obligation to the sales agent or distributor. This means that the producer could end up with a big bill if the film is successful - even before it receives any profits! The same applies when box office bumps are promised to lead actors. Lower budget films tend to use original score, but if producers use music that is pre-recorded and "featured" in the film then they must ensure it is clearable for an affordable price before shooting.

What advice would you offer a film maker making their first feature?

Abby - I think the most important thing is to get your first film made. The first is normally the hardest, and the second is usually a lot easier to get off the ground. My other piece of advice is that although some producers finance their films privately, seeking traditional finance from the BBC, Film Four, Pathe etc can greatly help to improve your exposure and extend your contacts with the traditional film financing entities in the UK - it's never too early to start this process! There's quite a lot of loyalty within the British film industry, so if one of the traditional financiers funds your first film, it is likely to also finance your second. First time producers should try and get as much exposure as possible to commissioning executives such as David Thompson, Tessa Ross etc and heads of development. Also, try and attract names for cast if possible. This always helps to in getting the film distributed. The most important thing for a first feature is to get a theatrical release so that the film is reviewed and gains exposure. Also, it's important to forge good relationships with writers, actors and directors so that you can call on them again for your second film! Never underestimate how nerve-wracking and stressful the film making process can be. And don't forget to enjoy the shoot - that's what it's all about!

Marc Samuelson
Samuelson Productions

BEING A UK PRODUCER

Q - What is your job?

Marc - I think that the job of the producer is to be the person who makes everything else happen, though the role of the producer does vary from film to film. There are executive producers, who are really just investors. This happens, in the UK, where endless tax funds have required their principles to take credits in the way of the Americans, where anyone who puts in financing, gets an executive producer credit. The kind of producer that I am, originates projects, develops projects, assembles the team, usually including the director, oversees the production, the post production, and all the way through marketing and distribution. I think the industry would be healthier if there were more properly experienced and trained hands on producers. Quite frequently when a film has been a disappointment, it has been because there hasn't been sufficient creative tension between the filmmakers and the producer.

Q - Creative tension is an interesting way of looking at it. Have you had any experiences where that tension has caused problems?

Marc - I think the problem of being a director is that your only limitation is your imagination. There aren't really any boundaries. That is fine in some ways and a disaster in others because there is nothing to rub up against. You can go off in any creative direction in a limitless degree. I am not talking about budgets or money here, but genuinely creative things, like the tone of the film or the casting. If there is nobody who shares your vision of the type of film you want to make, and has enough power to be able to argue and provide that creative tension, then even the most talented directors can go too far in a certain direction. It's like a grit in an oyster. If you have the right set up, then you don't necessarily have the director or the producer having the final word - if they are both good at their jobs and decent people, they will find a compromise that is the optimum position, or at least, it is the best way to reach the optimum position. The situation where the director is a hired gun and the producer is calling all the shots would be just as unhealthy. One of the reasons we don't have empowered producers in this country is because it is such a small cottage industry. And secondly, the financiers of the film don't understand the role of a producer and disempower them whilst not doing anything to the director's position. This doesn't help the director. The best thing a director can have is a producer that completely supports them and is able, with withering honesty, tell them what they think about the decisions that are being made. Within the safety of the family, those decisions can be argued through and will end up being extremely robust. So when they end up in the real world, they are that much more robust because they have been argued through, instead of it being one person's vision.

Q - So being a good producer is like being a good parent, giving considered boundaries to their director?

Marc - Yes, other than the pejorative "paternal" aspect. There is an inverse of it as well, which the producer is trying just to achieve the budget and needs to be pushed by the director as well. There are some producers that are much too focused on delivering the budget, and there is that old saying that no one ever went to see a film because it came in under budget. Whereas I think that a really good producer, would like to deliver every film with one pound left in the kitty, with everything else up on the screen. It is a particularly useful analogy when you have a newer director and a more experienced producer. The best is when both are experienced, have been through the wars and appreciate that they are each other's best friend and ally.

Q - Do you ever mentor or take on film makers who have little experience?

Marc - Yes. I have ended up mentoring people in that role for a bunch of different reasons. On a number of projects, the financiers have asked me to become involved to help make sure everything goes fine, and in other instances, the producer or the director are relatively inexperienced and they have asked me to get involved. It is a role that is extremely enjoyable and it is a good way to make sense of a business equation that doesn't otherwise work. I don't like this expression, but it is the 'monetising' of my experience and all the hard work that has gone into twenty years of working. When I am not fully immersed with my own production, there is time to offer support on someone else's project. A few times it can be awkward, which has always been when I have been put onto something by the financiers, because they don't feel secure with the team making the film - usually they have good reason to feel that way. But when the team asks me to be involved, we end up with a very strong, very enduring friendship and more projects often follow.

Q - How much should a new director relinquish the putting together of a project to the producer?

Marc - There are some unsuccessful directors who think they should not be making phone calls. All the ones that are any good are able to simultaneously reach for what you might call high art in their craft, as well as embrace and assist in the sometimes slightly embarrassing and "down and dirty" way of, getting the money together. If you have chosen to express yourself artistically, then it is much cheaper to either write something because all you need is a word processor or paint something. But if you want to make a film, then it is going to cost you hundreds of thousands or millions of pounds to achieve it. So the directors that make it are not embarrassed or ashamed of the business side, and understand that it is part of the process. A lot of people want to be a director, but a hell of a lot don't and I think that the essential reason why it wouldn't work for me, is that I like to concentrate on a lot of different things. I enjoy the business side and the creative side and immersing both sides of my brain. But in particular, what I like about producing over directing is that I am able to self-start. I don't have to wait for the phone to ring and it being my agent saying do I want to audition for this or for that. I want to be the person making the calls.

Q - What skills do you think a young producer needs to hone in order to be successful?

Marc - Being absolutely ruthless with yourself as to who is the audience for the film and how is it going to work is everything. Looking back in my extreme old age now (laughs), the biggest and most important decision is the first, which is the conceptual decision. As I get older, I get pickier. I have stood at the back of so many test screenings and wanted to kill myself because the project that I love and have worked on for a year, or ten years, is playing and the bums are shifting around in the seats. And I am thinking what is the point of all of that because the audience doesn't care enough. I have also been there when they have cheered at the end and that is much better. So making films for the audience is definitely the way for me.

Case in point, (mentions a recent high profile film), I don't know who that is for. And no-one has been able to give me a straight answer. Is it a kid's film for adults? Does that work? It is what the Americans call a 'tweener'. It falls between groups. That can be a problem. I look at some of the films that I have made, some of which I am very proud of, and I don't know who they are for. *Gabriel and Me* would be a great example of that. It is a beautiful film. Wonderfully directed and acted, but it is a film where no one is sure who the audience is. A very very hard lesson learned, at great cost to the investors and two years of work.

Q - So if you are going to make a film with a marginalised audience, you have to bring the budget down?

Marc - Correct. It is empirical and it is capitalism. The people who put the money up have a pretty shrewd idea as to what audiences there are out there. But then there are twists. The very obscure project that attracts the humongous star - that can change everything. Look at *The Hours*. It starred Nicole Kidman, so that means a whole different level of budget and potential box office. Imagine, *The Hours* starring some fantastic actress, but not a star, then you would have to make it for a different budget. Then you can get a really interesting paradigm, which is to try to make the film for a relatively low budget, but with big stars in it because they are taking a risk with you. That is the kind of thing that we have to do in this county. We have to be smart.

Q - Who are the key groups of people that you think a good producer should be plugged into?

WHAT NEXT?

Marc - The number one thing is to form relationships with distributors, both here and elsewhere in the world. If any distributor is willing to take a risk on your film, put money into it or buy it, then you are already three quarters of the way there. Most projects that have a pretty good script and a pretty good director and a decent cast can easily achieve half their budgets via tax breaks and subsidies. If they have any sort of value to them, you should be able to borrow 20%-25% of the budget from a bank against projections of international sales. But after that, you grind to a halt because you really have to have some distributors coming in to invest in the film - taking some genuine hard risk. There are hundreds of 50% financed films, but they won't get the other half because that is the really difficult part. When the tax breaks were at their height, there were so many people saying that they were almost there with 70%-80% of their budgets, but it was all soft money. Sometimes as little as 15% hard money would drive 85% soft money. That is changing as things are becoming more difficult. You need more than 15% hard money, you need 40% hard money. The interesting thing is that I find that distributors are very open and if a fantastic script or package arrives, they are very open to it. They probably won't pay for it until it is delivered. They don't care about production and if it doesn't get made properly, then they don't have to pay for it. They can dictate quite astoundingly tough terms. Nonetheless, these can be your best friends. And they will give the best feedback, straight from the horse's mouth. Anyone who has had a meeting with a top quality distributor knows that in a very polite way, he/she will tell you exactly what he thinks about your project. And it will be infuriating because it is almost always right, and will have laser beamed in on the weakness in the package or the project, and he probably won't invest until you fix those problems.

Q - So the problem is that new producers think of the project from the beginning to the end, and not from the end to the beginning?

Marc - That's exactly right. If a green producer rang me and said that I have this interesting project with all of these actors attached, that would be fantastic. But if he also said, and I have a UK distribution deal and I have two other territories pre-sold, an American deal and I have 40% of the budget from those - I am absolutely sure I could put the rest of the finance together in about three seconds. The problem is that most people come in and say that they have tax deals and private investors and 60% of the budget, and could you find the other 40%, which is the same thing as saying please find 100%. If everyone thought from the end, the beginning would take care of itself.

Q - Are there any other kinds of people new producers should be cultivating relationships with?

Marc - The talent agents, but I think that if you have a fantastic project and you are clever and do your research and home in on a particular director whom you really want who isn't obvious or who is up and coming, you can get the agent onboard. The agents will always be open to that and you don't necessarily have to be best friends with them. At worst, they will say that you are inexperienced and that they want you to team up with an experienced person to keep an eye on you. There is a strange contradiction in the industry, where, on one hand, I'm sure it seems like a very closed book to a lot of people - it is a really small enclave because the number of people that actively make British independent films is around a hundred strong - but on the other hand, it is incredibly open. And if you arrive with a really great project, even if it is a really great concept, then it will be embraced. People don't really care where stuff comes from. You don't really have to know them.

Q - Do think that if no one wants to produce your script, then it is probably crap?

Marc - Yes. To expand on it, it is either crap or it is good, but there isn't a clear path to an audience. The question is not, can you please do me this favour? The question is, I want you to buy this for big money and then spend even more big money on marketing it, into the millions perhaps. It better be really, really good for them to roll the dice. 99% of everything that is around is not good enough, and I include myself in that. I have made one and a half movies a year for fifteen years. But those one and a half films are on top of a revolving stack of fifteen projects that haven't been made because they are not good enough.

Q - Where would you tell a producer to go in the world, where they can experience some part of the film business that they would not get in London?

Marc - Los Angeles, where it is possible to live illegally or cheaply, and to get a job in the photocopying department of the script room in the garage of an agency. That is all fantastic knowledge and experience. New York is interesting because there is quite a feisty independent industry there where people are scrounging together no budget movies. If you can somehow tap into that, that

After completing a film, you can experience a great sense of loss, as well as elation. Your film experience is probably more valuable than the actual film asset itself! So take advantage of that experience and the opportunities it creates.

1. Most new film makers put so much into their first film, there is nothing left when they are done. Try and plan ahead, have projects and ideas ready to move once your film is complete. Almost everyone you meet will say, 'so what's next?' You want a great answer.

2. Try and be self critical when you look at the film. Let the little problems go, the production issues, the lack of coverage, the occasional bad acting. That's all related to budget and time. Look at your story and how well you told it. What can you learn from the mistakes you made?

3. If you are a director, talk up your writer and producer in meetings. Everyone will assume you, the director, was responsible for the film entirely, which is nonsense, so spread the good vibes.

4. Take meetings with people you could not get to see before. With a movie under your belt, most people will be intrigued to see what you are doing next and to see if they might get involved.

5. Understand that you are only 'hot' for a short period, so whatever you are going to do, get on with it.

6. Anyone can dash out and make a movie, but after your first, you will realise just how hard it is to make a great movie. Also, if your first film fails, you are then a 'failed film maker' and not a 'talented and unproven new comer'. You may find it harder to find investors for a second film.

can be interesting. London, because it represents 95% of the film making industry in the UK. So rather than change the world, if you want to have a career you have to sort of go along with how things are. Most of the other European countries have interesting industries. The question is, will it speed you up in terms of making your way in the UK industry? But, for example, if you are up for living in Copenhagen, then there is a small film industry that you could hook into there too.

Q - Do you think that if you had tried to take on 'Stormbreaker' fifteen years ago it would have been disastrous due to your lack of experience at that point?

Marc - I wouldn't have been allowed to make it, and if I had, it would have been disastrous, yes. For sure, there were a load of things I would have completely fucked up. I wouldn't have been nearly as rigorous with the development of the project. I wouldn't have been as witheringly commercially minded and thought about the audience as I did. I wouldn't have assembled the same team. I wouldn't have been able to get the rights to the book. I think the biggest problem facing British producers is that we don't do enough. The same thing is true of directors. We have people whom are considered major directors and who have only made four films. In the heyday of the industry, in the '30's or the '50's, people in the studio system were making four films a year or more. And if you look at the career of Howard Hawkes, well he should have been good because he was making three or four films a year, every year. Many of them were not good, some were among the greatest ever made. *'Tom And Viv'* was the first feature film that I did myself and that was ten years ago now. I look at the mistakes that I made on that and slightly cringe. I would have done it better now. I think the same thing is true for directors.

Q - What is it that you have learnt from 'Stormbreaker'?

Marc - I have learnt that it is very hard to make a $40m film with no studio behind you. You have no one behind you and there is no one to go to if you screw it up and go over budget. I have learnt that you can find fantastic collaborators among the financiers, such as the aforementioned Nigel Green. He's the nightmare negociation going in but, once the deal was done, he has become a fantastic collaborator and great sounding board. I have learnt that there are amazing people out there at every level, as far as the crew is concerned. I have learnt that you can get almost any actor you want if the project is really good. It's not really about money, although you have to have a reasonable amount. I have learnt that you have to budget your CGI with an amazing amount of care because it can go wrong and make all of your financial problems on a film set look like petty cash.

Q - Do you think new producers are shocked by how tough people negotiate for what they want in this business?

WHAT NEXT?

Survival GUERILLA FILM MAKER SAYS!

Traditionally, many people in the film business have personal wealth, not that it's soooo much money that they can do anything they like, but enough to not have to work most of the time. We all need a roof over our heads and food on the table. So how, as film makers, do we do that? Especially in light of the overwhelming statistics that show new film makers movies don't perform. So if we discount the possibility of making enough money from your film, what other survival options are there?

Below are some tried and tested options, the only caveat being that these should not be (though often end up being) new careers. They should be small businesses or freelance jobs that you can dip in and out of. Ideally, these should also be, on some level, creative endeavours, or you will probably go stark bonkers. The final point to make is that, whatever you choose, don't enjoy it too much or you will find yourself years down the line without having made a film (and we include ourselves in this!)

1. High End Corporate Video
Making training and internal films for companies has been done by most film makers. They like your 'I made a movie and can also make your training video...' approach, and we like the fee that we can get away with. The downside is that it's often very dull and you have to work with people who have little, if any, creativity.

2. Job In The Business
Any paid job on a film set is better than working behind a bar or stocking shelves in a supermarket. You get to be around the film making process all the time, and that will inspire you, aswell as build contacts. Good and easy jobs (given your experience having made a film) include production work, assistant direction etc., and if you have the skills, editing and sound recording are also good professions to develop as a backup.

3. Training
Your experience making a film will make you a good teacher. With so many media courses popping up everywhere, you should be able to get some freelance work doing days here and there, working with students. It can be demoralising and frustrating at times, as well as inspiring and well paid. Best of all, at the end of the day you walk away from it.

4. Low End Video
The main market here is wedding videos, which pay quite well. The upside is that with your knowledge of film, you should be able to make the best wedding video in the world. The downside is that the pay is bad, the pressure high and the business will take a great deal of time to build. It's a good back burner, but most give it up over time.

5. Commercials and Promos
If you can get the work, great! Directing or producing promos and commercials will give you great showreel material, get you learning your craft more, and probably pay you obscene amounts of money. The business is notoriously high pressure and often people come out the other end so burned out, there isn't much left of them. Some people manage to make the leap from commercials to high end drama, and when it works well, it's possibly the very best way to do it.

7. Creative Work
Be it designing websites, working as a graphic designer, writing advertising copy... the list is endless. Most of these new media jobs will be driven by a knowledge of computer technology and specific programs. Buzz word names we have all heard are Photoshop, Flash, Dreamweaver, After Effects.... Having a basic knowledge of these programs, and others (if computer work turns you on) will serve your job prospects well.

6. Any other job
Best avoided, but if you need to, start by asking for work at the video shop. Better working there than the supermarket! Try and sneak a laptop in so that in downtime you can surf and do research, write emails, and even scribe your screenplay. It's all about how you use your downtime.

7. Property
Sadly, most people who have some financial stability, do it by owning a number of properties. It's no fun, but it is about as strong a business as there is, and once it's up and running, keeping it going can mean minimal work compared to the overwhelming domination of a nine to five job.

Marc - Yes, they are merciless. They will restrict the amount of money that it costs them to get the film, by any means that they can, and it is not personal. They will put you up against the wall and beat you until you get to the point where the film won't happen and then they will close the deal.

Q - What advice do you have for a producer when they are being beaten with that stick?

Marc - I think they should try to draw a line at the things that really do matter and the things that really don't matter. Don't give away the things that don't matter up front. If you go into a negotiation with the theory of 'here is my bottom line and it is really my bottom line', then you must understand that people, psychologically, need to feel that they have chipped and chipped away and achieved something. So always go in with something that isn't your bottom line, so they can feel that they have beaten you up and you can feel that you have walked away with the film intact. It is a bit of a dance. Also if you can have more than one bidder for each section of the financing investment, that is extremely important. If there is competition, it gives everyone a sense of what the deal should be and it keeps people honest.

Q - What are the common mistakes that filmmakers make?

Marc - I think making films for themselves. I know that is what I did for the first part of my career and sort of got away with it because they were sort of things people wanted or they worked enough. It is difficult because if you always chase the commerciality and what you perceive the market to be, then you end up making the wrong films as well. So you have to have something that makes you passionate - sometimes for irrational reasons - and you have to be able to answer a question from a distributor along the lines of 'who is the audience and how do I sell this?' You need to give them an answer. You can't say that it is their problem. The best advocate for a film is its producer. I think a mistake that I see a lot of people make is going down interesting directions creatively, but directions that don't have any relation to the market. You might devote a year and half of your life to something that nobody wants to see and what is the point of that? And you usually only make enough of a fee to break even. I also think that you should find big projects. A £7m film is roughly the same amount of work as a £20m film, except that your fee is three times as much. It seems obvious, but then you have enough gas in the tank to know that you don't have to make something for a year and a half. It gives you time to make better choices. It gives you more credibility.

Q - What advice would you give a new producer?

Marc - Be more tenacious than everyone else. I also feel that producers need to be hands on at every level of the process. People often ask me why I am on the set around the production. That infuriates me. If you are a creative producer, you cannot separate the execution of the film from the development and all the rest of it. And no-one teaches a producer how to be on the set. Amusing and obvious things like where to stand, simple things like that, but also how to relate to the director. How not to overstep and drive the director mad so they cannot do their job properly, but at the same time being sure that the film is getting made in the way that you saw it. You are the one who has the original idea of how the film should be and you should definitely have an idea in your head of how the financiers see the film. It is a difficult balance, but I do think that producers should feel empowered and confident to be more hands on. If you have the right relationship with the director that would be welcomed instead of resisted. I have been there for both ways and welcomed is better, but resisted is not necessarily a disaster. That way you get the grit in the oyster. But non-enjoyable film sets have produced excellent films. It is difficult because we are British and we all like to be nice to each other. For example, every day of the shoot, you should arrive half an hour before the call so you are there for those crucial conversations over a bacon and egg roll with the director and others, so you know exactly what the issues of the day are. Then you can have influence over them and you can say, '*I don't think that matters*' or '*let's cut that and use the money to solve this problem*'. You can really steer the ship that way. If you are not working the hours, you cannot expect to be treated with respect. You should be there before everybody else and you should be there after everyone else. And you should let everyone see you right there by the camera. Talk to everybody and enable everybody to talk to you about things, because if you are scary or intimidating, or can't be bothered when there is bad news, then no-one will tell you bad news and you and your film will suffer as a result.

Walking the walk as I call it, is very rewarding, and you get a better film out of it. Almost all films expand to fill the available space, but they don't quite fit. So almost always you are having a conversation at four or five in the afternoon about how you are going to get the day done. Are we going to go for an hour of overtime, which is very expensive and crews don't like to do? Should the last six shots of the day be given a quarter of the time that the first six shots got? That's mad. But if it is the case, then those first six that you schedule had better be the most important. You need to invest yourself to that degree. You invested yourself in the script to that degree, so why not? A lot of producers are uncomfortable on the set because there is a lot of science they can be blinded by, and there is a lot of jargon and bullshit. If you get enough "goes" as a producer, you can start to understand how it all works. For instance, now I can look at a schedule and see what four days are going to be the hardest to pull off. That is very important and rewarding.

Charlotte Kelly
Casarotto Ramsay

GETTING AN AGENT

Q - What is your job?

Charlotte - I represent writers and directors. In terms of what I do, it's both creative and practical. From the creative viewpoint it's about advising, guiding and focusing clients on their strengths. We also introduce people who might be useful eg. producers, financiers etc. From a practical point of view it's about doing deals and contracts, sometimes we also help with packaging.

Q - Because of your position, you have your finger in pies that a new film maker might not have access to?

Charlotte - Yes. Production companies often don't have time to seek out new film makers and can be inundated by new hopefuls. The agent acts as a filter. A development executive is likely to take you and your project much more seriously if you are represented by an agent.

Q - How do film makers get an agent?

Charlotte - Obviously you need to have made a film to showcase your talents. If you're at film school, then you will have a graduation and usually they'll invite agents. We also see new film makers at film festivals and more often than not, you get to hear a buzz about a film, read something that gets you interested, or get a recommendation from someone in the business who you trust.

Q - What if somebody sends you a showreel saying 'would you represent me'?

Charlotte - We do look at unsolicited tapes but often the best way to get agents to see your work is to set up a screening. Present your work seriously and professionally. Agents are looking for professionalism and talent, but mostly originality. Obviously I need to know that I can sell the film maker, but that doesn't mean they have to be overtly commercial, although I need to feel that I know where and who I can sell the particular talent. Personality also counts for a lot as eventually a writer or director will have to sell themselves. An agent can only get them into the right place at the right time. A lot of agents want to build longterm relationships, so you want to enjoy working with that person and get on with them. I think the most important thing is originality.

Q - We made two commercial films for what we perceived to be a commercial market place and then we made Urban Ghost Story with the attitude that we didn't care about the commercial marketplace. The movie itself might not have been very successful, but it really opened doors to new opportunities.

Charlotte - Yes, because it's fresh and original. It's a unique film with a unique voice and that's what people are looking for. Second guessing in my experience doesn't work - you have to remain faithful to your belief in the story, it's really important to try and retain your integrity.

Q - Part of the psychology with people who finance films, especially at the studio level, is that they're still going to make the same movies but they want to find people with different voices so they look like new or different movies?

Charlotte - Absolutely. I think there's always the Holy Grail of what will clean up at the Box Office in any year. We saw lots of *Blair Witch Projects*, but the thing about *The Blair Witch Project* was that it's completely and utterly original and because it's micro budget they just did it. You can't repeat that.

Getting An Agent

GUERILLA FILM MAKER SAYS!

1. If you are in business with a partner, discuss how you will deal with an imbalance of power / opportunity when success arrives.

2. Invite agents to a screening of your film and explain that you are seeking representation.

3. Don't sign with the first agent you meet. Find a person you like, who understands your tastes and what you want to do. Find someone who will represent you accurately.

4. Don't go for the biggest agent, go for the agent that is right for you and your needs.

5. The agent won't get you work, they will just get you into a room with the people who can offer the work. You have to deliver on the promise.

6. Arm your agent with press clippings, copies of your film and showreels.

7. Listen to your agent. If you have chosen wisely they will mentor you and help you through the new world of the film business. It is not the same world as the low budget one, so open your mind to learn.

8. If you have made a well received first film, everyone will be watching the second to see if you deliver on the promise of the first. A good agent will steer you towards the kind of work that will showcase your strengths and away from work that will be disappointing.

9. Keep in touch regularly. If you haven't spoken to your agent for several weeks, give them a call to remind them of you, to get yourself fired back up and chat about any new opportunities that might have arisen.

Q - What kind of agent would you recommend to new film makers?

Charlotte - It depends on your personality. If you're new you may want somebody who's going to work with you, give you time and help you make the films you want to make.

Q - How does the commission work?

Charlotte - I believe there are variations but we usually take 10% plus VAT of all the money earned by a client. Any agent or manager asking for money up front should be avoided.

Q - You don't actually have cash to give film makers straight away?

Charlotte - No, we aim to help clients get jobs that pay but we also work with clients to help raise finance for their own projects for example, by introducing them to potential sources of film finance.

Q - Do producers have agents?

Charlotte - Yes, sometimes. A producer is most likely to have an agent to do a deal for them - for example, with a studio or a financier, or to help them raise finance for their project.

Q - What are the advantages and disadvantages of having an agent?

Charlotte - I'd have to say I can't see any disadvantages unless you're with the wrong agent. The advantages are that you've got somebody out there talking about you, focusing on you, introducing you to a world that you might find difficult to get into, protecting and advising, and always trying to get the best deal. In many ways it's a partnership.

Q - What is the most important selling tool once you've signed a client?

Charlotte - If you've made a film, people need to see it and I'd much rather people saw it on the big screen but often this is not possible so

CASAROTTO RAMSAY & ASSOCIATES LIMITED

Charlotte Kelly

National House 60-66 Wardour Street London W1V 4ND

Telephone: 020 7287 4450 Fax: 020 7287 9128

Email: charlotte@casarotto.uk.com

WHAT NEXT?

Networking

Making your first film is often about 'just doing it' with the available resources. But after that first film, the industry will become more available to you, making contacts and relationships valuable assets. Getting information from tight lipped sources, getting hard to reach talent to read your work, persuading negative commissioning editors to put your project into production and working deals to keep the budget down are some of the main jobs for any producer. These tips may seem predatory or sleazy, but hey, it is moviemaking.

1. Form as many contacts as possible. This can be people you do business with daily, or through social events like industry parties. People do favours for those that they know.

2. Get on the phone and stay on the phone. Find out the latest news and gossip about projects, talent and the needs of production companies, financiers and broadcasters. The more in the know you are, the better game you can talk.

3. Set breakfasts, lunches, drinks and dinners with people you want to meet. Pick fun places to go so that you are associated with an upbeat, friendly feeling.

4. Research the person that you want to talk to and their company / clients, and try to fit their strengths to your needs.

5. Have a plan when you talk to people. Know what you want to get out of a meeting or phone call so that the other person does not feel like you are wasting their time.

6. Use connections that you have already made to get introductions to new people. A phone call placed on your behalf can make a stranger more open to listening to you.

7. Do activities outside of work with your contacts (some of which will hopefully become your friends), such as going to sporting events, movies, parties and weekend trips. It gives you shared memories and you have something to bond over.

8. Create customer loyalty by using the same hire companies over and over again. They are more likely to cut deals with people that they know personally.

9. Join organisations like Shooting People and the NPA, communities for networking. Later on you can join BAFTA too.

10. Be respectful to assistants. They have lousy jobs and low pay, but they are the gatekeepers to their bosses. Further, they may soon be the next person in power that can help you.

you will then target the ones who didn't make it to the screening by sending out tapes; so plenty of VHS tapes and DVD's, both PAL and NTSC are useful. For example, with *Urban Ghost Story*, having a print in LA was important. It means producers, agents, lawyers and executives can screen the film whenever they want to see if you are suitable for a project. They all have access to 35mm theatres so they will get to see it on a big screen too. If you can afford it, have more than one print of your film. It's also a good idea to know what your next project is (ie. what you want to make - it doesn't necessarily have to be in script form) because everybody will want to know about it. To an extent you also have a "sell by date"; it doesn't mean that if you don't get your next film off the ground within the year that you aren't going to make another, but you should take advantage of being hot.

Q - Is it common for new film makers to have unrealistic expectations and become disillusioned with their agent?

Charlotte - A lot of this business is about personalities. It's also about communication. If you're not happy with how things are progressing with your agent, do something, talk about it, work with your agent, have a brainstorming session, come up with ideas. This is a partnership. However sometimes the fit is wrong. You can always change agents - it happens on both sides.

Q - Going from micro budget film to the professional world where you get paid is a shock - how much can you earn?

Charlotte - Yes it can be a shock but a very nice one! Mostly the budget will dictate what a writer or director can earn. There are many variables but as a very rough guide, you might command between 2% and 5% of a film's budget plus a share of the films profits (e.g. if it's a £3.5m feature and you've made one good film already, you could be earning anywhere between £100k and £150k plus a share of the film's profits). In any case there will usually be a ceiling on the fee. It obviously makes a huge difference if your film has been a real hit at the box office. So it's a hard question to answer but the likelihood is that you could personally earn more on your second film than it cost to make your first!

Q - Do film festivals and awards help?

Charlotte - They definitely help to raise the profile of a filmmaker, especially festivals like Sundance and Cannes. If you win an award at either of those you're likely to become hot property. Other festivals are good too and any award might get you a few inches in Screen International and Variety. But beware, you can become a festival junkie as well, so it's important to keep focused on your next film and not on travelling the world on other peoples expenses for too long.

Q - How does the LA thing work, you're a UK agent but there's the rest of the world?

Charlotte - We're not just agents for the UK because we represent clients from all over the world, including Canada, Australia and Europe; we deal directly with producers, studios and TV companies worldwide. We co-represent some clients, mainly with LA based agents. In that case, we split commission (usually between 12.5%-15%) with the other agent and work together for the client. As well as agents we also work with lawyers and managers, particularly in the US.

Q - Do you have any comments for a young film maker who made a hit movie with a DV Camcorder suddenly finding themselves on the set of a $15m studio picture where the crew are seasoned professionals, perhaps twice the age of the director?

Charlotte - It can be very daunting. I'd say make sure you surround yourself with experienced and supportive heads of department, and producers. And just be incredibly well prepared and sure of what you want. Listen to people and get everyone on your side.

Q - What are the common mistakes you come across?

Charlotte - I can think of three mistakes in particular that we've come across here at Casarotto. Firstly, directors or writers who are hungry to make their film, make agreements without thinking about it and more often than not, find that they've signed something away that could have been of benefit to them. If you're going to have an agent you might as well use them and let them do the deal for you. A new film maker might have creative talent but sometimes they don't fully appreciate their true market value. Secondly, two people work on a screenplay together without making an agreement as to how they will split any payment that they might receive. This can be the end of many a friendship so put everything in writing even if it's just a simple letter setting out your mutual understanding. Lastly, many a micro film maker promises their cast or crew a position on their next film. However, if it's a financed feature you might not be in a position to fulfill that promise so be careful about making promises. This obviously doesn't mean that you should forget those who helped you when you started out.

Q - What advice would you offer?

Charlotte - Make the film you really want to make. It's the only time that you won't have people interfering with your vision and it's the only way anyone's ever going to get to know what your voice is like. So have faith in yourself and your instinct on the one hand and on the other hand, do remember to ask yourself is anyone going to want to finance this film and is anyone going to want to watch this film?

WHAT NEXT?

Anonymous
The art of the blag

SCHMOOZING

Q - So you've made your first film and you've come out the other end feeling emotionally drained and you really need to get into the world where the 'real' film makers live. Where should you start to hang out, what clubs should you join?

Anon - Off the record, I am not a member of any club, although I will say that I do frequent many clubs. There's Soho House - I used to get in by saying my name at the door with great conviction, sometimes kissing the cheek of the door-lady. One time I got called up on it - *are you a member?* and I said *yes, of course,* so they said, *well, can we see your card?* and I say *sorry, I forgot my card* and they said *can we look you up on the computer?* and I said *sure* and I told them my real name. Of course I wasn't on the system though someone did share my last name so I pretended that he was my brother. That didn't quite work and then they said *well, what colour is the membership card?* and because the membership card in Cannes was silver, I said *silver* and they said *ah, no* so I said *well what colour is it?* and they said *purple* and I said *well, mine's silver.* In the end it was really embarrassing, especially as I had three actors in tow – I made up a story *look, I have been shooting till 5am this morning, I just want to come to a nice quiet place to drink with my actors,* and the long and short of it is that I got booted out. The up side is they now think I am a member because they recognise my face, but don't quite remember from where. I could join if I wanted to but it's terribly overpriced, I just have an aversion to paying for something when I know I can get it for free. Paying to go to a pub just seems such a waste of money although some might argue that it is the place to meet people in the industry.

Q – What about the Groucho Club?

Anon – Groucho's is slightly more up market, more A list celebrities and important industry people. Groucho's is hard to get into unless you know someone. And you can't buy a drink in Groucho's unless you are a member. Beware, the average price of drinks at both places is more expensive than normal pubs.

Q – How do you get invited to those all important media parties where deals get struck?

Anon – For the first two years in Cannes I wasn't invited to anything. I don't know who gets officially invited, nor how they get invitations, it's a mystery to me but it is important to go. Normally I would have to blag my way in any way I could - scaling fences, crawling through windows, elaborate scams pretending I was related to the film maker. Another very simple way which seems to work every time is approaching the doorman in great haste and saying *oh, I'm terribly sorry I left my coat inside* at which point they usually let you in. What you want to avoid is being escorted in by some six foot beefcake to look for it. The way that I usually dealt with that was to go to an empty chair and shout, *oh, my God my jacket's missing! My friend must have taken it, let's look for him together.* So he gets really bored and after a while says *when you've found it come on out.* Once you are in the party there is another queue inside trying to get into the VIP lounge. The jacket scam is very good for that one. Hopefully you will have started to rub shoulders with executives, solicitors, agents and the like. You need to develop relationships with these people as they have a direct line into the business and they can keep you informed of who is doing what. They also tend to get invited to all the top functions and sometimes have spare tickets. Even so, when you get into a party, if you don't know the people in the first place it is hard to know who to go up to and speak to. I find the best way of meeting people in Cannes for instance, is to stand outside the Petit Carlton and the Petit Majestic at 3am in the morning where you find yourself stood next to drunken acquisitions executives from big studios and the like.

Q - What trade magazines should you get?

Anon - The most popular UK trade magazine is Screen International, which at £2 a pop can be pricey - hey, you can always read it at the newstand. Screen tells you what is happening in the business right now, what films are in production, plus lots of fluff about the business in general. Screen Finance is also a very good publication, aimed at the financial section of the market. It is a well-constructed newsletter created through an arm of the Financial Times, but it's really expensive, so find someone who subscribes and raid their offices after they have read it. You must arm yourself with knowledge – so read the trades and become familiar with who's doing what. A problem that is very apparent at Cannes is that people just turn up and call themselves 'producers' when they don't know a thing about how the industry works. We all have ambitions and dreams of doing it and you have to start somewhere, but if you are going to call yourself a producer, then at least know how a film works.

Q - Have you ever gate crashed a premiere?

Anon - Many, although one stands out in my mind. I had seen *The Mask of Zorro* while at the Deauville Film Festival. I enjoyed the film and the party afterwards was an event in itself. When I heard about the big London premiere, followed by a swank party at the Criterion, I though it might be fun to try to blag my way in. I thought I'd give it a try so I called the London press office and announced with great conviction that I am a film maker, and I would like tickets to the party. Without a moment's hesitation I was refused. There's nothing like rejection to fuel one's perseverance. I now had a mission - to get tickets to this party. I needed a way of approaching them where there would be no possible way of them turning me down - and how could they turn me down if I worked for the company? Not only that, but what if I was actually an executive from the upper echelons of the studio in LA? A while back I had sent a script to Universal in Hollywood with the hope of someone actually reading it. Several weeks later the script was returned with a rejection letter. I had kept the letter, so scanned the letterhead in colour and made a replica. I also had a database of executives working in Hollywood, found one, the "Executive Vice-President of Business Affairs", filled in his name and personal phone extension number and wrote a letter which read something like...

"Dear Maggie - I am writing on behalf of Mr Smith, Executive Vice-President of Business Affairs for Universal Studios here in Los Angeles. Mr Smith will have a brief stopover in London on his way to Paris this Thursday. Please could you arrange for his name to be placed on the guest list for the post-premiere party of The Mask of Zorro. Should you need to contact Mr Smith blah blah blah..."

I printed it out. It looked perfect. I had to be careful of what time I faxed the letter due to the time difference and from what machine I faxed it as most fax machines send out a fax ID. Also, I didn't want the press officer contacting the LA office, so I gave a convenient London fax number, my mum's! With these things solved, I sent off the fax and sat back, thinking I'll just show up at the party. Imagine my surprise when that very day a fax came for me from the London Press office!

"Dear Mr Smith - your secretary faxed me yesterday and told me you would be stopping in London for business. We are delighted that you will be coming to the post-premiere party. Would you also like to come to the Gala Charity premier in the presence of HRH, the Prince of Wales? Unfortunately, your secretary forgot to mention what hotel you were staying at. However if you contact me, I can arrange to have tickets biked over. Yours faithfully..."

OK - firstly I am not staying at a hotel and secondly, I'm not who I say I am. How in hell was I supposed to get her to bike these tickets to a legitimate hotel like the Dorchester, for a fictional guest that would not be arriving? I have a friend with a public school accent who I convinced to help me out. Luckily he is a member of an exclusive club in Mayfair, so I got him to call the press office in his best Queen's English...

Late night drinking clubs are a haunt for film makers. Hard to get membership, hard to get into, but a place where important people hang out. This inconspicuous doorway is Soho House (upper left) at 40 Greek St, 0207 734 5188, and the Groucho Club (lower left) 45 Dean Street, 0207 439 4685.

WHAT NEXT?

"Yes, I am the general manager of the 'blah blah' club and I'm calling on behalf of Mr. Smith who is tied up in meetings all day. He's asked me to call you to confirm that he will be attending the Gala Premiere and asked if you could send the tickets to his suite here..."

"Sure, we'll bike them over..." Nervously I turned up at my friend's club, of course he wasn't the manager, he was the doorman. And lo and behold, the tickets had arrived.

I went to the premiere in black tie and when I arrived there were film crews relaying the video to the screens inside the cinema - where hundreds of studio executives were watching everyone's entrance. Simultaneously there was a man commentating on all the entrants, and pointing out the well known faces and executives. At any moment I was waiting for the announcement, *and coming in now is Mr Chuck Smith, Vice-President of Business Affairs for our LA office.* Thankfully, that didn't happen. I had great seats, several rows up from Prince Charles and the Sultan of Brunei. I also noticed that the tickets were numbered by the press office - and the seats were assigned - which presumably meant that someone, somewhere, had a list of where everyone was sitting. Again, I nervously waited for a lady with a clipboard to come up to my seat and introduce herself, *Mr Smith, how nice to finally meet you and put a name to the face, when are you off to Paris? By the way, I called your office today and how funny that you're still in LA...*

Q - Isn't that immoral, no illegal?

Anon - Yes, it is illegal to pretend to be someone else in order to get into a party. Morally it was wrong, but have you ever tried to get invited to one of those things, it's damn hard. At the end of the day I wasn't trying to defraud anyone of anything, I was just seeing how far I could get. You have to be prepared to do almost anything at times. My first feature had a very small budget. I did everything I could to save costs. I remember one incident when an agent asked me to bike over the script so her celebrity client could have a look. *Oh, sure, I'll bike it over today* would be my normal response. Of course I couldn't afford to bike over a script every time an agent asked me, so I got into the habit of dressing up as a bike courier and delivering it myself! I would dress up in all the kit, have shades and clip board and put on an Ozzie accent. The things you do!

Q - What is the key to survival in the industry?

Anon - You must have passion for your craft and ask yourself why you are in this business. Ambition is all very well, but a grounded sense of passion and commitment to the art itself is the single most important quality you must have. Yes, the drive for money, success and power might have ramifications, but commitment and belief in your art should come first. You have to be determined and thick-skinned and eventually your perseverance will pay off. Someone, somewhere will recognise your talent...eventually. Don't give up!

Decide if you are a person who is into the business for the fun, if you are, leave now - or if you are a person in the business for life - recognise it's a marathon. No-one really knows what's good. The single biggest problem is that people don't have faith in their own judgement of what is good. It's easier and less of a risk to just say no. Know you can do one of two things – continue to try and convince somebody to take an interest in your project, or you can take control of your destiny and go do it yourself. And why not? My suggestion is, be motivated and do it yourself. On my first feature I went straight to a company I knew had money and got them to write me a cheque – that cheque funded my film and I did it without going to the BBC, Ch4 or any of the usual suspects that end up rejecting projects from people they don't know. Like everyone else, I have a huge file of rejection letters, and if I gave up during all those times, I'd be flipping burgers by now.

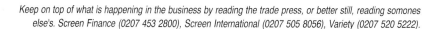

Keep on top of what is happening in the business by reading the trade press, or better still, reading somones else's. Screen Finance (0207 453 2800), Screen International (0207 505 8056), Variety (0207 520 5222).

Elizabeth Ingold
MGM Senior Exec (former)

Q - What is your job?

Elizabeth - My job is to look for new projects for the studio, either in screenplay or book form or by way of a pitch or remake idea. We either option or buy the ones we get excited about. If the material is not ready right away then we begin the development process. We usually do a couple of drafts with the original writer, or sometimes we hire a new writer if we want a different take on the writing. When we're happy with the quality of the script, we begin to attach a director, cast etc. Then we have a budget made. If it's a movie we ultimately want to make, we "greenlight" it. From then on, I supervise the pre-production and production processes, making sure we stay on the agreed budget and schedule. After principle photography ends, the director works with the editor to create his or her cut of the film. After we see the director's cut, the film is tested in research screenings which may determine if and how the film is re-cut. Finally, the film is marketed and distributed, I'm less involved at that point of the process, as we have departments internally that handle those aspects.

Q - What size projects are you looking for?

Elizabeth - It's hard for us to make movies for $6million and below because of the unions and because our overhead goes into the budget. When a major Hollywood studio says "low budget", it usually means $8 - $20million. More of the movies we do fall into the $50-$60million range with the occasional $90-$100million film.

Q - What do you look for in new filmmakers?

Elizabeth - I look for someone who can tell a story. I see a lot of music videos, commercials or shorts that are flashy and stylish. The director may use cool lenses and neat special effects but not possess the ability to tell a good story. I need to know if that filmmaker can hit all the dramatic beats and draw in an audience. It helps if I can see a feature the new filmmaker has made. While dramatic structure is a priority, it is also important that the filmmaker be able to pull good performances out of the actors. When watching a sample film, I am less concerned with production value because most films by new talent are made on such meagre budgets.

Q - How do you see their movies if you've heard good things?

Elizabeth - When an agent or a colleague that I trust asks me to take a look at a filmmaker's new material, I will have them send me a tape or set up a screening. And since I'm constantly flooded with new material, I remember the projects that really stand out.

Q - What mistakes do new filmmakers hired by the studios make?

Elizabeth - Studios don't hand a new filmmaker a cheque for $8million and say OK, go make your movie. Filmmakers must understand that there is a certain amount of bureaucracy they will have to contend with when making a film for a major studio. When we make a movie that will open on 1000 or more screens, a certain level of casting is required to attract such a large audience. This is not to say that a director cannot fight for a certain actor but he or she should keep the studio's casting interests in mind. New filmmakers must realise that a studio wants to reach a very wide audience. While we don't want to discourage individual style, we need the filmmaker to be aware of what type of material is or isn't commercial. We often see independent filmmakers who prefer a darker sensibility to give a film mood and texture or who use film stocks that are not necessarily right for studio pictures. However, independent fimmakers can also bring a lot of special qualities to a project. They tend to know many creative tricks and shortcuts and tend not to have as bloated a sensibility as many Hollywood directors do.

Q - Should a new filmmaker pitch a film that is in the same genre as their independent feature?

Elizabeth - If he or she directed a successful independent horror movie, the studio will most likely look at that film as a sample for the horror/thriller genre. If this filmmaker wanted to do a romantic comedy however, his or her past work won't be of much help. The director should consider directing a romantic comedy independently to show his or her range.

Q - What advice would you offer?

Elizabeth - When making your first independent feature, worry about creating a dramatic and focused story, more than anything else. A good story rises above flashy production design or unique look. Many new filmmakers make the mistake of choosing style over substance. Be careful when signing with an agent. Find someone who believes in you and has the time to promote you. Realise that as a first time director for a studio, you're still going to be working on a limited budget. While the budget will be more than you're used to in the independent world, it still won't be the big Tom Cruise vehicle. It's important to understand the studio's sensibility. While our aim is to produce movies that appeal to a large audience, we don't necessarily look for ordinary material. American Beauty, for example, was a unique film and was also very successful. A film, which achieves this sort of balance, is what the studio ideally wants to produce.

WHAT NEXT?

Todd Hoffman
B·WCS Agency

GETTING AN LA AGENT

Q - What is your job?

Todd - I represent writers and directors and help them figure out how to navigate their careers, find employment opportunities for them, get their movies made and be a cheerleader for them. Because I have a past in independent producing, I have an expertise in piecing together independent finance. Studio financing is getting increasingly complex these days so if you can bring additional pieces to the puzzle, it makes it easier for the studios to say yes when they are saying no more frequently.

Q - What should a film maker coming from the UK look for in a US agent?

Todd - Passion. Most people think it's better to have an agent at one of the top six or seven agencies rather than a one person agency outside of LA. But if that one person outside of LA is willing to wake up and turn on their lights every day and think that you are the second coming and there is someone at CAA who is kind of willing to maybe take you on in a hip pocket situation because you might hit one day? I'd think twice about signing at CAA. Because at the end of the day people respond to passion. It's all about excitement and you can't fake that. People are represented by people, not agencies.

Q - Roughly how many clients does an agent have?

Todd - Most have 60. Some have up to 70. I wouldn't be able to do that. I think that my head would spin. I tend to have between 25-30 and that is plenty.

Q - Is there a danger of getting lost at the bigger agencies?

Todd - Yes. When they have large actors and actresses and huge directors making sometimes several million dollars in commissions for them every year, those are the people who would get attention instead of the journeyman writers and baby writers and directors. That said, smart agents at all agencies are going to find new talent and take a shot on them. If you do sign at one of the top five or six agencies, the key is finding somebody who not only tells you *'I have time for you',* but one who actually does.

Q - What is the difference between agents and managers?

Todd - People know why they need an agent. Our charge is very obvious. We can find and negotiate for jobs. We can navigate the waters to help clients move from point A to point B to all the way through their professional careers. Managers typically have very different charges. Some managers act very much like agents. They say it is so competitive out there that you can not have enough voices out there screaming your name and I agree with that. Other managers don't want to go after jobs for clients because that is the agent's job. These guys work with the client to ensure that when they go up for the job they have a better chance of getting the job. At the end of the day if the client feels that their life is better with that person serving them, it is a value added. If a manager brings an extra job to the table every year or every two years, then essentially they have paid for themselves. Since I have a background in development and producing I don't think of myself as a typical agent who is out there booking and schmoozing until 1 a.m. in the morning. I love getting involved in the development process and producing so I do things that may be seen as more associated with what a manager might do. Hopefully that makes me seem different and better. But they might want someone else who is always only going after writing assignments.

Q - How do you find film makers?

Survivers Guide to LA

GUERILLA FILM MAKER SAYS!

1. Rent a car. LA is a city built for the car. You can turn right on a red light as long as the route is clear, park in the same direction as the traffic and don't expect people to indicate when they change lanes. Valet parking is nearly everywhere so don't panic when you pull up outside a restaurant and they take your car keys.

2. Jay walking (crossing the road at a non designated point) is illegal and you could get an on the spot fine.

3. LA is not a late night city. There are late bars but few and far.

4. Tipping is expected. Waiters - 15%, Bartenders - 10-15%, Valet parking - $1-2.

5 Get your internet sorted so that you are in touch over email. A laptop with wireless is essential.

6. Foreign exchange - the easiest way to get cash is from an ATM so don't forget your cards or pin numbers.

7. It's Cell phones not mobiles. Have your cell phone turned international or rent one whilst you're out there. Buy a telephone card at the airport, they are cheaper than pay phones, you can use any phone and they can be topped up at any time from your credit card.

8. Buy the film trade mags. Hollywood Reporter and Daily Variety. Pick up LA Weekly and The New Times Los Angeles, free weeklies that tell you what's going on in town.

9. Eating is cheap. Shopping malls have food courts with a wide variety of cheap but good fast food. Dining out is also pretty good value unless you want to be ultra hip and trendy and eat in exclusive places.

10. Set up your meetings before you arrive, you don't want to waste any valuable time in LA making phonecalls and setting up meetings for the next few days.

11. Stay in town. There are plenty of motels that are cheap and cheerful, especially mid town. Santa Monica and Venice Beach can be great places to stay but it's pricey.

12. Check out the film bookstores - it's a town for film makers so there are books galore on the subject.

13. Do the LA thing whilst you're there, Rollerblading and people watching on Venice Beach, Universal Studios, Disneyland.

14. Check out the movie theatres. American audiences are much more enthusiastic and don't fear airing their opinions in a theatre. Almost as entertaining as the film itself.

15. Dress to impress. LA is a town where everyone looks great, don't go to meetings in your grotty old jeans and holey T shirts.

16. Flights - shop around for the cheapest as prices vary. It's a long flight, usually about eleven hours, a long time if you aren't used to long flights. LA is eight hours behind the UK, so our late afternoon is their morning.

17. Set up an online phone service with Skype or similar service. You can then setup and make calls from your laptop using wireless internet in Starbucks or anywhere you can get wireless. You can also setup an answerphone on that line.

18. Make friends. You will need floors and sofas to sleep on. Being a Brit in LA can get you further than you would imagine, so tweak that accent and claim to have met the Queen.

19. Take photos of yourself at the studios and the Hollywood sign. You can use this as great PR back in the UK should you have to make another low budget Brit film.

Todd - Generally through referrals from managers, lawyers, people in the community such as producers or development executives or through other clients. We get many query letters and blind submissions and, by law, we have to return them. We can only accept referrals, which goes back to relationships and trust. If a friend of mine calls who I know has good taste calls me and says I just read this great script, it is a lot better than if someone from Mississippi writes me and says I have a great script.

Q - So if someone comes from the UK, it helps to have an agent or producer recommend them?

Todd - Absolutely. And often they use the film festivals as a way to introduce their clients. I also try to go to Sundance every year and Toronto. But also in terms of looking at new talent, the Los Angeles Film Festival is something that people increasing go to. South By Southwest is a good one as well.

Q - If a film maker is approached by an agent at a film festival, what is the best way to handle the situation?

Todd - The best advice I would give is to not sign at the festival. Anyone who is interested in you at a festival is going to be interested in you in a week or two. People can get caught up in the fury of the festival and that is ultimately what agents and managers are hoping for. Their main charge is to make contact with you, and wow you. Remember, though, that in the best possible world the decision to choose and agent and a manager is something that you would do once in your career. You wouldn't choose a husband or a wife after one rushed blind date, why would you do that for your business? It is exciting when people want you, but that doesn't mean that you have to sign immediately. Agents and managers will just want you more if you tell them to politely hang on. But there is a balance. You can't drag it on too much or else they might eventually get upset. You should make a decision if you are seeking representation, you should do it with clarity, but not in overdue haste. Do your research on that agency and see who their other clients are. Also don't necessarily do what your UK agent wants you to do. There may well be an agenda that your agent has. If they want you to go to a specific agency, ask them why. Maybe they put all their clients with that agency. So is that good for you or for them? Ask the tough questions. You only have one chance in your career when you are signing to ask the tough questions. And without being a jerk about it, there's no better time to ask than at the signing process.

Q - What are you looking for in a film maker?

Todd - There are two main things that I look for. One involves their body of work and the second is the film maker themselves. The body of work or the film has to be extraordinary or show incredible promise. If it doesn't, then the person that I want to sign better have that 'it' factor. By that I mean an unbelievable charisma that when they walk into a room you just want to be around them, that makes you shut up and listen to what they have to say. If their film is extraordinary, then they don't necessarily have to have that 'it' factor. If they have both, jump on it fast. If they are a nice person and their film is just OK, then there's no way to sign them. You can't. Putting careers in motion takes too much time and energy and it is too hard so you have to take your shots wisely. You can't go with good because good doesn't cut it anymore.

Q - Are there any personality traits to have in order to wow someone in the room?

Todd - I think it is a fine line between having a commanding presence and an overwhelming presence and I think getting a job in our business is at times as much a political process. You would like to think that the best person gets the job, but many times it is the person who is the most adept politically who gets the job. Or the person who is the best pitcher gets the job and in a studio setting you have to talk to a lot of people. Due to this being a great communicator is essential.

Q - What advice do you have on pitching projects?

Todd - It has been my experience that producers and studios don't want a director to come in and say, *'I love this script, it is ready to shoot,'* and then tell them how to shoot it. They always want to know that there is something to do and you are going to come in and make it better - that without your help the movie is going to suffer. The people who go in and talk text first, and only text, are the people who get the most consideration. If you walk into the room talking about lenses you are going to lose them because they want to talk the script they have just come off of a year to five years of development on. I like to talk about it in concentric circles moving outward. The story and characters are the inner most circle. Next, is there any personal attachment that you have to the story and why. Then, what is wrong with the story and what are your thoughts for making it better. And then after you spend 10-30 minutes talking about that and engage them, you can start moving out and talk about the look and the feel you envision. Invoke other movies to get them into your frame of reference. Then the next circle out is an hour into the meeting when you discuss casting. Now you have them hooked and you can talk about why you like Tom Hanks for a role. And they understand why Tom Hanks because you have spent 20 minutes talking about this lead character.

Q - Is it a good idea to have a screenplay ready to go after you finish your first feature?

Todd - Yes. People always want to know what you want to do next, so it is good to have at least one on the shelf. And yet you don't want to have six on the shelf because people don't want to be overwhelmed. They don't want you to back up the truck and say here are six projects, pick one. They want you to say, *'I want to make this one.'* They want to know what you are passionate about. And it is better to have a script than an idea that you have to pitch.

Q - Should your script be in the same genre as your movie?

Todd - It certainly helps. It is generally accepted thing that people here like to put you in a box so that they can figure you out. There are directors like Gore Verbinski who refuse to be put in a box. He says, *'I am a director, I direct.'* And he does different movies of different genres but that is the exception not the rule. The toughest thing to do would be to make a really, really scary movie and then make your next one be a broad comedy, which was the problem that the people who made *'Blair Witch'* ran into. As you get more successful, you can branch into other genres. So if you are a comedy person, after a while do an action-comedy, then do an action one, dropping the comedy.

Q - What is the process for getting a script out to market?

Todd - Each script is different and needs its own selling strategy. So a broad comedy has a selling strategy where you don't really need to get a director or an actor attached because each studio is going to want to do it their own way and they could make it with one of fifteen guys. So on that script you would take it out to multiple producers and try to get them to take it in to the studios and hopefully get a bidding situation. If the writer has a real meaningful drama where the studios don't buy them as often, then it might make more sense to try and get an element attached before going out to sell it.

Q - Are these producers based at the studios or do they have deals with distributors?

Todd - Either or. It is easier to go with producers who have first look obligations with the studios because there is a pre-existing relationship. If there is somebody that we think would get the material but doesn't have a first look deal, that is fine as long as they have a relationship.

Q - How difficult is it to get a script sold if you are attached to direct it?

Todd - It takes a little extra time unless there is an amazing awareness of the director and a want to employ that person. Like Danny Boyle - he has come off a few good movies and everyone knows and wants him. Let's say he's written a script and an agent says, *'I have a Danny Boyle script and he wants to direct it.'* That is one case where things can go quickly. But for a new director coming out of the UK, the process goes slower because you have to get people to read your script and like it. Then you are going to need to show them your finished film. Then we are going to have to set up a meeting, hopefully a lot of meetings with different studios so they can sit and listen to your view on how they would direct this movie. In some ways, you would loose some of the auction frenzy, but the point isn't to make as much money as possible, it is to move your career forward and get the movie made. I take the marathon approach - slow and steady wins the race. I truly believe that talent wins out in the end and there is plenty of money to be made down the road. You don't need to cash in with your first studio movie and you can't because first time studio directors don't make a lot of money, but they get their first chance. But one of the great things about the studio system is that studio

Useful LA Addresses

GUERILLA FILM MAKER SAYS!

British Consulate-General
11766 Wilshire Blvd, Suite 1200
Los Angeles, CA 90025-6538
Tel: (310) 481-0031
Fax: (310) 481-2960
www.britainusa.com/la

Film Independent (Find) – (The Los
Angeles division of IFP)
8750 Wilshire Boulevard, 2nd Floor
Beverly Hills, CA 90211
Tel: (310) 432-1200
Fax: (310) 432-1203
www.ifp.org (NY, Chicago, Miami,
Minnesota, Seattle),
www.FilmIndependent.org (LA)
A cool organisation that is a one-stop shop
for information on film production in Los
Angeles. They have other locations in New
York (see NY section), Miami, Minneapolis,
Seattle and Chicago.

Filmmakers Alliance
453 Spring Street, 7th Floor
Los Angeles, CA 90013
Tel: (213) 228-1152
Fax: (213) 228-1156
www.filmmakersalliance.com
Similar to the IFP, but more focused on the
actual production side of things.

The Writers Guild (WGA) – West
7000 West Third Street
Los Angeles, CA 90048
Tel: (323) 951-4000, (800) 548-4532 (for
toll free outside Southern California)
Fax: (323) 782-4800
www.wga.org
The WGA has an alliance with several
writers' organisations from around the
world including The Writers Guild of
Great Britain. They have some great
information on their website for writers.

**The Producers Guild of America, Inc.
(PGA)**
8530 Wilshire Boulevard, Suite 450
Beverly Hills, CA 90211
Telephone: (310) 358-9020
Fax: (310) 358-9520
www.producersguild.org
info@producersguild.org
A relatively new organisation for US
producers. While you can't join them
unless you have done US productions,
they have loads of good information on
navigating the Hollywood maze.

**Directors Guild of America
(DGA)**
Los Angeles Headquarters
7920 Sunset Boulevard
Los Angeles, California 90046
Tel: (310) 289-2000, (800) 421-4173 (toll
free for outside of Los Angeles)
Fax: (310) 289-2029
www.dga.org
The DGA welcomes independent
filmmakers and even has special events
for them to try to get these people to join.
Like the PGA and the WGA, they too have
a wealth of information on getting through
the Hollywood system. They have
locations in New York and Chicago.

**EIDC – Entertainment Industry
Development Corporation**
7083 Hollywood Blvd, 5th Floor
Hollywood, CA 90028
Tel: (323) 957-1000
Fax: (323) 962-4966
www.eidc.com
Grants all permits for shooting in Los
Angeles.

directors can go from a little bit of money to a lot of money fast if they do well.

Q - What is the chance of getting an 'open directing assignment' off your movie?

Todd - It is tough, but it is not impossible. Studios want to go increasingly with the tried and trested film directors and not the newcomers. They would rather pay somebody $5m US who is going to bring in a huge cast or pay somebody scale and do something unique. In some respects, people off of first films, video directors, commercial directors, short film directors have come along at a time when studios are more open to those possibilities. It is a numbers game because the studios make fewer films there are less open assignments. And you have to do so much work to prepare for one of these jobs to hold your own in the room and be impressive. And it may not be about that job. It is about going into a room where you have one chance in one hundred. But if you impress them, they might remember it and call you back on another job because you were so well prepared. This time you might be in a better position to get it.

Q - Sometimes foreign film makers are seen as first time film makers because they have not made a studio film yet.

Todd - It just depends. If it didn't have a US release or a sizeable box-office, it might be seen that way. But the woman who made *On A Clear Day*, which was picked up by Focus, is not looked at as a first time film maker. Icon financed her movie for $10m US and now she is going up for studio movies.

Q - After the deal is done with the studio and production starts, what is the agent's role then?

Todd - I am there through all of it as a partner. I'm there whenever there is a problem. I think a good agent is somebody who helps navigate the process or solve problems whether it has to do with casting, or dealing with media buys the week before your movie opens and talking to the marketing department and trying to clarify their strategy. There is a limit, though. An agent isn't somebody who is going to go into the star's trailer and try and coax them back to the set if there is a problem.

Q - What is an agent's commission?

Todd - 10%.

Q - What would be a standard writing and directing deal a first timer coming from the UK or Europe could expect?

Todd - If it is a spec script then it is what the market can provide - from $50,000US to $1 million US. If we are talking about your first writing assignment and you don't have a quote, then most likely it is going to be 'scale' which is around $70,000US to a top range of around $125,000US. As for directing, your first film here, the agent tries to get scale plus 10%, which is around $175,000US. And this gets you into the Director's Guild if it is a studio movie.

Q - Can producers have agents?

Todd - Yes. Not a lot of them do, but some people like Brian Grazer who works with Ron Howard who is repped at CAA, Brian and his company, Imagine is repped there. Typically producers think they don't need it because it might in some way prevent them getting material from other agencies.

Q - What is packaging and do all agencies do it?

Todd - The definition is to take a script and get all the acting and directing elements together from one agency, and then present it to financiers. From my experience it is more of a myth than a reality. It is a really exciting signing tool that the five bigger agencies use when they want to seduce clients.

Q - Many UK directors complain that the world doesn't open up for them once they get an agent. They expect things to happen and they don't?

Todd - They may well be at the wrong agency. But then again it may be them. And most likely it is a mixture of the two. You shouldn't expect the world to open up when you sign with an agent. You should continue to work it just as hard as before because nothing in this life is given to you. And agents like to work with clients who work as hard as they do. The more things you have going on the better. And things will happen sooner. Those who wait for the agent to call, find themselves either lucky or unlucky. Better to create you own luck by generating material. I look at it like the client is the CEO of their own company and a CEO would never sit around and do nothing. The talent is in charge and moving their career forward and the agent takes their direction. That said, a good agent is going to look for interesting opportunities and talk to their clients frequently and send them scripts. And if someone is interested in working in the Hollywood system, they have to make frequent trips here and really invest in being here. I have a director in Milan who comes quarterly. And he has to because it is an out of sight out of mind mentality. There is a sexiness to not being here, but if you are never here it doesn't work.

Q - What are common mistakes that film makers make?

Todd - Successful film making starts in pre-production and not doing the prep work hurts. If you don't hire really good people around you, you won't necessarily fail, but it is so much easier to succeed if you have great people supporting you. Get a great DP, 1st AD, and producer. Then you don't have to yell and scream because you have people doing it for you. Also, you cannot let yourself be a pawn in the system. You have to be strong and not be thankful just to be called up to the show. You have to know that you can prove it without being arrogant or pushy. People respect people who respect themselves and aren't just pushovers.

Q - What advice would you give to a film maker?

Todd - Sign with me.

Paul Nelson
Mosaic Media Group

GETTING AN LA MANAGER

Q - What is your job as a manager?

Paul - Ultimately, it is procuring employment for clients, creating employment opportunities and proactively guiding them in their career.

Q - What is the difference between a manager and an agent in the US?

Paul - There is a lot of crossover between the two, but the primary difference on paper is that a manager has the ability to produce and an agent has the ability to negotiate. A manager traditionally has about 10% of the amount of clients that an agent has so you have that much more brainpower going into each client for gaining employment and creating opportunity.

Q - How many clients would a manager have as opposed to an agent?

Paul - It's totally across the board, but a lot of literary agents in Hollywood have anywhere from 40 to 80 clients. It is astounding at the big agencies how many they actually represent. And they keep signing people. And it is a little more focused on the bottom line. Managers usually have about 10 to 20.

Q - What do you do on a day-to-day basis for your clients?

Paul - Every day is different. The most common thing I do is take requests from studios, producers or financiers, to have my clients look at their material. Sometimes this comes along with an offer of employment and sometimes they want to consider them and put them in with a handful of people that they like for the project. I also deal with offers of employment from these same people for my clients. Also, in terms of open directing assignments, a studio will call us and say, *'Hey will you read this script for all your directors and tell us who you think would respond to this material?'* So I try to read everything that is out there and decide which projects match my clients' goals. If I find something that does, I send it to them in order to gauge their interest and then respond to the sender with my client's decision.

Q - Would you advise a film maker coming out to the US to seek both at the same time?

Paul - I am biased and I think you should first find your manager, because it is more of a personal relationship, and they know every agency in town and whom you might match up best with. It may seem confusing as to why you are paying out an additional 10% for both, but you need to look at it as an investment in your career. You now have another person looking for opportunities for you. It's another person to help get multiple things into development, who has different connections, all of which adds up to more meetings. I think there is nothing better than a strong agency and manager working together.

Q - Would you agree that in the UK, managers are not like they are here?

Paul - I think in the UK, because there are fewer resources in finding money for the films, the British representatives act as a manager / agent. In Los Angeles it is so unruly because there are so many different ways to find financing for your film, and so agents are limited in how much time they are able to put into this area. Managers are able to keep on trying to find new opportunities because they have fewer clients.

Q - Should you find a lawyer at the same time?

Paul - I think that you only need a lawyer once a project comes along. I always recommend getting an attorney because their 5% can make a deal worth more than 5%, so you are getting your value. Generally, director's deals are more complex than a writer's deal in the beginning.

Q - What are you looking for in a film maker?

Paul - I like directors that have a specific style and you kind of look at their film and they are inventive, visionary and they are doing something that you haven't seen before. Obviously, they would have the ability to work with actors, create great performances and tell a great story.

Q - What is the best way to approach a manager?

Paul - The best way is through a UK agent or a producer - someone in the business that has a good reputation that we have a relationship with. Blindly submitting is definitely harder.

Q - Do you consider people who have made short films?

Paul - Absolutely. It is all about the talent. I have worked with short film directors before. One of them, Robert Luketic, did a short film from film school in Australia and has gone on to do *'Legally Blonde'*. There is a prime example of an industry person telling me about a film maker. An executive at Miramax saw his short at the Aspen Comedy Festival where his film premiered and told me about him.

Q - Do you pick up people off international festival circuits?

Paul - Most people in the Hollywood system are only going to hear about film makers from the high profile festivals, such as Sundance, Toronto and Cannes. But winning the London Film Festival is definitely a plus and is great calling card.

Q - How important is it to have a good relationship with your manager?

Paul - Hugely, because you are talking to that person more than anyone. You have to know that creatively you are in synch because they are your voice box. They are you. So you want to know that that person is representing your interests in the way that you want.

Q - What are open directing assignments?

Paul - They are when a studio buys a script or buys a pitch and they develop it to the point where they say we are going to hire a director on this piece of material. There might be an actor attached, but most times it is just a script.

Q - What kind of open directing assignments could a film maker who has made a moderate film in the UK expect to get?

Paul - Open directing assignments are difficult to land. Generally, the directors who get them are people who have critical acclaim due to a visionary approach or have done well at the box office. Someone who hasn't had either of those would have the best chance of getting employment here by either writing a new movie or acquiring the rights to a piece of material and work with other writers and attach themselves. Open writing assignments are even more difficult because it is kind of like being a movie star. There are so few of them and generally studios want somebody that they have worked with before.

Q - How important is it for someone to come out here armed with scripts?

Paul - There are two things in that. Some writer / directors that are new to the business, say those coming out of Sundance, all they want to do is direct their own material. And that is great. And if you can keep on getting your material greenlit, that is fantastic.

WHAT NEXT?

However, it is hard to set up your own material repeatedly. I would say to those people, be open to reading everything that comes your way. And be diligent about the reading. Read quickly and give your representation a reaction on what your feelings are. There might be a great concept in the script, but you hate the characters, the dialogue is terrible. And what I would say is meet on that project and see if they are completely open to revamping the script. Maybe they bought the script and they don't like it either and they like you enough as a writer / director, that they could have you rewrite the script.

Q - Should a film maker keep their next movie within the same genre as their last movie?

Paul - Ultimately, if you are inspired to do something completely different then you should follow on that impulse. But, it is definitely harder to get a film financed if you do a complete 180° from the genre you are known for. If you have material that you control it is a little easier, but I would say it tends to be a little easier when you make a splash in a certain genre to follow it up with the same thing.

Q - Does it help to have talent attached?

Paul - It depends on the project, but a lot of times you will find that studios want to know what actors you are going to get in this movie. But at each studio there are different actors they respond to. New Regency might love Hilary Swank and Disney doesn't for instance. So you have to do research and the studios are fickle and every week they may change their ideas on who excites them.

Q - Can a manager help with funding?

Paul - I would say that a manager could help even more than an agent because like I said before, sometimes an agent will have a spec script or something the director wants to direct and they want to go to those nine places. A manager might have more time to actually find independent resources.

Q - What is the standard commission for managers?

Paul - 10%.

Q - What kind of money can someone expect to make on his or her first studio film?

Paul - On a first time studio film, a director will make about $200k. Generally you do not see breakage in this, but maybe you can get $350k if you are in a position where they really want you and maybe you aren't so keen, so they come after you. Writing can be across the board. If three studios want your script and it is the first script you have ever written you could sell it for $1m!

Q - What are common mistakes that you see foreign film makers make in coming over here in either getting their career going or making a film?

Paul - I think the big mistake is to take a movie because you are offered it. This usually happens because there is excitement about you from studios and you jump into the thing that is in front of you. You are committing a year of your life to this film so you want to make sure that you have a creative impulse for it - that it is something you feel good about. There is a French film maker who made 'Ma Vie En Rose', which I absolutely loved. Then his first Hollywood film was 'Passion Of Mind', which was a very well regarded script, but the movie did not turn out very well. Sometimes in Hollywood you are as good as your last film, and this kind of took him out of the system as far as being considered for other open directing assignments. Another mistake I see is not taking yourself off projects when they are not going well. If you are developing a script with a studio and they are pushing to make the film and you don't feel like the script is ready, then sometimes it is best to gracefully bow out. Lastly, sometimes people think they have the appetite to work in the American system, which can be very corporate, and they get here and they don't respond well to it.

Q - What advice would you give a film maker coming out here?

Paul - Take as many meetings as you can. Get advice from producers and agents. If you are seeking representation and you have

Useful NY Addresses

British Consulate-General
845 Third Avenue, New York, NY 10022
Tel: (212) 745-0200
Fax: (212) 754-3062
www.britainusa.com/ny/

IFP-NY
104 West 29th Street, 12th Floor, New York,
NY 10001-5310
Tel: (212) 465-8200
Fax: (212) 465-8525
www.ifp.org

Writers Guild of America, East
555 West 57th Street, Suite 1230
New York, NY 10019
Tel: (212) 767-7800
Fax: (212) 582-1909
www.wgae.com

The Directors Guild – East
Directors Guild of America
New York Headquarters
110 West 57th Street
New York, New York 10019
Tel: (212) 581-0370, (800) 356-3754
Fax: (212) 581-1441
www.dga.org

PGA East Chapter
100 Avenue of the Americas, 11th Fl.
New York, NY 10013
Tel: (212) 894-4016
Fax: (212) 894-4056
Email: PGA-NY@producersguild.org
www.producersguild.org

MOFTB - The Mayor's Office Of Film,
Theater & Broadcasting
1697 Broadway, Suite #602
New York, NY 10019
Tel: (212) 489-6710
Fax: (212) 307-6236
www.nyc.gov/html/filmcom
Grants all permits for shooting in NYC.
Can help with police, fire, parking and
traffic control.

Shooting People
www.ny.shootingpeople.org
The UK film networking network, now
available for filmmakers in New York.

Film and Video Arts
462 Broadway
Suite #520
New York, New York 10013
Tel: (212) 941-8787
www.fva.com
Similar to the IFP's, but more grass
roots oriented. They have lots of
information, relationships and even
educational classes on filmmaking.

Kodak in New York occasionally hold
free events or paid workshops. Log onto
their website to find bulletins of when or
where: www.kodak.com

---

the opportunity to meet several agencies, meet them all because even if you know an agency is not the right one for me, you are going to learn something in every one of those meetings. Make sure if you are signing with a person that you feel creatively, you are in synch, you can speak to on a day to day basis and they have long term goals in mind. I think another trap that directors fall into is that they get hired on to an open directing assignment, and they limit themselves to working only on that job. They are so focused in getting that one movie made that they stop taking other meetings. You can make one movie a priority, but at the same time a lot of these movies get close to being made, but not greenlit and then a year later you haven't worked. So you always want to have multiple things in development. If you can develop with more than one studio, do it. If you can develop on your own with other writers or yourself, do it. You want to keep as many balls in the air as possible so it's more your decision of what movie to make versus being in a panic to make that one movie that you've been completely focused on. You also might get to a point where the studio might want to cast their choice instead of your choice, and if you have multiple projects in development and a chance to direct something else, you can leverage the movie into getting made. You will walk if it doesn't get greenlit.

Adam Kaller

Behr, Abramson, Kaller

GETTING AN LA LAWYER

Q - What do you as an entertainment lawyer?

Adam - The traditional entertainment lawyer is someone who is an expert in the motion picture and TV business, who understands intellectual property rights. Someone who you would bring a deal to and they would review the agreements and make comments on them. On the other end of the extreme is the super-agent type lawyer. He doesn't do much of the paperwork at all. He has underlings who handle that for him or her. So this person acts more like a dealmaker or broker using his relationships to sell and package material. They do all the things an agent does without necessarily being an agent, yet having the background of a lawyer to make deals in a way most agents can't. Then there are things in between. Some lawyers like to act more like managers. Most of the people who are successful are more of the super-agent type, but you have to be careful because you don't want to act like an agent because then you are not really a lawyer anymore and you don't want to step on the toes of the agents.

Q - So there is a danger of clashing with the agents?

Adam - Well, not really clash. You work collaboratively. They have relationships that are far and wide and you have relationships that are far and wide. And if you add a manager to the mix, between the three of you, there is almost nothing that can't be reached or done or attacked in a unique way. It may be that all three people know the same creative executive, but all three have a different relationship. One of those relationships may be a bad one. One may be a really good one, but too close, too personal to call upon. We don't want to be in a position where our relationships are put in a place where we shortchange our clients, which sometimes happens. So the more people you have working for you, the better it is for the clients. You just have to make sure everyone has their egos in check and work together.

Q - Should a UK film maker coming to the US, get the whole package of a manager, an agent and a lawyer?

Adam - Yes. I just went through this with someone coming over from the UK. He had a manager and an agent in the UK. He hasn't taken an agent in the US and he is interviewing me to be his lawyer and the question that came up was, *'Do I need and agent here?'* And the answer is absolutely. You should keep both. The UK agents get nervous because they know when they come over here, the big agencies here start acting for their clients so the UK agents start thinking that they are useless save for booking jobs in the UK. But the more successful you get in the States the more you end up staying in the States. It is a hard dynamic and the agencies struggle with it because they want the constant supply of new talent from the British agencies so they cannot alienate the UK agents. But the clients naturally, over time if they are successful in the States, don't see a need for the UK agent. For the client, you have to have people here on the ground doing everyday business in the entertainment business you want to be part of. It is a relationship based business and if you don't have people working for you that are connected to that system, then you might as well be sending scripts from the UK on your own.

Q - What is the best way for a UK film maker to find a US lawyer?

Adam - I think I would start with the US agencies because they are easy to pick up on the internet. They all have websites - CAA, ICM, Endeavor, etc. Those agencies have a much bigger presence than any law firm. And all of them have tremendous relationships with all the law firms. And you would want to make sure that your agents were comfortable with the lawyers that you selected. The downside is that the agents are getting way more submissions that the lawyers are. So if you can find us, we can do great things for you. If I get a piece of material and I respond to it, I can get it to any agent and it will come to them in a totally different way than if it is a straight submission. They have done business with me and respect me and if I like it, then they will definitely take a look. I don't get them a lot, but some people get a list of all the entertainment lawyers in LA and they send a query letter about their script. If it were clever and well-written and catches your eye and doesn't take more than ten seconds to read, then I would take a look at it.

Q - Do you go to film festivals?

Adam - Yes. A lot of lawyers these days go to festivals looking for clients. They go to Sundance, Toronto, Berlin, Cannes, they go everywhere. It is very competitive among the lawyers. I do it, too.

Q - Are there any basic problems about a UK film maker coming over to the US to work on a studio film?

Adam - The biggest problems are immigration issues where you don't have the appropriate visas, etc. The truth is the major studios have a pretty good system. If you are coming over to make one of their movies, you are getting an H-1 visa or whatever you need. If you are doing an independent film, you have to get to the right entertainment attorney. One guy that has made a name for himself doing this is Ralph Ehrenprise. The studios use him a lot. When it comes to film making you have to provide a unique service that other people cannot be providing. And as a writer, director or an actor that is a no-brainer. It is not like you are hammering nails into wood. There are taxation issues. If they render services in the US, then they are subject to taxes here. They need to know if they want to create a loan out company to try and shelter some of that income.

Q - There is a paragraph in many contracts that states that someone is unique to their job. Is that what you were talking about?

Adam - That is different. That paragraph relates to the waiver of injunctive relief. When you make a deal with a studio and they get in a fight with you, they may fire you and not pay you. They breach the contract. You say, *'I am going to sue you for money and injunctive relief'*, which is a court order to say you must do something. And what we are talking about is either getting the studio to stop making or distributing that film. The problem is that the studio probably has committed millions of dollars to making the film and advertising it. And you come along and they owe you $30k, you can get an injunction to stop everything until you get paid. The studios know this so in every contract that an artist will sign it will say, *'I waive all my rights to injunctive relief.'* And all that stuff about uniqueness is pretext to that waiver. So you can't stop them. And that goes for the rights, too. The contract says we have your rights no matter what. And if you are right, then we have to pay you money, but you cannot stop us under any circumstance.

Q - Is there any way as a new film maker that you wouldn't get fired in a certain number of days?

Adam - There are two concepts that you have to understand as a director. There is *'pay or play'* and *'pay and play'*. *'Pay or play'* means we will either use your services and pay you or not use your services and pay you. But we don't have to use your services. We can pay you money and send you home. So let's say we a make a pay or play directing deal for you for $250k and a week into production the studio loses complete confidence in you. They fire you and pay you $250,000. Most people are saying I am *'pay or play'* and what most studio contracts say is yes, you are *'pay or play'*, which means we can get rid of you whenever we want, but when do we have to pay that $250k? Anytime between when you sign that contact and when they *'elect to proceed'*, they can fire you without cause. They don't owe you $250k. You only get that money if they *'elect to proceed'* to production and that often means the first day of shooting. Sometimes they will say you become *'pay or play'* when they approve the final screenplay, approve the final budget, when the bond is in place, when we are irrevocably and irreversible *'pay or play'* to the two top principle leads and we have notified you of a start date. When those five things happen, you are deemed *'pay or play'*, but then it will say in any event, when we start shooting, you are *'pay or play'*. And all those things will never be satisfied until they are shooting, so it is a way to make people feel better, especially lawyers, so they feel they are getting something special. But they aren't. If all five of those things happened, at most, it would be a few days before principle photography started.

Q - So what is 'pay and play'?

Adam - *'Pay and play'* means you must pay me and you must use my services. You can get that in the independent world a lot because usually the director and the writer are the same person and the writer-director has written something that is personal and that a studio is not going to make. It is a person's particular vision and they are doing it for $50k or whatever. They say, *'Fine. I will do it for no money, but you cannot make my script without me directing it'*. Now the same thing applies with respect to the payment. Just because they say you are *'pay and play'* doesn't mean they have to pay you. It could mean that, but you wouldn't be guaranteed your fee until they started shooting. Then they would have to pay you as if you were *'pay or play'*, but they couldn't fire you. There is a hybrid to that, which is to be *'pay and play'* for the first week or two of principle photography and that happens fairly often. So you are *'pay or play'* in every deal you enter. You are *'pay and play'* when you have the leverage. Sometimes if you come in and you say, *'we have the script, we have the budget, we've got Brad Pitt and I am the director. And if I am not the director, then you are not making the movie.'* The studio will sometimes say, *'fine.'*

Q - What would be a typical deal for a first time director in terms of money?

Adam - Anything over scale plus ten percent is a bonanza. So you can expect a development deal of $25k paid $12.5k upon signing and $12.5k if they elect to proceed or abandon the project and DGA scale plus ten percent, which is about $175k or so. Now, they will demand optional pictures. Usually two or three. The only play in those negotiations is if you can cut it to one or cut them out entirely by directing another picture for somebody else first. So you make a deal with Warner Brothers and they give you scale plus ten for the first movie, $300k for the second movie and $600k for the third optional movie. But if I do a movie for Disney before I do your movie, then your options are canceled. The whole theory behind options is that if the studio gave you your shot and spent all this money when you were nobody, then we want something in return if you are successful at a set price, which is what an option is. But if another studio steps up and takes the risk, and they will have their own options, then WB options are canceled. It doesn't always work. Sometimes we cannot get this in the contract.

Q - It is funny because people in the old days used to get three picture deals with studios and would be thrilled. Now it sounds like a burden.

Adam - Inexperienced people say that they happily made a three picture deal but they don't know what it means. There are some companies that would say they were not giving you optional pictures, but they would guarantee your next two movies. The problem is they can be brutal in the way they allow you to make those movies. They put you in a position where they own you and they aren't going to honour the contract. So in the optional picture context, most of the companies out there have an unwritten rule that we are not going to stand in your way if there is another movie you want to make, despite our options, if we don't have anything we want you to make. So everyone is operating under that premise, but occasionally some disreputable companies can interfere and muscle in on your new deal. Or they could be vindictive and prevent film makers from doing other movies out of spite or to renegotiate deal terms. Always quid pro quo, it was never easy. So multi-picture deals are a bad sign in my eyes. I had one client who spent years trapped in this system, never able to make a movie. Getting paid, but unable to make a movie.

Q - Do the options mean anything since the industry changes so fast?

Adam - So many things can happen that some guarantees that the studios make are unreal. For me it is always better to make the deal for the movie you want to make now. But in the future? I am doing one now. I am trying to figure out a development deal for what would be someone's fourth movie? Who knows? What if the first movie makes $250 million domestically. What if it reinvents the genre? What if it is the most important film ever? Suddenly I have made a deal that makes no sense. The studio is happy. People also tend to get hung up on them about how much they are. It is kind of irrelevant because when you go to make that optional picture, hopefully you will be in a position where your marker rate far exceeds the option price. You might be a $2 million director, but they have you for $500k. They won't admit this, but they know they will not get you to do it for the option price. But they do have the right to force you to do it for that price. But you know it is an artistic endeavour and you feel like you have a gun to your head and you are being screwed, the chances that you are going to direct a good movie for them is slim and they know that, too. So what happens is you don't get your $2 million, you get $1.25 million. So you are both better off and all is good. They are typically renegotiated.

Q - How long does the deal process take?

Adam - Longer than anyone ever thinks. The deal process from the time you get the call saying they want to make a director deal to the time the deal is concluded, if it is a simple deal, is a week to ten days. Sometimes I have done a deal in ten minutes - that is rare. Usually there is a lot of back and forth. Complicated back ends for big directors can go on for a month. Once the deal is done, then the documentation process starts and that varies from studio to studio. Some are quick and others are grossly understaffed. Usually the talent lawyers react quicker than the studio business affairs lawyers. Depending on the lawyer that can take a month to six months and meanwhile no one is getting paid. What is even more important for people to understand is that even if your deal is done, you may not get paid until someone else's deal is done. If they need the rights on a piece of material from someone else before you can start working on it, so you have to wait.

Q - How long is it from when you do sign to when you actually get paid?

Adam - Within ten business days.

Q - Is there anyway for a British first time studio film maker to come over here and get final cut?

Adam - None. Not unless they are the most important director that ever lived in Britain. It is hard for people here to get it in a meaningful way. There may be ten who can. However, in the independent world there are no rules. You can get anything you want. If someone is eager enough to make your movie, then you can get them to turn over final cut.

Q - How often does a claim come against a film such as copyright infringement?

Adam - Every single time. It is just the nature of the beast. Ideas are not that unique and almost everyone has had one and at some point a crackpot has sent it in to a studio and that person is waiting for the movie to come out and just before it does, they hit you over the head. Sometimes they are right. *The Dukes Of Hazzard* had a claim against it where Warner Brothers had to pay $17.5 million dollars to the original rights owners. *The Dukes Of Hazzard* TV series apparently spun off from another lesser-known movie or TV series that these guys owned that WB never acquired the rights to. They sued and got and injunction to stop the release of the film. WB settled as soon as the injunction came out. Wrote them a cheque for $17.5 million and good-bye. It happens between studios, too, but less often. As writers, the studio's insurance should cover you - give you indemnity. But if you actually did plagiarize, then you are going to be on the hook for a lot of money.

Q - What advice would you give a film maker coming to the US?

Adam - It is a very different culture and system in Hollywood than the UK system or any other. You have to devote yourself to understanding the rules and principles of this system and applying them to yourself. Study how you get yourself from wannabe film maker to film maker. Know what agents do, what lawyers do, what managers do. Know how studios receive material. Know what it means to take a spec out. Understanding the language of the business so you can work within the system. You have so many strikes against you when you say you are a director and no one knows who you are. You want millions of dollars from them and their jobs are on the line. Don't make it more difficult. Completely understand what it is you are asking them to do and how other people typically ask for it to be done. Ask yourself what is important to them. What do they want me to say? My favourite expression in this business is *99% of the people can say 'no' but only 1% can say 'yes'*. It is a cliché, but it is true as to what is going on around here. And people exercise that *'no'* power a lot. You have to understand how the chain of command to that *'yes'* person is and how to work it. Otherwise you are waiting for lightening to strike and that is not a good way to go about any business.

Jeremy Bolt
Producer

BREAKING INTO HOLLYWOOD

Q - As a first time British filmmaker, what are some good tips for getting meetings in Hollywood?

Jeremy - However suspicious filmmakers, particularly European ones, will be of agents and representatives, today a number of the agencies represent producers, projects and production companies act as a kind of vetting facility for executives. You will stand a far greater chance of getting a meeting with an intelligent executive if you go through an agency, and for the price of 10% or a packaging fee, it is worth initially getting some kind of representation either for yourself or your project here. I think to try to cold call, unless you're coming off a big critical success at one of the festivals or a low budget hit in your local market, is going to be difficult. In fact, if I had known that when I started out with 'Shopping', I probably would have gone straight to ICM in LA and said, please represent us and the project. But big headed as I was back then, I thought we could do it without help. One of the things you learn as you produce more, is, that getting movies made requires an awful lot of help from an awful lot of sources. It's so difficult to get movies made.

Q - If you didn't have representation and didn't have a film behind you, perhaps the advice is to get something made to approach agents with?

Jeremy - If you're a director then yes, you're not going to get a shot unless you've got something to show for yourself. If you're a nobody and you have a project that you want to pitch to a studio, the first thing to do is to submit it to an agency, and the agency will read it and get coverage and see if they want to represent it. You can also send it into a studio, but unless it gets great coverage you won't get a meeting. To get a meeting simply because 'Hello I'm Joe Schmo, I'm a nobody but I want to pitch you a project', it won't happen. I mean, I won't even take that meeting. I don't have time. It's not rude, it's simply there aren't enough hours in the day and there are a thousand projects out there. However on a positive note, the thing that there's a huge shortage of, is good material. And an agency will pick up on good material. It takes one 'consider' (script report aka coverage) from one reader and your project begins to get traction. And then you'll be invited in, and then the agency will potentially ask to represent the project and then you'll start. I just feel that through an agency or a manager with real credibility and standing, that's how I would approach this town. The agencies are the dynamo that drive it. If not an agent or manager, then another producer. You need somebody or something to vet you in terms of Hollywood and legitimise you. Because unless you're somebody's son or you have a famous surname, I mean my surname helped me when I first came out here because everybody thought I was related to Robert Bolt. Of course I'm not, but I wasn't very quick to tell them that! I didn't think he, God rest his soul, would mind helping a young filmmaker!

Q - Is it a good idea to build up relationships with writers and get your hands on many scripts?

Jeremy - Absolutely, I would never come out here with just a pitch. What is a pitch? Everybody has great ideas. What people need are scripts. You come out with a script and maybe some illustrations, a clear concept, an intelligent and informed idea of budget.

Q - What are some things to bare in mind in preparation for a meeting with a studio exec?

Jeremy - I would only ever pitch one project, which is true in Europe or in America. He or she has probably got, at the most, thirty minutes. I would be aware of his or her recent successes. I'd make sure that the studio doesn't have projects that are in a similar area. Remember he or she will be looking for reasons to say no, not to say yes.

Q - What are the Do's or Don'ts in a meeting with a studio exec?

Jeremy - Don't talk too much. When the executive starts talking, listen. Do not get emotional or critical of anyone or anybody. You have no idea who they know and who they don't know and when you're a nobody, you need as many friends as you can get, so there's no point inadvertently making an enemy. And be very courteous, it's amazing how far good manners will get you in this town.

Q - Are there any personality traits that are attractive to studio execs?

Jeremy - Confidence. I always like people who talk quite concisely and quietly - not quietly, but slowly. I don't like people who come in and hit me with a thousand words per minute, I get overwhelmed. Remember the executive has so much going on in his mind. He needs a very clear simple concept. Remember though you won't get the meeting, unless either the agents have said this is a brilliant talent or he's read the script and he's really interested. So I wouldn't be too defensive, too nervous. As I said in the beginning, I very much doubt you will ever get a cold meeting with any executive who has any value.

Q - Is there anything that you think would make you stand out in that meeting? That exec has twenty pitches a day say, so how do you make a difference?

Jeremy - A clear commercial concept. No vagueness. No grey area drama. Paul (Anderson) my business partner is really one of the best pitchers I've known and has a great reputation for being good in a room here, and he's successful because he speaks clearly, slowly and simply. And his concepts are very simple to follow.

Q - Would you say it's a good idea to bring pictures into meetings?

Jeremy - Definitely. To be honest, we do that a lot with projects. On *Alien Vs Predator*, Paul did these phenomenal illustrations that I know played a strong role in giving him traction on that project at Fox. Spending a bit of money on some illustrations is a very good idea. As a director it shows you have an interesting eye. You have to remember that unless it's a very senior level executive, the junior executive is going to have to pitch this internally, so if you can present it in a simple memorable form with pictures that you can leave, it makes his or her job much, much easier and you should only really be interested in making their job easier. Anything that shows your dedication is always a good thing.

Q - How much latitude does a studio give a producer when they're doing their first film, in production and post?

Jeremy - If it's a relatively new team in terms of the director and the producer and the studio is a hundred percent financing it, they will not give you a great deal of latitude. You just have to hope that you get clear direction from the studio and you have a strong executive who can filter through notes and present them to you in a simple way. Because what you want to avoid are contradictory notes. But no, understandably, they're not going to just let you get on with it. I mean, to be honest, they never do that.

Q - If you're a new producer or producer/director team, do they team you up with a producer who's more experienced?

Jeremy - I haven't experienced that but I do know that does happen. And again I wouldn't show any resistance to that, I would simply be thankful for the support. On the studio lot they have their five or six really expensive deals and those deals need to pay for themselves and they need to feed those mouths. So if it gets suggested that you go to one of these very experienced five star producers, I would agree to it, because it means the chances of your film getting made just went up a little bit. And then it's about how you figure it out with that Producer. And remember that producer is probably so busy that he or she won't be able to be there the whole time, so they won't necessarily steal your thunder.

Q - Do producers get branded in a certain genre?

Moving to Hollywood

GUERILLA FILM MAKER SAYS!

The No. 1 consideration before moving is 'how do I get a visa to enable me to live and work in the US?' It isn't easy. There are a variety of visas to look at, as a visa exists for practically every letter of the alphabet! The two main temporary visas that can help lead to a green card (permanent residence) are the O-1 and the H-1. The O-1 is when you're an 'alien with exceptional ability' and the H-1 is if you have a degree. Both last for 2 or 3 years and can be extended. There's a lot to do to prepare for this and although it is possible to download the forms from the US government (http://uscis.gov/graphics/) and do it yourself, it's best to get a professional immigration lawyer. Not only are they familiar with how all the questions should be answered but also lawyers who specialise in immigration will be known to the INS and so the process may well move quicker.

Social Security Number: Once you have a visa and you're in the US, you can apply for a social security number. It's only then that you will be regarded as a normal person and be able to live a normal lifestyle with things that you have always taken for granted.

First stop after getting a number, is to get a driving license. This is super important as this is used as ID and America is a place where you need to have ID on you at all times (a passport does not always work). Your next step should be health insurance, or you'll find yourself paying the equivalent of £500 for each doctor's visit, and then tens of thousands of pounds if an accident occurs. (Just buying a simple bottle of wine can be a major problem without recognisable ID...a passport sometimes just doesn't cut it).

Credit rating: Forget that great relationship you built up with your UK bank manager, as now having moved country, it's as though you're 18 again, and you must start to build up your credit rating.

Once the practicalities are over, you'll find it easy. Americans are extremely friendly, they love the English and there are many ex-pats there who can give you advice. Join one of your closest film networking organisations and schmooze, schmooze, schmooze! If you ever feel a little homesick, there are plenty of British pubs and curry houses to keep you happy!

Jeremy - Absolutely.

Q - And does that make it more and more difficult if you're trying to do something different?

Jeremy - Yes and the way to overcome that is to work with a director who's proven in that new area. Personally I would pursue a genre and focus on it initially and try to become successful in that genre. I think it's very dangerous to become too eclectic before you've had really one or two hits. I think it's helpful if they go, well you're the horror guys. We focused on video games. It means we have credibility when it comes to that genre, which means it helps us get movies made in that area. If Paul and I suddenly declared that we wanted to make romantic comedies, it would be a lot harder. So it's all about making your life easier and I think pick the area that you like the most and focus on it.

Q - Even if you stuck to one genre, is it a good idea to team yourself up with many writers or directors in that genre, or just the one. For instance, you've lined yourself up with your partner Paul and you do projects together?

Jeremy - If you look at the most successful producers, there is always a period where they've worked with the same director for a period of years and I think you have to learn from history. So with Larry Gordon, it was Walter Hill. Obviously I've benefited from Paul. Andrew MacDonald works with Danny Boyle in the UK. Lawrence Bender works with Tarantino. It's a really tough business and it's tremendously helpful to have a business partner, somebody that you can trust.

Q - How does the financial success affect you as a producer making the next movie? Say, if you have a film that's critically acclaimed but it flops at the box office?

Jeremy - If it's critically acclaimed and it cost a lot of money and it doesn't make any money, then you're in trouble. It doesn't matter if it was critically acclaimed unless it begins to make money over time, like a *'Blade Runner'*, in which case you will ultimately reap tremendous reward but it will take a few years. Generally, unless it's a movie of low budget, and its critically acclaimed but it doesn't really connect or make too much money, then it won't harm you.

Q - So if a big budget movie didn't get great reviews and didn't do well financially...?

Jeremy - In this town, what matters is if it makes money. If you've made a film that's been so well received, it buys you two or three flops. Ultimately what you want is a film that makes a lot of money and is critically well received. If you achieve that, you'll find that you can withstand two or three flops. If you make a film that just makes a lot of money, it'll be very hard to recover from one flop.

Q - What would you say are the big differences between the way films are made in Britain and the way they're made by the studios in the US? Do you think there's still that 'art-house' based thought that goes into making films in the UK or do you think that's become less and less nowadays?

Jeremy - I think it's becoming less. It's very hard to make high concept low budget films. There's only a certain number of scenarios that will work. And on a low budget film, also, nobody is really making much money so I found that everyone is a little nicer in Europe. There's a little more of the kid gloves approach. Here, if it's a studio movie, everybody's probably being quite well paid, so if there's a problem you better bloody listen. So it becomes much more about managing the studio and making sure that the information the executive is giving you is clear and you trust it. Then it's making sure the marketing department is giving enough energy to your project and spending enough P&A. Then, making sure you have the right weekend. In Europe it seems to me, that those things aren't always interconnected. Half the time, you don't even have a distributor when you make a low budget film, so it's hard to see the beginning and the end in one fell swoop. In Britain it's an achievement just to get a decent release, but here it's not about the release it's about getting a number one movie.

Q - How much control, as a producer, do you get at a studio in choosing the release date?

Jeremy - I would imagine Jerry Bruckheimer, or I would hope Jerry Bruckheimer, gets a lot of control. But on my level I don't really get much control at all. In fact I'd say we have no control. We can voice an opinion and if they like us, they'll listen to it. I think there are very few producers who have that level of power and very few directors.

Q - Is that the same case with marketing?

Jeremy - Yes, definitely. But my view is you look at the films the marketing department have done and you trust their judgement, and if you don't, in a very diplomatic way, you try to convey your point of view. The other thing is the marketing department tend to test their trailers and their posters. So you do get external responses which, if you're a little worried about a trailer and a poster, can be very comforting to hear, *'it's just tested very well'.*

Q - What advice can you give to British producers who've decided to come out to Hollywood to give it a go?

Jeremy - I think you need to set yourself some deadlines so you don't go insane. And if you haven't achieved them, you need to sort of go back and regroup. One of the important lessons to learn is to know when to give up on a project. One of the interesting things is a project that may appear to be wonderful when you're sitting in London, out here, may soon lose its glow. There's something in the air here, a different sensibility in Hollywood or America, to Europe. When that happens and you can't get traction, drop the project. You have to be very brutal with your own children unfortunately. Otherwise you'll spend an awful lot of energy and time trying to turn a movie into a reality when actually the bottom line is you'd probably have been better off putting your energy into something else that was more achievable. I think a labour of love project is an indulgence for a young producer, I think you need to just get a movie made. Labours of love are for successful, middle aged or even old age. I'm always distrustful when someone comes in and says this is a passion project. It usually means it's commercially unviable.

Q - Do you prefer shooting in Europe or Hollywood?

Jeremy - I've only shot one movie in America and that was *'Soldier'* which was great because it's very comfortable. Personally I'm one of these producers who enjoys a challenge, so the harder the shooting conditions, the better for me. I'd probably be very happy to shoot a film in the Antarctic. I just came back from 8 months in China, in the middle of China, not in Beijing or Shanghai, which was an extremely arduous experience, but I loved every minute of it. So the easier it is, the less happier I am. Which actually is probably why I'm a producer!

WHAT NEXT?

Gabrielle Kelly
Film maker

A BRIT IN THE USA

Q - What are the main differences in the mentality between making films in the UK / Europe and in the US?

Gabrielle - One thing that always strikes me is how much more money is spent in the UK in making shorts. There is a funding structure there for this that just doesn't exist here in America. Many of my American students envy Europeans because of this. However, while it's good to be in a country that subsidises your craft and enables a filmmaker to express their voice, it does give you a very unreal view of the market place of what we call here in LA 'show business'. It's not called 'show art'. A short here in LA is a calling card for a director, to get you your feature and to get your name on the map. I'm also always aghast when I hear what the budgets are of these short films made in Europe. As people in the States don't have that financial support, the budgets are generally pretty modest. Living in a city such as LA, you are in a production matrix where you tend to get support via deals made with great craftsmen. So you can make a short that looks like it cost $100,000, but it actually costs much less. And, you don't have to be an expert on sound or lighting or effects because you can find someone who is. However, wherever you're from, give me wobbly camerawork and bad production design anytime for a good story and good acting.

Q - Do you think in the States people are more aware of the business side of film making and therefore are more conscious about making something commercial so they can make their money back?

Gabrielle - Completely. I do see much longer shorts coming out of Europe which are far more difficult to sell or to screen at festivals where you hope to get attention so to move on to your feature.

Q - How are film makers perceived by the industry in both Europe and the US?

Gabrielle - In Europe, if you are a film maker, then you are a film maker. You can make a film, any kind of film, any kind of genre. But in the US, you tend to get pigeon-holed as a horror director or action director or comedy director depending on what they first see you as. This goes for writers as well. So when US film makers make a short or write a script, then do so knowing that they are making a calling card to get them into a certain genre or to get them an agent or manager. For example, *'Meet The Parents'* started out as a short and became a very successful movie. The director didn't get to direct it, but he made a good deal and has a successful career comedy. I think the reason is, because movies in the US cost so much, the studios are less likely to take chances on people crossing to new genres. Angela Robinson, who directed her short *'D.E.B.S.'* went on to direct the feature version, and even though it wasn't successful, she went on to direct *'Herbie: Fully Loaded'*.

Q - How do you compare the communities by size?

Gabrielle - The US market is so much larger than anything in Europe. Just as an example, Sundance received over eight thousand submissions for its shorts program. There are so many more people doing it here so it makes it tougher to get noticed. However, there are more movies being made. In Europe, the business is much smaller so you have to be really good to get anywhere. There are fewer agents and producers there.

Q - Is it easier to put a feature film together in Europe or in the US?

Gabrielle - As with the shorts, Europe offers so many more resources for finding funding than in the US. There are so many national tax breaks there such as sale and lease back in the UK, where you can get a good portion of your budget. In the US, this doesn't exist and therefore you have to go with more commercial stories that will be accepted by the studios. That said, in the US, you can write a commercial story, go buy a camera at Circuit City, shoot the film in thirty days and return the camera. I know someone who did this recently and they then made a deal with Blockbuster who is going to spend $3 million to advertise and promote the film. I can't unfortunately tell you its name! But it has actually opened theatrically these last few months to rave reviews.

So making films is easier here and you can do it for less money, but, my friend's story aside, it's the distribution portion that provide the overwhelming nightmare stories. Five thousand films were made in the US last year that did not get distribution, so people are turning to other ways of getting them out there, even if it is selling them off their own website. But then you need even more skills as a filmmaker and need to be your own machine, or you need more alliances. You need to be a producer, a web designer and a promoter / sales agent to get it out to the mass audience. Or you try to self distribute by going to the smaller city theatres yourself and you pay for your film to be screened. Say you get some good buzz and you then broker it to theatres across America, if you reach a critical mass, you will then get calls from Lion's Gate and Blockbuster who will take it on themselves because you have proven it can be profitable. Due to this, the producer becomes much more important as he or she can take on a lot of this footwork. Or nowadays there's a possibility of cell phone distribution. What if you made a three minute short film and you sold it to Sprint in the US, or Orange in the UK, to play on your mobile phone? You could have a new phenomenon on your hands with millions of people watching your funny, sexy, different and innovative short. Then before you know it, you could suddenly have a three picture deal with a studio! It's not too far fetched. Two days after the London bombings, in America, the FCC - America's communications regulators, will now accept as broadcast journalism footage that you shoot on your mobile which you can deliver to a news station. We are now all filmmakers and journalists.

Q - What advice would you give a European film maker who has made a feature in Europe and then wants to come to the US to work in the studios?

Gabrielle - The toughest thing is actually getting to the US and getting meetings. If your film comes out in Europe and makes a splash, chances are some agent, manager or producer will see it and if it is any good, contact you, sign you up and fly you over for meetings. But if this doesn't happen, if you are a producer or distributor, you can join programs where they bring out people to LA. But you have to have some money because you can only get a 90-day visa to come to the US and you can't work here on that. There are other avenues too that you can go down. I judge the Hartley-Merrill Screenwriting competition. Two guys from Ireland won it this year and Hartley-Merrill set up meeting for them in LA. If you are just Joe Film Maker who is just coming out here, then you have to get the phone numbers for people you want to meet, and besiege them to try and get a meeting. You do have an advantage because you are not from here and that makes you a bit intriguing, but getting into the studios is tough because they generally want someone pushing you or that you've come in from a personal contact. You could also come here to find representation, but you have to plan it carefully by prepping their work. I'd advise you to set up meetings from Europe rather than just turning up hoping for the best. The indie filmmaker in America is in many ways much worse off than their counterpart in Europe. They do have their support systems for indie filmmakers such as the IFP (Independent Feature Project) but you're really in the business like everyone else and it's sink or swim. My main advice would be to network. Get out and show people your material, build relationships from the UK and then ask for favors when you want to come over. It's all business here in LA. It's all about selling. You need to create a buzz about yourself in some way to get them excited. If you come out here and haven't done very much, then you're going to find it very hard.

Q - Is there an ex pat networking community for film makers in the US?

Gabrielle - No. The closest there is to it, is BAFTA and the London Film Council Office. But no, there's no place where you can show up and hang out with other filmmakers. BAFTA LA has more members in Hollywood than it does in London, but it's rather strict on new members joining. You have to be in the business for 4 years and it's now very difficult to get into the LA division. The London Film Council would hopefully be more helpful. Santa Monica in Los Angeles is a huge ex pat community where you can bump into a British film maker in The Kings Head Pub or over at the continental shop on Wilshire Boulevard where you can pick up an LA based ex pat newspaper and a Galaxy bar.

Simon Graham-Clare
UK Film Council US

THE UK FILM COUNCIL IN LA

Q - What is the role of the Los Angeles Film Council (UK) office?

Simon - The LA office is set up to service the US industry and to promote the UK film industry here in America. That means, we disseminate the policies of the UK Film Council to US film makers and provide them with information of UK film services. These services could be details on tax breaks, finding British talent - whether that's finding a British DoP or a co-producer or whether you want the UK as a place to make films. In addition we supply information to the US industry to both encourage co-production and highlight British talent. This will include sending out British trade magazines such as *Factory* and *British Cinematographer* to the Hollywood community, letting them know who and what is out there. My role is to cultivate and nurture relationships in the US primarily with producers and agents. This is principally a people business and relationships with our contacts are incredibly important.

Q - How directly can you help a British film maker coming out to LA?

Simon - We can only assist the filmmaker if they have been recommended to us by the UK Film Council. For example where there is a requirement for a US partner, in say the Development Fund, and they need a production company or some other resource, I can assist. We are not an information bureau for UK film makers visiting LA. We are also not able to set up meetings or introduce UK film makers to studio execs etc., unless requested by the UK Film Council in London. On occasion I have supplied online reference tools and explained the difference between an agent and a manager etc. However it is not the norm.

Q - If someone is in talks with the UK Film Council to fund their project, but needs some US information to help the process along, can they come to you?

Simon - Yes if they are in the US. However, if they are in the UK it would be the UK Film Council that would make the recommendation to us. I am able to suggest potential US equity partners and co-producing partners, however again, the approach must come from the UK Film Council in the first instance. If the project is a UK film and is submitted by a film maker in the US then we will arrange coverage here and help them with their application and supply potential UK co-producing partners information.

Q - Do you put on any screenings of British films to the US industry?

Simon - Yes. We produce, in conjunction with BAFTA-LA, a series of screening British films that, at the time of screening, don't have US distribution. Over the last three years we have screened twenty UK films that fall into this category. BAFTA-LA has approximately 1200 voting memberships for the BAFTA awards therefore it is important these films are given a fair chance. These films are also shown to our key contacts over here, which might possibly help the films find distribution in the US.

Q - Can individual film makers approach you on this?

Simon - Usually the contact is made through British sales agents who let us know which films don't have US distribution. But an individual can bring their film to us directly. A selection committee of BAFTA-LA voting members is formed and from the eligible films a small number are chosen to screen. A film must have a UK release date to qualify.

Q - What about for short films?

Simon - For shorts, we've hosted a UK short films showcase; produced an evening of Academy Award nominated UK shorts, assisted British short film makers in attending short film festivals here in the US and given our US contacts a DVD compilation of award-winning UK shorts (where we include on the DVD the film makers' contact details).

Q - What do you do to help British filmmakers, who haven't made a film using one of the UK Film Council Funds?

Simon - We offer several things that could help but all are programmes that are offered through the UK. For instance, we work with Skillset on their program, Inside Pictures, which is an annual event of a three week course for fourteen people for two weeks in the UK and one week in the US. On the LA side of things we put them in front of panels of US executives. So one panel might be US agents and managers and the fourteen people get to ask them questions. Then we might take them around to different facets of the US industry. We'll take them to studios, independent companies, home video departments with studios, the trade magazines such as Variety - all to give them a thorough overview of the industry over here. If someone wants to get involved they would apply to the UK Film Council in London. We also work with IFP New York's No Borders program and that is usually attended by someone from London. We bring film makers out to New York for that. We also get involved with the AFI Festival by bringing films and film makers out for that. I think this year it is called EU New Faces and that person's film will be in the AFI festival. The AFI chooses a selection of films of emerging film makers and then the Film Council chooses one and sends them to the US. We bring film makers out who are nominated for Academy Awards and have Q&A's with them. The audience for these is usually a mixture of agents, managers, production executives, organisation members like IFP who's west coast branch is now called FIND (Film Independent).

Q - What events do you offer in the US to the UK industry?

Simon - Throughout the year we host a number of events in Los Angeles ranging from special screenings, lunches to promote emerging talent, and receptions. It is always advisable when visiting the US to enquire with us what networking opportunities are available to UK film industry visitors. For smaller sales agents, we offer, through our work with the Film Exports Group (which is the government's strategy of stimulating and supporting film exports) an office at the AFM at the Loew's Hotel which they can use as an umbrella office. We kit out the office with all the screens and audio visual aids, receptionist, telephone and faxes etc. for their use. We also have Showcase. Supported by UK Film Council US, UK Showcase is an opportunity for the US movie making industry to connect with representatives from over fifty film service companies during November 8th and 9th in Hollywood. So that would be with the guys who run Studios, Labs, post production facilities etc. It also has seminars and conferences over two days which include information on how the tax benefits work etc. It comes with free access and free parking and it's free to register online. For more information, visit www.showcase.uk.net.

Q - What is the Diversity and Inclusion Department?

Simon - That's the UK Film Council's program to help achieve a more diverse workforce behind and in front of the camera across the film sector. It also ensures that equality and diversity commitments are fully integrated into every aspect of all core UK Film Council activities. So a part of this programme would entail our office researching 'best practice findings' on this from the US industry, feeding back intelligence on specific programmes and events in the US and connecting with 'urban' film making communities as part of our everyday working practice. Within this, events are also included such as one we're putting together right now that will highlight women film makers from the UK. It would be an afternoon event where we would bring UK female film makers to the US and get them in a room with key contacts.

Q - If someone wanted to shoot in the UK, what can you do for them?

Simon - We would meet with them to determine which projects could potentially be shot in the UK. We would give initial advice and information and then forward to the UK Film Council's British Film Commissioner, Steve Norris, and his inward investment team. We also have an extensive information library on financial incentives, crews, locations, co-producers, legal and accountant contacts, co-production treaties etc. including numerous directories such as our directory on UK Co-producers which lists the production companies, what countries they've made movies with before, and the budget ranges they have worked with. We would also add them to our email list of open invitation to attend UK Showcase.

WHAT NEXT?

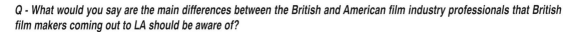

BAFTA in the USA

BAFTA has two locations in the US that serve as a bridge between the Hollywood and British production and entertainment business communities. Like the UK office, the US branches provide members with screenings with Q&As with the film makers, social events such as the Annual Britannia Awards, the BAFTA Film Awards Brunch and the Annual Garden Party. They hold seminars on film topics such as finance and music and educational outreach programs as well. If you're a member of BAFTA UK already, then it's worth giving them a call to find out what benefits you can get either in LA or NY and for what period of time. However, as of October 2005, BAFTA LA has capped it's membership and is closed to new membership. Speak to BAFTA LA if you'd like to be put on a list for when openings become available.

BAFTA-LA
8533 Melrose Ave. Second Floor
West Hollywood, CA 90069
Tel: (310) 652-4121
Fax:(310) 854-6002
www.baftala.org

BAFTA-East Coast
31 West 56th Street, New York, NY 10019
Tel: (212) 258-265
www.baftaeastcoast.com

Q - What would you say are the main differences between the British and American film industry professionals that British film makers coming out to LA should be aware of?

Simon - In business Americans are more direct. They are precise and concise because everyone is so busy. Of course there will be niceties when you first sit down in a meeting, but be conscious of the fact that the person has other meetings behind yours. First impressions go a lot further. Also Americans prefer to have personal contact - meeting face to face. America is a 'can do' culture, particularly in Los Angeles...*the land of opportunity*.

Q - Can you help or advise film makers getting visas to come out to work in the US?

Simon - No.

Q - What advice would you give a film maker who is coming out to the US?

Simon - There are six main things a British film maker can do to help him or herself. First, prepare: there are a number of religious and public holidays, festivals and markets throughout the US calendar year so make sure you research before you plan your trip. Second, plan - know why you want to come and what you want to achieve and who you want to see. Time goes really quickly here because it's a social environment. Third, research: there are a number of valuable information tools accessible via the web, HCDonline, In Hollywood/Studio Systems. Make sure you research the company you are visiting, have the correct spelling and pronunciation of the individual's name and it is always advisable to get to know the assistant as they are your ticket in to seeing your US contact. Fourth, Communication: make sure you have a US cell phone and if not make sure your UK cell works here and is on your business cards. Fifth, Getting around: you will need a car and be prepared for traffic in LA anytime of the day, so allow plenty of time to reach your destination and find parking. Do not outstay your welcome - the average first meet in LA is twenty minutes, get to the point within that time. It is better to leave them wanting more than ejecting you from the room. Always use an internet map device like Mapquest to find a hotel that is centrally located so that you can get to your meetings on time. I have known people that have booked hotels that are so far out that it takes so much energy and effort to get to where they need to go. Sixth, Follow up - ensure you always follow up after your meeting with a phone call email or letter. Also FYI, when speaking to a US executive it is customary for their assistant to also be on the line.

CASE STUDIES

THE LIVING SPIRIT STORY

PROLOGUE

Filmmakers and authors of this book, Chris Jones and Genevieve Jolliffe met at Bournemouth Film School in 1989. Chris, born and bred in the North of England, had started making amateur horror films on Super 8mm many years earlier. His first triumph, an unashamed homage to the films of George Romero and the *Evil Dead*, an immense success at his college. After 'bluffing' his way into film school, he began work on what he believed would be his greatest film yet, *Rundown*, a sci-fi thriller. Genevieve was inspired and terrified at an early age, by the black & white classic, *Dracula. Star Wars* quickly followed and she knew that she wanted to make movies. She started out working in the industry, attending markets such as the Cannes Film Festival and dabbling in animation before travelling the world with her Nikon and Super 8mm camera. When she attended film school, she quickly became frustrated by the lack of inspired leadership and was eager to make a movie. After meeting, Chris and Gen decided to make *Rundown*, Chris' graduation film, but too many obstacles were put in their way. They decided to leave the film school, Chris after two and a half years, Gen after only six months. Neither of them made a movie or shot a single frame of film while at the film school.

Note - The interviews in this section were performed between 1994 and 2005.

ACT 1

THE RUNNER

Q - How did Living Spirit Pictures come about?

Gen - Film School, at the time we were there, was about making depressing TV style drama, full of pessimism, about minority issues - anything that involved a social problem. They didn't want to do anything that strayed from that formula, there was no variety, just one particular kind of film and if you didn't fit into that, then you didn't get a film made. When we came out of film school we just wanted to do something that was BIG. The frustration of film school had built up in us to such a degree that when we considered what to make, there was one thing we really wanted to do - blow everything up! We were both fans of *Aliens* and *Die Hard*, so we knew that we wanted to make an action thriller.

Chris - I was in my third year at film school, Gen was in her first. We teamed up and decided to make a film school project together. I was taken onto the film school course as a director and I was supposed to be directing a film that year. I put forward a script that I had written in my first year and had been developing ever since, about a game show in which contestants were killed. After endless script development meetings with the staff, it became apparent that this was not going to happen in the form that I wanted. It wasn't going to be the sci-fi action-adventure that I wanted to make. Gen felt the same.

One night we sat down and thought - What would happen if we didn't actually make this movie at film school? We'd worked out a budget of around £14k, went down the list and calculated that the film school offered us a crew (which in any case we could persuade to work with us) and equipment (which would cost us £4k if we had to hire it). So, in reality, all the film school could offer was a quarter of the budget in equipment hire and some serious headaches (and they got to retain the copyright!)

We still had to raise £14k and if we could raise that, we could raise £14k and make the film outside the film school. We decided to leave film school, set up our own company and make the film the way we wanted. London was out of the question as it would just be too expensive to live there so we decided to set up in the North of England, in Cheshire, so that we would be a big fish in a small pond.

Q - Is that when you approached the 'Princes' Trust'?

Chris - We found that we were eligible for the PYBT (The Princes' Youth Business Trust, an organisation headed by HRH Prince Charles which helps young people with big ideas but no money). We put our application through and got a soft loan of £3k and a further £2k a year later. This enabled us to get all our business equipment, computer, fax, letterheads, all that kind of stuff. And so Living Spirit was born.

First Assistant Director, Lisa Harney on 'The Runner'... after 5 weeks shooting at 3 a.m. in a Manchester ghetto. It's all a bit much.

Q - Why the name Living Spirit Pictures?

Gen - We wanted a name to express the way we planned to run our business and make movies. Everyone seemed to like it, even the strange people who still ring us and ask if they can join our religious cult!

Q - Did you start a formal company?

Gen - Yes, we were no longer in the playground. We took an accountant's advice and started a Limited Company (US laws differ here). There is so much to running a company and it is very expensive. Read some books on starting a company, they're a lot cheaper than advice from a solicitor or accountant.

Q - After you began trading, what was at the top of the agenda?

Image Copyright Jon English

(above) A production sketch for Rundown, a game show on which contestants are hunted and killed - the script was very developed when Chris and Gen left the film school. Due to problems with special effects, the project was eventually binned in favor of The Runner

Gen - The movie. We were at home, planning the film, looking at the reality of the project. We had a script for a forty-five minute film costing about £18k and had sent off details to potential investors. We weren't sure what to expect, maybe one or two replies. Every single one wrote back and offered finance, saying - *'if you make a movie, we will put in some money... but why a short?'* we were also asked. We started thinking, maybe they're right. £18k is a lot of money for a short - why don't we double it to make a 90 minute film costing £36k. Naively we believed that to be the equation. We're not going to sell a forty five minute film. But we could sell a ninety minute film and suddenly, a much larger market was opened up to us. No longer would we be confined to TV - but now the feature market, including cinema, video, TV, satellite and cable, and now DVD.

Q - Were you nervous about skipping the short film stage?

Chris - Yes of course, but we were no longer in film school, we had to pay the rent and put food on the table. I have spoken to many filmmakers who say - *'I'll make a feature film next but I've got to do another short and learn a bit more'*. And I say *'What do you need to learn?'* You'll learn three times more if you make a feature film and regardless of how much you mess up, you'll still be able to sell it. More than likely you'll make some money back too. If you don't, so what! Make another one'. You've just got to go for it!

Gen - I think you've got to be prepared to take the risk - we were prepared to do that, to plunge in head first. We realised that if we wanted things to happen, we couldn't wait in the hope that Hollywood would give us a call and offer us *Jurassic Park 9.*

Q - Have you chosen the projects you have undertaken on commercial viability?

Chris - We've talked a lot about how we choose the stories we make into a film. Anyone who has seen *The Runner, White Angel* and *Urban Ghost Story* would agree that they are all very different. And you can see a linear progression in our experience, each one gets substantially better than the previous. We're aware of commerciality, we have to be. However, no matter how much we ever thought we were being hard nosed business people, it all boiled down to one thing - *'what did we want to make?'*

(left) In order to convince investors, some pretty dodgy artwork was created. We couldn't afford a model, so Gen had to step into the role for these shots.

When we made *The Runner* we were into movies with serious muzzle flash, semi automatic weapons and lots of explosions - and we did just that. It turned out to be a pretty dreadful movie but we blew a lot of things up. I guess in context, *The Runner* is a knee jerk reaction to the inhibitions of film school. It felt VERY decadent.

Q - Did you have problems talking to people at the top?

Gen - To begin with we did - it depends on your approach. Many young filmmakers, particularly those fresh out of film school, are arrogant, and assume that they have an unwritten right to freebies, discounts and will get offered the best projects. We didn't feel that way and chose not to be arrogant and reasoned that we were more likely to get help if we asked politely.

(above) To prove to EGM that Living Spirit had what it takes, they produced a short two minute action packed trailer. This was a very successful course of action to take as it convinced everyone the picture was going to happen.

Q - How did people in the industry react to these two young upstarts?

Chris - At the time the industry was depressed and didn't seem to understand what we were doing, we were so far removed, we were almost a cottage industry. It was obvious that if we wanted to make movies in the UK then it was up to ourselves to generate our own projects. We've just had to do it with the limited means at our disposal, with whatever talent that we had, and on a micro budget. Risk it all and hopefully at the end of the day it will all come together. We were in a *need-to* situation.

Q - Are there any filmmakers who have been a source of inspiration?

Gen - We knew the story of Sam Raimi and *The Evil Dead* and after we saw a documentary on its making... about how he shot a promo on S8mm, then would visit doctors and dentists etc., get out his 8mm projector, pin a bed sheet to the wall, and show these potential investors what he wanted to make - and these people put money in. He was only eighteen. We thought *'Wow! Maybe we could do this!'*

Q - You tried to get investment for The Runner from several sources, but because you had no real track record, you didn't get very far. How did you eventually get things going?

Chris - We met a company called EGM Film International based in Cardiff, Wales. We said, *'Hey! We're young filmmakers and we've got this idea for a film.'* We showed them a promo tape of films (made by other people) and they were very impressed. We had a one page synopsis which we had written the night before because we thought that we should look like we knew what we were doing. And they said, *'We'll make this but we need to shoot in three weeks time. If you're not going to be ready then the whole show is off.'* We said *'Of course, we're poised'* and we walked out of the office thinking, *'great, we've got this chance to make a feature, but what are we going to do? We're shooting in three weeks time and we don't even have a script!'*

Like most things on *The Runner*, the script was written on a need-to basis. We'd been floundering about, trying to make this great movie and just never got around to putting words on paper. Now we had a real big problem.

(above) Screen hero Jack Slater as portrayed by Terence Ford... The Man, The Myth, The Legend, The Brother...

(below) Ford in action...

(below) Paris Jefferson and Andrew Mitchell - Heroine and Villain. Andrew gave such a psychotic interview that Living Spirit nearly rejected him - as it happened, he turned out to be one of the best things about the film.

Gen - We said we'd fax them the budget, so we had to go out and buy a fax machine! EGM had said, *'we don't want to spend over £40k'*, but we knew it would cost more. We said, *'we need £140k'* and they said, *'we'll give you £40k'*. We said *'Okay, we'll send you the budget tomorrow'*. We consulted our figures and saw that we really had to spend at least £100k. They said - *'No! No! We'll give you £60k.'* We knew that once they committed funds, they would have to finish the film. So we just agreed. We didn't waste much but it actually costs a certain amount of money to blow up half of North Wales, so we spent a lot on pyrotechnics, bullets and all sorts of things - the budget escalated to £140k, exactly what we thought!

Q - With only three weeks pre-production, no money and no script, how did you manage to get everything going?

Chris - We rang a few friends and asked *'What are you doing for the next couple of months? Do you want to come and live at our house and make a movie?'* Everybody said yes and moved in. About thirty people in all. It was great. There were very few problems. Lots of relationships sprung up between various crew members, perhaps because the work was so crisis ridden, everyone needed a shoulder to cry on and it all got rather steamy at various points. I am really surprised there were no *Runner* babies!

I suppose there was a tremendous sense of camaraderie, that no matter what was asked of anyone, they would do it. I've often felt as if I now know what kind of team spirit troops must feel before they go into battle for the first time (not that our job is anywhere near as demanding).

Q - The screenplay usually takes months of development?

Chris - Yes, we had to write a script, good, bad or indifferent. We had to have ninety pages of words to give the actors, to say on the day. Neither Gen nor myself could afford the time to divorce ourselves completely from the much needed three weeks of pre-production. Mark Talbot-Butler, the editor of the film, seemed to be capable of writing a screenplay, so we commandeered him. He did a commendable job when you consider that this was his first screenplay, and the timescale involved. There was simply no development process. When it came to the point where we were shooting, I would walk on set, be given my pages of the script, hot from the photocopier, and read it for the first time. I'd think *'Oh! So that's what we're doing!'* and Gen would read it and see that there were three helicopters needed and she'd say to me, *'Give me three hours',* and off she would go and come back with three helicopters. Really, she did get three helicopters. It was incredible.

There were so many screw-ups because we were totally unprepared. It was a serious crash course, and I emphasise the word crash, in how not to make films. We learned so much. At the end of the day the film was pretty bad. It looked and sounded great and consequently sold, but it's many years on and we still haven't nor expect to receive a penny.

Q - How did you get a cast crazy enough to be involved in this movie?

Gen - We put an ad in the actors newspaper *The Stage* and received sack loads of CV's and photos. It really was sackfuls. The postman once brought three sacks up to the front door and then he informed us that he wouldn't deliver to the door but would leave it all at the back gate. We sifted through these replies and thought, there can't be this many actors in the world, let alone the UK - we sorted them into two piles, *Looks OK, Doesn't look OK*. Then sorted the *Looks OK* into two piles, *Done Film Work, Haven't Done Film Work*. It still took a few hours to short-list, and the list wasn't very short, but it did cut down our work load.

Q - So what did you do about the lead actor?

Chris - Tough man Jack Slater had to be played by a star - but we couldn't afford a star - so we got the brother of a star.

Gen - We rang up a few agents and told them who we were and what we were doing. One agent came back to us and said *'What about Terence Ford?'* We'd not heard of him. *'Well he's done some TV and a movie.'* Still we weren't impressed. Then she said, *'he's the brother of Harrison Ford'*. We thought great! Apparently Terence had read the treatment and liked it, so he rang up and Chris spoke to him (we couldn't afford to fly out to audition him). *'He sounds cool'* said Chris.

Chris - They sent us his CV which was pretty unimpressive with regard to feature film work, but his photo was good. He looked like a younger, more rugged version of his brother. We felt we had found our lead actor. He was Harrison Ford on a budget. We offered Ford a fee of five grand. EGM took over at that point. We said Harrison Ford's brother's interested. Their ears pricked up and they gave him the job. Gen picked him up from the airport and brought him to the studio (which was actually our garage). When we first met, I feared we might have problems as he had lost a lot of weight and his hair had silvered. His photo had portrayed him as a much more rugged and tough looking actor. As he was Harrison Ford's *younger* brother, we all imagined someone like Harrison Ford ten years ago. In fact, they were only separated by a few years so looked about the same age.

Gen - We didn't have much choice. We'd spent loads of money on his flight and were about to start shooting. We'd have to change him a bit. Dye his hair for a start.

Chris - We had cast another guy in the role of the villain, he was an American living in the UK. A week into shooting, he didn't turn up. We thought *'where is our villain?'* Gen got on the phone to his agent and found out that he was on holiday in Turkey and didn't want to come back. So, here we were, I was on set and Genevieve came up to me and said, *'we have a problem with shooting McBain tomorrow* (the villain), *well, he's on holiday in Turkey and he's not coming home.'* I said *'fine, OK',* because I had become used to this kind of crisis every twenty minutes. I relied on the company slogan - *'Gen'll fix it!'* Anyway, that night I returned to the production office and there were two photographs on the production office wall, one of this rather delicate looking actor from Amsterdam and the second, slightly less delicate, living in London.

Gen - They both looked like models.

Chris - The one in London was a friend of the lead actress and she suggested him as he could play American, so we decided to interview him. We asked him to take the train up to Cheshire and we gave him an interview. This is an interview that took place at two-thirty in the morning after a long day's shooting, with the whole crew asleep in this house. We had twenty bunk beds in our living room and there I was in one of the bedrooms with fourteen people farting and snoring giving an interview to this guy who must have thought, *'Oh my God! What am I doing here?'*

The blind leading the blind! (above) Cameraman Jon Walker, who had never shot a film before The Runner, was one of the most experienced crew members!

Gen - The other actor from Amsterdam had said, *'whatever happens, I will come over from Holland for an audition'* and I said, *'we can't afford to pay for you to come over, and if you don't get it, then I'm sorry, it's your tough luck!'* And he said *'that's fine, I'll get it! I'll get it!'* So I drove to pick him up from Manchester - he didn't have enough money to fly, so he had spent thirty hours on a ferry and train. It was maybe three o'clock in the morning when we got back and it's straight upstairs to do the audition.

Chris - He was quite good looking and very pleasant. We took him into a room full of bunk beds and asked, *'what would you like to read for us?'* He replied in a strong Dutch American drawl, *'Okay man. I don't want to read no words. I've prepared my own interpretation of the part. Do you want to hear it?'* We agreed. A pause before he suddenly exploded into this incredible, violent, one-man play about killing babies in Vietnam. I was sitting on the bed thinking *'we cannot employ this guy, he will murder us in our beds. In fact, I'm going to double lock my bedroom door tonight!'* Mark, the editor and writer, was sitting next to me, and he was equally terrified while watching this performance with dinner plate eyes. We left the room.

'Oh my God. What are we going to do? This guy's completely insane' I said and Genevieve is hyper, saying *'He's great. He's so energetic!'* The other actor, the one from London was more bankable, a little more secure. We knew he would at least read the words on the page (when they were eventually written). Then there was the method maniac who might have been a little more exciting on the screen, but I just couldn't get over the paranoid thought that he might actually kill us all. We couldn't decide so we promised to tell them in the morning after sleeping on it. So, the Dutch actor had to sleep on the kitchen floor, since there was no space anywhere else. In the morning, we decided not to give him the part. We said *'We're going with the other actor'* - he was devastated.

Gen - You shouldn't admit this.

Chris - It's fine now - but for some reason, something said *'this man's not as loony as I thought he was.'* It was something he was projecting in the hope of getting the role, and I had this gut feeling, *'hire him quick!'* I dragged Gen out of the room and said *'I think we should take him'.* She said *'you spent all night saying we can't'* and so we had another debate and decided to go with the psycho Dutchman. I went out and said *'you've got the part! That was just a test to see how you'd react!'* And he bought it. He really believed me.

Q - What happened with the crew?

Gen - Most of the crew were very young, and everyone was inexperienced. I suppose we were all cheap labour. The crew got nothing but a £5 donation from EGM, halfway through the film. One day, Geoff, one of the partners in EGM, came in with a brown envelope of used notes and handed them out. Actually, he ran out, so a few crew members didn't even get a fiver.

Q - With thirty five people living in your house, what was it like?

(left) Endless paperwork, contracts, accounts - the bane of every guerilla producers life.

Chris - We lived in this one cottage, at least eight people to a room, mixed accommodation. We sectioned off half of the main room. That was the office. The other half was the bunking quarters. One bathroom, one toilet, no shower, no washing machine and we shot like this for over a month. We ran out of locations, so we built a lot of them in the garage, in our back garden. And it was hell on earth. But it was great and everybody loved it. We could ring every one of those crew members and say *'there's a reunion'*, and everyone would be there. The only way I can explain it is like this. Sometime during the shoot I remember being driven around North Wales, I'm not entirely sure where and I'm not entirely sure how many hours we'd been out there, I just sat in the van, looking across this dark landscape and tried to remember what it was like to sit down in front of the TV at night and relax. I had completely lost contact with that side of my life. And it felt that we could do anything we wanted to. Really, seriously weird.

(above) Windmill Cottage - Living Spirits' base in Cheshire. Served as hotel, kitchens, locations, studios, indeed everything for the thirty strong crew and production of The Runner. "We were evicted three weeks after shooting, but at least we got the movie in the can."

Q - How did you deal with preparing locations with so little time?

Gen - The general order of business was *'what are we going to do today? We've got to do this or that scene and we'd better do this tomorrow...'* And so we'd sort out the locations a day in advance, two days if we were lucky. The money situation just made things worse - on the first day of principal photography the backers didn't turn up. We had to carry on without them but we didn't have any money to get the food. Occasionally, we ended up in deep trouble - I remember one time, we drove for hours, a whole crew and cast in convoy, to a mine in the middle of Wales. When we got there, they wouldn't let us in. And that was one of the times when we had actually *got* permission!

Chris - That's right. We were about to do the final scene in the film - the climax of the movie. As usual we were trying to set up the shoot the day before and Gen was zooming across North Wales to find a mine in which to shoot. She found a brilliant one in Llan-something. We got to the mine/power station and took all the kit in. It was like driving into a Bond set. The middle of this mountain had been quarried out. There were houses, office buildings, everything *inside* the mine. Roadways, traffic lights and cars parked inside the mountain. We shot for two days without any problems, and on the third day we had to film in another location. Come the morning of the fourth day, we returned to the mine and there was a new guard on the gate who said *'You can't go in'*. We protested... *'We have clearance'*. But we weren't going to get in, no amount of bribery could budge this guy. It transpired that the original guard had been sacked for letting us in as part of the mine was a top secret Ministry Of Defence nuclear air raid shelter. It was so high level that even the guard who had let us in didn't know it was there!

Gen thinks *'Okay we've been filming in a high security establishment and we're not getting back in. We've got to finish our movie. What are we going to do?'* So, she gets back into the car and zooms off to find another mine - and she did! The next day the convoy drove 100 miles into what seemed like the heart of darkness. It's raining like a waterfall and all we can see is wet black slate. It's so depressing. We arrive at the mine entrance and unload the gear. Everyone is soaked. We check out where we can film and it is a half mile walk underground with the equipment. We have twelve hours to shoot the last 15 pages of the script for our action-packed adventure, the most action-packed sequence in the whole film. And I'm thinking - *'Let's go for it. Lets go for it! We're going to finish it!'*

Five hours later, we're still lugging *IN* all the gear. Eventually it's all in. We're about to go for the first shot. It's taken five hours to set up. Terence is there. Lead actress, Paris is there. I rehearsed. I called for silence... Then we realised there were no guns. This was the big shoot out. The armourer says *'I'll go and get them.'* Fifteen minutes later the guy comes back looking kind of sheepish and says *'I don't know how to tell you this, but the guns are in the back of the prop girl's car.'*

And I said *'fine, then get them.'* Then he says *'But the prop girl has gone back to Cheshire twenty minutes ago.'* The props are on a four hundred mile drive, with no cell phone, and we have got six hours to shoot the climax to our movie! The next thing I can remember is being woken up by Jon Walker, the DP. Apparently, I'd just fallen asleep on a large rock. Both body and mind had gone into retirement - for a short time I was in a vegetative state.

(above left) Things got pretty nasty on set.... A good rule was, 'Never argue with the director when he has a gun...'

(above right) The mine in Wales - a great location, but unfortunately, it turned out to be a secret Ministry Of Defence Nuclear Air Raid Bunker.

Gen - Then it got worse. We had a massive argument with the cast. It became apparent that we weren't going to finish the film that night. Also we had been rushing to finish the film because the lead actress, Paris Jefferson, had said she had to fly off in the morning so that she could get to another shoot somewhere in Europe.

We knew this was the last day we had with her and we were running out of time, and we'd lost the guns - it was absolute hell. Then Paris says *'well, why don't we all come back tomorrow?'* - *'But you're not going to be here tomorrow!'* I reply. *'Oh, no. I can be here if you want me to be.'* Shocked, we blew up at her and had a massive argument with all the actors. Everyone took sides, mainly against us. It all got pretty heavy and enemies were made. Most of us made up later, but there were still a few grudges floating around. In retrospect, Paris was quite within her rights, it's just the insanity of low-budget filmmaking creates a crazy atmosphere. Our executive producers, John and Geoff, had gone off to America by then and were out of contact. So, we decided to pack it all in and come back in a month when we had the guns, the mine and the actors. Then we'd finish *The Runner*.

Chris - Tensions between cast and crew always ran high. It has to be said that a lot of the time the actors were quite right. There was such hell going on, they couldn't help but snap, because they spent ninety percent of the time just waiting for us to decide what to do. And everybody was ill with flu. However, one day we had a real medical shock. I was shooting on set and Gen came up to me and says...

'...Have you heard? Terence is dead. He's just been air lifted to Bangor Hospital. He's dead. What are we going to do? Can we write around it? It was like something out of Fawlty Towers!'

We'd got so used to problems that the concept of our leading man being dead was simply another obstacle to overcome. What had actually happened is that Terence was ill, the doctor had given him a sick note and sent him to bed. By the time we heard about it, the rumour mill had changed it to *'Terence is*

(left) Three choppers for free in as many hours...

dead!' The entire production was thinking *'What is going to happen?'* while Terence is wrapped up in his bed with a hot water bottle and a dose of aspirin. That was a bad day.

Gen - I remember my state of mind at that time. I had been told that Terence was in the morgue - it was some kind of Welsh joke by the hotel owner. So I was racing through the narrow winding roads at a hundred miles an hour, thinking of ways we could write him out of the story without it looking too crazy. I wasn't bothered that he might be dead - all I wanted was to make sure that the film didn't suffer! That is the degree to which we were all affected by the insanity of low-budget filmmaking. It gets into your blood and takes over your soul, I guess that's why it feels a little like going to war.

We were staying in a tiny Welsh village, where the villagers thought that this kind of joke was really funny. The other joke they played on us was potentially more serious. Someone rang the hotel telling them that they had planted a bomb. So we had the police round, searching everyone's room. I remember being in dreaded fear that the police were going to check my room, because that morning I had just taken delivery of a crateful of semi automatic weapons from our armourer, AND a fake bomb for the bomb scene. Luckily they didn't check my room.

Q - The Runner *has many action sequences with one breathtaking high fall. How did you get stuntmen involved?*

Gen - The week before filming, we received lots of phone calls because we were trying to find actors and crew. I got a call from a guy called Terry Forrestal who said he was a stunt man and wanted to help. I said *'Yeah, great, great'* thinking he was another karate expert from down the road who wanted to get into the business.

Terry said *'I've been working on Indiana Jones, this, that and the other and I used to do James Bond'.* He reeled off a list of a hundred A list movies. I asked for his CV and said I'd get back to him. You have to understand that we had taken so many weird phone calls from so many wacky people that we were cautious. Then his CV arrived, and I looked at his list of movies - it looked like my video collection! I realised - this guy's for real! Immediately, we rang him up and arranged to meet. He was so keen and wanted to do everything he could to help us out. Everything was possible. In fact, he was so enthusiastic that he wanted to do more stunts than were in the script!

Chris - Terry had read the script and saw the bit about the high fall, *'how are you going to do this? Well, we'll probably dress the actor up and jump off a low point onto some cardboard boxes. Ten feet or so. You know, we'll cheat it. It'll look all right...'* And he said *'No, no. You need a proper stunt. I'll do a high fall for you.'* And I said *'How high is high? 15 or 20 feet?'* - *'Oh no'* he said, *'I'll do a ninety foot high fall for you'* He pointed to this house in the distance which seemed pretty big and explained, *'it's about that, and a half again'.*

I was stunned. So we went on this location scout in North Wales to find a cliff from which he could jump without killing himself. Finally we found a cliff. On the day he just turned up with his airbag man, blew the bag up and jumped off the cliff. Well, in fact there were two high falls. We co-ordinated this with Terry. The first one was off the cliff into the airbag. The second, the more dangerous was off the cliff into the water. On each stunt attempt we had three cameras. Two would have done the job but we really wanted three.

(above left) Stuntman, Terry Forrestal, considers the jump he is about to make. (below left) The crew, roped off above, prepare for the final shot as the sun sets.

So we had three cameras set up and shot each stunt twice. We ended up with six separate shots, all in slow motion so that they would cut together to make it look like the fall lasted for ever. Well, the actual high fall lasts for nine seconds in the movie - a serious amount of screen time for somebody to be hurling towards earth at two hundred and thirty five feet per second. So it gave the impression of an immense fall which really did get gasps in the theatre.

To be honest, one of the best things about *The Runner* is that stunt and even Terry considered it one of the best falls he's ever done. I think he meant in the way it comes across on screen. He'd done other, more dangerous falls, much higher but somehow they don't look as dangerous. Perhaps the circumstances were never quite as wild as on this shoot. We were totally into Sam Peckinpah and action movies, so we wound the slow motion dial until it wouldn't go any further - no matter how fast the film was whizzing through the gate, Terry still went flying through frame.

Gen - And there was, as with all stunts, a real sense of danger. When Terry jumped into the lake he said '*If I don't come up after five seconds, either I've hit my head on the bottom or I'm dead*'. It was a very long five seconds.

Q - Once you had the film in the can, was it all down hill?

Chris - Not really, we had to fix all the problems we had given ourselves during the shoot. A good example is the firing range scene - there are shots in that sequence from five different locations, shot at seven different times, with up to seven months separation - piecing it together was a logistical nightmare. Mark Talbot-Butler edited the film after we finished shooting. Unfortunately, we were evicted from our house for having thirty five people living there which broke the terms of our tenancy. This meant that we had to put most of the work in Mark's court - he had to go off and do a lot of the cutting on his own, locked in his attic. It was all very rushed.

EGM wanted the film ready for the MIFED film market in Milan which took place in October and we therefore made sure it was done. This really compromised the movie. We only had about seven weeks post-production. A great deal of energy was spent getting the picture to look good, the audio to be full and rich, and to make sure the cuts flowed. But at no point do I remember sitting down to ask whether the story was actually working. This neglect meant we had a good looking, great sounding, boring movie. And even then, the sound was rushed with effects still being edited while we began dubbing. Mark didn't even have an assistant. He was in his Mum's attic with a Steenbeck

The International Sales booth for The Runner *at the Milan Film Market 1991. Visiting a sales market is an invaluable experience.*

(editing machine) working eighteen hours a day. No pay, no nothing. Each time I saw him, he began to look a little weirder - not surprising really.

While Mark was cutting away, we were working on the score with an old school friend who had done the music for my amateur Super 8mm Zombie films. He had gone on to play in a local band and was excited by the prospects of being involved in a *real* film. He had to fake an illness and take time off work to spend seven days at his keyboard. There was no music budget, so we had to create that big orchestra sound with some synths and an Atari computer locking it all together. It worked out really well, the music was pacey and dynamic - and recorded in our front room. When John Eyres (one of the Exec producers) came to view the final cut, he wasn't particularly happy. He wanted some stuff cut out. We agreed but never cut the scenes out. He wanted to remove the helicopter rescue at the end of the film, because it said RAF on the choppers (giving away the fact that the film was shot in the UK and not in the USA as claimed).

(above) Cast and Crew of The Runner at the London Premiere - A great night!

Q - How was the premiere?

Chris - Everyone clapped, but it was hollow polite clapping. I think people were amazed that we had managed to get it made, a film that looked and sounded good. But what a dreadful story.

Gen - It was the achievement, rather than the actual film that was applauded. The audience were saying well done for getting this far. We were caught up with it all. We didn't get nervous. We just enjoyed it.

(above) The Living Spirit team for The Runner - *Left to right, Chris Jones - Director, Genevieve Jolliffe - Producer, Mark Talbot Butler - Screenplay & Editor, Andrew Mitchell - Actor and Jon Walker - Cameraman.*

Chris - At the time we thought that it was the best movie ever made. We talked like we were old time movie moguls. It was terrific! Sadly though, we were not yet aware that we had actually made a really crap film. But at the time, that didn't matter - it was OUR premiere!

Gen - However, we do have people coming up to us who saw *The Runner*, saying how much they like the movie, how they've gone out and bought their own personal copy of the film. *The Runner* aspires to big budget movies and isn't like the majority of low budget 'quirky' movies that get made.

Q - How much did The Runner make you?

Chris - To date, not a single penny. Living Spirit did not make the proverbial 'fortune' out of *The Runner*. What happened to us, and what happens to most first time feature makers, is that we got caught with a standard distribution deal. Basically, EGM financed the film and acted as the sales agents. They received thirty five percent commission plus all expenses before they started to recoup their investment. This meant that they got all their money back, plus thirty five percent commission, plus expenses, before we would even see a penny. It means we will never get paid, never ever, which

means that we'll never be able to pay our cast and crew which means it's a bit of a downer really. This is a very common story that many filmmakers tell.

Gen - We were very naive when we took the film on. Our attitude was - *'Let's do the film, We've got three weeks. Let's just do it, get our foot in the door rather than just sit on our butts'.* So, when the contract came, we had a lawyer go through it, and he advised us not to sign it. But at the end of the day, we thought, well, we have a choice here. If we sign it, there is a possibility that we could get ripped off. If we don't, the film may never happen. So we went with it. I am very glad we did, it gave us a track record and a showreel. Most important was the experience, *that* was invaluable. If you have nothing to lose, just go for it.

Q - How do you feel about it all now that it is ancient history?

Chris - We went with it and got the chance to make a film. We got to go mad in North Wales, with Hollywood stuntmen, bombs, guns and a bunch of actors - it was a fair trade off. My only regret is that nobody got paid - I guess and hope that everyone was rather philosophical about it. For many of the crew, the experience was worth more than the money.

(top) The final poster for The Runner, complete with splendid action movie style chromed logo and blazing background. (above) Living Spirit are presented to HRH Prince Charles after receiving their award.

Gen - A lot of the crew members were either still at film school or had just left and had never worked professionally on any kind of film. I remember at the first production meeting, Chris asked who had worked on a film before. It was quite a shock when only two people put their hands up. The average age was 19/20. There was even a 14 year old - I felt old at 19.

Q - Can you protect your rights as filmmakers on the first film?

Gen - The main problem you're facing is that it IS your first film. You are so desperate to make it that you will sign anything. If it comes to the crunch, I would advise anyone to sign because what is important is that you make the film. Just make sure you invest none of your own money or money that you are responsible for and therefore reduce your losses. If you can make your first movie without losing anything, then go for it because nobody is going to give you free money and nobody's going to invest in you because you've never made a film before. It is easy to be completely shafted, everyone

from Tobe Hooper to Steven Spielberg has been ripped off, and not just on their first films. I think it is the nature of the business. Once we had finished *The Runner*, we had a lot less trouble making *White Angel*. We had more control and simply refused to sign anything unless we had total control.

Q - I believe you are in the Guinness Book of Records.

The Runner is available in the US under the title Escape from... Survival Zone (often on eBay). If you get the chance to view it, we would recommend you don't! It really isn't worth an hour and a half of your life! Check out the trailer at www.livingspirit.com instead, you'll see everything worth looking at in under 90 seconds then.

Gen - Yes, Britain's youngest producer for *The Runner*. I was 19, not so young when compared with American filmmakers.

Q - Because of your connections with the Princes Trust, did you invite the Prince of Wales to the screening?

Chris - We actually won an award - the PYBT award for Most Tenacious Business Of The Year. There was a special award ceremony with a screening of *The Runner* at the BAFTA theatre in Piccadilly. HRH came along and presented the award.

Q - Did HRH see the film?

Chris - He saw some of it but he couldn't watch it all because he had other appointments on the schedule. He said it looked a little too violent for him.

Q - How did your second film, White Angel, come about?

Chris - Obviously, after *The Runner*, we wanted to make another film. *The Runner* had crippled us so much that we didn't have any funds left. The only way we could possibly get out of the great financial hole we were in was to make another movie! We decided to make what we considered to be the most commercial film possible, shooting with the least amount of money. *White Angel* was conceived the same day that we saw *Henry, Portrait of a Serial Killer (*in a grimy cinema) We thought it was a great movie but it was too offensive for a wider audience. However, we thought we could make something with the same feel, but not quite so graphic - and turn it into a taut thriller.

Gen - We also saw *Silence of the Lambs* and felt that we could do something similar, that was more contained, and not awash with gore. Also we didn't think that Hannibal Lecter gave a true portrayal of a serial killer - sure, he was a terrific character which the audience had a love hate relationship with - but he had been glamorised for the movie. We researched real serial killers, reading lots of books, for example Dennis Nielson's biography, *Killing For Company* by Brian Masters. We became fascinated by the British serial killer and his peculiarities. Admittedly, most of our research was very lightweight, we didn't want to start making psychological assumptions, merely chart the actions of a killer. The closest that we came to real research was through my uncle who worked at a top security prison and he would tell us of his encounters with the infamous Yorkshire Ripper. We also saw some home movie footage of Dennis Nielson which gave us the idea of using video taped interviews.

Chris - Many people appear to have a morbid fascination with the serial killer. The motivation seems so meaningless, and it's now a cliché, but it could be the person next door. Audiences like to dip into horror, to experience the shocks and come out of the other side unharmed and emotionally purged.

Q - What are you looking for in a no-budget script?

Gen - We knew the limitations of our location, so we developed our story from that single point. We were looking for containment, to keep the majority of the story in one place. The production office would be there, all the facilities such as makeshift changing and make-up rooms, a kitchen and equipment store. The location was inside the M25 (the major freeway around London), at the end of the tube (underground line), we could even see the station from the front door of the house! This meant that the cast and crew could be given a monthly underground pass, and therefore their travelling expenses were minimal. The location was also close to shops, parks etc., and all the other locations required in the screenplay were within five minutes walking distance. It worked quite well.

Ellen Carter fights Steckler in the climactic scenes of White Angel.

Chris - Where we went wrong with *The Runner* is that the production was sprawling, shooting in locations that were hundreds of miles apart. That would eat up our shooting time. We had to put people up and pay for hotel rooms, catering, travelling etc. The number of principal cast was five, far too high. This in itself was very expensive which is why we limited the principal cast in *White Angel* to two, with Don Henderson (a well known TV actor in the UK) bobbing in and out (we actually only shot for two days with Don).

Q - So **The Runner** *was a good exercise in how NOT to make a low-budget film?*

Chris - Yes, after *The Runner* we sat and looked at the budget to see where the money went. A lot was spent on American actors, flying them over, making them comfortable and getting them in front of the camera. So, we said, *'what has Britain got to offer?'* We have great actors and we knew that if we could find one, who was willing to do it for virtually nothing, on the assumption that they will get paid eventually (and also receive a percentage), then we were onto a winner. We made a conscious decision to try and get a really good, classical actor, and Peter Firth filled that bill.

On the other hand we felt that we had to have a North American in the film, or we would be in the position where the Americans may not want the film because it doesn't have that American feel. And we had heard stories about other British films like *Gregory's Girl, Trainspotting* and even *Mad Max* from Australia, being dubbed for the American market. We knew that *White Angel* had to sell in the US as in financial terms, the American market represented a huge slice of world sales. In retrospect, we were being over cautious. If we could have persuaded a great British actress like Helen Mirren to play Carter, it may have improved sales and I think it would have been a better film. The Americanisation of the lead female character (Ellen Carter who was played by Harriet Robinson) felt inserted into the story. Having said that, Harriet does have a quality that people like - I don't think we could have made a better choice with a North American.

Q - Why genre subjects?

Chris - Most low-budget filmmakers don't choose a genre because they've sat down and clinically thought, *'now if we make a sci-fi thriller, the Japanese market is going to like it'*. I think most first time filmmakers make the kind of film that they really want to make. Either that works or it doesn't. With *The Runner* we wanted to blow as much up as we could - we wanted to throw as many people off cliffs as possible - we wanted to create mayhem because we loved *Die Hard* and similar Hollywood movies. Low-budget filmmakers story choices seem to be a product of their youth. More than anything, on your first film you get the chance to do whatever you want. More than likely, the money will come from someone who knows nothing about filmmaking. You've

(left) The house used for the primary location in White Angel *had to double up as both production office and set. Ruislip outside central London was the perfect location and was steeped in suburbia.*

got so little money at risk that you can go out on a limb, and in retrospect, we could have been more daring with some aspects of *White Angel* - to arouse much more controversy.

Q - The script idea is rooted in the idea of a very British murder?

Chris - We said let's make this film British. As British as *The Long Good Friday*. The intrinsic Britishness emerged during script development. We didn't start off saying, let's make a film about a VERY British serial killer. We said let's make a film about a serial killer in Britain, and the true British angle came out when we started on the research, and also with the involvement of Peter Firth. He manipulated the script in the way that we wanted him to. The scripts that we've produced are functional. They get from A to B without showing too many of the footprints in the wet paint (we hope!). Peter Firth took the screenplay and changed Steckler from this mid Atlantic, generic psychopath and brought the character into the English home. Many of the mannerisms in the film were invented by Peter. A number of people have been surprised by this. They think everything in the film comes from the director or writer, when in essence, the director, writer and producer are merely the people managing the creative talent. Actors have the last say by virtue of their own perform-ance.

Peter Firth as the mild mannered serial killer, Leslie Steckler. Peter's experience brought a new dimension to an otherwise run of the mill screen killer.

We felt Peter's ideas were good. You know on set whether something is working or not. For instance, we agreed with Peter to use the recurrent theme of *'would you like a cup of tea?'* as one of the main angles in the film. It was there in the script, but Peter made much more of. Each murder was followed by a *'cup of tea'*. Even the way Steckler dresses, the top button of his shirt being fastened was Peter's idea. There was a conscious decision to make Peter this out of date character, in so much as the film is set in the nineties, but everything about him is stuck in the seventies. He wears those trousers and that neck tie that only weird people still wear. He was very much stuck in that vein, and of course, clothing charity shops were the best place for him to shop. This is what people of quality bring to a production. An experienced and talented actor will bring so much to any story, and it's worth moving heaven and earth to engage their services. From a marketing point, everyone always thinks that big actors cost big bucks. This isn't necessarily so, and their mere presence in a film will enhance it's value.

Gen - We had seen so many movies about serial killers, but nothing that really explained why they do what they do. We wanted a more realistic approach, looking into what urges these people to do it - movies had shown these killers in a kind of glamorous light, rarely exploring why. We thought that the British serial killers were more interesting. The frightening thing, was how these killers really blended into society - how normal they looked... what fascinated us most was, *could it be the guy living next door to you?*

Q - The killer next door seems to be a concept which keeps coming up?

Chris - Yes, we decided that the screenplay should take the serial killer living next door right to its logical conclusion, to create a killer who is actually very likeable as a human being. We never see him murder except in small details*, and when it does happen, it has a kind of humour to it rather than horror. Therefore, apart from his memories of various crimes, we never experience Steckler, the serial killer. But we do see Carter kill and she is not the serial killer, which in turn is an interesting slant. Several people have mentioned that Carter was a bit of a cold character and that they liked Steckler. This is exactly what we wanted. Some people seem to like this different slant on the killers. At the end of the day if you get two

Peter Firth and Don Henderson - great British actors are worth every penny or percentage you pay them. They will bring quality and experience to any production.

killers together in a house and get them to talk about killing it's going to be strange, it's going to be funny, it's going to be horrifying and it could get very nasty. We wanted to get that seething atmosphere into the house, *lock the doors and see what happens...* Some of the elements from the screenplay we lost in the shoot. For instance, the heating was supposed to have gone insane during the film so that it was always hot in the house. We wanted a pressure cooker. We wanted claustrophobia. That is something that harks back to the needs of a low-budget film. You need to look at what you've got and turn that into an advantage. We had a small location, so we thought, let's make it claustrophobic.

Q - Had you seen the British serial killer film 10 Rillington Place?

Chris - Yes, a long time before we made *White Angel*. After *White Angel* was completed, we saw the film again and were pleased, and to some extent shocked, by the similarities. There weren't any conscious similarities when we were making it. I don't know whether Peter had seen it but he had done research into serial killers. I remember Harriet asking Peter whether he had a defined idea of how he was going to play the character and he said *No, I don't have a clue, I'll tell you how I'm going to play it on the last day of photography.* And you could see it sometimes when he was unsure how Steckler would react. He had in him that ability to say, *I'll try this out and if it doesn't work, then fine.* This was a very valuable asset to have.

Q - A serial killer moves in with an undiscovered murderer. Where did that idea come from?

Chris - I don't know really, I guess by a process of development from a single concept. What we did is play around with this single concept. For example, we want to make a film about a serial killer. We have to make it in one house. We can't have him just going out and killing people because that would be tough to shoot, so we introduce a woman to get a male / female thing going and keep it in the one place. What could she be? Well, if she knows he's a serial killer, maybe it's his wife, but then it's obvious. Maybe she can be a crime writer, an expert on serial killers and he wants her to write his story. That's good. But why would she do it? Well, maybe she murdered her husband, bricked him up in the wall of the house and got away with it. Maybe the serial killer finds the body and blackmails her? Then, they're both murderers. Hey! That's a good idea. Before you know it you have a rough hook on which to hang your structure.

Gen - Then you write the first one page synopsis, give it to your mates and ask what they think - *well, this is good, this is bad - OK.* Turn it into a two page synopsis. You keep building and building. What we like to do is to write it as a novella first, or at least

Polaroid photos are one of the only times we see Steckler's victims. It is amazing how multi talented your crew can be when pushed.

* In order to secure deals later, extra scenes of sex and violence were shot and added.

a thirty page short story. When that reads well, then you've got something. It is structured very heavily. We have two plot points which come thirty minutes from the beginning, thirty minutes from the end and we have a sixty minute centre section. So, we have act one at thirty minutes, act two which is sixty minutes and act three at thirty minutes. And in addition, in the middle of act two we have a mid point. If you watch any good Hollywood feature, you'll see that they often stick to this common structure. When editing, what usually happens is that you end up cutting some of the junk out of the middle where it gets too wordy and slow. You also trim stuff from the start of the movie so you get going much faster. Then the movie should end up at around ninety minutes.

In a scene cut from the final film, Ellen Carter has recurring nightmares about her husband's body trying to escape from it's living room wall tomb.

Q - What are the plot points in White Angel?

Chris - We spend the first ten minutes setting up the various stories which combine to form the main plot and characters. Ellen Carter has killed her husband and hidden the body - she has *'got away with murder'*. She is a crime writer who studies mass murderers. There is a serial killer in London killing women who wear white, and the killer may also be a woman. Mild mannered Steckler is probably the serial killer, he cuts up newspapers and has dead bodies in his living room after all! He moves in with Carter as a tenant. And all the time, the police are closing in as they have a fingerprint on a hammer that was left at the last murder scene...

The plot is completely set up in the first ten minutes or so, and then we had a framework in which to work. The fingerprint on the hammer is the time bomb waiting to go off which gives the movie a sense of impending doom and momentum.

Plot point one is where Steckler says *'I am the White Angel and I want you to write my story'*. Up until that point he has been getting on with his life, Carter has been getting on with hers. We've been setting up various parts of the story. But at that point, the film changes direction. It sheers off at ninety degrees. Carter's life is totally destroyed. Steckler's is totally fulfilled because he's got the writer he wanted to do his book. We then spend the next forty minutes of the movie exploring this theme of writing the book and what Carter is interested in. The mid-point of the film is where Carter interviews Steckler and he says about his wife, *'she deserved to die, the world is a better place without her'*. In the same scene, Steckler turns the interview around to Carter and she says of killing her husband, *'he deserved to die... the world's a better place without him'*. And she realises that she has said the same thing as Steckler, therefore it questions the *differences between them*. It's a subtle mid-point but it is a character point when Carter suddenly realises that she is essentially the same creature, a human being with the ability to kill. The rest of act two develops this theme - her attempts to poison him etc. Plot point two is where Carter finds out (wrongly) that her friend, Mik, has been killed by Steckler. She finds the glasses covered in blood - that's a pinch point - just before plot point two.

The exact position of plot point two is where she sees the blood and the knife in Mik's flat and comes home to find Steckler burying the body in the garden. Again, at this point, the film sheers off at an angle. Carter is no longer interested in writing the book. She has one thing on her mind and one thing only. To kill Steckler. To get him off the face of the planet. She can't turn him in to the police because she'll go down for murder. So she plots an elabourate plan which the audience discovers as it happens. This leads us to the climax and twist in the tail. Most people like a good twist, it lets them leave the theatre feeling fulfilled in a strange sort of way. However, it can often backfire and make the audience feel cheated. We are not saying *White Angel* is the greatest screenplay ever written, but it does work as a thriller. Some people say the story was *'gripping'*, which is a real compliment when you consider the constraints under which the film was made.

(above) *The hammer in* White Angel *was the device which provided the plot and twists. This evidence would eventually lead the police back to the killer, and straight back to Ellen Carter for the final twist.*

(left) *The original premise for* White Angel *explored the differences between murder and manslaughter through the eyes of two killers.*

Q - So the treatment was extremely detailed before you wrote the script?

Gen - Absolutely. *White Angel* wasn't a short treatment. I think that the final version was twenty five pages. It is important that you can write this kind of treatment and you know the structure (page eight is plot point one and on page twenty two you have plot point two, with the mid point on page fifteen). We structure everything, so when writing, you don't lose control of your characters, nor will the story lose its direction. Every scene has got to move the story onward to its final conclusion - otherwise you may be boring your audience. You have around two hours to get everything across, and leave no loose ends.

Chris - Screenplays and stories are all about mystery and exploration. Many film makers are obsessed by character, *'let's stop the movie and have a talky scene where the character confesses that he's shot a kid in a back alley ten years ago'* - this is often resolved later in the film, and I find it divisive and obvious. For me, a movie is about getting on to the next scene. One of the interesting things that we did on *White Angel* was when we finished the first rough cut we went back and started to cut the end out of many scenes, and some of the middle. What originally was a well structured scene now felt unbalanced, not finished. The audience felt there was more, that they were not being told everything. This is not a hard and fast rule but it is a good guide - *don't tell your audience everything!* It keeps them wanting more.

Q - There is a great deal of video footage used. Was this in the script?

Chris - Yes. There were two reasons for the inclusion of video tape footage. I'm from the amateur filmmaking scene and while I started on Super 8mm, VHS soon became a medium that was very accessible. I loved the way that in science fiction movies of the eighties, video footage was heavily used, (e.g. *Aliens*). It always looked grainy and really gaudy and I thought it was great. What an image. So, wouldn't it be great to get Steckler's monologues on video tape because that is a format that is much more *'real'*. People understand that film is drama but the news is *'real'*. People believe video images. In the film, Steckler gives interviews, and I thought, if we can do the interview on tape, then we have a five minute take in one. Five minutes of the film translates to about six percent of the final product. We had fifty five rolls on which to shoot this film. I was fully aware that to get a five minute monologue in one film take, which is what I wanted, was going to be difficult. So we shot it several times on video tape and then transferred the final result to film (by filming it off a TV screen).

So you have a chunk of your film finished with a cutting ratio of one to one which is pretty damn good. The cutting ratio is how much stock you shoot in comparison with how long your film is. If the film is to be one hundred minutes long and you shoot one thousand minutes of stock, then you would have a cutting ratio of ten to one. Most low budget feature work is between eight and twelve to one. I think we shot *White Angel* on four and a half to one. It's all about preventing waste. Don't do endless takes. I learned on *The Runner* that take one is often very similar to take fifteen. Often in the editing room your can hear your voice calling *'Take four. Loved it darlings!'* and you wonder why you got that far - there was nothing wrong with takes one to three. If you've got the shot and your cameraman says that it's fine and the gate's clear - go with it. It saves you time and it saves you *stock and it saves you money.*

Gen - We had seen the effect of video images in films like *Henry - Portrait of a Serial Killer* - where it was pretty nasty - and the reason it was more horrific than seeing the other killings on film, was simply because it was shot on video tape. It was real. It's like seeing the news - the images can be shocking.

Q - Some writers chose an imaginary cast when working on a script, to give characters life. Did you do this?

Chris - Yes. When Steckler's character was formed I had Jeremy Irons in mind. For Carter, the female lead, I only had one person in mind. No chance of getting her, of course. A 1970's Jane Fonda! It helps you 'see' them in the scene when writing.

Q - When you started pre-production you had very little money, why didn't you wait until you had your full budget in place?

Chris - Mainly because we would have had to wait forever. We had worked out that it was possible to make a feature film for less than ten thousand pounds and we looked at how we made *The Runner* and where the money went. There were obvious things like film stock, processing, camera gear, things that you cannot avoid. You can get a good deal, you can get discounts, you can get some things for free, but there is always going to be an expense. There are however, other expenses that you can avoid or minimise. The reason why *The Runner* went over budget was that it was set in lots of locations, so out of a twelve hour shooting day, you'd spend a quarter of it driving between A and B, and then another quarter loading and unloading the vans... We lost thirty to forty percent of our time through location changes. *The Runner* was filled with events that just wasted time through ignorance or lack of forward planning. *White Angel* was going to be different.

Gen - The rules for low-budget scripts are all cost related. Money is the one thing you have little control of because on a no-budget film, you don't have it. The big expense we had on *The Runner* was crew and accommodation expenses. That took £15k to £20k out of our budget. On *White Angel* we decided to shoot in London and buy everyone an underground pass. It cost about £25 a week to get cast and crew to and from location.

White Angel was based in one house and there are very few scene changes - this minimised time wastage and allowed us to finish the film in eighteen shooting days as compared with nearly forty on *The Runner*. From *White Angel's* point of view the two golden rules we had were, minimise locations AND shoot where the cast and crew can spend the night at home and not at our expense. This saves money in other ways. For example, if we wrapped early, we may not have needed to provide a meal in the evening. So, we'd not need catering that night. Catering is one of the areas where basic expenses can't be avoided, and it is actually a bad idea to skimp on it. If you feed your cast and crew well, you'll get twenty percent more out of them. You have to feed them something so why not make it good! A low-budget shoot needs good food to look forward to. Out in the rain, or the cold, good food keeps the spirits up.

When creating a character it helped a great deal to visualize a certain actor playing that part.

Q - What would be an average menu?

Food is always an issue. More than likely, you won't be able to afford a food wagon. On top of good food, remember cast and crew will need tea, coffee and water at all times, and a warm dry place to sit down and eat.

Gen - We didn't supply breakfast because everyone lived in London and we looked at it as coming to work. Lunchtime, we would provide sandwiches, easy food that could be served from a cardboard box anywhere. For the evening meal, we'd always do something hot, baked potatoes, stews etc. Warm, stodgy food with plenty of carbohydrates to keep people going. We'd also send out chocolate bars to break up the times between meals and even persuaded a local bakery to give us all their cakes that were left unsold at the end of the day. Once a week, we provided beers. It is the same idea as getting chocolates etc. You give people beer and they think, this isn't so bad and it holds the team together.

Q - Where were all the meals prepared?

Gen - There just wasn't room in the kitchen, so Mark Sutherland, the set constructor, found a skip outside a pub which was being refitted. He pinched the old bar and set up 'Steckler's Diner' in the garage. Meals were prepared and consumed in the garage and it was pretty squalid - the caterer had a simple gas fired stove, but still managed to feed thirty mouths, twice a day. I guess the crew named it 'Steckler's Diner' because sometimes we just didn't know what was in the stew!

Q - From a production point, what advantages did White Angel present?

Gen - We had a film set in suburbia, a location that would be cheap to shoot in, which would be near central London so that we could get the cast and crew to it easily. It was set in the present, so actors could wear their own clothes, or we could buy stuff from the charity shop, down the road. I'm not joking. We had a deal with Oxfam (UK charity shop). It cost us a fifty pounds for all our costumes in the film. And it worked. At the end of the day, when you have £10k to make a film, two and a half goes on film stock, one and a half on cast and crew because you've got to give them something.... and before you know it, the whole budget has gone on essentials. Therefore, £50 quid for costumes. At each production meeting, Mark Sutherland, our production designer, would proudly announce that out of his total budget of £100, he was going to spend another forty pence on nails. He couldn't get them for free and was quite distressed about this.

Chris - He became notorious for going around dumpsters. The dumpster is a production designer's supply base on a low-budget shoot. Another man's junk is a production designer's dream.

Q - How detailed was the budget?

Gen - Very. We had to know where every penny was going to go. We worked out what we thought the entire production was going to cost -

White Angel *publicity shot - Sexy girl, big gun, blue light - this kind of image is about as far removed as possible from the attitude of many (but not all) UK based production companies and institutions. This was a problem for Living Spirit as we couldn't afford to hire a model,so Louise Ryan, from the set construction team, kicked off her overalls and boots, and slipped into something slinky...*

everything - even down to the gas and phone bills. Then we started to work out what things we actually needed to pay for to get the movie in the can - we just couldn't raise the entire budget before we shot, so we concentrated on getting the movie shot. Eventually, we narrowed our list of essentials down to around £11k. We knew we might need more than this, but once the snowball is rolling down the hill, it is difficult to stop it.

Chris - You spend months just trying to get this thing going, and then a few days before the first day of principal photography, the production runs itself - it's as if you have built a huge machine, and all you need to do is maintain it to ensure it doesn't stop working. If you get to the first day of shooting, you'll probably make it all the way to the finish line.

Gen - First of all, we concentrated on getting the right house that was cheap. Then we could start sorting out everything else. We rented the house in Ruislip, West London, and based the production there. Most of the film would be shot there and the production office would also operate from one of the upstairs bedrooms. Then we visited all the hire companies and I spoke to them about the film, and of course, getting free deals. I told them who we were and that were trying to... *'make a career for ourselves, we are young filmmakers, the film is very low-budget, and we need the best deal ever - please, please, pretty please...'*

Remember that any initial deal is the quote they probably give anyone. No one pays full price. Tell them how little you have. Get a quote. Look at your budget and decide what you can afford. Then ring them back and try to make a deal. They can only say no. I used to ring up, say a lighting company and say, *'look, I've got five hundred, can you do it for that?'* It is also important to pick a time to shoot your movie when you know that there is less work around in the industry. Then you will receive better discounts. You must make sure that you tell them exactly what you want and for how much. This is all I can afford, and I need an all in deal, all the equipment, all the accessories, all the gel, all the spun - ask if there are any hidden extras, or if you pay extra if you go overtime, what about broken bulbs. And get a quote that lays everything out in detail. The best deal to get is always an *'all in'* deal.

Q - And what about cast and crew?

Gen - You've most probably started thinking about who would be an ideal cast for your film, and you may have been speaking to agents who have been asking for the kind of money that is completely impossible - ask for their help and support. Again, it is best to be straight with these people and not to attempt to deceive them. If an actor likes the script and wants to do it, their agent will probably be unable to stop them.

Q - How did you budget for crew wages?

Gen - We put the crew on deferred payments. We agreed to pay their expenses so that they wouldn't be out of pocket. The film was shooting in London so we concentrated on people who could get the tube (subway) rather than paying fuel expenses which are harder to estimate before shooting. Also, we always over budget for expenses because there are tiny elements that you just don't expect. Somebody can't get the tube. The shoot runs after tube hours or someone rings up and has to get a taxi for some reason. That money has to come from somewhere so it is best to over budget on transport.

Q - Crew members need to eat and pay the rent, how do you deal with these very serious problems?

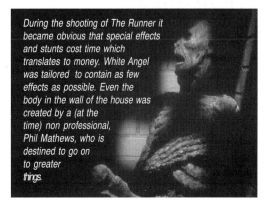

During the shooting of The Runner it became obvious that special effects and stunts cost time which translates to money. White Angel was tailored to contain as few effects as possible. Even the body in the wall of the house was created by a (at the time) non professional, Phil Mathews, who is destined to go on to greater things.

(left) All the night-time sequences for White Angel *were shot during the day with the windows covered by black trash bags. A routine is very important if the cast and crew are going to perform to the best of their abilities with limited resources.*

If money is tight, the basic Super 16mm Camera, Tripod, Lens, DAT, Mic and stock is all that is needed to make a cinematic quality feature film... And of course there are many new digital options. Oh you will also need and a script and cast and... (below left) Jane Rousseau, camera operator for White Angel.

Chris - What we did on *The Runner* was very different from *White Angel*. On *The Runner*, we couldn't pay anybody anything and we didn't want to do this again, because people have to live. So, what we did on *White Angel* was to cover everyone's expenses, a tube ticket everyday and everyone received £50 a week, to keep them on beer and cigarettes. On top, we offered a deferred payment so that when the film was sold, they would receive their wages. This would be more than they would have got since they have to wait years for it - and don't kid yourself by promising money in two weeks. There is also a very good chance that they will *never* get paid. Selling a film is a long process. You've got to be straight with people. This is the money we've got - they can say *yes* or *no*. And make sure you pay it to them and reward them with good catering.

Q - What's in it for them?

Chris - Mainly experience at your expense. Many UK pro filmmakers earn money through commercials, television etc. but they usually want to make movies. There are also a lot of new students being turned out from film schools - take advantage of their enthusiasm and give them responsibility. In my experience, most people will deliver if you give them the opportunity to do so. There is a debate about deferred films - *are they ethical?* Well, almost all big budget features take advantage of free labour by taking on free runners or office assistants - we are doing the same, but giving them greater opportunity and experience, and a possible fee if it all works out. At the end of the day, everyone can say no. As a rule, if you can pay someone, do it, you will get a better worker, and no nasty phone calls two years down the line if you were not able to pay as promised.

Q - What shooting elements proved a problem later?

Gen - Something hit us when we were doing the effects on *The Runner*. The sheer quantity of stock needed to shoot action and effects. So on *White Angel*, we deliberately had very little stunt work or effects. By remaining in London, there was another saving. Because we were near the facilities houses, anything could be dealt with by a phone call and a quick trip in the truck. For example, if a camera went down, it was easy to get a replacement without costing much time or money. Also, we were close to the labs and could view rushes every day. When we were shooting *The Runner* up in North Wales, the camera did go down and it was a serious problem. We had to call London to get a new camera delivered, and then wait for them to courier it up to us. With transport on location, always expect your trucks to break down - they always will! They'll get stuck in mud, stuck in snow, completely fail or crash. We had a few crashes - no-one was hurt, seriously at least. People get in too much of a hurry. This is one of the problems of low-budget filmmaking. Safety. Everybody knows there is a limited time scale. The production team is rushing to and from the set. Props must get to the set or the crew is sitting about waiting - so the foot goes on the accelerator and you speed along winding roads.

LIVING SPIRIT PICTURES
Present

WHITE ANGEL

EVERYONE HAS A DARK SIDE

(left) The original artwork on the cover of the White Angel investment proposal. With virtually no material, we tried to make it look as much like a shocker of a movie as possible.

(below) The involvement of TV and Film faces such as Don Henderson help solidify the project in the eyes of potential investors.

On *The Runner*, I remember nearly losing my life when I was driving at 100 mph on a busy winding road on my way to the set. A truck pulled out in front of me at the last minute and the brakes made a horrific noise - luckily I am still around. It is incidents like this, when you realise that although it's important, is it really worth losing your life for a movie?

Q - What was the total you needed to make White Angel?

Gen - The grand total was about £85k. We didn't raise all the money at once. Initially we could only raise £11k and we thought, either we hang around waiting for all the rest or we take a risk and shoot it with what we have. The cast and crew were working on deferments and we could just about do it if we shot for eighteen days. Once we had the movie shot, we could show investors what they would be investing in, and it worked, it was much easier to get people to part with money when they could see where the other money had been spent. A lot of people think they need the full budget to make the movie but I would say, if you can't raise it all, and it's your first movie, just go for it. Once you've got something there, then people are more likely to put money behind you because they see you are not just talking about it but actually doing it. We both know a lot of people who have been waiting years to get their first movie off the ground because they haven't managed to get their two million budget yet - *dream on!*

Q - How did you approach investors?

Gen - We approached people who we thought might have a bit of money stashed away, and asked if they were interested in investing it. We also approached people who might be specifically interested in investing in films. Lots of people want to be a part of the film business, it's something to talk about over drinks. Starting with the local area, we made a list of doctors, dentists, lawyers etc. and sent letters off to them, working our way from A-Z. Obviously this can cost a lot of money, sending out letters etc., so we decided to make a short-list of firm contacts, people who we'd met or people to whom we could get an introduction. Also, news of *White Angel* travelled by word of mouth. We would meet a lawyer and he would be really keen so we'd send a full package of information. We'd have a second meeting and he'd say *'I've got this friend and she's interested, would you like the number?'* We had more success that way, rather than by cold calling.

Q - What's in an investment proposal?

Gen - We put a package together that would include a synopsis of the film, a brief of the budget, a breakdown of their investment and the returns that they could expect. The returns were calculated on the cost budget rather than the total budget. For example, if we were making a movie for £200k but only needed £100k to cover all immediate cash costs on the film (the remaining £100k would be on deferred payments) the investment percentages would be calculated from £100k. This meant the deal was even more interesting and showed we didn't want to waste a penny. Once initial investment monies are recouped i.e. all investors get their money back, deferments are then paid (cast, crew, facility houses

WHITE ANGEL Schedule Breakdown

1991

October
Commence writing screenplay. Begin to attract finance.

November
First Draft Complete.

1992

January
Approx. $15k raised. Decision to shoot in February is made. Casting and pre-production move into top gear.

February
Principal photography begins and lasts 21 days.

March
Begin editing, continue day jobs and continue raising production finance.

May & June
Several small reshoots to patch some of the holes left in the main shoot. More investment comes in.

September
First fine cut complete.

December
Fine cut complete. Begin track laying sound and music.

1993

February
Final mix at dubbing theater. Negative is cut and labs begin very long process of printing.

March
Labs damage the master negative. Living Spirit recall cast for reshoot of damaged stock. Re-mix quickly.

April
First Prints viewed. Publicity gearing up for Cannes. London based sales agents view the film. No one bites.

May
Cannes - meet several companies who all express an interest.

July
Re-edit film and remix as it needs tightening and there are some sound problems.

August
Pilgrim Entertainment signed as sales agents for one year.

September
Premiere at the Montreal Film Festival. Goes down well. German, Korean and US companies express interest and negotiations start.

October
UK premiere at London Film Festival. Plan for an April theatrical release funded with money expected from Germany, Korea and US.

December
Korean and German deposits paid.

1994

Jan - March
Publicity for theatrical release.

April
Theatrical release. Film performs badly due to opening on bad weekend. Deals with US and Korea fall through. PANIC.

June - December
Pilgrim fail to deliver any deals. Publicity works a bit too well and Chris and Gen spend short time in police cells. Chris and Gen lose home.

1995

January
Labs threaten court for monies owed. Living Spirit sack Pilgrim. Feature Film comes on board to handle the video release.

Feb - March
Video release begins publicity. New version with more sex and violence is edited to help bolster sales.

April
A song, performed by local band, is included in the new edit. It's later discovered to be owned by the Elvis Presley estate and carries a price tag of $1.5m. Re-edit - AGAIN!

May
Video release.... Film performs poorly.

September
Living Spirit approach and secure new sales agent, Stranger Than Fiction. They are confident of making sales.

1996

February
White Angel is sold to Benelux, Italy and several far Eastern territories. Monies as yet have not been received.

1999

January
White Angel is recut after the experience of 'Urban Ghost Story', taking out seven minutes of 'nothing', tightening the action and drama. The first director's cut in history to be shorter than the original!

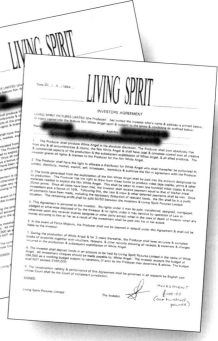

Investors in White Angel were given simple contracts that were one page long. Good for us and good for them.

etc.) Once the film has broken even (paying back the total budget of £200k) then all monies received from that point are deemed to be profit. Monies are returned and are split 50/50 between the production company and the investors. Therefore, the investors provide £100k and the deferred cast and crew provide the other £100k. The first sales would repay the investors back their £100k, then the deferred £100k would follow. The remainder would be split 50/50 between the production company and investors - an investor who put in £10k would receive 10% of the 50% split (5% of total profits).

Q - How did you confirm an investment?

Gen - We provided a simple contract, two or three pages and as long as they were happy, they would sign it. We had all the control. The only thing that they would be doing is putting their money in and receiving reports from us on the progress of the film. For them it was a risky investment but they knew it, and wanted to do it. There are many payments that must be met while in the sales process, all of which eat into any potential returns, such as making delivery and marketing. These figures need to be nailed down wherever possible. Obviously, they are deducted from any sales and that will push the investors profits further away, but there is nothing that can be done about this. Without your delivery items, you won't be able to give your film away - it's like a car without an engine.

Q - Did investors give the money up front?

Gen - We didn't cash flow the payments because our budget was so small, but if someone wished to invest a larger amount, say £50k, then we would have linked that in with a cash flow prediction. We didn't do this on *White Angel* because the money was raised in instalments anyway, so there was no need. We were almost doing a cash flow without knowing it. As soon as we had shot something we invited the investors down to the set, showed them around to prove that we were filming something and they met the lead actors. It creates the buzz and raises more money in itself. Once the filming finished we then concentrated on raising money to finish the film. We cut a trailer and showed that to investors - we kept the trailer short and punchy, left them wanting more.

(above) The bank vault was nothing more than a metal door with cardboard security boxes painted grey. Little white stickers were added to give the impression of key holes.

(below) After producing The Runner, the production of White Angel ran smoothly and without hiccup.

Q - How long did it take to raise all the money?

Gen - One of the big problems with no-budget filmmaking is that if you raise money in instalments you often take time off from finishing the film, so the film takes longer to produce. We were still raising money nearly a year after we shot it.

Q - So, you must finish shooting?

Gen - Yes. It's vital to cover the screenplay as thoroughly as you can. You don't know if your lead actor could die, get awkward, move out if town... This could cause major problems. Even if you have to drop *close up cut-aways* during the shoot, do it in order to cover the main action and the screenplay. I know several other movies that were shot over, say ten

consecutive weekends, but I guess the cast must have been made up from either friends or actors who lived locally. I wouldn't like to do it that way, but it is an option. Once we had completed shooting *White Angel*, we had no problem raising money for post- production. People could see what was there. They could watch it to see how it was working, see it was working well and put more money in. Not rushing the film allowed us to have a few test screenings, reshoot the ending and polish the feature as a whole. To check that everything was in place and that the story was going as planned - and that people were going to be gripped. It's better to do this than rush the post production only to discover your problems when you are sitting in a cinema with a crowd of two hundred people on the day the movie opens.

Q - Control is important. Why?

Gen - On *The Runner* we had given the final cut to the distribution company, they had a lot of say in the picture because they had put all the money in, in one lump sum. At the end of the day the film was not the film we wanted to make. The producers kept changing the film, trying to force the material to be more commercial, sacrificing the characters and the story, and they rushed post to get the film to the Milan film market - we ended up with a film that we felt didn't make too much sense. With *White Angel* we didn't want a situation to arise where people whose opinions we didn't agree with had a creative say in the process - *wouldn't it be a good idea if her head exploded?* etc. We wanted to keep control so that it would end up as the movie we wanted. That's not being possessive. It comes back to the writing stage where we will involve quite a few people to discuss the project, and screenings where we ask the audience to criticise the final result.

Q - What were your main legal questions?

Gen - The main contracts are for your actors and your crew. Especially, with the actors, you have to make sure that everything is in there. You have to have total control, to make certain that you can do anything that you want with the picture, reshoots and with the publicity afterwards. You do not want an actor refusing to do something because it's not contractual and they then request more money. The price that you have agreed to pay includes everything. The music contract is also very important to nail down. The composer composes the music and you have permission to use it in the film. You think everything is fine, however, there are other hidden problems. There are mechanical and synchronisation rights along with publishing/performing rights that all have to be cleared. Mechanical reproduction is perhaps the most important for low-budget films since a good deal of money is recovered through video. If a buyout is not agreed, money is payable on every single copy of the video reproduced worldwide and it comes out of the producer's pocket. On *White Angel* we covered all such rights and no further payments are to be made. Anyone buying this film will ask to see these contracts and not having them in place might prevent any sales occurring.

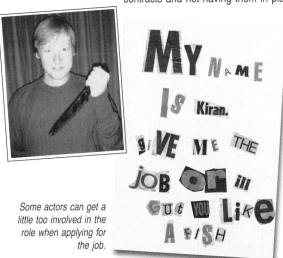

Some actors can get a little too involved in the role when applying for the job.

Q - Did you use a lawyer?

Gen - We used a lawyer on *The Runner,* but not an entertainment lawyer. This was a problem because the film industry is very specialised and needs a legal expert, which is expensive. In the US, with it being such a litigious society I recommend that you have an attorney look over any and all contracts. Yes, it may be expensive but many organisations offer free or cheap counselling. In the end you'll end up saving money and a lot of headaches.

Q - What did the schedule for White Angel look like?

Gen - The schedule was 20 days, with a day off each week, so that gave us 17 shooting days. We made sure we never had more than a 12 hour day. If you start running into long hours because you are trying to cover ground, you will pay for it further down the line. A crew can only work *so long*, and we said, no more than twelve hours a day. Only the producer works longer. In fact, the producer never sleeps! When I schedule, I look at locations first, making sure I shoot all the scenes around a certain location at the same time. This saves time getting in and out of a location. Try to bunch an actor's scenes together so you use them for the least possible time. It's not possible to make everything work, but minimising

Peter Firth liked the screenplay very much and had experience of low budget films - he accepted with little hesitation. Harriet Robinson was a little more unsure - she had no experience of low budget film making, but once she heard Peter was involved, it tipped her mental scales in our favour.

waste will save money. It's like putting a massive jigsaw together when you don't have the cover of the box to tell you what the picture looks like. If you have a star who is costing you money, there is no doubt that they should become the priority. We also decided to shoot in February as this was a lean time for rental companies in the UK and we were able to get great deals.

Q - What was the worst day?

Gen - I can't think of a *'worst day'* on *White Angel*. I can think of several on *The Runner* but you see, *White Angel* profited from the disasters on the first film. We learned from our considerable mistakes. On *White Angel*, we knew the ropes, we knew how to shoot a movie for little or no money. In a way it was quite dull because, from a production point of view, we got it right. We did lose one location and had to make a bank out of absolutely nothing. There is a scene in the film where Carter goes to a bank where all the evidence against her is locked in a safety deposit box. So Carter gets through the reception and into the bank vault. We had planned to use a real bank which was agreed, but they pulled out at the last minute. Someone found a gutted bank that we could use. There was nothing in there, and it was like a warehouse, but it did have the vault door intact. We decided to paint deposit boxes on the wall and we all worked on it, painting away through the night and half an hour before shooting in the morning it was finished. The paint was still wet in the shot! To be honest, that was not a real disaster. Filmmaking breeds this kind of situation. If you can't handle that, you shouldn't be making films.

Q - Were there any problems shooting on location?

Gen - Nothing above the run of the mill stuff like weird people hassling the cast and crew, or the weather. One thing to consider when looking for locations is the sound. Filmmaking is always biased toward the image, but we had real problems with one or two scenes because we shot near an airport. We also had real problems in an apartment where kids were running about upstairs - this really held us up.

Q - How did you find working with the actors?

Gen - Actors tend to flock together, as do the crew, and sometimes this can generate a *them and us* situation which can be unhealthy. There were a couple of incidents that proved problematic for the production team. For example the lighting for the scene might take longer than expected and the actor might have gone for a walk or something. We did lose all our actors on one occasion. We had told them that the set up was going to take a little time so they decided to go off together. We had a room for them but they weren't there. The whole crew had to search the town, and they were found having an dinner in the local restaurant. It was a bit of a heart stopper at the time. On *White Angel*, none of the actors really put pressure on us, they were all great. But on *The Runner*, we had terrible problems with the cast, clashes of interest, egos, impatience, frustration (from both them and us of course) - it was a volatile pot of angry energy.

Q - How did you go about casting the movie?

Chris - We never finished the screenplay to our satisfaction and were still rewriting the script on the set, but when it was in a position where we felt - this will work, and we had our £11k in the bank, we had to start casting. First, we put ads in *The Stage* and *PCR* (UK casting papers and newsletters). As usual, we received sackfuls of mail. The ad said *'Wanted. Sophisticated Psychopath'*. We got some very strange letters back! One was from a guy who had pasted his reply from pieces of newspaper and enclosed a photograph of himself, hooded in black, holding a carving knife. It read *'Give me the role or I will kill you!'* I looked quite hard for the sophisticated angle in this guy's approach but I couldn't quite see it. We also had photos of naked girls saying *'give me the role and I'll make your dreams come true!'* It's very strange. A few people are either very determined or very desperate. I even had one woman come to the house and offer to take a shower with me in exchange for the lead role. Deadly serious.

So, you have to be careful how you deal with actors and be as fair as possible. We broke the replies down into a short list of fifty, then to twenty five and initially interviewed them all. We found a church hall in West London, which cost ten quid for the day, and was heated by a thermonuclear burner in the centre of the room. It had two settings. Off and meltdown. You couldn't hear yourself shout when it was on. So, we spent the day alternating between ice and fire. We ran through the actors and they were all slightly inexperienced professionals. We realised that no-one had what it took to fill the role so we started thinking about classic, British actors.

We knew that we needed someone with quality and ability. So, we went to the top. We approached top British agents. We liked the idea of Michael Caine but he wasn't available or interested, and another famous actor we approached seemed to warm to the idea. We said that we were young filmmakers trying to make British movies, we needed support. He liked the idea so we sent him the script. Two days later we received a phone call and he absolutely destroyed us, *'the script is complete crap! What you are doing is immoral. You're destroying the British film industry by making this sort of crap!'* He just decimated us. We were shattered. This great British actor who I'm not going to name, poured cold water over our entire concept. Eventually I said, *'well, it's obvious that we're not going to be working together* - and he said - *why don't you make something beautiful and wonderful like* Baghdad Cafe?' and I said *'what's* Baghdad Cafe?' I'd no idea what he was talking about. I wanted to make *The Fog* or *Halloween* or *Return of the Living Dead Part IV*. He asked *'why are you making this kind of film?'* I replied, *'because I like it!'* We went around in circles.

Q - Can an agent stop an actor from doing a low-budget film?

Chris - By virtue of not even telling an actor a film is being cast, an agent can stop an actor getting involved. However, the bottom line is that if the actor wishes to do a film, then they will do it regardless. You have an advantage as a no-budget

When trying to attract a star cast on a low budget film, the screenplay is without doubt the most valuable asset a production company can offer an actor

filmmaker. Your screenplay should be different from typical scripts that are going around - more than likely it will be rough around the edges, maybe contain some clichés, but it will hopefully have a bit of energy about it and originality. At the end of the day, actors want to work, to stretch themselves artistically, even experiment. They like to do things that are different, that might win awards or get some attention, and low-budget productions are famous for this.

Q - What about approaching the top actors?

Chris - Always start at the top. Do not start at the bottom because you will undersell yourself. We tried Michael Caine and got a resounding NO, but at least we tried.

Q - And how did Peter Firth get involved?

Chris - His agent was helpful, although we never told anyone what the budget was. We always said that it was under a million. The fact that we had £11k in the bank was a closely guarded secret. I'd seen *Lifeforce*, possibly one of the worst movies ever made (although I loved it!), where Peter Firth runs through the streets of London and saves the world from a plague of space vampires! I was aware of his Oscar nomination for *Equus* and his work on *Tess*. We also knew of the Brit low-budget film *Letter to Brezhnev* that was a huge success here in the UK. We were interested. His agent offered us the usual £25k per week deal and I said *would it be possible for Peter to just read the screenplay?* He was sent the script and he called me - he liked it - he understood what low-budget meant, and after a discussion over the treatment of the violence in the film, he agreed that he would like to be involved. I filled the agent in on the fact that we didn't have any money. A certain chill entered the negotiations. She said, *I have to say that this is not what we are in to.* Then I got this phone call from Peter who said, *whatever my agent says, I do want to do this movie. You guys just work it out with my agent and come to an agreement. I just want to do it.* We paid him what we could afford and gave him a deferred payment and a percentage so he might get more once the movie was sold - his agent was fine (as with all the cast and crew, no extra payments were ever made as the film never broke even).

Don Henderson was originally thought of as the gangster, Alan Smith, from whom Carter gets the gun. The role of Inspector Taylor was available and one night I suggested to Gen that Don should be Inspector Taylor. Now, we paid Don more than we could really afford but his agent was being a real stick in the mud and we ran out of time. But Don was a great chap. He's the best. I

(above) Not all performances require highly skilled thespian abilities...

(right) This isn't a desperate attempt to raise much needed funds, it's the multi talented crew helping out as the cast!

never really had to direct Peter, he just hit his mark and delivered the goods. Occasionally he would look to me to see if he was going down the right alley, or I would ask him to emphasise something, but that's about it. There was one scene with Peter and Don. What a dream it was. One take. Perfect. It was that simple.

Q - So, it's a false economy to use method actors?

Chris - It can be. If time is short and there just isn't money to get it right, it's better to get a scene covered than half the script covered electrifyingly well - half a script doesn't make a feature film. Peter didn't need to immerse himself in the character to play Steckler - he didn't need to keep a knife in his inside pocket, or follow women home from work, just to see how it felt. It's great if you're Daniel Day-Lewis in a multi-million dollar movie. Time is a luxury we did not have. People who have lots of experience in front of the camera know what it takes to play the lead in a film, they know about pacing a character, knowing when to say - no, we don't need another take. I remember a scene with Don Henderson - I ummed after a shot and he said - *'no, that was fine'.* I'd never come across an actor who didn't want more screen time. Don knew that he couldn't give any more so why waste time and money doing another take.

Q - Stars often won't sign until the last minute?

Chris - We were shooting before Peter actually signed. Principal photography had started. Peter only became involved two days before we began his scenes. It was very tight. That is a problem but it is one of the burdens of having no money. You have to keep a reserve in mind in case your star can't or won't do it.

Q - Did you have to wait until the last minute?

Chris - If an actor says *'I want to do this film',* there are usually a couple of provisos. They might want the dialogue altered to suit them, or a say in the co-star. You have a choice then, to say yes or no. They will only sign at the last moment, just to make sure they don't get that call from Spielberg after they are signed to some low-budget thing. As you get close to shooting the chances become more remote of that call coming and *your* chances get better.

Q - Main cast professionals. Minor cast are friends?

Because the location where White Angel was shot appeared to have been taken over by drug dealers, the house had to be rebuilt in minute detail - in the garage! - (right) how the garage looked in the final film.

Chris - Every crew member of *White Angel* appears in the film. Genevieve actually plays four different characters. A classic example - we were shooting a late night scene with an actress who was to play a prostitute, but she didn't turn up so Gen put on the wig etc and did the scene. I'm in it as a forensic expert. It's unavoidable, but it makes the film very personal and saves you a whole heap of money. Why employ the services of a professional *'extra'* to stand around. When you've got £10k, you're not going to waste a single pound when anyone can do it. Get friends and relatives. Get them to pay to be in it. Get them to invest money in the film and you'll give them a role. One guy paid a thousand pounds to play one part in *White Angel* (unfortunately, we had to cut him out). But be aware that they might be crap, although this guy was pretty good, so audition them and see if they can act. Have a backup plan, don't rely on non professional actors to be able to deliver.

Q - Did you give him back his thousand pounds?

Chris - No.

Q - What about crew. How do you get the best people possible people?

Chris - The initial crew was myself (the director), and Genevieve (the producer). Jon Walker, the DP who shot *The*

The crew for White Angel *looks large when everyone is standing together, but every department was honed down to the absolute minimum required to get the job done quickly and efficiently.*

Runner, and he was also involved with the script for *White Angel* and we have a very good working relationship. For the rest of the crew we sent the feelers out - people who knew people who knew people. We had some experienced professionals come in. They said how much they wanted. Then, we'd say *'I'm sorry - Can you do it for this?'* Sometimes we got a yes, but mostly a no. We had very few industry names involved. What we did get was intense dedication from a crew of relatively inexperienced people. Everyone who was there, wanted to be there, and that got us through the rough stuff. Our experience in production pacing also saved the production from disaster.

On a film school project, the crew could work anywhere between three and seven days, and for 18 hours a day. That's fine for film school, but you can't work people like that for anywhere near as long as it takes to shoot a feature film. You can run a film crew into the ground in the first week but by the third week you will pay severely.

A classic example is the production designer on *White Angel*, Mark Sutherland. He'd never been near a movie in his life but he became famous for getting the job done. Sometimes he'd have stupid deadlines. The house where we shot White Angel had three bedrooms upstairs, and two small rooms downstairs. One of the upstairs bedrooms was the production office, another was a bedroom for the production team and the other was make-up and wardrobe. So, no bedroom scenes could be shot upstairs. Downstairs there was a living room and a back room. The backroom became the store room. So, apart from the hall and kitchen, we had one room in which to shoot - this room would have to change, when required, into the front room, backroom, all three bedrooms and anything else that was needed.

Day one - it was dressed as Steckler's bedroom. Overnight, Mark tore that down and built Carter's bedroom. Day two - we shot Carter's bedroom. It was torn down overnight and replaced with the living room including one huge hole in the wall. Virtually, the entire film was shot in that one room and we never waited for the set to be finished. Mark always got the job done on time and under budget. Everybody would pitch in and pick up a paintbrush. Once a film begins shooting, it's like a rolling ball - difficult to stop - It's just a matter of how quickly and how well it will be done.

Another example of Mark's flexibility came when we had finished the film and we had a test screening where the audience offered suggestions. The one thing that was clear is that the ending was wrong. In the original ending, Steckler shuffles in after being stabbed, shot, bashed etc, straps Carter into a chair and starts drilling into her head with a dentist drill. It was a great bit of *Friday 13th* style movie hokum, but everyone seemed to feel that it was the end of a different movie - it just didn't fit. So we decided to re-shoot the end. We returned to the house where we shot the original footage. Unfortunately, in the interim, drug dealers had taken over this house and wouldn't let us within a thousand yards of it! So, Mark Sutherland came up with the idea of a set. But where could we build it? In our garage of course. So, we built the hallway and part of the living room in the garage at the front of our house. We painted the walls, put wallpaper up, built false windows and re-shot the whole end section of the film. The actors were very good and never said anything, I guess they were used to our peculiar ways. I must admit that when I said to Peter *'let's go to the studio.'* I think he was expecting something different from our garage. I remember him walking in - he was very impressed and said this is fine. But he did say it was one of the strangest places he'd ever had to shoot. No-one ever knew and we got away with the cheat.

Q - Everyone seems to do a bit of everything?

Chris - People like to put filmmakers in boxes. This person is an editor, that person is a designer. Most filmmakers are just that. People who love making films. Everyone would like to direct but most don't expect to be doing that to start with. So, you get this crossover where everyone can do everyone else's job. One day the sound man was ill so Jon Walker took over and recorded sound as well as lighting the film. That's a tremendous asset. Whatever shit happens (and it always does) you can deal with it.

Q - Did you ever over crew?

Chris - We just made sure there was enough crew to do the job. For instance, we had two make-up artists which was a conscious decision. The film is about two characters who were needed for shooting almost every day - with two make-up artists we were ready to shoot half an hour earlier every day. That was worth it.

Q - You say it was a small crew, but the credits do seem to be quite extensive?

Gen - Yes, if you have a low-budget picture it's a good idea to make up about fifty fictitious names in your titles, especially if you only have 15 or maybe 20 people working on the team - it makes your movie look more expensive. A few extra credits can also stretch the length of your film if it is a little on the short side. Chris edited the film and I edited the sound. We chose to use pseudonyms to make it look as if we could afford an editor and sound editor.

Q - Was the main reason for editing the film yourselves financial?

Gen - Yes, it was mainly because we couldn't afford to get anyone to cut it for us, so we thought why not do it ourselves. Plus we wanted to learn the process of editing.

Q - What were the main difficulties in editing?

Chris - Objectivity. Staying objective on something that firstly, you wrote, then directed, saw the rushes, sunk up, rough cut, fine cut - It's like the third part of a triathlon. Just being objective about material, *'should that scene have gone or should it have stayed?'* - and keeping the energy up while being wracked by paranoia. Technically, we didn't know what we were doing, we'd never cut anything before, so we

Harry Gregson-Williams wrote the score for White Angel. *He then went on to write the scores for* Antz, Armageddon *and* Enemy of The State!

just had to start on day one, with *oops how do we edit film?* and learn by our errors.

Q - Did you find there was trouble keeping the story-line running through it?

Gen - No, it was obvious when things either weren't working or when the pace was slow. We actually didn't shoot too much, our cutting ratio was 4 or 5 to 1 so we didn't have too much material with which to go crazy.

Q - Did you storyboard?

Gen - No. At the time we thought it to be a waste of resources for a low-budget picture, although our next picture, *Urban Ghost Story,* utilised storyboards. *White Angel* was also restricted by the locations and many times, the rough shooting script that

The final mix can be a harrowing event and there is no space for perfection. Make all creative decisions in advance as a five minute discussion about a bird sound effect could cost you $60!

Chris had worked out had to be scrapped because it just couldn't be done in the location we found, or because we just ran out of time and money and ended up shooting the scene in a single wide shot just to cover the action and plot.

Q - How did you decide the final cut for White Angel?

Chris - We had about 95 million different final cuts - this is going back to being objective, because you're so damn close to the thing. We were really happy with our first final cut and had begun track laying and getting ready for the dub when our cameraman, Jon Walker, came round and took a look at it. We were saying *'Isn't it brilliant...!'* but he reckoned we could lose some stuff. We went through the film slowly and Jon's point of view made us sit up and think about it differently. We ended up cutting about 12 minutes out of what we thought was our final cut - we neg cut, printed it at a running time of 100 minutes and we went to the Montreal Film Festival and watched it with a full audience - they enjoyed it but it was quite obvious more needed to come out.

When we returned to the UK, we thought let's have another fine cut - we went back and cut another 6 minutes out, called that the final movie - re-premiered it at the London Film Festival and everything was going swimmingly. Then only 5 to 6 months later, we decided that we had to do yet another re-cut for the international market, to make the film more sexy and violent. We cut out 10 minutes, put some other stuff back in - all this is about 3 years after the film was shot in the first place! We needed more *'oomph'* so we re-shot stuff, got Harriet back, with a completely different hair cut and reconstructed the film yet again. All the new stuff was shot on Hi8 video and helped give it a much more seedy and voyeuristic look - we are kind of pleased with it now.

Gen - We also had an audience test with our first rough cut. We arranged a screening at some offices where the staff agreed to stop behind to watch the film - they were all complete strangers and we wanted to see what effect it had. They came back with - *'well we thought it was great in this part, but maybe too slow in the middle',* so we decided we could chop out more in the middle. That was also the dreaded point when we discovered that the ending of the film was wrong and we had to go back and reshoot that.

Q - The music is a strong part of White Angel. How did you decide on a theme?

Gen - There were certain composers whose music we liked a lot, for instance Bernard Hermann who did some of Hitchcocks' most famous movies, and we felt that *White Angel* needed a Bernard Herman type score, with mystery, intrigue, suspense and a big orchestra feel. When we initially started out, we were going to have computer synthesised sounding music - then we found Harry Gregson-Williams who could pull off a brilliant *'orchestral sounding'* theme and we jumped on him. He could take a few musicians and turn them into what sounded like the London Symphony Orchestra.

Chris - At various stages during the editing, we cut a lot of music from other films into *White Angel* in order to make it feel more like a finished movie. We used a lot of *Basic Instinct* - that had the right tone and pace. When it came to the music being composed by Harry, we said, listen to this, this is kind of what we want - and then he took all of what that music was *'saying'* and regenerated it in his own original way and worked in his own theme and composition. At the end of the day the music doesn't sound anything like what we originally wanted, it sounds better as it is a completely original interpretation of the film. Dubbing on other music just helped everyone focus on what we were aiming at. We also considered using out of copyright music because it's free. You don't pay copyright on the musical notes, only on the performance and recording. There were loads of music libraries and we could have used anything, from Brahms to Beethoven with a full orchestra for about £230 per thirty seconds. That's world-wide rights. The problem was finding the right music to fit the scenes. If you're doing *Amadeus Part 2*, then you're fine, but not a serial killer thriller.

Q - Sound mixing is where it all comes together, how did that go?

Chris - Most of the sound in *White Angel,* apart from the dialogue, has been recreated in the studio, and by the studio, I mean our front room, not a £2k a day studio. Most low-budget films suffer from poor sound and we were determined that *White Angel* was at least going to sound good.

Q - How does the sound mixing process work?

Chris - We ran through the whole movie and we added an effect for every single little thing that happened, be it somebody

putting a cup down, somebody scratching their face, whatever it was, we add an effect - all those sound effects were then track laid into place. We ended up with I guess about 12 - 15 tracks of sound - 2 music tracks, 2 dialogue tracks, 3 or 4 effects tracks which would be stereo as would be the music, 2 Foley tracks, 2 or 3 atmosphere tracks - which would be background sound, and then on occasion 1 or 2 extra tracks for when we had problems or when there was a heavy sequence. All those tracks are then premixed, we mixed the 2 dialogues into one, the 2 music into one, the effects into 1, the atmos into 1 - we end up with 4 or 5 different pre-mixed tracks being atmos, music, dialogue, effects whatever, and those were finally mixed into one Dolby mix master, which is when it sounds great.

The final telecine is an invigorating yet terrifying experience. It is the very last stage of production and once traversed, the film is technically completed. However, it is hellishly expensive and fraught with potential technical errors.

Q - How did you prepare for the final mix?

Chris - We had a hell of a time as we weren't ready for it. We had a new computer system on which the sound was laid and three days before the mix we found out that it was all out of sync! We had to start from scratch and re sync every effect. We worked solidly for three days and nights, I had never done that before and I hope never to do so again. We were still cutting hours before the mix but we got there. Fortunately we had been good about track laying and everything was pretty much covered so there weren't any panicked cover up jobs.

Q - What was it like in the dubbing theatre?

Chris - Great, it's where everything comes together. It's dark, it's loud and there are lots of plush sofas and free coffee. The only down side is that it's so expensive and there is always this urgency to get to the end of the picture. There is absolutely NO room for perfection in a low-budget mix. We paid about £200 per hour and mixed for two days, the second day we went late into the night. Big overtime, so I guess we needed three days. I would recommend a minimum of three days and five is better, that would give you time to cover the M&E mix as well. If you're not prepared, you're going to have a terrible time, so have everything track laid, know your movie inside out, and just go for it.

We had some pretty bad camera noise which the mixer managed to filter out - not all of it though, so we added a loud mechanical printing press sound over the top. Don't believe that you can get rid of 100% of a noise, unless you're prepared to cut it out completely (dialogue and all). There are amazing things possible at the dub but it all takes time, if you have a 2 hour movie, it takes you 2 hours just to go through it, and you have to go through it at least twice, once for pre-mixes and then your final mix, so you've lost 4 hours just in screen time, never mind changing tapes. All this and there's still only 8 hours in the working day.

Q - What is the M&E mix?

Gen - The M&E is the Music and Effects Mix. When you're selling overseas, the buyer will want a copy of the soundtrack without the dialogue so that they can dub over in their own language. To do the M&E mix is quite easy, all the mixer has to do is to pull the dialogue tracks out - if you've properly track-laid it and there's good foley, there shouldn't be any problems. The problems with the M&E mix come when you're deciding on what format to mix. Full M&E in stereo or split Music and Effects? We did both in the end but the one we use most, if not all the time is the traditional split Music and Effects, music on track one, everything else on track two.

We also ran headlong into a problem at the telecine. While the video format we chose (DigiBeta) could take four tracks of sound, (the full stereo mix on tracks 1 & 2, the M&E mix on tracks 3 & 4), we couldn't lay it all down at the same time - we had two separate mixes, two tapes. We ended up having to telecine it once and then re-run the whole lot for the M&E mix - that added a huge amount to our telecine budget straight away, and like the dub, it's damn expensive to start with.

(right) Midnight faxes from Hollywood did prove to be a tremendous giggle and ego boost, but ultimately bore no sales. However, it was good to establish contacts and worth noting that even small obscure British productions do get noticed by the major players.

The Haymarket in central London on the wet Friday morning of the theatrical release for White Angel. *How cool is that!*

Probably the easiest way to deal with this now is to separate everything. Get the telecine down onto DigiBeta and just concentrate on getting the picture right. Then go to a sound facility, or even the sound department at the telecine house, and get them to transfer your full stereo mix to tracks 1&2 of the DigiBeta, then the M&E to tracks 3&4 of the DigiBeta. You'll also need to ask them to pass both mixes through a compressor limiter as the mix you have may well be too dynamic for TV and video. Just make sure they keep the audio levels legal. If you have mixed in Dolby Digital that complicates things even more as you will be dealing with Magneto Optical disks.

Q - By the time you do the dub do you have a sales agent?

Gen - We didn't, but we did speak to a sales agent to see what they would want. By that time you should have sales agents interested enough for them to explain to you what they would require.

Q - What happened about foley?

Gen - We had an amazing woman called Diane Greaves do the foley - the foley is where someone adds all the sounds that an actor makes just moving around. She would add the leather creak in a jacket, the footsteps on gravel, the sitting on sofas. Diane would make a sound for pretty much everything that happened on screen. She would watch the film through and then do all the foley in one pass! She truly was amazing. We foleyed the whole picture in one very long day and it made all the difference in both the full dub and especially the M&E mix.

Q - What was the first print like?

Chris - The first 35mm print we saw wasn't great - the sound disappeared half way through, it was really dirty and it was a bit of a nightmare as some cast members were present. At the very last stage there was an accident in the lab and our neg was ripped. We didn't have any insurance so had to go back and reshoot! Thank goodness there were no actors in any of the shots that were damaged or that could have turned into a nightmare.

Q - Did you have any problems with the telecine?

Gen - Yes, firstly we produced a widescreen telecine which no distributor could use, so we had to do another. We mastered to D1 and the film was supposed to fit, but the tape ended fifteen seconds before the final end credit, so we had to recompile on another D1 tape! We would master to DigiBeta now. The sound was not compressed in advance so we had to do another sound dub and lay the M&E down at the same time. The first print we got out of the lab was too dark so we had a battle with the lab to make up a new S16mm print with the printer lights increased to give a brighter image. So yes, we had some problems, it all got fixed eventually but it cost an arm and a leg in both time and money. This seems to be very common. Every new filmmakers has some horror story about the labs.

Q - What was the first thing you did once you completed the film?

(right) Glossy sales brochures were out of the question so a full color A3 sheet was pasted up with photos and a synopsis of the film - the torn paper effect was in keeping with the serial killer theme. The results were color laser copied and laminated. They turned out to be both cheap and effective. Go crazy with your color printer. But remember, it's GOT TO LOOK GREAT!

Gen - Slept for a week.

Chris - Yeah but when we got our own VHS of the film we literally drove home at 100mph ran into the living room, put it on the telly and watched it. We'd spent the past two years seeing this film in bits (as it was cut on film and not an Avid) and we didn't know what it looked like all strung together with full sound

Q - What was it like?

Gen - Quick, it seemed to fly through. It was brilliant.

Q - How did you approach selling the film once it was completed?

Chris - We didn't have a sales agent or a UK distributor on board. Miramax had made a few phone calls to ask what this strange film called *White Angel* was about, and a few of the big players like Paramount and 20th Century Fox faxed us at three in the morning (UK time), which was quite fun, but essentially we had to start from scratch. We set up meetings with five sales agents and sat them down to watch *White Angel* - the idea was that we would then field the offers from those meetings.

Gen - We couldn't afford screenings at a theatre where everyone would sit down and watch together, so we decided it would be better to give everyone their own individual screening in a small studio - we set up a really good sound system and monitor, dimmed the lights and let the film do the job. We sat outside, between the door and the elevator so there was no chance of them making a swift exit.

Chris - The reactions we got were mixed. First of all, one company didn't turn up and we had to drop a tape off with them. Another watched it and left 5 minutes before the end saying it was too long and didn't have enough scope for them. Another said they would get back to us (they didn't). The Feature Film Company saw it and liked it but ummed and aahed.

Finally, Miramax saw it and visibly liked it a lot - obviously Miramax is THE biggest distributor and sales agent of low-budget independent features in the world, and the fact they were interested was very exciting.

Gen - Their UK acquisitions rep thoroughly enjoyed it. She told us that she believed *White Angel* could be a hit at the up-coming Cannes Film Festival - Peter could win awards and we would win Best Film. She was sure Miramax could do a great deal with it. We talked about advances etc.

Chris - We were very specific about what we wanted - a big cash advance to cover the budget and to pay the cast and crew, and that was all we wanted. We said we needed an advance of £450k against all rights, which was double what we needed, and that we wanted an answer quickly. She said, *'No problem, I think we can probably do that and I can give you an answer in 48 hours!'*

Gen - She told us that she was flying to New York for the weekend to see Bob and Harvey, and that she would like to take a copy of the film, and get back to us on Monday. She did get back to us, telling us that they had seen it but they hadn't got an exact answer yet, *'but we're all really positive about it'.* However, as we ran up to Cannes the channels of communication dried up, even after this amazing amount of interest and promises. When we tried to contact her, our calls would either be directed somewhere or she was *'out of the office'.* This was a little weird after she had been so positive. Then we got a letter in the post, saying *'thanks very much, but we're not interested...'* And it was pp'd by somebody else! Remember, this was after the intimation that we were going to get a very large cash advance with world-wide distribution, and we would pretty much win the Palm D'Or!

Chris - The basic message is to take everything you hear with a pinch of salt, keep your options open, hassle for the money, and don't let the situation rest, pursue it. If you can't speak to the person, and they say they are still thinking about

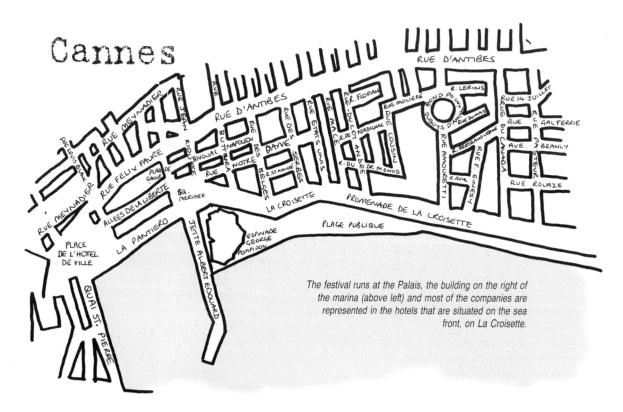

The festival runs at the Palais, the building on the right of the marina (above left) and most of the companies are represented in the hotels that are situated on the sea front, on La Croisette.

(right) The British Pavilion at the Cannes Film Market - a hotbed of moaning filmmakers basking like beached lobsters in the sun! The American Pavillion is a great place to get a placement if you want to do Cannes for free, though you will need to work long hours.

(below right) The hotel corridors at Cannes are packed sales booths all adorned with hard sell posters for a dizzying array of low brow B movies.

it, then you are in an awkward situation - they may still be thinking about it, or they may be giving you the run-around. However, if they really are interested, they will come up with an offer within 7 days, and anything over 7 days, then I think you have to say, well thank you for the interest but really we want to show it to somebody else now.

Q - Six weeks later you went to Cannes - did you take a print with you?

Chris - No, we didn't have a print then as we had shot on S16mm and making the 35mm blow up was going to be costly. We didn't want to incur any extra costs yet. We took 40 tapes of the film (telecinied from the S16mm answer print) and 40 tapes of the trailer that we had cut the night before. We also put together some sales literature that was literally cut and pasted together and printed on a colour laser photocopier before being laminated - it cost us about £100 to do 50 of these brochures, but they looked really good. When we got to Cannes, people were impressed and thought we had spent thousands on the marketing!

Q - How did you gain entrance to the festival?

Gen - The easiest way at that time to gain access to the market was to turn up with a business card and two passport photos, calling yourself a producer. We waited in a hot sweaty line at festival accreditation to get our pass that got us into everywhere we needed to go. It now costs about •85 to enter if you have not applied in advance – so do it in advance! www.cannesmarket.com.

Q - If you had to sum up Cannes in one sentence what would it be?

Gen - Hot, blisters, hard work, expensive, bullshit, pornography, free drinks, little pieces of strange food on plates which you eat lots of because you can't afford to eat properly.

Q - Did anyone show an active interest in the film?

Chris - Yes, we rented an apartment outside Cannes and drove in every day, which worked out quite well as it was quite cheap to do that. We targeted every single world sales agent, visited all the hotels and every stand and told them that we had made this feature film called *White Angel* which was *terribly good*, and would they want to see the trailer, and would they like to keep a copy, and would they like a copy of the sales literature, here you are and thank you very much, gave them a business card and took one of theirs.

Gen - We felt we had to see who was who, and what kind of films they did, so that we would know who to target. It was difficult to see the top people like Fox, Paramount or Universal etc., but everybody else who would have been impossible to see if you walked into their offices in LA, would be willing to see you in Cannes, especially if you have a film.

Q - So Cannes is a great place if you have a film to sell?

Chris - Cannes is an experience which brings the film sales business into sharp focus.

Gen - It is also about finding out which companies do what, learning the marketplace, meeting people either in their sales suites or at parties.

Q - What happened when they saw your trailer?

Gen - We would walk in to their suites, chat to them about the film, show them the trailer and get some feedback - yes, no or maybe. Those who were interested asked to know if we were going to have a screening back in LA after Cannes. No company made an offer there and then.

Chris - The problem is that sales agents are not at the market to acquire product but to sell their product, so it's one of the worst places to go to get a sales agent. Cannes is about the only place a filmmaker can go, and know that anyone who is anyone in the film industry is within one mile from where they are standing. That in itself can make getting a meeting doubly difficult, and you have to be very persistent - most people are booked up before they even leave for the airport!

Gen - Out of the 100 people we saw, 80 of them were not the type of people who would pick up *White Angel* - they would go for schlock horror, movie rip offs, ninjas, family drama, porno - it can be pretty sleazy, but hey *'it's all product!'* Films of quality seem to be sold independently, behind closed doors or not at the market at all.

The only company who showed a real interest was Beyond Films. Being an Australian company they felt more in tune with our way of thinking, and because we knew that they had picked up another low budget UK film, we felt there was more of a connection. At the time, their big success had been *Strictly Ballroom*. A week after Cannes we set up a screening for them in London - we felt everything was riding on this so we hired a screening room in Soho and sat their rep down to watch it in a theatre. He liked it. Beyond made an initial offer of something like £8k and then upped it to £25k and finally up to £75k, which was structured over a period of three years. The delivery requirements were quite horrendous and they wanted the film for a term of fifteen years.

We were concerned because of our experience on *The Runner* and the idea of handing the film over to Beyond for fifteen years with a staggered (over years) advance that wouldn't cover our minimal budget didn't sit too well. We had immediate debts that needed to be met so we offered them a £300k buy out for all rights, but they didn't go for it.

Q - In retrospect, would it have been a good idea to take the deal?

Chris - Now that we know what we know, and don't forget they were leaving the UK to us, it would have been a good idea - just to get rid of the film. The thing to remember is that we were acting in the best interests of the investors and the company, we felt at the time that we couldn't accept what we considered a low offer when the film had only just been completed. The other thing is that we did believe in the film, we were confident we had a very high quality low-budget film. It is a hard decision to make and I guess one gets more experienced - what do you do if you believe your product is worth much more than your initial offers? How long can you wait before you have to take one? There are no hard and fast answers, only twenty twenty hindsight. I don't think you can ever get it totally right, but you can let go and move on to your next film.

Q - When you were faced with delivery requirements, was there anything that you didn't know about?

Chris - We knew about basic delivery requirements because we had done *The Runner*, so we knew about the immediate things like the Music and Effects mix or colour slides and that kind of thing. What we weren't prepared for from Beyond was the 25 page fax of the most unbelievable requirements, even down to things like alternative out takes on original master negative. Half of these we just didn't have and couldn't get - I'm sure they thought it was necessary but for a low-budget picture, some of the requirements were totally out of the question. Most companies had this kind of list, some differing slightly - but when it comes down to it, if they wanted the film, they would compromise as long as the main elements are in place, and that's no mean feat!

Gen - The one thing that we didn't know about at the time which came as a big shock was the Errors and Omissions Policy (E&O) - an insurance policy which insures the producer and distributor against all sorts of weird legal actions, such as a person saying that the film is based on their brother - the only thing was that this would cost around £7k!

Q - So have a good idea of what you need to deliver and say there it is, take it or leave it?

Chris - If you can't afford to make full delivery, then yes, but you do have to be sure of what the sales agent really does need to sell the film. There are a lot of things that don't actually cost a lot that are on the delivery list, like having the proper contracts with every one involved, waiver forms, release forms, chain of title, legal documents proving the country of origin. All of these are cheap to get together, but they do take time. A delivery list will usually say 75 high quality B&W photographs and 75 high quality colour photographs. With the best will in the world you're not going to have that many good quality pictures on a low-budget film, it's just not going to happen.

Q - Apart from Beyond, was there any other interest?

Gen - At Cannes we went to an attorney's party and started chatting to two brothers, Simon and Andrew Johnson who had made a film called *Tale Of A Vampire*. They told us how they had sold the film themselves to a US company, turned a healthy profit and managed to hold onto the UK rights. We felt they were on our wavelength. It appeared they had gone through the same process we were going through and had frustratedly decided to do it all themselves, and they had come out on top. They were very interested in teaming up with us, because we all shared the same goals.

Chris - At the point of us turning down Beyond, Simon and Andrew (of Pilgrim Ent.) told us that they could guarantee deals with America and Japan through their contacts. They only wanted a three month window and ten percent so we decided to let them have a crack. After all they had been successful with their film. Sure enough, within months we did have several deals on the table including a deal memo from Trimark who wanted the US rights plus Canada for US $120k advance plus extras which would top it up to roughly $250k.

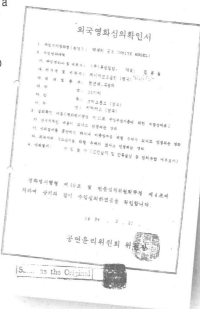

Q - How did the American deal come about?

Chris - Michael Cole from Trimark acquisitions had seen the film at the Montreal Film Festival in September where we had four totally packed screenings. He sat in on our last screening with an amazing audience, and negotiations began. Because of their prior relationship with Trimark, we allowed Pilgrim to take over negotiations and they came up with the deal memo. Because of the Montreal screenings we started to get a lot of offers, Germany came in as we stepped

Is this the Korean equivalent of the BBFC's certificate banning White Angel *from public viewing, or is it an insurance form, or even the back of a Korean cornflakes box? We sure didn't know.*

White Angel premiered at the Montreal Film Festival where it was very well received. The festival paid for the shipping of the print, one flight and accommodation for four in a five star hotel.

off the plane from our return. We had to decide what to do, whether to extend our agreement with Pilgrim as sales agents or to carry on the negotiations ourselves. We decided to extend the agreement and to leave all the negotiating to Pilgrim. The German deal happened and we actually got some money.

Q - How much was Germany?

Gen - Roughly £62k which was paid in three lump sums. Pilgrim took a slice off the top, about half was used to pay off debts and running costs, and the remainder was used to finance our UK theatrical release. Korea also came in at this point with an offer of $35k which we took. So at that point, we had nearly $350k signed, sealed but not delivered.

Chris - Firstly it would take weeks and weeks to negotiate a deal. The one thing that was really infuriating was that somebody would make an offer, and then you wouldn't be able to contact them until they came back from their three week holiday or whatever - time just goes by. And because you can't sit across a table from these people, you had to call and get through their secretaries who weren't speaking the same language - certainly, in Korea, that became a nightmare. Whatever we did, we just couldn't get an answer.

Q - Were you ready to deliver once a deal was signed?

Chris - Aside from making up the clone master tape, and patching up a few problems with the M&E, yes. The problem we had with the US is that Pilgrim negotiated what they called minimum delivery i.e. all you need to sell and exploit the film. Trimark agreed and signed in a deal memo, and then changed the goal posts in the long form agreement. They asked for additional items that we didn't have, so we then had to go back to them saying we don't have these, and we've already agreed that you don't need these. Because we only had a one page deal memo that was not specific, they simply stood firm and stated that the detailed delivery list must be completed if they are going to take delivery. One major problem was that in the delivery list they mentioned the master 35mm negative - of course, we had shot on S16mm. While this obviously made no difference to Trimark in terms of quality, they could use it to stall the deal.

Q - Did Trimark have a copy of the film?

Gen - They had a copy for about five months - it's a tricky situation because they said that everyone in the company needed to see it for them to finalise. They could have used that time to show the film to their prospective buyers and field their responses - basically get a commercial assessment of that product. Ultimately we couldn't agree on the delivery items and they refused to take the film.

Q - What happened with your Korean deal?

Chris - After paying the £6k deposit, the company who acquired the rights just disappeared off the face of the earth for six months. After the American Film Market they got back to us and explained that the film had been banned as it had 'immoral

White Angel attended several festivals and picked up several awards. Each time Living Spirit would use the award for publicity, even if neither Chris or Gen attended the festival. (right) A picture of Gen taken in her back garden as she accepts a best 'production' award. The picture made it to several magazines.

ℱantastic 𝔅urgos 1994

WHITE ANGEL

Premio Feliciano Vitores
Mejor Opera Prima

social values' - they faxed through the certificate of 'banning' (which for all we know could have been an insurance form) and asked for their deposit back. We told them that we had spent it and it was their problem if the film had been banned. Now, not only had we gone stale on the US deal but we had also lost the very considerable balance of the Korean deal.

Q - If you made another film, what could you do differently, how would you overcome this problem?

Chris - You can't. The only thing you can do is make a film that will make the buyers go mad i.e. make a good film, give it to the sales agents and let them go for it. Hopefully you can trust the sales agent, but at the end of the day you can never really be sure - if a sales agent screws up, there's very little you can do as you have assigned the rights to them. I've never heard of any filmmaker being really happy with their sales agent on their first film.

Gen - I suppose try and get a reputable sales agent and build up a relationship to make them want your next film.

Q - So you make a loss on your first film in order to make your second film and get it right then?

Gen - I think our problem was that because we didn't get any money back from *The Runner*, we just didn't trust any other sales agent with *White Angel* - that was the main reason that we went with Pilgrim. In retrospect, it was a mistake.

Chris - The basic problem is that selling a low budget indie film is very difficult. When you're making deals to territories for a few thousand dollars, those few thousand dollars are instantly eaten up on expenses. What could end up happening is that the basic sales merely cover the cost of attending markets in the first place - it's a vicious circle. There really is very little you can do except make as good a film as possible and maybe speak to an agent before setting out - find out what they think they will be able to do with the project before it is committed to film.

Q - How do you get a film into a festival?

Chris - First of all you need to find out which are the best festivals, and where they are, when they are and apply at least 3 months in advance.

Gen - For Cannes, it is hard to get into the festival but you can screen the movie by hiring a theatre when you get there - many low-budget films do this to generate a buzz about the movie. For a festival like Sundance you have to make sure that they have seen the film by the end of July and obviously the earlier the better. So really you're looking at nine months. The film only ever has one world premiere so it's important to use that on the best festival you can get - pass it around and field the offers - a good sales agent will advise you which are the best festivals to go for. In some respects we blew the premiere of *White Angel* at the Montreal Film Festival. If we knew more about it, we would have premiered at the Toronto

UK 1993
Scr: Chris Jones, Genevieve Jolliffe
Leading players: Peter Firth, Harriet Robinson, Don
Henderson, Anne Catherine Arton
Rt: 92 mins
UK Dist: Living Spirit Pictures

White Angel
Dir: Chris Jones

15 MON 16.00 & 21.00 ODEON WEST END 1

White Angel heralds the arrival of two young, talented filmmakers: producer Genevieve Jolliffe and director Chris Jones. More a film about serial killing than about a serial killer, *White Angel* offers a novel and very British view, whilst dealing with the complex (subtle?) differences between manslaughter and murder. Leslie Steckler (Peter Firth) is a soft-spoken dentist who rents a room in Ellen Carter's (Harriet Robinson) house. She is a successful writer on criminal psychology who is being hounded by the police in connection with her husband's disappearance. Meanwhile, London is in the grips of a serial killer, 'the White Angel', and the dentist and the writer become entangled in a dangerous game of blackmail. The plot is full of surprises, twists and turns (all best left untold) that keep you on the edge of your seat, relying on powerful psychological devices and avoiding unnecessary gore. In many ways it's a first in its chilling (fictional) portrait of a very British way of serial killing. Mesmerizingly good, and a triumph of British independent production. *Rosa Bosch*

Festival (which followed on from Montreal) as it has a reputation for being a buyers festival whereas Montreal is a bit more arty.

Q - Do they pay for you to attend the Festival, how does it operate?

Chris - Send a VHS tape with the application form to the festival co-ordinator, they will then come back to you with *'no we don't want it thank you very much'*, or *'yes, we would like to invite you to attend the Festival'.* They will then invite the film and probably one member of the filmmaking body which is usually the director, and may possibly invite an actor or the producer as well. Normally the Festival will cover the hotel bills of anybody who can get to the screenings (who is directly related to the film). If it's an international festival, your flights can be paid for by the Festival and for festivals in the US, it depends on the festival and how profile your film is (they may even pay for all shipping of the prints). Essentially the filmmaker should try not to spend a single penny to attend a festival but that isn't always the case. There are SO many films being made now that it is getting tougher and entry fees are going to get more common and much higher.

Gen - Watch out for small print - sometimes a festival will say that the producer must take care of the return shipment of the print, which can prove to be expensive.

Chris - We got inundated with requests to attend festivals and it became impractical to attend them all. At a festival in Puerto Rico we met a top sales agent who charges $300 on top of ALL expenses. If a festival comes to us now and we don't want to go, they can have the film for $300 plus all expenses. And the money comes directly to the production, not the sales agent.

Gen - I wouldn't recommend adding a fee if it's a festival you want to attend, particularly if they've agreed to pay for your flight, accommodation and a weeks stay in their country. But if they are asking to screen your film, and they're not going to accommodate you, or you don't really feel as though their festival is going to do much for the film - it's a small festival in the middle of nowhere - then, if the festival wants your film, they will have to pay for it.

Q - Did you find Film Festivals to be useful in the process of selling films?

(top) Great reviews at the London Film Festival, helping create a false sense of security.

Gen - Yes, it's a FREE showcase for your product and it can create a profile for your film. If you enter a film and win Best Film or Best Actor, it creates a bit of a buzz about the movie, you get publicity and it becomes an 'award winning film'.

Q - Which Film Festivals did White Angel attended and has it won any awards?

Gen - *White Angel* attended 13 film festivals around the world - Montreal, London, Ankara, Sao Paulo, Puerto Rico, two in Rome, Mannaheim, Emden, Valenciennes, Burgos... and we won two awards - Best First Film at Burgos Fantastic Film and Best Actor for Peter, at Valenciennes. I remember I got a phone call about a terrific film Festival that I should attend, give some lecture, go on TV and generally be a high profile British filmmaker. I said fine, where is it - *'Oh, it's the Gaza Strip Film Festival.'* There was a very long pause. Eventually I was persuaded to go. I was even going to be sneaked across borders with guards being bribed! The whole trip got called off a few days before because some tourists were murdered and the Gaza Strip was closed down. That was pretty weird.

Q - Do the festivals expect you to promote the film?

Chris - Yes, usually local press and radio, sometimes TV. The worst TV interview I had to do was in Turkey where I had been lined up for an interview at the local station (this is during the film festival AND their heated leadership elections). When I got there I was more than a little concerned as it was surrounded by razor wire and I had to pass through metal detectors and sniffer dogs to get in - I realised they were looking for bombs and weapons! Suddenly, it dawned on me, I was going on state TV - exactly the kind that was hated by the extremist terrorists of that country. I was then informed that my interview was going to be live, and it was out to 47 million homes at prime time 7pm! The interview was nerve racking as it descended from chit chat about movies to hard hitting political rhetoric - I kept saying, *'I'm sorry but I don't know anything about the political situation in your country'* - which was then translated into a three minute speech! The last thing I wanted to be was a Westerner telling the natives what to do in their own seemingly fractured, fundamentalist religious country. After it was over, both Gen and myself were thanked, passed back out, through the metal detectors, past the sniffer dogs and razor wire before being dumped on a dark and cold Turkish roadside.

Gen - The movie *Midnight Express* comes to mind.

Q - How did the London Film Festival come about?

Gen - The London Film Festival is one of the major UK festivals and White Angel was selected to play as the centrepiece film. It was screened in Leicester Square and it was great.

Q - Was this good for the film?

Chris - Yes. At the time it seemed to crystallise what we thought - firstly, we've got a great film, and secondly, it was very commercial. This small film was suddenly put right up there, next to *Remains of the Day* in Leicester Square. We got a lot of press and a very high profile. Suddenly we felt that it was all going to happen right here and right now. We felt very confident that the film was going to be a hit.

Gen - And remember, at this time we were negotiating with America, Korea, and Germany - signed deals were on the table, it's just the money still hadn't come through.

Film Festivals are a great place to win awards. This gets distributers, broadcasters and sales agents interested, and as a bonus you get to collect strange figurines mounted on marble blocks.

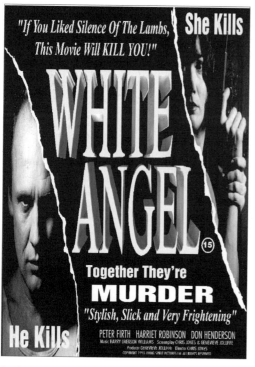

"If You Liked Silence Of The Lambs, This Movie Will KILL YOU!"

She Kills

WHITE ANGEL (15)

Together They're MURDER

"Stylish, Slick and Very Frightening"

He Kills

PETER FIRTH HARRIET ROBINSON DON HENDERSON
Music HARRY GREGSON WILLIAMS Screenplay CHRIS JONES & GENEVIEVE JOLLIFFE
Producer GENEVIEVE JOLLIFFE Director CHRIS JONES
COPYRIGHT 1993 LIVING SPIRIT PICTURES LTD ALL RIGHTS RESERVED

Q - What about the UK theatrical release?

Gen - The theatre manager of the Odeon Cinema at Leicester Square told us that he liked *White Angel* - *'it had an amazing effect on the audience'* - and that he would like the film to be screened at his theatre. He told us that if Rank Film Distributors picked it up then he would get it - he had a few colleagues at Rank that he would put us in touch with and put a good word in for the picture. We decided to get in contact with Rank Film Distribution who requested a private screening there at their offices. They laid on sandwiches and wine, all the razzmatazz, and had four or five of their people viewing the film. They told us they loved it, thought it could work very well and they wanted it.

Chris - They made an offer of something like £25k advance against a UK theatrical plus half of the UK video. After several discussions and haggling we got that up to £65k. In reality we believed that if we took that deal we would never see more than the £65k offered, and I still believe that, although it was still a very good deal. Rank guaranteed to do a P&A spend of around £70k, which again sounds a lot, but it's not huge. It would have ended up going out in five theatres with a lot of advertising. We did the math and felt we could make more if we did the release ourselves, so we turned down the deal, which I think was a shock for them. In hindsight we should have taken the deal, we still wouldn't have broken even but we would have been a hell of a lot closer. Out of everything we ever did, I feel that turning down that deal was the only real and stupid mistake we made.

Gen - That said, the money Rank were offering would mean that we still would be unable to pay the cast and crew. As the German, Korean and US deal which totalled $350k were about to come in, we thought that we could afford to take a risk to make more by self distributing. Pilgrim did their own release with *Tale of A Vampire* and did extremely well, certainly better than Rank's advance. We watched *Tale of A Vampire* and in comparison, we felt *White Angel* was a superior film and would therefore do better. It doesn't actually work like that as we later found out. It's more to do with marketing, the type of film and timing - but at the time, we didn't know that.

Q - So you decided to release your film theatrically, so what is involved in doing that?

HAYMARKET
(Piccadilly Circus / Tube) 071- 839 1527

ADVANCE BOOKING
081-970 6016 (Bkg fee)

WHITE ANGEL (15)
In Dolby Stereo
Sep Progs 2.15, 5.15, 8.15

RESERVOIR DOGS (18)
In Dolby Stereo
Sep Progs 1.20, 3.45, 6.10, 8.40

KALIFORNIA (18)
In Dolby Stereo
Sep Progs 1.50, 4.10, 6.30, 8.50

Gen - Firstly we had to decide how wide we were going to release, on how many screens and work a budget out accordingly. Because of Pilgrims experience with *Tale Of A Vampire* we took a lot of their thoughts on board and they wanted to open quite wide. Initially we were going to open in three theatres only, but they had a screening with the exhibitors who offered them more screens - everybody liked it which meant that it would be picked up by the multiplexes. So our three screens then developed into fifteen scattered around the country in the major cities, which increased our advertising budget. The other thing we had to do, was to get hold of a theatrical booker to actually get the film in the theatres, someone who knew how the system worked.

(above)There was so little money for the release that the film's poster had to be put together on a PC by Chris, using Photoshop and Quark Xpress. (left) White Angel may have opened at some top London cinema venues, but due to a number of factors, it didn't last long so the whole exercise became a very expensive PR campaign for Living Spirit.

(right) EPK - The electronic press kit contains shots taken during filming, very roughly edited interviews with key cast and crew plus several clips from the completed movie. It should be delivered on Beta SP and is vital if any TV coverage is to be expected. (lower right) The old 'director pointing' press shot - it was actually taken a week before the London Film Festival in a front garden.

Q - Who is the booker?

Chris - The booker is the person who engineers and schedules the booking of screens and the moving of the prints. For instance, they will tell you the dates that your film will be screened, and the dates that the film will be moved from one theatre to another. With 15 prints we would move from 15 theatres to another 15 theatres, moving around the country until, hopefully, we had covered every major town.

Q - What happened about publicity?

Chris - We had to hire a publicist, but a lot of the publicity we did ourselves, and eventually we became quite good at getting newspaper interviews, radio and TV. We discovered that telling the occasional white lie or even complete outright lie would always be good for publicity - always managing to get a good column in a newspaper. That was a good way of generating interest around the film.

Q- Do you think the London Film Festival's good press had an effect?

Chris - It's fair to say that having the London Film Festival putting us on a plinth and using the phrase *"mesmerisingly good and a triumph of British Independent Production"* perhaps nurtured a false sense of quality in our film that actually may not have been there. It certainly raised the expectations of the critics as what they actually got was a standard, commercial, ultra low-budget thriller. One interesting thing is that almost ALL the magazines gave us fair to good reviews while the *'daily newspapers'* unanimously slaughtered us.

Q - In retrospect, would it have been a good idea to take some of these people out to dinner and tell them how you made the film, win them over so to speak, instead of hyping the film out of proportion?

Gen - Yes, because the journalists who we did sit down with and have long chats with were the people who gave us favourable reviews, and all of them were loyal enough not to mention the budget (as we had asked them not to). The problem here was that we were in essence sitting between two goal posts and we were stretched to the limits. We didn't have the financial resources to schmooze people, nor did we have the contacts in the first place. We didn't have the power to demand a favourable or non committal review, (or we'll pull £10k worth of advertising from your mag for instance), and you read a lot of non committal reviews! Quite simply, we didn't have the resources to do the job properly within the set time frame. That's the job of a distributor.

Chris - I think the problem with the *White Angel* release was partly the film itself. We aspired to a big budget style film with very little money. When you see a thriller up there on the screen, people expect Bruce Willis, blue light and a lot of gloss. We didn't have all that. What we had, was a TV style film that was a competent thriller and we were actively marketing it as an 'A' movie super duper thriller.

"White Angel is stylish, slick and often very frightening - everything you don't expect from British movies"
SELECT MAGAZINE

"Unpretentiously gripping and solidly commercial, White Angel deserves more than a little glorification"
Mark Wyman - FILM REVIEW

"A chillingly impressive film. White Angel is so scarily sinister, it makes Psycho look like an old Ealing comedy."
Sam Steele - NME

"A cracking thriller with plenty of edge-of-the-seat tension. and more twists and turns than a Dune sandworm"
VIDEO WORLD

Chris - To some degree, a film appears to be valued at it's perceived cost. If you go down to a used car salesman and say 'how much is this car?' and he says '£1,000'. Then you ask 'how much is this other one?' and he says £10 - they may both look the same but you'll think there is something wrong with the £10 one. And it's the same with films. Why go and see a film if it only cost £50k to make when you can go and watch Bruce Willis in a film that cost $70m, or another film that has been critically acclaimed? Why bother going to see this small independent thriller? So on the one side of the coin you want to get on top of the building and shout 'you won't believe what we made this film for' but at the same time you know when you do that you devalue the film, which is exactly what top UK TV critic, Barry Norman, did on his TV film show. He criticised the film, which is fair enough, he's a critic and it's his job. But one particular comment absolutely destroyed us. And that comment was '...this is no more than a 90 minute student film.' Why bother going to see a 90 minute student film, when you can go and see a 90 minute 'real' film. If he had panned the film it would have been one thing, however he put a value on the film and consigned it to the bargain basement.

Q - So you claimed not to be low-budget, but fairly low, you claimed to have made the film for just under a million?

Chris - The phrase we used, was that the film cost less than a million, which is true!

Q - In retrospect, do you think you should have been straight?

Chris - I don't know. I think a lot of critics may have thought where did all the money go, but then again, we never said it cost a million, just under a million. It is impossible to gauge how much of an effect the bad reviews had, they sure didn't help, but I'm not so sure they damaged us terribly. Most people seem to ignore critics. There were probably other factors other than the reviews that helped the film fail at the box office.

Gen - There were other things, like when we booked our opening weekend, we didn't have six months leeway to book in reviews with the big glossy magazines, so we lost a lot of publicity there. The youth magazines could fit us in as they had a quicker turnaround, and luckily we got in there with some great reviews. And we just couldn't afford TV advertising.

Q - Would it have been a good idea at the time of production to have got more journalists involved?

Gen - We did attempt to do that. UK film magazine *Empire* were interested, they came on set for a day and spent another day taking photos - it seemed to go well. But nothing came of it. They never used it in the magazine. Unless you have a star, or really great angle, most journalists aren't interested.

Q - In terms of the prints and advertising, how important do you think the poster is?

Chris - I believe they are absolutely vital. It's the only point of sale where you can make your movie look like all the other Hollywood major movies - we made the name as big as we could on the poster so that people would remember it. Two small ads were placed in the London Evening Standard, probably two inches by three inches over the weekend of the release, which cost us around £5k (and the Evening Standard isn't even national). 5000 A1 full colour posters cost us £2k. You can see how cost effective posters are.

Q - You had a fairly wide UK release with the film but it didn't go very well, what happened?

Gen - The big thing that went wrong, was that we released on a dreadful weekend, one of the worst weekends in the year. We had no control with the theatrical booker and were naive about the distribution side of the industry. We only found out afterwards by actually visiting the theatres, usually to help promote the film, and talking to the managers. They all said, *'why did you pick this weekend? This is one of the worse weekends in the year'.* Oops.

Q - What weekend was it?

Gen - It was the weekend immediately after the Easter Break. Everybody had gone to the cinema the week before and there were box office records, but the following weekend, our weekend, they were all going back to school, back to college, back to work after their Easter break. Unfortunately nobody wants to open on that weekend, but because we didn't know, there we were in that slot.

Chris - If we had gone with a reputable distributor, or taken the Rank deal, they would have said, we're not having that weekend, forget it. So again we learnt. But in retrospect we now know all these things, which we wouldn't have found out if we had gone the other way.

Q - It occurs to me that films have a short shelf life?

Chris - The film only gets one premiere, people can only hear about it for the first time once - that's the point to hit. If the American deal had been made through a reputable sales agent, the sales agent would, firstly, have a relationship or, secondly, the clout to say *'put up or shut up'.* If that deal hadn't happened, something else would have come into place. But because it hung about on the shelf, nothing happened and *White Angel* was old news.

Q - So the belief you had in the film from the London Film Festival was one of the downfalls?

Gen - It inflated our perception of the value of the film. In our own minds we believed it was worth much more.

Q - Do you feel that sales agents, international buyers etc, are out there to rip you off?

"this occasionally laughable and often inept British thriller from young hopefuls... hard to take seriously"
Wally Hammond
TIME OUT

"It's crass and amateurish, and looks as if it was shot for about threepence-ha'penny..."
DAILY MAIL

"I had a bad feeling about this one even before the opening credits had rolled because its young director, Chris Jones, gave a grovelling speech at the premiere begging us to like his movie"
Julian Brouwer
HARINGAY INDEPENDENT

"aaaaargh!"
Alexander Walker
THE TIMES

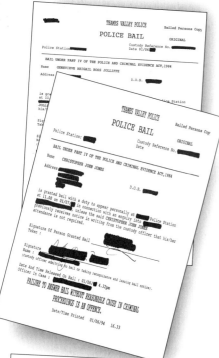

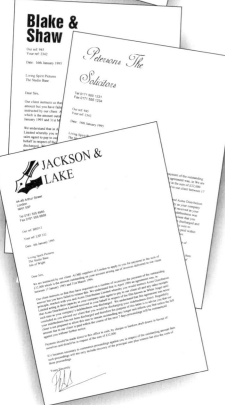

Chris - It's not that they're out to rip you off, but again, it's the inherent problem of having a low-budget film. It's not worth very much, and it's not worth anybody's trouble to sell it. And even if they do sell it, they'll never make enough money to make any real profits, and probably just cover their own expenses. The advice I would extend to a new filmmaker is to get to the best sales agent you can, get to the best distributor you can, get as much money up-front as you can, and write the rest off. Do not assume you'll ever get anything else back. Try and get an advance that covers your debts because your investors may never get paid anything else. The rest is really up to the performance of the film and whether the sales agent is honest. If you cling on to it, you're dead in the water anyway. Psychologically, write it completely off the moment you have completed the film, don't hang around, get going on your next picture or your first film will become a millstone around your neck. That's what happened with *White Angel*.

Q - What other problems did you encounter?

Gen - We had unexpected events that occurred after our theatrical release which delayed our entire process.

Chris - Basically the film was released and the press were saying how amazingly well we were doing and that we were making loads of money. In real terms we were doing terribly badly. At that point we also lost the US deal and the Korean deal. Suddenly, from having around $350k coming in to us we found ourselves high and dry owing £30k from the losses on the UK theatrical release, which was pretty much paid for by the German deal. Not only had we lost all our deals but we had also lost all the money that we had made.

At this very point... (long pause) ...we had a bit of bad luck. We had just got back from the Cannes Film Festival and at seven o'clock in the morning the doorbell rang. Three of us were living in this house. Myself, Gen and another friend. I went downstairs and eight policemen barged in, and arrested all of us, searched the entire house, drawers, shelves, floorboards - you name it, they searched it - and impounded all our Living Spirit files, floppy disks and equipment.

Gen - This also included sifting through my underwear, reading my diaries, looking through photo albums... They discovered the fake gun that we used for the film and there was a flurry of excitement... *"weapons possession sir - we got em!"* I entered our office to see three policemen holding the gun on the end of a pencil, examining it in every detail. I pointed out that it was a replica used for the film - pause - *"oh yes, of course, we knew that"*...

Chris - Basically, they believed we had been making lots of money without declaring it. At that point we had applied for benefit from the government as

(top) The arrest warrant for Chris and Genevieve. (bottom) And so the floodgates opened as solicitors, undersheriffs and bailiffs made Living Spirit their business...

we had absolutely no money to live on, especially with everything falling through. They had read all the press and seen the publicity and believed that we were not entitled to that benefit, firstly because the newspapers said we were doing well, and secondly, they couldn't believe that a film company could make and release a film *AND* be broke. Obviously if they read this book they may see things differently. Anyhow, we were taken down to the police station, shoved in a cell, belts and shoelaces taken off to make sure that we couldn't hang ourselves, read our rights - the works.

Gen - That was if you were wearing a belt and shoelaces, and not still in your nightshirt like myself!

Chris - They closed the cell door and it felt like they were throwing the key away. That was it! We asked them to call a lawyer which they finally did, and a few hours later, which felt like days, the lawyer turned up. He asked what was going on as he was used to representing murderers and rapists - and we certainly didn't look like the murderers or rapists he usually dealt with. It was really bloody horrible at the time. We didn't know what the hell was going on. He told us he would sort it out and we would be out immediately. It didn't quite work that way.

Gen - Eventually we were given our interrogation where all our positive attributes as filmmakers, bullshit, bending the truth, running through the wet paint etc, became indicators of criminal intent. They were quite sure that we had committed serious criminal fraud and continued what we felt were ludicrous lines of questioning. And remember, at this time we are surrounded by a bunch of pretty hefty police officers in a room with a tape recorder and pretty much being shouted at. When you hear about it, you always think I would do this or that, but until you have been put in a cell and had your entire life and home opened up in minute detail, you just can't appreciate what it's like.

Anyhow, we were released on bail to appear in one month for an interrogation, sorry, interview! We couldn't leave the country, so it was a damn good thing we had no festivals to attend and in fact, as everything to do with the film or Living Spirit was in the police station, we couldn't actually do very much apart from watch our future go down the tubes. Our bank managers and investors got letters from the Police, asking for information relating to Living Spirit, ourselves and fraud. Our poor friend who lived with us, and who has nothing to do with making films, was considered to be an accomplice in our big operation. They went and interrogated our landlord, not surprisingly we ended up being thrown out of our home a few weeks later. We were all in this together according to the police. It was astounding.

Q - So how did this all happen?

Chris - Quite simply, they had seen some of our press, wondered what on earth a big film company's directors were doing claiming benefit, put two and two together, got three million and decided to jump on us. They even had press clippings we didn't have, so they must have done a lot of research! They confused off shore bank accounts belonging to my brother, who at that time lived in Germany, with me - they also confused Gen's father's credit card with me - they thought I had about six different identities! Slowly, it became apparent that what they thought was a big fraud operation was actually a couple of people who were completely broke trying very hard to make the best of a very bad situation - and they had just made it infinitely worse.

Q - How long did it take them to solve this case?

Chris - About four months to assess everything and to say *'No, we're not going to press any charges'*. Two months after that we got all our information back. So all in all, six months, after which we got heavily 'fined' by the tax office for not having completed our returns on time - we couldn't as we did not have our own paperwork!

Gen - And that was the end of it - but it had created a ripple effect that, combined with the failure of the film at the Box Office and the falling through of all the international sales, crippled us for twelve months or so. During that twelve months, Pilgrim Entertainment did zero business - we couldn't chase them because our plate was more than full just picking up the pieces. One month after we were in the clear, Rank (labs not distribution) to whom we still owed £30k, sent us a letter saying pay us within 48 hours or we will force you into liquidation. We then had to start negotiating how we were going to get out of this hole. At that point, we decided the best thing to do was to terminate the agreement with Pilgrim Entertainment and take the film ourselves to find new UK distributor and international sales agent. Within days we had The Feature Film company on board to handle the UK video, satellite and TV through Polygram. We had some interest from some international sales agents but couldn't nail anything down. But the UK video was a new source of real cash that could come in for us. We had been made homeless and had no money at all. We were entitled to benefit but just didn't want to take it as the last time we did, we ended up in a police cell. We ended up living with my parents for nearly a year.

Q - When was your video release?

Chris - We had to do yet another re edit of the film to put more sex and violence in which would make the film a lot more commercial and had even thought of retitling the film for the international sales market as *Interview with a Serial Killer*. With a new edit and a new title, we could in some respects reinvent the film for international sales. But with regard to the UK video, it didn't perform particularly well, I don't think that's a reflection on anything apart from the fact that the market was particularly depressed. We did business, I think we sold somewhere between 2,500 to 3,000 units but at the end of the day we only got around £7k which doesn't do much more than put a dent in Living Spirit's debts. We were hoping that we could continue with making more international sales. When Rank sent us the attorney's letter giving us 48 hours we decided to fight, to work as hard as we could to make good the debts. Pilgrim also owed Rank from the UK release but they decided to simply go bankrupt.

Q - In all of this you could have opted for bankruptcy, why didn't you do that?

Gen - We felt a moral responsibility to everybody involved, particularly the investors. When this whole thing happened with Rank, our first reaction was fair enough, we'll go from minus £27k to zero overnight by going under. What a really good way to clear your debt? But it was also a big slap in the face, a big failure and failure doesn't make you sleep well at nights. Not that we've had a great deal of success either, but we didn't want to accept failure and lie down and die, they would have to kill us off with extreme prejudice. We were legally advised to fight it and let them force us into liquidation, but the real reason was that we didn't want to write that letter to our investors and have to say *'Dear investor, thanks for your money, by the way, we've given up on it, and we've gone into liquidation'*. That would have been too difficult a letter to write. That may not be good business sense - maybe a good businessman would say, *'Oh well, it's a bad deal, get rid of it and move on'*.

Q - In either of your past lives do you think you did something that meant that White Angel went through what you could say is the most unlucky curve of all - not only were you practically made bankrupt, your release went totally wrong, you spent time in prison - but then a real life situation was discovered within 20 miles of where you made the film?

MOVIE OF HORROR

PAT CODD
Showbiz Editor

SERIAL killer West visited a film set - to watch scenes from a movie about a mass murderer.

And there are bizarre coincidences between White Angel and the real-life mass murderer whose wife Rose is now facing 10 murder charges.

Scenes were filmed just yards from West's front door in Cromwell Street, Gloucester, six months before his arrest.

Director Chris Jones said: "It's chilling, particularly as the coincidences were stunning - bodies buried in the wall of the house and garden, 12 young female victims and family members being murdered."

And in the film the killer writes his biography.

West penned his own - eerily entitled I only Ever Loved An Angel - before his suicide in jail in December.

Chris - Yes! Would you believe it! We were on a plane coming back from the Ankara Film Festival, just a few weeks before the film's theatrical release and we heard rumours of a serial killer in Gloucester (where we lived) and my first thought was *'the film must be really getting out there, people are even talking about it on the plane!'* - I didn't realise that it was a REAL serial killer they were talking about. When we found out that it was reality, it was a huge shock. Initially, Fred West was only accused of two murders, but then the body count started growing and we began to worry that the press would jump on us. The story broke on Easter day '94 - *Serial Killer Film made yards from Fred West House - chilling parallels - possible collusion between filmmakers and mass murderer!* Many of the big newspapers carried a small column about it and we tried to play it down. It was a very bizarre occurrence. I think what is most bizarre, when you refer back to when we talk about the screenplay and what we say about why people find serial killers fascinating, that *it's the man next door...?* Well for us, it ended up that way! We used to park our car outside his front door when we went into town! That was very chilling and brought everything into sharp focus - as we were making a piece of fiction, just down the road it was happening in reality!

What was frustrating is that we were being accused of being sick *'cash in'* filmmakers by the people who were printing the story saying *'Sick Fred West Film Made In Front Garden'.* Actually, the only people making any money out of this story were the people selling the newspapers! We pointed out that the film had been completed and premiered at the London Film Festival before Fred West was known to anyone outside family, friends and his unfortunate victims. We had to defend the film and say *'well it's not that sick and nasty',* which diluted the impact for the theatrical release of the film. I couldn't say, *'it's a real shocking, real blood and gutsy thriller',* because the press would say, *'isn't it a bit sick releasing the film the same time as all these revelations about Fred West?'.* What could we do? We couldn't afford to put off the release, we were four weeks away and it was all moving - we were in a no win situation.

Q - Why did you decide to write this book?

Gen - We wanted this kind of book when we started up, a book that gave other people's experiences - showing where they got it right, and where they didn't. There's nothing better than your own experience, but hearing somebody else's really helps and I'm sure we've had a few bad experiences that can be avoided by other filmmakers.

Chris - The other reason why we wrote the book is that it's about the only way we could make money out of our experiences now. That's the tragic reality of the whole situation. It has also been a catharsis too!

Q - What basic advice would you give to somebody about the attitude it takes to make low-budget films?

Chris - There are two kinds of new filmmakers who will go out and attempt to make a film. One is somebody who thinks they want to do it but will lose their nerve, the other is the kind of person who actually believes, quite literally, that they are a genius and that they have no possible way of failing. Quite honestly when we started out we believed ourselves to be mini geniuses, it was absolutely impossible to fail! That is intrinsic to a low-budget filmmakers psyche, it's the only thing that will get you to do these ridiculous things that will destroy your life and financial standing.

It could be the man next door - in Living Spirit's case, it literally was, in the form of serial killer Fred West.

'Stylish, Slick and Very Frightening...'

Living Spirit Pictures Present

WHITE ANGEL

Gen - Most new filmmakers, ourselves included, are never prepared for the chaos that will happen after having made the film - making the film is actually the easy thing, dealing with it afterwards is the difficult thing. My basic advice would be, if you can pay yourself, pay yourself and don't put your own money in. Not because you don't believe in the project, but because if it all goes wrong you won't be left so high and dry that you cannot function for several years.

Chris - The other thing is to get out as quickly as possible and start on the next project - don't be too concerned about quality, turnover is much more important. Quality will come later, with experience and serious budgets.

Gen - For a first film, you should make the kind of film you want to make as later you may not have that luxury - many other fingers will be in your pie, each with an opinion.

Q - So to make a film you need to be an optimist, but also a realist?

Gen - You need a vast quantity of optimism, dedication, self will, self motivation, and I believe, honesty and integrity. Those are the things that allow you to get it done properly. The moment you finish the film, take off your director/producer cap, and put on your sales agent cap, or *'now I have to go and make this business work'* cap, then you need to replace your optimism with pessimism and realism - put on your accountancy cap, look at the figures and take as much money as you can, as and when you can, and as quickly as you can. Treat it as a hundred yard sprint. After a hundred yards, kick it into touch and move on, because after a hundred yards you're not going to get any more.

Q - What would you advise the balance between the budget for the actual film production and film sales be?

Chris - It's inevitable that new filmmakers are focused on getting to day one of principal photography and aren't too concerned about things like screenplays or casting - it's just *get the movie shot!* It's an insane desire to shoot and then deal with the chaos that you have created for yourself. With the best will in the world, I don't think that a new filmmaker is going to say, *'well I've got my £100k to make the film, but I'm not going to make it now, because I need another £100k to sell the film afterwards'.* All I can suggest is be aware of it, know that you are going to have problems and say *'I know that I can make the film for £100k, but the real budget is going to be £200k after I have fixed all the problems, paid my rent, been to a few festivals and made delivery to a sales agent'.* If at the end of the day the film doesn't sell you'll never make any money, you'll never pay your investors back and you'll have this millstone around your neck for several years. At which point either everyone will get bored and go away or they'll sue you and you'll be made bankrupt.

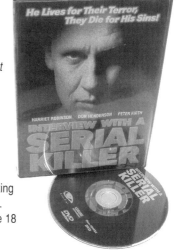

He Lives for Their Terror, They Die for His Sins!

HARRIET ROBINSON   DON HENDERSON   PETER FIRTH

INTERVIEW WITH A SERIAL KILLER

Gen - Get your screenplay to a sales agent and say *'I have this screenplay, this is the cast I'm thinking about, this is the budget I'm thinking about, what are your ideas?'* And they'll give you a fair appraisal of the films commercial value.

Q - Test your idea out first and be aware that if you are going to make any money you've got to sell it afterwards?

Gen - When we talk about making money out of it, it's nothing to do with profit. Sure, we would all love to have our own yacht in the Caribbean, but what we're talking about is making enough money to pay people back what they have put in and to pay for your rent and food. Any film is going to take at least 12 to 18 months of your life. Who is going to pay for those 18 months?

Chris - Nobody would buy a house for £200k if they didn't know they could pay the mortgage - making a film for £200k is like buying a house and you've got to know that you can pay that mortgage, or you'll lose that money and get repossessed. It's a hard reality. It's naive to assume you're going to make a lot of money. However, if you are prepared to enter the arena and say, *well I'm going to lose it all, and if I do, I don't care*, then great, go for it. *And if I lose it all, I can still survive and start again.* Low-budget filmmaking is designed to launch careers, it isn't about getting rich quick.

Gen - However, I think we've been spectacularly unlucky.

Q - Maybe you are just talentless?

Chris - I think we had better end the interview here!

End of interviews 1996

Chris and Gen completed White Angel *and after being arrested, spent two years as freelance journalists while they worked themselves out of debt. It was during this time that Living Spirit worked on the screenplay for their third feature,* Urban Ghost Story *and wrote the first edition of this book (UK edition). It's worth noting that in the few years between* White Angel *and* Urban Ghost Story, *digital technology had moved on so far that non-linear editing was the best way to edit, and digital features are being made on considerably smaller budgets than the £11k it cost to shoot* White Angel.

White Angel *is available on DVD in the USA, under the title,* Interview With A Serial Killer. *If you want to buy a copy, buy it from us at www.livingspirit.com so that we can make some money from the sale. If you buy from somewhere like Amazon, we will get zip!*

Q - How did the idea of Urban Ghost Story (UGS) come about?

Chris - I had seen a documentary on TV about a real poltergeist case and it was really scary. We had always wanted to do a ghost story but the genre felt overpopulated, so we decided to make this ultra real version of a paranormal tale. We originally said it would be like *The Exorcist* if Brit social realist director Ken Loach had made it. We wanted to capture that spooky feeling of late night ghost stories, where not too much happens, but because it's real, it's that much scarier.

Gen - I had some experiences with the paranormal as a kid, my grandmother was a medium, and I loved horror, so it seemed like an obvious choice. Right from day one we wanted 'real' poltergeist stories and experiences to be the focus of the drama in the movie.

Chris - Yeah, we even hung out with spiritualists and ghost hunters. It was heaps of fun.

Q - You swapped roles - why?

Gen - Chris directed *The Runner* and *White Angel,* and I directed *UGS*. When we left film school we agreed that we would split everything down the middle, directing and producing.

The original image put together by Chris with Photoshop conveyed Urban Ghost Story *as a horror movie. Printed on 1000 postcards for $100 it gave the film a glossy but cost effective presence in Cannes prior to shooting.*

We'd both wanted to direct and it's just the way that the chips fell that Chris directed *The Runner* and *White Angel*. So after producing twice I felt ready to direct.

Chris - In some ways it was a real problem for us. We had two movies behind us, and the first edition of this book (in the UK) which was doing well, but when people read the script for UGS and liked it, we then had to say oh, *'and Gen is directing...'* This was usually a problem as Gen had no real directorial experience, she was young and female, which all seemed to go against us.

Gen - This was all compounded by the fact that a lot of people didn't 'get' what the story was about. We had one company who was interested but wanted to change the end so the tower block was built on a gateway to hell - we just had to say, *'guys, you just don't get what we want to do...'*

Chris - One of the problems we just haven't managed to get over is that of development. We have searched high and low for scripts written by new writers and they are either very poor, or already snatched up by a bigger production company. That means we have to write ourselves, and that means we have to fund that too. And I don't care what anyone says, writing a great 120 page script takes months, maybe years if you can't work on it full time.

Gen - We were disillusioned about what we had made too. *White Angel* and *The Runner* were both genre films, and while *White Angel* was quite good, it still pretty much failed commercially. So we decided to just make a movie that we wanted to make, throw caution to the wind and just do it.

Chris - In some ways it has failed commercially again, but this time it's been a critical success which has meant some very exciting things are now happening.

Q - How much work did you do on the script?

Chris - We spent about 18 months writing but at the same time, we both had to do other work to keep afloat. It was a hard film to write because so much of it was just feel and not plot, it never was a film about a ghost being exorcised. The problem was always audience expectation of a ghost story. We knew the film wouldn't deliver the shocks that a mainstream audience would expect and that it was too paranormal for your average art film fanatic. So we just said, to hell with it, we fall between two posts, but it's a story we want to tell.

Gen - It was so frustrating to have sales agents tell us that there just weren't enough *'blue light'* scenes, or effects. That said, all the actors loved it because it had rich characters for a film that still had a commercial slant.

Chris - We were also taking a risk making the lead a 13 year old. What if she couldn't act?

Q - Why in a tower block?

Chris - We wanted an oppressive and interesting backdrop and a tower block just seemed like the obvious choice. It's cold, dark and scary.

Concept paintings by Alex Fort helped convince all parties at the table that the production was being helmed by a creative team with vision.

Gen - Glasgow seemed like a good location as the accents are so much more lyrical than say Southern English. I also liked the landscape, it felt dramatic, fresh and new. Setting the movie in southern England/BBC land would have been disastrous, it needed an edge.

Q - Where did the money come from?

Gen - We had produced a budget for £800k, set a date, and said whatever we had on that date, we would shoot with. We tried all the usual places but got nowhere - the usual answers were; *'we don't get what it's about...', 'It's too paranormal for us...', 'It's not paranormal enough for us...', 'Who's directing? She can't do it, she has no experience...', 'What about Chris directing instead, then we'd finance it...'*

Chris - It was really hard standing by your agreement when someone is offering you the money if I just cut Gen out of the loop and direct myself. It got Gen down a lot because she felt so devalued. So we stood by our guns, and no industry money came our way.

(right) Just photocopying a 120 page screenplay on a low budget feature is costly, time consuming, not to mention back breaking. DP Jon Walker helps out just weeks prior to the shoot. (left) The tower block was conceived as a character in the movie, with a life of its own, organic and mechanical. It wasn't in Glasgow, but a short drive from the studios where Living Spirit were based in London.

Gen - Just when we were about to crumble we got this call out of the blue from one of the investors in *White Angel*. His name is Dave and he said that he felt we had been in training on the other two films and now it was time to do it properly. He got a few of his friends together and collectively they put in £220k. This was great, we worked out that we could shoot the movie for that, quite easily actually, but continued to try and get more industry money. Dave then became our Executive Producer.

Chris - The money also meant that we could take an office at Ealing Film Studios in West London, which then meant we were taken seriously by the business... *'yeah, it's Chris here from Living Spirit, we're at Ealing Film Studios and blah blah blah'* - it just made us sound so much better. The room we hired was about the best value we have ever got out of anything - although we are situated next to the boiler room and when they switch on, the office makes a sound like the Millennium Falcon starting up and shudders continuously! It's just a great way to look bigger and more serious than we might be.

Q - Did you take the project to Cannes before shooting?

Gen - Yes, Chris did some artwork on the PC and we did some postcards and printed up a pile of scripts. We hawked it around but again, no-one seemed to understand what we were making and why. The best thing that happened was that we met David Thewlis and Amanda Plumber at a party, who were, weirdly enough, the two actors we wanted for the two adult roles. They both turned the film down eventually, but we did get the script to them and they did read it.

Chris - Cannes was great for getting in the mood, but for actually getting the film made, it didn't really help.

Q - What happened when you took the office at the studios?

Months of casting and sending out screenplays led to the very best cast we could have imagined. Left to right, Nicola Stapleton, James Cosmo, Heather Ann Foster, Jason Connery, Billy Boyd, Stephanie Buttle, Andreas Wisniewski and Elizabeth Berrington.

Chris - We had a friend called Carmen who had worked as a production coordinator on *White Angel* and she was between jobs. We convinced her to come and help out in the office for next to nothing and that made a real difference. Living Spirit suddenly had a consistent voice on the phone and it sounded like we had a secretary. Carmen acted as a filter, making sure we didn't get distracted by unimportant calls, and she also arranged heaps of production things too.

Gen - Because we had set a date, we had some cash and a script we believed in, we absolutely knew the film was going to happen. The only questions left were exactly how much money we would have when we got to photography, and just how good the movie would end up being. The freight train started to move down hill and we both knew it wouldn't be long before it would be impossible to stop it.

Chris - It was a great time.

Q - How did you get the cast involved?

Gen - I spent months interviewing actors. Cathy Arton, who had worked on both *The Runner* and *White Angel* stepped in as our casting director. She dealt with agents brilliantly which meant I only needed to see if the actor was the right person for the job. She made a big difference as she would always make interesting suggestions and find a way to get to the actors.

Chris - What was most interesting was that Gen seemed to make really good short lists, but because she was so close to it all, when she came to make the final decision on who would be the best person for the part, we all had to go by our gut instinct. I wasn't as involved in the casting, so when it came to decision time and there was a lot of *umming* and *ahhing* going on, I usually had a gut feeling based on fresh new impressions. Although Gen made a brilliant choice with Heather, the young girl from Glasgow playing the lead.

Gen - I went to Glasgow in Scotland and met about 100 young actresses whom Cathy, our casting director, had found. Heather was the 7th girl I saw and she just shone out immediately. Her dad was a cameraman too, so there was no need to explain how the business worked, they understood.

Chris - We had discovered that all sorts of laws exist for working with kids, all of which were a pain in the butt, so we moved the shoot forward so that we could shoot in the summer holidays and set a shoot date, August 18th. Then

Dave Hardwick, Executive Producer for Urban Ghost Story, *was the only person who believed in both Chris and Gen and the movie itself.*

we discovered that Scottish kids go back to school weeks before English kids - on August 18th, so we were just as screwed! So we had to adhere to all the laws and get a professional minder and all the rest of the stuff, which was very expensive.

Q - Did you have any problems with unions?

Chris - Astonishingly yes. BECTU, the technicians union blacklisted us. Even after blacklisting, they couldn't tell us why we had been blacklisted, even though we were named for months in their magazine. I asked them to substantiate their position, but they didn't, and never have. It didn't really cause much of a problem for us, just made us look like crooks.

Q - How much did you pay the crew?

Chris - About £100 a week, plus food. It's not much I know but everyone did it because they wanted to be there, everyone was getting a break - art directors got to do production design, gaffers got to operate camera etc. And because everyone was on the same money, there were no squabbles, no-one felt less or more important than anyone else - DP, production designer, runner, editor - everyone got the same deal and there was a real team spirit.

Q - But those aren't union rates?

Chris - Who said it was a union film? And what right does a union have to blacklist a company without backing up any claims? Then the thing with the agents happened. We were about a week from shooting when an agent called me and said to me - quote, *'you've just fucked yourself! I'm pulling my actors and you'll never work in the industry again - goodbye!'* I couldn't believe what I was hearing. How arrogant to think that they had the power to tell anyone whether they could work in 'their' industry or not. Then it happened with another agent and another. In the space of an hour, we lost most of our cast, except for Jason Connery's agent who stood by us.

Q - What was wrong with them?

Chris - The Personal Managers Association (PMA), is a group of agents in London who meet regularly behind closed doors. What transpired is that they had got hold of a letter written (for prospective investment) by our investor, Dave, in which he said Low Budget Films don't pay their deferred fees. It's a fact, deferred fee movies don't work. That's why we decided not to make UGS with deferments, but that just didn't matter. I couldn't even get hold of the PMA, they seemed to be more like a secret society than a group of agents who want to encourage new filmmakers. Anyway, the agents just didn't believe that we were not crooks and insisted that we make the film using the unionised *'PACT Equity registered low budget scheme'*. I just want to say clearly and categorically that because we were forced to use the *'PACT Equity registered low budget scheme'*, we ended up paying the cast 35% less than what we had anticipated. Even so, I was humiliated by the butt licking that I had to go through in order to get our cast back - but I did it.

To crown it all, a top agent who represented a major actor whom we had agreed would play a part in UGS then said, *'yes I know it's registered low budget, but... don't tell Equity and hire my actor as a producer then you can give them an extra £40k deferred fee as well'*. I had already been in hot water with Equity and as this proposed practice was strictly forbidden under union rules, I was damned if I was going to jeopardise it all again, so I just let it slide. Weeks later, this guy wrote to me with all sorts of wild accusations, again telling me that I would never work in the industry in the future. Where do they get these people?

Q - Did you get your cast back?

Chris - Yes, and you can imagine their faces when we told them that Equity, Agents and the PMA had collectively forced us to effectively negotiate their fees down by 35%!

Q - How did you find working with actors?

Gen - Because the production ran so smoothly, nights were early and days relatively short, tempers never frayed. Initially I was daunted by directing and thought that it would be obvious that I had never done it before, but no-one noticed so it was fine! I spent a lot of time talking to them about their characters and they seemed to get the idea that there was a cohesive idea behind what I wanted to get. And because everything had been storyboarded in great detail, I didn't need to spend so much time working on the camera.

Q - Did storyboards help?

Chris - We had never storyboarded before but this was a great experience. Weeks before shooting we could argue out the best ways to cover a scene. Gen would normally say *'I want to do this'*, I would say *'no we can't afford it, why not do this?'*, then she would say *'how about that way then?'* and before you knew it, we had the most creative and cost effective way of shooting a scene on paper. This didn't happen on *The Runner* or *White Angel* and it shows.

Gen - Alex Fort drew many of the story boards, but we ran out of time and stick figure sketches with camera placement diagrams took their place. It's amazing when you look at the boards then at the shots, just how closely they match. There were times when I turned up on location without any idea of what the location would look like. So I'd have to make it up there and then and looking back, these scenes didn't work as well as the ones that were storyboarded, they just weren't planned out.

Q - Did you shoot on location?

Gen - We couldn't afford to shoot in Glasgow, so we shot all the tower block scenes just down the road in West London. We used our tried and tested rule of finding all the locations as close as possible to the main unit as practical. Then we shot all the interiors on a set at the studios. Because we were shooting in London, the local council wanted thousands for us just to stand out on the pavement with a camera. So we just lied, told them we weren't going to do any shooting, then just did it. No-one ever had a problem and there was not a single complaint.

Q - How did you find working on a set?

Gen - First of all it was Stage 4 at Ealing Film Studios, which wasn't a sound stage, more like a big shed. And some days

we were on the flight path with Heathrow airport so that every 90 seconds we'd stop shooting and wait for a plane to fly over, then when it rained we couldn't record sound because it had a metal roof. Other than that it was great. We cut a great deal with the studio which got us the stage, green room, production office, changing rooms etc., and there were on site bathrooms and a canteen so catering wasn't an issue. From a production point of view it was a dream come true. The actors liked it too because there was parking, they could go somewhere quiet to relax, and there were virtually no night shoots. Very civilised.

Q - What happened about catering?

(left) The beginning of the compromise. An unhappy Genevieve argues for her shots, against Chris who constantly says 'no, it's a half page scene, we don't need to do it in eleven shots!'

URBAN GHOST STORY STORYBOARDS

Sketched by Alex Fort

SCENE 7 - INT. NIGHT - LIZZIE'S BEDROOM
Lizzie sits up and looks around bedroom as she hears noises in the dark.

SCENE 5 INT. NIGHT - HALLWAY
Lizzie walks down the grim hallway in the tower block.

SCENE 65 EXT. DAY - WALL
Lizzie angrily walks along whilst reading the newspaper.

SCENE 42 INT. NIGHT - LIVING ROOM
Slow motion dolly into Lizzie and Alex sit on a sofa as a policeman kneels down to question them.

SCENE 12 INT. DAY - KERRIE'S FLAT
Lizzie and Kerrie look down into the cot where little Jack is asleep.

Artist Alex Fort worked with Gen and Chris to storyboard Urban Ghost Story. The storyboards allowed Gen to communicate to every member of the cast and crew, just what was needed throughout each day. It also ensured that what was shot would actually 'cut' once in the edit suite. Overhead camera diagrams were also used to illustrate where actors and the camera would move during a shot. Management of anywhere between 500 and 1000 storyboard images is an issue not to be underrated.

(Left) Stage 4 at Ealing Film Studios, West London. An effects stage with no real sound proofing. Ideal for Urban Ghost Story as it was based at a studio facility, came with green rooms, production offices, storage, bathrooms, canteen, parking etc. It was cheap, BIG and all other locations needed were a short drive away. (Below) It may look convincing on film but it is just plasterboard, plywood, paint and wallpaper.

Chris - Because we were shooting at the studios we were able to give everyone £5 per day and they could feed themselves at the canteen. On the very odd occasion when we were on location, one of the production team would go to the local supermarket and buy sandwiches and buffet type food and everyone was happy. Aside from tea and coffee, we always had cold water on tap because the stage wasn't air conditioned and it was the height of summer. With all the lights turned on what was supposed to be a freezing cold Glaswegian flat was more like a furnace and dehydration became an issue. In retrospect it's amazing how much we spent on water, nearly a thousand pounds!

Q - Who built the sets?

Chris - When Gen was casting, I was crewing. I met this wild guy called Simon Pickup who seemed to me to be bonkers. But he had extraordinary passion and a vision. I wasn't too sure about his vision, if it was doable, but I felt that if we were going to build sets, they should be as unique as possible. Simon designed a fantastic set for the film, and gave every ounce of energy in his body to make the film as good as possible. Mark Sutherland, from *White Angel,* came on board as the construction manager, and together they made it happen. A BBC designer came on set one day and proceeded to tell us that what we were doing wasn't the way to do it, it couldn't be done for the money we had, and it was impossible. Well Simon and Mark proved him wrong.

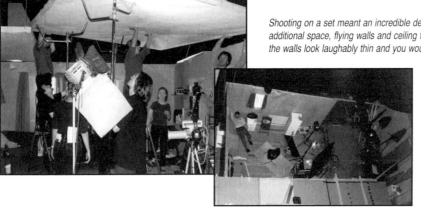

Shooting on a set meant an incredible degree of control over lighting, additional space, flying walls and ceiling for better access. In the pictures, the walls look laughably thin and you wouldn't ever believe that in the movie they look convincingly like two foot thick concrete. We also had a little help from the neighboring, bigger budget dumpsters that were on the studio lot. Many of the sets in UGS were built from junk pulled from BBC drama dumpsters. Many of the sets in UGS were built from junk pulled from BBC drama skips.

(top) A typical 2nd unit pickup. On the day, we were running late, the baby in the scene was tired and crying and it was unbearably hot. We ended up with no reverse shot of the store keeper, so the following day, the actor was brought back, a tiny set was mocked up and the 2nd unit picked up the shot.

(middle) Working with kids could present a nightmare scenerio. Fortunately, Heather Ann Foster was probably the most profesional cast member!

(bottom) Actress Heather Ann Foster aged 13 (left), with actress double Niki Ball aged 23 (right). We couldn't get a picture of them stood together wearing the same clothes as we only had one set!

Gen - The level of detail in the sets meant that we could shoot anything, and in close up detail. Walls could be moved, and there was a floating ceiling so lights could be suspended from above. The big problem was that it took longer to build than we expected, so they were still hammering weeks into the shoot. Just as they completed the build we had to rip it all down. One problem we found was that you need lots of space around your set so that you can get lights or a skyline backdrop far enough away to be acceptable. We built the set right up to the wall at times and that was a mistake. The more I think about it, I can't think of a single drawback to shooting on a set. I guess if there isn't time to paint and dress it properly, it might look a bit crap and then it's self defeating. Because you make the sets, everything is bigger, which means there is more space to work in and the actors aren't so restricted. If you look at UGS, it has to be the biggest council flat in the history of Glasgow!

One big problem, literally, was Andreas, who played Dr Quinn, was just too, well, big! And his head would often pop off the top of the set. We had a cunning solution which was to put him in a wheelchair, but that was a little too mad scientist, so we just got him to sit down whenever we could.

Chris - We also built a few tiny sets, just corners of rooms or walls. Again, this meant that we kept the equipment, cast and crew all in one place.

Q - How did you approach the style of the film?

Gen - With *The Runner* we'd gone for a glossy look, with *White Angel* we'd gone for a social realist look that ended up looking a lot like TV. For *UGS* we knew we would still have a limited lighting budget but more than we'd had before. Myself, Chris and DP Jon Walker, who had shot both *The Runner* and *White Angel*, all got together and decided on the 'look'.

Combined with shooting in a studio with complete control over the sets allowed us to create a style with which we were all happy. It's hard to quantify the look but we wanted it to look a lot like Luc Besson's *The Professional*. We wanted it to look cinematic and not televisual, so we used a lot of slow motion, long lens shots, fast cutting and ultimately, although this wasn't planned, put it through a bleach bypass at the labs. The costume and sets were another area that we wanted to control in order to create this look. Simon Pickup and Mark Sutherland, with their crew of die hard set dressers, had created this beautifully detailed set that just meant we could shoot in every direction. Early in the shoot a costume for our lead man was a problem. I hadn't had time to collabourate with costume designer Linda Haysman on everything as there just wasn't time or money. Actors often ended up wearing their own clothes which isn't always the best idea as you don't have much control and personal preferences start to come into play.

(left) Micro Set - To plug the hole that had appeared because of the opera subplot, we needed to shoot three new scenes with Lizzie listening to her walkman in the bathroom. The sets had long gone so Chris Burridge built a micro set, simply two sheets of plywood with tiles, a pipe and toilet seat that was screwed into a wooden box. The frame was kept tight and the illusion, helped by dripping water sound effects, was sealed.

Chris - On the first day of shooting with Jason Connery it all went well except I was unhappy with his costume. I thought he looked too dressed up and less like the bit of 'rough' I expected. This 'look' had been a compromise between what Jason was comfortable wearing, budget restrictions and what he had brought with him in his bag. As I was not literally at the coal face directing I was able to stand back and note that the costume was just not quite right. Gen had gone through the whole day and noticed the costume but because it was early on in the shoot and there were other seemingly bigger issues, it just didn't seem like an immediate problem.

This is where a creative producer is useful because the costume issue didn't seem too dramatic at the time but in retrospect it would have changed the dynamics and tone of the film and was actually very important. Linda adapted the costume that night after persuading DP Jon Walker to relinquish his trousers, giving the dressed down 'look' everybody agreed was right.

Gen - Ironically we ended up using these first scenes in the final cut of the movie to create a new story thread where Jason Connery's character comes back at the end of the film, sometime after the main story has finished. The obvious costume difference implied a change in character and a passing of time. Quite funny considering it was a screw up!

Q - You mention bleach bypass - what is this?

Chris - Bleach bypass is a process in the labs where the film isn't put through the bleach bath. It makes the blacks and dark areas of the film almost impenetrable and it adds a kind of rich feel to the image. It's very subjective and is only used in the theatrical version of the film, but it didn't half make it look great. *Se7en* used it in the cinema for instance.

Q - What did you shoot it on - S16mm or 35mm?

Gen - Even though we had £200k and could have afforded 35mm we chose S16mm. This was because we had a 13 year old girl in the lead and we didn't know if she would be a one take wonder or a take twenty six disaster. In fact she was fantastic. It was also because we had learned from our other films that coverage is paramount. It's a lot like the way Hollywood shoots films, we just wanted to burn stock like there was no tomorrow and we knew that if we shot on 35mm we wouldn't be able to do that.

Chris - We reasoned that audiences were not interested in whether a film was shot on S16mm, 35mm Kodak or Fuji, they were just interested in whether the story and characters were engaging. So we

George the handyman, a prominent character played by Richard Syms. During a test screening we discovered that the audience believed he was the father of a loan shark character who turned up later. This wasn't the case and we ended up having to cut the character to avoid this confusion.

let go of 35mm and embraced S16mm and truly did burn stock! It was the right decision and I know that the film wouldn't have been as good if we had shot on 35mm. We would have crisper shots, but fewer shots and diminished coverage.

Q - Did you use a second unit?

Gen - Yes. One of the things that was different with *UGS* from our other movies were that there were an enormous amount of characters. That combined with the fact that our young actress was legally only allowed to work for a few hours a day meant that often we had to have two cameras running on set. The second camera was usually free and roaming and would grab snippets of anything interesting when it could. A lot of the time, Chris would be directing the second unit while I was on set doing the main unit, which freed me up to forget about doing close ups of newspapers or hands putting a cup down and concentrate on the drama and the actors.

(above) A large main unit and small 2nd unit ensured maximum coverage.

Chris - The other advantage was that I was able to use a stand in for Heather (Niki Ball) and shoot large portions of scenes with her, then Gen would come in with the lead actress, shoot her close ups, then move on. Because we were cutting as we shot I was able to isolate sequences that needed a cutaway to bridge two shots that weren't cutting comfortably and then go and shoot them, or shoot a cutaway to help cut the middle out of a dialogue scene that wasn't quite working - basically invent tiny segments of drama to help with the overall pacing of the movie. Even though we shot for only four weeks, because we pretty much had two units going almost all of the time, it enabled us to nearly double the amount of shots that we were able to achieve had there only been a single main unit.

Q - When did you edit?

Gen - Because we had a budget we were able to hire an Avid which we installed in a room 50 yards from Stage 4 where we were shooting. Our editor, Eddie Hamilton, was fresh out of the corporate video world but loved movies. He appeared to have limitless energy and showed us a short film he'd cut called *Hallraiser,* about a mad axe murderer in a hall of residence at a university. We recognised a kindred spirit who was born from a love of *Star Wars*, so we gave him the job even though he'd never cut drama before. It was a brilliant decision because Eddie's technical expertise, creative knowledge, combined with his almost super-hero like energy levels meant that by lunch time each day he'd already cut the previous days dailies. This meant we could watch the scenes over lunch and plan how we would plug any holes or problems, or just feel damn fine about how good we thought it was looking. We also let the actors look at some scenes which boosted their confidence.

Chris - You have to be careful with this because one of the actors often became unconfident after seeing themselves. I don't know why because they were fantastic. The upshot of having this Avid and Eddie cutting away, aside from plugging holes in scenes, was that by the end of the shoot, Eddie had pretty much cut the whole movie. So within a couple of days of wrapping we actually sat down and watched the movie.

Q - How did it look?

Gen - Terrible. It was the most depressing experience of my life. It was a mess, all over the place, full of holes and it just didn't flow. My directorial debut was a disaster!

(left) Even though there were seven cameras on set, it was camera four, running at 250 fps, with a 500mm lens operated by Jay Polyzoides that was the one that produced the shot that gets the gasps in the cinema.

Chris - I believe all movies are like that and the editing process is designed to smooth everything out and fine tune the story. Editing is an interesting stage because when you think about it, if there's a problem with the script, the editor has to fix it. If there's a problem with the acting, then the editor has to fix it. Problems with the camera, then the editor has to fix it. And so much of post production is just making something that doesn't work into something that does work. And after a few drinks, the cut didn't seem as bad as we thought, but we knew we had a lot of work to do. We discovered there were a lot of holes we hadn't seen and we almost immediately planned a quick re-shoot weekend where we shot an extra 50 or so shots without any actors. These were things like exteriors of buildings etc.

Q - So you held test screenings?

Gen - Yes. The first one was with a few friends and whole sequences were still missing, like the car crash at the end of the movie, so it lacked punch, but we were just trying to find out if people understood the story mechanics that were going on underneath the hood of the film. We isolated a lot of problems and did another re-cut, then we had to plan the stunt sequence which Terry Forrestal co-ordinated for us. Once we had this footage and cut it in the whole movie came to life. To be quite honest, none of us expected the crash to be as spectacular as it was.

Chris - So we had another test screening, this time for a large group of 30 or so people who we didn't know. It was quite an eye opener as we discovered that all our friends had been, on the whole, fairly generous with their criticism. We weren't really interested in finding out whether people liked it or didn't like it. There's nothing you can do about personal taste, we just wanted to know whether the story was working and we discovered all sorts of problems.

Gen - I hated the screening because everything that I knew was wrong with it seemed to glow like a beacon. It was

demoralising listening to what people were saying after Chris had stood up after the film and said to the audience so 'tell me what's wrong with it?' - after the invitation to tear it apart, they didn't lose much time. In retrospect this was brilliant because all the problems became apparent, and every problem had a solution, so we were able to go back and fix them all. So while the process might have been demoralising, in the long run it was the best thing to do.

Chris - We discovered all sorts of strange things. When you write a script and make a film, you create a kind of road map for the story, the idea is that the audience never knows what's round the next corner - the problem is that sometimes you think they're driving along one road when actually

(upper left) Stunt Co-ordinator Terry Forrestal takes charge . (lower left)To flip the car before hitting the stationary car a pipe ramp was bolted to the floor and greased up. Terry checks the trajectory meticulously as he will be in the car when it hits at 60mph.

they're off on a completely different road because of the way they've interpreted what they've seen. This happened in UGS with two characters - George was a character who was cut because everybody thought he was the father of the money grabbing loan shark. To everyone involved in the film it was an astonishing revelation that anyone could even consider this, yet there we were with thirty people all saying it to us. So we made some brutal cuts and George hit the cutting room floor. It was an important lesson to learn that no matter how confident you are in your own story, you need to show it to people to test out whether it's working on a purely mechanical level. Do they understand who is who and what relations they have and do they understand where they are being led by you the filmmaker. If they don't, invariably they get confused and bored and will fall asleep. And we've all seen films where we don't really understand what's going on, or something in the fabric of the story seems very odd, this is probably because you're thinking one thing when the director thinks you're thinking something else.

Gen - We began fine cutting the movie. Even though Eddie was like Buzz Lightyear with inexhaustible batteries, the whole process began to wear his enthusiasm down. Chris and I argued vehemently in the cutting room, often over frames, or the slightly different delivery of lines, and it was very hard work - not just exhausting but it was a spiritual and emotional marathon.

Chris - Because of the fact that three re-cuts of *White Angel* had happened in the past, each time vastly improving the film, I was adamant that there wouldn't be a single frame in the movie that wasn't absolutely essential. This of course flew in the face of what Gen wanted because she was so in love with the nuances and detail that would inevitably require a few extra frames here and there. Eventually we agreed on a cut and after a test screening we felt sure that it was the right one. It felt lean and mean and everyone was happy. I was sure that the horror of re-cuts as we'd had on *White Angel* would never happen.

We had a test screening for some industry people at Polygram. They came out and said it was good but it was too slow. I just couldn't believe it! I'd argued so aggressively to cut, cut, cut! I was sure there was nothing in there that could be taken out. But I knew from experience that even if you're sure, you could be wrong. I went to see Gen, who was recuperating with her family... *'they're all wrong!'* she exclaimed, *'but what if they're not?'* I argued. For eight hours we fought until Gen dug her heels in explaining that it's her art, her film, and nobody was going to *'fuck with it!'* Some time later, I'd secretly arranged for Eddie to drop by to argue the case for a recut of the first 25 minutes, the part of the story with pacing problems. Gen was still opposed, but intrigued to see what would happen if we did cut 15 minutes. An hour later and we'd done it. Having been away from the movie for a few weeks it was incredible to see how baggy it was. The three of us sat in the cutting room with our jaws on the floor saying *'why on earth did we leave all that junk in? - I can't believe we didn't cut it out before - It's so much better - Oh my God... !'* That's the cut that we released, short at 86 mins, but we felt it's better to have a well paced shorter film than a long baggy affair.

Q - UGS uses a famous bit of opera, why and how did that come about?

(above) Danielle Da Costa, stunt double for Heather Ann Foster, wearing oversized costumes and wig, prepares to make her leap from the 13th floor whilst attached to a fan descender.

Gen - We knew we had to get the key sequence at the end of the film right. The car crash formed the pivotal question in the audience's mind, *'what happened?'* - it was also the moment that Lizzie remembered just what did happen, as she faced death falling from a window thirteen floors up in her tower block.

Chris - We broke this out and did it eight weeks after the main shoot. We knew this one would be hard and fast and wanted to have as much energy as possible, plus half of it was a night shoot. It was shot over two days with seven cameras, some running in extreme slow mo. When we got the footage back and Eddie cut the sequence together it was jaw dropping. It was at that moment that I said, *'I don't know how or why, but we should put opera over this sequence, how can we do it?'* I found an old opera CD and I listened to all the famous tracks, until I heard one that seemed perfect. We put it on the Avid and watched it with the pictures. There was stunned silence as everyone in the room knew that we absolutely must use this opera music.

Gen - The challenge was to work out a way where we could plausibly use this music without it being self indulgent. Perversely this worked in our favour as part of the screenplay's problem had always been what reason was there for Lizzie to conveniently remember *what happened in the crash?* at the end of the movie. We used the opera as a kind of acoustic memory that Lizzie has, and when she finally hears it in all it's glory, it triggers a series a mental flashbacks. We then shot three new scenes to explain it's presence.

Chris - Again this shows that with low budget films as you don't have enough money to write the script and go through as many drafts as is needed, you end up being forced to shoot before you're actually ready. The secret to making this work is to treat the editing as yet another screenplay revision and not be afraid to go back and re-shoot or invent entirely new characters, subplots, scenes etc.

Q - How did you do the joy riding car crash sequence?

Gen - Terry Forrestal, the stunt coordinator on *The Runner,* came back to do *UGS*. He now had even bigger movies under his belt and he really did it as a personal favour. There were two sequences - the car crash and the high fall out of the tower block. From a stunt point, the car crash was very dangerous but essentially a fairly run of the mill stunt, a car hits a pile of sand, flips over, skids to a halt and explodes. You could probably see this kind of stunt in a TV drama. The reason this sequence worked so well in *UGS* and why it looked much more impressive was because of the quantity and the diversity of coverage. We had seven cameras, all running as fast as they could so that they would slow down time on screen (slow motion). The main camera was on a very long lens about quarter of a mile away and this was running at nearly 300 fps, which meant that when the car flew through the air it slowed down so much that visually it looked stunning and smacked of John Woo! It was a very exciting night and even though the crash seemed to happen over just one or two seconds, it felt like an eternity before Terry was pulled from the wreck.

The mix of spooky story, urban setting and social realist with a slash of Hollywood treatment made Urban Ghost Story *an odd movie. A hit with the critics, film festivals and Hollywood executives, all of whom respond to it's unique qualities, but a failure with international sales as buyers just don't know what label to put on it, Ghost Story or Social Drama?*

(right) Directing is a physically rigorous job. Lack of sleep, mental exhaustion, severe backache, poor diet and a crisis of faith are common. (below right) Nightmare compromise.The pharmacist heist scene - it's the first day of shooting, it's the hottest day of the year, the location is a tiny pharmacy with customers coming in and out, there's no air conditioning and the lights make it like an oven, you are behind schedule, the baby is going mad... and it's a really complicated scene. It was eventually shot hand held and the sheer spontaneity of the way in which it was filmed actually helped the scene. Second unit picked up a missing shot the following day and the scene was saved.

Chris - Then came the explosion with special effects man Dave Beavis. He had a limp which was vaguely worrying considering he was blowing something up for us, but we knew his credentials and felt confident. We set up all the cameras as he rigged the car to explode. Just before we started the cameras I asked him *how far away do we need to be safe? -* he coolly took three paces back and said *here's safe.* So we called action, the cameras started and Dave pressed the button - BABOOM!!! - I was hit by a blast of heat and then my hair stood on end as I watched a wall of flame come at me with terrifying speed. I glanced over to Dave who was casually scratching his chin as though nothing had happened. I looked over my shoulder at the crew but they weren't there, they were twenty yards away, and running! There were a lot of expletives. None of us had any idea how big the explosion was going to be, but whatever we had imagined it was at least three times bigger. It was a splendid experience! As Jason Connery put it, *'how unlucky for Lizzie to steal a car only to find that there are 40lbs of semtex in the trunk!'*

Gen - The next day we had to do the high fall out of the building. What was supposed to happen here was Lizzie was to be holding on to some pigeon wire attached to the side of the building thirteen stories up, the wire would give way and then she would drop - again coverage and slow motion made this scene work as well as it finally did. In fact this wasn't as dangerous in terms of stunts because the stunt girl, Danielle, was on a very thin cable and was dropped several floors as the pigeon mesh came away from the building. Still the moment that she came away and dropped was absolutely riveting. Even though you know it's a stunt and she's on a wire, and that there's a crash mat at the bottom, it still looks like somebody jumping out of a twenty story window! Two people screamed involuntarily which helped seal the tension on set. There was a guy walking his dog some forty feet away who hadn't seen the film crew and looked round when he heard the commotion only to see what he thought was a young girl falling out of a thirteenth floor window and screaming! We had to stop him ringing the emergency services and calm him down with a cup of tea!

Chris - In Cannes a couple of people came up to me and said *'how did you do that stunt... with the crash and falling out the window that must have cost at least half a million dollars?'* I wryly smiled and said yes, it was a small portion of our budget that was well spent. In fact this entire sequence, with Union rates, including paramedic and the emergency services, the fire service, six extra cameras, pyrotechnic effects, location fees, cars to crash, special wire rigging etc. all came in under £20k. Sure it's a lot of money but for what we got it was the best money we've ever spent.

Q - What did you learn directing UGS?

Gen - It's so exhausting! You have to keep your mind on everything all the time, constantly thinking on your feet. The other thing that surprised me was the physical rigors of directing. Unlike producing, you never have a chance to stop, there is always a line of people queuing up to ask you questions and the only time that your brain can actually stop is when you switch off the lights to go to sleep, even then your mind is buzzing over the days rushes and thoughts on the day to come.

The most disappointing thing about directing is the constant compromise that you have to suffer, camera movements are never quite as good as you visualise, actors deliver performances differently from the way you imagined and there's just not enough time, money or daylight to get what you want.

Chris - There was a funny moment on the first day when I was driving Gen home, She was very depressed and I said *'what's wrong?'* and she said, *'the actors, why couldn't they just act... better?'* First days are always dreadful, and actors tend to do things differently from the way you imagined, but that isn't necessarily bad work.

Gen - In a strange sort of way these compromises become your allies because it allows the other creative people around you, as long as you have chosen carefully, to flourish and bring something new to the movie. We tried to work with the most talented creative people we could find and then let them loose within rigid parameters so that they could produce their best work but at all times it stays true to the spirit, vision, story and style of the movie. There are times when the compromise is difficult to swallow but you have to ask yourself if I go for another take or another shot is it really going to improve what I want? It's easy to go for take after take in vain, hoping that the camera move will somehow get better or the actor will somehow do it differently. There's no hard rule here but I learnt to trust my instinct and not to waste time on something if it isn't working. I knew that I had a second line of defence in the form of Eddie in the cutting room, and he could work wonders with those scenes that I didn't think were working, as long as I had enough coverage.

Chris - Gen always says to me that there is one scene in the middle of the movie that she hates and regrets the day we shot it because I forced her to shoot it quickly the way that she did, because we were so behind schedule. Again with no rules and just opinion, there is no answer aside from the fact that Gen tends to forget about the other times where compromises were made and the compromises didn't show. You have to accept that some scenes will be disappointing and you'll end up hating them.

Q - Did directing ever get the better of you?

Gen - Yes, two thirds of the way through the shoot there was a day that I got so overloaded, stressed, hungry and frazzled that I became sick and I had to stop for a few hours and go and lie down. Fortunately because Chris is also a director and close to the project it was just a matter of him stepping on set and continuing to direct one full scene so we didn't fall behind. Interestingly, although we're not going to tell you what scene it is, you can clearly detect a different directorial style and strangely when I saw it I thought *'My God! That scene's great, I wouldn't have directed it that well!'*

Chris - Then again when I saw some of the scenes that Gen did I said *'My God I wouldn't have done it that way and it works so well!'* Interesting how other peoples interpretation is surprising and that surprise makes it better.

Q - Chris, how did you approach producing?

Chris - My approach to producing was very different from that of Gen's during *White Angel* and *The Runner.* Gen had taken the

The poster for Urban Ghost Story wasn't at all what we expected, but it was different, suggested there was more to the film than just a spooky tale, and it was bold. The red hue made it stand out when fly-posting and everyone seemed to remember the name of the movie.

(left) It looks great in the photos and on TV, but Cannes is often exhausting, hot, sweaty, and downright expensive.

(below) Chris, with fellow film maker Simon Cox, try to sell a concept to Troma, agents for Killer Condom. Their movie, The Breath Of Death - The Killer Fart.

(bottom) Jason Connery was 100% behind the movie and spent much of his time in Cannes promoting Urban Ghost Story. On this occasion he is doing a live link for Euro channel Sky News. Getting your cast behind your film is extremely valuable because journalists are always up for an interview with an actor, they're just prettier than us film makers!

weight of production on to her shoulders and had taken every single problem as a personal challenge. I on the other hand, being lazy, decided that I would delegate everything, and I mean everything. I had a really good team of production people around me and I told them that the only time that I wanted to hear from them was if we were about to be shut down, somebody was going to die or there is some impending disaster, otherwise, they would fix it. I also developed a peculiar condition called producers cramp which manifested itself in the inability to sign checks! Because I didn't pay anything until after the shoot, I didn't have to keep track of money, and because I didn't have to deal with the thousands of production problems that occurred, my brain stayed clear. Consequently I was able to keep tabs creatively and I became for want of a better description, the cast and crew therapist. Crew members would regularly come to me and bemoan some compromise or condition that they had had inflicted upon them and I would say *'there there, I understand and I care'*. They'd get it off their chest and we'd get on with it. I didn't realise how important this role was in terms of team building but it meant that everybody's gripe was heard and if something could be done about it, it was. Consequently from a production point of view, I wasn't stressed, I could deal with *real* problems in a level headed way and everything ran pretty much smoothly.

Q - Were there any major problems?

Chris - I don't know, the production team dealt with it.

Q - How did you get the music for UGS?

Gen - Harry Gregson-Williams had done the music for *White Angel* and then went to Hollywood to do movies like *Armageddon* and *Antz.* As *White Angel* had been Harry's first feature film and because of personal contacts we really wanted Harry to do *UGS* and Harry wanted to do it too. Unfortunately, the meagre music budget we had was severely outweighed by Jerry Bruckheimer and *Enemy of The State*, so Harry had to graciously bow out, but did suggest his brother might do a good job.

Chris - We decided to have a look at a bunch of other composers but bizarrely enough Rupert, Harry's brother, was indeed the best choice. He tapped in to the style of

music that we wanted, something contemporary and upbeat. It was important not to give it a Hollywood thriller sounding score and equally we couldn't just pack it with Brit pack band songs. I think the music is one of the strongest elements in the film because it is so left field from what you would imagine from a movie called *Urban Ghost Story*, set in Glasgow, and yet it seems to work so incredibly well.

Gen - We were also very specific with Rupert about where and how much music we were going to use and in comparison with our earlier films there isn't that much music in the whole movie, probably around 25 minutes. The music was composed of samples, electronic instruments and wherever possible, real performers. We recorded it over Christmas and all of us all got very severe food poisoning from a dodgy curry. The last thing you want to do when you're up against a deadline is to spend a day chucking your guts up, it's not what you call creatively inspiring.

Q - So you completed all your post production. When did you start to talk to sales agents and distributors?

Chris - After we'd recut the movie, we set up a screening in London, with high hopes because we knew that *UGS* was the best film that we'd made. One thing that had surprised me during earlier screenings is that at the end of the movie, people were in tears because they had found the resolution emotionally moving. We never expected people to cry at the end, but the combination of Heather's performance, the lighting, the music and the story worked so well that everybody started sniffling. We were starting to get a sense that the movie we had made actually looked like one thing, i.e. a ghost story, but was actually another thing, i.e. a story about guilt and redemption. This dichotomy was at the heart of the problems we were going to have as we tried to sell the movie. *'Is it a ghost story? Is it a social realist drama?'* We always said that it was a ghost story in a social realist world and that was it's unique position.

Gen - So the distributors watched it, all smiled and passed on it because they didn't know what box to put it in. In the absence of any good reviews or press they also didn't know whether people would take to it or not. Only one company was interested, Stranger Than Fiction, who were already acting as our sales agents for *White Angel*. We were very excited because they were about to sign a deal where they were going to have an influx of cash, which meant that they would have a high profile at Cannes and our movie would be their number one product.

Chris - We had run out of cash and the labouratory processing bill meant that we owed the lab about twenty grand. We were eager to get sales so we signed with Stranger Than Fiction and they began putting together all the bits. A design agency put together a poster, which was not what either of us had imagined, yet it seemed really fresh and original and we liked it a lot. So we went with it. It was bold red and very eye catching, which meant that when we fly posted in Cannes, it really stood out. The poster definitely worked for the movie and it also conveyed a sense that there was perhaps more to this than just a simple spooky tale.

Gen - We'd already cut a trailer for *UGS* which we liked, but Stranger Than Fiction asked for another one, and this time they said *'make it look like Die Hard with ghosts'*. So Eddie, who is already energetic to start off with, was caffeined up and locked in a cutting room for a day only to emerge eight hours later, eyes bloodshot and hair crazy, explaining *'it's done'*. We watched it and somehow Eddie *had* made it look like *'Die Hard with ghosts!'* It wasn't exactly a fair representation of the film but it was big and ballsy.

Q - What happened when you took UGS to Cannes?

Chris - We wanted a big push at Cannes so decided to take a few friends down with us, all of whom had worked on the film. All in, there were six of us and we were determined to make sure that everybody in Cannes had heard of *UGS*. Every morning we would go up and down La Croisette and fly post anything that didn't move - cars, telephone boxes, railings, Hollywood movie posters. Within a few hours they'd all have been taken down because it's illegal, so in the afternoon we went and fly posted again. The posters were just the red coloured image that we had decided on for the film and its simplicity and boldness really worked in our favour. After a couple of days everyone we bumped into would say, *'Oh yeah I've heard of that film Urban Ghost Story'*. It was very labour intensive and damned hot but worth it.

Gen - We had three screenings which we tried to pack - the first was hard, but the second and third were full and the buzz on the street was that UGS was a cool movie. We approached every company and gave them an invite to come to the screening. It's really hard work knocking on so many doors, sensing rejection, but it has to be done.

Q - Did you pitch new projects when you were there?

Chris - One of the fun things we decided to do was to see how far we could get by talking the talk. Myself and fellow filmmaker Simon Cox decided to give it a try. We went to the Noga Hilton Hotel, targeted the companies who make and sell American style B movies, swaggered in, pitched, told them that we had half of the $2m budget already in place. Of course we didn't but it was really an exercise to see how far you could get with bullshit. Within an hour, we had an Anglo-Canadian co-production for a science fiction thriller that we hadn't even written, budgeted at $2.2m, to be shot in Wales and post produced in Canada. Clearly we couldn't pursue this because we didn't have the $1m that we claimed we had, neither the screenplay or even the desire to make it! But it did show how quickly you can put something together if you have something that you want to do and a bit of cash. We also dropped in on Troma, who had their new movie, *Killer Condom.* Over dinner that night we came up with a concept for a new movie for them and the following day went and pitched it. It was called *The Breath of Death the Killer Fart.* We'd already constructed a story that held water. The guys at Troma got excited and again we talked the talk, but really didn't want to make an end of the world movie about an evil doctor and his Killer Fart potion!

Gen - One major distinction from our previous Cannes visits is that because we had a film that was screening, we were perceived as credible filmmakers. We were invited to parties and dinner and got to hob nob with fairly important people on a more level playing field than we'd ever experienced before. One of the reasons we also got a lot of coverage was because Jason Connery also came down to Cannes and worked very hard with us to get as much good press and exposure as possible. It's really important to have positive and constructive support from your cast as they represent the glitz that Cannes is really all about.

Q - Did you sell the film?

Chris - Yes, one far eastern company from a small territory came to look at the trailer that Eddie had cut, the one that makes it look like *Die Hard.* They got very excited and bought the film on the spot. A couple of months later we

(above) Concept paintings by Alex Fort for the Werewolf movie.

(over page) a six inch maquette sculpted by Phil Mathews all helped illustrate what Gen wanted to achieve with the werewolf movie.

(right) Another Hollywood project that appeared was The Crow Part 4. *Chris and Gen met with Ed Pressman for* The Crow *franchise and pitched a concept about a blind samurai nun. They liked it a lot, suggested some changes, but like so many projects, they passed as they didn't see a female Crow as viable.*

discovered that they were going to do a 15 print theatrical release and we were opening against *Armageddon!* It was *Urban Ghost Story* vs. *Armageddon!* I started to wonder whether the guy had actually seen the film. A week later I discovered that he hadn't and when he finally watched it he had a bit of a panic attack because it wasn't the horror movie he thought it was, and that even worse, *'it wasn't even in English but in Scottish!'* The next contact I had was when he asked me if I wanted to buy back 15 prints as he was unable to open the film.

Q - Did you premiere the film at a film festival?

Gen - We chose Edinburgh as our World Premiere because UGS is a Scottish movie, the people at the festival liked the movie, Jason lived quite close and the timing was right. We wanted to make a big impact and from the outset wanted to promote ourselves as filmmakers as well as the movie. We wanted the whole world to hear about *Living Spirit Pictures, Urban Ghost Story, Chris Jones* and *Genevieve Jolliffe.* We hired a publicist who cost us a couple of grand but in terms of what we got it was well worth spending as we had full pages in daily newspapers, excellent write ups in magazines and plenty of TV. Because of the work load in the office, Chris decided to stay behind in London for the first couple of days while I went ahead to do the press. As soon as I stepped off the plane it was interview after interview and before either of us knew it, the story ceased to be about *'Chris, Gen, Living Spirit* and *Urban Ghost Story'* and became *'hot new attractive female young film director makes startling debut film.'*

Chris - Suddenly Gen was everywhere in the press and I was mentioned in the fine print, if at all. It was the first time that either of us realised just how the world views the filmmakers, the producer is ignored and the director is given all the credit. Everybody thinks that the director is the only person who made the film. Whether they've heard of the auteur theory or not, they believe it. Sure the actors acted in it, but the producer, writer, editor, cameraman etc - were all pawns in the director's grand view. It's sad because there is so much creative talent involved and yet only one person is recognised.

Q - How did the screenings go?

Chris - We had a great response and Q&A session afterward. But then something else happened which neither of us were prepared for. As we were being whisked away from the theatre my cell phone rang. It was an agent who had seen the film and wanted to meet up with Gen. Then the phone rang again and it was another agent again wanting to meet with Gen. On the one hand it was exciting because this was a fantastic opportunity and at last we were being taken seriously by the business, but on the other hand, it was a real downer as clearly they were only interested in the *'hot new attractive female young film director who made a startling debut film'.* The positive press had really worked for Gen, but not for me. Whenever an agent would even consider me in the equation, they'd take a look at *The Runner* and *White Angel,* then say *'well they're not as good as UGS, clearly Gen is the one with the talent'.* Of course they aren't as good, we didn't know then what we do know now and the next film we make will be better than UGS! It's common sense. But they and the industry in general, just kept on coming back saying well we don't care what you tell us about collabouration, Genevieve is *'the hot new young attractive female film director who made a startling debut film'.*

Gen - It was difficult because we are both filmmakers and had hoped that one day we would get agents and a chance to move into the bigger playground. Here was this opportunity for me, but it was quite clearly for me alone. It caused a lot of friction between us.

Q - So did you sign with an agent?

Chris - After meeting several agents, Gen met up with one back in London and they got on like a house on fire. She really understood what Gen wanted to do with her career and seemed like she could open doors in Hollywood. Within days, and out of the blue, a FedEx landed on Gen's desk. It was a big studio werewolf movie budgeted at $15m, and they were looking for a hot shot new director. They'd seen *UGS* in Hollywood as we had a print out there. We can only surmise why they liked it, but it's probably because it felt like a unique slant on a ghost story. So Gen read the script and got back to them and before anyone knew it she was on a plane to LA being given the red carpet treatment.

Every film will have it's premiere. Make the most of it as it will probably be one of the best nights of your life.

Gen - We put together some concept sketches and asked Phil Mathews, an old effects buddy from *White Angel,* to mock up a werewolf model. Armed with this I marched into the office of the studio head and did the talk. The moment I landed and had my first meeting in LA, I started to get calls from all the other studios wanting to meet me. Hollywood seems to be constantly in search of new talent. The project still hasn't been made, with either myself or another director, and may never happen. I think this is part of the way of Hollywood movies, so many films seem to so nearly happen but falter before the final hurdle. This has happened several times with other projects too. It's really frustrating because I put all my personal projects on pause while I threw everything at these movies and at the end of the day you just have no control over your own destiny. It was also difficult because the opportunities were clearly for me and whenever I tried to bring Chris in, it just seemed to weaken my position.

Chris - When Gen got back from LA we had to have a heart to heart and accept that she was going to go first and that wherever possible I would be standing right behind her on her coat tails. I had to accept that that was the way the business works and because Gen and myself had gone through so much over the last few movies I knew that come hell or high water I could trust her. If you're in a film partnership with another person, I can't stress how important it is that you have a very frank and open minded discussion about what will happen if one of you suddenly gets an unbelievable opportunity, but that opportunity excludes the other. Gen and I had many unpleasant arguments which really boiled down to my frustration at the fact that other people were marginalising me as a filmmaker. It was out of Gen's hands and I just had to come to terms with the fact that we're a partnership and that if she's going to get an amazing opportunity then hopefully I will be there for the next amazing opportunity. No matter how we looked at it we just couldn't turn away from Hollywood over the question of who gets the glory and who gets to go first.

Gen - A few months later we went to LA to present ourselves as more of a team and pitch our personal projects.

Chris - This was amazing because we'd spent so long complaining that we were ignored by the film industry, and there we were sitting in DreamWorks pitching. It became clear that the only thing stopping us from making a movie was the fact that we didn't have a fabulous screenplay that was ready to go.

Q - Did you meet Steven Spielberg when you were at DreamWorks?

Chris - Yes. We had a wonderful chat.

Gen - You said *Hi* and he said *Hi* back!

Q - So is it that easy to get to meet people in LA?

Gen - Yes and no. If you've made an interesting first film you can take advantage of their perception that you might be the next Tarantino or *Blair Witch.* Ideally this is the point at which they will say *'so what have you got next?'* And you'll put that

120 page script on their desk. They'll have seen the film because they have their own 35mm screening rooms and they'll say *'we can see from your film that you have talent but this film is too small for us, what have you got next?'*

Chris and Gen in the Hollywood Hills prior to their meeting at DreamWorks.

Q - So you are starting to meet more important people who could help your career in LA?

Chris - Yes, since we've started to schmooze with more important filmmakers we've found ourselves in a strange new world. Once we were taken out for dinner to the poshest restaurant that I'd ever been in. I needed to go to the bathroom so I excused myself and went to the gents - as I walked in I was hit by opulence, the bathroom was polished marble. While peeing I looked at the urinal and said to myself, *'this has got to be the nicest urinal that I've ever peed in, there's all this water sprinkling down, it's made of marble and oh look there's even coins in the bottom'*. I look over my shoulder to see a row of normal urinals and realised with horror that I was pissing in an ornate fountain!

Q - How about people in the UK film industry?

Gen - Before I knew it, I was sitting at a table next to Nik Powell at the First Annual British Independent Film Awards for which I'm nominated as Best Director and Chris is nominated as Best Producer. We're up against films like *Elizabeth, Nil by Mouth,* and *My Name Is Joe*. We had no expectations and we didn't win, but it was another indicator as to how slowly and surely we were working our way into the British Film Industry. The deep irony here is that just as we're breaking into the British film industry both of us can't help thinking about Hollywood.

Q - Did you take UGS around the festival circuit?

Gen - Because *UGS* is an original film it started to get invited to heaps of festivals. Being a hard up filmmaker, when you get offered an all expenses trip to somewhere like Korea or Australia it's hard to turn it down, especially if you love travelling. I spent a good part of eighteen months in airport lounges, sat at dinner tables with important dignitaries, many of whom I don't even know how to pronounce their names. This all sounds great but the problem is that I haven't spent the time I should have spent on writing my next screenplay and whenever anybody says *I've just seen Urban Ghost Story, what's next?* I had to fall back on *'I'm writing and I'll let you have a copy when it's completed'*. I would have been in such a good position if I could just drop that screenplay on their desk, there and then.

Chris - It became a running joke. Whenever Gen went to a festival she'd spend the week before pontificating about how much great work she'd do on her screenplay while abroad in those foreign exotic lands, writing on her laptop and generally living the lifestyle of an ex pat creative.

Gen - Of course when you're on the plane you're asleep and when you're in an exotic place you want to go out and sample exotic food and drinks, see the world and meet the people. The last thing you want to do with your five days is work hard on that screenplay.

Q - Do distributors see the film at festivals?

Gen - Yes and there's no reason why, if you're so motivated, you couldn't cut some kind of deal. If you want to do this though, you really need to think about contacting all the distributors before the festival, sending them flyers and press packs, even a DVD trailer, then when you get to the festival you'll need to do fly posting, a lot of press and make sure that you have both NTSC and PAL tapes and DVD's for distributors who missed the screening. Don't leave this to your sales agent or it might not get done. You'll also meet other filmmakers and possible future work partners.

Q - Is it hard to keep going?

Chris - Fitting everything in is a real problem because amongst developing your new projects, dealing with sales and distribution, going to film festivals etc., you have to do things like answer the phone, do accounts and empty the waste paper basket, never mind have a life! Making a film generates an enormous amount of stuff to deal with and you shouldn't underestimate how much hassle that is. If you can find someone you can trust, delegate as much as you can, because the window of opportunity after you've finished your film can be short and you mustn't be tied down by the hum drum day to day of running a business. You need to be out there pitching and selling yourself as aggressively as possible.

Gen - This problem is exacerbated by the fact that you'll probably be broke and not able to pay an accountant to do your books, and then you have to do stuff like meet with the bank manager because you need a loan. All of this crap is labour intensive, stressful and generally counter-creative.

Q - How has UGS done?

Chris - It took us a while to secure a UK theatrical deal. At UGS's first Cannes market, Germany bought the film and a few other much smaller territories were snapped up too. Unfortunately our sales agent Stranger Than Fiction was not supplying us with the financial information that we needed so we were finding it very difficult to keep tabs on how well or how badly the film was doing. We had calculated that they owed us over £30k and it was becoming very frustrating because STF were not making contact with us - no return of phone calls and no response to faxes.

The sales agent/distributor dynamic with new filmmakers always seems to be fraught with discontent. Every low budget or new filmmaker we have met has complained about their sales agent and distributor. I think it's fair to say that selling a low budget film is very difficult and that unless you make something fiercely original or blisteringly good it's unlikely that your project will financially succeed. Even if you have made such a good, film there is still a very good chance that it will fail.

Eighteen months after the first sales, we finally got a meeting with Grace Carley who had by then left STF. I think she felt bad about what had happened, and I know there was some serious mismanagement that was out of Grace's hands. No one seemed to know what had happened with our film. No one would produce accounts or contracts and we eventually just had to sever ties. STF did legally give us the film back and we received a few thousand pounds from them. The problem is if you don't know which countries they sell your film to, what are you going to do? There was no one left to take legal action against and so we cut our losses.

Gen - We then made a deal with Lise Romanoff of Vision Films in California to handle all our world sales. She actually sends us checks. Admittedly not big ones as STF seemed to have done so much damage previously. She also sends us a report via FedEx ever 12 weeks detailing deals, the balance and a check if there is one due! So we now seem to have a reputable sales agent representing the film.

Chris - One thing new filmmakers tend to get very upset about is making sure that they have everything contractually tied up. It's just worth stressing that even if you have a strong contract, if somebody wants to breach that contract, or is forced to breach that contract by their own circumstances, they can and may well do so. A simple example of this is with our sales agents STF who, even though they were contractually obliged to supply us with information, simply didn't.

Gen - Again, it's a common story that the filmmaker ends up in some kind of dispute with the sales agent or distributor. It's very sad when you consider that every other person in the filmmaking process, from the camera rental companies to the

actors, the caterers to the dubbing mixers, have all bent over backwards with their generosity to help you make your film only for it to end up not getting the exposure it deserves because there are so few sales agents and distributors to go to in order to sell your film. It really does beg the question why not sell the film yourself?

Q - What have you learned from UGS?

Gen - When opportunity knocks you've got to be ready, you mustn't be distracted. If you're in a filmmaking team be prepared to face an imbalance of reward and remember the producer doesn't get the attention. If Hollywood is interested, have your next project ready. Don't have too much fun travelling the world with festivals. Get on to your next screenplay and your next movie. We've both learned that you need certain things, talent not being at the top of the list, but energy and enthusiasm being of paramount importance, original ideas and the ability to tell familiar stories in a different way, but probably the most important factor is your ability to get on with people and nurture your contacts. One strange thing is that you've probably spent years being ignored by the industry, then suddenly you're considered for twenty fully funded films where you'll earn more in ten weeks than you have in the last ten years. It's a quandary. Do you accept the first one that comes along or wait for the right one? It's difficult when you've been struggling for so long. Also you can't wait too long as people will lose interest in you.

Chris - One important thing is that UGS was a film that we wanted to make, not for a market, but for selfish personal reasons. Thereby it's unique and interesting, and that's what seems to get people excited. They don't want this movie, but they do want you to make one for them. We were also very lucky as we found Dave, our Executive Producer, who was the only person with the vision and belief and the ability to equip us so that we could make the movie. Without Dave we might still be on the phone and sending scripts out.

Gen - It's been echoed by other filmmakers that we've interviewed in this book, but if there's one thing you should do, it's MAKE THE MOVIE YOU WANT TO MAKE! Sometimes I wonder if making films is actually a curse. The strange thing and this is something that some people just don't understand, is that we just have to make movies. I've often thought of what it would be like to have a more normal job with a regular pay cheque, especially when I had those days of running out of coins for my electricity meter and water leaking through my living room ceiling into my cold downtrodden London flat. But whenever I lost the faith, I'd go to the movies and the magic that happens on the silver screen is like a drug, I'm elated and addicted all over again.

Chris - Filmmaking isn't taught, it's caught! If filmmaking was a sport, it wouldn't be football, swimming or the hundred metre dash, it would be a marathon. More than anything, I've learned that going the distance is the most important thing. Some of your friends and peers will be able to run the marathon as though it's a hundred meter dash, the very lucky ones get helicoptered to the finishing line, many of your friends will fall by the wayside exhausted and disillusioned, but if you've got the stamina you'll make it to the finish and anyone who makes it to the finish, is a winner.

Q - How did the film finally do with UK sales?

Chris - You would think that we should have had our quota of bad luck wouldn't you. We made a deal with a company called Visual Entertainment, for a UK theatric and Video/DVD release. They gave us the whole spiel, how they were going to do amazing things blah, blah, blah! We went to their offices, large and plush, and they had some other good titles and we felt confident they were the ones for us. A date was set for the theatrical release and a plan made. We would release on two prints only and move them around the country. We would target specifically the theatres we wanted and work hard at getting great, localised PR. We had an excellent publicist who got us tons of coverage and reviews, most of which were glowing. I don't think we even got a single bad review. We opened extremely well in central London, and had a packed weekend. We also did well in Glasgow too. We were held over for a second week in both cities. One thing that worried me though was that I was doing everything for the release and the guys at Visual were doing very little. Every time I made a request they gave me an excuse. I was concerned that the poster was not strong enough, but they refused to do a new one for instance. And they asked me to handle all press too.

A week into the release, they told me they were so happy, they wanted to rush the DVD out. That seemed odd but I let it go. We made a great DVD with tons of extras and really cool documentaries, and we put a lot of effort into it. But all the time, Visual were screaming to move the release date forward! I was starting to smell a rat. The DVD was released and five days later I found out that they had gone bust, taking our money with them.

Gen - There we were again, having done everything, only to find the distributor going under and leaving us with nothing.

Chris - What was most upsetting was the fact that one person at this company had really seduced us, been our friend, and when the shit hit the fan, didn't even bother to call to tell us. In time I have dug around and discovered that there is an elusive character behind this company and many other failed video distribution companies. I can't name names for legal reasons, but he is as elusive as Keyser Soze!

Gen - A new company came to our rescue, ILC. Time will tell how we get on with them. We got the TV rights back and immediately cut a deal with David Wilkinson at Guerilla Films, who then made a great deal with the Universal Channel here in the UK. Then, believe it or not, before we got fully paid, the Universal Channel went under! Universal!

Chris - David, being the excellent distributor that he is, managed to control the damage though, and cut a new deal with the Sci-Fi Channel and ultimately we got back pretty much all our losses.

Gen - No matter what we seem to do, the awful truth is that whatever we got upfront is all we ever seemed to get. Due to this, you do ask yourself, why not self distribute? At least then, you're the one in charge. There's a lot to learn when you self release a film, and that can be a benefit of doing it, IF you have the time to devote to it and the incentive.

Chris - I guess that we all want to make films and not necessarily distribute. It's much more fun working with actors and cameras, dreaming up ideas and sitting in a cutting room etc., than it is shipping DVDs or arranging for trailers to screen in a theatre three weeks before the film opens, or keeping inventory of your VHS stock. We want other people to do those jobs. The problem, it seems to me, is that bar a few honest small distributors such as David Wilkinson at Guerilla Films, you just can't trust anyone. David is now releasing both *White Angel* and *Urban Ghost Story* on DVD for us in the UK.

Q - Did UGS see a release in the US?

Gen - The film was picked up by a New York distributor, Panorama Entertainment, who wanted to start with a small theatrical release and then hopefully move to more screens around the country. Panorama wanted to focus on getting the film out to US film festivals, so we could drum up the publicity and then through that we'd get interest from the theatres. Not being in the US at the time and the fact that it would be very difficult to handle the campaign from London, we decided to follow their strategy.

In our contract with Panorama, we had a clause that the film would be released in three of the top one hundred markets. We thought that this would be fine and we all hoped that this would certainly be beginning with either New York or LA - both, however extremely tough markets to open in. The film was released in Monterey (supposedly a very independent market), Savannah (we had played in the film festival there) and somewhere in Louisville, Kentucky. With the first release in Monterey, I was told that there was a publicist on the case, but when I flew out to California a week before the release, I discovered that no publicity had been done for the film and in fact it was opening that Friday and nobody had been contacted. I immediately flew up to Monterey and started trying to get interviews all over the place, trying to persuade the press to put it in the next day's paper - anything to try and publicise the film so people might know something about this movie rather than just seeing the title up in lights. But, it was too late. The limited press that there is in Monterey did do several articles, but they came out several days after the release, and of course the figures on the first night and the consequent two nights are vital to whether a film is pulled or not. We were pulled. With Savannah, we received more press as reviewers had seen the movie at the Savannah Film Festival. We had positive reviews, but we had very little in the way of paid print or radio advertising and the film was pulled. In Louisville, I found out that the film had screened before I could get there, so it was gone before I had a chance to do anything. The theatrical release was very disappointing.

Chris - Panorama told us that they were having difficulty with the film because, as it was Scottish, it was deemed to be a 'foreign film' and therefore exhibitors were not interested. Both Gen and I were burnt out with dealing with the US release and combined with what we were still experiencing in the UK, we could not handle the thought of fighting for a better or longer American release. A mistake maybe, but very difficult to deal with constantly when you're in a country miles away.

Gen - I was also in the process of moving to the US and that in itself was eating up much of my time. There soon came a 'shouting match' between Panorama, ourselves and our investors as we tried to do the best for the film. People wouldn't talk to each other, it was kind of ridiculous as though we were back in nursery school. Panorama then told us that the 'right' deal had come along, one that offered the same type of benefits as the other company. We thought it sensible for the movie and for our investors to continue on the path we had started out on. The deal took several months to get into place and finally we nailed it down. April 27th 2004 *Urban Ghost Story* saw its US DVD release. Finally it's out there!

Chris - And a year and a half later, we finally got some money in from the DVD release! We both fell off our chairs we were that surprised! It's actually done pretty well but with fees being taken off for advertising/marketing etc. and then commissions, it's not a huge amount, but the point is, we actually got a cheque!

Q - So what is next?

Gen - I've been out in LA for a while now and I love it. When I first came over I got a big US agent on board, ICM, from whom I hoped to get work. However, after a year and only a few meetings, I was incredibly frustrated. I was a small fish in a big pond and the larger clients took precedence over me. However my agent did come up with a good solution. She introduced me to a manager who had fewer clients but a fair amount of clout. He would handle my day-to-day meetings and pretty soon he got a production company to pick up one of my pitches. That was my first experience of doing a pitch to the studios. We spent a long time refining a very precise 20 minute pitch to go out on the town. It was great fun to do in terms of meeting people and letting people know that you're out there, but was again frustrating when you realise that you really do need to have more credits behind you to get anyone to buy straight off a pitch. The same response came back each time - "I love it! So when can we read the screenplay?" So I had to make a decision…is this the one to start writing? However, there was something to consider on this…the movie pitch was a horror that went back to the '70s way of thinking - it didn't pull any punches and had a shocking ending. An ending that seemed too much for the studios sensibility at this time. So, do I start writing this screenplay knowing that it might be difficult to sell to the studios? Or do I focus on something new that would not have as many problems? Wanting to persevere in the studio system, I opted for something new.

I've always had an idea to do a vampire movie with American cheerleaders because, well, they are kinda like vampires. I wrote it with my now husband, who was my boyfriend at the time, and we had it done within three months! Then I had a falling out with my agent and we parted ways. But my manager hooked me up with a new agent, who when I met, I knew in my gut that he was the best person to represent me - and the two of them took the script out onto the spec market. My agent and manager split the town up into certain territories, meaning studios and funding bodies. All the producers we sent it to, loved it and took it to their territories but unfortunately they passed, mainly because it was a mixture of horror and comedy and they were confused on how to market it. But fortunately, one producer wanted to work on it with us and after doing a bunch of rewrites, a table read and getting some actresses attached, Warner Bros. optioned it. They wanted an experienced writer to come onboard to polish it up and fortunately the person who we thought would be the only person in the world that we would want to rewrite our movie, got the gig! As the director I got to oversee the rewrite which was a blast, a huge learning experience and an honour AND I made a great friend in the process! Now we are waiting for Warner Bros. to give it the greeenlight. Many scripts get picked up by the studios but will they actually make the movie? It's always hurdle after hurdle…and as you continue to work on giving the film life, it can drive you mad waiting. So, we moved onto writing the next one. If only we had a stack of scripts already written, it would make things soooo much easier!

Q - How was your experience with Warner Bros.?

Gen - Fantastic! I'm lucky to have a great producer behind me who's persistent and in love with the project. Not only that, we have a great executive at the studio who got the movie from the get go. Many filmmakers worry about the film being taken out of their hands by a studio and having no control, but my experience has been the contrary.

Q - How different is the LA world from the UK?

Gen - There are two main differences. First, in the UK, if you make one type of genre movie, that doesn't necessarily pigeon hole you into making that kind of movie. In LA, they like you to stay within a certain genre because they know what they're getting for their money. The only way you can move from genre to genre is to either have a lot of power or make one of your films be a combination of genres (which can be difficult to sell) and move to the other genre script after that. I found this out when I tried to get a romantic comedy script going, but I kept hearing 'aren't you a horror director?' So, I started coming up with more horror ideas, which I'm a great fan of anyhow, and all of a sudden more doors started to open. I suppose there is one other way to get out of a certain genre and that would be to make a movie independently again, but then again once you go for a studio picture, they'd probably pigeon hole you into that genre! The second major difference is that in the UK I struggled hard against a 'can't do' attitude, whereas in the States, everyone wants to make a movie and everyone says, "I love it!" Even if it's a bunch of bullshit, it's at least easier to get out of bed every day when you are talking to people with a positive attitude.

Q - What advice would you give new filmmakers out there?

Gen - Make sure you have the ideas coming, one after the other! You need to be constantly pushing product out onto the marketplace and not to get tied up trying to set up one particular project that is proving difficult. You never know which one is gonna hit or is right for that moment. Also for those out there about to embark on your first studio meeting - remember to be prepared, be passionate and know your vision inside out. Producers and studio execs see that passion and feed off it. Also take as many meetings as you can - get to know people and build up your relationships with them so that they soon know your name inside out. And lastly, don't expect to be an Oscar winning filmmaker over night. It will most likely take a lot of time and for numerous reasons but remember it's those reasons that will make you ultimately a better filmmaker. Just remember to keep the passion and the determination and you will succeed.

Chris - What I have learned is that now, after three features, it just isn't worth going through the hell of making another film unless the screenplay is great. That's not true for everyone. I think a new filmmaker with little experience should throw caution to the wind and just go do it, in a smart a way as possible of course, but make the movie now. How else can you learn? Very recently my father died, and I became acutely aware of how short life is. So get on with it, and that's for both you and me.

Neil Marshall
'Writer and Director'

DOG SOLDIERS

Q - How did you start film-making?

Neil - I walked out of *Raiders of the Lost Ark*, when I was 11, and decided I wanted to make films for a living. It was a combination of seeing that at the cinema, and later watching *The Making of Raiders* on TV. Off the back of that, my best mate and I got hold of his mum's Super 8 camera. It was the classic story that we just started making these crazy *Raiders* homages and ludicrous Super 8 films and sticking them together with tape. We were always trying to figure out how to do special effects, like gun shots for example, we would get a microscope out and scratch onto the surface of the film to create a muzzle flash.

Q - Many people had similar experiences, in terms of making films on Super 8, and then putting it in front of friends and relatives. What advice would you give to somebody who is at that stage of film-making, where they think they kind of like the idea of being a film maker, but they are stuck with a camcorder. What can you learn about film and story telling with those home tools?

Neil - We learnt everything really. You learn how to structure a film, how to shoot stuff, then start piecing it together in some kind of order. You learn how to go back and then shoot it in a different way next time. You learn about framing, and what you should try to frame out, or frame in. I think the most important thing that I learnt was editing. It's all very well going out there and shooting stuff, but you must be able to put it into some kind of coherent order. It was difficult to do that with Super 8, but I think nowadays it's easier and more flexible with a digital camera - it can teach you the nuts and bolts of film-making, and if you can't learn that from a camcorder, then you are not going to learn anything.

Q - Let's zoom forward 15 years, there you are on the set of 'Dog Soldiers'. . . Do you still feel like that Super 8 film-maker?

Neil - Well yes, to a degree, because I ended up editing 'Dog Soldiers' myself. I'd spent 8 years prior to that as a freelance editor and I think it's the best training that I could have got for going onto a feature set, because I'd worked with and watched so many other directors. While shooting 'Dog Soldiers', I was editing in my mind, and so I could walk onto the set and say *'I want that shot, that shot and that shot'*, and someone else would say and *'what about this shot?'*, and I'd say *'I don't need it! I've got the sequence, that's it, let's move on.'* It also applies to the storyboard as well, and before that, even the script as I will visualise and edit in my head while writing.

Q - Did you go to Film School?

Neil - I went to Newcastle Polytechnic to do a Media Production course and graduated in '92. The most important thing I learnt was self reliance. It's up to you to use your own initiative. The course was angled towards making artistic statements and I wanted to make this 20 minute zombie film, and they weren't having any of it. I ended up having to do 'guerilla style', where I handed in a fake script to the tutors and they approved that, and then I went off and filmed an entirely different film. When it was all done, one of the tutors stood up and championed my attitude towards the whole thing. But there were a lot of frowns and all this *'you shouldn't be doing this kind of stuff'*. I heard that they changed the rules of the course the following year to prevent anybody from doing the same sort of thing again. So I apologise to that year...

Q - But they will find their way I guess...

Neil - Exactly. You will always find a way, so it was a great experience, and I came out with a 20 minute film which got me work.

Q - How did 'Dog Soldiers' come about? Did you doubt its ambition or how it would be received by the British film industry?

Neil - I can honestly say that I never had a single doubt going into it, and I had sheer, brut, stubborn determination to get through it. I think the fact that a lot of the British Film Industry was dead set against it at the time just made me more determined to pull it off. Especially when the attitude was it's too ambitious, nobody wants to see horror movies! Now, of course they are like *'Oooh give me Horror!'* The genesis of it goes back to 1995, when I wrote and edited a low budget deferral film in Newcastle, called *'Killing Time'*, and that was kind of a disaster from start to finish. It was a nightmare shoot for 4 weeks, nobody got paid, but it was a fantastic learning experience. The production manager on that was a friend of mine from college, a guy called Keith Bell, and we basically sat round the set and said *'OK, we can do this better, and we can do it where everybody gets paid!'* I came up with the idea of *'Dog Soldiers'* and I just started writing it, and 5 years down the line, the money came together. Throughout that period, we were re-writing the script, taking it to every source of finance in the UK, who came back saying *'Not our cup of tea', 'Too ambitious, too many special effects for a 1st time director'* etc. That just strengthened our resolve to get it done.

Q - How many script revisions did you go through?

Neil - I think the draft that we shot of *'Dog Soldiers'* was something like the 16th draft, but the redrafts were not major over-hauls. If we had filmed the 1st draft it would have been shit! I don't go round quoting Robert McKee much, but I would say that one of his rules of script-writing is absolutely true - *'thou shalt re-write!'* Re-writing is the key, always re-look at your work again and again and again and again. You will always think of something better, or you will think of something that could be changed to improve it.

Q - What was the budget?

Neil - The budget was £2.3m. That came together by chance more than anything, the story has achieved some sort of legendary status about the Arkansas Spinach millionaire who bailed us out at the last minute. We had looked everywhere - we were going to go to the Isle of Man and do it there, and then that fell through, we were going to go to Canada, and we were like 2 weeks away from getting on the plane, then that fell through because they were making another werewolf film, which turned out to be *'Ginger Snaps'*. So we looked right across the world, then finally the script and a big drawing of the werewolf were taken to the AFM in Los Angeles, the film market out there, where we met an Arkansas Spinach millionaire, a guy called David Allen, whose dad had made the family fortune in the '50's by canning spinach and putting *'Pop-eye'* on the label. It made them millions and his son inherited the money and he wanted to invest in feature films. He was a big horror film fan, and he had always wanted to do a werewolf movie, and then we came along, and he saw the picture, grabbed the script and that was that. He came on board with money out of his own pocket. I think he put up about $2.5 million of the total budget.

Q - It's interesting you mention about your Arkansas millionaire, because one of the questions I always get is 'How do you find these people?', and my answer is, you don't find them, they find you. You have got to be out there doing it, like it's going to happen, and they are magnetically attracted to you.

Neil - That was very much the case, we found the location Luxembourg and we found pre-sales, but the main source of the money, that got the ball rolling on this film, found us. It was kind of a mini-miracle.

Q - How did you get a sales agent?

Neil - It was in the wake of the shoot of *'Killing Time'*. We had finished on the Saturday night, and on the Sunday morning, I went straight into the edit suite and I cut a 30-second trailer, which was to go off to MIFED in Milan on the Monday. Victor Films was the sales agent on this and sold the film to Colombia Tristar on the basis of that trailer. So when it came to *Dog Soldiers* we thought well, we've got nothing to lose, we might as well take it to them, and they remembered the fact I'd had this trailer, so they knew I could do the business. They came on board *Dog Soldiers* in an unofficial capacity, no contracts were signed, no money exchanged hands, but they agreed to be the sales agent on it. It was them who took it to AFM, getting them on board was a life-saver.

Q - How did you find the integrity of the whole sales experience?

Neil - Dodgy! There's not much you can say about it really, it is what it is, it's the sales end. In the case of *'Dog Soldiers'*, no contracts were signed and no money exchanged hands. It was a leap of faith.

Q - What was it shot on?

Neil - It was shot on Super16. Off the back of *'Lock Stock...'*, which was also shot on Super16, and that allowed us to work very fast and shoot an action film in 6 weeks.

Q - Because of the nature of 'Dog Soldiers', you are in a battle of coverage. You need to be able to shoot and shoot and shoot.

Neil - Absolutely. It would have been nice to do it on 35mm, but the price of processing when getting as much coverage as possible in so short a time would have crippled us. The transfer quality is pretty good, it's a little bit grainy, but it's not terrible, and once you've put it onto DVD, then you'll never notice. It was fine, I had absolutely no problem with Super16. Everything is just so much quicker compared to 35mm.

Q - If you were shooting today would you be considering HiDef?

Neil - No, I'd still do it on Super 16. I'm old fashioned, I like my film. There's definitely a place for HiDef and other films have used it amazingly well.

Q - How did you approach getting that quantity of effects, and pulling off credible werewolves?

Neil - From a very practical point of view. It's something I learnt from Ridley Scott, he says *'if you can do it for real, do it for real.'* I always wanted to put the effects in front of the camera and not do it CGI. We had a reaction against the CGI onslaught, especially with *American Werewolf in Paris*, where they went for CGI werewolves and I don't think it looked particularly good. So, I thought no, let's go back to basics, everybody's on the CGI route, let's go old school, let's go back to animatronics, and see what we can do. At the end of the day, you are giving something for the actors to react to, something to work with. On the level of our film, I just think it works so much better.

Q - Of course with your training in Super 8, and editing, you knew exactly how to shoot what perhaps on set, may have looked dodgy and actors may have been asking, 'are we going to get away with this?'

Neil - This is the thing, at the end of the day, it is a guy in a rubber suit. We shot loads of footage, trying to get the werewolves to look half decent. Sound and editing also helped seal the illusion. We had a lot of gore, and blood and guts and stuff, it was just so much better to do it physically, and we shot the film in chronological order too, so that made our lives a lot easier in terms of those who had their head ripped off, or their arm ripped off at any one time, so it helped with continuity issues.

Q - How important do you think sound is?

Neil - Sound is vital. It's half the picture, so you've gotta get that right. We had fantastic sound recordists. 99% of the sound in the film was what was recorded on set, and we didn't have the money to do loads of ADR.

Q - How did you find working with the actors?

Neil - That was the best experience of the whole film. I hadn't had much experience with actors before, so I was throwing myself in at the deep end, but we had such a great relationship. I knew what I wanted but I didn't know what was possible within those boundaries so they were constantly bringing ideas in, and yeah, some of the ideas that they came up with were shit, and some were great. It's my job to know the difference. It's their job to provide me with this ammunition, and so it's a really good creative collaboration. They were superb to work with and they were supportive of each other. We had highly experienced actors like Liam and Sean and Kev, and we also had people who hadn't done much, but they all looked after each other, and by the end these guys would have fought and died for each other. They became such a solid unit.

Q - Did you have an assembly editor cutting as you were shooting?

Neil - Not really. I thought I was probably going to sleep for 3 days at the end of the shoot, especially as you are coming down from the buzz of the shoot, which I absolutely hate. I came back on the Saturday night and the next morning I was up, and thinking, right what am I going to do, I need to be working on the film still! So I took one day off, and then on the Monday morning I was in the edit suite. I just thought I've got to get on with it, I've got to get busy, I've got to keep the ball rolling.

I got straight in there and just started cutting it together, from the first scene to the last. I think I'd done my first rough cut in 5 weeks, and then the process just slowed down. The American producer wanted to see all the cuts but wasn't in England to do it. So we had to transfer every cut to video, send it to London, then they would transfer it to NTSC and they would send it to the States. This took about a week, and then a week after that we get a huge great e-mail listing problems and changes like *'the sound is poor...'* and we'd have to explain that the sound is not mixed, concentrate on the pictures and story! Then *'Oh it's too dark!'* and we'd say *'It hasn't been graded yet!'* So that just dragged the whole process down, and then finally we get to some kind of agreement on it and we were able to lock the picture.

Q - Do you have any comments about diplomacy? Were your choices always the right choices for the story?

Neil - No, not all the time. It does help to have other people's opinions, especially at that stage, because you are so involved with it, you need to be a little bit objective. It depends on who the opinions are coming from, if it's an opinion that I respect, then yeah, I am more than happy to listen to it.

Q - When you slipped into the final phase of sales and distribution, how was that experience for you?

Neil - It was difficult to hand it over to the sales agent. But when Pathe, the UK Distributor came on board, that was a totally different and wonderful experience. I was involved right through the whole process, I had ideas for the trailer, how the poster should be. I think it's something that film-makers should have, it's pointless just making a film and not having a clue who is going to watch it, or how you are going to sell it. At the end of the day, it is a product for people to pay and go and see. So, I was well aware of the kind of film I was making, what the audience was. I had plenty of ideas, and Pathe were really responsive to that, and they ended up using my idea for the teaser trailers, which was to take the piss out of the army commercials which are in the cinema all the time. It was nice to have input, nice to be invited. They could have just said *'We'll do it, stand back'* but they didn't, they wanted to know our ideas.

Q - Without wanting to blow your own trumpet, how much of the success of the film is down to the fact that the film works very well for it's target audience?

Neil - I think Pathe saw in it what I had hoped to be seen. It was going to be a good Friday night, Saturday night movie, after the pub or a curry. That was the audience it was made for, and I think

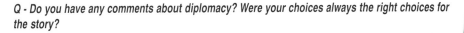
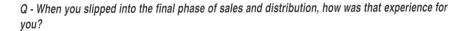
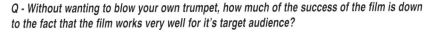

they registered that and thought OK, we'll go down that road. It was very deliberate. I set out to make a very commercial film with a very British sensibility to it. I didn't try and make a mid-Atlantic film, I didn't try and make something to appeal to the American market. Except in the fact that it's got action and gore and stuff like that, but it's also full of colloquial accents, and British humour and British dialogue, which I didn't expect them to get, and I didn't intend them to get. So it wasn't for them, I made it for our audience on a Friday or Saturday night down the multiplex. I thought there's a good audience there, there is an audience there that can turn a profit on a film like this. So, let's make a film for them, they deserve it.

Q - What are the UK figures for 'Dog Soldiers'?

Neil - In the UK *'Dog soldiers'* went out on 320 prints and Pathe spent £1m on P&A. It grossed £2.5m at the Box Office and over £5m on DVD.

Q - How's it done abroad?

Neil - It's done fine and sold theatrically to pretty much every country that it can, with the exception of the States. That's the toughest market to crack, and unfortunately, from what I can gather our American Producer was handling US sales, and he wanted a quick return on his investment so took the first deal that came along, which was Blockbuster video and the Sci-Fi Channel. It's done okay in the US despite not getting a theatrical release. It has a very strong following on the Internet. There are also some daft statistics, such as it's the second most popular British film in Russia, even. The alarming thing is that the most popular is *Notting Hill*!

Q - How has the money from the sales flowed back? Considering its domestic and global success, I have to ask, are you rich yet?

Neil - No, I haven't seen a penny in terms of profits. Both myself and co-producer Keith Bell deferred £10k of our fees until it broke even. Well, it's three years on now, and for it's success around the world, on video, DVD and TV sales it officially still hasn't broken even. And remember, the budget was only £2.3m. The distributor takes the biggest chunk. what's left over goes first to the investors (which is fair enough) then filters down. Consequently the film production gets very little, if any at all, at the end of it.

Q - Do you have any advice for a new film-maker about that equation, because a lot of new film-makers have the naïve notion that you make a film, you sell it, you get all this money back, you'll be able to pay it off, buy a yacht, retire . . .

Neil - Well, I think if you are in charge of it, if you remain in charge of the sales process, then yeah you might be able to do it that way. But that would only work on a smaller film, and on a smaller film you would get less money for it anyway. On a larger film, I'd say, get whatever you can up front. Get a fee for it and don't rely on profits.

Q - If you had been more involved in sales and distribution, would that have left any space for you to be working on your next film which as we talk now, is only a few weeks from shooting?

Neil - No, but it's not my cup of tea either. I'd rather just get a fee up front and make a film, and do the best job possible.

Q - Have you had any flirtations with Hollywood based on 'Dog Soldiers'?

Neil - Not really because it didn't get a theatrical release over there, so as much as it's got a big following over there now, especially through the DVD and the Internet, it's not taken entirely seriously because it didn't get theatrical. They are well aware of it, but I haven't been offered anything major from it.

Q - How have you found having 'Dog Soldiers' in your creative cache, in terms of making your next film?

Neil - It has helped enormously because it's a known film, even though it wasn't a massive success, it was a good success. It wasn't like *28 Days Later* in terms of Box Office, but everybody's aware of it. Its proved very popular within the festival circuit, which is a massive thing for horror and Sci-Fi, and such like.

Q - What did you learn on 'Dog Soldiers'?

Neil - I learnt to cast well, and to trust in your actors, and to work with them, not work against them, or let them work against you. I learnt the importance of character and humour within a plot. It's so easy to just make some action film where nobody cares about anybody. I've learnt to negotiate with financiers and producers, and maintain my vision, because at the end of the day that's what it's going to be. It's easy for them to put their tuppence worth in, but your name is going to be on it, as writer / director or whatever. So you have to accept some responsibility for that. It's not egotistical, it's to do with the fact that at the end of the day, I'm putting my neck on the line, so I'd rather it be my decision. If it's wrong, then fine, but at least it was my decision.

Q - What advice would you offer a new film-maker?

Neil - Be absolutely determined. For all the ups and downs, over 6 years, whatever it took to get *'Dog Soldiers' made*, there was never a point which I thought, this isn't going to happen. I always knew it was going to happen, it was just a question of when. If I'd known that it was going to be 6 years at the start, I still would have done it, because that 6 years allowed me to develop the script, got it to a better place. At that 6 year point, everything fell into place, we got the money, we got the cast right, we got the script right, and you can't account for that. So all I would say is, be determined, be stubborn, and know where you are going.

Edgar Wright
Writer and Director

SHAUN OF THE DEAD

Q - Where are you from and were you a film lover from a young age?

Ed - I was raised in and around Bournemouth and Poole, and my Mum and Dad took me to the cinema all the time. It was a handy drop-off to get rid of us for the afternoon when they were doing craft fairs and stuff! Some summers, my brother and I would see every single movie on release because it was cheaper to just leave us at the cinema than to hire a babysitter. I don't think I actually got a VCR until I was 16 because my mum and dad couldn't afford one for a very long time, but when I did, I started watching 6 films a day!

Before we actually got a video recorder, if something like *Piranha*, or *The Howling* was on at 3am, we'd stay up and watch the whole thing. From an early age I'd always been obsessed with films and I went through periods as a child and teenager of wanting to do different things. First, I wanted to be Han Solo, then I wanted to be Spiderman, then I wanted to be an actor, then I wanted to be a stuntman, a comic book artist, maybe an animator. I wanted to be an animator or comic book writer or artist until I saw a documentary called *The Incredibly Strange Film Show* by Jonathan Ross, about Sam Raimi and *The Evil Dead*. I've met Jonathan Ross since, and I said to him, *'Do you realise how influential that documentary series was?'* He said *'Oh fuck off, you make me feel so old!'* The truth is, it was a really influential series. I'd heard about *The Evil Dead*, and I'm not sure I'd actually seen it by that point. The documentary made me understand how *The Evil Dead* was made. This was something that wasn't just in the domain of grown-ups.

Q - Did you make any movies while growing up?

Ed - Around that time, my dad bought us a second hand Super 8mm camera. We started off doing Sesame Street-style animation 'stop frame', and moved on to simple live action dramas where we'd shoot the action then dub the entire thing later. That was amazing because it started this run of making films. The first one that I did was five minutes long and it starred all of my school friends. It was all based around that fact that one of my friends could do a really good Rolf Harris impersonation. So we made this film called *'Rolf Harris Saves The World'*. Rolf was like the John McClane character taking on these terrorists. We shot for maybe five days, and it was quite expensive because the Super 8mm reels would be £15 a go. When you used up eight of them, that is quite a lot for a 14 year old and it was all with my own money I'd earned from working at a supermarket. One friend had a 4-track, so I'd go round to his, and we'd do the soundtrack in one day. But that day my friend who could do the Rolf Harris impersonation was ill and couldn't make it, so I had to do it myself and my impersonation wasn't as good as his. It was like 'fuck!' The whole *raison d'être* of this entire film is now just rubbish. Still, the good thing about it was that I showed it at lunch breaks at school. Then we did a sequel, *'Rolf Harris 2: The Bearded One'* and that was half an hour long on Super 8. That took six to nine months to make because of all the trial and error involved. I'd get whole reels back black because I'd exposed it wrongly. I remember vividly having to shoot the same scene three times because I'd fucked up the exposure. I had also figured out that the more people who were in it, the more people would come and see it - all of their friends will come as well!

Also around this time I was quite lucky, I was in the first year of 6th form, and there was a competition on *Comic Relief* about making a film about one of the causes. The prize was a video camera. Now I couldn't afford a video camera, so I made an animation about wheelchair access and I ended up winning the competition! It was really cool because it was like this thing that I had made in my bedroom with plastercine was played on *Comic Relief* on the BBC. So now I had this Video 8 camera, and it was all out then! The films started to balloon in terms of size. One was a western called *A Fistful of Fingers*. One was a superhero film called *Carbolic Soap* and there was a cop one called *Dead Right*. And with each successive one, the cast got bigger and bigger. Not that any of my immediate friends wanted to be actors, but it was just that they were my mates, and it was like *'you can be the Indian, you can play the cop'*. Then it would be like *'hey do you know there is this other guy, who, I know he is a prat, but he's a really good actor, I've seen him!'* I stopped showing them in the lunch hall and moved up to the main hall at the school. That really got me hooked because I was getting the audience's reaction. Not so much from gags, but from gore effects. You do the most hand-made gore effects and just getting people going *'Euurrrggghh!'* It is the best thing.

Q - You had a media course / film school education, how useful was it?

Ed - I went to the Bournemouth Art College, on the audiovisual course, and it was really good to be with like-minded people. In the summer, Bournemouth would be deserted, and because I was not very sporty or a big sun-lover, I would think *'Ok fuck it, I'm just going to lock myself in the edit suite all weekend, and all night if need be!'* I used to make compilations of film clips and stuff just to learn how to edit. I really, really love editing, and editing things to music and stuff. I really got it into my head that *'I want to be like Sam Raimi. I want to make a film when I'm 20, I'm going to do it, I'm going to make my own film'*. So I started shopping around with the stuff that I'd done. I had the idea of re-making *A Fistful of Fingers* on 16mm. I'd come up to London and met a couple of people through the NPA and Raindance which was good in terms of making some contacts.

I sent a draft of the new version to a couple of people, and I even sent it to Jonathan Ross. I was thinking he would realise how many people he has inspired. I got a rejection letter back from his secretary, along with rejections from everyone else. I was even more motivated by this, and thought *'well, we've done all these things on our own, we can just do this, and we just need to find some money to do it on 16mm'*.

Q - So where did the money come from?

Ed - I began work with a producer, Danny Figuero, but the money didn't come from the tiny in-roads into the London film scene that I had made. My mum, back in Somerset, happened to mention to a friend of hers, who was the editor of the local newspaper that I wanted to remake the film. I'd made a kind of corporate film for him before and he'd seen the films that I'd done. He had come into an inheritance so he put up the money, which was £11k. Not a lot of money in film terms, to us it sounded like a lot.

Q - To a non-film person, with a nine to five job, it is a huge amount of money to lose or gamble.

Ed - Yes. It came together really quickly. I realise now, how lucky we were. I literally finished my summer term at film school, wrote a draft of the script, and was then making it in August. It was crazy. It was powered on by its own naiveté and the enthusiasm of the people working on it. It didn't occur to me to cast any young actors in the area, so I just cast all my school friends again! And it turns out that the comedians that I work with now, like Simon Pegg, David Walliams and Matt Lucas, are all of my own age group and lived not too far away. They went to Bristol University and Simon came from Gloucester. It never occurred to me to think *'Oh I wonder if there are any good young actors out there'*, I just thought *'well, we will just use the same people as last time, it will be cool!'*

I pretty much used the same locations as before, and it was very much improvised. The crew was made up of people from my course, with other friends and a couple of people from London. The DP, Alvin Leong, was the first DP I had ever met, and I'd seen one thing that he'd done, and I thought *'great, you've got the job!'*

We had nowhere for anyone to stay, so we had loads of people just kipping on floors, and we shot for 21 days over the summer. During the whole lead up, I kept thinking it was going to collapse at any second. The other thing, which was the biggest shocker of all, was that thing of being slightly in awe of the process. 16mm was a professional format and we had limited stock, big cameras, and we couldn't afford to have dailies. So we did the entire thing with only one day of looking back at what we had done. You had to just go in and shoot and trust the process. It was difficult because before, when shooting on Super 8 or VHS, if we didn't get a shot, we'd say *'Oh we will go back and get that another morning!'* When we had finished shooting, and we started editing, it started to really hit me that I wasn't as happy with the rushes. That wasn't anybody's fault, it is more just my own naiveté. Before when I'd done stuff on video, I hadn't been so worried about continuity of light for instance, and we just got all the shots that we needed, whether it was sunny in one, and cloudy in another - it didn't matter. Now though, we are making a film, so we've got to wait for the sun to go under a cloud. At the end of it, even though it looked better, when I was editing it, I really started to get depressed as I felt like it had lost some of the spark of the original. There is something about re-making something, a comedy especially. On reflection, I kind of prefer the original video version!

Q - Where did you edit it?

Ed - I edited the film with another Bournemouth graduate, Giles Harding, at Pinewood. We didn't have an edit suite at Pinewood, but we did have a broom cupboard. For the first two days of commuting to Pinewood we were thinking, *'wow, Pinewood Studios!'* But then when you had to get three different buses to get there, and in the middle of winter it started getting dark at 4pm, and Giles didn't have a flat at the time, so he was sleeping on the floor, and we had no money, so we were making teas out of increasingly rancid milk - it became less glamorous! At the end of the process, I wanted to shoot more stuff because as we were editing I started to think of better jokes. I started to think *'fuck, he should have said that!'*

Danny had started to get other people to put in money, to essentially pay for the edit, the sound dub and we needed to do a music score. There was a composer/music lecturer at the college, Francois Evans, and he got his music class to perform and record an orchestral score for the movie. The score is probably one of the best things about it!

The assemble edit was 70 minutes long and too short really so my brother did an animated credits sequence, which turned out really nice and added to the running time. We also made a long end titles sequence too, adding to the length, but it was still too short. Then in the middle of the film, there was a campfire scene where at the end of the scene, the lead guy blew the fire out. So I thought *'Uh, I could put a scene there in darkness.'* So I filmed some black and I wrote a bit with just two people talking in the night. The end result was a 78-minute movie, and whenever I look at it, all I want to do is take it into an Avid and start tightening the whole thing up!

Q - What happened with distribution?

Ed - Blue Dolphin, a small distributor, picked it up because they could see that there was a spin on it in terms of it literally being a DIY Western made by teenagers in the country. Rather than make any claims like it being an amazing independent British comedy, it is essentially like a home movie on the big screen. To their credit, that angle got some magazine articles and it got reviewed everywhere - it got good reviews in *Variety* and *Hollywood Reporter*, but Empire gave it 1 star, which I was absolutely mortified about. I was so embarrassed, because I had collected Empire since Issue 1! When critics watched the film I decided to introduce it, and in one review the critic commented *'the young man who introduced the screening did not look old enough to attend the film, let alone direct it!'* It got released at the Prince Charles and got some OK buzz, but I kind of thought that I'd failed.

Around the same time that I'd been writing, I started to get in with some of the comedians coming through, and the first person that I met was Matt Lucas. He completely blew me away as a stand up comedian. I went up to him afterwards and said *'I'm writing a film and I think you would be really good in it and I'd love you to have a look at it'* So we got talking and then I told him that I'd done this other film, and it was on at the Prince Charles, and he said *'I'll go and see it with David Williams'.* They liked it and introduced me to their agent, ICM, who watched the film, read the reviews and signed me up. I then got into TV and started to learn what the fuck I was doing! I remember there was one other director that I knew who had done some independent things and he said to me *'Oh, we are losing you to TV...'* The thing is, I know that if I hadn't started doing TV stuff, I wouldn't have been able to get a second film off the ground.

Q - So it was the success of 'Spaced' that really lead to 'Shaun of the Dead', as opposed to the triumph of making an £11k film?

Ed - Yes. I was one of the youngest TV directors working at 21, and started doing comedy sketch shows. I progressed to bigger things, including shows like *French and Saunders,* where I learned huge amounts. *Spaced* then followed from that.

Q - One of the industry myths is 'This hot new, young filmmaker comes out and creates this amazing movie', but this wasn't your first attempt of making something. You've got maybe 30 or 40 hours of broadcast stuff behind you, and so there wasn't the pressure of immediate genius?

Ed - Totally. Spielberg is probably one of the few people I can think of who hit the ground running and kept on going. I remember thinking this at art college, that there was that pressure of the immediate genius thing, where you have got to do a film by the time you are 26, otherwise that's it! That is just not true though.

Q - How did Shaun of the Dead come about?

Ed - We did two series of *Spaced*, and I was really pleased with how it had come together, how it looked and the performances and the editing. But it left us all completely exhausted. Each series was 7 hours of airtime that took 18 months to make. It was really intensive. I started thinking that if we are going to be spending this much time doing something, why don't we do a film next instead of a third series? Around this time I'd started doing some music videos again. I'd always tried to keep my hand in with that as you could always try out stuff that you can't necessarily do on TV. There are things in *Shaun of the Dead* that I never would have attempted if I hadn't tried them in music videos first, like the long Steadicam shots, and things with choreography. We started writing and we shopped it around, but we figured that FilmFour was the perfect home for it because they had made *Spaced* as well.

It was interesting, after having done single half hours, to then write a feature screenplay again. Obviously approaching it in a much more serious vein than I had done previously, so we actually got quite anal about it. We read all the books on screenwriting, and there was one very good one called *'How Not To Write A Screenplay'* which was looking at it from a script reader's point of view. We watched films that we liked - not necessarily zombie films - but films that we liked structurally, or films that were tonally similar, and then we'd try to pick them apart by using the Syd Field paradigm (in Syd's screenwriting books). Pretty much it would always work, you would watch *The Birds* then draw a diagram and say *'Ok, what was the first plot point?'* We did that for maybe a couple of weeks - watch *American Werewolf In London*, or *Tremors*, or *Back to the Future*, and try and figure it out on the graph. So we started to formulate our own one. We did this big flip chart thing rather than do it on index cards. A page a scene. Not just ideas for what exactly would happen, but bits of dialogue, little doodles and stuff. So we did that whole thing where we worked out the plot by all the notes we had done so far and we were doing it round at each other's flats at first. Then we found that we needed to be in a specific space. So we got a little office on Berwick St., which had nothing except for a table, which was perfect in a way because there were no distractions whatsoever.

Q - How long did Shaun Of The Dead take to write?

Ed - The first draft took about eight or nine weeks. When we were finishing, September 11th happened and there was that feeling that nothing can be funny ever again, especially because we were writing this black comedy about the end of the world. We thought *'our script is fucked, nobody is going to want to see this anymore.'* Then I thought, *'actually no'*, a lot of the stuff that we had written

in the script was the kind of stuff that was born out by what happened in the wake of 9/11. Things like the first thing you do, ring your mum, your girlfriend, make sure everybody is OK. And also that strange kind of daze that sets in when, even like last week (London bombings in 2005), when people don't really know what to do and can't react in any other way than just carrying on sort of in a state of shock. As we were writing, things we had already written in there suddenly felt quite significant, even if it was only to us. So we handed in that draft and FilmFour liked it. Then over the next nine months we got through about five drafts and we got to the point where we were talking about casting, FilmFour announced it in Cannes, and then they collapsed! Paranoia set in and we asked ourselves *'What are we going to do? We probably*

can't even go back and do our TV show now as we've left it too long', and 'Oh shit what's this Resident Evil film coming out? What is this 28 Days Later film? Fuck! FUCK NO!' We want to do a British zombie film! Fuckers!' Then it occurs to us, their films are serious and ours is a funny one, so 'OK, it is fine!' We managed to get Shaun into turnaround and then shopped it around.

Q - Was it easier or more difficult to pitch it the second time around?

Ed - It was a different experience because now we were pitching a finished script. And a lot of people who had been interested in the original idea, passed on the finished script. That was like bringing you back down to Earth. Not mentioning any names, there had been maybe three other companies interested as well as FilmFour, who thought it was a really good idea and wanted to develop it. We went back to these other companies and we heard comments like 'Not funny enough, not scary enough', and someone else said 'Not what we were expecting'. Working Title, who originally had been the first people we pitched the idea to and were a little bemused by it, now expressed an interest. The good thing was that they were really into it. They really got the joke. And as it turned out, they were one of the few companies who could fully finance it. All of the other offers that we were having were lots of 'pulling people together' deals. It is better if you can get one person to do the whole thing, because if you have five different partners, every one of those companies is going to want their cut, so you actually end up with less money on screen.

Film Four had laid off loads of people, including Jim Wilson who was head of development, so we asked Jim to stay on as a producer because he had essentially developed the whole thing. So he worked with our producer, Nira Park as well as Natascha Wharton at Working Title. This uncertainty went on for six months and I was skint because I had to turn down jobs - I was offered a TV show, and it would have been a big job and good money. I said to the Producer, 'I'm really flattered that you have offered this to me, but I can't do it, because I'm trying to get my low budget film off the ground, and it might happen' and she said 'If I had a pound for every time I heard a director say that!'

Q - So what was the final budget of Shaun of the Dead?

Ed - It ended up being £4m. We had done various different budgets for different financial scenarios with better-known actors in it, or with it scaled down. People say 'Did it feel a lot different to doing TV stuff?' It didn't really feel that different to Spaced because the first series of Spaced was really low budget. The second series of Spaced had bigger budgets, but more ambitious scripts, so it just levels out, exactly the same again. Shaun of the Dead, bigger budget again, even more ambitious idea. So again it feels like you never have enough time, never quite enough money, always going home at the end of every day only getting through two thirds of your shot list. When we shot the exterior scenes, we were shooting in the summer and it was still like four seasons in one-day kind of weather. We had an American DP and he was amazed at how changeable the weather was. About 60% of the film is outside, set on the same day, so continuity is extremely important. I remember at some points with Shaun thinking, regardless of what extra budget you've got, or people around you, nothing can change that cloud going in front of the sun.

Q - How would describe your directing style when you are on set?

Ed - I tend to get very intense on set. I'm probably not the best director in terms of being a warm-up man. I relied on Simon Pegg to keep the crew entertained whilst I figure out what I was doing. So sometimes on set I can have a very unreadable face. Some directors at the end of a shot will go 'Woah! Great!', just to keep the energy up, but I will be stroking my beard at the end of every single take, so some crew members or cast are thinking 'Was that good? Was that not good? I can't tell?!' Usually it is about getting through the shot list, 'we've got to keep going, we've got to get this shot'. I'm sure that my method sometimes might seem unconventional, unorthodox and sometimes that doesn't inspire the greatest amount of confidence.

Q - How many shots were you doing a day on Shaun Of The Dead?

Ed - Some days we'd shoot 35, 40 slates, which having come from a TV show, was par for the course. You'd hear about people who had been on other features saying 'You have got to be happier than that, you've done 35 slates today!' With all films, Shaun is the sum of its parts and so with a lot of coverage, it is impossible to see how the whole thing is going to come together. Every now and again, you get a scene, which you essentially can play in one. The crew and actors really get into those. The bit where Dylan Moran gets ripped apart was essentially all on camera. So everybody who was there was thinking 'Wow that looked amazing', because it was all on camera, so you could watch back the tape and say *'Fucking hell that was great!'* On other scenes we would be darting around the shooting schedule so I would be very much *'I can't see the wood for the trees'*, and I'd be thinking about every single thing at the same time.

Q - When you started editing, did you think you had a winner on your hands?

Ed - I remember halfway through the shoot, Chris Dickens had been doing an assembly, and I'd look at it and think *'Oh shit that wasn't how I imagined it at all',* usually because it had just been put together in the order of the script. Simon watched the first assembly and it freaked him out because there was no music, sound effects and it was very rough. Everyone seems to go through this when they see the first assembly of any film. Working Title were very supportive and pretty hands-off, which is really nice, especially since it was essentially our first film. Eric Fellner at Working Title rang up at one point, and said *'Are you pleased with the dailies?'* and I was like *'Err'* and he said, *'you should be!'* That was the end of the conversation.

Q - Did you show any of the other cast the assembly?

Ed - Sort of. We were doing six-day weeks for nine weeks, which is absolutely punishing. Halfway through we cut together a couple of scenes, cool shots and out takes and made a little trailer and showed it to the crew. It was a great morale booster.

Q - Did you shoot anything chronologically?

Ed - The pub scenes were shot in chronological order. Some of the more emotional scenes in the film were shot when the cast and crew were exhausted. They almost hit the same point in terms of emotional exhaustion.

Q - Did you have a second unit?

Ed - For the most part we were doing 2nd unit as we went, and these are shots that are SO important. Close-ups of things, things that are going to completely power the editing along, any of the stunt stuff, we were doing it at the same time. Occasionally we'd have two cameras, but we were essentially doing stuff that was very time sensitive, but didn't necessarily involve the actors. We started to have two camera crews, with different call times. One crew would start at 8am, and the next crew would start at 9am. I'd work with the 8am crew for an hour, and by the time the other crew had started we'd already done eight shots of people closing curtains, knocking on doors and slamming money down. Chris Dickens, the editor, would tell us what he needed and we would shoot it. That is always a problem with independent films, not enough shots, and you can only edit if you have got the shots.

Q - Sometimes when you know exactly what you want you can accomplish more with a skeleton crew.

Ed - Absolutely. On the last day of the shoot, we were shooting dialogue stuff on the main stage and on the other side of the stage, and cut-aways on the other side of the stage in some other existing sets. Chris Dickens, our editor and our B Camera operator were doing shots of people zipping up, getting their tie, looking at their badge. We had everything ready Chris just did shot after shot. In between main unit shots I'd check Chris' shots and say *'OK that's a good one, let's do the next one'*. In the space of two days, we'd helped the edit enormously by adding 50 shots or so. That was the problem with *A Fistful of Fingers*, I was scuppered by the low budget. You can't cut out the scene because you can't afford to cut out the scene. You can't cut into the scene as you have no cut away shot to bridge the edit. What are you going to do? You can't really go into jump cuts unless it is the style of the film. These close-ups are really important. I remember I overheard some crew saying *'why are we doing*

a close-up of this?' and the other guy said *'oh, we did close-ups of everything!'* I was thinking, wait till you get in the edit, you need all this shit. There is not a single close-up shot that we didn't use. I could have easily shot another fifty shots, and they would all be in there.

Q - So tell me about what happened when the film was completed?

Ed - We did a proper test screening, which I had never done before. I had to cover my eyes! It was in High Wycombe, and it was a play out off the Avid and projected onto a massive screen. We didn't have all the shots from the end of the film where the army turns up, or the credit sequences, so the end was pretty lame. Also none of the effects were finished. The test screening went pretty well, though you could tell that some people in the audience had never seen a zombie film before, and that was really quite exciting. It was really quiet for the first twenty minutes, then people started to get into it, so that was cool.

We had done almost everything we could, without doing extra shoots, but we knew the end was still weak. Luckily the test screening results said the same thing *'What do you think of the ending?', 'I think it is a bit abrupt, the ending was a bit lame, it seemed to end really quickly'*. So Working Title said *'Write a really expensive version, an ideal world ending, write a medium one and write a lowish budget one'*. The big budget one was like *'OK, it has got a car smash in it, Lucy comes back as a zombie, Bill Nighy comes back as a zombie, there are more head shots, we do more stuff outside the Winchester, and we do all the army things'*. The second one is just the army turning up, and we do another crowd shot. The third one was literally just guns, and trucks pulling up, zombies being shot at, and we do this one shot with Pete's head exploding, which was the one bit we hadn't got. We found a shot, a wide shot where we could make it look like the storyboard version, and they said *'OK, low budget version!'* So they let us have two days on a stage, doubling for outside, with just some army extras and all the zombies we could get together for nothing. As many squibs (bullet hits) as we could do. We spent two days shooting guns cocking, people jumping out trucks, boots, squibs going off, as much as we could! Even though, the end is still a compromise and only 15 seconds long. But it antes up the ending enormously. If we hadn't have done that, fucking hell!

Q - Did the re-shoot effect your release date?

Ed - They had the release date set for 1st April, which UIP had said this was a good time for comedy. But we hadn't finished and we'd only just done the re-shoots in December, and you need eight weeks before it comes out for the press to see it. Suddenly, after all this time writing, shooting, and editing, you are in a race to meet this date. By the first press screening, we'd only got through grading half of it and many digital effects were missing. Even after we had done all that, Eric Fellner watched it again and said we needed one more belly laugh at the end! We actually realised we could film a new TV bit. So we came up with this idea of Vernon Kay interviewing Coldplay, because Simon knew them. We just shot that video and dropped it in. It was done eight weeks before it came out. They said we had to do this, otherwise we won't get any long lead reviews (magazines etc). So that was a really nerve-wracking experience because you kind of have to come out and make some apologies for the film. It had no end credits.

The first press screening was pretty cool and two thirds of them really liked it. Then we had it finished and then we had a bigger one in the West End with 400 people. We actually re-invited some of the original people and there was one reviewer from a magazine where I was particularly upset because one of the things that they criticised the film for was something that wasn't finished when they had seen it - they were saying *'where is the flying blood, where is the gore?'* There were two or three big gore effects still to go in when he had seen it, so at our final screenings when it was complete, I rang the PR company and said *'please re-invite that person to come and see it again properly with the finished grade and all the effects.'* He came and changed his review, giving it an extra star!

Q - Did you watch the screening with the audience?

Ed - I watched bits of it, but I get so nervous I couldn't actually sit through the whole thing. I suppose at that point we started doing quite a lot of industry screenings and getting some really nice responses back. This was weird because the release date was coming up and we'd only just finished it. We had no experience of doing the markets and film festivals. It was out, and it felt like it was still like wet paint. Still, we got good buzz from the press and especially on the internet. The week before it came out, I flew out to the States to the *Ain't It Cool News* people, because they had been really keen to see it. That was a really fun experience because I went over on my own, to Austin, Texas, to meet Harry Knowles. He asked if he could bring some people along. I said *'sure'*, and he brought fifty people! It was really cool because it was like we were with mates. We were in this cinema after midnight, so the rest of the thing had shut up and the owner of the cinema had come to watch too. Also around that time we showed it to George Romero. He really liked it, and that was really important for me and Simon. The greatest gift of *Shaun* has been getting to travel the world with it and go and do press in other countries. Especially with something that didn't really make any concessions to an international audience. We did a PR tour in the States, going through 17 different cities over a 4 week period. For the most part, people would get every single joke, and they appreciated it on that level.

Q - What kind of opportunities have opened up to you, and how do you decide to play those opportunities?

Ed - The world suddenly got smaller. We were meeting directors that we admired - heroes of yours that have responded to your film. Getting to meet your hero is an amazing thing. A lot of people in the States, and over here as well, responded to it. That is great in terms of getting lots of offers. The downside to it is you write stuff as well, so people ask what's next? We'd been working on the film for three years right up until release, and in the first interview you do, *'So, what's next?'* I had no idea. I hadn't done any writing since this. So that is the down side, and I think there are lots of people who get into that kind of hole. I've been trying to be proactive in terms of trying to write a couple of other things or getting someone to write something for me. I don't want to be in that position again, working for two years and then going *'Now what?'* They are obviously higher-level problems to have, and nothing to really cry about. People that do first films can get that festival fever, where you can do the festival circuit for eighteen months, or two years. You get to travel the world, but you might lose momentum in terms of getting the next one going. On the other hand, last time I met Sam Raimi through the film, he said I should travel the world whilst I've got a chance and I am young. I suppose we have been doing it, as we've not only been to the States now a bunch of times, but Australia, and New Zealand, which I'd never been to before.

Q - What mistakes do you think you made?

Ed - There were thoughts like *'I wish I'd got that other shot. I should have done that other angle now'.* That kind of stuff. On the end sequence there was supposed to be a lot more action, and it was supposed to get a lot more *Evil Dead*. That wasn't in the first draft, but with each draft we got bigger and bigger with the action.

I remember when we were on set, and we had to cut two days from the schedule, I just got a big marker and said *'cut all that out!'* Sometimes you have got to focus. There are lots of ways of working on set, in terms of not only directing everybody, not only leading the troops, but also keeping the crew going. Recently I was very honoured to see Tarantino directing a CSI episode. I was watching him direct, he's just brilliant in terms of he was just a little bundle of energy. We had lunch afterwards, and I said *'I should have been a bit more like that on Shaun.'* I tend to let the weight of the world show on my face. Sometimes that isn't good for morale. It is a difficult thing, sometimes you have really got to focus. I remember reading an interview with Brian de Palma, and he was questioned about being famously grumpy, the crew complaining that he didn't even say good morning, no chit chat, and he said, *'forgive me, but, these are films I have to have on my shelf for the rest of my life, if I lost concentration because I'm having a cappuccino with the gaffer at the start of the morning, then . . .'*

Q - Eddie Murphy once said he's worked on films where it has been a bundle of laughs, and other times it has been absolute hell, and you can not tell whether the film will be any good, or terrible based on the experience.

Ed - There is that other kind of school of thought, the tougher the shoot, and the harder everyone is working, the better the film is going to be. I don't think that is always true, but I don't think any film

where people having gone home early was necessarily going to be any good. The day that you go home early is the day that you become complacent. With a comedy as well, you can't get hung up on making the crew laugh. Especially if you are doing a lot of takes where on the first take you might get a giggle out of the grip, but by take ten, nobody is even smiling. It doesn't mean it is not funny any more.

Q - Equally what is funny on set, is not necessarily going to become funny when you see it on screen.

Ed - There are some comedy actors, who may be from a stand-up background, who when it gets to doing a second or third take, start changing the material because they kind of want to get that first reaction out of the crew. Sometimes it is good, and sometimes it is counterproductive. "You are a great improviser, but that thing you did in the first take, that is still the best". So that is an interesting thing, set dynamics. Lots of different performers working in lots of different ways. Especially if you have got an ensemble cast. You almost have to do strategies to think, *'Ok, they are best on their first take, the other performer needs a couple of takes to warm up. Do the other guy first, and then do him on the reverses because by then he will have learnt his lines.'*

Q - Do you think the making of movies are as mystical as they used to be?

Ed - No. I noticed a downside to DVD when we did the *Shaun of the Dead* disk. I'm really proud of the DVD that we did because we self-produced it, but I was thinking back in the '70's how a film like *Eraserhead* would come out and would be speculated over. It has been a cult film for like 10 years, 15 years, 20 years, and all through that time people speculate *'what is it actually about?'* But now pretty much within six months of a film coming out, everything you would ever want to know about that film, you can get off the DVD or internet. It removes some of the magic.

Q - What advice would you offer a filmmaker?

Ed - Try every aspect of it. I didn't really want to do my own camerawork, but I had to for my video films. I only did it as a means to an end, and I learned a lot about directing from using the camera. I was also forced to edit, which again taught me a lot. Then when you meet collaborators in your career, you can hand the responsibility to them, but you will have an understanding of what they do. Try and do your own stuff, rather than wait for it to come to you. Even when I did the AV course, at college, I did the stuff on the syllabus, but I nicked the equipment, and went off and abused the editing suite, and tried to do lots of extra curricular things. I watched all my favourite films, and tried to rip off the same shots on a video 8. I failed a lot, but I still learned through those experiences. The people who are now coming through the digital generation have an amazing opportunity. Everybody has non-linear editing facilities on their laptop so I think that the only thing to do is to get out there and do it. There are enough films where people have just done it. Look at *The Blair Witch Project*. No matter what people think of that film, nobody can ever take away from them that they made a cheap and simplistic film, and that it made maybe $200 million all over the world. That is incredible.

(Dan is on a mobile, on a conference call, going to the airport)

Q - What gave you the idea of a horror movie?

Dan - It was inspired by old dramatised documentaries like In Search Of... Bigfoot and we thought it would be cool to make a horror movie that was formatted like that. It made sense because it was just the cheapest thing for two broke film makers to do, we could shoot it on Hi8 and we didn't need any named actors to pull it off. We didn't want a single frame to look as though it was shot by a third person or have a convenient cutaway, it had to look absolutely genuine. We just held onto that realistic line and didn't deviate from it.

Q - Technically, how did you make The Blair Witch?

Ed - We cast it in New York and saw a bunch of people to get Heather, Mike and Josh. We shot for eight days during October '97 in the woods near Germantown, Maryland on Hi8 and 16mm b&w. Most of what you see in the film was actually shot by the actors. We sent the actors out into the woods and Dan and I directed them by remote control. We gave them little notes and talked to them every once in a while but tried to keep the contact with them to a minimum because we wanted them to feel lost, hungry, confused and tired. By the end of the shoot we started to give them less and less food, and this all helped in their performance, creating a reality that you can sense.

Q - Directing actors by remote control almost?

Dan - Yes. The first couple of days they were in the town, we just had them follow a map - so they were instructed to go to the quickie mart and interview whoever. We'd leave director notes in little canisters on the front seat of their car with new instructions for their characters and also logistics, like go down route 20 to the cemetery. Ed and I had scouted the woods for about three weeks so we knew where everything would happen, the camp sites, the stickmen, coffin rock etc. Once the actors were in the woods we gave them a handheld satellite GPS and we would give them the co-ordinates of the locations so they could find them without our intervention. When they'd get to these check points they'd have a set of directing notes for the next checkpoint and new batteries. They'd leave the exposed film and used video tapes and collect unexposed stock and blank tapes and finally leave a bicycle flag on a milk crate so that we knew they had been there. We tried to keep them guessing as to what would happen to them and constantly assess what their characters would know and do. We had a tent that was near all the locations as we wanted them to feel safe and they were always within radio contact so they could call us if there was an emergency. The shoot went remarkably well, nobody got sick, nobody twisted an ankle although all of us were running around for more than a week in the woods, it was pretty miraculous that none of us got hurt. The actors looked at it as being an opportunity for them to have full creative control over their characters within the parameters of what Ed and I created, but it is improvised. It took an immense amount of trust

Dan Myrick   Ed Sanchez
Directors, The Blair Witch Project

to allow them to shoot and improvise their lines and to trust our remote control directing techniques.

Ed - The biggest disadvantage with improvising was that we constantly doubted ourselves. We had no idea of what we were doing. Dan and I would be in the woods and we'd look at each other and say what the hell are we doing? We would look at the footage and sometimes it was really good and sometimes it was like, how are people going to sit through this film? We had no idea what we were doing but we were kept so busy with the machinery of trying to make the film that ultimately we didn't have time to think about it too much.

Q - Did anything ever go missing or go wrong?

Ed - Yeah, we lost one of the tapes, it disappeared for three days. A lot of things went wrong that actually ended up being good. One day it rained so heavily that we, the film makers, fell really far behind, so the cast just hiked out of the woods and knocked on someone's door explaining they were shooting a film. There's a really cool moment in the film where they're hiking through the woods, it's raining and they're all miserable. Then they turned off the camera and in reality they're suddenly in somebody's house drinking hot cocoa - funny.

Q - How long did it take?

Ed - We conceived it in '93, sat around for a while, then in the summer of '96 decided we were going to do it. Then we made it in '97 and '98.

Dan - We did about three weeks of pre production prior to principal photography, then we were in the woods for six days and two days in the town. By the wrap party everyone was really high as it had been a great experience to shoot a film this way and we knew nobody had shot a film like this before, it was unique and exciting. We returned to Orlando three months later and Ed and I started editing in between Planet Hollywood corporate videos to pay the bills. In June '98 we built the website, then in September '98 we finished the edit and got accepted to Sundance, went to Sundance and sold it to Artisan.

Q - What was the phase two stuff?

Ed - During the edit we shot this phase two footage, interviews with relatives etc, but we realised that we already had our movie and that it was what these kids had already shot in the woods. That footage was used on the website and integrated into Curse Of The Blair Witch that was made for the SciFi Channel. Curse was something Artisan wanted to do, a TV tie in with Blair. We came up with the idea and it was our chance to make the film that we originally conceived, to completely go the documentary route. It was a lot of hard work for very little money, but it was very rewarding, successful and we're really happy we did it.

Q - Were there any big disagreements in the cutting room?

Dan - I think the biggest thing was that we took two different approaches of how to incorporate this phase two stuff. I was going to try and integrate it through the story and Ed was going to try and build a prologue to the story. Ultimately we realised that neither worked and we just jettisoned it and held firm. That was an agonising decision for all of us at Haxan as you're going on instinct and you're battling the demons of doubt the entire time.

Ed - It's really tough to step back on a movie saying it's not working because take five is better than take three, so much of it is trusting your instincts, debating whether or not your instincts are worth a damn or not!

Q - How much was the Internet really responsible for the Blair phenomenon?

Ed - We'd just shown a clip from Blair on a TV show and the show's website got a lot of hits from people talking about the film and asking whether it was real or not. So we decided to put up a website, keeping up the idea that the film was real, that these three student film makers actually had disappeared and people started really digging it. What came out of the website was totally unexpected and I think it's largely responsible for what happened with the film. The film is a good film, I don't think it was a fluke, but the fact that it blew up like that is really a testament to how the Internet can be used. The Internet as a marketing tool for independent film makers is a powerful equalising tool.

Q - Did you anticipate how it was going to do?

Ed - We hoped for a success, but had no idea it would be as big as it was. We thought if we get a video or cable deal then that would be great. We didn't expect this to be in the theatres, we thought maybe we could do a limited arthouse run in three or four theatres but as far as

opening as big as it did, nobody ever dreamed that anything like that was going to happen.

Dan - Money is always a big obstacle for independent film makers and survival was hard at times. Fortunately, the film itself was implicitly supposed to look low budget so all the weaknesses of low budget films turned into our strengths.

Q - Where did the cash come from ?

Ed - From our credit cards, savings and John Pierson gave us almost half the budget that we needed for the initial shoot. We spent $22k to get the film in the can and then kept trying to raise money through private investors. Once we got into Sundance everyone kind of jumped on board and we got the money to take the film to print, then Artisan bought the film, fixed the sound, re-transferred it and did a couple of other things to it. The film you see in the theatres probably cost $500k.

Q - How did you get Blair into Sundance?

Dan - We had a 2½ half hour cut that we screened at our local arthouse theatre in Orlando. We had no idea what the hell we had so we had to show it to an audience and get their reaction. During this screening we met our executive producer Kevin Foxe, who just happened to be producing a movie there, and by fluke came along to the screening. He subsequently hooked us up with our biggest investor and said You guys are going to Sundance! and we're like Oh my gosh, who is this guy? We had no idea who he was but he seemed for real and he had a couple of films that had gone to Sundance before. Kevin has opened so many doors to people who have been instrumental in our success, publicists, agents, and the success of Blair Witch. Following the movie, three of the top agents at Endeavour flew to Orlando and signed us up. We didn't realise that that was such a big deal, we thought that was just what they did! Kevin orchestrated a pre publicity campaign and a lobbying group to get into Sundance so that when we sent the tape in, it actually stood out from the pile. We held a screening in New York where some industry people saw it, our website was starting to get a lot of hits, and the news that Endeavour had picked us up - all these things combined made Blair an interesting thing and the guys at Sundance wanted to see it. The movie has to work on it's own merit, but it gave us an advantage going in as we were more than just another film submitted.

Ed - Kevin was also the first person to suggest dropping the phase two footage, he said you guys have ruined the film, take it out! - and he was right.

Q - After your screening at Sundance, did Artisan pounce?

Dan - We screened Saturday night at the Egyptian and there was quite a bit of anticipation for the movie, built up by Endeavour and Clein & Walker (publicists) pushing it, plus the Internet presence. We had a packed house with a lot of distributors who we had met at pre screening meetings. It was a really good sign that 90% of the people stayed and we had a quick Q&A, then our agents talked to three or four distributors who wanted to meet the next day. We were really excited and we all went back to the condo, had a few beers, relaxed and about an hour later Artisan called. They said we want to get together, right here and now... So our agents, attorney and producers did an all night negotiating session with Artisan and by 6am the next day we had a deal with them, then the press craziness began. Artisan were gauging Blair Witch with what they did with Pi, which was about $3m at the box office. Because Blair was a little more approachable than Pi they were hoping it would take maybe $6m - $8m tops. We even made a bet with Artisan, because we're all foosball fanatics, saying that if we break $10m they'd have to buy us a brand new foosball table.

Ed - When Dan and I saw it at Sundance both of us agreed we could cut it down so we cut five minutes out. Artisan experimented with the ending, they wanted to make it more extreme, so we shot alternative endings but none of them worked and we ended up with the original ending. Artisan also urged us to do a new sound mix, so we did.

Q - Low budget filmmakers lament about the distribution nightmare as distributors often act as though they're not accountable. Is it any different at your level?

Ed - I can't comment on our experience with Artisan, but just about every film maker, even the big ones, have this same problem. We were recently talking to Barry Levinson and he said that distributors basically rip off film makers and you have to hire lawyers, accountants and you have to do audits - and that's just the way business is done. It's sad and I don't understand why, if you deserve the money, you can't get it as soon as the film has performed. They forget who made the film, that some people got together and sacrificed a lot, putting their heart and soul into making this movie. They forget that this is the reason why the film is in their possession in the first place and the reason that they're making money off it.

At this point, Dan gets on the plane and is cut off.

Q - What mistakes do you think you made?

Ed - When we were at film school Robert Rodriguez got the three picture deal at Colombia, that was incredible, that's making it! And that's essentially what happened to us, but having gone through it, I now think that it isn't such a good thing. We got a first look deal for two films from Artisan and I think that kind of deal is to be avoided at all costs. First look deals are an excuse for somebody to take your project and hold it hostage. The whole three picture deal can sometimes turn into a nightmare because they can turn into films that you don't want to make but you're forced to. We're all creative, at least for now, until we completely sell out. We're motivated by creativity and the first look deal has put deadlines or limitations on our creativity because they need to release a film at a certain time.

Q - What did you get right?

Ed - We did so many things right but it was pretty much out of luck. I built the web site because I didn't have a girlfriend at the time so I had a lot of time on my hands, and that took off. Originally we were going to get rid of Mike, he was the one who was going to end up dying first, but leaving Mike and Heather together formed a nice dynamic and it made the last third of the film different from the first two thirds. We also cut a lot of footage that we loved, the phase two footage, all the documentary stuff, and even though it hurt and Dan and I really had a hard time convincing ourselves to do it, it was the right decision.

Q - What advice would you offer new film makers?

Ed - Go to film school or a college with some practical media course. Learn about editing, lighting, camera, how to work with actors. If you've got a video camera, buy a computer editing system and make movies. It's something that Dan and I didn't have when we were young. Both Dan and I started making things before film school and when we went there, even though there were a lot of talented people in the school, there were only a handful of really good film makers because of the fact that we had already learned so much by making our own little films. I've been editing since I was 16 so I had learned and made my mistakes on a $5 VHS tape. Fellow students who were talented in their own way, were making mistakes on their films that cost them $150. I can't over emphasise this, learn on DV, learn how to edit and shoot, then move over to film or HD.

It's cool to be inspired by certain film makers, like Spike Lee or Kevin Smith, but don't go out and make another Clerks or Pulp Fiction and don't go out and make another Blair Witch! The fact that these films did what they did is because they introduced something new and fresh, something that people hadn't seen ever, or for a long time. So understand that this is the reason why all those films exploded out of Sundance and were a success. John Pierson puts it best, he says whenever a big independent movie comes out, for the next year and a half I get a hundred and fifty different versions of it. People are looking for something new, because most of the time Hollywood is not going to deliver that. If you're going to go out there and try and make a Hollywood film on $10k you're NOT GOING TO SUCCEED! So make you're own film and understand that you can't and shouldn't compete with Hollywood. Even if you had an unlimited amount of money, make the film you want to make.

Stacey Testro
Producer

Leigh Whannell
Writer and Actor

SAW

Q - What is your background?

Leigh - When I was a kid, my grandfather won a Beta video machine in a golf tournament and said, *"What am I going to do with this thing?"* So he gave it to my Dad. It was about the size of a fridge and I was instantly in love. I remember getting *Jaws* and was hooked on it from when I was five years old. I went through a film-obsessed childhood and took acting classes, performed in school plays and theatre outside of school. By the time I got to high school, I had a teacher that really turned me on to filmmaking more than acting. He introduced me to films like *Taxi Driver* and *Apocalypse Now*. And then I started getting excited about the other side of the camera. When I finished school, I decided that I had more of a chance to make it behind the camera so I went to University to study filmmaking. That's where I met James Wan. He was the only other filmmaker there who was more interested in *The Evil Dead* than Fellini, so we said we would make a film together one day. We finished Uni, went on separate jobs and five years later we still hadn't done anything about it. So we were sitting down one day and I said the only way we are going to make a film is to pay for it ourselves. That was when *Saw* was born. James and I were going to pay for it out of our own pockets. Try to get a *Blair Witch* thing going.

Q - How did you guys meet Stacey?

Leigh - I signed up with her agency in Melbourne when I was a kid. I went in and auditioned and was precocious enough to make an impression on her.

Stacey - Yes. Leigh wanted to be an actor when he was a teenager and he had been acting for some time when I met him. So, I started managing him. Then he decided to pursue the writing area after he met James Wan at film school and they became partners. Leigh recommended James to me as a potential client and I took him on. They had an immediate attraction to each other in so far as the type of movies they wanted to make. They always had many and varied ideas, were very diligent, proactive and to this day both have a great knowledge of the history of the industry. They were also very educated in the area of the films that they wanted to make.

Leigh - Stacey has been there the whole time and knows our whole story of how I was bitching that James and I had this goal and it wasn't happening and now she's seen us realise it. It's really good to have someone who's on your side and been there from the beginning.

Q - How did Saw come about?

Stacey - Our production arm set about developing an idea or two with Leigh and James and we made a trailer of one of their ideas. But as it turned out, it didn't go forward. And then James and Leigh really decided that they wanted to make a film and the only way they were going to do this was for them to write something for James to direct and Leigh to star. They came in the office one day and they talked about an idea which sounded great. They went and worked on the script for quite some time, really cultivating the plot and the characters, then came back and delivered the script of *Saw*.

Q - How long did it take you to write the script and how many drafts did you do?

Leigh - The first draft took awhile. When we first had the idea, I had never really written a script seriously before. I took a long time with the characters, writing bios for all of them, getting scene cards so I could have the whole script mapped out.

So the first draft took me nine months to get it where I wanted it. And I was working a full time job and I had a girlfriend at the time to whom I was giving a lot of attention. I was trying to squeeze in this scriptwriting, so it took awhile. I am glad I had that long with it. After that we did about four or five more drafts. The whole length of the process from coming up with the idea to shooting the film was about two years. Which is fairly quick. But that is how I write. I like to let things gestate. I'm not good at just vomiting out something in two weeks.

Q - How did the writing process work with James involved?

Leigh - I finished the script. I didn't want to show him anything. Once we had the initial idea, I made him wait for those long nine months. He had no idea what I was doing. I didn't want to tell him either. I just wanted him to read it, and I'm glad I did it that way. It gave me a glimpse into that feeling a writer can have when they are confident in what they are doing. I have never been able to quite capture that since. I am sure I will someday. I hope I will. Whenever independent filmmakers ask me how I did it and what was the secret, I feel like, well, I've been in that position as well. I would go to screenwriting seminars and what you really want to hear is, what is the shortcut? What you want Robert McKee to really do is lean over and say, *"Look, all this character and working hard stuff is bullshit. If you include a character named Agnes in your script, it will be guaranteed to be a million dollar blockbuster."* Human nature is the path of least resistance. You want the secret. You don't want someone to tell you, *"Well, the key to making it in Hollywood is hard work."* Christ. I didn't have to pay $500 to learn that. People were scribbling in their notebooks the fastest when Robert McKee said here are the three things you need in a thriller.

Q - So did you take a lot of Robert McKee's advice on board when you were writing Saw?

Leigh - It made me realise that when filmmakers ask me about the secret, I say if you are confident in the script you are writing, the script is where it starts and finishes. Of course, everything is important in film - it is a collaborative art. But you are telling a story and the scriptwriting is interpretive art. If you're 100% confident in writing it, you will not need to ask anyone the secret for writing it or you won't be worried anymore. With *Saw*, I wasn't worried for a second. When I first finished it, I gave it to one our friends who was an independent film producer and he hated it. I remember him really giving it to me and I wasn't worried in the slightest. That is how I knew I was confident in *Saw*. I always knew, and I can say this in retrospect, I always knew that *Saw* would get made. I never doubted for a second. I thought that it may take a while, which almost killed me because I thought I would be thirty-five by the time it got made. I would have been playing the doctor by then. But I always thought it would get made.

Q - So it was always the intention to have minimal locations and only a few actors for Saw?

Leigh - Exactly. The whole idea was born from the idea of what if two guys were chained up in this bathroom and couldn't leave. Therefore the whole film gets to take place in one room with these two actors. That is something that you can visualise. That is something you can afford. When I went off and wrote the script, I found that it was really hard to contain the film within this one room as it felt more like a play than a film. So I expanded it to the point where James and I wondered if we could really do it justice with the very meager funds we had available to us. It sort of bounced around as things do with these independent films. They get passed from person to person and maybe a producer is interested. And you come up with a plan B. But it sort of just landed in the right people's laps.

Q - Did you think about the commerciality of the story when you were writing it?

Leigh - Instinctually, we are pretty commercial anyway. We were never going to come up with a story that was an impenetrable art film. We wanted it to be something that we would see. I am very sort of concept based. I don't base films by who is in it. *'Ooo, the new Harvey Keitel film is out!'* That's not me. Obviously people do do that. It's the concept of the

film that appeals to me. The last film that I read the concept for and I said I had to see it, was *The Machinist*. It really intrigued me; it's concept - a guy who couldn't sleep for a year. So that's how we came up with *Saw*. I would write down my ideas as if it was a synopsis on the back of a DVD cover to see if would read intriguingly. I think I have it in a notebook somewhere. *'Two men wake up in an abandoned bathroom chained to a wall on opposite sides.'* It's fire in your belly when you have something good. You can't wait to get started.

Q - As their manager, what did you think when you read Saw for the first time?

Stacey - On first read, the script was tremendous. And very soon after this, there was a request of several producers via the Writers Guild in Australia who had a million dollars and wanted to make a low budget genre picture. So we sent the script to these two producers in Sydney and they immediately loved it. They took an option on it and unfortunately, they couldn't raise the money for it. It was a shame because it seemed that James and Leigh were genuinely going to get an opportunity to star and direct. So I started sending the script out of our LA office and the response was overwhelming to it as a spec. And I told James and Leigh that if the producers loved the script so much they are going to love them. But to amplify their position, we started talking about shooting a particular scene from the script to show their vision. They went away and thought about it and eventually decided to do it. We hooked them up with a great young DP from Melbourne, and told them to go away and come back to show us what they came up with.

Q - Did James have a collection of shorts or any other feature behind him?

Stacey - He had done some music videos and some shorts. But, the two of them lived, breathed and slept filmmaking so it wasn't a big task for them to go off and shoot the one scene. I really and truly felt that due to the reaction of the script, they had to be given the opportunity to really and truly be involved.

Q - Which scene was it?

Leigh - It was the jaw trap scene. It was shot like a Nine Inch Nails video. It looked beautiful. It was the perfect selling tool and within a week we had the deal stitched up to make the film.

Q - How much did you spend on the short and what did you shoot it on?

Leigh - It was about $7k AUS. So $4k US. We shot on 16mm and James edited it.
It was great. I played the guy who was strapped into the jaw trap. Without that, who knows? I asked the producer once before if we didn't have the short, would you have made the film? He said, *"That's interesting. We wouldn't have probably let James direct and you star, but we probably would have made the film."* You can see the scene on our special edition DVD.

Q - How long did it take to make the short?

Stacey - It wasn't long at all because I said to them that it was really worth getting this ASAP. They shot it in a day or two. They tried to get favours from everyone. I was on my way back to LA and James and Leigh were rushing to get this finished. I was so excited to see it when James delivered it to my house just before I left. I immediately put the DVD in and I was just so proud, overwhelmed and excited - I couldn't stand it! I hugged James and said that he had given me what I can really work with and there is no way anyone else is going to make this film except you two.

Q - What was the response?

Stacey - I took it to LA and handed it to a literary agent at Genesis called Ken Greenblatt. I didn't oversell it at all. Then I get this phone call about two hours later from the agent who said that I was the type of person who over-delivers and under-promises. I thought that was hilarious because it is completely the opposite of what that line really is. He really wanted to work with these two guys. Then it was this whirlwind. The eight-minute DVD went out to all the people who had the script all over LA. James was in Australia. Leigh was in London. I called them and said *'you're coming to LA',* this was June of 2003, *'and there are going to be a rush of meetings. You're going to meet on the basis of being attached as creative key personnel.'*

Q - How did Evolution Entertainment come on board as the producers?

Stacey - We had these meeting with studios, mini-studios and production companies. And the first meeting we had on the first day was with the head of production at Evolution Entertainment. These guys were really gung-ho and they really wanted to make this project. They promised that if they get the project then James would be the director and Leigh would star. That was really encouraging. Then, we went on all the other meetings and there were lots of different options in terms of opportunities and some deals were on the table. But in the end, it was Evolution's guarantee that James would direct and Leigh would star and a guarantee of certain amount of creative control in terms of casting and all the other important elements that sealed the deal. So looking at it as their manager, it was really the way to go to fulfill their creative goals. Even though there were a lot of attractive offers made, this one was head and shoulders above the rest. And then later that week, we were talking to lawyers and the deal was getting done. James and Leigh got back on a plane to Australia to pack their things, and while they were in flight, the film was officially put into pre-production.

Q - Did Evolution give you a lot of notes on changes to the script?

Leigh - Not many. The great thing about how they wanted to do it was that they just wanted to dive right into it. Now if you have $100 million dollars riding on a film, it has to be this vanilla fucking piece of shit. Evolution didn't want to fuck with the formula too much. They felt like they had stumbled onto this kind of gem. They felt like if they put their fingers in there, they would fuck it up. So they let us go. It was great!

Q - Were Cary Elwes and Danny Glover always in mind for the leading roles?

Stacey - Not at all. The film was originally going to be made in Australia. The only attachments were Leigh to star and James to direct. It was going to be low-budget, and it was going to be an opportunity to advance their careers. But it was a script of such high standard and written in a style that was very appealing to the American market, so it was possible to attract Hollywood stars. Once Cary Elwes and Danny Glover saw the short and read the script, they were convinced.

Q - So you wrote Saw knowing you were going to star in it?

Leigh - Yes. I was doing some acting over in Australia, but not as much as I would have liked which is precisely why we did *Saw.* So that was part of the deal of doing the film in America. Again, it comes down to the budget. If Evolution had spent more money, they would have said, *"We should really get Josh Hartnett for this role."* But because it was low budget, they could take the chance on me acting in it. It was awesome.

Q - What was it like acting with Cary Elwes and Danny Glover?

Leigh - It was awesome. These huge actors speaking lines that you have written - it's a huge honor. I did all my scenes with Cary and he was just a great guy. It was an all around good experience. From the writing process to the making of it through doing the publicity tour to the release, *Saw* was this blessed thing. It felt like our child that has grown up and has a life of its

own. I envy *Saw*, it's good luck. Everything works out with it. The company that released it was the right company, as they knew exactly how to market it.

Q - During casting, were Cary Elwes and Danny Glover keen right from the start?

Leigh - Yeah. It was the short that did it. That DVD is what got every one of the actors turned on to it. I'd always advise new filmmakers that if you can manage to get that script written and it's the one that you are utterly confident in and you love; take a scene from it and instead of spending $10,000 to make an inexpensive feature film and selling your script short, spend the money to make a very expensive eight minute demo reel. It will look good and it is such a good selling tool. A script is just pages with words on it. There is not much you can do to sex it up. Of course, if it's good it will stand out, but if you want it to stand out more in a crowded marketplace, you strap this little DVD to it. It will take you all night to read the script, but it will take you eight minutes to watch the DVD. If the scene makes them flip out like the scene from *Saw* did - I mean people flipped out. They said, *"That was the sickest thing I had every seen!"*

Q - When did you start principal photography?

Stacey - In July we did the deal, August we started pre production and September we started shooting. It was so fast. And that was one of the attractions, too. Everyone wanted to proceed and they didn't want to wait. It was private equity so the quicker the better that this could happen. James went back to Australia to pack and Leigh had a commitment for an acting job in Australia. When James came back to the US, he had visa issues and was up in Canada while the film was in pre-production. When he finally returned to LA, he hardly had any time for pre-production. He was doing casting via telephone. It was really tough. The whole thing was shot in Los Angeles in one big warehouse. We shot it in eighteen days and there was enough time to get it into Sundance. It was amazingly electric on set because there was a sense that everyone loved the script and project.

Q - Did any of the dialogue change during shooting?

Leigh - Of course there were some changes, but for the most part we stuck to what I had written. I found that because the shoot was so rushed, they really stuck to what I had on the page.

Q - What was the budget for the film?

Stacey - $1.1 million US. And theatrically in the US, it grossed $55 million US.

Q - Did you ever think that you were going to have problems with the violence as so many of the studios nowadays want PG-13 movies?

Leigh - When you're making an independent film you want to stand out. There is no use sitting on the fence. The reason the studios make these vanilla films is because they are trying to be all things to all people. The dream is to be *E.T* or *Titanic*. The dream is to have the old ladies, the middle aged ladies, the middle aged men, the teenagers, the kids, the babies - everyone to love the film. You get a market share of everything but you get these bland movies. When you're doing an independent film, I don't understand why anyone would fence sit? Then again, if you're such a great writer that you can make *Rushmore* or *The Graduate*, go for it. We did *Saw* because we wanted it to stand out. We wanted to make people go, *"Ugghhh, holy shit!"* For them to be scarfing in the aisles. We wanted to make a thriller, but we didn't want to make *Kiss The Girls*. We wanted them to be psychologically affected. We wanted people to be sitting around saying, *"Have you seen that film where the guy saws his foot off?"* I guess it is a very pointed way of getting people to remember your film. Sometimes films need a gimmick. *The Blair Witch Project, Run, Lola Run, Memento* - the films that stand out in the independent world are the ones that mainstream films cannot offer. So it might be valuable to spend time thinking about what can I do that isn't being offered by the mainstream at the moment. What is a bit taboo? As long as you are smart about it - it is easy to shock - it is harder to shock in a smart way.

Q - Did Lion's Gate see Saw at Sundance?

Stacey - Lion's Gate saw it just prior to going to Sundance 2004, and were made aware of the film before that. Right up until that point, there was no sale. People were excited to see it, but they were very much waiting for a finished product. Then just before Sundance, Lion's Gate acquired it and did an extraordinary job of marketing the film. Then it got into the Toronto Film Festival in September. Then it was released widely on Halloween, October 31st, 2004.

Q - Which do you love more - acting or writing?

Leigh - I love both of them, but they are different. At the moment, my desire to act is stronger because I haven't done that in so long. So the acting side of me is starving. It is a lot harder because it's not up to you. Unless you're writing your own films and plays and put them on yourself, you are relying on someone else's decision. It's like hoping to win the lottery. You are relying on a huge mixture of luck. Are you the right look? Are you the right age? Acting can be very soul destroying. I mean everyone reading *Hello Magazine* and hearing actors bitching about why they can't have a parasail without someone taking their pictures. And you're like, *"Oh, shut up. You break my heart!"* What you don't read about are the thousands of actors who are constantly rejected. Acting is a series of constant rejections. Unless you are lucky to be one of these actors that is constantly working, it's really soul destroying. I am getting to the point where I just want to write another film for myself because the chance of getting a part via auditioning is so slim.

Q - Even after the success of Saw?

Leigh - Yeah. You can't plan for anything in this industry. All you can do if someone is not giving you a job, is create your own job. Go and put on your own play. And if you're not a writer, find one. It is the only way to do it without going mental. Right now, I'm writing and developing ideas.

Q - Did you make any mistakes during the process that you learned from?

Leigh - Mostly the things came from me. I look back on some of the things that I did as an actor and maybe I would have made some different choices. Overall, obviously, it's not flawless, but I am proud of it and its flaws. I think it's a great film.

Q - What advice would you give to a new filmmaker?

Leigh - Look, I don't believe in all the film guide bullshit of pushing and pushing for your project to happen. If you have a great script and a great little scene shot to send out to five companies, you will get five calls. So, story, story, story is the key.

Julian Richards
Writer and Director

THE LAST HORROR MOVIE

Q - Back when you were a kid in Wales, what is it that made you want to make a film?

Julian - It was three experiences I had. First of all, my father had a Super 8 camera and we used to go on an annual holiday abroad. He used to film the holiday, send the film off to Kodak to be developed and they would come back a week later. It was like Christmas to unwrap the parcel and put the Super 8 film through the projector. Just the magic of seeing that, our life caught on film, was captivating. Then seeing him edit it, putting the Super 8 through an editing machine, cutting all the boring bits out, made me realise that I could actually have a crack at making a film myself with my school friends. Also I was a real horror maniac and I used to kick my parents out of the living room on Saturday evenings - usually because they would fall asleep and snore - so that I could watch the horror double bills on BBC2. So I combined that with the accessibility of Super 8 and made my first horror film when I was 13.

Also, I had an uncle, who in 1958, went to America to become a Hollywood star. He used to play for the Welsh rugby team and his nickname was Tarzan because he was one of the most athletic men on the field. He heard that they were auditioning for a re-make of Tarzan in Florida, so he went out there to audition, got short-listed, but eventually he didn't get the part. Another film was casting at the time called *The Wild Women of Wongo*, and they basically employed all the Tarzan rejects to play the men of Wongo! My uncle, Rex Richards, ended up playing King Wongo, and I grew up with this object of admiration of a guy from Wales who had gone to Hollywood and was living the American dream - albeit in one of the worst films ever made!

Q - How much do you think that crystalised in your mind the desire to be a success at an early age?

Julian - In working class, provincial Wales, we are more taken by the American dream than by anything else. And so, my desire to be a film maker was as much to do with my love of the American dream, as it was to do with my love and understanding of cinema. I think my perspectives have changed now.

Q - What do you think you get from film school in the best possible sense?

Julian - Well the great thing about film school is that you get put into a building with like-minded people, the same age as you. You get given all the equipment, and you can just go ahead and make your films with the guidance of the teachers. The courses that I did at Bournemouth were not really academic - they were very practical. It gave me the opportunity to work on a level that was much more professional than I had been doing with my Super 8 films. It was a step towards me being recognised by the industry as a professional, worthy of employing or financing. I think that in the long term, however, the fact that there wasn't an academic side to the process meant that, well, what's the use of a film maker who doesn't have anything interesting to say? At the end of the day, there is no easy answer, and there are many ways of achieving success, but I think the more weapons you have at your disposal, which includes having an academic as well as practical grasp of film making, the better.

Q - How did your first feature film come about.

Julian - The first feature film was *'Darklands'* and it is something that I had written way back in Bournemouth Film School in 1987. I'd been kind of tinkering with the script on and off right through to 1994 and I sent it out to a lot of companies who all wrote back and said *'We are not interested!'* At this stage I had established myself as a film maker to watch with my short film *Queen Sacrifice*, which won several awards. The problem was that people were a little bit confused by the fact that I had built up this reputation as the kind of director who would tackle a social realistic comedy drama like *The Full Monty*, but now I was presenting a horror movie at a time when horror movies were not in vogue. Things changed when the government introduced lottery finance, and there was lottery money available in Wales. I think my application for production finance to the lottery was the only one that came in that year, so there was little competition. I got £250k out of the lottery and matched that with private investment from Metrodome. Metrodome had established themselves as a producer of commercial British genre films with Paul Brooks as a veritable Roger Corman, who would take undiscovered talent and give them their first chance in feature films. So we made the film for £500k. I had written it with a bigger budget in mind, somewhere between £1.5m - $2.5m. So it was about making compromises work.

Q - What did you learn making 'Darklands'?

Julian - At film school I was in control of the shorts I made. I was in control of the casting. I was in control of the budget and the schedule. With *'Darklands'*, it was the first time I handed over control of the film to a producer. I found myself being forced to make compromises with casting, budget and schedule, which inevitably had a derogatory effect on the film. I also learnt that you really have to be careful about the crew you choose to work with because every film has its own constitution in terms of who the decision makers are and how those decisions get made. I learnt that it is important to go into a film as a director who has some influence on the production side of things and make sure that you are not turned into a Rumplestiltskin character, being asked to weave gold out of straw. I also learnt about the importance of script development. *'Darklands'* did go through a period of development, but in retrospect, I think it would have been a better film had I got another writer involved, which would have allowed me to become more objective to the material as a director. I also learnt how brutal the industry is. In the past I had ignored the whole business side of the process in terms of contracts and representation. I had to learn that very quickly in order to protect myself. I think going into the industry as an innocent, there are a lot of things you have to learn to protect yourself as you will work with people, particularly in the horror genre, who just don't have the same quality threshold as you have, or don't have the same moral and business ethics as you have.

Q - Were there any big shocks that hit you like a freight train during sales and distribution?

Julian - With *'Darklands'*, no, because I effectively gave away the project as soon as I started to direct it. I simply became the director and I wasn't really involved in any other aspect.

Q - Surely you made shit loads of money out of it?

Julian - Out of *'Darklands'*? No! I didn't make a penny - in fact I lost money. It was an extremely ambitious film for a £500k budget and, as I said, it was an exercise in making compromise work. During the shoot there were a couple of scenes that had been so terribly rushed that I wanted to re-shoot them, but the producers didn't have the money. So I funded the re-shoot myself without actually owning any of the film. I wasn't going to make anything out of it other than make sure that my reputation as a director wasn't jeapordised. So I went out, guerilla-style and re-shot several scenes at a cost of about £3k. Luckily, the actors were willing to come back for free and the producer turned a blind eye. In the end everybody was very pleased that I did it. That was the frightening aspect, if I hadn't have been willing to do that, the film would have been presented to the market and I don't think it would have been anywhere near as successful as it was.

Q - So all you got out of it was a directing credit, on something that at best you knew was as good as it could be based on the circumstances?

Julian - I agreed a fee of £20k with another £60k deferred, and I knew that I would never see the £60k. A week before shooting, the production had cash flow problems, and I was asked whether I would defer the other £20k, but the word deferral wasn't used - instead they called it a 'hold-back' which was presented to me as *'a corridor at the back end'* - a sort of guaranteed deferral. So, thinking I was helping everybody involved in making the film, I naively agreed - but eventually, I was only paid £2k, which was £1k less than what I spent on the re-shoots!

Q - How did the next film, 'Silent Cry' come about?

Julian - I didn't work for 5 years after that, partly because of the compromises that I was forced to make on *'Darklands'*. My agent at the time said had the film been 5% better, he could have got me my next feature gig, but despite my efforts to deal with all the curve balls thrown at me, my first feature film had fallen short. Meanwhile, I was developing a number of scripts with writers and one of those scripts was put on a script website. This was during the first year that the section 48 tax break funding became available and there was a company called Little Wing Films that found a way to use that to fund a whole slate of feature films. But these films had to be made immediately and completed by the end of the business year and they had got cold feet with one of their projects because it required extensive special effects work and therefore a protracted period of post production. So they shelved it and looked for a replacement project. They were actually fishing around on websites to try and find screenplays that were in an advanced state of development so that they could go into production within five weeks!

To get this into perspective, five weeks before shooting I was in the dole office, not the normal dole office, but the dole office you get sent to when you have been unemployed for several years and you feel like you are at the end of the line. I was in some horrible building in Neasden, surrounded by people that looked like they had just got out of jail. That's when I got the call... *'We've got £3m to invest in your film, but would you be ready to start shooting in five weeks?'* I seized it with every ounce of energy that I had left, and gave it my best shot.

Q - What did you learn on 'Silent Cry'?

Julian - The benefit of working with a team of people who are extremely professional, who have a high quality threshold and are there to support the director in everything that he wants to do. Well almost. It was the first bonded film that I had done, and therefore I didn't get a full choice of crew. Some of the crew members were imposed on me by the producers. I found that when those kind of decisions are made, they are made because they want to play safe, and sometimes playing safe is not the best way to make a good film. Sometimes you have to take risks, and I tend to be more of a risk taker. But you also have to give and take. Directing a film is not a totalitarian affair and the producer has as much right to contribute. *'Silent Cry'* is something that I was employed to direct. I could have quite easily been removed at any stage, and somebody else could have been brought in to complete it. I also learnt that the people behind the financing side were incredibly savvy accountants, who could maximise the tax possibilities, and gave a lot of new film makers a break.

Q - How did the film perform around the world?

Julian - When In-Motion Pictures presented the film at Cannes, they did a fantastic job with the posters and the marketing, but they were selling it as a TV film. They sold it to Australia, Indonesia, Malaysia, Scandinavia, Germany and it was screened on Channel 5 here in the UK. Unfortunately, In-Motion Pictures are now in the process of being taken over by another company, so *'Silent Cry'* is stuck in a state of limbo and I'm not sure who controls the rights, which of course is frustrating.

Q - Has it come out on DVD in the UK yet?

Julian - Not yet (2005). There are all kinds of theories as to why, but we don't really know. I don't think it has anything to do with the quality of the film. It is out on DVD in Germany, Scandinavia and Australia. There is now a trend in distribution where sales agents are going straight to TV. They are getting all the exposure and publicity from TV, then they will put it out on DVD. Also if cash flow is what you are interested in, the theatrical / DVD distributors are going to pay you a tiny minimum guarantee compared to the full buy out fees that a TV station might pay. In Germany, stations pay $120k for the TV rights, whereas a DVD distributor will probably give you, if you are lucky, $20k for the DVD rights. So there is an argument to sell it straight to TV. It is a better option if the film doesn't have the kind of theatrical potential that is required. To be honest, most European films, most non-Hollywood films, do not have the theatrical potential that is required.

Q - How much money did you make out of sales and distribution on 'Silent Cry'?

Julian - Again because I was a director for hire, I didn't make anything from sales and distribution because I don't own the film. But I got paid a handsome salary to direct it. It was that salary that I used to fund *'The Last Horror Movie'.*

Q - So I guess the lesson here is, no matter how you get your picture made, don't assume you are going to get any money out of the back end, so try and get paid up front?

Julian - Absolutely. You are only ever going to see money out of the front end of any deal. When a sales agent and a producer sell the film to the distributor, they get the MG - minimum guarantee. It may as well be the maximum guarantee! When the film is distributed, it goes through various other sub-distributors that take their share. The amount that trickles back to the distributor, and then trickles through the sales agent and back to the producer is negligible. It is easily consumed by P&A expenses. However, you could make the back end work. For instance, if I was directing a low budget film and there wasn't enough to pay me a decent salary, I would say *'That's fine, I'll accept the salary that you are offering, but I want Germany, and I will sell it to Germany myself.'* I have relationships now with several German distributors, and three of my films have been distributed in Germany successfully. I am confident that I am at least going to get a minimum guarantee from Germany, which would amount to what I would normally expect to be paid.

Q - So as each film utilised a bigger budget than the last, why did you choose to make a movie on a camcorder next?

Julian - Two reasons. I became frustrated with the film making process. The production designer on *'Darklands'* described it as being *'rail-roaded'*. You stick the director on a set of rail tracks and you keep them on there throughout the whole process. I couldn't take risks or do anything that they thought might undermine the project. Let's bring in the old guys with experience, like the DP, the editor, people who have a proven track record, so they can make the big decisions. You feel like you are on some sort of production line. It happened on *'Darklands'*. It happened on *'Silent Cry'*. I knew that I was better than that. I still hadn't been given the opportunity to show what I could do. I realised that the only way that I was going to do that would be to put my money where my mouth was and do something where I made all the decisions. At the same time, it had been a long term ambition to make a low budget independent horror movie inspired by *'The Texas Chainsaw Massacre'*, *'Night of the Living Dead'* and *'Evil Dead'*. I attempted to come up with ideas and scripts in the past that were derivatives of those films, and shoot them on 16mm. I still needed a good £200k to do it justice, and I could never raise that amount of money. Then digital film making came along, which allowed me to do it for £50k. I had £50k, my fee from *'Silent Cry'*, and what I considered to be a brilliant idea, so the timing was right.

I realised as a director that knowledge is power and you only really have the knowledge if you become a producer and understand what happens with the money. If you control the money side of things, it has an influence. You are therefore controlling the creative side as well because nobody can tell you, *'Oh we can't do this, because of this'*. You can turn round and say *'Well, actually we can!'* At the end of the day, that is what makes a good film - if the director is given enough space, enough room to do his thing. That is exactly what I did with *'The Last Horror Movie'*.

Q - What is the concept of 'The Last Horror Movie'?

Julian - The film is a video diary of a serial killer, but the serial killer has made the film to choose his next victim, and he does that by recording the film on top of an existing horror film, called *'The Last Horror Movie'*. The idea is that the next person who rents that film after the killer has returned it to the video store, gets followed by the killer, and becomes his next victim. So YOU, the unsuspecting viewer, think that you are going to watch one film, and five minutes in you discover somebody, the serial killer, has taped over it. He was there when you rented the film, followed you home, and you are the next victim. The idea was really born out of my desire to do something different with the horror genre and push the boundaries. It was an attack on the teen slashers of the 90s, and in many ways it deconstructs the genre. Ultimately, it is confronting the audience on a number of levels about why it is the audience likes to watch a horror film. As a horror film maker I always get asked *'Why do you make horror films?'*, and this is an attempt to answer that question. Also I think that people like to watch horror films because they know that what they are watching is second hand, it is safe, it is fiction. Some of the most powerful horror films push the envelope on realism. So you've got Orson Welles' radio broadcast of *'War of the Worlds'*, *'The Texas Chainsaw Massacre'* which was presented as a reconstruction of true-life events, *'The Blair Witch Project'*, which presented itself as real footage that had been found and edited together. I wanted to take that a step further. The best way that I could think of doing it was to not only suggest to the audience that what they were watching was real, but they were also now going to be directly threatened by the character within the film. They are no longer safe within the sanctuary of their living room watching the TV screen and thinking that they are watching fiction. The guy could be outside. I thought that is possibly as far as the genre, or at least that aspect of realism in horror could be pushed, apart from hiring somebody to actually kill a viewer! (laughs)

Q - How did you find working with a smaller crew, and what were the disadvantages when shooting it?

Julian - I think this type of film making has all the same values as the Free Cinema movement, the French New Wave, and the American New Wave where the Studio System self destructed and the film students and critics came out with their hand held cameras and started to produce fiction. Not within a studio, not on a set, but on the street. With digital it's the same, except you have even greater freedom because you can use available light. Suddenly, you don't need gaffers and grips, lights and generators. You can literally work with a documentary-sized crew, and that cuts down time and expense. What were the negatives? Very few, apart from the fact that with digital (DVcam / miniDV etc.) you do tend to have to shoot everything quite close. You can just about get away with mid-shots, but wide-shots tend to pixelate. You just don't have the definition. Also it works very well in dark interiors and available light situations. But when you are outside during daytime, especially if it is a bright, cloudless day, it can be a real problem trying to get a good image. I think that the ideal with digital, which Michael Mann did with *Collateral*, is that you take available lighting into account when you write the script and choose locations.

Q - What did you learn shooting it, making it?

Julian - Because we were shooting it as if it were a documentary, it was often shot in real time. I wasn't using my usual approach of breaking a scene up into shots and creating this jigsaw puzzle that would often be shot out of order and then reconstructed in the editing room. Instead, we were shooting every scene in one long developing shot. Everything happened in real time, and

that completely changed the whole emphasis of the process. Whereas before the actor would be reduced to being, as Alfred Hitchcock used to say, *'cattle you could push around on the set'* suddenly they became everything. Forget the actor hitting their spot. Forget the fact that the camera is out of focus. What matters is the performance. A film is only as good as its worst performance. We had some fantastic performances in *'The Last Horror Movie'*. We had a great idea, a great script and a great cast. None of the actors were stars, but they had talent. It proved to me that there is a lot of undiscovered talent out there. The question is how will I take what I have learnt from this type of garage film making and apply it to a more conventional way of making a film, where I have to break a scene up into 25 shots and create a jigsaw puzzle where nobody really knows what is going on except the director. I'm in favour of tilting the balance of power on the set, as much as possible towards the actor, which lends itself towards a realist school of film making. You can't apply that to every type of film, but it was a valuable lesson to learn how to get good performances.

Q - Did you have any budgetary concerns, did you stay on budget?

Julian - The budget started at £30k but went up to £50k by the time we had finished shooting. Mainly because the producer persuaded me that I needed more production value in the wedding scenes and also the murders, if the film was going to stand a chance of competing in the market place. *The Last Horror Movie* was designed to go straight to DVD and we only really needed to deliver a Digibeta, but I knew that the festival circuit was an important way of platforming the film, and that meant we needed a 35mm print. So we had to spend another £15k to get it up to 35mm. Then I realised there are so many festivals out there that one print isn't enough, so I spent another £1.5k on another print. With all the marketing, publicity and festival expenses, the project came in at £85k.

Q - So how was the film received by the market?

Julian - The first territory to go for it, and they went for it with gusto, was the US. The ideal scenario would have been to get the film into Sundance or Toronto, as those are the key festivals for this kind of film. I knew that if I broke America, then the rest of the world would follow. America sneezes and the rest of the world catches a cold, that was my plan! I knew that the distributor that I wanted was Lion's Gate, but they didn't respond and I didn't get into Toronto or Sundance because the festival programmers thought that *TLHM* was too similar to *Man Bites Dog*, which was disappointing. Then Fangoria put in a small offer, which was attractive as the theatrical costs were not crossed with DVD, so as far as the accounting is concerned, there is no way of eating up future DVD profits through theatrical expenses. Once America had gone for it, Tartan picked it up in the UK. We went on the festival circuit and played 50 festivals, and we won 14 awards, and slowly but surely all the smaller territories bought it.

Q - If you were to advise a new film maker about their contract with a sales agent, what are the clauses that you would say "Try and get this in"?

Julian - Sales agents will want to put themselves in first position to recoup their expenses. So however you funded your film, whoever you have got in first position, suddenly the sales agent checks in and says they are in first position. Chances are, even if it is remotely successful, the minimum guarantee payments will barely cover the sales agent's expense. So the sales agent is cash flowing its company on the revenue from your film. This might be acceptable of a film where everybody has been paid a union rate, but it's not acceptable for guerilla films when cast and crew have worked for free. When selling deferred payment films, I think the sales agent has got to bear in mind that it is just unviable to put themselves in 1st position. The best deal that you can strike is to just say, *'Look, let's do Pari Passu'*, where the sales agent takes 10% of what he sells the film for, against his expenses, and 15%-25% commission of everything. When you strike a deal like that, you don't need to put a cap on expenses because the sales agent should continue to sell the film, and every sale that they make, they are going to be spending money doing it, so they may as well repeat that 10%.

Q - It is in their interest to sell as much as possible?

Julian - Yes. I've also heard it advised that you have a performance clause in the contract where if they don't achieve those sales figures by a certain time, then you get the rights back. The other key thing is deliverables (all items needed by the sales agent to sell the film, also called the Delivery List). Sales agents have a generic list of deliverables that they will slap on the table and say *'OK, this is what we want from you, and if you don't deliver, you breach your contract'*. At the end of the day, most of the deliverables are unnecessary. If you are delivering straight to video, you need the basics. The distributor or sales agent may ask for the 5.1 sound mix broken down onto DA88, which is great for *Harry Potter*, but this isn't the same. I could have spent another £10k on providing the sales agent with all the deliverables on the generic delivery list, but I knew they would not be needed, and only if they were requested by the distributor, would I spend the money to make them available. That is one way of saving money. The other thing is that the sales agent will often employ a delivery company to deliver

to the distributors. The delivery company will charge the distributor a mark up fee, so why doesn't the producer do it instead? At least you would be getting some revenue back that is not going via the sales agent. However, the problem with this is that you have to be available to do the deliveries when it is required. Then you become a delivery company and not a producer. You have got to be aware of that.

Q - This is the age-old dilemma - you could control the sales yourself, but at what cost?

Julian - The real cost is what you become. You become a delivery company, a sales agent, a lawyer looking at contracts, and an accountant. Two, three or four years could pass by very quickly and you have no time to sit down and write your next script or develop your next project. So there is a price to pay. I suppose you have got to start somewhere, and the ideal thing is next time round, you will employ people or get interns to cover those things. The only way to learn is by doing it yourself. The one good thing I would say about me doing all this recently is I now understand the business of film more than I ever did. I'm not talking about making films, I'm talking about selling them, distributing them, exhibiting them, and how that reflects on the type of film, as a producer, you should be making. The problem with a lot of films is that they are made by people who have no understanding of that side of the business, and therefore they are hoping that it is going to find it's place in the market. Whereas if you have the experience that I've had, and you can say *'I know what distributor is going to buy this, I know what audience is going to come and watch it, which festivals it is going to play well at...'* You can look at an incoming project as a producer and say *'Yes, this is going to work.'*

Q - Because digital is so cost effective, so transportable, why not get on a plane and shoot your movie in downtown Milwaukee, making it an American movie? How would that have affected sales and distribution?

Julian - Our US distributor described *'Darklands'*, which was shot in Wales and cast with Welsh actors, as a foreign, art house film. Jo Blo in Milwaukee can't understand regional UK accents and even the Queens English can irritate. The only films that a mainstream US audience want to see are American films with American actors in them.

Q - How do you keep going from one project to the next?

Julian - That is the problem with being a film maker. Once you have finished your film, you are back where you started, and you have got to somehow pick yourself up and find the motivation to make the next one. It consumes a vast amount of your time. So I think yes, go out and do it, but make sure that the film is going to reward you in some way. More than just *'I've made a feature film'*, that is not enough. I've made a feature film that has got international distribution that has recouped the money that I've put into it. For that you need a good idea and a good script. That could be the easiest part because it is just you, your computer and your brain. That doesn't cost you anything.

Q - Given that film making is an antisocial and obsessive behaviour, what impact does that have on your reality in terms of interfacing with normal people?!

Julian - Ask my ex-wives! It is difficult, but I don't think it is as extreme as going to war, and coming back as one of those freaked out Vietnam vets. But when a film maker is not making a film, it becomes difficult to live a normal life. You are used to the adrenaline rush of getting out of bed in the morning with a real tangible purpose. It is very difficult to get out of bed in the morning when all you've got to grasp hold of is *'pie in the sky'* and you know the gargantuan effort it is going to take to make it reality. One of the great things about making a film, is the opportunities it gives you. I've spent the last two years traveling all over the world attending film festivals and premieres. I have been to about twenty-five different countries with *'The Last Horror Movie'* - some of those places I'd never been to before. The festival circuit is a great perk of the job, without which, film making might be a thankless task.

Q - What were your biggest mistakes in terms of career?

Julian - I wouldn't describe it as a mistake, but I tend to do things the way I want to do it. I find it very hard to be anything other than brutally honest. I can't pretend. I can't tow the line and compromise when I know that there is a better way of doing things. I think that has possibly created the wrong impression of me being 'difficult'. The reality is that it is not about me, it is not about my ego, it is about the film. I'm not interested in being a film maker. I'm interested in making good films. You could say that making *'Darklands'* with all the compromises involved, knocked my career back five years. You could say that that was a mistake. But without making *'Darklands'*, I wouldn't have had the showreel or experience to get *'Silent Cry'*, and without *'Silent Cry'*, I wouldn't have had the money to make *'The Last Horror Movie'*.

Q - What advice would you offer a new film maker?

Julian - Forget film. Embrace the digital medium with everything that you have got. Prove how good you are using that medium and regard it as the waste product of the process. Because at the end of the day, if you come out with something that is exceptional like Chris Nolan did with *'Following'*, it will launch you into another stratosphere. The problem is, new filmakers are still hankering after 35mm film, and it is just increasingly a more difficult goal to achieve. It is affordable to make your own feature film in your bedroom now, and make it as good as anything Hollywood is doing. So why not just do it? It really is as simple as that.

Steve Simpson
Writer and Director

THE TICKING MAN

Q - Did you have a passion for film when growing up?

Steve - I wasn't particularly interested in movies as a child. Not like Spielberg or Rodriguez who knew they wanted to be directors at twelve or something. In fact, looking back on it, the film thing kind of crept up on me. It was a subconscious thing from watching BBC2 and Channel 4 matinees on a Saturday afternoon or going and watching great old movies. The thing that actually got me to pick up a camera funnily enough was two people, Bruce Lee and Jackie Chan. As a teenager, I loved their movies and started doing martial arts. When I was 18, I became a stockbroker, but at weekends I'd get friends together and we would shoot martial arts movies. The fights were great, but the films looked like shit! I would watch all these martial arts movies - sometimes three a night - and they were usually terrible. But one time, there was this Japanese samurai movie on TV called *Kagamusha*. It was the first time I watched Kurasawa. I thought *'this is something else'*. I then started renting better things and got sucked into the whole concept of directing. By the time I was 23, I had directed my first movie, which was the first serious script I wrote. It was a very bleak character drama about someone who was conceived through rape. It was the polar opposite of what actually got me to pick up a camera in the first place.

Q - So did you go to film school?

Steve - No. My training ground was actually when I was a stockbroker / financial advisor. I set up a film making group, which I called *'Roaring Fire Films.'* I didn't want to call it Camera Club, or anything stupid like that. So I set up a group of people from different walks of life. Most of us had jobs, and at weekends and evenings we'd go out and shoot films. The first film I'd ever shot was fifty minutes long, and it should have been 35 minutes, but they didn't have non-linear editing then. The next one was eighty minutes long and should have been sixty minutes. They were kind of epic, period adventure movies. We'd make costumes and go out to ruined castles and film these action scenes. We filmed it in three months, which we just made out of evenings and weekends. Other people in the group would shoot other things and through a twelve-month period, we got a lot done. We didn't have editing, so we actually shot the equivalent of about three features. I think two of them haven't even been cut.

Through that time I was writing scripts and eventually when I moved to LA, I interned for Roger Corman Studios for six months. There were two things that struck me almost immediately. One of which was, I expected everyone who wanted to get into film in the entire world to be beating down his door to start there because as far as I was concerned, it was the only place to start. You get thrown in at the deep end. Within the first week I was working for all the executives. There are almost as many interns as paid staff in the office, so you could be working for the head of production, head of development, head of international sales, head of home video, all within the same week or in the same day. You really get a great sense of all different sides of the business. The thing that astonished me was that most of the interns didn't even know who Roger Corman is. They were just there for school credit. Only a handful of people arrived thinking this is my film school. It was the easiest place to start because he would take any free labour.

Q - I'm always surprised by the number of people who say 'I want to be in the film business, I want to make movies', but there is only a 1% or 2% of people who have the dedication to do it.

Steve - I absolutely agree with that. The second thing that grabbed me the most when I got over there was that I was 22, probably the youngest intern there. There were people there who were in their early thirties. There was another stockbroker, a guy who had a six-figure salary on Wall Street and a guy who was a programmer at IBM all working there for free just to get a grounding. We were obviously committed. The other thing that struck me when I went to Corman's was that I expected people to have been busily writing and filming on their own as I had. But, none of them had filmed as much as I had or written as much as I had. There was an assistant editor I worked with who was ten years older and had done the full directing programme at NYU. I'd directed and written more than he had! He was $60k in debt from his course, which he had to work any job he could to pay off. That really got me. The other thing was realising that Corman made things happen so easily. There are a lot of Corman stories, some of them are very embellished, but some of them are absolutely spot on.

He just filmed 'The Fantastic Four', which he'd been paid just over a million dollars to make. But for various reasons, it had to be shelved. Corman went down to the studio just towards the end of the shoot on a Friday morning, and said 'OK, we are going to make another picture.' They dusted down and re-wrote an old sci-fi script over the weekend, then on Monday, Tuesday, Wednesday they cast, then on the Thursday they were in production. It's all about perception, and how you choose to make it.

I only went out there for 6 months. A friend of mine, who was a successful TV Writer, wrote me a letter when he knew I was coming back saying 'Don't come back!' kind of like 'stick at it!' I think he thought I was coming back with my tail tucked between my legs. But I was coming back to shoot a feature that I had written set in Aberdeen. So I came back in May '93 and was firing out letters to try and get funding for a budget of half a million. And then a budget of $250k, then the budget kept shrinking to the point where it was what was just in my bank account! I had $17k sitting there to play with and I'd committed to a friend in LA who was going to come over and help me with a production. At this point I wasn't smart enough to have any sense of reality of the business and stupidity is one of the best assets you can have in this game, if you use it right!

Let's face it, if we had common sense we'd be doing something else. So I started setting up things, but I wasn't getting any response from anyone I was sending the script to. I didn't know where to get cameras, so I went into Grampian Television one day to speak to the guy who ran the facilities, to find out how much it would cost to rent some lights - and I came away with a deal where they were letting me have all the equipment I needed for nothing! Cameras, editing, full lighting store, sound everything! This guy, Eric Johnstone, who retired just shortly after, was just the most wonderful man and he made all the difference in the world, because I could never have afforded those things.

Then I had my DOP, Assistant Director, a Gaffer and a friend who effectively Associate Produced, who was Roger Corman's lawyer and he helped me with the legal work. They all came at their own expense to work on this film. I got some key crew from Edinburgh, people with a bit of experience. Nobody was shooting features in Scotland, so they were glad to get the experience. Then I had a bunch of people from my film group help out as well - all of which actually ended up with full time jobs in the film business. We just went and shot with that budget on 16mm.

Q - Tell me about 'Ticking Man' and the frustration you had with the multiple projects leading up to that?

Steve - One film I made, *Ties,* kind of worked. We won Best British Film at Cherbourg, and played at some good festivals. It was critically mixed, and the same with the audience, some people loved it and some people thought it was the biggest piece of shit. The truth was somewhere in between. Then after that, I'd go back and forth to LA developing other projects. I ended up shooting the opening to this promo for a project called *Pulse*. I got a lot of interest including having some very good sales companies wanting to handle it even before they'd read the script. For a while I was locked into that, and I wanted to shoot it on £250k because I could comfortably do it for that. Yet they wanted me to do it for a minimum of £750k because it needed to be bonded. It needed to be this, it needed to be that, which meant it needed a certain amount of estimates to come in, which could only be done with certain names. And a few years ago there were very few bankable actors in their 20's out of the UK.

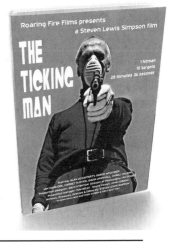

So, one got caught in this trap where we were literally a week or two away from production and the whole thing collapsed. So we were really frustrated and a friend of mine suggested that I pursue a documentary project. Some money manifested itself quickly, as did a DV camera and I flew to Indonesia and shot this little documentary. It was a wonderful experience. It was very liberating as a film maker. Then I had this project, 'The Ticking Man' that was written before, but the premise was slightly different. I had finance for it and I'd gone to the States to find an American lead for it. The premise revolves around this mass shooting incident in Scotland in a tiny little community. When I was in LA looking for cast, the Dunblane massacre happened, so we immediately said *'OK, we've gotta forget about this project.'* Years later, I realised this was a perfect project for digital, low-budget film. It's got quite a scope in terms of locations and the actual idea. It's all daylight, outdoors in Scotland where you can get amazing locations for nothing. So I dusted it down, and just started casting and I just started going for it.

In the meantime, I thought I'm going to fire an application into Scottish Screen, just for the hell of it. There was no way in hell they were going to give me money for it, but I might as well, so I put it in for only £25k, which is a level where it didn't have to be approved by a committee. It was a very functional script that worked well for an exciting, strong movie, but as a read it was pretty lame because I wrote it to be shot, not to be read. I got the coverage back from them and it was the worst coverage I'd ever had. I wrote back a letter taking the piss out of their coverage, and funnily enough John Archer, who was head at that point, came up to me just after he had resigned, and just commented on how he really loved the response I gave to their coverage. I basically just undermined their readers. They couldn't understand if there was dramatic potential in this film about a bunch of people being massacred in a rural place in Scotland. What is more dramatic?

Surprisingly they gave me the award. I think they might have thought, well for £25k we don't have to hear from him for a while! So I had another private investor put up £5k, then I'd put £5k in-kind on the table in terms of equipment that I had, and I deferred the rest up to £95k, which is mostly my cast and crew fees and my fees. Everyone was paid off the top, and they were paid a living wage the whole time. The cash cost of the film excluding VAT was £35k. We went and shot for 18 non-consecutive days. The bulk of it was shot over two and half weeks, and there was some bits that I did after that depending on people's availability. It went very smoothly for the most part, except for a couple of actors you would want to put over your knee and give them a good spanking. The rest of it was a dream, except for the Scottish weather. One day for example we shot 13 pages in 9 hours, and not in a way where one felt the material was being compromised. The crew was so small that we could move very fast, I had a DOP, Sound Recordist and Boom Op, and two people in the production office, other than myself.

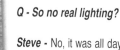

Q - So no real lighting?

Steve - No, it was all daylight. One scene where there was somebody hidden in a cupboard under the stairs, we just used a torch! That's what the character had, and it worked. It was very liberating. We moved fast, and everyone had a fun time. There is one thing that is very true about low budget, which I found on my first film, which is feed the crew well. I think that's the thing, if nobody is getting paid, don't insult them by feeding them badly. Then again, I feel that people on a low budget spend too much money on proper catering. It's one of those ailments that actually creates a high cash budget. So if you are paying them a decent enough wage, so long as everyone feels like they are in it together, and they are not making a piece of shit, they are totally happy with lesser food - just wholesome and filling. That way they are not eating their wages.

Q - So from a production point of view, you conceived a screenplay that could be made very cost effectively?

Steve - Kind of, although I have to say that I've never written a script with a budget in mind. I just come up with ideas that I love, that could be done on a very low budget. Before *The Ticking Man*, I'd produced a 40 minute film called *Frog* for a very good friend of mine. It's a dark fairy tale, and we shot it for about £12k on film, over 18 days. We had animatronics, and every set was built from the ground up. Even to the point where the cutlery around the table was hand designed and the crockery was hand painted. Nobody got paid. It looked amazing, really amazing. Nobody in their right mind would have made it on low / no budget, but it is that thing if you are just prepared to spend the time and graft.

I think there was a revolution in people's minds, in '93 when we all saw *'El Mariachi'*. He was doing gags in that film, whether it be the sliding down the bar, or shooting things, it felt more exciting than a big budget movie. He wrote it around the things that he had, but he wasn't thinking small and I think that's the key thing.

Q - You shot Ticking Man *on DV?*

Steve - Yes, a VX2000, though I would probably shoot on an HD DV format now.

Q - From a production point of view, what mistakes do you think you made?

Steve - On *Ticking Man* the only thing that I look back on as a real pain in the arse thing is purely a dispute I had with an agent where they were being unreasonable. Apart from that, I don't really have a problem with anything. I actually like a sense of chaos on set, in a way, because I have a very short attention span. So when I get swamped by something it really makes me perform well. The funny thing about the way I work is that I write, produce and direct simultaneously. I know a lot of people produce and direct up until the point they start shooting, then the production team just gets swamped by the production responsibilities. I also effectively become my own AD because when you are wearing both hats, you naturally become so aware of the schedule. My feeling as a director is the moment you start getting behind, you start shooting yourself in the foot elsewhere.

Q - How did you approach post-production?

Steve - I already had an editing system so I just edited myself. The problem for *'Ticking Man'*, and this is back before Avid XpressDV came online, was that I was editing on Premiere – the movie was over 85 minutes and there were over 2,300 edits, including split-screen sequences that went up to larger split-screen sequences - split maybe over a minute and a half and comprised over 200 components with at the most 18 components on the screen at one time! That's just a lot of graft, laying it all out. It got to the point where the project became so large that Premiere couldn't handle it, and it started crashing a lot. On the new project, the sequel to *Ticking Man,* which is in post at the moment, I've been using Avid XpressDV the whole way. It's been so solid. It's not as complicated a project though, but even then, just the fact that you can take the project straight into Symphony suite is a major bonus.

Q - How important do you think post is?

Steve - Post-production is by far the longest commitment, or it should be. The biggest mistake low budget films make is rushing post-production because that is where you can rectify so many things. I had an actor fall ill the night before shooting the climax, which we were shooting at a castle right the way across Scotland. I had to postpone it, and we picked up a few weeks later. Because of people's availability, we could only do one day, which involved six hours driving within that day. I ended up shooting a nine minute long climax within that day, with only an hour and a half to shoot the absolute climax of the scene. I was doing single take stuff, bang it off, rush things forward, blah, blah, blah, and at the end of it I didn't think I had remotely enough. Then I started cutting it and really made things happen to the point where the most disastrous things became the most beautiful things on screen. I did it through effects I was using, changing time and stuff. Even down to the point that, I'd have a single frame where I'd have three different characters doing an action thing within each side - shooting it in a single take. The timings of them wasn't really working with the other events that were going on, so I'd split the screen and I'd re-time them in the edit. So I'd end up with my perfect take that we never covered on set.

Q - How important is sound?

Steve - The other thing that I think is forgotten, even more in low budget film, particularly if you are doing a genre film like action or horror, is sound design. Sound designers are the ones that if someone's got a very low budget, end up not getting the salaries that they might merit or deserve. The sound designers are potentially the ones who are hammered the most because they are the ones working with the most expensive equipment. In the market place, people will forgive a film a lot of things, but if it's an action movie, it needs to sound like an action movie. So we spent a long time in sound design. I ended up going in and track-laying the film myself at John Cobban's Glasgow studio. He'd let me in at nights, I would track lay until very late and then crash on the floor. He was so supportive. We spent a lot of time on it, so the film sounds good. It really has a big sound, and really helps suck an audience in as well.

Q - When you sit with an audience watching independent films, there is no bigger indicator of 'I am a cheap film' than the sound being bad. Do you agree?

Steve - We actually took it a little bit to the extreme. We decided that because of doing International M&Es, we did all of the dialogue in post-production. Not out of fixing problems, but out of stylistic choice. So every footstep was fully foleyed. We actually ADR-d most of the dialogue in the film because a problem with DV is that if you do on-board sound, it's a bit hissy. I would personally recommend recording on a different unit, which is cleaner sounding. So we ADR-d most of the film, out of creative choice, and it worked really well, and managed to tweak some performances which was good. What I ended up doing when I shot *Retribution* (the sequel) was that I decided with the sound designer that all I was going to shoot was guide track on location. That really freed us up even further and even saved money in terms of sound recordists. I'd occasionally have somebody

hold a boom pole, then we would replace all the dialogue in post. The end result just sounds so good, so layered and so deep.

Q - So how long would it take to do a low budget feature, ADR, with all the actors, all the performances from beginning to end?

Steve - To have done the whole thing on *'Ticking Man'* would have taken about two weeks including getting all the elements together. It normally works out about a page an hour to shoot, just when you break down their lines. With *'Retribution'* the sequel, it's got way more dialogue, and it worked out at more or less four weeks. What I've done with the sequel is set aside somewhere in the region of 16% of the budget purely for the sound design, which is a good percentage. If my sound designer was charging his book rate, I'd be paying quite a bit more than I am. The fortunate thing is that he really gets much more out of doing this kind of project, because it's much more creatively satisfying than doing yet another crappy short. I'm very fortunate to have him.

Q - Are there any advantages to using camcorder style camera and shooting ultra light?

Steve - I really stripped things down in *'The Ticking Man'*, but with the sequel *'Retribution'*, I've done it even more. With *'Ticking Man'* I ended up shooting quite a lot of pick-ups myself in the edit - very simple things like *'OK now I want shot of a hand pulling a pin out of a grenade.'* So I'd go out into my garden, find a similar background, my hand doubled for about five characters in the film. I put a lot of pick-ups and that is the great thing about DV - you don't have to get a camera shipped up from London.

Also, when I started shooting the sequel, I started shooting it before I had confirmation of finance because one of the lead actors was on contract with the RSC. He got a week's holiday, and I got him up and shot all of his stuff within a few days - most of the time it was just me and him. The stuff looked good, so I became confident that I could shoot the sequel, so I didn't get a DOP in. Also, actors develop a particular relationship with the DOP that is separate to the director and I wanted to experience what that was like. The moment I knew we had it, the actors knew we were onto the next set up, because they were just following me. I'd just pick up the camera and walk and they would follow me. So the speed that we could move was fantastic. We'd average maybe 8/9 hours of a shooting day on the sequel, and I typically got between two and two and a quarter hours of footage in the can within that time. So it's a very efficient operation, a lot of locations, a lot of turnover of scenes, it was a very complicated script in the sequel. I'd have a couple of

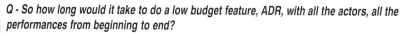

production people just preplanning stuff, packing boxes and stuff. You can have so much fun, particularly because in the sequel everyone was getting quite nicely paid. To the point where, no matter what my budget was, I'd always try and minimise the amount of resources on set at the time, because it's a great feeling the intimacy you have with characters.

Q - One thing actors do get concerned about is how they look. How did you take care of make-up and wardrobe? Or did you just let them deal with it?

Steve - I was fortunate I guess, none of the actors came across as particularly vain. The funny thing is on my first projects, whenever I had make-up people there, I always hated what they did. I always thought it looked fake. I like stylised naturalism where you put the audience into a situation that feels real and then stylistically pushing it to the point where everything amped up. So we didn't have make-up. Traditionally, because film in it's primitive days needed so much light to look good; make-up was needed to make people look even human under all those lights. Whereas, if you want somebody to look real, nowadays, the camera does that. The only thing that I had make-up-wise in the sequel was a character with a lot of bruising on his face for most of the film. A friend of mine taught me how to do that so I did it myself.

Q - How many edits did you do and did you test screen it? Did you think it was working from the start?

Steve - I do everything more or less myself. Not because I'm a dramatic control freak, because I do love opinions. I've had people come in, sit down and watch things, give me an opinion, and go OK, and then literally just cut four minutes out. But with the *Ticking Man,* from quite early on I could see that it worked in terms of what it set out to do. For me it was a case of making it tighter and tighter. Sometimes it was a case of *'Well, I don't quite like that character as much in terms of he is always dreary'*, or I could go in and find takes where he was a bit lighter tone.

Q - Would you suggest editing a film yourself if you are pressed for budget?

Steve - Yes, if you can edit, but give yourself time. The main thing is, don't be overly excited about the world seeing it, because if they see it too early, you can blow the whole thing. Only let the world see it when it is ready. The thing that I've found from my first feature was that if I'd spent a bit more time over it, if I'd invested more time before going into production, and got a few more elements right it would have made a massive difference. Likewise in post.

Q - So let's move into the final chunk of the film making process: sales and distribution.

Steve - The actual film making is the easiest part as far as your sanity is concerned. The sales side, on my first feature, it got to the point where I didn't promote the film as much as I could have because I knew it was on an uphill battle. It was a very serious drama with no cast that half worked. With *'The Ticking Man'*, it was kind of a bit different, partly because it was a genre film. It was exciting and tense, it was pushing a lot of the right buttons for the audience even though I had a no name cast. It was a high concept movie. Something that somebody in Hollywood could throw me a lot of money to remake as a studio film. So when it premiered at the Montreal Film Festival, it got an amazing response from the audience. I had a few sales companies ask to see it after it played there.

The funny thing is, I'd sent copies of it to a handful of companies back here, and the thing I find about the UK is, it's the hardest place to get people to watch anything! I don't know what the hell these people do with their jobs! I had four sales companies phone me up to see it after Montreal. Three were in the States and one was in Canada. At the same time, no one in the UK was getting back to me except for a couple of the biggest companies that I sent it to. I knew they weren't going to handle it, but just thought it would be nice for them to see it anyway. They were American companies, and it was their London offices. So I had these four offers, and we ended up going with a sales company in Canada.

Q - Have they made any sales?

Steve - Yes. They got six sales within four weeks of handling it, and they've got a few more since then. Although it started to tail off.

Q - Have they been sending you reports? Have they sent reports?

Steve - They have. They are timely-ish!

Q - Crucially, the $64m question, have you got any cash out of them?

Steve - Yes. I got a small advance.

Q - How has the UK done?

Steve - I've set up a deal where it should be released by the same UK distributors as *'Retribution'*.

Q - In terms of your future career, has the film presented any opportunities that have been exciting or surprising?

Steve - It's funny because the moment *'The Ticking Man'* was done, I decided to go ahead and do the sequel. The sequel is entirely different, the first one is an action thriller, this is a straight on thriller. What I haven't done yet is go out to LA, and done the rounds with *'The Ticking Man'*. Because it's such a stylised film, it could potentially establish me, in terms of doing a much bigger films. It is something that people would watch and say *'This guy should be directing thrillers!'* But there is much more to me than thrillers. I'm doing a feature length political documentary of the American Indians that I've been shooting for six years for example. In

terms of future things, the good thing is now I've got a body of work that works on it's own terms. Because they are stripped down budgets, and they are so financially sound, my whole business plan is based around financially viable film making, whatever the budget. If somebody gives me $10m, I will make a film that's going to compete with $50m movies.

Q - In terms of having these pictures behind you, is it easier to get a call returned?

Steve - I think that certainly the speed in which the sequel came together financially indicated that I'd crossed a line, and that was great. I know having the combination is going to take it a stage further again. There is dialogue going on right now about other projects, some exciting ones, one set in Nicaragua, one set in the States, which I am writing, but they are still my projects, which can be done whichever way.

Q - What was the budget?

Steve - The final spend on *Ticking Man* was £30k on the production, and then there was another £5k that came in to cover the sound design. So £35k to deliver.

Q - What is the single biggest mistake that you've made?

Steve - My single biggest mistake probably was on *Ties*, going into production too quickly. If you hear from quite a few people that the script is not ready then seriously re-look at it. I think that shooting your first script without having written any others is a mistake, in the sense that you learn a lot a as writer through writing different things. I had written four or five scripts when I did my first one. The biggest mistake ultimately with *Ties*, was that the exposition was boring.

Q - What advice would you offer a new film maker?

Steve - It's not as scary as you think, but you might need therapy at the end of it!

Q - What is your background?

Claire - I studied an advanced GNVQ in Media studies and then got a broadcasting degree. That's where I met my business partner and co-producer of Fakers, Todd Kleparski. We both wanted to make movies so we decided to make shorts where we used our student loans to do so. I also helped produce some National Film School shorts which was an invaluable education.

Q - How did Fakers come about?

Claire - A year after university, I was selling film stock in Soho, trying to get a foot in the door when Richard Janes, the director of Fakers, turned up and said 'I've got £250k, and a script, do you want to produce it?' So, I said "Yes!" We had to raise more money, at least £850k and we finally got a total of £550k. All the money was privately invested. It was all people who knew people, who wanted to invest though the EIS scheme and who understood the risk, believed in the script, and believed in the director. The final budget however came out to just over £1m including post.

Q - What is the Enterprise Investment Scheme?

Claire - It's a government fund that was set up for high-risk small businesses. The key word is 'high risk', because most people can't get an investment if they are high-risk business as it's not attractive to investors. So the government does this so that investors get a little bit back in a tax break. The investors buy shares but they can't sell their shares in the first 3 years and the company can't release any dividends / profits in the first 3 years. If the company has made a profit, they can buy those shares back at a different price. But you can't give those guarantees in your business model or else you are not classed as high risk because you are giving a guaranteed exit route. It's all regulated by the SCEC (Small Company Enterprise Centre), so you have to get your prospectus approved. The SCEC are brilliant. If you've got any problems, you just go to them. You don't need a big, expensive accountant to do it. You can do it yourself; you just have to work with the SCEC.

Q - What did you shoot on, and how long did it all take?

Claire - We shot on 16mm anamorphic and did post via the digital intermediate route. We saved 70% of lighting and camera budget by dropping from 35mm to a 16mm budget. We shot for 10 weeks, had no real re-shoots but did take a break for Christmas coming back for a week in Spain. Post took 8 weeks in total and when a prospective investor who was going to invest half a million vanished, we shut down editing. We went to Cannes and met the Future Film Group, who told us about their super sale and lease back with equity investment, so we could procure 20% of the budget, which was just enough to get post-production done. Some of the original investors chipped in as well.

Q - How did you find Distribution?

Claire Bee
Producer of Fakers

Claire - We contacted all distributors and to fulfil the wishes of some eager buyers, we did show some the off-line edit which was definitely a big mistake. We eventually had a big screening and Content, who are part of ContentFilm in New York, saw it and have been our sales agents since.

Q - So as yet how much money have you got from them?

Claire - Zero as yet! I think Fakers has made about $260k worth of sales from the smaller territories like Scandinavia, Russia, Portugal, Greece and a theatrical in Japan. But the big territories like France, Germany and America wouldn't bite because it's a UK film and if it didn't have a sale in it's own territory, then why should they take it? So the UK theatrical release became the golden apple. We soon signed up with Guerilla Films and had to raise a further £35k for the P&A as well as getting Content to release the UK rights back to the producers for us to do the deal.

Q - If I had said to you before Fakers, here's a million pounds, what would you now make in hindsight?

Claire - I would have made a horror movie or a romantic comedy - something that was much more defined in its genre. The problem with Fakers is that it's a commercial film, but it doesn't have the usual commercial bells and whistles like a big star attached. It doesn't fit in the art-house market at all either because that audience wants something that is totally different, something thought provoking and not purely entertaining.

Q - What advice would you offer a producer?

Claire - It's weird doing this interview, because your book helped like you wouldn't believe! If you are starting from scratch, I would have some sort of job to fall back on to be able to pay the bills. Get the best crew you can, make sure you know what you are saying to investors. Don't say, 'you will have your money back in a year.' It's a really small industry; so don't play people off each other - especially facility houses, post-production houses and crew. If you can't secure that person for that much money, then you can't secure them and finally, spend more time on the script!

NOTE - full interview on the CD

Jake West
Writer and Director

FROM RAZOR BLADE SMILE TO EVIL ALIENS

Interview begins in 1999

Q – Why did you want to get into movies?

Jake – I always loved movies and from an early age it seemed to be an exciting thing to do. I loved horror movies and was influenced by directors like Sam Raimi and Peter Jackson. I was inspired by that fact that for low budget film makers, horror was always a good solid starting point for a career.

Q – You are an editor – is that how you got into the film business?

Jake – At film school I edited a lot of people's stuff for them and learnt a hell of a lot through the editing process. That has proved invaluable in the making of my movies.

Q – 'Razor Blade Smile'- it's a black PVC shrink wrapped bare breasted vampire with machine guns thing – how did, um, why?

Jake – I wanted to do a vampire movie in a way I hadn't seen before and to not hold back. I have always been interested in the fetish scene, it's a look that is very striking and when you photograph it, it looks brilliant. Vampires are seductive creatures and a nineties vampire would wear rubber rather than lace or velvet – it just seemed a natural progression of vampire eroticism to take the sexy contemporary clothing and dress them in it. After I decided on a female vampire I asked what would they do with their time? Well they're good at killing people, OK so make them an assassin...

Q – How long did it take to write the screenplay?

Jake – A year and twelve drafts as I knew it was important to get right. To begin with it was funded by the fact that I was editing and directing, stuff like film trailers and pop promos. I had to tailor everything in the story to the fact that I knew I had very little money to make the movie - some of the earlier drafts were better, but I had to cut out some of the bigger set pieces and shrink everything down to a do-able size.

Q – How much money did you have to go on initially?

Jake – It was a 23 day shoot and we shot it for £16k, £12k of which was mine. The rest was split between my Dad and two other film makers, Will Jeffrey at Maverick Media and Rob Mercer. We got it in the can for that £16k although I couldn't afford to process it at that point so we didn't see anything until much later - that was quite scary.

Q – What about the crew and how they worked under pressure?

Jake – It was a small crew, about eight people, sometimes less, all of whom were hard core and I could really trust. There was me, Jim Solan the DOP, James Pilkington the gaffer, my ex-girlfriend did all the costume, make up and bits like catering. Neil Jenkins was the Production Designer, an old film school friend. We had loads of sound recordists which was a pain, and a few days we had to shoot mute as there was no recordist. We had a special effects and make-up guy who didn't work out too well, especially as it's a horror movie, the effects and gore should have been outrageous.

Q – You said your ex-girlfriend – did the movie kill your relationship?

Jake – Yeah it did. I don't think it was the movie, I think that my obsession with film making would have killed it anyway. My first love was film making, and my second love was my girlfriend - I couldn't get any balance on it, I was completely obsessed. On a low budget you answer to no-one and I enjoyed that freedom. You also tend to try to do everything and work as hard as possible, but after a week, or even just a few eighteen hour days, you get very worn down. I was up all the time and just about managed to get through it, but it was a strain on a lot of other people. Because everyone was very dedicated it was ultimately a very enjoyable shoot.

Q – What happened about casting?

Jake – I spent three weeks casting, sifted through thousands of CV's and saw forty people for the lead role of Lilith Silver. Ultimately I chose Eileen Daly as she was both the right actress for the part and incredibly dedicated. She was really fit and up for anything I threw at her, whether it was sex scenes or gunfights. She was fantastic.

Q – How did you approach shooting?

Jake – When working on such low footage ratios, there were times that I had to prioritise - there were some scenes that I absolutely had to get spot on, so I would spend two or three days shooting them, then there were other scenes where we literally spent ten minutes shooting them, often without sound unless there was dialogue. We could only afford a few takes at best, and even then if there was a problem with take one, I would move the camera angle for take two so that at the end I had an enormous amount of angles from which to cut.

Q – What did you shoot on?

Jake – Standard 16mm. We blagged most of it from production companies so we didn't have a choice. It was all Kodak, but we mixed all speeds - even so it looked great in the end.

Q – How long did it take to edit?

Jake – A year mainly because I cut on BetaSP in the evenings and weekends. I did have access to Avid suites but I didn't want to spend my time re-digitising whenever I had to move to a new suite. On tape, all I had to do was collect my tapes and relocate and I could carry on making creative decisions straight away. Usually I would work as an editor during the day, then at night I would cut my movie. So for about six straight months I didn't see anybody. I became like a vampire and was quite sickly. It's not good for you, but I was so dedicated to the project, by any means possible I would get it done.

Q – Did being an editor by trade help?

Jake – If I was a director who didn't have the ability to edit my own film then I don't think I would ever have got it done in the first place - it was always going to be a film with a fast editorial style. Many low-budget films are very slow, master shot after master shot and little or no action. I didn't want to make that kind of movie.

Q - What happened when you completed the cut?

Jake – Before I completed the cut I took two promos to Cannes to raise completion money. At this point we still only believed it would go out on video - never theatrically - so we were only looking for £20k. Finishing on film is a lot more expensive and certain things like a blow-up, sound mix, Dolby licence all cost a fortune - it's a nightmare.

You really have to be ready for Cannes and we made sure we were - we set up all our meetings in Cannes before we went by going through Variety and Screen and highlighting all the companies who liked this kind of movie. We had business cards, flyers and postcards made up, all with the address of where we were staying. I had cut a two and a half-minute trailer and a twelve-minute promo with a temp sound mix. As I had been cutting film trailers for years I really knew how to make what I had look even better - so I cut a world class trailer and I was really proud of it. We spent £1k doing all that stuff.

Q – So you are on the plane to Cannes with your trailers and flyers - what was going through your mind?

Jake – I didn't know what to expect - it was the first time that I had gone with a film and I knew that it would be crazy. I'm quite a social sort of character so I was looking forward to the parties too. I was never embarrassed to talk to people, so even if we did not get the money to finish the film I was determined to enjoy it. I think it was 'don't expect too much, don't be naïve, and keep your fingers crossed'. People are always looking for something interesting by new filmmakers and because of films like *Blair Witch, El Mariachi, Bad Taste* and *Evil Dead,* there is a tradition of new filmmakers churning out interesting work even though there are budgetary restrictions.

We put our flyers out in the hotels and all the places where the big companies had their flyers. We used the British Pavilion as a meeting point and place to leave and pickup messages. Most of the people in the British Pavillion weren't very helpful and turned their nose up at a vampire film - they just weren't very helpful with my project. So it was kind of well, *hey guys, if that's your attitude then that's fine*. I was very unhappy about that attitude, so when I did actually get completion money, to a certain extent it was two fingers up to some of those people. There were other people who were really supportive - mostly other film makers who had already made a first film. A lot of the people who had never made films were telling me how I should make the film and I thought *hold on, why am I taking advice from you? What have you done other than corporate videos – I don't think so pal.*

Q – So did you cut a deal at Cannes?

Jake – We did get a lot of interest from a German company but they really wanted to screw us in the deal and were taking too long. Over the following months, simple things like speaking different languages and not having top lawyers really made it hard work.

In the meantime, through Raindance, Elliot Grove had mentioned the movie to Wendy Striech at Manga as she was looking for projects. She saw the trailer, liked it, contacted me and we met. Even though it looked like Manga were going to take the movie, things went really slowly again - we were hanging around for six months twiddling our thumbs, waiting for the contract and money. I hadn't completed the cut so I thought I might as well carry on and finish the movie in the meantime.

Q – So how much did they stump up?

Jake – They needed a detailed budget outlining everything we needed, including the money I and the other investors had already put up. They wanted to do a theatrical release too so that meant a 35mm blow up. That lot came to about £160k. It was very expensive to blow up because I had 250 optical effects, loads more than an average movie. There were also 40 digital effects so there was nearly 300 effects shots in the movie.

Q – This was Jurassic Park on low budget!

Jake – Oh, no *Jurassic Park* had about 500 shots, and they were 3D. Because I had only ever thought the film would exist on video, I did lots of effects which on video are pretty much free. But when you go to film, all those things like making a shot half speed, making colour into black and white, special dissolves and wipes - they all cost shit loads of cash on film. And it took four months of my life too. It was hell. The digital effects were much easier though, done by Cinesite who I had a relationship with because of the promos I had done. They were great.

Q – What happened about the release in the UK?

Jake – The budget we had also included a $50k prints and ads budget. We demanded that money before signing with Manga so that we knew the movie would get out there. Then we knew there would be posters and ads in the magazines. Seeing our posters on the underground was like a fucking dream come true! Too many low budget films get released without advertising which is a mistake. If people don't know a film is released, they won't go and see it. I think it made a small profit of £3k. Even though it went out in some great theatres, it only played late night screens which restricted the audience to hard core fans. I pleaded with the distributors for evening screenings too, but they didn't want to know. I think that was a mistake.

Q – What were the reviews like?

Jake – Mixed - brilliant and awful. The more mainstream the reviewer the less they generally liked the film - and it hurts when you read a bad review. Some of the horror mags were great though, I mean really great reviews - the best I think was in Variety, fucking corking.

The movie was claimed to have cost just under £1m which I believe raised the expectations of reviewers. It's clearly micro budget in places and that just made us look a bit stupid. We felt we should have been honest about the budget and people would then have been more favourable. I mean, shooting a film for less that £20k is pretty special and it doesn't happen very much. People were saying at the time – oh, you had a million pounds for that, you had loads of money – and I'm like 'fucking hell guys, we got it out there, don't complain'.

Q – How did it do on video?

Jake – Good - it got into all of the main video shops with five or ten copies per store. We were number 13 in the video chart! And internationally it's been sold to Japan, France, Australia, and a lot of Asian countries. I think that most major territories have been sold.

Q – So, the big question – have you made any money?

Jake – (laughs) The film isn't in profit, no. I'm supposed to get quarterly reports but I have only had one so far, and this was before a lot of the sales had happened. According to the sales agent, the film has to make $500k before it goes into profit. But we did get that small advance so I made my investment back. So investor wise, we have all been repaid and I got back the money that I spent.

Q – Would you recommend deferments?

Jake – If you can pay people up front, even if it's a token fee, then do it. I did deferments because my budget was so small and I only had eight crew members most of whom were friends. Out of the advance they got about 20% of their deferments which is more than I think they expected.

Q – What mistakes did you make?

Jake – I knew that the film was going to be compromised from a writing point of view. Earlier drafts of the script were actually better but I just had to keep dropping the best bits. As soon as you write 'the set blows up' then you are going to have to re-write that scene – this I know! The bits I was most disappointed by were the make-up effects - there should be blood all over the fucking shop, it should be spurting out of people's necks, the kind of stuff that the fans like. I had to cut round it and that really pissed me off. In my mind the film was a lot gorier, and it should have been. One thing that I was pleased with was the lesbian scenes. I made that as strong as I could, without being pornographic - and the BBFC didn't demand any cuts! On the sex front I think I pushed quite hard, I haven't seen a micro-budget film with as much sex in it.

Q – Are you pleased with the way the movie turned out?

Jake – Well, I couldn't ask for any better than it is within the constraints of how it was made. I would throw down the gauntlet and say that I do not think that anyone could have made a better film under the same restrictions. I am sure that I could do better now, with a bigger budget, so for a first step it was all right.

Q – What advice would you give to a new filmmaker?

Jake – Don't do anything until you are happy with your script. It has to be a blueprint of what you are going to do. The other thing is to know how much you are capable of as a filmmaker. I have spent my life making little action movies and horror films on video so moving quickly and shooting entirely from the hip came very easily. Other film makers might have problems squeezing so much in without experience.

I think you need to be obsessed. I have never met a successful filmmaker who was not obsessed by film making. I really think that when you meet people your passion comes across - when you see interviews with people like Steven Spielberg, they are kids. If I am a bit of a geek, then that is all right – hey I have a life too!

INTERVIEW CONTINUES IN 2005, 5 YEARS ON FROM PREVIOUS INTERVIEW

Q - Since we last spoke, what has happened with 'Razor Blade Smile'?

Jake - In the UK, we have done a two-disk DVD set because the original DVD of *Razor Blade Smile* was really poor. It was never marketed as an *El Mariachi* style film, though your book revealed the truth. Anchor Bay bought out Manga, who distributed it. I do DVD extra work for Anchor Bay and when I heard that they had the rights to *Razor Blade Smile*, I pitched them a two disc set with a genuine making of, behind the scenes, deleted scenes and audio commentary to kind of put the record straight. I put my short film *Club Death* on there too, which at 30 minutes, isn't that short! It has a lot of the same actors and props as *Razor Blade Smile* and there is a feature about the journey between the two films. None of the features are a slap on the back kind of thing, they show how we actually achieved the making of the films. New film makers would probably find it useful.

Q - Have you seen any money from the release of this new DVD?

Jake - We haven't seen anything! The only money that we've seen from *Razor Blade Smile* was when we got the advance and paid some of everyone's deferred salaries. The plus side was that I did get my £12k investment back - the money that I put in personally. But seeing as how it took three years to make, it wasn't a well paid job.

Q - Would you have been able to make your second movie without doing Razor Blade Smile?

Jake - No. It was the stepping stone that got me to the next film. And it landed me my next investor because he was actually in the first film! My investor for *Evil Aliens* was managing a band called The Rain and I needed some extra gunmen for the scene on the rocks in *Razor Blade Smile*. So I asked the guys in the band because I had shot two pop promos for them. Their manager was a guy called Quentin Reynolds who loved film making and wanted to be a gunman, too. And he looks like a hard nut! So without that movie, I wouldn't have met him and got my next investment years later.

Q - What genre is Evil Aliens?

Jake - It is a tongue *through* cheek, *splat-stick* sci-fi/horror picture in the vein of *Evil Dead 2*. It is not an out and out comedy, but you can't take those kind of films seriously as people's arms do not come straight off like that in real life.

It is about an alien abduction that takes place on a remote Welsh farming island. The island is only accessible by a tidal causeway and therefore the only way you can get there is at low tide. A farm girl is abducted and impregnated by aliens and her boyfriend is killed, but no one believes her. Everyone thinks she is doing it for attention and a TV show with dying ratings picks up on it and sends off a TV crew to investigate. And being a Soho media crew, they think it is a load of bollocks because they have spent years looking into these things. So they start faking their own evidence to make the show exciting and then the real aliens show up and they are trapped on this farm and have to use farm weaponry to survive. They can't escape because of the tide so they use everything from hoes to combine harvesters to defend themselves.

Q - Who wrote the script?

Jake - I came up with the concept and wrote the script. I spent a year working on the idea and came up with a whole bunch of concept art. One thing I found when seeking investment was that when you do anything with aliens, the first question they ask is, *'what do the aliens look like?',* which is a good point because they might think they are going to be HR Giger style aliens, whereas mine are more practical due to the budget. I worked with my production designer on *Razor Blade Smile*, Neil Jenkins and we came up with designs for the aliens and their technology. It also helped with writing the script because it gave me ideas and changed what I originally wanted to do. So we had a visual package and a treatment - and used that to coax investors with the idea that if I found an investor, I would finish the script. This way I didn't waste six months of my time writing a script that wasn't going to get made. One guy I used to work for wanted to develop it, but most people didn't want to make a splat-horror, they wanted to make a serious *X-Files* alien abduction film. I wanted to make a love letter to my teenage years, to the films that I loved and there are not too many film makers these days who make that kind of stuff here. To make something with no social comment, just pure entertainment.

Q - What was the approximate budget?

Jake - It was under £1m, though right now I can't disclose the actual budget - maybe in the next edition of this book! We had a real crew this time and it was made professionally as opposed to *Razor Blade Smile*, which was made in an amateur way.

Q - How did you raise the finance?

Jake - We had one investor, Quentin Reynolds. He asked how much money we needed, so I came up with a number that wouldn't scare him off. I wasn't sure how I could pull the film off for that number, but I knew there were some emerging technologies like Hi-Def that would help, even with the effects. So I could not ask for £3.2m as you are not going to get that from one investor, and if there are many investors, the deal gets complex and it can take years. So I said a reasonable figure and because he wasn't a film maker he trusted that I could do it for that amount, especially after seeing that I made *Razor Blade Smile* for nothing. I think he knew I was going to be a safe bet.

Q - How did your background as an editor help with squeezing every penny out of your budget?

Jake - It took over a year to do the post on *Evil Aliens*. We had 152 digital effects shots. I don't think I would have been able to do it if I didn't have the editing background that I have, which gave me the confidence to know that I could do it.

Q - What was the time-table from getting the finance to being on set?

Jake - I got a call from Quentin just before Christmas in 2002 and we met up on January 2nd 2003. I hadn't seen him for years. He wanted to know what I was up to and I said was trying to raise money for a film. This was a friendly meeting so I didn't have anything on me to show him, but he said he might be interested in getting involved. So I pitched it and gave him the pack with the art and he wanted to know how much I needed. I told him I didn't have a budget yet and that the script still needed to be written. He said he was really interested in it and would give me a call later to discuss it. I thought that was the last I would see of him. Later that day he called me and asked what I needed to get the script

written and work out a budget. I told him that to do that, I would have to stop my editing work and concentrate on the script for three months. He said he would drop off a cheque the next day, which is fucking magic! And he was true to his word, dropped off the cheque, I put it into the bank and wrote two drafts of the script. I went to producer Tim Dennison to get it budgeted, and I explained how I intended to do it, because when you read it there are a lot of effects and it could have cost millions. I delivered the script to Quentin and he loved it. He greenlit it. Then once Tim and I had a budget that we were confident about, he started bankrolling the picture to go into pre-production. We had twelve weeks of prep, including a lot of work on the prosthetic elements and the aliens.

Q - Did you always intend on shooting HD or was Super 16mm or 35mm ever a possibility?

Jake - Because of the many effects in post, HD was the only affordable option. I had never worked in HD, but kept tabs on what Robert Rodriguez and George Lucas had been doing with it. And especially Rodriguez made me feel like it was the right choice. By this time, I had a visual effects supervisor named Llyr Williams who I had worked with before on smaller projects and we worked out that we would have to work at 2k resolution if we were going to ever go back to a film print. We figured out a way to use *3D Studio Max* (3d computer software), which he already had, and I could integrate and composite the shots using *Combustion*.

Q - Did you have any name cast in the film?

Jake - The only names in terms of casting are Norman Lovett from *Red Dwarf* and he only did a cameo for a day. We had TV presenter Emily Booth who did bits here and there and I cast her as a cable TV presenter. The real star of this film is the concept.

We paid equity minimums, but that is really fucking low and I actually felt embarrassed. But still, people shouldn't be afraid to go union if you have little money because it is affordable. I would have liked to have had someone like Simon Pegg in the film, but I don't think he would have done it.

Q - How long did casting take?

Jake - We spent two months casting the film. I wanted to make sure I got actors that were really willing to go with the genre, who were willing to be really uncomfortable on the shoot. They were going to be covered in gore. They were going to be shooting at night. They were going to be cold. All of the things actors hate. For the people playing aliens, I went for people with martial arts and dance training skills - movement based people who weren't afraid to throw themselves around because we couldn't afford stunt people. And we got a great bunch of aliens who made it fun and went for it. If you get moaners, that kills your schedule. I also thought about if this group of actors would get on with each other and we did three days of read throughs so I had a chance to bin people who were not working. But everyone got on well. A lot of credit went to Tim who had things organised, so the actors knew that if we said something was going to happen it did.

Q - How long did you shoot for?

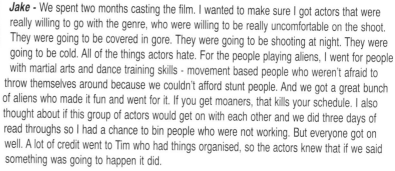

Jake - We had five weeks of principal photography, which is quite a reasonable time period. We needed a real working farm with farm equipment because I had to make crop circles, so we bought a section of field to do that. So we shot three weeks on the farm and then three or four days in Dorset for the island location. We built our own stone circle there called *The Devil's Teeth* which became a character in itself. We even got a helicopter in to do some aerial shots for POV of the UFO's. Most producers would have said no way, but Tim said he would look into it and the people that owned the farm knew a helicopter pilot. So we got a helicopter for the price of the fuel! We hung out of a helicopter with no proper rig, and got seven or so shots. Because we were over private land, we were able to get it done without special permissions. Then we went to Halifax where we built our spaceship and farmhouse interiors. We had to build it on a raised set in order to get the trap door, *Evil Dead,* style of shooting. We went to Halifax because my set designer John Bentley is based up there and could get cheap labour. We also took over an old meat packing plant, so we had this huge space to work in.

Then two months after my first edit, we booked a one week, eight man crew to do a reshoot, 2nd unit style. We also spent a few days in Wookie Hole because we needed some underground caverns. And a day on a beach out in Somerset. So there was a lot to do, but we had a small crew and since I had done my edit I knew exactly what I needed to pick up. And there was some blue screen work that we had to do as well.

Q - Did you find you were able to increase the story density in terms of more shots?

Jake - Yes. And also because we shot so many months later, everyone was fresh. Five weeks was the longest shoot I had ever done and after three weeks I was really tired. By the fourth and fifth week the whole crew is sort of dead on their feet. At that point the work rate does tend to go down, especially on low budget stuff when you are working really long hours. So by the time we got to that week, we were supercharged. We had the experience of the long shoot behind us and a small crew meant you could work faster. We got loads done.

Q - Was the HD equipment reliable on set?

Jake - We had zero problems with it. We shot at 25p, using the cheaper HD750, so it didn't do 24p. Which doesn't really matter because working in the UK with PAL, I could lay off all my edits and run them through a video projector. 24p is a pain whereas 25p is a breeze. Many new film makers make the terrible mistake of shooting 24p in the belief that it somehow has more theatrical potential, and they end up spending much more in post needlessly. Shoot 25p, it will save you loads of money and headaches.

Q - How did you deal with sound?

Jake - We recorded it separately because, although in theory the sound quality is good enough to go to HD tape, the truth is that you have your sound crew locked into the camera all the time. And we were using a lot of grip equipment, cranes and dollies so you didn't want leads going into the camera. Also, if you are shooting on a long lens, your sound guys are right up next to where the actors are. It was much easier to go onto DAT, and actually we went right onto hard disk, which was great.

Q - Did you record an audio guide track?

Jake - Yes. The great thing about HD is that you can take sound as a guide, just using a mic on the camera. Remember it's just a guide and not used in the final film. The thing that I missed most was slow motion though we could do some slow motion in High Definition post. It looks great, but it is not like you can do bullet time slow motion or John Woo style slow motion. That is one of things that will get better with HD.

Q - Did you stay on budget and on schedule?

Jake - Yes. It was something that I learned how to do from working on *Razor Blade Smile*, on friends' films and on commercials. On *Razor Blade Smile* I wrote, directed and produced the film and had to go to the cash point and pay the actors! On *Evil Aliens*, Tim Dennison, who is a very experienced line producer was able to create a great schedule and stay right on budget. The investor couldn't believe that we came in on schedule and on budget. There was no more money if we fucked up. And the biggest nightmare was weather. If it rained on us, we would have lost

precious days. But that was the summer of 2003 where we had almost no rain. We only got rained on once, which stopped us for three hours. That was luck.

Q - Were there any real problems on the shoot?

Jake - Not really. The film gods were smiling on us. Then again, we were really organised and that all came down to Tim. *Razor Blade Smile* was amateurish. We didn't know what we were doing and it was always chaotic. On *Evil Aliens* it went like clockwork. It also helped to have trained professionals working for us. Having worked at the micro-budget level, my key crew and I were very keen to implement the lessons we learned. Some of the crew didn't like the way we worked because they were very industry orientated, and they didn't like that we were shooting HD. But for me, I got to see my rushes as they were being shot and knew exactly what the lighting was going to be like when I was editing. There was no guesswork. There are no nasty surprises working in HD, and as a director that really empowers you in a way that I never felt with film. On *Razor Blade Smile* I couldn't even afford to process the film until two months after shooting.

Q - Did you edit the film?

Jake - Yes, but I didn't edit on set even though I had my laptop there. I didn't have time. I think there can be a danger in some directors editing their film because they can be self-indulgent. I am quite hard on my material and there are whole scenes that I just cut. I think I can do that because I am a working editor and get paid to do that. I don't get precious with my material. I think Alfred Hitchcock said, *'Any director that doesn't understand editing isn't a real director.'* You shape the film in the editing room, but my editing skills made me stronger on set because I knew what I needed. Actually, what really helped get what I need was being able to communicate better with my actors, which is something that I learned on *Razor Blade Smile*. I had much more trust in my actors on this one. I still need to get out on more sets and watch other people do it to learn more.

Q - Let's talk about post. Why did you avoid 24p?

Jake - Shooting 24P is where the mistakes begin for many new film makers. 24 frame processes are difficult to keep track of and watch when editing in PAL (UK etc) world. It's different if you are in the USA and using NTSC, and 24P makes sense then. At the end of the day, there is no real discernable difference between 25P and 24P. The four percent speed difference is not noticeable to most people, though musicians do notice it. Also if you shoot at 24P you are going to have to make the four percent compromise when you go to DVD anyway, so musicians will then moan about the DVD release instead! People who are hard set on 24p are letting the technology overwhelm them because here in the UK it presents more problems when you can shoot 25 fps and be PAL compatible. And here's another benefit. If you shoot at 25 frames, your film will run a little bit longer in the cinema, by a few minutes.

Q - What technology did you use for post?

Jake - The kit that I was using was a little troublesome because things were in flux. We finished shooting in mid-October and then I had to set up my post facility. I bought an Apple G5 and an HD card to capture the video. Though I had done a lot of research, no-one had used them at that time. I had to get an external RAID storage system too because the only way to play HD back in real time is to have fast drives. It has to sustain 200 megabytes per second. The RAID cost about £8.5k. In all we spent £20k on post equipment, but it was budgeted for, and so now we own it. I edited the whole fucking project in my flat!

The 3D effects process started at the compositor's house, using five computers. And then he brought them round to my flat and we hooked up all the computers in my front room. I was doing the compositing and he was doing the effects and we did it for a year. It got fucking hot. My landlady who lives upstairs was concerned because the bill had gone up by 1000% on the electricity!

The way it worked is I down converted all my rushes to DV, stuck them on a Firewire drive and then I could edit them at DV resolution without having to match back to HD until I had locked the edit.

Q - So you did what ten years ago would have been called an offline edit followed by an online re-conform at HD res?

Jake - Yes, except it was at broadcast DV quality when 'offline'. It was not like working on an old Avid at AVR3, with blocky images. So I spent four months getting the edit locked down and then I started the effects process. At the end of that, I mastered to HD, which took about two and half days. So the offline was through Final Cut Pro on a G5 editor with a Cona card and a RAID.

Another thing to note is that on the night shoots, we shot two cameras because we had limited 'night' at that time of year. Everything was storyboarded and two cameras saved so much time. You couldn't do that with film cameras because the stock is so expensive, but on HD a tape costs £50. In the end, I had forty-four hours of rushes. I had my DV offline and then just captured in all the rushes by hiring an HD deck for the day and kept popping the tapes in and out. Then I cut in all my effects shots, which we did at HD resolution.

Q - What about all the grading?

Jake - I did all the grading and all the titles in Final Cut Pro and it looks amazing.

Q - How did it feel knowing that you can do this all at home?

Jake - It was great, but what happens is that you have to know how top post production facilities places like The Mill work. I've worked with colourists so I know how to draw in colors. I worked with my DP and we made little garbage mattes and all the stuff that you can do at The Mill, but you just do it slower at home. We spent two weeks grading the film, whereas at The Mill you could do it in two days. You have to take on the responsibility to do these things. I think a lot of director and producers think that they should get someone else to do it. They don't have enough trust in their own abilities. Keep in mind, this was new technology at the time and no other film maker I knew had done it. I didn't know it was going to work, but I believed in myself and everything worked. And it worked like a dream. And it is only going to get better.

Q - What happened about the sound?

Jake - Sound was always a high priority since it is a horror movie. We had a budget for sound, but we didn't know where we were going to go and we wanted someone good. We went to all the sound facilities in London, spoke to the owners, told them what we were doing and our budget, which was a reasonable sum for what we needed done. In the end we did a deal with Richard Conway at Videosonics. They are really good guys. They had just done *Alien Versus Predator,* so I had a lot of those guys working on my film. We got about twelve weeks of sound design and two weeks of mixing. And they did an outstanding, top job. It was mixed in Dolby Digital 5.1 with Richard Wells' score. Every reel that I gave them was a Quicktime movie, which then came out of their computer and was video projected. And it came straight off a hard disk so I didn't even have to go to tape for them. So if I had any changes in the cut, I could just upload the changes in the effects shots to a Firewire drive, stroll up the road and hand it to them. The technology is so powerful and you have to master it. I think this is why producers are more afraid of technology than directors because they spend all day on the phone and not hands on with the machines. And if things go wrong they feel at the mercy of the technology and the people who use it.

Q - So the movie is completed now?

Jake - Yes. We went back out to 35mm on a an Arri 2k res scanner, and it looks gorgeous. It cost £20k.

Q - And one HD master is good all world distribution?

Jake - Yes. You don't have to make NTSC or PAL versions. You don't have to break apart M&E mixes. They can take that HD master and they can make whatever they want from it. If they want a DigiBeta dub in Poland, they can do it. There was one complication when we were doing our Dolby Digital mix and put it back onto HD. The Sony format only has four tracks of audio and Dolby has six tracks. So we had to get a Panasonic HD5 deck in. It is the same specs picture wise, but it has more audio tracks. I was surprised at how efficient the technology was and that how now low budget film makers can make movies that look great. You have so many options now of delivering a film unlike ten years ago - DV, HDV, HD all are viable. There are some film purists out there because HD doesn't quite look like film, but lighting and lens selection can close those gaps.

Q - And of course it does always come back to a good story told well.

Jake - Yes, it is always about the story. Because of the effects and the story, HD was the right choice. To make the same film on 35mm, it would have cost three times as much and there would have been no difference in the story.

Q - You didn't have to go through the typical story of selling your film. You didn't have to go to all the markets?

Jake - Yeah. It was very surprising. We set up three screenings in London, projected from the HD master. It looked as good as it could ever look and sound. We invited all the acquisition people from the UK and the US companies with UK offices. I cut together a trailer and only half of the invitees showed up. And the people that did come liked it and serious offers came in. We went with the best offer, which was ContentFilm, which is Ed Pressman's company who did *The Crow* and *Batman*. They gave us an advance on the UK and on the US and agreed to do a theatrical release. I don't know what size that is going to be. They repped it for the world as a sales agent and in Cannes they were selling it and it was their top selling film. It was the only film from ContentFilm that made Screen International Top Thirty Sales List.

Q - So are you rich yet?

Jake - Not yet. I will tell you in a year's time. We are still doing the delivery requirements for many of the territories. The investor should make his money back by the end of the year and for the first time in my life it looks like I could make some money out of one of my films. My confidence levels here are much higher than they have ever been after the lessons learned on *Razor Blade*. I have a proper deal looked over by lawyers, as I am as protected as I or anyone could be, so as long as everyone is honourable and pays the money as they should. Let's hope that's how it plays out.

Q - How have festivals received it?

Jake - At the moment the film has only played in one film festival in San Francisco. I went there and this was the first paying audience to see the film and I was nervous as hell. It was a genre audience and they went nuts for it. It's the only time in my life where I've ever had a standing ovation. They put on an extra screening of the film due to popular demand. I stayed an extra day in San Francisco for that screening. Some people came to see the film three times! So I am very confident that it will work with a horror audience and I'm sure it will crossover if the distributor advertises it properly. We are now waiting on a few more festivals including Toronto's Midnight Madness slate.

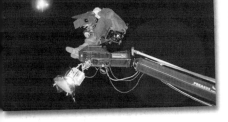

Q - Has Hollywood come knocking?

Jake - Not yet. We had some inquires from places like Paramount Classics after the screening and a brilliant write up in Variety.

Q - Do you have an agent as a director?

Jake - No but I am looking to get one. I was speaking to a friend who got picked up by ICM, which is a big company, and he was telling me that sometimes you can feel ignored if you are with a big agency. If I were to get an agent, perhaps I would want a smaller agent who will give me more time.

Q - What mistakes do you think you have made?

Jake - There weren't many. We had to fire one person, which is not a nice thing to do. They weren't pulling their weight. He was there specifically to do gore effects. By day three all of the blood that he had made had run out and he told us that was all the blood for the whole shoot. And I told him that this was a splatter film and he needed to be making gallons per day. He was just obstructive. So it was just normal production stuff. There were no real tragedies on the film.

Q- What advice would you offer a new film maker?

Jake - If you want to be a film maker, just go and do it. The digital technology is out there, you just have to get a camera and shoot stuff. Set yourself up with an editing program, they are under a grand now. That is how you start learning how to make movies. And then you will find out if you like film making without having to spend too much money. After that, it's all passion and obsession. I don't think I have ever met a successful film maker that was not obsessed with the craft.

Allan Niblo
Vertigo Films

FOOTBALL FACTORY

Q - What is your background?

Allan - I actually started working in a bank and my mates and I quit on the same day to be in a punk band full time. We traveled all over America and ended up in California where I met John Cassavetes at a party in Malibu. It was quick, but just meeting him for those few minutes inspired me to get into film making. When I got back, I got into European films and then signed up for a three-year film course at Newport film school. I got my degree, found out that camerawork was what I was strongest in, and signed up to the National film School. I Did a DP course there, graduated, started shooting stuff, but knew I wanted to do a little more by using my finance skills to produce a film.

Q - What was it like making that transition?

Allan - It was a baptism by fire. When I was a cameraman I was teaching at a film school. I came across a kid named Justin Kerrigan whose work I really liked and I said we can make a film together. He wanted to go traveling after he graduated and I thought he would never come back, so I promised we could make his script, *Human Traffic*. But of course, every person in the British film industry rejected it. They said we didn't have enough experience and the script was non commercial. My producing partner Renata S. Aly and I managed to raise £340k, and we were thrown into the deep end. I didn't have a line producer, an accountant, nothing. I had one lawyer who gave some advice. We rolled up our sleeves and did absolutely everything ourselves. And it did really well. It made about £2.2 million at the UK box office.

Q - Did you see any of that money back?

Allan - We did the stupidest of deals. Again, it was a situation where we shot the film and cut it, but we didn't have enough to finish it. We were looking around for completion money. We showed it to Madonna in LA, and she loved it, as did others, but nobody wanted to buy it. Eventually, Irish Screen bought it and wanted to complete the film to very high standards. It actually cost more to complete the film than to shoot the film. And in the process of raising the completion monies we sold off all the rights, DVD, everything, to them. All I cared about at that time was just finishing this unfinished movie on my shelf, and getting my original investor his money back.

Q - Knowing what you know now, how would you structure that deal differently?

Allan - Ah, hindsight is a beautiful thing, I wouldn't have sold off the rights. But we had no option. No-one wanted to buy it and we had to finish it and Irish Screen showed a lot of commitment. The other thing that hurt us badly was that we could not make the best deals with distributors because even after it was completed, nobody wanted to distribute it. Every single UK Distributor rejected it. And we had all these kids coming out of screenings telling us it was fantastic and how much they loved the film. *'That is my life up there'* they said. And still, no offers whatsoever, it was down to the last distributor left, Metrodome, who made a paltry offer two weeks after we screened it to them. They made an offer of a twenty print release, no minimum guarantee and back end terms that were not too good. Metrodome took a thirty percent fee on DVD, plus the sub-distributor took a further fifteen percent fee. So forty-five percent had already gone from DVD right off the top and that was all before the costs and expenses kicked in. It would have to make millions for us to see our money back. To be fair to them they really got behind the film once it gained momentum and great press and eventually they put it out on 200 screens with a decent P&A. As I said, it was a baptism of fire from beginning to end of the film.

Q - How did Football Factory come about?

Allan - After *Human Traffic,* I read the novel and the hairs stood up on the back of my neck. Then whilst I was teaching at film school I screened *The Firm to the students*. Most of these students were younger and had never seen it, not even on TV. And they got really excited about it so I knew that a film about that culture would translate well to the screen. Nick Love, who ended up being the director, unknown to myself at the time, was trying to get the rights for the book. He was working with Working Title at the time. In the end, the rights went to me, but on one condition: I had to take the director that was already attached, a friend of John Kings, the writer. I tried for three months to convince John King that this guy was not the right director for the film. But he didn't go for it. So, I realised this was the only option if I wanted to make the film, even though in my heart, I knew this was wrong. I was proved right when we had to shut down production on the first weekend of the shoot because the rushes were so bad. It was heart-breaking. Closing down a film is the hardest thing we, that is me and my producing partner James Richardson, had ever done. We were torn up morally because this was something that could ruin this directors career, and he was actually a really nice guy, but we had to do it, we owed it to ourselves, the investors and the book.

Q - How much money did it cost you?

Allan - It cost almost half the budget. £500k was the budget and it cost £210k to get that first week in the bag. So there was £290k left. Our financiers were going crazy. The agents were going crazy. It was like a war-zone. So we eventually convinced the financiers that we could still make the film at the same quality level for the amount of money left, that is £290K. I went to Nick Love, who had made *Goodbye Charlie Bright*, and I knew he was familiar with this culture. Nick had been in development hell for a couple of years and when we met up he was actually selling Christmas trees on the King's Road for a living. We found him and said we are shooting in April. It is mid-December. You have until then to write a finished script on this book, prep and cast it because we start shooting 20th April. After the Christmas period Nick wrote a brilliant script in a week, he had it all planned in his mind and we shot it word for word. We then got about the same amount of money to finish the film which raised the production values in post production and gave us a great soundtrack.

Q - There were some piracy issues with Football Factory.

Allan - Yeah. A pirate got out from a top facility on Wardour Street we believe. We had only ever done one copy of the film so we know where it came from and who did it, and it was one of the trainees. And I think it was done innocently. The kid really liked the book and the film and wanted to show it to some friends. It was a temporary version that the editor had done, not even the director's cut, to show the financiers. And within the week, I was getting calls from people who had seen the film, famous people even. I even got a call from my Dad saying his mates had seen it! A survey was done and it was estimated that 800,000 copies had been sold.

Q - So who was ultimately responsible for selling it illegally?

Allan - It was a network. It must have hit every pub in the UK. I was offered it on three separate occasions in my local. My own film! It was very much a pop culture film and people were buying it for £10. It seriously damaged the theatrical release, because all our core audience had seen it and our core audience was not necessarily a cinema going audience but then again it probably served as a good marketing device for buying the good quality DVD.

Vertigo Films
Allan Niblo - Producer

The Big Room Studios
77 Fortess Road / London NW5 1AG

T / +44 (0) 20 7428 7555
F / +44 (0) 20 7485 9713

www.vertigofilms.com

Q - How did the film perform on DVD?

Allan - It performed fantastic. To date it has sold 400,000 copies.

Q - Do you think shooting films for lower budgets with independent finance is a better model than larger budgets at more established places?

Allan - No, they are just different experiences. We are shooting a movie for The Weinstein Company in October and that has a bigger budget but still utilising the strict "no waste" policy that we are passionate about. *The Football Factory* was a labour of love and was an amazing shoot. There were no problems whatsoever. Everyone was in it together at the same level. Everyone got paid £500 per week across the board. Everybody got great experience and can now go on to the next level, which is the great thing about making these lower budget films. They are real platforms for people to excel.

Q - With Rupert Preston you had an in house distribution company. How did that work?

Allan - The dream idea was to have everything in house from finance to distribution so that we could control the revenue streams and we could then make the next films on our terms. And that is pretty much what is happening. The exhibition network is very a tight network and hard to break into. Rupert has worked with them for years and knew who to talk to. He became available and we made him a partner in the company. He wanted more out of life than just distribution. He wanted to be part of an outfit that was making films and have a say on how they were being made and importantly thinking of "distribution" before the film was shot. So this gave us some power in the industry and I never wanted to be in the situation that I was in with *Human Traffic* again, where we had a film we worked so hard on and really believed in it and still no one wanted to distribute it. That is painful! And being your own distributor excited all the other distributors. So when we did *It's All Gone Pete Tong*, which we could have done in house, all the offers we got from the other distributors were too good to turn down. We actually rejected everyone on the first pass saying we were going to do it ourselves and then they came back to us with better offers we couldn't refuse.

Q - So Redbus came in with the offer. How much did they set aside for P&A?

Allan - They came in with a decent spend and it went out on 270 prints.

Q - But with all of that, the film didn't perform as well as it should have theatrically. What do you think happened?

Allan - That is a great question. It might be that cult films like this can only make so much money at the box office no matter how much money you spend in P&A. The film took in £800k, which is a lot more than most British films, but it was the exact same as *The Football Factory* and *24 Hour Party People*. Another thing that came up was that based on the poster, most people didn't know what the movie was. Some people heard it was cool, indie, award winning and others thought it was going to be a trashy Ibiza program. So basically, the marketing failed in that respect. We never found our full audience theatrically. Having said that, I think this is a perfect film for DVD. Warner Brothers is releasing the DVD and I think we are going to have a big audience there just like *The Football Factory* and that will be the true measure of its success. It's a film I'm very proud of.

Q - Did you get an advance?

Allan - We were offered an advance of £500k and we didn't take it. In retrospect, we should have. But we were feeling bullish. We had just won the Toronto film Festival. Ben Stiller called up to say it was the funniest movie he had seen in years. The director is working on Ben Stiller's next film. So it was getting a big buzz. What we did instead of the advance was negotiate an enormous back end percentage. I can't say what it was exactly, but it completely reversed the normal distribution deal.

Q - How did Human Traffic come about?

Justin - At the end of film school I was knackered and wanted to get out of Cardiff and travel. Me and my best mate were talking about packing our bags, going out seeing the world and getting some sort of life. I was still in contact with Allan over the summer holidays and that's when he convinced me that the time was right to make a film. So I thought why not? and wrote down everything I knew. The film was very personal, about my sexual insecurities, social prowess, anxieties and frustrations and I just wrote as honestly as I could about me and my friends. One of the characters, Jips, was something that I went through and I wanted to see that represented, I basically made a film that me and my friends wanted to see. I also wanted to see a representation of the club culture in which me and my friends were immersed.

Justin Kerrigan
Director - Human Traffic

Q - How long did it take to write the screenplay?

Justin - I had a first draft within a few months but I kept on rewriting for about a year.

Q - Do you think that one reason your film was successful is that you wrote purely from personal experience?

Justin - I guess so. I didn't want to make somebody else's film. The scenes were taken from reality, my reality anyway. I didn't want the film to have a final climax at the end, with a death or something like that, I wanted it to be real.

Q - Did you get support from the industry?

Justin - No, we couldn't get any financial support out of Britain whatsoever, nobody would touch it because it was about recreational drug taking and they saw it as immoral. They wouldn't go near it. They were like, it sounds great; but no thanks.

Q - Did you have enough money to shoot properly?

Justin - We had almost no money to shoot it with, so little that we only got two thirds in the can so editing took much longer. I can say that most of the time making Human Traffic I was signing on. A bit more money came in during the closing days of editing so we could complete. It was mostly through private investors outside the UK that my exec. producer Renata S. Aly had convinced, who I don't think ever read the screenplay nor saw the finished film. There were a lot of holes in the film and we had to re-jig it, then add some more voice-overs to make it flow. I just know I've not made any money from it.

Q - What happened about casting?

Justin - I didn't want big names to put on the poster to fit into a market slot, the characters had to be right. We had a great response and interviewed up and coming actors for three months. There are also people in HumanTraffic who've never acted before, all my friends were in it and all the extras were clubbers - we'd put flyers in clubs and ads in music magazines and we'd get bus loads every day of these clubbers, just off their heads ready to party, it was crazy.

Q - Did you have lots of problems on the shoot, especially with it set in clubs etc?

Justin - Loads of problems all the time man. The end shot when they're walking down the street, that's the busiest street in Cardiff. We did a night shoot on a Sunday and it was pissing down, then it started to clear at about five in the morning. We never had permission to close the roads but we had permission to hold traffic and before we know it, it's Monday morning rush hour and we've got cars everywhere. We're holding traffic on every corner and we start filming "go, go, go!" The extras who were clubbers were great, we kept them in clubs for 14 hour days, feeding them sandwiches and promising them a bottle of beer, but it soon started to get a bit dangerous and we'd have half crazed clubbers banging on tables shouting Beer! Fags! Beer! So I'd be up on the podium trying to calm them down and at the same time keeping them going for the next clubbing scene by promising the booze is coming! It was mad.

Q - There's a lot of music in the film, did you have problems?

Justin - It's almost wall to wall music throughout but that was stereotypical of a weekend with me and my friends. Walking home from work you'd be listening to a walkman, getting into the car you'd listen to a track, you get home and get ready and you put your music on, you go out to the pub and there's music, then to a club and to a party. There's music all the way through, you can't escape it. I started asking, 'is this tune part of the story? Is this tune part of the atmosphere? is the tune helping us understand the characters?' So it took ages going through thousands of tracks. My producers got Pete Tong involved to help with the film. He wanted to be a part of it because it's his scene and he was able to bring in stuff that we needed. He'd come in with a selection of tracks, we'd talk about what I was looking for and listen to the tracks, sometimes they'd work sometimes they wouldn't. When we were dubbing we had new tracks in only a week before the film actually came out, so it was a real rush. We'd dub all day, finish, go upstairs talk to the music editor then we'd come back and dub some more, then crash out in the dubbing theatre overnight.

Q - At the point of post producing the film did you have a sales agent or distributor on board?

Justin - Winging it on self belief man. A rough cut of the film was taken from the Avid, without the proper sound but music was added to it. Everyone, including Madonna and her company, saw it, and everyone turned it down. So I was fuck! I knew it was a bad idea to take it over without being properly finished. It just didn't feel right. We took it to all the distribution companies but they all wanted us to take out the drug elements and turn it into a love story. They just didn't get it. We had to cut out ten minutes for the US release as they didn't understand the slang dialogue.

Q - How did Metrodome, the UK distributors, get on board?

Justin - I was ecstatic that we eventually found a distribution company that would take us. I was into films like Buffalo 66 which they were distributing so it was excellent man, this is going to have some kind of real life! We were thinking we were going to have a few prints, as up until then their biggest release had been 18 prints, but they started Human Traffic on 175 prints! We did loads of publicity but because this film was a big financial leap of faith for Metrodome, when the money came in over the opening weekend they kept it thinking great, it worked, stay tight, instead of pouring it back in which we would have liked to have seen. It took about £3.5m.

Q - How did Miramax become involved?

Justin - Two people who deal with submissions at the Toronto Film Festival took a shine to it and said, yes we'll have it. This was our opportunity to get our film some kind of distribution, small art house release, at least something. So we went over there, feeling like a real fish out of water, but on the day of the screening I went down and Kevin Smith's film was playing at the same time, and both his and my movie were sold out. I was as nervous as hell but it went down really well. Afterwards, I had an hour's kip back at the hotel, then the phone rang and it was

"The last great film of the nineties"

Human Traffic

the weekend has landed

my agent saying 'Harvey Weinstein is watching the film as we speak can you get your arse over there!' I asked him if he was going to be there and he said no, Harvey wants to meet you alone. I was oh Fuck! I go up there and I was shaking and thinking whoa, I'm going to meet the Don of the industry. I had a couple of glasses of wine to cool down, rang him from the lobby of the Four Seasons Hotel... We enter and Harvey comes in, full of praise for the film, he loves it and tells me it reminds him of when he was young. Negotiations began and within two hours they'd bought it! It was amazing to see Harvey in action. Our sales agents were there doing the deal and there was a moment when it looked like it wasn't going to happen and I was thinking Fuck Man go for it! then Harvey just said Oh fuck it, ok we'll go with it and I just put my hands up in the air screaming Yes! Room service! get the fucking booze in!!!" I couldn't believe it!

Q - What did you get right in the story?

Justin - Sexual insecurity, the feeling of a weekend, an authentic portrayal of people on ecstasy, the whole course of the up and the down, friendship, paranoia. If I had Jip dying at the end I feel sure that we'd have got financial support, but it would have been a real cop out. If the moral lesson is if you take drugs you'll die then it's inaccurate to the clubbing world.

People take drugs, they have a good time, they do get paranoid, it's down to the individual whether they use or abuse drugs, and I wanted to fairly and accurately portray that world.

Q - What mistakes do you think you made?

Justin - I tried to do too much. Complicated shots that took too long. Not being able to finish it. Not being able to give it the ending that I was supposed to give it. I learnt so much. But I'm glad it happened. At the time it was like shit man, this is the only film I want to make, this is it, it hasn't been done before blah blah blah. I came out gutted at the end. When I finished it I came down to London and ended up going to a doctor for an allergy problem. I sat in his office and he asked me lots of questions and then it came to the last one and he asked how do you feel? So I told him and went on a ten minute monologue about my film. There was this cold silence. Before I knew it I was being interviewed in a room full of psychiatrists when all I had gone in for was a dust allergy! As soon as I got a distributor I was all right again, I was cured!

Q - Have you made any money out of it?

Justin - Fuck all. Not a sausage. The people with the money make the money - that's the deal. What blew me away is that cinemas take three quarters of the box office before you see anything. Then the distributor, sales agents, the investors, deferments, and it goes down the line. So is there any chance that you could lend us a quid to get home?

Q - What advice would you offer a new film maker?

Justin - Don't listen to anyone! (laughs) No, listen to people and take their advice but don't get too led by it so that you think so much about it that you lose focus. Have people around you who help you keep in focus. My Dad used to keep telling me to keep at it until you get it and he was right.

Q - In retrospect, do you regret not distributing it yourself?

Allan - No. In our hearts we thought this was going to be a small, cult movie that would be on one hundred screens. We didn't want to spend a lot on P&A. But when a distributor comes in and says they are going to spend a lot of money on it, put us on three hundred screens and we will be all over the TV, it is exciting. And the film was in profit before the UK deal was even done. At Toronto, we sold it to every country including the USA.

Q - You didn't handle foreign sales. Is that something you might want to incorporate into the company?

Allan - Yes. It is a very difficult job, sales. It is not just getting the film sold. It is also chasing the foreign distributors up for payment, which is an absolute nightmare. A deal is done at Cannes or Toronto and it sometimes takes a year and a half to get the money. Having said that, the amount of commissions that we have given away if you count them up over *The Football Factory, The Business* and *It's All Gone Pete Tong* we spent over £1 million on sales commissions. Just imagine if you had that in the bank account. You could go hire some very impressive people and go to film festivals and sell. Plus, then we would hold onto the rights of the films and make lots of money from re-licensing them every seven years or so. It is very difficult but overall I would say that we have made the right decision working with sales agents like Hanway and Content. They are impressive and served our films very well.

Q - How did the movie with The Weinstein Company come about?

Allan - I first met Harvey when I did *Human Traffic*. Miramax distributed it in the US and gave Justin Kerrigan a three-picture deal. Then he liked *The Football Factory* and *It's All Gone Pete Tong* and Miramax then bought the *The Business for the USA* . We built up a relationship with him - hung out with him. Harvey came up with *Harry He's Here To Help,* which was a remake of a French film that had done really well there. It is a Hitchcockian thriller. We applied all the Vertigo principles to keep the costs down whilst budgeting and allowed no wastage. We will then use all our own equipment, as we own a set of HD cameras and lenses, edit suites and other equipment so we can go out and shoot tests when we feel like it. We bought them with production money and they have paid themselves back after two films. So by using these things, even though Harvey's film has stars in it, we would be able to keep to the budget. He was impressed by that.

Q - What kind of deal did you get?

Allan - We get fees in the budget, so we are more like producers for hire. We are to shepherd it and build up the relationship with the director who is Robert Rodriquez's prodigy - a guy called Jonathan Jakubowicz who made his first film *Sequestro Express* for a tiny budget. It is an amazing film set in Venezuela and Harvey Weinstein bought that film. So what Vertigo gets out of in addition to fees, is a working relationship with a director to watch and hopefully we will do other things with him.

Q - Does it bother you not being able to retain any of the rights?

Allan - There are lots of ways to look at it. One we get a fee in the budget. Two, our profile is stronger by releasing through The Weinstein Company, which is good for the company. Three, the relationship with the director. Four, if it goes well, that will mean more projects. So yes, we would have liked to hold onto the rights, but he is without doubt one of the best distributors around, a very sharp businessman and why is he going to give away a territory? We got the flat deal and that was fine. Maybe after a few films together, we could talk about holding onto rights.

Q - Does Vertigo want to stay with the niche British films or move into larger Hollywood type films?

Allan - We have had offers from Hollywood and have absolutely rejected all of them. We love what we are doing. We love the excitement of screening in front of our core audience. We want to increase our brand, as there is only one other brand in the UK, Working Title. There aren't that many worldwide. Maybe Miramax or Killer films. They have real strong brands. We want to do that in the UK and make real strong, cultural, entertaining films in the UK. There is so much talent here. So many young film makers who are getting passed by.

Q - Why is that? What is wrong with the system?

Allan - The system is only as good as the people who run the system. Every system has its faults and by defintion the word "system" to me implies that there is some factory like process churning out films, sheep mentality. *Lock, Stock* does well and now everyone wants to find the next *Lock, Stock*. Or *Sliding Doors* does well - let's make twenty romantic comedies that fail. The system did not want to make *Human Traffic* or *The Football Factory* or *Its All Gone Pete Tong* and they are probably better films for that reason.

Q - Do you finance all of your films?

Allan - It varies. We usually co-finance. For *The Business*, we put up one quarter of the budget. Our financing partners were Rockstar Games, famous for *Grand Theft Auto* and we have done two films with them.

Q - That is unusual. Most people who put equity into films will never do it again.

Allan - Yes. Only one in thirteen films in the UK make a profit. That's eight percent. And that is only the films that get released, there are many many more that get no release whatsoever!

Q - What advice would you offer other film makers?

Allan - If you are making your film independently, then you have to be one hundred percent pragmatic on how you can get that film made. Which a lot of people are not. So there is option A of going to the Hollywood Studios like Warner Brothers and hoping they are going to give you $60 million to make it, which is highly unlikely. If they love your script, chances are it will sit around for two years and your passion and energy will slowly be eroded in development hell. Seen it so many times. It is so critical to have that initial energy and ignition in order to get a film made. So the next choice is to make it for the traditional price of a UK film - £4m. So you go to the UK film Council, BBC, then you package it and get the rest of the financing. You have to weigh in what the risks are of wasting your time or investing your time i.e. judge whether the project will go into development hell or not. Then you look at the statistics and they are staggeringly against you. So again, you have to think very pragmatically. What choices exist, can you make it for £500k, and if you can't do that, what can you find, can it be made for that, is there a way of doing it? The cost to make films keeps coming down. You can save huge amounts on post-production and sound these days, by doing it yourself on your own computer. Also, when films start to project digitally, you will be able to take all the 35mm costs out of it. Another piece of advice I would say to directors is to keep shooting when you are in development hell. A test for a film. A short. Workshops. Anything to get you into that headspace of finding the nugget that will inspire you and hence the financiers that what you are doing is worthy!

Note - this interview was conducted before Memento, Insomnia and Batman Begins

Q - How did you both get into the film business?

Chris - I've been making films on super 8mm since I was a kid. It's been an organic process, doing whatever I could with whatever was available. Emma and I didn't study film at uni, but there was a great film society where we'd make shorts every year from the proceeds of screening second run films. We had a camera, a roll of 16mm and you'd have to make a three minute film from that. It was much better than film school where you can end up making only a ten minute film after two years.

Emma - We had a budget for five short films a year, so we had a bidding process where people write their scripts and a committee decided who will make them. It was really cool, because there was no discipline, no course tutor, people literally just went out and did it. We made a feature length project in the final year which was about 80 minutes but it didn't get finished as we just didn't have the resources.

Chris - Once I've made a film I move on to the next, usually at the same time I move into a new flat so I can use it as a location, hence I moved a lot!

Q - How did Following come about?

Chris - We made an 8 minute film about a burglary, shot in B&W on 16mm costing us £200. When I wrote Following, one of the things going on in my head was we can make an 8 minute movie for £200 so that means we can make an 80 minute movie for £2k. As it turns out that was pretty much what we did. With Following we tried a much more compromised way of working, black and white, entirely hand held.

Q - How much money did you raise before you started shooting?

Chris - I didn't raise anything, I had a job and I was receiving regular pay cheques for the first time in my life. I would spend half on my rent and the other half on film stock and processing. Whatever I had, I'd work out how much footage I could shoot that week. I shot over 14 weekends, shooting 15 minutes of footage a day. That would be enough, theoretically, to get the film made. I knew that if we ran out of money we could just stop for a couple of weeks. I was not going to process anything because that was expensive, I was just going to keep shooting.

Emma - The key to Following was that it was not like any other film, there was not a conventional budgeting stage. We could get the equipment for free, the only thing we paid for was the stock, processing and the odd bit of catering.

Q - How big was the crew?

Chris and Emma Nolan
Director and Producer
'Following'

Emma - There was a core of about 6 to 10 people. Each weekend the actors would be consistent but the crew would be whoever was around. Everyone had worked together in some combination so it worked really well. That was the thing about our group of friends, instead of hanging around drinking coffee all Saturday long, we would just get together and make movies.

Chris - You have to know every job as well as the people that you are working with, then you don't have to fit around everyone's schedules and can do it yourself. One of the things I don't do is work with experienced people on low budgets. I've listened to people who say you've got to get a good sound guy, you have got to get a really good DoP - I don't agree with that, we would never have got our film made if we had worked with people more experienced than ourselves, for a start they demand a whole new level of equipment which we just couldn't provide.

Q - What disadvantages were there in the way you shot?

Emma - Finding actors to commit for that period of time, that's why there are so few characters in the film. One of our actors shaved his hair off mid shoot which was a bit of a nightmare.

Chris - I brought Jerry Theobald in as a producer as he's the main actor and in every scene. I wanted him to be part of the process. I wasn't prepared to say to the actors this is a great opportunity, we're going to make it with this one, but instead I said we're going to have a lot of fun making this film and make it as good as we can.

Q - How did you cut it?

Chris - It was pretty weird if I think about it. I didn't even sync up any rushes for about six months. We had shot without actually seeing anything, I would check through it and make copies of dats but that was it. I managed to get editing help from my friends from uni, those who had gone into the film and TV business, doing transfers, syncing up, one ended up cutting the movie. I found a place that was prepared to give me a little time to learn the machines for free, and beyond that I had to start paying for it. I rented the machine over a weekend for £100 and over three weekends I did the rough cut.

Q - So how much did it actually cost?

Chris - We finished the film creatively and had a pretty good sound mix. We got accepted into the San Francisco film festival and that's when we started looking for money to complete. We'd spent £3,500 to that point. You can creatively finish your film for literally hundreds of pounds, it's just a question of time and effort.

Emma - The fact that we were in a film festival meant it was a lot easier for us to go to people and ask for cash, so we asked friends to help out.

Q - When you finished it on tape did you have a festival strategy?

Chris - We sent a lot of tapes out and one of the judges at a very prestigious festival liked it. Even though we didn't get into that festival she recommended it to San Francisco. My experience this far with the festival world has been that I have never got in to a festival that I have applied for, or where we've had to pay an entry fee, the film needs to be invited.

Q - Did you get good reviews in San Francisco?

Emma - The reviews got better and better. At the time of the first ones we were happy to get even bad reviews! We went to the festival without having thought about publicity, we made the press pack only because the festival asked us for one, we didn't have a particular strategy in mind and I think that we were very lucky that we got the good reviews - actually that we got reviews full stop.

Chris - The only festivals we have ever got into are the ones that had somehow heard of us, then invited us and waived the fee. Festivals have so many submissions a year and there's this belief that if you get your film made, you'll get it into festivals, but it really isn't the case. You need to find some way of getting in there.

Q - So when you got it accepted in San Francisco you suddenly needed a print?

Emma - Yes, the first time we saw our print was the first screening in San Francisco! We were already in America so our lead actor brought it out with him on the plane straight from the lab.

Chris - We had four screenings in four venues and technically each screening was perfect. We then went to Toronto with the same 16mm print and every screening had a problem. That's when I realised that 16mm is a terrible way to screen in Festivals - they roll in their old 16mm projector and you can get terrible sound problems although the picture is all right. 16mm is a very unreliable format for projection, every time you watch it you're on tenterhooks because something could go horribly wrong.

Emma - We managed to create a buzz with our reviews, but afterwards it is a little bit of well what are we going to do next? That's when we discovered that there were festival scouts attending all the festivals who then invite you to the next one.

Q - When did Next Wave Films become involved with top up funds?

Emma - We met them just after we did San Francisco and sent them a tape. They liked it and helped us position the film for Toronto and format a strategy.

Chris - I had always wanted to do a 35mm print, partly because we had already seen what could happen with 16mm and also because we wanted to do a good sound mix, so Next Wave came in and we finished the film on 35mm doing the sound mix in London very, very cheaply.

Q - So how much did Next Wave end up putting into the film?

Emma - We don't really know yet as there are all kinds of associated expenses, the blow up alone cost $40k. They also worked out a festival strategy and organised a publicist which was an enormous help as Toronto is such a huge festival and it's easy to fall between the cracks. Also when we were shooting the film we didn't take stills which was a big mistake.

Chris - They also helped create an image for the film. We went back and took the exact still that we needed two years after filming! You need at least one image that expresses the film.

Q - Isn't black and white stock more expensive?

Chris - There's this myth that it's more expensive but it's not. People talk about using short ends but I insist on buying new stock as I can't accept the risk of the stock being damaged.

Q - Did you change the film in the editing process, from the point of the screenplay?

Chris - Not much, although there's a few structural changes toward the beginning and the end. There's a point where the film stops being a linear story about two thirds the way through. It was scripted in a fragmented way and in the editing we made it less so, to give people time to get into the story. Also I knew that we could stop making the film halfway through and I could make a film from what I had because it doesn't have a conventional story - it could have been a half hour film with certain elements removed.

Emma - Apart from the creative reasons that Chris had for making this story with that kind of narrative, it was actually very helpful to us as we were making this during weekends over a year. So any continuity problems weren't as obvious.

Q - How was the film received?

Chris - The structural element of the film has divided critics, but every now and again, a reviewer will say it's a good film but it's almost ruined by a pointless structure. I can see why they might say that but what they're not acknowledging is that they wouldn't be reviewing the film if it didn't have that kind of structure as it wouldn't even exist. Your film has to have something that's different from mainstream to get out there, you have to be adventurous, do whatever it takes to get your film noticed. In our case, it was the structure of the story that seemed to stand out.

Q - They'd probably be more accepting now because of film makers such as Steven Soderbergh hitting the mainstream with films like Out Of Sight and especially The Limey?

Chris - Most reviewers saw the film just before these films came out, and the majority of them liked the structure saying it's an interesting thing about the film. Certainly the American low budget indies realise this but it seems England doesn't and there are a lot of films coming out of the UK where there's still the attitude that you can make a Hollywood movie for $2m but there's no place for them, nowhere for them to go and no one to buy them. We've just spent millions of dollars on our next movie, but in Hollywood terms it's low budget, so it still has to be a clever film to be different otherwise it goes straight to video. Nobody's going to give you credit for doing a car chase but more cheaply.

Q - You got a theatrical release in the UK and US, how did that do?

Chris - It was a limited release. We released in a prestigious theatre in New York and in the NuArt in LA. We got great reviews but didn't have much money to advertise. Since then we've had three prints playing in various cities around the US. There is a kind of myth that the film will sell itself and people buy into that. In England we got amazing coverage but they did one print and stuck it in a theatre that was a hundred seater, and there was no poster.

Q - Have you made any money from Following?

Emma - No. But doing the Next Wave thing was very good. It was far more valuable for the film, the theatrical has benefited everyone although not financially. For instance Lucy who plays the blond, is now going off to do an Eric Rohmer film.

Q - How did Hollywood react to you and the film?

Chris - Everyone here in the US will watch the film if you can get it to the right people. Getting it into festivals helped getting an agent but nobody's going to offer you your next film, they will send you scripts, but you have to have YOUR next film ready. Before San Francisco I met with a few agents who wanted to look at what I wanted to do next, so I sent them my latest screenplay which I'd spent a year doing and one of them agreed to take me on.

Q - Any words of advice for new film makers?

Emma - Just do it and don't get hung up on the whole process of the ins and outs of film making, strip back all of that stuff and just concentrate on the film.

Chris - Don't say we'll fix it in post. I was once told that you could filter out anything, but you can't. We've just finished mixing the sound on Memento here at Universal and you can still hear when there is bad sound and you can't do anything about it. However you have to make a film with whatever resources you have. Treat making that film, however you're making it, not as a means to an end, but as the best film you're ever going to make. If you're making it for money, then you're never going to do it and it's never going to be any good. Do something you believe in, something you love, and enjoy it.

Ryan Lee Driscol
Film Maker

MAKING A KILLING

Q - When did you know that you wanted to be a film maker?

Ryan - As a ten-year-old watching *Star Wars*. A bit of a cliché, but I knew it was what I wanted to do for the rest of my life. My world was my local Odeon. I started making films when I was bought a Super 8mm cine camera. The beauty of Super 8mm is that it is film and it is expensive. So three and a half minutes would cost so much that it made you very economical with your shooting. I had a one-track mind, to be a film maker, except when I was four and wanted to be a train driver. The Super 8mm stuff lead to the Screen Test programme, where I sent in a film I made which won, and a minute of that got shown on the BBC. How I wish now I could get something on for one minute of prime time air! My prize was two rolls of Kodachrome film and I went on and made two other films.

Q - Did you go to film school?

Ryan - Yes. I went to the University of Westminster. I didn't fair as well as I liked. In this transitional world between Screen Test and the real world, I realised that there was a lot more competition and a lot of louder voices than my own.

Q - You became a professional film editor. What was that like?

Ryan - I did a one-year course in film production at the Northern School of Film and Television and that was a great course. I progressed much better there because I specialised in editing, which is what I was good at, with an eye on directing at a later point.

Q - Do you think that editing is a good training ground for directors?

Ryan - Yes. I've done a few documentaries recently and it surprised me that some of the directors can shoot material, but cannot assemble the material.

Q - Was Making A Killing *the first film that you directed?*

Ryan - No. Previously, I directed a film called *Grave Mistakes*, which was a real learning exercise. It starred Andrew Lincoln, who had just come off a programme called *This Life*. I invited him to audition for this thirty minute piece which was to be a sort of trial run for a feature. It was shot for £3k but it never got shown anywhere, probably because I didn't promote it very much.

Q - What was it like working with well known actors, as a new film maker?

Ryan - Directors like to build up what they do, but I think that professional direction is easier than say, writing, because if you have a good cast, you don't have to do very much. If you have a good DP and crew, it is going to make your job a lot easier because they will suggest a lot of good things. I've often wondered what the conductor of an orchestra does sometimes? I am sure they are doing more than they appear to be doing, but I wonder if they wandered off and had a cup of tea if the orchestra would get to the end of the piece at the same time. If you cast correctly, I think you are fifty percent of the way there with directing.

Q - How did Making A Killing come about and what did you think it would achieve?

Ryan - I thought it would achieve a small theatrical release. Get decent press and maybe a Jonathan Ross type review on TV. Then people would have heard of it and it would get a decent TV and DVD release and so on. Interestingly enough, one of my inspirations was *White Angel,* because I felt it hit many of the right boxes for a first film. For example, it was more or less all set in one house. The standard of acting was high. It had good twists and turns and kept me intrigued. I have a copy of it on my shelf. I really think new film makers, or fledgling film makers, should look at other peoples' films who are doing it with a certain level of success.

Q - What were your budget / script concerns, in order to keep the film manageable?

Ryan - From a script point of view it was the performances - one actor interacting with another actor as opposed to fireworks and action. No big scenes that cost a lot of money. I already had the idea to make a small, intimate film because, although I was inspired by *Star Wars*, I also like films like *Death And The Maiden* and *Sexy Beast.* Quite small psychological studies that I thought worked well as films. It was shot in two locations that were very close to one another, a five bedroom house that we used as a studio and on the other side of the road was a three bedroom cottage. I worked out that if we dressed the rooms sufficiently differently enough, those two places could handle the whole film. We did borrow someone's cellar for a scene, but it was essentially a one location film. We cut down transportation costs tremendously.

Q - Did you write it?

Ryan - Yes. The actual writing wasn't too painful, but I must say that I have many awful unfinished scripts under my bed. Writing is a whole different ballgame. It takes a long time to learn how to be an adequate writer, let alone a good one. The criteria for me is that the script has to be a page turner. You have to get to the end. Not get up and get a cup of coffee, read it all the way through to find out what happens. A tip I would give screenwriters, is to find someone that you trust and who will give you an honest answer and read out your idea. Verbalise it. Don't have a piece of paper in front of you. Get to know your idea so well that you can just say it. You find out if your idea has legs by looking at their face. You will see if anything excites them or confuses them and if you are really lucky they might even chip in. Also, you might find out that by the time you get to the end, you have forgotten a whole subplot or sequence and that is probably because it was never necessary in the first place.

Q - So they shouldn't get bogged down with dialogue at this point?

Ryan - Right. The dialogue isn't going to make it great at this point. Often, I find that dialogue is the last thing to do. What is important is the building blocks - the characters and the story, which is what the audience will latch on to. Also, if you don't have great dialogue and you have great actors, they will help you. I understand the philosophy that you rewrite and rewrite and rewrite, but don't do it without showing it to anyone. Someone might say that they only liked the film because of the ending and they guessed the ending on page twenty, and so you are sunk. You could have avoided this by giving that person a half page synopsis ages ago. Although your script is your blueprint, you should avoid investing huge amounts of time without getting a response from people you trust.

Q - What is the plot of Making A Killing?

Ryan - It's a psychological thriller in the vein of *Shallow Grave*. It has a little bit of dark humour bubbling up underneath. I always say that if you cannot say the plot in one sentence, then it is not high concept enough for people to get. As independent film makers we don't really rely on the art of the pitch. People go by our enthusiasm. That said, *Making A Killing* is always difficult for me to say in one sentence because it relies on a lot of twists and turns.

Q - That is interesting because films like that tend to take chances and aren't formulaic. It sometimes attracts big name actors who are tired of the same thing.

Ryan – Yes, with independent filmmaking you have a chance to be controversial or edgy. I think my film is certainly quirkier than the norm. So you can push the limits. You run the risk that people will run away of course but that is part of the game.

Q - So what is the plot of Making A Killing?

Ryan - Right! (laughs) It's about three friends who decide to con a hard-nosed insurer out of some life insurance money with fatal results. A British *Blood Simple*, if you will.

Q - Did you produce it?

Ryan - Yes, though I would not recommend it, unless you are an egomaniac. You have to be slightly mad to do something so ambitious. Actually, on a low budget film under £10k it becomes necessary to keep control of costs. One thing to do is to get a good line producer and production manager, and I did have that. But at the end of the day, if you are working on how to get the best shot and someone shoves a chequebook in your face, it destroys everything.

Q - What did you do about casting?

Ryan - I learned from my short film that professional casting is the key to success, and people have commented that they were surprised at the calibre of acting in the film. Part of the stress of it is that professional actors do not understand that, even though it looks like a real film, with a lighting truck out front, your budget is really tight. And the actors start going, *'One more for me,'* and you can't because you don't have the filmstock. You know you already have it and there is a slight conflict there because the actor is used to a certain way of doing things. It is a hard thing to get around. Of course you can give it to them and not run the camera! With HD it is slightly different as stock is cheaper, though you still need to keep up the pace to get all the shots.

Q - What format did you shoot on? How long did you shoot for?

Ryan - Super 16mm, which I am very comfortable with. It looks like film because it is film, unlike some digital films I have seen. We shot for four weeks, with the last week running to nine days! We had to get the film done. On the first day, which was a night shoot, we were shooting the first killing and we wanted to get it right. So we spent a long time setting up the lights, getting the track ready. And I wasn't worried because I figured we would pick up steam as we went along as people got to know one another. But at the end of the evening, we had shot the scene and it was fine, but we had only shot one page of a hundred page script. I got nervous. My AD had a word with me and said you either need to raise more money or you have to stop production and get back what you can. It was his job to wake me up and bring me down to reality. This was my big ambition to make a feature film and I had spent a lot of money at that point. I felt it would be disastrous to stop and I told him that we just have to keep going and reschedule. And we did. We made up time with the dialogue scenes between two people where we could shoot six pages a day.

Q - Do you think it is important for the director to do the schedule?

Ryan - Yes. I was quite religious about breakdown sheets. It was useful because you can do it in the relative calm period of pre-production, whereas when you are on the set and there are one hundred and one things to think about - you cannot focus. I had a folder for each week and I could shuffle around scenes based on how much we had shot. That was a big help.

Q - What was the budget? Did you stay opn budget?

Ryan - It was initially going to be £60k and it slowly moved up to £100k because to get the kind of actors I wanted and to get the image quality I wanted, the crew, the equipment, things slowly escalated. You forget that if you overshoot on a day and no one can make it home, you are going to have a thousand quid taxi bill. We also went over-budget because we went over-schedule. Certain costs came up that I hadn't expected. Taxis. The crew ate a lot of snacks! You cannot deny poorly paid people at least good food. We got a huge amount of receipts for things that people wanted, which I thought was fair for them to have, and that came to thousands!

Q - Did you edit it yourself?

Ryan - I did at home on my home editing system. I also edited the sound myself with a plan to take it to a sound studio for them to sweeten it - and they said, *'Why, it's already terrific!'*

Q - What were the difficult things about the sound?

Ryan - We had several sequences where the conditions for getting clear sound were not ideal. There were scenes in a pub that was next to a road and you could hear the traffic in the dialogue. You can post-dub the sound, but I am not keen on doing that. It looks like a bad Japanese film. I ended up editing out most of the traffic so you only hear it on dialogue bits. Then the software had some sweetening tools where I could make it sound tinny and get rid of the traffic. I mixed in stereo and did my own M&E as per requirements. It is easy as long as you track lay properly.

Q - Did you finish on tape only?

Ryan - We really didn't plan post fully and because of that ended up spending £6,000 on re-transfers. Now that would not happen as I would plan in detail exactly how we would do every stage.

Q - I'm surprised that your editing experience didn't cover those pitfalls.

Ryan - Yeah, me, too. Hindsight is a wonderful thing. Now I would shoot on Super 16mm at 25 fps, transfer the rushes to DVCAM, for off-lining and HD for on-lining and grading. Then I can transfer the HD to 35mm if I need to at a later date. One of the frustrations at the moment is that we are just on the cusp of digital cinema distribution (2005). If you make your film on a tight budget and you want to get a release, the financial effort of moving your film from tape to film is going to set you back tens of thousands of pounds. And if you don't have a 35mm print it is difficult to get your film into festivals. So I look forward to the day when all theatrically released films from *Making a Killing* to *War Of The Worlds,* are the equivalent of putting a DVD into a player and the film begins. Then we are all equals.

Q - Did you do the grading at home or at a lab?

Ryan - At a lab. It is possible to do it at home, but in my experience, if you do, it will fail international sales quality control. So you can be low-budget to a point, but if you are ambitious then you need to spend money at the end to tweak it and make it look professional and meet exacting professional technical standards.

Q - How did you get your final sound onto Digibeta tape?

Ryan - The sound came off my PC onto a Digibeta machine that we hired. They are heavy! And I transferred while watching the levels so they didn't peak too high and distort. We had a great composer named John Paxman who on his home setup, created a cinema like score. It had depth and gave the film a lot of production value.

Q - What happened with the release of the film?

Ryan - Aspirations are a wonderful thing. You have to lie to yourself to make movies because they are so difficult to do. There was a point in the edit suite where I looked at my film, and I thought it's a TV movie. A good TV movie, but nonetheless, a TV movie. My initial ambition was a small three print London release, but the scale of the film and the production value could only compete with a TV drama or TV murder mystery. It could not, however, compete with even a finely made independent film like *Lock, Stock And Two Smoking Barrels.* You can make a great film, but it might not be what the general public perceives as a great film for cinema release. It's because good isn't good enough, it has to be amazing. Go to Amazon.com and see *Murder By Design (US title).* And there a few reviews, ok one that I wrote myself, but others by actual Americans who cannot believe that they had not heard of the film before. That is who we are

making films for, not the average person who goes into Blockbuster and is expecting *Spiderman* and is disappointed. You are making if for someone who can accept the lower production value and likes your story and tone. I got an e-mail from someone in Kentucky last week who said they really liked my film and wanted to get an autograph! That is someone appreciating your efforts.

Q - When the film was completed who did you show it to?

Ryan - I sent 70 copies to sales agents. 60 to America and 10 to the UK. And I waited. And I waited. And reality began to sink in. William Goldman has a saying from *Adventures In The Screen Trade* that *'no one in the film business knows anything'.* I think that something similar can be said for low budget films arena, which is *'no one cares'* - which is harsh. But it makes sense as there are much bigger films out there. Maybe we can change it to, *'no one cares unless they can make money out of it'.* People also say they

like to discover the next Guy Ritchie, but they only ever say it after the event. They never say it before the event unless the cash register starts ringing and you start getting publicity.

I wasn't hearing back from any of the US international sales agents so I decided to focus more on the UK ones. I decided to screen my masterpiece to different UK sales agents, one at a time, and the first person who says yes, gets it. I rented out the screening room at De Lane Lee, which cost £350, but if they go for it, then it would be worth it. At that point, it seemed like the most important money I could spend. One

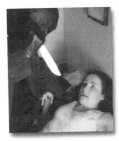

company, with a good reputation with low budget films, came to see it and I sat in a café across the road with my girlfriend procrastinating over whether to sit in on the screening or not. So we decided we hadn't seen the film in a while so let's sit in. It was awful choice. The film looked great and it sounded like a real movie. But as it unfolded, I sensed that it wasn't doing it for them. I heard them mumble something about 'good' but I wasn't sure if it was *'it isn't very good'* or *'it's very good'.* They watched the whole film and they said they would talk to me the next day. I heard nothing. A week came and went and I didn't hear anything. Two weeks came and I didn't hear anything. This is a pattern in the film industry where people don't get back to you. Or they don't want to say 'no' because if the film became a success and my boss heard I said 'no', then I am going to be in the firing line. So I

phoned her up and she was very polite and told me that you really can't get away with that level of film at the moment. And I understood that she meant that it didn't look like something that people expect from a cinema release and then she gave me the number of her TV sales arm. She did say that she was surprised that there were no other distribution companies there. And in hindsight, it makes sense to get more people at one screening as it is cheaper and it creates a buzz. Competition! It also moves things along faster.

Q - TV has become so good recently, it being a TV movie is not such a bad thing?

Ryan - It is unlikely that I will get a BBC sale though. Switch on BBC on a Monday night at 11 PM and you will see an American movie of the week about an underage abortion. And you think that surely the public would rather see my film than that film because it is British and it is quirky and different from what they are used to. I would kill for the 11 o'clock slot! The only reason they are showing the US film is because they wanted *Spiderman* and the only way to get *Spiderman* was to buy forty-nine other US B-movies. That is the frustration of TV. It is a good venue for low budget films, but they are not embracing it, even though it will cost them so much less to buy my film than all those films due to the professional fees and red tape.

Q - Just before you completed the film, did you do any major re-edits?

Ryan - Yes. One of the good things that happened, when we got our world sales agent was that they looked at the film and they said if it doesn't grab the attention of the buyers in the first five minutes we are sunk, because it doesn't have the stars or big set pieces to attract them. So we needed to spice up the beginning. So I reshuffled the murders so it grabbed you much more quickly.

Q - So you got a sales agent?

Ryan - We took on an American International sales agent who gave us a minimum quota of all the territories they will go for. Of course, there is no way they can guarantee that they will sell Japan for

$50,000. So three years down the line we have sold to US DVD for $25k, to Thailand for $3k, to Middle East pay TV for $2k. The world sales agent takes twenty percent of that and we take the rest. We have a possible $20k sale to Germany - maybe. Guerilla Films has taken it over in the UK. Although rental and retail DVD sale have been good it will probably only generate a four figure sum return. It might also get a UK TV sale of £10k. So you are talking about three to four years down the line of getting a third of your cash budget back. The horror is that some people would say that is a success! Over a longer period of time, you can claw back all the money you spent and make a small profit, but it doesn't support what I wanted, which was a successful little film business where you make enough money to live and eat and plough into your next film.

Q - If you could go back and change anything, what would you do to make it more of a commercial success?

Ryan - Its two drawbacks are that there are no stars in it; someone with box office value. Not just Tom Cruise, but anyone who people want to see. A comedian who wants to make a transition from TV to film, for example. Someone who has a ready made audience. What you really want is a Ewan McGregor or Jude Law calibre actor to read your script, which is possible. We did have a named actor who read the script, liked it and the agent said pencil him in. Then they found out what our weekly fee was. I was willing to pay the experienced actors £1k a week, which is a lot of money on a low budget film. The agent said that £1k was his daily rate, wished us well, and walked away. I was determined to start the production on a certain day so I did not take the time to go back to the actor and tell them what their agent had said in an effort to sway their artistic side.

Q - Do you think if you had come up with £20k for that actor that you could have recouped that in sales later on?

Ryan - It is difficult to say. There are so many factors needed to make a successful film. I was in Cannes and having a drink with a guy who had a £2 million film with Rutger Hauer in it. He is a star of a certain magnitude with pulling power and he couldn't get the sales amounts he needed to get his money back. I would feel more comfortable with a star actor in at least a cameo role than not having one at all. It helps get sales agents to take you seriously.

Shooting in a house is problematic. You can't get far enough away from the actors. What you get is a lot of mid shots, two shots and close ups. You don't get those wide shots that give it a sense of scope. So it ends up looking like TV because that is how they shoot TV. Whereas those films that end up in cinema, like *Shallow Grave,* have gone into a studio with huge sets. It looks bigger and hyper-real. And in the cinema, you usually want to see that. There was a mistake made when the film started off as one size and slowly shifted to another size. I thought at first that we were going to shoot a forest scene guerilla style, with someone running off into the forest, and without getting permits. When we actually shot it, I forgot to get permits and when we arrived, there was a huge Arri truck and lights everywhere. Two patrol people came walking along and I realised it looked like Hollywood had come to town. I told them that we had permission and wrote them a cheque immediately, which is a good way to smooth out stepped on toes. You have to think about everything all the time. As for sales, we have a good relationship with our agents, but they do seem to be new kids on the block. If you have to choose between sales agents, go for the biggest one because you need a bit of a lift.

Q - Why did they re-title it in America?

Ryan - They thought that *Making A Killing* was too tongue in cheek. So they changed it to *Murder By Design*, which I thought was OK. I think they thought it would sound like Sandra Bullock's *Murder By Numbers* and get people sucked in that way.

Q - What advice would you give a new film maker?

Ryan - I woke up one day sweating and saying to myself, I know that I can make a film, certainly as good as what I see on TV, and some of them in the cinema. If you feel that you have the burning desire to do it, you must do it. You must persevere. You must believe in yourself. You must think that you have something to offer, but you must also listen to the people who have gone before you and take on board the good and bad points they went through. Do not put your head in the sand because failure is very common in this game and that goes for well-established people too. It is a long arduous process, but it is rewarding and you should enjoy all of the experience!

Chris Kentis and Laura Lau
Film makers

OPEN WATER

Q - What are your backgrounds?

Chris - I went to NYU Tisch film school. I decided when I finished there to go into post production rather than working in production. I got jobs as assistant editor and I eventually went to a trailer company and became a trailer editor. That's where I met Laura and we then made a short film together.

Laura - I went to Columbia University for creative writing and ended up going into more of the producing side, but always wanted to write. I left the trailer company in order make the short with Chris and then we wrote a couple of scripts together and then we made a feature film together in 1997 called *Grind*. And then we had a child.

Chris - Best production we've had!

Q - What was the budget of 'Grind'?

Laura - $200k and it all came as private investment, mainly through family.

Q - What did you shoot 'Grind' on?

Chris - We did *'Grind'* the traditional way shooting on 35mm film with a full crew. It was a major learning experience for us and it was very much guerilla style even though we had SAG actors and it was a union shoot. It was still very much an indie film.

Laura - We shot it in 25 days. And as far as the outcome, we were thrilled because the film got a theatrical release. It did really well for our actors. Both Billy Cruddup and Amanda Peet. It was their first films. It was like graduate film school and everything we learned from it, enabled us to make *Open Water*.

Q - How did you come up with the subject matter for Open Water?

Chris - As soon as *Grind* was done, Laura was pregnant with our daughter and made a conscious decision to be a full time mum. Terrible for me because I was on my own writing. I really had to learn to write then and push myself!

Laura - It also meant that we didn't want to take on a huge production. We wanted to do things in a very small, intimate, family kind of way. We wanted to work in a way where we could include Sabrina, our daughter, and with the advent of digital technology, this was possible.

Chris - That was a big thing. I became aware of this technology from the Dogme '95 film, *Celebration* and *Breaking The Waves*, which were shot with digital video prosumer cameras. It was my first awareness of that and it was incredibly exciting. I remember reading that top directors like Steven Spielberg wanted to make a Dogme film. But what it meant was that we could challenge ourselves and try to work in an intimate fashion where we can control everything and wear a lot of hats. We also felt that digital imparts a very distinct feeling, so we wanted to find a story that would be well suited to the medium and take it to place where we haven't seen it. Laura and I have been recreational resort scuba divers for a decade, and I always brought a video camera along for shooting underwater. I would then cut together home videos and documentaries. But because we were divers, I had this awareness of a story in 1998 that I read in a dive newsletter about a couple from Louisiana who were off the Great Barrier Reef and got left behind. When I read that at the time, I couldn't stop talking about it because as a diver I found it compelling. What could be scarier? Also, I always wanted to make a film about the sinking of the USS Indianapolis. In 2001, when we started looking at this digital technology, everything clicked together. Here is a chance to explore a lot of the themes, do the Indianapolis on a small scale and take the technology somewhere it has never been before with a story that could benefit from this. And it kind of fit the mold of challenging ourselves as far as story telling. I didn't know if it was going to work. Working in digital video you get a sense of immediacy and realism from the look and we didn't want to light it and pretend to make it look like 35mm. We wanted to embrace this look, which meant unknown actors. This is a challenge because they were basically going to be the only characters in the movie. They are going to be in one location, they don't have any real props and they are just shoulders and head up. So can we hold an audience's attention with that and even more so, can we keep them on the edge of their seat?

Q - Did you have a problem finding actors who would be willing to be in the water for the whole duration?

Laura - We live in New York and there are so many actors here, it wasn't too hard to find people. We were very clear about how we were going to work and what the parameters were going to be. We knew that we were going to be working with no crew, so we told the actors that they were going to have to do their own hair, make up and costumes. We were going to shoot family style and literally it was Chris and me, my mother, his dad and my sister, who's a lawyer. And my mother and Chris' dad came along mostly to babysit our daughter. Very different from *Grind* where we did have quite a few problems with a large crew.

Chris - As a director it is important to have the skills to be able to deal with a lot of different personalities and the conflicts on a day-to-day basis of a large shoot. But this was a chance where it was just all the good stuff. There was no revolt because they didn't like what craft services had, or so and so is not getting along with such and such. This was all the good stuff. It was shooting. It was story. It was working very closely collaborating with the actors. Everybody has a say. Everybody had an opinion. No one had to be afraid to voice their opinion and believe me, they weren't. This was the way we wanted to work and it was a wonderful creative environment.

Q - What was the process with the script? Did you sit down with the actors?

Chris - I was familiar with the story of the USS Indianapolis and I did a lot of research which is so easy now on the internet. Then it just poured out of me and I wrote the first draft in six days. Laura got back from a trip and we started working together. Once we got it to a certain place, we stopped because we knew we were working with unknown actors and we wanted to collaborate with them. So we did not get too far into character.

Laura - Then once we cast the film, we spent a lot of time with the actors discussing what kind of characters they were interested in playing. What kind of relationship they were interested in exploring. Then we went through the script again and we wrote dialogue specifically tailored for those characters.

Q - How long was that process?

Chris - A month or so. I would sit down and in three or four days write something based on that and give it to Laura and she would sit down and rewrite it! We would go back and forth and that is how the process worked. But it is interesting how much filmmaking is such a process of refinement. You have a script and you are constantly working on it draft after draft to get it so tight - to the point where you think it is perfect. Then you start shooting and you realise all the fat that is still on that script and then when you get into editing it's suddenly like you see all the other mistakes. It's a constant process of refinement.

Q - Did you sit down and do a budget and was it self financed?

Laura - That is exactly what we did. We came up with a budget and because we had made *Grind* we understood the kind of insurance we needed and why we had to be careful to clear logos and to make sure that we got all the releases and clearances that we would need.

Q - You mentioned insurance. Was it a problem getting as you were shooting in water with sharks?

Laura - No, we had insurance, but we were working with an expert, Stuart Cove, who'd done many many films with sharks so we knew we were in good hands. And whenever you do work like that there are waivers that you have to sign anyway as these are the exact same waivers that you sign anytime you go diving. And again, we were very clear in the casting process making everyone aware we were shooting with sharks. If we had stars, we wouldn't have been able to get insurance. This was the advantage of doing it guerilla style.

Chris - There were many aspects of this film that had to do with our conscious decision of turning things that would normally be seen as deficits into assets. Making this film in a very typical Hollywood way would have been very difficult - even with the marketing aspects of it. We wanted to do something that Hollywood isn't very interested in doing right now. They want everything to be computer generated. When I turn on cable TV and see a film from the '70's or '80's and you know that those are not computer generated effects, you are kind of invested or at least there is a sense of awe of how did they do it? Now no-one ever asks that because we know it is a computer manipulating pixels. Not to say that there aren't a lot of gifted artists, but I think that there is a gratuitous use of that and so we thought this was a way to sneak in and give the audience an experience that no one's really provided. That is why we wanted to work in the open ocean and work with real sharks.

Q - Where did you shoot?

Laura - We wanted to disguise the location purposely so we shot in many locations. We shot in the Bahamas, the Grenadines, the Virgin Islands and Mexico.

Q - Could your actors scuba dive?

Laura - Blanchard had done a while ago and although they didn't have to be certified, in order to be safe, we wanted to make sure they were. So we had them certified in New York.

Q - Did you have any problems with the actors over that?

Laura - We made sure that we wouldn't have problems as we were very upfront about it and it had all been part of the audition process. When we were in the call back stage, we took our actors to a pool and had them dive. Of course, everyone was saying it would be no problem. But you can tell if someone is really comfortable or not.

Q - Most movies would have had CGI sharks but you went with real sharks swimming underneath and around the actors...

Laura - That's right. In fact, Stuart Cove, the shark wrangler, said that he had never worked with the actual actors before, he had always worked with stunt doubles

Chris - But what was interesting talking to Stuart was seeing how many big films he had done where he would come work with the sharks and when the movie came out, they had erased all the sharks and put computer ones in. It was key to us to work with real sharks. We spent a day and a half working with Stuart for the shark shots and they were carefully mapped out with a specific shot list. We did that very early in the shoot and we matched to those shots later because we had to be prepared. In the water you can't suddenly move around or flail your arms around or yell because you run the risk of confusing the shark and you could have a pretty severe accident. All the actor performance stuff happened months later in a different part of the ocean.

Q - It was only a day and half with the shark wrangler?

Chris - We originally scheduled one day and it was one of the first days of the shoot. We had done an earlier shoot with the other sea creatures. So we started the shoot and we went out to the Bahamas and what a miserable start! A lot of this film was shot on weekends and on vacation time because I worked my full time job and they didn't know I was making a film - so needless to say, time was precious. I had it all booked with Stuart ahead of time. And that morning at 7am I show up at his dock and it's all cloudy. I went to the desk and they said Stuart went to the mainland. He wasn't there! They looked at their books and they had nothing written down. I couldn't believe it. Luckily I found Stuart and we cleared it all up, and then it started raining. We went out in six or seven foot seas - huge swells and pouring rain. I will never forget when we were going out thinking what the hell am I doing? I am out of my fucking mind. I took our savings and this is what I did? We went out to our main site, which was close to shore and there were problems there. The sharks weren't coming in so we had to go way further out past this part of the ocean called the Tongue of the Ocean where there is this 6000 foot drop. And this was Blanchard Ryan's first experience with sharks. Daniel was like me, for whatever reason he didn't have a shark issue. Blanchard is what you would refer to as a normal person. And what I should have really done is taken these guys on a shark dive because being underwater with sharks they are not nearly as threatening for some reason as being on the surface, which is what we wanted to exploit in the film. So here we pull up to this site and fifty sharks are around. I jumped in and Daniel jumped in and we expected Blanchard to jump in and she did do just that, but she was pretty frightened. Eventually the weather cleared and we were able to move inland and halfway through the day we started to get our shots. But we realised that we needed another good half day in order to get all of our shots.

Q - Did you have any problems with the sharks?

Laura - No, we didn't. The only thing that happened was there were too many sharks and in a lot of scenes we only wanted one shark or two sharks so it was more tricky to separate the sharks.

Chris - Also if the film was going to unfold in a realistic and authentic way we couldn't have too many sharks.

Q - So was that real fear we saw on Blanchard's face?

Laura - We didn't know until it was actually time to get into the water that she was afraid of sharks. If we knew, she wouldn't have been cast. And I think she overestimated her own confidence for the situation so when she was actually faced with getting into the water with sharks, it was very difficult for her. We just reassured her as we didn't want her to be miserable. We just wanted to make her as comfortable as we could. But at the same time, we were committed. We had already done some shooting and she knew she had a job to do. So she got in there and did it, but she really was very frightened of the sharks.

Q - How long was she in the water with the sharks for?

Chris - Actual water time was about four to six hours, but not all at once. Even with Blanchard being terrified and having to deal with it, we did not lose one second to that. She did what she had to do. I'll never forget her coming out of the water and I would be looking at the shot and she would say, "Chris, did you get what you wanted." And I'd say, "It's pretty good." And she would just suit up and get right back in the water. She was totally professional.

Q - What was it like working with Stuart Cove?

Chris - Stuart's great. The first thing is you sit with this guy and he starts telling you stories from twenty years of working with sharks. He told us a story of how a shark ripped the scalp off his head and then showed us his scars. It was like sitting down with Quint from *Jaws*.

Laura - He had such confidence. Everything seemed so easy and it was more a question of solving the puzzle of getting the sharks that we wanted. There was never any sense of anxiety or fear. He's a professional and a master at what he does. And instead of just throwing money at a problem, we got inventive. And Stuart was very smart that way. Always trying different ways to solve problems. Using things on hand as rigs, a piece of wood or a piece of plastic, constantly looking at a situation trying to figure out solutions.

Chris - I think Stuart had fun and was into it because from what I have seen of sharks in film, 90% of the time they are shot under the water. And as I said, as a diver, I don't find that particularly threatening.

Laura - In fact, Stuart said he had never worked with the sharks on the surface before.

Chris - And we wanted to exploit that *what you can't see is more frightening*. Let the imagination work. I have been underwater with sharks and I'm there chasing them around! But I have been on the surface waiting on a boat when all of a sudden, out of nowhere, there's an explosion of water and a tail, and then it's gone. It's very disconcerting. We wanted to capture that, as the key to the film was to capture everything from the point of view of these main characters. Our hope was that the movie was going to work when the audience members would put themselves in the place of the characters and experience the film in that way and ask themselves what they would do at any given moment. And we also wanted to portray shark behaviour in a more realistic way. Experts from Shark Week have agreed that we have achieved exactly that, as well as leaders in the dive industry, the presidents of PADI and NAUI.

Q - Jaws is such a classic and terrifying in itself but shooting on DV as a home video really captured more of a reality to the story...

Chris - I love *Jaws*. It's a brilliant movie and so we didn't want to go there. But we never saw this as a shark film. If we were going to tell the story accurately, they were going to be an element that had to be dealt with, and the most logical thing seemed to be to work with the real thing if we could do it in a safe manner.

Q - On your DVD you say that you used a cage at one point...?

Chris - It was kind of funny because we never used a cage for the bulk of the shoot. What happened is once the film was acquired by Lion's Gate, there was an opportunity to go in and get one or two more underwater shots. Some underwater shots I hadn't been too thrilled about. Particularly for the lightning scene, I wanted the shark to come a little closer than the one I had. We called Stuart and he said let's use a cage. This seemed really safe because I have been in the water with these sharks and they were bumping into me like crazy.

There was bait in the water and tuna blood. So I got in the cage and we are baiting the sharks to come as close to me as possible because we wanted them to attack the cameras. Then a big, old shark came along and barrelled his way right into the cage! We are talking about a space the size of an elevator and all of a sudden I was trapped in the cage with an angry shark. So what I thought would be the easiest thing that I ever did became the most dangerous thing I ever did.

Q - Were you advised on what to do in that situation?

Chris - You don't really think. You just go on instinct and try to push this thing away with your camera and you get out!

Q - Did you have any problems shooting on and in the water?

Laura - Well, we had some problems with water getting everywhere, but the biggest issue we had was with matching. Water is always changing in terms of the current, its colour and the light. For example, when it is really clear and bright blue skies, the water becomes really harsh looking. Chris being an editor, really understood what coverage we needed, so we shot with two cameras the whole time and with that, combined with a fantastic boat captain and mother nature really cooperating with us, we really only lost two days to good weather.

Chris - And we also had a very concrete plan about how we wanted to use mother nature and use the palette of the ocean and how it changes. We wanted to begin the film with the very inviting aqua marines and cobalt blues and then go to silvers and eventually to blacks and red. So we were always doing print outs of what we had to make sure we could match. Traditionally it's very well known that working underwater can be a disaster and had we been a regular film crew with a hundred people and huge giant rigs, I can see how it would be a nightmare.

Laura - That is certainly an advantage of being guerilla. We could just pick up the anchor and go. And sometimes we would be shooting and you could see the storm cloud coming and we would have about twenty minutes to get in and go!

Chris - There's a scene were Daniel gets bit and she is checking him which we did in one take. There was a storm coming in and we had black water that was really active. We had enough time for a couple of takes and I remember having the cameras there and I couldn't believe it when we were shooting how everything fell into place. I said we got it. And everyone was like, how could we get it? This is the biggest scene in the film! Another thing that we did was constantly being inventive by building different rigs to capture the right shot. I wanted to shoot right at water level, but the gear just didn't exist. So I went to Office Depot and I bought this file box and converted that into a housing rig so that we could put the camera right into the water. I took the plastic box and I cut a hole in it. There is a German company that makes these ports for underwater, so I bought one of those and glued it in and then I put in different stuff for sound. All so I could get the camera right there in the water with the actors.

Q - What camera did you shoot on?

Laura - The Sony PD-150 and the VX-2000. The great thing about those cameras is that they both look like consumer cameras. We would just go out and get in the water and shoot and no one paid any attention to us. We could get crowd shots. We didn't get permits, we probably should have. If we were at a hotel location, then we would get a clearance or ask them for permission. But shots in a market and on a beach, we just stole those shots.

Chris - The cameras are lightweight and so unobtrusive that it looked like we were on vacation. Everyone else there was on vacation. It was perfect. Also as I knew I was going to edit on Final Cut Pro, we were constantly creating these edit bins of cutaways by shooting shots of birds, sky shots, water shots, helicopters...I don't know how many times Laura saved my ass because she shot something amazing. The amazing thing about shooting digital is that you can just shoot, shoot, shoot. We could do pickup shots here in Manhattan. On every single film that is made there is going to be pick up shots. I'll never forget on *Grind* what a pain in the ass it was getting that together. We only did one short afternoon of re-shoots and you've got to deal with unions, crew, actors, film and processing. And when I saw these Dogme Films and these new DV cameras I was thinking you get an idea, you pick up the camera and you shoot it.

Laura - We could just to the roof and shoot a sky shot. Long into post if we needed a shot, the actors would just come out and just do it because they were all living in New York. Blanchard's hair length changed over the three years that we made the film, so we had to get real clever about gel in her hair and putting up in a bun so it looked seamless.

Q - It took you three years to make the film?

Laura - Yes, between the conception of the idea to the finished product. It took longer than it should have done, not just because I was still working but because a year into the film, with only two weeks from getting everything finished shooting, Daniel blew out his knee playing volleyball. He had to have reconstructive knee surgery. It was a year before he was well enough to shoot again. The shoot was so rigorous. The actors were tethered to the boat but they were swimming the whole time so they had to be in amazing shape. And even a year later it was hard for him. His leg would hurt and we would have to ice it.

Q - How far off the mainland were you?

Chris - I think it was about twenty miles in 1500 feet of water.

Laura - One thing that we forget is how physically grueling shooting on the ocean is. The boat is constantly rocking, there is current to deal with, and the sun beats down on you.

Chris - It was funny because Laura did all the shooting from the boat. The actors were always in the water. I shot underwater and on the surface of the water and from the boat. Laura would be on the boat and at the end of the day, she couldn't wait to get in the water. The actors couldn't wait to get into the boat. I was the only one who knew it was miserable everywhere!

Q - How many trips did you go down to the Caribbean with everyone to shoot?

Chris - Six or seven. A lot of those were short weekends. We had two times that were big chunks of a week or more. As you can imagine I called in sick a lot on Mondays and Fridays.

Q - Did you have any problems shooting in these different places?

Chris - No. I contacted the Bahamas Film Commission very early on in the process. Before we started this, we needed to know if we could do it. I never would have gone ahead with this if I hadn't contacted Stuart Cove so I could get those shots. And it was the same with the Bahamas Film Commission. They were very helpful. I went down there and did several scouts in the islands, so not only were there not problems, they pointed me in the right direction.

Q - What was the editing process like? Did you edit between shoots?

Chris - I was working on the film 24/7 except for my day job. All the time between shoots I was editing and adding things. We were always refining and rewriting.

Laura - We added the opening scenes to the film pretty late. It was the fall, September. We didn't like what we had shot so we went out and got those.

Chris - That was Laura. She fought for a long time to have an opening scene to establish the characters. We had our little test screenings where friends and family assemble a group ten to twenty people who didn't know us and we would hand out questionnaires. One thing when you do every job on a film, you have no objectivity whatsoever, so we were very aware that we needed some way of seeing if this was becoming the kind of movie we wanted to make. And after doing so, it seemed that we needed something up front.

Q - When did you finish the film and when did you submit it to Sundance?

Laura - We actually had a cut of the film that we showed at the Hamptons Film Festival. Coming out of that, our rep said you have to apply to Sundance. But we had blown our premiere and thought we would never get into Sundance.

Q - Who was your rep? And how did you find her?

Laura - Ronna Wallace. We brought her on before the festival. Her advice at the festival was to enjoy the screening, lay low and hope no one important sees it because it wasn't finished. But it turned out Variety was at one of the screenings, which was horrible!

Chris - Yep, we were having a wonderful time at the Hamptons. The audience was loving it - screaming, reacting so well. It was the last night, and our last screening. And this woman comes up to me at the end of screening and says, *"I'm Ronnie Shieb of Variety and I am reviewing your movie. Will you be having a 35mm print anytime soon because I want to be fair?"* I explained that we wouldn't. I couldn't believe it! It was so not fair. I only had an output right from my Final Cut Pro machine! We were not even out of the gate! I thought we were dead.

Q - But you got a fantastic review.

Chris - Lo and behold a wonderful review. So we decided to apply to Sundance and we got in. We then brought on our attorney, Sue Goldstein, who was with us on *Grind*.

Laura - People advised us that you don't need to spend the money to do a film out. At festivals it is OK to project video and at Sundance that year, half the films were being projected on video. It is probably more than half now. So we put money into getting a good master.

Chris - It is foolhardy to go to film now.

Laura - Once the film was acquired, it was tricky getting a good film negative out of our original because there is a lot of constant movement on the screen due to the water. But we worked with Heavy Light Digital who had done the film out for Morgan Spurlock's film *Super Size Me*. They figured out some techniques in our movie and wished they could have used it in *Super Size Me*. The way the labs work in New York is they help each other out. They'd send a test out and say, what ideas do you have to solve this problem.

Chris - I was impressed with Heavy Light Digital as they were so concerned with the film being the best it can be, they would talk to anybody. They were inventing stuff to get it on film.

Q - Was there anything in the colour correction process that you really wanted?

Laura - Absolutely. As Chris was saying before we wanted to use mother nature. So in terms of pushing the consistency of the water, we did that in post. The lightning scene was created in post as it was shot day for night.

Q - How much control did you have with Lion's Gate in completing the film after they acquired it?

Laura - Lion's Gate was really great. They knew we made film ourselves so they let us complete the film. We did the colour correct, we did the film out, we timed the print, we supervised everything.

Chris - It was probably a bit of a learning curve for Lion's Gate as well because their department heads from marketing and legal would call up to talk to our department heads which is me and Laura, there's nobody else. Every single still, I had to pull from the picture. I cut the trailer. Every aspect of the film, even after it was acquired, we were able to oversee. Now that is not to say that we didn't work with some really talented wonderful people thanks to Lion's Gate. For instance Glenn Morgan who was our sound editor and Graham Revell, our composer.

Q - What kind of score did you have at The Hamptons and how did Graham Revell come about?

Laura - A lot of the music that we picked was old and mono so once we had a stereo mix we realised that the music was a little thin. Lion's Gate suggested that Graham Revell come on and he loved the picture. We were a little worried because we didn't want it to go into a genre direction. Graham understood that. He said that he loved the silences in the film and that is when we knew that we were on the same page.

Q - It was very haunting score. Almost religious.

Chris - Yes, all the songs are the exact same ones that were in Sundance. But Graham bolstered the score that I created. He used it as a steppingstone and totally understood what I was after and created something that was his.

Laura - And we really worked on it in the mix. We took the ambient effects and drums that Chris created and we would add that to what Graham did. He knew that we were looking for something elemental.

Chris - He and his brother Ashley were the ones at the mix. It was exciting to have access to this kind of talent.

Q - Did you have to clear a lot of rights for the music you used originally?

Laura - I don't think we went and got festival clearances, but we were very aware after making *Grind*, where we spent a good amount of money on music rights, not to do that on this film. We purposely picked really obscure music.

Chris - It was a creative choice first. One piece was recorded in Fiji in 1948. I loved this music as it spoke to me and we just didn't want to take the film in a genre direction.

Q - When during Sundance did Lion's Gate approach you?

Laura - It was really fast. The festival opened on a Friday and we had four or five screenings planned. We had a screening Friday night, Saturday morning and another on Sunday afternoon. Coming out of the Saturday morning screening Lion's Gate made their offer. So all of the other companies had to scramble because they figured they would make their offers coming out of our Sunday screening. There was this bidding war that happened on Saturday and we decided to go with Lion's Gate.

Chris - I will never forget that Saturday night. We came out of the screening and we met the Lion's Gate guys. I had to go do a Robert Redford thing and when I came back, that's when Laura told me about Lion's Gate and the offer and the numbers. Then we went to the war room. Ronna and Sue and Andrea our attorneys, these chain smoking women, were in this room in this cloud of smoke, and they all had cell phone to their ears. And I am hearing these numbers going around, "One million? You are not even in the game, pal." I thought, are they working on another movie? Then I am hearing nasty stuff - the threats! One of them said, and how is this for a cliché, *you are never going to work in this town again!* It was really shocking.

Q - Did you have a sales agent at the time?

Laura - No. Our rep, Ronna, with Sue Bodine, acted as our sales agent. They were fantastic.

Q - How much did Lion's Gate pick it up for?

Chris - $2.5 million. It cost us $120,000 which was financed just by the two of us and we released in August later that year.

Q - Were you guys surprised with the response?

Chris - Everything from the Hamptons on was a surprise and a shock because this film was truly a labour of love. It was really about the experience for us. Could we pull it off? Once the film was completed before we went to any festivals, I remember screening it for the actors and they loved it. This was what it was about and anything after that was just gravy. So to find out that Lion's Gate was going to release this on 2700 screens and the film was then released in 70 countries and it made about $31 million in the US, and $27 million in the world. To think our little video project has gone on to do what it has, is phenomenal.

Laura - It did well in the UK. It was #1 in box office theatrically and on DVD sales and rentals. And our opening weekend in the US was $18m, I think! We're the filmmakers so we know less than anybody, we only know what the distributor tells us and according to the distributor it's still in the red!

Chris - We're teasing of course.

Q - Did you go overseas and do publicity?

Larua - Yes. Because we shot the film with a lot of unknowns, a lot of the publicity focused on us. Doing the film and then the publicity it's been pretty full time but we traveled a lot and it has been a lot of fun.

Q - Did agents come knocking at your door?

Laura - After we sold our film on the Saturday, we were so happy. We thought we had the whole festival ahead of us. We can go see all these movies. We can go skiing. Fortunately, we hired a publicist, Jeremy Walker. On Sunday, he came to us with five pages of press that were interested in us and between that and meeting with agents, suffice to say for the whole week we did not see a single film nor go skiing!

Chris - It was crazy. We get into Sundance and two days later they are leading me into a room and there is Isabella Rosellini and Kyle McLachlan and they are sitting in a chair and they told me to sit down. I thought I

was keeping it warm for someone. Next thing I know there is a guy with a microphone in my face and they are taking my picture. And it continued like that for a year and yes, we did get an agent.

Q - After getting your agent, did you find that the doors were now being thrown open to you?

Laura - Yes. We were getting scripts every week and it is exciting that people want to work with us. Different producers, production companies and studios are looking for projects to do with us. But because we had made a film before and we have been at this for a long time, we were really clear about how we wanted to work. We both want to write and direct our own work.

Chris - We are working on our own projects and have several studio projects as well. There is a learning curve there because we are used to having control and we like it that way.

Q - What would you say are the common mistakes that new filmmakers make?

Laura - Not getting the proper releases. Not making sure that legally you are doing the right thing. Not making sure that all your contracts are in order up front. For actors or working with friends, you need to have contracts. The information is there on the internet or in books. Get your nuts and bolts down.

Chris - From a creative prospective, *Grind* was so much trying to make a movie that looked like a movie. I think a lot of filmmakers start to do that and I really think it is about trying to find your own voice. Also, you must think outside the box. I think people get caught up with trying to work with the latest equipment and the like. We had a certain amount of money and we had to do it with the resources we had. It's a challenge to be innovative. Always ask yourself, what do you have to bring to this? What's my voice?

Q - What advice would you give to new filmmakers?

Laura - This is your life at the same time. People forget that you need to have a balance and treat other people with respect and integrity. Behave in a way that is fair. Everything that you do is a reflection of who you are.

Chris - It's true. No one can predict what is going to be a hit. Any film that you make as a writer/director you are dedicating at least two years of your life to. And you can't do it worrying about the outcome. It is what you do in between.

Laura - Also when making a movie, ask yourself what do I want to see next? What will be interesting? And that is the barometer. Do not think *what might be commercial* or *what might audiences like?*

Chris - Yes, but there is a balance too. You want to put yourself in the seat of an audience member. Am I going to feel ripped off here or pissed off?

Laura - Also never capitulate any part of the process. Always engage people about whatever you are doing, whether it be renting equipment or talking with actors.

Chris - It is very easy to get intimidated and cowed as a first time film maker when you are working on a set with people who are much more experienced than you. You start questioning yourself. But you must remember that you're putting your own voice to it. You must stand your ground without being an asshole.

Q - Chris, do you still work at the trailer company?

Chris - I do! Once you work full time and are able at the same time to write, direct and edit a movie, then you feel you can take on anything and everything! And I love doing it.

Stuart Fletcher
Producer

INFESTATION

Q - Flash back 20 years - you are sat back at school in Wigan, in the Northwest of England, which as I know, is a provincial town with a cotton and coal industry heritage... and you say 'actually I want to make Hollywood movies', what was the response to that, and how did you come to that choice?

Stuart - I've had a love affair with movies for a long time, and you mention different things to different folks, and often you get ridiculed. People say *'It's just not a goer, think about it practically, forget it!'* I'd take that on board, bury it for a while, and then it would just resurface a few years later. I bummed around after I failed my exams, and it was when I was in my mid 20's, fed up with working in a shit hole of an office, selling life insurance, that I thought I should go and do a degree in Media. So at 27, I finally got to go back to Art College in Carlisle.

Q - Tell me how 'Infestation' began.

Stuart - It started with me going to Art College, where I met up with Ed Evers-Swindell. I produced and co-wrote, and he directed and edited our graduation film, which was a 20 minute short based on this slightly futuristic idea of a post-apocalyptic world. We used a lot of techniques like blue screen and CGI and learnt a huge amount, which we later implemented in *'Infestation'*. We achieved everything we set out to do, which for us was important, to have a realistic goal which we kept in sight at all times. The film won some awards, we graduated and went our separate ways. I went back to the North West and got a job as a video technician, and before we know it, a few years had passed. Then out of the blue Ed rang and said *'I've got an idea, I've found this amazing location, do you want to come and have a look?'* The germ of *'Infestation'* was that location he'd found in North Wales - a derelict holiday village from the 70's where a tornado had come through and wiped it out, and it had been left to rot for 20 years. We then took our two main characters and the situation from the student film, and turned it into a feature film. The short was always a feature film really and we had crammed too much into it. We were able to learn from all the simple mistakes that we made on the student short version, and incorporate those lessons into the feature.

Q - So your student film was really a trial for the bigger movie?

Stuart - Yes. You think *'OK, we've gone up a big hill with the student version, and we've come down that hill - there were a few mishaps, but we didn't fall off it into a crevice and die. So now we can take the same rules and apply them to the mountain.'*

Q - Did you think of taking the project to big industry players?

Stuart - There wasn't ever really a discussion about a real budget, it was always a micro budget film. What I've learnt as a filmmaker is to write to what you've got - and we had this location. We were able to adapt the story, break a few of the rules, and still make what we thought was going to be a good action film. The momentum came from the fact that the location was going to get knocked down, so that was actually a very good catalyst for us.

Q - How did you go about casting? Did you get any named actors?

Stuart - We used the people from the first film. We used some friends and some unknown actors who did a pretty good job. The cast we eventually used were great. You need to consider if they will be reliable for the long haul on a micro budget film. You can't pin people down, as you are not paying them properly, so you have to cast using your instinct, and if they have passion for the project. We picked up one person who was scheduled to do two days filming and they didn't turn up for the second. We also found that there is a huge difference between a properly trained and experienced actor and a non-actor. I would always hire trained and experienced actors if possible.

Q - Would you go along with the notion, that if everyone understands what journey they are on, then you don't have problems, it is only when you big up your production, and people think they are going to get luxury, when they have to sit in a derelict block of flats while they eat cheese sandwiches for lunch?

Stuart - Absolutely. That goes back to picking the right people. Sure you have to get them excited to get them on board, but you can't over sell it. If people see a film crew, they assume your pockets are full of money. We kept that in check by saying *'we are just local boys trying to make good'*. People were cool about that, whether it was Liverpool or North Wales, wherever we were filming.

Q - Is it as an advantage, shooting in places where there has not been much prior production? Certainly not London?

Stuart - Yes. There is a huge benefit to doing what we did. No one wants to give you anything in London. In the rest of the country there are amazing locations, amazing people who would be excited to be on board, and just do it for the buzz. For instance, we got the Mersey tunnel for free, and the guards hung out so they could watch some women in black leather pants running around, and doing high kicks and stuff. They were happy with that, and we didn't have to pay a penny! You wouldn't get that down here.

Q - You chose to shoot on mini-DV?

Stuart - Yes, we used the Sony PD150.

Q - How did you do the sound?

Stuart - For the first 10 days in Wales, it was recorded on DAT. How much of that DAT sound ended up on the film, I don't know because for international sales reasons, we actually chose to do an awful lot of ADR and replace local accents with American ones.

Q - Other low budget film makers have chosen to record a guide track only, and replace ALL the sound in post production. Do you think that's a good plan?

Stuart - Definitely, as long as you do a test to figure out how to do it. It is a bloody lot of work to do it afterwards, but it allows you to do a lot of set ups when shooting and you can work very quickly.

Q - How big a crew did you use?

Stuart - Around 12 people.

Q - How did you approach catering?

Stuart - Ed's nan and mum made sandwiches. If your crew gets hungry and tired, you need to feed them, but without catering to their every whim. That means help and preparation.

Q - What were your major budgetary expenses?

Stuart - We spent more on catering, insurance, security, greasing palms, than film making equipment. It is about having friends in low places - that's so important, and it is over-looked. Stuff like props and sets we did ourselves, and it didn't cost much aside from materials.

Q - So what was the budget?

Stuart - We started with £1k for ten days shooting, which is totally do-able. Ed's mum was doing the catering and putting people up in her big house. When you take those kind of things out, and the catering being done in-house, you can keep your costs way down. The big cost of our first week was insurance. We were able to get some props for no money and we had some costumes already. Then it kind of just went from £1k to £5k, and we paid for it all out of our own pockets, never claiming travel expenses or phone calls - so there are two ways of looking at our budget. Because it took such a long time to make and we were able to pull in a lot of favours, it should have easily cost £350k. We also got some investment from a Welsh businessman.

Q - In total how much cash did you spend?

Stuart - Definitely significantly less than £350k!

Q - How long did it take you to edit the film?

Stuart - Editing began a few days after we did the first 10 day shoot. We foolishly thought we could do this in a few weeks of spare time. We also thought we had shot the majority of our film in the first 10 days of shooting, and that it was only going to take another 5 or 6 weekends of shooting here or there to finish the film. Actually it took 6 years.

Q - Looking at the overall story editing process, what did you learn when you put scenes together?

Stuart - We were all keen not to do the things that Hollywood is doing at the moment, which is just spectacle without emotion. We wanted to make a spectacular action film but we realised that if there is no emotional connection with the characters, you've got nothing. We wanted the audience to go on a journey with the main characters, and to actually give a shit about them. If there was anything that we were all agreed on, it was that.

Q - Did you find removing stuff improved a scene?

Stuart - Definitely. Most new film makers think that you have this script, and not a word of it is going to change. It is the absolute opposite of that if anything! You are always crafting and refining it, and that generally means taking stuff out. Occasionally it is going to mean putting stuff in, which we did as well. It is more like a sculptor working with something, and refining it. You are allowing creative people to collaborate and to add lines or take them out. Again, that is about picking the right people to work with. We were really keen not to make our first feature a baggy film. We looked at stuff like Cameron's 'Terminator' - the first two thirds of the film is exposition and it shouldn't work, yet as it is all done while they are fighting or on the run, it does work. We thought, right, whenever we have got to give some exposition, it has got to be during a fight scene or when something exciting is going on.

Q - It is a very interesting point though, if you have got a page of what is potentially dull dialogue, get them to do something exciting while saying it.

Stuart - Yes. But of course it's best if the scene is so strong in the first place you do not need to resort to these kind of tactics.

Q - Post-production sound is one of the areas you spent a lot of energy getting right. What did you do? How did you approach that?

Stuart - We managed to get help from The Creative Partnership, in downtime, where we did our 5.1 mix and all our ADR. It was a very long process and everyone was in at the deep end, but we got it done.

Q - How long did that process take?

Stuart - Colour grading and the sound mix has taken seven months, going backwards and forwards. It sounds really good in 5.1 and it has absolutely been worth it. I didn't have a problem editing at home with low end kit but for final mastering I needed to know that it had been done as professionally as possible, on a properly calibrated system.

Q - So you can do almost all of the work at home, apart from the very final mastering because it is going out to be broadcast?

Stuart - Yes. It's essential. We mixed the sound in a multi million pound studio and colour graded and mastered the picture on a top end *Smoke* machine. It's all state of the art kit being driven by experts who do this day in, day out. I didn't want the final master to be sub standard so that when we made sales it was rejected on technical grounds. You will need to deliver your final film on something like DigiBeta, or perhaps even HD, which you can't just hook up to your home edit system.

Q - How did you find the process of the colour grading, was it a revelation what you could do with it?

Stuart - It was. While you may have the kit and software to do it, do you have the experience to make sure it will pass all quality control checks in distribution? Now I realise just how much scope you can have with colour grading in post, I wouldn't light scenes to be so contrasty. If you are building a set and it is only half built, you have got to be specific where you put your pools of light so as to hide problems. The issue with some of the way *'Infestation'* was lit is that I allowed too much to get too dark, which means in post colour grading we had very little control - the detail is just not there - and the same is true if it is over exposed, the detail is not there, so no amount of grading is going to pull it back.

Q - So don't ever crush your blacks, and try to avoid burning out over 100% white?

Stuart - Yes. Almost shoot it clean and do the colour effects afterwards. We were doing it in camera as we didn't know what we could do later. I don't like it when people say *'Just shoot it, we will fix it in post'*. You have got to get it close to what you want on the day, just don't crush the blacks or over expose. It may look a little flat, but once you get into a professional colour grading suite, you will be thankful you shot it that way.

Q - So the idea is you know exactly what you are going to do in post, as opposed to shooting and hoping you will be able to fix it with the expensive toys in post production?

Stuart - Absolutely.

Q - Visual effects, your film is crammed with them.

Stuart - Yes, it has 70 effect shots, which is quite a lot for a micro budget film. We used Andrew Whitehurst, a freelance CGI artist who has worked on loads of films. He did it at home on his own equipment. It took a long time as Andy would work during the day on big films and on our film at night. It was scary because if these shots didn't work, the whole film didn't work - so we were sweating until we got our first tests. We filmed an awful lot of stuff thinking we hope this is going to work - but with the effects, we had no choice, they had to work! It took two years to do all the shots.

Q - Once you completed, and you thought we have got to sell this film, what did you do?

Stuart - We always expected the film to be good, we wouldn't have started out if we thought it was going to be rubbish. But the strange thing is you get shy about showing it to somebody, and wonder if it is in fact no good. You are so close you tend to lose perspective. We showed a trailer to some sales agents and screened part of the movie. People were really excited about it and at one point there was a bit of a bidding war. That fired us up to finish the film. We went back to Cannes the next year and we got a sales agent even though the film was still incomplete.

Q - What kind of deal did the Sales Agent offer you?

Stuart - They were taking the usual 20% plus expenses.

Q - So you have made this £350k movie, for much less than that in cash terms, and it probably looks like it cost a million, and you got a great Sales Agent selling the world - surely everyone has got their money back and you are rich?!

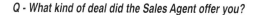

Stuart - No, not at all.

Q - How long has it been being sold for now?

Stuart - We made contact with our sales agent in Cannes last year and so far we have sold in five territories - nothing amazing yet, territories like Thailand and Russia, though we do have interest from the USA and from Anchor Bay in the UK. Sales is a long haul.

Q - You took a DV camera, a bunch of mates, and several countries in the world have bought your film! That's amazing!

Stuart - I know, it's mad! That is one perspective on it. There are other perspectives which are equally true - it has taken us a long time to do it, we didn't just get up one morning and go out with our DV cam and do it. What we lacked in experience and budget we made up for in determination and a huge investment in time.

Q - When it came to delivering to the Sales Agent, were you surprised by what you had to give them in order for them to sell it?

Stuart - Our problem there was we hadn't done any production stills. That was an issue. Don't take stills yourself, have someone who has got an interest in photography do it for you or you will over stretch yourself. Get them to shoot loads of stills on a top end digital stills camera.

Q - In terms of your video masters did you do the music and effects mixes and trailers and all that stuff, did that take more time and energy than you thought?

Stuart - All the video masters and things like the M&E mix were handled by the guys at The Creative Partnership in down time, which is why it took so long. There were a few heart stopping moments when we thought we had screwed it all up, but we would just keep going and fix it. This business is all about staying power.

Q - Do you think part of the success of your chosen post production route is that you made allies in powerful places? They may not have been powerful people, but they are in powerful institutions with technology that can massively augment your film?

Stuart - Yes. Their involvement had a huge impact on the quality and professionalism of the final product. It was like the difference between a Rolls Royce and a Fiat.

Q - A common mistake that new film makers will make is that they have no game plan - it is always going to be finished someday, just not tomorrow... So there is a lack of momentum?

Stuart - Yeah. It has been quite a painful and long process, though I'm glad we did it the way we did. Knowing what I do now, it makes me think long and hard before I jump into the next relationship - because that is what it is, you are having a relationship with this thing. I haven't got the energy to do it the *'Infestation'* way ever again! Thinking about the next project makes me reflect on a big issue though - we stepped outside of the rules of the game to get *'Infestation'* made, and that was cool, it meant we could do all these wonderful things really cheaply. We've had to step back into the system as far as Sales Agents and markets are concerned. I've realised that for the next project I need to be within the system.

I picked your book up six years ago and it was really helpful. And I remember thinking at some point of making this film, wouldn't it cool if we got in *The Guerilla Film Makers Handbook!* And here we are!

Q - What has been really gratifying is that many film makers have used the book as a tool to get motivated and educated and used that to make their film. You are not the only one who has said that reading the case studies helped them bring what felt like a dream, into being. And what's really cool is that I hope some film makers in a far flung town, light years from the film industry, will read your case study and realise that they can actually do it too, and that they may well be a case study in the next edition!

Stuart - What goes around comes around!

Q - Your path seems to be a fairly common one for people who are raised in towns that are far flung from London or the film business. My experience was very similar, and not only do people say 'you are mad, you are crazy', they actually didn't even understand what I was talking about, they just didn't get it. So you are always 10 years behind the game when you look at people who are born and bred in the film business, and they were on set at 15. Where as you and I were throwing rocks at greenhouses! What advice would you give to some kid sat in a town that feels like it's the furthest point from the film industry in the UK, who thinks they want to make movies, but maybe Mum and Dad will say 'Get a REAL job'?

Stuart - I'd just say go and do it! It is important to listen to people, to a degree. Then again, I'd say I listened to people too much. So if you really feel strongly, go and try it. You come to crossroads in life and most people are paralysed by that. I say go down the path that you think is going to take you to a happy place, give it a try, there is no disgrace in going down that road only to find that it didn't take you where you thought it was going to. There is no shame in turning back or taking a different path. The worst thing you can do is to continue on a path that you know isn't right for you, just going along with what others say you should do. For me, that is failure. Worse still is when you sit at the crossroads and are afraid to take a choice and you just stagnate there. If film making is something you think you want but don't know where to start, I'd say just try it, get your hands on a camera and make something. Don't worry about buying a camera, get hold of someone else's and save the money, or get a job where they have equipment. It is all about kit when you are starting out, you've gotta have it, otherwise you can't make a film. You can write a script sure, but you are not a film maker until you have a camera and somewhere to edit it.

Q - Essentially the biggest hurdles facing any new film maker are financial. That is assuming you are a statistical average, as you and I are - we are not rich, we don't come from a family within the film business - so how do you survive financially? Also it's about breaking free of 'safety' and how quickly you can adopt the risk-taking mentality. I realised that if I did all the things that my parents suggested I do, which were all very sensible, all I'd end up with at the end of the day is a really nice coffin, instead of a cheap coffin. So what the hell?!

Stuart - Absolutely. Life is much better if you can do something you really enjoy with a passion. It is not worth selling your soul to get into the industry, you see people going in that way, but maybe they had no soul to start with. Take that risk.

Q - What mistakes did you make?

Stuart - No huge mistakes. We are all still friends, just about (laughs)! I guess we just underestimated the time and scale of the project, but we just dealt with it.

Q - What advice would you offer a new film maker?

Stuart - Get yourself in with decent folk, who are also interested in what you are doing. It is a collaborative industry. Don't just sit around, go and do it. Don't worry about having the latest camera or technology, use the best that you can get, but don't procrastinate. I know what it was like when I graduated and I didn't have a camera or access to one, I had no kit, I had no money, I was on the dole, and I had all these great ideas! It is massively frustrating, but you have got to look at what you do have, and use that. There are always great reasons why you shouldn't make your movie. Success lies in the act of taking action now.

Jeremy Bolt
Producer

FROM SHOPPING to HOLLYWOOD

This interview takes place in three parts, 1996, 2000 and 2005. It starts with the interview in 1996.

Q - Why did you decide to make films?

Jeremy - When I was 12 I saw *The Elephant Man* and was overwhelmed by the experience. Whilst having a cigarette behind the bike shed after the film I discussed with my friend what we were going to do with our lives, he was talking about running ICI and I thought I'd quite like to make films and thought I'd be a director. When I was eighteen I made a film of the Salome story which was absolutely disastrous, a kind of soft porn epic in Southern Turkey. I realised then that my talents lay in the ability to persuade people to do things, and that my skills lay in production rather than direction. I'm grateful for that experience because I didn't waste any more time trying to be Stanley Kubrick.

Q - How did that film in Turkey lead on to Shopping?

Jeremy - I left University with the goal of becoming a producer and started to work for Ken Russell as a runner, then assistant, then became associate producer on some of the films he made for the South Bank Show. It was an amazing apprenticeship in production. Whilst working for Ken Russell, I went to a party and met a beautiful girl - I was chatting her up, and this other guy was chatting her up. So we were both sort of competing for her interest, but she wasn't interested in either of us and we ended up chatting each other up. I said to him that I wanted to be a film producer, I was a fan of Ridley Scott, *Lethal Weapon* and *Die Hard* and I really loved action movies. He said I should meet this young director/writer called Paul Anderson. I met up with Paul and we got on extremely well, we had the same taste. He had a treatment which was inspired by the joyriding that was taking place in Newcastle, Paul's home town. I said to him, *look I haven't got any money, but if you write the script then you can direct it and I'll produce it*. That's how it began. It took us four years but we managed to pull it off, with a lot of lying and luck.

Q - What was the budget?

Jeremy - £2.3m which was a lot for a first time young director. It couldn't be made for less because there's a lot of action in the film. We had tremendous support from Ch4 and David Aukin, without whom we couldn't have made the film. The money came from Ch4, a German company called WMG, a Japanese company called Kazui and Polygram. Ch4 were the first to be interested and then the others came on board.

Q - And you put that deal together with your limited experience and track record?

Jeremy - Yes. I was persistent and had a desire to learn. I'm very suspicious of the mystique of the producer. There is nothing particularly difficult about doing these deals if you have a reasonable understanding of business. What is hard about this business is the energy level required, the persistence, the will to make the film. It's extremely difficult to pull everything together and you need tremendous self belief to keep yourself going. The rest is your own creative judgement which you either have or you don't.

Q - There are a lot of new film makers thinking of making their first film for £25k for instance. From your experience with Shopping, would you say that it's a good idea to forget £25k and aim for £2m?

Jeremy - It's a good idea to do a low budget film and then work up. When I was 23 I line produced a film for £800k called *Turn Of The Screw*. That was an important part of my education as it gave me the confidence to negotiate deals and to operate in the film world. It also gave Ch4 and the Completion Bond company the confidence to let me produce *Shopping*.

Q - Were there any problems in the making of Shopping that you didn't expect?

Jeremy - Editing. First time directors and producers tend to leave too much in and kill the pace of the film. They should just let the film go and let the editor cut it because they'll probably do a better cut. The final cut wasn't as good as it could have been. Since then, we've cut 15 minutes out and it's a much better picture. You need to give yourself as much time as you can in post production.

Q - How did Shopping perform in the UK and internationally?

Jeremy - Badly. We made a film that was confused as to what it was. It didn't know whether it was a moralistic drama about the dangers of youth-crime and joy-riding or whether it was an out and out action movie. From the beginning, you have to be absolutely clear about who the market is. The classic American distributor comment is *It's not New Line and it's not Fine Line - it's somewhere in the middle.* Well that's really helpful, thank you! I think that's something to do with a lack of confidence to say *I am making a horror film* for example. We had £2m to make something as entertaining as *Lethal Weapon,* and perhaps in retrospect, we didn't have enough confidence in ourselves to state that clearly.

Q - You didn't have the balls to put on the screen what you really wanted?

Jeremy - Absolutely. Now we would say *this is what we're making.*

Q - What happened after Shopping?

Jeremy - We had a truly remarkable experience. We made a film that didn't work but have done extremely well out of it. I think we sold ourselves very well, particularly Paul. We got two very important people, a manager and an agent into Paul's life in America. They watched *Shopping* and saw potential. At The Sundance Festival, Paul's manager, Phyllis Carlisle (also a producer) got him *Mortal Kombat*, a concept film in need of a director. Peculiarly, directors appear to be an amazing rarity in America.

Q - Is it advisable after a first film to get an agent and a manager?

Jeremy - Yes, you need a lawyer and an agent, or an agent and a manager, you don't need three. Think about who you want to represent you and why you want them to represent you. The relationship I have with Phyllis has ultimately benefited Impact Pictures, even though I had nothing to do with *Mortal Kombat*. Effectively we had eighteen months apart, but we remained a strong unit, partly because of our friendship and trust, but also because we have people in our lives who want us to be together and present us as a team.

Q - And more importantly you're actually being paid to be filmmakers, whereas most filmmakers in Britain aren't?

Jeremy - Yes, completely right. However, you must be strong enough to allocate time to make the films you want to make and not be completely sold on the money that exists in LA. You must have another life. In fact it makes you more attractive to the Americans. They love it if you say *I'm sorry I'm not available during that period, I'm producing this film over in Europe.* I think it's important for a film producer not to be entirely reliant on one director. I think it takes the strain off that director's talent and it makes the producer feel as though they have value in themselves and that they're not just on the coattails of this extraordinary blazing talent.

Q - Is being English a major advantage in America?

Jeremy - You should be as English as you can. Arrogance is always bad news, but it's important to have an English accent, they like that. What you shouldn't do is try and be American, you should try and maintain your Englishness. For many American film makers, the great directors have all been English, Lean and Hitchcock are the names that come up most in Hollywood.

Q - How did you physically get over to the States to meet agents and managers?

Jeremy - I had a girlfriend whose mother was very wealthy and at that time Virgin Airlines had just launched - if you flew upper class you got a free economy ticket. So her mother kept coming over and giving me these free economy tickets - Paul and I both went to America on my girlfriend's mother effectively. My girlfriend was very important because her mother had this fabulous house in L.A and that's where we used to stay.

Q - How do you relocate over there?

Jeremy - When a company employs you to work for them in America they will give you what's called an O1 visa which is much better than a Green Card. A Green Card means you are taxed in America on your worldwide income, even if you've already been taxed in the UK for any income you've earned there. Whilst trying to raise money, we came in as visitors and could stay for up to six months. There's a huge ex-pat community in LA and somebody's bound to know somebody who's got a floor or a couch - it's completely acceptable in LA to get a call from a penniless filmmaker and put them up for a few days. In those few days you then have to lie. The agents in L.A are constantly trying to find the next Paul Anderson or Danny Boyle - you just call up and lie, *I've just made this extraordinary film for the BFI, would you like to have a look at it?* cut off the titles, pass it off as your own and go and show them something. You also try and time it so it's around lunchtime so you can get a free lunch. You do that with CAA, William Morris, UTA and ICM and you create a bit of buzz about yourself and get four free lunches. That's how you begin. Then you say *I've got a lot of other films which I've left at home, but this is my latest work* - you must have an amount of charm to get away with it. With Paul, I used to say that he had directed lots of television, *Shopping* was his first feature and that I would send videotapes - but of course you never do, and they never ask for them, they just make a note - *he's done other stuff.*

Q - Should a new filmmaker go to L.A before they have made a film?

Jeremy - They should go to LA to try and raise money because I think the experience of being exposed to the industry there is very inspiring. It's not as intimidating as it sounds and it also makes you want to achieve it more than ever. If you have something to show, it will be a lot better for you. You will get turned down by a lot of places and that can be quite tough.

Q - What are the major bonuses of working in the States?

Jeremy - The money to actually have a life and do what you love and not feel that anybody who gives you money is doing you a

favour. Everybody here is so grateful to the BBC and Ch4 when they are given money to make a movie. What they fail to realise is that those companies exist to make product for the public. We almost feel like saying, *well, I'm sorry, but I have to ask you for money,* it's that apologetic attitude. In America it's *Fuck you, I'm going to be the next Tarantino and you should give me money because I'm going to make you money.*

Q - What are the major drawbacks?

Jeremy - People can be insincere in America. It's difficult to identify who in a company has the power to say yes or no. Often you are dealing with people who don't have that power and they're quite frightened for their jobs so they will not commit either way. You tend to get a kind of *yes, maybe,* and you can be strung along. They won't say *No,* because you could be the next *Reservoir Dogs,* and they won't say *Yes,* because you might not be. It's difficult and you have to learn to discriminate between who is really interested and who's not interested. Also, if they think they are doing you a favour they will screw you to kingdom come. You have to make them think that you could go across town to Warner Brothers and do the deal there - you have to use leverage. Fear is the overwhelming atmosphere in LA, you have to make them frightened that they are going to lose the project unless they commit to you. It just doesn't exist here in the UK because there are only one or two companies who do make films, so it's not surprising that you are grateful when one of these companies does give you money.

Q - What do you think are your biggest mistakes?

Jeremy - I think we should have had more courage in our convictions when we made *Shopping,* we should have trusted our instincts to make what we believed in and stand by it.

Q - What do you think were your best decisions?

Jeremy - To keep the machine running, not to stand still, to keep selling ourselves and keep telling the world that we believed in what we made, even when we had made a film that didn't work. Also, we got two people in our lives who could really help us to keep moving.

Q - Do you have any final advice or tips?

Jeremy - At the end of the day, nobody really knows anything, it's all about perception. Even if you have made a film that does not actually work, you must still sell yourself as though you have made the greatest film ever. Don't deny the problems and learn from the experience, just don't apologise for it. The moment that you are perceived as being apologetic for what you have done, you're weak and you sell yourself short.

End of interview 1996. Interview continues Feb 2000.

Q - As Paul was your partner and a 'hot' director, how did you stay attached to Soldier and Event Horizon?

Jeremy - *Soldier* was a film we made with Jerry Weintraub. It was an extraordinary experience as he's one of the largest characters in this industry. From his point of view he did not feel that he needed me in the early stages, he just wanted Paul as the director. Obviously Paul wanted me to work on the film which put me in a difficult position. As a producer with a directing partner you have to get on board the project without upsetting all the other parties who probably don't trust you at first, and that potentially weakens your partner's position too.

Once we had got over the hurdle of me being around he thought that I was a nice guy and competent and I was very respectful of his experience, which wasn't hard when you consider what he has done. The question was in what capacity was I going to work. After a meeting with Paul he asked Paul to leave the room and he sat down with me and started talking in his thick New York accent which makes him sound like the Godfather, which is very effective because you start feeling that you won't get out of there alive and you will probably end up with the fishes. He said *well, what I think we should do, Jeremy, (Godfather voice) is we should go for a walk on the beach and discuss this credit issue* so at this point I say *Jerry I will take whatever you think is appropriate* and he says *(Godfather voice) good, good, I'm glad you see it my way.* I actually ended up with a co-producer's credit which was actually appropriate and we now have a great relationship.

Jerry is a remarkable man and has taught both Paul and myself a great deal. He was a very necessary part of the process of working at Warner Bros. which is I imagine very much like working at the BBC. It's such an old corporation and nothing is as it seems - there are many layers and it takes time to work out where the power lies and how to get to that power. You really need a Godfather like Jerry Weintraub in your life if you are going to work there.

Event Horizon was a very different experience with Larry Gordon who is also an institution in Hollywood. He was open to me being involved, mainly because we were shooting in the UK and he needed a man in London to run it. Again I had this awkwardness of negotiating myself on board. So I just did the hard work and it eventually paid off when I had this extraordinary phone-call about a month before shooting where Larry made me a full producer with him on the film because he had seen how important it was in the process. He called me up and told me that he felt *just like the Queen knighting somebody, rise Sir Bolt, you are on my card, we are going to share my card, how do you feel about that?* I never imposed myself and I had accepted what was offered me. I think this is the way to play those sorts of situations, let them see how good you are and let them reward that.. and take the risk.

I think that at a certain point your director has to say to the powers that be *I want my partner involved in this process* and he has to say it with some emphasis. Then he is going to have to rely on the personality of the partner to negotiate the part. When we went to Hollywood it was as though we had nothing and we were very grateful and listened as much as possible, talking only as much as we needed and did not swagger. As a result the doors that had opened stayed open. Certainly we came across as guys who were going to be easy to work with. I think that people should listen more than talk in these situations. I came across as somebody who was not going to try to steal Larry's or Jerry's credit, I was going to be working with them in the mix and I was respectful of who they were. At the end of the day I have got forty years of this business left in me, they are probably in their last few movies and there is plenty of time for my glory. You have to keep your ego in check, the minute you start listening to your ego you will probably fall foul of them.

Q - So your partnership with Paul is important?

Jeremy - I think that as a producer one of the ways to juggle as many balls as we need to do in order to survive is through partnership. One of the reasons that our partnership has lasted as long as it has is that there is no insecurity, there is only trust, and it has been proven. A producer director relationship is rather like a marriage, if one party becomes possessive the bond is likely to suffer and break. We are both very relaxed, I don't think he would like it if I got into a relationship with another action director but I do work with other directors with different talents.

Q - Is it hard existing here in the UK and in LA?

Jeremy - Last year I did 14 round trips and my doctor told me that I was jet-lagged for the whole year. It was at least a trip a month and I would have perhaps one week out of every month where I was stable, so I only had twelve weeks of stable sleep out of the fifty-two. It became very unhealthy and I developed asthma and various other allergies, so I wouldn't recommend it. Actually most of the films that I saw last year I saw in planes which is rather tragic for a film maker, seeing the next big movie on a three inch screen going over Greenland.

Q - How do you feel about Event Horizon and Soldier in terms of how they turned out as movies, how they were received and their performances?

Jeremy - I love them both and am very proud of them. I love *Event Horizon* because of the pull back from the daylight space station which I think is one of the best visual effects ever shot. I love *Soldier* for the final fight scene and people who saw it on Sky and video rave about it.

Event Horizon has become a cult film so I am less harsh on the selling of that because it reached an audience. It didn't cost as much as *Soldier* but I think that the script needed more work and it shows. We had built up this incredible feeling of Evil and then had to deliver on the promise. You spend two hours building this thing up and then - *shit, what is it?* Ultimately the audience was disappointed. I think Paramount should have let us re-shoot the ending and if they had we would have made them another $20-30m. When the audience realised where we were going with it people just lost interest in the third act. Anyway I am very proud of the film, I love it, and I learnt a great deal.

Soldier was mis-sold. It was sold as an eighties action movie, in an eighties movie style, a big head on a poster, it looked like *Universal Soldier* but with Kurt Russell, so the audience thought that they had seen it all before. In fact it was a 1983 script and we didn't update it enough. Again we learnt great lessons. It was certainly good enough to have been theatrically released here but it wasn't because when a movie does

Jeremy and Paul on the set of 'Soldier'

not perform well in America, the studios try to stop the bleeding. No matter whether it is a good movie or not, they will just stop the theatrical releases and put it out on video so they don't get the P&A cost. As a result it is doing very well on video and it has not cost them that much. It's not a reflection on the film, it's a reflection of how badly it performed at the American box office.

Q - How easy is it to deal with having made a $70m flop?

Jeremy - Being English I deal with failure better than success, but as Rudyard Kipling said about Triumph and Disaster *treat those two imposters just the same*. You just have to keep focused and try to do good work. I think that if you have not done your own work, or if you have not worked hard then that is your own funeral. For me film is war and I am very comfortable being at war. If it became peaceful then I would probably go into a terrible depression and take up landscape gardening. So I relish the combat, as does Paul. If you are going to fail, fail huge, because at least then people hear about you and at the end of the day, that's what matters.

Q - How did the studios react to you when it was a failure?

Jeremy - In the industry the perception about *Soldier* was that it was wrongly sold. Although it was our mistake to try to do the thing in the first place as it was an old fashioned concept. Therefore I doubt that we will be making a movie at Warner's for the foreseeable future because of the shareholders - to spend a lot of money again with Paul does not make sense to them. However, Tom Cruise has stuck with us on *Deathrace 3000* which was a project set up before the release of *Soldier*. Nobody pointed a finger at us and said you're irresponsible, bad film makers - we haven't gone to film jail yet. You rise out of it by not being bitter or resentful. As film makers yourselves you know that 90% of this job is war wounds from which you have to recover and pick yourself up, go over the top and hopefully through the barbed wire.

Q - What lessons have you learned from these two Hollywood movies?

Jeremy - Trust your instinct, do not listen to anybody if your instinct says they are wrong. If someone, like your financier, has trust in your instinct but you do not, then not only are you letting yourself down but you are also letting your financier down.

Q - What advice would you offer someone whose first film was moderately successful and they are thinking of going to Hollywood for 'that deal'?

Jeremy - Stick to the ground, or genre, in which you have worked. It will be easier to sell yourself and your project if you have already proven yourself, even if it is only in a small way. For example if you have done short film comedies, make a comedy. If you have done a first feature and it is a horror film, pitch another horror film. Do not move too far away from the genre in which you first proved yourself.

End of interview 2000. Interview continues Oct 2005

Q - How have things been for you since Soldier?

Jeremy - We were in film jail for a bit of time after *Soldier*. *Soldier* was a big disaster. We made some films in Europe, we were very proud of, did some TV and then really we had a new lease of life by going back to basics and the beginning with video games. We did *Resident Evil* and I'm interviewing directors for the third movie now. In addition to that, we've just finished another video game movie, *DOA* and Paul directed *AVP*. Now we're setting up his next movie. We have an overhead deal with Constantin, one of the most successful companies in Europe which enables us to speak to all the US Studios without having to be caught up in all the studio politics which is terrific. We're in a really strong position and I think we're better filmmakers. I think we probably had to fail as big as we did with *Soldier* to be in this position.

Q - How long did it take after Soldier to get back?

Jeremy - We were probably in the doghouse for about two or three years. And you know, that's when it's very good to have a partner. The business is very unforgiving. We'd had some success prior to that but we didn't have the level of success that could withstand the failure of *Soldier*. Paul and I are very proud of the film but unfortunately commercially it was a disaster in America.

Q - So when you came back with Resident Evil?

Jeremy - It was great! People were *'wow, they're back!'* rather than just getting back or *'that's really clever - they made that for not a lot of money'*. It's a huge video game. It's grossed $millions on DVD after a solid theatrical release, the second one made even more. Then Paul directed *AVP* which was a huge hit for Fox.

Q - Did it take a while to actually get Resident Evil happening after the failure of Soldier?

Jeremy - Interestingly, not that long. Paul wrote a bloody cracking script. Constantin are not a Hollywood studio, and they need to make movies. Once they had a good script, they just charged ahead. So it was probably only a two year process for us. Once we commit, we've got quite good at turning them into movies fairly quickly. We're very focused. When we first started out, we got a little distracted by too many projects, and now we have a much tighter development slate and we're much more brutal with projects.

Q - You say that you had to fail to get to the success that you have now. Is there anything else that you've encountered since then that could have been avoided or you've learned from?

Jeremy - What, like my gambling problem?! (laughs). I think you have to see through and accept the very seductive layer of bullshit that is smothered across these hills that I'm looking at. Hollywood is very, very seductive and that is quite dangerous.

Q - I know many filmmakers who get easily sick of the Hollywood bullshit and others that get sick of the negativity of England and would rather have the bullshit...

Jeremy - I think that's right. I now have a very profound respect for making a commercially successful film, which is something I've learned over ten years of making films, and I know for a fact that I didn't know how hard it was ten years ago. It is just as hard to make a successful commercial movie as it is to make a great art house movie in my opinion.

Q - What advice would you now give to filmmakers and new producers in general?

Jeremy - Be pragmatic. What you need to get in the game, is to get a movie made. Look at what is working, don't go out there saying your movie is *Lawrence of Arabia*, *The Elephant Man*, *Brief Encounter* or *Rear Window* - see what's working, see if you can get something that works in that genre, then you'll be able to sell it commercially because you'll be able to say, look, I can cite these examples of these kind of movies that have worked recently. Therefore with the right budget, there's a chance this could get a shot. I would say you have to be very commercially minded. And once your movie is greenlit then you can pour your emotion and your passion into it. You need to make a good movie, but initially I think you have to be really pragmatic.

Also see Jeremy's interview in the 'What Next' section

LEGAL TOOLKIT

READ THIS FIRST...!
LEGAL DISCLAIMER

THE LEGAL TOOLKIT - NOTES

Limited Company or Partnership?

If you are an independent producer you will need to set up a limited company through which to contract both with financiers and artists in order to give yourself the necessary protection. The limited company can be structured as a joint venture or more usually governed by a shareholder's agreement. You and your fellow producers can effectively act as a partnership in terms of sharing income i.e. profits, if that is what you intend to do. It is a very good idea to enter into an agreement which sets out rules for the conduct of the business of the company as between the directors and/or shareholders. It is particularly important to consider how outside work is to be treated i.e. whether the fees a company director receives for his services on an outside project are to be paid into the company, or to be retained by him personally.

A company is treated as a separate legal entity and it is liable for any contractual obligations, warranties and undertakings it enters into. Therefore, if a company is in breach of any of it's obligations, it and not the company's officers (the directors and secretary) will be liable (unless the company's officers have acted fraudulently or wrongfully). If the company has, for example, an obligation to make a payment under the terms of an agreement and it is unable to do so the company may be wound up by it's creditors. This means the assets of the company are gathered in and paid out to those creditors. But the company's directors will not be personally liable for the company's debts (unless the director has acted or traded unlawfully or wrongfully) and the director's personal property is untouched by the winding up.

This is an important source of protection to the individual. It is particularly useful in the film industry where even though the expenditure on a film may not be high, the liabilities and damages payable to contracting third parties could be considerable.

The downside of having a company is that you must comply with the Companies Acts in relation to how you run and administer the company. In certain circumstances, if you do not comply with the law eg. filing accounts at Companies House, your company can be struck off the register. It can be restored to the register but not without expense and inconvenience.

If you trade as a partnership, you are personally responsible for the contractual obligations, warranties and undertakings of the partnership. If you or your partners do not meet those financial obligations and they are over £750 you can be made bankrupt by a creditor. If you are adjudged bankrupt your personal property

including your home (but excluding tools of your trade) can be sold off to pay the creditor.

As a partner you are jointly and severally liable for the debts of the partnership. Unless you agree otherwise, if your partner binds the partnership to pay money to a third party, the third party can come after you for all of that sum (not just half of it, if for example, there were two partners).

A partnership is governed by the Partnership Act 1890 and there are very few legislative rules regarding the conduct of partnerships.

Company Directors and the Law

Role of Company Director

Directors are agents of the Company and as such occupy a fiduciary position in relation to the Company. All powers entrusted to them are only exercisable in this fiduciary capacity (see Sec. 2).

Since directors have control of the Company's business and assets, the law requires them to act honestly in what they consider to be the Company's best interests, not their own.

If the directors are also majority shareholders or if they represent the majority shareholders, they must not manage the company so as to unfairly prejudice the minority shareholders.

There is also a general duty on the directors to have regard to the interest of employees as well as shareholders.

Directors should also have the interest of the creditors particularly when the Company is insolvent (or nearly so) as well as all (sometimes instead) of the interests of the shareholders.

Fiduciary Duty

The directors are under a fiduciary duty which requires them to act in good faith and with loyalty to the Company (akin to a trustees' position).

They should not permit a conflict to arise between their personal interests and those of the Company and should disclose any interest of any kind, whether direct or indirect in a contract with the Company (including any loans or guarantees).

A director's powers are given to them under the Articles of Association and such powers shall be used for the proper and primary/substantial purposes for which they are given.

They should take proper care of the Company's property and should not appropriate such property, failing which they will be accountable to the Company for any personal gains obtained including from knowledge or opportunities of investment which they obtained as directors (unless the Company agrees otherwise).

There is a general prohibition on companies making loans, guarantees, etc. available to directors over £5000 (or £20,000 in certain other circumstances).

Standards of Performance / Duties of Care Diligence and Skill

A director is under a duty of care, diligence and skill owed to the Company. He must show an acceptable degree of such care, diligence and skill as would be displayed by a reasonable man.

If a director has a certain skill e.g. accountancy, he is required to show proficiency in that skill as would be reasonably expected of a competent member of that profession.

A director is not liable for errors in judgement (but is liable for his own negligence and may be held accountable of any loss arising from such negligence).

A director may accept (without making investigation) information provided by an apparently reliable source e.g. a co-director or senior employee.

He should attend a board and general meetings whenever possible.

Directors as Employees

A director is not necessarily an employee of the Company (although he is liable to Schedule E income tax and National Insurance contributions on his fees.)

A director who is also an employee should not vote at a board meeting to approve his own contact of employment and (unless the Articles provide otherwise) cannot be counted in the quorum for that purpose of that vote.

Accounts and Records

The directors must prepare a profit and loss account in respect of each financial year of the Company with a balance sheet as at the last day of that financial year reflecting a true and accurate position of the company at the relevant date.

The directors must lay a copy of such accounts before the Company in general meeting and file the same with the Register of Companies within certain time limits. The accounts must include directors' and auditors' reports properly signed.

TOP 10 POINTS TO LOOK OUT FOR IN ANY AGREEMENT

Here are some broad considerations which you should give to any agreement. Of course, each circumstance will require more specific attention. If your liabilities under the agreement could involve you in substantial expense, seek legal advice.

1. Ask yourself first what interests you need to protect and are they sufficiently protected.

2. Do you have any existing contractual obligations to other people and if you enter into this agreement are you going to be in breach of those existing contractual obligations?

3. What are your liabilities in this agreement and if things go wrong, what are you liable for? Look out for clauses which make you personally liable even though you may be contracting through a company i.e. are you being asked to give a personal guarantee for a loan which is being made to your company?

4. What is the agreement asking you to do and is it reasonable and within your power to deliver or achieve?

5. If you are required under the agreement to do something ask to change any reference to your using your "best endeavours" to "reasonable endeavours".

6. If you are providing your own original work or any intellectual property owned by you under the terms of the agreement what happens if the project does not go ahead? Do you have the chance to regain or repurchase your property?

7. If you are due to receive any royalties or profit share under the agreement make sure the other party has an obligation to collect any revenue derived from the film or project, that they must show you their books and you have the right to audit those books. Check also that your share of Net Profits (as defined in the agreement) is as agreed i.e. are you receiving a share of the Producer's net profits or a share of all net profits?

8. What are the possible sources of income to you from the film or project and are all those sources being exploited and if so are you getting a fair share of that income?

9. What sort of controls do you have over the conduct of the other party? Are the promises they are making under the agreement sufficient to cover your interests? What happens if they are in default of their promises?

10. Remember that if the agreement is being provided by the other side, the terms will be very much in their favour. This does not mean that they are necessarily trying to stitch you up, this is just business.

The directors must maintain a register of directors and their interests as well as minutes of all board and general meetings.

Copyright

Copyright is in fact a bunch of rights that attaches to the owner of the copyright in certain types of intellectual property (as defined in the CDPA 1988) i.e. literacy, artistic, dramatic and musical works and derivative works including film, sound recordings and published work. The right of copyright rests first in the author or creator of the work (there are some exceptions to this). To qualify for copyright protection the work must be original to the author and not a copy. The bundle of rights given to the creator of the work are set out in the CDPA 1988 and these rights may not be exercised by another without the permission of the author or owner. The restricted acts are:- copying, issuing copies to the public, performing, broadcasting, transmitting by cable or adapting the work.

The rights of copyright rest automatically in the author. There is no requirement of notice or registration. In order to provide evidence of creation, an author may send, for example, a screenplay to him/ her self in an envelope which is kept sealed so the postmark on the envelope provides evidence of the date of creation.

Copyright exists in artistic, musical, literacy and dramatic works for 70 years after the end of the year in which the author dies. For Film it lasts for 70 years after the death of the last to die of the director, scriptwriter, dialogue writer or composer of commissioned music for the film. For sound recordings, broadcasts, performances, cable transmissions, it lasts 50 years from the end of the year in which the performance etc. was made or made available to the public. The CDPA 1988 has been amended recently to harmonise copyright duration throughout Europe and important changes, including the revival of copyright in certain works, have been made. Any dealings with Copyright works should be checked with your solicitor.

Options, Licences & Assignments

OPTIONS

An option over a piece of work is an agreement by the owner of the work not to dispose of the work to a third party for a specified period of time in consideration of the purchaser (i.e. a producer) paying a fixed amount of money. This may be a nominal amount of £1 or a commercial sum negotiated between two parties. If the purchaser exercises the option the owner agrees to assign or licence some or all of the rights in the work to the purchaser. An option is necessary for a purchaser so they can develop a project based on a piece of work without the fear that some other party is doing likewise. An option grants the producer the right to develop a project based on the work to see if it is worth acquiring the work or certain rights in the work, or obtaining permission to exploit all or some of the rights in the work.

An option may be taken over a screenplay or more usually over an underlying piece of work such as a novel or a stageplay. The owner of a novel is only likely to grant an option over the work for the specific rights necessary to make and exploit a film or films.

It is advisable to annex the licence or assignment to the option agreement with the terms set out and agreed. If you enter into an option and do not agree the terms upon which you will acquire the rights in the work, this is an agreement to agree and may not be enforceable. It also leaves you very vulnerable when it comes to negotiating the terms for any licence or assignment.

LICENCES AND ASSIGNMENTS

A licence is a permission given by the owner allowing you to do certain acts without infringing copyright in their work. Frequently, when you are dealing with published literary works the owner or their agent will only wish to grant you a licence to those specific rights in the work that you need to make and distribute the film. You usually need to acquire ancillary rights (i.e. the video, CD-Rom, book of the film) to make the film commercially attractive and viable, but the owner may insist that they participate in income from this source.

A licence fee is payable, usually upon first day of principal photography. This fee can be calculated by reference to a percentage to the budget with a minimum and maximum fee cited. The advantage to the owner of this is that if the film is taken up by a Hollywood studio, for example, and the studio pumps in huge sums for the film, the owner is a direct beneficiary of this. A licence can be for a specific period of time or in perpetuity subject to negotiation. A licence can be exclusive or non-exclusive. If it is exclusive, the owner cannot sell the rights (or otherwise dispose of them) to any one else. If you are making a film you must insist upon an exclusive licence as obviously you (and certainly not your financiers and distributors) do not want a competing product out on the market.

An Assignment is a transfer of ownership from the owner to you. Copyright in a work can be broken down into specific rights and those rights can be sold separately. Therefore, you can buy the film rights in the work and the owner can retain the publishing rights or stage rights (as is usually the case). If you are commissioning a script or treatment or engaging creative talent (directors, actors, composers) then you must ensure you own out right all their copyright in their work or performance and this will be affected by an assignment of rights. As with a licence, it is usual for an assignment to set out those rights which are being transferred.

In both licences and assignments there is usually a turnaround provision which allows the owner of the work to re-acquire it if the film or programme does not go into production within a specified period of time.

Where work is owned jointly by two or more authors/owners you must obtain an assignment from both or all of them, as one joint author/owner acting alone does not have authority to assign rights in the work.

Writers Agreement

If you commission a writer to write a screenplay you must enter into a written agreement with him in which the writer assigns or licences their rights in the screenplay to you (they may assign/ licence all their rights or only the specific rights you require i.e. film and ancillary rights). If you do not have this written assignment of rights or an exclusive licence, the writer will remain the owner of the screenplay and could sell the screenplay to another person.

A writer may be a member of the Writer's Guild (of the UK or America) and you should clarify with them in the first instance the status of the agreement i.e. whether it is a Guild agreement or not.

If it is a Guild agreement then you should refer to the appropriate Guild to confirm the minimum payments have been complied with.

A writer's agreement must most importantly contain a waiver of moral rights (see Glossary). Without this it will be very difficult to both raise finance and distribute the film.

Usually the writer's fee is broken down into several payments so that they receive part of their fee on commencement, part on delivery of the first draft, part on delivery of the second draft and the final sum on completion. For a film where many re-drafts and polishes may be required, it should be made clear in the agreement that the fee includes payment for such further re-drafts. A Film Producer will usually want a complete buyout to avoid having to make residual, repeat or fees in the future (the Guild agreements provide for minimum payments for repeats etc.).

The Producer must have the ability to engage another writer to work on the script if the work produced by the writer is unsatisfactory. If you are the Producer you need to negotiate a right of cut off which allows you to engage another writer to write, for example, the second draft without being obliged to make any further payment to the original writer.

You will need the writer to warrant the screenplay is his and he has not assigned or licensed it to any other person and that it is not defamatory, libellous etc. The writer should give an indemnity to you for any breach of warranty or undertaking provided in the agreement.

It is unusual for a scriptwriter to retain any rights in the work, but where a writer is also an author they will often wish to retain novelisation rights and occasionally the stage and radio rights. As these rights are of little commercial interest to the film producer (except perhaps any 'making of' book), producers usually are happy to allow this, provided they retain a participation in any income derived from such exploitation. A hold back on the exploitation of the rights retained for a number of years is often negotiated so that a stage play or book based on the same treatment does not compete with the film.

Glossary Of Contract Terminology

ABOVE THE LINE - the portion of a film budget that covers creative elements and personnel i.e. story, screenplay rights, producers, directors and principal members of the cast.

ACCRUALS - the accumulation of payments due.

ANCILLARY RIGHTS - other subsidiary rights i.e. the right to make a sequel, soundtrack, computer game etc., merchandising, video, novelisation.

ACQUISITIONS - purchases.

ARBITRATION - an informal method for resolving disputes (by finding the middle ground) which is usually quicker and less expensive than litigation. Usually an arbitrator is agreed in advance by the parties or chosen by the head of an appropriate professional body i.e. Institute of Chartered Accountants etc.

BELOW THE LINE - accounting term relating to the technical expenses and labour involved in producing a film.

BREACH OF CONTRACT - failure of one party to fulfil the agreement.

BREAKEVEN - the point when sales equal costs, where a film is neither in profit nor loss.

BUY OUT - this term is used in relation to the engagement of artists where no repeat, residual or other fees are required to be paid to the artist in relation to any form of exploitation of the film or programme.

BEST ENDEAVOURS - means you have to do all you can including incurring expense in order to carry out your relevant obligation under the agreement.

CAP - a ceiling, upper limit. Try to cap expenses in sales agents agreements.

COLLATERAL - assets pledged to a lender until the loan is repaid. i.e. with a bank loan a house can be put up for collateral.

COMMISSION - a percentage of specified amount received for services performed.

CONTINGENCY - money set aside for unanticipated costs.

CREDITOR - one to whom monies are owed.

CHAIN OF TITLE - contracts and documents that hand down the copyright to the present owner.

CROSS COLLATERALISE - this is where a party, usually a distributor, will offset losses in one area against gains in other areas. If you are a producer you will want to resist this.

DEAL MEMO - a short version of the contract, giving the principal terms of the agreement which can be legally binding - check carefully if this is the intention.

DEFERRAL - delay of payment of a fixed sum which is all or part of payments for cast and crew and other services, usually paid out of receipts from the film after the distributor or financier has taken their commission/fee/expenses or been repaid their initial investment (plus a %).

DISTRIBUTION EXPENSES - there is no set definition for this term but things to watch for are that the expenses are reasonable and relate directly to the film. It should not include the distributor's overheads and any expenses payable by the distributor to third parties should be negotiated on the best commercial terms available.

DISTRIBUTION FEE - this is usually between 30-50% of income received. You should try and negotiate a sliding scale for the fee which reduces as the income from the film increases.

ERRORS AND OMISSIONS - insurance protection covering against lawsuits alleging unauthorised use of ideas, characters, plots, plagiarism, titles and alleged slander, libel, defamation of character etc.

ESCROW - monies or property held by a third party for future delivery or payment to a party on the occurrence of a particular event or services rendered.

EQUITY - the interest or value an owner has in a property but where they have no legal ownership in the property.

FAVOURED NATIONS - meaning that the contracting party will be given treatment on an equal footing with others that the other party deals with. i.e. could refer to placement of billing requirements, or profit participation.

FORCE MAJEURE - this term is usually defined in the agreement. Generally it means any event which is outside the control of the parties to the agreement i.e. act of God, fire, strike, accident, war, illness of key persons involved in the production, effect of elements etc.

GROSS DEAL - a profit participation for the producer or others in the distributor's gross receipts (unusual).

GROSS RECEIPTS - this term is usually defined in an agreement to mean all income received from the exploitation of the film by the distributor before any deduction of the distributor's fees and expenses but sometimes it is expressed to include the deduction of such fees and expenses.

INDEMNIFY - in essence to secure against loss and damage which may occur in the future or to provide compensation against any loss or damage.

INDEMNITY - a promise to make good any loss or damage another has incurred or suffered or may incur. It may not always be appropriate to give an indemnity.

IN PERPETUITY - to exist forever.

INDUCEMENT LETTER - this is required where a party, usually an artist, director or individual producer, contract through their company (for tax reasons) rather than as individuals. A Producer and/or financier will require the individual to provide personal warranties and undertakings in relation to the ability and authority of their company to state the artist/director/producer will render their services. The letter will also confirm that they have granted the relevant rights to the company which the company then grants to the producer under the principal agreement of engagement.

INSOLVENT - where one has liabilities that exceed their assets.

JOINT VENTURE - a business by two or more parties who share profits, losses and control.

LETTER OF INTENT - a written communication expressing the intent of a person or company to perform whatever services that they provide. This may not be legally binding.

LIBEL - a false and malicious publication which defames one who is living (it may not be printed for that purpose - you don't have to show malice in UK libel law).

LICENSOR - one who grants a license.

LIMITED RECOURSE LOAN - a loan which may only be repaid through specified sources of income i.e. income derived from the exploitation of a film.

LABORATORY ACCESS LETTER - this is an instruction to the laboratory to release the negative of the film to named distributors and is required where more than one distributor is being used.

MORAL RIGHTS - this is a general term used to describe a bunch of rights which belong to the author of a copyright work. These so called "moral rights" derive from the European principle, which was asserted most forcefully in France and Germany, that an artist has the right to protect their work even if it is the property of another. England only recognised authors "moral rights" in 1988 by the incorporation of those rights into the Copyright Designs and Patents Act. See ss77-79 The right of paternity (i.e. to be identified as the author), the right of integrity (i.e. for the work not to be treated in a derogatory way), the right to object to false attribution. These rights may be waived by the author and in nearly every case they are. A distributor would not find it acceptable for an artist to be able to prevent the distribution of a film on the basis that their moral rights had been infringed. In France and Germany an author cannot by law waive these rights.

NEGATIVE COSTS - total of various costs incurred in the acquisition and production of a film in all aspects prior to release. Includes pre production, production, post production costs.

NET DEAL - a distribution deal where the distributor recoups all it's costs and collects all it's fees before giving the producer the remainder of the film's revenue.

NET PROFIT - there is no set definition of this term as in every case there will be much debate about what may or may not be deducted from the gross receipts to arrive at the net profit. The definition of net profit in any agreement should be looked at very carefully to ensure inter alia expenses and commissions are not being deducted twice i.e. once by the distributor and again by the sub distributor etc.

OUTPUT DEAL - a contract through which one party delivers it's entire output to another party. i.e. a distribution agreement between a production company and a distribution company in which the distributor commits to distribute the films that have been or will be produced by the producer.

PARRI PASSU - means on a like footing i.e. everyone is to be treated in an equal fashion. For instance, on distribution of net profits everyone gets an equal amount irrespective of their contribution.

PRO RATA - means that, for example, if an artist is entitled to payment on a pro rata basis then if they receive a weekly fee for 6 days work and the artist subsequently works only 3 days the artist would receive half the weekly fee i.e. the weekly fee would be pro rated according to the amount of time the artists services were engaged.

PER DIEM - a daily payment. It is usually used in the context of an artist's daily expenses.

PRODUCERS SHARE - means the net sum remaining to the Producer after deductions of distribution fees, expenses (or other deductions that are agreed) and after other profit participants have received their share. The producers share of net profits may be shared with other third parties.

PROFIT PARTICIPATION - percentage participations on net profits.

REASONABLE ENDEAVOURS - this is less onerous than best endeavours and simply means you will make a reasonable effort to carry out your obligations.

RECOUPMENT - when the costs and expenses of a film production are recovered from the film's revenue i.e. when production costs have been recouped.

RENTAL AND LENDING RIGHTS - these rights are contained in Directive no. 92 and 100 EEC and have been brought into effect in the UK by regulations which amend the CDPA 1988. The principle behind the changes is that with the development and expansion of video and other similar forms of distribution, an artist should share in the income derived from this commercially important area. However this is of concern to producers and distributors who do not wish to have a continuing obligation to make payments to artists and so all agreements contain a clause stating that the artist recognises that the payment due to the artist under the agreement is adequate and equitable remuneration for these rights and they assign all such rights to the producer. There is uncertainty as to whether such a clause will be legally binding on an artist as the right to remuneration for rental rights is expressed to be unwaivable and this issue has yet to be considered by an English Court.

RESIDUALS - payments for each re run after initial showing. In the case of guild or union agreements minimum residual payments have been agreed.

ROYALTIES - payments to a party for use of the property calculated as a percentage of a defined amount (i.e. net income from video sales).

THEATRICAL RELEASE - exploitation of the film in the cinema as opposed to on television or video etc.

TURNAROUND - e.g. a screenplay development situation where the purchaser or licensee of the property has decided not to go forward with the production or if the production is not screened or does not begin principal photography within a specified time the owner or licensor can serve notice on the owner/licensee so that the screenplay can be re-acquired by the owner/licensor.

VENTURE CAPITAL - financing for new ventures that involves some investment risk but usually offers a share of any profit - there is usually a high premium paid for such investment reflecting the risk taken by the investor.

WAIVER - a relinquishment or surrender of particular rights

WARRANTY - a promise by one party that the other party will rely upon. i.e. in a distribution agreement a producer may warrant that the filming is of a particular quality and standard.

LEGAL TOOLKIT AND FORMS

Option Agreement

(for previous work)

This is a guideline only and should not be relied upon without taking legal advice.

THIS AGREEMENT is made as of the .... day of 20.....

BETWEEN

............................(hereinafter called "the Owner")
of .... of the one part

AND

...........................(hereinafter called "the Purchaser")
of................................... of the other part.

WHEREAS

(A) The Owner is the absolute owner free from encumbrances except as hereinafter mentioned of the entire copyright and all other rights throughout the world in an original literary work entitled "..............................." (hereinafter called "the Work") written by........................... (hereinafter called "the Author") which expression shall if the Author and the Owner are the same person be construed as a reference to the Owner.

(B) The Owner has (as is witnessed by the Owner's execution of these presents) agreed to grant to the Purchaser the sole and exclusive option to acquire by way of partial assignment of copyright, the sole and exclusive film and other rights hereinafter referred to for the consideration and upon and subject to the terms and conditions hereinafter contained.

NOW THIS AGREEMENT WITNESSETH as follows:-

1. In this Agreement the following expressions shall unless the context otherwise requires bear the following meanings:-

"First Option Sum" : . ...Pounds (£..................)
"Second Option Sum": ....Pounds (£...................)
"First Option Date" : A date ....from the date hereof
"Second Option Date": A date................following the First Option Date

2. (a) In consideration of the immediate payment by the Purchaser to the Owner of the First Option Sum (the receipt of which sum the Owner hereby acknowledges) the Owner hereby grants to the Purchaser the sole and exclusive option (hereinafter called "the First Option") exercisable by notice in writing to the Owner in the manner hereinafter mentioned at any time on or before the First Option Date to purchase from the Owner by way of partial (or full) assignment of copyright the sole and exclusive rights in the Work as more particularly specified in the form of the Deed of Assignment ("the Deed") annexed hereto and by this reference made a part hereof for the sums and upon and subject to the terms and conditions set out in the Deed.

(b) The Owner agrees to grant to the Purchaser a further sole and exclusive option (hereinafter called "the Second Option") upon the same terms and conditions as for the First Option provided that the Purchaser pays the Owner the Second Option Sum on or before the First Option Date. Such further Second Option shall be exercisable by notice in writing as aforesaid at any time on or before the Second Option Date.

(c) Not withstanding anything to the contrary herein contained the First Option Period and (if applicable) the Second Option Period shall be extended until such time as the Owner has provided the Purchaser with evidence of it's title to the rights expressed to be granted in the Deed sufficient to enable the Purchaser if the Purchaser should require to obtain errors and omissions insurance in respect of such title upon customary terms.

3. The sums paid to the Owner pursuant to Clause 2 above shall be non returnable in any event and shall be deemed to be paid in advance and on account of the sum payable pursuant to Clause 2 of the Deed.

4. (a) The Owner hereby warrants that the Owner is the absolute owner free from encumbrances (save as expressly provided in the Deed) of all such rights in the Work as are referred to in the Deed.

(b) The Owner agrees and undertakes during the subsistence of the aforesaid option periods not to dispose of nor deal in any way with any of the rights in the Work which are the subject of the options hereby granted.

5 (a) The Purchaser agrees and undertakes not later than ten (10) days after the exercise of the applicable Option to submit an engrossment in the form of the Deed to the Owner for signature and further agrees agrees forthwith upon signature of the same by the Owner to pay to the Owner in exchange for the executed Deed the consideration therein expressed to be immediately payable.

(b) In the event that the Purchaser fails to submit an engrossment of the Deed to the Owner for signature within the time limited as aforesaid the consideration in the Deed expressed to be immediately payable shall become due and payable forthwith upon the expiration of the said period of ten (10) days without prejudice to the right of the Purchaser to call upon the Owner at any time thereafter to execute an engrossment of the Deed.

6. The Purchaser shall be entitled to write or cause to be written film treatments and/or screenplays and/or adaptations of the Work and undertake so-called pre-production work for the purpose of enabling

the Purchaser to decide whether or not the Purchaser wishes to exercise any of the options hereby granted and in connection with the financing production distribtution and exploitation arrangements for the film or films to be based on the Work.

7. The notice in writing referred to in Clause 2 hereof shall be deemed to have been duly and properly served if addressed to the Owner and sent by prepaid post or if sent by telex or if sent by facsimile transmission to the above address or any subsequent address duly notified to the Purchaser and the date of service shall be deemed to be the day of delivery in the normal course of posting if posted or the day of sending such telex if telexed or the day of sending such facsimile if sent by facsimile.

8. The Purchaser shall be entitled to assign the benefit of this agreement to any third party but shall not thereby be relieved of it's obligations hereunder.

9. (a) All sums mentioned herein are exclusive of any Value Added Tax that may be payable thereon.

(b) All sums payable to the Owner hereunder shall be paid to the irrevocably appointed Agent at it's address above whose receipt thereof shall be a good and valid discharge therefore.

10. This agreement shall be construed and shall take effect in accordance with the laws of England and subject to the exclusive jurisdiction of the English Courts.

AS WITNESS the hands of the parties hereto or their representatives the day and year first above written

SIGNED by...
in the presence of:- ....

SIGNED by...
For and on behalf of:-..
(if a limited company)

in the presence of:-..

Deed Of Assignment
(Original Screenplay)

This is a guideline only and should not be relied upon without taking legal advice.

This Deed is made the .... day of .... 20........

BETWEEN

(Name, address) (hereinafter called "the Owner") of the one part

and

(Name, address) (hereinafter called "the Purchaser") of the other part.

WHEREAS

A) The Owner is the absolute owner free from encumbrances except as hereinafter mentioned of the copyright and all other rights throughout the world in and to the Treatment and Screenplay entitled.......................... (hereinafter called the "Work") written by......................... (hereinafter called the "Author", which expression shall if the Author and the Owner are the same person be construed as a reference to the Owner).

B) The Owner has agreed to grant and assign the Producer for the consideration hereafter mentioned the (specify applicable rights) rights in the Work throughout the world as hereinafter more particularly mentioned.

NOW THIS ASSIGNMENT WITNESSETH

1.1. In consideration of the payment by the Purchaser to the Owner of the sum of ....Pounds (£..........) (receipt whereof the Owner hereby acknowledges) the Owner with full title guarantee hereby assigns and grants to the Purchaser (specify applicable rights i.e. all rights) (including but not limited to copyright) of whatever description whether now known or in the future existing in and to the Work TO HOLD the same unto the Purchaser absolutely throughout all parts of the world in which copyright in the Work may now subsist or may be acquired and during all renewals, revivals and extensions thereof and thereafter (in so far as may be or become possible) in perpetuity and except as herein expressly provided to the contrary free from all restrictions and limitations whatsoever including (but not by way of limitation of the generality of the foregoing) free from all so-called "Authors rights" or "droit moral" and any similar right now or hereafter accorded by the laws prevailing in any part of the world (including but not limited to any rights pursuant to sections 77 and 80 of the Copyright Designs and Patents Act 1988) and the Owner hereby expressly waives any so-called "Authors rights", droit moral and any such rights.

FILES ON THE DISK

1.2. Without prejudice to the generality of the assignment of rights in Clause 1.1 above, the Owner hereby confirms and agrees that the assignment of rights hereby made to the Purchaser includes any and all rights of communication to the public by satellite, cable re-transmission rights and any and all rental and lending rights, whether now or hereafter known or existing in any country of the world, in and to the products of the Owner's services hereunder and/or the Film (as hereinafter defined) and/or copies thereof and/or any part or version or adaptation of any of the foregoing.

2. (a) As further consideration for the rights hereby granted the Purchaser hereby agrees to pay to the Owner
(i) upon the first day of principal photography of the first or only film made in exercise of the rights hereby granted and not being part of a television series or serial (hereinafter called "the Film") the sum of (£...............................)

(ii) sums from time to time equal to (...................) Percent (....%) of the Net Profits (as defined below) of the Film.

For the purposes of this Deed the expression "Net Profits" shall have the same meaning as is accorded thereto in the principal production finance and distribution agreements for the Film.

2. (b) The Owner agrees that the consideration payable to the Owner in accordance with the provisions of this Agreement takes into account and includes a payment in respect of all rights of communication to the public by satellite, cable, re-transmission rights and any and all rental and lending rights as referred to in Clause 1.2. hereof and that the said payment constitutes equitable and adequate consideration for the assignment of satellite, cable and rental and lending rights, and constitutes and satisfies in full any and all rights which the Owner has or may at any time have to receive equitable, adequate or other remuneration for the exploitation by satellite and cable and the rental or lending of the products of the Owner's services and/or the Film and/or copies thereof and/or any part or version or adaptation of any of the foregoing. Without prejudice to the provisions of this Clause nothing in this Agreement shall prevent the Owner from being entitled to receive income under collection and other agreements negotiated by recognised collection societies under the laws of any jurisdiction PROVIDED THAT this does not imply any obligation or liability on the part of the Purchaser regarding the collection or payment of such monies.

3. The Owner hereby represents, warrants and undertakes to and with the Purchaser that:-

a) the Owner is the Owner and Author of the Work which was and is wholly original with the Author and nothing therein infringes the copyright or any other rights of any third party

b) copyright in the Work subsists or may be acquired in all countries of the world whose laws now provide for copyright protection and that

the Owner and the Author have not and will not at any time hereafter do authorise or omit to do anything relating to the Work whereby the subsistence of copyright therein or any part of such copyright may be destroyed or otherwise impaired.

c) the rights hereby granted are vested in the Owner absolutely and neither the Owner nor the Author or any other predecessor in title of the Owner heretofore assigned, licensed, granted or in any way dealt with or encumbered the same so as to derogate from the grant hereby made and that the Owner has a good title and full right and authority to make this Deed

d) the Work does not constitute a breach of any duty of confidence owed to any party and does not breach any right of privacy and does not contain any libellous or defamatory statement or matter or innuendo of or reference to any person firm company or incident

e) the Owner will indemnify and at all times keep the Purchaser fully indemnified from and against all actions, claims, proceedings, costs and damages incurred by or awarded against the Purchaser or any compensation paid or agreed to be paid by the Purchaser on the advice of counsel agreed between the parties hereto (and in default of such agreement within one month from the time such agreement is sought then a counsel decided by the President for the time being of the Law Society) in consequence of any breach, non-performance or non-observance by the Owner of all or any of the covenants, warranties, representations and agreements by the Owner contained in this Deed

f) the Owner will and does hereby authorise the Purchaser at the Purchaser's expense to institute prosecute and defend such proceedings and to do such acts and things as the Purchaser in it's sole discretion may deem expedient to protect the rights granted by the Owner to the Purchaser hereunder and to recover damages and penalties for any infringement of the said rights and insofar as may be necessary in the Purchaser's reasonable view to use the name of the Owner for or in connection with any of the purposes aforesaid and the Owner shall in any such proceeding afford the Purchaser all reasonable assistance the Purchaser may require at the expense of the Purchaser in instituting prosecuting or defending such actions unless the said action is occasioned by some breach or non-performance by the Owner of any covenants or warranties herein contained.

4. For further securing to the Purchaser the rights hereby granted the Owner hereby undertakes with the Purchaser that the Owner will at the request and expense of the Purchaser do all such further acts and things and execute all such further documents and instruments as the Purchaser may from time to time require for the purpose of confirming the Purchaser's title to the said rights in any part of the world and the Owner hereby appoints the Purchaser it's irrevocable attorney-in-fact with the right but not the obligation to do any and all acts and things necessary for the purpose of confirming the Purchaser's title at the expense of the Purchaser as aforesaid and to execute all such deeds

documents and instruments in the name of and on behalf of the Owner which appointment shall be deemed a power coupled with an interest and shall be irrevocable.

5. The Owner hereby grants to the Purchaser the right to use and authorise others to use the name, biography and likeness of the Author when exploiting or dealing with the rights hereby granted provided that the Author shall not be represented as personally using or recommending any commercial product other than films or other products of the rights hereby granted based upon the Work.

6. The Purchaser shall not be obliged to exercise any of the rights of copyright and other rights in and to the Work or any part thereof granted unto the Purchaser hereunder and if the Purchaser shall not exercise any of these said rights the Purchaser shall not be liable to the Owner in any manner whatsoever.

7. The Purchaser shall be fully entitled to negotiate and conclude agreements for the sale performance licensing and other commercial exploitation of the rights hereby granted upon whatever terms the Purchaser considers fair and reasonable and shall not be obliged in any way to seek the approval of the Owner in connection therewith and the Purchaser gives no warranty or representation as to the amount (if any) of any receipts that may arise.

8. a) In the event of a film or films being based upon the Work the Purchaser shall give the Author a single card credit on all copies of any such film or films issued under the control of the Purchaser in the form: Screenplay written by .... provided however that no casual or inadvertent failure by the Purchaser to accord the Author credit as aforesaid shall be deemed a breach

b) the Purchaser will incorporate in it's agreements with the distributors or broadcasters of such films as aforesaid a provision obliging such distributor or broadcaster to accord such credits to the Author but the failure of any distributor or broadcaster to accord such credits shall not constitute a breach by the Purchaser hereof provided however that if the Purchaser shall be notified of such failure the Purchaser shall use all reasonable endeavours but without incurring material expense to ensure that such failure is remedied by such distributor or broadcaster (as the case may be)

9. All rights assigned by this Deed shall be irrevocable under all or any circumstances and shall not be subject to reversion rescission termination or injunction in case of breach of the provisions of this Deed by the Purchaser including failure to pay any part of the consideration other than the sum payable under clause 1 hereof. The Owner's remedies shall be limited to an action at law for damages or for an accounting (if applicable). The Purchaser shall not be liable for damages for breach of contract (except for payment of consideration) unless the Purchaser has been given reasonable notice and opportunity to adjust or correct the matter complained of and the same has not been adjusted or corrected within a reasonable time following the notice aforesaid.

10. Any notices required to be served hereunder shall be deemed to have been duly and properly served if addressed to the Owner or Purchaser as the case may be and sent in a prepaid envelope or if sent by facsimile transmission to the above address or any subsequent address of the Owner or Purchaser as the case may be duly notified to the Owner or Purchaser respectively and acknowledged and the date of service shall be deemed to be the date of delivery in the normal course of posting if posted or the date of sending if sent by facsimile.

11. All sums mentioned herein are exclusive of Value Added Tax that may be payable thereon.

12. The Purchaser shall be entitled to assign the benefit of this Deed to any third party but shall not thereby be relieved of it's obligations hereunder.

13. This Deed shall be construed and shall take effect in accordance with the laws of England and subject to the exclusive jurisdiction of the English Courts.

IN WITNESS WHEREOF the Owner and the Purchaser have executed this Assignment and is hereby delivered as a Deed the day and year first above written

SIGNED as a DEED

by:..

in the presence of:...

Executed as a DEED by:...................................... (Limited) acting through it's two Directors/Director and Secretary

FILES ON THE DISK

Actors Agreement

This is a guideline only and should not be relied upon without taking legal advice.

(MAIN AGREEMENT)

Dated:

PRODUCER: ("the Producer")
Address:

ARTIST: ("the Artist")
Address:

FILM TITLE: ("the Film")

ROLE: ("character")

1. Services: Producer hereby engages Artist as a performer in the Film portraying in the role described above (as said role may be changed or rewritten at Producer's discretion).

2. Start Date: It is presently contemplated that read through day will commence on....................and rehearsals will commence on......................and that principal photography shall commence on................... provided however Artist's services shall commence no later than....................subject to events of force majeure. Artist agrees to remain available and not accept another engagement which would conflict or interfere with Artist obligations hereunder.

3. Guaranteed Period of Engagement: Term: The term of Artist's engagement hereunder shall commence on the start date and continue subject only to the provisions for suspension and termination set out in Exhibit A hereto for a minimum period of .... (.....) weeks ("Guaranteed Period of Engagement") and thereafter for the period necessary to complete all continuous services required by Producer from Artist in connection with principal photography of the Film. Artist shall perform additional services prior to and after the term in accordance with the provisions of clause 4 hereof.

4. Additional Services: The Artist shall on written notice from the Producer perform additional services ("Additional Services") on .... or such other or additional day notified to the Artist by the Producer in connection with principal photography of the Film.

5. Further Services: If the Producer requires the Artist's services after the Guaranteed Period of Engagement and not for any Additional Services the Artist shall if so requested by the Producer render such further services ("Further Services") which shall include without limitation dubbing and post-synchronisation subject to the Artist's prior professional engagements.

6. Basic Compensation: Subject to the provisions of this Agreement and provided that Artist shall keep and perform all covenants and conditions to be kept and performed by Artist hereunder Producer agrees as full compensation for services rendered and for all rights granted to the Producer hereunder to pay Artist as follows:-

(a) Guaranteed Compensation: For the Guaranteed Period of Engagement, Artist shall receive the sum of .... pounds (£........) payable as to .... pounds (£.......) following the first week of rehearsals inclusive of the read through day and .... pounds (£..........) following the ....weeks of rehearsals and as to the balance following the end of the first full week of Artist's services in principal photography of the Film. Such payment shall be made to Artist care of (..............). If the Artist renders Additional Services, Artist shall receive..........pounds (£.......) for each day after which he attends at the request of the Producer and renders services hereunder. If the Artist renders Further Services, Artist shall receive a further sum (if any) to be negotiated in good faith between the parties for each day or part day (if any) upon which he attends at the request of the Producer and renders services hereunder.

7. Credit
(a) If Artist shall keep and perform all covenants and conditions to be kept and performed by the Artist hereunder and if Artist appears readily recognisable in the Film then Artist will be accorded credit in the main titles of the Film on all copies of the Film issued by or under the control of the Producer and in all major paid advertising excluding the customary industry exclusions. The size type and placement of such credit shall be at Producer's sole discretion.

8. Transportation and Expenses: From the commencement of principal photography until the expiry of the Term, Producer shall provide Artist with .... transportation facilities (state what these are if any and whether other expenses will be paid).

9. Conditions: Artist's engagement hereunder is subject to Producer obtaining standard cast insurance for Artist at normal rates.

10. References: The term of Artist's engagement hereunder shall be as set forth in this Main Agreement and in Exhibit "A" attached hereto which is incorporated herein by reference. In the event of any express inconsistency between the provisions of this Main Agreement and the provisions of Exhibit / a the provisions of this Main Agreement shall control.

IN WITNESS WHEREOF the parties hereto have executed the within Agreement as of the date first set forth hereinabove

(insert name of Producer)
By:..
Duly authorised officers:..
Accepted and Agreed to:..

EXHIBIT A

1. The Artist hereby

(a) warrants that the Artist is not under any obligation or disability which might prevent or restrict the Artist from entering into this agreement or from giving the undertakings or fully observing and performing the terms and conditions of this Agreement or granting the rights and consents referred to herein

(b) gives all such consents as are or may be required under the Copyright Designs and Patents Act 1988 or any re-enactment consolidation or amendment thereof or any statute of like purpose or effect for the time being in force in any part of the world including but not in limitation of the foregoing all consents under Part II of the said Act in order that the Producer may make the fullest use of the Artist's services provided by the Artist hereunder and furthermore the Artist hereby irrevocably and unconditionally waives all rights relating to the Artist's services in the Film to which the Artist is now or may in the future be entitled pursuant to the provisions of Section 77 80 84 and 85 of the said Act and any other moral rights to which the Artist may be entitled under any legislation now existing or in the future enacted in any part of the world

(c) warrants that the Artist is a "qualifying person" and the performance of the Artist is a "qualifying performance" within the meaning of the Copyright Designs and Patents Act 1988.

2. The Artist undertakes that the Artist shall during the subsistence of and subject to the terms and conditions of this Agreement as where and when required by the Producer:-

(a) perform and record the Artist's part

(b) attend for tests conferences fittings rehearsals and the taking of still photographs and other arrangements

(c) dress, make up and wear the Artist's hair (subject to prior consultation with the Artist) as directed by the Director and generally comply with all decisions of the Producer concerning the manner in which the Artist shall render the Artist's services hereunder and be portrayed and presented

(d) render the Artist's services hereunder willingly and to the utmost of the Artist's skill and ability and as directed by the Producer both in connection with the production of the Film and for publicity and other purposes connected therewith Provided Always that nothing in this sub-clause and sub-clause (c) hereof shall be deemed to require the Artist to recommend or endorse any commercial product other than the Film and any commercial gramophone record of the sound track of the Film or to engage in any publicity or other activities for any such purpose (but without prejudice to Clause 5 hereof).

3. The Artist further undertakes:-

(a) that the Artist will comply with all reasonable and notified directions, regulations and rules in force at places where the Artist is required to render services hereunder (including in particular regulations and rules relating to smoking and the taking of photographs) and will comply with the orders given by the Producer of it's representatives from time to time

(b) to keep the Producer informed of the Artist's whereabouts and telephone number from time to time prior to and throughout the engagement

(c) that the Artist will use the Artist's best endeavours to maintain a state of health enabling the Artist fully and efficiently to perform the Artist's services hereunder throughout the engagement and that the Artist will not take part in any activity which might interfere with the due and efficient rendering of such services or which might invalidate any such insurance as is referred to in the preceding sub-clause

(d) that the Artist shall not at any time pledge the credit of the Producer nor incur or purport to incur any liability on it's behalf or in it's name.

4. (a) The Artist hereby acknowledges that all rights whatsoever throughout the World in or in any way attaching to the Film and all photographs and sound recordings taken and made hereunder (including all rights of copyright therein and in any written or other material contributed by the Artist and all such rights therein or in such material as are or may hereafter be conferred or created by international arrangement or convention in or affecting any part of the World whether by way of new or additional arrangement or convention in or affecting any part of the world whether by way of new or additional rights not now comprised in copyright or otherwise) shall belong absolutely to the Producer and the Artist with full title guarantee assigns and grants the same to the Producer throughout the World and throughout all periods for which the said rights or any of them are or may be conferred or created by the law in force in all or any parts of the world and all renewals, revivals and extensions of such periods the Producer may make or authorise any use of the same and may exploit the same in any manner but only in and in connection with the Film

(b) the Artist hereby acknowledges and agrees and confirms that the Producer shall be entitled and it is hereby authorised to adapt change take from add to and use and treat in every way all or any of the products of the Artist's services rendered hereunder and to use reproduce and perform and broadcast and transmit the same with or as part of the work of any other persons and synchronised or not with any music or other sounds or motions as the Producer considers necessary or desirable

(c) for the avoidance of doubt the assignment of rights set out in this Clause includes all satellite cable rental and lending rights ("the Rights") and the Artist agrees that the remuneration payable pursuant to this agreement includes and constitutes equitable and adequate consideration for the assignment and exploitation of the Rights and to the extent permitted by the law the Artist waives the right to receive any further remuneration in relation to the exploitation of the Rights.

5. The Producer shall be entitled by written notice to the Artist given at any time to suspend the engagement of the Artist hereunder (whether or not the term of such engagement has commenced) if and so long as:-

(a) the production of the Film or the operation of any studio involved in such production shall be prevented suspended interrupted

FILES ON THE DISK

These sample contracts & documents have been created for your general information only. The copyright owner, the authors of this book & the publishers cannot therefore be held responsible for any losses or claims howsoever arising from any use or reproduction.

postponed hampered or interfered with by reason or on account of any event of force majeure, fire, accident, action of the elements, war, riot, civil, disturbance, sickness, epidemic, pestilence, national calamity, act of God, or any actual labour disputes (including strikes, lockouts or withholding of labour of any kind whether by the direction or with the support of any trade union or other body or otherwise) or illness or incapacity of the Producer of the Director of the Film or any principal artist or principal technician or any cause (apart from those hereinbefore specifically referred to and whether or not similar thereto) not reasonably within the control of the Producer or
(b) the voice of the Artist shall become unsatisfactory in quality or tone
(c) the Artist shall be reason of any illness or physical or mental incapacity or disability be unable in the opinion of the Producer fully to render the Artist's services hereunder or to devote sufficient of the Artist's time ability and attention to such services or
(c) the Artist shall fail refuse or neglect duly to render willingly and to the utmost of the Artist's skill and ability the Artist's full services hereunder or shall fail, refuse or neglect fully to observe or comply with any of the Artist's material obligations under this Agreement or with any of the terms thereof.

6. Upon any suspension of the engagement of the Artist hereunder
(a) such suspension shall be effective from the date of the event giving rise to such suspension and shall continue for the duration of such event and for such reasonable period thereafter as may be necessary for the Producer to make arrangements to commence or resume production
(b) the Producer shall during the period of suspension cease to be liable to make any payments of remuneration to the Artist hereunder (or to pay for or provide accommodation or living expenses if the suspension is due to the Artist's default or refusal) save such instalments of remuneration as shall have become due and payable prior to the suspension and the period of engagement hereunder shall be extended by or (if appropriate) the commencement of the Artist's engagement shall be postponed by and the dates for payment of any further instalments of remuneration hereunder shall be postponed (or further postponed as the case may be) by a period equal to that of such suspension
(c) all rights of the Producer in respect of services rendered by the Artist and in all the products thereof previous to such suspension and the benefit of all consents granted hereunder shall not be affected and accordingly shall be or remain vested in the Producer.

7. The Producer shall be entitled by written notice to the Artist given at any time to terminate the engagement of the Artist hereunder (without prejudice to any other rights and remedies available to the Producer hereunder)
(a) if any suspension under the provisions of paragraph (a) of clause 6 hereof shall continue for 28 (twenty-eight) consecutive days or 28 (twenty-eight) days in the aggregate or more
(b) if any suspension under the provisions of paragraph (b) or (b) of Clause 5 hereof shall continue for 2 (two) consecutive days or 3

(three) days in the aggregate or more
(c) at any time in the circumstances referred to in paragraphs (d) or (f) of Clause 5 hereof (whether or not the Producer shall have suspended the Artist's engagement under the provisions of Clause 5 hereof) subject to the Artist being given the opportunity to rectify any default if capable of rectification within 24 (twenty-four) hours of the Producer giving notice of such default

Provided however that if any suspension under the provisions of paragraph (a) of Clause 5 hereof shall continue for six weeks or more then the Artist shall be entitled to terminate this engagement by seven days' written notice to the Producer unless by the expiry of such notice the Producer shall have terminated such suspension but the Producer shall not be entitled to terminate this engagement for the same event subject however to the right of the Producer to suspend or terminate the Artist's engagement for other proper cause including but not limited to the occurrence of a different event (even though of the same nature as a previous one) of force majeure in accordance with the provisions hereof

8. In the case of termination of the engagement of the Artist under the foregoing provisions or by the death of the Artist
(a) such termination shall be effective from the date of the event giving rise to the termination or (if there shall have been a prior suspension) from the date of the event giving rise to the suspension from which such termination arose
(b) any claim which the Producer may have against the Artist in respect of any breach, non-performance or non-observance of any of the material provisions of this Agreement arising prior to such termination or out of which such termination shall arise shall not be affected or prejudiced
(c) the Producer's title to and ownership of all copyrights and all other rights in or in connection with the services rendered by the Artist up to the date of such termination and in all the products of such services shall not be affected and such rights shall accordingly be or remain vested in the Producer
(d) payment to the Artist of the instalments of remuneration due and payable to the Artist up to the effective date of such termination shall operate as payment in full and final discharge and settlement of all claims on the part of the Artist under this Agreement and accordingly the Producer shall not be under any obligation to pay to the Artist any further or other sums on account of salary or otherwise

9. The Artist undertakes at the expenses of the Producer to execute and procure the execution of any document which the Producer may consider necessary for the purpose of carrying into effect the arrangements made by this Agreement or any of them including in particular any documents required to vest in or confirm any rights of copyright or other rights in the Producer

10. The rights and the benefit of all consents granted hereunder to the Producer are irrevocable and without right of rescission by the Artist or reversion to the Artist under any circumstances whatsoever

FILES ON THE DISK

11. Credit will be given only
(a) if Artist appears recognisably in the Film as released
(b) if this Agreement has not been terminated for the default of the Artist

No casual or inadvertent failure to comply with credit requirements shall be deemed a breach of this Agreement. The sole remedy of Artist for a breach of any of the provisions of this clause or of the Principal Agreement shall be an action at law for damages, it being agreed that in no event shall Artist seek to be entitled to injunctive or other equitable relief by any reason of any of the breach or threatened breach of any credit requirements, nor shall Artist be entitled to seek to enjoin or restrain the exhibition distribution advertising exploitation or marketing of the Film

12. All notices served upon either party by the other hereunder shall be delivered by hand at or sent by pre-paid recorded delivery letter post or by facsimile addressed to the respective addressed hereinbefore contained or any subsequent address duly notified and if delivered by hand shall be deemed to have been served five days after posting and if sent by facsimile shall be deemed served 24 hours after receipt of the facsimile (and facsimile notice shall be confirmed by post). A copy of all notices to the Artist shall be sent to the Agent (if any)

13. The Artist shall treat as confidential and shall not disclose to any third party (save to the Artist's professional advisors whose dissemination of such information they receive shall be limited to use for business purposes i.e. quotes for services or as may be required by law) the provisions of this Agreement or any confidential information concerning the Producer or the Film or it's distributors which may come to the Artist's attention in connection with the Artist's engagement hereunder or otherwise

14. For the avoidance of doubt, it is expressly agreed between the parties that this Agreement and the provision of Artist's services in connection with the Film, is not subject to any collective bargaining agreement or guild or union regulations and the compensation paid to the Artist under clause 6 of the Main Agreement represents full and complete consideration for all of the services of the Artist hereunder and all rights assigned and granted by the Artist in the products of those services.

15. This Agreement shall be governed by and construed in accordance with the laws of England and subject to the exclusive jurisdiction of the Courts of England.

Accompanying Notes

MAIN AGREEMENT
Clause 3: The Producer needs to ensure the actor is around for a fixed number of weeks and because the actor agrees to make him/herself available for that period the producer must pay accordingly.

Clause 4: Additional services are during principal photography.

Clause 6: Further services are post production services where the artist will be available subject to other prior engagements. Sometimes a producer can negotiate a certain number of so called "free" days (3 is the norm) where the artist will render Additional or Further Services for free. This gives the Producer more leeway but is only appropriate on big productions. The fee for Further or Additional Services can be agreed in advance and it is customary for the fee to be a daily rate calculated as a pro-rated amount of the weekly sum.

EXHIBIT A
Clause 4(c): See Glossary of Terms. This may not be legally effective but at present all relevant contracts include such a term.

Clause 7: The periods of suspension giving rise to the entitlement of the Producer to terminate the agreement are subject to negotiation.

Note 1: It should be made clear whether or not the terms of the agreement are going to be governed by the appropriate Equity agreement or not. Many actors, or more likely their agents, will insist on the application of Equity's terms as Equity has negotiated residual and royalty payments on repeats, video etc. with PACT. However if the project is a film intended for theatrical release you should negotiate a complete buy out of the Artist's performance rights wherever possible. A buy out will be expected by most sales agents, financiers and distributors as they will not want the trouble of having to account to the artists and more importantly, any residual payments will be seen as a drain on the revenue of the film.

Note 2: Deferments. If the fee or proportion of the fee is to be deferred, there should be further provisions that should also be mentioned, i.e. that the Deferment will be pro rata and pari passu with all other deferments to persons, providing services to the Film, after which all deferments to companies and firms should be met. All deferred sums are payable in first place from receipts received by the Producer from the exploitation of the Film subject to the recoupment of the production and post production cost of the Film only. It should be emphasised that the Deferment is a contingent amount and is only payable to the extent sufficient receipts are generated. It should also be mentioned that the Producers will use their reasonable endeavours to procure that their auditors or any other firm of Chartered Accountants appointed, will provide an audited detailed statement of all transactions relevant to the production and the income generated which should be made available to the artist and/or representatives by a specified date.

N.B. Due to legislation, BECTU argue that it is possible that using deferred paments is unlawful.

Note 3: A Daily Rate is usually calculated at 1/7th of the weekly rate.

LEGAL TOOLKIT AND FORMS

FILES ON THE DISK

Note 4: If the artist is a so called star they may insist upon a share of net profits.

Note 5: Work exists on bank holidays unless otherwise stated in the contract or accompanying schedule.

Note 6: Credit. The size and placement of the credit (billing requirement) is usually negotiated between the parties.

Note 7: Material. The artist will sometimes ask for the right to select the photographs of themselves to be used and this is usually granted subject to certain restraints.

Note 8: If an actor or their agent is concerned about the ability of a production company to make the payments due to the Artist, they may ask for all the monies due under the agreement to be paid to a third party to be held in an Escrow Account and paid out in accordance with the agreement under the terms of the agreed Escrow arrangement.

Performers Consent

This is a guideline only and should not be relied upon without taking legal advice.

From: *("the Performer") of (address)*

To: *(name of company) ("the Company which shall include it's successors assigns and licensees)* of *(address)*

Dated: *(date)*

Dear Sirs

(Name of film) (the "Film")

In consideration of the sum of (£ *amount*) paid by the Company to the Performer (the receipt of which the Performer acknowledges). The Performer irrevocably and unconditionally grants to the Company all consents required pursuant to the Copyright, Designs and Patents Act 1988 Part II and all other laws now or in the future in force in any part of the world which may be required for the exploitation of the Performer's performance contained in the Film, whether or not as part of the Film, in any and all media by any manner or means now known or invented in the future throughout the world for the full period of copyright protection pursuant to the laws in force in any part of the world, including all renewals, reversions and extensions.

This letter shall be governed by and construed in accordance with the law of England and Wales the courts of which shall be courts of competent jurisdiction.

Yours faithfully

(signature of Performer)

Accompanying Notes

Note 1: The Performer's Consent form is specifically for, and only relates to the Performer and their performance. The performers do not own copyright as such in their performance (there is none) but their consent is needed to exploit their performance.

Note 2: Consideration must be given in any contract. A contract requires an offer, acceptance and consideration. It is a legal necessity. ("Consideration" does not have to be money, it can be provided by, for example, giving up a legal right).

These sample contracts & documents have been created for your general information only. The copyright owner, the authors of this book & the publishers cannot therefore be held responsible for any losses or claims howsoever arising from any use or reproduction.

Release Form

This is a guideline only and should not be relied upon without taking legal advice.

From: *(name of individual)* of *(address)*

To: *(name of company) ("the Company" which shall include it's successors, assigns and licensees)*

of *(address)*

Dated: *(date)*

Dear Sirs

(Name of the film) (the "Film")

1. In consideration of the sum of £1 (*or any other amount*) now paid by the Company to me (the receipt of which I acknowledge) I warrant, confirm and agree with the Company that the Company shall have the right to exploit any films, photographs and sound recordings made by the Company for the Film in which I feature, or any literary, dramatic, musical or artistic work or film or sound recording created by me or any performance by me of any literary, dramatic, musical or artistic work or film or sound recording included by the Company in the Film in any and all media by any and all means now known or invented in future throughout the world for the full period of copyright, including all renewals, revivals, reversions and extensions.

2. I irrevocably and unconditionally grant to you all consents required pursuant to the Copyright, Designs, and Patents Act 1988 Part II * or otherwise under the laws in force in any part of the world to exploit such performances.

3. I irrevocably and unconditionally waive all rights which I may have in respect of the Film pursuant to the Copyright, Designs and Patents Act 1988 Sections 77, 80, 84 and 85**.

4. I consent to the use by the Company of my name, likeness, voice and biography in connection only with the Film.

5. The Company may assign or licence this agreement to any third party.

6. This letter shall be governed by and construed in accordance with the law of England and Wales and subject to the jurisdiction of the English Courts.

Yours faithfully

(signature of the individual)

* the "Performers Rights"
** the Moral Rights of an author

These sample contracts & documents have been created for your general information only. The copyright owner, the authors of this book & the publishers cannot therefore be held responsible for any losses or claims howsoever arising from any use or reproduction.

Accompanying Notes

FILES ON THE DISK

Note 1: The release form covers any work created by the individual. This form is more comprehensive than the Performer's Consent which does not contain an assignment of copyright (as there is no copyright as such in a performance) and covers an assignment of any artistic material contributed by the individual to the producer.

Note 2: Consideration must be given in any contract. A contract requires an offer, acceptance and consideration. It is a legal necessity. ("Consideration" does not have to be money, it can be provided by, for example, giving up a legal right).

LEGAL TOOLKIT AND FORMS

FILES ON
THE DISK

Crew Agreement

This is a guideline only and should not be relied upon without taking legal advice.

Dated:

PRODUCER: ("the Producer")
Address:

CREW MEMBER:("the Crew Member")
Address:

FILM TITLE:("the Film")

1. Services: The Producer hereby engages the Crew Member and the Crew Member undertakes and agrees to render to the Producer his/her services (hereinafter called "the Services").

2. The Period of Engagement shall commence on or about .... (hereinafter called "the Start Date") and shall continue until the earlier of;
a) completion of the Film in all respects ready for delivery to the principal distributor of the Film
b) termination of the Crew Member's engagement pursuant to the provisions of this agreement

3. Payment: Subject to the provisions of this Agreement and the observance and performance by the Crew Member of all his obligations under it the Producer shall pay to the Crew Member the sum of .... per week/ day (or a fixed amount), for all services rendered by the Crew Member in respect of the Film and for all rights in the products of such services
b) all sums payable to the Crew Member under this agreement are exclusive of Value Added Tax ("VAT"). The Producer shall pay such VAT as is properly charged by the Crew Member promptly following receipt of the Crew Member's tax invoice.
c) the Producer is expressly authorised by the Crew Member to deduct and withhold from all sums due to the Crew Member all deductions (if any) in accordance with local laws and regulations from time to time applicable
d) all sums payable under this clause 3 shall be paid directly to the Crew Member, whose receipt shall be a full and sufficient discharge to the Producer.
e) the Crew Member acknowledges that the remuneration provided under this clause 3 shall be inclusive of all guild and union minimum basic fees, overtime and all residual repeat and re-run payments, direct or indirect employment and like taxes and state governmental and/or social security contributions.

4. Expenses: All payments of pre-approved expenses to the Crew Member will be issued on a weekly basis by the Producer on provision of relevant invoice therefor.

5. Duration of Filming: The filming week shall be a 6 day week where the Producer may nominate such 6 days as in any week but the Crew

Member shall not be required to work more than 7 consecutive days without receiving the next consecutive day off. A Filming day will not exceed 14 hours inclusive of meal breaks. Any hours worked in excess of the said 14 hours will at the Producer's sole election either be carried over to the following day or a payment of a pro rata hourly rate shall be paid to the Crew Member on the pay day next falling due.

6. Rights/Consents: 6.1 The Crew Member with full title guarantee assigns and grants to the Producer the whole of the Crew Member's property right, title, interest in and to the Film and the entire copyright and all other rights in and to all products of the Crew Members services in connection with the Film including all vested future and contingent rights to which the Crew Member is now or may hereafter be entitled under the law in force in any part of the universe for the Producer's use and benefit absolutely for the full period or periods of copyright throughout the universe including all reversions, revivals, renewals and extensions created or provided by the law of any country. The Crew Member undertakes to execute all such documents and takes all such steps as may from time to time be necessary to secure to the Producer the rights in this clause 6.1.

6.2 The Producer shall have the right to make, produce, sell, publicly exhibit, lease, license, hire, market, publicise, distribute, exhibit, diffuse, broadcast, adapt and reproduce mechanically graphically electronically or otherwise howsoever by any manner and means (whether now known or hereafter devised) the Film and all products of the Crew Member's services throughout the universe; to permit any third party to exercise any of such rights in the sole discretion of the Producer.

6.3. The Crew Member hereby irrevocably and unconditionally waives all rights relating to the Crew Member's services in the Film to which the Crew Member is now or may in the future be entitled pursuant to the provisions of Section 77 80 84 and 85 of the Copyright, Designs and Patents Act 0f 1988 and any other moral rights to which the Crew Member may be entitled under any legislation now existing or in the future enacted in any part of the world.

7. Crew Member's warranties: The crew member hereby warrants, undertakes and agrees that;

7.1 the Crew Member is free to enter into this agreement and has not entered and will not enter into any arrangement which may conflict with it.

7.2 The Crew Member will render his/her services in willing co-operation with others in the manner required by the Producer and in accordance with the production schedule established by the Producer.

7.3 The Crew Member shall not without consent in writing of the Producer issue any publicity relating to or otherwise reveal or make public any financial, creative or other confidential information in connection with the Film or the terms of this agreement or the business of the Producer and will not knowingly commit any act which might prejudice or damage the reputation of the Producer or inhibit the successful exploitation of the Film.

7.4 The Crew Member is in a good state of health and shall use his/her best endeavours to remain so during the continuance of this agreement.

7.5 The Producer shall have the right to make the Crew Member's services available to third parties and the Crew Member will co-operate fully with such third parties and follow all lawful directions and instructions of such third parties.

7.6 The Crew Member shall at all times throughout his/her engagement keep the Producer informed of their whereabouts and telephone number.

7.7 The Crew Member will not on behalf of the Producer enter into any commitment contract or arrangement with any person or engage any person without the Producer's prior written consent.

7.8 The Crew Member shall willingly and promptly co-operate with the Producer and shall carry out such services rendered by the Crew Member as when and where requested by the Producer and follow all reasonable directions and instructions given by the Producer.

7.9 The Crew Member shall attend at such locations and times as are reasonably required by the Producer from time to time.

7.10 The Crew Member shall comply with and observe all union rules and regulations and all the formal agreements, rules and regulations relating to safety, fire, prevention or general administration in force at any place in which the Crew Member shall be required by the Producer to render any services.

7.11 Upon the expiry of earlier termination of the Crew Member's engagement, the Crew Member will deliver up to the Producer all scripts, photographs and other literary or dramatic properties all film materials and all other properties, documents and things, whatsoever which the Crew Member may have in the Crew Member's possession or under the Crew Member's control relating to the Film.

7.12 The Crew Member shall indemnify the Producer and keep it fully indemnified against all proceedings, costs, claims, awards, damages, expenses (including without limitation legal expenses) and liabilities arising directly or indirectly from any breach of the Crew Member's undertakings, obligations or warranties hereunder.

8. **Credit:** Subject to the Crew Member rendering their services under the terms of this agreement, the Crew Member shall be given credit on the Film. The Producer shall determine in it's discretion the manner and mode of presentation of the Crew Member's credit. The Producer shall not be obliged to accord credit to the Crew Member in any other method of advertising or publicity. No casual or inadvertent failure by the Producer or any third party to comply with providing credit, and no failure by persons other than the Producer to comply with their contracts with the Producer shall constitute a breach of this Agreement by the Producer. The rights and remedies of the Crew Member in the event of a breach of this clause 8, by the Producer shall be limited to the rights (if any) to recover damages in an action at law and in no event shall the

Crew Member be entitled by reason of any such breach to enjoin or restrain or otherwise interfere with the distribution, exhibition or exploitation of the Film.

9. **Producer's liability:** The Producer shall not be liable for any loss of or damage to any clothing or other personal property of the Crew Member whether such loss or damage is caused by negligence or otherwise howsoever except to the extent that the Producer receives compensation from an insurance company or other third party.

10. **Waiver:** No waiver by the Producer of any failure by the Crew Member to observe any covenant or condition of this agreement shall be deemed to be a waiver of any preceding or succeeding failure or of any other covenant of condition nor shall it be deemed a continuing waiver. The rights and remedies provided for in this agreement are cumulative and no one of them shall be deemed to be exclusive of the others or of any rights or remedies allowed by law. The rights granted to the Producer are irrevocable and shall not revert to the Crew Member under any circumstances whatsoever. In the event that the Producer terminates or cancels (or purports to terminate or cancel) this agreement or any other agreement entered into by and between the Producer and the Crew Member (and even if such cancellation or termination or purported termination or cancellation is ultimately determined by a court to have been without proper or legal cause or ultimately determined by such a court that the Producer committed any material breach of any such agreement) the damage (if any) caused to the Crew Member thereby is not irreparable or sufficient to entitle the Crew Member to injunctive or other equitable relief and the Crew Member shall not have any right to terminate this agreement or any such other agreement or any of the Producer's rights hereunder.

11. **Insurance:** The Producer may secure in it's own name or otherwise at its own expense life accident health cast pre-production and other insurance covering the Crew Member independently or together with others and the Crew Member shall not have any right, title, or interest in or to such insurance. The Crew Member shall assist the Producer to procure such insurance and shall in timely fashion submit to such customary medical and other examinations and sign such applications and other instruments in writing as may be required by the insurance company involved.

12. **Condition precedent:** As a condition precedent to any and all liability of the Producer, the Crew Member shall at the Crew Member's own expense apply for and assist the Producer in applying for and do all such things as may be necessary in support of any application for the Crew Member's membership of any trade union, labour or professional organisation or guild and/or for passports, visas, work permits or other matters necessary to enable the Producer to make use of the Crew Member's services. If as a result of such application being refused, revoked or cancelled the Producer shall be unable to make use of the Crew Member's services this agreement shall be deemed null and void and without effect and without liability whatsoever on the parties save that the Crew Member shall repay to the Producer any sums previously paid to him/her pursuant to clause 3.

FILES ON THE DISK

13. Suspension: The Producer shall be entitled by written notice giving reasons for such suspension to the Crew Member at any given time, to suspend the engagement of the Crew Member hereunder (whether or not the term of such engagement has commenced) if and so long as:-

13.1 The production of the Film is prevented, suspended, interrupted, postponed, hampered or interfered with by reason or on account of any event of force majeure, fire, accident, action of the elements of war, riot, civil disturbance, sickness, epidemic, pestilence, national calamity, act of God or any actual labour disputes, or illness or incapacity of the Producer or the director of the Film or any principal artist or principal technician or any other cause not reasonably within the control of the Producer.

13.2 The Crew Member fails, refuses or neglects duly to render willingly and to the utmost of the Crew Member's skill and ability, the Crew Member's full services or that the Crew Member fails, refuses, or neglects fully to observe or comply with, or perform any of the Crew Member's obligations under this agreement.

13.3 Suspension shall commence from the date of the event giving rise to such suspension and shall continue for the duration of such event and for such reasonable period thereafter as may be necessary for the Producer to make arrangements to commence or resume production of the Film.

13.4 During this period of suspension, the Producer ceases to be liable to make any payments of remuneration or provide accommodation or living expenses if the suspension is due to the Crew Member's neglect, default, disability, incapacity or refusal) save such payment Instalments as shall have become due and payable prior to the suspension and the period of engagement shall be extended or the commencement of engagement shall be postponed by an equal period to the suspension.

13.5 All rights of the Producer in respect of the services rendered and products of those services thereof by the Crew Member previous to the suspension shall not be affected and shall remain vested in the Producer.

13.6 If the Producer pays any remuneration to the Crew Member during any period of suspension arising pursuant to clause 13.2, then the Producer may require the Crew Member's services hereunder without additional payment to the Crew Member for an equal period to the suspension during which the Producer paid remuneration to the Crew Member.

14. Termination: The Producer shall be entitled (but not obliged) by written notice giving reasons for the termination to the crew member given at any time, to terminate the engagement of the Crew Member hereunder (without prejudice to any other rights and remedies available to the Producer hereunder) if:-

14.1a suspension continues for 3 consecutive weeks or 4 weeks in the aggregate or more, according to clause 13.1, or

14.1b at any time in the circumstances referred to in clause 13.2,

14.1c the Crew Member does not fulfil their respective obligations under this Agreement.

14.2 **In the case of termination** of the engagement of the Crew Member under the foregoing provisions or by the death of the Crew Member

14.2a such termination shall be effective from the date of the event giving rise to the termination or (if there shall have been a prior suspension) from the date of the event giving rise to the suspension from which such termination arose

14.2b any claim which the Producer may have against the Crew Member in respect of any breach, non performance or non observance of any of the material provisions of this Agreement arising prior to such termination or out of which such termination shall arise shall not be affected or prejudiced

14.2c the Producer's title to and ownership of all copyrights and all other rights in or in connection with the services and all other rights in or in connection with the services rendered by the Crew Member up to the date of such termination and in all the products of such services shall not be affected and such rights shall accordingly be or remain vested in the Producer.

14.2d payment to the Crew Member of the instalments due and payable to the Crew Member up to the effective date of such termination shall operate as payment in full and final discharge and settlement of all claims on the part of the Crew Member under this agreement and accordingly the Producer shall not be under any obligation to pay to the Crew Member any further or other sums on account of remuneration or otherwise nor shall the producer be under any liability whether by way of damages or otherwise for any inconvenience or loss of publicity or other loss suffered by the Crew Member by reason of the termination of the Crew Member's engagement hereunder (but the provisions of this paragraph shall not affect the Producer's rights referred to in clause 14.2b.

15. Conflict: Nothing contained in this Agreement shall be construed so as to require the commission of any act contrary to law and wherever there is any conflict between any provision of this agreement and any statute law ordinance or regulation contrary to which the parties have no legal right to contract then the latter shall prevail but in such event the provisions of this agreement so affected shall be curtailed and limited only to the extent necessary to bring them within the legal requirements.

16. Assignment: The Crew Member expressly agrees that the Producer may transfer and assign this agreement or all or any part of the Producer's rights under it. The Agreement shall inure to the benefit of the Producer's successors, licensees, and assigns but the Producer shall not thereby be relieved of it's obligations.

17. Self employed status: The Crew Member warrants to the Producer that the Crew Member is self employed and is not considered to be an employee of the Producer and the Crew Member warrants to the Producer that he/she is personally responsible for all tax, national insurance and/or other taxes levied by the inland revenue (or relevant tax authority if working abroad). The Crew Member shall provide evidence of their self employed status to the Producer. The Crew Member indemnifies and holds harmless the Producer for any liability to pay local or governmental taxes arising from the Crew Member's engagement.

18. **Notices**: All notices served upon either party by the other hereunder shall be delivered by hand at or sent by prepaid recorded delivery letter post or by facsimile addressed to the respective addressed hereinbefore contained or any subsequent address duly notified and if delivered by hand shall be deemed to have been served five days after posting and if sent by facsimile shall be deemed served 24 hours after receipt of the facsimile (and facsimile notice shall be confirmed by post).

19. This Agreement contains the full and complete understanding between the parties and supersedes all prior agreements and understandings whether written or oral pertaining thereto and cannot be modified except by a written instrument signed by the Crew Member and the Producer.

20. Nothing contained in this Agreement shall or shall be deemed to constitute a partnership or a contract of employment between the parties.

21. This Agreement shall be construed in accordance with and governed by the laws of England whose courts shall be the courts of the competent jurisdiction.

IN WITNESS WHEREOF the parties hereto have executed the within Agreement as of the date first set forth hereinabove

(insert name of Producer)

By..

Duly Authorised Officers..

Accepted and Agreed to:

....

*VAT number or NI no. if applicable:

Accompanying Notes

FILES ON THE DISK

NOTE 1: Deferments. If the fee or proportion of the fee is to be deferred, there should be further provisions that should also be mentioned, i.e. that the Deferment will be pro rata and pari passu with all other deferments to persons, providing services to the Film, after which all deferments to companies and firms should be met. All deferred sums are payable in first place from receipts received by the Producer from the exploitation of the Film subject to the recoupment of the production and post production cost of the Film only. It should be emphasised that the Deferment is a contingent amount and is only payable to the extent sufficient receipts are generated. It should also be mentioned that the Producers will use their reasonable endeavours to procure that their auditors or any other firm of Chartered Accountants appointed, will provide an audited detailed statement of all transactions relevant to the production and the income generated which should be made available to the crew member/ and or representatives by a specified date.

N.B. Due to legislation, BECTU argue that it is possible that using deferred payments is unlawful.

NOTE 2: Payment. It should be made clear whether or not this agreement is a non guild or union agreement. Clause 3 (e) refers to a buy out.

NOTE 3: Expenses: The travel arrangements to and for the set are usually the responsibility of the crew member. However if on location, the crew member is provided with accommodation and travel expenses depending on the budget of the Film.

NOTE 4: Self employment: It is necessary that if the crew member is self employed, the producer receives written confirmation and evidence to prove their status. Otherwise responsibility falls upon the Producer who could be heavily penalised for not paying on time and be subject to the danger of prosecution.

FILES ON
THE DISK

Composers Agreement
(Original Score)

*This is a guideline only and should not be
relied upon without taking legal advice.*

THIS AGREEMENT is made the ....day of ....20....

BETWEEN:..
*(hereinafter called "the Company" which expression includes it's
successors in title licensees and assigns)*

AND...
(hereinafter called "the Composer")

WHEREAS:

The Company is currently engaged in the production of a film called
"..............." ("the Film") and wishes to engage the services of the
Composer to write compose and arrange the Music and record the
Recordings (as hereinafter defined) to be included in the Film upon the
following terms.

NOW THEREFORE IT IS HEREBY AGREED AS FOLLOWS:-

1. The Company hereby engages the Composer and the Composer
undertakes to make available his services as hereinafter provided
(hereinafter called "the Services") on the terms and conditions herein
contained:

1.1. The Composer shall compose and arrange the music ("the Music").
1.2. The Composer shall perform and record the Music ("the
Recordings") and shall record the Music in a first class recording studio
to a commercial and technical quality suitable for the synchronisation of
the Recordings made therefrom in timed relation with the Film and for
the reproduction therefrom of Records for sale to the public. The
Composer shall deliver the Recordings to the Company on or
before.......................20.....
1.3. The Composer acknowledges that the soundtrack for the Film shall
include certain music and recordings thereof ("the Licensed Music")
written and recorded prior to the date hereof and owned or controlled by
third parties. The details of the Licensed Music are specified in Schedule
A hereof and in rendering the Services hereunder the Composer shall
take account of such Licensed Music to be included in the Film and such
Licensed Music shall not be deemed to be Recordings or Music
hereunder. The Composer shall arrange clearance and pay all necessary
fees for all Licensed Music.

2. The Composer hereby agrees, warrants and undertakes with the
Company that:

2.1 The Composer will render the Services hereunder to the full extent of
his creative and artistic skill and technical ability.

2.2 The Music and the Recordings will be wholly original to the
Composer and will not infringe the copyright or any other like right of any
person firm or company.
2.3 The Composer is free to enter into this Agreement and that he has
the unencumbered right to grant to the Company all of the rights and
Services hereby granted and that no prior contract or agreement of any
kind entered into by the Composer will interfere in any way with the
proper performance of this Agreement by the Composer.
2.4 The Composer will execute do and deliver all such acts deeds and
instruments as the Company may at it's own expense from time to time
require for the purpose of confirming or further assuring it's title to the
rights assigned or intended to be assigned hereunder.
2.5 The Composer will indemnify and hold the Company harmless
against all claims costs proceedings demands losses damages and
expenses arising out of any breach of any of the warranties and
representations and agreements on his part contained in this Agreement.
2.6 That no material composed by the Composer recorded on the
Recordings will in any way infringe the rights of any third party.
2.7 That the Composer hereby grants to the Company (and it's licensees
and assignees) on behalf of the Composer and any person whose
performances are embodied on the Recordings the requisite consents
pursuant to the provisions of the Copyright Designs and Patents Act
1988 or any similar legislation throughout the world in order that the
Company and it's licensees an assignees shall have the fullest use of
the Composer's and such persons services hereunder and the products
thereof.
2.8 That the Composer and all other persons who have performed on the
Recordings hereby irrevocably and unconditionally waive any and all
moral rental lending and like rights the composer and such persons may
have pursuant to the Copyright Designs and Patents Act 1988 or
otherwise in respect of the Recordings the Music and the performances
embodied thereon.

3. In consideration of the agreements on the Company's behalf herein
contained the Composer with full title guarantee hereby assigns (subject
to the rights in the Music vested in the Performing Rights Society Limited
("PRS") and it's affiliated societies by virtue of the Composer's
membership of PRS) to the Company and it's successors in title (and so
far as the same has not been completed at the date hereof by way of
immediate assignment of future copyright) and for the full periods of
copyright and all renewals and extensions thereof throughout the world
("the Territory") whether now or hereafter existing the entire copyright
rental rights and all like rights whether now or hereafter existing in the
Recordings and the product of the Services and all Masters thereof and
the Composer hereby grants to the Company (it's licensees and assigns)
the exclusive right and licence to use the Music in synchronisation with
the Film and to use the Music as incorporated in trailers therefor and to
record broadcast transmit exhibit and perform for an unlimited number of
times and otherwise distribute and exploit by sale hire or otherwise in all
and any media (including videos) the Music as part of or in
synchronisation with the Film or trailers therefor or upon Records
incorporating all or part of the soundtrack of the Film for the full period of
copyright and any and all renewals and extensions thereof throughout

the universe TO HOLD the same unto the Company absolutely throughout the Territory.

4. The Composer hereby grants to the Company (and warrants and undertakes that it is entitled to make such grant):

4.1 The irrevocable right to issue publicity concerning the Composer's Services and the product of the Services hereunder including the right to use and allow others to use the names professional names likeness, photograph and biography of the Composer and all musicians featured on the Recordings in Connection with the Music, the Recordings and/or the Film and the exercise of the rights granted hereunder.

4.2 The right to decide when and/or whether to commence cease or recommence the production of Records embodying the Recordings on whatsoever label and the right to fix and alter the price at which such Records are sold.

4.3 The right to licence grant transfer or assign without having to obtain any further consent from the Composer all or any of it's rights (including without limitation any or all of it's rights in the Recordings and the Music) hereunder and the benefit of this Agreement to any third party.

5. The Composer hereby further authorises and empowers the Company at the Company's expense to take such steps and proceedings as the Company may from time to time consider or be advised are necessary to protect and reserve to the Company all rights hereby granted or expressed to be granted to the Company and the Composer hereby further authorises and empowers the Company and hereby appoints the Company his Attorney to institute actions and proceedings in the name of the Composer (but in any event at the Company's expense) or otherwise in respect of the infringement or violation of any of the rights hereby assigned or granted or expressed to be assigned or granted.

6. The Composer shall at the Company's request and expense take such steps and proceedings as the Company may require and to execute all or any further documents to vest in the Company and/or to renew and extend any and all rights an/or copyrights assigned or agreed to be assigned hereunder and which are or may hereafter be secured upon the Music and the Recordings or any part thereof and after such renewal or extension to transfer and assign to the Company the rights herein granted for such renewal or extended term. In the event that the Composer shall fail so to do within 7 (seven) business days of receiving a request therefor the Company is hereby authorised and empowered to exercise and perform such acts and to take such proceedings in the name and on behalf of the Composer and as the Attorney-in-fact for the Composer.

7. As full and final consideration for the Services hereunder and for the grant of rights in respect of the Music and the Recordings contained herein and for the physical tapes and for all expenses incurred by the Composer in arranging the Recordings the Company shall pay to the Composer the

7.1 The sum of £......(.......pounds) payable on signature hereof (receipt of which is hereby acknowledged).

7.2 A royalty in respect of Records reproducing only the Recordings sole paid for and not returned and the said royalty shall be calculated upon the Royalty Base Price of each such Record at the rate of 7% (seven percent) ("the Royalty Rate") and subject as hereinafter appears.

7.3 The remuneration payable to the Composer by the Company pursuant to clauses 7.1 and 7.2 in respect of the Services is and shall represent full and final consideration for the Services and the entire product of such Services and the rights granted to the Company hereunder and shall include any and all residual repeat rerun foreign use exploitation and other fees and payments of whatever nature due to the Composer or the Composer by virtue of any guild or trade union agreement and any and all payments due to the funds of any guild or union or other similar taxes and state and government and social security contributions. No further or additional payment shall be due from the Company to the Composer in respect of any of the foregoing or by reason of the number of hours in a day or days in the week in which the Services shall have been rendered or for any other reason whatever.

7.4 The Company shall ensure that mechanical royalties are payable to the appropriate collection society and/or publisher in respect of the sale of Records embodying the Music.

8.1 In respect of a Record reproducing the Recordings and also recordings not the subject of this Agreement the royalty payable to the Composer shall be that proportion of the Royalty Rate which the Recordings reproduced on such Record bear to the total number of recordings reproduced thereon.

8.2 No royalties shall be payable upon promotional Records given away free goods Records sold or distributed under any arrangement for the sale of deleted Records promotional Records Records for which the Company is not paid Records sold at a discount at 50% (fifty percent) or more from published price audio-visual Records.

8.3 If in any agreement made between the Company and the Company's licensees or assigns the royalty payable to the Company by the Company's licensees or assigns or the basis upon which such royalty is calculated shall be reduced (including all reduced rate half rate terminal reductions and royalty free provisions) then the royalty and Royalty Rate payable to the Composer shall be reduced by a like proportion.

8.4 The Composer shall have the first option to produce any soundtrack Record of the Film upon terms to be agreed if the Company in it's sole discretion decides to release such a Record. The costs of editing, remixing and converting the Recordings produced for the Film for the purpose of reproducing the Recordings upon Records shall be treated as an advance against the first recoupable from any and all royalties due to the Composer hereunder pursuant to clause 7.1.

9.1 The Company shall supply to the Composer within 90 (ninety) days after the end of June and December in each year a statement showing the latest information received by the Company during such half year period as to the number of Records sold and the amount of royalty due to the Composer. The Company shall be entitled to establish a reserve for potential returns of Records apparently sold in any half year in a reasonable quantity. The Company's liability to pay royalty to the Composer hereunder shall be limited to the amounts thereof actually received by the Company and the Company may deduct and retain from any sum payable to the Composer hereunder any withholding taxes required to be deducted by any government or law.

9.2 The Composer hereby directs the Company to make all payments due to the Composer to (name of agent if any) whose receipt thereof shall be a full and sufficient discharge of the Company's obligations in respect of such payments.

10.1 The Company shall accord the Composer on all positive prints of the Film made by or to the order of the Company a main title credit on a separate card substantially in the form "Original Music by".

10.2 The Company shall instruct the distributors and exhibitors of the Film to accord the Composer credit as hereinabove provided on all prints of the Film issued by such distributors and exhibitors but the Company shall not be liable for the neglect or default of any such distributors or exhibitors so long as it shall have notified the distributors of the credit to which the Composer is entitled hereunder.

10.3 The Company shall use it's best endeavours to afford a credit to the Composer upon all paid advertising for the Film subject to the distributor's usual credit exclusions.

10.4 In respect of soundtrack Records of the Film the Company shall accord the Composer a credit in the form "Original Music by" on the back cover and label of the Record save that such credit shall appear on the front cover and label of the said Records if 50% (fifty percent) or more of the Recordings featured on such Record were performed by the Composer and a credit "Produced by Stephen Warbeck" if 50% (fifty percent) or more of the Recordings featured on such Record were produced by the Composer on the back cover and label thereof but otherwise on the same terms and conditions as set out in this clause.

10.5 No casual or inadvertent failure to accord the Composer or any other party credit hereunder shall constitute a breach of this Agreement by the Company and/or the Composer's remedies in the event of a breach shall be confined to recovery of damages.

11. The Composer acknowledges that it and the Composer has prior to signature hereof received independent expert advice on the contents hereof to enable him to understand fully the terms of this Agreement.

12. In the event of a breach of this Agreement by Company the Composer shall not be entitled to equitable relief or to terminate or rescind this Agreement or any of the rights granted to Company herein or to restrain enjoin or otherwise impair the production distribution advertising or other exploitation of the Film the Composer's sole remedy being an action at law for damages if any.

13. For the purposes hereof the following words shall have the following meanings:

"Record" - shall mean vinyl records, compact discs, tapes, cassettes, CDI, CD Roms or any other device or contrivance whether now know or to be invented in the future reproducing sound alone (with or without visual images) but excluding videocassettes, videotapes and/or videodiscs embodying the Film.

"Recordings" - shall mean the original sound recordings or combination of recordings recorded hereunder and embodying the Music or any part thereof (whether on recording tape lacquer wax disc or any other material).

"Master" - shall mean a 2(two) track stereo Dolby tape recording fully edited equalised and leadered and of a first class standard suitable for synchronisation with the Film and the reproduction of Records therefrom.

"Royalty Base Price" - shall mean the retail price upon which royalties payable to the Company are calculated by it's licensees and assigns (net of packaging allowances and sales taxes).

"Copyright" - shall mean the entire copyright and design right subsisting under the laws of the United Kingdom and all analogous rights subsisting under the laws of each and every jurisdiction throughout the world.

14. All notices writs legal process or any other documents served under or in respect of this Agreement shall be addressed to the party to be served at the address of that party hereinbefore appearing or at such other address for service as may be notified by each to the other in writing and shall be sent by registered letter or recorded delivery in which event such notice shall be deemed to have been received 3 (three) days after the posting thereof.

15. This Agreement shall be exclusively governed by English law and the High Court of Justice in England shall be the exclusive Court of Jurisdiction. Nothing herein contained shall constitute or create or be deemed to create or constitute a partnership between the parties hereto.

AS WITNESS the hand of the parties the day and year first before written

SIGNED by.....................................(.............................)
for and on behalf of........................(.............................)
in the presence of:..........................(.............................)

SIGNED...(.............................)
in the presence of ....(.............................)

Accompanying Notes

Clause 1.3: The Composer (or sometimes the Producer) has to arrange for the use of pre existing music that is incorporated in the soundtrack and arrange and pay for licences to use any such music.

Clause 3: A Composer cannot assign his/her right to receive payment from PRS and they remain the beneficiaries of any income paid to the PRS, which is a collection society for musicians. The Composer must specifically grant the right to allow the music to be played in sync with the film. This is a specific right. This agreement only allows the Producer to use the music for this purpose and does NOT allow the Producer to publish the music.

Clause 5: This gives the Producer the ability to take any legal action to prevent a third party using the music for their film if the Composer does not agree to do so.

Clause 6: A "further assurance" clause is used in contracts where a grant or licence of rights is made. This ensures the producer has all the necessary documents to perfect their right or interests in the licence or grant of rights.

Clause 7.2: A Composer will often get a royalty from any records made whether the Producer acts as the music publisher or whether they negotiate a deal with a third party. This royalty obligation must be made clear to any publisher as the Producer is primarily liable under this type of agreement to make any such payment to the Composer.

Clause 7.4: Mechanical royalties are paid to MCPS and are due when the records are sold.

Clause 8.1: The Composer gets a proportion of the royalty rate according to the proportion of his/her music incorporated on the recording i.e. if there were 6 tracks and only 3 were the Composer's music he/she would get half the royalty.

Clause 8.3: If the Producer assigns the Composer's agreement to a third party (i.e the distributor/financier) and under it's deal it gets a lower Royalty Rate then the Composer agrees to accept that lower rate.

Clause 8.4: The Composer is given the chance to arrange the music for any record produced.

TOP 21 POINTS TO LOOK FOR IN A SALES AGENT/DISTRIBUTION AGREEMENT

1. An Advance: Rarely given, usually only if the Film needs completion money, in which case the Sales Agent may take a higher commission.

2. No. of Years for the rights to be licensed to the Sales Agent/Distributor: From 5 to 35, standard is 5-10 years.

3. Extent of Rights being requested by Sales Agent/Distributor: i.e. worldwide, worldwide exc. domestic, worldwide exc. America, etc. to be negotiated between the parties.

4. Fees/rate of commission: Usually between 20 - 25%. Sometimes 30% depending on extent of input by Sales Agent/Distributor and this should be limited so that the Distributor takes only one commission per country.

5. Ownership: Make sure you, the producer, will still own the copyright to the Film - not applicable if you are selling the film to the Distributor. If you are licensing the rights to certain territories you will remain the copyright owner.

6. CAP on Expenses: Make sure there is a maximum limit on expenses and that you are notified in writing of any large expenses i.e. over a specified amount.

7. Direct Expenses: Make sure that overheads of the Distributor are not included in Distribution expenses and will not be added as a further expense.

8. Sub Distributor Fees: Make sure that these fees are paid by the Sales Agent/Distributor out of it's fees and not in addition to the Distribution expenses.

9. Consider you position on Net Receipts: i.e. monies after Distributor has deducted their commission and fees subject to any sales agreements you enter into with a Distributor.

10. Errors and Omissions Policy: See if this is to be included in the delivery requirements as this could be an added unexpected expense.

11. Cross Collaterisation: Where the Distributor will offset expenses and losses on their other films against yours. You don't want this.

12. P & A (Prints and Advertising) commitment from the Distributor: Negotiate total expenses that will be used on P & A in the contract i.e. a fixed sum.

13. Domestic Theatrical Release: Negotiate what print run is expected, and in what locations.

14. Distribution Editing Rights: Limit for only censorship requirements although if you are dealing with a major Distributor this will not be acceptable.

15. Producer's input in the marketing campaign.

16. Trailer commitment: Will this be another hidden additional cost? Make sure theatres have this in plenty time.

17. Release window: Get Distributor to commit to release the film within a time frame after delivery of film to Distributor.

18. Audit Rights: The Producer has the rights to inspect the books re: the distribution of the film.

19. If the Sales Agent intends to group your film with other titles to produce an attractive package for buyers, ensure that your film is not unfairly supporting the other films or that you are receiving a disproportionate or unfair percentage.

20. Make sure that the rights revert back to the Producer in case of any type of insolvency or if the Agent is in material breach of the agreement.

21. Check the Delivery requirements very carefully.

SALES AGENCY AGREEMENT

BETWEEN:

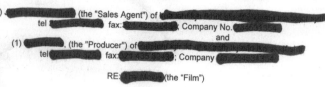

(1) _____ (the "Sales Agent") of _____
tel _____ fax: _____; Company No. _____
and

(1) _____, (the "Producer") of _____
tel _____ fax: _____; Company _____

RE: _____ (the "Film")

DEAL TERMS

1. The Producer hereby appoints the Sales Agent as its sole and exclusive sales agent for the Film and the Sales Agent accepts such appointment in accordance with this Agreement.

2. The particulars of the Film are as set out in Schedule A and the Producer undertakes to make and deliver the Film in accordance with such particulars.

3. PAYMENTS : Address for Payments of sum due to Producer: _____

4. DELIVERY DATE: The Producer shall effect delivery by no later than 07/01/2000 of the items set out in the attached Schedule B.

5. RANK FILM LABORATORY: The Sales Agent shall have full access to all materials delivered to the laboratory in accordance with the Laboratory Access Letter set out in Schedule C.

6. TERRITORY: the World - Holdbacks - none

7. MEDIA RIGHTS GRANTED: the Sales Agent is appointed sole and exclusive agent in respect of all distribution rights in any and all media including but not limited to theatrical, non-theatrical, all forms of TV, video on demand, cable, satellite, all forms of video, and ancillary rights such as airlines, hotels, schools but excluding soundtrack, music publishing and merchandising rights throughout the Territory.

8. TERM: Commencing on the date hereof until the expiry of the end of the year which is 30 years after Delivery of the Film pursuant to this Agreement, that is 2029.

9. Sales Forecasts - attached as Schedule D.

10. COLLECTION ACCOUNT: A sales collection account shall be established by the Sales Agent with Barclays Bank or a third party Collection Agent appointed by the Producer shall open a collection account (the "Collection Account"), from which the Sales Agent shall be paid its Sales Fees and Distribution Expenses in accordance with this Agreement.

11. The Sales Agent is authorised by the Producer to enter into sales/distribution contracts and sign AFM International Rights Distribution Agreements (Short Form Version) (aka "Deal Memos") in the name of and as the disclosed agent for the Producer.

12. This Agreement shall be deemed to include the Deal Terms, Standard Terms and Conditions and the Schedules annexed hereto. In the event of any discrepancy between the Deal Terms and the Standard Terms and Conditions the terms of the Deal Terms shall prevail.

THIS AGREEMENT is executed by the parties hereto this 7th day of January, 2000.

BY: _____   BY: _____

For and on behalf of PRODUCER   For and on behalf of _____

STANDARD TERMS AND CONDITIONS

1. DEFINITIONS

1. The following terms shall have the following meanings in this Agreement:-

"Business Day" - means a day (other than a Saturday) when banks are open for business in the United Kingdom;

"Collection Account" - means the separate trust account held at the Bank pursuant to the Collection Agreement or if no Collection Agreement the bank account opened by the Sales Agent for collection of Collected Receipts;

"Collection Agent" - means the bank selected to manage and operate the Collection Account (if any);

"Collection Agreement" - means the agreement (if any) to be entered into between the parties hereto governing the receipt, administration and disbursements of Receipts;

"Collected Receipts" - means Receipts generated by the exploitation and distribution of the Rights in the Film in the Territory to the extent actually received by the Collection Agent or the Sales Agent net of deduction of any withholding, sales or similar taxes and all costs and expenses of remittance and conversation and less any part or parts thereof which comprise (i) the payment or reimbursement by Local Distributors in respect of the cost of delivery materials supplied to Local Distributors and any freight or insurance costs in connection therewith (ii) prizes, subsidies or aid (iii) cable re-transmission fees (iv) any amounts paid to the Sales Agent by way of returnable deposits or advances or which are otherwise subject to a condition requiring repayment in any circumstances until the same become non-returnable (v) recoveries from infringements;

"Delivery" - means the delivery and acceptance by the Sales Agent of the items listed in Schedule B hereto and the laboratory letter in the form set out in Schedule C produced and completed in accordance with this Agreement to the Sales Agent at such locations as Sales Agent may specify.

"Distribution Expenses" - means the aggregate of all costs, expenses and charges incurred by the Sales Agent in providing its services hereunder including without limitation, the cost of release prints, replacements, re-recording, preparation or trailers, processing, repairing, packing, shipping, transportation, insurance, advertising, publicity, personal transport, living and incidental expenses for promotion, administration and negotiation purposes, printing and distribution to trade, all advertising and screening costs, novelties, personal appearance fees, telexes, faxes, mailing, courier, pro-rated share of convention costs, auditors, photography, all import and export fees, levies, licenses, tariffs, duties, censorship expenses, costs incurred in connection with cuts, editing, dubbing, lengthening, modifying of the Film, attendance at any and all exhibition of the Film, all costs in connection with reparation of foreign versions, amounts allocated in connection with checking accounts, collection and costs of security and maintaining copyright, any royalties or profit or any other financial participation's, reuse fees and transmission fees, cost of delivery materials not provided and costs of taking, defending and settling any and all legal actions, claims, allegations, disputes, controversies, causes of action.

["the Fee" means the finder's fee to be paid to the Sales Agent for finding finance for the Film, of an amount equal to [£   ] payable on completion of financing or first day of principal photography whichever is the earlier in accordance with a Finders/Executive Producer Agreement;]

"Film" - means as described in Schedule A, a film or films or programmes and associated sound-tracks whether made for theatrical release, television or any other media based on the Screenplay;

"Licensing Distributor" - means a distributor or licensee to whom the Sales Agent grants the right to exploit the Film by means of any of the Media in any part or parts of the Territory;

"Local Agreement" - means an agreement with a Local Distributor for the distribution, sale and exploitation by such Local Distributor of the Film by means of any of the Media (as set out in the Deal Memo) in any part or parts of the Territory;

"Receipts" - means receipts to be paid to the Collection Account by Local Distributors and any advance or minimum guarantee on account thereof together with al prizes, subsidiaries or aid, all cable transmission fees, blank tape levies and other similar collections and recoveries from infringements;

"Rights" - the sole and exclusive right in relation to the Film and all parts or versions thereof (now or hereafter existing) in all formats, sizes and gauges, to exhibit, sell, reproduce, transmit, broadcast, project, perform, distribute or exploit in any manner relating thereto in all media now or hereafter known, including the Media (as defined herein) including without limitation theatrical exhibition, all forms of television exhibition (including without limitation network, syndication, cable television, "Pay TV" MDS DBS, pay per view, satellite, toll and closed circuit television and referred to as "Television Rights") video-on-demand, video cassettes or discs, videograms, laser discs, 8mm cassettes, and all similar electronic or mechanical devices (whether now known or hereafter created and referred to as "Video Rights"), non-theatrical exhibition including without limitation use of exhibition in aircraft, military and government establishments, libraries, schools, hospitals, churches and other institutions (referred to as "Non-theatrical Rights") and to make arrangements and enter into agreements with sub-licensees, sub-distributors or any other third party in respect to any or all of the above rights, and the right in the Sales Agent's sole discretion to do or authorise others to do the following with respect to the Film:-

(a) make foreign language versions and cut, edit and insert dubbed and synchronised versions of the Film; and

[(b) use the title and insert the Sales Agent's logo and credit onto the Film and to change, revise, cut, edit and adapt the title and Film as Sales Agent shall determine in its sole discretion; and]

(c) advertise, publicise and promote the Film with other materials or alone and to have sole discretion as to the content, design and frequency, advertising/publicity agency and other such arrangements and for these purposes to publish synopses and excerpts and use all and any copyright material included in the Film and to broadcast for promotional purposes by radio, television or other means parts of the Film and to create, exhibit, and distribute trailers incorporating material from the Film and to use the names biography reproductions of the physical likeness and photographs of any person contributing to or performing in the Film and to use exerpts of the Film on the internet for promotional purposes;

[(d) grant and permit the exercise by third parties of the right of first negotiation and matching last refusal in relation to the right to make remakes, serials, prequels and sequels based on or derived from the Film;]

(e) enter into, alter and conclude and cancel all contracts for the distribution, lease, licence, exploitation, exchange, rental, sale, sub-distribution, grant, authorisation, barter or assignment of all or any rights granted herein to Sales Agent and to collect payments adjust and settle disputes relating thereto.

"Sales Fees" - means [twenty five per cent (25%)]of Collected Receipts;

2. APPOINTMENT
The Producer irrevocably appoints the Sales Agent through the Territory for the Term as the Producer's sole and exclusive agent to exhibit, distribute, broadcast, licence, subdistribute, market, exploit, sell, advertise, publicise, perform, dispose of, turn to account and otherwise deal in or with the Film and the soundtrack thereof and to license such rights to others and/or any part thereof or rights therein or thereto in such manner and in and by such Media (now known or hereinafter devised) as the Sales Agents may in its sole discretion determine.

3. SALES AGENTS OBLIGATIONS
Subject to this Agreement the Sales Agent agrees to use its reasonable efforts to distribute and exploit the Film throughout the Territory in its sole business judgement. The Sales Agent shall use reasonable endeavors to sell the Film for the prices set out in Schedule D provided however the Sales Agent makes no representation to the Producer or any third party that such prices are attainable.

4. DELIVERY
The Producer shall deliver those items listed in Schedule B namely: the completed Film, free of any and all liens, claims and encumbrances (other than any customary lien by a Completion Guarantor to secure payment of amounts expended to complete production of the Film) fully cut, edited, scored and ready for release in all respects, and complying in all respects with all of the material specifications, approvals, terms and conditions, shall be fully delivered to the Sales Agent or to the laboratory as the Sales Agent shall designate, at the Producer's sole cost and expense on or before the Delivery Date, time being of the essence. Delivery shall not be deemed complete until all items in Schedule B have been delivered which items shall be of first class technical quality suitable for commercial exploitation.

5. PRODUCER'S WARRANTIES
The Producer warrants and represents with the Sales Agent as follows:-

(a) that the Film and all material delivered hereunder shall be of first-class technical quality suitable for exhibition, broadcast, transmission, distribution and dissemination to the public throughout the Territory;

(b) that upon execution hereof the Sales Agent shall be the sole and exclusive agent in respect of the Film throughout the Territory and all obligations and commitments which in any way affect the exploitation of the Rights shall have been fully paid and satisfied;

(c) that the Film will not violate or infringe upon the rights of any person, firm or corporation including without limitation, copyright, moral rights of authors, performers rights, trademark rights and such use or exploitation shall not constitute a libel or slander upon any person, company, entity or from material delivered hereunder, shall not contain unlawful material and the Producer warrants it has conducted a title search and know of no reason or adverse claim which would prevent or cause liability by reason of the use of the title;

(d) there are no claims and no litigation is pending or threatened which will adversely affect the Rights and the Producer has not granted and will not hereafter grant any licence, assignment, charge, lien, mortgage or encumbrance whatsoever to any person, firm or corporation in respect of the Rights or material or rights granted hereunder to Sales Agent and will not appoint another agent or otherwise dispose of or deal with the Film in any rights therein in the Territory and the Film and Rights are free from all charges, mortgages, liens, claims and other encumbrances.

(e) the Film shall be based on the Screenplay and the Producer shall upon the Sales Agent's request supply to the Sales Agent copies of all agreements forming the chain-of-title by virtue of which the Producer has acquired the rights in the Screenplay and the Film;

(f) that all persons contributing copyright material used in the Film have waived their moral rights;

(g) that there are no third party restrictions that may be imposed in respect of the exercise of the Rights granted hereunder nor any residual, reuse or use fees or payments due (including without limitation profit participation) or that can be claimed other than those disclosed to and approved in writing by the Sales Agent before Delivery;

(h) in respect of any musical recording or composition used or recorded in the Film the Producer has obtained and will throughout the Term maintain irrevocable assignable rights and licences to record, reproduce, transmit, perform and exploit the same alone and in synchronisation with the Film throughout the Territory for the full period of copyright payments for recording the dialogue, sound effects and music in the Film and for the use of the Rights therein has been paid by the Producer on or before Delivery save for monies payable to performing rights societies;

(i) copyright in the Film and in all copyright material incorporated in the Film or upon which the Film is based is and shall remain valid and subsisting throughout the Term in the Territory;

(j) the signature and execution of this Agreement has been authorised by all appropriate persons on behalf of the Producer; and

(k) On reasonable notice from the Sales Agent at any time, the Producer shall supply the Sales Agent with all documents and other information required by the Sales Agent in its discretion with respect to evidence of compliance or otherwise by the Producer of its warranties, undertakings or agreements contained herein.

6. PRODUCER'S UNDERTAKINGS

The Producer hereby undertakes with the Sales Agent as follows:-

(a) at their own expense to effect Delivery of the Film including without limitation all items listed in Schedule B hereto, fully titled, synchronised and ready for immediate exhibition not later than Delivery Date;

(b) at the request of the Sales Agent to do all such further acts and execute all such further documents as may from time to time be required by the Sales Agent for the purposes of assuring to the Sales Agent the rights granted hereunder. If the Producer fails to execute the said documents within seven (7) days the Producer hereby authorises the Sales Agent to execute such documents and all costs incurred by the Sales Agent pursuant to the execution shall be borne by the Producer;

(c) to defend, indemnify, save and hold harmless the Sales Agent, its assignees, representatives, successors licensees, affiliates, subdistributors, employees, officers, directors, shareholders, agents and independent contractors from any and all loss, damage, liability and expense including without limitation, reasonable legal fees and court costs (whether or not litigation is actually commenced), which may be incurred as a result of or in connection with any breach or alleged breach of any representation warranty or undertaking of the Producer hereunder;

(d) upon signature Producer shall supply to the Sales Agent originals duly executed of the following documents referred to in Schedule B:

> Short Form Assignment;
> Certificates in French;

(e) to pay the Sales Agent upon or within 10 (ten) days of a request therefor the Sales Agent's reasonable costs of performing any other services which the Sales Agent may perform at the Producer's request;

(f) that the Sales Agent shall be entitled to include its customary presentation credit on the negative and all positive copies and/or prints of the Film and all tracks and promotional material in respect of the Film, and to authorise its agents, licensees, subdistributors, designees and assignees to include their respective presentation credits and logos in a like manner in their respective territories;

(g) to effect a world-wide Errors and Omissions Insurance Policy for the Film with an insurance company acceptable to the Sales Agent for such sum as the Sales Agent shall consider appropriate and effective for a minimum period expiring 3 (three) years from the Delivery of the Film to the Sales Agent, such insurance shall not be cancellable without notice to all loss payees and additional insured parties and shall name the Producer and the Sales Agent and any third parties notified by the Sales Agent including any relevant distributors and their bankers (inter alia) as additional insured parties.

7. CREDIT

(a) Producer shall deliver to the Sales Agent for approval a full and detailed list of final screen and advertising credit requirements and the Sales Agent shall comply therewith provided that the Sales Agent shall not be liable for any error, neglect or default on the part of the Producer in the preparation and delivery of such list and the Producer shall defend, indemnify, save and hold the Sales Agent harmless against any loss, liability, damage, cost, debt or expense incurred by the Sales Agent, its affiliates, sub-distributors, licensees, assigns, representatives, agents, employees, officers, directors, shareholders and independent contractors as a result of or in connection with any such error, neglect or default.

(b) No casual or inadvertent failure by the Sales Agent nor any failure by its licensees or assignees to comply with the provisions of this clause shall constitute a breach hereof and in any event the Producer's remedy and the Producer shall ensure that any remedy of any third party providing services or goods (including initial limitation copyright) shall be limited to damages and the Producer nor any third party shall be entitled to equitable (including without limitation injunctive relief) relief or termination of this Agreement.

8. COLLECTION

8.1 The Sales Agent shall collect all initial distribution deposits payable by distributors under Licensing Agreements and will retain these until the production financing is agreed. It will be at the Sales Agent's sole discretion to release this deposit to the production at any earlier date. The Producer shall not be liable, responsible or accountable for such deposits whilst they remain under the control of the Sales Agent. [As part of the production loan documentation, the Producer shall arrange for a Collection Account to be set up into which all such deposits shall be paid to the extent that they have not been applied towards the cost of production of the Film and into which Collection Account Receipts shall be collected from the sale, exploitation and distribution of the Film and from which all the financial entitlements of the Film shall be administered and disbursed to all interested parties pursuant to the terms of the Collection Agreement.] or [The Sales Agent shall set up a Collection Account into which all Receipts shall be collected and monitored in accordance with this Agreement].

8.2 It is acknowledged by the parities that all Licensing Agreements shall provide for the payment of all monies and other consideration payable thereunder directly into the Collection Account. In accordance with the terms of the [this Agreement/Collection Agreement,] the Collection Agent shall pay directly to the Sales Agent the Distribution Expenses, Sales Fees and reimbursements it is entitled to receive hereunder out of the Receipts actually received and deposited in the Collection Account provided that no sums shall be disbursed from the Collection Account before a completion guarantee has been issued in connection with the production of the Film or, if earlier, commencement of photography of the Film, without the written consent of the Sales Agent, and the Producer. In the event that the Producer or the Sales Agent receives any sum which constitutes Receipts directly, the Producer or the Sales Agent (as the case may be) shall hold such sums in trust and shall immediately deposit such sums into the Collection Account.

9. ACCOUNTING

(a) Sales Agent agrees to keep available during normal business hours for inspection all usual books of account relating to exploitation of the rights in the Territory and all costs and expenses incurred for a period of 2 (two) years after monies relating thereto are contracted and the Producer's authorised accountants shall be entitled to inspect such books not more frequently than once in any calendar year upon reasonable notice and at Producer's expense.

(b) Sales Agent shall prepare statements of account made up to the end of every calendar period, which period is defined as every month for the first two (2) years from delivery and every quarter for the next two (2) years and every six (6) months for the next two (2) years, and thereafter six (6) monthly only when sales income is received, (herein referred to as "Statements") and shall send such statements to the Producer within thirty (30) days following the end of the period to which they relate.

(c) Statements shall be deemed conclusively true and accurate if not disputed in writing by Producer within one (1) year after being delivered to Producer.

10. APPLICATION OF RECEIPTS

Subject to Clause 8 above Receipts shall be paid into the Collection Account and together with any interest thereon shall be paid and applied in the manner and order set out in Schedule E hereto (which shall be reflected in the Collection Agreement, if any);

11. EDITING AND TITLE

The Sales Agent shall be entitled throughout the Territory during the Term to authorise others:

(a) to use the Film's title or any translation thereof of the Film in connection with the distribution exhibition exploitation advertising and any others uses thereof to change the said title and to use any other title in any language to designate the Film but no warranty of Producer shall be applicable to (any of) the said changed title;

(b) to arrange or commission the subtitling and dubbing of the Film in any language spoken in the Territory and make subtitled and dubbed language versions of the Film for use in the Territory;

(c) to make such changes to the Film as may in the Sales Agent's good faith judgement be necessary for censorship and other regulatory purposes for time segmenting purposes for airline versions and for the interpolation of commercial advertising. If the Producer is available (having strict regard to the Sales Agent's distribution exigencies) to undertake such changes then the Producer will (at their own expense) be offered the first opportunity to undertake any such changes;

12. PRESS AND PUBLICITY

12.1 The Producer will fully co-operate with the Sales Agent to assist with any and all promotional activities including co-ordinating the presence of the cast and director, subject to their availability.

12.2 Each party shall have the right to release individual corporate publicity releases without the consent or approval of the other, but agree to show such releases prior to their distribution.

13. BREACH BY PRODUCER

In the event that Producer is in material breach of any of its obligations hereunder which is incapable of remedy or is in material breach of its obligations hereunder including failure to deliver the Film to the Sales Agent in accordance herewith and fails to cure correct or remedy such breach within thirty (30) days after service of notice specifying the same or in the event that at any time prior to the Delivery Date the following events occur:-

(a) liquidation or bankruptcy proceedings are commenced against the Producer and are not withdrawn within twenty-one (21) workings days;

(b) the Producer shall petition for or consent to any relief under any bankruptcy reorganisation receivership administration, and administration receivership liquidation compromise or arrangement or moratorium statutes whether now in force or hereafter enacted;

(c) the Producer shall make an assignment for the benefit of its creditors or;

(d) the Producer or any other party shall petition for the appointment of a receiver administrator, administrative receiver liquidator trustee or custodian for all or a substantial part of the Producer's assets and the Producer shall not cause him to be discharged within 60 (sixty days from the date of appointment hereof.

14. EFFECT OF BREACH

14.1 The Sales Agent shall be entitled to terminate this Agreement with immediate effect by giving notice in writing to the Producer provided that such termination shall not affect or prejudice the rights and remedies of the parties hereto arising prior to the date of such termination. Such termination may relate to this Agreement as a whole or only to the country or countries of the Territory in respect of which the breach complained of occurs as the Sales Agent in its discretion may elect.

14.2 If the Sales Agent terminates this Agreement pursuant to any right so to do, the Sales Agent shall be released and discharged from all further obligations under this Agreement; provided, however, that the Sales Agent shall have the continuing right to receive and collect all and any Sales Fees, Distribution Expenses, Fees, Profit Shares or otherwise to which it is entitled, and if it shall so elect, to service any or all subdistribution or license agreements with respect to the Film or any rights therein or thereto entered into by the Sales Agent with Local Distributors or third parties prior to the date of such termination. Subject to any claims or damages from the Sales Agent, the Producer shall be entitled to receive its share of Receipts, if any, therefrom for the remainder of the term of such agreements (and for so long thereafter as Receipts if any, shall continue to be derived therefrom).

15. BREACH BY SALES AGENT

This Agreement may be terminated in whole by the Producer if:

(a) the Sales Agent acts in material breach of the Sales Agency Agreement or any other agreement relating to the production of the Film and fails to cure such breach within thirty (30) days of the Sales Agent's receipt from the Producer of written notice of such breach;

(b) the Sales Agent makes an arrangement or composition with its creditors;

(c) if any judgement is obtained against the Sales Agent which substantially affects its credit and financial standing in relation to the Producer and is not discharged without thirty (30) days of such judgement being obtained unless the Sales Agent (as appropriate) shall appeal against such judgement within the time allowed for appeal;

(d) if any distress, execution, sequestration or other process is levied or enforced upon or sued against any chattels or property of the Sales Agent and is not discharged within thirty (30) days;

(e) if the Sales Agent is unable to pay its debts within the meaning of Section 123 of the Insolvency Act 1986 or any statutory modification or re-enactment thereof for the time being in force;

(f) if a petition for liquidation is presented or an order is made or any effective resolution is passed for winding up the Sales Agent except a resolution for reconstruction or amalgamation the terms of which have previously been approved in writing by the Producer (such approval not to be unreasonably withheld or delayed) or an order for the winding up of the Sales Agent which is paid off or otherwise discharged within thirty (30) days;

16. EFFECT OF TERMINATION BY PRODUCER

The Producer shall be entitled to terminate this Agreement with immediate effect by giving notice in writing to the Sales Agent provided that such termination shall not affect or prejudice the rights and remedies of the parties hereto arising prior to the date of termination and the Sales Agent shall continue to be due any outstanding Sales Fees, Distribution Expenses or Fees. Such termination may relate to this Agreement as a whole or only to the country or countries of the Territory in respect of which the breach complained of occurs as the Producer in its discretion may elect.

17. EXPIRY OF TERM

Upon expiry of the Term or upon termination of this Agreement the Sales Agent shall enter into no further arrangements licences or contracts for the exploitation of the Rights or any of them and the Rights shall thereupon revert to the Producer provided that rights of agents, sub-licensees, sub-distributors and exhibitors (sub-licensees) under agreements entered into by the Sales Agent prior to the expiry of the Period (sub-licensees) shall remain unaffected and shall continue until the expiry or exhaustion of the rights granted to them under the sub-licensees and the Sales Agent shall remain solely entitled to collect and account for all further Receipts and to retain the Sales Fees and Distribution Expenses.

18. NOTICES

Any notice required to be served on either party hereunder shall be in writing given or delivered in writing personally by registered prepaid first class mail or by telex or fax to the said party at its address aforesaid or such other address of which it may hereafter give notice to the other party in writing. Any notice sent by registered prepaid first class mail shall be deemed served forty eight (48) hours after it shall have been so sent. Any notice sent by telex or fax shall be deemed served upon telexed or faxed answerback or acknowledgement of receipt.

19. PARTNERSHIP

Nothing herein contained shall constitute a partnership between or joint venture by the parties hereto. Neither party shall hold itself out contrary to the terms of this clause and neither party shall be or become liable by any representation act or omission of the other contrary to the provisions hereof.

20. ASSIGNMENT

The benefit of this Agreement shall not be assigned in whole or in part by the Producer without the prior approval of the Sales Agent.

21. WAIVER

No waiver express or implied by one party hereto of a breach by the other party of any of the provisions of this Agreement shall operate as a waiver of any preceding or succeeding breach of the same or any other provision of this Agreement.

22. PRIOR AGREEMENTS

This Agreement shall supersede and cancel all prior arrangements and understandings between the parties relating thereto whether oral or in writing. No modification hereof shall be valid or binding unless in writing and executed by both parties hereto.

23. FORCE MAJEURE

Notwithstanding anything to the contrary contained in this Agreement if for any reason beyond the control of either party either party shall be delayed in or prevented from performing any of its obligations under this Agreement then such non-performance shall be deemed not to constitute a breach of this Agreement. If this Agreement cannot be enforced or performed according to its terms for a period in excess of six (6) months it shall be deemed to have terminated at the end of such six (6) month period provided that if any such reason shall apply in respect only of one or more countries of the Territory such termination shall apply to such country or countries only.

24.LAW

This Agreement shall be governed by and construed in accordance with the Laws of England and the parties hereby agree to submit to the non-exclusive jurisdiction of the English Courts.

SCHEDULE A

Film Title:
Running Time: 120 mins
Language Recorded in: English
Director:
Principal Cast:
Calendar year in which Film is to be completed:
Screenplay by:
Budget:
Delivery Date: 04/09/2000

SCHEDULE B

DELIVERY REQUIREMENTS

FILM ELEMENTS TO BE DELIVERED:

A.	FILM ELEMENTS	
1.	Release Print	Deliverable Item
2.	Original Negative	Access Item
3.	Internegative - 2 copies	Deliverable Item
4.	Interpositive - 1 copy	Deliverable Item
5.	Sound Negative	Access Item
6.	Dolby or Ultra Stereo	Deliverable Items. If picture is to be exhibited with a Dolby or Ultra Stereo soundtrack, the following materials, items 6a to 6e must be delivered in additionto all other materials.
a	One 35mm four-track magnetic master of the final stereo domestic dub.	Access Items
b	One 35mm optical Dolby two-track Dolby master from the final domestic dub.	Access Items with Interpositive
c	A copy of the executed license agreement between the Producer and Dolby or Ultra Laboratories	Deliverable Item
7	One 35mm four track magnetic master of the final stereo domestic.	Deliverable Item
8	One 35mm optical	Delivery Item
9	Six (6) Track Stereo Soundtrack	Access Item
10	Check Print/Answer Print	Deliverable Item
11	Video Mastering Print (aka Low Contrast Print)	Deliverable Item
12	Magnetic Sound Master ("Three Stripe")	Access Item
13	Textless Title Backgrounds	Deliverable Item
14	Music Tapes	Deliverable Item
115	Coverage Materials	Access Item

TRAILER ITEMS (90-270 seconds duration):

1.	Compositive prints - 3 -	Delivery Item
2.	Negative prints -	Access Item
3.	Textless internegative print	Access Item
4.	Mag sound master	Access Item
5.	Mag M/E track	Access Item
6.	Other trailer materials	Access Item

VIDEO AND AUDIO MATERIALS

A.	NTSC master - Digital Beta and/or D1*	Deliverable Item
B.	PAL Master - Digital Beta and/or D1*	Deliverable Item
C.	Viewing Cassette - PAL and NTSC	Deliverable Item
D.	Reference Cassette	Deliverable Item
E.	Music and Effects Audio Track	Access Item

PROMOTIONAL MATERIALS

1. "PROMO REEL"
    Promotion cassette master - Beta SP or 3/4"
    (i) Promotion cassette consists of 3 to 15 minutes summary of the film (with dialogue and/or narration) or
    (ii) series of sequences from the Film, which capture the "flavour" or "essence" of the film

2. PROMOTION CASSETTES
    20 PAL VHS and 10 NTSC VHS copies

3. ELECTRONIC PRESS KIT (EPK)
    (approximately 30 minutes duration)
    Master Digi Beta (PAL and NTSC) and
    2 Beta SP PAL and 2 Beta NTSC and
    20 VHS PAL and 20 VHS NTSC

    EPK consists of at least two of the three items listed below:

    (i)   Trailer
    (ii)   Promo Reel
    (iii)   Interviews shot on camera with
            - 3 to 6 of leading actors
            - director
            - producer
            - special guest artistes (if any)
            - DOP/writer/music/novelist

4. 4 - PAGE BROCHURE 4 COLOUR
    (layout and content according to Sales Agent's approval)

5. POSTER (portrait size)

6. Campaign for print advertisements

7. Free access to art work for items (4) and (5)

RECORDS AND DOCUMENTATION

A.	Records and Documentation	
1.		Deliverable Item
2.	Combined Dialogue and Action Continuity	Deliverable Item
3.	Final Footage Record	Deliverable Item
4.	Final Main and End Credits	Deliverable Item
5.	Title Materials	Deliverable Item
6.	Paid Ad Credits	Deliverable Item
7.	Video Packaging Credits	Deliverable Item
8.	Dubbing and Subtitling Restrictions	Deliverable Item
9.	Residuals Materials	Deliverable Item
10.	Music Licence	Deliverable Item
11.	Music Licence Materials	Deliverable Item
12.	Synopsis	Deliverable Item
13.	Cast and Technical Personnel List	Deliverable Item
14.	Publicity Materials	Deliverable Item
15.	Promotional Materials	Deliverable Item
16.	Black/White Stills and Negatives - 10 different scenes	Deliverable Item
17.	Colour Still and Negatives and Colour	Deliverable Item
18.	Rights Agreement	Deliverable Item
19.	Service Agreements	Deliverable Item, if requested
20.	Rating Certificate	Deliverable Item, when available
21.	Certificate of Origin - 10 copies	Deliverable Item
22.	Final Certified Statement	Deliverable Item, if available
B.	Certificate of Insurance	Deliverable Item
C.	Chain of Title Documentation	
1.	Title and Copyright Reports	Deliverable Item
2.	Copyright Reports	Deliverable Item
3.	Anti-piracy Documents	Deliverable Item

RECORDS TO BE DELIVERED OR ACCESSIBLE TO THE DISTRIBUTION IF REQUESTED

A.	Script Supervisor's Notes	Access Items, Deliverable upon request
B.	Editor's Line Script	Access Items, Deliverable upon request
C.	Daily Film Code Shoots or Book	Access Items, Deliverable upon request
D.	ADR and Wild Line Recording Logs	Access Items, Deliverable upon request
E.	Conductor's Score of all music recorded for the Film	Access Item
F.	Music Scoring Logs	Access Item
G.	Music Re-recording Cue Sheets	Access Item
H.	Sound Effects Re-recording Cue Sheets	Access Item
I.	Dialogue Re-recording Cue Sheets	Access Item
J.	Negative Cutter's Key Sheets	Access Item

PROTECTION ELEMENTS

A.	Picture Elements	Access Item
B.	Sound Elements	Access Item
C.	Video Masters	Access Item
D.	Audio Recording, Tracks and Masters	Access Item
E.	Other Film Elements	Access Item
F.	Work Materials	Access Item

SCHEDULE C

Laboratory Access Letter

SCHEDULE D

Sales Forecasts

SCHEDULE E

Recoupment Schedule

As witness the hands of the duly authorised officer on the day, month and year first above written.

SIGNED
BY: ▬▬▬▬▬▬▬

For and on behalf of PRODUCER

SIGNED
BY: ▬▬▬▬▬▬▬

For and on behalf of ▬▬▬ LIMITED

Production Forms

On the following pages are several documents used in the production office, on set or in the cutting room. They are a guide, not an absolute, and copies of most can be found on the DVD accompanying this book. They are saved in MS Word format.

Actors Day out of Days - This checklist shows when an actor is on set or not. The information is taken from the Production Schedule. It is used for anyone who needs to know which actors are on set on which day.

Call Sheet - This is handed out to all cast and crew the day before the shoot day it represents. It is created by the 2nd AD and deals with the cast's pick-up, arrival and on-set times and any other relevant departmental information.

Production Checklist - Created by the Production Office as a checklist prior to principal photography and for putting the budget together.

Continuity/Edit Notes - Filled out by the Continuity person and should state all and every detail about the shots, usually as a sheet per shot and can include photographs and diagrams. These are later handed to the Editor as a guideline for putting the rough assembly together.

Petty Cash Expense Report - Must be handed out any time petty cash is issued to keep track of how much money each department is using and how much you have left. It also reminds crew members that they are accountable for any money spent on behalf of the production.

Daily Progress Report - Completed by the 1st AD and usually sent to the Production Office if the shoot is away from the office. Forwarded to Financiers and the Bond Company. It shows exactly how much has been shot on what day, how long it took and who was involved.

Script Breakdown Sheet - The 1st AD should break down every scene of the script to extract what is needed, where it takes place, day or night etc. - essentially, everything needed to shoot the scene.

Locations Checklist - Produced by the Locations Manager, this is a list of things that must be done in advance of the production moving to a location. It also provides useful information for the 2nd AD for the Call Sheets.

Movement Order - Produced by the Location Manager as travel directions. It should also include train times, when possible. Usually attached to Call Sheet for the day it refers to. This is an example only and could include photocopied maps with highlighted routes.

Sample Schedule Page - A single page from a schedule to illustrate the type of information and layout that works. Programs like Movie Magic make producing a schedule easier and it is available for both Mac and PC.

Sound Report - Filled out by the Sound Recordist and sent to the lab, copies also sent to the Editor. Details takes, technical problems and other illustrative information.

Music Cue Sheet - Produced for international sales to detail where and how the music is used in a film, also who own what in terms of publishing and copyright etc.

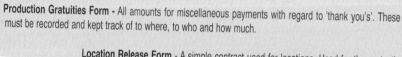

Production Gratuities Form - All amounts for miscellaneous payments with regard to 'thank you's'. These must be recorded and kept track of to where, to who and how much.

Location Release Form - A simple contract used for locations. Used for the protection of both the producer and the owner of the location. Increasingly, locations are becoming harder to negotiate as production has increased dramatically in the last few years.

Product Release Form - Used when commercial products are featured in shot. It's what a corn flakes manufacturer would sign if you used their cornflakes in the movie.

FILES ON THE DISK

LEGAL TOOLKIT AND FORMS

ACTORS DAY OUT OF DAYS

Mad Dog Movies Production Company	Bank Holiday Production Title	Date 17 · 1 · 02
		6 · 1 · 02 version Script Date
Claire Roper Producer	John Oldman Director	Emma Smith / Paul Edwards Prod. Manager/Asst. Director

Rehearsal - R	Hold - H
Started - S	Travel - T
Worked - W	Finish - F
On Call - C	

Day Number: one
Date: 17 · 1 · 02
Day of the Week: Monday

No.	Character	Cast Member
1	EMMA DUGGAN	JOSIE FELLOWES
2	CHRIS KERR	HARVEY WILLIS
3		
4		
5		
6		
7		
8		
9		
10		
11		
12		
13		
14		
15		
16		
17		
18		
19		
20		

No.	M	T	W	T	F	S	S	M	T	W	T	F	S	S	M	T	W	T	F	S	S	M	T	W	T	F	S	S
1	X	X	X	S	R	C	C	W	W	W	W	X	C	X	W	W	R	W	W	C	X	X	X	X	X	X	X	X
2	S	R	W	W	W	C	C	X	X	X	W	W	C	X	W	W	X	W	X	X	X	W	W	W	X	X	X	X
3																												
4																												
5																												
6																												
7																												
8																												
9																												
10																												
11																												
12																												
13																												
14																												
15																												
16																												
17																												
18																												
19																												
20																												

Production office
PM: Emma Smith
23 Movie Avenue
Guerilla Town
KP12 9DR
Tel: 01555 123456
Fax: 01555 123455

Mad Dog Movies
Bank Holiday

Unit office
Loc. Mgr: David Moore
Portacabin 8
Guerilla Indus. Estate
Mob: 555 1234

Date: Monday 17th January 2002
UNIT CALL: 08:00
Breakfast will be on set at 07:30
Estimated Wrap: 18:00

Director: John Oldman
Producer: Claire Roper   Mob: 555 2468
1st A.D. Paul Edwards   Mob: 555 4321

WEATHER: Fine and Dry day, frost in morning, sunshine, a little cloud in the afternoon, light winds

Location 1: Int of Emma's Office at the Industrial site
Location Contact: Mr Bill Travers Tel: 01555 456123

NO SMOKING ON ANY SET

Scene No	Scri pPg.	Int./ Ext.	Description	Story Day	Day/ Night	Pages	Cast
9	5	Int	EMMA'S OFFICE Establishing shot	Day 1	Day	1/8 pgs	
3	1	Int	EMMA'S OFFICE Chris walking towards Emma's office, through window	Day 1	Day	2/8 pgs	1, 2
1c	1	Int	EMMA'S OFFICE Emma and Chris first conversation	Day 1	Day	1/8 pgs	1, 2

NO:	ARTISTE	CHARACTER	PICK –UP TIME	ON SET TO REHEARSE	M/UP/COST	TURNOVER
1	Josie Fellowes	Emma	08:15	08:30	08:45	09:00
2	Harvey Willis	Chris	08:15	08:30	08:45	09:00
SUPPORTING CAST/EXTRAS						

REQUIREMENTS	
PROPS:	Chris's bag & coat, Emma's mobile
ACTION VEHICLES:	Chris's car
MAKE-UP & COSTUME	As per Charlotte and Zoe
CAMERA DEPT:	As per James
CHAPERONE:	NONE
MEDICAL:	Casualty at Queen Victoria Hospital Tel: 01555 654321
CATERING:	Breakfast on set from 07:30, Lunch at 13:00, Tea break at 16:30
RUSHES:	To be given to Barry to take to Metrocolor drop off

ADVANCE SCHEDULE TUESDAY 18th JANUARY 2000							
Scene No	a.o.b.	Script Pg.	Int./ Ext.	Description	Story Day	Day/ Night	Pages	Cast
1d		1	Ext	INDUSTRIAL ESTATE Montage of estate for title sequence	Pre-Story	Day	1/8 pgs	
20a (i)	high crane	10	Ext	INDUSTRIAL ESTATE High shot of Emma & Chris walking through estate	Day 3	Day	1 2/8 pgs	1, 2
20a (ii)	stunt	10	Ext	INDUSTRIAL ESTATE Fight scene between Chris & guard	Day 3	Day	1 2/8 pgs	2, 7,

Call Sheet No 1 Monday 17th January 2002

FILES ON
THE DISK

LEGAL TOOLKIT
AND FORMS

PRODUCTION CHECKLIST

Date *17 . 1 . 02*

Mad Dog Movies
Production Company

Bank Holiday
Production Title

CAST	✓
Deal memos	☐
Contracts signed	☐
Wardrobe fitted	☐
Special make-up	☐
Hair/wigs	☐
Dialogue coach	☐
Stand-ins	☐
Stunt/doubles	☐
Musicians in Picture	☐
Children & licences	☐
Chaperone/tutor	☐
Extras/crowd	☐
Livestock or Animals	☐

KEY CREW	✓
Contracts signed	☐
Wardrobe - special	☐
Armourer	☐
Make-up & body make-up - special	☐
Hair - special	☐
Props - discuss	☐
Stunt Co-ordinator	☐
SPFX co-ordinator	☐
Action vehicles co-ordinator - Special	☐
Greensman - special	☐
Script supervisor - script timing	☐
Paramedics	☐
Unit Nurse/Health and Safety/First Aid Box	☐
Technical advisors	☐
Handlers or Wranglers	☐

CAMERA	✓
Equipment ordered - extra cameras	☐
Film ordered	☐
Video assist	☐

SOUND	✓
Equipment ordered	☐
Stock ordered	☐
Walkie-talkies	☐
Pa system	☐

LOCATION / STUDIO	✓
Dressing rooms	☐
Police	☐
Parking	☐
Firemen & fire permits	☐
Location permits	☐
Heaters/air conditioning	☐
Tables & benches	☐
Location facilities	☐
Hot & Cold water	☐

GRIP	✓
Equipment ordered	☐
Generator - special	☐
Crane	☐

FOOD & DRINK	✓
Breakfast	☐
Lunch	☐
Dinner	☐
Snacks	☐
Tea & Coffee	☐

LABS	✓
Contact address & tel	☐
Rushes drop off/Collection	☐
Special process	☐

MISCELLANEOUS	✓
Petty cash	☐
1st AD Sheets (script breakdown)	☐
Transportation and Lunch Lists	☐
Release forms	☐
Call sheets	☐
Movement orders	☐
Production reports	☐

VEHICLES	✓
Motor homes/caravans	☐
Vehicles - picture or standby	☐
Honey-Wagons/Toilet facilities	☐
Water wagon	☐
Buses/coaches	☐
Trucks	☐

FILES ON THE DISK

CONTINUITY/EDIT NOTES

17 · 1 · 02
Date

Mad Dog Movies
Production Company

Bank Holiday
Production Title

/ **Page**   / **of**

Production No. 1.

		SCENE	SLATE
WEATHER Sunny, dry, windy, cold, no clouds		14	26
LOCATION Unit 8, Penvale Indus Estate			

CAN ROLL	SOUND ROLL	Circle whichever appropriate						CAM INFO	
5	7	(INT) / EXT	(DAY) / NIGHT	(SYNC) / MUTE	(WILD) / (TRACK)	LENS 16	DISTANCE 5'	STOP T 2.8	SP FILTERS Wratten

SHOT DESCRIPTION

Emma meets Chris for the first time at the Indus. Estate.

TAKE	DUR	REMARKS (if ng)	CONTINUITY NOTES (inlc. Costume/props/dialogue etc)
1	0.5sec	ng	boom in shot
2	2mins	✓	fire " I'm looking for Emma Duggan"

FILES ON THE DISK

DAILY PROGRESS REPORT SHEET

17 · 1 · 02	Bank Holiday	1	1
Date	Production Title	Page	of

John	Mad Dog Movies	Paul Edwards.
Director	Production Company	1st AD

Started: 17 · 1 · 02   Finishing Date: 17 · 2 · 02   **Scene Nos:** 14, 16, 24
Scenes scheduled:

Days to date: 1   Location: Perivale   Scenes shot today:

Scenes part shot:

Remaining Days: 27   Weather: Sunny cold dry   Scenes not shot:

TIME   SCRIPT:

Call time: 08 · 00
1st set up completed: 08 · 30
Lunch break: 13 · 00 to 14 · 00
Supper break: n/a to n/a
Breakfast break: n/a to n/a
Unit wrap: 16 · 30
Total hours: 7 1/2 hrs

	total scenes:		pages:
	scenes deleted:		pages:
	scenes shot to date:		pages:
	scenes remaining:		pages:

	No of setups	mins	no of pickups	mins	no of retakes	mins
Prev:						
Today:						
Total:						

ACTORS (s-start day, w-days worked, sb-standby, c-call, s-set, f-finish)   CROWDS

Name	s	w	sb	c	s	f	rate
Josie Fellowes	X						
Harvey Willis							

PICTURE NEGATIVE   SOUND

	exposed	N.G.	Print	waste
Prev.				
Today:				
Total:				

STILLS - COLOUR/B&W:

ARRIVALS:
TRANSPORT:
CATERING:
PROPS:
EFFECTS:
XTRA CREW:
ABSENTEES:
REMARKS:

FILES ON
THE DISK

EXPENSE REPORT FOR PETTY CASH

Mad Dog Movies _____ Bank Holiday _____ B7610
　　Production Company　　　　　Production Title　　　　Petty Cash Voucher No.

Larry Nash _____ Art Department _____ Amanda Roberts.
　　Crew Name　　　　　　　　Department　　　　　　　Issued by

Entered into Accounts	Checked by Accountant	Approved by Production Manager
Amanda Roberts	Amanda Roberts	Clare Roper
Date: 27 · 1 · 02.	Date: 17 · 1 · 02	Date: 17 · 1 · 02.

Crew Only		Accountant Only	
Petty Cash Advance Received	£300	Receipts Paid	£250
Total Receipts	£250	Cash in Hand	£ 50
(Over or Under)	£50.	Total	£300
Crew Signed: Larry Nash.		Accountant Signed: Amanda Roberts.	
Date: 17 · 1 · 02		Date: 17 · 1 · 02.	

Date			Company/Payee	Purpose	Cash/Cheque		Amount	
31	12	01	SUPER HIRE	KITCHEN FURNITURE	✓		£ 200	00
16	01	02	STUDIO + TV HIRE	PAINTINGS	✓		£ —50	00
							£	
							£	
							£	
							£	
							£	
							£	
							£	
							£	
							£	
							£	
							£	
							£	
							£	
							£	
							£	
							£	
							£	
							£	
							£	
							£	
							£	
							£	
							£	
							£	
							£	

FILES ON
THE DISK

SCRIPT BREAKDOWN SHEET

17·01·02   Bank Holiday   /   /
Date   Production Title   Page   of

John   Mad Dog Movies   Clare Roper
Director   Production Company   Producer

17	Chris takes Emma's dog out
Scene Number	Scene Description

CAST NOS	CAST/CHARACTER	INT/EXT	DAY/ NIGHT	W/R	M/U
1	Josie – Emma	INT	NIGHT	As per B	Chris sweat
2	Harvey – Chris				

STAND-INS	CROWD	LOCATION	ART DEPT/CONSTRUCTION	GRIPS
n/a	n/a	Outside Indw in Emma's Hse	Dress Emma's Kitchen and hall	Long track hall

CAMERA	LIGHTING	EXTRA EQUIPMENT	ACTION VEHICLES

TRUCKS/TRAILERS	EXTRA CREW	PROPS/ANIMALS	SFX/WEAPONS
		Emma's Dog called Bertie	

MISC

"Bertie" will be on set from 14·00 hrs. While he is here he will be the most important person on set. Best behaviour, as as soon as he arrives we will need to shoot.

FILES ON THE DISK

LOCATIONS CHECKLIST

Production Company: _Mad Dog Movies_
Production Title: _Bank Holiday_
Producer: _Claire Roper_
Director: _John Silman_

Date _17.1.02_
Location Manager: _David Moore_
Prod. Manager/Asst. Director: _Emma Smith / Paul Edwards._

Location	Contact Tel & Fax No.	All Dates Required	Release Form Issued	Release Form Returned	Schedule A Issued	Police Informed	Movement Order	Nearest Hospital Casualty	Meter Readings	Elec. Source	Rooms & Green Room	Parking
Int. Church	Rev Michaels	13th Feb 02	yes	yes	yes	yes		Ealing 567078	n/a	main church	yes	very limited

FILES ON
THE DISK

A. O. B.   sdc - Steadicam   indpt unit - unit works seperately   2nd unit: Works simultaneously   ngt shoot: night shoot   Day 3a - Extra story day

Shooting Schedule No......

Movie Title

Scene No A.O.B	Scrpt Pg	Int/Ext	Description	Story Day	Day/Night	Pages	Cast
15	9	Int	Boys' Flat LIVING ROOM — Joe comes back from pub, smokes joint, leaves room	Day 1	Day for Night	1 6/8 pgs	2, 4
18	12	Int	Boys' Flat LIVING ROOM — Bob relights joint, having put Joe to bed	Day 1	Day for Night	1/8 pgs	4
68a*	54	Int	Boys' Flat LIVING ROOM — Lady 1 in business attire. Long stare then slaps Bob.	Day 5	Day for Night	1/8 pgs	4, 25
52	43	Int	Boys' Flat BATHROOM — Douglas experiences the mirror	Day 3	Day for Night	1 pg	3
107	79	Int	Boys' Flat BATHROOM — Joe flossing, Bob discussing Alison	Day 10	Day for Night	1 1/8 pgs	2, 4
130	94	Int	Boys' Flat BATHROOM — Alison and Joe being coupley and cleaning teeth in harmony	Day 15	Day	3/8 pgs	2, 5
End of Day 1			Monday 23rd August 2002			4 4/8 pgs (4.5 mins).	
25	16	Int	Boys' Flat LIVING ROOM — Joe tells Bob that he hallucinated last night	Day 2	Day	1 4/8 pgs	2, 4
32	24	Int	Boys' Flat LIVING ROOM — Sitting in flat with their angels, having cups of tea	Day 3	Day	4/8 pgs	1, 2, 3, 4
42	29	Int	Boys' Flat LIVING ROOM — Bob teaching Audrey what dancing is, interrupted by Joe	Day 3a	Day	2 4/8 pgs	1, 2, 3, 4
50a	41	Int	Boys' Flat LIVING ROOM — Reaction shot of Audrey hearing this news through Joe's head	Day 4	Day	1/8 pgs	1
75	57	Int	Boys' Flat LIVING ROOM — Joe and Alison sit, she talks of newspaper story	Day 6	Day	7/8 pgs	2, 5
84	62	Int	Boys' Flat LIVING ROOM — Joe tells them all that Audrey has gone, reactions	Day 7	Day	1 2/8 pgs	2, 3, 4, 5
End of Day 2			Tuesday 24th August 2002			6 6/8 pgs (just under 7 mins)	
49a	41	Int	Indian restaurant (mocked up in house) — Bob admits to Joe that he thinks that he is in love with Audrey	Day 3a	Day	4/8 pgs	2, 3
50b	41	Int	Indian restaurant (mocked up in house) — Joe's reaction, battle to order with Waiter 1	Day 3a	Day	1 4/8 pgs	2, 3, 10
50c	43	Int	Indian restaurant (mocked up in house) — Finally order with Waiter 2	Day 3a	Day	4/8 pgs	2, 3, 11
50d	43	Int	Indian restaurant (mocked up in house) — Joe and Bob fooling around with the orange peel, waiters reactions	Day 3a	Day	4/8 pgs	2, 3, 10, 11
End of Day 3			Wednesday 25th August 2002			3 pgs (3 mins).	

FILES ON THE DISK

David Moore
Location Manager

Date *17 · 2 · 02*

Mad Dog Movies
Production Company

Bank Holiday
Production Title

16 · 1 · 02
Script Date

Claire Roper
Producer

John Oldman
Director

Emma Smith
Prod. Manager

Movement Order No *3*...

Location 1: (*story location*)

Address: *Flat 7, White Angel Road, Guerilla Town KP3 1PD.*
Tel: *01555 123333*
Contact there: *Mr. Jones.*

Directions by Car: (see attached map)

This is off the A3, take the Guerilla Town turn off and the road is the second on the left, and on the right hand side.

Trains:

Paddington : 07.30   07.45   08.00
Guerilla Town: 07.45   08.00   08.15

Buses:

The number 37, please call london travel line on 0345 484949.

Parking:

Generator: *In car park, in bay no 7.*
Catering Truck: *In car park, in bay no 8.*
Dining Bus: *In car park in bay no. 10*
Honey-Wagon: *In car park, in bay no 1.*

Facilities:

Toilets: *Cast to use ones in flat 7. Crew use honey wagon.*
Green Room: *The second bedroom in flat. look for signs.*
Crew Room: *The fourth bedroom. look for signs.*
Dressing Rooms: *First bedroom in flat.*
Make-up/Wardrobe: *First bedroom in flat.*

NO SMOKING, FOOD OR DRINK ON SET PLEASE!!!!!!

FILES ON
THE DISK

SOUND REPORT

ROLL No.

PRODUCTION COMPANY	PRODUCTION TITLE	PROD. No.	DATE

TAPE SPEED

3.75	7.5	15

DOLBY NOISE REDUCTION

A	B	C	SR	OTHER OR NONE

RECORDER MAKE & MODEL

CAMERA FORMAT

35mm	16mm	VIDEO

PILOT Hz

50	60

NR TONE

TONE REFERENCE LEVEL

RECORDING FORMAT

CAMERA SPEED FPS

24	25	30	PAL	NTSC

DIGITAL SAMPLE RATE

44.1	48

USER BITS

:   :   :

USER BIT COMMENTS

AUDIO TIME CODE PPS

24	25	30	29.97

TRANSFER TO:

35mm	16mm	R-DAT	OTHER

RECORDER MAKE & MODEL

SLATE	TAKE	FOOTAGE or TIMECODE	MONO or STEREO	CHANNEL 1	CHANNEL 2

PRINT CIRCLED TAKES ONLY

mcps | PPL | PRS
GIVING MUSIC ITS DUE

LICENSOR APPROVED MUSIC CUE SHEET

Important Note

The correct completion of this cue sheet is a strict condition of the granting of the broadcast licences by the various copyright owners and agencies. The shaded sections indicate essential items of information which **must** be supplied in all cases. The unshaded sections signify information which should be supplied if it is available.

Please turn to the reverse side of this form for explanatory notes, a key to the standard codes, and helpful telephone contacts should you require any further assistance.

Production Details

Film Title	AN URBAN GHOST STORY	Production Co.	LIVING SPIRIT PICTURES '97 LTD	Country of Origin	UK	Trailer /Promo/ Full Programme (T/P/F)	F
Episode Title	-	Production No.	-	Production Year	1997	Tx Time	
Episode No.	-	Director	GENEVIEVE JOLLIFFE	First Tx Date		Film Duration	90'
Film/Item No.	-	Principal Actors	Jason CONNERY	Channel		Music Duration	28'40
Alternative Title(s)	-		Heather Ann FOSTER				
			Stephanie BUTTLE				
			James COSMO				

Music Details

1. Music Cue Title and ISWC No. (if known)	2. Composer(s) Author(s) Arranger(s) CAE No(s) (If known)	3. Publisher(s) CAE No(s) (If known)	4. Performer(s) / Video/Record Title	5. Catalogue No. and Label	6. ISRC No.	7. Music Orig. Code	8. Music Use Code	9. Music Cue Dur.	10. Video Clip Dur.
"Vesti la Giubba" from "I Pagliacci"	Leoncavallo	Public domain	Cornel Staura World of Opera	2120.2007-2 Electrecord/ Selected Sound Carrier	-	C	F	0'18"	-
1M1 The Day I Died	Rupert Gregson-Williams CAE: 263121401 Guy Edward Fletcher CAE: 161847559	Living Spirit Pictures 97 Ltd/ Trackdown Music Ltd CAE: 269 127 448	Rupert Gregson-Williams Guy Edward Fletcher	-	-	X	B	0'30"	-
Clyde 2 Jingle	Muff Murfin	Happy Face Music	Muff Murfin Clyde 2 Jingle	-	-	?	F	0'05"	-
1M2 Suicide?	Rupert Gregson-Williams CAE: 263121401	Living Spirit Pictures 97 Ltd/ Trackdown Music Ltd CAE: 269 127 448	Rupert Gregson-Williams	-	-	X	B	0'24"	-

Page 1 of ..6....   Cue Sheet Compiled By ..LIVING SPIRIT PICTURES 97 LTD...Cue Sheet Supplied By . TRACKDOWN MUSIC   Date Supplied ....

FILES ON THE DISK

PRODUCTION GRATUITIES FORM

Bart Holiday   12th Feb 02.

Production Title   Date

Date	Item	Amount
9th Feb	Payment to gym next door to location use of power	£40.00
11th Feb	Payment to neighbour of location uses of power + water	£50.00
20th Feb	Bottle of whisky for use of location	£15.00
1st March	Wrap party misc.	£100.00

LEGAL TOOLKIT AND FORMS

FILES ON THE DISK

LIVING SPIRIT

LOCATION RELEASE

● Living Spirit Pictures Limited, Ealing Film Studios, Ealing Green, Ealing, London, W5 5EP ●
● Tel 020 8758 8544 ● Fax/Messages 020 8758 8559 ● mail@livingspirit.com ● www.livingspirit.com ●

From: *(name of company)* of *(address)*
To: *(name)* of *(address)*
Dated: *(date)*

Dear Sirs

(name of production) (the "Film")

This letter is to confirm the agreement with us in which you have agreed to make available to us the following premises (the "Premises") *(address)*.

1. The premises shall be made available to us on a sole and exclusive basis in connection with the Film on *(date)* (the "Dates").

2. You agree to make available to us the facilities in Schedule A on such days as we require on the Dates.

3. We shall be entitled to use the Premises as we may require on the days on giving you reasonable notice and as are negotiated in good faith between us but subject to the same terms as this agreement and on any additional days. You understand that we may need to return to the Premises at a later date if principal photography and recording is not completed on the Dates.

4. We have notified you of the scenes which are to be shot on or around the Premises and you confirm and agree that you consent to the filming of these scenes and you confirm that you will not make any objection in the future to the Premises being featured in the Film and you waive any and all right, claim and objection of whatever nature relating to the above.

5. We shall be entitled to represent the Premises under it's real name or under a fictional name or place according to the requirements of the Film.

6. We shall be entitled to incorporate all films, photographs and recordings, whether audio or audio-visual, made in or about the Premises in the Film as we may require in our sole discretion.

7. We shall not <u>without your prior consent</u> (not to be unreasonably withheld or delayed) make any structural or decorative alternations which we require to be made to the Premises. We shall at your request properly reinstate any part of the Premises to the condition they were in prior to any alterations.

8. We shall own the entire copyright and all other rights of every kind in and to all film and audio and audio-visual recordings and photographs made in or about the Premises and used in connection with the Film and we shall have the right to exploit the Film by any manner or means now known or in the future invented in any and all media throughout the world for the full period of copyright, including all renewals, reversions and extensions.

9. We shall have the right to assign, licence and/or sub-licence the whole and/or any part of our rights pursuant to this agreement to any company or individual.

10. We agree that we shall indemnify you up to a maximum of £*(amount)* against any liability, loss, claim or proceeding arising under statute or common law relating to the Film in respect of personal injury and/or death of any person and/or loss or damage to the Premises caused by negligence, omission or default by this company or any person for whom we are legally responsible. You shall notify us immediately in writing of any claim as soon as such claim comes to your attention and we shall assume the sole conduct of any proceedings arising from any such claim.

11. In consideration of the rights herein granted we will pay you the sum of £*(amount)* on *(date)*.

12. You undertake to indemnify us and to keep us fully indemnified from and against all actions, proceedings, costs, claims, damages and demands however arising in respect of any actual or alleged breach or non-performance by you of any or all of your undertakings, warranties and obligations under this agreement.

13. This agreement shall be governed by and construed in accordance with the law of England and Wales and subject to the jurisdiction of the English Courts.

Please signify your acceptance of the above terms by signing and returning to us the enclosed copy.

Signed..

ACME FILMS
Ealing Film Studios, Ealing Green, London W5 5EP
020 87588544
mail@guerillafilm.com

NON-EXCLUSIVE LICENCE FOR USE OF MATERIAL IN AN ACME FILM LTD PRODUCTION

DATE: 12 NOVEMBER 2006
LICENSOR: ULTIMATE CORN FLAKES, for UCFlakes Ltd, The Address, Somewhere
LICENSEE: ACME FILMS of Ealing Film Studios, Ealing Green, London W5 5EP

AGREEMENT:

1. The "Material" shall be:

2. **Use of** ULTIMATE CORN FLAKES, **(Scenes 34, 89 & 90)**

3. The "FILM" in which the material will be included is titled 'ROCKETBOY' and it shall be an **ACME FILM LTD film**

4. The "Licence Fee" shall be £1.

5. The "Licence Period" shall be in perpetuity.

6. The "Territory" shall be the World.

7. The "Rights" shall mean the right to record, copy, reproduce, broadcast, transmit and perform all or part of the Material for and/or in connection with the production, exploitation, promotion and/or advertising of the Programme throughout the world by all means and in all media whether now known or hereafter discovered or developed (including without limitation broadcasting by television and inclusion in cable programmes).

8. In consideration of the Licence fee, the Licensor grants to the Licensee a non-exclusive licence in respect of the Rights for the Material to be used in the Programme for the duration of the Licence Period.

9. The Licensor agrees that in further consideration of the Licence Fee, the Material as incorporated into the FILM hereby licensed for use in all theatric, and televisual media including, but not limited to videogramme and multimedia.

10. The Licensor warrants that it is the sole owner of, or controls all copyright and other rights in the Material, that all consents required under the Copyright Designs and Patents Act 1988 have been obtained and that the Licensee is not responsible for any payments other than the Licence Fee. The Licensor will indemnify the Licensee in the event of any loss or damage to the Licensee arising from a breach of this provision.

11. The Licensee is entitled to assign the benefit of this Licence.

12. This Licence is subject to English law.

Registered Office : Ealing Film Studios
Company Registration No : xxx xxxxx   VAT No : xxxxxxxx

LEGAL TOOLKIT
AND FORMS

INDEX

INDEX